ISBN 978-0-331-67771-3
PIBN 11084137

57th Congress, 1st Session. } HOUSE OF REPRESENTATIVES. { Document No. 621.

BULLETIN

OF THE

OF THE

DEPARTMENT OF STATE.

No. 4.

MARCH, 1894.

WASHINGTON:

CONCURRENT RESOLUTION OF CONGRESS.

CALENDARS OF CORRESPONDENCE OF THOMAS JEFFERSON, JAMES MADISON, AND JAMES MONROE.

Resolved by the Senate (the House of Representatives concurring), That there be printed and bound in cloth 4,000 copies of each of the following bulletins of the Bureau of Rolls and Library of the Department of State, namely: Calendars of the Correspondence of Thomas Jefferson, James Madison, and James Monroe; 1,000 copies for the use of the Senate, 2,000 copies for the use of the House of Representatives, and 1,000 copies for distribution by the Department of State.

Passed May 10, 1902.

Extract from U. S. Stats. at Large, 24th Cong., 2d Sess., c. 33, 1837.

[CHAP. XXXIII. An Act making appropriations for the civil and diplomatic expenses of Government for the year eighteen hundred and thirty-seven.

*   *   *   *   *   *   *   *   *

For the purchase of the manuscripts of the late Mr. Madison referred to in a letter from Mrs. Madison to the President of the United States dated fifteenth of November, eighteen hundred and thirty-six, and communicated in his message of sixth December, eighteen hundred and thirty-six, thirty thousand dollars.]

CHRONOLOGICAL RECORD OF THE LIFE OF JAMES MADISON.

1751, March 16. Born at Port Conway, King George County, Va.; son of Col. James Madison and Nelly Conway.

1771. Graduated from the College of New Jersey.

1776. Elected to the Virginia assembly.

1778. Member of the executive council of Virginia.

1780–1783. Delegate to the Continental Congress.

1783. Advocated establishment of system of general revenue.

1786–1788. Delegate to the Continental Congress.

1787. Member of convention for forming the United States Constitution, and taking prominent part in the debates.

1789–1797. Member of Congress; a Republican and moderate opponent of Washington.

1793. Refused the post of Secretary of State vacated by Jefferson.

1794. Married Dorothy Todd.

1798. Author of "Resolutions of 1798" protesting against increase of power of Federal Government.

1801–1809. Secretary of State.

1808. Elected President of the United States.

1809, March 4. Inaugurated President.

1810, May. Decree of nonintercourse with Great Britain.

1812, June 18. Declaration of war with Great Britain.

1812. Reelected President of the United States.

1814, December 24. Treaty of peace signed at Ghent.

1817, March 4. Retired to private life at his farm at Montpellier.

1829. Member of the Virginia convention to amend the State constitution.

1836, June 28. Died at Montpellier.

ADAMS, CHARLES FRANCIS.

1835, October 13, Montpellier. Acknowledging letter of September 30, with a copy of "an appeal" from the new to the old Whigs. Claims of the Senate for a share in the removals from office and for the legislative authority to regulate the tenure. [Copy.] "Private." 8°. 3 pages.

ADAMS, JOHN.

1814, December 17, Washington. Acknowledging letter of 28th November. Returns letter from J. Q. Adams of October 27, 1814. The fisheries question. Original views of Congress to the common rights to fish in waters three leagues from the British shores. Policy of the British cabinet in our negotiations consists in consuming time. Our envoys beginning to overcome prejudices. [Copy.] 4°. 4 pages.

1816, October 12, Washington. Acknowledging receipt of letter of 4th September. Dr. Freeman's short visit. Adams's expressions on the course of Madison's administration are very gratifying. [Draft.] 4°. 2 pages.

ADAMS, JOHN (Mayor of Richmond).

1824, October 17, Montpellier. Acknowledging letter of 12th. Regrets he can not accept the invitation to the reception of Lafayette. His tribute of respect and gratitude to Lafayette. [Draft.] 4°. 1 page.

ADAMS, JOHN QUINCY.

1787, September 17. Completion of the Journal of the Federal Convention of 1787, furnished by Madison. [Draft and copy.] fol. 4 pages. 4°. 3 pages.

St. Petersburg.

1810, October 16, Washington. If Adams wishes it, he will be recalled from his mission, and gives instructions relative to guard against any misconstruction which may be made on his departure. [Copy.] "Private." 4°. 3 pages.

1811, November 15, Washington. Acknowledging letters of February 8, April 19, June 3, and August 17. Trusts his diplomatic situation may be less incommodious than was at first found. Count Pahlen presents his letter of leave. He goes to Rio Janeiro. The "Chesapeake" affair. Pretensions of Great Britain. The matter before Congress. Our merchant vessels to arm in self-defense. [Draft.] "Private." 4°. 3 pages.

ADAMS, JOHN QUINCY.

Washington.

1817, December 23, Montpellier. Acknowledging letter of 15th. Mr. Adams's interviews with Mr. Bentham. Opinions on his works. Letters from Governor Plumer and his son. Question of publication. [Draft.] 4°. 2 pages.

1818, August 7, Montpellier. Acknowledging letter of 25th ultimo, with copies of Dr. Mayhew's sermon. Origin of the subject of American independence, in Albany, 1754, on proposal of the British Government to pay advances for the colonies by a parliamentary tax on them. Letter from Franklin on its unconstitutionality. The merit of independence declared in 1776, traced to individuals. [Draft.] 4°. 2 pages.

1819, May 18, Montpellier. Acknowledging letter of 14th in behalf of Mr. Cardelli. [Draft.] 4°. 1 page.

1819, June 7, Montpellier. Acknowledging letter of 1st. Speech of Col. Hamilton on 18th June, 1787, in which was sketch of a plan of government for the United States. [Draft.] 4°. 1 page.

1819, June 27, Montpellier. Acknowledging letter of 18th. Returns a list of yeas and nays in the convention. [Draft.] 4°. 1 page.

1820, June 13, Montpellier. Acknowledging a letter accompanying copy of printed journal of the Federal Convention. Corrects an error therein. [Draft and copy.] 4°. 3 pages.

1822, October 24, Montpellier. Acknowledging letter of the 11th and a copy of Adams's "Collection of Documents." The treaty of Ghent a lasting monument of the ability and patriotism with which it was negotiated. [Draft and copy.] 4°. 2 pages.

1827, December 9, Montpellier. Thanking him for copy of his message. An able document. [Draft.] Scrap of paper.

1829, February 24, Montpellier. Acknowledging letter of 21st, with a pamphlet containing Adams's correspondence. Governor Plumer's letter. Hamilton's agency in a project for severing the Union. Not to be believed. [Draft.] Strip of paper.

1829, March 13, Montpellier. Acknowledging letter of 1st inclosing letters to Mr. Bacon. Remembers an interview with Mr. Bacon in 1808 and conversing on the discontent and menacing crisis produced by the embargo in the Eastern quarter. Mr. Jefferson's anachronisms. [Draft.] Strip of paper.

1831, September 23, Montpellier. Thanking him for copy of his eulogy on life and character of Monroe. A just and happy tribute. [Draft.] Scrap of paper.

Quincy.

1834, July 30, Montpellier. Acknowledging receipt of copy of his intended speech on the "Removal of the Deposits." Very able and impressive. Has received a letter from George Joy, of London, containing an incident in the career of Lafayette. Mr. Joy's papers on "Orders in Council." [Draft.] Scrap of paper.

ALBEMARLE, AGRICULTURAL SOCIETY OF.

1822, October —, Montpellier. Address of the society respecting their wish to provide for a professorship to be incorporated into the University of Virginia. The means proposed. [Draft.] fol. 4 pages.

ADLUM, JOHN.

1823, April 12, Montpellier. Acknowledging receipt of a letter and two copies on the "Cultivation of the Vine," with a bottle of Tokay. His opinion of American wines. [Draft.] 4°. 1 page.

ALDEN, TIMOTHY.

1824, February 18, Montpellier. Acknowledging receipt of the resolution of the trustees of Allegheny College, with printed copy of its library. Congratulations and thanks. [Draft.] 4°. 1 page.

ALGIERS, DEY OF.

1816, August —, Washington. Acknowledging letter representing the capture of two vessels of war by the U. S. squadron and not restored according to promise. Explains how he was mistaken. The policy of the United States is peace, but war rather than tribute. The U. S. consul and Commodore Chauney authorized to terminate difficulties. [Draft.] 4°. 2 pages.

ALLEN, WILLIAM.

1824, May 6, Montpellier. Inclosing an obligation complying with a condition stated in a correspondence of Allen's with Governor Barbour. [Draft.] 4°. 1 page.

AMBLER, J.

1783. Series of questions relating to the State of Virginia. fol. 1 page.

ANDERSON, ELBERT.

1816(?) no year, October 22, Montpellier. Bears testimony favorable to his agency in supplying the Army in the late war. [Draft.] Strip of paper.

APPOINTMENTS.

Not *dated.* Power of the President to appoint public ministers and consuls in the recess of the Senate. [Memorandum.] 4°. 4 pages.

ANNAPOLIS CONVENTION.

1788. Address read in the convention at Annapolis respecting proposed alterations in the Constitution. 4°. 1 page.

ARMSTRONG, JOHN (Secretary of War). *Washington.*

1814, August 20, Washington. Notice on proposed consolidation. Asks him to suggest the names of those most fit to remain in service. [Draft.] Scrap of paper.

ATWATER, CALEB.

1823, April —, Montpellier. Acknowledging letter of March 18, with copy of a bill providing for common schools in Ohio. His views on the subject. [Draft.] 4°. 1 page.

AUSTIN, BENJAMIN. *Boston.*

1815, March 7, Washington. Acknowledging letter of 23d in behalf of Republican members of the legislature of Massachusetts on the return of peace and complimenting him on his instru-

AUSTIN, BENJAMIN.
mentality in accomplishing it. His views on the policy to be pursued. [Draft.] 4°. 2 pages.

AUSTIN, JAMES T. *Boston.*

1832, February 6, Montpellier. Acknowledging letter of 19th January. The services of the late Vice-President Elbridge Gerry. Had a high esteem and regard for Gerry. Was an active, able, and interesting member of the convention of 1787. Madison in his eighty-second year. [Draft.] Scrap of paper.

AZUNI, ——. *Genoa.*

1817, October —, Montpellier. Acknowledging receipt of three copies of his book on Piracy. [Draft.] 4°. 1 page.

BAILEY, THEODORUS.

1796, January 5. Respecting a conveyance of land. Articles of agreement. 4°. 2 pages.

BANKS, LINN, and others.
Madison Court-House, Va.

1834, August 18, Montpellier. Acknowledging letter of 1st, writing him in the name of Democratic Republicans to a public dinner to be given on 23d to Hon. J. M. Patton, the Representative in Congress. His age and debility will deprive him the pleasure of accepting. Strip of paper.

BARBOUR, JAMES (Governor of Virgina).

1814, June 16, Washington. Acknowledging letter of 13th. Great Britain to send a greater force to United States. The measures to be taken to meet it. In absence of knowledge of designs of the enemy the State governments to be prepared for emergencies. [Draft.] 4°. 4 pages.

BARBOUR, JAMES (Senator). *Washington.*

1820, February 14, Montpellier. Acknowledging letter of 10th. Decided majority in one house against an unrestricted admission of Missouri. His views thereon and suggestions. [Draft.] 4°. 2 pages.

1820, November 25, Montpellier. A tribute to the worth and political career of Mr. T. Coxe. [Draft.] 4°. 2 pages.

1823, December 5, Montpellier. Acknowledging letter of the 2d. Views on a resolution to be proposed to the Senate advising a treaty of cooperation with Great Britain against an interference of the allied powers for resubjugating South America. [Draft.] 4°. 2 pages.

BARBOUR, JAMES, and JOHN HENSHAW.
Bank of Virginia.

1824, May 6. Power of attorney to William J. Roberts of Fredericksburg, to execute a note in the bank to James Barbour for renewal. [Copy.] fol. 1 page.

BARBOUR, JAMES.

1824, May 7, Montpellier. Acknowledging letter of 2d. Thanks him for papers inclosed. Has signed and forwarded them to Mr. Allen and Mr. Roberts. Renewal of note at bank. Receipts of tolls on turnpike stock. The weather and crops. [Draft.] 4°. 1 page.

BARBOUR, JAMES. *London.*

1828, December 18, Montpellier. Acknowledging letter of September 29. Barbour's views of the market and harvest in Great Britain. The price of wheat in Virginia. The new president and the course to be steered. Stormy questions and baffling expectations. The ferment in South Carolina respecting the tariff. [Draft.]
Strip of paper.

1829, February 6, Montpellier. Acknowledging letter of November 13. The Duke of Wellington the mainspring of the cabinet in a more friendly policy towards this country. Trusts that Barbour may succeed in bringing about satisfactory arrangements in points of controversy. Our trade with the West Indies. The flour markets in Virginia. The views of the new President unknown. The proceedings of South Carolina and Georgia about the tariff. Revision of constitution of Virginia. [Draft.] 4°. 2 pages.

BARBOUR, JOHN S.

1820, April 21, Montpellier. Acknowledging letter of January 27. Instructions respecting rents due by Mr. Ward. Private business about land and rents. [Draft.] 4°. 1 page.

BARKER, JOHN (Chairman). *Philadelphia.*

1810, February 21, Washington. Acknowledging letter of 17th, inclosing an address and resolutions adopted by Republican citizens of the First Congressional District of Pennsylvania, touching our foreign affairs. [Draft.] fol. 2 pages.

BARLOW, JOEL.

1809, February 7, Washington. His selection to fill the approaching vacancy in the Department of State. [Draft.] 4°. 2 pages.

Paris.

1811, November 17, Washington. The British orders in council. Nothing but a termination of the war will reopen the continental market to British products. Nothing done in Congress to meet British hostile attitude. Merchant vessels may be permitted to arm in self-defense. France evades correction of outrages. The "Chesapeake" outrage. Independence of Spanish America. [Draft.] "Private."
4°. 4 pages.

1812, February 24, Washington. Acknowledges receipt of dispatches. Views on the subject of the commercial treaty with France. Vagueness and delays on part of France. Changes and securities are necessary for a friendly reciprocity. [Draft.]
fol. 4 pages.

1812, August 11, Washington. Cipher dispatch of this date. Shameful conduct of France on subject of decree of April, 1811. Departs from the declaration to General Armstrong of which the enforcement of nonimportation was the effect. British orders in council to be revoked. Great indignation directed towards France. A double war the shortest way to peace. [Draft.] fol. 2 pages.

1812, August 11, Washington. Cipher dispatch.
fol. 2 pages.

BARNETT, WILLIAM. *Elberton, Ga.*

1809, March 15, Washington. Acknowledging letter of 10th February, inclosing proceedings of a

Barnett, William.

meeting of citizens of Elbert County, expressing confidence in the General Government respecting our foreign relations. [Draft.] 4°. 1 page.

Barney, Joshua, and others. *Jamaica.*

1794, May 1, Philadelphia. Acknowledging letter of March 13th, with inclosure in which American masters of vessels detained in Jamaica express their sentiments on Madison's resolutions in Congress on 3d January. Expresses sympathy with the victims of depredations. [Draft.] 4°. 2 pages.

Barry, W. T.

1822, August 4, Montpellier. Acknowledging letter of June 30. Appropriations by the legislature of Kentucky for a general system of education. Views and suggestions. [Draft.] 4°. 8 pages.

Bascom, H. B.

1827, July 23, October 22, and November 10, Montpellier. Acknowledging several letters relating to a new college at Union Town to be called after his name. Some suggestions, also acknowledging the honor of such a connection with the institution. [Drafts.] 3 strips of paper.

Bassett, George W.

1833, April 30, Montpellier. Acknowledging letter of 25th, requesting his company at the laying of the corner stone of a proposed monument to the memory of the mother of Washington. His advanced age and indisposition prevents his acceptance. [Draft.] Strip of paper.

Bates, Stephen.

1831, January 24, Montpellier. Acknowledging letter of 31st October, with a pamphlet. Is ignorant of the true character of Masonry, never having been a Mason. Never regarded the institution as dangerous, noxious, or important. [Draft.] Strip of paper.

Beasley, Frederic.

1824, December 22, Montpellier. Acknowledging letter of 13th. On the system or polity for the University of Virginia. [Draft.] 4°. 3 pages.

1828, November 20, Montpellier. Has received copy of tract on the proofs of the "Being and Attributes of God." Reflections on the subject. [Draft.] 4°. 2 pages.

Bentley, William.

1809, December 27, Washington. Acknowledging letter of 11th. Inclosing a letter to General Stark expressing his esteem for him. [Draft.] 4°. 1 page.

Salem.

1816, December 28, Washington. Is gratified at the kindly sentiment expressed in a letter to Mr. Crowninshield. In retiring it is a great satisfaction to make way for a successor who enjoys, as he merits, the confidence and affection of his fellow-citizens. [Draft.] Half sheet. 1 page.

Bernard, Simon, General.

1831, July 16, Montpellier. Acknowledging letter of 12th. Regrets that he is about to leave this country. Is a gratifying recollection that Madison had a part in obtaining for the United States

BERNARD, SIMON, General.

his invaluable aid in the defensive system so well matured and extensively executed. [Draft.]
Scrap of paper.

BIDDLE, NICHOLAS.

1823, February —, Montpellier. Acknowledging letter of 9th, accompanied by a copy of Biddle's agricultural address. On the diminutive size of the Roman farms. [Draft.] 4°. 2 pages.

1827, May 17, Montpellier. Thanks him for his "Eulogium on Thomas Jefferson." Corrects an error in the notice of a revised code of the legislature of Virginia. [Draft.] Strip of paper.

1827, May 31, Montpellier. Acknowledging letter of 27th. Incloses a oopy of the revised Code of Virginia. [Draft.] On strip of paper.

BIGELOW, ANDREW.

1809 (?) no date, Washington (?). His sermon on the 6th January on the election. He thinks Bigelow's letter overrates his (M.'s) services. Is anxious for the preservation of the Union and success of the constitutional experiments. [Draft.]
8°. 1 page.

BILLS PAYABLE.

1806, Washington. Canceled acceptance of draft in favor of Thomas Tingley, drawn by Nicholas Voss, dated July 8. Also Madison's note, payable to John Cox, dated September 24. Canceled.
2 strips of paper.

1806, December 30, Washington. Acceptance of Fulwar Skipwith's draft. 4°. 1 page.

BILLS PAYABLE AND RECEIVABLE.

1806, November 22, New York. Draft on Madison by James H. Eakin in favor of James Eakin.
1806, July 23, Washington. Madison's note in favor of John Cox.
1807, March 6, Georgetown. William Gordon & Co.'s draft on W. Gordon & Co., Fredericksburg, in favor of Madison. All paid. 3 strips of paper.

BINNS, JOHN, and others. *Philadelphia.*

1813, February 11, Washington. Answer to a communication in behalf of naturalized citizens born in the British dominions. It will be the duty of the executive to employ just means to enforce the respect due from the enemy to rights of those defending their adopted country. [Draft.]
4°. 1 page.

BIRKBECK, MORRIS.

Not dated. Acknowledging letter of 18th September. No encouragements to emigrants to this country unless they bring some special addition to our stock of arts or articles of culture. The Government can not dispose of public lands other than in the ordinary way. [Draft.] 4°. 2 pages.

BLAKE, JAMES H. *Washington.*

1817, March 4, Washington. Acknowledging the expressions of regard and respect of the citizens of Washington on his retirement from public office. [Draft.] 4°. 1 page.

BLOODGOOD, ABRAHAM. *New York.*

1809, September 24, Washington. Acknowledging the address of the Republican committee of the city

BLOODGOOD, ABRAHAM.

and county of New York of 15th approving of Madison's measures respecting foreign relations. [Draft.] 4°. 1 page.

BALLS, ———.

1834, March 18, Montpellier. Inclosing a sum to discharge the account of William F. Gray, with directions about applying surplus of check. Strip of paper.

BOTTA, CARLO. *Paris.*

1817, January —, Washington. Acknowledging receipt of a copy of "Camillo." Regrets he does not understand Italian to do justice to its merits. His "Storia della Guerra d'America" to be translated. [Copy.] 4°. 1 page.

BOWDITCH, NATHANIEL.

1827, May 4 and June 18, Montpellier. Respecting the filling of a vacancy of a professor's chair in the University of Virginia. [Draft.] 2 strips of paper.

BRANNAN, JOHN.

1823, July 19, Montpellier. Acknowledging letter of the 4th, with a volume containing the official letters of the military and naval officers during the late war. Opinion of the volume. [Draft.] 4°. 1 page.

1825, September 7, Montpellier. Acknowledging letter of 31st August. Consents to be a subscriber to a translation of the travels of the Marquis de Chastellux in the United States during the Revolutionary war. [Draft.] Strip of paper.

1825, September 26, Montpellier. Acknowledging letter of 16th. Corrects some errors in the author's book relating to late Bishop Madison. Act of the legislature of Virginia on subject of slaves. [Draft.] Strip of paper.

BRECKINRIDGE, JAMES.

1827, August —, Montpellier. Respecting the filling of a vacancy in a professorship in the University of Virginia. [Draft.] Strip of paper.

1827, November 27, Montpellier. Introducing Jesse B. Harrison, of Lynchburg, who offers himself as successor to Mr. Long in the professorship of ancient languages in the University of Virginia. 4°. 1 page.

BRIDGE STOCK.

No date, 1835 (?) Notes on a scrap of paper relating to a deed of trust and directions about conveying bridge stock.

BRIGGS, DR. R.

1823, September 13, Montpellier. Acknowledging letter of 5th, relating to Briggs' recommendation of Mr. Reynolds as successor to Mr. Long in the University of Virginia. [Draft.] On strip of paper.

BROCKENBROUGH, A. S.

1827, October 29, November 24, and December 2, Montpellier. Acknowledging several letters. Report of the visitors to the University of Virginia. Reduction of number of hotels and appointment of keepers. [Drafts.] 3 strips of paper.

BROOKE, FRANCIS.

1828, February 22, Montpellier. Acknowledging receipt of his nomination by the convention at Richmond as elector for next President of the United States. Gives his reasons for declining the honor. Suggestions as to conducting the contest. [Draft.] 4°. 2 pages.

BROWN, JOHN. *Kentucky.*

1785, August 23, Orange. Acknowledging letter of 12th July. Communicates his ideas towards a constitution of government of the State in embryo (Kentucky). fol. 7 pages.

1788, October —, New York. Remarks on Jefferson's draught of a constitution for Virginia. 4°. 13 pages.

1835, May 16, Montpellier. Incloses a letter for Mr. Butler; also one to him unsealed that he may read the contents. [Copy.] Scrap of paper.

BURR'S CONSPIRACY.

1807, January 23. Notes of Ballman's conversation with the President, on Burr's conspiracy, in Madison's writing; Madison being present at the interview, at the President's request. fol. 10 pages.

BUTLER, MANN.

1834, October 11, Montpellier. Acknowledging letter of 21st ultimo. Recollections of what passed between John Brown and himself in 1788 on the overture of Gardoqui to create an independent State of Kentucky and enter into an arrangement with Spain for exportation of their products to New Orleans. Can give no information that is not published relative to General Wilkinson's official investigation. [Draft.] 4°. 1 page.

CABELL, JOSEPH C.

1819, July 26, Montpellier. Acknowledging letter of 10th. Allowance of interest on the debt from the United States. The Massachusetts claim in Congress not valid. The objection to the Virginia claim will arise from the bearing of the precedents. The justice of interest. [Draft.] 4°. 1 page.

1827, January 13, Montpellier. Concerning the University of Virginia. The sale of a bust and pictures to the assembly mentioned in Jefferson's and Randolph's letters. Old documents relating to the Virginia assembly and proceedings of the convention of 1776. [Copy.] 4°. 2 pages.

1827, February 7, Montpellier. Acknowledging letter of 24th. Matters relating to the University of Virginia. Two discontinued hotels to be again in hands of former keepers. [Draft.] 8°. 1 page.

1827, March 18, Montpellier. Acknowledging letter of 12th. Failure of the Virginia legislature to do what was due to the character of the State and memory of Jefferson. Views on the tariff. [Draft.] 4°. 4 pages.

1828, September 18, Montpellier. On the constitutionality of the Houses of Congress to impose a tariff for the encouragement of manufacturers. [Draft.] 4°. 11 pages.

1828, October 5, Montpellier. Acknowledging letter of 27th. Thinks that his (Madison's) views on the

CABELL, JOSEPH C.

tariff and the powers of Congress should not be published at present. The Presidential election absorbing all attention. [Draft.]
Strip of paper.

1828, December 5, Montpellier. Acknowledging letter of November 20. Corrections to Madison's remarks on the tariff and suggesting explanations of Jefferson's letter to Mr. Giles on assumptions of power by the General Government. [Copy.]
4°. 2 pages.

1829, January 5, Montpellier. Acknowledging letter of December 28. Contemplated convention for revising the constitution of Virginia. Basis of representation. Provision for rights of property. Matters concerning the University of Virginia. [Draft.] 4°. 2 pages.

1829, February 2, Montpellier. Acknowledging letter of 29th January. Fears confirmed that nothing can be done for the university on account of prevalence of fever. Explanations of his letters relating to the tariff. [Draft.] 4°. 3 pages.

1829, February 13, Montpellier. Constitutional powers of Congress in relation to the tariff. [Draft.]
4°. 2 pages.

1829, March 19, Montpellier. Acknowledging letter of 13th, with a pamphlet containing two letters of Jefferson. Recommends publishing them. Gross misstatements and misconstructions about Madison's letters to Cabell on constitutional powers of Congress relating to the tariff. The malady at the University of Virginia. [Draft.]
4°. 2 pages.

1829, August 16, Montpellier. Acknowledging letter of 5th. Cabell's view of the Virginia doctrine in 1798-'99 is essentially correct. Wishes certain revisions to guard against misconstructions. Jefferson's authority on constitutionality of the tariff. Provision in Constitution for deciding controversies concerning boundaries of rights and power. The position taken by South Carolina and Virginia. [Copy.] fol. 2 pages.

1829, September 7, Montpellier. Acknowledging two letters of August 30 and September 1, with copy of Virginia proceedings in 1798-'99 and the letters of "Hampden." Views on the constitutionality of the tariff. Disorganizing doctrine of rights of States to withdraw from the Union. [Draft.]
4°. 3 pages.

1829, October 30, Montpellier. On the constitutional power of Congress to impose duties and restrictions on imports in order to encourage domestic productions. His views on protective duties. [Draft.] 4°. 4 pages.

1830, May 31, Montpellier. Acknowledging letter of 26th. Has never concealed his opinion of the nullifying doctrine of South Carolina. Jefferson's correspondence proving he had nothing to do with Kentucky resolutions of 1799. Monroe's feeble health. Small 4°. 2 pages.

1831, September 16, Montpellier. Acknowledging letter of 29th ultimo. Absurdity of nullification. [Draft.] Strip of paper.

1831, October 5, Montpellier. On the controlling jurisdiction of the Supreme Court of the United States

CABELL, JOSEPH C.

over the State courts. Judge Pendleton's views corroborating his own, opposing the nullifying power of a State. [Draft.] Strip of paper.

1832, December 27, Montpellier. Acknowledging letter of 22d. Correspondence with Judge Roane with regard to powers of the U. S. Supreme Court in relation to State courts. Mr. Pendleton's views. [Draft.] 4°. 2 pages.

1832, December 28, Montpellier. Acknowledging letter of 22d. Rectifying certain errors in previous correspondence. The Virginia resolutions of 1798. His views on constitutional questions; on internal improvements, tariff, etc. [Draft.] 4°. 2 pages.

1832 (?), no date, Montpellier. Notes on letters to Cabell on the tariff and the constitutional powers of Congress. [Draft.] 4°. 2 pages.

1832 (?), no date, Montpellier. Emendations and erasures in previous correspondence, evidently for purpose of publication. [Memorandum.] Strip of paper.

1833, April 1, Montpellier. Acknowledging letter and documents. Judge Roane's correspondence. Calhoun's speech charging Madison as inconsistent. Refutation of the charge of being a nullifier. Relations between the Federal and State governments. [Draft.] fol. 4 pages.

CALDWELL, CHARLES.

1825, July 22, Montpellier. Acknowledging a letter. Gives instances of longevity in his farm and vicinity. Instances of extreme heights. [Draft.] 4°. 2 pages.

1826, September 20, Montpellier. Thanks him for his copy of "Elements of Phrenology." [Draft.] Strip of paper.

1826, November 23, Montpellier. Acknowledging letter of October 11. Concurs with him in rejecting the idea that there is no road from nature up to nature's God, and that all knowledge of his existence is derived from oral tradition. [Draft.] Strip of paper.

CAMBRELING, ——.

1827, March 8, Montpellier. Thanks him for copy of his speech on proposed increase of duty on wool and its manufacture. Madison's views on the principle of a tariff. Supply and demand. Balance of trade. Predicts the supremacy of British navigation will be transferred to United States. [Draft.] 4°. 1 page.

CAMPBELL, G. W.

1814, November 2, [place not stated]. On a call from the House to inquire into causes of late military events in this district. Hopes no information Campbell can give in relation to Madison will be withheld. Is anxious for an investigation, as he is implicated in a charge. Conversation with General Armstrong probably referred to. [Draft.] "Private." 4°. 2 pages.

CAPELLANO, ANTONIO. *Baltimore.*

1817, September 8, Montpellier. Acknowledging letter of 5th. Engagements will deprive Madison of the pleasure of seeing him at Montpellier the present month. Refers him to Mr. Lee. [Copy in Madison's hand.] 4°. 1 page.

CARDELL, WILLIAM S. *New York.*

1820, March —, Montpellier. Acknowledging letter of 4th, with a copy of an address on a "National Philological Academy." Madison's views and cordial wishes for the success of the projected academy. Declines the proposition to use his name as a nominal functionary. [Draft.] 4°. 2 pages.

1821, January 19, Montpellier. Acknowledging letter of 12th, with a copy of a circular on the subject of "American Academy of Language and Belles Lettres." His good wishes for the success of the institution. [Draft.] 4°. 1 page.

CARDELLI, ANTONIO.

1819, November 4, Montpellier. Acknowledging letter of October 29. Orders a bust of Jefferson. (Signed J. M.) [Draft.] Scrap of paper.

CAREY, MATHEW.

1820, February 11, Montpellier. Acknowledging letter of January 26, with copies of addresses of the Philadelphia societies for protection of national industry. The vindication of Ireland. [Draft.] 4°. 2 pages.

1821, May 26, Montpellier. Acknowledging letter of 16th instant. Observations on political economy. Capital and labor. [Draft.] 4°. 4 pages.

1821, December 12, Montpellier. Acknowledging letter of 1st. Can not give him the desired information relative to the balance of trade with Great Britain previous to the Revolution. Remarks on the subject. [Copy.] 4°. 3 pages.

1822, February 21, Montpellier. Received the copy of "Appeal to Common Sense and Common Justice." Madison's views on the tariff. Believes in legislative encouragement to a certain extent of domestic manufactures. [Draft.] 4°. 2 pages.

1824, March 10, Montpellier. Acknowledging letter of February 28, with a pamphlet. Madison's views on the tariff. [Draft.] 4°. 1 page.

1825, May 12, Montpellier. Acknowledging letter of 22d April. Subject of internal improvements. Roads and canals. Carey's remarks on the cotton trade very opportune. [Draft.] Strip of paper.

1831, July 27, Montpellier. Acknowledging letter of 21st, with copy of address to citizens of South Carolina. Strange doctrines and misconceptions prevailing in that quarter. Disastrous consequences of a separation of States. [Draft.] 4°. 1 page.

CARTWRIGHT, JOHN.

1824, no date, Montpellier. Apologizes for delay in acknowledging his volume on the English Constitution. Advantages of two legislative chambers. Is pleased that Great Britain is relaxing their prejudices against the United States. [Draft.] 4°. 2 pages.

CATHCART, JAMES LEANDER.

1806, May 19, Washington. Certificate as to services of Cathcart to the Tunis ambassador during his visit to the United States. [See letter from J. L. Cathcart to Madison, August 11, 1834.] [Copy.] 4°. 1 page.

CATHCART, JAMES LEANDER. *Madeira.*

1811, May 21, Washington. Acknowledging receipt of parcels of wine from Madeira. Orders some more. [Draft.] 4°. 1 page.

Washington.

1821, September 23, Montpellier. Acknowledging letter of 18th. Regrets his unfortunate want of success. Bears testimony to his fidelity and capacity in Government employ. If it can be useful will cheerfully do what he can. [Draft.] 4°. 1 page.

CAZENOVE, A. *Alexandria, Va.*

1821, April 30, Montpellier. Relating to his supply of wines. Declines purchasing foreign woolens and linens. Prefers having them manufactured at home and from his own materials. [Draft.] 4°. 1 page.

CHANCERY SUIT.

1830, October 1. Answers of persons interested in a suit by Madison against Fanny Bell and others. fol. 5 pages.

CHAPMAN, REYNOLDS.

1821, January 25, Montpellier. Acknowledging letter of 16th. A plan for reading history. [Draft.] fol. 1 page.

1831, January 6, Montpellier. Acknowledging a letter inclosing a manuscript of J. M. Patton. Constitutionality of the tariff. Internal improvements. Roads and canals. Madison approves of a tariff for the encouragement of manufactures. [Draft.] 4°. 3 pages.

CHARLTON, THOMAS U. P. *Savannah.*

1815, June 19, Washington. Acknowledging letter of 5th with the address of the mayor and city council of Savannah on the conclusion of peace. [Draft.] 4°. 1 page.

CHAZOTTI, STEPHEN.

1821, January 30, Montpellier. Thanks him for his tract on the culture of vines, olives, etc. Importance of the matter. [Copy.] 4°. 1 page.

CHECKS.

1806, Washington. Nineteen canceled checks on office of discount and deposit, Washington, from May to August. 19 strips of paper.

CHEW, JOHN.

1800, February 14, Orange, Va. Acknowledging letter of October 20, 1799. Chew's claim to land in Kentucky. [Draft.] fol. 1 page.

CLAIBORNE, FERDINAND L. *Mississippi Territory.*

1809, August 10, Washington. Acknowledging address of July 5th, expressing friendly confidence in his principles and views, by the representatives of the Mississippi Territory. [Draft.] 4°. 1 page.

CLAIBORNE, Wm. C. C.

1804, February 20, Washington. Instructs him to bring about the removal from New Orleans of Morales. [Press copy.] "Private and confidential." 4°. 1 page.

1804, August 28, Virginia. Acknowledging letters of 12–14th July. Conduct of Spanish officers at New Orleans. Instructs him to not allow them to

CLAIBORNE, WM. C. C.

affront the authority of the United States. Their longer stay left to [his] judgment. Respecting a chain of post-offices. Discontent of Spanish Government at Madrid at act of Congress organizing a revenue district on the waters of the Mobile. [Draft.] 4°. 2 pages.

1804, August 30, Virginia. Appointing Claiborne governor of Territory of Orleans. Incloses his commission, also commissions for two judges. [Draft.] 4°. 1 page.

C——K, G.

1830, August 3, Montpellier. Acknowledging letter of 10th ultimo. Is unable to aid him in his application for advice and assistance in his patriotic undertaking. [Draft.] Scrap of paper.

CLARKSON, CROLIUS.

1819, December —, Montpellier. Acknowledges copy of the address of the Society of Tammany. Want of economy in use of imported articles a cause of present embarrassment. Balance in foreign commerce against us, hence the call for specie. Views on the address. [Draft.] 4°. 5 pages.

CLAY, HENRY.

1824, April —, Montpellier. Has received his speech on "American Industry." Views on the tariff. [Copy.] 4°. 3 pages.

1830, October 9, Montpellier. Acknowledging letter of 22d September. The rescue of the Resolutions of Kentucky in '98 and '99 from misconstructions led Madison to the task of vindicating the proceedings of Virginia. The nullifying doctrine. [Draft.] Scrap of paper.

1832, March 22, Montpellier. Acknowledging letter of 17th. Opinions on the tariff. In its present form a source of discontent. Serious effects threatened. Consequences of a Southern convention. Threats of disunion. [Draft.] "Confidential." Strip of paper.

1833, June —, Montpellier. Acknowledging letter of May 28. Madison's opinion on the retention of the land bill by the President. A compromising tariff will avoid a renewal of the contest between the North and South. Progress in manufacturing. Improvements in machinery. The future of Virginia. Rapid exhaustion of the soil in cultivating tobacco. [Draft.] 4°. 2 pages.

1835, January 31, Montpellier. Acknowledging copy of Clay's report on our relations with France. It is able and laudable in its object of avoiding war without incurring dishonor. [Draft.] 4°. 2 pages.

CLOWES, TIMO.

1827, June 19, Montpellier. Acknowledging letters of May 4 and 25. Matters connected with the University of Virginia. [Copy.]

COCKE, J. H.

1827, August 3, September 5, October 21, November 2, 15, and 19, December 4 and 9; 1828, February 9, March 9, April 4, Montpellier. Eleven letters relating to the University of Virginia. Filling of vacancies, etc. [Drafts.] 10 strips of paper.

COGSWELL, WM. Rev.

1834, March 10, Montpellier. Acknowledging letter of 18th. Claims no credit for being the "writer of the Constitution of the United States." It was not the offspring of a single brain. Apologizes for not acknowledging two pamphlets. His extreme age. Criticises Cogswell's sermon. [Drafts.] "Private." Strip of paper.

COLES, EDWARD.

1823, May 23, Montpellier. Acknowledging letter of April 25, on the question of filling vacancies to office during recess, not only of State governments but of the Federal Government. [Draft.] fol. 1 page.

1830, November 8, Montpellier. Acknowledging letter of 4th. The judicial power of the United States. The relation between Federal and State Courts. [Draft.] 4°. 2 pages.

1831, June 28, Montpellier. The claim of the new States to the Federal lands within their limits. He always viewed the claim as just. Private business matters. The crops and prospects of prices. [Draft.] 4°. 2 pages.

1834, August 29, Montpellier. Acknowledging letter of 17th. Has withdrawn from party agitations because of the debilitating effects of age and disease. The charge of the President's claiming a power over the public money. Removal of the deposits. Strictures on the President's proclamation. Does not think that nullification is less dangerous than the popularity of the doctrines of the President. The discontent of South Carolina is susceptible of contagion in the Southern States. [Draft.] 4°. 3 pages.

1834, October 3, Montpellier. Acknowledging letter of 15th September. Remits a check, being the proceeds of a sale of some slaves to kinsmen to whom they gladly consent to be transferred. [Signed J. M.] [Draft of a dictated letter.] 4°. 1 page.

1834, October 15, Montpellier. Acknowledging letter of 15th. Comparative danger from the popularity and example of the President and the doctrines of South Carolina. The bank, tariff, and nullification discussed at length. Innovation in the Senate for a discretionary regulation of the terms of offices. Removals and appointments in diplomatic and consular situations. [Draft.] 4°. 4 pages.

COLMAN, HENRY.

1826, August 25, Montpellier. Colman's oration on the 4th of July. Criticises a passage therein. [Draft.] 4°. 2 pages.

COMEGYS, CORNELIUS. *Kent County, Md.*

1809, March 21, Washington. Acknowledging letter of 16th, inclosing proceedings of the Democratic citizens of Kent County, Md., and expressing thanks for kind mention of himself in those proceedings. [Draft.] 4°. 1 page.

COMMITTEE OF CITIZENS PEYTON, GRIMES, AND OTHERS.

1832 (?), no date, Montpellier. Declining an invitation to a dinner to be given to John M. Patton, Representative to Congress. Is gratified at the attention. His sympathies for the Republican party. [Draft.] 8°. 2 pages.

CONFEDERACIES, ANCIENT AND MODERN.

Not dated. A copy, in Madison's handwriting, of a description of the ancient and modern confederacies. 18°. 40 pages.

CONGRESSIONAL COMMITTEE.

1782, July 5. Report of the committee consisting of Madison, Duane, and Clymer relative to revision of the instructions of Mr. Adams (minister to England) respecting the proposed treaty of peace with the United Provinces. [In Madison's handwriting.] fol. 2 pages.

CONSTITUTION OF THE UNITED STATES.

1787 (?), not dated. Prefatory sketch and scraps belonging to the debates on the Constitution. 4°. 16 pages.

CONSTITUTION, AMENDNENTS TO.

1789. Notes for a speech in favor of amendments of the Constitution by Congress, giving reasons for urging the same. 8°. 2 pages.

CONSTITUTIONAL DRAFTS.

1787 (?), not dated. Notes on constitutional drafts. fol. 2 pages.

CONSULAR ACCOUNTS.

Not dated. Memorandum respecting consular accounts. Recommendations. 4°. 2 pages.

CONTESTED ELECTIONS.

Not dated. Notes, in Madison's hand, of a contested election. 4°. 1 page and strip of paper.

CONVENTION, FEDERAL, 1787.

1787. Notes, in Madison's hand, entitled "Originals of appendix to debates in the convention of 1787" including copy of a letter from Gen. James M. Varnum to Gen. Washington, June 18, 1787, respecting the action of the Rhode Island legislature, also a letter from John Brown and 12 other citizens of Rhode Island to the chairman of the Federal Convention, dated May 11, 1787. 4°. 8 pages and strip of paper.

1787. Introduction to the debates of the Federal Convention. In Madison's handwriting. 4°. 5 pages. 8°. 12 pages.

1787, May 28. Observations on a plan of government submitted to the Federal Convention in Philadelphia by Charles Pinckney, delegate from South Carolina. fol. 3 pages.

1787. A collection of memoranda, notes, drafts of speeches, reports, etc., without date or sequence, relating to the convention of 1787 in Philadelphia. Many of the papers written at a subsequent period. 31 pieces and 4°. 14 pages.

COOLIDGE, MRS. E.

1830, April 8, Montpellier. Acknowledging letter of 20th, with the anticipated review of the published correspondence of her grandfather. Compliments the author. [Draft.] Scrap of paper.

COOLIDGE, JOS., JR.

1827, June 8, Montpellier. Acknowledging letter of May 28. Vacancy in the chair in the University of Virginia lately filled by Mr. Key. [Draft.] Scrap of paper.

COOPER, THOMAS.

1810, September 4, Washington. Acknowledging letter of 19th August. Has transmitted his request to Mr. Warden in Paris. [Draft.] 4°. 1 page.

1824, March 22, Montpellier. Has read Cooper's pamphlet on the tariff. His views on the subject. [Draft.] 4°. 2 pages.

1826, December 26, Montpellier. Acknowledging letter of November 15, with copies of lectures on political economy. Impossibility of accounting for the support of a family on the minute farms of the Romans as alleged. Lectures on civil government by Cooper. The term "National" in contradistinction from the term "Federal." [Copy.] 4°. 3 pages.

CORPORATION OF CITY OF NEW YORK, COMMITTEE OF.

1826, May 31, Montpellier. His views relating to the Erie Canal. Acknowledges receipt of a gold medal presented by order of the common council. [Draft.] 4°. 1 page.

COX, JOHN.

1806. Canceled notes payable to John Cox, dated March 19, 1806, and May 21, 1806, respectively. 2 strips of paper.

COXE, TENCH.

1819, February 12, Montpellier. Acknowledging letter of 2d instant, with printed addition to his memoir relating to cotton. Great Britain intent on supplanting our cotton staple in her markets. Anticipates fall in prices of cotton, tobacco, and grain if peace continues. [Draft.] 4°. 2 pages.

1820, March 20, Montpellier. Acknowledging letter of 7th. Had written to the President on the subject of Coxe's son. Our vacant territory an outlet for the unfortunate part of our population. Cultivation of the vine. Cotton and cotton fabrics. Contest with Great Britain for reciprocity in the West India trade. [Copy.] 4°. 4 pages.

1820, November 4, Montpellier. Acknowledging letter of 12th October. Politics. Allegations on the Southern ascendency. Erroneous ideas. Asks to procure for him certain debates of Congress and other public pamphlets. [Copy.] 4°. 3 pages.

1823, February 21, Montpellier. Acknowledges two letters. Has forwarded them to Mr. Jefferson. Has grounds for believing that with himself he will take no part in the coming Presidential election. [Draft.] small 4°. 1 page.

1823, March 1, Montpellier. Mr. Jefferson returns Coxe's two letters and papers, annexing a line requesting Madison to answer on account of a lame hand. He will abstain strictly from the Presidential election, not even expressing a sentiment on the subject of candidates. [Draft.] Strip of paper.

1823, October 12, Montpellier. Acknowledges a letter inclosing a printed pamphlet about an asylum. Indignation at the outrage committed by publication of private confidence. [Draft.] 4°. 1 page.

COXE, TENCH.

1823, November 3, Montpellier. Acknowledging letter postmarked October 27. Thanks him for dispensing with answers to Coxe's letters. Sensible of his kindness in repelling attacks on Madison. Coxe's solicitude for the memory of Franklin. [Draft.] 4°. 1 page.

CRANCH, W. *Washington.*

1835, July 25, Montpellier. Acknowledging receipt of letter of 20th, informing him of his unanimous election as president of the Washington National Monument Society, in the place of the late Chief Justice Marshall. Takes a deep interest in the association and accepts the appointment. [Draft.] 8°. 1 page.

CRAWFORD, W. H.

1815, no date, Washington. Instructions in filling blanks for the execution of the proclamation relative to squatters on lands ceded to Gen. Jackson. (Memorandum attached relative to the above, signed W. H. C.) [Draft.] 8°. 1 page. 4°. 1 page.

1816, June 21, Montpellier. Returns letter of General Gaines with the papers connected with it. Amicable negotiations may put an end to all difficulties. Distressing case presented by Gen. Cass. [Draft.] 4°. 3 pages.

1816, September 21, Montpellier. Acknowledging letter of 19th, relative to squatters on public lands. Practicability of obtaining by just means everything from the Indians. The fort on the Chattahoochie. If Spain will not prevent attacks on us we must defend ourselves. [Draft.] 4°. 1 page.

1816, September 23, Montpellier. A confidential communication received from Monroe, made by Col. Jessup. Onis's intriguing at New Orleans. Gen. Jackson is apprised of the apprehensions of Gen. Jessup. His intelligence is communicated to the Secretary of the Navy. [Draft.] 4°. 1 page.

1817, February 3, Washington. Returns papers inclosed to Mr. Crawford relating to resumption of specie payments. Negotiations and arrangements with delegates from banks in New York, Philadelphia, Baltimore, and Virginia. [Draft.] fol. 1 page.

1817, April 24, Montpellier. Acknowledging letter of 18th. Thanks him for some lupenella seed, which he will plant. British affairs are approaching a paroxysm. But for the terrors of the French revolution there would be a radical change in the monarchical system. The Whig party will be divided. [Draft.] 4°. 2 pages.

1820, February 12, Montpellier. Acknowledging letter of 12th with a medal from Count Marbois. Asks Crawford to make his acknowledgments for this token of his polite attention. [Draft.] 8°. 1 page.

1821, February 15, Montpellier. Recommending Mr. Hackley for an appointment in East Florida. [Draft.] 4°. 1 page.

1824, April 13, Montpellier. Acknowledging letter of 8th. Incloses copy of a letter relating to the resignation of Eustis. The mission to France

CRAWFORD, W. H.

was unsolicited on Crawford's part. Thanks him for the volume of "Diplom. Française." [Draft.] 4°. 1 page.

1824, October 1, Montpellier. Returns the volume of the "Histoire Génerale de la diplo. Française." Account of the Mission of Rayneval. The view taken by Mr. Jay. [Draft.] 4°. 2 pages.

CRESSON, ELLIOTT.

1829, April 23, Montpellier. Gives sample of his handwriting for Cresson's album. [Draft.] Strip of paper.

CREYON, JOHN M. *Columbia, S. C.*

1809, October 17, Washington. Acknowledging receipt of the resolutions of the citizens of Columbia of 20th September, approving of the measures of the Government respecting foreign relations, and pledging support. 4°. 1 page.

CROCKETT, G. F. H.

1823, November 6, Montpellier. Acknowledging letter of September 24. Madison's views on capital punishment. [Draft.] Strip of paper.

CROKER, Mr. *London.*

Not dated. Observations (intended to be printed) by Madison on Mr. Croker's remarks in the British House of Commons on the American war. Relating to blockades and impressment. fol. 2 pages.

CROWNINSHIELD, B. W.

1814, December 15, Washington. Mr. Jones retiring, Madison sends a nomination to the Senate of Crowninshield as his successor in Department of Navy. Hopes he will accept. [Draft.] 4°. 1 page.

1815 or 1816, not dated, Washington. The frigate Congress, Captain Morris, to proceed to Gulf of Mexico, where he will take command of the New Orleans station. Instructions to protect our commerce and communicate and cooperate with officers commanding land forces to repel and defeat invasion by foreign armaments. [Draft.] 4°. 2 pages.

1816, June 27, Montpellier. Acknowledging letter of 25th. Returns letter from Mr. Kerr. It is due to Captain Porter to disbelieve anything impeaching his character without proof. Instructs the Secretary of the Navy to furnish Porter with an opportunity for every necessary explanation. [Draft.] 4°. 1 page.

1816, August 22, Montpellier. Instructions as to the regulation of affairs with the Dey of Algiers. [Draft.] 4°. 1 page.

CUSHING, CALEB. *Washington.*

1836, February 9, Montpellier. Acknowledging letter of 3d, inclosing a copy of his speech on the right of petition. Is unable to supply the difficulty in understanding a passage in his (Madison's) speech in the first Congress. His memory can not supply the meaning. [Draft.] 4°. 1 page.

CUTTING, Dr.

1822, December 7, Montpellier. Acknowledging note of 30th January last, with a little tract of Mr. Law on the subject of finance. Views on the subject. [Draft.] 8°. 1 page.

CUTTS, ——.

1818, March 14, Montpellier. Acknowledging letter of 5th. Corrections in the publication of a revised edition of the "Federalist," by Mr. Gideon. [Draft.] 4°. 2 pages.

CUTTS, RICHARD D.

1835, September 12, Montpellier. Acknowledging letter of 5th, asking Madison's advice on the choice of a profession. The legal profession desirable. [Draft.] 4°. 2 pages.

DADE, LAURENCE T., and others. *Orange.*

1832, June 29, Montpellier. Acknowledging an invitation to a festive celebration on the 4th July. Declines on account of indisposition and sends a toast. [Draft.] Strip of paper.

DAILEY, WILLIAM.

1834, July 20, Montpellier. Acknowledging letter of 10th. Respecting a claim for public service at the time Jefferson was Governor of Virginia. [Copy.] Scrap of paper.

DALLAS, A. J.

1795, August 23, Orange. Acknowledging letter of 3d. Madison's opinion on the treaty with Great Britain 1794 called "Jay's Treaty." fol. 7 pages.

1807, November 6, Washington. Detained letter from Admiral Berkley to Mr. Erskine. Complaint of Mr. Erskine in strong terms for the detention. [Press copy.] "Private." 4°. 3 pages.

1816, April 9, Washington. Acknowledging letter of 8th, communicating his purpose of resigning from the Treasury Department. Asks him to prolong his functions to a date indicated in his letter. Will carry away with him Madison's testimony of his invaluable services to his country. [Draft.] 4°. 1 page.

1816, July 4, Montpellier. Acknowledging letter of 29th June. The currency. Attempt to remedy the difficulties. Depreciation of Treasury notes. Hopes the State banks may enter into the means of reestablishing the proper currency. [Draft.] 4°. 2 pages.

1816, July 27, Montpellier. Acknowledging letter of 23d. Current business of the Department. Our trade with Bermuda. [Draft.] small 4°. 2 pages.

1816, August 25, Montpellier. Acknowledging several letters relating to the Treasury proposition and the decision of bank deputies at Philadelphia. Madison's opinions on the subject. [Draft.] 4°. 4 pages.

1816, September 15, Montpellier. Acknowledging letter of 11th. Business of the Treasury Department. Offer of Commodore Porter relative to site for Observatory. Proposal made to Mr. Clay bearing on the completion of the Cabinet. Matters connected with the Library. The weather and crops. [Draft.] 4°. 4 pages.

1816, September 27, Montpellier. Acknowledging letters of 20th and 21st, referring to the general state of the finances, which is satisfactory. Mr. Clay declines the War Department. [Draft.] 4°. 2 pages.

1816, October —, Montpellier. Acknowledging letter of 1st. The vacancy in the War Department. Has invited Mr. Lowndes to accept it. [Draft.] small 4°. 2 pages.

DALLAS, A. J.

1816, October 15, Washington. Mr. Crawford to enter the Treasury Department. The letter offering the War Department to Mr. Lowndes missed him. Improbability of Colonel Jessup's information relative to the Spanish squadron. [Draft.]
4°. 1 page.

1816, November 11, Washington. Asks him to prepare a statement relative to finances and condition of the Treasury to insert in his message to Congress. [Draft.] 4°. 2 pages.

DALLAS, GEO. M.

1817, March 6, Washington. Acknowledging letter of 26th February. Is pleased to learn of his intention to write the life of his father. If Madison's name as associated with his fathers adds any value to it, is not disposed to withhold it. [Draft.]
4°. 1 page.

DAVIS, J. A. G.

1829, September 29, Montpellier. Acknowledging letter of 21st. Thanks him for his offer in his own name and that of the rector of the university, of his services in preparing the report for the literary board. [Draft.] 8°. 2 pages.

DAVISON, MOSES, and others. *Cincinnati.*

1836, February 20, Montpellier. Acknowledging letter inviting him to a public dinner on the 4th of March to celebrate the expiration of the charter of the United States bank. Declines to participate. [Draft.] small 4°. 2 pages.

DEARBORN, HENRY.

1812, August 9, Washington. Acknowledging letter of 3d. Instructions relative to the campaign in Canada. Hull preparing an attack on Malden. [Draft.] 4°. 4 pages.

1812, October 7, Washington. Acknowledging letter of 30th September. The state of the war. Dearborn's success in producing apprehensions at Montreal. Instructions. [Draft.] fol. 3 pages.

1813, August 8, Washington. Acknowledging letter of 24th July. Madison's esteem and regard have not changed. Dearborn's retirement. [Copy.] "Private." 4°. 1 page.

1815, March 4, Washington. Nomination of Dearborn to be Secretary of War. Contrary to expectation the Senate did not concur, in consequence the nomination was withdrawn. [Copy.]
4°. 2 pages.

DEBLOIS, LEWIS.

1822, August 29, Montpellier. Acknowledging letter of July 23. Expresses regret at his business distress. Advises him as to the course to pursue under insolvent laws. If relief is not to be obtained from the courts, an appeal to Congress should be made in respect to the case. [Draft.]
fol. 1 page.

DECLARATION OF INDEPENDENCE.

1783, January 1. Copy of the original draft of the declaration by Jefferson. [In Madison's handwriting.] fol. 4 pages.

DE LA MOTTE, JACOB. *Savannah.*

1820, August —, Montpellier. Acknowledging letter of 7th, with his discourse on the history of the Jews. [Draft.] 4°. 1 page.

DEW, THOMAS R.

1833, February 23, Montpellier. Acknowledges letter of 15th January, with copies of pamphlets on the "Restrictive System" and "Slave Question". Views on emancipation. [Draft.] 4°. 2 pages.

DODDRIGE, PHILLIP.

1832, June 6, Montpellier. Acknowledging letter of 1st and copy of his speech on Congressional privilege. His rheumatism prevents a thorough consideration of the subject. [Draft.] 4°. 2 pages.

DOUGHERTY, Mrs.

1819, February 13, Montpellier. Acknowledges letter of 4th. Is not surprised at the misfortunes of Shorter. His bad habits. Sends check for $20. [Draft.] Strip of paper.

DRAKE, DANIEL, Dr.

1835, January 12, Montpellier. Has received copy of the "History, Character, and Prospects of the West." His views. [Draft.] 8°. 1 page.

DRAYTON, JOHN.

1821, September 23, Montpellier. Acknowledges receipt of a copy of memoirs. Is valuable not only to those who are interested in local details but a fund for materials for a general history of the American Revolution. [Draft.] 8°. 1 page.

DUER, W. A.

1833, September —, Montpellier. Acknowledging letter of 28th August, inclosing outlines of his work on the constitutional jurisprudence of the United States. Concerning the University of Virginia. [Draft.] 4°. 2 pages.

EARLY, PETER (Governor). *Milledgeville, Ga.*

1814, December 18, Washington. Acknowledging letter of 2d, with resolutions of the legislature of Georgia, expressing their dissatisfaction of the terms of peace demanded by the enemy. [Draft.] 4°. 1 page.

EATON, J. H.

1833 (?), not dated. Respecting money advanced by John H. Eaton to Duff Green, editor of the "Telegraph," a Jackson party newspaper. [Copy.] 4°. 2 pages.

ECCLESTON, PLANTAGENET.

1810, no date. Acknowledges receipt of a medallion of Gen. Washington. [Draft.] 4°. 1 page.

EDWARDS, PIERREPONT.

1806, August 4, Washington. Acknowledging letters of 30th and 31st ultimo. Proceedings in the case of Smith & Ogden. [Draft.] 4°. 2 pages.

ELLIOTT, JONATHAN.

1826, November 25, Montpellier. Acknowledging letter of 21st. Gives him a list of the proceedings of the State conventions on the Constitution of the United States in Madison's possession. [Draft.] 4°. 1 page.

1827, February 14, Montpellier. Acknowledging letter of 12th, with copy of a volume of debates of the State conventions on the Constitution of the United States. Sends him copy of debates in the Pennsylvania convention and of the two North Carolina conventions. [Draft.] 4°. 1 page.

ELLIOTT, JONATHAN.

1827, November —, Montpellier. Acknowledging letter of 12th, respecting debates of the State conventions on the question of adopting the Constitution of the United States. [Draft.]
Scrap of paper.

ENGELBRECHT, JACOB.

1825, October 20, Montpellier. Referring to a letter of October 20, 1825, in which was ascribed to Dr. Franklin some verses which, on critical examination, proves to be an imitation of his handwriting. Asks him to return the letter. [Draft.]
small 4°. 1 page.

1827. June 20, Montpellier. Correcting a statement made in his letter of October 20, 1825, as to the handwriting of Dr. Franklin. It was in imitation of it. [Draft.] 8°. 1 page.

ERVING, GEORGE W. *Madrid.*

1805, November 1, Washington. Sends by Mr. Smith instructions for his conduct at Madrid. The impression made on this country by Spain's proud and perverse conclusions to the endeavors of Monroe and Pinckney to adjust our differences, should be faithfully reported to her. England's foolish depredations on our commerce.
[Press copy.] 4°. 3 pages.

EUSTIS, WILLIAM.

1809, March 7, Washington. Inclosing commission as Secretary of War. [Draft.] 4°. 1 page.

1809, August 30, Montpellier. Expedient that the commander-in-chief of the territory of Orleans should be at the seat of Government. Requests instructions be transmitted to that effect. Copy of correspondence between the Navy Department and Capt. Porter inclosed. [Draft.]
4°. 1 page.

1812, December 4, Washington. Acknowledging letter of 3d. Eustis's purpose to resign. Pays his tribute to his worth and zeal. Asks his official continuance until replaced by a successor.
[Draft.] 4°. 1 page.

1813, November 12, Washington. Acknowledging letter of 7th. Relating to an appointment of collector at Boston. [Draft.] 4°. 1 page.

1814, September 28, Washington. Offers Eustis to name him to the Senate as envoy to United Netherlands. [This draft of a letter is written on same page with one addressed to Governor Tompkins of same date.] [Draft.] 4°. 1 page.

1814, December 15, Washington. Has nominated him as minister to the Netherlands. [Draft.]
4°. 1 page.

The Hague.

1816, May 12, Washington. Acknowledging letters of August 10 and December 9. The Dutch humiliation. Baron de Nagel on the violation of local sovereignty in case of impressed seamen. The allies in restoring Louis to the throne have compelled him to indemnify sufferers from spoliations of Napoleon. Efforts will be made by the United States to obtain indemnities due. Standing armies of Great Britain and Russia. The peace of Paris not auspicious as to its duration.
[Duplicate.] 4°. 6 pages.

EUSTIS, WILLIAM.

1817, March —, Washington. On consultation with Mr. Monroe it was understood that Eustis's stay in Holland would be prolonged for purpose of negotiating a commercial treaty. Monroe's friendly disposition toward Eustis. Madison's intention to retire to private life at his farm. Introduces William Preston. [Draft.] 4°. 2 pages.

1819, July 6, Montpellier. Thinks Eustis should not bury in silence his knowledge of interesting events relating to American history. Asks him to pay him a visit. 4°. 2 pages.

1823, May 22, Montpellier. Acknowledging letter of 10th. Congratulates him on the triumphant vote which restores a prodigal sister to the bosom of the Republican party and his election as governor. Remarks on the distinctions of the Republican and Federal parties. [Draft.] 4°. 2 pages.

1823, June 14, Montpellier. Acknowledging letter of 6th and his address to the legislature of Massachusetts. Strictures on the Federalists of New England. [Draft.] 4°. 2 pages.

EVANS, ROBERT J.

1819, June 15, Montpellier. Acknowledging letter of 3d. Madison's views on the extinction of slavery in the United States. Should be gradual, equitable, and satisfactory to the individuals immediately concerned, and consistent with the existing and durable prejudices of the nation. [Draft.] 4°. 9 pages.

EVANS, THOMAS. *Accomac County, Va.*

1809, May —, Washington. Acknowledging receipt of a copy of the proceedings of a meeting of citizens at Accomac Court House of 1st, approving of the measures of the President respecting the late negotiations with Great Britain. 4°. 2 pages.

EVE, GEORGE.

1789, January 2. Madison's views on the amendments to the Federal Constitution. [Draft.] 4°. 3 pages.

EVERETT, EDWARD.

1822, March 9, Montpellier. Acknowledging letter of February 14th. Madison's opinions on a book sent him by Everett and his brother on "Europe." [Draft.] 4°. 1 page.

1823, February 18, Montpellier. Acknowledging letter of 9th Views respecting Jay's treaty. [Draft.] 4°. 4 pages.

1823, March 29, Montpellier. Acknowledging letter of 2d. Jay's treaty. Virginia University. Harvard theological professorships. Sectarian seminaries. Rumors of Madison's being engaged in writing a political history. Profits of authorship in England and United States. [Draft.] 4°. 4 pages.

1823, November 26, Montpellier. Acknowledging letter of October 30th, accompanied by a treatise on population and combating the theory of Malthus. Madison's views on the subject. [Draft.] 4°. 2 pages.

1825, April 22, Montpellier. Acknowledging a letter informing him of his election as honorary member of the Bunker Hill Monument Association. His acknowledgments. [Draft.] Strip of paper.

EVERETT, EDWARD.

1825, July 19, Montpellier. Acknowledging receipt of a copy of his oration at Concord on 19th April. Is pleased with it. [Draft.] Strip of paper.

1827, June 3, Montpellier. Thanks him and his brother for their work on "America." Corrects an error where it is stated Washington wavered in his mind upon the Constitution. Madison testifies from his own knowledge that on the contrary signed it with cordiality and was anxious for its ratification. [Copy.] 4°. 1 page.

1828, June 1, Montpellier. Acknowledges receipt of copy of speech on February 1. Policy and practice of diplomatic missions. [Draft.] Strip of paper.

1830, April 2, Montpellier. Incloses letter to Mr. Sparks. Thanks him for Webster's and Sprague's speeches. Debates on Foote's resolutions. [Draft.] Strip of paper.

1830, August 5, Montpellier. Thanks him for copy of his address on the centennial anniversary of the arrival of Governor Winthrop at Charlestown. Also for his able speech on the Indian subject. [Draft.] Strip of paper.

1830, August 20, Montpellier. Acknowledging letter of 11th. Respecting the Virginia resolutions of 1798 and Kentucky of 1799. The question of Jefferson's authorship in which the term "Nullification" appears. [Draft.] 4°. 2 pages.

1830, August 28, Montpellier. Acknowledging a letter in which he refers to the "Nullifying Doctrine" advocated as a constitutional right, and the proceedings of the Virginia legislature in 1798-'99. Madison's ideas on the subject. [Draft.] 4°. 6 pages and a strip of paper.

1830, September 10, Montpellier. No proof that Mr. Jefferson wrote the draft of manuscript of the Kentucky resolutions of 1799 in which the term "Nullification" appears. [Draft.] Strip of paper.

1830, October 7, Montpellier. Acknowledging letter of 28th September, with copy of North American Review bearing on debates in conventions of States. Corrects an error in his printed letter. Mr. Everett errs in saying that Madison wrote the greater part of the "Federalist." The greater part was by Col. Hamilton. [Draft.] Scrap of paper.

1832, May 30, Montpellier. Acknowledges receipt of Mr. Doddridge's speech on subject of Congressional privileges. The judicial act of 1789. [Draft.] Strip of paper.

1833, August 22, Montpellier. Thanks him for copy of his 4th July address at Worcester. [Draft.] Strip of paper.

1834, October 22, Montpellier. Acknowledges receipt of copy of the eulogy on Lafayette. Mr. Binney's speech. [Draft.] Scrap of paper.

FARRAR, —— (Professor).

1827, May 4, and June 18, Montpellier. Relating to the vacancy in the University of Virginia caused by the resignation of Mr. Key, professor of mathematics. [Drafts.] 2 strips of paper.

1827, June 7, Montpellier. Acknowledging letter of May 17. Thanks him for copy of volumes on astronomy [Draft.] Scrap of paper.

FEATHERSTONHAUGH, G. W.

1820, June —, Montpellier. Acknowledges letter of 1st, with a pamphlet containing an "Address from the Board of Agriculture of the State of New York to the County Societies". [Draft.] 4°. 1 page.

1820, December 23, Montpellier. Acknowledging letter of 7th. Relating to agriculture. Formation and food of plants. Chemistry. [Draft.] 4°. 2 pages and strip of paper.

1821, March —, Montpellier. Thanks for first volume of memoirs published by the agricultural board. Remarks on the chemical doctrine with regard to elements of organized matter. [Draft.] 4°. 2 pages.

1821, April 5, Montpellier. Acknowledging letter of March 19. Opinion as to the reception of his new edition of his agricultural work in the South. [Draft.] 4°. 1 page.

1826, March 11, Montpellier. Acknowledging letter of 25th instant (sic), and the volume of Agricultural Memoirs. The new breeds of cattle. [Draft.] 4°. 1 page.

1828, March 13, Montpellier. Acknowledging letter of February 28. Congratulates him on his return from across the ocean with his geological spoils. Importance of the knowledge of geology. [Draft.] Strip of paper.

1833, December 8, Montpellier. Acknowledging letter of 6th. Public attention in Virginia turning toward the mineral resources of the State. [Draft.] Strip of paper.

FENDALL, P. R.

1833, June 12, Montpellier. Acknowledging letter of 6th about the exhausted state of the treasury of the Colonization Society. Sends him $50. [Draft.] Strip of paper.

FINCH, JOHN.

1824, June —, May 13, 1828, and June 20, 1829, Montpellier. Three letters acknowledging copies of Finch's "Tertiary Formations," "Celtic Antiquities," "Physical Geography," and "Boundaries of Empires." The views on his ingenious speculations. [Drafts.] On 3 strips of paper.

FLETCHER and TOLER (Editors Lynchburg Virginian).

1827, October 10, 14, and 31, Montpellier. Three letters correcting statements on published articles on the powers of Congress to regulate trade. [Drafts.] 4°. 1 page and two strips of paper.

FLORIDA CLAIMS.

Not *dated.* Recommendation in Madison's handwriting of taking possession of Florida. 4°. 1 page.

FOORD, JAMES. *Milton, Mass.*

1812, May 18, Washington. Acknowledging receipt of the memorial of the inhabitants of Milton on the subject of vaccination. Has had the interesting papers inclosed therein distributed. [Draft.] 4°. 1 page.

FOOT, SAMUEL A., and others. *New York.*

1834, December 20, Montpellier. Declines an invitation of the New England Society of New York to a dinner on the 22d to celebrate the anniversary of the principles and virtues of their Pilgrim Fathers. [Draft.] 8°. 2 pages.

FRANCIS, JOHN W.

1831, July 9, Montpellier. Acknowledging letter of 4th. Noticing the death of Monroe. A hero and patriot. Madison's affection for him. [Draft.] Scrap of paper.

1831, November 7, Montpellier. Acknowledging letter of 28th October. Thanks him for his address to the Philolexian Society of Columbia College. Madison's friendly relations to Chancellor Livingston and Monroe. Their negotiations for the transfer of Louisiana. [Copy.] small 4°. 2 pages.

GAINES, EDMUND P. (General).

1826, November 15, Montpellier. Acknowledging letter of October 16. Madison's recollection too faint to relate what passed at an interview in reference to his court-martial. Commends Gen. Gaines's purpose to authenticate and preserve truths connected with his conspicuous services against traditional injustice. [Draft.] 4°. 1 page.

GALES, JOSEPH.

1821, June 26, Montpellier. Acknowledging letter of 22d. Mr. Jay's desire to obtain his political essays in newspaper form. Madison declines the offer to make of the Intelligencer the medium for contradicting erroneous published suggestions. [Drafts.] 4°. 1 page.

1821, August 26, Montpellier. Acknowledging letter of 20th, with extracts of notes from the convention of 1787, in a New York paper. Views about a proposed publication. [Draft.] 4°. 2 pages.

GALES & SEATON.

1818, February 2, Montpellier. Acknowledging letter of January 26. Approves of the proposed work on a legislative history of this country. Will contribute any suggestions as to the sources from which materials may be drawn. [Draft.] 4°. 1 page.

1833, August 5, Montpellier. Acknowledging letter of 29th July. Lloyd's debates. Suggestions where debates of that period may be found. [Draft.] Strip of paper.

GALLATIN, ALBERT. *Washington.*

1810, January 26, Washington. The sword purchased by Mr. Livingston for the State of Virginia. Its cost, and suggestions as to the balance being paid by the State and not by the United States. Memorandum on the back by Mr. Harrison relative to the same. small 4°. 1 page.

1810, August 29, Montpellier. Acknowledging letter of 8th. The Treasury deposits decreasing. Relief to the banks. The French decree releasing American property in Holland. [Draft.] 4°. 1 page.

1813, August 2, Washington. The painful manner in which the Senate has mutilated the mission to St. Petersburg. Explanations and instructions. [Draft.] "Private." 4°. 5 pages.

1817, March —, Washington. Resumption of specie payments. Struggle of our manufacturers. High price of agricultural products. Proposed reciprocation of British West India navigation. Anticipations of retirement to his farm. [Draft.] 4°. 2 pages.

GALLATIN, ALBERT.

1827, April 9, Montpellier. Relative to salaries of professors in the University of Virginia. Qualifications for applicants for vacancies. [Draft.] Strip of paper

1829, July 13, Montpellier. Introduces Mr. Rives, who is about to embark for France. [Copy.] Strip of paper.

GALUSHA, JONAS (Governor of Vermont).

1812, November 30, Washington. Acknowledging letter of 7th communicating a resolution of the general assembly of Vermont pledging their coöperation with the General Government and nation in the present contest with England. [Draft.] 4°. 1 page.

GANO, A. G., and others. *Cincinnati.*

1835, March 25, Montpellier. Acknowledging letter of 13th, inviting him to a celebration by the native citizens of Ohio on the anniversary of her first settlement in 1788. Is obliged to decline. [Draft.] Strip of paper.

GARNETT, R. S.

1824, February 11, Montpellier Acknowledging letter of 5th instant, with copy of the "New Views, etc." Criticism of the work. [Draft and copy.] fol. 2 pages. 4°. 2 pages.

Washington.

1821, February 20, Montpellier. Acknowledging receipt of the report of the Committee on Agriculture. [Draft.] 4°. 1 page.

GEDDES, JOHN. *Columbia, S. C.*

1813, December —, Washington. Acknowledging letter of 18th inclosing the address of the South Carolina legislature approving the war and of Madison's public conduct. fol. 2 pages.

GIDEON. JACOB.

1818, January 28, Montpellier. Acknowledging letter of 19th. Sends him a copy of the Federalist, first edition. Corrections for the second edition suggested. [Draft.] 4°. 1 page and strip of paper.

1818, February 20, Montpellier. Acknowledging letter of 12th. Relative to a proposed new edition of the Federalist. [Draft.] 4°. 1 page.

1818, August 20, Montpellier. Acknowledging letter of 15th, with copy of Gideon's edition of the Federalist. [Draft.] 4°. 1 page.

GILES, W. B.

1827, September 8, Montpellier. Acknowledging letter of 4th. Is unable to comply with his request to supply him with copies of the journals of the general assembly of May, 1779 and 1782. [Draft.] Strip of paper.

GILMER, THOS. W.

1830, September 6, Montpellier. Acknowledging letter of August 31. The expediency of promoting public education at the public expense of youths of distinguished characters whose parents are poor. [Draft.] 4°. 1 page.

GILMORE, THOMAS W. and others. *Charlottesville.*

1834, June, —, Montpellier. Acknowledging letter in behalf of citizens of Albemarle to partake of a dinner on the approaching Fourth of July. He is obliged to decline from debility and indisposition. [Draft.] 4°. 2 pages.

GILPIN, HENRY D.

1827, October 25, Montpellier. Acknowledging letter of 9th, with Gilpin's life of Thomas Jefferson. Corrects some errors. Sends him a manuscript reviewing the state of parties during the earliest proceedings of Congress. [Draft.] 4°. 1 page.

1828, January 10, Montpellier. Acknowledging letter of 4th. Does not object to the use of his name in the dedication of his work. [Draft.] Scrap of paper.

1828, January 14, Montpellier. Prefers he use some other name in the inscription of his work. [Draft.] Strip of paper.

GILPIN, JOSHUA.

1822, March 11, Montpellier. Acknowledging letter of February 8, and a little volume on the Delaware and Chesapeake Canal. Thinks well of it. [Draft.] 4°. 1 page.

GLASS, FRANCIS.

1821, April 8, Montpellier. Acknowledging letter of March 3. Would prefer that he would dedicate his "Life of Washington written in Latin for the Use of Schools" to some one who has a more critical knowledge of the language. [Draft.] 4°. 1 page.

GOLDSBOROUGH, ROBERT H.

1835, December 21, Montpellier. Acknowledges letter of 15th with some tobacco seed. Remarks on the culture of tobacco. [Draft.] 8°. 1 page.

GRAHAM, GEORGE.

1827, April 5, Montpellier. Acknowledging letter of March 31, with report of committee on the charges against Graham. Groundlessness of the charges. Asks Graham to procure for him a copy of certain papers relating to origin of the "Constitution of Virginia" and "Declaration of Rights." [Draft.] Strip of paper.

GRAHAM, JOHN.

1813, August 28, Montpellier. Acknowledging letter of the 26th. The letter from Turreau, the French minister, to R. Smith. Attempt to cover a rudeness. [Draft and transcript.] 4°. 7 pages.

GRAY, W. F. *Fredericksburg.*

1823, May 24, Montpellier. Acknowledges receipt of several reviews. [Draft.] Strip of paper.

1823, October 24, Montpellier. Thanks for collecting a sum which will settle his account with him, and the surplus to remain on account. [Draft.] Strip of paper.

1828, December 16, Montpellier. Sends $30 to balance account. Directions as to commissions. [Draft.] Scrap of paper.

GRIMKE, THOMAS S.

1828, January 15, Montpellier. Thanks him for a copy of a report on the question of reducing the laws of South Carolina to the form of a code. Madison's opinions. [Draft.] small 4°. 2 pages.

1833, January 10, Montpellier. Acknowledges receipt of his letter to the people of South Carolina. Comments on the same. [Draft.] Strip of paper.

GRIMKE, THOMAS S.

1833, August 10, Montpellier. Thanks him for "Oration on 4th July" and his letter on temperance. The subject of autographs. 4°. Strip of paper.

1834, January 6, Montpellier. Acknowledging letter of last August. Sends Grimke autographs of distinguished Americans. Reasons for not sending more of them. Errors corrected in Mr. Grimke's pamphlet relating to the formation of the Constitution of the United States. [Draft.]
4°. 2 pages and strip of paper.

GURLEY, R. R.

1831, December 28, Montpellier. Acknowledging letter of November 21. Madison's views on the principles and measures of the Colonization Society. [Draft.] 4°. 2 pages.

1833, February 19, Montpellier. Acknowledging letter of 12th, informing Madison of his election to office of president of the American Colonization Society. Sensible of the honor, but his advanced age and impaired health leaves him inadequate to the duties of the station. [Draft.]
4°. 1 page.

1833 (?), no date, Montpellier. Acknowledging letter of 31st, requesting a letter of introduction for Mr. Brooks to the friends of American Colonization Society in England and France. [Draft.]
Strip of paper.

HALL, EDWARD. *Salem County,* N. J.

1809, March 18, Washington. Acknowledging receipt of the proceedings of the Republican delegates of the several townships of the county of Salem on the 3d, approving of the measures of the General Government at the present crisis of our foreign relations. [Draft.] 4°. 1 page.

HAMILTON, A., respecting.

1826, January 25, Montpellier. Remarks on an extract from Hamilton's report published in the Richmond Enquirer on the constitutionality of the bank. [Draft.] 4°. 1 page.

HAMILTON, ALEXANDER, JR. (?).

1831, July 9, Montpellier. Acknowledging letter of June 30. The death of Monroe. Their long and uninterrupted friendship. [Draft.]
Strip of paper.

HAMILTON, J.

1828, December 13, Montpellier. Thanks him for copy of his speech on October 21. Does not concur in its doctrines. Sends Hamilton pamphlet edition of the alien-sedition acts and the Virginia and Kentucky proceedings. [Draft.] Strip of paper.

HAMILTON, PAUL.

1812, December 31, Washington. Acknowledging letter of 30th, signifying his purpose of retiring from the Navy Department. [Draft.] 4°. 1 page.

HARRISON, GESNER, Dr.

1828, August 10, Montpellier. Incloses appointment as professor of ancient languages in the University of Virginia. [Copy.] Scrap of paper.

1828, August 10, Montpellier. Appointment as professor of ancient languages at University of Virginia. [Copy.] 8°. 1 page.

HARRISON, JESSE B.

1828, August 15, Montpellier. Acknowledging letter 3rd. Relative to the vacancy in the chair of languages in the University of Virginia. [Draft.] Strip of paper.

HARRISON, W. H.

1821, February 1, Montpellier. Acknowledging letter of 22d January. Madison's opinion of the character of Gen. Pike. [Draft.] Strip of paper.

1830, June 5, Montpellier. Acknowledging copy of Harrison's remarks on charges made against him during his diplomatic residence in Colombia. [Draft.] Strip of paper.

HASSLER, ——.

1828, March 6, Montpellier. Thanking him for a copy of the "Popular Exposition of the System of the Universe." Wishing him success for the work. [Draft.] Strip of paper.

HAWKINS, W. (Governor.)

1812, January 4, Washington. Acknowledging letter of 26th December, inclosing resolutions of the general assembly of North Carolina declaring their readiness to cooperate in vindicating the violated rights of our country. [Draft.] 4°. 1 page.

HAY, GEORGE.

1823, August 23, Montpellier. Acknowledging letter of 11th. The present method of voting for President. Madison's remarks on Mr. Hay's suggestions. [Draft.] 4°. 4 pages.

HAYNE, CHARLES EATON.

1832, August 27, Montpellier. Acknowledging letter of 12th. Remarks on "nullification." [Draft.] small 4°. 2 pages.

HAYWARD, WILLIAM. *Talbot County, Md.*

1809, March 21, Washington. Acknowledging letter of 14th covering an address from the Democratic Republican citizens of Talbot County, Md. [Draft.] 4°. 1 page.

HERTELL, THOMAS.

1829, December 20, Montpellier. Acknowledging letter of 11th November with a copy of his "Expose." The task of abolishing altogether the use of intoxicating drinks. [Draft.] 4°. 2 pages.

HILL, MARK L.

1820, April —, Montpellier. Acknowledging letter of 7th. Remarks on the Missouri question. [Draft.] small 4°. 2 pages.

HILLHOUSE, JAMES. *New Haven.*

1811, May 24, Washington. Acknowledging receipt of the petition of the inhabitants of New Haven, representing the inconveniences resulting from the existing nonimportation law and soliciting that the national legislature may be speedily convened. Explains and defends the position of the Executive. [Draft.] 4°. 4 pages.

1830, May —, Montpellier. Acknowledging letter of 10th, with a pamphlet containing the proposed amendments of the Constitution of the United States. Opinions and remarks thereon. [Draft.] 4°. 2 pages.

HINDE, THOMAS S.

1829, August 17, Montpellier. Acknowledging letter of July 23. Is not writing a history of our country. Some of his correspondence and manuscript connected with public transactions may contribute materials. The criminal enterprise in the west in Jefferson's administration. A statement of the facts may be in Madison's possession. [Draft.] Strip of paper.

HOFFMAN, DAVID.

1832, June 13, Montpellier. Thanks him for copy of a lecture delivered at University of Maryland. The distinction between bench legislation and judicial interpretation. [Draft.] Strip of paper.

HOGE, MOSES.

1820, April 22, Montpellier. Acknowledging copy of the laws of Hampden-Sydney College in which he finds his name as trustee. Declines accepting. [Draft.] 8°. 2 pages.

HOLLAND, EDWIN C. *Charleston.*

1822, November 30, Montpellier. Thanks him for his interesting pamphlet. [Draft.] Strip of paper.

HUMBOLDT, BARON VON.

1833, March 12, Montpellier. Introducing Prof. Hoffman, law professor of University of Maryland. [Draft.] Strip of paper.

HUMPHREYS, DAVID.

1813, March 23, Washington. Acknowledging letter of 19th February. Madison expresses regret that an opinion should prevail that "an alliance with France and a systematic exclusion of commerce" were entertained by the administration. Has no fears that the Union is in danger. [Draft.] 4°. 3 pages.

HUNTINGTON, EBERD.

1818, January 4, Montpellier. Acknowledging letter of 30th December. On the question whether the proposition to commute half pay was suggested by Congress to the Army or by the Army to Congress. [Draft.] 4°. 2 pages.

HURLBERT, M. L.,

1830, May —, Montpellier. Acknowledging letter of April 25th. Opinions and remarks on the pamphlet sent him relating to the proposed amendment of the Constitution of the United States. [Draft.] 4°. 2 pages.

INDIANS.

1812, Washington. Address or *talk* to a deputation of Indians of the different tribes, showing them the advantages of burying the hatchet between the tribes and assuring them of his friendship and protection. [Draft.]
fol. 4 pages and strip of paper.

INGERSOLL, C. J.

1814, July 28, Washington. Acknowledging letter of 18th. The armed neutrality of 1780. Maritime law. The question of "free ships, free goods". [Draft.] 4°. 5 pages.

1817, January 21, Washington. Acknowledging letter of 16th giving intelligence of death of Mr. Dallas. His virtues, endowments, and services. [Draft.] 4°. 1 page.

INGERSOLL, C. J.

1818, January 4, Montpellier. Acknowledging letter of 25th ultimo. His task of making a historical review of the late war. Will contribute to the stock of materials from his papers. [Draft.]
4°. 2 pages.

1825, November 8, 12, and November 17, 1827, Montpellier. Madison's views and opinions on several pamphlets sent him on political matters. [Drafts.] 3 strips of paper.

1830, January 8, Richmond. Acknowledging letter of December 26. Exercise of executive power in cases referred to without the intervention of the judiciary, as warranted by the law of nations. The debate on the case of Robbins. The convention at Richmond. Their projects. [Draft.]
Strip of paper.

INGERSOLL, C. J., and others. *Philadelphia*.

1830, October 13, Montpellier. Acknowledging an invitation of the "Penn Society" to their anniversary dinner on the 25th. Declines the invitation and offers a toast. [Draft.] Scrap of paper.

INGERSOLL, C. J.

1831, February 2, Montpellier. Acknowledging letter of January 21. State power to make banks. Asks whether the Federal power as it has been exercised is preferable to that proposed to be exercised by President Jackson. [Draft.]
4°. 2 pages.

1835, February 12, Montpellier. Received Ingersoll's view of the "committee powers of Congress". The task will be worthy the most skillful hands. [Draft.] Scrap of paper.

1835, December 30, Montpellier. Thanks him for his pamphlet comprising his address at New York. Freedom of external commerce; that it be universal, and peace perpetual among nations. [Draft.] 8°. 2 pages.

INGERSOLL, C. J., by J. C. PAYNE.

1836, May 14, Montpellier. Mr. Madison too indisposed to write himself. (He died in June.) He dictates his views on free goods and free sailors on neutral vessels. [Draft.] 8°. 2 pages.

JACKSON, ANDREW.

1835, October 11, Montpellier. Acknowledging letter of 7th with letter and medal from Mr. Goddard. The temperance subject. [Draft.]
Scrap of paper.

JACKSON, J. G.

1821, December 27, Montpellier. Acknowledging letter of 9th. Regrets circumstances have interfered for arrangement of his papers relating to his public life. The convention for forming the Constition. Reflections on republican form of government. [Draft.] fol. 4 pages.

JAY, PETER AUGUSTUS.

1833, August 14, Montpellier. Acknowledging letter of 8th. Rectifying an error, a misprint of the name Jay for Joy. [Draft.] Scrap of paper.

JEFFERSON. *Governor of Virginia*.

1780, December 13, Philadelphia. Jointly with Theodorick Bland asks instructions from their con-

JEFFERSON.

stituents respecting claims to the navigation of the Mississippi. Virginia's claims in case of the concessions of Congress to Spain. [Copy.]
4°. 3 pages.

1783, February 11, Philadelphia. Acknowledging letter of 31st January and 7th instant. Congress occupied on projects for valuation of land. Adams's letters to Congress remarkable for vanity and prejudice against French court and venom against Dr. Franklin. [Draft and duplicate.]
4°. 5 pages.

1783, February 13, Philadelphia. Sends copy of the King's speech which presages a speedy establishment of peace. Critical uncertainty.
4°. 1 page.

1783, February 15, Philadelphia. No vessel to sail until suspense is removed produced by the King's speech. If Jefferson's embarkation is wished by Congress, a French ship may be obtained by the Chevr. de la Lucerne. 4°. 2 pages.

1783, February 18, Philadelphia. Acknowledging two letters of 14th. Tokens of preliminaries of peace. Apprehension of tricks by the British court. Jefferson's mission. 4°. 2 pages.

1783, April 22, Philadelphia. Acknowledging letter of 4th. Report on funds, etc., passed Congress. Nice and interesting questions produced in the interval between preliminary and definitive treaty. The system for foreign affairs is not digested.
4°. 2 pages.

1783, May 6, Philadelphia. Acknowledging letter of 21st April. A portion of this letter in cipher. Letters from Lafayette and Carmichael show that Spain has become tractable since acknowledgment of our Independence by Great Britain. Boundaries of Florida. Navigation of the Mississippi. Appointment of a minister to Great Britain.
4°. 2 pages and a slip of paper.

1783, May 13, Philadelphia. (This letter mostly in cypher. Deciphered in handwriting of Jefferson.) Marbois's complaint of ungenerous proceeding of the British against individuals. The project for a treaty of commerce with Great Britain reported. Supposed terms. Interview between Washington and Gen. Carleton relative to evacuation of posts by the British. 4°. 4 pages.

1783, May 20, Philadelphia. Acknowledging letter of 7th. Territorial cession of Virginia.
4°. 2 pages.

1783, August 11, Philadelphia. Reserve of our foreign ministers concerning the definitive treaty with Great Britain. Congress at Princeton undecided as to their ultimate residence. The Commander-in-chief expected there. The budget of Congress. Action of different States. fol. 2 pages.

1783, September 20, Princeton. Acknowledging letter of 31st ultimo. The territorial cession. Question of the permanent seat of Congress. Negotiations for the definitive signing of the peace. Contrariety of interests. No decision yet by Congress on any of the branches of the peace establishment. 4°. 4 pages.

1783, December 10, Orange. Conversation with Mr. Mason on the impost and territorial cession. Commerce of this country in a deplorable state. Madison not yet settled in the course of law reading. Buffon's theory of central heat. Diameter and form of the earth. fol. 2 pages.

1783 (?), not dated. Fragments of a cipher letter. 3 scraps of paper.

1784, March 16, Orange. Acknowledging letter of 20th. Can not apprehend any difficulties in the delay of ratification of the peace. Cession of territories of States. Madison's intentions respecting establishing himself in his profession near Mr. Jefferson. 4°. 9 pages.

1784, April 25, Orange. Acknowledging letter of 16th March. Cipher relating to Mr. Mazzei and his proposed visit to Mr. Jefferson. His hatred to Franklin. Thinks favorably of Mr. Adams. Hatred to England. Queries respecting the treaty and other political matters. Subterranean city discovered in Siberia formerly populous and magnificent. [Translation of cipher in Jefferson's hand inclosed.] 4°. 3 pages.

1784, May 15, Richmond. Acknowledging letter of 7th, with a pair of spectacles. Hears of Jefferson's appointment to Europe. Asks permission to make use of his ideas in the revisal of the State constitution. 4°. 2 pages.

1784, July 3, Richmond. Reviews the proceedings of the general assembly now adjourned. fol. 4 pages.

1784, August 20, Orange. Acknowledging letter of July 1. Jefferson embarkation from Boston. Adjournment of the Virginia legislature. Amendment of the State constitution. Views and opinions on commerce and on foreign relations, boundaries and trade on the Mississippi. [Original and draft.] 4°. 12 pages.

1784, September 7, Philadelphia. Tour to the Eastern States proposed. Meets Lafayette, who has been visiting Mount Vernon; may accompany him on his tour. Converses with him on subject of the Mississippi. Suggests mediation of France with Spain in our behalf. 4°. 2 pages.

1784, September 15, New York. Has abandoned his plan of going further East. Lafayette in New York; is going on a trip with him to Fort Schuyler. Receives in New York a continuation of marks of cordial esteem and affection. Rumor that Indians have surprised and plundered Fort Michellemackinack, occupied by the English. 4°. 2 pages.

1784, October 11, New York. His trip with Lafayette to Fort Schuyler and the Oneida Nation. Interview with the Indians. Occupation by the British of the posts of Niagara, etc. fol. 2 pages.

1784, October 17, Philadelphia. Relates by cipher (which is deciphered by Jefferson) the particulars of his tour with Lafayette in New York State. Interviews with Indian chiefs, etc. 4°. 4 pages.

1785, January 9, Richmond. Detailed account of the proceedings of the Virginia general assembly. fol. 8 pages.

1785, April 27, Orange. Acknowledging letters of November 11 and December 8. Receives pamphlets on animal magnetism, the last aeronautic

JEFFERSON.

expedition, and phosphoretic matches. Commissions for purchase of books. Tax on transfers of land. Convention in Kentucky. Shares voted Gen. Washington by the assembly for opening rivers. Remarks in cipher on Lafayette, France, and Spain. 4°. 8 pages.

Paris.

1785, August 20, Orange. Acknowledging letter of March 18. The machinations of Great Britain with regard to commerce causing distress and noise in Boston, New York, and Philadelphia. Internal trade. Lafayette's character, etc. Local intelligence. 4°. 4 pages.

1785, October 3, Philadelphia. Conversations in New York with Virginia delegates on the affairs of the confederation. Madison's views and opinions. 4°. 4 pages.

1785, November 15, Richmond. Acknowledging letter of May 11. Matters relating to the University of Virginia. 4°. 2 pages.

1786, January 22, Richmond. Acknowledges receipt of books. Close of the session of ninety-seven days of the assembly. Details of the proceedings. 4°. 10 pages.

1786, March 18, Orange. Acknowledging letters of September 1 and 20. Plan for the capitol at Richmond. Proposed plan of meeting for a commercial convention. Prices of products. 4°. 5 pages.

1786, May 12, Orange. Acknowledging letters of February 8 and 9. Jefferson's notes printed in France will no doubt be translated, so suggests his giving out the original. Houdon's statue. The changes in late elections. Internal situation of Virginia worse. Remarks on natural history and Buffon's works. Describes certain strange American animals. 4°. 6 pages.

1786, June 19, Orange. Acknowledging letter of October 28, 1785. The poor of Europe. Political economy. Natural history of the mole and weasel. [Draft.] 4°. 4 pages.

1786, August 12, Philadelphia. Ride through Virginia, Maryland, and Pennsylvania. The crops. The Potomac at Harper's Ferry. Works on the Potomac to improve navigation. Paper money in the States. Appointment of deputies to Annapolis. Purchase of land suggested, in company with Monroe, on the Mohawk. Asks Jefferson's cooperation. 4°. 7 pages.

1786, December 4, Richmond. Acknowledging letter of April 25. Resolution of the assembly unanimously adopted to appoint commissioners to the convention in Philadelphia to devise means to render the Constitution adequate to the exigencies of the Union. Details of proceedings in the assembly. The weather and crops. 4°. 4 pages and newspaper cutting.

1787, February 15, New York. Proceedings of the Virginia assembly. Action of the States relative to the convention for amending the Constitution. Navigation of the Mississippi River. 4°. 4 pages.

1787, May 15, Philadelphia. Meeting of the convention. Among the arrivals is Gen. Washington. Received with acclamations. 4°. 1 page.

JEFFERSON.

1787, June 6, Philadelphia. Meeting of the convention 25th ultimo, Gen. Washington in the chair. Names of deputies. Mr. Adams's book excites attention. The scheme for paper money.
4°. 4 pages.

1787, July 18, Philadelphia. The sitting of the convention. Is unable to disclose their proceedings. Paper money ceased to circulate. Distress brought on the poorer classes. Popular rage. The wheat harvest. Corn and tobacco.
4°. 2 pages.

1787, September 6, Philadelphia. General propositions agreed on in the convention; in cipher translated. Disposing of public lands by Congress. Situation of affairs in Virginia. 4°. 2 pages.

1787, December 9, New York. Acknowledging letter of September 17. The procuring of fruit and other trees for Mr. Jefferson. Proceedings in the convention for adopting the Constitution. Virginia politics. 4°. 7 pages.

1788, February 19, New York. Acknowledging letter of October 8, and receipt of a watch. The proceedings of the convention for the adoption of the Federal Constitution. 4°. 4 pages.

1788, April 22, Orange. Elections for the convention for ratifying the new Constitution. State of parties. Views and opinions. 4°. 4 pages.

1788, July 24, New York. Acknowledging letters of December 20 and February 6. Ratification by Virginia of the new Federal Constitution. Proceedings of other States. 4°. 4 pages.

1788, August 10, New York. Proceedings in Congress for putting Government in operation. Place of meeting. Second convention. The Federalist.
4°. 4 pages.

1788, August 23, New York. Convention of North Carolina. Proceedings of Congress on the seat of Government. Second convention. 4°. 3 pages.

1788, September 21, New York. Report of the committee in Congress and resolution supporting the free navigation of the Mississippi. Project of another general convention. Seat of Government. Primitive structure of language. The question of Jefferson's outfit. [With copy of resolution.]
4°. 6 pages.

1788, October 8, New York. Incloses letters from Washington to Jefferson and Lafayette. Reports that Lafayette is in the Bastile, and another, heading a revolt. Law in Pennsylvania for election of general ticket. Candidates for President and Vice-President. 4°. 3 pages.

1788, October 17, New York. Jefferson's outfit. The States which have adopted the Constitution. Candidates for Vice-President. Opinions on Hancock and Adams. General views on politics.
4°. 9 pages.

1788, December 8, Philadelphia. Probability of commencement of the new Federal Government next March. Washington and Adams to be President and Vice-President. Elections under the new Government. The questions which divide the public. Talk of another convention. Count Moustier's unpopular behavior. His liaison with

JEFFERSON.

Madame de Brehan. Patrick Henry's opposition to Madison. 4°. 6 pages.

1788, December 12, Philadelphia. Elections in Pennsylvania to Congress. 4°. 2 pages.

1789, May 9, New York. Acknowledging letter of January 12. First number of Congressional Register. Discussions on impost in the House. Discriminating duties Rum and molasses. New York steeped in Anglicism. Titles to both President and Vice-President condemned by unanimous vote of House. 4°. 3 pages.

1789, May 23, New York. Introducing Mr. Colden. The President's inaugural address. Question of title. Adams and R. H. Lee in favor of titles. Their project unsuccessful. Moustier, the French minister, more acceptable. Madame de Brehan. General character of the Congress. 4°. 3 pages.

1789, May 27, New York. Acknowledging letter of March 15. The Executive Departments. Jay, Livingston, or Hamilton for foreign affairs. Knox, War Department. The bill of rates passed the House not yet come from the Senate. Discriminations in favor of nations in treaty. Action towards Great Britain. Moustier more acceptable. His commercial ideas liberal. Madame de Brehan. 4°. 4 pages.

1789, June 13, New York. Tardiness in complying with Jefferson's desire to come home. Mr. Joy returns to London. Proposed amendments to the Constitution. 4°. 2 pages.

1789, June 30, New York. Permission for Jefferson to visit America. The Federal business necessarily tardy. No precedent for legislative action. Regulation on duties. Discrimination. On our commerce with Great Britain. [Part of this letter missing.] 4°. 4 pages.

1790, January 24, New York. The business of Congress. The plans of revenue and militia. Hamilton's report on revenue. Anxiety for Jefferson's acceptance of the appointment by the President. 4°. 3 pages.

1790, February 4, New York. Acknowledging letter of January 9. On contracting and providing for public debts. Discussion of Jefferson's theory on the subject. [Copy.] 4°. 5 pages.

Philadelphia.

1791, May 1, New York. Claims of Mazzei against Dorkman. Freneau as translator. Menaces against Washington on subject of the bank. Sentiment of Rufus King adverse to conduct of Great Britain. 4°. 3 pages.

1791, May 12, New York. Mr. Adams's anti-republican discourses. 4°. 1 page.

1791, June 23, New York. Acknowledging letter of 21st. Proposed trip to the eastward. French regulations on tobacco. Hostility to England. Attack on Payne in a Boston paper under name oi "Publicola." 4°. 2 pages.

1791, June 27, New York. Col. Smith's conversations with the British ministry. Mr. Adams's attack on Payne. His anti-republican doctrines. Undecided about going to Boston. 4°. 1 page.

JEFFERSON.

1791, July 10, New York. Acknowledging letter of 6th. Jefferson's commission for maple sugar. Bank shares advanced. The public debt. Abandons his visit to the East. 4°. 2 pages.

1791, July 13, New York. Mr. Adams unpopular in Boston. "Publicola" probably the manufacture of his son. Special action in the bank stock. British politics. 4°. 3 pages.

1791, August 4, New York. Speculation in stock and scrip. 4°. 1 page.

1791, August 8, New York. The public debt to be taken up at next session. The probable cause of the movement in bank stock. 4°. 2 pages.

1792, June 12, Orange. Acknowledging two letters. Jefferson's negotiations with Mr. Hammond, the British minister. Virginia politics. Drought in Virginia. 4°. 4 pages.

1792, no date, Orange. Conversation with Col. Beckwith, relative to military supplies to the Indians by the British Government. 4°. 4 pages.

1793, April 12, Orange. Acknowledging letter of March 31. Thinks the President dissatisfied with the fiscal administration of Hamilton. Politics in Virginia. Feeling in regard to the execution of Louis XVI. Agricultural. 4°. 3 pages.

1793, May 8, Orange. Acknowledging letter of April 28. Proposition for annulling the treaty with France. The weather and crops. 4°. 2 pages.

1793, May 27, Orange. Advises him at the present condition of foreign affairs to not retire from his public position. American sentiment towards France and Mr. Genet. About plows. 4°. 2 pages.

1793, June 13, Orange. The apostacy of Dumourier. His support by the army. The hopes of France lie in the discordant views of her combined enemies. Remarks on the President's proclamation of neutrality. The weather and crops. 4°. 4 pages.

1793, June 17, Orange. Acknowledging letter of 9th. French affairs. Dumourier's treason. American sympathy with the French revolution. Weather and crops. 4°. 3 pages.

1793, June 19, Orange. Favorable anticipations for the harvest. Criticisms on the anglified complexion charged in the President's proclamation of neutrality and disregard to the stipulated duties to France. Jefferson's plan for a house. 4°. 4 pages.

1793 June 29, Orange. The weather and crops. Animadversions on the President's proclamation of neutrality. Search on American vessels for French goods while British goods are protected by the neutrality of our bottoms. 4°. 2 pages.

1793, July 18, Orange. Acknowledging letter of 7th. The publication of "Pacificus." Conduct of Genet, the French minister. The crops and weather. 4°. 2 pages.

1793, July 22, Orange. Acknowledging letter of 18th. Sentiments of W. C. Nicholas and Ed. Randolph on French affairs. Madison preparing a reply to "Pacificus." 4°. 2 pages.

JEFFERSON.

1793, July 30, Orange. Acknowledges letter of 21st. Preparations for answer to "Pacificus." Difficulties of the undertaking. Virginia politics. About new plows. 4°. 2 pages.

1793, August 5, Orange. Acknowledging letter of July 28. Conduct of Genet, the French minister. Answer to "Pacificus" by "Helvidius." 4°. 1 page.

1793, August 11, Orange. Acknowledging letter of 3rd. Relating to the answers by "Helvidius" to "Pacificus." Asks Jefferson's assistance in the matter. 4°. 3 pages.

1793, August 20, Orange. Acknowledging letter of 11th. Relating to the last number of "Helvidius's" answer to "Pacificus." The drought in Virginia. 4°. 3 pages.

1793, August 22, Monroe's. The hurry in the last answer of "Helvidius" to "Pacificus." 4°. 2 pages.

1793, August 27, Monroe's. Politics in Richmond. Mr. Wythe drawn in. A change in his political sentiments. The indiscretions of Genet. 4°. 2 pages.

1793, September 2, Orange. Acknowledging letters of 11th August and 18th instant. Sketch of resolution relative to the cultivation of friendship with France. The course of Genet. Conversation between the President and Jefferson. 4°. 6 pages.

Monticello.

1794, March 2, Philadelphia. Acknowledging letter of February 15. The "Madison resolutions." Calumnies of the British party in New England. Unfriendly features of the British policy toward the United States. The scheme to blockade the Mediterranean. Genet superceded by Fauchét. Anonymous letter charging the Eastern States with supplying British armaments in West Indies. 4°. 4 pages.

1794, March 9, Philadelphia. British instructions of November 6. Retaliatory measures suggested. Frigates to protect commerce. Wholesale military executions at Toulon. fol. 3 pages.

1794, March 12, Philadelphia. British seizure of American vessels in the West Indies. fol. 1 page.

1794, March 14, Philadelphia. Sedgwick's speech in Congress. Designs of the faction which use him as their organ. His immediate prompter. fol. 1 page.

1794, March 26, Philadelphia. Passage of the embargo bill in the House. Eastern losses in the West Indies. Charleston people excited. Hanging and burning in effigy of Smith, Ames, Arnold, Dumourier, and the devil *en groupe.* fol. 1 page.

1794, March 31, Philadelphia. Question whether the ways and means should be referred to the Treasury, passed the House. fol. 1 page.

1794, April 14, Philadelphia. The measures proposed in the House retaliatory to British outrages in the West Indies. Hamilton spoken of as minister to Great Britain. 4°. 2 pages.

1794, April 28, Philadelphia. Acknowledging letter of 3d. The nonimportation bill passed the House. Disappointment of Hamilton at not being ap-

pointed minister to Great Britain. Jay's appointment. British instructions of January 8.
4°. 2 pages.

1794, May 9, Philadelphia. Acknowledging a letter. Influence of aristocracy, anglicism, and mercantilism in New England. The people deluded into "following when Washington leads."
fol. 1 page.

1794, May 11, Philadelphia. Taxes. Employment of the House. Effect of Jay's appointment to Great Britain. The embargo still in force.
fol. 2 pages.

1794, May 25, Philadelphia. Repeal of the embargo. State of public opinion. fol. 1 page.

1794, June 1, Philadelphia. Ineffectual efforts to get a powerful military establishment. Bill for punishing certain crimes, including that of selling prizes. fol. 2 pages.

1794, November 16, Philadelphia. Acknowledging letters of October 30 and November 6. The innovation of a standing army will be attempted. The elections in several States. European affairs.
4°. 3 pages.

1794, November 30, Philadelphia. Attack on republicanism through Democratic societies. The President's speech. Answer of the Senate.
4°. 4 pages.

1794, December 21, Philadelphia. Acknowledging letters of 9th, 12th, and 20th. Crops and the weather. The attack on constitutional rights in the blow leveled at the "self-created" societies. The elections in several States. fol. 2 pages.

1795, January 11, Philadelphia. Bill in the House for revising the naturalization law defeated. Our revenue from trade increased. The French everywhere victorious. Nothing final yet from Jay. He is expected to accomplish much. Virginia politics. fol. 2 pages.

1795, January 26, Philadelphia. Acknowledging letter of December 28. Nothing received from Jay and Monroe. French victories. House of Representatives on the military establishment. The public debt. Hamilton's report on the subject. Hamilton to retire to private life. fol. 1 page.

1795, February 15, Philadelphia. Acknowledging letter of 5th. Official account of the signing of the treaty by Jay is not yet received, the public not knowing the particulars except what is gleaned from private sources. It is not considered as satisfactory. Not much in our favor. Elections in New York and Massachusetts. The military establishment in Congress. fol. 3 pages.

1795, March 23, Philadelphia. Acknowledging two letters, inclosing one for Mr. Christie, the President, and Mr. Randolph. The treaty with England not yet made public. The French less respectful to our rights on the seas.
4°. 3 pages.

1795, August 6, Philadelphia. Remonstrances against the Jay treaty. fol. 1 page.

1795, October 18, Orange. Copies extract of a cipher letter from Monroe relative to American residents connected with British merchants, and hostile to

JEFFERSON.

France. State election in Pennsylvania, hinged on destruction of treaty and anti-treaty candidates. 4°. 2 pages.

1795, November 8, Fredericksburg. The crops. Mr. Randolph's publication. 4°. 1 page.

1795, December 6, Philadelphia. Acknowledging letter of November 26. The meeting of Congress. Candidates for Speaker of the House and vacant departments. French political news. 4°. 1 page.

1795, December 13, Philadelphia. Acknowledging a letter covering one to Mon. Liancourt. Incloses the President's speech on the treaty with Great Britain. Answered by the Senate. By the House to-morrow. High price of flour. 4°. 2 pages.

1795, December 27, Philadelphia. Mr. Randolph's pamphlet. Remarks on the President's speech on the treaty. The situation perplexing. Monroe's letters speak encouragingly of French affairs, and is mortified at the rumors of ratification of Jay's treaty. High price of flour. 4°. 2 pages.

1796, January 31, Philadelphia. The original of the British ratification of the treaty not yet arrived. The treaties with Spain and Algiers ditto. The Ways and Means Committee investigating the revenues and our wants. The excise system unproductive. Gallatin sound in principles and indefatigable in his researches. The navigation project of Gen. Smith. fol. 2 pages.

1796, February 7, Philadelphia. Acknowledging letter of January 24. Aspect of British affairs more lowering. Sedition bills, bounty on foreign wheat and flour. Detention of the armament for the West Indies. Accounts from France auspicious. Fears that unrestrained exportation of breadstuffs may threaten scarcity in our country. Advocates an embargo. fol. 2 pages.

1796, February 21, Philadelphia. Relates to a business agent. Provision for the daughters of De Grasse. Bill for selling Western lands. British treaty not yet before the public. The Spanish treaty in hands of Senate. The Algerian treaty. Friendly influence of France. fol. 2 pages.

1796, February 29, Philadelphia. The treaty with Spain adjusts boundary and navigation satisfactorily, a question whether it clashes with the British treaty. Curious features in the Algerian treaty.. The President's birthday celebrated with unexampled splendor. The compliment of adjourning was rejected; vote 50 to 38. Last year 13 nays. fol. 1 page.

1796, March 6, Philadelphia. Ratification of the Algerian and Spanish treaties. Reflections on the British treaty by Jay. The carriage tax. Its constitutionality. Flour $15 per barrel. fol. 2 pages.

1796, March 13, Philadelphia. On the subject of a kitchen stove. Discussions in the House on the treaty with Great Britain. The proposition to call on the President for papers. The constitutional right of Congress in relation to treaties. The British armament in the West Indies. This will augment the price for provisions. Flour $15. fol. 1 page.

JEFFERSON.

1796, April 4, Philadelphia. Acknowledging letter of 6th. Settlement of Mazzei's business. Post-roads. Refusal by the President of the call from the House for the treaty papers. Tone of the message improper and indelicate. Letters from Monroe relating to French news. 4°. 4 pages.

1796, April 11, Philadelphia. Acknowledging letter of March 27. Discussion in the House asserting their right to judge of the expediency of treaties, stipulating on legislative subjects, and the use made of a call for papers. Discussion on the treaties. fol. 1 page.

1796, April 18, Philadelphia. The Spanish, Indian, and Algerian treaties. The British now depending in Congress. Opponents of the treaty. fol. 1 page.

1796, April 23, Philadephia. Incloses debates on the British treaty. The subject still going on in the House. fol. 1 page.

1796, May 1, Philadelphia. Acknowledging letter of April 17. The treaty question brought to a vote. Its passage. fol. 2 pages.

1796, May 22, Philadelphia. The Republican cause much crippled by the passage of the treaty with Great Britain. Gloomy letter from Monroe. France prefers an open enemy to a perfidious friend. Fears a rupture. Categorical steps on the part of France towards us, anticipated. fol. 2 pages.

1796, December 5, Philadelphia. Not certain the choice of the electors. Adams's enmity to banks and the funding system. Adet's note. Alienation feared. The policy of the Executive unknown. 4°. 2 pages.

1796, December 10, Philadelphia. Result of election still unknown. Pinkney probably will have the greatest number of votes, Adams second. Answer to the President's speech. fol. 1 page.

1796, December 19, Philadelphia. Returns not entirely in of the election. Jefferson if elected to Vice-President should not refuse to serve. Madison's opinions on Adams's course relative to France. Answer to the President's speech. 4°. 2 pages.

1796, December 25, Philadelphia. Still uncertain the results of the election. Probability of Adams's success. No foreign news. Distrust of the French Government towards our Executive. Probable dissatisfaction of the Spanish Government. Alliance with England to cause a rupture with France. Financial distress. fol. 1 page.

1797, January 8, Philadelphia. Acknowledging letter of December 17. Probable election of Adams by 71 votes and Jefferson 68. Suggests the necessity of Jefferson's presence before adjournment to be qualified as Vice-President. The special message of the President on our affairs with France not yet made. Nothing from Monroe on his recall. 4°. 2 pages.

1797, January 15, Philadelphia. Acknowledging letter of 1st, inclosing one to Adams unsealed. Has concluded to delay delivery of it for reasons mentioned. Our relations with France. Hamilton's treachery to Adams. 4°. 4 pages.

JEFFERSON.

1797, January 22, Philadelphia. Acknowledging letter of 8th. Fears of a rupture with France. Nothing from Monroe or Pinkney. Rumors of a new envoy to France. His own name mentioned. Thinks there is no truth in it. 4°. 2 pages.

1797, January 29, Philadelphia. Acknowledging a letter inclosing one to Mr. Tazewell. War with France and alliance with Great Britain talked of. Inconsistency and weakness of the Executive. Nothing known of the mind of the President-elect. Madison does not anticipate much that is consoling from him. fol. 1 page.

1797, February 5, Philadelphia. Acknowledging letter and giving notice of his going to Philadelphia. Nothing to alleviate the crisis. The French continue to prey on our trade. The British, too, not desisted. Difficult to decide on the course to pursue. Bill for collecting proposed taxes on land. 4°. 2 pages.

1797, February 11, Philadelphia. The mode of conveying notice of Jefferson's election. Adams to ask advice of Senate on the question of offices held during pleasure, are or are not vacated by the political demise of his predecessor? Conjectures as to its meaning. 4°. 2 pages.

1797, August 5, Orange. Acknowledging letter of 3d. Promises to converse with Monroe on the subject of his recall. Suggestions as to alterations of certain passages in a petition relative to functions of grand jurors. 4°. 3 pages.

1797, August 24, Orange. Monroe's correspondence with Pickering relative to his recall from France. Blount's and Liston's conspiracy.

1797, October 20, Orange. Incloses a pamphlet of Monroe's. Curious specimen of the folly of its author. Rhetorical artifices. Exaggerated complaints. Unfair and virulent persecutions of himself. Malignant insinuations against others, including Jefferson. 4°. 1 page.

Philadelphia.

1797, December 25, Orange. Private business in which Monroe is concerned. Cold weather unpromising for crops. Liston's plot. Envoyship to France. Monroe's publication. The President's prerogative of proroguing the legislature. 4°. 2 pages.

1798, January 21, Orange. Acknowledging letter of 3d. The attack on Monroe's publication. Its enormous price an obstacle to an extensive circulation. The Amherst memorial on glebes and churches. Unfavorable accounts from our plenipotentiaries. The British treaty places difficulties in adjusting negotiations. 4°. 3 pages.

1798, February 12, Orange. Acknowledging letter of January 24. The difficulties of the British treaty interrupt our negotiations in Paris. Monroe's publication. 4°. 3 pages.

1798, February —, Orange. Acknowledging letters of 7th and 8th. Public opinion on subject of arming. May save us from the rash measures of our hot-headed Executive. Comparison of our President with his predecessor. Debates in Congress relative to Lyon and Griswold. fol. 2 pages.

1798, March 4, Orange. Acknowledging letters of February 15 and 22. Tazewell's speech in defense

of his proposition to associate juries with the Senate in cases of impeachments. The affair of Lyon and Griswold extremely disgraceful.
fol. 3 pages.

1798, March 12, Orange. Acknowledging letter of 2d. Nonattendance of the Adamites at the celebration of Washington's birth night. Repeal of the stamp act. Weather and crop. fol. 1 page.

1798, April 2, Orange. Acknowledging letters of March 15 and 22. The President's message a development of his violent passions and heretical politics. Trusts Congress will not echo them.
4°. 3 pages.

1798, April 15, Orange. Acknowledging letters of 29th March and 5th and 6th instant. The President's speech. Extraordinary conduct of Talleyrand. Its unparalleled stupidity. Our foreign affairs. Question of Executive prerogatives in declaring war. The President's objection to City of Washington. 4°. 4 pages.

1798, April 29, Orange. Acknowledging letter of 19th. Improper views of the Executive party relative to our affairs with France. Conversation with Monroe. fol. 1 page.

1798, May 5, Orange. Acknowledging letter of April 26. Success of the war party mortifying. Dispatches by Sydney an effectual antidote. Object of Jay's treaty to draw us into a quarrel with the enemies of Great Britain. fol. 1 page.

1798, May 13, Orange. Acknowledging letter of 3d. The management of our foreign relations. The credit given to Adams for a spirit of conciliation with France is wonderful. fol. 1 page.

1798, May 20, Orange. Acknowledging letter of 10th. Materials for building a new house. The alien bill proposed in the Senate a monster. Criticises the President, whose language to the young men of Philadelphia is abominable and degrading.
fol. 2 pages.

1798, May 27, Orange. Acknowledging letter of 17th. Continuance of the session is expected to favor the success of the Executive projects in the legislature. 4°. 1 page.

1798, June 3, Orange. Acknowledging letter of May 24. Our relations with France. The hot-headed proceedings of Mr. Adams not well relished in the cool climate of Mount Vernon. fol. 1 page.

1798, June 10, Orange. Acknowledges letter of 31st. The law for capturing French privateers. Bill suspending commerce with the French dominions. If it passes the French Government will be confirmed in the suspicion begotten by the British treaty. Mr. Adams's assault on Monroe.
fol. 2 pages.

1798, December 29, Orange. The President's speech. The answer of the Senate cooked in the same shop as the speech. Our affairs with France. Alien and sedition laws. fol. 2 pages.

1799, January 12, Orange. Respecting the alien bill.
fol. 1 page.

1799, February 8, Orange. Acknowledging letter of January 16. Fears there is tampering with the

JEFFERSON.

mails. The question of publishing the debates of the convention. fol. 2 pages.

1799, December 29, Richmond. Proceedings of the Virginia legislature. Foreign events. Course of the Executive and our envoys. fol. 2 pages.

1800, January 4, Richmond. Incloses copy of resolution moved by Mr. Giles, to which he will add instructions on subject of the intercourse law so injurious to price of tobacco. fol. 1 page.

1800, January 9, Richmond. Proceedings of the Virginia legislature. 4°. 1 page.

1800, January 12, Richmond. Proceedings in the Virginia legislature. Mr. Giles's resolution. 4°. 1 page.

1800, January 18, Richmond. Proceedings of the Virginia assembly. Bill for increased pay of members passed. Wrong in principle. 4°. 1 page.

1800, February 14, Orange. Bill before the assembly of Virginia for drawing jurors by lot. French affairs. The destiny of the revolution transferred from the civil to military authority. A lesson to us of the danger attending intrigues between political and military leaders. Heavy snowstorm in Virginia. 4°. 1 page.

1800, March 15, Orange. Acknowledges public documents. Bill respecting the election of President and Vice-President. small 4°. 3 pages.

1800, April 4, Orange. Acknowledging letter of March 25. The electoral bill. fol. 1 page.

1800, April 20, Orange. Agreeable information from our envoys to France. Trusts that she will come to a proper adjustment with us. 4°. 2 pages.

Monticello.

1800, September —, Orange. The negotiations of our envoys to France. Conjectures as to their silence. Reasons attributed. 4°. 2 pages.

1800, October 21, Orange. Introduces Mr. Altson, of South Carolina. Conjectures as to the vote of some of the Northern States in the approaching election for President. 4°. 1 page.

1800, November —, Orange. Difficulty of negotiations in Paris. Delays carved out by the Executive and favorable moment lost thereby. Accounts from South Carolina rather ominous (relating to pending election). small 4°. 2 pages.

1800, December 20, Orange. Uncertainty of the election. Probability of its devolving upon the House of Representatives. Probability of a Republican President and Vice-President. 4°. 2 pages.

Washington.

1801, January 10, Orange. Acknowledging letters of December 19 and 20. Grounds for complaints of the post-office for delays. The election probably to be thrown into the House of Representatives. Desperate attempts to strangle the election of the people. The French convention. Pretensions of Great Britain. fol. 4 pages.

1801, February 28, Orange. Acknowledging letters of 1st, 12th, and 19th. Death of Madison's father. Consequently his departure for Washington delayed. Conduct of Mr. Adams unexpected. Throwing difficulties in the way of his successor. Appointments to office. Fortunate results of the election. Efficacy of the public will, without military force to abet usurpation. fol. 2 pages.

Monticello.

1809, March 19, Washington. Asks Jefferson's intentions relative to Mr. Latrobe. Accounts from Paris. No change in affairs. Occurrences and prospects in Spain. 4°. 1 page.

1809, March 28, Washington. Acknowledging letter of 24th. Letters from Erving at Cadiz. Spanish affairs. Irugo at Cadiz. His mills. 4°. 1 page.

1809, April 9, Washington. The ministry of Great Britain shaken with respect to this country. The catastrophe in Spain the cause. Great dread in England of our perseverance in the embargo. Faux pas of Erving about an arrangement between Iznardi and Hackley about a vice consulate. Notice by the Department of State of its nullity. 4°. 3 pages.

1809, April 24, Washington. Acknowledging letter of 19th. Result of advances made by Great Britain. Adjustment with this country becomes essential. Their hope to embroil us with France. Commercial sufferings of France's allies. Prohibition of the trade with St. Domingo. Cession of the Floridas. 4°. 2 pages.

1809, May 1, Washington. Acknowledging letter of April 27. Mr. Gallatin's conversation with Turreau, who professes to be confident that the French decrees will be repealed. Our commerce with Spanish America. Cuba a cardinal object with Napoleon. The school of adversity may teach Great Britain the policy of arrogant pretentions changed to conciliatory moderation towards the United States. 4°. 2 pages.

1809, May 30, Washington. Acknowledging letter of 22d. Hopes Jefferson will make use of his services at any time relating to money arrangements or other matters. Federal cant on our foreign relations. The British cabinet thrown them off their center. The leaders soured towards England and less disposed to render our interests subservient to hers. 4°. 3 pages.

1809, June 12, Washington. Accounts from Great Britain. The new orders. Opinion as to her policy. 4°. 2 pages.

1809, June 20, Washington. Acknowledging letter of 16th. Mr. Erskine's explanation of the repeal of British orders of April. Great Britain may fulfill what its minister stipulated, but if she means to be trickish it will frustrate the proposed negotiations. The question likely to agitate Congress will be on the bill which opens our ports to French as well as British ships of war. 4°. 2 pages.

1809, June 27, Washington. A letter from Gen. Armstrong noticing an improvement in plows and a new machine to take the place of the spinning wheel. New French regulations. Bill passed the Senate of nonintercourse with France. The House rejected a motion to discriminate in favor of British ships. 4°. 2 pages.

JEFFERSON.

1809, July 4, Washington. Sends him the skin of an animal belonging to the Rocky Mountains. Renomination of J. Q. Adams for Russia. 4°. 2 pages.

1809, July 7, Washington. Incloses a letter from Mr. Short on his way to St. Petersburg. Relaxation of the commercial policy of Napoleon. Inconveniences felt in France from the want of external commerce. The blockading system irksome. 4°. 2 pages.

1809, July 23, Montpellier. Acknowledging letter of 12th. Objections to the arguments of Mr. Short relating to our foreign commerce. Arrival of M. Daschkoff. 4°. 3 pages.

1809, August 3, Montpellier. Goes to Washington to consult with heads of departments on questions of our commercial relations with England. Instructions to Erskine. Our affairs with France unchanged, owing to the absence of the Emperor. 4°. 3 pages.

1809, August 16, Montpellier. The President's proclamation. Our commercial relations with Great Britain. Enforcement of the nonintercourse act against her explained, should adverse criticism occur. Erskine may not be able to defend himself on charge of exceeding instructions. He may make, however, a strong case against Canning. 4°. 4 pages.

1809, August 23, Montpellier. Mr. and Mrs. Gallatin and Madison propose going to Monticello. Russia and Holland adhere with vigor to the means of excluding British trade. Colonial produce, even Dutch, in neutral vessels to be warehoused in Holland. 4°. 2 pages.

1809, September 11, Montpellier. Jackson (British minister) expects to be in Washington on Friday. Letters from Mr. Pinkney. Conversation with Canning respecting colonial trade. Canning rather distrusts Jackson. Introduces Mr. Palmer, a Chinese scholar. 4°. 2 pages.

1809, October 6, Washington. Dupont de Nemour's contribution to the execution of his project of education. Jackson (British minister) deficient in requisite instructions. 4°. 2 pages.

1809, December 11, Washington. Monroe's willingness to have taken a seat in the cabinet. Lafayette urgent on the subject of his land titles which are required as the basis of a loan. Actions of Congress. J. G. Jackson wounded in the hip. 4°. 2 pages.

1810, April 23, Washington. Acknowledging letter of 16th. The House endeavoring to pass a bill providing for a conditional repeal by either of the belligerents of their edicts, laying in the meantime an addition of 50 per cent on present duties on imports from Great Britain and France. Information from Great Britain and France has a promising aspect, but not definite. 4°. 3 pages.

1810, May 7, Washington. Arrival of the merino sheep. It is not known what has passed between Wellesley and Pinkney. Nonintercourse and French restrictions. New York and New England rallying to the Republican ranks. 4°. 2 pages.

JEFFERSON.

1810, May 25, Washington. Acknowledging letter of 13th. Relating to an importation of merinos. Our negotiations with France and Great Britain. Lafayette's extravagant expectations. Value of his land grants and amount of his debts.
4°. 3 pages.

1810, June 4, Washington. Acknowledging letters of May 25 and 30. Respecting the papers in the Batture case. The great drought in Virginia.
4°. 3 pages.

1810, June 15, Washington. Official communications from France and Great Britain. Obnoxious refusal of Great Britain to comply with the reasonable course of ending the predatory edicts of both nations. [Not signed.] 4°. 1 page.

1810, June 22, Washington. Pedigree of imported merinos. Armstrong's picture of French robbery. The original sin against neutrals lies with Great Britain. Prepares to depart for his farm. Will send copy of Cooper's "Pennsylvania Judge," his masterly opinion on the sentence of a foreign admiralty court in a prize cause. 4°. 2 pages.

1810, July 17, Washington. Acknowledges letter of 13th. Merino ewes and lamb. Will send him Moreau's Memoirs. 4°. 2 pages.

1810, July 17, Washington. Convention of 1787. Hamilton's plan of a constitution. Asks if Jefferson has it, and wishes a copy. 4°. 2 pages.

1810, October 19, Washington. Acknowledges letter of 15th. Rumors of steps taken by France towards reconciliation. Great Britain's mock blockade. Congress will not be disposed to submit. Irreconcilable to honorable neutrality. The crisis in West Florida. Question of our taking possession of the country to the Perdido. Would be resented by Spain. The vacancy in the judiciary. 4°. 4 pages.

1810, December 7, Washington. Nothing new from abroad. England's blockade. She may abandon it. The vacancy in the judiciary. Lincoln, Grainger, and John Q. Adams. Views of New England and the South. Yazooism in the Supreme Bench. Rodney's loss of furniture and books by shipwreck. 4°. 3 pages.

1811, March 18, Washington. Report that the Prince Regent had appointed his cabinet. Lord Holland prime minister. Probable change in policy toward the United States. Question of the repeal of orders in council. The subject of blockades. Napoleon's want of money. Difficulty in understanding his meaning towards us. Our prospects not flattering. Appointment of Warden as secretary of legation resented by Armstrong. 4°. 4 pages.

1811, April 1, Washington. Hostility of Gen. Armstrong to Mr. Warden. Monroe appointed Secretary of State. Mr. Smith declines the mission to Russia. The charge of Wilkinson's privity with Burr. Indications from France rather favorable. Little to be hoped for from England.
4°. 2 pages.

1811, April 19, Washington. Acknowledges letter inclosing extract from Armstrong's letter relating

JEFFERSON.

to Warden. Armstrong's inconsistency. Return of Pinkney expected weekly. Convalescence of the King. His cabinet inflexible in its folly and depravity. Nothing official from France. Indications of renewal of trade. Symptoms of war between France and Russia. 4°. 2 pages.

1811, May 3, Washington. Acknowledging letter of April 24. Jefferson's expostulations with Duane for his attacks on Gallatin. Erskine's statement of Gallatin's favorable disposition toward England, although denied, reiterated by Duane, who, though a friend to liberty, is a slave to his passions. The nonarrival of Pinkney. Reports from France of repeal of the decrees. 4°. 3 pages.

1811, June 7, Washington. Duane's attacks on Gallatin. Occurrence between Rogers and the British ship of war; repetitions of them will probably end in open rupture. The state of parties in Massachusetts. Great Britain determined against repealing her orders, and Bonaparte equally so on the destruction of her commerce. The blockade of England not continued in force. 4°. 2 pages.

1811, July 8, Washington. Acknowledging letter of 3d. Turpitude of the conduct of Mr. Smith (late Secretary of State). The case of Mr. Ewing relative to salaries for the three offices in London centered in him. The character of the mission of Mr. Foster from Great Britain unable to conjecture. 4°. 3 pages.

1812, February 7, Washington. Acknowledging receipt of several letters. Intelligence from Great Britain indicates an adherence to her mad policy towards the United States. Measures by Congress to invade Canada. Wilkinson's defense. The weather and earthquakes. 4°. 2 pages.

1812, March 6, Washington. Acknowledging letter of February 19. Congress gives proof that they do not mean to flinch from the contest to which the conduct of Great Britain drives them. [The signature of this letter cut off.] 4°. 1 page.

1812, April 3, Washington. Acknowledging letter of March 26. The British cabinet prefer war with us to a repeal of their orders in council. Bill before Congress for embargo. Madison's views of the measure. Probable passage of the embargo bill. 4°. 3 pages.

1812, April 24, Washington. Acknowledging letter of 17th. Large amount of produce in the hands of merchants, farmers, and millers. Difficulties attending the embargo. The holders of produce will be secured good prices. Mr. Barlow's instructions exceeded. Mathew's acts in East Florida. 4°. 3 pages.

1812, May 25, Washington. Incloses letters from abroad. Our relations with France. Nothing done towards adjustment of difficulties. Speculations on a possible triangular war with France and England. Might hasten a peace. 4°. 2 pages.

1812, June 22, Washington. Incloses a paper containing the declaration of war. Action of the Federalists in Congress in protest against the war. Assassination of Percival; question in England as to his successor. The Prince Regent ruled by Lady Herbert. 4°. 2 pages.

JEFFERSON.

1812, August 17, Washington. Acknowledges letter of 10th instant. Seditious opposition of Massachusetts and Connecticut. The volunteer act leaves us dependent on the militia. Endeavors to secure the maritime frontier and penetration into upper Canada. Expedition of Hull. Hopes to redeem Michilimackinac. Change in England relative to the orders in council. Unpopularity of the war in England. Pressure of the non-importation act. Proposal of the local authorities at Halifax sanctioned by Mr. Foster, the British minister, to suspend hostilities. Activity of the Indians against our frontiers.
fol. 4 pages.

1812, October 14, Washington. Acknowledging letter of 2d. Office of surveyorship sent to Mr. Meigs. Military crisis near Fort Defiance. Our best hopes for the campaign rest on Harrison. He will probably regain Detroit. Will soon know the views of England in regard to peace. The State elections not favorable to the administration. The doubtful States. fol. 3 pages.

1813, January 27, Washington. Puts Jefferson on his guard about Dr. T. Ewell. The undercurrent in Congress against us. Bonaparte and army in serious danger in Russia. Wellesley's party attack the ministry for not prosecuting the war more vigorously against us. The harvest and finances.
fol. 1 page.

1813, March 10, Washington. Acknowledging letters of 8th and 21st ultimo. The conduct and character of the late commander at Halifax, as inspector-general. Mr. Randolph named to the Senate for command of a regiment. His acquirements. The disaster to Napoleon's army in Russia. No despondence in Paris. Will surmount his difficulties. Exultation in England. Favorable disposition of Emperor of Russia to us.
4°. 3 pages.

1813, June 6, Washington. Abilities and learning of Dr. Waterhouse. Persecutions of his enemies. At present no position for him. The suggestion of protecting the trade of the Chesapeake by gunboats. The Secretary of the Navy, his opinions; also Commodore Barney's suggestions.
4°. 3 pages.

1814, May 10, Montpellier. No information from our envoys to the Baltic. The British Government should send negotiators to meet ours, but whether in the spirit of ours is the question. The New York election crushes the project of the Junto faction. Our difficulties in procuring money without the odium of heavy taxes. The idea of armistice has no foundation. The harvest. The Hessian fly. 4°. 2 pages.

1814, October 10, Washington. Acknowledging letter of 24th ultimo. Jefferson's proposition to supply loss of books by Congress, reported favorably. Madison's views on finance. Dispatches from Ghent. The fisheries question. The situation of Sacketts Harbor critical. 4°. 3 pages.

1814, October 23, Washington. Acknowledging letter of 15th. The variance of ideas relating to "ways and means." Situation of Sacketts Harbor. The campaign in Canada. 4°. 2 pages.

JEFFERSON.

1815, March 12, Washington. The causes and character of the late war with Great Britain. Mr. Dallas. European affairs. But for our peace with England a war with Spain would have opened on us. 4°. 4 pages.

1817, February 15, Washington. Extreme cold weather. Mr. Pinkney leaves Naples. Mr. Gallatin's demands of indemnity. Delay in Spanish negotiations. Bad prospects for harvest in Europe and here. The compensation and claims laws in Congress. Reciprocity in the West India trade. Roads and canals bill. 4°. 4 pages.

1819, February 12, Montpellier. Inclosing a printed memoir by T. Coxe. Prospect of an early and satisfactory close to the negotiations with Spain. 4°. 2 pages.

1819, March 6, Montpellier. Acknowledges letter of 3d, with seeds. Matter concerning the Virginia University. Denies newspaper articles giving his and Jefferson's opinions on the conduct of Gen. Jackson. 4°. 2 pages.

1819, October 25, Montpellier. Inclosing specimens of various seeds of grain and garden seeds from Madrid. 4°. 2 pages.

1820, December 10, Montpellier. Acknowledging letter of November 29. The law terminating appointments. 4°. 2 pages.

1821, January 7, Montpellier. Views taken of the act of Congress vacating periodically executive officers. Typhus fever in Madison's family. 4°. 2 pages.

1821, September 20, Montpellier. Acknowledging letter of 16th. The tax on imported books. Considers it an impolitic and disreputable measure. 4°. 3 pages.

1821, November 10, Montpellier. Acknowledging letter of October 30. Has interlined a slight change in Jefferson's petition to Congress in view of the protective tax on foreign books. 4°. 1 page.

1821 (?), not dated. Proposed application of the funds of the University of Virginia. Statement showing how the loan of $60,000 can be met. 4°. 1 page.

1822, March 5, Montpellier. Acknowledging letter of February 25. The new society for the benefit of Indians. Views as to its expediency. 4°. 3 pages.

1823, January 15, Montpellier. Acknowledging letter of 6th. Mr. Gerry's letters on the subject of a cause of rupture with France. Madison's opinion of what a history of parties should be. Judge Johnson's letter respecting the organization of the Supreme Court. 4°. 3 pages.

1823, June 27, Montpellier. Respecting the authorship of Washington's farewell address. Judge Johnson indebted to Jefferson for remarks on the definition of political parties. The boundaries between the General and State governments. The question whether the judicial authority of the United States be the constitutional resort for determining the same. 4°. 7 pages.

1823, September 6, Montpellier. Acknowledging letter of August 30. The people of Spain and Portugal need light and heat from American example before they can contend with the armies, intrigues, and bribes of their enemies, the treachery of their leaders, their priests, and their prejudices. The question of the origin of the declaration of independence. fol. 1 page.

1823, November 1, Montpellier. Returns to Jefferson the letter of the President. Concurs in the President's views respecting the advances of the British Government in cooperation in the great struggle of the epoch between liberty and despotism. The French invasion of Spain and the struggle in Greece. The extension of British commerce to her former colonies. 8°. 2 pages.

1823, November 11, Montpellier. Acknowledging letter of 6th. Respecting the salary of professor of law in the University of Virginia and Madison's preference for Mr. Gilmer. The British cabinet skittish on the very business propo-ed to us by them. 4°. 2 pages.

1823, December 18, Montpellier. Respecting Mr. Gilmer, professor of law at the Virginia University. His proposed trip to Europe. [Signature cut off.] 4°. 1 page.

1824, January 14, Montpellier. Acknowledging letter of 7th. While recognizing the qualifications of Dr. Cooper for a place in the Virginia University, dreads impairing the popularity of the institution on account of his enemies. Respecting the proposed amendments of the Constitution relating to Presidential elections. 4°. 2 pages.

1824, May 20, Montpellier. Acknowledging letter of 16th. Respecting the removal of the college from Williamsburg. 4°. 1 page.

1824, August 16, Montpellier. Purchase of books for the University of Virginia. [With draft affixed.] 4°: 1 page. 8°. 2 pages.

1824, September 10, Montpellier. Respecting the purchase of theological works for the library of the Virginia University. List of works appended. 4°. 1 page. fol. 3 pages.

1824, December 31, Montpellier. The proposed removal of William and Mary College from Williamsburg. 4°. 3 pages.

1825, January 15, Montpellier. The law professorship of the Virginia University. Mr. Tucker requires time for deliberation. His rival pursuits. The proposed removal of William and Mary College. 4°. 1 page.

1825, February 7, Montpellier. Acknowledging letters of January 12 and 15. The judicial appointment of Mr. Barbour lessens the chance of him for the University. Mr. Tucker also out of reach. The roads and canals bill and Missouri cases. 4°. 2 pages.

1825, February 8, Montpellier. Mr. Cabell succeeds in defeating the project of removing William and Mary from Williamsburg. Chance slender of Mr. Barbour's accepting the place of law professor at the University. Question of text-book for the law school. 4°. 3 pages.

1825, December 28, Montpellier. Acknowledging letter of 24th. Views on the question of "Roads and Canals." 4°. 4 pages.

JEFFERSON.

1825, February 17, Montpellier. Acknowledging letters of 12th and 15th. Matters connected with appointments at the University of Virginia. Political sentiments of Chancellor Tucker. [Draft.] Strip of paper. 2 pages.

1826, February 24, Montpellier. Acknowledging letter of 17th. The law professorship at the University. Embarrassment of Jefferson's estate. Madison's bad crops oblige him at present to live on borrowed means. Madison's great interest in the University. Internal improvements. Reminiscences of mutual friendship and political harmony. 4°. 3 pages.

JEFFERSON'S works.

Not dated. Prospectus Jefferson's works in Madison's handwriting. [Draft.] 4°. 1 page and strip of paper.

JOHNSON, CABELL, LOYALL, and BRECKINRIDGE.

1827, March —, Montpellier. Circular addressed to the visitors of the University of Virginia on the resignation of Prof. Key. [Draft.] 4°. 1 page.

JOHNSON, CHAPMAN.

1827, November 4, December 9 and 18, Montpellier. Three letters. Matters concerning the University of Virginia. [Drafts.] 3 strips of paper.

1828, March 24, Montpellier. Acknowledging letter of 8th. Selection for the professor's chair of natural philosophy in the University of Virginia. [Copy.] 4°. 2 pages and strip of paper.

1828, August 10, Montpellier. Acknowledging letter of 3d. Matters connected with the University of Virginia. Dr. Patterson the professor of natural philosophy. [Copy.] 4°. 1 page.

1827, December 1, Montpellier. Jesse B. Harrison offers himself as successor, to Mr. Long, as professor of ancient languages in the University of Virginia. Recommendations from various persons. [Draft.] 4°. 1 page.

JOHNSON, EDWARD. *Baltimore.*

1815, April 22, Washington. Acknowledging the congratulations of the Republican citizens of Baltimore on the return of peace. [Draft.] fol. 2 pages.

JOHNSON, WILLIAM.

1825, May 6, Montpellier. Acknowledges receipt of a copy of "Life of Major-General Greene." His appreciation of the valuable work. [Draft.] Strip of paper.

JONES, WILLIAM.

1814, April —, Washington. Acknowledges his letter tendering his resignation as Secretary of the Navy. Madison's regrets. [Draft.] 8°. 1 page.

JOY, GEORGE.

1807 May 22, Washington. Acknowledging letter of February 10. The treaty signed by the British and our commissioners not received the approbation of the President. The impressment question. [Draft.] 4°. 4 pages.

1810, January 17, Montpellier. Acknowledging letter of 10th. Anxiety that our country be kept out of the vortex of war Fears that there is no choice but between absolute disgrace and resistance by

JOY, GEORGE.

force. British orders restricting trade of neutrals. The case of the Chesapeake. Impressment of seamen. [Draft.] 4°. 4 pages.

1817, August 15, Montpellier. Acknowledging letter on subject of his wish to be translated from Rotterdam to Amsterdam. The President being absent. his friendly offices can not be used until his return, [Drafts.] 4°. 1 page.

1821, November 21, Montpellier. Acknowledging letter of February last. Is unable to furnish Mr. Joy with a copy of his "Conciliator." Growing consequence of this country in Europe. The harvest and crops. [Draft.] 4°. 2 pages.

1822, August 10, Montpellier. Acknowledging letters of January 2 and 9. Britain's juster views of her monopolizing attempts with regard to navigation between her colonies and the United States. [Draft.] 4°. 2 pages.

London.

1834, September 9, Montpellier. Acknowledging letters of June 4 and 11. Incident in the life of Lafayette. Mr. Adams's obituary memoir of him. The orders in council. Our embargo. Our declaration of war. Circumstances attending, detailed. For sake of humanity it is hoped that England will put an end to impressment at home. [Draft.] 4°. 2 pages.

KEILSALL, CHARLES. *London.*

1817, October —, Montpellier. Acknowledging receipt of the "Phantasm of an University." No national university in the United States. A central institution now on foot in Virginia. Architectural plan. [Draft.] 4°. 1 page.

KENNEDY, JOHN P.

1834, July 7, Montpellier. Acknowledging letter of June 19, with copy of discourse on life and character of William Wirt. Condition of Madison's eyes and general debility. Panegyric of Wirt. [Draft.] Strip of paper.

KENNEY, THOMAS T. *Essex County*, N. J.

1809, March 18, Washington. Acknowledging address of the Republican citizens of Essex County, approving of the measures of the President touching foreign relations. [Draft.] 4°. 2 pages.

KING, MILES, Rev.

1816, September 5, Washington. Acknowledging letter of June 29. Declines all correspondence relating to religious subjects. Appreciates his pious motives and thankful for his kind solicitude for his future happiness. [Draft.] 4°. 1 page.

KERCHEVAL, SAMUEL.

1829, September 7, Montpellier. Acknowledges letter of August 27. Thanks him for pamphlet containing Jefferson's letters to him (Kercheval). Declines on account of his health and time to state on what points he did not concur with Jefferson. [Draft.] Strip of paper.

KING, WILLIAM. *Maine.*

1819, May 20, Montpellier. Acknowledging letter of 10th. Proceedings of the Virginia legislature in reference to the separation of Kentucky into an independent State. [Draft.] 4°. 3 pages.

KEEMLI, JOHN. *Philadelphia.*

1810, January —, Washington. Acknowledging receipt of the address of surviving revolutionary characters of Philadelphia, and incloses answer expressing his gratification of their approval of his measures. [Draft.] fol. 2 pages.

LAFAYETTE.

1785, March 20, Orange. Acknowledging letter of December 15. The navigation, and the States which are ultimately to be established on her borders, of the Mississippi. The policy of the United States respecting the control of the same. Appointment of John Jay as Secretary of Foreign Affairs. No successor appointed of Benj. Franklin. Inland navigation. Judicial system. [Draft.] 4°. 4 pages.

1806, February 21, Washington. Acknowledging letter of October 8. Regrets to be unable to procure a loan. The banks have very limited means and the writer has no influence with these institutions. Great demand for money for private enterprises. Mr. Du Plantier charged with the location of Lafayette's land. [Draft.] 4°. 2 pages.

1820, November 25, Montpellier. Acknowledging letter of July 22. Progress of reformation in Europe. The Missouri compromise. The question, thought settled, reproduced by a clause in the Missouri constitution distinguishing between free blacks and whites. Finances and commerce in this country not in satisfactory state. Low prices of products. Tonnage bickerings. [Draft.] 4°. 4 pages.

1821, not dated, Montpellier. Acknowledging letter of July 1. Lafayette's sentiments on the French budget. Dissappointed that the Emperor Alexander defends arbitrary power against national reforms. His unparallelled armaments. His interference in Naples' domestic struggles. Russia's gigantic growth. Great Britain's ascendancy on the ocean. Ultimate ascendancy of United States. Negro slavery a blot. [Draft.] 4°. 4 pages.

1824, August 21, Montpellier. Welcomes him to America. Hopes to see him at his own house while in America. [Draft.] Strip of paper.

1824 (?), not dated. Toasts suggested for the Lafayette dinner (in Madison's handwriting). fol. 1 page.

1826, November 26, Montpellier. Acknowledging letter of August 28. The death of Jefferson. His family left destitute. Ill success of the lottery and subscription. Hopes that the legislature will aid. Proposed publication of Jefferson's manuscripts by his executor. South American affairs. The Greek equipment at New York. Miss Wright's experiment in Tennessee concerning manumission. [Draft.] 4°. 6 pages.

1828, February 20, Montpellier. Acknowledging letter of October 27. Condition of the Jefferson estate. Struggle of the Greeks. Hopes for the best. The extravagancies of the presidential election. Affection of this country for Lafayette. The Jackson party confident, and faint hopes of the Adams party. Miss Wright returned to Tennessee. Her benevolent schemes. Her disregard for prejudices. Amalgamation, etc. Condition of the Virginia University. Improvement in discipline. [Draft.] 4°. 2 pages.

LAFAYETTE.

1829, June 15, Montpellier. Acknowledging receipt of letter of January 28. The liberal policy of France contrasted with the frowns of England relating to the Greek cause. The hopes of the result of the publications of the Jefferson memoirs towards benefiting the estate. Their translation into French. Le Vasseur's account of Lafayette's visit to United States. Introduces Mr. Rives, United States minister. [Draft.]
4°. 2 pages.

1830, February 1, Montpellier. Acknowledging letter of September, 29. On the convention at Richmond and the proposed amendment of the constitution of the State. Morbid sensibility on questions relating to abolition of slavery. [Draft.]
4°. 2 pages.

1830, December 12, Montpellier. Acknowledging letter of July 10. "The three glorious days of July." Substitute for the dethroned monarch. Confidence in Lafayette's patriotic discretion. The constitutional monarchy adopted, may be necessary to actual condition of France. Our system on the boundary between general and local government. South Carolina. [Copy.]
4°. 2 pages.

1831, August 3, Montpellier. The anomalous doctrines of South Carolina. Gross exaggeration on subject of the tariff. People in South Carolina more disposed to calculate the value of the union by the consequences of disunion. The effects produced on our political horizon are but local and transient. The American interest in the fate of Poland. [Copy.] 4°. 2 pages.

LANGUAGE, INNOVATION IN.

Not dated. Causes of innovation in language. Notes in Madison's handwriting. 4°. 1 page.

LATROBE, ———.

1818, July 24, Montpellier. Acknowledging letter of 8th. Speculations of different authorities on the origin of Greenlanders. [Draft.] 4°. 2 pages.

LAW, THOMAS.

Year not dated, January 27, Montpellier. Acknowledging receipt of his address before Columbian Institute on paper currency. [Draft.]
Strip of paper.

LEA, ISAAC.

1828, April 3, Montpellier. Acknowledging letter of March 30. Is unable to recollect anything about the expedition of Capt. Wilder in 1772, for the discovery of the North Pole. [Draft.]
Strip of paper.

LEE, CHARLES CARTER.

1831, May 17, Montpellier. Acknowledging letter of 9th, inclosing a long one from his father. Their old friendship. Thanks him for his kind sentiments. [Draft.] Strip of paper.

LEE, HENRY.

1783, June 21, Philadelphia. Jefferson's leave to visit this country. Short will act as chargé during his absence. [Copy.] 4°. 1 page.

New York.

1786, November 9, Richmond. Indelicacy of the situation in which Gen. Lee is placed. [Copy.]
4°. 1 page.

LEE, HENRY. *Alexandria.*

1786, November 23, Richmond. Explains misapprehensions relating to recent elections in Virginia. [Copy.] 4°. 3 pages.

1787, October 4, New York. Acknowledging letter of September 8. Remarks on the question relating to the proposed seat of Government. [Copy.] 4°. 4 pages.

1788, November 30, Philadelphia. Acknowledging letter of October 29; also 19th instant. Proposition to share in a speculative purchase. Proceedings of the convention at Richmond. [Copy.] 4°. 4 pages.

1789, January. View of the advantageous situation at Great Falls of the Potomac. 4°. 3 pages.

1790, April 13, New York. Acknowledging letter of March 4 and 9th instant. Discovers in them strong signs of dissatisfaction of public prospects. Does not feel the same despondency. Report of the Secretary of the Treasury. Discussions on assumption of State debts. Public debt a curse to a Republican Government. [Copy.] 4°. 4 pages.

Richmond.

1791, December 18, Philadelphia. Acknowledging letter of 8th. The western disaster. Measures for reparation of the calamity not yet disclosed. Suspected relation of Indian hostility to the western posts .the subject of free conversation. Disavowal by Hammond of encouraging hostilities. Thomas Pinkney to be minister to London. Representation bill. 4°. 3 pages.

1792, January 1, Philadelphia. Declines to ask a favor of Mr. Hammond at Mr. Marshall's request. The apportionment bill suspended. The post-office bill. Appointments to foreign courts. Pinkney to London, Morris to Paris, and Short to The Hague. The disturbances at Hispaniola. Report of the Treasury on manufactures. [Copy.] 4°. 3 pages.

1792, January 29, Philadelphia. Acknowledging letter of 17th. Discussions on the western defense not yet over. [Copy.] 4°. 1 page.

1792, February 12, Philadelphia. Acknowledging letter of July 29. Disagreements of the Senate on the military bill. Thinks the measure of the assumption of State debts will be carried. [Copy.] 4°. 2 pages.

1792, March 28, Philadelphia. No nomination made for a new commander for the military establishment. Inquiry as to cause of western calamities. The representation bill by the Senate. The mint bill passed the House. Proposition for stamp of head of the President for the time being disagreed to, as a feature of monarchy. Distresses of the island of Hispaniola. [Copy.] 4°. 4 pages.

1792, April 15, Philadelphia. The nominations for general officers all confirmed except Wilkinson. The rage for speculation in New York. An earthquake inevitable. The President exercises his power of checking the unconstitutional course of Congress. Invalid pensions. 4°. 3 pages.

LEE, HENRY (author).

1824, April 22, Montpellier. Acknowledging receipt of a volume and critique on Judge Johnson. If any injustice has ever been done to the memory of Gen. Lee, a vindication can be but gratifying to an old friend and distinguished revolutionary hero. [Draft.] Strip of paper.

1824, May —, Montpellier. Acknowledging note of 4th. Madison would willingly contribute lights on the subject of a new edition of Lee's father's memoirs, but during the period of the Southern war, his abode was in Philadelphia, as delegate to Congress and not in correspondence with any of the actors or spectators therein. [Draft.] 4°. 1 page.

1824, June 25, Montpellier. Acknowledging letter of 18th. On the proposal of a new publication under title of American Gazette and Literary Journal. Thinks it concedes too much to a remedial power in the press over the spirit of party. Illustrations and examples. [Copy.] 4°. 3 pages.

1824, August —, Montpellier. On the subject of biographies. Is unable to furnish material except from his private files, which are destined to a posthumous period. 4°. 2 pages.

1825, January 14, Montpellier. Acknowledging letter of 6th. Expresses a laudatory opinion of a printed sheet sent him. As a political disquisition a critical review does not lie in the compass of a letter. Obligations of a Representative to his constituents. In what degree a plurality of votes is evidence of the will of the majority. These remarks not for the public. [Draft.] 4°. 2 pages.

1825, January 31, Montpellier. Is satisfied of the fact that the movement of the Southern army from Deep River to the Santee, in the campaign of 1781, was suggested by Lee's father. Reasons for the belief. [Draft.] 4°. 1 page.

1825, November 29, Montpellier. Acknowledging letter of 19th. Commends the purpose of Lee's proposed work on the campaign of Niagara in 1814, and naval achievements in the Mediterranean. Will supply from his private files such papers as may be desired, if designated. [Draft.] Strip of paper.

1827, February —, Montpellier. Acknowledging letter of 2d. Events of the war of 1812. Plan of the campaign. Appointments of officers. Their characters and capabilities. The Cabinet. [Draft.] 4°. 6 pages.

1827, September 24, Montpellier. Acknowledging letter of August 24. Can not inform him on the cause of delay attending the order to Gen. Jackson of July 18, 1814, having no recollection or access to documents. Hopes the occurrence may be rightly traced. [Draft.] 4°. 1 page.

1833, August 14, Montpellier. Acknowledging letter of June 5. Corrects an error in reference to a misprint of "Jay" for "Joy." Had Lee consulted the correspondence of his father with Madison, would have found that he was one of the harshest censors of the policy and measures of the Federal Government during Washington's first term. [Draft.] "Private." Strip of paper.

LEE, HENRY (Author).

1833, November 26, Montpellier. Acknowledging letter September 15. Incloses to Lee his father's letters to Madison, as requested. Madison's feeble health. [Draft.] Strip of paper.

1834, March 3, Montpellier. Acknowledging letter of November 14. Gives reason for declining a position in Washington's Cabinet and accepting one in Jefferson's. Appended is a short note to Ch. Carter Lee, in which is inclosed a letter to him from his brother. [Draft.] "Private." Strip of paper.

LEE, HENRY, notes on.

1811, November 8. His views on Government financial measures, as expressed in his correspondence at various times. Scrap of paper.

LEE, JOHN H. *Kentucky.*

1831, January 1, Montpellier. Acknowledging letter of November 12. Mrs. Willis and Madison thank him for his attending to the troublesome business relating to a disputed title. [Draft.] Scrap of paper.

1831, June 12, Montpellier. Incloses an answer by Mrs. Willis to Lee's letter of April 13. Concurs in her request that Lee will be governed by his own judgment relative to buying or selling land to settle a disputed title. [Draft.] Scrap of paper.

LEE, R. B.

1819, August 5, Montpellier. Acknowledging letter of 2d, with copy of Lee's Fourth of July oration. The existing tranquility and harmony in public feeling a just subject of congratulation. [Copy.] 4°. 2 pages.

1825, April 20, Montpellier. Acknowledging letter of 15th. As requested, will not fail to write to Judges Duvall and Todd on the subject of his letter. [Draft.] Strip of paper.

LEE, RICHARD H.

1784, December 25. Proposition to empower Congress to collect impost in Virginia as soon as 12 States unite in the scheme. Objections. Projects for the Continental Convention. Union of the States essential to their safety against foreign danger. [Extract, not signed in Madison's hand.] 4°. 1 page.

1785, July 7, Orange. Acknowledging letter of May 30. Advocates the separation of Kentucky from Virginia. Arrival of Mr. Gardoqui, to adjust matters relating to the navigation of the Mississippi. Our commercial relations with Spain and Great Britain. The weather and crops. [Draft. Signature cut off.] 4°. 3 pages.

LEE, R. H. JR.

1824, February 9, Montpellier. Acknowledging letter of January 24. Respecting the memoirs preparing for the memoir of his grandfather (R. H. Lee). Madison hesitates to furnish material for publicity before looking over the letters he desires sent him. [Draft.] 4°. 2 pages.

1824, March 11, Montpellier. Returns letters sent for inspection, with a view to publication. Sees no objection except, perhaps, in a doubtful passage which may touch personal feelings. [Draft.] Strip of paper.

LEE, WILLIAM. *Washington.*

1817, September 8, Montpellier. Incloses letter from A. Capellano and his answer. Does not wish his bust in marble on account of the expense. [Extract in Madison's hand.] 4°. 1 page.

LEGISLATIVE AND JUDICIARY.

1833 (?), not dated. Memorandum on the supposition that the legislative and judiciary departments are coordinate. [Draft.] Scrap of paper.

LEHRE, THOMAS.

1828, August 2, Montpellier. Acknowledging letter of July 21. Is pained to find Lehre confirming the spirit of disunion prevailing in South Carolina. The awful consequences such a separation portends. [Draft.] Strip of paper.

LEIGH, B. W. *Washington.*

1836, May 1, Montpellier. Acknowledging receipt of copy of his speech of April 4 and 5. The expunging question. A preservation of the original journals of Congress should be kept in a known spot. Copies get dispersed. [Copy.] Scrap of paper.

1836. On the subject of Mr. Leigh's letter to the general assembly of Virginia respecting the obligation imposed on a representative by instructions of his constituents. small 4°. 5 pages and strip of paper.

LEONARD, JONATHAN. *Canton, Mass.*

1829, April 28, Montpellier. Acknowledging letter of 10th, with a copy of the "History of Dedham". [Draft.] Strip of paper.

LEVINS, THOMAS C. *New York.*

1827, June 19, Montpellier. Acknowledging letter of June 14. The subject will be laid before the visitors of the University of Virginia. [Draft.] Strip of paper.

LEWIS, ROBERT. *Fredericksburg.*

1824, November 10, Montpellier. Acknowledging letter of 8th, inviting him in behalf of the citizens of Fredericksburg to a dinner to be given to Gen. Lafayette, and which he is obliged to decline. [Draft.] Scrap of paper.

LEWIS, SAMUEL S.

1829, February 16, Montpellier. Acknowledging letter of 3d. Appreciates the compliment tendered him in electing him a member of the "Washington College parthenon." [Draft.] Strip of paper.

LIST, FREDERICK.

1829, February 3, Montpellier. Declines to subscribe to a proposed work relating to legislation for encouragement of domestic manufactures. [Draft.] Strip of paper.

LITTELL & HENRY. *Philadelphia.*

1821, October 18, Montpellier. Acknowledging letter of September 24 Approbation of the proposed edition of Blackstone, accompanied by a comparative view of the laws of the United States and of the several States. [Draft.] 4°. 2 pages.

LIVINGSTON, EDWARD. *New Orleans.*

1822, July 10, Montpellier. Acknowledging letter of May 19, accompanied by a copy of Mr. Livingston's report to the legislature of Louisiana on the subject of a penal code. Appróval of the work with suggestions. Immunity of religion from civil jurisdiction. [Draft.] 4°. 5 pages.

Washington.

1824, April 17, Montpellier. Thanks him for copy of his speech on internal improvements. Observations on the question of canals. Uncontested authority of Congress over the territories. [Copy.] 4°. 3 pages.

1825, December 27, Montpellier. Acknowledging letter of March 13. Hesitates to make suggestions on Livingston's work on the penal code of Louisiana, as the author desires. The hazard of substituting compound technical terms for new ones. [Draft.] 4°. 2 pages.

1830, May 8, Montpellier. Acknowledging letter of April 29. The coincidence of the proceedings of the Virginia legislature in 1798 and 1799, with the nullifying doctrine. The interpretation of the same. [Draft.] 4°. 1 page.

1833, January 24, Montpellier. Acknowledging letter of 19th inst. Gives permission to the publication of his remarks on Livingston's speech on Foote's resolution respecting the resolutions of the Virginia legislature in 1798–'99 on the nullifying doctrine. [Draft.] Strip of paper.

Paris.

1834, August 2, Montpellier. Acknowledging letter of February 8. The decrepit state of Madison's health. Thanks Livingston for his outline of the condition of France. Death of Lafayette. Its influence on the future game of parties. Party spirit rages in the United States. No where more so than in Virginia. [Draft.] 8°. 2 pages.

LIVINGSTON, R. R. *New York.*

1795. August 10, Orange. Gloomy views on the treaty with Great Britain. A ruinous bargain, a disqualification to make a good one with any other nation. [Copy.] fol. 4 pages.

Paris.

1804, February 7, Washington. Livingston's correspondence with Monroe. Question whether they should remain private or placed on files of the office. Bill pending in Congress for the government of Louisiana. Reasons for not sending Livingston a letter of leave. [Press copy.] "Private." 4°. 3 pages.

1805, July 5, Washington. Acknowledging letter of June 29. Congratulates him on his safe arrival from abroad. Spain struggles against our demands and France has her views in defeating the negotiation. Should our disputes with Spain involve France and throw the United States into the British scale she may promote an adjustment of our affairs with her ally. [Draft.] 4°. 2 pages.

LOMAX, Professor.

1827, September 10, Montpellier. Acknowledging letter of 6th. Respecting matters connected with the Virginia University. Is gratified at the increased number of students. [Draft.] Strip of paper.

LONG, Professor.

1827, September 8, Montpellier. Acknowledging letter of August 31. Long's retirement from the university. His proposal to try to supply the vacancy. 4°. 1 page.

1827, November 3, Montpellier. On the subject of Mr. Long's leaving the University of Virginia to accept a more eligible situation in London. Desires the arrangement may be made so that his departure may be delayed until a successor may be obtained. [Draft.] Strip of paper.

1828, January 4, Montpellier. Acknowledging a letter. Long's appointment to the Greek professorship at the London University necessitates his presence there on October 1. Will write Mr. Bingham that the difficulty is greater here than in England in procuring a successor. [Draft.]
Scrap of paper.

1828, January 7, Montpellier. Circular letter addressed to the trustees of the Virginia University relative to Prof. Long. [Draft.] Strip of paper.

LONGACRE, JAMES B.

1833, August 27, Montpellier. Acknowledging letter of 21st. In conformity with his request a friend will prepare a brief chronicle of Madison's career, with remarks and references, in order to preserve uniformity in Longacre's gallery. [Draft.]
Strip of paper.

LOVELL, JOHN E.

1832, March 31, Montpellier. Acknowledging letter of 22d. Respecting qualifications and accomplishments of Mr. Cardello for a position in the University of Virginia. [Draft.] 8°. 1 page.

LOWNDES, WILLIAM J. *Washington.*

1816, October 16, Washington. On resignation of Mr. Dallas, Secretary of the Treasury, he offers Mr. Lowndes the vacant position. [Draft.]
4°. 1 page.

LUDLOW, BENJAMIN. *Trenton,* N. J.

1812, July 25, Washington. Acknowledging receipt of the addresses of the convention of Republican delegates of New Jersey, approving of the war and promising support. Explains the causes of the war. [Draft.] large fol. 2 pages.

LYNCH, D.

1817, June 27, Montpellier. Acknowledging letter of 18th informing him of his election as member of the American Society for Encouragement of Domestic Manufactures. Accepts the honor and gives his views on the desirability of protection to domestic industry. [Draft.] 4°. 2 pages.

LYON, ISAAC S.

1834, September 20, Montpellier. Acknowledging letter of April 20. Is sorry that upon looking into the pamphlets he possesses is unable to find any that would supply the specified chasm. [Draft.]
Strip of paper.

MCCARAHER, A., and others.

1834, June 29, Montpellier. Acknowledging letter inviting him to a Democratic festival on July 4. Is obliged to decline and sends a sentiment. [Draft.] Scrap of paper.

McClure & Robertson.

1806, September 7, Paris. Falwar Skipwith's draft on Madison in favor of McClure & Robertson. Paid. 4°. 1 page.

McDuffie, George. *Washington.*

1824, January 3, Montpellier. Acknowledging letter of December 26. Inclosing copy of "a joint resolution" for amending the Constitution in the case of choosing a President and Vice-President, accompanied by a "report" on the same. 4°. 4 pages.

1828, March 30, Montpellier. Acknowledging receipt of copy of the report on the state of public finances. Theoretic views on the tariff. A nation that does not provide against the effect of wars and the policy of other nations on its commerce and manufactures exposes those interests to caprice and casualty of events. [Copy.] Strip of paper.

1830, May 8, Montpellier. Acknowledging receipt of copy of the late report on the Bank of the United States. Its merits discussed. [Draft.] Scrap of paper.

McIntosh, John. *McIntosh County, N. C.*

1809, October 28, Washington. Acknowledging receipt of the resolutions of a meeting of the inhabitants of McIntosh County of September 25, approving of the measures of the President in the present state of our foreign relations. [Draft.] 4°. 1 page.

Mackay, ——.

1820, September 1, Montpellier. Incloses a bill on Mr. Maury for £100, to cover an advance on account of shipment of tobacco. [Signed J. M.] [Draft.] 4°. 1 page.

1821, January 7, Montpellier. Accident to the saw in his mill. Asks him to attend to it. Also to the sale of his flour. [Draft.] Strip of paper.

1821, February 20, Montpellier. Has received a saw for his mill. As it is defective he will return it and wishes to be sent another. [Draft.] 4°. 1 page.

Mackay & Campbell. *Fredericksburg.*

1820, December 29, Montpellier. Acknowledging a letter of 18th, respecting the transferring an account with Maury & Latham, of Liverpool, to Mackay & Campbell. On shipments of tobacco. [Draft.] [*See* letter from Mackay & Campbell dated 18th. Letters to Madison.]

1821, July 21, Montpellier. Acknowledging letter of 19th. Incloses a draft on Maury & Latham. Gives instructions as to proceeds. [Draft.] 4°. 1 page.

1821, October —, Montpellier. Returned the note covered by letter of 4th, signed. Articles of furniture marked R. Cutts, for himself. [Copy.] 4°. 1 page.

1821, December 18, Montpellier. Private financial matters. [Draft.] Strips of paper.

McKenney, T. L.

1825, May 2, Montpellier. The efforts to civilize the Indians. The American and British conduct towards them contrasted. Policy pursued during the late war. Sends a copy of the "Talk" of a deputation of Indians at the commencement of the war. [Draft.] Strip of paper.

McKENNEY, T. L.

1825, May 14, Montpellier. Acknowledging letter of 10th. The "Talk with the Indians" vindicates our Government from unprovoked and unfounded charges. [Draft.] Strip of paper.

1826, February 10, Montpellier. Acknowledging letter of 4th. Review and opinions of the article in the North American Review concerning the Indians. Gradations from the most savage state to the advanced one in Mexico and Peru. [Draft.] 4°. 2 pages.

1826, March 27, Montpellier. Acknowledging letter of 18th, with a document on the civilization of the Indians. Its moral and intellectual merit. [Draft.] Strip of paper.

McLEAN, JOHN. *Washington.*

1824, February 2, Montpellier. Acknowledging letter of January 28. Views on the publication of the archives of the Revolution. Discretion to be used concerning confidential matter in correspondence. [Draft.] 4°. 1 page.

MADISON, AMBROSE. *Orange.*

1791, January 2, Philadelphia. Acknowledging letter of December 19. Excise on distilled spirits of this country will probably take place. Also duties on imported rum. Private business. 4°. 1 page.

1791, May 19, New York. Acknowledging letter of 9th. Business matters. 4°. 1 page.

1795, March 1, Philadelphia. Directs his brother to forward inclosed letter to Mr. Fontaine, containing remarks relating to public subjects, to be made use of on election day. Illness of Mrs. Madison. Private business. fol. 1 page.

MADISON, JAMES, Senior. *Orange.*

1769, September 30, Nassau Hall. Acknowledging receipt of a letter. The annual commencement. Conferring of degrees. Events at the college. fol. 2 pages.

1770, July 23, Nassau Hall. Acknowledging letter of June 4. His expenses at college. On the engagement of a tutor. Sends measure of neck and wrists for shirts. The merchants of New York break their resolution to not import. Their letters asking cooperation burned by the students in the college yard. The new students all dress in American cloth. 4°. 2 pages.

1771, October 9, Princeton. Acknowledging letter of September 25. His desire to remain in Princeton the coming winter. Private family matters. 4°. 2 pages.

1776, June 27, Williamsburg. The negotiation and sale of a bill of exchange. Not known when the convention will adjourn. Rumors that 7 ships have come to the aid of Dunmore. small 4°. 1 page.

1777, March —, Orange. Cure of one of the members of the family by bleeding. Arrest of one Benjamin Haley as a disaffected person and adherent of King George. fol. 2 pages.

1778, January 23, Williamsburg. Takes lodgings with his kinsman, Mr. Madison (afterwards Bishop). Shoes, etc., collected for the army. Mr. Madison (senior) will be informed what to do with them.

MADISON, JAMES, Senior.

However inconvenient it is to continue to be lieutenant of the county suggests it would have an unfriendly aspect on the execution of the draft to resign. 4°. 2 pages.

1778, March 6, Williamsburg. Relating to money matters and purchase of books abroad. Burgoyne's disaster creates a fermentation in England. Parliament refuses to grant supplies for carrying on the war. Arrival in North Carolina of a rich cargo. Arrival at Martinique with 7,000 tents from France to the grand army. 4°. 3 pages

1779, June 25, Williamsburg. Acknowledging receiving £2,000 from Mr. Hunter. The horse sent Madison by his father in meager plight. Sends newspapers. 4°. 1 page.

1779, December 8, Williamsburg. The assembly adopts no plan to comply with requisitions from Congress. The tax on tobacco. Depreciation of our money and rise of produce. New arrangements in the college. 4°. 3 pages.

1780, March 20, Philadelphia. Progressive depreciation of paper currency. Schemes for raising money to carry on public measures. Recommendations by Congress to the States. small 4°. 1 page.

1781, August 1, Philadelphia. Sends him a barrel of sugar and a bag of coffee. The proposed mediation of Russia in the dispute between England and Holland. Gen. Washington's preparations against New York. French fleet at Rhode Island. Reports that orders for the British troops in Virginia under Cornwallis to sail to New York. High prices of tobacco and other articles. fol. 3 pages.

1782, February 12, Philadelphia. Disappointment in not receiving money. The legislature has made no provision for the subsistence of the delegates. 4°. 2 pages.

1782, March 30, Philadelphia. Purchase of books. Unless the assembly decides and allows on the accounts of the delegates, will be obliged to sell a negro to meet arrearages. Rumors that Great Britain will suspend offensive war against us to direct their whole resources against France. Their artifices. fol. 2 pages.

1782, May 20, Philadelphia. The anxiety on account of West India news. Continental money passes at a great discount. His colleagues returned home, but as it is a crisis which calls for a full representation from every State he will stay. The state of his finances low. 4°. 3 pages.

1783, January 1, Philadelphia. Negotiations for peace with Great Britain said to be going on. Mr. Jefferson to depart soon in order to give his aid in case it be in season. 4°. 1 page.

1783, February 12, Philadelphia. Reports prevalent on the subject of peace. The most favorable evidence of their truth is the material fall in price of imported goods. small 4°. 1 page.

1783, May 27, Philadelphia. Acknowledging letter of 16th. Buying of books for Mons. Joseph. Joseph Chew's position and expectations. No information respecting the definitive treaty and bill for opening trade with United States. 4°. 2 pages.

MADISON, JAMES, Senior.

1783, June 5, Philadelphia. Sends papers containing arrangements made by the British ministry. Sends pamphlets of Congress on subject of revenue, etc. Will go to Virginia before fall.
4°. 1 page.

1783, August 30, Princeton. The definitive treaty not yet come over. Sir J. Carleton notifies Congress of his reception of final orders for evacuation of New York. Gen. Washington in Princeton on invitation of Congress to be consulted for provisions necessary for security in time of peace. Question of final residence of Congress. Princeton too crowded for business or ease.
fol. 1 page.

1783, September 8, Philadelphia. Acknowledging letter of August 22. Shall return to Princeton tomorrow. Respecting the disposal of his slave Billy. Does not wish to punish him by transportation for coveting that liberty for which we have paid the price of so much blood and proclaimed so often to be right and worthy the pursuit of every human being. 4°. 2 pages.

1784, May 13, Richmond. Sends him a pair of spectacles. Jefferson an associate with Franklin and Adams, appointed by Congress in forming commercial treaties and will proceed immediately to Europe. Jay returns to America and will be Secretary of Foreign Affairs if he will accept the offer. 4°. 1 page.

1784, June 5, Richmond. Private business matters. The house of delegates have agreed to postpone the June tax till January. The senate may require one-half to be collected earlier. 4°. 1 page.

1784, June 15, Richmond. Private business. The senate have ratified the postponement of the taxes till the last day of January. Possibly an intermediate tax will be essential. small 4°. 2 pages.

1784, June 24, Richmond. Private business. Abortive efforts in the assembly for amendment of the constitution and fulfilling the treaty of peace in the article of British debts. small 4°. 1 page.

1784, September 6, Philadelphia. Arrived in company with Lafayette, who proceeds north as far as Boston, from thence to the Indian treaty at Fort Schuyler, and from thence to Virginia. He wishes Madison to accompany him. He may do so. 4°. 1 page.

1784, November 27, Richmond. The bill for confirming surveys against subsequent entries negatived by a large majority. Vote in favor of general assessment. Vote passed for circuit courts. Private business. fol. 1 page.

1784, December 3, Richmond. Vote in the Virginia assembly in favor of circuit courts. The Indian treaty at Fort Stanwix. The commission to proceed to Fort Pitt to hold another treaty. The British still hold the Northwestern posts in justification of breach of the peace in Virginia and New York. small 4°. 1 page.

1785, January 6, Richmond. End of the tedious session. Acts which have passed. Incloses act for incorporating the Episcopal Church, the result of much altercation. fol. 2 pages.

MADISON, JAMES, Senior.

1785, November 18, Richmond. Business matters. Public credit has more friends and paper money more adversaries. Names of the Delegates to Congress for 1786, R. H. Lee, Wm. Grayson, James Monroe, H. Lee, jr., Edward Carrington, and Carter Braxton. 4°. 1 page.

1785, December 24, Richmond. Miscarriage of the assize scheme. Reform of the county courts. Bill for payment of British debts. Price of tobacco. Bill for establishing religious freedom. Business matters. small 4°. 3 pages.

1785, December 27, Richmond. Acknowledging letter of 24th. Private business. 4°. 1 page.

1786, November 1, Richmond. Discussion in the assembly relative to paper money. Opposition to it. Commotion in Massachusetts. Shay's rebellion. The discontented prefers to aim only at reform of their constitution. 4° 2 pages.

1786, November 16, Richmond. Indents will continue to be receivable. A bill pending to make tobacco receivable for taxes. 4°. 1 page.

1786, November 24, Richmond. The house of delegates passes a bill making tobacco receivable in the tax. small 4°. 1 page.

1786, December 12, Richmond. Inclosing a paper stating the mode and terms in which tobacco is made a commutable. Repeal of the port bill. District courts bill differs from the assize. Taxes on articles of luxury. Proposition that another convention be authorized in Kentucky to decide the question of independence. 4°. 2 pages.

1786, December 17, Richmond. Acknowledging a letter. Private business. fol. 1 page.

1787, February 25, New York. Refusal of Connecticut to comply with the requisition of Congress. Payments of the Federal Treasury are ceasing everywhere. People's minds losing confidence in our political system. 4°. 1 page.

1787, April 1, New York. Acknowledging letter of 17th. The convention for adopting the new constitution. Rhode Island refuses concurrence. Hopeful views. fol. 1 page.

1787, May 27, Philadelphia. Failure of the deputies to assemble for the convention. Gen. Washington in the chair. 4°. 2 pages.

1787, July 28, Philadelphia. Acknowledging letter of 9th. Private matters relating to his slave Billy. Nothing known of the proceedings of the convention. Civil war in Holland. Many are flying to England. Sale of western lands. Treaties with Indians. Indian confederacy under Brandt. 4°. 2 pages.

1787, August 12, Philadelphia. Assembling of the convention. Absence of deputies from Rhode Island, New Hampshire, and New York. Great drought in Virginia. 4°. 1 page.

1787, September 4, Philadelphia. Acknowledging letter of July 9. Convention not yet broken up. Proceedings unknown. Spirit of insurrection shows itself in Greenbrier County. Thinks the report exaggerated. Drought in that part of the country. 4°. 1 page.

MADISON, JAMES, Senior.

1787, September 30, New York. Act of the convention for forming the new Constitution forwarded to the States. Reception problematical. 4°. 1 page.

1788, January 20, Richmond. The friends of the Constitution are confident of superiority. The final question will decide the contest in a few days. The judiciary bill. 4°. 1 page.

1788, July 6, Richmond. Sends two copies of the Federalist. Is just setting out northward 4°. 1 page.

1788, July 27, New York. The Constitution ratified by the Virginia convention. North Carolina not yet heard from. 4°. 2 pages.

1788, August 18, New York. Acknowledging letter of 9th. The new Constitution. Only two States oppose it, Rhode Island and North Carolina. 4°. 2 pages.

1788, September 6, New York. The antifederalists exerting themselves for an early convention. Congress not yet settled the place for meeting of the new Government. 4°. 2 pages.

1788, December 18, Alexandria. On his way home. small 4°. 1 page.

1789, February 24, Mount Vernon. Unparalleled badness of the roads. Shall delay his departure for New York a few days. 4°. 2 pages.

1789, July 5, New York. The business in Congress. Bills imposing duties on imposts and tonnage. The distinction between nations in treaty and those not in treaty. Great Britain on same footing with the most favored nation. Bills for colleeting impost and regulating coasting trade. Amendments to the Constitution. fol. 2 pages.

1790, February 27, New York. Incloses papers giving proceedings of Congress. The proposed assumption of State debts. Fluctuations of stock. High price of grain. 4°. 2 pages.

1790, May 2, New York. The high price of tobacco and grain likely to continue. The influenza prevalent. fol. 1 page.

1790, June 13, New York. Incloses a few grains of rice from the South Seas. Question of the future seat of Government. fol. 1 page.

1790, July 31, New York. Acknowledging letter of 9th. The funding bill passed the two Houses. The provision for the State debts postponed to next session. It will probably consist chiefly of duties on rum distilled in the United States and a few imported articles. Expects the adjournment in a week. [Signature torn of.] 4°. 3 pages.

1790, August 14, New York. Shall remain in New York a few weeks for the pleasure of Jefferson's company as far as Orange. fol. 1 page.

1790, November 28, Philadelphia. Private business. 4°. 1 page.

1791, January 23, Philadelphia. Peace between Great Britain and Spain. Sad accounts from France. The excise bill opposed. Thinks it will pass. The Kentucky bill will probably pass. The

MADISON, JAMES, Senior.

bank bill will not go through this session. The militia and western land bill wait for the conclusion of the excise bill. fol. 1 page.

1791, February 13, Philadelphia. Acknowledging letter of January 31. The excise bill not yet passed the Senate. Bill for incorporating a bank passed both Houses. Bill for admitting Kentucky has become a law. Vermont applying for same privilege. Bill for selling western lands before the House. 4°. 2 pages.

1791, July 2, New York. Acknowledging letter of May 29. His tour with Jefferson an interesting one. Denies having been concerned in the Yazoo transaction; thinks it disgraceful. No probability of war between Great Britain and Russia. A minister from Great Britain expected soon. 4°. 2 pages.

1791, October 30, Philadelphia. Arrival of Mr. Hammond the minister from Great Britain. His public character not yet announced in form. The subject of his mission only known to the Executive Department. 4°. 1 page.

1791, November 13, Philadelphia. Family concerns and business matters. 4°. 3 pages.

1791, December 3, Philadelphia. Acknowledging letter of November 12. Private business. Apportionment of Representatives still with the Senate. fol. 1 page.

1791, December 10, Philadelphia. Acknowledging letter of November 26. Private business. Bill for apportioning Representatives returned by the Senate with alteration. [Signature cut off.] 4°. 1 page.

1792, March 2, Philadelphia. Private business. Bill for the western defense settled between the two Houses. Representation apportionment still depending in the Senate. The militia bill in the House. Probable adjournment next month. 4°. 1 page.

1792, March 15, Philadelphia. Acknowledging letter of February 1. Changes in the representation bill in the House. The House taken up with the Georgia election. 4°. 2 pages.

1792, March 30, Philadelphia. The representation bill passed both Housess. The mint bill passed. Assumption of State debts. St. Domingo remains in distress. 4°. 1 page.

1792, April 17, Philadelphia. Col. Wadsworth, of Connecticut, wishes to be sent him a barrel of peach brandy. fol. 1 page.

1792, April 27, Philadelphia. Congress to adjourn May 5. Private business. fol. 1 page.

1792, May 7, Philadelphia. Adjournment postponed till 9th. Private business. 4°. 1 page.

Healing Springs.

1792, July 6, Orange. Private business and family matters. 4°. 1 page.

Orange.

1792, November 6, Philadelphia. Senate and House. Session opened by a speech from the President. Nothing new from France. 4°. 2 pages.

MADISON, JAMES, Senior.

1792, November 23, Philadelphia. Private business. small 4°. 1 page.

1793, November 25, Dumfries. Abatement of the fever at Philadelphia. The legislature will meet there at once. Private business. Accounts from Europe say that the carnage of the British and allied troops was dreadful. The Republican forces advancing to recover Toulon. fol. 1 page.

1794, February 21, Philadelphia. Acknowledging letter of January 27. Subject of dispatches of our minister to Great Britain unknown. Infers that there is nothing agreeable in them. Commercial propositions in Congress. Proposition for a fleet to blockade the Algerines. Arrival of French ships in Chesapeake Bay. fol. 2 pages.

1794, March 10, Philadelphia. Acknowledging letter of February 17. Genet superceded by Fauchet. Depredations on our commerce by the British. The commercial resolutions. The bill for six frigates. Recapture of Toulon confirmed. fol. 2 pages.

1794, April 7, Philadelphia. No action yet taken on the sequestration of British debts. Motion made that all trade with Great Britain be stopped until the treaty be executed and late depredations paid for. 4°. 1 page.

1794, April 21, Philadelphia. Jay appointed minister to Great Britain. The proposition for enforcing our demand for redress by making our market a condition is favored by a majority, but eastern members violently opposed. Martinique surrendered to the British. Success of the French in Europe. fol. 1 page.

1794, April 25, Philadelphia. Acknowledging letter of 11th. Business matters. The nonimportation law agreed to. Its passage through the Senate doubtful. The embargo continued till May 25. fol. 1 page.

1794, May 4, Philadelphia. Private business. Nonimportation bill rejected in the Senate. They rely on the mission of Jay to sue for satisfaction. House of Representatives occupied with new taxes to defray expenses of the naval armament. fol. 2 pages.

1794, May 19, Philadelphia. Acknowledging letter of 5th. Discontent as to the excise tax. The embargo not to be continued. Price of flour. fol. 1 page.

1794, June 6, Philadelphia. Acknowledging letter of May 26. Private business. Monroe about to sail for France as minister. 4°. 1 page.

1794, November 10, Philadelphia. The first communication from Jay was dry and equivocal on the part of Lord Grenville. It is thought that the mission will not be without effect. French successes alarm the British. The naval equipment of Denmark and Sweden. Monroe's reception by the national convention. Private matters. fol. 1 page.

1794, November 17, Philadelphia. Accounts from Europe. Irresistible force of the French armies and the distresses of their combined enemies. Nothing official or private from Monroe. From

MADISON, JAMES, Senior.

England the information, though not decisive, is favorable to United States. fol. 1 page.

1794, December 14, *Philadelphia*. Acknowledging letter of 24th November and 3d instant. Private business. High cost of living. Prices of all things 50 per cent higher than last year. 4°. 3 pages.

1795, February 23, *Philadelphia*. Jay's treaty not yet come to hand. Conjectures of the newspapers. Private business. Contradicts reports that he declines being a candidate in his district in March. fol. 1 page.

1795, November 8, *Fredericksburg*. Private business. 4°. 2 pages.

1795, December 27, *Philadelphia*. The President's speech, with the answers of the two Houses. The ratification of Jay's treaty in England. Great scarcity of breadstuffs in Europe. Everything tranquil in France and the new Constitution likely to have an auspicious commencement. Flour $14 per barrel. 4°. 1 page.

1796, January 17, *Philadelphia*. The treaty not yet laid before Congress. Gen. Smith's resolution as the groundwork of a navigation act, will draw into view the subject of the treaty. French checks on the Rhine exaggerated. Britain uses every pretext for riveting the yoke on the people. Scarcity of bread. The British Government parrying this calamity by encouraging importations and prohibiting their use for other purposes than food. 4°. 2 pages.

1796, February 21, *Philadelphia*. News from Europe. The Constitution is promising in France. Aspect of things threatening in England. Provisions dear. Flour $14 in Philadelphia. The treaty still as it was and that with Spain not arrived. That with Algiers is before the Senate. 4°. 1 page.

1796, March 6, *Philadelphia*. Acknowledging letter of February 8. Private business. The Spanish treaty ratified by the Senate. The navigation of the Mississippi. Boundaries defined, etc. The British treaty laid before the House of Representatives. Referred to committee. No question yet been taken on it. fol. 1 page.

1796, March 13, *Philadelphia*. Acknowledging letter of February 24. Friendly suit for adjusting his share in lands held in the name of his late brother. Agricultural and matters relating to his farm. The House of Representatives discussing the British treaty. The majority will vote that Congress has a constitutional right to refuse to execute it. The British armament in the West Indies. fol. 3 pages.

1796, April 11, *Philadelphia*. Acknowledging letter of March 28. Purchase of a chariot. Proposition calling for papers refused by the President, concerning the treaty. The Spanish treaty will be provided for. The British will hardly get through the obstacles to its passage, particularly in seizures of our vessels and seamen. fol. 1 page.

1796, April 25, *Philadelphia*. Business matters. The treaty question not yet decided. Probably the majority will be against carrying it into effect

MADISON, JAMES, Senior.

when the Executive will give no information and the British continue to rob our vessels and impress our seamen. fol. 1 page.

1796, no date, Philadelphia. Congress will be summoned to meet on May 25 ensuing. Gen. Pinkney not admitted by the French Government and placed in a mortifying position. Failure of negotiations for peace between France and Great Britain. State of things between us and France not satisfactory. fol. 1 page.

Healing Springs.

1796, August 10, Orange. Work proceeding on the new mill. Family and farm news. 4°. 1 page.

Orange.

1796, November 27, Philadelphia. The election for President. The general prospect is that the chance is in favor of Adams. Remonstrance of Mr. Adet. Unless harmony is restored the consequences will be serious. Spain and other powers may concur in her measures against us. Agricultural and household affairs. 4°. 2 pages.

1796, December 19, Philadelphia. Agricultural, household, and private business matters. fol. 1 page.

1796, December 25, Philadelphia. Acknowledging letters of 11th and 12th. Business matters and agricultural. Extreme cold weather. Adams will be President and Jefferson probably Vice-President. fol. 1 page.

1797, January 15, Philadelphia. Acknowledging letter of 2d. Matters relating to his farm. fol. 1 page.

1797, January 22, Philadelphia. Acknowledging letter of 8th. Matters relating to his farm. Sweeping system of captures adopted by the French, particularly in the West Indies. The Spaniards their allies. The communication to Congress by the President more likely to widen than to close the breach between the two republics. fol. 1 page.

1797, January 29, Philadelphia. Agricultural matters. House of Representatives resolved on a direct tax. Dreads the possibility of a foreign war. Efforts of British partisans who blow the coals of enmity to France and who openly recommend war with her and an alliance with England. 4°. 2 pages.

1797, February 5, Philadelphia. Acknowledging letters of January 10 and 23. Farm business. Nothing occurs to alleviate the crisis with France. Failure of English negotiations with France for peace. fol. 1 page.

1797, February 13, Philadelphia. Acknowledging letters of January 16 and 30. Farm matters. fol. 1 page.

1797, February 19, Philadelphia. Farm business. Prospects of peace in Europe. The French continue successful with their armies. Debates in Congress about taxes will probably end in increase of duties on sugar, molasses, tea, etc. fol. 1 page.

1797, March 12, Philadelphia. Declines to be a candidate for election to the assembly. Private business matters. The temper of France towards the United States not favorable. Their resentment the fruits of the British treaty. fol. 2 pages.

MADISON, MRS.

1814, August 29, Washington. After the burning of Washington. Giving directions as to her movements. [The first portion of the letter cut off.] [Signed J. M.] 4°. 1 page.

MADISON, WILLIAM.

1829, March 25, Montpellier. Respecting the invitation of delegates of his senatorial district to represent it in the convention to propose amendments to the constitution of the State. [Draft.] Strip of paper.

MARBOIS, BARBÉ. *Paris.*

1803, November 4, Washington. Acknowledging letter of 21 Prairial. The formal approbation of the late treaty by every branch of our Government. It is to be hoped it establishes perfect harmony between the two countries. Full reliance is placed on the reciprocal disposition of the French Government. Agreeable recollections of public and private nature. [Draft.] 4°. 4 pages.

No date. Acknowledging volume relating to the equestrian statue of Henry IV, with one of the medals. France is happy in having had a King worthy of national devotion. [Draft.] "Not sent." 4°. 1 page.

MARTIN, THOMAS, Rev.

1769, August 10, Nassau Hall. Is affected at hearing of Martin's misfortune. Describes his situation at college, his occupation and prospect. fol. 2 pages.

MASON, GEORGE. *Williamsburg.*

1826, July 14, Montpellier. Acknowledging letter of 6th. Gives the origin of the "Memorial and Remonstrances against Religious Establishment." [Draft.] 4°. 1 page.

1827, December 29, Montpellier. Acknowledging letter of 10th, with copies of remonstrances in favor of religious liberty. Approves of his project in writing a biography of his ancestor, Col. George Mason. Gives information as to the share Mason had in preparing the Declaration of Independence, Declaration of Rights, and the Constitution. [Draft.] 4°. 2 pages.

MASON, J. M. *New York.*

1810, February 5, Washington. Acknowledging letter of January 29. Can not furnish at present the form of a constitution delineated by Gen. Hamilton, neither papers relative to the convention. [Draft.] 4°. 1 page.

MAURY, JAMES. *Liverpool.*

1803, November —, Virginia. Bill of lading 21 hogsheads of tobacco shipped per *Atlantic* for Liverpool for sale. 8°. 1 page.

1822, September 28, Montpellier. Acknowledging letter of July 20. Change of the British Government in her colonial policy. The United States will meet Great Britain and other nations in a liberal and reciprocal system. The season and crops. Great drought. [Draft.] small 4°. 2 pages.

1823, March 24, Montpellier. The speech of the French King against the independence of Spain. Much interest expressed to know the course of the British Government. Bad crops in Virginia. [Draft.] 4°. 1 page.

MAURY, JAMES.

1828, April 5, Montpellier. Acknowledging letters of March 29 and 31. Gives reasons why Mr. Maury's advice to the tobacco planters will not be followed. The tariff. Cotton and silk manufactures. Unsatisfactory accounts of the prospects of the Monticello family. Failure of the lottery scheme. Publication of the Jefferson manuscripts. [Draft.] Strip of paper.

1830, December 10, Montpellier. The new constitution of Virginia. Discontent in South Carolina with the tariff. Is not supported in her violent doctrines. Sends copy of President's Message. [Copy.] 4°. 2 pages.

MAURY, W.

1819, December 24, Montpellier. Acknowledging letter of 4th. Agricultural matters. The tobacco culture. [Draft.] small 4°. 2 pages.

MAYO, ROBERT, and WILLIAM A. BARTON.

1823, March 31, Montpellier. Acknowledging copy of an address in behalf of the Juvenile Library Company of Richmond. Commends the laudable activity of its founders. [Draft.] 4°. 1 page.

MAZZEI, PHILIP.

1781, July 7, Philadelphia. Acknowledging receipt of letters of December 7 and November 30. A narrative of military operations and state of our finances. Barbarity of the enemy in the South. [Copy.] 4°. 11 pages.

MEADE, JOEL K. *Washington.*

1820, October 17, Montpellier. Acknowledging letter of 12th. Madison's views relative to the project of a lottery in aid of educating indigent youth. [Draft.] 4°. 2 pages.

MEADE, R.

1828, June 3, Montpellier. Acknowledging letter of May 27, inclosing letters from Dr. Cooper and Mr. Duponceau, recommending a candidate for the classical professorship of the University of Virginia. [Draft.] Strip of paper.

MERRY, ANTHONY. *Washington.*

1804, September 3, Virginia. Acknowledging letter of August 25. Regrets that sanction is given to impressment of seamen from American vessels. Further discussion with him (the British minister) not advantageous. The subject will probably be seen in a more satisfactory light by the counsels of Great Britain, which may indicate a disposition to cherish friendly relations. Irregularities charged against French ships of war will be investigated. [Draft.] 4°. 3 pages.

1806, January —, Washington. Acknowledging a letter stating that His Majesty has directed a discontinuance of the blockade at the entrance of the Elbe and Weser. These communications considered as friendly to the commercial interests of the United States. It is the only light in which they can be reconciled with the true principles of blockade and unquestionable rights of neutral commerce. [Draft.] 4°. 1 page.

MOORE, GABRIEL.

1832, March 31, Montpellier. On the subject of the Loyal Company, in which his father (Madison's) was interested. [Copy.] 4°. 1 page.

MORRIS, ANTHONY.

1827, May 28, Montpellier. Acknowledging letter of 7th, covering a letter from Judge Peters, relating to the Fellenberg institution. Returns the letter as requested. [Draft.] Strip of paper.

MORSE, JEDEDIAH, Rev. *New Haven.*

1822, February 16, Montpellier. Acknowledging letter of 16th, with printed constitution of a society for the benefit of the Indians. [Draft and copy.] 4°. 3 pages.

1823, March 8, Montpellier. Acknowledges, with thanks, receipt of copies of "The New System of Modern Geography" and "Ancient and Modern Geography." [Draft.] Scrap of paper.

1823, March 28, Montpellier. Answers to questions propounded by the Society for the Amelioration and Gradual Abolition of Slavery, a printed copy of which is appended. Requests that any use be made of the answers it may be done without reference to the source furnishing them. [Draft.] 4°. 2 pages, and printed fol., 3 pages.

MONROE. *Trenton.*

1784, November —, Richmond. Acknowledges a letter with a cipher. Arrival of Gen. Washington and Lafayette. Both addressed and entertained. Proceedings of the House. fol. 1 page.

1784, November 14, Richmond. Congratulations on his escape and safe return to Trenton. The Indians unquiet. Spaniards charged with spurring them on. The House of Delegates to urge treaties with the Southern Indians and negotiate with Spain touching the Mississippi. Other proceedings of the Virginia legislature. fol. 1 page.

1784, November 27, Richmond. Acknowledging letter of 15th. Umbrage given to the commissioners of the United States by the negotiations of New York with the Indians. fol. 3 pages.

1784, December 4, Richmond. The proposition for establishing circuit courts in Virginia. Propositions in favor of the fourth article of the treaty of peace by Mr. Jones. Other proceedings in the legislature. Busts of Lafayette. small 4°. 2 pages.

1784, December 17, Richmond. Assize law defeated in house of delegates. Reform of the county courts proposed as substitute. Proceedings of the Virginia legislature. 4°. 2 pages.

1784, December 24, Richmond. Acknowledging letter of 14th. Rejection of the proposition to empower Congress to carry into effect the imposts as soon as 12 States would agree to it, on the ground that Rhode Island would be an inlet for clandestine trade, and other reasons specified. Extradition act for certain crimes passed. Bill for assize courts passed the Senate. small 4°. 2 pages.

New York.

1785, January 8, Richmond. Acknowledging letter of December 18. Foreign appointments should be unfrequent. The variance between United States and Great Britain; the latter's internal affairs Her disregard for our treaty. Our relations with Spain. Our title to the free use of the Mississippi. Proceedings of the Virginia legislature. fol. 3 pages.

MONROE.

1785, March 21, Orange. Acknowledging letter of February 1. Mr. Jay's letter to Congress. Affront put upon him by Congress, as Minister of Foreign Affairs. The advances which Kentucky is making towards independence. 4°. 2 pages.

1785, April 12, Orange. Acknowledging letter of March —. Appointment of Adams as minister to Great Britain. Thinks him well fitted. Hopes it has removed obstacles to the establishment of Jefferson to the Court of France. General assessment. Inconsistency of the Presbyterians respecting it. 4°. 2 pages.

1785, April 28, Orange. The elections in Virginia. The question of coinage in Congress, and weights and measures. Advocates more uniformity. 4°. 2 pages.

1785, May 29, Orange. The mode of surveying and selling the territorial fund. Dispossession of the British of the western lands. Navigation of the Mississippi. Separation of Kentucky from Virginia. A state actually set up in the back country of North Carolina. Interferences of antiquated bigotry countenanced by the legislature. 4°. 2 pages.

1785, June 21, Orange. Bill for establishing the Christian Religion. Warm opposition to it by the people. Commissioners from Georgia to demand of the Spanish governor of New Orleans the ports in the limits of that State and settlement of the boundary. An outrage on the Federal Government. Commercial discontents. Our trade completely monopolized by Great Britain. Its remedy. 4°. 2 pages.

1785, August 7, Richmond. Acknowledging letter of July 26. Proposed change of the ninth article of the confederation. Views in detail respecting the question, whether the power of regulating trade should be vested in Congress. 4°. 3 pages.

1785, December 9, Richmond. The question in Congress of confiding to it a power over trade. Proposed convention from States to Annapolis to deliberate on the state of commerce. Proceedings of the Virginia legislature. 4°. 2 pages.

1785, December 24, Richmond. Proceedings of the Virginia assembly. Bills for establishing religious freedom. British debts. The proprietary interest in the Northern Neck, and for reforming the county courts. 4°. 2 pages.

1785, December 30, Richmond. Proceedings in the Virginia assembly. Changes in the bill relative to British debts. Reform in county courts. fol. 2 pages.

1786, January 22, Richmond. Acknowledging letters of 19th December and 7th instant. Adjournment of the Virginia assembly. Digest of its proceedings. 4°. 3 pages.

1786, March 19, Orange. Acknowledging letters of February 11 and 16. Congratulates Monroe on his marriage. Joint purchase of land. Relative to the Annapolis Convention. 4°. 2 pages.

1786, April 9, Orange. Acknowledging letter of March 18. Purchase of land. The conduct of New Jersey. The opposition of New York to the im-

MONROE.

post is likely to be overcome. Power of Congress to regulate trade. 4°. 2 pages.

1786, May 13, Orange. Acknowledging letter of April 28. Purchase of land. Two conventions sitting at same time, an odd appearance. Embarrassment of Congress. Elections in Virginia. Inroads of savages in Kentucky. 4°. 2 pages.

1786, June 4, Orange. Unexpected circumstances have prevented his making the journey with Monroe as anticipated. Is obliged to postpone it. Disinclination of Kentucky to a separation. Condition of planters and merchants. Advocates for paper money. The finances of the country. 4°. 2 pages.

1786, June 21, Orange. Acknowledging letter of May 28. This letter, mostly in cipher, relates to his views on the navigation of the Mississippi and settlement of claims and accounts of States. 4°. 3 pages.

1786, August 15, Philadelphia. Incloses a letter for Mr. Jefferson in which he proposes his joining himself and Monroe in a purchase of land on the Mohawk. Conversation with Mr. Wilson on the Annapolis Convention. 4°. 3 pages.

1786, August 17, Philadelphia. Acknowledging letter of 14th. Madison's opinion on the action to be pursued in Congress on the subject of the navigation of the Mississippi. [This answer was copied on the letter from Monroe, dated August 14, 1786, on file in letters from Monroe.] [Copy.] 4°. 1 page.

1786, September 11, Annapolis. Acknowledging letters of 1st and 3rd instant. The convention at Annapolis. A proposition to break up the meeting and intimating the expediency of extending the plan at another time and place. 4°. 1 page.

1786, October 5, Philadelphia. Acknowledging letter of 2d instant. Navigation of the Mississippi. Abuses of majority rule. The purchase of land on the Mohawk. 4°. 3 pages.

King George.

1786, October 30, Richmond. The navigation of the Mississippi will be defended by the Virginia legislature. Appointments to office from Virginia. 4°. 1 page.

Fredericksburg.

1786, December 21, Richmond. Acknowledging letter of 16th. Has heard nothing from any of the other States on subjects of the Federal convention. The bill for district courts. 4°. 1 page.

Richmond.

1787, April 19, New York. The business of the Mississippi will come to a point in a few days. Proposition to remove the Government to Philadelphia. Objection to the movement. fol. 2 pages.

Virginia.

1789, May 13, New York Acknowledging letter of April —. The impost the subject of deliberation. 4°. 1 page.

Fredericksburg.

1789, August 9, New York. Acknowledging letter of July 19. The purchase of land on the Mohawk.

MONROE.

Proposed discrimination between foreign nations. Compensation for members of Congress. President's Message on Indian affairs and militia. 4°. 3 pages.

1790, April 17, New York. Acknowledging letter of 5th. The purchase of land on the Mohawk. The House of Representatives on the revenue business. Assumption of States debts. The eastern members avow a determination to oppose all provision for the public debt that does not include this. 4°. 2 pages.

1790, May 19, New York. The President has been critically ill. Commercial relations with Great Britain. Assumption of State debts. 4°. 1 page.

1790, June 1, New York. Acknowledging letter of 19th. Assumption of State debts still pending. Commercial and navigation. Residence of the seat of Government. The President has been at the point of death. Recovered. 4°. 2 pages.

Charlottesville.

1793, September 15, Orange. Conduct of Mr. Genet. Action of the Anglicans and Monocrats. Their animosity to France. England's war on our commerce by intercepting uncontraband articles bound to unblockaded ports. small 4°. 1 page.

1793, October 29, Orange. Proceedings of public meetings in Virginia. small 4°. 1 page.

Paris.

1794, December 4, Philadelphia. Acknowledging letter of September 2. Account of Monroe's arrival and reception. The prevailing idea is that the mission will be successful. The whisky rebellion in Pennsylvania. The question of a standing army. Scheme to connect the Democratic societies with the rebellion. The President's pointed reply to the Senate. The election. 4°. 7 pages.

1795, March 11, Philadelphia. Extracts from Monroe's official correspondence printed in New York papers on Jacobin Society. Political use made of them in questions agitated on the President's denunciation of Democratic societies. The treaty with Great Britain in hands of the Executive. Particulars unknown to the public. Complaints that reasons are not given for its suppression. fol. 2 pages.

1795, March 26, Philadelphia. Acknowledging letter of December 18, 1794. Mr. Swan much embarrassed in his operations by the high price of wheat and flour. Conjectures as to the terms of the treaty with Great Britain which are not yet made public. Questions as to its inconsistency with treaty with France. 4°. 3 pages.

1795, December 20, Philadelphia. Acknowledging letter of September 8. Madison's views on the effects of the Jay treaty. France continues to be friendly notwithstanding the treaty. A magnanimous conduct on the part of France will conduce to her interest. [In cipher, with its translation.] 4°. 13 pages.

1796, January 26, Philadelphia. Acknowledging letters of October 23 and 24. Conjectures as to the action of Congress on the British treaty. Conclusion of the treaty with Spain. Terms as yet un-

MONROE.

known. Scene produced by the French flag. The President's harangue grating to the British party. Edward Randolph's vindication on his resignation. [Mostly in cipher, with translation.] 4°. 7 pages.

1796, February 26, Philadelphia. Comments on the British treaty. The Algerine and Spanish treaties before the Senate. Pickering, Secretary of State, and Charles Lee, Attorney-General. The President will not serve beyond the present term. Bills before Congress. Refusal of the House to adjourn on the President's birthday. Rumors of Monroe's recall. [Mostly in cipher.] 4°. 4 pages.

1796, April 7, Philadelphia. Acknowledging letters of January 12 and 20. Harsh letter of T. Paine to the President. No suspicious that Monroe countenanced it or had knowledge of it. Rumors current that Monroe is to be recalled. Insinuations of Monroe's being engaged with Skipwith in speculations in Paris. Purchase of Chantilly. Cautions him, as his enemies lay hold of slightest pretex. fol. 3 pages.

1796, April 18, Philadelphia. Proceedings in Congress relative to the British treaty. The country stirred up to join in petitions to carry the treaty into effect. The Spanish, Algerine, and Indian treaties decided on separately and bills ordered for carrying them into effect. fol. 2 pages.

1796, May 14, Philadelphia. Full account of the proceedings in Congress and general observations on the British treaty. Bill passed the House prohibiting the sale of prizes in our ports. It is generally understood that the President will retire and Jefferson and Adams be candidates for the office. [Mostly in cipher.] fol. 3 pages.

Charlottesville.

1797, December 17, Orange (?). Acknowledging letter of 10th. Financial matters of private nature. The spirit and views of the Monarchical party. small 4°. 3 pages.

1798, February 5, Orange. Quotes from a letter of Jefferson that Talleyrand states that our envoy's pretentions are high; that possibly no arrangements can be made, but there will be no declaration of war by France. Bemonville has hopes of an accommodation, and that he will be a diplomatic envoy. The Spanish minister and the Executive. Altercations. fol. 2 pages.

1798, June 9, Orange. Acknowledging letter of 8th. The base attack of Addison. Monroe's publication will place vile calumniators in their true light. Advice to Monroe respecting the course to pursue in relation to his demand to the Executive for reasons of his recall. small 4°. 2 pages.

Albemarle.

1800, May 23, Orange. Acknowledging letter of 15th. The sedition act. The vote for disbanding the Army. 4°. 1 page.

Richmond.

1800, November 10, Orange. Acknowledging letter of 6th. Apprehensions as to state of politics. Charleston anti-republican. The coming election for President and Vice-President. fol. 1 page.

MONROE.

1800, November 10, Orange. Respecting the Presidential election. No fears of a surprise that would throw Jefferson out of the primary station. More apprehension of a tie that would appeal to the House of Representatives. fol. 1 page.

1800, December —, Orange. Acknowledging letter of 16th. Inquietude as to issue of the election. The project of a State bank. 4°. 1 page.

1801, May 6, Washington. Acknowledging letters of March 11 and 12. Livingston not to embark on his foreign mission till the ratification of the treaty in France arrives here. Mr. Callender's fine. 4°. 2 pages.

1801, June 1, Washington. Acknowledging letter of May 23. The implacability of Callender. Reasons for his irritation. Disappointment in not procuring the post-office. Rejection of a matrimonial scheme. Remittance of his fine. Mediterranean trade in jeopardy. Louisiana ceded to France. 4°. 3 pages.

Albemarle.

1801, July 25, Washington. Probability of the ratification of the convention with France. The British Government in disposition more favorable to us. Peremptory orders to their cruisers to abstain from captures. Friendly cooperation in the Mediterranean. 4°. 2 pages.

Richmond.

1801, October 24, Washington. Acknowledging letters of 11th and 15th. Procuring a sword for the heir of Gen. Campbell. Negotiations for settling difficulties under the sixth article of the British treaty. Seizures by the Spanish in the Mediterranean. Progress of public sentiment towards the administration. 4°. 2 pages.

1802, January 19, Washington. Acknowledging letter of 14th. Subjects depending between the United States and Great Britain. Unaccountable tergiversation shows itself in the leaders of the British cabinet. 4°. 2 pages.

Paris.

1803, March 1, Washington. Matters concerning Louisiana. Suggestions as to the object of Monroe's mission. Bill for the benefit of Lafayette, granting him land for military services. The Beaumarchais claim. "Private" 4°. 4 pages.

1803, April 20, Washington. The Spanish Government promptly corrected the wrong done by its officer in New Orleans. The navigation of the Mississippi. Elections in New England running against the administration. The affair between the President and Walker has had a happy eclaircissement. Grant of land to Lafayette. 4°. 3 pages.

1803, May 1, Washington. Inclosing letter for Lafayette. Conflict between England and France scarcely avoidable. To be hoped we may turn it to our interests. Monroe's arrival critical for the purpose. Orders from Spain for restoration of the deposit. The elections in the States. "Private."

4°. 4 pages.

MONROE. *London.*

1803, October 10, Washington. Spain's remonstrance against our acquisition of Louisiana. Yrujo is given to understand that we shall not withhold any means necessary to secure our object. Instructs Monroe in his negotiations with Great Britain to insist on their instructing their naval officers to abstain from impressment and respect our jurisdictional rights. 4°. 3 pages.

1804, January 18, Washington. Instructions on subject of a convention with Great Britain for preventing impressment. Monroe's outfit to London. St. Domingo in the hands of the negroes. Great Britain will not aim at monopoly of trade there. Merry (British minister) expresses dissatisfaction of his Government against the memorial of Mr. Livingston. "Private." 4°. 3 pages.

1804, February 16, Washington. The question of etiquette respecting precedence of foreign envoys at the table of the President. Explains difficulties arising from the pretensions of Merry, the British minister, sustained by Yrujo, the Spanish minister. Disgusting manners of Mrs. Merry. Merry's refusal to dine with the President and Madison's answer to Merry's note of refusal. [In cipher, with a translation.] "Private." 4°. 8 pages. fol. 3 pages.

1804, March 8, Washington. Acknowledging letter of November 25. British ministry candidly acknowledge the justice and fairness of our treaty obtaining Louisiana. Bill in the Senate on impressment postponed. The Executive does not wish to resort to any means which may interrupt harmony. Conversation with Merry on the subjcet. French prisoners taken from American vessels. Monroe's proposed mission to Madrid. "Private." 4°. 4 pages.

1804, September 3, Virginia. Acknowledging letter of August 25, with copy of a new form to the Government of France. Gen. Armstrong succeeds Mr. Livingston at Paris. Proofs of our friendly relations to France under its new form. (Empire.) 4°. 2 pages.

1804, November 9, Washington. Acknowledging letter of August 24. Instructions as to his mission to Spain. West Florida essential to the United States, both as to the Mississippi and trade through the Mobile. The boundaries to be defined, it is hoped with the aid of France. South American claims. Yrujo's conduct such as to require his recall. Mr. Pinckney's recall. The Prince of Peace will claim special attention. He governs the court absolutely. Dreadful mortality in New Orleans. 4°. 3 pages.

1804, December 3, Washington. Captain Dutton goes to Spain with dispatches. Spain lays aside certain reinforcements for Florida. She does not wish to quarrel with United States. Monroe's negotiations in London. "Private." 4°. 3 pages.

London.

1805, September 24, Philadelphia. Decision in the admiralty courts of Great Britain alarms the merchants. Instructions to Monroe. "Private." 4°. 2 pages.

MONROE.

1806, January 13, Washington. Recalls his letter to Monroe on 8th instant, and to consider it canceled. "Private." 4°. 2 pages.

1806, March 11, Washington. Proceedings in Congress. Posture of things with Spain and Great Britain. Opposition to Armstrong and case of ship *New Jersey*. The matter concerning Yrujo (the Spanish minister) and Miranda. Outcry against the Executive as violating the law of nations. "Private." 4°. 6 pages.

1806, May 17, Washington. Acknowledging letter of March 11. Difficulties in settling details in negotiations. Mr. Pinkney goes out with the joint commission with instructions. Negotiations with Spain will be governed by prospects of peace or war between Great Britain, and France and Spain. Schisms in the Republican party. "Private." 4°. 4 pages.

1806, June 4, Washington. Departure of Mr. Pinkney with dispatches. Communications of the British minister relative to the blockade of four German rivers. Good will expressed by Mr. Fox of the King towards the United States. Relinquishment of the Grand Menan Island. Elections in Massachusetts and New York. "Private." 4°. 4 pages.

1806, November 28, Washington. Departure of Merry (British minister). Intercepted dispatches of Yrujo. A copy desirable if possible to get one. Proclamation of the President against a military enterprise in the West. Severance of the western country from the Atlantic States espoused. General sentiment will not countenance it. [In cipher, with a translation.] "Private." 4°. 5 pages.

1807, March 20, Washington. Suggestions of course to pursue in negotiations with Great Britain. The President writes instructions by this conveyance. Difficulties in closing the bargain on the terms which she insists on. The impressment question. The President and all are impressed with the difficulties which Monroe contends with and satisfied with his faithfulness and ability. 4°. 3 pages.

1807, May 25, Washington. The painful task of the President to withhold his sanction to the treaty. Hopes that further efforts may succeed. Question whether the new British cabinet will recall. Mr. Erskine from his station here. 4°. 2 pages.

1807, July 25, Washington. The British squadron on receiving the proclamation fell down to the capes. They continue to defy the proclamation by chasing merchant vessels arriving and departing. The public mind settling itself into a determined stand. Preparation for war is proclaimed at every meeting. The reparation for the insult must be such as to satisfy the just feeling. Hopes the British Government will recognize and not evade it. 4°. 3 pages.

Richmond.

1808, January 5, Washington. Still uninformed of the circumstances detaining Mr. Rose (British minister) on board the frigate. 4°. 2 pages.

1808, February 6, Washington. Acknowledging letter of 3d. Apologizes for delay in sending copies of papers, and transmits them. 4°. 1 page.

MONROE.

1808, March 18, Washington. Acknowledging letter of 5th. Mr. Rose's mission abortive. The terms of the satisfaction he had to offer entirely inadmissible. He will depart without delay.
4°. 2 pages.

1808, March 21, Washington. Asks for the joint letter of Monroe and Pinkney relating to impressments in negotiations with Great Britain in 1806 to be communicated to Congress. [With press copy.]
4°. 4 pages.

1808, March 30, Washington. Acknowledging letter of 26th. Communications to Congress relating to the mission to Great Britain, 1806. The paper relating to impressments is wanting. Asks to correct the omission. Incloses paper containing the correspondence with Mr. Rose produced by his mission. 4°. 1 page.

1808, April 18, Washington. Acknowledging a letter with papers, now returned, relating to correspondence bearing on the mission to London in 1806 having been transmitted to Congress and for publication. 4°. 2 pages.

1811, March 20, Washington. Tenders him the position of Secretary of State and wishes for as early reply as possible. "Private and confidential."
4°. 2 pages.

1811, March 26, Washington. Acknowledging letter of 23d. Is pleased at Monroe's acceptance of the appointment as Secretary of State. Madison's views as to what is expected in the conduct of this position and the association of labors in promoting the country's interests. Particularly the adjustment of differences with Great Britain. "Private." 4°. 4 pages.

Washington.

1817, August 22, Montpellier. Acknowledging letter of July 27. Thinks Monroe will be repaid for the fatigue and inconveniences attending his Northern tour from the harmony of sentiment so extensively manifested. Asks for position as consul at Amsterdam for Mr. W. Taylor, and for other persons for other places. 4°. 3 pages.

1817, November 29, Montpellier. Acknowledging letter of 24th. The question of roads and canals. The expediency of Congress being vested with powers. The overflowing treasury. Suggests lessening taxes excepting the still tax. [Draft.]
4°. 2 pages.

1817, December 9, Montpellier. Commends the President's message. Recommendation of repeal of taxes, and subject of amendment of the Constitution happily shaped. Suppression of the establishments at Amelia Island. 4°. 1 page.

1817, December 27, Montpellier. Acknowledging letter of 22d. Views on the constitutionality of the measure on roads and canals. 4°. 4 pages.

1818, May 21, Montpellier. Acknowledging letter of 18th, inclosing the Moscow document. The equivocal conduct of Great Britain in relation to Spanish America. The position taken by our commissioner relative to the independence of Buenos Ayres. The character and views of the Emperor Alexander wrapped in mystery.
4°. 4 pages.

MONROE.

1818, July 18, Montpellier. Acknowledging letter of 13th. The revolution in South America. Will disapprove of measures unnecessarily involving in it a danger of war. Tardiness in acknowledging independence of Buenos Ayres. Mr. Rush's conversation relative to McGregor's scheme for acquiring Florida. [Draft.] 4°. 2 pages.

Highland.

1818, October —, Montpellier. Acknowledging letter of September 27. Can not join Monroe at meeting of the visitors at the university. Communications from Mr. Rush. Great Britain anxious to secure our trade. The renewal of the existing treaty not desired unless coupled with reciprocity in the colonial trades. Jealousy of Spain in connection with our South American trade. [Draft.] 4°. 2 pages.

Washington.

1818, November 28, Montpellier. Acknowledging letter of 23d. Direct trade with Great Britain increasing. Growing respect for us among the great powers of Europe. The work of emancipation of South America. Question of impressment. Impressment and peace are irreconcilable. The possession of Canada of no use to Great Britain in case of war, and when at peace of equal value whether a British colony or American state. [Copy.] 4°. 4 pages.

1819, February 13, Montpellier. Acknowledging letter of 7th. Death of Gen. Mason. Spanish affairs and Florida. Jackson's conduct is invulnerable to complaints from abroad. His zeal and patriotism. The university. [Draft.] 4°. 2 pages.

1819, September 6, Montpellier. The claim of Capt. O'Bryan. Documentary evidence having been burned in 1814, wishes some evidence from personal recollections. 4°. 1 page.

1820, February 10, Montpellier. Acknowledging letter of 5th. Admission of Maine and Missouri. The Missouri compromise. "Migration or importation". When the ordinance of 1787 was passed interdicting slavery northwest of the Ohio, Congress had no authority to prohibit importation of slaves. [Draft.] 4°. 2 pages.

1820, February 23, Montpellier. Acknowledging letter of 19th. The Missouri question. Thinks Congress can not restrict slavery in the territories. An uncontrolled dispersion of slaves throughout the Union favorable to emancipation. Inflammatory conduct of Rufus King. [Draft.] 4°. 2 pages.

1820, November 19, Montpellier. Acknowledging letter of 16th with the message. The Missouri question. Diplomatic transactions of Mr. Correa. Tench Coxe desires office. His merits and services. Prevalence of typhus fever in Virginia. [Copy.] 4°. 4 pages.

1820, December 28, Montpellier. Acknowledging letters of 18th and 23d. Probable acquisition of Florida. The Missouri question likely to be settled. Tench Coxe. Dr. Eustis. Tenure of office. Encroachments on the executive powers of Government. [Copy.] 4°. 4 pages.

MONROE.

1822, May 6, Montpellier. Anduaga's reproaches at the delay of recognition of Spanish America. How to prevent further delay. Our sympathy with their cause and that of Mexico. An appeal to Europe. Views of Russia. Appointment of ministers. Is a public minister an officer in a strictly constitutional sense. A hard winter. The Hessian fly. [Copy.] 4°. 3 pages.

1822, May 18, Montpellier. Acknowledging letter of 12th. Nominations of officers in the Army to take rank from certain dates. British practice as to filling military vacancies. Origin of brevets. Effect of political relationship in the Cabinet. The President too sanguine as to party spirit. [Draft.] 4°. 4 pages.

1822, September 24, Montpellier. Acknowledging letter of 16th. Query, if the Senate has a right to vary the date at which, according to the nomination of the President, an appointment is to take effect. [Draft.] 4°. 2 pages.

1823, February 13, Montpellier. Acknowledging letter of 3d. Thanking him for his kindness to his nephew. The constitutional question of roads and canals. [Draft.] 4°. 1 page.

1823, June 9, Montpellier. Mr. Morris's claim for expenses incurred when employed in a confidential mission to Spain. Bears testimony to his intelligence, integrity, and respectability. [Draft.] 8°. 1 page.

1823, October 30, Montpellier Intentions of the Holy Alliance to aid Spain in subduing her colonies. We should endeavor to defeat the crusade. British cooperation fortunate for us. Canning's proposal to Mr. Rush. Interest of more weight with Great Britain than principle. The Spanish cause and that of the Greeks. Canning's disclaimer. [Copy.] 4°. 3 pages.

1823, December 6, Montpellier. Acknowledging letter of 4th, and copy of the message. Canning's reserve mysterious and ominous. He should not have withheld his intentions from Mr. Rush. Commends his message. [Draft.] 4°. 1 page.

1823, December 26, Montpellier. Acknowledging letter of 20th. Alienation between Great Britain and the continental powers. Canning's croaking at the Liverpool dinner. We must not appear to be Britain's satellite. An expected Congress of nations. A den of conspirators. The course taken by France. [Draft.] 4°. 2 pages.

1824, February 4, Montpellier. Application of Mr. Wagner to publish the archives of the Revolutionary Congress. [Draft.] 4°. 2 pages.

1824, February 5, Montpellier. Acknowledging letter of January 26. Respecting the dates of Gen. Jackson's commissions. [Draft.] 4°. 1 page.

1824, April 10, Montpellier. Acknowledging letters of March 27 and April —. Submits recommendations which he can not sometimes decline to receive. Dr. Torry, professor of chemistry. Mr. Cabell's and Virginia's claims for advances made during the last war assigned to the University of Virginia. The message approved of. The compact with Georgia. Reciprocity in trade. Madison's relations with Livingston friendly. [Draft.] 4°. 2 pages.

MONROE.

1824, August 5, Montpellier. Acknowledging letter of 2d. Convention with Russia. The advances of France towards a compromise with Columbia. The determination of Great Britain not to permit foreign interference between Spain and South America. [Draft.] fol. 2 pages.

1824, December 16, Montpellier. Acknowledging letter of 13th. The message. Effect of lessons taught by the United States. The tree of liberty and its fruits. Trusts Monroe's claim for reimbursement and compensation will be successful. Regrets the delay in receiving his outfit obliged Monroe to part with his land near Charlottesville. [Draft.] 4°. 1 page.

Oak Hill.

1827, September 22, Montpellier. Letter received from H. Lee respecting the provincial order to Gen. Jackson of July 18, 1814, authorizing him to take possession of Pensacola on certain conditions. [Draft.] Strip of paper.

1827, October 29, Montpellier. Acknowledging letter of 3d. Correspondence about supplies to the Army in 1814 at New Orleans. Had not read Jackson's life. Seizure of Pensacola. Vacant chair in the University of Virginia. [Draft.] Strip of paper.

1827, November 16, Montpellier. Acknowledging letter of 2d. Supplies to the Army in New Orleans in 1814. The prohibitory letter to Gen. Jackson. Authorship of the "Farmers" papers. [Copy.] 4°. 2 pages.

1827, December 18, Montpellier. Acknowledging letter of 10th. Relative to the proposition to place Madison and Monroe on the ticket of one of the candidates in the approaching election. Their desire to be neutral and keep aloof from political matters. [Draft.] Strip of paper.

1828, January 23, Montpellier. Acknowledging letter of 18th. Surprised to find his and Monroe's names on the electoral ticket contrary to the decided terms in which he declined. Awkwardness of the situation. Question as to what is best to do. Professor Long and the Virginia University. [Draft.] 4°. 1 page.

1828, February 26, Montpellier. Acknowledging letters of 13th and 15th. Has received notice of his and Monroe's electoral nominations. Unaccountable delay in giving them notice. Awkwardness of the position. [Draft.] Strip of paper.

1828, March 20, Montpellier. Acknowledging letter of February 23. Their electoral nominations. Meeting of visitors of the University of Virginia. Vacancy in the chair of natural philosophy at the university. Candidates. [Draft.] Strip of paper.

1830, May 18, Montpellier. Acknowledging letter of 13th. Advises him not to resign as visitor to the university. Hopes he will be present at the meeting of visitors. The Virginia convention. Jared Sparks on the negotiations for peace. Rayneval's statement. Jay misled about the course of the French Government. Franklin's excellent conduct. [Draft.] Strip of paper.

MONROE. *New York.*

1831, April 21, Montpellier. Fears the climate of New York will not suit Monroe. Sum voted by Congress may prevent sale of his estate. The long and uninterrupted friendship of the two ex-Presidents. Madison 80 years old. Suggests Oak Hill as an occasional residence. Age the cause of microscopic writing and slower and shorter steps. [Draft.] Strip of paper.

MOUSTIER, COUNT DE (French Minister).

1788, October 30, New York. Answers to queries of the French minister relative to trade with the French colonies with Virginia.
4°. 5 pages. fol. 3 pages.

NATIONAL DEBT.

Not dated. Respecting the national debt. Problem of Pike corrected by Elliott. fol. 1 page.

NEUVILLE, HYDE DE.

1818, December 9, Montpellier. Acknowledging letter of 3d. Congratulates him on the evacuation of France by the occupying armies. [Draft.]
4°. 1 page.

1828(?), December 19, Montpellier. Has read with pleasure his speech. Its intrinsic merits. [Draft.]
Strip of paper.

1829, June 15, Montpellier. Introducing Mr. Rives, who goes to Paris as our diplomatic representative. [Draft.] Strip of paper.

1830, July 26, Montpellier. Thanks him for two pamphlets received. One entitled "Discours d'ouverture prononcé à la séance générale etc.," and the other "De la question portugaise". Sends De Neuville copy of the new constitution of Virginia. [Draft.] Strip of paper.

Washington.

1816, July 17, Montpellier. Acknowledging letter of 12th. Gratifying to be assured that the French nation cherishes friendly dispositions to our country. [Copy.] 4°. 2 pages.

New York.

1819, November 17, Montpellier. Acknowledging letter announcing his expected departure for France, followed by the intelligence that he is to remain. Begs him to accept a sincere return of his good wishes. [Copy.] fol. 1 page.

NICHOLAS, GEORGE W.

1823, July 13, Montpellier. In response to a letter from his father, informs him of matters respecting horse-breeding. [Draft.] fol. 1 page.

NICHOLAS, JOHN. *Geneva, N. Y.*

1813, April 2, Washington. Acknowledging letter of 11th. Reviewing the conduct of the Executive at the opening of the war. Importance of striking a blow before reinforcements could arrive. Hull's disaster. The mediation of Russia. The only power in Europe which can command the respect of France and Great Britain. Friendship of the Emperor for the United States. [Copy.]
4°. 3 pages.

1816, May 30, Washington. Acknowledging letter of 20th. Respecting an appointment to office. [Copy.] 4°. 2 pages.

NICHOLAS, JOHN.

1819, January 4, Montpellier. Acknowledges receipt of a copy of his agricultural address. Question of a tax on distilleries combined with a prohibition of foreign spirits. The ox giving way among the farmers to the horse. Prefers the ox. [Draft.] 4°. 2 pages.

NICHOLAS, WILSON C. *Richmond.*

1814, November 25, Washington. Acknowledging letter of 11th. The conduct of New England is the source of great difficulty in carrying on the war. Lamentable tardiness of the legislature in applying relief. fol. 1 page.

1816, October 5, Montpellier. Acknowledging letter of 30th. The desire to appoint Mr. Armistead to a Government office. Leaves it to the heads of departments. Relating to banks and return to specie payments. [Copy.] 4°. 4 pages.

NOAH, M. M. *New York.*

1818, May 15, Montpellier. Acknowledging receipt of letter of 6th. On freedom of religious opinions and worship. Is glad to learn of the closing of his accounts while employed in his mission abroad. Noah's religious views being known was not the motive of his recall. [Draft.] 4°. 1 page.

NORTH CAROLINA, BAPTIST CHURCHES OF.

1811, June 3, Washington. Acknowledging receipt of the address of the Baptist churches on Neal's Creek and on Black Creek, N. C., approving of his objection to the bill containing a grant of public land. His views on the practical distinction between religion and civil government. [Draft.] 4°. 1 page.

NORTH CAROLINA GENERAL ASSEMBLY. *Raleigh.*

1813, December 11, Washington. Acknowledging memorial of November 29, representing the exposure of North Carolina to danger on the seacoast and asking protection of the General Government. Due attention will be paid to the appeal, but regard must be had to the comparative practicability and probability of attempts on particular States and places. [Draft.] 4°. 2 pages.

NULLIFICATION.

1833(?), not dated. On the doctrine of nullification. Scrap of paper.

O'CONNOR, THOMAS. *New York.*

1819, June —, Montpellier. Declines to subscribe to the periodical work (the "Globe"), of which O'Connor is editor. Scrap of paper.

ORR, BENJ. G. *Georgetown.*

1802, June 28, Washington. Acknowledging letter of this day. Madison's suggestion respecting the case of the negro Plato. 4°. 2 pages.

OTIS, GEORGE ALEXANDER.

1820, July 3, Montpellier. Acknowledging letter of June 20, with copies of translations of Pradt's Europe for 1819, and first volume of Botta's History of our War of Independence. The merits of the latter work. Hopes Mr. Otis will meet with encouragement in his translation. [Draft.] 4°. 2 pages.

OTIS, GEORGE ALEXANDER.

1820, December 29, Montpellier. Acknowledging letter, with the second volume of the translation of Botta's History. Merits of the work. [Copy.] 4°. 2 pages.

1821, January —, Montpellier. Acknowledging letter of 4th. On the translation of Botta's History. [Draft.] 4°. 2 pages.

PAGE, FRANCIS.

1833, November 7, Montpellier. Acknowledging a letter and printed petition to the assembly in behalf of the heirs and representatives of Gen. Nelson. Strip of paper.

PANNILL, MCRAE, and POLLARD, Captains.

1823, June 28, Montpellier. Acknowledging letter of 17th. Declines to participate in the celebration by the Petersburg Volunteers on the national anniversary. [Draft.] 4°. 1 page.

PATTON, JOHN M.

1834, March 24, Montpellier. Commends his speech on the "Virginia Resolutions." Controversy on the removals from office. The power claimed by the Senate. Tenure of office. [Draft.] "Confidential." Strip of paper.

PAULDING, JAMES K. *Washington.*

1818, July 23, Montpellier. Acknowledging letter of 16th. Returns a copy of the "Federalist" and gives a memorandum respecting the origin and authors of it. [Draft.] 4°. 2 pages.

1827, March 10, Montpellier. Acknowledging letter of February 28. His views on his pamphlet respecting abuses in incorporations in New York and legislation respecting bequeathing of property. Respecting banks. [Draft.] 4°. 2 pages.

1831, April —, Montpellier. Acknowledging letter of 6th. Furnishes Mr. Paulding certain data towards his biographical undertaking. Sketches of Franklin, Jefferson, John Adams, and Hamilton. Allusion to the "Federalist." 4°. 2 pages.

1831, April —, Montpellier. A publication entitled "Plan of Government proposed by Charles Pinckney in the convention of 1787." Its marvelous identity with one entitled, "Observations on the Plan of Government submitted to the Federal Government, etc." [Draft.] Strip of paper.

1831, June 6, Montpellier. Concerning a small pamphlet of Charles Pinckney printed at the close of the convention of 1787. [Draft.] Strip of paper.

1831, June 27, Montpellier. Acknowledging letter of 20th, and the volume of pamphlets containing that of Charles Pinckney. Corrects an impression that he had in view a history; it was simply a preservation of materials, of which he was a recorder. Strip of paper.

1832, January —, Montpellier. According to promise, incloses him a sketch. [Draft.] Strip of paper.

PENDLETON, EDMUND.

1780, September 19, Philadelphia. Admiral Rodney at Sandy Hook with 12 sail of the line. It is said the French fleet is somewhere on the coast. Re-

PENDLETON, EDMUND.

enforcements from England. Reports of the embarking of troops for Virginia or South Carolina. Prizes of the Quebec fleet carried into New England. Mortality in Philadelphia. 4°. 1 page.

1780, September 26, Philadelphia. Ternay is yet unreenforced. Graves at sea, and Rodney with 10 ships of the line at the Hook. State of uncertainty and speculation. fol. 1 page.

Caroline, Va.

1780, October 2, Philadelphia. Acknowledging letter of 25th ultimo. Still unable to gratify hopes of any prospect of a successful issue of this campaign. Reports of the approach of the French fleet groundless. Spanish operations against the Floridas, The apostacy and plot of Arnold. fol. 2 pages.

1780, October 10, Philadelphia. Acknowledging letter of 1st. The situation of the English and French fleets. Reports of the large embarkation from New York. Hopes Virginia will not be their destination. Execution of André. The contempt of our adversaries for Arnold on account of their loss of André. fol. 2 pages.

1780, October —, Philadelphia. Acknowledging letter of 8th and 17th. Descent from Canada by way of Lake George of troops, tories, Canadians, and savages, probably were intended to take advantage of the consternation expected to result from Arnold's treason. Troops embarked from New York destined for Virginia or South Carolina. Capture of a British fleet confirmed. fol. 1 page.

1780, October 17, Philadelphia. Seizures of Jamaica prizes by the *Saratoga;* their subsequent loss in a fog. Baron Steuben reports an embarkation from New York, but no confirmation of it. The capture of the British fleet by the Spaniards considered as a certainty. fol. 1 page.

1780, November 14, Philadelphia. Acknowledging letter of 6th. The enemy's numbers less formidable. Inroads of the enemy in the frontiers of New York distressing and wasteful. Burning of Schoharie with great loss of grain. Sailing of Rodney from New York. Exchange of prisoners. fol. 2 pages.

1780, November 21, Philadelphia. Acknowledging letter of 13th. Arrival of the English fleet. Destination of the New York embarkation unknown. Conjectures. The projected junction between Leslie and Cornwallis frustrated by the volunteers at King's Mountain. John Adams at Amsterdam reports the British will make the Southern States the scene of an active winter campaign. fol. 1 page.

1780, December 5, Philadelphia. Acknowledging letter of November 27. Letters from Jay and Carmichael state no reliance to be made on Spain for cash. Her credit and finances not adequate. No distrust on part of the King. Portugal agrees to shut her ports against English prizes. Reports of the fate of the Quebec and Jamaica fleets effect the price of stocks. Violent tempest in West Indies. 4°. 2 pages.

1780, December —, Philadelphia. Acknowledging letter of 2d. No news of the fleet which lately left

PENDLETON, EDMUND.

the Chesapeake. News confirmed of neutrality of Portugal. Dismasting of the *Ariel*, Capt. Paul Jones, with supplies, which will prolong the sufferings of our Army. Change in the French ministry. small 4°. 2 pages.

1780, December 19, *Philadelphia.* Acknowledging letter of 11th. Sufferings of the Virginia militia ascribed to the commanding officer. Embarkation from New York to the Southern States. Encounter between Tarlton and Sumpter. Tarlton's loss and wound. small 4°. 2 pages.

1780, December 26, *Philadelphia.* Acknowledging letter of 18th. The Danish declaration. Report that Arnold has gone up the sound with 4,000 troops toward New London. fol. 1 page.

1781, January 2, *Philadelphia.* Another embarkation from New York with 2,500 troops. Their destination supposed to be the Southern States. Uneasiness as to this accumulating force, with small means of defense. Want of money for subsistence and clothing. Combined force at Cadiz 68 ships of the line. fol. 1 page.

1781, January 23, *Philadelphia.* Discontent among the German troops in New York. Desertion of 200 from Long Island to Rhode Island. The British minister proposes to Parliament to allow trade with us for all kinds of goods except linen and woolen. Conjectures as to the reason of the assembling of so great a force in Cadiz. Arnold's hostile reception. fol. 2 pages.

1781, February —, Philadelphia. Acknowledging letter of 5th. Reports of intended departure of the enemy. Exchange of prisoners. Case of C. Taylor. England's strenuous exertions in the article of money for the current year. Parliament votes large reenforcements. Blockade of Gibraltar. The garrison in great distress. fol. 2 pages.

1781, July 31, Philadelphia. Acknowledging letter of 23d. Congratulates him on the safety of his estate from the ravages of the enemy. Mediation tendered by Russia in the dispute between England and Holland. Washington's preparations against New York. Col. Willett's success over a party from Canada on the frontiers of New York. fol. 1 page.

1781, September 18, *Philadelphia.* Acknowledging letter of 10th. Reports of the success of our fleet in the Chesapeake. Preparations at New York for some movement. Supposed to be against this city. Success of the parricide Arnold against New London. Selfish projects of Spain. Washington and Rochambeau in Virginia. A relief to the militia. 4°. 3 pages.

1781, October 2, *Philadelphia.* Acknowledging letter of September 24. Sufferings of the British fleet on their visit to the capes of Chesapeake. Malignant fever in New York. False reports of large reenforcements to the British to buoy up their sinking hopes. They give up Cornwallis as lost. The obstinacy of Great Britain and fidelity of our ally. Legislation in Virginia. fol. 3 pages.

1781, October 9, Philadelphia. The judiciary question on the property of Virginia seized by Mr. Nathan. Mr. Adams's memorial to the States general. 4°. 1 page.

PENDLETON, EDMUND.

1781, October 16, Philadelphia. Acknowledging letter of 8th. The enemy have no hopes of relieving Cornwallis unless by some desperate naval engagement. The superiority remains on the part of our allies. fol. 2 pages.

1781, November 27, Philadelphia. Acknowledging letter of 19th. Washington's arrival on his return to the North River. The military establishment for the next year. Calumnies on Virginia for her deficiency in proportion of men. Successes of Great Britain's enemies not likely to impede our negotiations for peace. fol. 2 pages.

1781, December 11, Philadelphia. Election of Harrison as governor of Virginia. Requisitions of Congress on the States for $8,000,000. The quota of Virginia. Mr. Moore elected president of Pennsylvania. fol. 1 page.

1781, December 25, Philadelphia. Acknowledging letter of 16th. Confirmation of the success of Commodore Johnstone in taking Dutch East Indiamen. The danger of the British possessions in the East. The honorable acquittal of Jefferson. His ability and zeal for his country. fol. 1 page.

1787, January 9, Richmond. Acknowledging letter of 9th. Proceedings in the Virginia legislature. The revised code. The present rage for high duties. The seditious party in the East becoming formidable to the Government. Communications with the viceroy of Canada. 4°. 4 pages.

1787, February 24, New York. Dispersion of the insurgents. Shay's rebellion in Massachusetts. The approaching convention for revision of Federal articles. Existence of parties both for monarchy and partial confederacies. 4°. 3 pages.

1787, April 22, New York. Acknowledging letter of 7th. No signs of return of the insurgent spirit in Massachusetts. The elections. Change in rulers of that State. Convention of States for ratification of the Constitution. Proceedings in Congress. Our violations of the treaty of peace. Disposing of Western lands. Our affair with Spain on delicate footing. 4°. 4 pages.

Bowling Green, Va.

1787, May 27, Philadelphia. Proceedings of the convention. States composing it. 4°. 2 pages.

1787, September 20, Philadelphia. Incloses copy of the proposed constitution. Difficulty of tracing a proper line of demarkation between national and State authorities. 4°. 1 page.

Edmundsburg, Va.

1787, October 28, New York. Acknowledging letter of 8th. The new Constitution. Clause exempting vessels bound to or from a State from being obliged to enter, etc., in another. Conjectures as to what States will agree to the Constitution in the convention. 4°. 2 pages.

1788, February 21, New York. Acknowledging letter of January 29. The simple question in the proposed constitution is whether the Union shall or shall not be continued. The objects of the opposers. Events in France which may almost amount to a revolution. The want of union in the Dutch Confederation the source of their calamities. 4°. 3 pages.

PENDLETON, EDMUND.

1788, March 3, New York. The convention of New Hampshire adjourned without any final decision on adopting the Constitution. Its influence on other States. 4°. 2 pages.

1788, October 20, New York Acknowledging letter of 6th. The light in which the temporary seat of Government is viewed. Foreign intelligence. War likely to spread farther. France occupied with her internal fermentations. Lafayette in the Bastile. 4°. 3 pages.

1789, April 8, New York. Examination by Congress of the ballots for President and Vice-President. Unanimously for Washington and a sufficient number for Adams. Speaker of the House Muhlenburg. Intelligence from England. The King's disability. Prince of Wales regent. 4°. 2 pages.

Bowling Green, Va.

1789, April 19, New York. Acknowledging letter of 7th. Preparations for reception of the President and Vice-President shortly to arrive. The House of Representatives occupied with the impost. Health of the King of England. The case singular and perplexing as respecting the reins of government. 4°. 2 pages.

1789, May 17, New York. Acknowledging letter of 3d. The question of imposts. Proposition for putting Great Britain on the same footing as our allies prior to a treaty. Popular sentiment opposed to it. fol. 1 page.

1789, June 21, New York. Acknowledging letter of 9th. Removals from office discussed. Tenure of office. fol. 2 pages.

1789, July 15, New York. Acknowledging letter of 3d. The judiciary bill. Removals from office. The act imposing duties. 4°. 3 pages.

Williamsburg, Va.

1789, August 21, New York. Constitutional amendments. The judiciary bill. Mr. Pendleton's introductory discourse in the convention at Philadelphia. fol. 1 page.

Bowling Green, Va.

1789, September 14, New York. The judiciary bill. Question of the permanent seat of Government. The Eastern States opposed to the Potomac. fol. 1 page.

1789, September 23, New York. The judiciary bill. The location of the permanent seat of Government undecided. Accounts from France. The King has thrown himself finally on his people, recalled Neckar, dismissed the troops, and given a carte blanche to the National Assembly to make a constitution. Tumults in Paris. Lafayette at the head of the militia. fol. 2 pages.

1790, March 4, New York. Reapportionment of representation. Report of the Secretary of the Treasury. Certain objections. Assumption of the State debts. The great work of France likely to be carried. All Europe aroused. Light chasing darkness and despotisms, an emanation from the establishment of liberty from the new world. 4°. 3 pages.

PENDLETON, EDMUND. *Virginia.*

1790, April 4, New York. Assumption of the State debts. Proceedings in Virginia during the crisis of the stamp act. 4°. 2 pages.

1790, April 13, New York. Acknowledging letter of 2d. Defeat of the bill for assumption of the State debts. 4°. 1 page.

1790, May 2, New York. The assumption of the State debts not abandoned. Hopes of its final success. Prevalence of influenza. 4°. 2 pages.

1791, January 2, New York. Questions on the treaty of peace. Col. Hamilton's plan of a bank. Excise bill. Militia bill and a plan for disposing of the the public lands. Convention between Great Britain and Spain. 4°. 4 pages.

1791, February 13, Philadelphia. Arguments in favor of the bank. The excise bill. The owners of stills to pay tax on their capacity. Bills for admitting Kentucky and Vermont. Bill for selling public lands will probably go through. The militia bill problematical. Arguments against the bank. 4°. 2 pages.

Bowling Green, Va.

1791, December 18, Philadelphia. Congress occupied by the representation bill. Communications between Mr. Hammond (British minister), and the Executive. Disavowal of encouragement to Indian hostilities. Thomas Pinkney to be our minister to Great Britain. The French revolution. The King accepts the constitution. 4°. 3 pages.

1792, January 21, Philadelphia. The Representation apportionment bill before Congress. A motion for reviving it in another form. Means for protection of the Western frontiers. Hamilton's report on manufactures. fol. 2 pages.

1792, February 21, Philadelphia. Acknowledging letter of 8th. The bill concerning election of President and Vice-President, and eventual successor to both passed both Houses. New apportionment bill. small 4°. 3 pages.

1792, March 25, Philadelphia. Acknowledging letter of 14th. Passage of the representation bill. Hamilton's report on the new duties on trade. The funding system. Assumption of State debts. The militia bill before the Senate. Failure of Duer, of New York, the prince of speculators. 4°. 2 pages.

1792, April 9, Philadelphia. The President's veto on the representation apportionment bill. Bill for assumption of the remainder of State debts before Congress. The Committee on Ways and Means discussing the Western defense. Bankruptcies resulting from Duer's failure. fol. 2 pages.

1792, November 16, Philadelphia. The President's message. Passages relating to the excise discussed. 4°. 2 pages.

1792, December 6, Philadelphia. Acknowledging letter of November 28. The State of affairs in France. Combination against the revolution. Greater danger from the follies and barbarities prevailing in Paris. The newspaper tax. The contest between Adams and Clinton for Vice Presidency. Query, whether Jefferson will remain in his public station. fol. 2 pages.

PENDLETON, EDMUND.

1792, December 10, Philadelphia. New report from the Treasury Department. The proposition for new taxes. fol. 1 page.

1793, February 23, Philadelphia. John Taylor, successor to R. H. Lee, in the United States Senate. Inquiry into the administration of the Treasury Department. Affairs in France and rest of Europe. 4°. 3 pages.

1795, January 8, Philadelphia. Acknowledging letter of 30th. No communications from Jay or Monroe as to their negotiations. House of Representatives engaged on the naturalization law. Renunciation of all who have borne hereditary titles. Influx of foreigners and aristocrats. fol. 2 pages.

1796, February 7, Philadelphia. Acknowledging letter of January 6. The carriage tax. Jay's treaty. The treaties with Spain and Algiers. British bounty on importation of foreign wheat. Flour $14 per barrel. fol. 2 pages.

PEPOON, BENJ. F.

1833, May 18, Montpellier. Acknowledging letter of 13th. The rapid growth in the States of population, wealth, and power tending to weaken the ties which bind them together. Happily these tendencies are not without counter tendencies, which he enumerates and discusses. [Draft.] 4°. 2 pages.

PETERS, RICHARD.

1807, September 5, Washington. The desertion of seamen. Distinction between deserters from merchant ships and from ships of war. [Copy.] 4°. 4 pages.

1818, August 15, Montpellier. Acknowledging letter of July 30. Thanks him for the "Notices for a young farmer." Has read it with profit. Discusses the question of spontaneous productions. Cheat is deteriorated wheat. The kind of wheat said to resist the Hessian fly. [Draft.] 4°. 4 pages.

1819, February 22, Montpellier. Thanks him for copy of an agricultural almanac and memorial. Is pleased with his scheme of a "pattern farm." Mr. Rawles's address on immigration. Our law of naturalization. [Draft.] 4°. 2 pages.

1823, February 22, Montpellier. Respecting an agricultural address. Corrects an error. Strip of paper.

1824, December 1, Montpellier. Returns copy of agricultural almanac. Attentions to Lafayette. [Draft.] Strip of paper.

1826, September 8, Montpellier. Acknowledging letter of 1st. Has not lost his interest in agriculture, but does not retain the activity required for it. Reminiscences of the Revolutionary times. Death of Adams and Jefferson. [Draft.) 4°. 1 page.

PEYSTER, FREDERICK.

No *date.* Acknowledging letter of July 19, with volumes containing "The published collection of the New York Historical Society." Merits of the work. [Copy.] 8°. 2 pages.

PHILADELPHIA SOCIETY OF ARTS. *Philadelphia.*

1811, January 28, Washington. Acknowledging letter of 27th, communicating Madison's appointment as patron of that institution. Accepts the appointment. [Draft.] 4°. 1 page.

PICKERING, TIMOTHY.

1825, September 17, Montpellier. Acknowledging letter of 7th, inclosing copies of the "New England Farmer." Concerning agriculture. [Draft.] 4°. 1 page.

PICKET, ALBERT, and others.

1821, September —, Montpellier. Acknowledging a letter. As to the establishment of a female college. [Draft.] 4°. 1 page.

PINKNEY, WILLIAM. *Washington.*

1814, January 29, Washington. Acknowledging letter of 25th, conveying resignation as Attorney-General. Hopes he will prolong his functions until a successor is provided. [Draft.] fol. 1 page.

PLEASANTS, ROBERT.

1791, October 30, Philadelphia. Acknowledging letter of June 6. The militia bill. Bill for abolition of slavery. Declines, for reasons given, why he should not present it. His views as to the expediency of such an application to the Virginia assembly. 4°. 2 pages.

PLUMER, WILLIAM, JR. *New Hampshire.*

1815, July 14, Washington. Acknowledging letter of June 8. Plumer's meritorious undertaking in preparing a history of the late war. No doubt the officers of the Department will be ready to contribute proper information for an undertaking so meritorious. [Draft.] 4°. 2 pages.

PLUMER, WILLIAM (Governor of New Hampshire).

1818, August 10, Montpellier. Acknowledging letter of July 28. Congratulates him on his return to private life. [Copy.] 4°. 2 pages.

1819, June 20, Montpellier. Acknowledging letter of 8th, with copy of his address to the New Hampshire legislature. [Draft.] 4°. 1 page.

POMEROY, SAMUEL WYLLYS. *Brighton, Mass.*

1820, February —, Montpellier. Acknowledging letter of 7th, with agricultural pamphlet. Dairy farms. Superiority of oxen over horses for drafting purposes. [Copy.] 4°. 2 pages.

Boston.

1821, July 21, Montpellier. On the culture of flax. Samples of flax in the several stages of its preparation by a newly-invented machine. [Draft.] 4°. 1 page.

PRESTON, FRANCIS.

1823, June 2, Montpellier. Acknowledging letter of May 15. Controversy as to the distribution of the laurels gained in the memorable battle of King's Mountain. [Draft.] 4°. 1 page.

PRICE, JOHN H. *Richmond.*

1809, September 26, Washington. Acknowledging letter of 18th, communicating the unanimous resolution of the Washington and Jefferson Artillery under his command in case the exigencies of their country should call for them. [Draft.] 4°. 1 page.

PUBLIC ROADS.

1772. Respecting an act of the Virginia legislature for opening and keeping in repair public roads. fol. 1 page.

RAMSAY, DAVID. *Charleston.*

1809, September 20, Washington. Acknowledging receipt of resolutions of the meeting of citizens in Charleston, of the 5th, approving of the measures of the President in respect to our foreign relations. [Draft.] 4°. 2 pages.

RANDOLPH, BEVERLY (Governor).

1789, August 22. Madison's bond for £200 to insure the payment of £100 due from him to the State of Virginia. Inclosing receipt of £100 of P. Southall, State treasurer. [Signature of bond cut off.] fol. 1 page. 8°. 1 page.

RANDOLPH, EDMUND. *Richmond.*

1782, November 5, Philadelphia. The question of the territorial cession of New York. Intercession from the Count de Vergennes to Washington in favor of the life of young Asgill. The desire of the King and Queen. The Army to go into winter quarters. fol. 2 pages.

1782, November 10, Philadelphia. Asgill set at liberty. Washington to call on Gen. Carlton to pursue the guilty. fol. 1 page.

1782, November 12, Philadelphia. Lord Howe not sailed from the channel and has but thirty-four ships. fol. 2 pages.

1782, November 12, Philadelphia. Resolution to renew the appointment of Jefferson as minister for negotiating peace. Asks him to prepare Jefferson for the intelligence. fol. 1 page.

1782, November 14, Philadelphia. Notifying him of the appointment of Jefferson as minister to negotiate peace. fol. 1 page.

1782, November 19, Philadelphia. Acknowledging letter of 8th. Official notification of Jefferson's appointment. Avidity of Western people for the vacant lands and for separate governments. The impost thoroughly blasted. Perversity of Rhode Island. Controversy between Pennsylvania and Connecticut. fol. 3 pages.

1782, November 26, Philadelphia. Virginia proposes to pay in tobacco the demands of Congress instead of cash. Captives returned from Canada. Debates on the exchange of Mr. Laurens for Cornwallis. Obstinacy of Rhode Island in rejecting the impost. Report of evacuation of New York. Col. Hamilton in Congress. fol. 4 pages.

1782, December 2, Philadelphia. Determination of Livingston, Secretary of Foreign Affairs, to resign. Question as to his successor. Opportunity for Jefferson to sail for his mission in a French ship. fol. 2 pages.

1782, December 3, Philadelphia. Perplexities and projects touching the old paper money and relative interests of the States. [Translation of cipher in letter of December 2.] Controversy between Connecticut and Pennsylvania. Bill in Pennsylvania against erecting a new State within its charter limits. A new cipher. fol. 4 pages.

1782, December 10, Philadelphia. Pennsylvania about to pay her own citizens creditors of the United

RANDOLPH, EDMUND.

States out of Federal requisitions. Deputation to Rhode Island to enforce impost of 5 per cent. Resignation of Livingston as secretary of foreign affairs. His successor. The British fleet effected the relief of Gibraltar. fol. 2 pages.

1782, December 17, Philadelphia. Reasons given by the Rhode Island legislature for refusing to concur in the impost. Respecting the admittance of Vermont. Gen. Greene refers to Congress to show necessity of a code for captures and recaptures on land. Letters from Franklin and Jay. Commissions issued by which some obstacles are surmounted. Spain and our Western territory. fol. 3 pages.

1782, December 24, Philadelphia. Arrival of the *Danae* with money for the French army. Commission empowering Mr. Oswald to treat with commissioners from the thirteen United States. Adams concludes treaty of amity with Holland. Constantinople partly destroyed by fire. Havoc suffered by French and Spaniards in their attempt to storm Gibraltar. States receding from their duties to the Union. fol. 2 pages.

1782, December 30, Philadelphia. Acknowledging letter of 13th. Sensations excited by the repeal of the impost by Virginia. Arrival of Jefferson, who is preparing for his mission. Deputation from the Army to Congress. Capture of the ship *South Carolina* by the British. fol. 2 pages.

1783, January 7, Philadelphia. Acknowledging letter of 27th. Effects of repeal of the impost by Virginia. Her resolution against restitution of confiscated estates. Grievances laid before Congress by the deputation from the Army. fol. 1 page.

1783, January 14, Philadelphia. Evacuation of Charleston. Views given by deputation from the Army. Rule of apportionment or valuation of lands impracticable. fol. 1 page.

1783, January 28, Philadelphia. Acknowledging letter of 15th. General funds for paying United States creditors, the Army, etc. A case which justifies disobedience of instructions Petitions for a new State in Pennsylvania. Criticism on the text of the treaty with Netherlands. 4°. 3 pages.

1783, February 4, Philadelphia. General conviction in Congress of the necessity of a continental revenue for discharge of continental engagements. Repeal of the impost by Virginia. 4°. 2 pages.

1783, February 11, Philadelphia. Acknowledging letter of 1st. Valuation of lands. Congress full of abortive projects. Reasons for resignation of Mr. Livingston, Secretary Foreign Affairs. Rumors of peace. 4°. 2 pages.

1783, February 13, Philadelphia. Dawn of peace. Cloud gathering in the Army not likely to be dispelled by the rays of peace. 4°. 1 page.

1783, February 18, Philadelphia. Acknowledging letter of 7th. Repeal of the impost by Virginia. Valuation of lands. Further tokens of approaching peace. In consequence of which the departure of Jefferson suspended till further orders of Congress. 4°. 3 pages.

RANDOLPH, EDMUND.

1783, February 25, Philadelphia. Recommendation of impost to be renewed. Rumors of violent purposes in the Army. Seizure of clothing for British prisoners. Consequences of disunion. 4°. 4 pages.

1783, March 4, Philadelphia. Congressional discussion on the provision for public debts. Resignation of R. Morris, superintendent of finance. 4°. 1 page.

1783, March 11, Philadelphia. Acknowledging letter of 1st. Delay of official information in notifying the progress of negotiations of peace. The plan for revenue before Congress. 4°. 2 pages.

1783, March 12, Philadelphia. Arrival of preliminary articles] of peace. Dr. Franklin and Count de Vergennes. Franklin's vigor of intellect. Astonishing at his age. Asks to retire from public life. Mr. Adams transmits his resignation. 4°. 3 pages.

1783, March 18, Philadelphia. Acknowledging letter of 7th instant and 22d ultimo Checks to confidence in the preliminary articles of peace. Dispatches from Washington on the discontent of the Army. His conduct does honor to his prudence and virtue. 4°. 3 pages.

1783, March 24, Philadelphia. Confirmation of peace. 4°. 1 page.

1783, March 25, Philadelphia. Settlement of the preliminaries of a general peace. Critical state of the Army. Deplorable prospect had war continued. Plans for revenue. 4°. 2 pages.

1783, April 1, Philadelphia. Acknowledging letter of 22d. Alarming defection of States from the means of supporting the confederacy. Necessity of exertions by its friends. Tone of Carlton and Digby on the notification of preliminaries and the recall of American cruisers. That of Digby surly and indecent. 4°. 2 pages.

1783, April 8, Philadelphia. Acknowledging letter of March 29. Hostilities continue on our commerce. Revenue plan before Congress. Number of inhabitants, instead of land, the basis, deducting two-fifths of slaves. Compromise of wide opinions. Satisfaction of the Army at the glorious event and the act of Congress commuting half pay. Jefferson's mission suspended. 4°. 2 pages.

1783, April 10, Philadelphia. Hostilities stopped. Different construction as to the time they were to cease on our coasts. 4°. 1 page.

1783, April 15, Philadelphia. Carlton importunate for discharge of prisoners and restitution to Loyalists. Variety and contrariety of interpretation of the import of the preliminary treaty. 4°. 2 pages.

1783, April 22, Philadelphia. Questions under the preliminary treaty. Whether laws prohibiting British commerce during the war are repealed or not. Term of enlistments. Revenue plan passed in Congress. 4°. 1 page.

1783, April 29, Philadelphia. The definitive treaty is said to be transmitted to the two imperial courts for their approbation before signature. Shel-

RANDOLPH, EDMUND.

burne so pressed by the unpopularity of some of the terms that he could not prevent a vote in the House of Commons declaring them disadvantageous and dishonorable. Probably change in ministry. Propositions relative to our national debt to be forwarded to State legislatures. 4°. 1 page.

1783, May 6, Philadelphia. Acknowledging letter of April 26. The proclamation of peace contains exceptionable passages. Spain dismisses her hauteur and reserve to us since the British acknowledgment of our independence. Interview between Washington and Carlton for arrangements for carrying stipulations of the provisional articles into effect. 4°. 2 pages.

1783, May —, Philadelphia. General views of the national policy in relation to commercial treaties and of England particularly. fol. 4 pages.

1783, May 27, Philadelphia. Inquires the pulse of Virginia as to the revenue plan of Congress. Rhode Island's views in the case. 4°. 2 pages.

1783, June 10, Philadelphia. Construction of the epochs to limit captures. Virginia's instructions as to commercial treaties. Revocation of Mr. Adams's power. Mr. Livingston resigned from Secretaryship of Foreign Affairs. Cession of territory by Virginia. 4°. 3 pages.

1783, June 17, Philadelphia. Acknowledging letter of 4th. Definitive treaty not yet arrived. Furloughing of troops. Mutinous remonstrance. Embarrassments as to the peace establishment. Nominations for Secretary of Foreign Affairs. fol. 3 pages.

1783, June 24, Philadelphia. Revolt of the soldiery at Philadelphia. Their grievances, want of pay. Afflicting state of public affairs. 4°. 2 pages.

1783, June 30, Philadelphia. Conduct of the Pennsylvania executive as to the revolt. Soldiers give up their leaders. Removal of Congress to Princeton. 4°. 3 pages.

1783, July 8, Philadelphia. Acknowledging letter of June 28. Case of Nathan. New England troops detached for quelling the mutiny in Philadelphia. The residence of Congress. 4°. 2 pages.

1783, July 15, Philadelphia. Inquiry into the mutiny. Address of Philadelphia citizens declaring their loyalty to the Government. 4°. 1 page.

1783, July 21, Philadelphia. Court-martial on the parties to the late mutiny. Address to Congress signed by the citizens of Philadelphia. 4°. 1 page.

1783, July 28, Philadelphia. Address to Congress from citizens of Philadelphia. Question of the seat of Government. 4°. 3 pages.

1783, August 12, Philadelphia. Hawkin's account of Dana and the Russian Government. Temper of Massachusetts as to the revenue propositions of Congress. Statue to Washington voted by Congress. fol. 1 page.

1783, August 18, Philadelphia. Maneuvers in Congress as to returning to Philadelphia for seat of Government. Impost and half-pay. Officers of the

RANDOLPH, EDMUND.

Eastern States threatened with total loss of their pay. fol. 2 pages.

1783, August 24, Philadelphia. Gen. Carlton notifies Congress of his having received orders for the evacuation of New York. Insinuates that there is no government in the United States. 4°. 1 page.

1783, August 30, Princeton. Monopolizing views of Great Britain respecting commerce. The same reported as to France. Revenue plan adopted by Pennsylvania. Cramped situation at Princeton. fol. 2 pages.

1783, September 8, Philadelphia. Acknowledging letter of August 30. Delay of the definitive treaty. Conciliating efforts of Philadelphia. Opposition of New England to half-pay increasing. Abuse of Virginia land warrants. fol. 3 pages.

1783, September 13, Princeton. Continued difficulties with Great Britain as to commercial stipulations. The experimental purposes against the United States. fol. 1 page.

1783, September 20, Princeton. The Virginia cession of lands. France has fixed on l'Orient as a free port for the United States. 4°. 1 page.

1783, September 30, Philadelphia. The French minister's coach and six. Questions of maritime law. fol. 2 pages.

1783, October 13, Philadelphia. Particulars of the votes on the temporary and permanent seat of Government. fol. 3 pages

1784, March 10, Orange. Acknowledging letter of January 27. Commencing on a course of law reading. Destined to the State legislature. Remarks on surrender of criminals by one State to another. 4°. 4 pages.

1785, March 10, Orange. Acknowledging letter of 12th. Extract from Jefferson's letter showing the state of affairs in Europe, and views of Great Britain towards the United States. 4°. 1 page.

1785, July 26, Orange. Acknowledging letter of 17th. Legislation in Virginia on clerical misdemeanors. Washington's negotiations with Maryland. Letter from Lafayette about France and the Mississippi. Remonstrance against the general assessment prepared at instance of Col. Nicholson. Law reading continued. Dislike to its practice. Dependence on labor of slaves. 4°. 3 pages.

1787, March 19, New York. Acknowledging letter of 1st. Informs him where he can procure copies of certain documents. 4°. 1 page.

1788, April 10, Orange. Acknowledging letter of February 29. Objections in Massachusetts. Tendency of conditional ratifications or a second convention. Desperate measures of Patrick Henry. 4°. 3 pages.

1788, November 23, Philadelphia. Acknowledging letters of 3d and 10th. Unfriendly complexion of the Virginia assembly. Antifederal views. Madison prefers a seat in Congress to Executive office; aware of obstacles to either in House of Representatives or Senate. 4°. 3 pages.

1788 (?), not dated. Memorandum of an account and balance due Madison. Strip of paper.

RANDOLPH, EDMUND. *Williamsburg.*

1789, March 1, Alexandria. After the election. Prospect before Madison in the new Congress. 4°. 3 pages.

1789, April 12, New York. Acknowledging letter of March 27. Votes for Vice-President. Different ideas as to imposts. Amendments attainable. British debts and taxes. 4°. 3 pages.

1789, May 10, New York. Acknowledging letter of April 22. Gen. Washington's acceptance of the Presidency. Difference between Senate and House of Representatives as to titles to President and Vice-President. 4°. 3 pages.

1789, May 31, New York. Acknowledging letter of 19th. Slowness of business in Congress resulting from its novelty. Removals from office by the President alone. fol. 2 pages.

1789, June 17, New York. The Indian bill. The pro and con on the Executive's power of removals from office. fol. 2 pages.

1789, June 24, New York. Printed debates on the question of removals from office defective and erroneous. Jefferson's leave to come home. Illness of the President. The danger over. fol. 1 page.

1789, July 15, New York. Acknowledging letter of June 30. Decision as to the power of removal by the President alone. Concurrence of Randolph, Pendleton, and Monroe. The impost bill as finally passed. fol. 1 page.

1790, January 31, New York. The suggestion of the President to institute a national university. Madison recommends Williamsburg as a proper situation. small 4°. 3 pages.

1790, March 14, New York. Assumption of State debts. Secretary of Finance's report simplified. 4°. 2 pages.

1790, March 21, New *York.* Acknowledging letter of 10th. Discrimination between original and actual holders of State-debt certificates. Hostility of Cabell and Strother. Debates on the Quaker memorial. Assumption of State debts. Arrival of Jefferson. 4°. 2 pages.

1790, March 30, New York. Acknowledging letters of 15th and 18th. Recommitment of resolution on the State debts. 4°. 1 page.

1790. Memorandum of letters written to Edmond Randolph from May 1, 1782 to 1790 on various subjects. 4°. 3 pages.

1792, September 13, Orange. Acknowledging letter of August 12. Respecting Freneau's newspaper and calumnious charges against Madison. [Copy.] 4°. 3 pages.

Not dated. Queries and notes on the common law of England and Virginia at the time of the Declaration of Independence. 4°. 15 pages.

RANDOLPH, JOHN.

No date. In reference to Randolph's assertion as to Florida and the alleged expression used by Madison that France wanted money and must have it. [Draft.] "For the public if found expedient." 4°. 1 page.

RHEA, JOHN. *Tennessee.*

1816, June 1, Washington. Acknowledging letter of November 24. Rhea's appointment by Treasury Department to receive subscriptions for the National Bank and by the Secretary of War a commissioner for treaty with the Choctaw Indians. [Draft.] 4°. 2 pages.

RICHMOND ENQUIRER.

1826, January 25, Montpellier. Remarks by Madison on extract from Hamilton's report on the constitutionality of the bank. [Draft.] 4°. 1 page.

RIKER, R.

1827, March 26, Montpellier. Acknowledging letter of February 26, with Colden's memoir on the New York canals. Merits of the publication, with specimens of the new art of lithography. [Draft.] Strip of paper.

RINGGOLD, TENCH.

1831, July 12, Montpellier. Acknowledging letters of 7th and 8th. The death of Monroe. Tribute to his memory. Monroe's pecuniary affairs. [Copy.] Strip of paper.

RITCHIE, THOMAS.

1821, September 15, Montpellier. Acknowledging letter of 8th, on the subject of the proceedings of the convention of 1787. Materials for the publication of the same. The labor of making an exact digest and transcripts. Will then be better able to decide on their publication. [Draft.] "Confidential." 4°. 2 pages.

1822, July 2, Montpellier. Correspondence with H. G. Spofford respecting a prospect to write a gazetteer of Virginia. Asks his opinion. [Draft.] fol. 1 page.

1822, August 13, Montpellier. Acknowledging letter of 7th. Attempts to pervert the historical circumstances relating to the draft of the Declaration of Independence. Mr. Jefferson was the author, and in obedience to Virginia's instructions to her delegates, the motion for independence was made. [Draft.] "Confidential." fol. 1 page.

1825, December 18, Montpellier. Acknowledging letter of 10th. Distinctions between assumptions of power by the General Government in opposition to the will of the constituent body, and assumptions by the constituent body through the Government as the organ of its will. The alien and sedition acts. Roads and canals. [Draft.] 4°. 4 pages.

1830, May 24, Montpellier. Corrects an error in the Enquirer referring to "Helvidius" on the proclamation of neutrality. [Draft.] Strip of paper.

RIVES, WILLIAM C.

1827, May 29, Montpellier. Acknowledging receipt of a copy of his speech on February 25 in House of Representatives. The subject argued with ability. Strip of paper.

1828, December 20, Montpellier. Acknowledging letter of 17th. Views on an article in the "Southern Review" on the power of States or sovereignty of the people. Also on the power of Congress to regulate trade and encouragement to manufactures. [Draft.] Strip of paper.

RIVES, WILLIAM C.

1829, January 10, Montpellier. Acknowledging letter of December 31, 1828. On the power of Congress to regulate trade. Madison's and Jefferson's views. [Draft.] 4°. 2 pages.

1829, January 23, Montpellier. Acknowledging receipt of newspapers containing explanatory remarks on two letters relating to the power of Congress to encourage domestic manufactures. Madison's notes and memoranda with references to papers in refutation of misrepresentations. [Draft.] 2 strips of paper.

1833, March 12, Montpellier. Acknowledging letter of 6th. Views on the doctrine of nullification and secession. [Draft.] 2 strips of paper.

1833, March 12, Montpellier. Copy of the foregoing. 4°. 4 pages.

1833, August 2, Montpellier. Acknowledging letter of July 28. Thanks Rives for his friendly acts in relation to attacks leveled against the Virginia deputies to the convention of 1787. [Copy.] 4°. 1 page.

1833, October 21, Montpellier. Acknowledging letter of 4th, and inclosing notes and references on the convention of 1787, and a defense of charges against his political actions and misrepresentations. [Draft.] 8°. 17 pages.

1834, February 15, Montpellier. Acknowledging receipt of his speech on the "Removal of Deposits." Strip of paper.

1836, April 19, Montpellier. Acknowledging copy of his speech on March 28. The preservation of original journals of the legislature. Republication of journals of the House of Delegates. Increasing pressure of his infirmities. [Draft.] Strip of paper.

1836, January 26, Montpellier. Possible intervention of England by friendly offices to adjust a controversy in France. [Copy.] Strip of paper.

ROANE, SPENCER.

1819, September 2, Montpellier. Acknowledging letter of 22d. Interpretation of the Constitution bearing on the latitude of national jurisdiction with that of local government, citing the judgment of the Supreme Court in the case of McCulloch *v.* State of Maryland. [Copy in Madison's handwriting.] 4°. 4 pages.

1821, May 6, Montpellier. Acknowledging letter of April 17. On the judicial powers of the United States in respect to local legislation. [Copy in Madison's handwriting.] 4°. 6 pages.

1821, June 29, Montpellier. Acknowledging letter of 20th. The papers of "Algernon Sidney," on the arguments against the suability of States by individuals and against the projectile capacity of the powers of Congress within the "10 miles square." [Copy in Madison's handwriting.] 4°. 4 pages.

ROBBINS, ASHER. *Rhode Island.*

1818, August 8, Montpellier. Acknowledging letter of July 17. Robbins's criticism on the address to the agricultural society of Albemarle relating to the theory of Tull. [Copy.] 4°. 3 pages.

ROBBINS, ASHER.

1832, March 21, Montpellier. Mr. Robbins's speech on protection of American industry received. [Draft.] Scrap of paper.

ROBERTS, JONATHAN.

1828, February 29, Montpellier. Acknowledging letter of 15th. The motives which induced Madison to decline to take part in the present political contest. [Draft.] 4°. 1 page.

ROBERTS, WM. J.

1824, May 6, Montpellier. Incloses a power of attorney. Asks him to write, specifying the means needed for the purpose. [Draft.] 4° 1 page.

ROBERTSON, JAMES, JR.

1831, March 27, Montpellier. Acknowledging letter of 8th. Respecting the draft of the resolutions offered in 1798 to the Virginia assembly. Views on the historical work in which Mr. Roberts is interested. 4°. 1 page.

1831, April 20, Montpellier. Acknowledging letter of 3d. On constitutional points. Disuniting and nullifying doctrines. Admittance of new States. [Copy.] 4°. 2 pages.

ROBERTSON, JOHN.

1836, May 23, Montpellier. Acknowledging copy of speech in the House of Representatives. Commends it, particularly in the part which relates to the distribution of public lands. [Draft.] 8°. 1 page.

ROCHESTER, N. (chairman). *Hagerstown, Md.*

1809, March 17, Washington. Acknowledging letter in behalf of citizens of Washington County, of 6th, approving of Madison's measures in the present situation. [Draft.] 4°. 1 page.

1810, January 31, Washington. Acknowledging letter of 25th, inclosing the unanimous resolutions of a meeting of citizens of Washington County on the 20th, approving of the course taken by the Executive with respect to the British minister. 4°. 1 page.

ROGERS, THOS. J.

1826, January 16, Montpellier. Acknowledging letter of 5th, with 3d edition of Rogers's biographical remembrances. Its merits. [Draft.] Strip of paper.

ROMAINE, BENJAMIN. *New York.*

1822, January 26, Montpellier. Acknowledging letter of 11th, with two pamphlets. Comparison of a constitution with that of the United States. [Draft.] Strip of paper.

1829, April 14, Montpellier. Acknowledging letter of March 30, with pamphlets. Views of a particular party during the period from 1803 to 1815. Constitutional reforms. [Copy.] Strip of paper.

1832, November 8, Montpellier. Acknowledging copies of Romaine's pamphlet on State sovereignty. Commends it, although he differs with him in some points. [Copy.] Strip of paper.

ROSE, H. and others.

1790, August 13, New York. Session of Congress closed. Assumption of the State debts. Question of the seat of government. [Circular.] 4°. 2 pages.

ROSE, ——— (English minister).

1808, February 16, etc. Notes on Rose's negotiations on our grievances against Great Britain respecting impressments and the Chesapeake affair. [Mr. Madison's handwriting.] 4°. 6 pages.

RUSH, BENJAMIN.

1790, March 7, New York. Acknowledging letter of February 27. On the proposition to discriminate between the original and purchasing holders of certificates of the public debt. Influence of the location of the seat of government. [Draft.] 4°. 2 pages.

RUSH, RICHARD.

1817, June 27, Montpellier. Acknowledging letters of 18th and 20th instant Illiberal and impolitic course of Correa in assuming a guardianship of our character in Europe. The British doctrine of blockades. South American affairs. [Draft.] 4°. 3 pages.

London.

1818, July 24, Montpellier. Acknowledging letters of January 14 and May 2, with publications. Hopes that Rush's negotiations may aid in friendly arrangements on fair conditions. Our commerce with Great Britain. [Draft.] 4°. 5 pages.

1819, May 10, Montpellier. Acknowledging letter of December 13. Respecting purchase of some books. The late treaty with Great Britain. To be regretted that all questions at variance were not adjusted. The perplexed situation of moneyed and mercantile affairs. The multitude and mismanagement of banks. England and France making themselves independent of the United States in encouraging self-subsistence in their colonies. [Draft.] 4°. 5 pages.

1820, August 12, Montpellier. Acknowledging letter of September —. The trial of Queen Caroline. Britain's effort to force a reciprocity in the West India trade. Want of adequate markets for our abundant supplies. [Draft.] 4°. 4 pages.

1820, December 4, Montpellier. Acknowledging letter of August 20. Contraction of bank discounts and fall in produce. The Missouri question and tariff agitation in Congress. [Copy.] 4°. 3 pages.

1821, April 21, Montpellier. Acknowledging letter of November 15. Godwin's attack on Malthus detailed at length. [Draft.] 4°. 8 pages.

1821, November 20, Montpellier. Acknowledging letter of June 21. Godwin's last work. Increase of population in the United States. Black and white. The Emperor Alexandria. His character. The power of Russia. The trident will ultimately belong to the Western hemisphere. Prevalence of typhoid fever in United States. The last year's productions of the soil. [Draft.] 4°. 2 pages.

1822, May 1, Montpellier. Acknowledging letter of March 6, with several publications. Criticisms upon them. Jefferson; his remarkable vigor. Our country laboring under the fruits of pecuniary follies. The balance of trade against us. Living beyond incomes. The crops and harvest. [Draft.] 4°. 4 pages.

RUSH, RICHARD.

1823, July 22, Montpellier. The state of Europe. The tranquility and prosperity of our country. The animated contest for the next presidency. State of the crops and prospect of prices. The Hessian fly and chinch bug. The ardor and emulation in promoting objects of improvements. [Draft.] 4°. 4 pages.

1823, November 13, Montpellier. Acknowledging letter of September 10. The slave trade. Great Britain's motives. The allied powers and the South American provinces. Navigation of the St. Lawrence. The Mississippi. Canada not wanted by the United States. [Draft.] 4°. 4 pages.

1824, April 26, Montpellier. Introducing Francis W. Gilmer, whose object in visiting England is to secure professors for the University of Virginia, the buildings being finished and about to commence operations. [Draft.] 4°. 2 pages.

1824, February 27, Montpellier. Acknowledging letter of December 28. Sends him extract from Linguets "Observations sur l'ouverture de l'Escaut." In reference to the navigation of the Mississippi. [Draft.] Scrap of paper.

1829, January 17, Montpellier. Acknowledging letter of 10th. The tariff question. [Draft.] Strip of paper.

1831, no date, Montpellier. Acknowledging a publication and is particularly interested in an article subscribed "Temple." The Whig party in England. [Draft.] Strip of paper

RUSSELL, JONATHAN. *Paris*

1811, July 24, Washington. Acknowledging letter of January 2. Sketch of a convention arranged between Russell and Marquis Almanara. [Draft.] Strip of paper.

1811, November 15, Washington. Acknowledging letter of June 10. Unfriendly language held by Mr. Pinkney against Mr. Russell. The reports are not confirmed. Delicate situation in which Russell is placed. Importance of obtaining from French Government confirmation of repeal of its decrees. Their mixed character relating to Great Britain and United States. [Draft.] 4°. 2 pages.

SAY, J. B.

1816, May 4, Washington. Acknowledging a letter and copy of treatise on political economy. Commends the work. [Draft.] 4°. 2 pages.

SCHAEFFER, Rev. F. C.

1820, January 8, Montpellier. Acknowledging letter of December 30, with copy of report of the committee to the managers of the Society for the Prevention of Pauperism in New York. [Draft.] 4°. 1 page.

1821, December 3, Montpellier. Acknowledging letter of November 19 and copy of address at the ceremonial of laying the corner stone of St. Mathews Church in New York. Commends his pious zeal, benevolence, and liberality. [Draft.] Strip of paper.

SCHOOLCRAFT, HENRY R.

1822, January 22, Montpellier. Receives copy of a memoir on the fossil trees and remarks on the importance of investigations in geology. [Draft.] 4°. 1 page.

SCOTT, ROBERT G.

1824, October 6, Montpellier. Acknowledging letter of 27th. Regrets to be unable to accept the invitation in behalf of the volunteers of Virginia, to join them and other citizens at Yorktown, in celebrating the anniversary and expressing gratitude and affection for Lafayette. [Draft.] Strip of paper.

SCRIPTURE TEXTS.

Not dated. Notes on Scripture texts. fol. 4 pages.

SEDGEWICK, THEODORE, JR.

1831, February 12, Montpellier. Acknowledging letter of January 27. Answer to queries about Mr. Livingston (formerly governor of New Jersey), and the part he took in the convention of 1787, and his politics. [Draft.] 4°. 2 pages.

SENATE OF THE UNITED STATES. *Washington.*

1813, July 6, Washington. Dictated draft in response to a communication from the committee appointed by the resolution of the Senate, authorizing them to confer with the President on the subject of appointments to office. 4°. 3 pages.

SHELBY, ISAAC (Governor of Kentucky).

1813, August 12, Montpellier. Acknowledging letter of July 18. The bravery and patriotism of the citizens of Kentucky and Shelby's military services. A call on them will depend on events and success of Gen. Harrison and his wants on Lake Erie and below Ontario. [Draft.] "Private". 4°. 2 pages.

SHERMAN, CONVERSE.

1826, March 10, Montpellier. Acknowledging letter of 3d, with copy of Webster's prospectus of his dictionary. Commends the plan. [Draft.] 4°. 1 page.

SIMONS, ROBERT.

1795, December —, Philadelphia. Acknowledging receipts of a letter with a memorial to the House of Representatives. [Draft.] 4°. 1 page.

SIMPSON, JAMES. *New York.*

1806, August 25, Washington. Acknowledging his letter respecting the wreck of the brig *Indefatigable* on the coast of Morocco, and capture of her people on board, by the Arabs, who offer them for ransom. Although it is a question whether this vessel was American, admitting that the crew were United States citizens, humanity pleads in favor of them. 4°. 2 pages.

SKINNER, J. S. *Baltimore.*

1822, July 3, Montpellier. Thanking him for a sample of tobacco sent him in a letter of this date, and regretting his inability at present of sending him a sample of Virginia leaf of the same description. [Draft.] Strip of paper.

SKINNER, TIMOTHY. *Litchfield, Conn.*

1809, March 22, Washington. Acknowledging receipt of resolutions of a meeting of Republicans of the town of Litchfield. [Draft.] 4°. 2 pages.

SMITH, BERNARD.

1820, September —, Montpellier. Acknowledging letter of 6th. Hesitates to give his views, to be publicly used, on an approaching political question in which a local bias might be suspected. [Draft.] 4°. 1 page.

SMITH, ELISHA.

1831, September 11, Montpellier. Acknowledging letter of August 24. On the constitutionality of the bank of the United States. [Draft.] Strip of paper.

SMITH, ———.

Not dated. Order for pecan nuts and various other articles. Strip of paper.

SMITH, Mrs. MARGARET H.

1830, September —, Montpellier. Acknowledging letter in which he is asked to relate some reminiscences of the early relations between Jefferson and himself. Relates an anecdote of Jefferson's views on a hereditary head of government. [This letter remarkable for the microscopic handwriting, Madison being 81 years old.] [Draft.] 4°. 2 pages.

SMITH, ROBERT.

1811, April —, Washington. Memorandum of conversations with Robert Smith respecting a rupture mentioned in the "Aurora" of April 5 between himself and Smith, Secretary of State, and subsequent resignation of the latter. [Signed J. M.] 4°. 16 pages.

SMITH, SAMUEL H.

1826, November 4, Montpellier. Acknowledging letter of October 25, in which he asks Madison's assistance in preparing a memoir of Jefferson. Refers him to sources published and manuscripts in possession of T. Jefferson Randolph, legatee. [Draft.] 4°. 4 pages.

1827, February 2, Washington. Acknowledging letter of January 24, with copy of biographical memoirs of Jefferson delivered before the Columbian Institute. Proceedings of the general convention of 1787. Thinks a publication of them, posthumous as to others as well as to himself, may be more delicate and useful, since no personal or party views can then be imputed. [Draft.] Strip of paper.

SNYDER, SIMON (Governor of Pennsylvania).

1809, April 13, Washington. Acknowledging letter of 6th, with act of legislature to be laid before Congress. The Executive is unauthorized to prevent the action of a decree of the Supreme Court, but enjoined by statute to carry into effect such a decree. [Copy.] 4°. 2 pages.

Lancaster, Pa.

1810, July 5, Washington. Acknowledging letter of June 9, inclosing the resolutions of the general assembly of Pennsylvania, approving of the course of the Executive touching the insolence of the British minister and promise of support. [Draft.] 4°. 1 page

SOUTHARD, SAMUEL L.

1825, May 4, Montpellier. Thanks him for copy of his address before the Columbian Institute. Recommendation for establishment of a university in the District of Columbia. [Draft.] Strip of paper.

SOUTH CAROLINA AND GEORGIA, STATES OF.

Not dated. Notes in Madison's handwriting relating to Huet's history of those States, recording events prior to 1773. fol. 3 pages.

SOUTH CAROLINA LEGISLATURE.

1812, January 8, Washington. Acknowledging the address of the South Carolina legislature respecting our foreign relations. Madison explains the condition of affairs and justifies the course to be pursued. [Draft.] 4°. 2 pages.

1812, October 10, Washington. Acknowledging the joint addresses of the senate and house of representatives of the State of South Carolina approving of the war and promise of support. 4°. 1 page.

SOUTHWICK, SOLOMON.

1821, April 21, Montpellier. Acknowledging letter of 12th, with copy of address on the opening of the apprentices' library. The importance and usefulness of libraries. [Draft.] 4°. 1 page.

SPARKS, JARED.

1827, May 30, Montpellier. Acknowledging letter of 22d. Respecting correspondence with Gen. Washington. [Copy.] 4°. 3 pages.

1827, August 6, Montpellier. Mentions a private conveyance if Sparks wishes to communicate to persons in Boston. [Draft.] Scrap of paper.

1828, January 5, Montpellier. Acknowledging letter of December 29 and August 25. Offers Sparks a letter of introduction to Mr. Maury of Liverpool. The Washington letters. Little inaccuracies sometimes, when written in haste, does not derogate from his greatness. On the first assembling of Congress, no one thought of independence, but reestablishment of colonial relations. [Copy.] 4°. 4 pages.

1830, April 8, Montpellier. Acknowledging letter of March 8. Congratulates Sparks on his success in obtaining materials for his history. Washington's letters to Madison which do not appear on his files. Is afraid to trust them by mail. [Draft.] Strip of paper.

1830, October 5, Montpellier. Acknowledging letter of July 16. Draft of an address prepared for Washington in 1792. A copy sent Mr. Sparks. Reference to Delaplaine's biography of Mr. Jay. [Draft.] Strip of paper.

1831, June 1, Montpellier. Acknowledging letter of 24th. Reference to a pamphlet by Governor Morris. Other unofficial writings by him. Madison now the only survivor of signers of the Constitution. [Draft.] Strip of paper.

SPOFFORD, H. G.

1822, December 5, Montpellier. Acknowledging letter of November 25. Discovery of a process giving great purity and cheapness to steel and iron. [Draft.] 4°. 1 page.

SPRING, Rev. S.

1812, September 6, Montpellier. Acknowledging letter of August 26. Is gratified at hearing from an old college friend. Is surprised at the opposition to the war declared against Great Britain. The way to make the war short and successful is to convince the enemy that we are united. This letter to be considered private. [Copy.] 4°. 3 pages.

STARKE, JOHN (General).

1809, December 26, Washington. Expresses his esteem and the sense he has always entertained of his character and the part he bore as a hero and patriot in establishing the independence of our country. [Copy.] 4°. 2 pages.

STATES, SOVEREIGNTY OF.

1830 (?), not dated. On subject of sovereignty of States and the Union. [Draft.] Strips. 7 pages.

STATE CLAIMS.

1783 and subsequent. Notes and memoranda in Madison's handwriting respecting claims before the commissioner of accounts between the United States and individual States.
small 4°. 4 pages. 4°. 2 pages. fol. 2 pages.

STEVENSON, ANDREW.

1826, March 25, Montpellier. Acknowledging receipt of a copy of his speech. Points out an error of fact into which Stevenson had fallen as to the meaning of "national" in the proceedings of the convention of 1787. The origin of the convention. 4°. 2 pages.

1827, May 2, Montpellier. Acknowledging letter of April 28. Madison anticipates a visit from Stevenson. The colonial policy of Great Britain at war with reciprocity. The question discussed in Congress in 1794 divided the two political parties. [Draft.] Strip of paper.

1830, November 27, Montpellier. Acknowledges letter of 20th. Relating to the history and determining the import of the terms "common defence and general welfare" as found in the text of the Constitution, by the convention which formed it. [Draft.] Scraps of paper and 4°. 18 pages.

1830, November 27, Montpellier. Acknowleging letter of 20th. Explanatory of the letter to Mr. Stevenson of this date relating to the term "common defence and general welfare" as found in the Constitution. [Draft.] "Private."
Strip of paper.

1833, February 4, Montpellier. Acknowledging letter of January 29. On nullification and secession. [Draft and copy.] 4°. 7 pages.

1833, February 10, Montpellier. Acknowledging letter of 8th. The doctrine of secession. [Copy.]
4°. 2 pages.

STOKES, MONTFORD (Governor of North Carolina).

1831, July 15, Montpellier. Asks him to accept a copy of Lawson's History of the Library of North Carolina. [Draft.] Strip of paper.

STONE, DAVID. *Hope, near Windsor, N. C.*

1810, January —, Washington. Acknowledging letter of 1st covering the address of the general assembly of North Carolina who have unanimously expressed their approbation of the course pursued by the Executive in relation to foreign insults and aggressions. [Draft.] 4°. 2 pages.

STORROW, S. A.

1828, March 9, Montpellier. Acknowledging letter of February 18. Respecting a packet from Mr. Sparks, with directions as to transmitting it. [Draft.] Scrap of paper.

SUFFRAGE, THE RIGHT OF.

1787. Draft of a speech of Madison before the convention of 1787 at Philadelphia on the right of suffrage. 4°. 10 pages. fol. 1 page.

SUMNER, W. H.

1823, June 20, Montpellier. Thanks for copy of Sumner's letter to Mr. Adams on the "importance of militia." [Draft.] Strip of paper.

TARIFF.

1834 (?), not dated. Notes on the tariff. [Draft by amanuensis.] small 4°. 1 page.

TAXATION, DIRECT.

1788 (?), not dated. Memoranda in Madison's writing relating to the necessity of direct taxation. 8°. 1 page.

TAYLOE, JOHN. *Washington.*

1820, December 4, Montpellier. Answer to letter of 1st instant, complying with a request to send a proxy for voting for directors of the steamboat *Washington.* (Unsigned.) 4°. 1 page.

TEACKLE, LITTLETON DENNIS.

1823, February 12, Montpellier. Acknowledging letter of 4th, with the copy of a bill to provide for the public instruction of youth and to promote the interests of agriculture. [Draft.] 4°. 2 pages.

1824, June —, Montpellier. Acknowledging letter of 8th, indorsing the plan of a work entitled "Political Economist." Commends it. [Draft.] Strip of paper.

1826, March 29, Montpellier. Acknowledging letter of 22d, inclosing copy of the law providing for primary schools. Congratulates him on the foundation thus laid. [Draft.] Strip of paper.

TEFFT, J. K.

1830, December 3, Montpellier. Acknowledging letter of November 27, with one from Rev. Mr. Sprague. Sends, as requested, a number of autographs of distinguished Americans. Asks him to send him certain numbers of "The Georgian", containing notes of the Federal Convention of 1827. [Draft.] Strip of paper.

TENNESSEE GENERAL ASSEMBLY. *Nashville.*

1811, December 10, Washington. Acknowledging letter of November 23, covering an address approving of the measures of the General Government touching the wrongs inflicted on our country by Great Britain, and promising support. Respecting the navigable streams proceeding from the neighborhood of Tennessee and secured to the United States. [Draft.] 4°. 2 pages.

THOMSON, GEORGE. *Kentucky.*

1825, June 30, Montpellier. Acknowledging letter of 3d. The sad financial condition of Kentucky. The irregularities to which the legislature has resorted. Lafayette's visit to this country. Jefferson's bequest to his country. [Draft.] 4°. 2 pages.

THRUSTON, JOHN BUCKNER.

1833, March 1, Montpellier. Acknowledging letter of February 27, with Judge Cranche's Memoir of President Adams, and Thruston's Latin epitaph,

THRUSTON, JOHN BUCKNER.

embracing the coincidences in the lives and deaths of Adams and Jefferson. Difficulty of conveying modern compositions into ancient languages. Anecdote of the Frenchman's rendering "preserve" into "pickle"—"God pickle you." [Draft.] Scrap of paper.

TICKNOR, GEORGE.

1825, April 6, Montpellier. Acknowledging letter of March 29, with engraving of Lafayette. Description of the Virginia University. [Draft.] Strip of paper.

1825, May 2, Montpellier. Acknowledging receipt of copy of Life of Gen. Lafayette. [Draft.] Strip of paper.

1825, December 1, Montpellier. Acknowledging letter of November 21, with copy of Ticknor's "Remarks Concerning Howard University." [Draft.]

TIFFEN, EDWARD (Grand Sachem). *Chillicothe, Ohio.*

1811, June 23, Washington. Acknowledging letter of 14th, addressed in the name of the Tammany Society of Wigwam No. 1, Ohio, approving of the Executive's measures touching our foreign affairs. Expresses his gratification. 4°. 1 page.

TOMPKINS, D. D. (Governor of New York).

1814, January 25, Washington. Acknowledging letter of 3d. Barbarities of the enemy on the Niagara frontier. Suggestions as to remedies. [Copy.] 4°. 2 pages.

1814, September 28, Washington. Mr. Monroe, having been appointed Secretary of War, offers Governor Tompkins the appointment to fill the vacancy in the Department of State. [On same page is a copy of a letter to William Eustis, offering to name him to the Senate as minister to the United Netherlands. [Draft.] 4°. 1 page.

1814, October 18, Washington. Acknowledging letter of 6th and 8th. Although appreciating the important reasons why Tompkins declines to accept the place of Secretary of State he regrets his refusal. [Draft.] 4°. 1 page.

1814, November 12, Washington. Acknowledging letter of 5th, covering the unanimous resolution of the legislature of New York on the terms of peace proposed by the British commissioners at Ghent. [Draft.] 4°. 1 page.

TORREY, JESSE.

1822, January 30, Montpellier. Acknowledging letter of the 15th, with a copy of The Moral Instructor. The volume is useful to others than children. The plan of free libraries does credit to Torrey's benevolent zeal. [Draft.] 4°. 1 page.

TOULMIN, HARRY (Judge).

1810, September 5, Montpellier. Acknowledging letter of July 28. On the employment of force to arrest the enterprise against Florida. [Draft.] 4°. 1 page.

TOWNSEND, C. C.

1831, December 18, Montpellier. Acknowledging letter of 3d. Jefferson was not author of the Kentucky resolutions of 1799. The meaning attached by the term "nullify" by Jefferson. He never as-

TOWNSEND, C. C.

serted the right in a single State to arrest the execution of an act of Congress. [Draft.] 4°. 3 pages.

TRACIE, M. L.

1827, September 15, Montpellier. Acknowledging letter of 11th. On the appointment of a successor to Prof. Long, of the University of Virginia. [Draft.] Scrap of paper.

TRADE AND SHIPPING.

Not dated. Notes and memoranda relating to trade and commerce in the United States. 12° 12 pages. 8°. 2 pages.

TREATY WITH GREAT BRITAIN.

1789 (?), not dated. Suggesting delay in negotiations until the arrival of Jefferson, whose views may throw light on the subject. [Not signed, but in Madison's handwriting.] fol. 1 page.

TREATY, DEFINITIVE.

1794, not dated. Notes, in handwriting of Madison, for a speech on Jay's treaty. Also, on reverse of the paper, notes on same subject. fol. 2 pages.

TRIST, NICHOLAS P.

1826, July 6, Montpellier. Acknowledging receipt of letter of 4th. Tribute to the memory of Jefferson. His worth and the undiminished friendship for the period of fifty years. [Draft.] 4°. 1 page.

1827, February 7, Montpellier. Acknowledging letters of January 31 and 1st instant. Matters concerning the University of Virginia. Proposed gymnasium and dancing hall. Vacancies in professorships. Merits of applicants. [Draft.] 4°. 2 pages.

1827, March 2, Montpellier. Acknowledging letter of February 21. Returns the lucubrations of "Regulus." Observations on the distinction made between the authority of a constitution and that of public opinion. The difficulty in supplying a successor in the university should Mr. Key retire. [Copy.] 4°. 2 pages.

1827, April —, Montpellier. Explanation of Mr. Key's determination to leave the university. Mr. Owen on the present condition of Great Britain. The panacea for the distresses of her population. [Copy.] 4°. 4 pages.

1827, June 12, Montpellier. Acknowledging letter of 8th. The question of successor of Mr. Key in the University of Virginia. Correspondence with Jefferson. [Draft.] Strip of paper.

1827, August 4, Montpellier. Acknowledging letter of July 30. Ineffectual search for a morceau in Franklin's works. Letter from Gallatin respecting the vacancy in the professor's chair at the Virginia University. [Draft.] Strip of paper.

1827, November 3, Montpellier. Papers in Mr. Spark's hands, to be sent to Madison, not received. Wishes information. [Draft.] Strip of paper.

1827, December 24, Montpellier. Respecting supplying vacancies in professorships in the Virginia University. Correspondence of Jefferson. [Draft.] small 4°. 1 page.

TRIST, NICHOLAS P.

1828, January 26, Montpellier. Acknowledging letter of 18th. Madison's letters to Jefferson. The Treasury report. Encouragement to manufacturers. The public lands. Decline in price of land in Virginia. Emigration. [Draft.]
4°. 2 pages.

1828, April 23, Montpellier. Acknowledging letter of 17th. License of the press. Jefferson's letter to Mr. Norwell on that subject. [Draft.]
Strip of paper.

1829, March 1, Montpellier. Acknowledging letter of April 24. Transmittance to Mr. Randolph of copies of Jefferson's letters to Adams, senior, and Madison. Corrects the text in a letter. The term "contracts" in the Constitution. [Draft.]
Strip of paper.

1829 (?), no date, Montpellier. Inclocing a statement of the faculty of the University of Virginia on the subject of the fever prevailing. [Draft.]
Strip of paper.

1830, February 15, Montpellier. The alien and sedition laws. On the assertion of a right in the parties to the Constitution of the United States individually to annul the acts of the Federal Government. [Draft.] 4°. 6 pages.

1830, February —, Montpellier. Respecting Virginia documents of 1798–'99. Corrects Trist's impression that the doctrines of self-government were not understood at the commencement of the contest with Great Britain. [Draft.]
Strip of paper.

1830, June 3, Montpellier. Acknowledging letter of May 29. Is surprised at the construction put in the President's message on the veto in 1817 against the power of Congress as to internal improvements. Correspondence relating to the doctrine of nullification. Virginia gave no countenance to it. Jefferson had nothing to do with the Kentucky resolutions of 1799. [Draft.]
Strip of paper.

1830, September 23, Montpellier. Acknowledging letter of 21st. Question of the instrumentality of Jefferson in the Kentucky resolves of 1798–'99 in which the terms "nullification and nullifying" appear. [Draft.] Strip of paper.

1831, May 5, Montpellier. Acknowledging letter of 2d, with a treatise on mental physiology. Changes in the Cabinet. [Draft.] Strip of paper.

1831, December 21, Montpellier. Returns newspapers in which there is a sad sample of pulpit authenticity, justice, and delicacy. That which relates to Madison he declares to be wholly untrue respecting his abandoning the study of the Bible, while the Secretary of State thinks the preacher is insane. [Draft.] small 4°. 2 pages.

1831, December —, Montpellier. State rights. Doctrine of nullification. [Draft.]
4°. 4 pages, divided into 8 columns.

1831, December —, Montpellier. Duplicate of the foregoing. [Draft.]
4°. 4 pages, divided in 10 columns.

1832, May 29, Montpellier. Views respecting the tariff. [Copy.] 4°. 2 pages.

TRIST, NICHOLAS P.

1832, May —, Montpellier. Acknowledging letter of 8th. Has been ill with a bilious attack and rheumatism. Refuting the attacks on Jefferson. Hopes something may be done with the tariff and arrest the headlong course of South Carolina. The alternative presented by the dominant party there is monstrous and can not be sustained. [Copy.] fol. 2 pages.

1832, December 4, Montpellier. Acknowledging letter of November 28. The attack on Calhoun in a newspaper entitled "A Friend to Truth." The ordinance of the convention in South Carolina (nullification). The course of the Federal Government to effect means of defeating it. His microscopic handwriting. [Draft.] Strip of paper.

1832, December 23, Montpellier. Acknowledging letter of 19th. The doctrine of secession. The nullifiers make the name of Jefferson the pedestal of their collossal heresy, who was ever closely and emphatically against them. Notes in evidence of same. [Copy.] small 4°. 2 pages.

1833, January 18, Montpellier. Acknowledging letter of 11th. Reaction in South Carolina. Doctrine of nullification losing ground. [Draft.] Strip of paper.

1834, August 25, Montpellier. Acknowledging letter of 20th. Jefferson's letter to Madison relating to the resolutions of 1898–'99. Letter from Monroe to Jefferson more emphatic in antinullifying language. Journal of House of Delegates in 1898–'99. [Copy.] 4°. 2 pages.

TRUDEAU, CHARLES. *New Orleans.*

1809, July 23, Washington. Acknowledging the address of the citizens of New Orleans of June 6, with the sensibility due to the kindness of their expressions towards himself. [Draft.] 4°. 2 pages.

TRUMBULL, JOHN.

1835, March 1, Montpellier. Recollections of what passed between them as to the revolutionary subjects for paintings provided for by Congress. [Draft.] Strip of paper.

TUBERVILLE, G. L.

1788, November 2, New York. Acknowledging letter of October 20. On the project of another general convention. [Draft.] 4°. 4 pages.

TUCKER, HENRY ST. GEORGE.

1817, December 23, Montpellier. Acknowledging letter of 18th, with report on roads and canals. Although he does not concur in the report that the consent of States can enlarge the jurisdiction of the General Government; he does not permit this difference of opinion to diminish his esteem for the talents and confidence in the motives of its author. [Draft.] 4°. 1 page.

TUCKER, GEORGE (Professor).

1829, July 20, Montpellier. Incloses him copy of the original draft of the constitution of Virginia. [Draft.] Strip of paper.

1830, April 30, Montpellier. Acknowledging letter of March 29. The purpose of Mr. Tucker in writing a biography of Jefferson. Madison thinks Tucker

TUCKER, GEORGE (Professor).

will do full justice to the subject. Paper relating to Ceracchi, a sculptor. His importunities. Concerning the Virginia University. [Draft.] small 4°. 2 pages.

1831, October 17, Montpellier. Correspondence between Judge Pendleton and R. H. Lee, deposited in the Virginia University. The judiciary bill. [Draft.] Strip of paper.

1833, July 6, Montpellier. Incloses answers to two letters from Jefferson. Objections to the power of treaties made by the States. Jefferson's remark that the Constitution of the United States forms us into *one State*. [Draft.] Strip of paper.

1836, June 27, Montpellier. Acknowledging letter of 17th. The value he puts on the mark of respect in a dedication to himself of Tucker's "Life of Jefferson." [Draft by amanuensis.] 4°. 1 page.

TUCKER, ST. GEORGE.

1826, December 23, Montpellier. Acknowledging letter of November 22. Thanks him for extracts from the legislative journals. [Draft.] Strip of paper.

1826, December 30, Montpellier. Acknowledging receipt of letters and papers. Merits of the edition of Laws of Virginia. [Draft.] 4°. 1 page.

TURREAU, Gen. (French minister).

1805, April 4, Washington. Edict by Gen. Ferraud, commander-in-chief and captain-general at St. Domingo, denouncing as pirates all persons on board vessels, allies or neutrals, from ports in Hispaniola occupied by rebels, or 2 leagues from such port, and sentencing them to death. Contrary to laws of nations, and asks the minister to communicate with Ferraud to deviate him from his alarming purposes. [Draft.] 4°. 4 pages.

TYLER, JOHN (Governor).

1804, November 3, Washington. Notifies him of having drawn a bill on him in payment for a sword voted by Virginia to Gen. Campbell. [Draft.] 4°. 1 page.

1826, August 4, Montpellier. Acknowledging letter of March 31, with copy of his (Tyler's) oration on the death of Jefferson. [Draft.] Strip of paper.

18—, no date. Respecting a speech of Tyler's, February 6, 1833, relative to the Federal Convention of 1787, Madison corrects statements calculated to do injustice toward the Virginia deputies. [Draft.] 6 strips of paper, numbering 11 pages.

UNITED STATES GOVERNMENT.

1829, September —, Montpellier. Outline of the compound government of the United States. [Draft.] 4°. 3 pages.

UNIVERSITY OF VIRGINIA.

1826, December 16. Report of the visitors at the Academy respecting examinations of students and adoption of plans of professors, accompanied by a statement of the faculty. [Copy.] 4°. 2 pages.

1827, March —, Montpellier. The resignation of Mr. Key. The propriety of his being present at the

UNIVERSITY OF VIRGINIA.

examination. The question how to fill the vacated chair. [Draft of a circular.] 4°. 2 pages.

1827, May 27, Montpellier. Circular letter relative to filling a vacancy in a professor's chair, made vacant by resignation of Prof. Key. 8°. 1 page.

1827, September 21, Montpellier. Circular. On the appointment of Mr. Long to the Greek professorship in the London University. The question of retaining him against his inclination until 1829, the time his presence will be required. [Draft.] Strip of paper.

1829 (?), not dated. Concerning the fever at the university. Mr. Quincy, president of Harvard, asks information. Strip of paper. 2 pages.

UNKNOWN. *Richmond.*

1803, March 13, Washington. Respecting some furniture received from Monroe, and directions as to its shipment to Washington. Inclosing a list of the articles. [Draft.] 4°. 1 page. 8°. 1 page.

1805, May 29, Washington. In answer to a letter of 17th, in which allusion is made respecting the case of the acquittal of Judge Chase, stating it would be improper to pronounce for public use opinions of heads of departments. "Private." [Draft.] 4°. 2 pages.

New York.

1824, December 22, Montpellier. Fragment of a letter respecting a copy of a work on the "Pains of the Imagination. Scrap of paper.

1819, December 6. Private note. Sends back the correspondence with Cooper by the ladies who visited Mrs. Madison. 8°. 1 page.

1834, December —, Montpellier. On the subject of nullification. Views of Virginia in her resolutions of 1798-'99. [Draft.] 8°. 41 pages.

1834 (?). not dated. Acknowledging a letter from "A friend of Union and State Rights", inclosing essays. The proceedings of Virginia on the subject of nullification. [Draft.] Strip of paper.

1834 (?), not dated. His views on a majority government. Representative principles in modern government. [Draft.] Strips. 8 pages.

Not dated. Fragment of a letter describing a dinner at which nothing appeared on the table but American products. Portion, on back, of list of toasts. Scrap of paper.

Not dated. Opinion on the subject of the Supreme Court of the United States as a Constitutional resort in deciding questions of jurisdiction between the United States and individual States. [Draft.] 4°. 1 page.

VAN BUREN, MARTIN.

1820, March 27, Montpellier. Acknowledging letter of 15th, in which Madison's consent is asked for the publication of his correspondence in 1814, with the Vice-President of the United States, then governor of New York. Complies with the request. [Draft.] 4°. 1 page.

1820, no date, Montpellier. Regrets that the publication of Madison's correspondence with Governor

VAN BUREN, MARTIN.

Tompkins was preceded by that between Van Buren and himself. Apprehensive of wrong inferences. [Draft.] 4°. 2 pages.

1826, April 28, Montpellier. Acknowledging letter of 22d; also the paper containing Van Buren's observations on the depending modification of the Federal courts. [Draft.] 4°. 1 page.

1826, September 20, Montpellier. Acknowledging letter of August 30. On the proposition of amendment of the Constitution in respect to the question of internal improvements. [Draft.] 4°. 3 pages.

1826, October 15, Montpellier. Acknowledging letter of September 28, with a copy of the report of the Committee on Roads and Canals. On the construction of terms used in the Constitution relative thereto. [Draft.] Strip of paper.

1827, March 13, Montpellier. Acknowledging letter of 3d, covering report to the Senate on the "Georgia Business." Question of deciding, except by negotiation, questions between the Union and its members. A league with too many parties. To amend the phraseology of the Constitution. [Draft.] 4°. 1 page.

1828, February 21, Montpellier. Acknowledging his speech in behalf of the surviving officers of the Revolutionary Army. [Draft.] Strip of paper.

1828, May 13, Montpellier. Acknowledging a copy of the report to the Senate relating to the "Colonization of people of color." Points to an error of fact in Van Buren's observations on Foote's amendment. [Draft.] Strip of paper.

1830, June 3, Montpellier. Receives the President's message. The President has not rightly conceived the intention of Madison in his veto in 1817 on the bill relating to internal improvements. [Draft.] Strip of paper.

1830, July 5, Montpellier. Acknowledging letter of June 9. Subject of the discrepancy between the construction put by the message of the President on the veto of 1817 and the intention of its author. Views on the bill relating to internal improvements and the powers of Congress. [Copy.] 4°. 6 pages.

1830, October 9, Montpellier. Acknowledging letter of July 30. Remarks on the veto of 1817 of the bill on internal improvements. [Draft.] Strip of paper.

1835, February 18, Montpellier. Thanks him for a copy of Adams's oration on the life and character of Lafayette. [Copy.] Strip of paper.

VAN POLANEN, R. G.

1802, August 13, Virginia. Has communicated to the President of Van Polanen's appointment to another station. The President's assurance of the friendly disposition of the Batavian Republic and personal esteem for its representative. [Draft.] 4°. 1 page.

VAUX, ROBERT.

1827, February 21, Montpellier. Thanks him for a copy of his discourse before the Historical Society of Pennsylvania. The tribute to Penn, her great founder. [Draft.] Strip or paper.

VERPLANCK, G. C.

1828, February 14, Montpellier. Acknowledging letter of 5th, with copy of report to the High School Society of New York. It is gratifying, the increase of institutions for education. [Draft.] Strip of paper.

VIENNA AND ST. PETERSBURG, MEDIATIONS.

1782, April —. Communication in French, relating to the issue of the proposed mediation of Vienna and St. Petersburg. [Copy.] fol. 11 pages.

VIRGINIA CHARTERS.

Not dated. List of the charters granted to the State of Virginia. [Unknown handwriting.] 4°. 4 pages.

Not dated. A memorandum of the charters of the State commencing March 26, 1584. [In the handwriting of Madison.] small 4°. 5 pages.

VIRGINIA CONVENTION OF 1788.

1788. Memoranda for the convention of Virginia in 1788 on the Federal Constitution, with a copy attached. small 4°. 9½ pages. 4°. 11 pages.

VIRGINIA GENERAL ASSEMBLY.

1784. Address to the Virginia assembly remonstrating against the act of 1784 incorporating the Episcopal Church. [In Madison's handwriting.] [Copy.] 4°. 1 page.

1784, May —. Madison's proposition regarding the fulfillment of stipulations of the British treaty in the legislature of Virginia, at the May session of 1784. 4°. 3 pages.

1784, December 28. Resolutions touching the navigation and jurisdiction of the Potomac. [In Madison's handwriting.] Certified copy of the foregoing. [Draft.] 4°. 1 page. fol. 3 pages.

1784 or 1785. Draft of a proposed resolution touching the opening and keeping in repair of roads in Virginia and causing surveys to be made. fol. 1 page.

1787. Memoranda in microscopic writing by Madison, written previous to the convention of 1787, relating to the Federal Constitution. Strip of paper.

VIRGINIA, TREASURER OF STATE OF.

1787. Orders for amount due him for attendance as Member of Congress. 8°. 1 page. Strip of paper.

WALSH, ROBERT.

1819, March 2, Montpellier. Acknowledging letter of February 15, in which he intimates his intention to vindicate our country against misrepresentations propagated abroad. Madison's information respecting negro slavery, moral character, religion, and of education in Virginia. Variance between Hamilton's and Madison's statement relating to the "Federalist". [Draft.] 4°. 8 pages and strip of paper.

1819, October 16, Montpellier. Acknowledging letter of September 30, with copy of the "United States and Great Britain." A triumphant vindication of our country against the libels which have been lavished upon it. [Draft.] 4°. 1 page.

WALSH, ROBERT.

1819, November 27, Montpellier. Acknowledging letter of 11th. Intention of the framers of the Constitution relating to the "Migration and importation of persons". Prohibition of the slave trade. The Missouri question as a constitutional one. [Draft.] fol. 3 pages. 4°. 13 pages.

1820, January 11, Montpellier. Acknowledging letter of 2d, with a pamphlet on the Missouri question. Congratulates Walsh on the prospect of ample success to his patriotic and able performance in placing his vindication of the United States before the British public. [Draft.] 4°. 1 page.

1826, November 23, Montpellier. Acknowledging letter of 16th referring to the prospectus of the "American Quarterly Review". Approves of the undertaking, but on account of his advanced age fears he can not contribute much. [Draft.] Strip of paper.

1827, December 22, Montpellier. Acknowledging letter of 10th inviting him to contribute for the "American Quarterly Review". Has no time, owing to accumulated work since retirement from public service. Will, however, transmit a paper drawn up by Mr. Wilson, which was never printed, dated February 13, 1776. [Draft.] 4°. 2 pages.

1831, January 25, Montpellier. Pamphlet from two sons of the late Mr. Bayard vindicating the memory of their father against certain papers in the writings of Jefferson. Their filial anxiety is commendable, but they have done injustice to Jefferson by hasty and limited views from the evidence taken. Relates to Jefferson's election. Promises respecting appointments to office. [Draft.] 4°. 5 pages and strip of paper.

1831, January 31, Montpellier. Corrects a passage in a paper inclosed for the "National Gazette". [Draft.] Strip of paper.

1831, February 15, Montpellier. Acknowledging a letter of 10th. Conjectures as to the authorship of the vindication of Jefferson. Thanks Walsh for the offer of the "National Gazette" for any use he may have for it. [Draft.] Strip of paper.

1831, August 22, Montpellier. Tribute to the memory of Bishop Madison. [Copy.] Strip of paper.

WALTER, LYNDE, and others.

1821, January 24, Montpellier. Acknowledging letter of 15th. Views on the subject of a bankrupt act. [Draft.] 4°. 1 page.

WALTON, MATTHEW. *Washington County, Ky.*

1809, September 27, Washington, D. C. Acknowledging receipt of the resolutions of the inhabitants of Washington County, assembled on August 28, expressing confidence in the Government and pledging support. 4°. 2 pages.

WARDEN, DAVID BAILIE. *Paris.*

1810, September 1, Montpellier. Incloses a copy of a letter from Judge Cooper, of Pennsylvania. Takes pleasure in contributing to the object contained therein and authorizes him to draw for the required amount. [Draft.] 4°. 1 page.

WASHINGTON.

1783, April 29, Philadelphia. Acknowledging letter of 22d. The merits and talents of Mr. McHenry. Vacancies to be filled. Will take pleasure in taking McHenry's wishes and merits into consideration. [Copy.] 4°. 1 page.

1784, July 2, Richmond. Acknowledging letter of 12th. Action in the Virginia legislature towards recompensing the author of "Common Sense." [Copy.] 4°. 2 pages.

1784, August 12, Orange. Acknowledging letter of June 12. Question of the compensation for the patriotic services of Thomas Paine. [Copy.] 4°. 2 pages.

1785, January 1, Richmond. Acknowledging letter of December 28 The business before the legislature respecting the Potomac, James, and Ohio rivers. [Copy.] 4°. 2 pages.

1785, November 11, Richmond. Acknowledging letter of October 29. Proceedings of the Virginia legislature. Mr. Harrison elected to the chair. The revised code prepared by Jefferson, Pendleton, and Wythe. Subject of manumission of slaves. Distress of our commerce. [Copy.] 4°. 3 pages.

1785, December 9, Richmond. Acknowledging letter of November 30. Discussion in the legislature on commercial propositions. Other bills. Kentucky's formal application for independence. Terms of separation. [Copy.] 4°. 4 pages.

1786, November 1, Richmond. Rejection in the legislature of the question for a paper emission. The affair of the Mississippi. McHenry does not wish to be reelected governor. Edward Randolph and R. H. Lee are in nomination for his successor. [Copy.] 4°. 1 page.

1786, November 8, Richmond. Acknowledging letter of 5th instant. Bills following the vote against paper money. The selection of those to represent Virginia in the Federal Convention. Washington's name at the head. Randolph elected successor to Governor McHenry. H. Lee dropped from the delegation to Congress. [Copy.] 4°. 1 page.

1786, December 7, Richmond. Acknowledging letter of November 18. Washington's name can not be spared from the deputation to the meeting in May in Philadelphia. The question of ceding the Mississippi to Spain for 25 years. Financial schemes. Tobacco for a commutable in the taxes. A bill for establishing district courts. [Copy.] 4°. 2 pages.

1786, December 24, Richmond. Acknowledging letter of 16th. Virginia's deputation to the convention. Washington's observations on tobacco as a commutable in taxes. Financial questions. The revenue business. The rage to draw our income from trade. The port bill. Revised code. [Copy.] 4°. 2 pages.

1787, February 21, New York. Session of Congress. The number of States present. The question of the treaty of peace. Embarrassment of Congress respecting the convention to meet in May. The rebellion in Massachusetts extinct. The questions as to the proposed reform in the existing system of government. [Copy.] 4°. 3 pages.

WASHINGTON.

1787, March 18, New York. The plan of the Empress of Russia for a comparative view of the aborigines of the new continent and of the northeast part of the old. Appointments to the convention. The rebellion in Massachusetts. Disqualification of the malcontents. Relinquishment of Vermont by New York, and the question of admittance into the Union. Intentions of Congress concerning the Mississippi. [Copy.] 4°. 4 pages.

1787, April 16, New York. Acknowledging letter of March 31. Submits some outlines of a new system for discussion of the convention. Change in representation. Powers to regulate trade, taxing imports and exports, and fixing terms of naturalization. A negative on the legislative acts of States. National supremacy in the judiciary. Locality for seat of Government. [Copy.] 4°. 8 pages.

1787, October 14, New York. Transmits a pamphlet by Mr. Pinkney. Conjectures as to States in favor of and opposed to the act of the convention. Appointments of governor and secretary for the Western country and allotment of money for Indian treaties. [Copy.] 4°. 2 pages.

1787, November 18, New York. Acknowledging letter of 5th. Enthusiasm in Richmond in favor of the Constitution subsiding. Publication of the "Federalist". [Copy.] 4°. 2 pages.

1787, November 20, New York. Information from Europe. The Dutch in a wretched situation. The Turks and Russians begin war. No news concerning the convention. [Copy.] 4°. 1 page.

1787, December 7, New York. The Constitution will be adopted in Connecticut and New Hampshire; more opposition in Massachusetts. [Copy.] 4°. 1 page.

1787, December 14, New York. Proceedings of the assembly in Richmond respecting the act of the convention. [Copy.] 4°. 1 page.

1787, December 26, New York. New Hampshire agrees to call a convention to meet in February. Massachusetts uncertain. New Jersey adopts the Constitution unanimously. [Copy.] 4°. 1 page.

1788, January 14, New York. Nothing of importance from Massachusetts. Accounts from New Hampshire favorable. Nothing from South Carolina. Georgia's convention at Augusta. North Carolina postpones her convention to July. [Copy.] 4°. 1 page.

1788, January 20, New York. Count de Moustier, the French minister, arrived. European intelligence. Opposition in Massachusetts to the Constitution. Other States. [Copy.] 4°. 2 pages.

1788, January 25, New York. Acknowledging letter of 10th. Conjectures as to convention's proceedings. [Copy.] 4°. 2 pages.

1788, January 28, New York. Incloses extracts from a letter received from Mr. King from Boston giving the proceedings of the convention in Massachusetts. Impropriety of conduct of Mr. Gerry. His discussion with Mr. Dana. [Copy.] 4°. 2 pages.

WASHINGTON.

1788, February 1, New York. Uncertainty of Massachusetts in respect to the Constitution. Georgia and South Carolina seem favorably disposed. [Copy.] 4°. 2 pages.

1788, February 8, New York. The prospect in Massachusetts seems to brighten. Mr. Hancock, chairman in the convention. Conjectures as to other States. [Copy.] 4°. 2 pages.

1788, February 11, New York. The proceedings in the Massachusetts Convention. Mr. Hancock's propositions which Mr. Samuel Adams approves of. Probably the result will be favorable. [Copy.] 4°. 1 page.

1788, February 15, New York. Favorable result of the convention at Boston. No question as to the result in New Hampshire. [Copy.] 4°. 1 page.

1788, February 20, New York. Acknowledging letter of 7th. Accepts the position offered in the Virginia convention against his private inclination. Misinterpretations of a letter from Washington to Col. Carter. European intelligence. France's purpose of supporting her Dutch friends. [Copy.] 4°. 2 pages.

1788, March 3, New York. Proceedings in New Hampshire. She has not rejected the Constitution, but failed to accept it. Intended visit to Orange. [Copy.] 4°. 2 pages.

1788, April 10, Orange. Conjectures as to the results of the convention. [Copy] 4°. 2 pages.

1788, June 4, Richmond. Acknowledging letter of May 2. Proceedings of the convention at Richmond. [Copy.] 4°. 1 page.

1788, June 13, Richmond. Acknowledging letter of 8th. Appearances less favorable in the convention at Richmond. Letters from New York state the elections are adverse to the Constitution. [Copy.] 4°. 1 page.

1788, June 18, Richmond. Still undecided as to the Constitution. Mr. Henry's course. [Copy.] 4°. 1 page.

1788, June 23, Richmond. The Constitution got through by paragraphs to-day. To-morrow the proposition for closing the business will be made. Col. Mason's declarations. Mr. Henry's aversion to the Constitution. [Copy.] 4°. 1 page.

1788, June 25, Richmond. The final question of ratification passed. Subsequent amendments will attend the act. [Copy.] 4°. 1 page.

1788, June 27, Richmond. The convention adjourned. Incloses the act of ratification. Mr. Henry's declarations. [Copy.] 4°. 1 page.

1788, July 21, New York. Proceedings at Poughkeepsie. Congress deliberating on the arrangements for putting the new machine in operation. The times for choosing electors. [Copy.] 4°. 2 pages.

1788, August 15, New York. Acknowledging letter of 3d. The place for meeting still remains to be fixed. Rhode Island retired from Congress. Circular letter from the convention of New York. [Copy.] 4°. 2 pages.

WASHINGTON.

1788, August 24, New York. Acknowledging letters of 17th and 18th. The circular address of the convention of New York a matter of much regret. The difficulty in deciding the locality for the new Government. [Copy.] 4°. 4 pages.

1788, September 14, New York. The delay in providing for the commencement of the Government terminated. Time for electing electors and choosing the President. The meeting of the Government to be in New York City. [Copy.] 4°. 2 pages.

1788, October 21, New York. The struggle in France between the monarchy and aristocracy. Probably neither parties contain real friends of liberty. Visit of Count Moustier and Marchioness Brehan at Mount Vernon. Connecticut's Senators. Representatives to be voted for by the people. The vote fixing New York as the place of first meeting. [Copy.] 4°. 2 pages.

1788, November 5, New York. Asks Washington's advice respecting a purchase of land through which the canal at the Great Falls is to run and in which Col. H. Lee is interested. Politics in Virginia as expressed by her representatives in convention. Candidates for Vice-President. [Copy.] 4°. 3 pages.

1788, December 2, Philadelphia. Acknowledging letter of 17th. Elections of Senators in various States. Folly of Virginia in urging another convention. The policy of his presence in Virginia preceding the election of Representative in his district. [Copy.] 4°. 3 pages.

1789, January 14, Orange. Acknowledging letter of 2d. The election in Virginia for electors of President and Vice-President. Is canvassing his district and contradicting reports circulated against him. [Copy.] 4°. 2 pages.

1789, March 5, Baltimore. The electoral vote of Georgia and South Carolina. [Copy.] 4°. 1 page.

1789, March 8, Philadelphia. Assembling of Congress in New York. Project of George Morgan for establishing a colony beyond the Mississippi. [Copy.] 4°. 2 pages.

1789, March 19, New York. Conjectures as to the balance of parties in Congress. News from Europe. Progress in France towards a constitutional establishment and a coalition between king and commons against the nobility. [Copy.] 4°. 2 pages.

1789, March 26, New York. Inclosing a copy of George Morgan's invitation to his fellow-citizens respecting the establishment of a colony west of the Mississippi. [Copy.] 4°. 3 pages.

1789, April 6, New York. Quorum made up in the Senate. Also in the other House. Muhlenburg chosen Speaker of the House. [Copy.] 4°. 2 pages.

1789, November 20, Orange. Question of the residence of Congress. Proceedings of the Virginia assembly. Defeat of Henry's attempt to revive the project of commutables. [Copy.] 4°. 3 pages.

1789, December 5, Orange. Transmits a copy from the Virginia Senators to the legislature. Calculated

WASHINGTON.

to keep alive the disaffection to the Government. The revenue bill in the Virginia legislature. Tobacco and hemp proposed as commutables for taxes negatived. The fate of the amendments proposed by Congress to the General Government still in suspense. [Copy.] 4°. 4 pages.

1790, January 4, Georgetown. Has been ill with dysentery. The contest in the Virginia assembly on subject of amendments ended in the loss of them. Visit to Monticello. Jefferson's appointment as Secretary of State. [Copy.] 4°. 3 pages.

1792, May 5, 9, and 25. Substance of a conversation with Washington respecting the latter's intention of retiring from public life at the expiration of his term. [Copy.] 4°. 7 pages.

1792, June 21, Orange. Acknowledging letter of May 20. Queries to Madison: 1. At what time should a notification of his purpose to retire be made? 2. What mode? 3. Whether a valedictory address will be requisite or advisable? 4. Whether it should be annexed to the notification or postponed to his actual retirement? Annexed to this letter is a draft by Madison of an address suitable for the occasion. [Copy.] 4°. 7 pages.

1793, October 24, Orange. Acknowledging letter of 14th. Answers to queries to Madison: 1. Ought the President to summon Congress at a time and place named by him? 2. If the President has no power to change the place, ought he to abstain from all interposition? 3. Ought he to notify the obstacle to the meeting in Philadelphia? 4. What is the place liable to fewest objections? [Copy in Madison's hand.] 4°. 3 pages.

1793, October 24, Orange. Duplicate to the foregoing. 4°. 7 pages.

1794, February 8. Madison apologizes for not sending pamphlets from Sir John Sinclair for the use of Mr. Peters. Gives his reasons and will comply with the President's request. [Draft.] 4°. 1 page.

1796, December 1, Philadelphia. Returns the treatise on small canals, etc. Is not conversant enough with such subjects to decide on the merits of the plans and machinery, etc. But the author is entitled to much praise for his ingenuity and zeal for improvement. [Copy.] 4°. 1 page.

WATERHOUSE, BENJAMIN.

1822, June 22, Montpellier. Acknowledging letter of 9th, with a copy of his letter on tobacco and ardent spirits. Observations of the use of them. The disposition of Europe to use our tobacco rather than our wheat. [Draft.] 4°. 1 page.

1822, December 27, Montpellier. Acknowledging letter of 12th, with the "Botanist" and "Heads of a course of lectures." Adams's interest in the subject of natural history. Madison's address to the agricultural society. The professorships in the University of Virginia. [Draft.] 4°. 1 page.

1825, July 13, Montpellier. Acknowledging letter of June 30. The imbecility which occasioned Gen. Hull's downfall. Attempts to decorate him with artificial laurels. Gen. Dearborn's character a contrast to that of the mock hero of Detroit.

WATERHOUSE, BENJAMIN.

Question of Waterhouse's age being a detriment for public service abroad. [Draft.]
Strip of paper.

1829, March 12, Montpellier. Acknowledging letter of February 14, with his (W's.) inaugural discourse prepared in early life. His doubts of his own qualifications to criticise its Latinity. The eastern States during the war. [Draft.]
Strip of paper.

1831, May 27, Montpellier. Acknowledging letter of 9th, with the volume on the authorship of Junius. Has done full justice to his hypothesis. [Draft.] Strip of paper.

1833, June 21, Montpellier. Acknowledging letter of May 30, with a volume (subject not mentioned). [Copy.] 4°. 1 page.

1834, March 1, Montpellier. Acknowledging letter of 20th, with a copy of his "Public Lecture." A good medicine for bad habits. Mr. Madison and himself amateurs of the snuff-box. The good done by temperance societies. Concerning the Hartford Convention. [Draft.] "Private."
Strip of paper.

1835, November 28, Montpellier. On the subject of Dr. Pemberton, whose pupil he was. [Draft by amanuensis.]

WATSON, ELKANAH. *New York.*

1820, May 12, Montpellier. Acknowledging letter of 3d, with his work on canals and agriculture. [*See* letter of Watson to Madison, May 3, 1820.]
4°. 1 page.

WEBSTER, DANIEL.

1825, February 25, Montpellier. Thanks him for printed documents sent him during the session of Congress. These printed records are more convenient for future reference than the daily papers. [Draft.] Strip of paper.

1830, May 27, Montpellier. Acknowledging letter of 24th, with a copy of his speech. Has a full sense of its powerful bearing on the subjects discussed, particularly its overwhelming effect on the nullifying doctrine of South Carolina. Madison's views already communicated to Mr. Everett, to whom he refers Mr. Webster. [Draft.]
Strip of paper.

1833, March 15, Montpellier. Acknowledging Webster's speech against nullification and secession. Madison's opinions. A revolt against the principles of the Constitution leaves no choice but between anarchy and despotism. [Draft.]
Strip of paper.

WEBSTER, NOAH.

1792, no date. Answer to questions in Webster's letter of June 30, 1792, on labor and agriculture. [Copy.] 4°. 2 pages.

1820, January —, Montpellier. Asks for a copy of a letter to Webster in answer to one of August 20, 1804, asking information as to the origin of the change in the Federal Government which took place in 1788. [Draft.] 4°. 1 page.

WESTGATE, DAVIS. *Hancock County, Mass.*

1809, March 15, Washington. Acknowledging receipt of resolutions of February 23 of the inhabitants of the towns of Eden, Trenton, and Mount Desert, in the County of Hancock, to maintain the authority of the laws and the natural rights. [Draft.] 4°. 2 pages.

WHARTON, THOMAS I.

1826, November 14, Montpellier. Acknowledging letter of 6th, covering copy of his discourse on the landing of William Penn. [Draft.] Strip of paper.

1827, August —, Montpellier. Acknowledging copy of Wharton's oration on July 4. Describes the part he had in bringing about the first public proposal for the meeting of the convention for forming the Constitution. [Draft.] Strip of paper.

1828, May 5, Montpellier. Acknowledging letter of 18th, with a copy of the report on the penal code, etc. Praises the ability to what relates to the penitentiary discipline. [Draft.] Strip of paper.

WHEATON, HENRY. *New York.*

1823, October 15, Montpellier. Acknowledging letter of September 29 on the proposed biography of Mr. Pinkney. Will supply Wheaton with any correspondence which he may have to fill any chasms. Pinkney's letters do equal honor to his penetration and patriotism during his diplomatic service in Great Britain. [Draft.] 4°. 1 page.

1825, April 1, Montpellier. Acknowledging, through President Monroe, a return of letters of Mr. Pinkney, with Wheaton's letter of February 27. Commits them to Mr. Wheaton to use according to his discretion. [Draft.] 4°. 1 page.

WHEATON, JOSEPH.

1820, July 6, Montpellier. Acknowledging letter of 1st, concerning his appointment as Sergeant-at-Arms. His gallantry in the Revolutionary War and war of 1812 creditable to him as both citizen and soldier. [Draft.] [Signed J. M.] 4°. 1 page.

WHITE, E. D.

1832, February 14, Montpellier. Acknowledging receipt of "Remarks upon a Plan for the Total Abolition of Slavery in the United States." Points out an error in ascribing to Madison an opinion. [Copy.] Strip of paper.

WILLIAMS, C. D. *Baltimore.*

1820, February —, Montpellier. Acknowledging his letter with pamphlet on the circulating medium. Views on paper currency. [Draft.] 4°. 1 page.

WILLISTON, C. FENNIMORE. *Philadelphia.*

1836, March 19, Montpellier. Acknowledging letter of 9th. Can give no information. Does not possess a copy of the printed correspondence between Jeremy Bentham and himself on the "codification for the United States," nor the original manuscript. [Draft.] Scrap of paper.

1836, May 13, Montpellier. Acknowledging letter of 6th. Knows of no propositions to codify the laws of the United States on the plan of Mr.

WILLISTON, C. FENNIMORE.

Bentham other than those by himself. At Washington there are individuals from every State who can readily answer his inquiries. [Draft.] Strip of paper.

WINDER, WILLIAM.

1834, September 15, Montpellier. Excuses for delay in answering his letter, in which he wishes him to express his personal approval of his father's character and conduct at the battle of Bladensburg. Had an esteem for him and thinks the evidence on record and verdict of the court of inquiry will outweigh and outlive any injustice to him. [Draft.] Strip of paper.

WIRT, WILLIAM.

1828, May 5, Montpellier. Inclosing a letter from Mr. Eppes, recommending to his favor a young friend. Asks Wirt to return letters to Mr. Pendleton sent him some years ago. [Draft.] Strip of paper.

1830, October 12, Montpellier. Acknowledging letter of 5th. The cause of the Cherokees. [Draft.] Strip of paper.

1830, October —, Montpellier. Acknowledging copy of Wirt's address to the two societies of Rutger's College and his opinion in the case of the Cherokees. The plea of dispossessing Indians of the lands on which they have lived. The difficult problem of reconciling their interests with their rights. [Copy.] 4°. 1 page.

WOOD, JOSEPH.

1836, February 27, Montpellier. Acknowledging letter of 16th, asking information pertaining to a biography of his father-in-law, Chief-Justice Ellsworth. Of his public character he always regarded his talents of a high order. [Copy.] 4°. 2 pages.

WOODWARD, A. B.

1824, September 11, Montpellier. Acknowledging letter of 4th. Standard of measures and weights. Origin of the constitution of Virginia was with George Mason. The declaration of rights was from the same hand. The preamble to the Constitution was by Jefferson. [Draft.] 4°. 1 page.

WRIGHT, FRANCES, Miss.

1825, September 1, Montpellier. Acknowledging a letter to Mrs. Madison, with a printed copy of Miss Wright's plan for the gradual abolition of slavery. His observations and views. [Draft.] 4°. 4 pages.

PART II.

LETTERS TO MADISON AND OTHERS.

ACHESON, THOMAS, to MADISON. *Washington.*

1812, August 25, Washington, Pa. Defeat of Gen. Hull and army. Appeals for change in Department of War, and for prompt measures for defense on the unprotected frontiers. Readiness of the Pennsylvania militia. fol. 3 pages.

1812, September 1, Washington, Pa. The defeat and surrender of Gen. Hull's army. Possession of Detroit by the British. Is persuaded that good will come out of it. The nation will arouse from its apathy and carry on the war with vigor. Incloses report of the committee of safety, giving sketch of the spirit of the people. News of safety of frontier. 4°. 3 pages.

1813, no date, Washington County, Pa. Address of the officers of the Fourteenth division of the Pennsylvania militia acquiescing in the measures of the General Government in the prosecution of the war, and declaring their determination to support it with energy. 4°. 5 pages.

ADAIR, JOHN. *Washington.*

1809, January 9, Natchez. Giving information of the wishes and views of people of all classes in Natchez and the adjoining territories of Orleans and Florida. The Government has many enemies and very few friends there. Bonaparte their god. British intriguers gaining ascendency. 4°. 3 pages.

ADAMS, HERBERT & CO. *Washington.*

1816, April 30, Alexandria. Sends a pipe of Madeira received from that place for Madison, with the bill annexed. 4°. 2 pages.

1816, May 3, Alexandria. Acknowledging receipt of letter of 1st, with check in payment of a pipe of Madeira. 4°. 2 pages.

ADAMS, JOHN, to BARCLAY, THOMAS.

1788, November 4, Braintree. Gives his testimony as to the diligence, judgment, and integrity in all the public departments in which Adams has known him to act. [*See* Jefferson's letter to Barclay dated August 3, 1787.] [Copy.] 4°. 1 page.

ADAMS, JOHN (Mayor), and others, to MADISON. *Montpellier.*

1824, October 12, Richmond. Invitation of the citizens of Richmond to participate in the reception of Gen. Lafayette. 4°. 1 page.

ADAMS, JOHN QUINCY, to ADAMS, JOHN.

1814, October 27, Ghent. Extract of a letter describing the diplomatic skill employed by the British Government in delaying the negotiations with the American commissioners at Ghent. [Copy.] 4°. 1 page.

——— to CONGRESS.

1819, December 14, Washington. Extract from the Secretary of State's report to Congress of this date relating to the services of Mr. Cathcart on the Barbary coast. Recommends the liberal indulgence of the legislature to his claims. [*See* letter from John Rodgers to J. L. Cathcart, June 19, 1809.] [Copy.] 4°. 1 page.

——— to POLITICA, CHEVALIER DE. *Washington.*

1821, December 15, Washington. Introducing Thomas Munroe, jr., who wishes to proceed to St. Petersburg with a view of offering his services in a military capacity to His Imperial Majesty. [Copy.] 4°. 1 page.

———.

1821. Statement of the various appointments granted to him from 1794 to 1821. fol. 2 pages.

ADAMS, THOMAS B., to DUANE, WILLIAM.

1809, January 23, Orange C. H. Incloses draft on Madison for subscription to the "Country Aurora," which he discontinues. 4°. 1 page and scrap of paper.

——— to MADISON. *Washington.*

1810, June 18, Quincy. Transmits copies of J. Q. Adams's lectures on rhetoric and oratory delivered while professor at Harvard University. 3°. 1 page.

ADDISON, J. *Montpellier.*

1825, October 16, London. Answer to inquiries about the price of large terrestrial globes, with printed prospectus. 4°. 4 pages.

ADDISON, THOMAS G. *Montpellier.*

1830, August 20, Washington. Asking Madison's good offices in procuring for him office in Washington. Incloses some references. 4°. 1 page. fol. 4 pages.

1835, April 29, Cincinnati. Asks Madison's opinion whether the present United States Bank can be so amended as to suit the convenience and interests of the country without endangering the welfare of the people. 4°. 2 pages.

No year, May 22, Louisville. Incloses a communication relative to the tariff. 4°. 2 pages.

ADET, P. A. *Washington.*

1804, July 24, Nevers, France. Assurances of sentiments of attachment and esteem. Recommending to Mr. Madison's good offices Mr. Roux-Bordier, of Geneva, who is going to the United States to establish himself. [In French.] 4°. 3 pages.

ADLUM, JOHN. *Montpellier.*

1823, March 28, Georgetown, D. C. Sends Madison a bottle of domestic wine called Tokay. Gives points on the cultivation of the grape and what can be accomplished, knowing his disposition to promote all things that may be of advantage to our country. 4°. 4 pages.

AFRICAN ABOLITION OF SLAVE TRADE. *Montpellier.*

1821, July 20, Boston. Notice of transmittance of papers concerning abolition of the African slave trade. [Unsigned.] 4°. 1 page.

AGRICULTURE, AMERICAN BOARD OF.

1803, March 30, Washington. Object of the society. [Draft.] 4°. 3 pages.

AGRICULTURAL SOCIETY OF BERKSHIRE.

1814, November 4, Pittsfield. Tendering an inclosure. 8°. 1 page.

AGUIAR, MARQUIS DE. *Washington.*

1816, February 1, Rio de Janeiro. Introducing José Correa da Serra as minister plenipotentiary to represent Portugal in the place of José Manuel da Camara. [In Portugese.] fol. 1 page.

ALDEN, TIMOTHY. *Montpellier.*

1824, January 6, Meadville, Pa. Notice of transmittance of the catalogue of the library of Allegheny College, Meadville. 4°. 2 pages.

ALEXANDRIA, PROTESTANT EPISCOPAL CHURCH OF.

1800, December 1, Alexandria. Bill enacted by Congress concerning this church. [Copy.] 4°. 3 pages.

ALEXANDER J. ADDISON, and others to MADISON. *Montpellier.*

1831, January 3, Nassau Hall, Princeton, N. J. In behalf of a committee invites Madison to their commencement to address them, he being considered the father of the institute. 4°. 3 pages.

ALLAN, WILLIAM. *Washington.*

1813, March 21, Chatham. Is a prisoner of war on the British ship Nassau. Wants to be exchanged. 4°. 2 pages.

ALLEN, MONROE T. *Montpellier.*

1833, May 3, New Berne, N. C. Asks for a catalogue of the studies pursued before and after entering the University of Virginia. 4°. 1 page.

ALSTON, JOSEPH. *Washington.*

1812, May 17, Oaks, near Georgetown, S. C. Asks for the appointment of William S. Bennett to the office of Federal marshal. 4°. 2 pages.

ALSTON, WILLIS.

1815, March 2, Washington. Having determined to retire after the present session, wishes to be appointed one of the commissioners to ascertain and fix the boundary and carrying out the execution of the Creek treaty. 4°. 1 page.

1829, December 25, Washington. Approves of Madison's proceedings in the convention. 4°. 2 pages.

AMBLER, J. *Philadelphia.*

1781, December 22, Richmond. The deranged state of finances. Paper money reduced to specie at 1,000 for 1, and loan certificates given for them payable in seven years. The thirst for hard money. fol. 1 page.

1781, December 29, Richmond. Wishes Madison would write some articles to arouse the members of the Virginia assembly. 4°. 1 page.

1782, April 6, Richmond. Perplexing condition of Virginia finances. fol. 1 page.

AMBLER, J.

1782, April 20, Richmond. Financial matters. The allies of France in the capitulation of St. Kitts. Great numbers of flag vessels arriving from New York. Orders given to have them searched. fol. 1 page.

1782, May 11, Richmond. Financial matters. Complaints by the people of the burden laid upon them by the assembly. Want of specie. The land tax. fol. 1 page.

1782, May 18, Richmond. The lost preeminence of the British among natives. An union now with them impossible. Ineffectual efforts to sow dissensions among the States and separate us from our great ally. Rumors of a dreadful naval engagement in the West Indies. Great loss of our allies and capture of Count de Grasse. fol. 2 pages.

1782, no date. On the settlement of arrears due the delegates. Wishes him to send account of number of days he has served in Congress. Anxiety to learn what has become of the French men-of-war. fol. 1 page.

1782, August 24, Richmond. Settlement of arrears due the delegates. Madison's accounts. fol. 1 page.

1782, August 31, Richmond. Partial settlement of arrears due Madison as delegate. 4°. 1 page.

1782, September 16, Richmond. Confidently stated that the war will be pushed by Britain with redoubled vigor, and Virginia the object to be first reduced. Financial matters. 4°. 1 page.

1782, October 5, Richmond. Remits money to Madison. Report circulating that 60 or 70 of the Kentucky settlements are cut off, including Col. Todd. 4°. 1 page.

1782, October 12; 18; November 9; 1783, February 1; 8, Richmond. Five letters relating to accounts and remittances. 4°. 8 pages.

1783, February 8. Answer to certain queries relative to affairs of the State of Virginia inclosed in a letter of above date. fol. 2 pages.

AMBLER, J., to MADISON. *Philadelphia.*

1783, March 22; April 12; 19; May 3; 10; 17; 24; June 1; 7; 14; July 5; 1790, January 1; January 22, Richmond. Thirteen letters relating to accounts and remittances. 4°. 18 pages.

AMERICAN, AN. *Washington.*

1814, December 23, New York. Proposition to establish a national bank with $20,000,000 capital. To divide its capital at the end of a limited term, say fifteen years, but till then to pay no dividend. 4°. 2 pages.

"AMERICAN FARMER", EDITOR OF. *Montpellier.*

1822, July 3, Baltimore. Sends a sample of tobacco such as is sold in the Baltimore market, with the price. [Remarks at foot in Madison's handwriting.] 4°. 1 page.

AMERICAN VESSELS.

1794, Kingston, Jamaica. List of American vessels taken and brought into the port of Kingston in 1794, with notes showing what disposition was made of them and their cargoes by the authorities. [Statement by unknown person.] 4°. 3 pages.

ANDERSON, ELBERT, JR., to MONROE (Secretary of War). *Washington.*

1812, December 28, Washington. Proposals for supply and estimated cost of rations for United States troops. [Copy.] 4°. 3 pages.

1813, January 6, Washington. In answer to the request of the Secretary of War and Albert Gallatin, whether the writer could name a definite price for the rations at Montreal and Quebec. Location for the depot. [Copy.] 4°. 3 pages.

——— to MADISON. *Montpellier.*

1823, October 12, Westchester, N. *Y.* Incloses a new system of cultivation by Gen. A. Beatson. 4°. 1 page.

1823, October 12, Westchester. A retired army contractor. Reviews his services in the last war; sends him copies of letters written during that period. 4°. 2 pages.

ANDERSON, JOS. *Washington.*

1810, March 29, Washington. Transmits a resolution passed by the legislature of the Mississippi Territory in relation to George Poindexter. 4°. 1 page, and newspaper cutting.

1811, March —, Washington. Respecting nominations sent in by the President. 4°. 1 page.

ANDERSON, JOS., and others. *Washington.*

1813, June 10, Washington. Resolution of the Senate of the nomination of A. Gallatin as envoy and minister plenipotentiary to Great Britain, to negotiate a treaty of peace under the mediation of Russia. Referred to Anderson and others of the committee. [Copy.] 4°. 1 page.

ANDERSON, JOS. *Washington.*

1813, June 11, Washington. Incloses a copy of a Senate resolution. The committee will wait upon Madison any time he may appoint. (The resolution relates to the appointment of Albert Gallatin as envoy to Great Britain, to negotiate a treaty of peace.) 4°. 1 page.

1813, July 12, Washington. As chairman of a committee of the Senate to whom was referred the nomination of Albert Gallatin, as one of the envoys to negotiate a peace with Great Britain, asks Madison to appoint a time to receive them. 4°. 2 pages.

1814 (?), no date, Washington. Recommends as Attorney-General, George W. Campbell. His character and ability. 4°. 6 pages.

1815, February 9, Washington. Asks for the appointment of Capt. David Porter, U. S. N., as an officer of the Naval Board. His merits and services. 4°. 2 pages.

1815, March 4, Washington. Asks for the appointment of John Sevier as one of the commissioners for running the boundary line agreeably to the treaty made with the Creek Indians. 4°. 1 page.

1816, July 24, Washington. Solicits an appointment for William G. D. Worthington. His character, legal knowledge, and capacity detailed. 4°. 4 pages.

ANDERSON, LEROY. *Montpellier.*

1829, June 9, Portsmouth, Va. Proposal to Madison to subscribe to a work not mentioned. 4°. 1 page.

1829, July 4, Portsmouth, Va. Apologizes for his intrusion on Madison for soliciting his subscription to a "prospectus." 4°. 1 page.

ANDERSON, RICHARD. *Philadelphia.*

1792, August 27, Jefferson County, Ky. Solicits Madison's good offices in procuring for him the appointment to settle the accounts of the United States with Kentucky. fol. 1 page.

ANDERSON, SAMUEL T. *Montpellier.*

1823, May 22, Washington. Relates his services during the late war as naval storekeeper and asks him to use his interest in having justice done to his demands for a claim for commissions against the Government. fol. 4 pages.

1823, December 29, Washington. Renews his request to Madison to use his good offices in securing for him the just dues from the Government for his services. 4°. 5 pages.

ANDERSON, WILLIAM. *Washington.*

1807, February 24, Botetourt County. Application to the Government for appointment as a surveyor in the Western country. 4°. 2 pages.

ANDRÉ, FRANCIS. *Philadelphia.*

1794, March 25, Philadelphia. His views relative to tariff, taxes, and encouragement to manufactures and to find channels of trade without intervention of Great Britain. Wishes to draw attention of legislators to the encouragement of domestic industry. 4°. 4 pages.

ANDREANI, COUNT. *Washington.*

1808, March 11, New Orleans. Introduces Dr. Pendergrast. Andreani's project for ascending the Mississippi and Missouri frustrated by events in France and sickness. Intends trying the benefit of the springs in New York or Virginia. Wonderful progress of this country. [In French.] 4°. 3 pages.

ANGELEY, R. DE ST. JEAN. *Washington.*

1815, September 13, New York. Apologizes for not delivering in person two letters addressed to Madison. [In French.] 4°. 1 page.

ANNAPOLIS CONVENTION TO MARYLAND, PEOPLE OF.

1788. *See* Madison to Annapolis Convention, 1788.

ANONYMOUS, to MADISON. *Washington.*

1808, January 17, Philadelphia. Warnings of an anonymous writer on the "impending ruin" of these once happy States. The corruption from the gold of England. Traitors' instruments of English ambition and avarice, and the lawyers' instruments of both Britain and traitors. Means to employ remedies. fol.. 3 pages.

1808, July 4. Appeal for removing the embargo. The folly of attempting a paper war. Great Britain will never change her policy. Form alliances with other nations to restore the liberty of the seas, etc. 4°. 20 pages.

1809, October 18, London. Apologizes that weak health prevents his having answered numerous letters.

ANONYMOUS.

The state of Europe. Submission of Austria. Europe to be under the control of France. Infatuation and insanity in England. The conduct of the ministry with United States commissioners. Cunning of George Rose. Appointment of Mr. Jackson. The conduct of Erskine. England never under an administration so weak and contemptible. Embargo breakers. 4°. 4 pages.

1814 (?), no date. On the formation of a plan for the establishment of a national bank to meet the exigencies of the situation. 4°. 4 pages.

1814 (?), no date. Series of letters and notes relating to the embargo, and recapitulation of events culminating in the last war, with opinions and suggestions from an unsigned paper apparently from an Englishman. [Press copy.] 4°. 82 pages.

APPLETON, TH., to MAZZEI, P. *Pisa.*

1804, not dated, Leghorn. Respecting the unsatisfactory reasons that Mr. Barnes gives for not having been at his post in Sicily. 4°. 2 pages.

ARMSTRONG, JOHN, to WARDEN, DAVID BAILIE. *Paris.*

1808, August 24, Paris. Notifying Warden of his appointment as consul and agent of prize cases in the room of F. Skipwith, in Paris [See letter of Warden, D. B., to Madison, April 23, 1811.] 4°. 1 page.

1810, September 6, Paris. Asks explanation of Warden's remarks derogatory to Mr. Russel's character and appointment as chargé d'affaires, also that he (Armstrong) had deceived him (Warden) and that he had been set aside to make room for a damned Yankee at Armstrong's instance. Gives Warden an opportunity to deny these assertions or justify them as promptly as possible. [Copy.] 4°. 3 pages.

1810, September 10, Paris. Recalls Warden's attention to a question in his former letter which he (Warden) omitted to reply to in his letter of 7 pages asking him to select during their acquaintance any act of his (Armstrong's) which was inconsistent with private morals or public duty. Asks for an explicit answer, and when given will give the source of his information concerning Mr. Hunt. [Copy.] 4°. 2 pages.

1810, September 13, Paris. Notifying him that Alexander McRae is appointed to the office provisionally held by Warden. [*See* letter of Warden to Madison April 23, 1811.] 4°. 1 page.

——— to MADISON. *Washington.*

1812, October 26, Maysville, Ky. Trusts in the wisdom and magnanimity of Madison to conduct the country through the toils and calamities of war, Trusts peace will not be made until we obtain full and ample compensation for our wrongs. The State of Kentucky has furnished her quota of men and will furnish more when called on. 4°. 2 pages.

——— to LANSING, AB'M G. *Albany.*

1813, April 20, Washington. Acknowledging letter, inclosing one from Mr. Cutts. Informs him that Mr. Cutts was mistaken by seeing a newspaper article that Lansing had been appointed Quartermaster-General. 4°. 1 page.

ARMSTRONG, JOHN, to DEARBORN, HENRY.

1813, July 6, Washington. Order of the President to retire from his command until his health is reestablished, and until further orders. [Copy.] 4°. 1 page.

——— to ANDERSON, ELBERT, JR.

1823, August 12, Red Hook. Acknowledging letter of 4th. Testimony as to the conduct and satisfactory manner in which Anderson fulfilled his duties as Army contractor during the late war. Annexed letter dated July 8, 1813, giving Armstrong the contract. 4°. 3 pages.

——— to LEE, HENRY. *Washington.*

1825, December 6. Acknowledging letter proposing subject of a history of the campaign of 1814. Thinks well of it and will furnish materials. [Copy.] 4°. 1 page.

ARMY ACCOUNTS, COMMISSIONER OF, TO MADISON.

1790, February 10. Extract touching an allowance made to officers and soldiers on the new emissions received by them. fol. 1 page.

ARNOLD, THOMAS. *Washington.*

1815, February 14, Paris, Ky. Pedigree of horse "Speculator." [*See* letter from Canby, J. T., May 5, 1815.] 8°. 1 page.

ARWONTH, SAMUEL. *Washington.*

1813, December 3, Somerset County. Appeal for remuneration for the loss of his schooner captured by the British. fol. 1 page.

ATHERTON, BOOZ M. *Washington.*

1813, November 9, Westmoreland, N. H. Soliciting the appointment of tax collector for the county of Cheshire. fol. 2 pages.

ATWATER, CALEB. *Washington.*

1809, December 20, Sullivan, N. Y. The triumph of federalism in New York State attributed by the writer to Federal postmasters. Detention of Republican papers. Wishes a Republican postmaster and recommends one. fol. 2 pages.

Montpellier.

1823, March 18, Circleville, Ohio. Asks suggestions from Madison in respect to the introduction of a system of education in common schools. fol. 2 pages.

AUSTIN, BENJAMIN. *Washington.*

1813, February 14, Boston. Introducing his son Benjamin. 4°. 1 page.

1814, April 7. On the appointment of judge-advocate in a court-martial held at New London. Bad character of the person appointed. 4°. 3 pages.

——— and others. *Washington.*

1815, February 23, Boston. Congratulatory address in behalf of the Republican members of both houses of the Massachusetts legislature on the return of peace, and complimentary expressions respecting Madison's instrumentality in bringing it about. royal fol. 2 pages.

AUSTIN, CHARLES. *Montpellier.*

1824, August 30, Fredericksburg. Sends from Dr. William Shepperd a box of early white wheat imported from Spain. 4°. 1 page.

AUSTIN, JAMES T. *Washington.*

1811, July 11, Boston. Transmits pamphlets. 4°. 1 page.

1812, November 10, Boston. Offers his services as judge-advocate in the trial of Gen. Hull. 4°. 1 page.

1815, February 14, Boston. Asks for the position of Comptroller of the Treasury. 4°. 1 page.

Montpellier.

1832, January 19, Boston. Asks information connected with the services of the late Vice-President Gerry in the convention for forming a constitution, in view of a revised edition of his biography. 4°. 1 page.

AYDELOT, BENJAMIN. *Washington.*

1816, April 5, Westport. Bill for cloth, cotton, etc. 4°. 1 page.

Montpellier.

1819, May 20, Corydon, Ind. Incloses a bill to a young man representing himself as a relative of Madison's, which was unpaid. 4°. 1 page.

AZUNI, D. A. *Washington.*

1816, May 8, Genoa. Sends him a copy of his work on the means of extirpating Barbary pirates. [In French.] 4°. 1 page.

BACHE, RICHARD. *Montpellier.*

1818, January 8, Philadelphia. Incloses a proposal to the public. His motive is to put an end to newspaper war in Pennsylvania and abolish all personal and private abuse. 4°. 1 page.

1818, April 10, Philadelphia. Returns a pamphlet, the writing on title-page is that of his father or of B. Franklin. 4°. 1 page.

1825, July 21, Philadelphia. Meets Mr. Tod at the dinner given to Mr. Rush. 4°. 1 page.

BACON, E. *Washington.*

1809, March *1, Washington.* Recommends Gideon Granger to be the head of one of the departments composing the Cabinet. [Private.] 4°. 1 page.

——— to GALLATIN, ALBERT.

1812, October 13, Pittsfield, Mass. Complaints on the management of Army concerns. Want of clothing and pay for the soldiers. 4°. 2 pages.

——— to SIMMONS, WILLIAM. *Washington.*

1814, April *18, Washington.* Acknowledging letter of 14th, with the account of T. Buford, late deputy-commissioner of purchases. Instructs Mr. Simmons (accountant of War Department) in relation to settlements of accounts of officers. [Copy.] 4°. 6 pages.

——— to MADISON.

1814, April 30, Washington. Is to be absent, if the President approves, for a few weeks. 4°. 2 pages.

1814, April 30, Washington. Respecting the appointment of principal assessor of the district tax for the eleventh collection district of Massachusetts. Recommends James Prince. 4°. 3 pages.

BAGOT, CHARLES. *Montpellier.*

1817, August 26, Washington. Will avail himself of Madison's invitation to visit him at the beginning of September with Mr. Antrobus. 4°. 4 pages.

BAILEY, —. *Washington.*

1802, April 27. Inquires of the Secretary of State how much it cost the late and present administration to pay Algiers from 1796 to 1801. 4°. 1 page.

BAILEY, FRANCIS. *Washington.*

1811, November 6, Philadelphia. Approves of the tone of the message. 4°. 1 page.

1812, January 2, Philadelphia. Asks for a Government position. 4°. 1 page.

BAILEY, THEODORUS. *Washington.*

1805, June 18, New York. In behalf of Gen. Armstrong, at Paris, the writer asks to have newspapers sent him. 4°. 2 pages.

BAILLIE, GEORGE. *See* British Treasury.

BAILLIE, JOHN, to MADISON. *Washington.*

1809, September 25, McIntosh County, Ga. As secretary of a meeting of citizens of McIntosh County, expressing sentiments relative to the disavowal by the British Government of overtures and arrangements made by their minister. Approves of the measures of the administration and promises support. fol. 2 pages.

BAINBRIDGE, A.

No date. Complains of having been badly treated, and claims his liberty and property. 4°. 1 page.

BAINBRIDGE, WILLIAM. *Washington.*

1817, March 27, Boston. Incloses a letter to the Secretary of the Navy respecting a claim, and to remove unfavorable impressions the President may have formed. 4°. 1 page.

——, CROWNINSHIELD, B. W. (Secretary of the Navy.) *Washington.*

1817, March 27, Boston. Acknowledging letter of 21st, informing him of the President's decision against his claim to the command of the navy-yard at Charleston. Thinks the President is mistaken in regard to his predecessor's having decided against it, and gives reasons for such a belief. [Copy.] 4°. 3 pages.

BAKER, JAMES, to MADISON. *Washington.*

1816, August 8, Norfolk. Asks for Government employment. small 4°. 3 pages.

BAKER, JOHN, and others. *Philadelphia.*

1795, December 2, Portland. A memorial signed by himself and other citizens of Portland requesting compensation for losses sustained from British piracy or license for retaliation. fol. 1 page.

BAKER, JOHN MARTIN, to JEFFERSON. *Washington.*

1808, December 28, Washington. Asks for temporary employment. 4°. 1 page.

BAKER, JOHN MARTIN, to MADISON. *Washington.*

1810, February 22, Cagliari. Interview with the King of Sardinia, who expresses friendly sentiments toward the United States. Soliciting the appointment of navy agent for Sardinia. 4°. 3 pages.

1810, February 22, Cagliari. Duplicate of the foregoing. 4°. 3 pages.

1811, September 28, Palma, Island of Majorica. Letter to the collector of port of discharge of the schooner *Ruthy*, with Capt. Hink's receipt of some articles shipped to Mr. Madison. fol. 2 pages.

1816, May 15, Bordeaux. Shipped by the brig *General Ward* a case of wine. 4°. 2 pages.

Montpellier.

1819, May 3, Georgetown. Acknowledging letter of April 20. Thanks him for his friendly mention of his work. 4°. 1 page.

BAKER, RICHARD BOHUN, to DRAYTON, JOHN (Governor of South Carolina).

1810, July 20, Sullivans Island. Sends two cannon balls fired by the British squadron against Fort Moultrie in 1776 or 1780. (*See* Drayton, John.) 4°. 1 page.

BALDWIN, CH. N., to MADISON. *Washington.*

1811, June 26, New York. Asks his assistance in support of a periodical work. Scrap of paper.

BALDWIN, DANIEL. *Washington.*

1809, September 18, Newark. Advocates a descent on Canada. Though maimed by wounds got under the walls of Quebec, is willing to die for the cause of his country and offers his services. fol. 1 page.

BALDWIN, THOMAS. *Washington.*

1817, February 13, Boston. Introducing Senator Morrill of New Hampshire. Sends Madison Marshman's "Clavis Sinica." 4°. 2 pages.

BALL, B. *New York.*

1788, December 8, Fredericksburg. Desires Madison's return to Virginia to canvass his district prior to the election as the course to pursue to secure it. 4°. 3 pages.

BALL, ISAAC. *Washington.*

1809, March 30, New York. Asks his subscription to the third edition of a literary work. 4°. 2 pages.

1809, April 11, New York. Acknowledging letter of 4th, authorizing his name to appear as subscriber to the second edition of the "Animal Economy." 4°. 1 page.

BALLARD, JAMES HUDSON. *Washington.*

1813, March 8, Washington. The writer, son of a revolutionary officer, asks for Government employment in Army, Navy, or a clerkship. 4°. 2 pages.

BALLARD, ROBERT. *New York.*

1789, March 5, Baltimore. Asks for appointment as Federal clerk of the court. States his antecedents. 4°. 3 pages.

BALLARD, ROBERT. *Philadelphia.*

1790, December 25, Baltimore. Asks for further allowance for fees as port surveyor at Baltimore. 4°. 3 page.

1792, April 1, Baltimore. Asks more compensation as surveyor of the port of Baltimore. 4°. 3 pages.

No date, Baltimore. Inadequacy of his fees as surveyor of the port of Baltimore. Details of his expenses. fol. 3 pages.

BALLINGER, JOHN, to TOULMIN, HENRY.

1810, November 3, Baton Rouge. A summary of the causes and effects of the revolution at Baton Rouge. large fol. 3 pages.

BALMAIN, ALEXANDER, to MADISON. *Philadelphia.*

1794, December 8, Winchester. Acknowledging letter of the 23d, with the President's speech. Expresses his opinions. fol. 2 pages.

BANCROFT, EDWARD, DR., to JEFFERSON. *Paris.*

1785, November 18, London. Asks Jefferson's good offices in assisting Mr. Paradise in accelerating the payment of £1,000 due to him on the securities of the State of Virginia. 4°. 2 pages.

BANKHEAD, JAMES, to ARMSTRONG, JOHN.

1813, March 8, Georgetown. His nomination for the command of a regiment was suspended without any apparent cause. Wishes Armstrong's good offices for the situation in the adjutant and inspector's department with rank of colonel. 4°. 4 pages.

——— to MADISON. *Washington.*

1813, March 13, Georgetown. Incloses a letter from the writer to Gen. Armstrong, and not hearing from him asks for employment at Norfolk, as that place is threatened with invasion. 4°. 1 page.

BANKS, GER. *Richmond.*

1785, October 28, Stafford County. Will confer with Madison on the confused and unhinged situation of the Government on November 4, at Richmond. [Notes by Madison on outside.] 4°. 1 page.

BANKS, HENRY. *Montpellier.*

1827, October 27, Frankfort. Has prepared a memorial to Congress relating to events of the Revolution. His early acquaintance with Madison. Matters relating to his brother, John Banks. fol. 1 page.

1829, September 22, Virginia. Printed proposals for the publication of a paper at Frankfort, Ky., to be called the Western Volunteer. 4°. 1 page.

Montpellier.

1829, October 29, Frankfort. Solicits subscription to a periodical entitled the Western Volunteer. fol. 2 pages.

BANKS, LINN, and others. *Montpellier.*

1834, August 1, Madison Court-House, Va. Invitation of citizens of Boone County to a dinner to be given to Hon. J. M. Patten on the 23d. 4°. 1 page.

BANKS, WILLIAM. *Washington.*

1808, January 1, Culpeper County. Asks Madison's signature respecting a revaluation of his house, to be insured. fol. 1 page.

BARBER, ABRAHAM. *Washington.*

1812, May 19, West Stockbridge, Mass. Wishes the appointment as captain in the Army. Has applied before but received no answer. Could raise a company in a very short time. 4°. 1 page.

BARBOUR, GABRIEL. *Washington.*

1812, February 19, Georgetown. Asks for a lieutenancy in Mr. Ball's company if he accepts a captaincy. Barbour's consenting to accept a lieutenancy will not prevent Madison's giving him a captaincy. small 4°. 2 pages.

BARBOUR, JAMES. *Washington.*

1802, January 17, Garrard County, Ky. Respecting the reversal of a judgment of the county court by the Federal court on some surveys caveated by George Wilson. small 4°. 1 page.

1807, December 11, Richmond. Asks his opinion on the resolution passed in the Virginia house of delegates to compel the President on application of two-thirds of both Houses of Congress to remove a judge. Also, whether a two-thirds vote in a State legislature can recall a Senator. Can State legislatures give the General Government aid in the approaching crisis? 4°. 2 pages.

1811, May 29, Orange. Asks that a post-offiee be established at Barboursville as a convenience to a multitude of people. 4°. 2 pages.

Washington.

1812, January 29, Richmond. Transmits the proceedings of the Virginia general assembly concerning the measures of the General Government connected with our foreign relations, and advocating a declaration of war and offering support. 4°. 1 page. large fol. 4 pages.

Washington.

1812, March 30, Richmond. The threatening position of our foreign relations. Asks advice of the course to pursue in Virginia. Her position as relates to arms and readiness in the event of war. His desire to cooperate with the General Government. 4°. 3 pages.

1812, July 18, Richmond. The measures to be taken connected with the defense of the State. Defenseless state of the maritime frontier. The complaints of the inhabitants of that section and how to relieve their distress. Governor Barbour sends Hon. C. K. Mallory to confer with Madison. 4°. 3 pages.

1813, January 19, Richmond. Recommends George Hay to fill the vacancy caused by the death of Judge Tyler, of district judge. 4°. 2 pages.

——— to ARMSTRONG, JOHN. *Washington.*

1813, May 7, Richmond. Importance of the position of Fort Hood as a defense of James River and protection of Richmond and Petersburg. Improvements that are essential in repairs and supplies. Asks that Gen. Armistead be instructed to inspect and report. 4°. 3 pages.

1813, October 4, Richmond. Referring to a promise respecting an inspection of some engineer of Fort Hood and it not being complied with, urges the importance of its position, and that prompt and efficient measures be taken to place it in a respectable state. [Copy.] 4°. 3 pages.

BARBOUR, JAMES, to MADISON. *Washington.*

1814, February 17, Richmond. Transmitting copy of resolutions of the Commonwealth of Virginia requesting the President's attention to the present condition of the fortifications of Fort Powhatan. 4°. 9 pages.

1814, January 13, Richmond. The possible consequences of the revolution which has recently occurred in Europe. The overwhelming force, as stated, of England to be sent to this country. Asks what measures should be adopted for the security of Virginia. 4°. 2 pages.

1815, February 8, Washington. His wish that his friend Col. Valentine Johnson be appointed to the place to which Mr. Jenkins was nominated in the Senate. 4°. 1 page.

Montpellier.

1818, April 11, Washington. Sends a paper with his remarks on a navigation bill which will probably pass. 4°. 1 page.

1820, February 10, Washington. The Missouri question. His views and those of others in regard to compromise. 4°. 3 pages.

1820, December 13, Washington. Has acted on Madison's recommendation to press the claims of Mr. Coxe on the President. The admission of Missouri. Hopes of the ratification of the treaty with Spain. Strange pretext of France of our violation of the treaty of Louisiana. 4°. 3 pages.

1821, January 8, Washington. Informs Madison of a fine saddle horse which he can buy. 4°. 1 page.

1823, December 2, Washington. Sends a copy of Cunningham's letters. Henry Clay elected Speaker of the House. Personal hostility to his brother Philip. Mr. Crawford's health. The message to be delivered to-day. Will refer to the interference of the allied powers in the internal concerns of the Spanish colonies. 4°. 3 pages.

1823, December 7, Washington. Settlement of a financial matter between himself and Madison at the bank. 4°. 2 pages.

1824, February 14, Washington. Acknowledging letter of 11th. Relating to private financial matters. Meeting to nominate for President and Vice-President. 4°. 2 pages.

1824, May 2, Washington. Relates to some private business. 4°. 2 pages.

1824, November 10. Concerning the expected visit of Lafayette to Orange. 4°. 1 page.

1824, November 14. Preparations for the reception of Gen. Lafayette. 4°. 1 page.

1825, January 4, Washington. Conference with the Virginia delegation respecting the prosecution of Madison's claims in Congress. Prospects flattering. Conjectures as to the Presidential question. The candidates. 4°. 3 pages.

1827, May 5, Washington. Search in the War Department for papers desired by Madison resulted but in one letter, viz, Armstrong to Jackson, May 28, 1814. 4°. 1 page.

1828, January 14, Washington. On Madison's call to the Anti-Jackson Convention. Urges him to ac-

BARBOUR, JAMES.

cept the call. His influence will make faction dumb. 4°. 2 pages.

1828, September 29, London. His voyage across the Atlantic. His impressions of the country and people. Cost of living among the operatives of mills and peasantry. The weather and crops. 4°. 3 pages.

1828, November 13, London. Acknowledging letter of 22d. The weather and harvests. Prices of products. The effects of the tariff in Liverpool. The great wealth of England. Englishmen's homes. Sufferings of the poor. Sympathy with the Turks. Conversation with the Duke of Wellington. He is favorable towards America. 4°. 6 pages.

BARBOUR, JOHN S. *Washington.*

1815, June 30, Richmond. Foreclosure of a mortgage. 4°. 2 pages.

Montpellier.

1818, April 18, Orange. The foreclosure of a mortgage. Recommends Madison to be the purchaser. 4°. 1 page.

1818, May 29, Culpeper. Action of the chancery court in relation to a mortgage sale. 4°. 2 pages.

1819, April 30, Fredericksburg. The case of the mortgaged lands in Fauquier County decided in Madison's favor. 4°. 2 pages.

1819, October 3, Fredericksburg. The rents and profits of the lands in Fauquier County. 4°. 1 page.

1820, January 27, Fredericksburg. Accounts of the chancery court relating to rents of land in Fauquier County. 4°. 1 page.

1820, May 1, Fredericksburg. Decrees of the chancery court respecting the Fauquier County lands. 4°. 3 pages.

———, to MACON, EDGAR. *Orange.*

1823, March 23. Respecting fees of the clerk and marshal and his own fee due from Madison. 4°. 1 page.

1823, May 24. Relating to statement of a claim of Madison. small 4°. 2 pages.

———, to MADISON. *Montpellier.*

1829, October 26, Richmond. Promises to pay a note, inclosed to Madison, when due. 4°. 1 page.

1830, March 9, Washington. Is ready to pay the note due to Mr. Madison, but does not know where it is deposited. Will send the money where Madison directs. 4°. 2 pages.

1830, March 18, Washington. Acknowledging letter of 15th. Will send money in care of Col. Barbour. 4°. 1 page.

1830, March 31, Washington. Reasons for delay in sending money. His sick wife. Remits $100 through Col. P. P. Barbour. Sends copy of South Carolina's exposition and protest. 4°. 1 page.

BARBOUR, MORDECAI. *Washington.*

1809, March 26, Petersburg. Thinks of going to Kentucky, Tennessee, and the Mississippi country, and for the second time, being unsuccessful on his first application, asks for Government employment. 4°. 2 pages.

1812, June 5, Petersburg. Asks for an appointment in the army as colonel. Incloses recommendations from some of his friends. 4°. 2 pages.

1812, June 28, Petersburg. Asks to be appointed colonel of a regiment. His experience in the Revolutionary war. small 4°. 2 pages.

BARBOUR, PHILIP, to BARBOUR, JAMES. *Culpeper County.*

1780, December 22, Fort Jefferson. The Spaniards assuming to be masters of the Mississippi to the mouth of the Ohio. Is asked by the inhabitants to go to Congress to represent the situation. Fertility of the country, and desire of the people to become American citizens. 4°. 3 pages.

———, to MADISON. *Washington.*

1809, June 8, Henderson, Ky. Asks for the extension of the privilege granted by Governor Harrison for the search for salt water in the neighborhood of the United States Saline. 4°. 2 pages.

BARBOUR, P. P. *Montpellier.*

1822, December 10. Concerning a pensioner having been stricken from the roll and not reinstated by the Secretary of War. The subject before the House of Representatives. 4°. 1 page.

1826, March 28, Frescati. Legal opinions. 4°. 2 pages.

1829, March 21. The delegation of Louisa County will call on Madison to inquire whether he will serve as member of the convention if elected. 4°. 1 page.

1829, March 24. Asks for instructions in answer to queries in the Enquirer to Madison and the other nominees for the convention. 4°. 1 page.

BARD, DAVID. *Washington.*

1809, January 24, Washington. Requests the appointment of Alfred Balch as bearer of dispatches to Europe. 4°. 1 page.

BARING BROS. & CO., to BARKER, JACOB. *New York.*

1815, October 12, London. Notifies Barker of the sale of stocks. fol. 1 page.

1815, October 25, London. Relating to sale of American stocks. Expects to see lower prices. 4°. 1 page.

———, to TODD, JOHN P. *Washington.*

1817, May 20, London. Acknowledging a remittance. Sends his account showing a balance due him. 4°. 4 pages.

BARKER, JACOB, to MADISON. *Washington.*

1811, July 1, New York. Respecting duties imposed on cotton imported into England in American vessels while English vessels can procure good freights. Restrictions by our laws should be removed. 4°. 1 page.

BARKER, JACOB.

1812, February 24, New York. Incloses the Prince Regent's speech. Hears that the British Government has determined to repeal their orders in council. 4°. 1 page.

1812, May 12, New York. Sends English papers. The nonimportation law presses hard on England. Popular feeling against the ministry if the orders in council are not repealed. Renewal of the charter of the East India Company. Senator Pope's proposition to rescind the Declaration of Independence. 4°. 2 pages.

1813, August 13, New York. Uneasiness in the Republican party of appointments of nonresidents to offices in the city. Recommends changes in some prominent positions. 4°. 3 pages.

———, to JONES, WILLIAM. *Washington.*

1813, September 23, New York. Acknowledging letter of 18th. Recommending John Haws to fill the position occupied by Weston, expected to be removed. Inclosing letter from Thomas Hazard, jr., on same subject. 4°. 3 pages.

———, to MADISON. *Washington.*

1814, March 24, Washington. Proposes that if Congress adjourns without establishing a national bank, that he can place about $10,000,000 in London, Paris, Amsterdam, and Hamburg. Will go to Europe and sell the stock on his own account to raise the money. Such a contract should be kept private. 4°. 2 pages.

1815, December 26, New York. Asks Madison to inquire into the proceedings at law against him by the United States on account of some bills of exchange furnished Treasury Department in 1814. Requests that the 29 suits now pending be consolidated into one. Suggests the means of proceeding. 4°. 5 pages.

———, to ANDERSON, JOSEPH, (Comptroller of the Treasury).

1815, December 26, New York. Reviewing his contract with the Government of a loan of $5,000,000. Requests that the proceedings at law against him on account of some bills of exchange be consolidated into one suit to save the enormous expense to him and indorsers. 4°. 6 pages.

BARKER, JOHN, to MADISON. *Washington.*

1810, February 17, Philadelphia. As chairman of a meeting of citizens of the First Congressional district of Philadelphia, sends an account of their proceedings and resolutions sustaining the President in his course in treating with the Government of Great Britain, and condemning their acts of insult and injury on our citizens and flag. 4°. 1 page. large fol. 5 pages.

BARLOW, JOEL. *Washington.*

1806, May 13, Washington. Gives reason why it would be better to send a private ship to Tunis with presents and the ambassador instead of a public ship. Objects to a permanent naval establishment in some island in the Mediterranean. His reasons. 4°. 3 pages.

1809, no date. Congratulates him on his election. The political status. His views. Expected that Madison would have offered Barlow the place of Secretary of State. His extreme solicitude for

BARLOW, JOEL.

the best good of his country is his first motive for seeking the place. 4°. 4 pages.

1809, May 9, Washington. Describes the "Encyclopedia methodique" which he has to dispose of. small 4°. 2 pages.

1809, June 9, Washington. Sends him the "Encyclopedia methodique" with the bill and statement. 8°. 1 page. 4°. 3 pages.

1809, June 13, Washington. Sends him books marked by Madison. Offers him the French Biographical Dictionary in 9 volumes. 8°. 1 page.

1809, July 6, Washington. At request of Col. Swan, incloses a letter toMadison which should have been addressed to the Secretary of the Treasury, asking for suspension of a decision. 4°. 1 page.

1810, April 25, Washington. Mr. Carey desires an interview with the President on the subject of Mr. Tench Coxe, whose office will probably be vacated. His character and merits. 4°. 1 page.

1811, June 12, Washington. Bill of wine. 4°. 1 page.

1811, December 5, Paris. Introduces Mr. Correa going to the United States. 4°. 1 page.

1811, December 19, Paris. Apologies for detaining the frigate. Diplomatic audience with the Emperor. Marked friendly attention to the American minister. The points to be conceded in the treaty negotiations. Probability of a war between Russia and Turkey. fol. 3 pages.

1811, December 30, Paris. On claims due our citizens against France, and the boundaries of Louisiana. The attitude of Spain, France, England, and the United States. "Private." fol. 12 pages.

1811, no date, Paris. Sketch of a convention of boundaries of Louisiana. [Draft.] fol. 5 pages.

1812, January 1, Paris. Doubts as to his instructions about framing a treaty of commerce. Will discuss and arrange articles of a treaty, but must have special authorization to conclude and sign. "Private." fol. 1 page.

1812, January 17, Paris. Project of a treaty of commerce presented to the French Government by the minister plenipotentiary of the United States. [Draft.] fol. 19 pages.

1812, March 3, Paris. Mr. Serrurier's zeal intemperate and style of writing little suited to his station. His favorite talent of complaint. Barlow's ob servations to the Duke in relation thereto, who assured him would have their proper weight. Barlow anxious to remove the cause of war with Great Britain. Sends documents. Suggests dispensing with special messengers when public ships are sent. A ship's officer will do as well with less cost. "Private." 4°. 3 pages.

1812, March 3, Paris. Duplicate of the foregoing. fol. 3 pages.

1812, March 5, Paris. Endeavors to impress as much as possible instructions received relating to the conduct of France since the repeal of decrees. The affair of East Florida. The Duke at work on the treaty. 4°. 1 page.

BARLOW, JOEL.

1812, April 15, Paris. Incloses an account of the affair of corruption in the War Office, from the "Journal de l'Empire." Count Czernicheff, aid to the Emperor Alexander, seems to have acted clumsily in this thing. fol. 1 page.

1812, April 22, Paris. Lafayette's sale of his Point Coupée lands. The uncertainty of the Emperor's actions respecting indemnity for spoliations. The Duke still at work on the settlement to accompany the treaty of commerce. Detains the *Hornet*, hoping in some measure to defeat the cause of war with Great Britain. 4°. 2 pages.

1812, April 22, Paris. Duplicate of the foregoing. fol. 3 pages.

1812, May 2, Paris. His object has been to remove the cause of war with England. The object of the French Government is directly contrary. Question of repeal of the decrees. "Duplicate." fol. 2 pages.

1812, May 12, Paris. Respecting the French decree. Attitude of France in our war with England. Conference with the "Duke." fol. 2 pages.

1812, July 14, Paris. Introduces Mr. Nancrede, a naturalized citizen of the United States, who will impart what he knows about the conduct of Aaron Burr while in Paris. Is well acquainted with Burr's projects. 4°. 1 page.

1812, July 22. Offers to procure him the additional livraisons of the Encyclopedia wanting in Madison's set. 4°. 1 page.

1812, September 26, Paris. Acknowledging letter of August 11. Difficulty of negotiating with the Emperor, who is absorbed in the Russian war. Consideration of the proposed treaty. Indemnity for spoliations. Has faith that we will ultimately succeed with the Emperor. Burr's project for dividing the United States between France and England was not disliked by either Government. Speculations on Napoleon's projects and career. fol. 9 pages.

BARLOW, THOMAS B. *Washington*

1819, December 18, Fredericksburg. Report in the case of Madison *vs.* Strade completed in favor of plaintiff. Bill for report charged to plaintiff. 4°. 1 page.

BARNARD, HENRY. *Washington.*

1807, October 15, Cape of Good Hope. The importance of a consul at this place. The former consul having resigned, he offers his services to fill the office. [Memorial.] fol. 3 pages.

BARNES, JOSEPH, to CLYMER, GEORGE. *New York.*

1789, August 23, Philadelphia. Acknowledging a letter with certificate from the secretary of state of New York, for enrolment of pamphlets containing drawings of an invention of Rumsey's. Experiments since tried are satisfactory. Asks his aid for a bill to secure the invention before Congress adjourns. 4°. 3 pages.

BARNES, THOMAS (President), to MADISON. *Washington.*

1812, November 19, Mississippi Territory. Resolutions of the general assembly approving of the conduct

BARNES, THOMAS.

of the General Government in declaring war against Great Britain and promising support. [With duplicate.] fol. 3 pages.

BARNETT, WILLIAM. *Washington.*

1809, February 10, Elberton, Ga. As chairman of a committee of citizens, expresses approval of the measures of the General Government. 4°. 4 pages.

BARNEY, JOSHUA, and others, *Philadelphia.*

1794, March 9, Kingston, Jamaica. A letter signed by ship masters in Kingston expressive of their gratitude for the speech made by Madison before Congress January 3, on resolutions to obtain redress for injustice of foreign nations respecting our commerce and seizure of our property in foreign ports. fol. 3 pages.

1794, March 13, Kingston, Jamaica. From American master's of vessels forcibly detained, transmitting to Madison an address thanking him for his speech of January 3, respecting redress of grievances towards the sufferers from the injustice of foreign nations to our commerce and illegal seizure of our property. fol. 2 pages.

——, to SMITH, SAMUEL. *Baltimore.*

1802, November 22, Baltimore. Recommending Mr. O'Mealy to be consul of the United States at Havre. Complains that the present consul issues certificates to foreigners as being Americans. Incloses a certificate of J. Holmes to that effect and giving an instance. 4°. 3 pages.

——, to JONES, WILLIAM. *Washington.*

1813, July 4. Defense of Chesapeake Bay. Number of the enemy's vessels on this station. Avowed object of the enemy, the destruction of the city and navy-yard at Washington, the city and navy-yard at Norfolk, and the city of Baltimore. Gives his views and opinions and a plan of offense and defense. 4°. 9 pages.

1814, April 13, 20, May 1, 11, Chesapeake Bay. See William Jones's letter to Madison, dated June 6, 1814, lettered F. [Extracts.] fol. 2 pages.

BARRON, JAMES, to SECRETARY OF THE NAVY. *Washington.*

1836, not dated, Philadelphia. Recommends that Mr. King, who is employed at the navy-yard, should receive more pay for his work. [Copy.] fol. 1 page.

BARROW, WM., to BEDFORD, J. R. *Nashville.*

1810, June 4, West Florida. See Bedford, J. R., July 4, 1810. [Copy.] fol. 1 page.

1810, August 5, Bayou Sara. See Bedford, J. R., August 26, 1810. [Copy.] fol. 2 pages.

1810, September 11, Bayou Sara. Acknowledging letters of August 14 and 24. Proceedings of a convention of inhabitants of West Florida and the question of their independence and ultimate destiny and asking advice. [Copy.] 4°. 3 pages.

1810, October 10, West Florida. Acknowledging letter of 5th. Taking of Baton Rouge and declaration of independence of the inhabitants. Details of the action. Convention in favor of becoming a

BARROW, WM.

part of the United States. Desire that the United States take possession. [Copy.]
4°. 3 pages.

BARRY, JAMES, to CROWNINSHIELD, GEO. & SONS.

1807, June 22, Teneriffe. Relating to a voyage to India. Prospects of the vintage. All wines in American vessels must go to India direct from America. [Copy.] 4°. 2 pages.

BARRY, W. T., to MADISON. *Montpellier.*

1822, June 30, Lexington, Ky. On the plan of establishing schools and academies in Kentucky.
4°. 3 pages.

BARTON, W. *New York.*

1789, August 26, Philadelphia. Has communicated his reasons to Mr. Page for declining the acceptance of the office offered by the President. Would like the place of assistant to the Secretary of the Treasury. 4°. 3 pages.

Washington.

1814, June 6, Lancaster, Pa. Incloses the prospectus of literary work. 4°. 1 page.

BASCOM, H. B. *Montpellier.*

1827, March 19, Union Town, Pa. Is instructed to say by the board of trustees of Madison College that in consideration of Madison's public and private worth they have called the institution lately established by his name. 4°. 1 page.

1827, June 26, Union Town, Pa. Intention of the trustees of Madison College to create an agricultural department. Asks Madison's views.
4°. 1 page.

1827, October 19, Madison College. The promising condition of this college. A library and necessary apparatus needed. The agricultural department excites interest. Asks Madison's frequent advice.
4°. 1 page.

BASSETT, BURWELL. *Washington.*

1813, July 30. Relative to appointment of principal assessors and collectors in Virginia. Persons recommended. 4°. 3 pages.

1814, March 6, Williamsburg. Respecting the situation of the lower country of Virginia. Position of the enemy. Their want of provisions. Suggestions for defense of Richmond.
4°. 12 pages.

BASSETT, GEO. W. *Montpellier.*

1833, April 25, Fredericksburg. Invitation to assist at the laying of the corner-stone of the monument to be erected to memory of the mother of Washington by the President. 4°. 1 page.

BASSETT, JOHN.

No *date.* Has completed a translation of Dr. Vanderdonk's Natural and Topographical History of New Netherlands. Asks whether there are any Dutch records in Virginia relative to their country. fol. 2 pages.

BATES, STEPHEN. *Montpellier.*

1831, October 31, Boston. Sends inclosed a pamphlet on subject of Free Masonry. Appeal of the writer to procure the destruction of the institution.
4°. 9 pages.

BATON, BENJAMIN SMITH. *Washington.*

1810, January 30, Philadelphia. Introduces his nephew, who holds a commission in the U. S. Navy. 4°. 1 page.

1810, May 20, Philadelphia. Respecting an expedition planned by him through the northwest parts of the United States and adjacent British Possessions, and exclusively directed to objects of science, especially botany, zoology, and mineralogy. Wishes Madison's assistance to remove obstacles to the procuring of the necessary passport for Mr. Nuttall, who is not a naturalized American citizen. 4°. 4 pages.

1810, May 21, Philadelphia. Declares that Mr. Nuttall desires to be an American citizen but has not resided here long enough to get out naturalization papers. As the object is purely one of science (the expedition to the Northwest) trusts that he can procure necessary papers for his protection. 4°. 1 page.

1813, April 20, Philadelphia. Asks to be appointed to a vacancy in the Mint. 4°. 1 page.

BATTOILE, H. *Washington.*

1811, August 16, White Sulphur Springs. Wishes to procure from Madison's manager, Mr. Gooch, a pair, or a ram of his broad-tail sheep. 4°. 1 page.

BAYARD, JAMES. *Montpellier.*

1833, January 18, Philadelphia. Incloses a work on the Constitution of the United States, intended for the use of colleges and schools. Asks Madison's approbation of it. 4°. 1 page.

BAYARD, J. A. *Washington.*

1812, April 14, Wilmington. Respecting the appointment of a district judge. Mr. Rodney declines it. Offers information as to legal characters in Delaware. 4°. 2 pages.

BAYLOR, FRANCES. *Washington.*

1807, July 16, Newmarket, Caroline County. Asks Madison to have forwarded, by Government means, a letter addressed to Opelousas, La., as there are no postal facilities to that part of the country. 4°. 3 pages.

1807, November 20, Newmarket. Asks to put some letters under cover to Governor Claiborne, who will forward them to their destination. 4°. 1 page.

BAYLOR, JOHN. *Washington.*

1790, February 20, Newmarket, Va. Asks for the settlement of accounts of his brother George, an United States officer in the Third Light Dragoons. 4°. 1 page.

BAYLY, THOMAS M. *Washington.*

1814, January 11, Accomac. Lieut. Geo. D. Wise is directed to stop at Washington and inform the President of the situation and force of the enemy on Fauquier Island. 4°. 1 page.

BEAN, PHINEHAS, JR. *Washington.*

1810, January 4, Newport, N. H. An account of the writer's distresses with an appeal for relief, accompanied by certificates of his character. fol. 3 pages.

BEASLEY, FREDERIC. *Montpellier.*

1824, December 13, *Philadelphia.* Asks for the system of government of the Virginia University and to send him documents which may enlighten him in the matter. 4°. 3 pages.

1831, March *17*, *Trenton.* Asks Madison's good offices towards his appointment to the presidency of the college at Lexington, Ky. 4°. 3 pages.

1831, March *28*, *Trenton.* Thanks Madison for his prompt attention to his request made in his letter of 17th. Relates incidents in his past life and injustice done him. 4°. 4 pages.

BEASLEY, R. G. *Washington.*

No *date.* Applies for the consulate at Bordeaux. Relates his past services. [Signed R. G. B.] large fol. 3 pages.

1813, May 6, London. Informs him of a scheme for smuggling goods into Bath, the collector having given facilities for a cargo valued at £20,000, entered for so many dollars. "Private." 4°. 3 pages.

BEATTY, JAMES. *Montpellier.*

1819, *February 11*, *Baltimore.* Has received a box of seeds from Hamburg, and asks instructions how to forward it to him. 4°. 1 page.

1819, *February 25*, *Baltimore.* Acknowledging letter of 23d. Sends sample of wheat and a box of seeds, per schooner *Delight*, for Fredericksburg. 4°. 1 page.

BECKLEY, JOHN. *New York.*

1789, March *13*, *New York.* Wishes the appointment of clerk to the House of Representatives. Gives reasons why he relinquishes his business at home. 4°. 2 pages.

Orange.

1792, *August 1*, *Philadelphia.* Statement of the claims of Virginia. Urges that the accounts be presented. Republican views progressing. Tumultuous proceedings in Lancaster in opposition to the conference. Candidates for the Vice-Presidency. 4°. 3 pages.

Virginia(?).

1793, November *20*, *Philadelphia.* Thinks there is no fear of contagion in Philadelphia. The yellow fever entirely disappeared. Thinks Madison and Southern members can return without danger. 4°. 1 page.

1795, *April 20*, *New York.* Private financial matters. Result of some State elections. Probable majority of Republicans in next House of Representatives. 4°. 1 page.

1795, *May 4*, *Philadelphia.* Has returned from New York. Been ill with fever and ague. 4°. 1 page.

Washington.

1803, *May 20*, *Philadelphia.* Respecting the purchase of a carriage for Madison. Annexing agreement dated May 16. fol. 1 page.

1804, *July 18*, *Washington.* Mr. Gregory offers to sell his carriage to Madison. 4°. 1 page.

1804, July *19*, *Washington.* Mr. Gregory accepts Mr. Madison's offer for a carriage. 4°. 1 page.

BEDFORD, J. R. *Washington.*

1810, July 4, Nashville. Incloses a letter from William Barrow respecting the situation of affairs in West Florida. Wish of the inhabitants to ultimately become United States citizens. fol. 3 pages.

1810, August 26, Nashville. Agitation in West Florida as to their declaring themselves independent of Spain, with the ultimate object of becoming part of the United States. With copy of a letter from William Barrow, of Bayou Sara, dated August 5, giving the sentiments of the inhabitants and action already taken. fol. 3 pages.

1810, November 8, Nashville. Details of the state of the country in West Florida and the probability of the interests of the inhabitants being linked with those of the United States. Inclosing two letters of September 11 and October 10 from William Barrow, giving information of the situation of affairs. fol. 3 pages.

BEE, THOMAS. *Washington.*

1801, March 19, Charleston. Declines the appointment as chief judge for the Fifth circuit court of the United States. Thinks he can be of equal service by continuing the station of district judge. small 4°. 1 page.

BELL, HENRY.

1799, April 9. Asks for letter of recommendation to the governor and council of Virginia for the appointment of superintendent of the State arsenals. 4°. 1 page.

BELL, JAMES M. *Montpellier.*

1821, September 25, Orange C. H. Asks Madison to use his influence to secure an appointment for his son, William Bell, at West Point. 4°. 1 page.

BELLINI, C. *Philadelphia.*

1782, March —, Williamsburg. Although he has suffered from the absence of the president of the college, he will be very glad to see Madison and his friends again. (In Italian.) (On back of a letter from Rev. James Madison to Madison, March, 1782.) 4°. 3 pages.

BENSON, PERRY (Chairman). *Washington.*

1813, September 8, Easton, Talbot County, Md. Proceedings of a meeting of citizens of Talbot County, approving of the measures of the General Government in respect to our foreign relations, and proffers their services in avenging the wrongs and to defend the rights of our injured country. 4°. 10 pages.

BENTHAM, JEREMY. *Washington.*

1811, October 30, London. Plan of a proposed work in the form of statute law (*Pannemion*) including a substitute (*succedaneum*) to foreign and unwritten law which remains still about our necks. This letter is alluded to in Appleton's American Cyclopedia. fol. 41 pages.

BENTLEY, WILLIAM. *Washington.*

1809, August 12, Salem, Mass. Relative to Gen. John Stark, the hero of Bennington. Asks Madison to gratify the old man by sending him a word of congratulation on the event of the celebration, of August 16, 1777. 4°. 2 pages.

BENTLEY, WILLIAM.

1809, December 11, Salem. Sketch of John Stark, the hero of Bennington. Incloses copy of a letter from Stark expressing his opinion of President Madison; also copy of a letter from B. F. Stickney, son-in-law of the general. 4°. 2 pages.

1810, February 1, Salem. Relates the pleasure Madison's letter to Gen. John Stark afforded the old hero. 4°. 2 pages.

1810, April 24, Salem. Madison's letter to Gen. Stark has served a good public service. Has saved New England. 4°. 1 page.

1810, July 2, Salem. Interview with Gen. Stark. His characteristics. Anecdotes. His portrait. 4°. 4 pages.

1811, May 17, Salem. Assures the President that in a great struggle the friends of Madison and of their country have done their duty. 4°. 1 page.

1813, August 19, Salem. States that the bodies of Capt. Lawrence and Lieut. Ludlow have arrived from Halifax. Preparations for their funeral. 4°. 1 page.

——— to GERRY, ELBRIDGE. *Cambridge.*

1813, September 18, Salem, Mass. Bad treatment of prisoners at Halifax by the British. fol. 1 page.

———, to MADISON. *Washington.*

1814, January 20, Salem. Asks for the appointment of a son of Joseph Wilson, who wishes to be a midshipman in the Navy. 4°. 1 page.

1814, May 27, Salem. Introduces Mr. Andrew Dunlap. 4°. 1 page.

1814, June 8, Salem. Wishes to obtain, if possible, the exchange of Capt. John Crowninshield, of the *Diomede*, for Capt. Bass, of the Liverpool Packet. 4°. 1 page.

1814, September 17, Salem. Gives Madison his pedigree Asks for commission as ensign for his brother John. 4°. 1 page.

1815, October 30, Salem. Recommends Joshua Dodge, of Salem, to the good offices of the President with the Secretary of the Navy in Dodge's behalf. 4°. 2 pages.

BERKSHIRE AGRICULTURAL SOCIETY. *Washington.*

1815, October 24. Certificate of honorary membership of this society. fol. 1 page.

BERMUDA HUNDRED.

1789, December 31. *See* Exports.

BEVERLEY, CARTER, to MADISON. *Washington.*

1808, June 22, Culpeper Co. Asks Madison's good offices to enable him to procure the contract for firearms for the Army. Will give necessary securities. 4°. 3 pages.

BICKLEY, ROBT. S. *Washington.*

1810, May 8, Georgetown. Bill authorizing the President to buy or build a house for public offices. Offers him a hotel for $10,000, with adjacent lots. fol. 1 page.

1810, May 18, Georgetown. Respecting the title to land and hotel offered for sale for Government offices. Urges prompt decision. 4°. 2 pages.

BIDDLE, CHARLES, to DALE, RICHARD (Commodore).

1805, September 7, Philadelphia. Asks if he understood that when Commodore Truxtun gave up the command of the Mediterranean squadron that he resigned his commission. [*See* Truxtun, Thomas, letter to Robert Smith of this date.] [Copy.] 4°. 1 page.

——, to TRUXTUN, THOMAS.

1805, September 7. States that his understanding was that when he, Commodore Truxtun, declined the command of the Mediterranean squadron that he had no intention of resigning his commission. [*See* letter of Truxtun to Robert Smith of this date.] [Copy.] 4°. 1 page.

BIDDLE, NICHOLAS, to MADISON. *Montpellier.*

1822, February 9, Andalusia, Bucks County, Pa. Sends, as mark of respect, a book on agriculture. 4°. 1 page.

1825, April 26. Acknowledging letter of 16th. Is obliged, by a decision of the bank, to decline to advance money on real estate for indeterminate periods. This rule was adopted and has been uniformly and strictly adhered to. 4°. 2 pages.

1827, May 10, Philadelphia. Sends Madison a pamphlet with his respects and regards—"Eulogium on Thomas Jefferson." 4°. 1 page.

1827, May 27, Philadelphia. Acknowledging letter of 17th. Thanks him for his correction of errors in the pamphlet on Mr. Jefferson. Will rectify the mistakes. 4°. 1 page.

BIDWELL, BARNABAS. *Washington.*

1807, June 27, Boston. Acceptance of the office of attorney-general of Massachusetts and the consequent resignation of his seat in Congress. 4°. 2 pages.

1808, February 19, Bennington, Vt. Query as to the consequences in case of rupture with Great Britain, of the status of Americans who have removed to Canada and become naturalized there, and sympathizing and cooperating with us. fol. 2 pages.

BILLING, W. W. *Montpellier.*

1832, January 3, Washington. Notifying Madison of taxes due the corporation of Washington before advertising the property to be sold. 4°. 1 page.

BILLINGS, E. B. *Washington.*

1814, May 25, Nashville. Complaints of arrest and trial for certain specifications and charges growing out of malevolence. His zeal is not confined to the company which he commands, but his country. 4°. 2 pages.

BILLINGS, JESSE L. *Washington.*

1809, September 22, Salem, N. Y. Inclosing an address of John McLean, chairman of the Republican meeting of citizens of Washington County on the 14th. 4°. 1 page.

BINES, MAXWELL, to RODNEY, CESAR A. *Wilmington.*

1804, December 29, Christian Bridge. Respecting the antecedents of a Mr. Watson, who is an applicant for the consulate at Martinique. fol. 3 pages.

BINGHAM, AMOS, to MADISON. *Washington.*

1814, September 9, North Stonington. Appeal for a reformation in 'the keeping of the Sabbath. Ramblings of a religious lunatic. fol. 4 pages.

BINGHAM, P. A. *Montpellier.*

1822, June 24, Rockville, Md. Sends Madison the prospectus of an important work. 4°. 1 page.

BINGHAM, WILLIAM. *New York.*

1789, April 25, Philadelphia. Thinks the President should furnish an opportunity, in a congratulatory address, of announcing the views of Congress to adhere to such principles as can alone do honor to the councils of a country, to be translated and published in all the languages of Europe. 4°. 2 pages.

1789, June 17, Philadelphia. Respecting the bill for the establishment of the impost. Its injury to public credit. [Signature cut off.] 4°. 2 pages.

BINNS, JOHN. *Washington.*

1808, July 7, Philadelphia. Request of Bernard Smith to controvert under oath a deposition made by one Gardner relative to publications printed in the Democratic press. Binns solemnly declares (declining a deposition) he has never received any article from Mr. Smith upon any subject which has appeared in the press. 4°. 1 page.

———, and others. *Washington.*

1813, February 11, Philadelphia. Memorial to the President from John Binns, William Smiley, J. W. Thompson, Francis Mitchell, John Maitland, and George Palmer, respecting the inhuman threat of the Prince Regent to treat prisoners of the U. S. Army and Navy, naturalized citizens, as traitors. Asks the course the Executive intends to pursue. 4°. 2 pages.

1813, April 20, Philadelphia. Recommendation of John Binns and other citizens of Philadelphia to appoint Elijah Griffiths treasurer of the Mint in the place made vacant by the death of Dr. Rush. [Ten signatures.] 4°. 1 page.

———, to INGERSOLL, C. J.

1813, April 24, Philadelphia. Respecting an appointment of Dr. James Rush. Can not recommend him, notwithstanding his qualifications, he having recommended another applicant. small 4°. 1 page.

———, to MADISON. *Washington.*

1814, July 11, Philadelphia. Popular dissatisfaction of Michael Liet as postmaster. His tampering with the mails and preventing important communications. 4°. 3 pages.

BIRCHETT, ROBERT, to GOODWYN, PETERSON. *Washington.*

1812, June 4, Petersburg. Testimony as to the good character, and merits, of Mordecai Barbour, a candidate for lieutenant-colonel's commission. 4°. 1 page.

BIRKBECK, MORRIS, to MADISON. *Montpellier.*

1817, September 18, Princeton, Md. Wished to remove with his family and some friends to Illinois and there establish themselves where he has entered a tract of land. Proposes to occupy north lands not offered to the public if permitted. fol. 3 pages.

BIRCKHEAD, ROBERT. *Washington.*

1813, May 7, Baltimore. The alarm and distress of the people in Baltimore. Useless to attempt to struggle against the inevitable. The people opposed to the war. Desires to make peace and arrest impending distress. 4°. 3 pages.

BLACK, J. R. *Washington.*

1812, June 3, New Castle, Del. Inclosing the sentiments of the Republicans of New Castle County, who express their determination to support the measures of the administration in the present crisis of our foreign relations. 4°. 4 cases.

BLACKFORD, ARTHUR, & CO. *Montpellier.*

1818, April 28, Isabella Furnace. Respecting an agricultural machine ordered by Judge Holmes, and asks instructions where to forward it. 4°. 1 page.

BLACKLEDGE, WILLIAM. *Washington.*

1812, March 20, Washington. Asks for the appointment of a correspondent, William Eaton, as baker for supplying the Army or Navy. Eaton informs the writer of the enlisting soldiers under unnaturalized Scotch and Englishmen. 4°. 2 pages and strip of paper.

1813, February 7, Washington. Solicits the appointment to some office of his friend, Capt. James Taylor, late collector of Ocracock. 4°. 3 pages.

BLAIR, F. B. *Montpellier.*

1832, October 25, Washington. Incloses a paper containing a letter ascribed to Madison. Asks if he wrote it. 4°. 1 page.

BLAIR, JAMES. *Orange.*

1797, April 25, Fredericksburg. Sends a list of articles received from Philadelphia for Madison. 4°. 2 pages.

BLAKE, GEORGE. *Washington.*

1814, February 16, Boston. Incloses extract of a letter to Blake from a friend in Washington. Trusts he will suspend any unfavorable impression against him before he has an interview with him in the course of eight days. 4°. 2 pages.

BLAKE, JAMES. *Washington.*

1801, June 15, Washington. Asks for the appointment of a consulate. 4°. 1 page.

BLAKE, JAMES H., to JEFFERSON. *Washington.*

1809, January 10, Washington. Wants Government employment. Incloses testimonials. 4°. 4 pages.

———, to MADISON. *Washington.*

1809, February 9, Washington. Inclosing testimonials in his favor. Wishes Government employment. 4°. 2 pages.

1809, March 10, Washington. Incloses additional testimonials. Anxious to get Government employment. 4°. 1 page.

1816, July 18, Washington. Transmits resolutions of the alderman and common council of this city to alter the canal so as to form a basin on the unappropriated public ground north of the Tiber, which can not be done without the consent of the President. 4°. 2 pages.

BLAKE, JAMES H..

1817, March 4, Washington. In behalf of a committee appointed by the general meeting of citizens of Washington expressing congratulations, mingled with regrets at the retirement of Madison from political life. fol. 4 pages.

BLAKWELL, PAGE & BLAKWELL.

1816, February 19, Pittsburg. Sends the President a pair of decanters manufactured by the writers from the materials taken from American soil. 4°. 1 page.

BLAND, THEODORICK, to JEFFERSON (Governor of Virginia).

1780, November 22, Philadelphia. Incloses a letter concerning the Indiana Company. Asks revision of instructions relative to navigation of the Mississippi should overtures from Spain be advantageous to the United States. [Certificate as to true copy September 30, 1820.] [Copy.] 4°. 4 pages.

———, to CONGRESS.

1783, February 20, Philadelphia. Motion for requisitions on States for such revenues as may be required for funding the public debt. 4°. 1 page.

———, to MADISON.

1783, June 22. Shall not quit his station whilst the majority of Congress trust their persons in the hands of a mutinous Army without support. Asks how matters stand respecting the determination of the Executive council. [Signature cut off.] 4°. 1 page.

1788, September 20. Certificate in favor of a claim for his interest in the capture of property of British refugees and negroes, and turned over to the quartermaster, in the year 1777. fol. 2 pages.

BLATCHLY, CORN'S C. *Washington.*

1815, May 6. Inclosing a pamphlet on the custom of war and proposing a remedy to end it. 4°. 1 page.

BLEDSOE, J. *Washington.*

1814, June 18, Lexington, Ky. Complains of the dismissal of good officers in the Army and the worst retained. Gives examples. Knows it was not the President's order, but thinks the Secretary of War will brew a storm which will shake the administration. 4°. 3 pages.

BLEDSOE, PECHY. *Philadelphia.*

1794, February 28, Fredericksburg. Sends him the claim of one Thomason for military service, with his discharge. Asks Madison to secure it. fol. 3 pages.

BLEIHEROLSEN, ——. *Richmond.*

1802, January 16, Philadelphia. Incloses a letter. Thanks him and Mrs. Madison for their hospitality and kindness when in Washington. 4°. 1 page.

BLOCHER, JACOB. *Washington.*

1813, May 30, Sumerset County. Protesting against the attempted change of the Cumberland road from its original location. 4°. 2 pages.

BLODGET, REBECCA. *Washington.*

1809, no date, New York. Petition in behalf of Aaron Burr. Prays the President to remove the prosecution against him. Appeals to his generosity and magnanimity, ignoring the justice or injustice of the prosecution. Appended is a short postscript to Mrs. Madison. fol. 3 pages.

BLODGET, S. *Washington.*

1810, April 11. Renewal of the charter of the United States Bank. Sketch of a new plan inclosed. 4°. 2 pages.

BLOODGOOD, ABRAHAM. *Washington.*

1809, September 16, New York. Inclosing an address by the general Republican committee of the city and county of New York, on 15th instant, approving the President's course and promising support. 4°. 5 pages.

BLOOMFIELD, JOSEPH, to RAISIN, SAMUEL.

1813, November 13, Washington. Instructions for protection of the inhabitants of Northern Neck and to oppose the enemy. [Copy.] fol. 2 pages.

———, to MADISON. *Washington.*

1815, June 6, Burlington, N. J. On the appointment of district judge of New Jersey in the place of Robert Morris, deceased. Recommends Joseph McIlvaine. 4°. 2 pages.

1815, June 7, Burlington, N. J. The candidates for district judge of New Jersey. Strongly recommends Joseph McIlvaine, as superior. [Confidential.] 4°. 8 pages.

BLOUNT, JOHN. *Washington.*

1803, July 22, Farborough. Recommends Mr. Benjamin Blackledge as commercial agent or consul at Guadaloupe. 4°. 2 pages.

BLOUNT, THOMAS, to GALLATIN, ALBERT. *Washington.*

1808, December 5, Washington. Believes in the statement of Lewis Leroy that he never intended to violate the laws of his country, and would be gratified if relief were extended to him. [Answer on same sheet. Copy.] fol. 1 page.

BLOUNT, WILLIE, to MADISON. *Washington.*

1812, March 1, Knoxville. Inclosing a report of a committee of the general assembly of North Carolina claiming the right of North Carolina to perfect titles on all claims to lands in the State of Tennessee not yet satisfied. 4°. 2 pages.

1812, March 6, Knoxville. Inclosing copy of an act of the general assembly of North Carolina touching certain lands in Tennessee. Asking to be advised of the course of proceeding which may be adopted by the General Government to secure the interest of such of the citizens of Tennessee as may be affected by the consequences growing out of that act. 4°. 2 pages.

Washington.

1813, April 29, Nashville. Incloses by request of the general assembly of Tennessee an address and resolutions. The war just and a vigorous prosecution until an honorable peace is necessary. 4°. 1 page.

BLUNT, E. M. *Washington.*

1811, June 28, New York. Incloses a copy of the Nautical Almanac. Its superiority over other almanacs. 4°. 2 pages.

1812, April 22, New York. Asks patronage for the Nautical Almanac. Errors in other similar publications. 4°. 2 pages.

BLUNT, JOSEPH. *Montpellier.*

1829, April 8, New York. Transmits the two first volumes of the Annual Register. 4°. 1 page.

1830, August 10, New York. Transmitting the third volume of the Annual Register. 4°. 1 page.

1830, September 27, New York. Acknowledges letter of 19th, inclosing payment for the Annual Register. 4°. 1 page.

BLUNT, WILLIAM. *Washington.*

1809, February 23, Eden, Hancock County, Mass. In behalf of the Republican society of this place, transmits resolutions of the citizens approving the measures of the General Government. fol. 7 pages.

BOAS, JACOB, and others. *Washington.*

1814 (?), not dated. Memorial of merchants and traders praying the removal of Gideon Granger from the office of Postmaster-General. 4°. 2 pages.

BOGGS, JOHN. *Washington.*

1814, September 20, Martinsburg, Va. Attributes the the disasters which has befallen this country to Sabbath breaking. Prays the President to proclaim a day of humiliation and prayer. 4°. 4 pages.

BOLLING, ROBERT, to GOODWYN, PETERSON. *Washington.*

1812, June 10, Petersburg. Thinks Congress will conduct us through threatening difficulties. Recommends to his and Madison's favorable notice Mr. Mordecai Barbour, who wants employment. fol. 2 pages.

BOLLMAN, ERICK, to MADISON. *Washington.*

1807, May 19, Alexandria. Returns a letter received under cover of one to Lafayette. When passing through Washington will call and see what satisfactory arrangements can be made relating to the business. 4°. 1 page.

1807, May 21, Richmond. Asks for letters in Madison's possession directed to him. 4°. 1 page.

1807, May 28, Richmond. Asks Madison to send him letters directed to him said to be in his possession. 4°. 1 page.

1810, December 23, Philadelphia. Transmits a copy of a production of the writers and asks him to review it. 4°. 1 page.

1815, November 28. Just arrived from Europe. Has a letter from Mr. Adams and asks when Madison can receive him. 4°. 1 page.

1816, January 17, Philadelphia. Transmits for Madison's approbation the copy of a pamphlet on the money concerns of the Union. 8°. 1 page.

BONNYCASTLE, C. *Montpellier.*

1834, July 21, University of Virginia. Improvement in canals, a subject connected with the School of Engineering. Asks for letters from Madison to Gens. Macomb and Gratiot. 4°. 1 page.

BORDLEY, J. BEALE.

1798, July 24, Philadelphia. Essays on husbandry transmitted. small 4°. 1 page.

BOSSAUGE & MASSON. *Washington.*

1810, August 10, Paris. Transmits a copy of Homer's Iliad translated from the Greek by the Archi-Trésorier of the French Empire. [In French.] fol. 1 page.

1811, July 5, Paris. Acknowledging letter and receipt of Homer's Iliad. Transmits, by same author, a translation of Jerusalem delivered. 4°. 1 page.

BOTANIC GARDENS. *Unknown.*

Not dated. Observations on a botanic garden and means for conducting it. fol. 6 pages.

BOTTA, CARLO, to MADISON. *Washington.*

1810, January 12, Paris. Transmits a copy of his work entitled "Storia della Guerra dell' Independenza degli Stati Uniti d' America." Trusts it will meet with his approval. [In French.] fol. 1 page.

1816, January 10, Paris. Transmits his poem of "Camillo." [In Italian.] fol. 1 page.

BOTTS, THOMAS. *Montpellier.*

1834, February 14, Fredericksburg. Inclosing his account as assignee to W. F. Gray, requesting an early settlement if convenient. 4°. 1 page.

BOUDON, DAVID. *Washington.*

1811, February 18, Georgetown. Solicits the position of drawing master should the plan of a military academy be established at Washington. [In French.] 4°. 2 pages.

BOURNE, GEORGE. *Washington.*

1809, April 22, Baltimore. Asks him to head the list of subscribers to his History of Jefferson's Administration. 4°. 1 page.

BOURNE, SILV. *New York.*

1790, June 28, New York. Opposition of some members of the House of Representatives to any emolument to consuls. Requests Madison to exercise his influence in support of such a gratuity and states his reasons. fol. 2 pages.

1790, December 1, New York. Is about to embark as consul at Hispaniola. Solicitous that the Government should more clearly specify the rights and powers of consuls and ascertain the *quantum meruit* of their services. 4°. 2 pages.

1809, June 21, Amsterdam. Direction to be given by Government to masters of vessels as to their destination. Information by the writer as to the decision of the Dutch Government in respect to the allowed articles admitted for sale. 4°. 3 pages.

BOWDITCH, NATHANIEL, *Montpellier.*

1818, March 30, Salem. Transmits a pamphlet. 8°. 1 page.

BOWIE, RALPH. *Washington.*

1801, March 24, York, Pa. His approval of the President's message. He and his friends trust there will be no general removals from office. 4°. 5 pages.

BOYD, J. P., to GERRY, ELDRIDGE. *Washington.*

1814, February 22, Boston. Thinks he has not been treated with the justice his services entitle him in the promotion of junior officers over him. Asks for the brevet rank of major-general, bearing date prior to those promotions. Appeals to the justice and candor of the high officers and Secretary of War. 4°. 4 pages.

1814, March 24, Boston. Military promotions of juniors over seniors. Claims notice of his services. Thinks he is entitled at least to a brevet. 4°. 3 pages.

——— to MONROE, JAMES. *Washington.*

1815, March 9, New York. The contemplated new organization of the Army. His anxiety of the possibility of his exclusion. His services in the last war. 4°. 4 pages.

BOYD, WASHINGTON, to MADISON. *Washington.*

1808, May 31, Washington. Notice of the city assessment on Madison's personal property. 4°. 1 page.

BOYDEN, JAMES. *Washington.*

1808, February 5, Baltimore. Forwards a bandbox to Mrs. Madison. 4°. 1 page.

BRACKENRIDGE, H. H. *Washington.*

1805, May 31, Carlisle, Pa. Sends him a continuation of his jeu d'esprit "Modern Chivalry." Recommends to his favor Capt. Richard Parker, of the Quartermaster's Department. large fol. 2 pages.

1813, May 1, Carlisle, Pa. Recommends to Madison's favor Francis Bailey, who wishes Government employment. Suggests the vacancy in the Mint caused by Dr Rusk's decease. 4°. 2 pages.

1814, January 15, Philadelphia. Requests the appointment of Francis Bailey as postmaster at Philadelphia. Sends Madison a copy of "Law Miscellanies," just published, and asks his approval. 4°. 1 page.

BRADFORD, ALDEN. *Montpellier.*

1831, April 9, New Bedford. Transmitted Madison in July last some remarks on Federal Government, and had received no acknowledgment. Importance of the question. Requests a return of the papers. 4°. 3 pages.

BRADFORD, JAMES. *Montpellier.*

1831, September 26, Washington. Referring to his acquaintances in the Richmond convention of 1829. Asks Madison to inform him whether his father, David Bradford, was inimical to the Government in the part he was forced to take in the whisky rebellion in 1794. Did those acts constitute treason? 4°. 3 pages.

BRADFORD, SAML. F. *Washington.*

1806, May 3, Philadelphia. On his transmittance of a book entitled "Cabinet of St. Cloud." If not of service to the Government it may afford amusement to Madison. 4°. 1 page.

BRADLEY, ABRAHAM, JR. *Washington.*

1806, August 22, Washington. At request of J. G. Jackson, has deposited $300 to Madison's credit in the bank. Receipt inclosed. 4°. 1 page.

BRADLEY, P. *Washington.*

1816, August 8, Washington. Remittance of $50, being a dividend of the Potomac Steamboat Company. 4°. 1 page.

Montpellier.

1818, July 16, Washington. Remits dividend of $50 of the Potomac Steamboat Company. 4°. 1 page.

BRADLEY, STEPHEN R. *Philadelphia.*

1797, February 18, Westminster. Col. Monroe's claim to land in Middlesex, New York State. The sum remains to be determined. fol. 1 page.

BRAMHAM, V. *Washington.*

1811, January 28. Profits of the collector's office. Asks if there may be an increase of emoluments. Leaves it to his judgment whether it were better to propose his appointment. fol. 2 pages.

BRAND, C. J. *Montpellier.*

1821, April 10, London. Sends Madison a copy of a treatise on the Rights of Colonies. 4°. 1 page.

BRANNAN, JOHN. *Montpellier.*

1823, July 4, Washington. Transmits a copy of his late work entitled "Official Letters of our Military and Naval Officers during the late war with Great Britain." The object of the compilation. 4°. 3 pages.

BRECKINRIDGE, JAMES. *Montpellier.*

1819, November 27, Fincastle. Acknowledging letter of 4th. Relative to the procuring of clover seed for Madison. 4°. 2 pages.

1820, January 16, Richmond. Concerning the forwarding of some clover seed. 4°. 1 page.

1820, January 17, Richmond. Madison's declining to receive the clover seed will put the writer to no inconvenience. 4°. 1 page.

1827, December 23, Fincastle. Appointment of a successor to Prof. Long at the University of Virginia. 4°. 1 page.

BREEZE, ARTHUR. *Philadelphia.*

1794, January 28, Whitestown. Difficulty of selling some land of Madison's on the Mohawk for cash. May do it on credit. 4°. 2 pages.

1794, April 11, Whitestown. Acknowledging letter of 22d ultimo. Description of the locality of land on the Mohawk belonging to Madison. Suggestions as to selling it. 4°. 3 pages.

1794, April 16, Whitestown. The writer's estimate of the value of Madison's land on the Mohawk. 4°. 1 page.

1796, December 17, Whitestown. Acknowledging letter of May 13. Sale of Madison's land. 4°. 1 page.

BRENNAN, J. *Montpellier.*

1825, August 31, Kingston. Solicits his subscription to a translation of the Marquis de Chastellux's travels in America. Its recommendation by Jefferson and Gen. Armstrong. fol. 4 pages.

BRENNAN, J.

1825, September 16, Kingston, N. Y. Acknowledging letter of 7th. Relative to his translation of the Marquis de Chastellux's work on America. Madison's correction of an error respecting his parentage. fol. 2 pages.

1825, October 18, Kingston. Acknowledging letter of September 26. Thanks Madison for corrections made in the translation of de Chastellux's work, as to his parentage. 4°. 2 pages.

1826, November 3, New York. Asks Madison to advance on his subscription to a work he is publishing. fol. 1 page.

BRENT, DANIEL, and others. *Washington.*

1801, June 25, Washington. The clerks in the Department of State remind the Secretary of the additional allowance of 15 per cent appropriated by Congress, and ask him to distribute it in just and reasonable proportions. 4°. 1 page.

1802, May 18, 21, 25, August, 25, 31, September, 3, 7, 10, 14, 21, and August 7, 1804. Detailed current business of the Department. [Series of 11 letters.] 4°. 18 pages.

——— to ARMSTRONG, JOHN. *New York.*

1804, August 6, Washington. The change in government in France. Question of the form of papers in absence of official notice of the change. [Press copy.] 4°. 1 page.

——— to MADISON. *Orange.*

1807, August 7, Washington. Interposition of Col. Newton to procure the discharge of our seamen detained on the British squadron. Other business of the Department. 4°. 1 page.

1807, August 10, Washington. The bomb-ketch *Etna* around from New Orleans with troops. Yellow fever on board, raging. 4°. 1 page.

1807, August 14, Washington. Victualling of the dispatch vessel *Columbine* at Norfolk. 4°. 1 page.

1807, August 16, Washington. Mode of communication between the British squadron and the British functionaries in the United States. Thirteen American seamen detained in the British squadron. 4°. 1 page.

1807, August 17, Washington. Obstructions to Spanish stores bound up the Mississippi. Governor Claiborne's explanation. 4°. 1 page.

1807, August 21, Washington. Mr. Cook's appointment to the agency at Martinique. Has sent orders for collecting information concerning John Strahan, a seaman. 4°. 1 page.

1807, August 23, Washington. Acknowledging letter of 19th. Maryland paper held by Mr. Howard considered worthless. 4°. 1 page.

1807, August 26, Washington. Department current business. Extract of letter relating to Spanish claims. 4°. 1 page.

1807, August 22, 31, September 10, Washington. Details of current business at the Department. [Series of 3 letters.] 4°. 3 pages.

1807, September 15, Washington. Acknowledging letter of 11th. Effect in England produced by the

BRENT, DANIEL.

President's message. Fears by Americans that an embargo would be laid on our shipping. 4°. 1 page.

Washington.

1815, September 6, Washington. Transmitting letters and documents from the Department of State. 4°. 1 page.

Montpellier.

1825, July 29, Washington. Introducing Mr. Rebello, chargé d'affairs of Brazil, who goes to Virginia. 4°. 1 page.

1828, August 9, Washington. Inclosing a letter from Mr. Laurence. 4°. 1 page.

1828, October 17, Washington. Acknowledging letter of 14th. Transcripts from records of the Department will be forwarded. Death of Richard Forest. 4°. 1 page.

1828, December 23, Washington. Sends copies from the records of the Department. 4°. 1 page.

1829, February 24, Washington. Asks for a testimonial to Gen. Jackson in reference to the position he holds in the Department, as to his conduct during Madison's administration. Wishes to be undisturbed in the change. Van Buren supposed to be appointed Secretary of State. Brent, though on the side of Adams in the contest for the Presidency, took no part. 4°. 1 page.

BRENT, ROBERT. *Washington.*

1808, November 17, Washington. Recommending Richard S. Briscoe to be justice of the peace in the first ward. 4°. 2 pages.

1811, April 25, Washington. Asks, as paymaster, liberty to deposit public funds in his hands, with the Bank of Washington. 4°. 2 pages.

Montpellier.

1813, September 7, Washington. Respecting the appointment of paymasters of the Army. 4°. 3 pages.

——— to GERRY, ELBRIDGE (Vice-President). *Washington.*

1814, August 18, Bath. Recommending Alexander Scott for the office of Secretary of the Senate. [*See* letter of Alexander Scott to Madison dated August 20, 1816.] [Copy.] 4°. 2 pages.

——— to ARMSTRONG, JOHN. *Washington.*

1814, August 19, Washington. Transmitting estimates for payment of the militia force commanded by Governor Shelby for services rendered in the expedition under Gen. Harrison in 1813. [Copy] fol. 5 pages.

——— to MADISON. *Washington.*

1814, November 15, Washington. Appointments of paymasters in the Army. 4°. 1 page.

——— to CRAWFORD, WILLIAM H. *Washington.*

1815, August 16. Estimates as paymaster in the Army, of the compensation per month required for the troops at the respective posts and stations of the North and South division of the Army of the United States peace establishment. roy. fol. 1 page.

BRENT, WILLIAM, to MADISON. *Washington.*

1814, February 12, Washington. Asks for remittance of fine imposed on Joseph Dougherty by court of inquiry. Did not wish to evade the law or avoid performing duty. 4°. 1 page.

BREWER, JOHN. *Washington.*

1817, February 12, Annapolis. Asking Government employment. large fol. 4 pages.

BRIDGES, ISAAC, to DEARBORN, HENRY.

1801, June 19, Boston. Wants the appointment of consul at Algiers. 4°. 2 pages.

BRIGGS, ISAAC, to MADISON. *Washington.*

1803, January 1, Sharon. Requests Madison's aid in causing an annual convention for the advancement for improvements in agriculture. fol. 2 pages.

1803, February 22, Washington. Record from the journal of the American Board of Agriculture. Isaac Briggs's plan of a constitution of the board. fol. 6 pages.

1803, May 17, Sharon. Introducing his brother, Joseph Briggs. small 4°. 2 pages.

1808, July 15, Baltimore. Introducing Matthew Witherspoon. Asks Madison to order some books from Europe. A list of same annexed. 4°. 2 pages.

1812, May 16, Triadelphia, Md. Importance of legislative action on various manufacturing enterprises in this country. Query as to convenient channels for collecting necessary facts. 4°. 2 pages.

1814, January 18, Triadelphia. Introducing William Paxson and William S. Warder. 4°. 2 pages.

Montpellier.

1817, January 4, Wilmington. Del. Introducing the widow of John Dauphin, a petitioner for relief. 4°. 2 pages.

1823, March 8, Sandy Spring, Md. Wishes to be appointed principal engineer by the board of public works of Virginia. Asks Madison's testimony as to his qualifications. 4°. 2 pages.

BRIGGS, ROBERT. *Montpellier.*

1821, July 5, Madison. Acknowledging letter of June 12. Sends statement of account. 4°. 1 page.

1823, July 26, Madison. Asks for settlement of account. 4°. 1 page.

BRIGGS, WESSON. *Washington.*

1814, June 6, Washington. Asks Madison's assistance in his claim on the Government. 4°. 1 page.

BRISTOW, MARY. *New York.*

1786, September 14, London. Asks Madison's good offices in behalf of a claim of her infant son on the Government. 4°. 2 pages.

BRITISH DEBTS. *Unknown.*

1795 (?), not dated. A statement of the precise rights of Great Britain resulting from the article of the treaty of peace which relates to private debts, intended to evince that the United States really exceeded the measure of favorable treatment which justice to Great Britain and the law of nations prescribed under the actual circumstances of the case, with notes. [Defaced by gnawings of miee.] 4°. 27 pages.

BRITISH TREASURY.

1714, September 29, Court of St. James. Warrant for £100 on the Commissioners of the Treasury signed by Geo. Baillie. 4°. 1 page.

BROBSON, JAMES, to DUVALL, GABRIEL.

1811, May 12, Wilmington. Explains his conduct as a public officer in the matter of a judgment obtained against John Bird as security for payment of duties. fol. 3 pages.

——— to MONROE, JAMES (Secretary of State.)

1812, August 12, Wilmington. Defends himself from accusations in Mr. Graham's letter, of neglect of duty as U. S. marshal, etc. fol. 5 pages.

BROCK, C. WILLIAM, to MADISON. *Montpellier.*

1821, May 25, Orange C. H. Reminds him of the non-payment of a fee bill. 4°. 1 page.

BROCKENBROUGH, A. S. *Montpellier.*

1828, June 17, University of Virginia. Notifying Madison of the meeting of visitors and wants to know his wishes respecting accommodations. 4°. 1 page.

1828, September 23, University of Virginia. Invites Madison and Mrs. Madison to his house during the meeting of visitors to the university. Extends the invitation to Col. Monroe. 4°. 1 page.

1827, no date, University of Virginia. Relating to the University of Virginia, number of students, etc. 4°. 1 page.

1829, April 10, University of Virginia. Asks advice on matters relating to the university. 4°. 1 page.

1829, June 29, University of Virginia. Providing for accommodation of visitors at the university. 4°. 1 page.

1830, March 10, University of Virginia. Relative to alterations and improvements at the university. 4°. 2 pages.

1831, July 28, University of Virginia. Complains of ill treatment on the part of the visitors as harsh, cruel, and unjust. Asks Madison's good offices to put things right. 4°. 7 pages.

BROCKENBROUGH, JOHN. *Washington.*

1814, February 28, Richmond. Recommending Robert Mills, of Philadelphia, as architect of public buildings. 4°. 1 page.

BROCKENBROUGH, LUCY. *Montpellier.*

1831, July 24, University of Virginia. Proceedings of the board of visitors in reducing the pay and emoluments of her husband's position in the university after his long services. Appeals to Madison in order to effect a remedy through his good offices. 4°. 8 pages.

BROCKENBROUGH, NEWMAN. *Washington.*

1812, May 4, Essex County, New Hall. Associates in Williamsburg in 1774. Fears the calamity of precipitation into war. Has confidence in Madison, and hopes he can avoid a conflict. Advises the abandonment of negotiations with either France or England, and that our merchants make their ventures at their own risk. 4°. 2 pages.

BRODNAX, W. H. *Montpellier.*

1833, May 24, Kingston. Acknowledging letter of 16th. Resignation of Dr. Dungleson of the professorship in the University of Virginia. Trusts that Madison's experience will enable him to make a selection of a suitable successor. 4°. 3 pages.

BROOKE, WALTER T. *Montpellier.*

1830, October 20, Washington. Asks information relating to the appointment of Walter Brooke and his commission in the Virginia State navy in the Revolutionary war. 4°. 2 pages.

BROOKS, ZACHARIAH, to INGERSOLL, CHARLES J. *Washington.*

1814, February 11, Manchester, Va. Complaints of frauds practiced by the Postmaster-General or his agents in contracts for carrying the mails. 4°. 3 pages.

BROOM, JACOB, to MADISON. *New York.*

1789, April 16, Wilmington. Congratulations on the adoption of the Constitution. Applies for appointment of collector at Wilmington. 4°. 2 pages.

BROOM, JOHN, to BURKE, THOMAS. *Loughburke.*

1787, May 16, New York. Copy of a letter inclosed in one to Thomas Burke relating to the death and disposition of property of John Burke, his brother. 4°. 3 pages.

BROUGHAM, HENRY (Lord), to MONROE, JAMES. *Washington.*

1811, November 1, London. Introducing Jeremy Bentham. His high character and learning. His design in proposing a code of laws for the United States. 4°. 8 pages.

BROUGHTON, EDWARD, to MADISON. *Washington.*

1812, September 21, Worcester County, Md. Incloses a copy of proceedings of the Republican citizens at a meeting at Snow Hill. fol. 1 page.

BROUILLET, MICHEL.

1810, June 30, Knox County, Ind. Deposition before a justice of the peace relating to the information he obtained while he remained in the Prophet's town as to the views, opinions, and measures of the Prophet, who is evidently bent on making war on the whites, being greatly exasperated by the cession of lands. [Copy.] 4°. 3 pages.

BROWER, GARRET. *Washington.*

1814, January 31, New York. Views of the writer on the campaign in Canada. [A specimen of curious orthography.] fol. 1 page.

1814, no date. Relative to the campaign in Canada. fol. 1 page.

1814, no date, New York. The campaign in Canada. The writer's invention for a bridge for passage of an army over narrow streams. fol. 1 page.

BROWERE, J. H. J., to MONROE, JAMES.

1825, September 12, Washington. Desires to make a portrait of Madison in his new method in sculpture of taking features. [This letter is directed to Madison on the outside, but is intended for Monroe.] 4°. 3 pages.

BROWERE, J. H. J., to MADISON. *Montpellier.*

1825, September 28, Washington. Acknowledging letter of 24th. Relating to a proposal to make a portrait (sculptured) of Madison. 4°. 3 pages.

1826, February 4, New York. Respecting criticisms on the writer's portraits in sculpture. Incloses verses on the artist's busts of eminent men. 4°. 6 pages.

1826, May 20, New York. Relates to the naming of his infant daughter. Wishes to know Mrs. Madison's Christian name, whether Dorothea, Dorothy, Dolly, or Doll, as the child will be named after her. small 4°. 2 pages.

Montpellier.

1826, June 24, New York. Has named his child Dolly Madison. Anticipates pleasure in visiting Montpellier. fol. 3 pages.

——— to MADISON and visitors of the university.

1826, July 17, New York. The death of Jefferson. Tribute to his memory. The writer's statue of Jefferson, for the common council of New York, described. Is willing to make a statue for the university, of any of its founders, in bronze or marble. fol. 7 pages.

BROWERE, J. H. J., and MRS. BROWERE, to MADISON. *Montpellier.*

1827 (?), no date. Proposes paying his respects to Madison and Mrs. Madison at Montpellier. 4°. 1 page.

BROWERE, J. H. J. *Montpellier.*

1828, July 26, New York. Proposes, on completion of his "National gallery of busts and statues," to exhibit them in various places anterior to their completion in bronze metal. fol. 3 pages.

BROWERE, J. H. J., and ELIZA C. M. *Montpellier.*

1833, April 29, New York. Acknowledgments of hospitality and favors received in years past. His national gallery of busts. Hindered from completing it. Fears of the collection being pirated. Proposes visiting Montpellier with his daughter. fol. 2 pages.

BROWN, ———, to JOHNSON, RICHARD M. *Great Crossing, Ky.*

1815, May 5, Washington. Narrative of the refusal of the Secretary of War to issue warrants for payment of sums due to Ward & Taylor, contractors for the Army. [Extract of a letter.] [Copy.] 4°. 2 pages.

BROWN, ETHAN A., to MADISON. *Montpellier.*

1821, January 26, Columbus, Ohio. Transmits a report. 8°. 1 page.

BROWN, JAMES, to CRAWFORD, WILLIAM (Secretary of War). *Washington.*

1816, April 23, Washington. Has been requested by Capt. A. W. Hamilton, to state what he knows of the characters of Drs. W. Flood and William E. Cochran, of New Orleans. Speaks in high terms of them. [Copy.] 4°. 1 page.

——— to MADISON. *Montpellier.*

1829, November 30, Philadelphia. Relates to some financial matters of the university. His intention to retire from public life. 4°. 2 pages.

BROWN, JOHN, and others to WASHINGTON.
Philadelphia.

1787. Copy, in Madison's handwriting, of a letter of J. Brown and twelve others to the chairman of the Federal Convention of 1787. [*See* Convention, Federal, 1787.] 4°. 2 pages.

——— to MADISON. *Orange.*

1788, April 9, New York. Sends Madison letters and newspapers. Proceedings of Congress. Is pleased at Madison's election for the convention. 4°. 1 page.

1788, May 12, New York. Acknowledging letter of April 9 and 21. Friends and foes of the constitution of Virginia. Sentiments of the people of New York respecting the new Government. 4°. 4 pages.

Richmond.

1788, June 7, New York. Acknowledging letter of May 27. Projected constitution of Kentucky. Objections of Col. Hamilton supported by the Eastern States. The writer's endeavors to remove the objections. 4°. 3 pages.

New York.

1788, August 26, Pittsburg. His arrival from the West. Bad state of the roads. Movements of the Indians. The action of Kentucky relative to their constitution and admittance into the Union. Movements of Brant and Indian warriors. fol. 2 pages.

1788, November 23, Danville, Ky. Acknowledging letters of September 24 and October 12. The convention of Kentucky meets at Danville. Determination to renew application to Virginia for an independent government and admission into the Union. The country much disturbed by faction and divided in political opinion. Asks Madison's views on a plan of government. Introduces Maj. Croghan. fol. 2 pages.

1795, June 8, Philadelphia. John Jay's election as governor of New York. Is expected in Philadelphia to give an account of his mission. Mr. Ardet, successor of Fouchet, minister from France, arrives in Newport, R. I. 4°. 1 page.

Washington.

1807, February 22, Washington. Note introducing Mr. Dufour, a Swiss immigrant, who has commenced the culture of wine in Kentucky. 8°. 1 page.

Montpellier.

1834, August 23, Frankfort. Introduces Mann Butler, who is engaged in writing a history of Kentucky. On the outside of this letter is a note from Mann Butler regretting that he can not visit Mr. Madison. 4°. 1 page.

BROWN, JACOB (Major-General). *Montpellier.*

1818, November. Acknowledging letter of 7th. Looks forward with satisfaction when agriculture will engage his whole attention. [Signature cut off.] 4°. 2 pages.

BROWN, OBEDIAH B. *Washington.*

1815, August 22, Washington. Transmits a paper from New Haven. Contents unknown. 4°. 1 page.

BROWNE, JAMES T. (assumed name). *Washington.*

1801, May 25, Brownlow. Advocating the purchase of an island of the West Indies called Bouriqueen, or Crab Island, as a naval station. Describes the island and its advantages. 4°. 6 pages.

BROWNE, WILLIAM. *Montpellier.*

1824, March 4, Fredericksburg. Asking Madison's good offices in procuring the appointment of William S. Stone as auditor to the navy-yard. His capabilities. 4°. 2 pages.

BRUNT, JONATHAN. *Washington.*

1809, April 24, Knoxville. A rambling, incoherent letter from a probable lunatic. The slavish devotion of men to personal domestic idols (female intriguers). fol. 4 pages.

1809, June 1, Knoxville. An incoherent and crazy letter, but amusing. fol. 3 pages.

BRYAN, JOSEPH. *Washington.*

1806, February 3, Washington. Barbary stallion sent by the Bey of Tunis. 4°. 1 page.

BRYCE, JOHN. *Montpellier.*

1829, September 14, Scott County, Ky. Introducing Robert W. Scott. 4°. 1 page.

BRYSON, JAMES. *New York.*

1788, March 12. Inclosing an extract from an ordinance of Congress relating to the employment of carriers of newspapers by the posts. Asks for an appointment in the post-office should a certain incumbent be removed. fol. 2 pages.

BUCHANAN, J. A., to SMITH, SAMUEL (General). *Washington.*

1807, no date, Baltimore. Arrival of the *Sidney.* Object of Mr. Rose's mission from Great Britain solely to atone for the attack on the *Chesapeake.* 4°. 2 pages.

BUCK, DANIEL, to MADISON. *Washington.*

1808, February 26, Norwich, *Vt.* The writer's views respecting the benefits to this country to be derived in consideration of the gigantic power of Napoleon, to amplify upon the provocations to a war against England and for her overthrow. 4°. 3 pages.

1809, February 24, Norwich, *Vt.* Europe being destined to the sway of one man, the writer advocates uniting with him for the destruction of England, so that the United States may control this continent. fol. 3 pages.

1811, July 4, Chelsea. The writer's views on the present condition of our affairs in relation to a probable conflict with England. Suggestions as to our cooperation with the designs of Napoleon. The South American Colonies. fol. 8 pages.

BUEL, SAMUEL. *Washington.*

1813, July 26, Washington. Had transmitted to the Acting Secretary of the Treasury communications to be presented to the President. Wishes redress for injustice to himself and others, and asks permission to lay the communication before him when his health and public business will permit. large fol. 1 page.

BUEL, SAMUEL.

1815, May 30, Washington. Complains of the injustice done him by the Secretary of the Treasury. 4°. 4 pages.

1815, June 27, Burlington. On the subject of his memorial. His object in writing is in vindication of his conduct. The unjust conclusions of the Secretary of the Treasury. Copies of letters with statements and observations bearing on his case. 4°. 12 pages.

BULL, EPAPHEAS, W. *Washington.*

1809, March 7, Danbury, Conn. The proceedings of the legislature are read with indignation by all friends of the administration. The people will support the General Government implicitly, immediately, and submissively. Wishes a letter from the President before the court sits. 4°. 3 pages.

BULLOCK, A. S., to JONES, WILLIAM. *Washington.*

1814, May 5, Savannah. (*See* William Jones's letter to Madison, dated June 6, 1814, lettered F.) [Copy.] fol. 1 page.

BULLUS, JOHN, to MADISON. *Washington.*

1811, May 4, New York. Inclosing a map for proposed canal from Lake Erie to the Hudson, with report of commissioners. 4°. 1 page.

BUMPASS, GABRIEL. *Washington.*

1812, March 20, Giles County, Tenn. Asks the President's advice and information touching the pretentions of North Carolina to issue grants on the vacant and ungranted lands west of the reservation. fol. 3 pages.

BURKE, R. *Washington.*

1801, June 5, Charleston. Introducing Mr. Brown, an Englishman of culture. 4°. 1 page.

BURKE, THOMAS, to BROOME (Alderman). *New York.*

1786, September 30, Loughburke. Asking information about his brother, John Burke. small 4°. 2 pages.

———, to BURKE, Mrs. THOMAS.

1787, August 4. (*See* Broome, to Thomas Burke, May 16.)

BURN, JAMES, to MADISON. *Montpellier.*

1824, February 23, Baltimore. Asks his aid in effecting the object in a letter inclosed, in reference to his son, James Madison Burn. 4°. 1 page.

1824, March 10, Baltimore. Acknowledges letter of February 3, and thanks him for his polite attention and kind wishes expressed in regard to his son. 4°. 1 page.

BURNET, DANIEL (Speaker of the House). *Washington.*

1814, January 11, Mississippi Territory. Memorial of the general assembly of Mississippi Territory praying the President and Congress to grant further indulgence to the purchasers of public lands and delay the enforcement of the land laws. 4°. 11 pages.

1814, December 29, Mississippi Territory. Unanimous resolution of the general assembly of Mississippi Territory repelling the aggressions and demands

BURNET, DANIEL.

of our enemy through the minister of the British Government to our ministers at Ghent, preferring a sacrifice of our lives and fortunes to the surrender of our rights. royal fol. 1 page.

BURNETT, ISAAC COX. *Washington.*

1801, October 10, Bordeaux. Complains of being superseded in his office by Mr. Lee without cause. Would accept the consulate at Lisbon. [Unsigned, noted as copy of Mr. B's letter.] [Copy.] 4°. 4 pages.

BURNLEY, HARDIN. *New York.*

1787, December 15, Richmond. Proceedings of the assembly at Richmond. fol. 2 pages.

1788, December 16, Richmond. Preparatory to election of Representatives to Congress it is thought advisable for Madison to be present in his district. Col. Monroe is also a candidate; his friends very active. Views and suggestions relative to the adoption of the Federal Constitution. An avowal of Madison's sentiments desirable. The Virginia legislature's proceedings. 4°. 3 pages.

1789, November 5, Richmond. Action of the committee on the amendments proposed by Congress. North Carolina said to have adopted the Constitution. 4°. 2 pages.

1789, November 28, Richmond. Business before the Virginia legislature. Question of the amendments proposed by Congress still in suspense. 4°. 3 pages.

Philadelphia.

1791, December 3, Richmond. The grant of land to Baron Steuben. The question of exemption of payment of fees. The Federal court in session in Richmond. Subject of British debts. fol. 2 pages.

BURRALL, CHARLES (Postmaster), to JEFFERSON. *Monticello.*

1814, March 6, Baltimore. The removal of Mr. Granger, Postmaster-General. Efforts made to remove subordinate officers. Asks Jefferson's good offices in having him (Burrall) retained in his office as postmaster in Baltimore. Relates his record for 14 years in that position. Sends a copy of his deposition relative to riotous proceedings in Baltimore. 4°. 3 pages.

Monticello.

1814, March 7, Baltimore. Inclosing an article from the "Whig" containing unfounded suggestions to his prejudice. Incloses a pamphlet containing his deposition alluded to in letter of 6th. 4°. 2 pages.

BURTCHETT, WILLIAM, to MADISON. *Washington.*

1816, July 5, Philadelphia. Appeal of a stranger and emigrant for a position in the Army, Navy, or any other occupation. 4°. 3 pages.

BURWELL, WILLIAM A *Washington.*

1805, December 14, Richmond. Character of the "Lynchburg Star." Its fitness for the publication of the laws of the United States. 4°. 1 page.

1809, February 17, Washington. The objections of Mr. Hull the supposed selection for the position of Secretary of War. 4°. 2 pages.

BURWELL, WILLIAM A.

1810, April 16, Washington. In view of the intelligence from Europe and other questions of national moment, he suggests the propriety of advising a message to continue the session. 4°. 1 page.

1813, February 19, Washington. Suggesting the appointment of Thomas M. Randolph for a colonel in the militia of Virginia. 4°. 1 page.

1814, March 21, Washington. Inclosing a letter from the president of the Farmer's Bank of Lynchburg. Attributes the evil (run on the banks) to the embargo and to defeat the loan. 4°. 1 page.

1815, February 1, Washington. Evils of the policy of defending Norfolk with the militia. Preferable to disband and dismantle the place if United States troops can not be spared. fol. 2 pages.

BUSHBY, WILLIAM. *Washington.*

1805, September 24, Washington. Appeals to Madison for his good offices that his place as painter on the public buildings may be retained. 4°. 2 pages.

BUTLER, MARIA. *Philadelphia.*

1793, November 23, Petersburg. Appeal of the widow of Gen. Butler for assistance from Congress. fol. 2 pages.

BUTLER, MANN. *Montpellier.*

1834, September 21, Richmond. The Spanish intrigues in 1788 to detach Kentucky from the American confederacy. Asks some points of Madison relating to that event and the views of Washington and Jefferson. Whether Wilkinson was connected improperly with Spain or Burr, and if Jefferson was satisfied with Wilkinson's fidelity. 4°. 4 pages.

BUTLER, PIERCE. *Philadelphia.*

1794, February 4. Highly approves of Madison's propositions in Congress. Let us combat Britain with every measure short of hostility. The seaports may exclaim, but the landed interest is with Madison. Suggests the policy of conciliating the Eastern members. [Signature cut off.] 4°. 2 pages.

1795, January 23, Charleston. Introducing Mr. Harper, a delegate from South Carolina. Butler's estimate of Harper's character and abilities. Mr. and Mrs. Monroe not pleased with their situation in Paris. No society. 4°. 2 pages.

Orange, Va.

1795, June 12, Philadelphia. Acknowledging a letter. Reading of the treaty in the Senate. Sends Madison a part of the document to read and send to Jefferson and to not communicate it further. A few copies only printed. Its constitutionality questioned. Its ratification problematical. 4°. 3 pages.

1795, August 21, Philadelphia. Acknowledging two letters. Underhand game playing with a view to injure Madison. The treaty signed and sent to England. Mercantile men's address controverting one presented against the treaty. President's of banks prominent in this. Coercing merchants who dread being refused discounts. Randolph's resignation. 4°. 2 pages.

BUTLER, PIERCE. *Federal City.*

1801, July 3, Philadelphia. Inclosing a letter from Dominick Hall, of South Carolina. Intense heat in Philadelphia. 4°. 1 page.

Washington.

1812, September 15, Philadelphia. Extract of a letter from the island of Great St. Simons. The President's intention of protecting the island by sending gunboats, not carried out. 4°. 2 pages.

1815, January 19, Philadelphia. In behalf of citizens of the seacoast of Georgia, requests permission, at their own expense, to replace buildings in the Bahama's destroyed by Capt. Thompson of privateer *Midas.* 4°. 1 page.

BYRNE, JAMES to GOODWYN, PETERSON.

Washington.

1812, June 5, Petersburg. In recommendation of Mordecai Barbour, a candidate for lieutenant-colonel. 4°. 1 page.

CABARET to MADISON. *Philadelphia.*

1787, July 4. Bill for binding books. [In French.] 4°. 1 page.

CABELL, JOSEPH C. *Montpellier.*

1817, August 22, Warminster. Returns papers respecting the nature of Atlantic coast climate. Subscriptions for the central college. 4°. 2 pages.

1818, February 16, Richmond. Sends Jefferson's bill on public education. Action of the assembly relative to it. They will do nothing for the central college. Views taken by delegates and others. Madison elected to the board of public works. 4°. 3 pages.

1819, July 10, Warminster. Methods for raising funds for the university. The debt due from the General Government. Extracts of letters inclosed respecting the interest paid by Virginia as constituting a claim against the United States Government. 4°. 4 pages.

1821, March 10, Richmond. The action of the legislature respecting the bill on public education. Matters relating to the university. Unpopularity of Dr. Cooper as president. 4°. 4 pages.

1823, April 16, Williamsburg. Conversations with Mr. Loyall on the plan and interior distribution of the library house of the university. 4°. 2 pages.

1825, April 6, Bremo. Conversation with Jefferson relating to the university. Mr. Barbour declines to accept the law chair. Difficulties in securing the position. Qualifications of Judge Carr, should he accept the appointment. 4°. 2 pages.

1826, November 23, Edgewood. Madison's report to the legislature. Offers to assist him in his second report in regard to the university. The expediency of finishing the buildings and discharging the debts of the university. The board unanimous as to the expediency of two additional professors —anatomy and natural history. Views as to professorships. 4°. 3 pages.

1827, January 24, Richmond. Acknowledging letter of 13th. Legislative action relative to the university and educational bill. Means suggested for reducing the debt of the university, etc. 4°. 2 pages.

CABELL, JOSEPH C.

1827, March 12, Richmond. Rising of the assembly. The writer's brother's insanity and death. Rejection by the House of the proposition to pay the university debt. Declines also to buy Jefferson's bust and library. The assembly pronounces the tariff unconstitutional. The writer's adherance to its constitutionality. Jefferson's letter. Asks Madison for information. 4°. 3 pages.

1827, October 25, Bremo. Concurs in the appointment of Dr. Thomas Jones, to fill the chair of natural philosophy in the university. small 4°. 1 page.

1827, October 25, Bremo. Suggestion to Madison that he write his views to the American minister in London to retain the services of Prof. Long another year, without loss to him in his promotion to his appointment in London. small 4°. 2 pages.

1827, December 15, Richmond. Death of Mr. Tucker. The university's claim for slaves carried off during the late war. Incloses a list of pamphlets of Judge Tucker in the hands of Chancellor Tucker. Prof. Long's usefulness to the university. 4°. 2 pages.

1828, January 12, Richmond. Urging him to reconsider his decision to decline to serve on the Presidential electoral ticket. Thinks he and Monroe should, under the circumstances, accept. 4°. 3 pages.

1828, March 1, Richmond. Sending him a loaned copy of first volume of Public Journals. 4°. 1 page.

1828, March 16, Williamsburg. Madison's appointment as visitor to the university. Opposition to the measure in the assembly to increase the lottery for the college. 4°. 3 pages.

1828, April 28, Washington. Acknowledging letter of March 27. Relative to the nomination of Dr. Jones's professorship. Trusts Madison's letter to Mr. Brougham will effect the desired arrangement as to Prof. Long. 4°. 2 pages.

1828, August 7, Warminster. Expediency of sounding Mr. Key as to the practicability of his return to the university to take the chair vacated by Mr. Long, of ancient languages. Importance of a price list of the library. 4°. 3 pages.

1828, September 2, Warminster. Acknowledging letter of August 18. On the subject of white wheat. Asks for the use of Madison's references on the tariff. 4°. 1 page.

1828, September 27, Warminster. Asks him to allow his letter on the tariff to be published. 4°. 1 page.

1828, October 10, Charlottesville. Madison's friends thinks his letter on the tariff should be published. It is not a party paper and defends principles to which he stands committed. It would do infinite good. If permitted, will publish it in the National Intelligencer. One hundred students in the unil versity. 4°. 2 pages-

1828, October 20, Edgewood. Acknowledging letter of 5th. Regrets that the publication of Madison's letter on the tariff is forbidden. Will make use of it after the election. 4°. 1 page.

1828, November 16, Edgewood. Acknowledging letter of October 30. Thanks him for his last letter on

CARELL, JOSEPH C.

the policy of the tariff, as a happy sequel to his first. Only regrets he was not allowed to give them to the public sooner. 4°. 1 page.

1828, November 20, Warminster. On the tariff. Mr. Jefferson's letter of December 26, 1825, on unfortunate production. 4°. 2 pages.

1828, November 26, Edgewood. Acknowledging letter of 22d. Corrects, as desired, portions of Madison's letters of September 18, and October 20. Goes to Richmond. 4°. 1 page.

1828, December 3, Warminster. Acknowledging letter of November 26. Asks Madison's wishes relative to the appointment of Mr. Davis to fill the place of Mr. Trist as secretary of the board of visitors of the university. Mr. Monroe's important paper. 4°. 1 page.

1828, December 28, Richmond. Acknowledging letter of 5th. Madison's letters published in the National Intelligencer. Producing a great effect. The question of proper basis of representation in the proposed convention. The office of secretary of the board of visitors of the university. Jefferson's bequest. 4°. 3 pages.

1829, January 29, Richmond. Acknowledging letter of 5th. Bill on the basis of representation. The tariff. 4°. 2 pages.

1829, February 24, Richmond. Acknowledging letters of 2d and 15th. Cabell's vote on the convention question. The tariff. The publication of Madison's letter. Tazewell author of pieces signed "Hampden." 4°. 4 pages.

1829, February 27, Richmond. Publication of the piece signed "The danger not over". Distribution of pamphlets containing Madison's letters. 4°. 2 pages.

1829, March 13, Williamsburg. An organized party in Virginia engaged in counteracting the Anti-Tariff party. The writer's exertions will be continued when his health permits. 4°. 1 page.

1829, March 16, Williamsburg. Gile's calumnies and misrepresentations. The publication of Madison's letters will destroy the effect. Asks for copies of letters on the constitutional powers or Congress to protect domestic manufactures. The President's message construed differently. Revenue duties. 4°. 2 pages.

1829, March 24, Williamsburg. Acknowledging letter of 19th. Madison's letters on the tariff. The effect of their publication. Thinks the tariff policy will be sustained through Jackson's administration. The enigmatical expression in his message on revenue duties. Will ask information of Madison to guide the writer in his researches in political history. 4°. 4 pages.

1829, May 14, Williamsburg. Acknowledging letter of March 4. Will postpone the copying of the letters sent him by Madison. 4°. 1 page.

1829, July 17, University. Regrets Madison's indisposition will prevent his visiting the university. Intends publishing Chaptal's two chapters on the tariff. 4°. 1 page.

1829, July 20, University. Extract of a letter from Richard Morris promising to see Mr. Pollard and get an answer to Madison's inquiry. 4°. 1 page.

CABELL, JOSEPH C.

1829, August 17, Edgewood. Inclosing a letter from Mr. Morris. 4°. 1 page.

1829, August 5, Warminster. Asking him to read an inclosed pamphlet from Cabell's pen, and inform him if his argument be sound respecting the Federal compact. 4°. 2 pages.

1829, August —. Anti-Tariff resolutions adopted by the legislature of Virginia at the sessions of 1825–'26, 1826–'27, 1828–'29. 4°. 2 pages.

Richmond (?).

1829, December 3, Richmond (?). Communicating with J. Randolph respecting letters in Jefferson's papers between the latter and Mr. Pendleton on the subject of the "Danger not over." States circumstances touching the subject of the convention. The basis of representation. Mixed and white. 4°. 3 pages.

Richmond.

1829, December 23, Williamsburg. Appointment of Judge Lomax. Respecting the appointment of Lomax's successor at the university. Suggests Judge Carr. Has written Mr. Slaughter, of the Senate, to examine the resolutions on the tariff. 4°. 2 pages.

Montpellier.

1830, February 7, Williamsburg. Acknowledging circular of January 30. Judge Lomax to combine the duties of the judicial office with his law lectures at the university. 4°. 1 page.

1830, May 26, Williamsburg. Touching Madison's expressed views on nullification. 3°. 3 pages.

1830, July 7, Richmond. Acknowledging letter of May 31. Incloses a letter of Gen. Cocke's. 4°. 1 page.

1830, August 3, Warminster. Inclosing letters relative to the place of assistant to the professor of modern languages. Qualifications of Col. La Pena. Mr. Hervé recommended by Lafayette and by the writer. 4°. 2 pages.

1830, October 8, Warminster. Dr. Blatterman's difficulties at the university. Nullification views. 4°. 2 pages.

1830, October 28, Edgewood. Respecting Dr. Blatterman and Col. Colonna at the university. Madison's letters to the North American Review on nullification has given great satisfaction. Mad conduct of the Southern States. 4°. 3 pages.

1831, March 3, Williamsburg. Acknowledging letter of February 9. Matters relating to the university. Proposal to augment the number of visitors. Political character of the university government. 4°. 2 pages.

1831, May 6, Williamsburg. Acknowledging letter of April 25. Dr. Patterson's dissatisfaction. His dislike to another professor, Dr. Dungleson. Will be a serious blow to lose these professors. Suggestions as to successors. 4°. 3 pages.

1831, July 20, University. Acknowledging letter of 11th. The visitors assembled at the university. Fears of losing Dr. Dungleson. Matters relating to the university. 4°. 2 pages.

CARELL, JOSEPH C.

1831, August 29, Warminster. Sends him a pamphlet in which he vindicates his course in the Virginia legislature on the subject of the Anti-Tariff resolutions of two years ago. Review of the writer's political course respecting Anti-Tariff and nullification. 4°. 8 pages.

1831, October 12, Edgewood. Acknowledging letter of 5th. The letters of Mr. Pendleton and R. H. Lee. A new and enlarged edition of the writer's pamphlet to be printed by resident citizens. 4°. 1 page.

1831, November 28, Warminster. Inclosing letters. Jefferson not the author of the second set of resolutions in the convention in Kentucky. Quotes Madison as authority for this fact. John Randolph's views on nullification. Assails the policy of the tariff but asserts its constitutionality. 4°. 3 pages.

1832, January 12, Richmond. Acknowledging letter of 2d. The course of Mr. Clay respecting the tariff. No important measures have passed this legislature. The subject of emancipation. Fears the subject will convulse us for years to come. 4°. 1 page.

1832, December 22, Richmond. On the subject of a motion in the house of delegates to print Madison's letters to the North American Review along with the report of 1799. Alleged change of Madison's opinions. Asks permission to print his letter to Judge Roane June 29, 1821, and to supply an omission in the writer's copy taken from the original. 4°. 2 pages.

1833, March 20, Warminster. Forwards copies of documents on the central improvement showing the course and direction of the writer's labors during the session. 4°. 1 page.

1833, March 27, Charlottesville. Returns Madison's letters to himself of December 27 and 28 as requested. Urges the publication of certain letters bearing on the tariff and nullification, and to enlighten the public on his views of particular constitutional questions. 4°. 2 pages.

1833, November 14, Warminster. The medical chair of the university. Dr. Magill. Scheme of the James River and Kanawha. Confident of the ultimate success of certain State improvements. 4°. 3 pages.

CABOT, SAMUEL.

1804 (?), no date. Opinion as to Mr. Cabot's salary. [He was commissioner to London to determine amount of British claims for violation of neutrality and American claims for illegal captures.] [Copy, unsigned.] 4°. 2 pages.

CADENA, MARIANO V. DE LA. *Washington.*

1811, January 26, New York. Presenting to the President a copy of a work entitled "Elements of the English Language." 4°. 1 page.

CADWALADER, THOMAS. *Washington.*

1812, May 30, Philadelphia. A piece of information in regard to the military state of Canada. This communication to be considered private. 4°. 2 pages.

CADWALADER, THOMAS.

1816, March 1, Philadelphia. Disbursing money received from the War Department in this district. Makes no charge for his services. Asks to be appointed commissioner of bankruptcy in the event of the passage of a bankrupt law. "Private." 4°. 1 page.

CAFFARENA, EDWARD. *Washington.*

1816, no date, Genoa. Ships a statue in alabaster of Napoleon crossing the Alps, by Henry Causici, scholar of Canova, by the ship *Gosport.* 4°. 2 pages.

1816, July 27, Genoa. Bill of lading of two boxes containing statue and footstall in alabaster per ship *Gosport* for Philadelphia. 8°. 1 page.

1817, July 12, Genoa. Has not heard of the reception of a statue of Napoleon sent Madison in July, 1816. Wishes an acknowledgment. 4°. 1 page.

Montpellier.

1820, December —, Genoa. Acknowledging letter of November 1, 1817. Apologizes for taking the liberty of sending Madison a statue of Napoleon. The original cost was $90, but will be satisfied with what he chooses to give. 4°. 2 pages.

CAINES, CLEM. *Washington.*

1811, April 2, St. Kitts. Assurances of his high esteem. Sends Madison his literary compositions. 4°. 1 page.

CALDWELL, CHARLES. *Montpellier.*

1825, June 16, Charlottesville. Longevity, size, and corporal strength and general efficiency of native Americans. Asks him to note whatever instances which may occur to him of individuals or families inclining towards gigantic size. Survivors of the Revolutionary Army. His object is to contradict statements abroad of influences of climate on the human race. 2°. 3 pages.

1826, October 11, Lexington, Ky. Acknowledging letter of 20th. The writers views on the science of phrenology. 4°. 3 pages.

1828, February 15, Lexington, Ky. Application to the legislature of Kentucky for additional funds for the Transylvania University. Asks what the general amount is given by Virginia to her university. 4°. 2 pages.

CALDWELL, JAMES. *Washington.*

1816, August 13, Philadelphia. Appeal for relief. 4°. 1 page.

CALDWELL, TIMOTHY, to MONROE, JAMES.

Washington.

1813, April 28, Philadelphia. Asks Monroe's good offices with the President in favor of the appointment of Gen. William Duncan as treasurer of the United States Mint. 4°. 2 pages.

CALHOUN, JOHN C., to MADISON. *Montpellier.*

1825, February 25, Washington. Introducing Mr Owen. 4°. 2 pages.

CALLENDER, E. *Montpellier.*

1823, February 16, Boston. On the cultivation of the olive. Plan of construction and management of the Virginia Agricultural College. 4°. 24 pages.

CALLENDER, E.

1825, June 12, Boston. Disappointed in not getting an answer to previous letter. The sensitive plant. How to find a spring of water by the aid of quicksilver. 4°. 2 pages.

1830, October 3, Camden, Me. The writer's disappointment in receiving no encouragement in opening an academy. Asks relief. small 4°. 2 pages.

CALLENDER, JAMES T. *Philadelphia.*

1796, May 28, Baltimore. Desiring occupation as a schoolmaster in the country. Asks Madison's aid in procuring for him some such situation. 4°. 3 pages.

Washington.

1801, January 23, Richmond. Wishing a situation under Government in the printing line. Sends Madison a newspaper. fol. 2 pages.

1801, April 15, Richmond. Denies statements made in a letter from Samuel H. Smith concerning himself. Gives his statement as to the probable origin of the story. [*See* letter of Samuel H. Smith to Callender, dated April 15, 1801.] 4°. 2 pages.

1801, April 15, Richmond. Appended to a letter from Samuel H. Smith relating to remission of a fine. Denies that the fine was remitted. 4°. 2 pages.

See SMITH, SAMUEL H.

1801, April 27, Petersburg. Expressing indignation in regard to an alleged promise of the President to remit a fine. Asks Madison's good offices in the procurement of the office of postmaster in Richmond. fol. 5 pages.

1801, May 7, Petersburg. Inclosing newspapers containing matters relating to the custom-house and of the official merit of Mr. Heath. Complains of ill temper and bad treatment of officials. fol. 2 pages.

CALLIS, W. O.

1784, August 9, Louisa. On the direction of the studies of the two sons of Mrs. Carr. small 4°. 1 page.

Philadelphia.

1790, December 20, Richmond. Claims one year's pay as a deranged (retired) officer in 1778. Is also entitled to bounty land. Asks Madison to make proper application that he may secure it. 4°. 1 page.

1791, October 29, Richmond. Inclosing a power of attorney to dispose of a land warrant. His claim as a supernumerary in 1778-'79. small 4°. 1 page.

1791, November 18, Richmond. Acknowledging letter of 10th. Thanks for his trouble and asks Madison to sell his land warrant. Proceedings of the house of delegates. 4°. 1 page.

1792, November 19, Richmond. Inclosing power of attorney to settle his claim for a full year's pay in 1778. Is chosen elector in his district to vote for President and Vice-President, and asks Madison's sentiments as a guide. 4°. 2 pages.

1792, December 2, Richmond. Acknowledging letter of November 25. Thanks Madison for his information respecting the competitors for the Vice-

CALLIS, W. O.

Presidency. Proceedings of the Virginia Assembly. 4°. 2 pages.

1792, December 9, Richmond. Acknowledging letter of November 27. Sends vouchers for his claim on Congress for back pay. 4°. 1 page.

CALVIN, A. *Washington.*

1813, February 17, New York. Commissioner of Foreign Relations favors the repealing the nonimportation act. Thinks starving the foe, nonimportation, and embargo is the best war measure. small 4°. 2 pages.

CAMBRELING, C. C. *Montpellier.*

1826, May 22, Washington. Sends Madison a gold medal commemorating the opening of the Erie Canal, presented by the corporation of New York city. 4°. 1 page.

CAMPBELL, ARTHUR.

1785, October 28, Washington, Pa. (?) Relating to the separation in Virginia. The fixing of boundaries. Has no fears that this country must eventually become a consolidated empire under one head and abolish different legislatures. 4°. 5 pages.

New York.

1787, January 2, Richmond. Important that the office of superintendent of the Southern Department should be filled. Suggests Col. Benjamin Hawkins, and, if not agreeable to him, will offer his own services. 4°. 2 pages.

1787, January 4. Commotions in Massachusetts. Importance of preparing the militia service. Conciliation of Indian tribes desirable. fol. 1 page.

1787, May 12, Washington County. Affairs of the Southern Department for Indian Affairs. The Spaniards and other intruders inciting the Indians to become our enemies. Is doubtful of the choice of the present superintendent. A company of U. S. troops should be stationed on the Tennessee above Cumberland Mountain. 4°. 2 pages.

——— to RANDOLPH, EDMUND. *New York.*

1787, November 20. Management of Indian affairs in the Southern Department. Incloses a few hints on the subject. 4°. 2 pages.

——— to MADISON. *Philadelphia.*

1796, January 24, Washington County. Offers his services in taking possession of the Western posts next summer with a select corps of riflemen. The treaty with Great Britain discussed. fol. 2 pages.

Washington.

1801, March 23, Washington County. Rejoices at the election of Jefferson. We should claim the right of the neutral flag, to have an injurious treaty with Great Britain amended, and be just to individuals. Now is the proper time to speak out. Asks for a position, as clerk, for the Rev. John Hargrove. fol. 3 pages.

1804, March 1, Washington County. Education of the Indians. A necessary measure. Question of the means of accomplishing it. Attempt of France, through her missionaries, to change the manners of Indians. Reading and writing must precede preaching. fol. 3 pages.

CAMPBELL, ARTHUR.

1807, July 11, Augusta. Schemes to counteract the hostile disposition of the British Government. Invasion of Canada. Asks him to interview Gen. Moreau. fol. 2 pages.

1807, August 27, Wythe. The hostile attack on our Atlantic coast. American citizens held on British men-of-war. No time to be composing resolutions. We should comply with the requisitions of Government in having our full quota of men ready for action. Suggests Gen. Moreau to take command of an expedition to Canada. 4°. 2 pages.

1808, September 5, Lee, Va. Sentiments of the people of Tennessee and Kentucky relating to the embargo. They ask why did not Congress embargo money as well as ships. British capital. No uniformity in the States in the recovering of debts. 4°. 2 pages.

CAMPBELL, G. W. *Washington.*

1814, April 30, Washington. Inclosures from the Treasury Department in relation to appointment of a principal assessor in the Eleventh district. 4°. 1 page.

1814, May 4, Washington. The loan of $10,000,000 effected. Account of the negotiation. 4°. 3 pages.

Washington.

1814, May 21, Washington. Inclosing memorial of officers in Jackson's army; also, a letter from Governor Blount. 4°. 1 page.

1814, May 22, Washington. Relative to a loan. Suggestion of Mr. Astor. Arrangements of Mr. Barker for paying the first instalment of the loan taken by him. Events in Europe baffle all calculations. 4°. 3 pages.

1814, June 6, Washington. Inclosing letters from D. A. Smith. The markets in England and continent for our public stocks. Also a letter from Mr. Astor. 8°. 1 page.

1814, September 26, Washington. Tendering his resignation on account of ill health. 4°. 2 pages.

1814, December 18, Nashville. Acknowledging letter of November 2. He complied with the inquiry of the House of Representatives as to the causes of late military events in Washington respecting the part Gen. Armstrong was to take, and Madison's conversation with Armstrong. 4°. 4 pages.

1826, June 18, Nashville. Introducing Mr. Cramer. 4°. 1 page.

CAMPBELL, HUGH G., to JONES, WILLIAM. *Washington.*

1814, May 21, St. Marys, Ga. *See* William Jones letter to Madison June 6, 1814, lettered F. [Extract.] fol. 2 pages.

CAMPBELL, JAMES, and others, to MADISON. *Washington.*

1810, February 12, Knoxville. Lottery to defray the expense of a library in East Tennessee College. Offers tickets to the President. 4°. 2 pages.

CAMPBELL, J. H. *Montpellier.*

1834, October 3, Columbus, Ga. Sends him address of the nullification party. Asks additional light

CAMPBELL, J. H.

on the report drawn by Madison and passed by the Virginia legislature. The State elections. The contest will be warm. fol. 1 page.

CAMPBELL, JOHN. *New York.*

1787, February 21, Pittsburg. Indignation and reprobation of the West respecting the cession of navigation of the Mississippi to Spain. Depredations of the Indians. 4°. 4 pages.

CAMPBELL, WILLIAM. *Washington.*

1812, March 22, Charleville. Flattery followed by advice as to the President's course to pursue in public affairs. fol. 2 pages.

CANBY, J. T.

1815, May 5, Washington. Purchase of a horse from Kentucky named "Speculator." Gives his pedigree by Thomas Arnold under date February 14, 1815. 4°. 1 page 8°. 1 page.

CANBY, WILLIAM.

1812, (?) No date. Iniquities of the people in this land and their blind pride, has brought on the dreadful scourge which threatens us. Sympathizes with rather than condemns well-minded rulers in their endeavors to govern a tumultuous and unholy generation. (Probably referring to the war just declared.) 4°. 1 page.

CANNON, ROQUIER.

1811, September 19. Passing certificate of Roquier Cannon, lieutenant of H. B. M. ship *Eagle.* fol. 2 pages.

CAPELLANO, ANTONIO. *Montpellier.*

1817, September 5, Baltimore. Wishes to make a marble bust of Madison and asks when he can visit him at Montpellier. 4°. 1 page.

CARBERY, H., and TAYLOR, JAMES. *Washington.*

1808, June 13. A mutual agreement that all differences between them are accommodated, Carbery declaring he had no intention of injuring Taylor, and Taylor retracting any expressions reflecting on Carbery. [Copy.] 4°. 1 page.

CARBERY, THOMAS, to GOLDSBOROUGH, C. W.

1813, January 19, Washington. Mr. Salvadora awaits official orders to relate to the President facts relative to powder, fearing the commodore will discharge him from the yard. 4°. 1 page.

CARDELL, W. S., to MADISON. *Montpellier.*

1820, March 4, New York. Inclosing a circular of a literary society. Asks that in case Mr. Jefferson declines being its president Madison will accept the office. 4°. 2 pages.

1821, January 12, New York. The organization of a literary institution and gives the names of the officers. Madison elected honorary member as a tribute of respect. 4°. 2 pages.

1821, May 2, Orange C. H. Will call on Madison to state the circumstances and prospects of the "American Academy of Language and Belles-lettres." 4°. 1 page.

CARDELLI, G.

1819, August 19, Washington. Forwarding busts of Jefferson, Madison, Monroe, and J. Q. Adams. 4°. 2 pages.

CARDELLI, G.

1819, October 29, Washington. Forwarding boxes containing busts with pedestals. 4°. 1 page.

1819, November 11, Washington. About a bust of Jefferson and two medals. Is working at the Capitol at carving. Wishes Madison to recommend him to his friends. 4°. 1 page.

1820, July 19, Washington. Sends Madison some busts. Leaves soon for a tour to New Orleans. [In French.] fol. 1 page.

CAREY, JOHN.

No date. Receives money for some books which he incloses. 4°. 1 page.

Philadelphia.

1795 (?), February 8. Requests him to send him a copy of his speech on the fishery bill. 4°. 2 pages.

1795, March 31, London. Sends a copy of the President's official correspondence. It is unfinished. Would like to complete the task if he could get some Government position to defray his expenses for a year or two, the time required. 4°. 2 pages.

CAREY, MATTHEW. *Washington.*

1812, August 1, Philadelphia. Corruption of the American press, especially that of New England. The Federals made tools of by the press by misrepresentation. The British restrictions in the Colonial trade. Sends a pamphlet on the subjcet. 4°. 3 pages.

1812, August 12, Philadelphia. It is an error to suppose that the determination of the leaders of the Federal party to dissolve the Union arose from the measures of the last administration. Suggests that any attempt to dissolve the Union be a high crime and subject to severe penalty. [Incloses a newspaper cutting showing the corruption of the press.] 4°. 5 pages.

1812, September 24, Philadelphia. Acknowledging letter of 19th. Corrects a misconception in a previous letter. Associations to frustrate Federalism. Any neglect to take every fair means to save the country from menaced ruin would be lamentable infatuation. 4°. 2 pages.

1813, January 25, Philadelphia. Associations to strangle treason as it exists, especially in New England, in the pay of England. A daring conspiracy. Employment of the press by a suitable management by Government to detect and expose the infamy of the corrupt press. Suggests the employment of Jonathan Russel with assistance of Mr. Coxe. 4°. 12 pages.

1813, December 15, Philadelphia. The state of parties in New England. The majority loyal, but the minority, under an excellent organization, bids fair to involve the country in civil war. The means suggested, an Union society to give the proper efficiency to the numerical force of the friends of the Government. 4°. 5 pages.

1814, February 19, Philadelphia. The writer's efforts for the past five years vain toward the union of the friends of republican government. The miserable minority in New England, owing to its admirable management, have lost Massachusetts,

CAREY, MATTHEW.

New Hampshire, Vermont, and Rhode Island to the Republican party. Had his suggestions been listened to it would have been saved. One more effort. Incloses a letter. 4°. 3 pages.

1814, September 14, Philadelphia. His attempt to harmonize the Federal and Republican parties has failed because Carey's simple measures were not adopted. Believes that the introduction of some Federalist of character, purity of intention, and talents into Madison's administration is the sole salvation tending to unite the country. 4°. 2 pages.

1814, October 30, Philadelphia. Complains that his correspondence with Madison for the last six years has disappointed all his expectations. Has begged him to give his plans a trial to conciliate political parties, and now we are on the verge of civil war and anarchy. It is barely possible Union societies may yet avert perdition. Incloses a constitution. 4°. 4 pages.

Montpellier.

1814, October 30, Philadelphia. Constitution of the Washington Union Society. 4°. 4 pages.

Washington.

1814, November 16, Philadelphia. Inclosing his letter of October 30, which he delayed sending, hoping we might escape the perdition that menaced us. We are gone past redemption. Madison might have avoided it had he not neglected his advice. Even now energy, decision, and fortitude at the seat of Government might save the destiny of eight millions of people. 4°. 2 pages.

1815, February 3, Philadelphia. Acknowledging letter of January 28. Is pleased at Madison's approbation of his work. Asks if certain indicated documents can be procured in Washington. 4°. 2 pages.

1820, January 26, Philadelphia. Inclosing a copy of the addresses of the "Philadelphia Society for the Protection of National Industry." 4°. 1 page.

Montpellier.

1821, May 16, Philadelphia. Sends by this day's mail a set of papers to prove the pernicious effects of our present policy for our agriculturalists. [Annexed is an advertisement of books for sale by M. Carey & Son.] fol. 1 page.

1821, June 26, Philadelphia. Acknowledging letter of May 26. Highly appreciates Madison's approbation of the writer's course of conduct. Our present policy impoverishes the country. A radical remedy for the distresses of agriculturalists. 4°. 4 pages.

1821, December 1, Philadelphia. Asks for information about the balance of trade between Great Britain and the Southern Colonies previous to the war. 4°. 1 page.

1822, October 3, Philadelphia. Advocating protection to manufactures. 4°. 3 pages.

1822, November 1, Philadelphia. Subject of the tariff, which he advocates. 4°. 2 pages.

CAREY, MATTHEW.

1822, November 12, Philadelphia. The injustice to our manufacturers. Selfishness of farmers. Plea for protection to manufactures. 4°. 3 pages.

1822, November 25, Philadelphia. Sends Nos. 2 and 3 of "Hamilton." Asks Madison to reflect on the subject. The wealth, power, and resources of the United States depends on our adopting the policy which has wrought wonders for Great Britain, France, and every country which has followed their example. 4°. 2 pages.

1823, September 21, Philadelphia. Sends documents to show the ruinous policy proposed for this country, whereby our resources are lavished in support of the industry of foreign governments. Asks information about tobacco. 4°. 1 page.

1824, February 19, Philadelphia. Sends three pamphlets. 4°. 1 page.

1824, February 28, Philadelphia. Sends copy of a recent pamphlet, which he hopes will be read attentively. Deleterious consequences of the proposed policy of this country. 4°. 1 page.

1824, June 5, Philadelphia. Recommending John Saunderson, a professor of modern languages. Should any opportunity of bettering his condition offer hopes Madison will bear him in mind. 4°. 2 pages.

1824, September 3, Philadelphia. Acknowledging letter of August 11. Relating to the tariff. Arguments in its favor. 4°. 4 pages.

1825, April 22, Philadelphia. Sends some of his recent publications. Asks materials for the "Annals." 4°. 1 page.

1827, October 5, Philadelphia. Sends 30 copies of an essay on a subject of vast importance to Virginia and Southern States. Requests Madison to circulate them. 4°. 2 pages.

1827, October 6, Philadelphia. An error in his essay on slave labor sent 5th. Wishes them destroyed and will send corrected copies. 4°. 1 page.

1827, December 13, Philadelphia. Acknowledging letter of 7th. Transmits essays. Has retired from business and devotes his time to endeavors to promote our National prosperity. 4°. 1 page.

1828, April 12, Philadelphia. Sends essays. Soundness of the Hamiltonian system of policy. 4°. 1 page.

1828, April 28, Philadelphia. Recommending, for the vacancy in the chair of classics in the university, Mr. M. L. Tracie. 4°. 1 page.

1829, February 16, Philadelphia. Sending a circular letter, annexed, relating to the publication of a series of essays, dated February 9, 1829. 4°. 2 pages.

1829, March 9, Philadelphia. Submitting a circular letter, annexed, requesting Madison to furnish him materials of a series of essays. 4°. 2 pages.

1829, November 1, Philadelphia. Sends copies of two essays on the protective system with a request to deliver them to members of the convention. 4°. 1 page.

CAREY, MATTHEW.

1829, November 27, Philadelphia. Sends essays on the protective system. His object is to allay fermentation existing in South Carolina and Georgia. 4°. 1 page.

1830, August 6, Philadelphia. Sends a series of papers on the tariff intended to dispel delusions under which many citizens of the Southern States labor. 4°. 1 page.

1831, July 21, Philadelphia. Sends essay exposing the fallacy and deception of the nullifiers of South Carolina. 4°. 2 pages.

CARLTON, MOSES. JR., to GERRY, ELBRIDGE. *Washington.*

1813, September 10, Wiscasset. Recommending Samuel Parker, of Salem, as district collector of direct taxes. 4°. 2 pages.

CARPENTIER, DENIS.

1796, ——— —, Paris. *Procès verbal* of commissary of police respecting the robbery of money belonging to the United States deposited with Fulwar Skipwith. [In French.] [*See* Pulwar Skipwith's letter of July 27, 1796.] 4°. 5 pages.

CARPENTER, THOMAS, to MADISON. *Washington.*

1806, November 8. Tailor's bill receipted 4° 1 page.

1810 (?), no date. Cost of cassimere (domestic) suitable for waistcoat and small clothes. 4°. 1 page.

CARR, D.

1802, June 21, Washington. Recommending Mr. Hanson to supply the place of Mr. Wagner. His unblemished character. 4°. 2 pages.

1807, September 11, Charlottesville. Wishes a certificate of citizenship and passport for Mr. David Yancy, who proposes going to Madeira for his health. 4°. 1 page.

CARR, FRANK. *Montpellier.*

1830, November 17, Charlottesville. Sends accounts of the bureau and proctor of the university, and a report for the president and directors of the literary fund. small 4°. 1 page.

1831, August 9, Charlottesville. Introducing Mr. Jacobs, principal of the Deaf and Dumb Asylum of Danville, Ky. 4°. 1 page.

1833, May 8, Red Hills. Inclosing certain papers asked for relating to the University. 4°. 1 page.

1833, November 30, Charlottesville. Sends, as rector of the university, voluminous reports to be forwarded under Madison's frank to Mr. Cabell, rector *pro tempore.* 4°. 1 page.

CARR, M.

1785, April 18. Relating to his two sons. Reasons why they have not been placed at school agreeable to Madison's appointment. small 4°. 2 pages.

1786, August 21, Monticello. Requesting Madison to give his approval of the change made in the course of reading of his son at school. 4°. 1 page.

CARR, PETER. *New York.*

1789, July 13. Relative to some money due Mr. Jefferson to be applied to the use of his brother and himself. fol. 1 page.

CARR, PETER. *Washington.*

1803, January 29, Richmond. Introducing William Brockenbroug. 4°. 1 page.

1813, March 17, Carr's Brook. Death of Mr. Barlow, late minister to France. Asks to be appointed secretary of legation. 4°. 1 page.

CARR, SAMUEL J. *Montpellier.*

1833, July 19, Washington. Asks for an autograph letter stating the condition of Madison's health. 4°. 2 pages.

CARRINGTON, EDWARD. *Philadelphia.*

1786, December 18, New York. Acknowledging letter of 4th. Is pleased at Col. Lee's reelection and deeply affected by loss of Mr. Jones from the delegation. Mr. Jay and the business of the Mississippi. The business of the convention. Dereliction of Massachusetts to be apprehended. 4°. 3 pages.

1786, December 27, New York. Intends going to Virginia. Recommends Madison to be there as early as possible. Incloses letter from Calonna, comptroller-general of finances of France. 4°. 2 pages.

1787, June 13, New York. Acknowledging letter of 10th. The writer's views and suggestions on the formation of the Federal constitution. fol. 4 pages.

1787, July 25, New York. Acknowledging a letter inclosing one to Jefferson which he will forward through care of Chevalier Jones. Action of Congress relating to Indian affairs and our Western territory. A general confederacy of all the tribes of the Six Nations. Treaties proposed. Precautions for defense. 4°. 4 pages.

1787, August 11, New York. Acknowledging letters of 3d and 8th. Mr. Turner's fitness for a seat on the bench. Indian affairs in Congress. Report of the convention. Suggestions that a convention by the people be held to accept or reject the project of the new plan of government. (Part of this letter missing.) 4°. 4 pages.

1787, September 23, New York. Schism in Virginia and New York in the convention. Proposition for essential alterations in the constitution. Action in Congress to consider the business of the convention. Opposition in New York. Col. Hamilton. 4°. 3 pages.

1788, January 18, Richmond. Speculations as to the action of States in respect to the adoption of the proposed constitution. 4°. 4 pages.

1788, February 10, Manchester. Sentiments in Virginia relative to the new proposed constitution. Mr. Henry's followers. The writer's opinion that Henry's views are a dismemberment of the Union. The writer's efforts for preserving the Union. 4°. 6 pages.

1788, April 8, Richmond. Acknowledging letter of March 3. The various sentiments in Virginia respecting the adoption of the constitution. 4°. 4 pages.

Orange.

1788, April 23, New York. Forwards packets from France. Proceedings in Rhode Island relative to the constitution. Will probably not adopt. 4°. 2 pages.

CARRINGTON, EDWARD.

1788, May 28, New York. Steps taken by Mr. Adams for negotiating a loan in Holland. British act of Parliament upon the subject of our trade with the different territories of that nation. Attitude of New Hampshire in respect to the constitution. 4°. 6 pages.

1788, May 31, New York. Ordinance of the Province of Quebec for regulating inland commerce with the United States. Our commercial intercourse with the West Indies. 4°. 3 pages.

Richmond.

1788, June 17, New York. Acknowledging letter of 6th. Satisfaction as to the prospect in Virginia relative to the constitution. The convention of New York at Poughkeepsie. Anti-Federalists received a shock from accounts from Virginia. Will probably adjourn without adopting the constitution. 4°. 3 pages.

1788, June 25, New York. Acknowledging letter of 13th. The convention of New York. Speeches of the chancellor for, and Mr. Lansing against, the constitution. 4°. 2 pages.

CARRINGTON, EDWARD, BROWN, J., GRIFFIN, C., jointly. *Richmond.*

1788, June 25, New York. Inclosing a letter from Ph. Schuyler and copy of one from Jno. Langdon to A. Hamilton, announcing the adoption of the constitution in New Hampshire. 4°. 1 page.

CARRINGTON, EDWARD. *New York.*

1788, October 19, Fredericksburg. Conversation with Washington at Mount Vernon on the probable politics of the Virginia assembly in respect to the Federal constitution. fol. 3 pages.

1788, October 22, Richmond. Conjectures as to the action of the assembly relative to the constitution. The election of Senator. Madison should be put in nomination. His own chances of election to the House. 4°. 4 pages.

1788, October 24, Richmond. The election decided upon as invalid. The writer's prospects in undergoing another election. Complexion of the legislature in respect to general politics and the Federal constitution. 4°. 6 pages.

1788, November 1, Powhatan. The spirit of anti-Federalism in the house of delegates. The writer's election still undecided. small 4°. 2 pages.

1788, November 9, Richmond. Election of R. H. Lee as Senator from Virginia to Congress. Reasons for Madison's defeat. Bill passed the Virginia legislature for election of electors of President. The disqualifying act. The voice of Virginia will be for Washington as President. Proceedings of the House. Election of a Representative to Congress. 4°. 7 pages.

1788, November 15, Richmond. Proceedings of the Virginia assembly on the subject of a convention. Bill for district elections of Representatives. Conjectures as to Madison's election. Suggests the publication of Madison's letter to Mr. Tuberville to give the lie to reports mentioned, and condemn the measure of a convention. 4°. 7 pages.

CARRINGTON, EDWARD.

1788, November 18, Richmond. Acknowledging letters of 4th and 6th. Sends journals containing drafts of letters on the subject of a convention. Passage in the House of the disqualifying act. Its object. Not yet ascertained who will be started against Madison in the election of Representative. Monroe may be the man. Expect no favors from him. 4°. 5 pages.

1788, November 26, Richmond. Monroe is to be Madison's opponent. Cabell and Strother combined in his favor. Monroe's political hostility. Reforms in the judiciary system. 4°. 3 pages.

1788, December 2, Richmond. Acknowledging letter of November 23. The coming election for United States Representative. Does not think it advisable for Madison to come to Virginia. Thinks Madison's election tolerably safe. Bill for reforming the judiciary. 4°. 4 pages.

1788, December 19, Richmond. Acknowledging letter of 10th. Does not think Madison's presence in Virginia will make any difference to the issue of the election. The candidates in other districts. Bill for reducing taxes one-third passed the house. 4°. 4 pages.

1788, December 30, Richmond. Has heard of Madison's arrival in Virginia. Advises him to give his attention principally to Culpeper and Spottsylvania. Those two counties will determine the election. The writer does not offer himself for his district. Bland is the only declared candidate. A push for declaring Clinton for Vice-President. 4°. 3 pages.

1789, February 16, Richmond. Acknowledging letter of January 20. Election of Adams for Vice-President. Congratulates Madison on his election to the House. Reflections on the politics of Virginia. 4°. 3 pages.

1789, February 20, Powhatan. Has given up any hope of getting into the House of Representatives on account of his Federalism. Enumerates his services to the Government in the war and since, and if it can be arranged asks Madison's good offices in procuring some Government appointment. Collector of customs at Norfolk would be a desirable berth. 4°. 3 pages.

1789, April 14, Powhatan. Acknowledging letter of March 19. Is gratified at Madison's friendly sentiments. The office which he mentioned in his last letter being filled, would be glad to be appointed to same other one which he is fitted for. 4°. 2 pages.

1789, May 12, Richmond. Acknowledging letter of April 8. Action in Congress relative to duties and tonnage, discrimination between our own and foreign bottoms. 4°. 2 pages.

1789, May 27, Powhatan. Acknowledging letter of May 8. The spirit of concession and accommodation in the House of Representatives. The motion of placing Great Britain upon the footing of the most favored nation is incomprehensible. A cold spring. 4°. 2 pages.

1789, July 30, Powhatan. Debates in Congress touching on the powers of the President to remove officers of the Executive Department. The writer's views. 4°. 2 pages.

CARRINGTON, EDWARD.

1789, August 3, Richmond. Acknowledging letters of July 20 and 22. The tonnage bill. Discrimination. Our natural advantages over Great Britain. The judiciary system as sketched by Mr. Granger. 4°. 2 pages.

1789, September 9, Richmond. Acknowledging letters of August 12, 26, and 28. Sentiments of the people of North Carolina. Their reconciliation to the Constitution. Representation discussed. The permanent position of the Government. Compensation of members. 4°. 5 pages.

1789, September 9, Richmond. Asking Madison's opinion on his acceptance of the position of the office of district marshal for Virginia, should it be offered him. 4°. 2 pages.

Orange.

1789, December 20, Richmond. Acknowledging Madison's friendly attentions. Has received a commission from the President of district marshal for this district. Will accept it. Business of the session of the assembly. Mr. Henry's speech. Subject of the amendments to the Constitution. 4°. 6 pages.

New York.

1790, February 5, Richmond. Acknowledging letter of January 24. Thanking Madison for his remarks concerning his appointment under the Federal Government. The plan for supporting the public credit. Great rise in grain. 4°. 2 pages.

1790, March 2, Richmond. Acknowledging letters of February 2 and 14. His views on the reports of the Treasury and War departments. The public credit and taxes. 4°. 4 pages.

1790, March 27, Richmond. On Madison's motion on the mode of treating the public debt. Assumption of State debts. 4°. 7 pages.

1790, April 1, Richmond. Asks to be informed what will be done in Congress in respect to the emoluments of the marshal's office. Enumerates the duties and the inadequate compensation. 4°. 3 pages. fol. 1 page.

1790, April 7, Richmond. On the Quaker memorial relating to emancipation in the House of Representatives. Assumption of State debts. 4°. 2 pages.

1790, April 30, Richmond. Acknowledging letters of 10th and 17th. Assumption of State debts. Thanking Madison for his observations on the establishment of the marshal's office. Incloses advertisement for assistants for taking the census. 4°. 4 pages.

1790, May 3, Richmond. Respecting the census. Penalties under which the people are compelled to render returns. [Asks him to take measures for remedy.] 4°. 2 pages.

1790, August 1, Fredericksburg. His tour upon the business of the census completed. Locality of the residence of the Government. The crops. fol. 2 pages.

Philadelphia.

1790, December 24, Richmond. Acknowledging letter of August 29. Resolutions of the Virginia

CARRINGTON, EDWARD.

assembly on assumption of State debts. The assembly agree to pay another year's interest on the military debt. The judiciary system. Incloses some money. 4°. 2 pages.

1790, December 25, Richmond. Recommends his friend, Mr. Giles, the successor of Col. Bland, a Representative of his district in Congress, to Madison's particular attention. 4°. 2 pages.

1791, February 2, Powhatan. Acknowledging letter of January 2. The excise bill. The use of banks. The national bank. small 4°. 2 pages.

1791, February 26, Richmond. Acknowledging letter of January 26. Sentiments of the people respecting the excise and banks. The census of Virginia. Claims for pay of assistants. 4°. 5 pages.

1791, April 20, Richmond. Acknowledging letter of February 27. Question of the constitutionality of the bank. The people becoming reconciled to the excise. The President leaves for Petersburg. The census. Decides to accept the appointment of supervisor. 4°. 3 pages.

1791, July 15, Richmond. Madison's return from a Northern tour. Completion of the Virginia census. The people being reconciled to the excise. Incloses a power to receive sums of money due him as marshal. 4°. 4 pages.

Orange.

1791, September 21, Richmond. Acknowledging letter of August 28. The excise becoming better understood and better liked as alternative for taxation. Visit to Southampton, in County of Isle of Wight, Va., on account of a riot against the collector. Bounty land of the Baron de Steuben. 4°. 4 pages.

CARRINGTON, PAUL, JR. *Washington.*

1812, July 17, Charlotte. Transmits copy of proceedings of the people of Charlotte at their courthouse. Coincidence of the people and Madison's sentiments. The freedom of the St. Lawrence may be gained with little loss of blood. His sons and nephews are equipped in volunteer companies, and are ready to march at a moment's warning. Incloses E. Carrington's speech to people of Halifax, July 4. 4°. 2 pages.

No *date, 1812 (?).* Representations respecting a law confiscating British debts. Vindicating himself from charges attempting to blacken his character. fol. 1 page.

CARROLL, DANIEL. *New York.*

1786, March 13, Annapolis. Proposition of the assembly of Maryland for a meeting of commissioners from all the States to adjust a general commercial system. small 4°. 2 pages.

1787, October 28, Georgetown. Acknowledging letter of 17th. Not a single member of the Virginia legislature but Patrick Henry who is not in favor of the new Government. Anecdote of Col. Mason. 4°. 3 pages.

1788, February 10, Georgetown. Conjectures as to the adoption of the constitution. 4°. 1 page.

1788, April 28, Georgetown. Acknowledging letter of 10th. Proceedings of the convention. Expected

CARROLL, DANIEL.

that this day will close the proceedings. Conjectures as to the vote. In a postscript states he hears the constitution had been adopted. Illuminations at Annapolis. small 4°. 2 pages.

1788, May 22. Acknowledging letter of April 10. Incloses the address of the minority of the convention. 4°. 1 page.

1788, May 28. A confidential letter respecting the elections in Maryland and misrepresentations made by prominent politicians respecting the framers of the constitution. The advocates of a "kingly government." A letter declared to be of Jefferson's relating to the constitution. fol. 3 pages.

1789, May 22. Returns estimates respecting a certain branch of the revenue. 4°. 1 page.

New York.

1789, October 4, Philadelphia. Question as to the permanent seat of Congress. 4°. 1 page.

Philadelphia.

1790, November 26, Annapolis. Incloses a copy of a resolution passed by the general assembly of Maryland respecting money to be advanced from Virginia and Maryland towards erecting public buildings. 4°. 1 page. fol. 1 page.

1791, April 6, Georgetown. Relating to the plan of the Federal City. Incloses articles of agreement (copy) of the proprietors of the land within the proposed limits. 4°. 3 pages.

1791, April 23, Georgetown Relative to the lines of the proposed Federal City. Maj. L'Enfant to give a description of the grounds within the limits. Change of property; its value since the purchase. fol. 3 pages.

1791, July 24. Georgetown. Matters relating to the Federal City. The census of Maryland. Addition to representation. fol. 2 pages.

1791, October 21, Georgetown. Sales of lots in various parts of the Federal City. 8°. 1 page.

1791, November 22, Georgetown. Asks Madison to subscribe for Mr. Freneau's paper. 4°. 1 page.

1791, November 25, Georgetown. Acknowledging letter of 25th. The house of Mr. D. Carroll, of Duddington, pulled down by L'Enfant's directions without consulting the commissioners. 4°. 1 page.

1791, November 29, Georgetown. Relating to the house of D. Carroll, of Duddington. Incloses a memorandum detailing the particulars of Maj. L'Enfant's action relating to the destruction of it. 4°. 3 pages.

1791, November 29, Georgetown. The demolishion of the house of D. Carroll, of Duddington, by Maj. L'Enfant. Action of the commissioners. 4°. 2 pages.

1791, December 12, Georgetown. Transmitting copy of the act of the Maryland assembly concerning the territory of Columbia and the city of Washington. 4°. 1 page

CARROLL, DANIEL.

1791, December 13, Georgetown. On the demolition of D. Carroll's house at Duddington. Maj. L'Enfant's letter. Action of the commissioners. 4°. 3 pages.

1791, December 20, Bladensburg. The law concerning the territory of Columbia. Fears that Charles Carroll, of Carrollton, will not be present at this session of Congress. Has written him urging the importance of his presence. 4°. 3 pages.

1791, December 21, Georgetown. Memorial from proprietors of land respecting D. Carroll of Duddington's house and in favor of Maj. L'Enfant. Transfers of property. Appointment of a clerk. 4°. 1 page.

1791, December 21, Georgetown. The representation bill. 4°. 1 page.

1791, December 26, Georgetown. Failure of the representation bill. The residence act attacked. A scheme for some wicked purpose. 4°. 1 page.

1791, December 30, Georgetown. Acknowledging letters of 20th and 25th. Charles Carroll, of Carrollton, intends going to Philadelphia on the 10th. The representation bill to be taken up. Illness of his aged parent. small 4°. 2 pages.

1792, January 5, Georgetown. Irritation in this session about representation. Business of the commissioners. 4°. 2 pages.

1792, January 8, Georgetown. Acknowledging letter of 1st. Commissioner's business with Maj. L'Enfant and Ellicott. small 4°. 2 pages.

1792, January 18, Georgetown. Acknowledging letter of 10th. The representation bill. Scandal to the effect that Mr. Brent had information given him of the extent of the commissioner's orders for the purchase of his quarries through the writer. Declares it to be an infamous slander. 4°. 2 pages.

1792, January 26, Georgetown. Steps taken to confound the perpetrators of the scandal about himself. Surmises as to action of Congress. Subject of the Federal City. Copy of a certificate from Mr. Brent denying he had any intimation from anybody of the price that the commissioners would give for his property. 4°. 2 pages.

1792, February 7, Georgetown. Acknowledging letter of 2d. Transmits letters for Mr. C. Carroll for their mutual information. 4°. 1 page.

1792, February 23, Georgetown. Acknowledging letter of 16th. The representation bill. Contest about the President of the Senate *pro tempore* and the Secretary of State for the time being. fol. 1 page.

1792, March 8, Georgetown. Acknowledging letter of February 28. Results of the negotiations with Maj. L'Enfant. The public buildings advancing. Exorbitant and unreasonable expectations of D. Carroll, of Duddington, and Robert Peter, may check the public good and do prejudice to themselves. Memorandum giving account of sales of property and prices given. 4°. 2 pages

1792, March 26, Georgetown. Business of the commissioners with the proprietors. Fears of disturbing the President in these matters. Conjec-

CARROLL, DANIEL.

tures as to the representation and assumption bills. 4°. 2 pages.

1792, March 29, Georgetown. The Maryland delegation against the assumption bill except one. Plans of the commissioners to locate the Government. 4°. 1 page.

1792, April 9, Georgetown. Acknowledging letter of 1st. Fate of the assumption bill. Accounts from France. 4°. 1 page.

Orange.

1792, June 27, Georgetown. Acknowledging letter of 12th. Sale of lots in the city of Washington to commence October 8. Hopes Madison may be present. Jefferson's desire that the assemblies of Virginia and Maryland build a few houses in the city. Affairs in France. Fears of Jacobins. Extinguishment of the public debt. 4°. 2 pages.

Philadelphia.

1792, August 17, Georgetown. Acknowledging letter of 24th. Is sorry to find Madison's hopes of the active cooperation of Virginia in forwarding the city of Washington are languishing. The writer's views of the political state of affairs in America. Reasons against Carroll's entering the stage as a legislator. Maryland politics. fol. 2 pages.

1792, October 1, Georgetown. Incloses a paper of Mr. Ross in answer to a speech of Mr. Mercer's. The elections to begin in a few days. Forrest will probably succeed Dorsey. 4°. 1 page.

1793, January 13, Georgetown. Acknowledging letter of December 11. Matters relating to the Potomac Navigation Company. The tax on horses. Success of the French against Brunswick. The situation of Lafayette. 4°. 3 pages.

1793, February 11, Georgetown. Acknowledging letter of January 27. Immigration of Irishmen. European affairs. 4°. 1 page.

CARROLL, HENRY. *Montpellier.*

1818, March 5, Washington. Solicits Madison's good offices with the President for an appointment in Missouri as register and receiver. His services in the mission to Europe as attaché during the critical period of the treaty. 4°. 2 pages.

CARROLL, JAMES, and others.

1834, February 16, Randolph-Macon College. Announcing, in behalf of the Franklin Literary Society, the election of Madison as an honorary member. 4°. 1 page.

CARROLL, JAMES CRAMSIE. *Washington.*

1815, October 18, Boston. On the adoption of a system of revenue laws. Protection of manufacturers. Duties on distilled spirits and wines. fol. 4 pages.

CARROLL, JOHN (Bishop).

1805, November 20, Baltimore. Acknowledging letter of 1st. The college will be ready to receive Madison's son on December 1. Private matters. 4°. 1 page.

1809, January 6, Baltimore. Introduces Rev. Mr. Richard, rector of parish of Detroit. Wishes en-

CARROLL, JOHN.

couragement in uniting the duties of his religion to education of settlers and Indians in that country. 4°. 2 pages.

1809, November 3, Baltimore. Introduces Julius de Menou. 4°. 2 pages.

CARSWELL, SAMUEL.

1810, February 9, Philadelphia. Mr. Macon's bill a violation of our treaty of cession of Louisiana. 4°. 2 pages.

1810, March 29, Philadelphia. Acknowledging receipt of letter February 23 and some hams. Frauds on the revenue. Seizures of importations of British merchandise. 4°. 2 pages.

1810, June 16, Philadelphia. On the keeping the post-office open on the Sabbath. Disapproves of it. 4°. 2 pages.

1811, January 28, Philadelphia. Respecting the United States Bank. Requests the appointment of W. J. Durand as surveyor of the port should Dr. Bache be removed. 4°. 3 pages.

1812, August 29, Philadelphia. Is obliged to decline the appointment of commissary-general on account of ill health. Mr. Clinton the instrument of dividing the Republican party. 4°. 3 pages.

1812, October 31, Philadelphia. Acknowledging letter of September 8. Election in the city and liberties of Philadelphia. Triumph of Republican principles. 4°. 1 page.

CARTER, CHARLES. *Philadelphia.*

1791, December 16. Acknowledging letter of 4th. Is pleased with his sons' situation, hopes Madison's aid will not be wanting. His sons will not lose the esteem of their acquaintances by being honest mechanics. 4°. 3 pages.

CARTER, C. H. *Montpellier.*

1834, May 21, Washington. Sends Madison copies of his letters to Gen. Henry Lee. Apologizes for the delay. 4°. 2 pages.

CARTER, LANDON. *Washington.*

1807, May 8, Cleve. Relative to an invention of a lock to be used in the construction of a carriage. 4°. 2 pages.

CARTER, LANDON.

1807 (?), no date, Rhodes' tavern. Has a letter from Col. Taylor and asks when he can procure an audience to bring a model of his invention. small 4°. 1 page.

1809, January 23, Cleve. Respecting papers deposited with Madison to take charge of. Requests him to destroy the papers. 4°, 1 page.

1810, February 19, Cleve. Invention of a new lock. small 4°. 3 pages.

1811, February 8, Cleve. Invention for gathering wheat. Asks to be informed of the probable annual amount of grain sown in the United States. small 4°. 1 page.

CARTWRIGHT, JOHN. *Montpellier.*

1824, February 29, London. Asks Madison to accept a production of the writer's pen entitled "England's Constitution Produced and Illustrated" as well as an "abridgment" thereof. 4°. 1 page.

CASS, LEWIS, to TIFFIN, E. (Surveyor-General.)

1815, July 21, Detroit. Negotiating with Indian chiefs interested in the lands sold at the treaties of Brownstown and Detroit. Requests that the surveyors be ready at the stipulated time. [Copy.] 4°. 1 page.

CATHALAN, STEPHEN, JR., to JOURDAN PÈRE, ET FILS. *Tain, France.*

1804, August 11, Marseilles. Acknowledging letter of 12 Messidor. Relating to a supply of Hermitage wine. Answer from Jourdan père, et fils to Cathalan relative to the same dated 28 Fructidor, year 12 (August 15, 1804). (In French.) [Copy.] 4°. 2 pages.

——, to MADISON. *Washington.*

1804, September 22; October 21; December 8; 1806, May 13; October 31; November 5; Marseilles. Nine letters relating to shipments of wine and business connected therewith. 4°. 21 pages.

1809, June 3, Marseilles. Duplicate of the foregoing with another note of October 12, annexed, relating to the pleasure of the acquaintance of R. C. Nicholas, who brought a letter of recommendation from Madison. 4°. 4 pages.

1809, June 3, Marseilles. Duplicate of the foregoing. 4°. 3 pages.

1809, June 3, Marseilles. Congratulating the President on his election, with a note annexed from Julius Oliver, joining in the same. 4°. 3 pages.

CATHCART, JAMES LEANDER. *Washington.*

1805, September 26, Washington. Application for the agency that is vacant at Nachitoches. His qualifications. 4°. 2 pages.

1808, June 22, Madeira. The recession of this island to Portugal. Sends a tub containing some grape vines for Mrs. Madison. 4°. 1 page.

1809, May 10, Funchal. Bill of lading of 4 casks and 2 hogsheads of wine, per brig *Madeira*, and consigned to Jacob Adams. 4°. 1 page.

1809, May 12, Madeira. Acknowledging letters of March 13 and April 28. Congratulating him on the election. Fills Madison's order for wine. The embargo interferes with his business. 4°. 3 pages.

1810, August —; August 13; August 17; 1811, July 22; September 12; September 18; 1812, February 28, Madeira. Nine letters relating to purchase and shipments of wine, with shipping papers, etc. 4°. 19 pages.

1811, July 2, Madeira. Proposes to change consulates with Mr. Jefferson, lately appointed to Lisbon. Jefferson seeks health and the writer emoluments, and as Madeira is much healthier, thinks a change would be desirable. 4°. 3 pages.

1811, September 18, Madeira. Incloses invoice of wines to be shipped by the *Dumfries* for Baltimore. Wishes to be appointed consul to Lisbon should there be a vacancy. 4°. 2 pages.

1815, August 7, Washington. Grateful to the President for appointing him consul-general at Cadiz. Business arrangements will prevent his acceptance. Asks the President to protract the nomi-

CATHCART, JAMES LEANDER.

nation of consul to Madeira, as it is well filled. Brought out 4 pipes of wine which the President can have, if wanted. 4°. 3 pages.

1815, September 5, Washington. Acknowledging letter of August 16. Has taken passage to Cadiz, where he means to establish himself and family. 4°. 1 page.

Montpellier.

1818, July 20. Recommendations of various persons of official position and distinguished merchants, for the post of Navy storekeeper of the contemplated Navy depot. His merits and long services. Appended is a letter from Commodore I. Chauncey, adding his testimony as to his worth and fitness. 4°. 4 pages.

1821, September 18, Washington. Reviews his public services in Algiers, Tunis, and elsewhere. He wishes Government employment, and asks Madison's good offices. 4°. 12 pages.

Washington.

1821, September 18, Washington. Respecting the neg lect of the Government under successive administrations to compensate him for his services, while, at the same time, giving proof of the approbation of the department to which he was accountable. Relates an anecdote of James II, of England, as applying to his case. [*See* letter of John Rodgers to Cathcart, June 9, 1819.] 4°. 2 pages.

Montpellier.

1827, January 17, Washington. The death of Jefferson deprives the writer of his only influential friend. Asks Madison's influence to obtain the position of translator to the Department of State. Incloses copy of letter of Jefferson in 1824, to Senator J. Barbour, recommending Cathcart; also inclosed a certificate from officers in the second comptroller's office. 4°. 5 pages.

1834, August 11, Washington. His claim against Government for services rendered the Tunis ambassador in 1805-6. Asks Madison's aid in presenting it by certifying to facts in the case. 4°. 6 pages.

CAUSTEN, JAMES H. *Montpellier.*

1827, January 1, Baltimore. Claims for French spoliation from merchants from Baltimore. Explanatory of the subject. fol. 8 pages.

1827, February 2, Washington. Acknowledging letter of January 9. Acquiesces in Madison's motives in declining expressing an opinion on the subject of French spoliation. 4°. 1 page.

CAZENOVE, A. C. *Washington.*

1810, June 6, Alexandria. Acknowledging note of May 30. An order for Madeira wine. 4°. 1 page.

Washington and Montpellier.

1810, June 19, Alexandria. Series of 33 letters dating June 19, 1810, to October 18, 1819. Relating to purchases and shipments of wines and groceries, and merino wool.

Washington.

1814, September 30, Alexandria. Sends check for wool purchased of Madison. Asks Madison's opinions and expresses his own on the acts of Congress

CAZENOVE, A. C.

now contemplated, viz, giving 100 acres of land to British deserters settling the same, and the issue of paper money. 4°. 3 pages.

1814, October 31, Alexandria. Introduces Mr. Manuel Torres. His plan of taxation calculated to relieve the United States from her pecuniary embarrassments. 4°. 1 page.

———, to DALLAS, ALEXANDER T. *Washington.*

1814, October 31, Alexandria. Introduces Mr. Manuel Torres. His new plan of finances and taxes. 4°. 1 page.

———, to MADISON. *Montpellier.*

1821, April 25, Alexandria. Acknowledging letter of 18th. Offers to buy some Lisbon wine in Philadelphia or Baltimore. Java coffee. Offers services to purchase Madeira. 4°. 1 page.

CAZENOVE, THEOPHILE. *Washington.*

1805, January 2, Paris. Introduces M. Maxime Godefroy. 4°. 1 page.

CHALAMET, CHARLES. *Montpellier.*

1834, February 11, Washington. His admiration for the history of America and of the war of 1812. It was not by force of arms that it was victorious, but the authority of Madison's name and confidence inspired by it. [In French.] 4°. 2 pages.

1834, March 3, Washington. Takes pleasure in Madison's approbation of his poetry. Incloses some verses, his tribute to Madison. [In French.] 4°. 6 pages.

CHAMBERLAIN, JAMES. *Washington.*

1811, July 4, Mount Locust. Appeal for assistance. Annexes an inventory of his property. fol. 5 pages.

CHAMBERLIN, WILLIAM A. *Montpellier.*

1834, November 17, Lockport. Asks for some incident in Madison's life in his own hand, that he may possess the handwriting of one so truly great and honorable. 4°. 1 page.

CHAMBERS, B. L. *Washington.*

1814, August 6, Georgetown, Ky. Suggests that Col. R. M. Johnson raise a division of mounted volunteers. His past services and gallantry at the battle on the Thames in Canada, October 5, 1813. 4°. 3 pages.

CHANCERY, COURT OF. *Unknown.*

Not dated. An enactment by the Virginia legislature in explanation of an act for establishing a high court of chancery. [The last part missing.] [Copy.] royal fol. 2 pages.

CHANDLER, JOHN B.

1810, May 25, Georgetown. Presenting a pipe and pouch from the speaker of the Creek Nation. 4°. 1 page.

CHAPMAN, CAPTAIN, and RALSTON, G. *Montpellier.*

1823, December 29, Orange C. H. Inclose letters and intend to pay their respects the next day. 8°. 1 page.

CHAPMAN, C. T., (Deputy Collector). *Washington.*

1810, November 12, Alexandria. Incloses certificates for three casks wine from Oliviera & Sons, of Norfolk, now on board sloop *Eliza Ann* for Washington. 4°. 1 page.

CHAPMAN, N.

1807, February 18, Philadelphia. Incloses a copy of a work which he is about to put into press. Asks his subscription. Asks for some specimens of American oratory. 4°. 2 pages.

CHARLTON, THOMAS U. P.

1815, June 5, Savannah. Address of the mayor and resolutions of the city council of Savannah congratulating the President on the conclusion of peace, and offering thanks and gratitude for his patriotism, energy, and firmness during the most unpromising periods of the contest. 4°. 6 pages.

CHARLTON, THOMAS B., to GALES, JOSEPH, JR.

1815, April 22, Savannah. The gallant services of Capt. Massias. Recommends him to Mr. Gale's good offices in doing justice to his merits through the Intelligencer. [Unsigned.] [Copy.] 4°. 2 pages.

CHASE, DUDLEY, to MADISON. *Montpellier.*

1824, September 7, Randolph, Vt. Introducing Henry M. Leeds and Benjamin P. Richardson. 4°. 1 page.

CHAUMONT, LE RAY DE. *Washington.*

1807, July 12, New York. *See* Le Ray de Chaumont.

CHAUNCEY, ISAAC, to JONES, W. (Secretary of Navy).

1814, May 30, Sacketts Harbor, U. S. Ship Superior. Informing of the capture of four of the enemy's boats at Sandy Creek, and about 200 prisoners. [Copy.] 4°. 1 page.

———, to CROWNINSHIELD, B. W. (Secretary of Navy).

1815, August 4, New York. Acknowledging letter of July 8. Declines the honor of a seat as commissioner of the Navy board which the President of the United States and Secretary of Navy tendered him. 4°. 2 pages.

1818, July 20, New York. *See* Cathcart, James Leander. [Copy.]

CHAZOTTE, P. S., to MADISON. *Washington.*

1815, September 26, Philadelphia. Author of a "new system of banking," presents copy of "A grand national bank." 4°. 1 page.

Montpellier.

1821, January 15, Philadelphia. Sends a pamphlet on the policy of introducing the culture of coffee, cocoa, vines, olives, capers, almonds, etc., in East Florida and Southern States. 4°. 1 page.

CHERIOT, HENRY. *Washington.*

1812, January 20, New York. Asks Madison if a book entitled "Jerusalem delivrée" was ever sent to him from Bossange & Masson, of Paris, by the care of Mr. Hamilton, bearer of dispatches. 4°. 1 page.

CHEROKEE TREATY.

1807, December 2. *See* Meigs, Return J.

CHEVALLIÉ, ———. *Richmond.*

1785, August 25, New York. Has a letter from Lafayette relative to a claim of his father Chavallié, of Rochefort, for a bill due to him from the State of Virginia in 1778. 4°. 2 pages.

CHEVES, LANGDON. *Montpellier.*

1820, January 14, Philadelphia. Acknowledging letter of December 20. Relative to an appointment of Mr. Corbin. 4°. 2 pages.

1820, February 7, Philadelphia. Introducing John Labouchere, son of the head of the house of Hope & Co., of Amsterdam. 4°. 2 pages.

CHEW, JOSEPH, to MADISON, JAMES, SR.

1745–'46, February 18, Annapolis. News of the Pretender's success. Creates confusion in all manner of business. Hears that Madison is to have a regiment of 1,000 men to guard the frontiers, would like to be with them. small 4°. 2 pages.

1749, September 6, Annapolis. Congratulates him on his marriage. Asks him to write to him to the care of Mr. Benj. Franklin, of Philadelphia. Relative to his employment in the Ohio company's affairs. Other schemes. Private personal matters. small 4°. 4 pages.

Orange.

1750, May 21, New York. Was unable to engage with Col. Lee, of the Ohio Company, on account of sickness. Is engaged in Boston in the mercantile business. Complains at not hearing from him. A piece of gossip in a postscript about a Mrs. Littlepage and Mr. Samuel Smith. small 4°. 2 pages.

——— MADISON, JAMES, Senior and Junior, jointly.

1796, December 2, Montreal. Gives power of attorney for the disposal of land in Bourbon County, Ky., to Robert Watts, revoking a power made to the Madisons as they are unknown to the person to whom the proceeds are to be paid. fol. 1 page.

1797, February 3, Montreal. Has secured to Sir John Johnson his land in Kentucky by deed to Robert and John Watts, of New York, to be sold within 18 months. Asks them to get the utmost the land will sell for. 4°. 1 page.

——— MADISON, JAMES, Senior.

1797, March 31, Montreal. Acknowledging letter of January 15. Relative to a debt to Sir John Johnson and expressive of gratitude in Madison and his son's successful endeavor to protect his interests in the sale of Kentucky lands against fraud and deception. His friends and relatives in Virginia. 4°. 4 pages.

CHEW, JOSEPH, to MADISON.

1783, November 6, New York. Gives directions about letters to be sent to him in London. Asks about the regulations with respect to trade by Congress. The demand for British goods in Virginia. Has written to Madison's father and wants his opinion how he will be treated should he go to Virginia. small 4°. 2 pages.

1797, March 31, Montreal. Acknowledging letter of February 28. Incloses a letter to Madison's father. Grateful for their assistance in disposing of his Kentucky lands. 4°. 2 pages.

CHEW, JOHN. *Richmond.*

1799, October 20, Montreal. Death of his father, Joseph Chew. Asks his assistance in disposing of land in Virginia. 4°. 2 pages.

Washington.

1803, December 25, Montreal. Alludes to a letter of February, 1800, in reply to inquiries about his father's claim to lands in Kentucky. Incloses a letter to Mr. Taylor. Is appointed secretary for Indian affairs. 4°. 2 pages.

CHICKASAWS, CONFERENCE WITH.

Not dated. Respecting a council to be held with American commissioners to settle disputes about boundary. fol. 2 pages.

CHISHOLM, HUGH, to MADISON. *Washington.*

1808, November 14, Montpellier. Reasons of the delay in making bricks. 4°. 1 page.

1811, May 26, Montpellier. Advice of a draft. Engaged in building Madison's house. 4°. 1 page.

1812, October 13, Charlottesville. Advice of a draft. 4°. 1 page.

1814, December 13, Charlottesville. Expects to be in Washington January 1, when he wishes Madison's account to be arranged for settlement. 4°. 1 page.

CHOUTEAU, PIERRE. *Washington.*

1808, December 10, St. Louis. Respecting the ceded territory by the Osages to the United States. Asks his aid in protecting his title to land in that territory. [In French.] 4°. 4 pages.

CHRISTIE, GABRIEL. *Washington.*

1802, January 5, Annapolis. Relative to the appointment of his son as consul at Madeira. 4°. 1 page.

1802, April 14, London. Wishes his son to be appointed consul at Madeira instead of Canton. The hatred of the British Government and people to America. Jealousy the cause. Mr. Pinckney, of our commission, the most prominent character. 4°. 8 pages.

1807, February 7, Baltimore. Loss of the brig *Jacob*, from Bordeaux, on which were sundry articles for the President and himself. Wines per the *Betsey*. 4°. 1 page.

1807, February 18, Baltimore. Arrival of the schooner *Three Friends*. The wines, etc., for the President and himself will be forwarded. 4°. 1 page.

1807, February 24, Baltimore. Has shipped the goods which arrived per *Three Friends*, a receipt of which is inclosed. 4°. 2 pages.

1807, May 30, Baltimore. Arrival of the ship *Catherine*, from Bordeaux, with wine. Asks Madison to send invoice to enable him to enter at custom-house. 4°. 1 page.

Washington.

1807, June 2, Baltimore. Bill of freight, drayage, duties, and storage on articles per schooners *Crispin* and *Three Friends*. 4°. 1 page.

Washington.

1807, July —, Baltimore. Bills and receipts relating to a shipment per brig *Betsey*, from Bordeaux, and

CHRISTIE, GABRIEL.

condemned at Guadaloupe, the articles having been reshipped from thence per ship *Catherine* for Baltimore. 7 papers.

1807, June 11, Baltimore. Sends bill of lading for 1 cask and 10 boxes arrived from Guadaloupe. 4°. 1 page.

CHURCHMAN, GEORGE. *Washington.*

1809, January 14, Lisle, Delaware County, Pa. Believes the welfare of our people and country may be greatly advanced. Trusts in the encouragement of our leaders to keep steadily in view the suffering cause of the oppressed African race. 4°. 3 pages.

CLAIBORNE, FERDINAND L. *Washington.*

1809, July 8, Washington, Mississippi Territory. In compliance with a resolution of the House of Representatives of the Mississippi Territory, incloses copy of resolutions expressing confidence in the measures of the administration. 4°. 1 page. fol. 1 page.

CLAIBORNE, WILLIAM C. C. *Washington.*

1803, July 26, near Natchez. The road through the Chickasaw and Choctaw country very insecure. Robberies and murders. Suggests two small detachments of regular troops to be stationed at suitable positions. Instigator to the crimes supposed to be Sam Mason, infamous by his crimes. Offers rewards for apprehending these robbers. Asks instructions. 4°. 2 pages.

1804, February 20, Natchez. Land speculation in which Manuel Texado conveys to Cato West a tract of land near Greeneville. Certified to by Claiborne as a copy of the original. The certificate is signed by Stephen Minor. [Copy.] 4°. 3 pages.

1804, March 24, New Orleans. Morale's residence in Louisiana objectionable. Describes him as an intriguing, designing, base man. His desire to be appointed Spanish consul. His intimacy with Laussat. "Private." 4°. 3 pages.

1804, March 24, New Orleans. Duplicate of the foregoing.

1804, March 25, New Orleans. Statement of facts from Stephen Minor on a conveyance of land from Manuel Texado to Cato West. Laws should be amended to prevent this species of speculation. "Private and confidential." 4°. 2 pages.

1804, March 25, New Orleans. Duplicate of the foregoing.

1804, April 14, New Orleans. Alluding to the writer's letter of January 2, representing the whole society (erroneously stated) as involved in profound ignorance. Regrets the publication, fearing it might break off the friendly feeling between Marquis de Casa Calvo and Governor Folch and himself. Departure of Gen. Wilkinson; his jealousy. Troops ordered to Louisiana. "Private." 4°. 4 pages.

1804, April 25, New Orleans. The Louisiana Bank. Claiborne's ordinance for its establishment censured by the Secretary of the Treasury. Explains his motives. His difficulties and embarrassments. Conciliation of public sentiment requires

CLAIBORNE, WILLIAM C. C.

expedients. Gen. Wilkinson will never undertake a duty in conjunction with another person. Three may accord, two never. "Private." 4°. 3 pages.

1804, May 12, New Orleans. Incloses letter from Matthew L on to his constituents. Considers it an imprudent circular, ungenerous and illiberal insinuations against our Atlantic brethren; will have no effect. Good order prevails in Louisiana. Prosperity of the country. Well pleased with the temporary government. "Private." 4°. 3 pages.

1804, May 23, New Orleans. Acknowledging letter of April 16. Vindicates himself from the charge of exceeding his powers in chartering the Louisiana Bank. Explains his motives. 4°. 8 pages.

1804, June 3, New Orleans. Edward Livingston's warm advocacy of the rights of Louisiana, and his disapproval of the measures of the Government in relation to this territory. Daniel Clark also inimical; his attempt to injure Claiborne. Experience has proved that conciliatory justice, called want of energy, was the wisest policy. "Private." 4°. 4 pages.

1804, June 29, New Orleans. Address of a small assemblage of citizens of New Orleans to Congress relative to local government. Edward Livingston's memorial. A translation in the French language. Thinks Livingston will be a troublesome member of our political society. Opinions on the Representative system for the Louisiana people. "Private and confidential." 4°. 3 pages.

1804, July 13, New Orleans. Edward Livingston's memorial to Congress. Fears it will create a spirit of discontent and render the temporary administration more arduous than it has hitherto been. Describes the three agents to bear the memorial, Messrs. Derbigney, Detrion, and Sauvé. Will send copy of the memorial next mail. 4°. 3 pages.

1804, September 27, New Orleans. Death of Mrs. Claiborne and little daughter. Will acknowledge officially the receipt of letter of August 30. "Private." 4°. 2 pages.

1804, October 1, New Orleans. Introduces Messrs. Derbigney, Sauvé, and Detrahan, with a request to present them to the President, as bearers of a memorial from citizens of Louisiana. 4°. 1 page.

1804, October 1, New Orleans. Mr. Crawford's invention of a cotton machine. Applies for a patent. 4°. 1 page.

1804, October 3, New Orleans. Departure of the bearers of the memorial of citizens of Louisiana to the President. Their high expectations. Probably some genuine patriotism among the signers, but it is feared it is tinged with foreign influence. The Louisianians are mild, pacific people, but credulous and easily misled by designing people. These agents' primary object will be the opening of the African trade. "Private." 4°. 2 pages.

1804, October 13, New Orleans. Question whether councillors will accept. Evan Jones resigns.

CLAIBORNE, WILLIAM C. C.

Fear the motives of the framers of the memorial are not pure. The fever rages in New Orleans and proves fatal. "Private." 4°. 3 pages.

1804, October 22, New Orleans. Relative to a pamphlet said to have been written by Derbigney. Calculated to awaken the attachment of the people of Louisiana to their late masters and increase existing discontent. Describing the characters of the agents of the memorialists. Increase of crime in Louisiana. Enfeebling the arm of the Executive. "Private." 4°. 4 pages.

1804, November 5, New Orleans. Exertions to induce councillors to decline. Mr. Daniel Clarke undoubtedly an enemy to the United States Government; is in the Spanish interests. Spanish force at Pensacola. No apprehension of disturbances should the memorial be rejected. "Private." 4°. 3 pages.

1805, January 4, New Orleans. The death of his private secretary and absence of his clerks delay the forwarding of general statements of public expenditures. Sickness in the city. Trusts the Government will be liberal in the compensation of the temporary governor. The Louisiana Bank. The want of the United States branch bank. Livingston and Clarke's successful speculations. "Private." 4°. 4 pages.

1805, October 15, New Orleans. Acknowledging letter of July 20. Location of a tract of land mentioned to Lafayette. Dispute as to title. Mr. Maurigny's claim. Will consult with Mr. Duplantin to promote the interests of Lafayette. "Private." fol. 1 page.

1806, March 3, New Orleans. Introducing Joshua Lewis, a land commissioner for Orleans. 4°. 1 page.

1806, October 27, New Orleans. The recrossing of the Sabine by the Spaniards owing to the debilitated state of their forces, and not to be viewed as evidence of a pacific disposition. Announcing his recent marriage. "Private." 4°. 3 pages.

1807, July 17, New Orleans. Imprudent conduct of Navy officers. Designing men exciting the prejudices of Louisianians against the Government. The charge of Judge Moreau to the jury not justified. Except intriguing Americans there is no want of respect to the law. The lawyers and printers the most restless, turbulent members of society with few exceptions. "Private." 4°. 3 pages.

1808, April 18, New Orleans. Edward Livingston's visit to Washington to confer with the President on the case of the Batture and the acts of Gen. Wilkinson and Gov. Claiborne. Livingston's efforts to make the American Government odious to the Louisianians. Hope that if Livingston be heard in support of his claims, the tribunal be composed by men of talents and integrity. "Confidential." fol. 2 pages.

1808, December 14, New Orleans. Candidates for the vacancy in the office of register for the district. Recommends Mr. Grymes or Mr. Robertson. Mr.

CLAIBORNE, WILLIAM C. C.

Johnson also deemed suitable for that office, or of being named a commissioner. "Private." fol. 3 pages.

1809, March 20, New Orleans. Incloses a letter from the lady abbess of the Ursuline Convent. Congratulates him on his elevation to the Presidential chair. fol. 1 page.

1809, December 17, New Orleans. Death of his second wife; her virtues and attractions. Asks leave of absence for a tour in the States. Unhealthy situation of the Government house. Deaths from yellow fever. Advises the sale of the Government house. fol. 4 pages.

1809, December 17, New Orleans. Duplicate of the foregoing. fol. 4 pages.

1811, October 8, New Orleans. His commission as governor expires on January 17. Requests to be a candidate for reappointment. Contemplated change in the Territorial legislature. Hears with regret, the probability of war with Great Britain. At such a crisis the nation will unquestionably be united and supported. fol. 3 pages.

1812, August 2, New Orleans. Enters upon his duties as governor of Louisiana. Assures the President of his desire to promote the views of his administration. fol. 1 page.

1813, October 23, Rapides, La. Assists in organizing a detachment of militia to be ready for an invasion. The Creek war to close soon. Gen. Claiborne usefully employed on the Mobile. His qualifications for commissioner. Success on the lakes. Opposition in the Senate to the embargo. Defeat of Revolutionists in Texas. fol. 4 pages.

1813, November 29, New Orleans. Attempts to organize a force to reenter Texas, to overthrow the government existing there. The governor's duty to put down violation of the laws of the United States. Introduction of quantities of contraband goods. Smuggling. Importance of suppressing it. Has issued a proclamation to that effect. Suggests Mr. A. L. Duncan as prosecuting officer for the United States. 4°. 4 pages.

1814, September 22, New Orleans. The fall of Washington City reported. It may be productive of good. Will revive the spirit of '76. Patriotic disposition of State of Louisiana. Additional auxiliary force needed. Has requested the governors of Kentucky and Tennessee to hasten reenforcements. The enemy intriguing with negroes, pirates, and smugglers. Interesting reports from Mexico. Independence of Mexico comports with the policy of the United States. Adds to the security of Louisiana. fol. 3 pages.

———, to MAZUREAU, STEPHEN, Attoney-General, Louisiana.

1815, February 24, New Orleans. Martial law in New Orleans enforced, to the injury of its citizens not in military service. Orders the attorney-general to reserve his official duties in New Orleans, to give aid to the civil magistrates and protect and avenge the injured laws of this State. fol. 2 pages.

CLAIBORNE, WILLIAM C. C., to MADISON.
Washington

1815, February 24, New Orleans. Report of the treaty of peace. Offers his congratulations. Unpleasant misunderstandings existing between Gen. Jackson and the executive authorities of Louisiana. Jackson's important services, but his violent character. Incloses a letter to the attorney-general of Louisiana to protect the interests of the people. fol. 2 pages.

1815, May 12, New Orleans. Introducing his friend, Joseph Saul, cashier of the Orleans Bank. His high character, services, and merits. fol. 2 pages.

1815, December 8, New Orleans. Acknowledging letter of October 1. Promises to secure some fruits and seeds of the Bon wood of Louisiana. Vacancy in the agency of Indian affairs. recommends Bartholomew Shaumberg to succeed the late agent. Reviews his conduct and services in the late war. fol. 3 pages.

CLARK, ABRAHAM.

1786, November 23, New York. The sentiments of the legislature of New Jersey. Sees, with satisfaction, Madison's name in the delegation from Virginia. fol. 1 page.

CLARK, BUSHROD W., and PARKS, G. D. A.
Montpellier.

1833, November 22, Lewiston, N. Y. Asks to be furnished with a sketch of the most prominent incidents of his life, to be published in autobiographies of our distinguished statesmen. 4°. 1 page.

CLARK, DANIEL. *Washington.*

1804, March 15, Bayou Sara, Mississippi Territory. Acknowledging letter of February 10. Is obliged to him for mention of his services. Asks that the papers from Mr. Morton be burned. 4°. 2 pages.

C——K, G. *Montpellier.*

1830, July 10, Frederick County, Va. From a boy who has enthusiastic admiration for Madison, asking him to devote occasionally, a moment of leisure to writing him a lecture. 4°. 3 pages.

1830, September 10, Frederick County, Va. Acknowledging reply to his letter. Though unsuccessful, he thanks Madison for his polite letter. 4°. 1 page.

CLARKE, JAMES, and others. *Washington.*

1816, March 31. Appeal of several persons located on Government lands for permission to raise crops this season. fol. 2 pages.

CLARK, JOHN. *Washington.*

1804, February 5, Orange, Va. Agricultural matters from Madison's overseer. fol. 3 pages.

CLARKE, JOHN.

1813, December 2, Richmond. Suggestions as to the carrying on of the war. Unmarried men to serve. Married men to procure substitutes in the militia and other suggestions. 4°. 10 pages.

CLARK, THOMAS.

1814, January 24, Philadelphia. Sends copy of second edition of the Naval History of the United States. Incloses proposals for the publication of a history of the United States. Asks Madison's patronage. 4°. 3 pages.

CLARK, THOMAS D. *Montpellier.*

1830, January 31, Springfield, Ala. Is collecting autograph letters of the Presidents. Asks him for his autograph letter. Gives a sketch of his own life. small 4°. 3 pages.

1834, September 12, Savannah, Tenn. Asks him to write him a letter. Lafayette's death. small 4°. 3 pages.

CLASON, J. *Washington.*

1813, December 17, New York. Smuggling by Swedes with forged papers. The Government defrauded of millions. Appeal for relief for seizure of his property by the British in 1805. 4°. 4 pages.

CLELAND, JAMES.

1809, November 24, Chambersburg. Appeal for aid from an insane person. fol. 4 pages.

CLINCH, D. L., to BUTLER, R., Adjutant-General.

1816, August 2, Camp Crawford. Report respecting the capture of a fort occupied by negroes and Choctaw Indians and its destruction. Inclosing schedule of property taken at the fort. 4°. 17 pages.

CLINTON, DE WITT, to MADISON.

1803, May 10, Newtown, L. I. Introducing John M. Goetschins. (Signature cut out.) 4°. 1 page.

1805, May 1, New York. Acknowledging letter of April 10. Correspondence relating to the enlisting of British seamen in our Navy. "Private." 4°. 2 pages.

1805, May 4, New York. Asks if the consul (Mr. Lee) at Bordeaux is to be removed or transferred to some other place. Desires to fill the vacancy by a friend. 4°. 1 page.

CLINTON, GEORGE, to GALLATIN, ALBERT. *Washington.*

1801, July 3, New York. Introducing Henry Hunt, of New York, who wishes to be appointed consul at some European port. 4°. 1 page.

COALTER, JOHN, to MADISON. *Montpellier.*

1828, November 23, Richmond. Fears the copy of the proceedings of the convention at Charlottesville sent to the Governor has miscarried. Asks him to communicate with the Governor. 4°. 1 page.

1828, November 29, Richmond. Has sent a copy of proceedings of the convention at Charlottesville to the governor. 4°. 1 page.

COBB, MATTHEW. *Washington.*

1811, October 29, Portland. Sends Madison a bill of exchange drawn by J. L. Cathcart at Madeira, with a request to pay the same into the Treasury and procure a check payable at Maine bank in Portland to his order. [Inclosed is the draft.] 4°. 1 page.

COBB, THOMAS W. *Montpellier.*

1826, January 19, Washington. Asks information respecting the boundary line between Georgia and Alabama. 4°. 3 pages.

COCHRAN, WILLIAM E., to HAMILTON, (Capt). *Washington.*

1816, March 5, Washington. Congratulating him on his patriotic and meritorious conduct in refusing to serve in the British army in which he held a commission when our war broke out. Will be glad to be of service to him towards the accomplishment of his desire to obtain a commission in the U. S. Army. [Copy.] 4°. 3 pages.

COCKE, JOHN H., to MADISON. *Montpellier.*

1827, January 9, Richmond. Acknowledging letter of December 27. The depravity of hotel keepers. The board of visitors at the university to be called together to get their views on the subject and the proper course to be taken. 4°. 2 pages.

1827, April 2, Bremo. Acknowledging letter of March 18. Prof. Key to leave the University. Question as to his salary. Difficulty in filling his place. Qualifications of suggested successors. Matters respecting the University. 4°. 3 pages.

1827, August 29, Bremo. Inclosing letters from Mr. Short respecting the vacant chairs at the University. Qualifications of Mr. Patterson. The tobacco crop prospects. 4°. 1 page.

1827, October 6, Bremo. Acknowledging letter of September 24, relating to Mr. Long's appointment in the University in London. His views on the subject. A note at foot of this letter from J. C. Cabell concurring in Gen. Cocke's views. 4°. 2 pages.

1827, October 12, Bremo. Dr. Patterson declining being a candidate for a vacant professorship, assents to appointment of Dr. Jones. The term of Mr. Long's engagement. 4°. 2 pages.

1827, November 13, Bremo. Order and regularity at the Virginia University. Relating to the hotel keepers. Mr. Bonnycastle and his astronomical instruments. 4°. 3 pages.

1827, November 22, Bremo. Appointment of Dr. Jones at the University. 4°. 1 page.

1827, November 29, Bremo. Hotel keepers and other matters connected with the University. 4°. 2 pages.

1828, February 14, Bremo. Respecting Dr. Jones at the University. Measures to be taken to secure the books against injury from dampness. Other improvements suggested. 4°. 3 pages.

1828, February 23, Bremo. Acknowledging letter of 9th. Proposal of the faculty of the University to shorten the term of chairman. 4°. 2 pages.

1828, March 29, Bremo. Acknowledging letter of 9th. Dr. Jones's claims. Discontent of the students by Mr. Bonnycastle's dissolving the natural philosophy class. Complaints against the expenses of the University. Suggestions. The new observatory. 4°. 3 pages.

COCKE, JOHN H.

1828, May 5, Bremo. Question as to appointment of Mr. Ritchie to the vacant chair of natural philosophy 4°. 1 page.

1828, August 23, Bremo. Acknowledging letter of 12th, inclosing one from Dr. Lomax, concerning the University. 4°. 1 page.

1829, May 23, Charlottesville. Acknowledging letter of 8th. Result of Dr. Harrison's investigation relative to the completion of "Stevens' Thesaurus." The successor of Dr. Long. 4°. 1 page.

1829, May 25, Charlottesville. Inclosing a corrected list of deficient numbers of the "Thesaurus." small 4°. 1 page.

1834, November 2, Charlottesville. Introducing Edward C. Delavan, of New York State Temperance Society. 4°. 2 pages.

1834, December 17, Bremo. Mr. Delevan and the temperanco cause. Promising appearance of the society and its influence. 4°. 2 pages.

COCKE, WILLIAM. *Washington.*

1808, December 4, Tennessee. Apologizes for his "arrogance" and wishes Madison to appoint John Quincy Adams as Secretary of State. 4°. 2 pages.

Montpellier.

1811, November 28, Knoxville. Introducing Col. Bernardo. small 4°. 1 page.

Washington.

1811, November 28, Knoxville. Introduction of Col. Joseph Bernardo. Attack of the Prophet on Gen. Harrison. The writer's impeachment by the house of representatives of Tennessee as judge of first district. Attributes it to no error of judgment, but to malice. fol. 2 pages.

COFFEE, WILLIAM J. *Montpellier.*

1819, December 23, New York. Has directed Mr. Coote to forward to him models in terra cotta. 4°. 1 page.

1819, January 25, New York. Proposes making a statue in plaster of Jefferson to be placed in the rotunda of the University of Virginia. The expense to be raised by subscription. 4°. 2 pages.

1820, May 3, Monticello. Incloses his account. 4°. 1 page.

COFFEY, WILLIAM A. *Montpellier.*

1823, August 19, New York. Incloses a copy of "Inside Out," a work of his own just published. Asks him to countenance his literary endeavors. 4°. 1 page.

COFFIN, ALEXANDER, JR. *Washington.*

1805, October 11, Hudson. Incloses a nut of the vegetable soap. Explains the method of using it. Also incloses a specimen of bird's nest from which soup is made. It qualities and effects. 4°. 3 pages.

COFFIN, ISAAC. *Montpellier.*

1817, May 17, Charleston. Asks him to procure some live wild turkeys and send them to Liverpool to the care of Thomas Earle & Co. 4°. 1 page.

COPPIN, ISAAC.

1817, December 22, Raley Castle, Durham, England. Acknowledging his present of two wild turkeys. Is much pleased, as they are much admired. Will send some pheasants to Mrs. Madison. Hints as to their breeding. 4°. 3 pages.

1819, June 10, London. Asks him to send him more wild turkeys, male and female. 4°. 1 page.

COFFIN, JARED. *Washington.*

1814, April 14, Hudson. Method of destroying insects in fruit trees of the writer's discovery. Asks how he can procure compensation from the Government for such a valuable discovery. fol. 2 pages.

COGHILL, JOHN. *Washington.*

1812, April 20, Paris. Is grateful to Lafayette for introducing him to Madison which has contributed to his becoming an American citizen. Has bought some land of Lafayette in Louisiana. Hopes to profit by the introduction. 4°. 3 pages.

COGSWELL, NATHANIEL. *Washington.*

1808, July 11, Newburyport. Incloses some Fourth of July orations. This town, which was the cradle of the Essex Junto, will support Madison's administration. large fol. 1 page.

COGSWELL, WILLIAM. *Montpellier.*

1834, February 18, Boston. Enjoyed his visit at Mr. Madison's. His subsequent visit at Monticello and the University. His opinions on the management of the University. The course prescribed in religious instruction. Religious liberty, etc. 4°. 3 pages.

COLVIN, J. B. *Washington.*

1805, January 5, Fredericktown, *Md.* Asks him to subscribe to the Republican Advocate. small 4°. 1 page.

COLDER, JOSEPH. *Washington.*

1804, June 12, Washington. Tells him of what he thinks is a mistake in Jefferson's "Notes on Virginia," and corrects it. 4°. 1 page.

COLEMAN, AMBROSE. *Washington.*

1801, October 15. Appeal for assistance. fol. 1 page.

COLEMAN, JOHN J. *Montpellier.*

1833, June 16, Nelson County, Va. Has some money for him which he can have by making a draft on him at Richmond. 4°. 1 page.

COLEMAN, SAMUEL. *Washington.*

1803, March 21, Richmond. Acknowledging letter of 13th. Will attend to the forwarding of some furniture left in Richmond by Col. Monroe. 4°. 1 page.

1803, March 24, Richmond. Incloses a letter opened by mistake, and suggesting the propriety of forwarding it to Monroe. 4°. 1 page.

1803, April 9, Richmond. Respecting the packing and forwarding plate and glassware and porcelain to Washington. 4°. 2 pages.

1803, May 24, Richmond. Acknowledging letter of 4th. Ships per schooner *Anna* some bales and cases of glass and china. Asks instructions about disposing of some wine. 4°. 2 pages.

COLEMAN, SAMUEL.

1803, May 24, Richmond. Ships per schooner *Anna* four boxes and a bale with directions to be handled carefully. 4°. 1 page.

1803, June 27, Richmond. Acknowledging letters of May 31 and 24th inst. Respecting the storage of some wine. Ill health of Col. Monroe. 4°. 2 pages.

1803, October 26, Richmond. Appeal for an office under Government. His services in the Revolution and small compensation. 4°. 3 pages.

COLEMAN, WILLIAM, to TUCKER, ST. GEORGE. *Williamsburg.*

1813, March 19, Williamsburg. States that British vessels had passed up to Newport News, and their barges had taken six vessels. Thinks this should be made known to the Executive. 4°. 2 pages.

1813, March —. Gives an account of an attack of nine of our gunboats on an English frigate near Hampton. 4°. 1 page.

COLLINS, CHARLES, to MADISON. *Washington.*

1811, December 25, New York. On the abstaining from the consumption of produce of slaves. Project of trading in such articles as do not interfere with religious scruples. Annexing printed remarks on prize goods. 4°. 3 pages.

COLMAN, HENRY. *Montpellier.*

1817, February 21, Hingham, Mass. Transmits the "Century sermon". Buckminster's sermons; their merits. Congratulates him on his retirement and compliments him on his administration. 4°. 3 pages.

1826, August 3, Salem, Mass. Accompanied by an oration. 8°. 1 page.

1830, July 24, Salem, Mass. The "Essex Farmers". Statesmen and intellectual men often retire from public life and devote themselves to agriculture. Examples. Book by the late Dr. Holyokè. Sends a biographical sermon. 4°. 2 pages.

"COLUMBUS."

1799, June 6, Virginia. Pamphlet consisting of a letter to a Member of Congress on the constitutionality of the alien and sedition laws signed as above. 4°. 48 pages.

COLVIN, J. B. *Washington.*

1806, November 27, Fredericktown. Project in forming a junction with the Baltimore American. Solicits his subscription and patronage. fol. 1 page.

1808, January 26, Washington. Asks of Madison a memorandum of the legislative addresses and others as approbatory of the President's general good conduct, as applausive of the act of embargo. 4°. 1 page.

1808, February 16, Washington. Incloses the "Enquirer." As the writer of this letter is Madison's advocate before the public, would like his views in respect to the article calculated to attract the attention of his enemies. 4°. 1 page.

———, to FORREST, R.

1809, December 5, Washington. The writer gives his testimony as to Mr. Forrest's efforts to promote Madison's elevation to the Presidency. 4°. 1 page.

COLVIN, J. B., to MADISON, Mrs. *Washington.*

1810, June 26, Washington. States that the sketch of Madison's life in Mr. Kingston's biographical dictionary was not by his (Colvin's) pen. He intends publishing in the autumn a biographical sketch of Madison's life. 4°. 2 pages.

———, to MADISON. *Washington.*

1811, November 26, Washington. Has received intelligence of a battle between Governor Harrison and the party of the Prophet. The Indians defeated and their town destroyed. The killed and wounded. The names of some of the killed. fol. 1 page.

1812, April 29, Washington. Solicits the appointment as consul in Tunis or Tripoli. Can silence any opposition in the Senate. fol. 1 page.

COMTZ, JOHN.

1796, February 28. Receipt of the clerk of the Land Office of a plat and certificate of survey and Register's fee per Joseph Chew's entry of land. 8°. 1 page.

COMYN, MR. Consuls, functions of.

Not dated. A paper in Madison's hand on the functions of consuls as defined by Mr. Comyn, with regulations touching French consuls extracted from the ordinances of marine. 4°. 1 page. fol. 2 pages.

"CONCILIATOR."

1807. [*See* letter of Joy, George, to Madison, dated October 5, 1807. London.]

CONDICT, LEWIS, to MADISON. *Montpellier.*

1831, March 3, Washington. Incloses a letter from Dr. McDowell. Nassau Hall in great need of pecuniary assistance. 4°. 1 page.

1831, March 15, Morristown, N. J. Appeals for aid for Nassau Hall. 4°. 1 page.

CONGRESS, ACT OF, to COOLEY, EBENEZER. *Louisiana.*

1828, December 21. A bill for the relief of Ebenezer Cooley, of Louisiana, relative to a tract of land located by Lafayette. [Copy.] 4°. 1 page.

CONGRESS, CONTINENTAL.

1780 (?). Proposed resolutions recommending the several States to pass laws enabling Congress to collect duties on imported articles to pay the interest and part of the capital of the public debt. [Draft.] fol. 2 pages.

1783, February 6, Philadelphia. Proposed resolutions to request the legislatures of the several States to pass laws requiring estimates of value of lands, buildings, and improvements, in order that Congress may proceed to make requisitions to defray expenses of the war, etc. [Copy.] fol. 4 pages.

CONGRESSIONAL COMMITTEE.

1782. Respecting the letter and report of Lieut. Col. Laurens to Congress concerning his mission to the Court of France. Report of the committee to whom it was referred, respecting the causes of the detention of the loans and donations obtained from France, censuring the United States minister in France in causing said detention. fol. 8 pages.

CONNECTICUT LEGISLATURE to MADISON.
Washington.

1812, September 1, Hartford. [*See* Griswold, Roger (Governor).

CONNOR, CHARLES.

1810 (?), no date. Representation setting forth his services in the Army of the United States during the Revolutionary war. The object of this application is to secure to him the benefit in land to which he is entitled for his services.
fol. 2 pages.

CONOVER, SAMUEL F. *Washington.*

1813, April 23, Philadelphia. Offers himself as a candidate for treasurer in the Mint. His testimonials accompanying. 4°. 1 page.

CONSTABLE, WILLIAM, to LAWRENCE, J.

1810 (?), no date. Gives the amount of clearances, annually, of his vessels. 4°. 1 page.

CONSTITUTION OF THE UNITED STATES.

1787, August 6. Printed and reported by the committee of five, consisting of Messrs. Rutledge, Randolph, Goshen, Ellsworth, and Wilson. [With a few notes and emendations in handwriting of Madison.] large fol. 7 pages.

1787, September 12. Printed copy, as reported by committee of revision, consisting of Messrs. Johnson, Morris, Madison, Hamilton, and King. [With a few marginal notes by Madison].
large fol. 4 pages.

1787, September 17. Printed copy, as finally agreed to by the convention, with Washington's letter to the President of Congress, submitting the same as President of the convention. [With notes in Madison's handwriting.]
large fol. 6 pages.

CONSULS, FUNCTIONS OF. [*See* M. Comyn.]

CONTEE, BENJAMIN, Dr., to MADISON.
Washington.

1808, October 31, Allen's Fresh, Md. Disclaims ever having expressed himself inimical to Madison. Is an old acquaintance and esteems him very highly and would vote for him, although his politics are adverse, perhaps. small 4°. 2 pages.

CONVERSE, SHERMAN. *Montpellier.*

1826, March 3, New Haven. Inclosing, for inspection, Webster's prospectus of his dictionary.
4°. 5 pages.

COOK, ORCHARD. *Washington.*

1809, January 20, Newburyport. Enumerating his losses by British capture and sacrifices in the cause of Republicanism and wishes to be appointed collector of Newburyport. 4°. 3 pages.

1812, August 11, Wiscasset. Address by the merchants of Wiscasset, requesting a cessation of arms. The administration would be more popular had Congress increased the Navy. 4°. 1 page.

1814, March 3, Wiscasset. The vacancy in the office of district attorney caused by the death of Silas Lee. Suggests the appointment of Mr. Pickman, John Holmes, or Mr. Preble, by request of officers of Government. The ingratitude of republics.

COOK, ORCHARD.

His long services not considered. His veneration for Madison. 4°. 4 pages.

1815, December 16, Wiscasset. Inclosing a newspaper containing remarks by Rev. Mr. Bentley, of Salem. 4°. 1 page.

COOKE, A. *Montpellier.*

1822, January 31, Fredericksburg. Inclosing his account. small 4°. 1 page.

COOKE, JAMES. *Montpellier.*

1822, January. Settlement of account with Mackay & Campbell. 4°. 1 page.

COOLEDGE, D. *Washington.*

1815, February 20, Concord, N. *H.* Congratulating the President on the peace. 4°. 1 page.

COOLEY, EBENEZER. [*See* Congress, Act of, December 21, 1828.]

COOLEY, E. *Montpellier.*

1829, April 28, Washington. Inclosing a statement of a claim for damages incurred and a bill for relief in connection with the transfer of lands to Lafayette in Louisiana, in which he is interested and proposes to enter suit for. 4°. 3 pages.

COOMBS, GRIFFITH. *Washington.*

1807, January 7. Bill of coal; receipted. Strip of paper.

COOPER, JOHN, to STONE, W. S. *Fredericksburg.*

1810, October 24, Norfolk. Receipt of one hogshead of wine from Oliviera & Sons. 8°. 1 page.

COOPER, THOMAS, to MADISON. *Washington.*

1810, July 9, Philadelphia. Acknowledging a letter approving Cooper's opinion on an insurance case. Incloses a newspaper cutting on the census. 4°. 1 page.

1810, August 19, Northumberland, Pa. Respecting the science of mineralogy. Deficiency in this country of its knowledge. The mineral resources of Pennsylvania. The importance of knowledge of chemistry and the manufacturing processes depending on it. Desires the President, through the ministers abroad, to procure the best foreign works on the subject. 4°. 3 pages.

1810, September 14, Northumberland. Acknowledging receipt of books The manufacture of glass. Difficulty in obtaining information owing to jealousy of the monopolists. Remarks on the census. Prejudices of the common, uneducated people. 4°. 3 pages.

1811, October 4, Northumberland. Respecting some books on chemistry and mineralogy. Removal by the legislature of Pennsylvania of his situation as judge. Will send account of proceedings in the case. Has been appointed to the chemical chair of Carlisle College (Dickinson College). 4°. 2 pages.

1813, February 18, Carlisle. Suggesting an analysis to be made of Congreve rockets, shrapnel shells, etc., captured from an English vessel. A plan of shell submitted thick enough to penetrate the hull of a vessel before exploding. 4°. 1 page.

COOPER, THOMAS.

1813, September 3, Carlisle. Applies for appointment of district collector of taxes in Cumberland County. 4°. 1 page.

——— to DALAS, JAMES. *Washington.*

1813 (?), no date. Incloses a letter and would like to be informed as to the emoluments of the situation at Carlisle College. 4°. 1 page.

——— to MADISON. *Washington.*

1814, November 16, Carlisle, Pa. Sends list of some books which he wishes Madison to order for him in France. 4°. 1 page.

1815, August 8, Carlisle. The health of Madison's nephew at the college. Course of his studies. Cooper thinks of practising law in New Orleans. Incloses a pamphlet. 4°. 1 page.

1817, January 17, Philadelphia. Death of Mr. Dallas. The loss to the public and his friends. Mr. Dallas's wish that should a general bankrupt law be enacted that Cooper be made one of the commissioners. 4°. 2 pages.

Montpellier.

1821, March 12, Columbia, S. C. His position as chemical professor at South Carolina College. His salary raised. Elected president of the college. Recommends Mr. Vauuxem as professor of chemistry and mineralogy to the University of Virginia. His character and merits. 4°. 3 pages.

1822, December 21, Columbia, S. C. Inclosing report of the state of his college. small 4°. 1 page.

1826, November 15, Columbia, S. C. Sends copy of his lectures on political economy. 4°. 1 page.

COOPER, WILLIAM. *Philadelphia.*

1794, May 12, Boston. Resolutions of the people of Boston on the general embargo imposed by the Government and their acquiescence, accompanied by a note of the town clerk. 4°. 2 pages.

Washington.

1814, November 3, New York. Detailing a plan for the destruction of the whole of the British naval force on the lakes, also Kingston, York, and Fort George, and seizure and holding any position on the St. Lawrence. Proposes to build a floating battery at Oswego. The facilities for so doing. fol. 5 pages.

COPELAND, E. JR. *Montpellier.*

1823, September 6, Boston. Asks orders relating to articles received from Marseilles and incloses letter and invoice. 4°. 1 page.

1823, September 27, Boston. Acknowledging letter of 15th. Incloses bill of lading and certificate of the custom-house for wine imported. 4°. 1 page.

1823, October 15, Boston. Asks Madison to remit a check for amount of invoice of wines, etc. 4°. 1 page.

1823, October 29, Boston. Acknowledging letter of 22d, covering a check for account of cost and expenses on wine per *Hershell.* 4°. 1 page.

COPPINGER, JOSEPH. *Washington.*

1810, December 16, New York. Proposes to form a company for the establishment of a brewery in Washington. Its benefits in counteracting the

COPPINGER, JOSEPH.

baneful influences of ardent spirits, and profits to holders of stock. Incloses list of his inventions. Also a letter of recommendation from William Du Bourg to John Couper is inclosed, dated November 8, 1809. fol. 3 pages. 4°. 4 pages.

1810, December 20, New York. Respecting his proposition to establish a brewery in Washington. Corrects some errors in his last letter. Benefits arising from the enterprise. 4°. 2 pages.

CORRIN, FRANCIS. *New York.*

1788, October 21, Richmond. Asks for copies of acts of Pennsylvania and Massachusetts respecting mode of choosing Members of Congress. Proposed method in Virginia. Preposition for a second convention of the States. Vanity of Virginians. small 4°. 2 pages.

1788, November 12, Richmond. Business of organizing the House of Delegates. Prejudices of Virginians. Henry's resolutions on the second convention. Substitute for them. Madison's absence felt. Ingratitude of the assembly. Bill for choosing electors for President. Promises to be a faithful correspondent. 4°. 5 pages.

Philadelphia.

1791, October 25, Richmond. The act of assumption and bank incorporation in the assembly. Question of apportionment. 4°. 3 pages.

1791, November 22, Richmond. The determination of Congress in respect to ratio of representation. Payment of British debts. Compensation for negroes carried away by British fleets and armies. The Trumbull divorce case. Overtures from Great Britain for a compromise touching British debts. 4°. 4 pages.

1791, December 15, Richmond. All the amendments to the Federal Constitution passed the Virginia Senate. Bill for arrangement of districts. Adoption of a resolution congratulating the National Assembly of France on the establishment of their new constitution. 4°. 2 pages.

1792, January 7, Richmond. Adoption of the amendments to the Federal Constitution in Virginia. Action of the assembly. The British debts. Arrangement of Congressional districts. The Pennsylvania demands on Virginia. 4°. 4 pages.

1793, February 29, Richmond. Asks Madison again to write to Judge Pendleton to intercede in Corbin's behalf in the ensuing election to Congress. 4°. 1 page.

1797, January 15, Blondfield, Va. The writer's dislike to slavery. Desirous of changing his residence. Asks for information respecting the cost of living in Eastern States and their laws respecting slaves, also expense of educating and matters respecting trade. 4°. 3 pages.

Washington.

1806, July 30, Georgetown. Asks the favor of an audience, and eventually his patronage. 4°. 2 pages.

1808, October 29, The Reeds, Va. Transmits a paper tending to injure Madison in the coming election.

CORRIN, FRANCIS.

Regrets its publication at present. Madison is assured that many Federalists will vote for him, knowing his attachment to the Constitution, and will not suffer it to be impaired during his administration. That he will be President of the United States and not of a party. 4°. 4 pages.

1812, April 6, The Reeds. Madison's policy in regard to the two great belligerents. Thinks he is still anxious to preserve peace with them both. Suggests the policy of making another appeal by sending an accredited agent to Great Britain. If he can be of service, will make the sacrifice and be that agent, and states his qualifications. Emoluments no object. 4°. 4 pages.

1812, September 13, The Reeds. Explaining his object in offering his services in a mission to England, as mentioned in a previous letter, which remains unanswered. 4°. 3 pages.

1813, July 11, The Reeds. Requests Madison to remind Gen. Armstrong of his promise for a commission for his nephew, Maj. Corbin, of King's Creek. His merits, and claim of his mother, whose husband and two sons are in active service. 4°. 3 pages.

1815, January 17, The Reeds. Solicits the appointment of his nephew, G. L. Corbin's son, to the West Point Academy. Also the berth of midshipman for Peter B. Randolph. The writer's son, Robert Beverly Corbin, now at college, will be well fitted to attend in the suite of one of our foreign ministers. 4°. 3 pages.

1813 (?), no date, The Reeds. His nephew, G. L. Corbin, being totally unfit for military service, on account of his wounds received at Hampton, is fully competent to any civil employment. Asks for the appointment of collector at Norfolk. 4°. 3 pages.

1815, January 30, The Reeds. Maj. G. L. Corwin will be flattered and honored by any military appointment, wherever his services or merit may entitle him. 4°. 1 page.

1815, July 5, The Reeds. Is importuned by Mrs. Corbin, of King's Creek, to remind Madison of the request made for the appointment for her son to Commodore Decatur's squadron in the expedition against Algiers. Complaints against the Post-Office Department. 4°. 3 pages.

1816, April 3, The Reeds. Calls his attention to the injustice of the orders issued to the collectors of Federal taxes and excise to receive none but Virginia notes. An *ex post facto* law which favors usurers and speculators at the expense of the people and no benefit to the Treasury. 4°. 4 pages.

1816, May 5, The Reeds. Would like to be appointed commissioner of the subscriptions to the Bank of the United States. 4°. 2 pages.

1816, May 17, The Reeds. Is pleased at the gratification of his whim by the President. (Commissioner of subscriptions to the United States Bank.) Rates of English exchange. 4°. 2 pages.

1816, July 29, The Reeds. Sends inclosed a statement of the subscriptions at Richmond to the United States Bank shares. 4°. 4 pages.

CORBIN, FRANCIS.

1816, October 20, The Reeds. Offers Madison a cask of port wine at cost if he wishes it. 4°. 3 pages.

1816, December 5, The Reeds. When the port wine arrives will send Madison a quarter cask. Transfers of stock to the Bank of the United States. Accuracy of settlements. Respecting the directors of the branch bank at Richmond. The country people, the largest subscribers, should have a choice. "Private." 4°. 4 pages.

Montpellier.

1817, April 29, The Reeds. Sends him a quarter cask of port wine. Congratulates him on his retirement from public life, followed, as he is, by the acclamations of his fellow-citizens and the consolations of an approving conscience. 4°. 4 pages.

1818, September 24, The Reeds. Symptoms of the gout prevents his visiting Montpellier at present. Is pleased with Madison's agricultural essay, though he expects no improvement so long as slavery exists. Remarks on the crops and prospeets. 4°. 4 pages.

1819, October 10, The Reeds. Intended visiting Montpellier, but was prevented by absence of his son. Does not dare to leave his plantation and his affairs to overseers. Gives his views at length on agriculture and its incompatibility with slavery. 4°. 8 pages.

1819, December 2, The Reeds. A letter from his eldest son, which he incloses, will inform him why he and Mrs. Corbin can not visit Montpellier at present. Deplorable condition of the banks. Losses of his income. Is obliged to attend personally to the fields instead of his ease with books and study. Named director of the United States branch bank at Richmond. 4°. 5 pages.

1819, December 25, The Reeds. Reasons why his wife and son can not, at present, accept the invitation to Montpellier. Numerous occupations prevent inclosing remarks on agriculture and domestic slavery, besides the danger of incurring popular odium. Doubtful if we ever shall be at liberty to think and speak as we please. 4°. 4 pages.

1820, January 18, The Reeds. Respecting the proposed appointment of the president of the board of directors of the branch bank at Richmond. Is congratulated at being appointed. Has received no intimation of it. 4°. 2 pages.

1820, November 13, The Reeds. The numerous guests at Montpellier prevented Mr. and Mrs. Corbin's visit. Attention to his plantation now prevents. Unprofitable state of affairs for agriculturists in Virginia. The evils of slavery. Desires to emigrate north. The profession of law vile and vicious. Despondency as to the future. Farming and slavery incompatible. 4°. 4 pages.

1821, March 3, The Reeds. Gout in the head and stomach, increasing family and expenses, with diminished income, causes the writer to write in a desponding mood as to the future of the country. Predicts the destruction of the Federal compact. The evils of slavery. Bankruptcy imminent. The tariff and taxes. 4°. 4 pages.

CORBIN, FRANCIS.

1821, May 18, The Reeds. Is concerned at Madison's loss of servants by a contagious disorder. Hears that Madison is writing a political history. Will supply him with facts which may have escaped his memory. Mr. Taylor's new book. Asks Madison's good offices towards an appointment of collector at Pensacola for Edward Randolph. His services and merit. 4°. 3 pages.

CORBIN, ROBERT B. *Montpellier.*

1821, May 1, The Reeds. Announcing the death of his father. Asks Madison as an old friend to write a sketch of his history. 4°. 2 pages.

CORLY, THOMAS M. *Washington.*

1813, March 17, Washington. Petition for assistance for procuring a situation in the Navy. fol. 1 page.

CORPREW, ELIZABETH REED. *Washington.*

1812, April 22, Portsmouth, Va, An incoherent letter respecting an alleged attempt to murder her. Complaints of being deprived of property. Evidently from an insane person. small 4°. 3 pages.

CORREA DE SERRA, J. *Montpellier.*

1810 (?), no date. Petition to the President to be supplied with: A recommendation to the Cherokee agent; some perfect fruits and seeds of bow wood from Louisiana, and a perfect skull of a buffalo. 4°. 1 page.

Washington.

1813, September 9, Philadelphia. His departure to Europe. Offers his services. Respecting Mr. Warden, consul at Paris, with an inclosure in which he suggests the advantage of conferring the title of consul-general to Mr. Warden. 4°. 2 pages.

1816, July 10, Philadelphia. Announces his appointment as Portuguese minister to the United States. Intends to present his credentials and respects as soon as rheumatism permits. 4°. 2 pages.

Montpellier.

1819, February 12, Washington. Acknowledging letter of January 9 with seeds of the Missouri orange. Sends a parcel of marrons (chestnuts). Report of Jefferson Randolph being stabbed by his brother-in-law. 4°. 2 pages.

CORNICK, JAMES. *Montpellier.*

1832, January 27, Norfolk. Inquires if Madison has among his papers anything relating to the Revolutionary services of his father, Lemuel Cornick. 4°. 2 pages.

COSMEAUX, LEKEEL. *Washington.*

1814, December 21, Boston. In view of the financial embarrassments of the Government he suggests a scheme of taxes on manufactures, horses, slaves, and cider. Destination of the *Constitution.* Spies in the departments. fol. 3 pages.

COTTON MILLS.

1815 (?), Paterson, N. J. List of cotton mills and its vicinity with the number of spindles employed in the same. Estimates of cost per spindle. [Unsigned.] 4°. 1 page.

COUPLAND, WILLIAM R. *Montpellier.*

1828, October 5, Langhorne's Tavern. Asks him if a piano which was presented to his daughter is in Montpellier or not. 4°. 1 page.

1833, December 10, Cumberland County. An order to deliver a piano to Mr. Shelton belonging to his daughter. 4°. 1 page.

COVINGTON, LEONARD, to BLAKE, JAMES H. *Washington.*

1808, June 2, Aquasco. Acknowledging letter of May 26. The desired position has been filled by the appointment of Mr. Brent. small 4°. 3 pages.

COWPER, JOSIAH, to MADISON. *Washington.*

1804, July 6. Memorandum of a draft in favor of Jonah Cowper on Madison. Also a weigher's certificate, February 11, 1807. 2 strips of paper.

Washington.

1804, September 28, Norfolk. Arrival of wine and cordials. Sends his account of duties paid. 4°. 1 page.

COX, JOHN. *Washington.*

1807, March *27.* Inclosing a paid draft on William Gordon & Co. 4°. 1 page.

1809, May 5. Sends him money for balance after paying a note, from the proceeds of a discount. Memorandum attached. 4°. 1 page.

Montpellier.

1828, February *1, Georgetown.* Petitions for the appointment of superintendent of the Capitol. Relates his services to the Government during the war and his subsequent ruin. Incloses letters of recommendation from Joseph Kent and J. C. Calhoun. 4°. 8 pages.

COXE, CHARLES D. *Montpellier.*

1820, October 20, Sidney, N. J. Asks his influence to be appointed to the head of the Marine Corps rendered vacant by the dismissal of Lieut. Col. Gale. fol. 3 pages.

COXE, TENCH. *New York.*

1787, September 27, Philadelphia. Incloses some comments on the Federal Constitution. Requests him to peruse them with Col. Hamilton, and, if they think it advisable, to publish them in Virginia newspapers. 4°. 3 pages.

1787, September 28, Philadelphia. Sends Madison the third number of the American Citizen. Proceedings in the Pennsylvania house of delegates respecting the calling a convention for the purpose of considering the new constitution, etc. 4°. 3 pages.

1787, October *21, Philadelphia.* Proceedings in the Pennsylvania assembly relative to the new constitution. Conjectures as to its success. 4°. 2 pages.

1787, December 28, Philadelphia. Explains a point connected with the new Federal constitution. The commercial powers of Congress. Advices from Georgia. Favorable to the new constitution. 4°. 2 pages.

1788, January 16, Philadelphia. Incloses copies of debates of the Pennsylvania State Convention.

COXE, TENCH.

Wishes them sent to Massachusetts for the use of their State convention. The letters of "Publius." 4°. 2 pages.

1788, January 23, Philadelphia. Speculations as to the decisions of various States respecting the adoption of the new constitution. 4°. 2 pages.

1788, January 27, Philadelphia. Views respecting the action of the convention of States respecting the new constitution. 4°. 1 page.

1788, February 6, Philadelphia. Apprehension as to Massachusetts' decision on the new constitution. 4°. 1 page.

1788, February 25, Philadelphia. Rumor of the adoption of the constitution in Massachusetts. Unanimity in Georgia. Constitution approved in England by the warmest friends of America. 4°. 2 pages.

1788, May 19, Philadelphia. The fate of new constitution is hastening to a crisis. The writer's views. 4°. 2 pages.

Richmond.

1788, June 11, Philadelphia. Probable acquiescence of Virginia to the new constitution. The course of South Carolina, New York, Massachusetts, and New Hampshire. Benefits of cotton to the United States. Cotton at Barbadoes. 4°. 3 pages.

New York.

1788, July 23, Philadelphia. Arguments of those opposed to the new constitution. Amendments suggested. Direct taxation. Representation. Cotton planting in Virginia. The place of meeting of the new Government discussed. 4°. 4 pages.

1738, September 10, Philadelphia. The "Publius" papers. The question of authorship. Efforts of those opposed to the new constitution to influence the elections of State and Federal representatives. Conjectures as to the next legislature of Virginia. Selection of Federal offices. Madison well qualified for minister of domestic affairs. 4°. 2 pages.

1788, September 26, Philadelphia. Authors of the "Publius" papers. Candidates for election of Senators. The election of Representatives and electors by one general ticket. °. 3 pages.

1788, October 22, Philadelphia. New Pennsylvania State legislature. Majority probably favor the constitution. Coxe's name on list for House of Representatives. He withdraws it. Maclay the agricultural Senator. Incloses an essay on manufactures. Returns from Jersey, Delaware, and Maryland favorable to Government. 4°. 3 pages.

Virginia.

1789, January 27, New York. Congress not yet assembled. Proposed candidates for Vice-President. The general complexion of the Pennsylvania legislature. Conjectures as to other States. 4°. 7 pages.

1789, March 16, Philadelphia. Introducing Col. Samuel Hanson. 4°. 1 page.

COXE, TENCH. *New York.*

1789, March 18, Philadelphia. Favorable termination of elections in Virginia. Religious liberty in the constitution. The public and separate State debts. 4°. 3 pages.

1789, March 24, Philadelphia. Incloses notes on our system of impost. Resolution in the Pennsylvania legislature countenancing the call of a State convention to alter its constitution. 4°. 3 pages.

1789, April 5, Philadelphia. Confides in Madison respecting certain overtures made him by prominent persons in Pennsylvania to enter public life. States his position and prospects and wishes Madison's opinion. 4°. 5 pages.

1789, April 21, Philadelphia. Respecting the affairs of the Western country. Navigation of the Mississippi. Internal improvements and manufactures. 4°. 6 pages.

1789, June 18, Philadelphia. Extract of a letter (copied by Madison), respecting the advantage of a canal cut at the Dismal Swamp in Virginia, and another at the head of the Delaware peninsula. 4°. 1 page.

1789, June 18, Philadelphia. Remarks on Madison's proposed amendments to the Federal Constitution. Internal improvements. Canals. Suggestion as to duties on cotton and other articles of commerce. Does not think the rates of impost too high. 4°. 4 pages.

1789, September 9, Philadelphia. Apprehension of dissension in respect to the Congressional residence. His views and suggestions. 4°. 4 pages.

1789, September 17, Philadelphia. Is informed by his friends that the Postmaster-General will be removed. He would like the position. Gives a sketch of his political life. 4°. 8 pages.

1789, September 20, Philadelphia. Acknowledging letter of 18th. Views relative to the Congressional residence. Conversation with Mr. de Marbois respecting trade with St. Domingo. Affairs in France. The grants of the King to the "Tiers Etat." Demands of France on our agricultural citizens for our crops. The Protestant Episcopal Church. 4°. 7 pages.

1789, September 28, Philadelphia. The appointment of Mr. Osgood as Postmaster-General. Question of the seat of Government. 4°. 2 pages.

1790, March 21, Philadelphia. Desires information as to the conduct of Rhode Island in not adopting the Constitution, with a view to publication. Standard of weights and measures discovered by an artist. Incloses the communication. Model for spinning flax, hemp, and wool by water, applies for a patent. Arkwright's cotton spinning mill described. Proposes appropriations of land by Congress to a fund to encourage manufactures. Constitution of Pennsylvania. Incloses a medal of the President. 4°. 6 pages.

1790, March 31, Philadelphia. His idea of a landed fund to encourage manufactures is an old one. An infringement of the Constitution. Rhode Island's object in not adopting the Constitution. Arrival of specie from Amsterdam. The begin-

COXE, TENCH.

ning of a tide of coin. Application to the Government on the slave trade. Incloses a paper on Spanish wool. 4°. 8 pages.

1790, April 6, Philadelphia. Incloses a further consideration of the affairs of Rhode Island. 4°. 1 page.

1790, May 4, Philadelphia. Asks Madison to engage a room for him at Mrs. Ellsworth's. Goes to New York to take the position of Assistant Secretary of Treasury. 4°. 2 pages.

Philadelphia.

1791, January 13, Philadelphia. Requests an interview on the subject of inquiries to be made at the Treasury. 4°. 1 page.

1791, January 14, Philadelphia. Incloses a paper of estimates relative to the proportion of foreign and American articles exported from Pennsylvania. Also returns of flour shipped from Philadelphia and respecting French trade. small 4°. 1 page.

1791, March 14, Philadelphia. Asks to be informed of the estimated amount of the debt of the citizens of Virginia to the British merchants. The debt of South Carolina. fol. 1 page.

Washington.

1801, April 3, Lancaster. Probable assignment of the office of supervisor of the revenue of Pennsylvania to Gen. Muhlenberg. Thinks he is not fitted for it at his time of life. Also the vacancy in the Senate arising from his leaving could not be filled by a Republican. fol. 4 pages.

Orange.

1801, March *24,* Philadelphia. Incloses a copy of State papers of Mr. DuPonceau illustrating important points of public law. Suggests that the present time to bring our affairs with England to a conclusion by the commissioners. Madison appointed as Secretary of State. 4°. 3 pages.

Washington.

1801, April 4, Lancaster. Respecting the situation of the people of Ireland. The alien law. Incloses a paper. "Private." fol. 2 pages.

1801, April 28, Lancaster. Introducing Mr. Jacob Meyer, former consul at St. Domingo. Is well informed on St. Domingo affairs, which need investigation. "Private." 4°. 3 pages.

1801, April 29, Lancaster. Applies for Government employment for E. Forman and Samuel White. fol. 2 pages.

1801, May 1, Lancaster. The information given by Jacob Meyer, late United States consul at St. Domingo, concerning certain schemes of American and British residents there. [Unsigned.] "Private." fol. 6 pages.

1801, June 11, Lancaster. Acknowledging letter of 5th. Has been unable to have an interview with the late consul at St. Domingo respecting the schemes mentioned in a previous letter. Observations on supposed jealousy of Coxe's influence. His services to the Republican party and experience entitle him to more consideration from the Government for position. 4°. 14 pages.

COXE, TENCH.

1801, June 22, Lancaster. Acknowledging letter of 6th. Has had an interview with Mr. Meyer, of St. Domingo, and has left everything upon the desired footing. Mr. Strickland's pamphlet on agriculture. English prejudices against our system. Divisions of land more successful and just than consolidation. Law of descent in different States. British claims in United States. "Private." 4°. 10 pages.

1801, October 17, Philadelphia. Transmits papers prepared soon after Mr. Randolph's resignation which may be useful in present negotiations with Great Britain. 4°. 2 pages.

1801, no date. Schemes of intriguers in St. Domingo. Danger of the proximity of European occupation. Reports that the French are to send them 20,000 to 30,000 men and England to provide ships for them. The peace in England not permanent probably. All opposed to republics. The monarchical party in this country. Probability of accession of Louisiana to France. Object of Great Britain in retaining Canada. "Private." 4°. 6 pages.

1801, no date. The plan of the sovereigns of Europe for the extinction of modern republics. "Private." fol. 1 page.

1801, no date. Reflections on the termination of war in Europe. The consequences of the revolution of the United States, and of the principles laid down in the manifesto of our independence, the first cause of it. 4°. 11 pages.

1801, no date. Confirmation of the suggested change of ownership of Louisiana and Florida. Mr. Monroe's negotiations tending to their cession to the United States. Reflections of Mr. Coxe on the measures the United States should adopt to diminish the sources of danger in our Southern States, in 7 articles. "Private." 4°. 8 pages.

1802, January 4, Philadelphia. Sends a book of tables, statements, and representations relating to our foreign trade. 4°. 2 pages.

1803, November 6, Philadelphia. Incloses some extracts from a French geographical work of 1741, showing the limits and boundaries of Louisiana and Florida. Uneasiness of the Spaniards relating to the boundaries. "Private." 4°. 5 pages.

1804, January 17, Philadelphia. Introducing Mr. Thomas Benger, who goes to Washington to procure a patent for the preparation of oak bark for dyeing. 4°. 2 pages.

1804, September —. Authorship of the paper signed "Graviora Manent" in the Freeman's Journal. Several foreign powers averse to our obtaining the country and waters west of the longitude of the Perdida. [Unsigned.] 4°. 1 pages.

1805, June 7, Philadelphia. Respecting a letter to Mr. Adams before the mission of Gerry, Pinckney, and Marshall to France. That paper may be of use in the subject of an arrangement with Great Britain now at war with France. The article in the treaty about impressments. Great Britain will not recede from it. 4°. 2 pages.

COXE, TENCH.

1805, June 18, Philadelphia. Acknowledging letter of 11th. Our trade with India under the treaty with Great Britain. 4°. 2 pages.

1806, June 8. The recent inroad of Great Britain on our neutral rights. Probable action of France relative to the embargo. Views as to our legislation. 4°. 4 page.

1806, no date. Considerations relative to certain articles of the treaty prepared in 1806. 4°. 17 pages.

1806, no date. Observations on the treaty with Great Britain. 4°. 2 pages.

1806, June 12. Incloses a paper relating to the British treaty. Consequences of our submitting to the blockade in our relations with European nations. 4°. 2 pages.

1806, June 20. Respecting the British blockade, etc. 4°. 2 pages.

1806 (?), no date, Philadelphia. Paper marked No. 3, respecting the temper of France and England towards each other. France's jealousy of our treaty of 1794. Existence of manufactures in this country. Statistics of commerce. Importance of the encouragement and protection to manufactures. Paper No. 4, advocating reciprocity. fol. 8 pages.

1806 (?), no date, Philadelphia. The trade with India. Our agricultural products should be protected. Our carrying trade. Prohibition of cotton goods not manufactured from our cotton. A paper showing the importance of protection to manufactures, etc. Paper marked No. 5. fol. 5 pages.

1806, November 4, Philadelphia. Tendency in Europe and America to the promotion of despotism, as alone adapted to the tranquillity of rulers and happiness of subjects. 4°. 3 pages.

1806–7, no date. Conjectures as to the influence and power behind Aaron Burr in his treasonable acts. "Personal and private." 4°. 2 pages.

1807 (?), January 11, Philadelphia. Sentiments of the Federalists respecting separation of the Union. Advises that the Government take immediate measures to frustrate Burr's dangerous measures. "Private." 4°. 3 pages.

1807, January 13. Information received concerning Burr's treason by Mr. Eaton. "Private." 4°. 2 pages.

1808, February 10. Incloses extract from a letter of Silas Dinsmore, Indian agent for the Choctaws. Information respecting Burr. "Confidential." 4°. 2 pages.

1807, February 13, Philadelphia. French retaliation against British transgressions on the rights of neutrals in the maritime department. Under present circumstances it is doubtful whether a treaty of commerce would be expedient, as it might arouse the hostility of the whole continent towards us. 4°. 5 pages.

1807, February —. Essay on the state of external affairs. Policy of our noninterference and abstaining from commercial treaties for the present with any of the belligerents. 4°. 16 pages.

COXE, TENCH.

1807, February 15, Philadelphia. Incloses notes on external affairs. Opinions of Federal merchants on the French decree of retaliation. The power of England to cut off our whole trade. 4°. 2 pages.

1807, February 20, Philadelphia. Transmits a copy of an examination into the subject of the spoliations of the neutrals. small 4°. 2 pages.

1807, March 1. A note not dated and signed "le premier de mars," stating that the accuser (Gen. Wilkinson) of Burr is the worst man of the two. A letter in cipher of the accuser. Speculations of the design for an imperial confederacy made up from part of the United States and Spanish territories. 4°. 1 page.

1807, March 2. Refers to a letter written 1st instant signed "le premier de mars," respecting Mrs. Allston, Gen. Wilkinson, and a cipher. Reasons given of Burr's serious ill designs. Misconduct of the press and of our political opponents. Hating Burr, they sigh for the objects they think he might have accomplished. "Private." 4°. 2 pages.

1807 (?), no date. Respecting papers sent Madison respecting Burr's designs without date or signature. Urges energy, activity, and vigilance of the administration. fol. 1 page.

1807, March 27, Philadelphia. The present critical state of our affairs. The British orders abrogating the written and customary laws of nations. Our duty to declare that the law of nations as settled by usage and treaty shall govern. Suspension of the nonimportation law. Speculations as to Burr's designs. 4°. 2 pages.

1807, April 1, Philadelphia. Acknowledging letter of March 27. Sends a rough draft of his views and suggestions on the subject of the treaty. 4°. 2 pages.

1807, April —. Relating to the drawback provision of the proposed treaty with Great Britain. (Marked No. 2.) fol. 4 pages.

1807, April —. Relating to the provision in the treaty with Great Britain relating to the East India trade. (Marked No. 3.) 4°. 4 pages.

1807, April —. Relating to Article IV in the proposed treaty with Great Britain touching upon our trade with British colonies in America. [Marked article No. 4.] 4°. 7 pages.

1807, April 2. Inclosing communications relating to the treaty with Great Britain in 1806. Rumors of a decisive action on the part of the French and Russian armies in which the Russians were defeated with great loss. 4°. 1 page.

1807, April 7. Memorandum of subjects of papers or correspondence respecting British blockade. [Draft.] 4°. 1 page.

1807, May 20, Philadelphia. Change in the English system in the East India trade. Its bearings on our cotton manufactures and commerce. Question of the rights of England and France to dictate to neutrals. 4°. 4 pages.

1807, May 22, Philadelphia. Reluctance of the Federal press to publish information of importance

COXE, TENCH.

to our countrymen. The prospects of restraints and impediments abroad affecting our legitimate trade. "Private." 4°. 4 pages.

1807, June 1, Philadelphia. Acknowledging a letter inclosing communication of January 5, 1804. Violations of treaties and French retaliations, and frequent and continued violations of the laws of nations. 4°. 3 pages.

1807, June 14, Philadelphia. Referring to his letter on impressments. Asks him if he will furnish him with a copy of the British Orders of 1793 to aid him in the preparation of a paper on the subject. large fol. 1 page.

1807 (?), June 28, Philadelphia. The trials to be held in New York. Statement of a short-hand writer who has received, anonymously, money to attend the trial and take notes. Query as to the sender. "Private." 4°. 3 pages.

1807, June 30. Conduct of the Federal party on the affair of the *Chesapeake* and *Leopard.* Meeting in Philadelphia on British aggressions. 4°. 2 pages.

1807, July 1, Philadelphia. Public meetings of Republicans and Federalists to discuss the British outrages and the affair of the *Chesapeake* and *Leopard.* 4°. 3 pages.

1807, July 2, Philadelphia. Crippling and dismantling of a British armed brig called the *Fox.* The feeling aroused by the affair of the *Chesapeake* and *Leopard.* 4°. 3 pages.

1807, July 6, Philadelphia. Impressment of seamen from the *Chesapeake.* Proclamation respecting the affair. Reorganization of militia. McPherson's corps. fol. 2 pages.

1807, July 21, Philadelphia. On the delivering up of British deserters. "Private." 4°. 3 pages.

1807, no date, 4, Philadelphia. Remarks on the position of Federalists in reference to impressment of seamen and giving up deserters. 4°. 3 pages.

1807, July 14, Philadelphia. Relating to William Griffiths Montgomery. 4°. 2 pages.

1807, July 31, Philadelphia. Importation of East India cotton into England. Consumption of American cotton. Our cotton manufacture. fol. 2 pages.

1807, October 9, Philadelphia. Incloses a paper for republication which the Government should know of. 4°. 1 page.

1807, no date. The present conditon of the world. The war between England and France. The arrogance of England in declaring she will not abandon the principles of her orders in council. France's retaliatory measures bear seriously on our commerce. 4°. 5 pages.

Washington.

1807 (?), no date. Rumor of Lord Selkirk's coming out to replace Mr. Erskine. Order of the British Government that no unmarried man will go out from England as minister. Desirous that treaty negotiations should be made in this country. (Signed C.) "Very confidential." 4°. 2 pages.

COXE, TENCH.

1808, March 24, Philadelphia. Asks for a copy of "external relations," just printed. Wisdom of the embargo measure. Figures giving the amount of our commerce. Improvements and manufactures invite serious consideration. 4°. 2 pages.

1808, August 5, Philadelphia. Applies for the situation of collector of Philadelphia. 4°. 3 pages.

———, to JEFFERSON. *Washington.*

1808, August 5, Philadelphia. Applies for the office of collector of Philadelphia. 4°. 2 pages.

———, to MADISON. *Washington.*

1808, October 4, Philadelphia. Respecting some abstracts from a paper mentioned in his unsigned letter. Our national character a subject of calumnies by various foreigners. "Private." 4°. 3 pages.

1808 (?), no date. Abstracts from a manuscript in French of a statistical account of the United States made up to January, 1808. Observations on the American people. Statements calculated to make the worst impressions in Europe. 4°. 5 pages.

1810, January 25. Submits a plan for the collection of statistics on tonnage and returns of immigration and other matters relating to shipping. 4°. 2 pages.

1810, May —. On home manufactures. The necessity of considering, fostering, and promoting them. [Not signed.] 4°. 6 pages.

1810, June 18, Philadelphia. Submits, in an inclosed paper, the dangers to our countrymen and to show the necessity of arming our whole free population. 4°. 3 pages.

1812, April 24, Philadelphia. Incloses copy of a paper exemplifying the mode in which manufacturing must support our agriculture and necessary to effective war. 4°. 2 pages.

1812, August 13, Philadelphia. Application for the office of superintendent of military stores. 4°. 3 pages.

1812, August 31, Philadelphia. Death of Mr. Mifflin, deputy commissary. Applies for his place. "Personal and private." 4°. 1 page.

1812, September 1. Solicits the appointment to the office of superintendent of military stores. Enumerates his services and neglect by the Government. 4°. 5 pages.

1813, April 20, Philadelphia. Intended negotiations at St. Petersburg for mediation. 4°. 7 pages.

1813, July 8, Philadelphia. Incloses a letter from F. Mulligan, who solicits the office of supervisor of the revenue. Suggests the President, lately recovered from illness, should reside in the summer months on the south side of the Potomac, it being healthier. 4°. 1 page.

1813, July 16, Philadelphia. Would like the appointment of commissioner of the revenue or collector of internal revenue. 4°. 4 pages.

COXE, TENCH.

1813, July 23, Philadelphia. Duties of a collector of internal revenue, an office which he solicits. 4°. 4 pages.

1813, September 2, Philadelphia. Office of commissioner of the revenues, etc. Growth of manufactures in New England. 4°. 3 pages.

1813, November 6, Philadelphia. Applies for the situation recently held by Gen. McPherson, who is just deceased. 4°. 3 pages.

1813, November 15, Philadelphia. Acknowledging letter of 8th, containing his commission for the office of collector of the district tax and internal revenues. The naval office also conferred upon him is thankfully declined. 4°. 4 pages.

No *date.* Outlines of a plan to remedy the mischiefs arising from the present Pennsylvania judiciary system. [Not signed.] [Copy.] 4°. 2 pages.

Washington.

1814, January 3, Philadelphia. Makes application for the office of postmaster at Philadelphia, made vacant by the death of Capt. Robert Patten. 4°. 2 pages.

1814, February 23, Philadelphia. Mentions a memorial he has made to the Senate of the United States. Subject not mentioned. Appreciates the President's goodness, and the honor conferred on him. 4°. 2 pages.

1814, March 10, Philadelphia. Accounts of Mr. Mifflin, the late deputy commissary. Refers to his memorial to the Senate. Is uncertain whether his office is to be continued. Mr. George Armitage. 4°. 4 pages.

1814, no date. Admission of new States and representation in consideration of slaves tending to create dissatisfaction in the Eastern States. Refers to the eleventh article of the confederation. (A memorandum.) Scrap of paper.

1814 (?), no date. Requests the perusal of a paper on the subject of the "Balance of Naval Power." Congratulates the President on the good effect of the frantic barbarian and impracticable menace of Admiral C. 4°. 1 page.

1814, August 30, Philadelphia. His four sons volunteer for the defense of his country, and offers his own services. Loyalty of the Middle States. Character of the general committee of 36 of Philadelphia. Unpatriotic remarks of Joseph Reed. Robert Wharton, a Quaker, on the military committee. his unpatriotic toast. 4°. 4 pages.

1814, September —, Philadelphia. Inclosing a paper on the British census in East Indies and a cutting from the Democratic press, giving a picture of the British nation. Showing how a few free aristocrats rule the immense population who have no votes. 4°. 6 pages.

1814, no date. Communications from the committee from the wards to committees of defense, inculpating the governor and General Government. Objections to furnishing the Government with copies. They should be open to them. "Confidential." 4°. 2 pages.

1814, December 12, Philadelphia. Asks for warrants of two sons as midshipmen in the Navy. Asks Mad-

COXE, TENCH.

ison's opinion on a work of his on manufactures, previously sent him. 4°. 4 pages.

1815, January 4, Philadelphia. Calls his attention to a request for warrants for his two sons for admission into the Navy. 4°. 2 pages.

1815, January 18, Philadelphia. Recalls a letter of resignation of the office of supervisor since being advised by the State attorney-general that there is no incompatibility in holding the office of clerk of the general quarter sessions. 4°. 2 pages.

1815, January 20, Philadelphia. The attorney-general of Pennsylvania has expressed a second opinion that there is an incompatibility between the office he holds under the State and United States, consequently it is impracticable to perform the duties of supervisor. 4°. 2 pages.

1815, January 25, Philadelphia. Grateful acknowledgments for the appointment of his two sons as midshipmen. Letter from his son at New Orleans expresses a determined spirit there of all classes in this crisis, that even if the enemy could obtain possession of New Orleans it could have no effect on the ultimate success of the United States. 4°. 3 pages.

1815, April 26, Philadelphia. Advocates the manufacture and distribution of firearms for the entire militia of the United States to suppress all kinds of hostility, whether of insurrection of blacks or incursions of Indians. 4°. 4 pages.

1817, February 8, Philadelphia. Memorial relative to the cultivation, sale, and employment of cotton. A call for legislative action. fol. 3 pages.

1817, February 25, Philadelphia. Respecting his memorial on the cultivation, etc., of cotton he adds a document as appendix. Recommends the nomination of three wounded young men in the Navy, including a son, to be lieutenants. 4°. 3 pages.

Montpellier.

1817, July 5, Philadelphia. Acknowledging letter of March 11, with inclosures. Reviews the subject of the great revolution in culture and manufacture of cotton. Legislative action desired. Calls attention to promotion of his son in the Navy. Increasing respect in foreign nations of the United States. fol. 5 pages.

1817, September 25, Philadelphia. Importance of legislative action to protect our cotton interests. Arrival of East India cotton in Philadelphia to be shipped to Marseilles. 4°. 3 pages.

1819, February 2, Philadelphia. Sends an addition to his original memoir on cotton. The changes from linen, silk, and woolen. Alludes to his other publications and reflections on the growing interest in natural science in this country. 4°. 4 pages.

1820, March 7, Philadelphia. Wishes to have his son reinstated in the Navy, from which he was obliged to resign on account of ill health. Reflections on the Missouri question. The vine culture. Remarks on his different publications. The cotton manufacture and trade. 4°. 4 pages.

COXE, TENCH.

1820, November 12, Philadelphia. Acknowledging a letter from Mr. Jefferson of October 13. Asks Madison's good offices with the President for public office. Reviews his past services in his writings and otherwise. 4°. 3 pages.

1820, December 28. Reflections on the Missouri question. Abolition of slavery and how the blacks can be disposed of with justice and policy. 4°. 4 pages.

1821, January 8, Philadelphia. Pennsylvania about to pass a final act of abolition, paying owners of slaves. His writings on the subject reviewed. Translations of articles from English reviews into German defaming United States. Ratification of the Florida treaty. Our increased exports. 4°. 3 pages.

———, to JEFFERSON and MADISON.

1823, January 31, Philadelphia. In view of the nomination of President for the next election, proposes, with Madison and Jefferson, to collect and publish papers showing the public the antirepublican sentiments of John Quincy Adams. 4°. 7 pages.

1823, February 1, Philadelphia. Continuation of the subject of his letter of 31st. 4°. 4 pages.

———, to MADISON. *Montpellier.*

1823, October 3, Philadelphia. Respecting the pamphlet of Mr. Cunningham. Mr. Pickering to come out in a paper with so broad a range as to bear unfavorably on Gen. Washington. Recollections of Coxe on the politics of the period. Does not fear any harm to the memory of Washington or to the Republican cause. fol. 3 pages.

CRACK, JEHU. *Washington.*

1814, April 12, New Orleans. In behalf of a society composed of draymen, boatmen, and mechanics, in which he (the president) is the only man of learning, expresses their patriotic sentiments as Republicans. Would like a snug place for which his talents would fit him for, under Government, worth $1,000 or $1,500 a year. fol. 3 pages.

CRAIG, ELIJAH. *Orange.*

1786, September —, Fayette County. Respecting a petition for a division of the county. Is desirous for equal representation. In behalf of his friends would like the new county to be called Versailles. fol. 1 page.

CRAIK, JAMES. *New York.*

1787, February 21, Alexandria. Settlement of his account for services in the Revolution now before Congress. Asks Madison's good offices. fol. 3 pages.

CRAMER, THOMAS. *Montpellier.*

1822, March 4, Winchester. Resolution of the Agricultural Society of the Valley to elect Madison an honorary member. Note added from Mr. Cramer announcing the fact. 4°. 1 page.

CRANCH, W. *Montpellier.*

1835, July 20, Washington. Informing Madison of his election as president of the Washington National Monument Association in the place of the lamented Chief-Justice Marshall. Project of the association. 4°. 2 pages.

CRANCH, W.

1836, February 4, Washington. Acknowledging letter of January 31. Plans proposed for the erection of the Washington monument. Its cost and location. The fund to be raised by voluntary subscription. 4°. 3 pages.

CRANE, GABRIEL. *Montpellier.*

1825, July 25, Wilmington, Ohio. As the agent of the Lord of Heaven and Earth he calls on Madison to send him $5,000 as an atonement for his violation of moral obligations. fol. 1 page.

1828, March 9, Waynesville, Ohio. In the name of the Supreme Divine Author of the Scriptures he calls on Madison for $2,200. (Probably insane.) 4°. 2 pages.

CRAWFORD, WILLIAM. *Washington.*

1811, November 30, Washington. Respecting an unintentional breach of etiquette, for which he makes excuses. 4°. 1 page.

1812, January 15, Washington. Incident in the testimony in the trial of Gen. Wilkinson before the court-martial. 4°. 2 pages.

1812, March 28, Washington. Respecting the critical situation of the country he would impress upon the President the importance of unity and energy, yet before we are committed to war suggests the propriety of delay by a short embargo, and see what conciliation may effect. 4°. 2 pages.

1812, May 2, Washington. Suggests that in view of the impatience of Congress to adjourn, and the danger of being precipitated into a course for which we are not prepared, that there be a recess. 4°. 2 pages.

1812, July 4, Washington. Disapproves of the selection for appointment to office in behalf of a member from Pennsylvania. 4°. 2 pages.

1812, September 7, Adams County, Pa. Urges a decision respecting some experiments in a discovery of Mr. Lloyd's. 4°. 1 page.

1814, January 17, Washington. Plan for raising $100,000,000, for the expenses of the Government. 4°. 3 pages.

1814, January 24, Washington. Plan for raising money for the Government expenses. 4°. 4 pages.

1814, February 12' Washington. Thinks peace should not be concluded with England until Upper Canada is ceded to the United States. Means by which it can be accomplished. 4°. 3 pages.

1814, March 31, Washington. Suggests a method of raising money to relieve the Government's financial embarrassments. 4°. 1 page.

Montpellier.

1822, September 6, Louisa. Asks for the loan of a ram of Madison's Cape breed of sheep. 4°. 1 page.

1826, December 10, Georgetown. Asks Madison's opinion as to the power of Congress to cede back the whole or part of the District to Maryland. 4°. 4 pages.

CRAWFORD, WM. H. *Washington.*

1812, May 25, Washington. Respecting filling the vacancy in a professorship of natural philosophy. Mr. Meigs recommended. 4°. 2 pages.

CRAWFORD, WM. H.

1812, June 30, Washington. Recommends C. S. Ridgely, of Maryland, for an appointment in the Army. 4°. 2 pages.

1813, March 3, Washington. Suggests the necessity of removing Gen. Wilkinson from the New Orleans station. Is untrustworthy and has a bad character. 4°. 3 pages.

1814, September 24, Washington. Law for relief of intruders on public lands of the United States. 4°. 4 pages.

1815, August 26, Washington. Asks for the decision of the President on the effects of brevet commissions in the staff on the peace establishment. [*See* letter of A. J. Dallas to Madison, dated August 26, on the same sheet.] 4°. 2 pages.

1815, August 26, Washington. Question of staff appointments and brevet commissions. [*See* letter of August 27, from A. J. Dallas to Madison.] 4°. 2 pages.

1815, December 11, Washington. Asks the President's approbation of the appointments of Thomas Hinds, brigadier-general of the militia of Missouri Territory, and Darby Noon, deputy commissary of purchases. 4°. 1 page.

1816, June —, Washington. Transmits proceedings of the court-martial in the case of Lieut. Wilmore, at Detroit, June 9, sentenced to be dismissed from the Army. 4°. 1 page.

1816, June 12, Washington. Incloses report of the age and qualifications of cadets of the Military Academy. Also the regulations prescribing the course of study and of instruction, as modified by the Department. 4°. 4 pages.

1816, June 18, Washington. Regulations to prevent the abuses practised in issuing provisions to the Indians. 4°. 3 pages.

1816, June 19, Washington. Applicants for the position of deputy agent made vacant by the death of Col. Hawkins. 4°. 1 page.

1816, June 22, Washington. Incloses a regulation for the government of the commissioners of claims on the quartermasters of the Army. 4°. 2 pages.

1816, June 26, Washington. Submits for consideration the instructions prepared to be sent to the commissioners appointed to treat with the Chickasaw Indians. 4°. 1 page.

1816 (?), no date, Washington. Respecting a letter of Gen. Gaines. Gaines suspects Hambly of agency in promoting hostility of the Seminoles. Measures contemplated. Strip of paper.

1816, July 2, Washington. Incloses Lieut. Gadsden's report on the fortifications to be constructed at Mobile and New Orleans. 4°. 1 page.

1816, July 9, Washington. Appointments to treat with the Chickasaws. Recommends Mr. Sharpe to fill vacancy. Remonstrance of Dr. Watkins against the appointment of Dr. Pinckney at Annapolis. The vacancy contemplated in the Cabinet. Opposition to Mr. Clay. 4°. 4 pages.

Montpellier.

1816, August 8, Washington. The vacancy in the Cabinet. Should Mr. Clay decline, Crawford would

CRAWFORD, WM. H.

prefer remaining in the War Department. The coming election. fol. 3 pages.

Washington.

1816, August 30, Washington. Suggests the appointment of the governor of Georgia, if he will accept it, to the Creek agency. The vacancy in the Cabinet. Will yield his objection to the exchange proposed in the vacancy to Madison's wishes. Mr. Bibb's disappointment at his defeat. Recommends him to Madison for some Government employment. "Private." 4°. 5 pages.

1816, August 31, Washington. Application of two soldiers in our service, British citizens, for release. Interview with Mr. Bagot (British minister), on the subject. 4°. 3 pages.

1816, September 7, Washington. Proposed appointments to office. Governor Posey's application in the Indian Department. Recommends it. Dr. Bibb declines the Creek agency. 4°. 2 pages.

1816, September 9, Washington. Letter from Gen. Smith respecting the equipment of vessels to cruise against the Spaniards. Arrival of a British vessel with Gen. Mina, contemplating hostilities against Spain. Conversation with Mr. Bagot about the two British deserters. Has directed an investigation. 4°. 4 pages.

1816, September 14, Washington. Request from the Indian agent to supply the Choctaws with a cotton gin and cards. Appropriations for supplying Indians with mechanical instruments. Expenditures. Demands from Detroit. 4°. 4 pages.

Montpellier.

1816, September 19, Washington. The laws forbidding intrusion upon the public lands. Destruction of the negro fort at junction of the Flint and Chattahoochie rivers. Report of Pensacola being in possession of the patriots. Accommodation effected with the Indian tribes, the Illinois and Sacs. 4°. 5 pages.

1816, September 20, Washington. The claims of Mr. Carroll for destruction of his buildings near the Capitol and Mr. Ringgold for his rope works. Sums awarded in favor of persons who may be insolvent and who are indebted to the Government. 4°. 4 pages.

1816, September 20, Washington. Claims of Whitman Knaggs, who was deputy Indian agent in 1812, and was captured. Claims pay and emoluments. Asks Madison's decision. 4°. 3 pages.

1816, September 26, Washington. Mortification of the corps of engineers at the delay in commencing the fortifications near the northern boundary. Reasons for the delay. 4°. 2 pages.

——— to JACKSON, ANDREW (Commanding Southern Division).

1816, September 27, Washington. Reports of an intended invasion by a Spanish force of the military department under Col. Jessup's command. Directs Jackson to adopt such measures as are necessary to meet the supposed views of the enemy. 4°. 4 pages.

——— to CROWNINSHIELD, B. W. *Washington.*

1816, September 27, Washington. Respecting the reports of the invasion of a Spanish force against

CRAWFORD, WM. H.

our Southern station, asks the Secretary of the Navy, in concurrence with the views of the Cabinet, to dispatch such armed vessel, now at his disposition, to cooperate with the land forces, to the Gulf of Mexico. [Copy.] 4°. 3 pages.

——— to MADISON.

1816, September 27, Washington. Incloses letters to Mr. Crowninshield and Gen. Jackson respecting the reported Spanish proposed invasion. Advisable that measures should not be taken to produce public excitement in anticipation of the report. 4°. 2 pages.

1816, September 28, Washington. Impression removed which Col. Jessup's communication produced respecting the invasion of New Orleans by a Spanish force. Proposition of Maj. Jameson for permission for certain Indian chiefs to visit Washington. fol. 2 pages.

——— to LEE, RICHARD B.

1816, October 21, Washington. Directions of the President respecting the act making provision for property captured or destroyed by the enemy while in the military service of the United States. [Copy.] 4°. 2 pages.

——— to MADISON. *Washington.*

1816, December 5, Washington. Asks Madison to delay his nomination as Secretary of the Treasury to the Senate for the present. (Note by Madison at foot.) 4°. 1 page.

1817, February 3, Washington. Memorandum respecting engagements made by the United States with claimants for indemnification for public lands in the Mississippi Territory on the cession of the State of Georgia. Incompatible with the rights and interests of the State of Georgia. A recommendation to Congress. Suggestions for the President's message. 4°. 5 pages.

Montpellier.

1817, April 18, Washington. Sends Madison lupinella seed from Baltimore. Mr. Adams's accounts of the gloomy feeling in Britain. Now on the verge of revolution. 4°. 3 pages.

1817, October 12, Washington. Was prevented from visiting Montpellier by the illness of his son. Sends Madison a parcel of the lupinella seed with directions for planting. The common locust seed as a food. Revenues from the customs. Condition of the Treasury. 4°. 4 pages.

No date. Inclosing a decision of the Secretary of the Treasury. The practice of the Department forbids the idea of reviewing the decisions of a predecessor. The papers in the case are returned to the agent of Mrs. Dauphine. [Memorandum.] 8°. 1 page.

Montpellier.

1824, April 8, Washington. Asks for a copy of his vote requesting Crawford to take charge of the War Department upon the resignation of Mr. Eustis. This is to refute slanders of his enemies. 4°. 2 pages.

CREDITOR FOR UNCLAIMED INTEREST.

1824. Account of accrued interest on a stock to credit of Madison. fol. 1 page.

CREYON, JOHN M. *Washington.*

1809, September 20, Columbia, S. C. Transmits as secretary, resolutions of a meeting of citizens of Columbia approving of the course of the President touching the late negotiations with Great Britain and promising support. 4°. 3 pages.

CRITTENDEN, J. J. *Montpellier.*

1828, November 17, Frankfort. Asks for the date of payment of the first installment of a covenant of Bell & Tapscott to Madison and Mr. Willis. 4°. 2 pages.

1830, March 5, Frankfort. Respecting a suit in chancery of Madison's and Mr. Willis's against Bell & Tapscott at the instance of John H. Lee, Madison's agent. 4°. 2 pages.

1830, July 21, Frankfort. Acknowledging a letter of 8th, inclosing $80 in satisfaction of claim. 4°. 1 page.

CROCKETT, G. F. H. *Montpellier.*

1823, September 24, Herndonsville, Ky. Sends a copy of his address to the legislature of Kentucky. Asks him for any hints or ideas in relation to it. 4°. 1 page.

CROGHAN, W. *Washington.*

1802, April 7, Jefferson County, Ky. Notifies Madison of bringing suits in chancery against him and Nellie Madison respecting land bought of his brother Ambrose, lately deceased. 4°. 1 page.

Washington.

1803, May 22, Louisville, Ky. Asks him to give him a deed of some property purchased by Richard Taylor and himself from Madison's brother Ambrose, in March, 1792, which land was sold as his and his brother's property. small 4°. 1 page.

CROLIUS, CLARKSON. *Montpellier.*

1819, November 29, New York. Transmits the address of the Tammany Society on the subject of national economy and domestic manufactures. fol. 1 page.

CROWNINSHIELD, B. W. *Washington.*

1814, December 26, Salem. Regrets that his health and domestic arrangements compel him to decline the acceptance of the office of Secretary of the Navy. 4°. 1 page.

1814, December 28, Salem. At the special request of his political friends he accepts the appointment of Secretary of the Navy if Madison has named no one since his letter of 26th. 4°. 1 page.

1815, February 8, Washington. Asks him to name the ships mentioned in an inclosed letter from Commodore Chauncey. 4°. 1 page.

——— to DECATUR, STEPHEN. *New York.*

1815, April 15, Washington. Appointment of Commodore Decatur to command the squadron to act against the Dey of Algiers. Gives instructions as to his movements. royal fol. 5 pages.

——— to MADISON. *Washington.*

1815, April 17, Washington. Incloses copy of orders to Commodore Decatur and asks Madison to suggest any alterations deemed expedient. 4°. 1 page.

CROWNINSHIELD, B. W.

1815, April 18, Washington. On the subject of building a steam frigate at Baltimore. 4°. 2 pages.

1815, April 21, Washington. Incloses papers and requesting Madison's sanction to dismiss a man from the United States naval service. 4°. 1 page.

1815, April 26, Washington. Acknowledging a note containing proceedings of the court-martial on Dr. Roberts. Has ordered a new court to be convened. 4°. 1 page.

——— to COMMISSIONERS OF THE NAVY. *Washington.*

1815, April 29, Washington. In attaching the Navy board to the Navy Department he will enjoy the benefit of the friendly and confidential cooperation of all its members. Invites their attention to sundry objects and to prepare rules and regulations which he enumerates. 4°. 4 pages.

——— to DECATUR, S. (Commodore.) *New York.*

1815, April 29, Washington. Directs the Commodore to delay the sailing of the expedition against Algiers until further orders. 4°. 1 page.

——— to MADISON. *Washington.*

1815, April 29, Washington. Inclosing papers relating to the fleet captured on Lake Champlain. News from Europe make it necessary to alter the destination of our squadron to the Mediterranean. 4°. 2 pages.

1815, May 1, Washington. Inclosing copy of a letter to Commodore Decatur and asks Madison's advice. 4°. 1 page.

——— to COMMISSIONERS OF THE NAVY. *Washington.*

1815, May 3, Washington. Transmitting letters for opinion and decision which he enumerates. 4°. 2 pages.

——— to MADISON. *Washington.*

1815, May 10, Washington. Commodore Decatur's anxiety to proceed on his expedition against the Algerines. Advises the purchase of the prize ship *Cyane.* 4°. 2 pages.

——— to RODGERS, JOHN (Commodore). *Washington.*

1815, May 18, Washington. Acknowledging letter of 16th, which appears to be founded on an erroneous opinion of the relation of the board of commissioners to this Department. Defines the duties of the Secretary in his communications with the board of commissioners. [Copy.] 4°. 3 pages.

1815, May 18, Washington. Duplicate of the foregoing. 4°. 3 pages.

Washington.

1815, May 23, Washington. Acknowledging letter of 19th. The tone and character of the letter unexpected and extraordinary. Will abstain from any altercation. The letter will be submitted to the President. [Copy.] 4°. 2 pages.

1815, May 23, Washington. Duplicate of the foregoing. 4°. 2 pages.

CROWNINSHIELD, B. W., to MADISON. *Washington.*

1815, May 23, Washington. Incloses correspondence with the commissioners of the Navy board. Asks Madison if the board shall control the Secretary or the Secretary to control the board. Monroe and Dallas sanction the Secretary's course.
4°. 2 pages.

1815, May 23, Washington. The extraordinary course of the board of commissioners of the Navy. Has closed all correspondence with them until he receives instructions from the President. Has been guided in this business by the advice of Monroe and Dallas. 4°. 1 page.

1815, August 14, Salem. Incloses a letter from Commodore Chauncey declining the offer of a seat at the Navy board. The frigate *United States* ready for sea and will sail to join the squadron in the Mediterranean. Attempts of Gallatin and Clay to make a commercial treaty. 4°. 2 pages.

1815, September 11, Salem. The seat in the Navy board has been offered to Capt. Stewart as directed. Peace made with the Dey of Algiers by the commissioners. The commercial treaty. Decatur thinks a respectable force should be kept in the Mediterranean. 4°. 2 pages.

1815, September 27, Salem. Acknowledging letter of 18th. Capt. Stewart declines the seat at the Navy board. Asks instructions. Question as to the precautionary force to be continued in the Mediterranean. Vessels preparing. Approves of the convention with Great Britain.
4°. 2 pages.

1815, September 28, Salem. Inclosing letter from Capt. Stewart declining a seat at the Navy board. To whom shall the seat be offered. Doubts if Decatur would accept it. Suggests captains Evans and Sinclair. Asks instructions.
4°. 1 page.

——— to VAN NESS, JOHN P.
Washington.

1815, November 16, Navy Department, Washington. Informs the commissioner of public buildings that the timber can not be spared, as the Navy has use for it all. [Copy.] 4°. 1 page.

——— to MADISON.
Washington.

1816, June 23, Washington. Incloses dispatches received from the Mediterranean. Reprehensible conduct of the Spaniards. The Dey seems disposed to quarrel. A fast-sailing brig to leave New York with provisions for the squadron.
4°. 1 page.

Montpellier.

1816, July 1, Washington. Acknowledging letter of June 25. The naval force sufficient at Gibraltar to protect us against the Dey of Algiers or to chastise his injustice. Instructions to be given to Commodore Chauncey. Destination of vessels.
4°. 2 pages.

1816, July 16, Salem. Regrets that he could not visit Madison as he had promised. Gratuity paid the boatmen of Commodore Chauncey's barge.
4°. 1 page.

1816, August 13, Salem. Mr. Coles to proceed on his message to Russia by the brig *Prometheus*. The

CROWNINSHIELD, B. W.

ship detained by Spaniards at Valparaiso has been set at liberty. Difficulty in getting a translation of the Dey's letter. 4°. 2 pages.

1816, October 2, Salem. Acknowledging letter of 23d, inclosing Col. Jessup's letter relating to Spanish affairs. The course to pursue if menaced by Spain. Disposition of our vessels. 4°. 2 pages.

CROWNINSHIELD, GEORGE, JR. *Washington.*

1812, April 21, Salem. Presents the President a small bag of white Sumatra pepper as a curiosity. Introduces Capt. Holton J. Breed. 4°. 1 page.

CROWNINSHIELD, JACOB. *Washington.*

1805, July 9, Salem. Asks if Curaçoa is blockaded; if so, when it commenced? 4°. 2 pages.

1807, April 17, Salem. Introduces Joseph Storey. His high professional character, his private life, and attachment to the administration. Asks Madison to introduce him (Storey) to the President. 4°. 1 page.

1807, April 19, Salem. Transmits commercial statements. Articles of the proposed treaty with Great Britain reviewed. 4°. 1 page.

1807, August 18, Salem. The late outrage on the Chesapeake. Views of the British Government and their merchants of a branch of the India trade. Criticises the provision of the treaty relative to it. The Eastern States will go with the administration in demanding reparation for their insults. 4°. 3 pages.

1807 (?), no date. The new British treaty criticised. Trusts it will be rejected. The explanatory note, given after the treaty was signed, insulting. The order in council worse than Bonaparte's decree. There is hardly a ship out not liable to be seized under it. 4°. 2 pages.

CROZET, A. *Montpellier.*

1830, October 7, Columbia, S. C. Offers himself as a candidate for tutor of modern languages at the University of Virginia. 4°. 1 page.

CRUGER, DANIEL, and others, to MEIGS, R. J. (Postmaster-General). *Washington.*

1816, February 1, Albany. Recommendation that Gerrit P. Dox be continued as postmaster in the city of Albany signed by Daniel Cruger and thirty-four others, members of the senate and assembly of the State of New York. fol. 1 page.

CUMMINS, EBENEZER H., to MADISON. *Montpellier.*

1820, December 13, Baltimore. Incloses an English history of the late war with critical notes by himself. Asks Madison's opinion of it. 4°. 1 page.

CUNOW, JOHN G. *Washington.*

1808, December. Memorial in behalf of the board of directors of the society of the United Brethren for propagating the Gospel among the heathens. A sketch of their labors in the Indian country since 1735. 4°. 6 pages.

CUSTIS, GEORGE W. P.

1808 (?) January 17, Arlington House. Incloses a lock of Smiths Island wool. Calls it American merino. 4°. 1 page.

CUSTIS, GEORGE W. P.

1808 (?) May 1, Arlington House. Meeting of the Agricultural Society. Premiums in sheep. Sends specimen of American manufacture. Invites Madison and the President to name a time when he will show them his sheep. 4°. 2 pages.

1808 (?) October 7, Arlington House. Testimonials from various quarters respecting the excellence of Smiths Island wool. Asks Madison to impart any information he may gather respecting this article in comparison with other samples. 4°. 2 pages.

1808 (?), December 4, Arlington House. Agricultural matters. Improvements in domestic manufactures. Raising of sheep, etc. 4°. 3 pages.

1810, May 31, Arlington House. Sends for Madison's inspection a Rambouillet merino sheep, lately received as a present from Chancellor Livingston, of New York. Has prepared specimens of foreign and domestic wools for Madison's private cabinet. Our country in no need of foreign resources. Its future prosperity. 4°. 3 pages.

CUTRUSH, JAMES.

1813, February 14, Philadelphia. Transmits the prospectus of a work. Madison's election as an honorary member of the Columbian Chemical Society. large fol. 1 page.

1816, December 7, Philadelphia. Considers his message as a masterpiece. Is pleased with his recommendation for the establishment of a national university. His views on the subject. 4°. 2 pages.

CUTTING, JOHN BROWNE. *Philadelphia.*

1796, January 26. Asks his opinion of a claim against the Government. 4°. 1 page.

1796, February 6. Thanks Madison for the investigation of his claim against the Government, and for his opinion. 4°. 1 page.

1796 (?), no date. Asks him to give a simple negative or affirmative to his written questions, on paper, in respect to his claim against Government. 4°. 1 page.

Washington.

1801, December 10, Antigua. Incloses a letter to the President. Congratulates Madison on his appointment as Secretary of State. About to embark for London. Offers his services. 4°. 2 pages.

Montpellier.

1822, November 30, Washington. Incloses an essay by Thomas Law. 4°. 1 page.

——— to TODD, P. *Washington.*

1825, April 8, Washington. A letter with a memorandum annexed to it respecting Madison's authorship of a memorial addressed to the Virginia legislature of 1785 protesting against the passage of the "bill establishing a provision for the teachers of the Christian religion," and establishment of the Protestant Episcopal Church. 4°. 3 pages. 8°. 1 page.

CUTTING, NATHANIEL, to MADISON. *Washington.*

1806, November 14, Baltimore. Has submitted the piece of ore given him by Madison for analysis. Has gone into the rope-making business. 4°. 2 pages.

CUTTING, NATHANIEL.

1809, June 13, Washington. His unsuccessful business in rope-making. Asks for Government employment not out of this country. His former services. 4°. 2 pages.

——— to SMITH, ROBERT (Secretary of State). *Washington.*

1810, November 27, Washington. Incloses copy of a project of a "new organization of the consulate of the United States within the empire of France." [This communication was inclosed in a note to President Madison.] [Copy.] 4°. 14 pages.

——— to MADISON. *Washington.*

1815, February 8, Washington. Solicits the appointment to the office of one of the Navy commissioners. Reminds Madison of his past services and capacities. 4°. 2 pages.

CUTTS, RICHARD, to LANSING, A. B. *Albany.*

1813, April 6, Washington. As superintendent-general of military supplies instructs the quartermaster-general to make a return of all the military supplies he had on hand according to law. [Copy.] 4°. 1 page.

1813, April 17, Washington. Acknowledging letter of 12th instant. Regrets the circumstance of his being called upon to render returns when his appointment as quartermaster-general had not been made as he had supposed. [Copy.] 4°. 2 pages.

CUTTS, RICHARD.

1831. Bill of taxes for the year 1831. Strip of paper.

——— to MADISON. *Richmond.*

1829, September 28, Washington. Introduces Mr. Agg, of Washington. 4°. 1 page.

DABBS, RICHARD. *Washington.*

1813, June 10, Oak Hill, Va. Requests the President to appoint a day for fasting, humiliation, and prayer to God to aid America in her struggle. small 4°. 3 pages.

DABNEY, WILLIAM. *Montpellier.*

1825, January 15, Richmond. Incloses a right to use his patent pump for drawing water from wells, the propelling power being gravity or weight. 4°. 3 pages.

DADE, FRANCIS. *Philadelphia.*

1790 (?), no date. Request to assist Col. Carrington in the settlement of his (Dade's) commutation. fol. 1 page.

DADE, LAWRENCE T., and others. *Montpellier.*

1827, June 24, Orange C. H. Invitation of citizens of Orange C. H. and vicinity to attend the celebration of American Independence anniversary. 4°. 1 page.

DADE, LAWRENCE T. *Montpellier.*

1827, July 5. Asks him to furnish him with the substance of his speech on the Fourth of July, in which he alludes to Governor Page, a Revolutionary patriot. small 4°. 2 pages.

1829, February 27, Richmond. Introducing Mr. Edgington, a delegate from Brooke County, in the general assembly. 4°. 1 page.

DADE, LAWRENCE T.

1829, June 22, Orange C. H. Wishes to be appointed auditor of the Treasury. Asks him to write a letter recommending him to the President. 4°. 3 pages.

1829, June —, Orange C. H. Incloses a letter of Judge Barbour. 4°. 1 page.

——— and others. *Montpellier.*

1832, June 25, Orange. Invitation of a committee of citizens of Orange to be present at the celebration of the Fourth of July, or, it unable to attend, to furnish a sentiment. 4°. 2 pages.

DAGEPAN, CHEVALIER. *Washington.*

1816, February 19, Mamaroneck. A letter in French, apparently from an insane person, supposing himself persecuted by English in Boston, intrenches himself in a tavern in Mamaroneck, and stands a siege. Finally "petrifies" his enemies. Wishes to establish a marine battery. 4°. 2 pages.

DAGGETT, DAVID. *Washington.*

1815, December 26, Washington. Petition for pardon of Aaron West, tried by court-martial for desertion; being apprehensive that he may be under sentence of death, he will call the next day and present the petition. 4°. 1 page.

DAILEY, WILLIAM. Montpellier.

1834, July 18, Chillicothe, Ohio. Is a colored man, and did service in the Revolutionary war. Asks his good offices in procuring him a pension. fol. 2 pages.

DALCHO, FREDERICK. *Montpellier.*

1819, August 13, Charleston, S. C. Proposes a work on the succession of American bishops of the Episcopal Church. Wishes to be furnished with a copy of Bishop Madison's letters of consecration in England. 4°. 2 pages.

DALE, RICHARD, to BIDDLE, CHARLES.

1805, September 7, Philadelphia. States that he understood that when Commodore Truxtun declined the command of the Mediterranean squadron, he did not resign his commission in the Navy. [*See* letter from Truxtun, Thomas, to Smith, Robert, of this date.] [Copy.] 4°. 1 page.

DALLAM, WM. S., to MADISON. *Washington.*

1811, May 1, Kentucky. Commendatory of Monroe. Is gratified that he has been appointed Secretary of State. 4°. 3 pages.

DALLAS, Alex. J., to COOPER, THOMAS. *Carlisle, Pa.*

1813, September 1, Philadelphia. Subscribes for the "Emporium." Approves of his application for an office, provided it does not detach him from the professorship. Advises him to apply directly to Madison. 4°. 1 page.

——— to MADISON. *Montpellier.*

1815, April 12, Washington. Sends sketch of a second letter to the general officers on the effects of the act of Congress on the preexisting military code. Jealousies and illiberality of officers, concerning promotions and changes. 4°. 3 pages.

1815, April 13, Washington. Organization of the Army. Appointments and changes. Charges against Gen. Izard. The Yazoo claimants. Jackson's inten-

DALLAS, ALEX. J.

tions to remove to Natchez. Gen. Gaines left in command at New Orleans. Popularity of Jackson. 4°. 3 pages.

1815, April 14, Washington. Letter from Gen. Jackson inclosed. Payment of his troops. British officers at Castine decline surrendering the post until orders are received from Halifax; also the command at Fort Niagara decline surrendering until orders are received from Gen. Drummond. 4°. 1 page.

1815, April 16, Washington. Gen. Macomb's acceptance of appointment to continue in the Army. Organization of the Army continues. Solicitude of officers. Finances of the War Department. Pay and discharge of men enlisted for the war. Paymasters making arrangements. 4°. 2 pages.

1815, April 19, Washington. Acknowledging letters of 14th and 16th. The President's selection of general officers. Gen. Ripley and the court of inquiry. Two cases of court-martial. Wishes Madison's decisions. Letter of instructions to board of officers altered. 4°. 3 pages.

1815, May 2, Washington. Bonaparte's return from Elba. Conjectures as to his intentions. Probable renewal of hostilities. Our Army should not be disbanded, neither our squadron sail, at present. Our commissioners abroad. Favorable time for arranging question of impressment. Report of board of officers in Army. 4°. 3 pages.

1815, May 2, Washington. Our commissioners were to assemble in London in February. The moment critical. England may be disposed to avoid a collision on the question of impressment. Delay of surrender of posts in Canada. Conjectures as to the stand England and France will make. 4°. 2 pages.

1815, May 3, Washington. Sends report of the board of general officers upon the organization of the peace establishment, the selection of officers, and a report for a general staff. 4°. 7 pages.

1815, May 4, Washington. Sends third report of the board of officers. Plan for establishing a Northern and Southern division of the Army. Accounts from France as late as March. Our squadron delayed. The surrender of Castine not accomplished. A serious difficulty. 4°. 1 page.

1815, May 5, Washington. Inclosing report of the board of officers on the organization of the Army. The news from France. Our commissioners to press our claims. Our affairs with Spain respecting the Floridas. Mr. Onis. Monroe's correspondence with Baker respecting the surrender of the Canada posts. 4°. 4 pages.

1815, May 9, Washington. Inclosing final report of board of officers. Our military arrangements will produce less discontent than was anticipated. 4°. 1 page.

1815, May 10, Washington. The board of general officers discharged. On the sailing of our squadron to the Mediterranean. The propriety of discharging the Army. 4°. 4 pages.

1815, May 16, Washington. On the disbandment of the Army. Treasury financial matters. 4°. 2 pages.

DALLAS, ALEX. J.

1815, May 20, Washington. Organization of the Army now completed. Rank of certain officers in the peace establishment. Livingston's attacks on Governor Claiborne. Indian affairs. Chain of posts on the frontiers proposed. Pirates and smugglers at Barrataria. 4°. 3 pages.

1815, May 23, Washington. Appropriations for subsistence and pay. Incloses a return of the quantity of gunpowder at the different posts. 4°. 4 pages.

1815 (?), not dated. Fragment of draft for the official "Exposition of the causes and character of the late war." Attributed to Mr. Dallas. [In Madison's handwriting.] 4°. 3 pages.

Washington.

1815, July 15, Washington. Maj. O'Connor's curious paper. His discontent. Expectation of the return of our commissioners. A suspicion that we shall have a commercial treaty. 4°. 2 pages.

Montpellier.

1815, July 16, Washington. Necessity of an explicit understanding with the British Government on the question of trade and intercourse between its subjects and our Indians. Suggests the propriety of issuing a proclamation ostensibly to quiet the minds of Indians, but really to convey the President's construction of the treaty of Ghent respecting the Indians. 4°. 2 pages.

1815, July 29, Washington. Acknowledging letter of 24th. Unaccountable silence of the commissioners. Respecting discriminating duties. Outrages committed by Barratarians. Suggests offering rewards for apprehension. Napoleon's chances. 4°. 3 pages.

1815, August 1, Washington. Incloses a sketch of a letter to Gen. Jackson. Difficulty in addressing him, and the nature of the subject, owing to his character. Arrival of the *Neptune* with Mr. Gallatin and Mr. Bayard. The other commissioners, Mr. Crawford and Mr. Clay, left in London. 4°. 2 pages.

1815, August 22, Washington. Compliance with request of the contractors of a British cartel ship to land and sell surplus stores. Current business of the Treasury Department. European intelligence. Napoleon's situation since his flight unknown. 4°. 2 pages.

Washington.

1815, August 27, Philadelphia. Answer to a request of the President to investigate a request of the Secretary of War respecting the effects of brevet commissions in the staff on the peace establishment. [This letter is written at the foot of a letter from W. H. Crawford, Secretary of War, to Madison.] 4°. 3 pages.

Montpellier.

1815, August 28, Washington. Acknowledging letter of 13th. Relief of distressed seamen in New York. Rumors of successes of our squadron in the Mediterranean. The blockade of Algiers. Edict of the King of Holland respecting duties. 4°. 2 pages.

Washington.

1815, September 5, New York. Views on the treaty with Great Britain. Disposition of the British

DALLAS, ALEX. J.

Government to conciliate the United States. Case of the sufferers at Dartmoor prison. Elevation of England and degradation of France. The trophies of France's conquests to be returned to their owners. Gallatin and the French mission. fol. 3 pages.

1815, September 12, *Philadelphia.* Acknowledging letter of 8th. The commercial treaty with Great Britain. Question of a special call of the Senate for its ratification. The President's proclamation conferring reciprocal commerce. 4°. 2 pages.

1815, September 25, Washington. Temporary loan due the State Bank of Boston discharged. Treasury notes rapidly mounting to par. [Signature and date cut off.] 4°. 1 page.

1815, no date. Powers of the commissioners of the Navy and Secretary of the Navy. 4°. 3 pages.

1816, April 8, Washington. Tenders his resignation as Secretary of Treasury. 4°. 1 page.

1816, June 26, Washington. Interesting intelligence respecting the Algerine business. Offensive conduct of Spain towards the United States. Seizure of whaling vessels under pretense that they sail without sea letters. Eastern merchants and underwriters ask that a frigate be sent to Lima to demand restitution. Armament of the lakes. 4°. 4 pages.

1816, June 27, Washington. Consideration of the Algerine case and the whaling vessels in the Pacific. Hostility of Mr. Daschkoff. Complaints against Mr. Eustervief and Kostoff. A high and decided tone as proper in the Baltic as in the Mediterranean. Treatment of Mr. Harris. Case of the schooner *Mary*. 4°. 2 pages.

1816, August 8, Washington. Conference with representatives from the banks of New York, Philadelphia, and Baltimore on resumption of specie payments. Preparing a report on the finances. 4°. 2 pages.

1816, August 11, Philadelphia. His solicitude respecting the conduct of the State banks, organization of the National Bank and disorder of the currency. 4°. 1 page.

1816, August 31, Washington. Acknowledging letter of 25th. The Treasury proposition for a partial renewal of payments in coin. Financial measures discussed. Public confidence in the National Bank. 4°. 5 pages.

Montpellier.

1816, October 1, Philadelphia. Wishes notice of a day on which he is to cease to act as Secretary of the Treasury. 4°. 1 page.

1816, November 14, Washington. Acknowledging letter of 11th. Wishes his report sent to Congress as explanatory to business which was transacted before Mr. Crawford's responsibility occurred. 4°. 1 page

1816 (?), no date. Opposition of the State banks to every measure for resumption of specie payments. Wishes a Cabinet decision on the measures to be adopted by the Department for collecting the

DALLAS, ALEX. J.

revenue in lawful money of the United States. The subscription to the National Bank.
4°. 3 pages.

1816 (?), no date. To issue notice to the State banks for the payment of Treasury notes due in New York. Delinquency of the merchants in paying duties. Question of their relief. 4°. 2 pages.

DALTON, TRISTRAM. *Washington.*

1809, March 11, Alexandria. Offers his congratulations on his election to the Presidency.
4°. 2 pages.

1814, May 26, Salem. Is unable to procure sureties for collector of the revenue. In appointment of a successor to him trusts that it may be done under the idea of resignation and not as removal. Would like to be postmaster, for which he can find ample sureties. 4°. 2 pages.

1814, December 1, Boston. Acknowledging receipt of his commission as surveyor and inspector of port of Boston and Charleston. 4°. 1 page.

DAINGERFIELD, JOHN. *Montpellier.*

1832, January 18, Tappahannock. Asks permission to testify as to Daingerfield's mother being the only heir of her uncle Willis. small 4°. 1 page.

1832, July 16, Tappahannock. Wishes to correct a mistake in his certificate of the heirship of his mother. She was the daughter of John Willis and niece of Henry. 4°. 1 page.

DANA, SAMUEL. *Montpellier.*

1818, February 6, Groton, Mass. On the agricultural society established in Virginia. Offers to send him publications from the Massachusetts Society. Compliments Madison on his retiring from public office after so severe a conflict crowned with so happy a peace. 4°. 1 page.

DANIEL, PETER V. *Washington.*

1814, July 14, Richmond. Francis H. Hooe much aggrieved at the sentence of the court-martial against him. The writer concurs in the opinion it was unjust under the circumstances. The accusers were to blame. fol. 1 page.

DAVIDSON, JOHN, and others. *Washington.*

1813, September 22, Washington. Petition of a committee appointed by the officers of volunteer companies on the subject of organization into a separate legion. 4°. 3 pages.

DAVIE, WILLIAM R. *New York.*

1789, June 10, Halifax, N. C. In view of the meeting of the Virginia Convention in November, asks Madison's opinion as to the amendments to be proposed to the constitution if adopted.
[Copy.] 4°. 3 pages.

——— to STEELE, JOHN.

1802, January 30, Halifax. Asks for his aid in procuring the appointment of Isaac Cox Burnett as vice-consul at Bordeaux. Also wishes the vice-consulship at Paris for his friend Mountflorence.
4°. 2 pages.

DAVIES, THOMAS.

1796, July 29, Paris. Certificate of T. Davies respecting the robbery of money belonging to the United

DAVIES, THOMAS.

States placed in the custody of F. Skipwirth. Sworn to before J. C. Mountflorence. [*See* letter of Fulwar Skipwith of July 27, 1796.]
fol. 1 page.

DAVIES, WILLIAM, to IRVINE, WILLIAM (General).

1792, June 26, Philadelphia. Advances of Virginia for purposes of naval defense and supplies of the Army prior to 1781. [Copy.] 4°. 3 pages.

DAVIESS, J. H., to MADISON. *Washington.*

1801, November 4, Frankfort, Ky. On the subject of Madison's Panther Creek lands near Green River.
fol. 6 pages.

1806, April 21, Yellow *Banks.* Acknowledging letter of February 4. Asks him to inform Mr. Gallatin that the money proposed to be paid to him was on private account. fol. 1 page.

DAVIS, ABIJAH. *Washington.*

1813, December 28, Millville, N. J. Sends him a copy of his American version of the Psalms of David. Recommends torpedoes to blow up enemies' ships. Curious interpretations of Scriptural prophecy.
fol. 1 page.

DAVIS, EDWARD E. *Washington.*

1812, July 31, New York. Unnecessary expenses incurred in the Army and Navy in employing incapable physicians and surgeons. He volunteers to come to Washington on one leg and cure diseases solely on account of his love of country. Signs himself as an Indian physician.
fol. 2 pages.

DAVIS, ELI SIMPSON. *Washington.*

1812, September 15, Abbeville, S. C. Respecting resolutions which he states has been forwarded respecting the sentiments of the citizens of Abbeville in support of the General Government in redressing the wrongs of our injured country.
fol. 1 page.

DAVIS, GEORGE. *Washington.*

1801, July 11, New York. Applies for the consulship of Algiers. 4°. 2 pages.

1801, July 24, New York. Incloses letters of recommendation to the President. 4°. 1 page.

1801, August 31, New York. Is offered a position on board the frigate *Chesapeake.* Before deciding upon it would like to know the President's views as to granting his request about a consulship at Algiers. 4°. 2 pages.

DAVIS, ISAAC. *Montpellier.*

1819, February 16, Charlestown, Pa. As a practical farmer, and who has been unfortunate in financial matters, would like employment by the Albemarle Agricultural Society. 4°. 3 pages.

DAVIS, MAT. L. *Washington.*

1808, May 16, New York. Mr. Main's appointment as consul for Tunis should not be made. His character and antecedents. "Private."
4°. 3 pages.

1812, July 14, New York. Incloses a letter from Mr. Strong, who wishes to be appointed consul at

DAVIS, MAT. L.

Lisbon. Davis's personal interest in this appointment. Strong's merits and qualifications. "Private." 4°. 2 pages.

DAVIS, T. A. G. *Montpellier.*

1829, August 21, Charlottesville. Reasons of delay in sending copy of proceedings of the visitors of the University. Offers his services in Madison's official duties. 4°. 1 page.

DAVY, WILLIAM. *Washington.*

1810, May 26, Philadelphia. Sends four volumes of Syms's Embassy to Pegue. After perusal to be returned. His son sails for Calcutta. 4°. 1 page.

DAWES, THOMAS, to MONROE, JAMES. *Washington.*

1817, February 1, Washington. Incloses a copy of a memorial of the Massachusetts Peace Society to Congress. 4°. 5 pages.

DAWSON, JOHN, to MADISON.

1785, July 20, Spring Hill. Asks Madison's good offices towards procuring for him the office of collector. fol. 2 pages.

New York.

1787, February 18, Fredericksburg. The approaching elections in Virginia. Candidates. The State divided on the new constitution. Virginia will probably go hand in hand with Massachusetts. 4°. 3 pages.

1787, April 15, Fredericksburg. Acknowledging letter of 1st. Wishes to cultivate Madison's acquaintance. The British debt in Virginia. Scarcity of hard money. Low price of negroes. The coming Virginia convention. Monroe elected to Congress. 4°. 4 pages.

1787, June 12, Fredericksburg. The prospect of a general convention of States. Discontent on south side of James River. Difficulty in collecting taxes. The law for incorporating towns. [The signature and date cut off.] 4°. 3 pages.

1787, July 14, Fredericksburg. The people in Virginia discontented. Petitions to make property receivable for payment of debts. Goes to the springs. 4°. 2 pages.

1787, August 5, Bath. Discovery of a very curious spring in Pennsylvania about 13 miles from this place. Describes its intermittent flow. 4°. 4 pages.

1787, September 25, Fredericksburg. Proceedings of the convention. Varieties of opinion. 4°. 3 pages.

1787, October 19, Richmond. Acknowledging letter of 2d. Proceedings of the convention at Richmond. 4°. 3 pages.

1788 (?), no date. Acknowledging two letters. Proceedings of the Virginia legislature. Duties on exports discussed. Petitions on repeal of the post bill. Conjectures as to the adoption of the new constitution. 4°. 4 pages.

1788, August 20, Fredericksburg. Rejection of the constitution by North Carolina. Adoption in New York. Proposed amendments. Baltimore spoken of as the seat of Government of the First Congress. 4°. 2 pages.

DAWSON, JOHN.

1788, no date, New York (?). Members from different States represented. Advices from the convention at Kentucky respecting navigation of the Mississippi. Negotiations between France and Spain respecting exchanging the Floridas for some of the French islands. Mr. Fox made Lord Holland. 4°. 4 pages.

1788, September 30, Fredericksburg. On the apprehension of Willet and Lindsey for counterfeiting Continental final settlement certificates. Persons of distinction involved. 4°. 3 pages.

1788, October 27, Richmond. Acknowledging letter of 15th. Proceedings in the house of delegates respecting Col. Carrington's seat. [This letter is almost illegible from the paleness of ink.] 4°. 2 pages.

1789, March 20, Philadelphia. Being short of money draws on Madison for 7 guineas. Apologizes for the liberty. small 4°. 1 page.

1789, June 28, Fredericksburg. Thanks for journals received. Hopes Congress will not adjourn before the alterations demanded by many of the States in the new Constitution are effected. The Mississippi navigation. Decisions of court of appeals on taxes. 4°. 3 pages.

1789, December 17, Richmond. Resolutions of the Virginia legislature on the permanent seat of the General Government. The amendments recommended by Congress taken up by the assembly. Ed. Randolph's plan for the State government. Dawson would not object to being appointed assistant to Mr. Jefferson, Secretary of Foreign Affairs. 4°. 3 pages.

1790, February 26, Richmond. Acknowledging letter of January 31. Mr. Hamilton's financial plans. Rumors of declaration of war by Prussia against Russia. The price of grain. Jefferson's expected arrival in a few days. 4°. 2 pages.

1790, March 14, Richmond. Acknowledging letter of January 31. Opinion in Virginia respecting Madison's discriminating plan respecting public securities. G. Nicholas appointed attorney for Kentucky. Charts of the Potomac sent to the Executive. No acknowledgment. 4°. 2 pages.

1790, April 13, Fredericksburg. Acknowledging letter of March 20. Vacancy caused by Grayson's death filled by John Walker, now on his way to New York. Determination of Congress on the assumption of State debts not approved of in Virginia. A wanton interference. fol. 2 pages.

1789–'90 (?), no date. Respecting the location for the seat of Government. Asks Madison's opinion. 4°. 2 pages.

1790, May 14, Richmond. Acknowledging letter of April 27. Appropriation by Congress to pay arrears to officers and soldiers in Virginia. Agent appointed to receive powers of attorney to collect. Assumption of State debts. Probability of adjourning to Philadelphia. 4°. 3 pages.

1790, no date. Speculations on the pay of officers and soldiers. Not so extensive as apprehended. Injustice of the measure of the friends of assumption of State debts. Private negotiations between

DAWSON, JOHN.

members and individuals about the seat of Government. Asks him to collect a debt due from Nath. Twining. 4°. 3 pages.

1790, March 22, Philadelphia. Question of seat of Government. Corrects some remarks about Madison calculated to injure him in public estimation. Applies for an appointment in the Treasury. Auditor or register. 4°. 4 pages.

1790, no date, Philadelphia. Asks Madison's good offices in any appointment worthy his attention. Suggests the place occupied by C. Baldwin, should he resign. 4°. 2 pages.

1790, no date. Question of the adoption of the location of the seat of Government. 4°. 2 pages.

1790, no date. The Virginia legislature passes an act granting 10 miles square to Congress for residence of Government. Discussions relative to residence. Mr. Coxe's desire for the office of Postmaster-General. 4°. 2 pages.

1790, July 4. Acknowledging letter of June 24. Question of the location of the seat of Government on the Potomac. Would like the appointment of one of the commissioners to settle the accounts of the United States with the individual States. 4°. 2 pages.

1790, July 7, Richmond. Introducing Mr. Austin, who is interested in the establishment of a shot factory. fol. 1 page.

1790, August 1, Fredericksburg. Acknowledging letter of July 24. Revival of the assumption of State debts. Renews application for office of commissioner in settling United States and individual State claims. 4°. 3 pages.

Philadelphia.

1790, November 7, Richmond. The Indiana claim. Division of the State into districts to elect Members of Congress. The Turnbull divorce case. 4°. 2 pages.

Orange, Va.

1792, June 23, Richmond. Asks Madison's opinion on the question on the number of electors in the next Presidential election. Can a member to the House of Representatives be elected in the room of Brown, who will be elected to an office in Kentucky? 4°. 1 page.

Philadelphia.

1792, November 12, Richmond. Candidates for Vice-President. Enemies of Clinton report that he is opposed to the Potomac as the seat of Government. Asks information. 4°. 2 pages.

1792, November 27, Richmond. Acknowledging letter of 21st. Incloses list of electors. All for Clinton as Vice-President except one. Conjectures as to other States. Bill of the general assembly establishing a bank at Alexandria. 4°. 2 pages.

1793, May 13. Arrival of Citizen Genet on his way to Philadelphia. Finds he is well informed, of agreeable address, and engaging manners. Thinks he will do honor to the Republic he represents. Rumors of a mob in Paris who have put to death Pieton, Condorcet, and others. 4°. 2 pages.

DAWSON, JOHN.

1793, December 6, Richmond. Anxiety to learn what direction the politics of the present Congress will take. The general assembly of Virginia to adjourn. fol. 1 page.

1793, December 22, Richmond. Acknowledging letter of 15th. General indignation at the restrictions of Great Britain against our commerce. 4°. 1 page.

1793, December 29, Norfolk. Has written to Col. Monroe relative to the arrival and continuance of a British frigate in this harbor. 4°. 2 pages.

1794, January 20, Richmond. Acknowledging letter of December 31. Situation of the French Republic very flattering. Approves of the resolutions offered relative to the Algerine business. Intimacy of the British and French consuls at Norfolk. 4°. 3 pages.

1794, January 21, Richmond. Introducing Francis Guade, esq. 4°. 1 page.

1794, January 23, Richmond. Acknowledging letter of 15th. Respecting the opposition made to resolutions offered by Madison in the House of Representatives by the party which is ever ready to sacrifice the interests of the country for advancement of individuals. 4°. 2 pages.

1794, February 12, Richmond. Probable success of Madison's resolutions in the House. Foreign intelligence. 4°. 2 pages.

1794, February 25, Richmond. Meeting of citizens to declare their opinions of their Representative's vote on Madison's resolutions. Wishes to know something about our new French minister. 4°. 1 page.

1794, March 2, Richmond. Acknowledging letter of February 21. Reports of the appointment of Fauchet's succeeding Genet, the French minister. Meeting of the militia companies of Richmond approving of Madison's commercial resolutions. 4°. 2 pages.

1794, March 24, Richmond. Changing of ground of the fiscal party in the House of Representatives. Agitation about prospects of war. The majority of our citizens would sacrifice everything to support the American character. Query as to conduct of M. Fauchet. 4°. 2 pages.

1794, March 27, Richmond. Inclosed in a letter to Monroe extract of one received from Norfolk, giving account of French successes on the Rhine. Hopes Sedgwick's plan of an army will not succeed. Should it, he recommends Capt. Alexander Quamer for an appointment. His services during the war. 4°. 2 pages.

1794, April 7, Richmond. Instructions of the British King to commanders of armed vessels, January 8. Violation of our commercial rights. Talk of war. The Parliament may wish it, but the people not. Many British subjects take the oath of fidelity to Virginia in anticipation of the passing of the sequestration bill. The French fleet to sail. Clear of the embargo. 4°. 4 pages.

1794, April 14, Richmond. Acknowledging letter of 7th. Language of Lord Granville not open and candid. Disappointment of the British court in

DAWSON, JOHN.

their expectation of success against the French, they may pursue a different tone of conduct toward us. fol. 2 pages.

1794, May 6, Richmond. Resolutions of the House prohibiting commercial intercourse with Great Britain rejected by the Senate. Causes discontent. The nomination of an envoy extraordinary. The selection a most improper one. 4°. 2 pages.

1795, January 18, Richmond. Report that France has made peace with Prussia. Also that the Duke of York has met with a severe defeat. 4°. 1 page.

1796, January 12, Richmond. Acknowledging letter of 30th. British agents openly purchasing horses to take to the West Indies. 4°. 1 page.

Orange.

1797, May 18, Philadelphia. The President's warlike speech. No accounts from Monroe, but expect him daily. The directory resolve to receive Mr. Pinckney. 4°. 1 page.

1797, June 4, Philadelphia. The resolution of the executive council to not appoint to office those of opposing politics for fear of impeding the movements of the Government. Answer to the President's speech by Congress, introducing the clause declaring France to be placed on footing as favorable as any nation. Bonaparte's brilliant successes may save us from a war. The rage of Europe against France. 4°. 3 pages.

1797, June 22, Philadelphia. Incloses papers showing the state of Europe. Confirmation of Gerry in the place of Dana, who declined commission to France. Hears nothing from Monroe. 4°. 2 pages.

1797, June 25, Philadelphia. Passing of a bill for the protection of commerce. Resolution laid on the table, authorizing the President in the recess of Congress to lay an embargo. 4°. 1 page.

1797, July 27, Philadelphia. No news from Europe. Monroe is here. Hopes to leave for Virginia in September. 4°. 1 page.

1797, August 13, Philadelphia. Acknowledging a letter. Fever prevalent in Philadelphia. A plot showing the perfidy of some of our citizens, the criminality of the British minister, and the partiality of our polite Secretary, and the sending an armed force by the British ministry to Pensacola in conjunction with American citizens and Indians against the cession of Louisiana by Spain to France. Accounts from Europe. Mutiny of the sailors on the Nore. 4°. 2 pages.

1797, September 7, Fredericksburg. Result of the inquiries of the committee. A bitter pill for the British minister, our Secretary of State, and their faction. Extraordinary movement in Philadelphia. Thirty-five thousand people left. Can not ascribe it entirely to the prevalence of fever. The recollection of 1793 and the governor's proclamation. 4°. 2 pages.

1797, December 10, Philadelphia. Report of the committee on Blount's affair. Not a French plot with Jefferson at the bottom. The papers now in

DAWSON, JOHN.

press. Our commissioners at Paris. The present directory probably friendly towards us. Success of France and increasing debt and revived commerce of Great Britain. 4°. 2 pages.

1798, March 4, Philadelphia. The disgraceful personal encounter between Griswold and Lyon in the House. Repeal of the duty on stamped vellum and paper. Debates on the appropriations for the foreign intercourse. Spain it is believed will run the boundary line according to treaty. 4°. 2 pages.

1798, March 20, Philadelphia. A printed circular letter with a written note at foot respecting the important, intemperate, and unconstitutional message of the President, which is referred to a committee of the whole on the state of the Union. [Pamphlet.] 4°. 1 page.

Orange.

1798, March 29, Philadelphia. The committee of the whole on the President's message of 19th instant, New England begins to move in opposition to the President's measures. 4°. 1 page.

1798, April 5, Philadelphia. Acknowledging letter of March 26. On the publication of the instructions of the President and the dispatches from our commissioners. Doubtful if this publication is favorable to peace. 4°. 1 page.

1798, April 12, Philadelphia. Incloses copies of communications from our envoy at Paris, published by the Senate, contrary to the sense of the House. Hopes that matters are in a train of accomodation with the commissioners. The expense for providing for internal defense. 4°. 1 page.

1798, May 8, Philadelphia. The land tax limited to one year, which will defeat the provisional army bill now under discussion. 4°. 1 page.

1798, July 5, Philadelphia. Resolutions passed for raising twelve additional regiments of infantry and six companies of horse. Second reading of the sedition bill. 4°. 1 page.

1798, November 24, Alexandria. On his way to Philadelphia. Asks Madison's opinion on the steps to be taken respecting Mr. Lyon and the encounter with Mr. Griswold. 4°. 1 page.

1798, December 9, Philadelphia. Incloses the President's speech. The tone much changed. We may still hope for peace. 4°. 1 page.

1799, January 2, Philadelphia. Acknowledging a letter with inclosures from Jefferson. Efforts to be made to repeal the alien and sedition laws. Now engaged on the bankrupt laws. Accounts from Europe if true are bad. 4°. 1 page.

1799, January 7, Philadelphia. Acknowledging letters of December 16 and 28. Criminal absence of members. Proposal to repeal the alien and sedition laws. The President has not communicated the dispatches relative to French affairs. 4°. 1 page.

1799, January 25, Philadelphia. The promised communications of the President on French affairs not yet made. Attempts made to censure Logan

DAWSON, JOHN.

for his trip to Europe. Engaged on the subject of the bankruptcy law. The sedition and alien laws. 4°. 1 page.

1799, February 5, Philadelphia. The alien and sedition laws. Petitions for their repeal. Query as to the successor of Mr. Tazewell. Georgia has appointed Baldwin. Hopes Madison will go into the Virginia legislature. Arrangements soon to be made for the election of President and Vice President. 4°. 1 page.

1799, November 28, New Brunswick. Conjectures as to the choice of candidates for the next election of President and Vice-President. 4°. 2 pages.

1799, December 12, Philadelphia. Acknowledging letter of 4th. The business of the Senate. Conjectures as to result of the next State election. Candidates for Vice-President. Thinks Clinton would be acceptable. Monroe's election as governor of Virginia. 4°. 2 pages.

1800, February 1, Philadelphia. The bankrupt law before the House. The legislature of Pennsylvania to agree on a mode for choice of electors. Bonaparte has brought about another revolution. Peace expected. 4°. 1 page.

1800, February 23, Philadelphia. Law prohibiting intercourse with France in the House of Representatives. The bankrupt law. Method of choosing electors in Pennsylvania not agreed on in the legislature. Report that the general ticket is not liked in Virginia. Asks Madison's opinion of a law before the Senate, constituting a tribunal to judge of the qualifications of electors. 4°. 2 pages.

1800, March 30, Philadelphia. Earnest requests that Madison should serve one more year in the legislature. Anxiety as to the elections in November. Proceedings in the case of Duane. 4°. 2 pages.

1800, May 4, Philadelphia. Success of the Republican ticket in New York city and State. Probably New Jersey will exhibit the same spirit. 4°. 1 page.

1800, July 28, Hagerstown. Election of State of Pennsylvania in October. Question as to course of North Carolina in appointing electors. 4°. 1 page.

1800, August 17, Baltimore. Efforts of the Federalists in Maryland. Their hopes of carrying the approaching election. 4°. 1 page.

1800, December 17, Washington. Accounts from the election in the different States. Efforts to prevent an election. Fears of their success. The States to be counted on as certain. The treaty with France before the Senate. 4°. 1 page.

1800, December 18, Washington. The votes of the States result in 73 for Jefferson and same number for Burr. Designs of the Federalists. 4°. 1 page.

1801, January 29, Washington. Acknowledging letter of 3d. The uncertainty of the result of the election of President by the House on February 11. The French treaty in the Senate. 4°. 1 page.

1801, February 12, Washington. Balloting for President still continuing in the House. Conjectures as to the meaning of the Federalists. 4°. 2 pages.

DAWSON, JOHN.

1801, March 21, Baltimore. About sailing for Europe. Intends returning in the fall. Trusts no attempt in his district will be made to his disadvantage during his absence. 4°. 1 page.

——— to SMITH (General). *Baltimore.*

1801, March 22, Baltimore. Asks for 6 copies of the President's speech printed on satin. Gives an order to settle his accounts. 4°. 1 page.

——— to MADISON. *Washington.*

1801, June 25, Paris. Delays strange and mysterious relative to ratification of treaty. Applications to offices of consul recommended by Lafayette and others. Tripoli declares war against the United States, supported by other powers of Barbary. Treaty between Portugal and Spain. The First Consul and the Pope. Invasion of England by France spoken of. 4°. 3 pages.

1801, August 5, Paris. Ratification of the convention. All intercourse between England and France prohibited. Fears in England of invasion. Reports that a Mr. Lee is appointed consul at Bordeaux. An unfit person. 4°. 2 pages.

1802 (?), no date, Washington. The Danish claim. Should be explained. 4°. 1 page.

1802, March 8, Washington. Respecting Skipwith's claim. Incloses statement of money expended, which he thinks the Government should pay. 4°. 2 pages.

1803, July 29, Baltimore. Is introduced to Jerome Bonaparte, who travels under the name of Mr. Dalbart. He is staying at Commodore Barney's. Bonaparte discontented with Picton who will be dismissed on arrival of Gen. Bernadotte. 4°. 2 pages.

1804, May 2, New York. Election of governor of New York. The result flattering to Mr. Lewis. 4°. 1 page.

1804, May 7, Philadelphia. Reports of the return of Monroe, Livingston, and Pinckney. If the administration thinks proper to appoint Dawson he would prefer France. Rumors of the death of the King of England. 4°. 1 page.

1805, October 9. Introduces Mr. Fuller, of South Carolina. 4°. 1 page.

1805, December 7, Washington. Incloses a letter from Mr. Poinsett, of South Carolina. Recommends him. 4°. 1 page.

1806, April 23, Washington. Asks Madison to lend him $100. 4°. 1 page.

1806, April 28, Fredericksburg. Introduces Mr. Morales, consul-general from the Batavian Republic for the Southern States. 4°. 1 page.

1806, May 28, Fredericksburg. Introduces Dr. Wellford with his daughter. 4°. 1 page.

1806, June 15, Fredericksburg. Incloses Madison $100 borrowed at Washington. 4°. 1 page.

1806, June 26, Philadelphia. Conversation with Governor McKeon, Mr. Dallas, Rodney, and others who are of the opinion Madison should attend the court in the Miranda case in order to remove erroneous impressions. 4°. 1 page.

DAWSON, JOHN.

1806, July 5, New York. Relates the contents of a letter he had seen from the Marquis de Yrujo, relative to the trial in the Miranda business. Thinks Madison should come on to attend it. 4°. 2 pages.

1807, June 28, Fredericksburg. Indignation meeting of citizens respecting the *Chesapeake* and *Leopard* affair. 4°. 1 page.

1808, November 29, Washington. Incloses a letter. As there is no Government vessel to sail for New Orleans advises the writer to take passage in a private vessel. 4°. 1 page.

1809, March 9, Fredericksburg. Recommends Mr. Pollard, of Virginia, who wishes to enter into service of his country. 4°. 1 page.

1810, June 20, Fredericksburg. Asks if Congress is to be convened during the summer. 4°. 1 page.

1812 (?), no date. Thinks the appointment of Federalists to command both the regiments in Virginia will cause discontent. 4°. 1 page.

DAWSON, JOSHUA, and others.

1816, October 24, Washington. Protest of citizens against the permission given by the President to Richard Forrest to occupy, as a stable, the house on southeast corner of G and Fourteenth street. • 4°. 2 pages.

DAWSON, JOSHUA.

1817, March 13, Washington. Testifies his respects to the late President and Mrs. Madison on their retiring to private life. 4°. 1 page.

DAWSON, MOSES. *Montpellier.*

1824, September 3, Cincinnati. Presents him with a copy of "A Historical Narrative of the Civil and Military Services of Maj. Gen. Harrison." 4°. 1 page.

DAY, BENJAMIN. *Washington.*

1802, September 20, Fredericksburg. Informs Madison that the British bark *Freedom* is lying at Tappahannock and wants freight. Will take tobacco. Incloses a circular. 4°. 1 page.

1804, February 10, Fredericksburg. Incloses bill of lading of tobacco shipped in the *Atlantic* with bill of shipping charges. 4°. 1 page.

1804, February 16, Fredericksburg. Acknowledging receipt of a draft and states a balance due him. 4°. 1 page.

1810, March 19, Fredericksburg. Incloses Anthony Buck's account, receipted. 4°. 1 page.

DAYTON, GEORGE.

No date. A paper signed J. D. giving an account of the position of affairs in Florida. Fear of a contest unless the Government sends an adequate force. 4°. 2 pages.

DEARBORN, H. *Washington.*

1802, September 10, Washington. Respecting the establishment of a trading post with the Choctaws. Incloses press copy of a letter to Governor Claiborne. 4°. 2 pages.

——— to CLAIBORNE, W. C. C. *New Orleans.*

1802, September 10, Washington. Acknowledging letter of August 6. Respecting the establishment

DEARBORN, H.

of a trading house with the Indians. Question of the location. [Press copy.] 4°. 3 pages.

——— to MEIGS, RETURN JONATHAN.

1807, February 28, Washington. The Secretary of War directs Meigs to ascertain the opinion of the chiefs of the Cherokees on the subject of Col. Earle's project of establishing a set of iron works with smith shops if a suitable site can be found and their consent to cede to the United States a tract of six miles square for the purpose. [Annexed is copy of letter from same to same, March 26, 1808.] [Copy.] 4°. 2 pages.

——— to MADISON. *Washington.*

1807, July 17, New York. Is to attend an exhibition of Mr. Fulton's for blowing up ships. Fulton's confidence in being successful. 4°. 3 pages.

1807, August 17, Washington. Attitude of the present British Government towards us and the course they will pursue respecting the conduct of Admiral Berkley. 4°. 2 pages.

——— to MEIGS, RETURN JONATHAN.

1808, March 26, Washington. Extract of a letter of above date respecting the non ratification of the Senate of the ceding of Cherokees of land to the State of Tennessee. [On same sheet of letter dated February 28, 1807, from and to the same.] [Copy.] 4°. 2 pages.

1808, October 29, Washington. Is authorized by the President to direct Meigs to demand of the Cherokee nation the prompt apprehension and punishment of Vann for the crimes by him committed on two American citizens, and to request Governor Sevier to grant the chiefs such military aid as they require. To also notify intruders to remove from the Indian lands. [Copy.] 4°. 2 pages.

——— to JEFFERSON. *Washington.*

1809, February 16, Washington. Asks for the removal of Mr. Simmons, accountant of the War Department. 4°. 1 page.

——— to MADISON. *Washington.*

1809, June 1, Boston. The result of the Massachusetts election. Conjectures as to the measures of the Federalists. Satirical remarks on the leaders. 4°. 3 pages.

1809, June 14, Boston. Certificate of importation of a pipe of brandy per ship *William* from Liverpool. 8°. 1 page.

1809, November 7, Boston. Col. Jonathan Russell, of Providence, desirous of appointment as a consul. 4°. 1 page.

1810, April 30, Boston. Incloses a sermon exhibiting a correct picture of New England Federalism. Question of the results of the next State election. Chances about equal. 4°. 2 pages.

1811, July 8, Boston. Sends a copy of his son's Fourth of July oration. 4°. 1 page.

1812, January 17, Boston. Acknowledging letter of 11. Does not desire military rank, but to prevent any unnecessary delay will accept such position and devote his talents as his country may demand. Requests that no measures may be taken about

DEARBORN, H.

the collectorship until he has a personal interview. 4°. 2 pages.

1812, March 21, Boston. Suggests the caution to be observed in appointing Federals to the higher grades in the Army. Scrap of paper.

1812, March 29, Washington. Recommendation that Col. Earle be allowed compensation for exploring the country and bringing on the treaty with the Cherokees or comply with the original intentions of obtaining a tract of land from them. [Copy.] 4°. 1 page.

1812, March 29, Washington. Statement of the proposition of Elias Earle to the establishment of iron works in the Cherokee nation in 1807 with the conditions. Recommends the fulfillment of the contract which was the cession of land on the Chickamauga. Elias Earle's explorations and services. [Copy.] 4°. 4 pages.

1812, April 4, Washington. Has written to the Secretary of War expressing his readiness to enter on the duties of his appointment. Takes it for granted that the office of collector of Boston will be kept open at present and himself to be replaced after the war in the same. 4°. 2 pages.

1812, June 12, Boston. Suggests the appointment of his son as collector of Boston so that the position may be restored to him should there be a short war. His sons merits and qualifications. The Republicans of Massachusetts desirous that the question of war be decided. The progress of recruiting. 4°. 4 pages.

1812, July 3, Boston. Suggests the advantage of gunboats on our coasts to protect our harbors. Immediate measures should be taken. Governor Strong will not turn out the militia. 4°. 2 pages.

1812, August 15, Greenbush. Acknowledging letter of 9th. His unpleasant position, owing to absence of orders in relation to Upper Canada. Will do his utmost to have an efficient army by the next spring. The treasonable conduct of the Tories. 4°r 4 pages.

1812, September 30, Greenbush. Predicts an unfortunate campaign unless the troops destined for Detroit and Niagara, aided by naval preparations, shall penetrate Upper Canada before winter sets in. Offensive operations against Montreal delayed. Hull's disaster. Urges action by Congress and the War Department for additional encouragements as to pay of volunteers. 4°. 6 pages.

1812, October 24, Greenbush. The unfortunate event at Niagara. Its origin, jealousy. Gen. Van Rensselaer, desiring to be relieved from command, has been directed to give it over to Gen. Smyth. Efforts made for reinforcing him. Hopes to surmount difficulties of a clumsy beginning by prosecuting the war with vigor. 4°. 4 pages.

1812, December 13, Albany. The necessity of raising additional regiments for offensive operations in order to take possession of Montreal in the Spring. A defensive policy recommended. Unpopular commanding officer at Niagara. 4°. 3 pages.

DEARBORN, H.

1813, February 14, Albany. Acknowledging letter of 6th. Gen. Smyth's unwillingness to request a court of inquiry. Question of a court-martial, His hopes in relation to an attack on Kingston. Defeat of Gen. Winchester. Advocates removal of Gens. Bloomfield and Smith to other posts and their places filled by more competent officers. Future army movements. 4°. 4 pages.

1813, March 13, Sacketts Harbor. On the appointment of officers for important commands. Will himself comply with any arrangement deemed expedient and be relieved from his present command. Preparations for the defense of Sacketts Harbor and the Navy. Difficulty in obtaining information of the movements of the enemy, and of their numbers. Congratulations on his reelection. 4°. 4 pages.

1813, March 22, Albany. Denies the intimation that his son-in-law, Maj. Wingate, Mr. Ilsley, the collector at Portland, and several others, had favored the Clintonian faction. 4°. 2 pages.

1813, April 7, Albany. New organization of the staff of the Army. Arrival of troops from Maryland and Pennsylvania to proceed to Lake Ontario. A new quartermaster-general. 4°. 4 pages.

1813, July 24, Utica. Resuming his command. Expected arrival of Maj. Gen. Hampton. Maj. Gen. Lewis to take command of troops at Sacketts Harbor. Intends retiring to his family near Boston and asks the satisfaction of an inquiry to investigate his conduct. [Signature cut off.] 4°. 3 pages.

1813, August 17, Roxbury. Acknowledging letter of 8th. On his suspension of command. Solicits a court of inquiry. 4°. 3 pages.

1814, June 6, Boston. Testifies to the character of Mr. Eakin as a public officer. On the next page is a letter from Joseph Bloomfield indorsing the general's opinion. 4°. 2 pages.

1814, June 17, Boston. Testifies as to the conduct of Gen. Boyd at the landing of our troops in Upper Canada near Fort George. Conspicuously firm, brave, and animated. 4°. 2 pages.

1814, September 6, Boston. Inclosing orders of Gen. Strong respecting the turning out of a body of militia to the Department of War. No provisions for defense for district of Maine. Asks for explicit orders. 4°. 2 pages.

1815, January 26, Troy. Great delay in the court-martial of Gen. Wilkinson for the want of the presence of the principal witnesses. [Unsigned.] 4°. 3 pages.

DEARBORN, H. A. S. *Washington.*

1811, October 14, Boston. Incloses a paper of N. Bowditch containing the result of his calculations on the orbit of the comet now visible. 4°. 2 pages.

1812, June 13, Boston. Solicits the office of collector of Boston, made vacant by the appointment of his father to the Army. Would desire, in the event of a close of the war, that his father should be reappointed as collector. 4°. 3 pages.

1813, September 13, Boston. Defends Mr. Rowson, a clerk in the custom-house, against the charge of

DEARBORN, H. A. S.

some meddling person and testifies to his loyalty and efficiency. His disgust at the conduct of Gen. Armstrong toward his father.
4°. 6 pages.

1814, March 16, Boston. Notice from the custom-house of the shipment of some wine, brandy, etc., received per brig *Wanderer*, and inclosing bill of lading. 4°. 1 page.

1814, March 24, Boston. Notice of arrival of brig *Rambler* with wine and sundries from Bordeaux, inclosing invoice, bill of freight, wharfage and drayage, and account for duties.
4°. 3 pages. fol. 1 page.

1814, March 28, Boston. Transmits a pamphlet written for distribution previous to the April elections, by A. H. Everett. 4°. 1 page.

1814, April 22, Boston. Sends account of duties and freight on some importations of wine and other things. Will take care of the articles until further orders. 4°. 2 pages.

Montpellier.

1824, August —, Boston. Sends some newspapers containing defense of his father against slanders.
4°. 1 page.

1830, December 6, Boston. Notifying Madison of his election as an honorary member of the Massachusetts Horticultural Society. [Broadside.]
4°. 1 page.

DE GRAY, MICHAEL. *Montpellier.*

1825, July 17, New York. Criticises the administration of Monroe in the extravagant honors and presents to Lafayette, when many of our countrymen (particularizing Daniel D. Tompkins) have been shamefully forgotten, who had done as much, or more, for their country in the late war. 4°. 4 pages.

DELACROIX, CHARLES (French Minister of Foreign Relations), to MONROE. *Paris.*

1796, October 7, Paris. Announcing the suspension of the functions of the French minister to the United States; also the decree that French armed vessels will act towards the United States as the English are suffered to do. Ordinary relations existing between the two nations will not be changed. [In French.] [Copy.] 4°. 3 pages.

DE LACY, JOHN D., to MADISON. *Washington.*

1803, October 14, New Orleans. Detailed statement of his hardships in his effort to induce the Indians, while a prisoner as a Spanish agent, to sell the whole of their possessions east of the Mississippi to the United States, and form for themselves a government west of the Mississippi to be ultimately annexed to the United States.
fol. 4 pages.

DE LA MOTTA, JACOB. *Montpellier.*

1820, August 7, Savannah. Asks him to accept a copy of a discourse relative to the history of the Jews.
4°. 1 page.

DELAPLAINE, JOSEPH. *Washington.*

1812, May 15, Philadelphia. Solicits Madison's patronage to the "Emporium of Arts and Sciences."
4°. 1 page.

DELAPLAINE, JOSEPH.

1814, November 18, Philadelphia. Portrait of Madison by Mr. Edwin, to be engraved by Mr. Jones. 4°. 1 page.

1816, January 31, Philadelphia. As the portrait which he had caused to be taken of Madison was not engraved, he now asks him to sit for Mr. Wood for a new one that he can use in his work. Asks Madison for a sketch of his life. 4°. 1 page.

1816, February 26, Philadelphia. Requesting Madison to sit for his portrait for Mr. Wood, with a view of having it engraved to be inserted in Delaplaine's repository of the lives of distinguished American characters, a prospectus of which is on the back of the letter. 4°. 3 pages.

1816, May 23, Philadelphia. Asks whether he had given Mr. Wood a sitting for his portrait. Is about to send another painter, Mr. Otis, to paint Jefferson, and who will paint Madison if he will be in Washington in June. [On the back of this letter is a printed prospectus.] 4°. 1 page.

1816, October —, Philadelphia. Acknowledging receipt of the sketch of Madison's life. Has sent him the first half volume of the "Repository." Asks Madison's approbation of it. 4°. 1 page.

1816, October 27, Philadelphia. Acknowledging letter of 22d. Complies with the request to not make use of his observations on Delaplaine's work until he has read it. 4°. 1 page.

Montpellier.

1818, June 22, Philadelphia. Acknowledging letter of 17th. Asks Madison to send the MSS. to which the letter alludes. 4°. 1 page.

1820, October 11, Philadelphia. Transmits a copy of a volume of poetry. Will send, when issued, an elementary book for the use of schools. 8°. 1 page.

1822, January 23, Philadelphia. Sends at request of Charles Mead, a book for the use of schools. Asks his approval of it. 4°. 1 page.

DELAVAN, EDWARD C. *Montpellier.*

1834, December 29, Albany. Sends him three declarations on parchment to sign and return to Hon. Walter Lowrie, secretary of the Senate. 4°. 1 page.

DELAWARE, STATE OF.

1798, January 23. An act to prevent aliens from voting at elections in this State, and for other purposes. [Copy.] fol. 3 pages.

DELIVET, PETER, to MADISON. *Washington.*

1813, May 26, Baltimore. Proposes a scheme for destroying the enemy's fleet in the Chesapeake, with drawings of his invention. fol. 8 pages.

DELOZIER, D. *Washington.*

1806, June 10, Baltimore. Respecting the tax on a lot in square 253, assessed to John Templeman. It was probably paid. 4°. 1 page.

DELPEAUX, ——. *Washington.*

1812, June 11, Philadelphia. Appeal of a refugee from St. Domingo, who has been unjustly imprisoned. Asks assistance. [In French.] 4°. 2 pages.

DENT, JOHN H., to JONES, WILLIAM. *Washington.*

1814, March 24, May 23, 28, Charleston. [*See* William Jones's letter to Madison, dated June 6, 1814, lettered F.] [Extract.] fol. 4 pages.

DE PEYSTER, FREDERICK, JR., to MADISON. *Montpellier.*

1832, July 19, New York. Transmits the published collections of the New York Historical Society. 4°. 1 page.

DERBY, RICHARD C. *Montpellier.*

1817, no date, Washington. Respecting a previous correspondence about a foreign appointment. His wealth added to the sum allowed by Government would enable him to live in a manner suitable to the dignity of the nation. His wife's intimacy with the King and Queen of Naples. Knows of a cipher impossible to decipher even with a key. 4°. 3 pages.

DERIEUX, P., to JEFFERSON. *Washington.*

1803, August 9, New York. Letter of friendship. [In French.] 4°. 3 pages.

——— to MADISON. *Washington.*

1804, July 23, Lewisburg, Greenbrier County. Sends a package of letters for Mr. Skipwith. Thanks for sending him letters received from France. Is unable to quit Greenbrier at present to establish himself where Madison and Jefferson recommended. [In French.] 4°. 1 page.

1805, May 19, Greenbrier C. H. Sends letters to be forwarded to France. Intends quitting Greenbrier for some seaport town where he can dispose of merchandise on commission which he expects from France. Asks Madison's good offices with Jefferson to procure him employment. [In French.] 4°. 1 page.

1805, December 15, Greenbrier C. H. His cousin sends him a small sum through Madison's hands, for which he offers excuses for the liberty taken. 4°. 1 page.

1806, March 27, Staunton. Acknowledging receipt of some money. Requests letters to be sent to Staunton where he now resides. 4°. 1 page.

"DESERT, THE."

Not dated. "Statement concerning a tract of land called 'The Desert' situated on, and adjoining to, Cape Henry, at the entrance of the Chesapeake Bay." [Writer unknown.] 4°. 8 pages.

DESFOURNEAUX (General), to MADISON. *Washington.*

1811, December 1, Chateau de Cezy, France. Asks permission that his wife, now in New York, may take passage in a Government armed vessel for France, she paying her passage. [In French. With duplicate and triplicate.] fol. 6 pages.

DEVEREUX, J. *Washington.*

1816, November 7, Washington. Sends Madison two tiger skins as a token of respect and gratitude. 4°. 1 page.

DEW, THOMAS R. *Montpellier.*

1833, January 15, William and Mary College. Sends a copy of his lectures on the restrictive system, with a pamphlet on the slave question. Asks Madison's opinion on the latter work without a view to publication. 4°. 1 page.

DICKENS, ASHBURY. *Washington.*

1815, March 14, Washington. Asks for the appointment of secretaryship of the commissioners of the Navy. If that is not practicable would like a position abroad or at home. 4°. 2 pages.

1816, March 26, Montarno. Asks for employment under the bill before Congress for constructing a board to settle claims on the United States for private property lost or destroyed in the public service. 4°. 1 page.

DICKINSON, THOMAS AND JOHN. *Philadelphia.*

1791, not dated. Certificates of debt to be sent to the office of Col. Lindsay. Strip of paper.

DICKSON, WILLIAM. *Washington.*

1809, September 11, Nashville. Inclosing resolutions adopted by a meeting of citizens of Nashville approving of the conduct of the President in promptly declaring and putting in force the laws of our Government to counteract the operation of the British orders in council, and pledge themselves to a strict observance of the nonintercourse laws. 4°. 1 page. fol. 1 page.

DIGGES, COLE. *Washington.*

1809, February 12, Richmond. Gives a narrative of his Revolutionary services and wishes for Government employment. Would like to be appointed commissioner of loans. 4°. 2 pages.

DIGGES, THOMAS A. *Washington.*

1812, February 9, Warburton. Requests some white thorn sets for a hedge. Also a few English papers. 4°. 1 page.

1814, August 30, Warburton. Anxiety the writer has felt for Mr. and Mrs. Madison by the disasters at Washington. Mentions the damage done to his place by the enemy. Condition of the fort there. List of the English vessels. small 4°. 3 pages.

1815, November 27, Warburton. Has not been in Washington since the day of conflagration, which he considers a happy day, as it broke party spirit and opened the eyes of many. Short crops of corn and grain. Good prices for tobacco. The chastisement of Barbary a happy climax to our marine warfare. 4°. 2 pages.

Montpellier.

1818, July 11, Washington. His family mansion nearly ruined by a hailstorm on May 21. Depredations on his farm by the soldiers at Fort Warburton. Can raise no crops. Intends raising tobacco. Claims against the War Department. Sends Madison some early seed wheat. Agricultural matters. 4°. 3 pages.

DILLEHAY, TH. L. *Washington.*

1812, December 26, Hagerstown. Has become the father of two sons to whom he has given the names of James Madison and Thomas Jefferson. Apologizes for the liberty of writing, but means no offense, and is very poor. fol. 1 page.

DILLINGHAM, JAMES, to LEE, WILLIAM. *Bordeaux.*

1813, October 6, Bordeaux. Certified copy of a receipt of two boxes of wine per schooner *Enquirer* marked for Madison, which he promises to deliver. fol. 1 page.

DILLON, ROBT. J., to MADISON. *Montpellier.*

1829, May 26, New York. Is a member of the senior class at Columbia College and asks hints on a question about State rights and Government usurpations, as he intends to make it the subject of his commencement dissertation. 4°. 1 page.

DINMORE, R., to LYON, M. *Washington.*

1803, January 13, Alexandria. Respecting the publication of the laws of Congress which he would like to have. fol. 1 page.

——— to MADISON. *Washington.*

1803, March 9, Alexandria. Incloses abstract of a letter from New Orleans, in which complaint is made of the intendant of New Orleans who refuses all privileges to Americans of landing at New Orleans, or any places on the river, and says he has authority of the King, his master. fol. 2 pages.

DINSMORE, JAMES. *Washington.*

1809, April 20; May 4, 16, 26; October 29; November 21, Montpellier. Private matters. House now building. [Series of 6 letters.] 4°. 8 pages.

1812, October 13, Park Mills. Acknowledging letter of September 25. Has drawn on Madison in favor of James Fitch for $600. 4°. 1 page.

DIXON, HENRY ST. JOHN. *Montpellier.*

1831, April 29, Abingdon. Asks if he ever was acquainted with John Dixon, one of the grantees of the Loyall Company. Claims a share as John's descendant. 4°. 1 page.

DIXON, THOMAS. *Washington.*

1809, September 6, Springfield, Tenn. Appeal for assistance to a man who had lost his leg and dying of consumption. fol. 1 page.

DODDRIDGE, P. *Montpellier.*

1832, June 1, Washington. Transmits a copy of his speech. Attributes to Madison the authorship of the judiciary act of 1789. David Daggett claims that it was Oliver Ellsworth. Asks explanation. 4°. 1 page.

DODGE & OXNARD. *Montpellier.*

1823, July 5, Marseilles. Transmits invoice of cost and charges of goods shipped per brig *Herschell* for Boston. 4°. 1 page.

DOHRMAN, A. H. *Washington.*

1809, March 4, Pittsburg. Congratulates Madison as President. Thanks him for services rendered. 4°. 1 page.

DONALDSON, THORBURN & CO. *Washington.*

1803, September 17, Norfolk. Incloses receipt for 13 cases wine from Bordeaux and account of charges. 4°. 2 pages.

DOOLITTLE, J. *Washington.*

1813, September 11, Washington. Incloses letters from Dupont de Nemours at Paris. Has been kept prisoner of war in England, being captured at Orient. Had secreted the papers now sent. 4°. 1 page.

DORSEY, BENEDICT. *Montpellier.*

1818, December 10, Philadelphia. Asks information relative to land in the Northwest Territory, known by name of Carver's land. 4°. 2 page.

DORSEY, J. *Washington.*

1808, March 10, Lancaster. Proceeding of the legislature of Pennsylvania respecting the subject of the United States road from Cumberland to the Ohio. 4°. 3 pages.

DOUGHERTY, JOSEPH. *Montpellier.*

1818, February 4, Washington. Jack Shorter's indisposition. Has taken care of him for years, but thinks all the expense ought not to fall on him. 5°. 1 page.

1819, February 18, Washington. Acknowledging letter of 16th, inclosing a check for $20, for which Jack Shorter is grateful. 4°. 1 page.

DOX, G. L. *Washington.*

1816, May 28, Albany. Incloses memorial of citizens of Albany advising his continuance in the office of postmaster in that city. fol. 4 pages. 4°. 3 pages.

DOYHAN, H. S. *Washington.*

1814, May 15, Washington. Complaint of a French cook who had been discharged by Mrs. Madison. [In French.] 4°. 4 pages.

D'OYLEY, DANIEL. *Washington.*

1809, January 14, Charleston. Dissatisfaction at the report that the late Governor Charles Pinckney is about to be appointed a member of the Cabinet. Incloses a pamphlet displaying Mr. Pinckney's character. 4°. 6 pages.

DRAKE, BENJAMIN. *Montpellier.*

1821, November 6, Cincinnati. Intending to write a biographical sketch of Tecumseh, asks Madison to inform him as to the nature of his alliance with the British Army and the tenor of his commission as a brigadier-general during the late war. 4°. 3 pages.

DRAPER, LYMAN C. *Montpellier.*

1833, May 9, Lockport. Is compiling a work to be entitled "The Lives of the Presidents of the United States." Asks Madison for a sketch of his life. 4°. 1 page.

1833, June 3, Lockport. Acknowledging letter of May 19. Asks him if there has ever been any sketches of his life published in books, periodicals, or newspapers and to mention them. 4°. 1 page.

1833, December 31, Mobile, Ala. Asks to be informed about Madison's ancestors, particularly his father. Also Madison's place of birth and date. 4°. 1 page.

DRAYTON, JOHN. *Washington.*

1809, April 12, Charleston. Presents Madison with a copy of his "View of South Carolina." Congratulates him on his election to the Presidency. 4°. 2 pages.

1809, December 1, Columbia, S. C. Transmits copy of his first communication to the legislature of South Carolina. 4°. 1 page.

1810, November 30, Columbia. Incloses copy of his first communication to the legislature of South Carolina. 4°. 1 page.

DRAYTON, JOHN.

1810, July 27, Charleston. Presents the President with a cannon ball and swivel shot which was fired into the Palmetto battery of Fort Moultrie in the year 1776 or 1780 by the British vessels of war, received from Richard Bohun Baker, who was engaged in that action June, 1776, as lieutenant. 4°. 3 pages.

1810, October 12, Charleston. Transmits a model for mounting cannon on a new construction invented by Jonathan Lucas, jr., of South Carolina. 4°. 2 pages.

1811, April 3, Hopeland, S. C. Applies for the office of District judge, which may be vacant, now occupied by Judge Bee, who is critically ill. 4°. 2 pages.

1811, April 3, Hopeland, S. C. Duplicate and triplicate of the foregoing.

1812, May 21, Hopeland, S. C. Has received his appointment of district judge. Will go to Charleston in a few days to enter upon his duties. Expresses his grateful thanks. 4°. 1 page.

1812, May 21, Hopeland, S. C. Duplicate of the foregoing.

1813, May 13, Charleston. In case Mr. Waring should not be appointed marshal of this district, recommends that Robert Bentham be appointed. fol. 1 page.

Montpellier.

1821, September 3, Charleston. Presents Madison with a copy of "Memoirs of the American Revolution," by himself. 4°. 1 page.

DRAYTON, S. *Philadelphia.*

1794, March 12, Charleston, S. C. As president of the Republican Society, of this city, and by their unanimous resolution, he expresses his approbation of Madison's conduct in the House of Representatives of the United States. 4°. 2 pages.

DUANE, J.

1781–'82 (?), no date. A paper unsigned, but in the handwriting of Duane, respecting the imprisonment of Henry Laurens in the Tower of London, and the criminal conduct of Great Britain in ignoring all the laws of nations in all her dealings with us. [Part of the document missing. Draft.] fol. 4 pages.

DUANE, WILLIAM. *Washington.*

1801, May 10, Philadelphia. Asks to supply the Department of State with stationery. Would like to undertake the furnishing of the library for Congress. Respecting the publication of the laws of Congress. Suggestions. 4°. 3 pages.

1803, August 3, Philadelphia. Asks for a copy of Lord Haurbury's answer to Mr. King's note concerning Louisiana. Feels the want of leading information upon which he could rely to rebut in his journal (the "Aurora") the incessant attacks of papers adverse to the Government. 4°. 2 pages.

——— to CAMPBELL AND BRITTON.

1805, March 27, Philadelphia. A printed handbill reflecting upon Mr. J. G. Jackson, M. C., touching the Yazoo claims. Some notes in writing (by

DUANE, WILLIAM.

Jackson) vindicating himself from unjust charges, and a note annexed from Campbell and Britton forwarding, by request, the handbill to Jackson. fol. 2 pages.

—— to MADISON. *Washington.*

1805, August 10, Philadelphia. Sends him a paper in which there is an article which he should see. 4°. 1 page.

1805, August 27, Philadelphia. Lanterns, used by the artillery service, ordered by a Frenchman in the service of the Spanish minister. Thinking the purpose may be hostile to the United States, the tinman, manufacturer, asks whether he should go on with the work. [Draft of Madison's answer on same sheet.] 4°. 2 pages.

1807, May 1, Philadelphia. Applies for permission to transcribe some papers of Franklin's political productions in the Department of State which may not be improper to publish. 4°. 2 pages.

1808, February 8, Philadelphia. Will propose with John Bioren to print an edition of the laws of the United States corresponding with Madison's suggestion. 4°. 3 pages.

1808, February 20, Philadelphia. Incloses information which he thinks had better be disposed of by the Department of State than in a newspaper. 4°. 1 page.

—— to W——, ROGER C.

1808, December 20, Philadelphia. Sends a volume of the laws of Pennsylvania to be presented to Madison and signify to him his intention to propose the printing of the laws of the United States in that form, to correspond with Tucker's Blackstone in size. 4°. 3 pages.

—— to MADISON. *Washington.*

1809, February 1, Philadelphia. Incloses a letter and draft in settlement of his personal affairs. Incloses a packet to be forwarded to Mr. Lyman, consul at London. 4°. 1 page.

1809, May 3, Philadelphia. Suggests the clemency of the Executive in the matter of the sentence of Michael Bright and others. 4°. 3 pages.

1809, November 1, Philadelphia. Introducing Christopher Fitzsimmons and Hugh Calhoun. 4°. 2 pages.

1809, December 1, Philadelphia. On the policy of the British Government and its hostile attitude towards us. Opinions as to what we should do. large fol. 5 pages.

1809, December 5, Philadelphia. His views respecting the institution of a national bank. 4°. 2 pages.

1809, December 8, Philadelphia. Means of raising a large sum, should the nation be involved in war, by a loan on the public lands. 4°. 3 pages.

1810, April 16, Philadelphia. Introducing his son, J. Duane, who visits Washington for the purpose of undertaking the publication of an edition of the laws of the United States. 4°. 1 page.

1812, August 6, Philadelphia. The intention of Mr. Carswell to decline the acceptance of the office of commissary-general. The duties and qualifica-

DUANE, WILLIAM.

tions of a fit man. Suggests Mr. C. Irvine, now superintendent of military stores. 4°. 3 pages.

1812, September 20, Philadelphia. Hull's disaster at Detroit. Conjectures as to how much the British Government calculates on disaffection in the maritime States. The writer's views and suggestions as to the most effectual means of defense. 4°. 7 pages.

1812, September 20, Philadelphia. Inclosing a letter of this date from and to the same. 4°. 1 page.

1814, February 22, Philadelphia. An effort made to impress upon Madison that his appointment of postmaster in Philadelphia is not approved by the community. Trusts the President will not give way to the clamors of demagogues. 4°. 3 pages.

1814, June 22, Philadelphia. Advocates the appointment of Dr. Leib as postmaster of Philadelphia. 4°. 3 pages.

1814, October 25, Philadelphia. Introducing Manuel Torres. Wishes to call the attention of his financial views to the Government. 4°. 1 page.

DUBOURG, WILLIAM, to COUPER, JOHN. *St. Simons, Ga.*

1809, November 8, St. Mary's College, Baltimore. Recommends Joseph Coppinger as a gentleman and inventor and entitled to confidence. [*See* Coppinger, Joseph.] fol. 1 page.

——— to MADISON. *Washington.*

1813, August 30, New Orleans. Acknowledging with thanks, his appointment as collector for the district of Mississippi. 4°. 1 page.

DUBUISSON, ———. *Washington.*

1815, February 12, Washington. States that he knows the means of forcing England to make a peace with the United States, on just and honorable terms, in less than eighteen months. [In French.] 4°. 4 pages.

DUER, WILLIAM.

1789. Estimates of revenue on imports, with memorandum of expenses of Government and foreign and domestic interest. With duplicate. fol. 3 pages.

1788, no date. Respecting the policy of electing John Adams as Vice-President. 4°. 2 pages.

1788, June 23, New York. Gives a short sketch of political prospects on the great question of the constitution. 4°. 2 pages.

1789 (?), not dated. Memoranda of estimates of revenue on imports. Also estimates by Mr. Sherman. fol. 3 pages.

DUER, W. A. *Montpellier.*

1833, August 28, Columbia College, New York. Transmits the design of a work inscribed to Madison. Will send a copy when issued from the press. 4°. 1 page.

1835, May 13, Columbia College, New York. Acknowledging letter of 15th. Madison's injunctions

DUER, W. A.

against publicity shall be observed in respect to certain papers and letters. 4°. 1 page.

1835, May 25, Columbia College, New York. Chancellor Kent wishes either the original or copy of a letter written to the writer's father with account of the proceedings of the New York State Convention of 1788. 4°. 1 page.

DUFRET, N. G. *Washington.*

1814, April 7, Philadelphia. Wishes Madison to state that the writer never sold or forwarded to him a work entitled "La Création du Monde," par Bécourt. The grand jury of Philadelphia has preferred an indictment against him as publisher thereof. 4°. 1 page.

DUKE, ALEXANDER. *Montpellier.*

1832, May 9, Hanover County, Va. Asks Madison's assistance in establishing him in business. Not pecuniarily, but by his advice and influence. fol. 3 pages.

DUMAS, HIPPOLITE.

1807, July 20, Philadelphia. Order of C. J. Tilghman and Judge Smith to release Dumas, imprisoned for desertion by the French consul-general, on a writ of habeas corpus. fol. 3 pages.

DUNBAR, JOHN R. W., to MADISON. *Montpellier.*

1834, December 29, Winchester. Sends a narrative of some experiments in galvanism. Also an essay on the nervous system and a memorial on the geological survey of the State. 4°. 2 pages.

DUNBAR, ROBERT. *Washington.*

1805, June 22. Bill for Irish linen; receipted. 8°. 1 page.

DUNCANSON, WILLIAM, to JEFFERSON. *Monticello.*

1816, August 5, Washington. Solicits his good offices in the procurement of a Government position in one of the departments or custom-houses. 4°. 2 pages.

DUNGLISON, ROBLEY, to MADISON. *Montpellier.*

1825, June 30, University of Virginia. Prescription for the swelled neck of a servant of Madison's. 8°. 1 page.

1825, November 11, University of Virginia. Introduces Mr. St. Aubyn and Mr. Hallam, from Cambridge, England. 4°. 1 page.

1826, June 22, University of Virginia. Mrs. Dunglison and himself propose to visit Madison. Contagion from whooping cough. 4°. 1 page.

1826, July 1, Monticello. Regrets that he can not visit Madison at present owing to the serious illness of Jefferson, which he describes. 4°. 1 page.

1827, August 27, Monticello. Incloses, for Mr. Payne, some vaccine matter with directions for use. 4°. 1 page.

1828, December 25, University of Virginia. Acknowledging letter of 22d. Will attend to the delivery of the books to the executor of Jefferson. Affairs of the university. 4°. 1 page.

DUNGLISON, ROBLEY.

1829, October 30, University of Virginia. Notes the absence of students with leave. 4°. 1 page.

1829, December 30, University of Virginia. The employment of a Boston firm for the purchase of books. 4°. 1 page.

1830, February 14, University of Virginia. About to lose Mr. Lomax, the law professor. Difficulty in supplying his successor. Examinations about to commence. 4°. 1 page.

1830, March 10, University of Virginia. Suggests that a list of officers and students be printed for distribution. Asks to be allowed to dedicate a work to Madison on which he has been engaged. Respecting a Mr. Willis, a student who is supposed to tipple. 4°. 2 pages.

1830, March 19, University of Virginia. Incloses a communication from Mr. Lomax. Thanks for being allowed to dedicate his medical dictionary to Madison. 4°. 1 page.

1830, May 24, University of Virginia. Expulsion from the University of Mr. Willis. Illness of his wife (Dunglison's). 4°. 1 page.

1831, April 18, University of Virginia. Is offered the professorship of the chair of anatomy in the institution at Baltimore after refusing the Miami University, at Cincinnati, and the Jefferson Medical College of Philadelphia. His new dictionary of medical science and literature is in press. Other works. 4°. 2 pages.

1831, April 20, University of Virginia. Should he resign his professorship, would like Mr. Davis, who would occupy his residence, to take carpets and other effects. 4°. 1 page.

1831, September 8, University of Virginia. Letter from Mr. Long respecting the affairs of the London University. 4°. 2 pages.

1831, October 11, University of Virginia. Wish of Mr. Brooks, an artist, to copy a painting of Jefferson, by Stuart, at the university. 4°. 1 page.

1832, June 28, University of Virginia. Hearing that Madison being ill will visit him on Sunday. 4°. 1 page.

1832, August 30, University of Virginia. Asks him to accept a self-pointing pencil. 4°. 1 page.

1832, November 8, University of Virginia. Forwards a treatise on cholera. If Madison has not received the second volume of Dunglison's on physiology, will send it. 4° 1 page.

1833, May 14, University of Virginia. Professor Davis wishes to occupy Dunglison's pavilion and grounds when he leaves the University. Asks to state this officially. Hopes to visit Madison. "Private." 8°. 2 pages.

1833, May 14, University of Virginia. Has received a communication from the University of Maryland appointing him professor in that institution. Tenders his resignation at the University of Virginia. 4°. 1 page.

1833, October 7, University of Virginia. His intention to leave on the 14th. Hopes to be able to take

DUNGLISON, ROBLEY.

leave of Madison and Mrs. Madison. If prevented, wishes to express his grateful acknowledgments of signal evidences of kindnesses and friendship. 4°. 1 page.

1834, July 31, Baltimore. Acknowledging letter of 26th. Prescribes for him a remedy for the itching sensation. 4°. 1 page.

DUNN, C. F., JR. *Washington.*

1812, October 31, Jamaica, N. Y. Applicant for office. "Confidential." fol. 3 pages.

1813, June 15, Jamaica, N. Y. After giving a record of his services renews his application for office. "Private." 4°. 6 pages.

DUNN, WILLIAM. *Washington.*

1809, March 15, Liberty, Va. Asks assistance. 4°. 2 pages.

1810, June 8, Richmond. Renews his application for assistance. fol. 2 pages.

DUPLANTIER, ——. *Washington.*

1805, September 3, Baton Rouge. Location of a land warrant to Lafayette in Louisiana. [In French.] Incloses a certificate of the register (J. W. Gurley) designating the locality, dated November 26, 1807. 4°. 5 pages.

1806, March *19, New Orleans.* Acknowledging receipt of land warrants. As agent of Lafayette is occupied in selecting the location of the cession. [In French.] 4°. 4 pages.

1806, April 17, New Orleans. Location of the cession of land to Lafayette. [In French.] 4°. 3 pages.

1807, September 25, Baton Rouge. The policy of selling a portion of Lafayette's land in Louisiana. Does not think it advisable to do so at a sacrifice. [In French.] 4°. 3 pages.

1809, July 25, 1813, January 28, May 15, New Orleans. Lafayette's lands in Louisiana. [In French.] 4°. 8 pages.

DUPONCEAU, PETER S. *Washington.*

1805, July 8, Philadelphia. Incloses notes on the history and motives of the British prohibition of the trade of neutrals with the colonies of her enemies. 4°. 1 page.

1805, July 15, Philadelphia. Incloses a continuation of his notes. 4°. 1 page.

1805, July 23, Philadelphia. Sends conclusion of his notes, with an appendix of documents and authorities. [Signature cut off.] 4°. 1 page.

1808, November 26, Philadelphia. Incloses a print received from New York under a blank cover. Sends extract of a letter from R. R. Livingston. 4°. 1 page.

1810, November 15, Philadelphia. Transmits a copy of his translation of the first book of Bynkershock's work. 4°. 1 page.

No date. Incloses a translation of a passage from Bynkershock 8°. 1 page, and scrap of paper.

DUPONCEAU, PETER S. *Montpellier.*

1818, June 10, Philadelphia. Incloses the prospectus of the first volume of the translation of the American Philosophical Society. 4°. 1 page.

1821, March 23, Philadelphia. Recommends as professor of chemistry and mineralogy of the Virginia University, Mr. Lardner Clark Vanuxem, of Philadelphia. 4°. 2 pages.

1824, September 13, Philadelphia. Acknowledging letter of August 14. His work on American common law. His views on the subject. 4°. 4 pages.

1825, May 21, Philadelphia. Introducing Count Charles Videre, of Turin. 4°. 1 page.

1825, November 5, Philadelphia. Informs Madison of his election as an honorary member of the Society for the Commemoration of the Landing of William Penn. 4°. 1 page.

1826, January 4, Philadelphia. Lafayette anxious to obtain a copy of Mr. Madison's report on the Federal Constitution. Unable to find it at the bookseller. Asks where a copy can be obtained. 4°. 1 page.

1826, January 17, Philadelphia. Acknowledging a letter and pamphlet containing Madison's report of 1798 for Gen. Lafayette. Remarks on Dupin's speech before the Cour Royale, of Paris, in favor of the editors of the Constitutionel, accused of attempting to subvert the Catholic religion. New book entitled "History of Democracy of the United States." 4°. 3 pages.

1828, October 25, Philadelphia. Lafayette's account of his journey through the United States being translated. Wishes a copy of the memorial which he drew up in opposition to the petition of ministers of the Episcopal Church to the Virginia legislature in 1784–'85. 4°. 2 pages.

DUPONT, E. J. *Washington.*

1809, November 3, Wilmington. Acknowledging a letter. Apologizes for the liberty his father has taken in sending through him the works of Mr. Turgot. His partner, Mr. Peter Baudry, will call on the President. 4°. 1 page.

1811, November 23, Wilmington. Acknowledging letter of 18th. Thanks him for the offer of conveying to his father letters and remittances. 4°. 1 page.

DUPONT DE NEMOURS, P. S. *Washington.*

1809, July 11, Paris. Congratulations on his succeeding to the position lately occupied by his friend Jefferson. Dupont's attachment to this country. His sons. His plan of education in the United States. Sends seven volumes of Turgot's works. [In French.] 4°. 2 pages.

1810, January 20, Paris. Acknowledging letter of December 3. Views on the system of education in America. 4°. 4 pages.

1811, July 4, Paris. Sends two manuscripts, one on finances of this republic and the other a plan of education. Asks if his correspondence with his sons can not be sent under official cover. Also, if remittances may not be sent by same means. [In French.] 4°. 3 pages.

DUPONT DE NEMOURS, P. S.

1813, February 10, Paris. Incloses a notice on the life of the late Joel Barlow. Congratulates the President on his reelection. Policy of Canada to seize the occasion to declare her independence. Mr. Doolittle the successor of Mr. Barlow. 4°. 3 pages.

1813, February 10, Paris. Notice of the life of Joel Barlow. [In French.] 4°. 1 page.

Washington.

1813, April 30, Paris. Alludes to his notice of the life of Joel Barlow. His intention of going to America to live. [In French.] 4°. 2 pages.

1813, October 23, Paris. Profits by Madison's kindness in sending his letters to his sons. [In French. Signature cut off.] 4°. 1 page.

1814, December 27, Paris. Interrupts and destroys a long letter on certain suggestions to be adopted by our Army, on hearing of peace. Efficacy of pikes. Camps and intrenchments. Is contented with the zeal of his sons. [In French.] 4°. 2 pages.

1815, May —, New York. Offers his person and intelligence to the service of the United States. [In French.] 4°. 1 page.

1815, July 25, Wilmington. Excessive heat and indisposition prevents his paying his respects. The system of education. Predicts the tendency of republicanism in Europe. [In French.] 4°. 3 pages.

1815, December 19, Washington. Sends a table. 4°. 1 page.

1815, December 28, Wilmington. Thanks him for appointing his grandson a midshipman. Sends Madison a copy of his work on Education. [In French.] 4°. 1 page.

1816, January 18, Wilmington. Sends him an essay on the question of manufactures now agitating Congress. Will endeavor to get it translated. [In French.] 4°. 1 page.

1816, January 18, Washington. An essay on agriculture and manufactures in the United States. [In French.] 4°. 18 pages.

DUPONT, VICTOR, to JEFFERSON. *Monticello.*

1815, not dated. States facts in support of the request made for a warrant of midshipman for his son Samuel Francis Dupont. His own services and those of his father described. 4°. 2 pages.

DURHAM, J., to MADISON. *Washington.*

1812, April 28, Windsor, Vt. Offers his services in the Army. Would not accept a commission, however, which would subject him to the command of any officer of recent appointment in the State of Vermont. 4°. 4 pages.

DUTIES ON IMPORTS. CONTINENTAL CONGRESS, RESOLUTIONS OF.

Not dated. Copy of resolutions recommending to the several States to pass laws enabling Congress to collect a duty on imported goods to pay interest on the public debt and officers necessary for collecting said duties, to be appointed by Congress. [Unknown handwriting.] fol. 2 pages.

DUTIES IMPOSED IN VIRGINIA.

1786. List of duties imposed by acts of Congress on tonnage, wine, spirits, etc. fol. 2 pages.

Virginia.

1787. Aggregate duties on tonnage of vessels and imported goods into the State of Virginia, between September 1, 1786, and July 20, 1787. fol. 2 pages.

Maryland.

DUTIES, RECIPROCAL.

Not dated. Proposed resolution to be offered before Congress respecting the admittance of vessels of any nation which shall admit those of the United States upon equal terms. [Fragment.] 4°. 1 page.

DUVAL, E. W., to MADISON. *Washington.*

1815, January 2, Washington. Incloses a letter which was unasked and unexpected, giving evidence of the good will of the writer towards him in bringing him to the notice of the President. 4°. 1 page.

Montpellier.

1822, September 8, Washington. Asks for a clerkship of the House of Representatives now made vacant by the death of Mr. Dougherty. fol. 3 pages.

DUVAL, WM. P. *Montpellier.*

1823, August 12, St. Augustine. Relating to Madison's nephew, Mr. Macon, who has distinguished himself in a murder case. The writer entertains high expectations of his success as a lawyer, and takes a great interest in him. 4°. 2 pages.

1826, November 14, Tallahassee. Col. Edgar Macon wantonly and cruelly persecuted by Judge Smith and the Government of Florida. Duval (governor of Florida), assures Madison that Macon is an honorable, frank, and independent gentleman, and he will support him. He must not believe injurious reports. 4°. 2 pages.

1827, February 11, Tallahassee. Acknowledging letter of January 11. The duel between Col. Macon and Judge Smith's son. Col. Macon's high character. Unfortunate propensity of indulging in drinking. The South a bad place for him. Suggests that Madison recall him to Virginia. 4°. 3 pages.

DUVALL, GABRIEL.

1800, April 28, Annapolis. The writer and J. T. Chace candidates for electors for President and Vice-President. Every exertion by the Government party to defeat Jefferson. The charges to effect it will be his Mazzei letter and irreligion. Asks if Madison can inform him of the circumstances which gave rise to the letter, and whether Jefferson wrote it. 4°. 2 pages.

Orange.

1800, June 6, Annapolis. Acknowledging letter of May 13. As Jefferson is silent about the letter to Mazzei it may be as well to say nothing about it since it is not certain he wrote it. Conjectures as to the results of the election. Rumors of the Executive to call the new legislature to appoint

DUVALL, GABRIEL.

electors. Exertions of Republicans to counteract it. 4°. 3 pages.

1800, October 17, Annapolis. Success of Republicans in the State election. Belief in Adams's being a monarchist inculcated by Mercer and himself interfered with by Jefferson's statement that Adams was a firm and decided Republican. The charge of Jefferson's irreligion subsided. 4°. 2 pages.

Washington.

1801, November 12, Annapolis. Report of a compromise between the United States and Great Britain as to the claims of the latter under sixth article of treaty of 1794. Asks information relative to it before it is made public. 4°. 2 pages.

1803, November 18, Washington. Respecting the newspaper, the "Expositor." 4°. 1 page.

——— to GRYMES, PHILIP. *New Orleans.*

1810, July 14, Washington. Acknowledging letter of May 21, respecting the claim of the United States against William Brown. Approves of the management of the claim. Authorizes Grymes to continue the agency and allows him a commission. fol. 2 pages.

——— to GALLATIN, ALBERT. *Washington.*

1810, August 15, Washington. Respecting the sale of William Brown's estate, purchased for the Government by Mr. Grymes. The wish of Mr. Jones to have it set aside. 4°. 3 pages.

——— to BROBSON, JAMES.

1811, May 24, Washington. Acknowledging letter of 12th. Brobson's conduct as marshal of the district of Delaware has not been censured. fol. 1 page.

——— to MADISON. *Washington.*

1812, March 24, Washington. Act of Congress relating to District judges. Asks reason for the change of the law. 4°. 2 pages.

1812, September 5, Washington. Expediency of asking Jefferson to be Secretary of State in this crisis, after filling the office of Chief Magistrate. Monroe's appointment to the command of the northwestern army would add lustre to his public character. Hull's victory over the *Guerriere.* 4°. 3 pages.

——— to TURNER, THOMAS. *Washington.*

1811, April 3, Washington. Relating to Samuel Hanson's accounts as purser in the Navy. [Copy.] 4°. 1 page.

DWYER, J. H., to MADISON. *Montpellier.*

1824, December 23, Cincinnati. Transmits a book intended for the promotion of the morals and intellect of the youth of America. 4°. 1 page.

DYSTER, JOSEPH JOSHUA. *Washington.*

1809, December 7, Washington. Describes an invention propelling ships and vessels of any description up navigable rivers against wind and tide, although effected by steam, differs with the practice and principles of the steamboat at present in use. large fol. 3 pages.

EARLE, ELIAS. *Washington.*

1812, April 6, Washington. Contract for furnishing iron and iron tools and a cession of land at the mouth of the Chickamauga for the works. Incloses letters from Gen. Dearborn, and copies of Gen. Meigs' letter to Secretary of War respecting the treaty of 1807 with the Cherokees.
4°. 2 pages.

EARLY, JOEL. *Washington.*

1802, December 7, Green County, Ga. Treaty with the Creek Indians. Peaceable temper of the Indians. Thinks that with a proportionate price the Agemulgy (?) and Tallahasse county could be easily purchased. 4°. 1 page.

EARLY, PETER (Governor). *Washington.*

1814, December 2, Milledgeville, Ga. Transmits a copy of resolutions passed by the legislature of Georgia disapproving the terms of the British commissioners at Ghent as the *sine qua non* upon which a treaty of peace may be concluded as insulting to the American character. 4°. 4 pages.

EASTBURN, JAMES. *Washington.*

1817, January 10, New York. Sends a prospectus of a course of publications which he wishes to publish with Madison's sanction. 4°. 1 page.

EASTBURN, ROBERT. *Washington.*

1813, January 11, New Brunswick, N. J. Is a decided Republican but advocates peace (he being of the Society of Friends) if it can be effected honorably. Congratulates Madison on his reelection.
fol. 3 pages.

EASTON, DAVID. *Montpellier.*

1822, January 14, Washington. Wishes positive evidence that Col. Harrison, when he retired from from the Army in ill health, in 1781, did so on furlough. His papers being lost, a knowledge of the fact will be beneficial to his daughters in establishing a claim. 4°. 2 pages.

EATON, WILLIAM. *Washington.*

1811, August 29, New York. Declares himself a good Republican. The awful situation of our country. Fears a war with Great Britain. Importance of Madison's reelection. Designs of the Federalists to take part with our enemies in case of war. Gives a sketch of his own life. Offers his services. Can give testimonials. 4°. 7 pages.

1811, October 25, New York. Trusts that in his message to Congress, he will not advise war measures, or the establishment of a large naval or land force. The militia ought to be the safeguard of republican government. 4°. 3 pages.

1815, November 29, Washington. Wishes to be postmaster at Albany. 4°. 3 pages.

1815, December 1, Washington. Thanks the President for presenting his application for the post-office in Albany, to the Postmaster-General.
4°. 2 pages.

1815, December 8, Albany. Has sent to the Postmaster-General recommendations. Hopes the President will look at them. 4°. 1 page.

1815, December 14, Albany. Urges his appointment as postmaster at Albany. His past political services. 4°. 2 pages.

EATON, WILLIAM.

1816, June 3, Albany. Asks the President to interest himself in appointing him postmaster at Albany. 4°. 1 page.

ECCLESTON, DANIEL BELTESCHAZZAR PLANTAGANET. *Washington.*

1810, January 1, Lancaster. Asks the acceptance of a medallion of Gen. Washington. 4°. 1 page.

1810, October 1, Lancaster. Acknowledging letter of July 18, respecting the exalted character of Gen. Washington. 4°. 1 page.

ECKARD, J. F. *Washington.*

1805, April 12, Philadelphia. Lately returned from Copenhagen, where he saw Mr. Olsen, who gave a letter and package for Madison which he incloses. 4°. 2 pages.

EDRINGTON, EDWARD. *Washington.*

1813, February 1, Staunton. Applies for a loan for which he offers good security. 4°. 2 pages.

1813, February 14, Staunton. Acknowledging letter of 8th. Thanks for his promptitude although his hopes are not fulfilled. Gives an anecdote in Latin of Louis XI, of France, apropos of his request. 4°. 1 page.

EDWARDS, ENO. *Philadelphia.*

1797, January 19, Frankford. Incloses letters from F. Skipwith. fol. 1 page.

——— to MONROE. *Albemarle.*

1798, April 21, Frankfort. Acknowledging letter of February 12. Relates what he knows of Monroe's patriotic conduct while representing the United States in Paris, particularly respecting a dinner given by Monroe on July 4, 1796, when it was stated by the latter's enemies, the health of the President was not proposed. Also respecting the conduct of Thomas Paine, which Monroe strongly resented, on account of his enemity to Washington. [*See* letter from Monroe of Pebruary 12.] [Copy in Monroe's hand.] 4°. 3 pages.

EDWARDS, H. W., to MADISON. *Orange.*

1807, July 29, New Haven, Conn. Summons by the clerk of the Supreme Court, Judge John Marshall, presiding, at New Haven, to testify in behalf of Azel Backus in a matter of controversy with the United States at Hartford, on September 17 next. 4°. 1 page.

EDWARDS, NINIAN. *Washington.*

1812, December 9, Kaskaskia, Ill. Incloses an address from the legislature of this Territory. fol. 1 page.

1813, January 16, Kaskaskia, Ill. Proposes measures to prevent and counteract Indian hostilities. 4°. 8 pages.

1813, December 12, Kaskaskia, Ill. Transmits a memorial from the legislature of this Territory. 4°. 1 page.

EDWARDS, PIERREPONT. *Washington.*

1806, July 30, New York. The conclusion of the trials of W. S. Smith and Samuel G. Ogden, and their acquittal. The Miranda expedition. The causes which have operated for producing the decision. 4°. 4 pages.

EDWARDS, PIERREPONT.

1806, July 31, New York. Causes of the acquittal of Smith and Ogden. State of political parties in New York. 4°. 4 pages.

1809, May 18, New Haven. Appointment of marshal. Proceedings of the court. Removal of Mr. Brainard. Among the candidates, Brainard is to be preferred. fol 3 pages.

1809, May 23, Bridgeport, Conn. The choice of candidates for the appointment of marshal. Mr. Seymour and Capt. E. Tracy. Seymour's character fair, but without energy. Tracy not deficient, but uncontrollable in temper. 4°. 3 pages.

EELLS, CUSHING. *Washington.*

1813, May 17, Norwich, *Conn.* Complains of the facility with which the English vessels on our coasts procure provisions from our vessels owned by the "peace men" in Connecticut. fol. 1 page.

EGREMONT, EARL OF, to BEDFORD, DUKE OF.

1763, March 1, Whitehall, London. Conversation with the Duke of Nevernois, on the subject of the Newfoundland fishery, referred to in the treaty of Utrecht and in the Definitive treaty of February 10, 1763. The insistence of the French that they had exclusive rights to the fishery until they were driven from America in the last (French) war. The writer's views and explanations. [*See* letter of Sir Stanier Porteen, to Lord Weymouth, not dated.] [Copy.] small 4°. 7 pages.

EILAND, ISAIAH, to MADISON. *Washington.*

1809, August 31. Ravings and ramblings of a religious maniac. 4°. 4 pages.

ELLERY, CHRISTOPHER. *Washington.*

1807, December 19, Provid*ence, R. I.* Introduces Mr. Charles Collins, collector of Bristol, and a friend of the administration. 4°. 4 pages.

1810, April 24, Pro*vidence.* Recommends as marshal of the district, Henry Wheaton, a gentleman qualified to honor his country and himself in a station much more exalted. 4°. 1 page.

1810, Nov*ember 20,* Pro*vidence, R. I.* Incloses a statement showing that the governor of the State is a despot and the lately chosen U. S. Senator, J. B. Howell, his tool. 4°. 2 pages.

1811, Oct*ober 21, Providence, R. I.* Incloses copy of a letter addressed to several members of the U. S. Senate, of the Republican party. 4°. 1 page.

——— to SENATORS OF UNITED STATES.

1811, Oct*ober 25, Providence, R. I.* Circular addressed to U. S. Senators of the Republican party, showing them the ineligibility of the Senator from Rhode Island, Mr. J. B. Howell, on account of his holding another United States office at the same time. In proof of which he incloses a certificate of the collector at Providence. 4°. 8 pages.

——— to MADISON. *Washington.*

1812, June 24, Provid*ence, R. I.* Bells tolling, shops closed, and flags at half-mast. Cause assigned, "the war." Agitation general. Rumors of action between frigates off Block Island. Love of country vanished from Federalists. Republicans, however, respond by firing of cannon. No draft-

ELLERY, CHRISTOPHER.

ing of militia. Exposed situation of Newport. Troops required. 4°. 4 pages.

1815, December 5, Providence, R. I. Introduces James Burrill as an advocate for cotton manufacturers. To petition Congress for protection. A suitable selection for advocacy of their interests. 4°. 3 pages.

ELLERY, WILLIAM, to HOWELL, DAVID. *Providence.*

1801, March 27, Newport. Is informed the President is to remove him from the office of collector simply because another wants the office. Wishes him to appeal to the President in his behalf and to consider his past services and unimpeachable honesty and fidelity. small 4°. 2 pages.

——— to MADISON. *Washington.*

1804, January 19, Newport, R. I. Is informed that he is to be removed from office of collector. Protests against it. His long life has been employed in the service of his country. Asks Madison's good offices with the President to be retained. 4°. 2 pages.

1804, November 16, Newport, R. I. Again asks Madison to exert his influence in not having him removed from office, as he hears efforts are being made among competitors for it. small 4°. 3 pages.

ELLICOTT, ANDREW. *Washington.*

1801, May 20, Philadelphia. Acknowledging letter of 8th. Relates the difficulties and discomforts he has undergone during his various engineering excursions, and extra expenses. His being obliged to sacrifice his personal effects. Never received anything but his salary. Mr. Anderson's accounts. 4°. 3 pages.

1801, July 15, Georgetown. Wishes to borrow the report and chart of our Eastern boundary. Wishes to obtain materials for compiling a correct map of the United States. 4°. 1 page.

1801 (?), no date. Memorandum giving dates of letters from Ellicott to Secretary of State from April 1, 1797, to March 23, 1800, with remarks opposite each letter in Madison's handwriting. 4°. 2 pages.

1802, March 26, Lancaster. Communicates a plan for an improved saw mill. The inventor, Moses, will ask for a patent. 4°. 1 page.

1803, January 12, Lancaster. Incloses astronomical observations which he wishes sent to our minister in Paris. Ellicott's letter of November 14, 1797, in cipher, giving an account of plan respecting the cession of Louisiana to France. Insufficient remuneration for his services while on the Southern boundary. Refusal of President Adams to receive him. Ellicott's refusal, on application of Gen. Wilkinson, to enter into the general outcry against Jefferson. 4°. 2 pages.

1803, May 20, Lancaster. Incloses a packet of astronomical observations for Mr. Delambre, a secretary of the National Institute of France, to be sent to Mr. Livingston, our minister to France. 4°. 1 page.

ELLICOTT, ANDREW.

1804, January 10, Lancaster. Incloses a parcel for Mr. Livingston for the French National Institute. New astronomical tables by Mr. Delambre. 4°. 1 page.

1805, October 2, Lancaster. Transmits a package directed to Mr. Armstrong containing astronomical observations for Mr. Delambre, of the National Institute of France. The political situation of Pennsylvania. The opinion that Duane, Clay, and Leib are in the full confidence of the President. 4°. 2 pages.

1806, December 21, Lancaster. Incloses a communication for the National Institute of France to be forwarded through the American minister to Paris. Has withdrawn from the political conflicts in this commonwealth since the reelection of Mr. McKean. 4°. 1 page.

1809, November 8, Lancaster. Gould's survey of the Dry Tortugas and Florida reefs, which, being out of print, suggests new impressions which Ellicott will undertake, as he has the best apparatus in this country for executing such work. 4°. 2 pages.

1810, November 14, Lancaster. Would like to continue to forward through the Department of State communications to the American minister to France for the Institute of France. Political intolerance in Pennsylvania under Snyder. Anecdote of the refusal of the legislature to allow Ellicott to use the telescope belonging to Government. Anecdote of Voltaire on intolerance. small 4°. 3 pages.

1810, December 8. Lancaster. Incloses a communication for the secretary of the National Institute of France to be forwarded. Criticisms on Madison's message to Congress. Suggests alteration of two expressions. The part respecting seminaries of learning should be put in the hands of every citizen of the nation. Quotation from Helvetius. small 4°. 1 page.

1811, March 9, Lancaster. Offers to carry dispatches to France should there be occasion. His friendship for Barlow, lately appointed minister. Offers support of his pen. small 4°. 1 page.

1812, June 3, Lancaster. Has just returned from determining the disputed boundaries between the States of Georgia and North Carolina. Wishes to forward astronomical observations made to the French National Institute through Mr. Barlow. 4°. 1 page.

1813, January 20, Lancaster. Attempts to injure Col. Hawkins. Has known him since boyhood and will come forward and bear testimony in his favor. small 4°. 1 page.

1813, August 10, Lancaster. Has been offered, by Gen. Armstrong, the position of professor of mathematics at West Point. If permanent, will accept, although the salary is too small. His apparatus of practical astronomy is extensive, sufficiently so for the use of the Navy. small 4°. 1 page.

1814, October 5, West Point. Introduces Harvey Brown, who wishes the appointment as cadet. Recommends him. Describes the flourishing condition of the Academy. Many students too young and uneducated before admittance. 4°. 1 page.

ELLICOTT, ANDREW, to COOPER, THOMAS.

1814, December 12, West Point. It is contemplated to add a professorship of chemistry and mineralogy to the Academy. Would advise Cooper to accept if tendered him. Extreme regularity of everything that is done here. Professorship of French now vacant. Wishes to obtain it for Mr. Berard. 4°. 1 page.

——— to MADISON. *Washington.*

1817, January 22, West Point. Introduces Capt. Douglass, of the corps of engineers and assistant professor of natural and experimental philosophy. Distinguished himself at the defense of Fort Erie. Deficiency in the mathematical and scientific branch of the art of engineering. Four assistants necessary. 4°. 2 pages.

ELLICOTT, N. *Washington.*

1813, November 27, Occoquan, Va. The next legislature of Virginia to be petitioned to open a road to Normond's ford. If Madison approves of it, will he give Ellicott a letter to each of the members from his county, stating his knowledge of its necessity? 4°. 1 page.

ELLIOT, JONATHAN. *Montpellier.*

1826, November 11, Washington. Asks to be furnished with his "Memorandum of controversies which have arisen in debating the merits of the Constitution," with a view of publishing them in a supplementary volume of his debates and proceedings of State conventions on the adoption of the Federal Constitution. 4°. 2 pages.

1826, November 21, Washington. Acknowledging letter of 15th. Asks the loan of volumes and pamphlets on the proceedings of States on the adoption of the Constitution. 4°. 1 page.

1827, February 12, Washington. Presents Madison with the first volume of a collection of debates in the State conventions on the adoption of the Constitution. Asks for the loan of pamphlets. small 4°. 2 pages.

1827, November 12, Washington. Will send the second volume of his debates on the adoption of the Federal Constitution. Asks information on the subject. 4°. 1 page.

1830, June 29, Washington. Sends Madison the third and fourth volumes of debates of the State conventions on the adoption of the Constitution. 4°. 2 pages.

1836, August 19, Washington. Acknowledging letter of July 7. His work on the Constitution. Would be glad to publish Madison's manuscript debates. Anxiety of the public to procure Madison's work on the Constitution. Copyright of the "Federalist." 4°. 3 pages.

ELLIOTT, J. D. (Commodore). *Montpellier.*

1834, October 10, Navy-yard, Boston. Sends Madison a cane from a piece of the frigate *Constitution.* 4°. 1 page.

ELLIOTT, ROBERT, JR. *Washington.*

1815, June 20, Baltimore. Finds that chaplains are not retained under the peace establishment. Does not complain, but having nothing but his talents to support a numerous family, would have been gratified had he been retained. 4°. 3 pages.

ELLEDGE, THOMAS. *Washington.*

1810, December 12. Compromise with the executors of W. Cocky about some land in Baltimore County. fol. 1 page.

ELLIS, THOMAS H. *Montpellier.*

1832, September 16, University of Virginia. Wishes to be released from one of the decisions of the members of the faculty as to his boarding place, as the law is construed too rigidly in his case. 4°. 2 pages.

ELSWORTH, DOROTHY. *New York.*

1790, August 13. Bill for board and sundries and balance of old account. small 4°. 1 page.

ELWELL, JONATHAN. *Montpellier.*

1821, March 26. Alleged seizure of his vessel (schooner *Hero*) and cargo and forced sale in 1811–'12. Bitterly complains of injustice done him by Congress in not taking the matter up and giving him relief. Apparently from a man crazed by his misfortune. fol. 8 pages.

EMLEN, SAMUEL, JR. *Philadelphia.*

1792, August 17, Philadelphia. Relative to a person in France, calling himself De Lormerie, who applied to Madison respecting a deed for a tract of land in Kentucky. Asks if the conveyance is in his possession and whether it was recorded. 4°. 2 pages.

EMMONS, RICHARD. *Montpellier.*

1828, May 25, Great Crossing, Ky. Is grateful to him for patronizing his first effort as an author. small 4°. 2 pages.

EMMONS, WILLIAM. *Montpellier.*

1828, March 30, Washington. Sends a set of the "Fredoniad" for Madison's inspection, trusting to the merits of the work and a liberal public. 4°. 3 pages.

1828, May 12, Washington. Acknowledging receipt of money from R. M. Johnson for a copy of the "Fredoniad," a work of his brother Richard Emmons. 4°. 2 pages.

Richmond.

1830, January 5, Richmond. Invites Madison to the Capitol. The subject to be introduced of a patriotic nature. 4°. 1 page.

Montpellier.

1830, December 15, Fredericksburg. Asks him to subscribe to the revised edition of Richard Emmon's great national poem. 4°. 2 pages.

1831, January 9, Richmond. As Madison does not subscribe to the second edition of the "Fredoniad," asks him to send the 4 volumes to Governor James Barbour, who has bought it 4°. 1 page.

ENGELBRECHT, JACOB. *Montpellier.*

1825, September 5, Fredericktown, Md. Asks for a letter in his own handwriting which he wishes to frame and preserve for posterity, as he has autographs of other distinguished men. 4°. 1 page.

1827, June 25, Fredericktown, Md. Acknowledging letter of 20th. Suggests that Madison write the letter to him, to be dated July 4. 4°. 1 page.

1827, October 12, Fredericktown, Md. Error in Madison's letter of October 20, 1825, which he re-

ENGELBRECHT, JACOB.

turned. As three months have elapsed and not hearing from him reminds him of his promise. 4°. 1 page.

1827, October 24, Fredericktown, Md. Acknowledging letter of 17th, inclosing one of July 4. Thanks him for the favor. 4°. 1 page.

ENNALLS, A. SKINNER. *Washington.*

1801, February 9, Baltimore. Acknowledging letter of January 31. Nonacceptance of a draft which he afterwards accepted and will pay at maturity. 4°. 2 pages.

EPISCOPAL CHURCH.

1784. [*See* Madison's address to the Virginia general assembly remonstrating against establishment of the Episcopal Church.]

EPPES, FRANCIS, to MADISON. *Montpellier.*

1827, April 2, Poplar *Forest.* Requests to be furnished with letters of introduction to friends in East Florida. 4°. 1 page.

1828, April 15, Tallahassee. Asks Madison's good offices with Mr. Wirt (Attorney-General), to appoint John K. Campbell, district attorney for Key West, The health, fertility, and delightful climate of Florida. 4°. 3 pages.

EPPES, JOHN W. *Washington.*

1810 (?), no date, Washington. Informs him that Col. Howard will accept the appointment, but desires the nomination should be delayed until the last days of the session. 4°. 1 page.

1810, January 18, Washington. The few troops remaining in New Orleans owing to desertions and deaths. Gen. Wilkinson's orders in disobedience of those from the Secretary of War in keeping the troops in a swamp. Public sentiment against Wilkinson. No confidence in him. 4°. 2 pages.

1810, March 24, Washington. Charges against Mr. Deblois, who solicits the appointment of purser. Was dismissed from the navy-yard under the Federal administration for peculation and frauds on the workmen. Can substantiate the charges. 4°. 3 pages.

1810, November 1, Cumberland. Papers relating to the proceedings of the convention confided to him by Jefferson. small 4°. 3 pages.

1810 (?), no date, Washington. The question whether it is better for the public interest that the nonimportation law should be at present pushed in the House of Representatives. Seizure and condemnation of American vessels under the Berlin and Milan decrees. small 4°. 2 pages.

ERSKINE, D. M. *Washington.*

1807, May 13, Philadelphia. Introduces W. Penn, a descendant of the founder, and son of Governor Penn, of Pennsylvania. 4°. 1 page.

1807 (?), May 27, New York. Acknowledging letter of 20th. Has no advices from England. Seems certain that Bonaparte has met with more resistance than he expected. 4°. 1 page.

ERVING, G. W.

1802 (?), not dated. Memorandum respecting British claims. [In red ink.] fol. 3 pages.

ERVING, G. W. *Washington.*

1807, March 24, Madrid. Accompanying duplicate of official letter No. 25. Negotiations with the Spanish Government. Condemnation of English property on board our vessels. The great part of this letter in cipher with no key to decipher it. Respecting the French campaign on Russia. Occupation of the Hellespont by the English fleet. [Duplicate.] "Private." 4°. 3 pages.

——— to JOY, GEORGE. *Copenhagen.*

1811, June 2, Copenhagen. Informs Mr. Joy that he has applied to the King requiring a suspension of all proceedings upon all American cases. [Press copy.] 4°. 1 page.

1811, June 5, Copenhagen. Acknowledging note of this date. Thanks him for his information on points of etiquette, but he is perfectly acquainted with them, but as minister can not make visits or send cards until he has been received by his majesty. [On same sheet as Joy's letter to him.] [Copy.] 4°. 1 page.

ESPIE, J. W., to LEE. *Bordeaux.*

1816, January 15, St. Foy, France. Sends to the President portions of his poem for his approval. Wishes to establish himself in some occupation in the United States. Asks Lee's opinion of locality in which to locate himself and family. [In French.] 4°. 3 pages.

EUSTIS, WILLIAM, to MADISON. *Washington.*

1809, March 18, Boston. Accepts the appointment of Secretary of War. 4°. 1 page.

1809, July 27, New York. Negotiations with Mr. Erskine, the British minister. Unexpected turn. Waits instructions. 4°. 1 page.

1809, September 10, Boston. Acknowledging letter of August 30. Instructions forwarded to Gen. Wilkinson to repair to Washington. The measures of the administration approved. fol. 1 page.

1809, December 4, Washington. List of appointments in the Army during last recess of Congress. 4°. 2 pages.

1809, December 18, Washington. Proposes for approbation, William Swan, captain First Regiment Infantry, to be appointed military agent for the Southern department, vice Andrew McCulloch deceased. 4°. 1 page.

1809, December 27, Washington. Proposes for the President's approbation Nanning I. Visscher, to be appointed captain in the regiment of riflemen. 4°. 1 page.

1810, April 9, Washington. Proposes Henry M. Gelham as ensign in Seventh Infantry. 4°. 1 page.

1810, April 12, Washington. It is not expedient to purchase the philosophical apparatus of Mr. Tatham. 4°. 1 page.

1810, July 11, Washington. Incloses a return exhibiting the several posts and stations occupied by the troops. Thinks the Indians will not commence hostilities. The movement of our troops on the Western waters. 4°. 1 page.

1810, July 12, Washington. Incloses copy of a letter from Governor Harrison. No apprehension of Indian hostilities. 4°. 1 page.

EUSTIS, WILLIAM.

1810, July 16, Washington. Incloses letter of Gen. Wilkinson requesting officers be ordered to Washington. Objections mentioned. Question as to Wilkinsons right to command. Asks special instructions. 4°. 2 pages.

1810, July 29, New London. Acknowledging letter of 17th. Movement of troops from Carlisle to Pittsburg. The attack on the *Vixen.* 4°. 1 page.

1810, August 19, Boston. Acknowledging letter of 10th. Col. Sparks's letter forwarded to Gen. Hampton with instructions to reinforce Fort Stoddert. Assemblage of troops at Mussel Shoals will defeat the contemplated expedition.
4°. 1 page.

1810, August 26, Portsmouth, N. *H.* Acknowledging letter of 16th. The disrespectful note is not by Mr. Prince, marshal. Colbert's letter to be communicated to Gen. Mason. Election of delegates to Congress. The publishing of Pinckney's private communication. 4°. 2 pages.

Montpellier.

1810, September 7, Portsmouth, N. *H.* Acknowledging letter of August 30. Question respecting the placing the territory of West Florida under the protection of the United States. The reinforcements of Fort Stoddert. Information contained in Col. Smith's letter. His dissatisfaction. Gen. Hampton orders Col. Smith to take command of troops in Tennessee. 4°. 2 pages.

1810, September 14, Portsmouth. Acknowledging letter of 7th. Instructions to Gen. Hampton and Col. Cushing predicated on apprehension for safety of public stores at Fort Stoddert.
4°. 2 pages.

1810, September 16, Portsmouth. Incloses copy of letter from J. Q. Adams. Accounts from the *Baltic.* Incloses instructions to Governor Holmes and commanding officer. 4°. 2 pages.

Washington.

1811, January 22, Washington. Appointments of officers in the Army during last recess of Congress.
4°. 2 pages.

1811, January 22, Washington. Proposes for the President's approbation a promotion and appointments to the Army. 4°. 1 page.

1811, January 31, Washington. Proposing for approbation of the President, appointments of officers in the Army. 4°. 1 page.

Montpellier.

1811, August 8, Washington. Submits proceedings of a general court-martial in the case of Lieut. Joel Lyon, of Third Regiment Infantry. The sentence appears to be just. 4°. 1 page.

1811, August 13, Washington. Acknowledging letter of 10th. Inclosing letter from Lieut. Voorhis. Business will prevent his visiting Montpellier. The armory at Harpers Ferry. Capacity for storing arms. The works in New York Harbor. Wilkinson says he will have the court-martial in Fredericktown. The Choctaw chiefs' proposed visit to Washington. 4°. 3 pages.

1811, August 21, Washington. Inclosing letters from Governor Harrison. Suggests that a movement

EUSTIS, WILLIAM.

up the Wabash be made with considerable force. Advises that Boyd's regiment be sent and that the visit from the Indian chiefs be postponed. 4°. 2 pages.

1811, September 2, Washington. Acknowledging letter of August 24. British aggressions. In case they are multiplied, will be obliged to adjourn the court-martial. The absence of so many field officers from the seaboard is particularly felt. Does not fear immediate acts of hostility will be authorized by the British Government. 4°. 1 page.

1811, September 11, Washington. Incloses a letter from W. Jones, judge-advocate, requesting instructions relative to the proceedings of the general court-martial. 4°. 1 page.

1811, September 14, Washington. Court-martial in Gen. Wilkinson's case. Inclosing letters of Gen. Gansevoort and William Jones, jr., judge-advocate. 4°. 4 pages.

1811, September 25, Washington. Acknowledging letter of 21st. Order issued by Gen. Hampton, directing attendance of officers at the court-martial of Gen. Wilkinson. Proceedings of the court-martial in the case of Surgeon's-Mate Huston. 4°. 1 page.

Washington.

1812, January 16, February 8, April 1, Washington. Officers proposed for the President's approbation. [Three letters.] 4°. 3 pages.

1812, April 9, Washington. The additional duties devolved by Congress on this Department renders it necessary that the Indian department should be transferred to some other department. Other alterations necessary. 4°. 1 page.

1812 (?), September 2, Washington. The companies required for Passamaquoddy. Gen. Dearborn's requisition complied with. Delays answer to Governor Strong. 4°. 1 page.

1812, September 5, Washington. Hull's defeat. The surrender of the posts and troops unnecessary. The capture of Malden was within the power of our troops. Movements of Gen. Wadsworth. Anxiety for Fort Wayne. Tecumseh's request of Gen. Brock. Gen. Dearborn's intentions. Inhabitants of Upper Canada acknowledging allegiance to United States. 4°. 3 pages.

1812, September 7, Washington. Expediency of detaining Indian chiefs as hostages. Report that Fort Wayne is taken. 4°. 1 page.

Montpellier.

1812, September 8, Washington. Letters from Gen. Dearborn and others, from the West, show that events of importance are daily occurring. Trusts Madison's return may not be inconvenient. 4°. 1 page.

Washington.

1812 (?), no date. Nominations in quartermaster's division to be made. 4°. 1 page.

1812 (?), no date, Washington. Thinks Gen. Lee should be made adjutant-general. 4°. 1 page.

EUSTIS, WILLIAM.

1812 (?), no date. Appointment of assistant deputy quartermaster to Henry Glenn withheld by Gen. Lewis. [Unsigned.] 4°. 1 page.

Washington.

1812 (?), not dated. Militia to rendezvous at Pittsburg. Harrison's call for one-month men. 4°. 1 page.

1812 (?), no date. Memorandum respecting enlistments of eighteen months. [Not signed.] 4°. 1 page.

1812, October 13, Washington. Requests the President to direct that $500,000, appropriated for the pay of the Army, be applied to defray further expenses in the quartermaster's department. 4°. 2 pages.

1812, October 29, Washington. Asks the President to direct that a sum appropriated for the pay of the Army, be applied to defray the expenses of the clothing department. 4°. 1 page.

1812 (?), not dated. Memorandum on the institution of a system for calling into the field commissioned and noncommissioned officers for instruction and discipline. [Not signed.] 4°. 1 page.

——— to SENATE and HOUSE OF REPRESENTATIVES.

1812 (?), not dated. Laying before Congress letters received from Governor Harrison reporting particulars of the issue of the expedition under his command. Dauntless spirit displayed by the troops. [Not Signed. Draft.] 4°. 1 page.

——— to MADISON.

1812 (?), not dated. Notes of a conversation with John Wait, a gloomy Federalist of Boston. [Not signed. Draft.] 4°. 1 page.

1812 (?), not dated. Recruits ordered to maritime posts, which retarded military operations on the northern frontiers. Surrender of the army and post at Detroit. Gen. Hull's conduct to be investigated by court-martial. Attack at Queenstown, near Niagara, by troops under command of Gen. Van Rensselaer. Defeated for want of support. Revision of the laws to supply defects in the Army and militia. [Draft.] 4°. 2 pages.

1812 (?), not dated. Memorandum stating the completion of defences on the seaboard, except New York and some other ports. [Not signed. Draft.] Strip of paper.

1812 (?), not dated. Completion of defences of the seaboard. Another season required to finish works on New York Harbor. Increase of supply of small arms. Condition of the Army. [Not signed. Draft.] 4°. 2 pages.

1812 (?), not dated. Fortifications for defence of the seaboard. Improvements in quantity and quality of small arms. Power asked of Congress to provide for arming and organizing the militia. [Not signed. Draft.] 4°. 2 pages.

1812 (?), not dated. Act of April, 1808, for raising for a limited time an additional military force. Orders issued to the executives of the several States to discharge their respective quotas under act of March 30, 1808. [Not signed. Draft.] 4°. 1 page.

EUSTIS, WILLIAM.

1812 (?), not dated. Gen. Cass's opinion respecting Pennsylvania troops at Pittsburg. [Not signed. Draft.] 4°. 1 page.

Washington.

1813, January 29, Boston. The bad management of the recruiting service. Indolence and incompetency of recruiting officers. Importance of a more vigorous effort. "Confidential." 4°. 2 pages.

1813, November 7, Boston. Acknowledging letter of 1st. Is grateful for the commission tendered him. He delays accepting it before Madison's views are known respecting the collectorship now held in trust for Gen. Dearborn by his son. 4°. 3 pages.

1813, November 21, Boston. Acknowledging letter of 12th. Offers his services. 4°. 1 page.

Washington.

1814, January 1, Boston. The failure of Wilkinson's movements toward Montreal. Primary object should be to fill positions with competent generals. Bounty to volunteers. Embargo a strong collateral aid. The medical department. In view of accident or resignation by Dr. Tilton would undertake to direct that department. 4°. 3 pages.

——— to GERRY, ELBRIDGE. *Washington.*

1814, February 14, Boston. Discontent of elder officers at promotion of juniors over them. Suggests a brevet in the case of Gen. Boyd. 4°. 2 pages.

——— to MADISON. *Washington.*

1814, December 21, Boston. Acknowledging letter of 15th. Expresses gratification at Madison's delicate attention. Will not decline the appointment (minister to Holland) should it be confirmed. [The signature cut off.] "Private." 4°. 1 page.

1815, January 14, Boston. Application of young Elbridge Gerry for position of secretary of legation to The Hague. His incompetency. Among other candidates is Mr. Alex. Hill Everett, of whom he speaks in high terms. Observance of fast day in Boston. 4°. 3 pages.

1815, January 15, Boston. Introduces Col. Eustis, of the light artillery. His services on the northern frontiers. "Private." 4°. 1 page.

1815, May 2, Boston. Suggests that one-half the force ordered for the Mediterranean may be sufficient to blockade Algiers, and after the expiration of a year to be relieved; thus giving an opportunity of training and disciplining officers and men. The return of Bonaparte. The frigate *Congress* waiting for men. Will be ready to embark. "Private." 4°. 2 pages.

1815, August 10, Hague. The enhanced respect of our nation since our successful conflict with Great Britain. Respecting an American seaman at Antwerp. Remedy promised. 4°. 3 pages.

1815, August 18, Hague. Acknowledging letter of May 12. Claim of impressed seaman in Holland for seizures and confiscations. Political situation of Holland. Comparison between foreign and United States governments. Strength of the latter. Hopes for the acquisition of Florida.

EUSTIS, WILLIAM.

In certain contingencies would like a Government position at home. 4°. 4 pages.

1815, October 9, Hague. Inauguration of the King at Brussels. Thinks the peace in Europe can not last long. The state of France threatens its interruption. Discontent and insubordination. Removal of the works of art. Alsace and Lorraine. Russian affairs. Return of the King of Prussia, leaving his legions in France. "Private." 4°. 2 pages.

Montpellier.

1818, December 27, Richmond. Respecting his tour in Virginia. 4°. 1 page.

1819, April 28, New York. Conversation with Dr. Mason respecting the draft of Washington's farewell address in Hamilton's handwriting. Interview with Van Wert, one of the men who arrested André, and the compensation offered for his release. Van Wert a well-to-do farmer in Westchester County. [Partly mutilated.] 4°. 3 pages.

EVANS, OLIVER. *Washington.*

1814, March 8, Washington. Invention of applying steam engines to propel war vessels constructed to glance off enemies' shot and throw hot water to prevent boarding. 4°. 3 pages.

EVANS, ROBERT J. *Montpellier.*

1819, June 3, Philadelphia. Convinced the time has arrived for the adoption of a plan for the eventual abolition of slavery. Asks Madison for such practical hints as may occur to him. 4°. 1 page.

1819, June 26, Philadelphia. Acknowledging letter of 15th. Thanks Madison for his views respecting the eventual abolition of slavery, which will not be made public, as requested. 4°. 1 page.

1819, December 31, Philadelphia. Incloses first number of the "Rural Magazine." Madison's interest in agricultural pursuits. 4°. 1 page.

EVANS, THOMAS. *Washington.*

1809, May 1, Accomac County, Va. As chairman at a meeting of citizens of Accomac County, he expresses their approbation of the President's proclamation, and promises to support and defend the administration. fol. 1 page.

EVE, GEORGE. *Washington.*

1807, November 24, Scott County, Ky. Recommending his acquaintance with Richard M. Johnson, a worthy young man. small 4°. 3 pages.

EWELL, JAMES. *Washington.*

1813, January 25, Washington. Inclosing letters recommending him to the Secretary of the Navy for an office in that Department. Submits them to the President first for his acquiescence. 4°. 1 page.

EWELL, MAXCEY. *Philadelphia.*

1791, February 21, Albemarle County, Va. His accounts against the Government. His papers forwarded to the Treasury. Asks how he may obtain them. His services during the Revolution and reduced condition at present. Hopes Madison will use his good offices. fol. 1 page.

EWELL, THOMAS. *Washington.*

1812, April 15. Having completed a manufactory for gunpowder wishes to obtain a contract from Government. Asks the President's recommendation. [Signature worn off.] 4°. 1 page.

1813, January 10. Order of the President countermanding an order of the late Secretary of the Navy to deliver materials for making gunpowder without any reference to Ewell. Fraud and misrepresentations by Charles W. Goldsborough. Trusts the President will avert the misfortune impending. 4°. 2 pages.

——— to JONES, WILLIAM. *Washington.*

1813, January —, Washington. Statement of facts concerning his contract for making powder and explains the transaction of disposing of a portion of material to be used. He is supported in his statement by an indorsement by the late Secretary of State, Paul Hamilton. [Copy.] fol. 4 pages.

——— to MADISON. *Washington.*

1813, January 20. Denies that he converted the nitre received in Philadelphia from the Navy Department into money. Gives a statement of the business and shows how he acted for the advantage of the Government in making an exchange. Trusts the President will not delay to suspend the violent method resorted to. 4°. 3 pages.

——— to COLES, WILLIAM E. *Washington.*

1813, January 27. Asks the secretary of the President to deliver an inclosed letter to Madison with a request to read it. 4°. 1 page.

——— to MADISON. *Washington.*

1813, May 21. Appeals to the justice of the President in protecting him from the acts of the present Secretary of the Navy. Injury done him in countermanding a contract for gunpowder. Asks him to order a trial of the excellence of his powder by an experienced and respectable officer. 4°. 3 pages.

1813, May 23, Georgetown. Injustice done him by the Secretary of the Navy. Urges the President to order a trial in the usual way to test the superiority of his powder over others. 4°. 3 pages.

Montpellier.

1823, November 7, Haymarket, Va. Inclosing copy of an oration. 4°. 1 page.

1824, December 12, Haymarket, Va. Inclosing prospectus of a work, entitled "The Virginia Family Physician." Applies for the position in the medical department of the University of Virginia. 4°. 2 pages.

EWING, F. *Washington.*

1814, January 27, Ewingville, Ky. Regrets the unwarranted opposition of the Northern clergy to the President's course. He is a Presbyterian minister and heartily approves of the war and took part in it as a soldier with his son. 4°. 3 pages.

EXCHANGE, BILL OF.

Not dated. Memorandum of an acceptance of Madison of £21, sterling. strip of paper.

EXPORTS.

1770. Exports from America to the southern ports of Europe in 1770, and to all parts of the world. [A memorandum in an unknown handwriting.] small 4°. 3 pages.

Charleston.

1787. List of exports of merchandise from Charleston from January, 1783, to November, 1787. 4°. 4 pages.

Bermuda Hundred.

1789, December 31. Statement of exports from the district of Bermuda Hundred from August 17, to December 31, 1787. 4°. 1 page.

EYBIEN FRÉRES & CIE, to MADISON.

Montpellier.

1821, April 2, Havre. Notifies Madison of the shipment from the King's garden, in Paris, of a box of seeds for the Rural Society of Virginia, of which Madison is president. [In French.] 4°. 2 pages.

"FABIUS," LETTERS OF.

1797. Pamphlet, entitled "Letters of Fabius in 1788 on the Federal Constitution, and in 1797 on the Present Situation of Public Affairs." [Title page mutilated.] 8°. 203 pages.

FAIRFAX, DENNY, to TAYLOR, JOHN.

Not dated. Memorandum respecting a claim for land in Virginia against that State. [As stated in the margin by Madison, this paper is in the handwriting of John Taylor.] 4°. 2 pages.

FARJON, SŒUR DE ST. XAVIER DE, to MADISON.

Washington.

1809, March 11, New Orleans. In behalf of the community of the Ursuline Convent of New Orleans, of which she is superior, congratulates the President on his elevation to the office, and as protector of instruction for youth she offers prayers to heaven for his happiness and health. [In French.] 4°. 2 pages.

FARLEY, ROBERT. *Washington.*

1813, September 6, Ipswich, Mass. Wishes to be appointed collector of this district. 4°. 1 page.

FARMER'S BANK OF VIRGINIA. *Montpellier.*

1825. Certificates of deposit May 20, July 5, August 2. Canceled check July 15. 4 strips of paper.

FARMER'S SOCIETY. *Washington.*

1802, May 8, Sandy Spring, Maryland. Certificate of membership of this society. 4°. 1 page.

FAUCHE, P. *Washington.*

1815, August 26, Paris. Introduces Count Reguaud de St. Jean D'Angely, who is going to the United States. [In French.] fol. 2 pages.

FAURE, STAS. *New York.*

1788, March 7, Havre. Notice of shipment of a case by the *King's Packet* for New York. 4°. 1 page.

FAY, DAVID. *Washington.*

1812, February 25, Bennington, Vt. Inclosing proceedings of a meeting of the Republican citizens of Bennington County, expressing sentiments of approbation and support to the Government in the present crisis. 4°. 10 pages.

FERNANDEZ, J. H., to NEWTON, THOMAS. *Norfolk.*

1808, June 22. Announcing the arrival of the *Osage* at Falmouth, having on board Messrs. Nourse and Lewis, after a detention of five weeks at l'Orient on account of having been boarded by a British privateer. Rumored departure of Gen. Armstrong from Paris. 4°. 1 page.

FICKLIN, JOSEPH, to MADISON. *Montpellier.*

1823, August 9, Lexington, Ky. Asks for the confirmation of Madison's views reported as expressed to Mr. Graves, respecting the Commonwealth Bank, and his approval of the measures taken to sustain our institutions of learning. 4°. 3 pages.

FIELDING, ROBERT. *Washington.*

1810, February 3. Bill for lanterns and candles for chariot. 4°. 1 page.

FINCH, JOHN. *Montpellier.*

1824, May 20, Philadelphia. Inclosing a literary work printed in the American Journal of Science. Has discovered certain fossil remains of sharks, crocodiles, and cetaceous animals on the banks of the James and York rivers. 4°. 1 page.

1828, May 1, Philadelphia. Submitting an essay on the boundaries of empires in which he attempts to prove that nature has erected barriers which nations can seldom pass with impunity. 4°. 1 page.

1829, May 10, Philadelphia. Inclosing a second essay on the natural boundaries of empires. 4°. 1 page.

FISHER, GEORGE (Speaker). *Washington.*

1812. Petition of the legislature of Illinois Territory to Congress for protection and remuneration for services of the militia. The isolated situation of the inhabitants exposes them to frequent incursions of savages who are instigated by British traders. fol. 4 pages.

1812, December 4, Illinois Territory. Petition by the general assembly of the Illinois Territory that a garrison of two companies may be erected at Peoria for protection against the savages, and that Capt. Wm. O. Allen be commandant. royal fol. 1 page.

FITCH, JOHN. *New York.*

1788, February 10, New York. Difficulties in perfecting and producing his invention of the application of steam for navigating purposes, for want of means. Asks Madison's good offices in Congress towards his project in making a steamboat of 50 tons to navigate the Ohio to Fort Pitt. Claims priority of invention. fol. 3 pages.

1788, February 11, New York. Asks Madison's patronage in reporting his petition to Congress. 4°. 1 page.

1788, February 25, New York. Explaining his proposition to Congress respecting his proposed plan of navigating the Mississippi from New Orleans to Illinois by steam. The economy of his method over any method now known. fol. 1 page.

1789, April 12, Philadelphia. Requests Madison's patronage respecting his claims to the invention of steamboats. He wishes exclusive rights by

FITCH, JOHN.

Congress to the enjoyment of his labor. Fears other applications, therefore takes this early time to present his petition. Copy of the petition inclosed explaining the whole matter.
4°. 6 pages.

FITZHUGH, DENIS. *Washington.*

1802, July 10, Georgetown. Asks him to forward deeds to William Croghan and Richard Taylor to Fredericksburg, as he leaves for Kentucky from that place. 4°. 1 page.

FLOOD, WILLIAM, to HAMILTON, A. W. (Captain).

1816, April 12, Washington. Complimenting him on the course he pursued in refusing a command by Gen. Pakenham during the late war. Hopes he will be rewarded by our country. [Copy.]
4°. 2 pages.

FOLCH, V., to FORT STODDERT, COMMANDING OFFICER OF.

1810, November 13, Pensacola. In view of the good intelligence existing between Spain and the United States, he asks his influence and every other means, to dissipate the hostile projects of Reuben Kemper preparing within the limits of the United States against His Catholic Majesty's possessions. [Copy.] fol. 1 page.

——— to SPARKS, RICHARD (Colonel).

1810, November 20, Pensacola. Transmitting copy of a letter to Governor Holmes, of Mississippi Territory, respecting the robberies and depredations made on the inhabitants of this district. Attached to this letter is another dated November 24, on same subject. fol. 2 pages.

——— to GAINES, EDWARD P. (Captain).

1810, November 25, Mobile. In consequence of negotiations pending for the acquisition of the Floridas, to show the good feeling existing between the Spanish and United States governments, he declares that no duties shall be levied or collected from citizens of the United States on merchandise within the district, including Pascagoula, and hopes our Government will assist by employing its forces to dissipate troubles. [Copy.]
4°. 1 page.

FOORD, JAMES (Town Clerk), to MADISON. *Washington.*

1812, March 9, Milton, Mass. Petition of Samuel Gile and others, inhabitants of the town of Milton, Mass., submitting to the President and Congress the expediency of provision being made to secure the armed force of the United States against smallpox infection by means of vaccination, which has proved efficacious in numerous cases.
large fol. 2 pages.

FORONDA, VALENTINE DE (Spanish Minister). *Washington.*

1808, July 27, Philadelphia. Transportation of Spaniards from Baltimore to Havana. Thanking Madison for the permission granted. [In Spanish.] fol. 1 page.

1808, July 29, Philadelphia. Asks for copies of proceedings of the last session of Congress. [In Spanish.] 4°. 1 page.

FORONDA, VALENTINE DE (Spanish Minister).

1808, July 29, Philadelphia. Notification of the abdication of Charles IV, of Spain, in favor of his son Ferdinand VII, and expressing his good will and friendship for the United States, with copy of the decree. [In Spanish.] fol. 2 pages.

1808, July 29, Philadelphia. Expulsion of Swedish vessels from Spain. [In Spanish.] fol. 1 page.

FORREST, RICHARD. *Washington.*

1807, August 14, Washington. Desertion of crew of the schooner *Wasp*, in England. Refusal of the British officers to give them up. Subsequently, a higher officer reprimanded the other and restored them. 4°. 2 pages.

——— to BARTON, ——— (Doctor). *Philadelphia.*

1810, May 17, Washington. Impossibility of complying with the request to furnish a passport to W. Nutall, as he is not an American citizen. 4°. 1 page.

POULTON, JESSE, to MADISON. *Washington.*

1810, February 6, Zanesville, Ohio. As chairman, records the proceedings of a meeting of the Democratic citizens of Muskingum County in approval of the President's course in refusing to hold further communication with Mr. Jackson, the British minister, expressing their confidence and promising support. 4°. 3 pages.

FOWLER, C. S. *Montpellier.*

1825, June 25, Washington. Asks Madison's wishes as respects the payment of a note, whether it be made payable in Washington or in Fredericksburg. 4°. 1 page.

FRAGMENTS.

Not dated. Five scraps of paper, being portions of letters. One signed Joseph Jones, and one in Madison's handwriting.

FRANCE.

1797. Questions by unknown writer concerning the possible grounds of dissatisfaction on the part of France against the United States. fol. 6 pages.

——— MILITARY SCHOOLS IN.

Not dated. A list of the different military schools in France. 4°. 3 pages.

——— MISSION TO.

1802. Contingent account of this mission from February to May, 1802. [A memorandum] 8°. 1 page.

FRANKLAND (FRANKLIN?), STATE OF.

1785. Resolutions in general assembly recommending a convention to be held in relation to the formation of a government and the conditions of their admission into the Federal Union. [Copy.] fol. 2 pages.

FRAZER, HUBBART, to MADISON. *Washington.*

1815, April 15, Baltimore. States that he enlisted for eighteen months, but the inspector-general declares he is returned in for five years. Wishes his discharge granted. small 4°. 1 page.

FRANKLIN, BENJAMIN, to BARCLAY, THOMAS.

1787, November 10, Philadelphia. Gives his testimony as to Barclay's conduct as consul while he (Frank-

FRANKLIN, BENJAMIN.

lin) was in France, in which his management of affairs was highly advantageous to the public. [*See* Jefferson's letter to Barclay, dated August 3, 1787.] [Copy.] 4°. 1 page.

FREEBORN, THOMAS, to MADISON. *Montpellier.*

1817, June 18. Regrets not being able to deliver in person William Thornton's letter of introduction. [On back of a letter of William Thornton's to Madison, of the above date.] 1°. 1 page.

FRENCH, BENJAMIN. *Montpellier.*

1832, April 3. Order to give to John Walker or John H. Price, the certificate given him for £36 for his pay as a regular soldier in the Army of the Revolution, and other papers establishing his claim. 8°. 1 page.

FRENCH, J. *Montpellier.*

1817, August 26, Fredonia. Asks if he has in his possession letters recommending the writer to appointment in a military position during the late war. If so, will he be kind enough to return them as an heirloom to his children, to show his patriotism. 4°. 3 pages.

FRENCHMAN, A. *Washington.*

1816, April 22, Richmond. Inclosing a paper (in French), being his views on banks in the United States. They should be abolished and a national bank, with branches in the principal commercial cities, substituted. Thinks the tariff rates should be augmented for articles of luxury, and a tax also assessed thereon. 4°. 5 pages.

FRENCH SPOLIATIONS.

[*See* American vessels in Kingston, Jamaica.] [*See* James Causten's letter to Madison, January 1, 1827.]

FRENEAU, PHILIP.

1772, November 2, Somerset County, Md. Giving a description of his occupation as a schoolmaster and poet. fol. 2 pages.

Philadelphia.

1791, July 25, Monmouth. Respecting the printing of his paper at Philadelphia, instead of New Jersey. Wishes Mr. Childs to be connected with him in the plan. 4°. 1 page.

1794, November 2, Monmouth. Solicits Madison's good offices in procuring the public printing for Mr. Francis Bailey. 4°. 1 page.

Philadelphia.

1795, May 20, Monmouth. Acknowledging letter of April 6. Mr. Bailey's services in the war. His experience as a journalist. Congratulates Madison on his marriage. fol. 2 pages.

1796, December 1, New York. Has formed a partnership with Thomas Greenleaf, in his two papers, the "Argus" and "New York Journal." Asks Madison to recommend him to Chancellor Livingston. fol. 1 page.

Washington.

1809, April 8, Philadelphia. Republication of his early poems. Congratulations on his election. 4°. 1 page.

1809, May 12, Philadelphia. Republication of his poems. 4°. 2 pages.

FRENEAU, PHILIP. *Orange.*

1809, August 7, Philadelphia. Completion of two volumes of his poems. Asks directions for sending them. 4°. 1 page.

Washington.

1815, January 12, Monmouth County. Retrospect of his life. Proposes the publication of additional verses. fol. 2 pages.

1815, March 3, New York. Intends writing a poem on the battle of New Orleans. 4°. 2 pages.

Orange.

1815, May 10, New York. Sends by Mrs. Anna Smyth, who intends going to Virginia, two volumes of his poems. Recommends Mrs. Smyth to his kind attentions. 4°. 1 page.

FROUTTÉ, ———, to JEFFERSON.

1787, June 27. Bill for French books furnished Mr. Jefferson. small 4°. 2 pages.

FULTON, ROBERT, to MADISON. *Washington.*

1809, January 28, Kalorama. Recommends in the formation of his Cabinet Joel Barlow, as Secretary of State. His talents as a writer and perfect acquaintance with European affairs and other qualifications. fol. 3 pages.

1809, February 9, Kalorama. Inviting Madison and members of the Senate and House to see experiments on harpooning and to investigate the principles of torpedo attack. 4°. 1 page.

1809, February 17, Bush Inn. The opposition of the majority of persons in the marine in France, England, and the United States, to experiments on the torpedo attack. Asks the temporary appointment of Mr. Barlow, as Secretary of the Navy, to promote the system which he considers as of utmost importance. fol. 2 pages.

1812, April 30, New York. Recommends Mathuren Livingston as second district judge in New York. The public printing now done in New York by papers hostile to the administration. 4°. 1 page.

1813, March 18, New York. Complains of unjust treatment of Governor Ogden, of New Jersey, as conspiring to break down his patent right to steamboats. Begs for Madison's protection. 4°. 3 pages.

1814, March 23, New York. Anxious to commence work on his steam floating batteries. Want of funds. Suggests making a loan giving guarantee of the Government. Is coming to Washington to defend his rights against the intrigues of Col. Aaron Ogden, of New Jersey, concerning steamboats. 4°. 2 pages.

1814, November 5, New York. Launching of the steam frigate. Describes it. Advantages for defense of ports. Figures proving economy in case of war. Suggests, in case of retirement of Mr. Jones, Secretary of the Navy, that he (Fulton) may temporarily succeed him to carry his views of the system of steam frigates into effect. 4°. 6 pages.

GAINES, E. P. (General).

1813, October 17, Detroit. General orders. Appointment of Gen. Cass to command troops in Michi-

GAINES, E. P. (General).

gan, and civil and military commander of the upper district of Upper Canada. Discharge of the regiment of militia from Pennsylvania. Complimentary remarks of the conduct of the Petersburg volunteers. fol. 2 pages.

——— to MADISON. *Washington.*

1815, April 17, New Orleans. Expressing gratitude and appreciation of the honor conferred on him by his unsolicited appointment to the brevet rank of major-general. 4°. 3 pages.

——— to JONES, ROGER (Adjutant-General). *Washington.*

1826, October 8, Cincinnati. Wishes to obtain from official source reference to the services of troops under Gaine's command during the late war with England. 4°. 16 pages.

——— to MADISON. *Montpellier.*

1826, October 16, Cincinnati. Inclosing copy of a letter to the Adjutant-General of the Army (Roger Jones), preparatory to a review of the principal occurrences of the late war with England in which he was immediately concerned. Injury done him by Mr. Crawford. Asks Madison's impressions of the letter inclosed and of his trial under court-martial. 4°. 3 pages.

GALES, JOSEPH, JR. *Washington.*

1815, June 19, Washington. Calls attention to an inclosed letter from Judge Charlton expressing favorable sentiments towards Madison. 4°. 1 page.

Montpellier.

1821, June 22, Washington. Acknowledging letter of 12th. Is unable to furnish copies of the National Intelligencer of the period desired, as they were burned by Admiral Cockburn in 1814. 4°. 1 page.

1821, August 20, Washington. Inclosing a cutting from the "New York Commercial Advertiser." 4°. 1 page.

GALES & SEATON. *Montpellier.*

1818, January 26, Washington. Inclosing copy of a letter to each member of both Houses of Congress. Asks Madison's views. 4°. 1 page.

1825, November 26, Washington Appointment of Mr. King to be minister to England and the desire by some that the nomination be rejected. Asks Madison for facts in his knowledge relative to certain publications of the "New York National Advocate." 4°. 1 page.

1833, July 29, Washington. Inclosing copies of the beginning of a work on the debates and proceedings of Congress. Asks for certain materials in Madison's hands to aid in the publication. 4°. 2 pages.

GALLATIN, ALBERT. *Washington.*

1801, no date, Washington. Memorandum relating to a pardon and matters connected with the Treasury routine. 4°. 1 page.

1801 (?), not dated. Fragment of a letter respecting appointments of collectors, etc. 4°. 2 pages.

1801, May 26, Washington. Reimbursements to Mr. Shaw for his advances to Portugese sailors. 4°. 2 pages.

GALLATIN, ALBERT.

1801, June 14, Washington. Inclosing papers relative to Priestmann's case. Remittance of forfeiture and the informer's pay. Agreement of the President to grant a pardon. Question as to his power to remit the forfeiture. fol. 2 pages.

1801, June 18, Washington. Respecting passes to be granted to vessels owned by United States citizens, navigated by Americans, but not built in the United States. Notes acts relating to passports and his construction thereon. 4°. 3 pages.

1801, November 5, Washington. On the policy of entering a suit against R. Cooper. The comptroller's and his own opinion. 4°. 2 pages.

1801, December 27, Washington. Inclosing a general outline of the list of public officers of the three departments, State, War, and Navy. Explains its classification. [Copy.] 4°. 2 pages.

1802, July 21, Washington. On the individual claims secured by the compromise with Georgia on grants by the British and Spanish governments. Memorandum attached respecting statements to be supplied by the Navy Department respecting deficits. 4°. 6 pages, and strip of paper.

1802, July 23, Washington. On commissions for offices of collector. [Private.] 4°. 2 pages.

1803, no date, Washington. Suggestions respecting Monroe's negotiations with France. Claims of United States citizens against France. Purchase of West Florida. 4°. 4 pages.

——— to SMITH, SAMUEL, (General).

1805, July 17, Washington. On finances. The tariff question. Policy of prohibition of English manufactures as a measure of retaliation. 4°. 2 pages.

——— to MADISON. *Washington.*

1805, August 6, New York. On the loan by the banks to Lafayette. Difficulties in the negotiations with Spain. 4°. 4 pages.

1805, August 12, New York. Situation of affairs respecting Spain and Algiers. The Algiers annuity. 4°. 2 pages.

1805 (?), no date, Washington. Mr. Harris declines going to France. Lieut. Leonard will go with the stock from New York. Asks for passport, stating he is bearer of dispatches to the American minister in Paris. "Private." 4°. 2 pages.

1807, August 15, New York. Martin and Ware not impressed, but deserters. News of the Russian defeat of June 14. 4°. 1 page.

——— to TURREAU, (General). *Washington.*

1807, January 17, Washington. Answer to note of 16th, stating that instructions from the President are necessary before he can purchase any bills. Asks him to write directing him in the President's name to purchase the bills to which he refers. [On same sheet with Turreau's letter.] [Draft.] 4°. 1 page.

——— to MADISON. *Washington.*

1808, August 9, New York. The Spanish vessel, prize to the British frigate *Hebe,* the cargo of which has been suffered to be landed in New Orleans. Laws on selling prizes in our ports should be examined. 4°. 2 pages.

Washington.

GALLATIN, ALBERT, to BLOUNT, THOMAS.

1808, December 5, Washington. Acknowledging letter of this date respecting a presumed infraction of the law prohibiting the slave trade. Is not authorized to interfere. The President only can afford relief. [On the same sheet as Blount's letter to Gallatin. Copy.] fol. 1 page.

——— to MADISON. *Washington.*

1808, December 21, Washington. Complaints respecting delay in issuing patents for lands. The cause lies in the Department of State. 4°. 2 pages.

1809, April 4, Washington. Actions of P. Manning, collector at Perth Amboy, render his removal necessary. Recommends Daniel Perrine his successor. Incloses memorandum respecting land office in Madison County, Mississippi Territory. 4°. 4 pages.

1809, June 15, Washington. Location of Virginia military lands in the State of Ohio. Suggestions submitted to the President. 4°. 4 pages.

1809, June 18, Washington. Locality of cessions of land of the State of Virginia. [Not signed. Copy.] 4°. 3 pages.

Montpellier.

1809, September 11, Washington. Intends making a short visit to New York. Thinks there is no necessity for Madison's return to Washington before October 10. Question of peace in Europe. 4°. 2 pages.

1809, October 28, Washington. Misbehavior of Benjamin Wall, marshal of Georgia. Investigations being made. Recommends his removal in favor of John Eppinger.
[Signature cut off.] 4°. 3 pages.

Washington.

1809, December 22, Washington. Appointment of J. Kelty Smith, Navy agent at New Orleans. As collector of internal revenues in Maryland, he was a delinquent. The amount due to the United States was assumed by his uncle, Mr. Kelty. Is compelled, with reluctance, to make this communication. 4°. 2 pages.

1810, January 26, Washington. Respecting swords purchased by Mr. Livingston for the State of Virginia. Remittance to pay for the same. Scrap of paper.

1810, no date, Washington. Location of Lafayette's land in Louisiana. [A memorandum signed A. G.] 4°. 1 page.

1810, May 2, Washington. Rejections of appointments by the Senate and recommendations of others in their stead. 4°. 2 pages.

1810, May 3, Washington. Act for the relief of Arthur St. Clair. Authority of the President necessary. [Signature cut off.] 4°. 1 page.

1810, May 28, Washington. Inclosing a form for signature empowering him to negotiate a loan with the United States Bank. Explanation of the loan. 4°. 2 pages.

Montpellier.

1810, July 16, Washington. Inclosing an act for the President's signature relating to duties. Depreciation of paper currency of Norway. 4°. 1 page.

GALLATIN, ALBERT.

1810, July 30, New York. Seeking a situation for Madison's nephew in a mercantile house. Advantages of New York for a mercantile education. A knowledge of acquirements requisite, as there are more candidates for occupation than there is employment. Suggestions to be followed. 4°. 3 pages.

1810, August 15, New York. Mr. Gelston refusing the appointment, recommends Joel R. Poinsett to be sent to Buenos Ayres as commercial agent. His qualifications. Suggestions as to his instructions. Questions of outfit. 4°. 4 pages.

1810, August 16, New York. Passport required for Mr. Poinsett to be designated as commercial agent to Buenos Ayres. 4°. 2 pages.

1810, August 17, New York. Gryme's correspondence respecting Mr. Brown's property. Resignation of Mr. Pease, of the office of surveyor of public lands south of Tennessee. Mr. Thomas's claims for the vacant office. 4°. 3 pages.

1810, August 21, New York. General alteration in the deposits of public money. 4°. 2 pages.

1810, September 5, New York. Difficulties respecting West Florida. The custom-house business of the districts of New Orleans and Mobile. 4°. 2 pages.

1810, September 17, New York. Papers received and delivered to Mr. Poinsett, who will sail for Rio Janeiro in two or three weeks. England will try to govern the Spanish colonies through a nominal Spanish regency and oppose revolutionary movements. She will attempt to take possession of Cuba. Her interests and prejudices may cause new sources of collision with us. Suggests that Erving be sent to Havana. 4°. 3 pages.

Washington.

1810, November 30, Washington. Inclosing a statement of the receipts and expenditures of the year ending September 30 last, with an estimate for this quarter. Necessity for placing the military school on a respectable footing. 4°. 3 pages.

1810, December 12, Washington. Depreciation of the Russian ruble. Importance of deciding on its fixed value to regulate exchanges and importations. [Signature cut off.] 4°. 3 pages.

1811, January 5, Washington. Request of Mr. Astor that his son-in-law, Mr. Benson, be permitted a passage on board the public vessel with Mr. Erving. Mr. Astor's message, that in case of non-renewal of the charter of the United States Bank two millions would be at the command of the Government, of his funds and those of his friends. His object not profit, but a wish to see the bank down. 4°. 1 page.

1811, January 17, Washington. Inclosing copies of the "laws, treaties, and other documents relative to the public lands." 4°. 1 page.

——— to GELSTON, DAVID. *New York.*

1811, February 25. Notice to collectors of ports. The charter of the United States Bank expiring, gives instructions as to deposits for collection. [Copy.] 4°. 2 pages.

GALLATIN, ALBERT, to MADISON. *Washington.*

1811, February 26, Washington. Charter of the Bank of the United States will expire March 3. Necessity for providing for collection of revenue bonds falling due after that day. Submits his views. 4°. 4 pages.

1811, March 22, Washington. Submitting plans relative to the business heretofore transacted by the branch bank at Washington, to be transferred to the banks of Columbia and Washington. The Treasury deposits and those of the officers of the War and Navy Departments. 4°. 3 pages.

——— to COLLECTORS OF CUSTOMS.

1811, October 7, Washington. Printed circular giving instructions to prevent the violation of the non-intercourse law, which forbids the importation of articles of British growth, produce, or manufacture, with written marginal notes. fol. 2 pages.

——— to MADISON. *Washington.*

1811, December 17, Washington. Inclosing a statement of the regular British force in Canada, transmitted by Mr. Astor. small 4°. 2 pages.

1812, January 31, Washington. An inclosed letter, being a statement of the proceedings under the act entitled "An act to regulate the construction of the Cumberland and Ohio Road." 4°. 1 page.

1812, March 17, Washington. Suggests the propriety of requesting the secretaries of the War and Navy departments to prepare estimates of probable monthly expenditures to the end of the present year, the law authorizing a loan having passed. 4°. 1 page.

1812, April 10, Washington. Inclosing memorandum containing information respecting the lands in Tennessee connected with the late proceedings on the part of North Carolina. [Covering two letters of Governor Willie Blount, with a report of a committee of the North Carolina senate and a copy of an act making further provision for perfecting titles to land within the State of Tennessee.] [*See* Blount, W.] 4°. 3 pages.

1812, no date, Washington. Mr. Eustis's aversion for Mr. Chrystie places him on the list of majors, while he has been recommended by all of the New York State delegation as lieutenant-colonel. Thinks the prejudice should be removed. 4°. 2 pages.

1812 (?), no date, Washington. Suggesting that orders be given for the protection of vessels from foreign ports while the British have inferior force on our coasts. Memorandum attached recommending the position of naval officer for New Orleans to Mr. Clay. 4°. 1 page, and scrap of paper.

——— to HAMILTON, PAUL. *Washington.*

1812, July 13, Washington. Note on the back of a letter addressed to Gallatin, Secretary of Treasury, declining to furnish the money on his order because it was not stated to be for the use of the Navy. Fortifications, etc., are placed under the control of the War Department. [*See* letter of P. Hamilton to Secretary of the Navy, dated July 12, 1812.] 4°. 1 page.

GALLATIN, ALBERT, to MADISON. *Washington.*

1812, July 21, Philadelphia. Recommending Pemberton Hutchinson to fill the vacancy of consulship at Lisbon. 4°. 3 pages.

1812 (?), no date, Washington. Recommendations to appointments to vacancies submitted. fol. 3 pages.

1812, October 11, Washington. Thinks that the suggested change of places (?) would be impolitic. 4°. 1 page.

1812, October 14, New York. Inclosing a communication, signed "A Friend to the Jefferson and Madison Administrations," criticising the recent proceedings of Mr. Sandford, district attorney, in libeling goods lately arrived from England. Suggests that it would be an act of justice to relieve importers and that the comptroller be instructed to write a circular to district attorneys disapproving the practice. 4°. 4 pages.

1812, November 1, Washington. Forfeitures of American property. Discrimination difficult. The profits of importers. Remedies suggested of unjust measures. 8°. 2 pages.

1812, December 11, Washington. Renews his recommendation that Mr. Hutchinson be appointed consul at Lisbon. 4°. 1 page.

1812, December 12, Washington. Disapproves of the permission to Gen. Armstrong to raise a volunteer force on different principles from those recognized by law and adopted elsewhere. 4°. 2 pages.

1812, no date, Washington. Inclosing a copy of the recommendation of the members of the New York delegation in favor of John Chrystie, and favoring his appointment as lieutenant-colonel in the Army. 4°. 2 pages.

1813, January 7, Washington. Inclosing the usual account of the contingent expenses of the Government for January 1 to December 31, 1812. 4°. 1 page. fol. 1 page.

1813, April 17, Washington. Inclosing copy of letter to the secretaries of War and Navy, which gives a general view of our fiscal situation for this year. 4°. 1 page.

——— to WAR AND NAVY, SECRETARIES OF.

1813, April 17, Washington. Receipts of the Treasury for this year and the amounts on which they may rely for their service of the Department. [Copy.] 4°. 4 pages.

——— to MADISON. *Washington.*

1813, March 5, Washington. Recommends cutting by the root militia expenses and of reducing the Western expenditure to what is necessary for defensive operations. Proposals for the loan. 4°. 2 pages.

1813, April 22, Baltimore. Approves of the wish of Gen. Armstrong to make an excursion toward the scene of action on our northern frontier. His military views more extensive than those of Gen. Dearborn. 4°. 1 page.

1812–1813, no date, Washington. Query, whether it is proper to enlist volunteers under the existing act for local and special services. [Unsigned.] 4°. 1 page.

GALLATIN, ALBERT.

1813, no date, Washington. Three memoranda relating to detachments of militia to assist in effecting the embargo on the lakes. Suggests the sending of seamen to the lakes from Philadelphia. Distribution of clothing and transportation. Recommends instructions to regimental quartermasters. 3 scraps of paper.

1813 (?), no date. Memoranda relating to: 1. Contract for supplies. 2. The recruiting service. 3. Local force. Statements of national expenses and resources. Question of loan. 4°. 3 pages.

1815, December 12, New York. Mr. Gelston goes to Washington about the damages recovered against him in the case of the *American Eagle.* His distressing situation and age. 4°. 1 page.

1815 (?). Memorandum respecting the appointment of Mr. Gallatin to treat of peace with Great Britain, and his second appointment at Gottenburg or Ghent in 1814, and his compensation and outfit with traveling expenses. 4°. 2 pages.

Washington.

1816, April 19, New York. Mr. Astor and the subject of the loan. Hopes Mr. Astor may be gratified. His subscription in April, 1813, when the Federalists of New York refused. 4°. 1 page.

1816, June 2, New York. Expects to sail by the *Peacock* on Wednesday following. Does not contemplate a long residence in France. 4°. 1 page.

1816, June 4, New York. Remittances to Barings for Todd's expenses. Rate of exchange. Requests that John Badollet may not be removed from office of land register at Vincennes. Will not be ready to sail before Friday. 4°. 3 pages.

1816 (?), no date. Inclosing a paper for the President's signature for authority to open a loan. fol. 1 page.

1816, August 12, Paris. Interview with the King, in which allusion was made to our former intimate alliance with France and the reasons they were disturbed. Discussions to open soon on subject of indemnities. Has met Lafayette and Humboldt. The British expedition against the Algerines. No news from our squadron. 4°. 3 pages.

1816, September 14, Paris. Wish of Mr. Lesueur, a civil engineer, to assist in the trigonometrical survey of the United States coast. Is fully competent. Asks instructions about his employment. Has seen Lafayette but once. Subject of indemnity. The crops. Expense of living in Paris dearer than London. 4°. 3 pages.

Montpellier.

1831, April 9, New York. Dissatisfaction at the appointments of certain officers of the incipient university at New York. Want of means. His health will not permit his visiting Madison. 4°. 1 page.

GALLOWAY, BENJAMIN.

1810, September 22, Hagerstown, Md. Appeal to the voters of his district to vote for him as Member of the House of Representatives of the United States in the place of Roger Nelson, resigned. His qualifications and patriotism and past services. 4°. 22 pages.

GALUSHA, JONAS (Governor), to MADISON.
Washington.

1812, November 7, Montpelier, Vt. Transmitting copy of a resolution of the general assembly of Vermont declaring their duty to support the declaration of war, and pledging their support to the General Government for a favorable result.
4°. 3 pages.

GAMBLE, JAMES. *Washington.*

1808, March 24, Philadelphia. On the employment of merchant vessels for the convenience of foreign correspondence during the embargo. Proposes to charter the ship *Susquehanna.* 4°. 2 pages.

GAMBLE, R. *Philadelpha.*

1796, April 4, Richmond. Approves of Madison's qualified amendment to Livingston's resolution in the House to carry the treaty with Great Britain into effect. 4°. 1 page.

1797, January 21, Richmond. Acknowledging letter of 15th, inclosing check for Mrs. Payne. Respecting revenue which has become necessary, and the mode of raising it. Favors the land tax as commerce is shackled. The merchant is the supporter of the present Government. The land owner should do his part. Trusts Madison will not refuse to serve again in Congress. fol. 3 pages.

1797, February 7, Richmond. Inclosing a power of attorney to draw from the Treasury a dividend, also directions where to pay it. fol. 2 pages.

Washington.

1805, June 11, Richmond. His son Robert about to sail for France. Would like to have some letters of introduction from Madison, also in case of difficulty to give a credit. 4°. 3 pages.

1807, March 7, Richmond. Asks for letters of introduction to persons in New Orleans for his son, who is interested in business engagements there.
fol. 1 page.

GANO, A. G., and others. *Montpellier.*

1835, March 13, Cincinnati. Invitation of a committee of native citizens of Ohio to celebrate the anniversary of her first settlement in 1788, and to partake of the hospitality of the city of Cincinnati. 4°. 1 page.

GANTT, THOMAS JOHN. *Montpellier.*

1821, August 23, Charleston. By a resolution of the '76 Association transmits a copy of Mr. Elliott's oration, delivered July 4; also that of Mr. Ramsay's, delivered last year. 4°. 1 page.

GANSEVOORT, P., to EUSTIS, WILLIAM.

1811, September 11, Fredericktown. Suggesting that one or two supernumeraries be ordered to attend the court-martial sitting in this place. Asks for the appointment of an assistant judge-advocate with a liberal allowance. [Copy.]4°. 2 pages.

GARDENEIR, B., to MADISON. *Washington.*

1812, May 16, New York. Speaks in high terms of Mr. Ogden Edwards, who has been mentioned at Washington for appointment as judge of this district. 4°. 1 page.

GARDINER, JOHN. *Washington.*

1809, May 23, Washington. Calling for the remainder of installments to a manufacturing company.
4°. 1 page.

GARDINER, JOHN.

1814, June 20, Washington. Suggesting that copies of the resolution of Congress, passed August 14, 1776, be printed on oiled paper and set afloat near the squadrons of the enemy in order to induce the men to desert to our country.
4°. 1 page.

Montpellier.

1817, October 29. Sends a map of the military bounty lands in the Illinois Territory, engraved for the use of the soldiers of the late army. 4°. 1 page.

GARDNER, GIDEON. *Washington.*

1814, January 4, Washington. Petition in behalf of the town and county of Nantucket to enable the citizens to fish and go whaling, it being their only means of subsistence, it now being contrary to the law of the embargo. Not a barrel of flour to be bought on the island. 4°. 1 page.

GARNETT, JAMES M. *Washington.*

1803, April 21, Essex, Va. Suggesting that the intention of the Government in giving Col. New a lucrative office, for the purpose of moving him out of Col. Taylor's way, would be impolitic.
4°. 3 pages.

GARNETT, ROBERT S. *Montpellier.*

1821, February 14, Washington. Transmitting the report of the Committee on Agriculture. [Acknowledgment of receipt by Madison on same page.] 4°. 1 page.

1824, February 5, Washington. Presents him with a copy of Col. Taylor's "New views of the Constitution." 4°. 1 page.

GAVRARD, WILLIAM. *Washington.*

1812, January 20, Opelousas, Orleans Territory. In reference to his claim as commissioner for adjusting land claims in the western district of this Territory, he asks Madison's good offices in the settlement of it. 4°. 3 pages.

1812, ——— ——— Opelousas. Invasion of the people of this State and adjoining territory into the Spanish province of Texas. Cowardly conduct of Gen. Hull in the surrender of Detroit. Has confidence in Madison's administration. 4°. 2 pages.

GARRETT, ALEX. *Montpellier.*

1817, June 24, Charlottesville. Title to the lands purchased for the Central College. 4°. 1 page.

1827, January 11, Charlottesville. Inclosing a check for balance due the University for the annuity, on the president and directors of the literary fund. Respecting the negotiation of a loan. [Memorandum at foot complying with a request, in Madison's handwriting.] 4°. 1 page.

1828, March 10, Charlottesville. Acknowledging letter of 4th. Inclosing a paper respecting various grants of money to the University of Virginia.
4°. 1 page.

1828, August 9, December 8; 1829, January 10, April 14, August 3; 1830, January 25, April 1; 1832, April 18; 1833, May 7, May 17, June 28, Charlottesville. Eleven letters. Financial matters relating to the University of Virginia. Remittances of checks for approval. 4°. 11 pages.

GARTLAND, JAMES. *Washington.*

1811, January 3, Philadelphia. Renewal of the charter of the United States Bank. His views on the subject, with statement of the results of the buiness of the bank. 4°. 3 pages.

GASSAWAY, JOHN. *Washington.*

1809, February 8, Annapolis. Sends the "Maryland Gazette," containing resolutions of a Democratic meeting expressive of their sentiments of the measures adopted by the General Government. 4°. 1 page.

HORATIO GATES. *New York.*

1787, November 26, Travelers Rest. An application to be made by Maj. Drumegole to Congress in behalf of the Cherokee Nation. Advocates a speedy, firm, efficient Federal Constitution. 4°. 1 page.

Philadelphia.

1794, February 3, New York. Congratulating Madison on his speech in support of Jefferson's report on the trade and commerce of the United States. Introduces Dr. Robertson, of Bath, England. 4°. 1 page.

1794, March 13, Rose Hill. Complimenting Madison on his reply to Smith, Ames, and Dexter. Approves Madison's plans respecting the Algerines. 4°. 2 pages.

1794, December 27, New York. Congratulating Madison on his marriage. Asks Madison's aid respecting land in Kentucky, taxes on which he never knew or heard of. Is fearful of losing it in consequence. 4°. 2 pages.

Washington.

1802, February 11, New York. Resignation of Gen. Armstrong in the Senate. Afflicted with rheumatism. Invites Madison to Rose Hill. 4°. 1 page.

1803, February 1, New York. Introducing Mr. Garnett. His literary and philosophic labors. Expresses satisfaction of Madison's measures. Is pleased at Monroe's appointment to France and Spain. 4°. 2 pages.

GAULLIER, J. F. *Washington.*

1801, August 2, Fredericksburg. Encouraged by the kind reception of the President at Monticello, he wrote to him asking a Government position, but not hearing from him in reply, asks Madison to remind him of the fact. 4°. 4 pages.

GAY, PAYTON. *Washington.*

1814, December 20, Boston. Wishes an appointment in the Army. Gives references as to his standing. 4°. 3 pages.

GEDDES, JOHN. *Washington.*

1812, January 29, Charleston. Acknowledging letter acknowledging receipt of the address of the South Carolina house of representatives transmitted on December 22. 4°. 2 pagos.

——— (Chairman).

1812, May 18, Charleston, S. C. Proceedings of a meeting of citizens of Charleston approving of the declaration of war and declaring their willingness to support of the Government. fol. 4 pages.

GEDDES, JOHN.

1812, September 26, Charleston. Transmission of the unanimous address of both branches of the South Carolina legislature approving of Madison's political conduct. South Carolina evidences a determination to support the Government in the prosecution of the war. Federal party opposes the member, Mr. Cheves, and bring forward Mr. Rutledge in opposition. The defeat of Gen. Hull may be productive of good in stimulating the citizens of the United States to carry on the war. Madison will receive the unanimous vote of South Carolina for his reelection. 4°. 3 pages.

1813, May 14, Charleston. The exposed condition of our seacoast. Defenseless state of Charleston. Congratulations on the success of our Navy. Delinquencies of public officers in Charleston, The confinement of the late Federal marshal. Recommends Col. Lehre to fill the vacancy. His integrity and qualifications. ["Private."] 4°. 3 pages.

1813, December 18, Columbia, S. C. Letter from the speaker of the house of representatives of South Carolina transmitting a resolution of both houses of the legislature expressing their confidence in Madison and his energetic prosecution of the war. 4°. 7 pages.

GELSTON, DAVID. *Washington.*

1802, January 13, New York. Acknowledging receipt of dispatches at the custom-house addressed to Mr. King and Mr. Lenox, London, and delivered to Mr. Christie. 4°. 1 page.

1802, April 12, New York. Acknowledging receipt of letter for Mr. King. 4°. 1 page.

1805, August 8, New York. Acknowledging letter of July 31, respecting a shipment of wine for the President and Mr. Madison from a vessel called the *Adventurer*, captured and carried into Halifax and then reshipped for New York. Inclosing a letter from Robinson & Hartshorn. 4°. 2 pages.

1805, November 7, New York. Respecting some wine shipped to the President and Madison and arrived in New York, to be reshipped to Alexandria. 4°. 2 pages.

1805, November 7, New York. Statement of duties on merchandise from Halifax for the President, Madison and Senator Butler. Statement of proportion of charges for each bill of duties, etc. Bill of lading brig *President* for Alexandria. 4°. 3 pages. 8°. 1 page.

1805, December 16, New York. Acknowledging letter of November 24, with remittance to pay duties. The balance still due from Mr. Madison on wine shipped from Marseilles. 4°. 2 pages.

1805, December 27, New York. Acknowledging letter of 24th, states balance due Madison in account. 4°. 1 page.

1807, April 3, New York. Regretting his inability to give the information desired. 4°. 1 page.

1807, December 4, New York. Arrival of a shipment of wine and other articles, which will be forwarded by first vessel. 4°. 1 page.

1807, December 19, New York. Inclosing Capt. Hopkins' bill of lading of wine. List of charges of freights and duties. Bill of freights receipted. 4°. 1 page

GELSTON, DAVID.

1808, February 2, New York. Has received from Mr. Lee, of Bordeaux, invoice and memorandum for sundries. Will forward by first opportunity.
4°. 1 page.

1809, May 11, New York. Has received bill of lading of wine, per the *Vestal* from Lisbon. Will forward it to Washington with bill of expenses.
4°. 1 page.

1809, June 9, New York. Acknowledging letter of May 15. Inclosing bill of expenses of wine.
4°. 1 page.

1809, June 9, New York. Bill of lading of wine, etc., per Schooner *Eliza Ann*, bound to Georgetown.
8°. 1 page.

1809, July 20, New York. Acknowledging letter of 26th, with a remittance. Anxious to hear of the arrival of wine in Washington. 4°. 1 page.

1809, November 20, New York. Has received a pipe of brandy and is not sure of the owner. If belonging either to the President or Mr. Jefferson, an order will be immediately attended to.
4°. 1 page.

1809, November 28, New York. Acknowledging letter of 24th, respecting a pipe of brandy. When it arrives in Boston will attend to duties, etc.
4°. 1 page

1809, December 12, New York. Has delivered to Mr. Forest the pipe of brandy. Incloses bill of expenses. 4°. 2 pages.

1810, March 5, New York. Acknowleding letter of 1st. Incloses receipted bill for subscription to the American Citizen. 4°. 1 page.

1810, May 21, New York. Has received by ship *Charles and Harriet* notice of shipment of a cheese, box of citron, and some olives from Cagliari. Will do the needful, and ship by first opportunity. 4°. 1 page.

1810, July 11, New York. Acknowledging letter of June 24, with remittance. Has received the hams and forwarded them to Chancellor Livingston. Incloses receipted bills. 4°. 1 page.

1810, October 5, New York. Has received from London a bill of expenses of a pipe of brandy.
4°. 1 page.

Montpellier.

1817, June 26, New York. Returns a letter addressed to Mr. Gill, he having left Halifax and his destination unknown. 4°. 1 page.

1824, September 4, New York. Respecting grains of wheat found in a package of goods from China. Result of his planting. Incloses a cluster.
4°. 2 pages.

1824, September 23, New York. Acknowledging letter of 11th instant. Incloses the collector's account.
4°. 1 page.

1824, December 22, New York. Respecting a copy of the proceedings of the late convention of this State. [The lower part, with signature cut off.]
2 slips of paper.

GEMME, C. D. *Washington.*

1809, October 28, Saintes, France. Congratulating the President on his election. 4°. 1 page.

GEORGIA. GENERAL ASSEMBLY. *Washington.*

1809, December 12, Milledgeville, Ga. Approving the conduct of the Executive of the United States towards Mr. Jackson, the British minister, and promising support. 4°. 5 pages.

1814, December 2. *See* Early, Peter (Governor).

GERRY, ELBRIDGE. *Washington.*

1804, February 5, Cambridge. Respecting copies of letters of Talleyrand to Gerry. Congratulates Madison on the happy state of our public concerns. Good dispositions of France and Spain in their conduct relative to Louisiana. Opposition of the Massachusetts legislature to the Federal Government. [Signature cut off.] 4°. 3 pages.

1806, February 19, Cambridge. The present state of Europe. Conjectures on the overthrow of Bonaparte by the allied powers. Dangers of a civil conflict. British depredations on our commerce. Suggests an embargo on our commerce and to make preparations for war. 4°. 8 pages.

1806, February 26, Cambridge. Irrational to attempt a competition with the great maritime powers in respect to a navy, but suggests an annual appropriation, to be increased in war, for the establishment of a navy to protect our coasts. 4°. 2 pages.

1806, March 13, Cambridge. Acknowledging letter of 3d. Respecting commercial restrictions or an embargo, the most effectual measure to be adopted. 4°. 1 page.

1807, June 19, Cambridge. Requesting an introduction for Mrs. George Blake to General Armstrong, our minister at Paris. 4°. 1 page.

1807, July 5, Cambridge. Acknowledging letter of June 27. The public curiosity to see a denouement of the treasonable conspiracy in the Mississippi Territory. Public indignation excited by the repeated destruction of our unoffending seamen. A state of war preferable to national insult and degradation. 4°. 1 page.

1809, May 20, Cambridge. Defense of Dr. Waterhouse against the endeavors to remove him from the direction of the Marine Hospital at Charlestown. Approval by all parties of Madison's public conduct. Predicts the downfall of party spirit. 4°. 4 pages.

1810, June 13, Cambridge. Defends George Blake, U. S. district attorney, against charges of his political enemies. 4°. 3 pages.

1810, September 22, Cambridge. The death of Judge Cushing creates a vacancy which he recommends to be filled by George Blake. His high character and qualifications. Proposes his son-in-law, James T. Austin, to fill the vacancy should there be one in the office of district attorney. fol. 3 pages.

1811, November 17, Cambridge. Has read the President's message with pleasure. His measures will unite all parties except British subjects and their partisans. Renews his request that Mr. Austin be appointed district attorney should the place become vacant by promotion of George Blake to the bench. 4°. 2 pages.

1811, December 27, Boston. Recommending Hull or Dearborn for Commander-in-Chief of the Army. "Confidential." 4°. 2 pages.

GERRY, ELBRIDGE.

1811, December 31, Boston. Introducing Richard Devens Harris, of Boston. 4°. 1 page.

1812, February 12, Boston. An endeavor to stop the Yazoo Company in Massachusetts from dividing their lands into small parcels and locating and dividing them. The policy of the Government of Great Britain to divide the U. S. Government and people on the question of war. Wishes the appointment of Mr. Azor Orne for a captaincy. 4°. 3 pages.

1812, February 25, Cambridge. Resolution of the legislature of Massachusetts respecting a supply of blankets and clothing. 4°. 1 page.

1812, April 16, Cambridge. Soliciting the office of collector of the port of Boston, made vacant by the appointment of Gen. Dearborn to a high military command in the Army. "Confidential." 4°. 2 pages.

1812, April 25, Cambridge. Letter from the Secretary of War relative to detaching 10,000 of the militia of Massachusetts. Has issued necessary orders. Appointment of officers. Incloses report of the Adjutant-General on the defects of the militia law. "Confidential." 4°. 3 pages.

1812, May 19, Cambridge. Acknowledging letter of 9th. Success of his measures respecting the appointments of Republican generals. Great anxiety for the final decision about declaration of war. Confidence in their ability to raise money. Plans for raising it. "Private." 4°. 3 pages.

1812, May 20, Cambridge. Madison has the entire confidence of the Republicans in this quarter. Results of the State election. Frauds in the election. "Private." 4°. 2 pages.

1812, June 12, Cambridge. Acknowledging letter of 3d. The House has declared for war. Trusts the Senate will use the same wisdom and fortitude. Inclosing duplicate letter to Jefferson, not having heard of his receiving the original. 4°. 1 page.

1812, July 5, Cambridge. War declared. The castle (*sic*) under command of a Federalist captain. May be carried by a *coup de main*. The governor refuses Gen. Dearborn his application for any part of the detached militia. There should be a law to provide for refractory governors. 4°. 2 pages.

1812, July 13, Cambridge. Col. Porter in command at Fort Independence. Extraordinary conduct of the governor of Massachusetts. Thinks every man in the State should be enrolled and equipped for support of the National Government. Also every recusant made known. The extraordinary proclamation for a fast justifies apprehensions of inimical character. Thinks the friends of the National Government are strong enough in Massachusetts to drive out every malcontent from the state. 4°. 4 pages.

1812, July 22, Cambridge. Interview with Gen. Dearborn, who agrees with him that nothing under present state of affairs could prevent the carrying of the castle by a *coup de main* of the enemy and sacking the town of Boston. Expresses great

GERRY, ELBRIDGE.

uneasiness. William Little a candidate for the office of commissary of prisoners. "Secret."
4°. 2 pages.

1812, August 15, Cambridge. Recommending the appointment of Dr. Waterhouse to any vacant medical office near Boston. His record. James Thomas asks the appointment of a suitable office in the Army. Several other applicants of the same kind, recommended as good men. Coalition of Federalists with the Clinton party. The pensioning, by Great Britain, of writers among us who overwhelm us with misrepresentations and falsehoods. "Confidential." 4°. 7 pages.

1812, August 24, Cambridge. Introducing Benjamin Homans, who wishes Government employment.
4°. 1 page.

1812, November 8, Cambridge. Incomprehensible conduct of Gen. Hull. Is mortified at having recommended him. Suggests, in case of Hull's trial, that James T. Austin be judge-advocate.
4°. 2 pages.

1812, December 12, Cambridge. Is pleased at the prospect of Madison's reelection. Congratulations on the brilliant success of our Navy. Asks if the new Congress will be convened. 4°. 1 page.

1812, December 19, Cambridge. Renews his inquiry if Congress will be convened after the election. His object is to know whether it will be requisite for the Vice-President to travel several hundred miles merely to be inaugurated to office. If an administration of the oath by a Federal judge is admissible. 4°. 2 pages.

1813, July 26, Cambridge. Thanks him for meeting his request. At the time prescribed will take the oath as Vice-President before the district judge and a circle of his friends. 4°. 1 page.

1813, February 9, Cambridge. Introducing John Appleton. 4°. 1 page.

1813, February 15, Cambridge. In introducing John Appleton it was not his object in recommending him as marshal, as Marshal Prince is as well (if not better) qualified to discharge the duties intrusted to him by the Government. George G. M. Micketts wishes the vacant office of consul at Lisbon. Recommends him. 4°. 2 pages.

1813, February 20, Cambridge. Acknowledging receipt of the certificate of William H. Crawford, president of the Senate *pro tem,* that he has been elected Vice-President of the United States. Accepts, with gratitude to the people, the distinguished office. Proposes to take the oath of office before the district judge. 4°. 3 pages.

1813, March 29, Cambridge. Although he has declined recommendations to office, he mentions Richard Cutts favorably. 4°. 2 pages.

1813, August 12, Philadelphia. Introducing Gen. Bloomfield. 4°. 2 pages.

1813, September 10, Cambridge. Announcement of the arrival of a minister from Sweden. Should one be appointed on the part of the United States, he recommends James Trecothick Austen, his son-in-law. His qualifications and merits.
4°. 4 pages.

GERRY, ELBRIDGE.

1813, September 21, Cambridge. Inclosing a letter from Mr. Carleton, also one from Mr. Wood, recommending for office, Samuel Parker. Also a letter from Dr. Bentley on the treatment of our prisoners. Mr. Farley's wish for office.
4°. 1 page.

1813, December 21, Cambridge. Is detained by sickness of Mrs. Gerry and two children. The public anxiously waiting the result of the closed doors of Congress. Recommends Capt. Frederick Conkling as deputy quartermaster-general. Respecting the embargo. 4°. 2 pages.

1814, March 5, Washington. Transmitting Gen. Boyd's and Mr. Eustis's letters respecting promotions over the general. Can give no opinion on the subject.
4°. 1 page.

1814, March 9, Washington. Lieut. Walter Coles wishes to be appointed captain in the new corps to be raised and apportioned among the States. Thinks he would honor the commission.
4°. 1 page.

1814, April 7, Washington. Inclosing a letter from Gen. Boyd on the subject of his rank. 4°. 1 page.

1814, April 18, Washington. Capt. David Townsend lost his leg in the last battle fought by our Army before it went into winter quarters, and the friends of Government think he should be rewarded for his services in the appointment of some position in the office of the staff department. 4°. 2 pages.

1814, June 10, Cambridge. Success of enemies of the administration in sapping its confidence in some of our meritorious officers. Defends charges against Marshal Prince, of Boston, a faithful and efficient officer. "Confidential." 4°. 3 pages.

1814, June 11, Boston. Inclosing a petition in favor of Gen. Boyd. He should be given the opportunity of establishing his military fame, and that he may rise superior to his personal enemies.
4°. 2 pages.

1814, June 25, Cambridge. Asking if the unparalleled events in Europe will require an earlier meeting of Congress or the Senate. Incloses a letter from Gen. Dearborn, recommending Capt. Joseph Lee.
4°. 1 page.

1814, July 17, Cambridge. Acknowledging letter of 5th. Approves of Madison's system of policy respecting a vigorous preparation for war. Incloses letters from the authorities of the town of Marblehead, respecting its defenseless state, and propositions about gunboats and applications for increased force to defend the forts. Also inclosed is application of Capt. Joshua Prentiss, for a command in the Navy. 4°. 4 pages.

1814, July 18, Boston. The death of Mr. Lovell, Naval officer of the port of Boston, makes a vacancy which he recommends be filled by Jonathan Loring Austen. 4°. 2 pages.

GERRY, ELBRIDGE, JR.

1814, December 4, Cambridge. Appeal for assistance owing to the death of his father, whose service to his country impoverished him and family. Asks for office. 4°. 1 page.

GHOLSON, THOMAS.

1809, December 15, Virginia. Withdraws his application for a Territorial appointment. 4°. 1 page.

GIBBON, JAMES.

1808, December 23, Richmond. Denies, emphatically, charges of a number of respectable characters lately sent in a paper to Washington, that he abused the President and the administration. 4°. 3 pages.

——— and others. *Richmond. (?)*

1829, November 19, Richmond. Invitation by a committee to attend a dinner given to James Barbour. 4°. 1 page.

GIBBS, ROWLAND, to BARKER, JACOB. *New York.*

1813, September 20, Fairhaven. Asks his influence in having the appointment of collector of New Bedford be given to John Hawes. 4°. 2 pages.

GIBSON & JEFFERSON to MADISON. *Washington.*

1808, October 5, Richmond. Incloses a bill of lading for coal shipped per the *Sally Ann,* with note of cost. 4°. 1 page.

1808, October 5, James River. Bill of lading of coal per schooner *Sally Ann* for Washington. 8°. 1 page.

GIBSON, PATRICK. *Washington.*

1805, May 14, Richmond. Sale of Madison's tobacco. 4°. 1 page.

1805 May 17, Richmond. Offers a price for his tobacco, but advises him to hold it. 4°. 1 page.

GIBSON, ROBERT B. *Washington.*

1816, July 18, Monroe County, Miss. Ter. Respecting a warrant (of which a copy is annexed) for the arrest of the robbers who stole a negro and some money belonging to himself. fol. 3 pages.

GIBSON, THOMAS. *Montpellier.*

1821, August 6, Fauquier. Asks information to be procured from Madison's mother (if living) respecting an estate said to belong to the Gibson family in England, of which there are heirs in Virginia. fol. 1 page.

GIDEON, JACOB, JR. *Montpellier.*

1818, January 19, Washington. Inclosing a list of several numbers of the "Federalist" about to be published, with a request for Madison to give the names of the authors to their respective numbers. [The list is filed with the letter.] 4°. 8 pages.

1818, February 12, Washington. Acknowledging letter of January 28, with copy of the "Federalist" with names of authors affixed as desired. Approves of certain suggestions made. 4°. 1 page.

1818, August 15, Washington. Presents Madison a copy of his edition of the "Federalist," and thanks Madison for his additions and revisions. fol. 1 page.

GILES, I. *Washington.*

1812 September 5, Newburyport. Approves of the administration. Incloses him some sermons proving he has friends even in this sink of Toryism. 4°. 1 page.

GILES, W. B. *Washington.*

1803, January 6, Amelia. Inclosing a letter from Col. Worthington, of Ohio, respecting the appointment of a district judge. Congratulates Madison and the President on the prosperous state of public affairs. Even the few Federals he sees are at a loss to criticise the message.
4°. 3 pages.

1805, no date, Washington. Inclosing copy of the clearance bill as about to be passed. fol. 1 page.

1811, November 25, Washington. Proposes accompanying Mr. Thomas Shore, of Petersburg, to call on Madison to make some representations respecting the collector of Petersburg, the office having become vacant by death of Shore's father.
4°. 2 pages.

Montpellier.

1827, September 4, Richmond. On advice of the council he requests him for the loan of two public journals of the general assembly to carry into effect the reprinting of those journals from 1776 to 1790. Incloses an order from the clerk of the council. 4°. 2 pages.

1827, December 7, Richmond. The general assembly desires the loan of several missing senate journals if he has them in his possession, for the purpose of publication.

——— to MADISON and MRS. MADISON, jointly.
Montpellier.

1829, August 10, Richmond. Inviting them to make the governor's house their residence while visiting Richmond during the meeting of the convention.
5°. 1 page.

GILL, VALENTINE, to MADISON, *Montpellier.*

1817, April 4, Halifax, N. S. Applies for occupation as a civil engineer. 4°. 2 pages.

GILMAN, NATHANIEL C. *Washington.*

1809, July 4, Marietta. Asks the loan of $200, and incloses his note for that amount. 4°. 2 pages.

GILMER, FRANCIS W. *Montpellier.*

1820, December 10, Richmond. Inclosing a letter from Mr. Correa to himself in which he wishes to express his sentiments of esteem and farewell, as he is about to leave the country. Also incloses copy of a treatise of his own. 4°. 1 page.

1824, April 9, Richmond. Asks for letters of introduction to our minister, Mr. Rush, and to Sir James Mackintosh, for a purpose exclusively literary.
4°. 1 page.

——— to LONG, GEORGE. *London, Eng.*

1824, September 28, London. A covenant entered in London between Francis W. Gilmer, attorney in fact for the University of Virginia, and George Long, appointing the latter a professor.
[Copy.] 4°. 1 page.

——— to BONNYCASTLE, CHARLES. *London, Eng.*

1824, October 1, London. Extract from a contract between Gilmer and Bonnycastle; the latter being appointed professor at the University of Virginia. [Copy.] 4°. 1 page.

GILMER, PEACHY R., to MADISON. *Montpellier.*

1828, April 18, Liberty. Sends a copy of the power of attorney from the University of Virginia to his late brother, Francis W. Gilmer. 4°. 1 page.

GILMER, THOMAS W., and BRAMHAM, THOMAS W., jointly, *Montpellier.*

1824, November 1, Charlottesville. An invitation of the standing committee of Albemarle County to attend the public dinner to be given Lafayette at the University of Virginia. 4°. 1 page.

GILMER, THOMAS W. *Montpellier.*

1830, August 31, Charlottesville. Plan of the University of Virginia for educating at the charge of the State a few select young men from the primary schools, and promoting them to the University. 4°. 3 pages.

——— to MADISON, WILLIAM.

1832, April 18, Charlottesville. Acknowledging letter of 13th. Annexes a transcript from the journal of the Loyal Company, relative to an assignment from Samuel Dalton to James Madison. Copies an entry made in July, 1753. 4°. 1 page.

——— and others to MADISON. *Montpellier.*

1834, June 9, Charlottesville. Invitation by the committee of the citizens of Albemarle to a public dinner on July 4. 4°. 2 pages.

GILPIN, H. D. *Montpellier.*

1827, October 9, Philadelphia. Inclosing a copy of a sketch of Jefferson's life. Should he discover any errors wishes him to correct them. 4°. 2 pages.

1828, January 4, Philadelphia. Thanks him for his letter relative to his sketch of Jefferson's life and particularly for a pamphlet sent him. Asks Madison's permission to dedicate the work to him. 4°. 2 pages.

GILPIN, JOSHUA. *Washington.*

1809, August 28, Philadelphia. Sends copies of papers published by the Chesapeake and Delaware Canal Company. 4°. 1 page.

Montpellier.

1822, February 8, Kentmore. Sends him copy of a new publication on the old subject of the Chesapeake and Delaware Canal. Thanks him for his favorable sentiments expressed towards him when he applied for the consulate in London in 1811. 4°. 3 pages.

1827, August 30, Kentmore. Introducing his son, who is about making Southern tour. 4°. 1 page.

GIMBREDE, THOMAS. *Washington.*

1812, March 3, New York. Sends him a print of the four presidents engraved by himself. 4°. 1 page.

GIRARD, STEPHEN. *Washington.*

1802, March 11, Philadelphia. Inclosing a memorial to recover a claim against France. Asks a letter of introduction to the U. S. minister, at Paris, for Joseph Curwen, his agent, in order to press his claim. 4°. 2 pages.

GIST, NATHANIEL. *New York.*

1790, January 27, Buckingham. A claim of which the President has full information. The money advanced him for expenses was returned to the Continental Treasury. fol. 1 page.

GLASS, FRANCISCUS. *Montpellier.*

1821, March 3, Lebanon, Ohio. Has written a life of Washington in Latin and asks Madison's per-

GLASS, FRANCISCUS.

mission to dedicate it to him. It is intended for the use of schools. [Written in Latin.] fol. 2 pages.

GLASSELL, ANDREW. *Washington.*

1810, August 14, Forthorwald. Recommends Edward Sims as a steward or overseer. 4°. 1 page.

1815, August 28, Forthorwald. Congratulates Madison on the close of the war. Recommends John Johnson, of Baltimore, as consul for St. Domingo. 4°. 1 page.

GLASSELL, WILLIAM. *Orange.*

1797, September 21, Fredericksburg. Asks Madison's good offices in procuring for Francis Taylor the office of collector of the port of Norfolk. 4°. 3 pages.

GLEN, HENRY. *Washington.*

1813, June 6, Schenectady. Wishes to be reappointed assistant deputy quartermaster. 4°. 2 pages.

GODEFROY, MAXIMILIEN. *Washington.*

1806, March 2, Baltimore. Introduces Monsieur de Mun. [In French.] 4°. 2 pages.

GOLDSBOROUGH, CHARLES W. *Washington.*

1809, May 8, Washington. Has appointed the son of Mr. G. Anderson to the Norfolk station. 4°. 1 page.

Montpellier.

1809, September 30, Washington. Transmitting paper from the Navy Department from a person of Columbian ambition; is persuaded he is not inferior to either of the great navigators he has mentioned. No fatigues can dishearten or dangers appall him in the execution of any duty assigned him by his Government! 4°. 1 page.

——— ——— (for PAUL HAMILTON).

1809, November 7, Washington. The Secretary of the Navy unexpectedly detained in South Carolina by illness in his family. Submits for the President's consideration matters connected with appropriations and deficiencies in several divisions of the Navy Department. 4°. 3 pages.

Washington.

1809, November 9, Washington. The Navy estimates for 1810 will be prepared before the meeting of Congress. Gives details of some urgent demands for vessels in commission, and suggests that the public service will be promoted by a transfer of funds from appropriation where they are not needed to the bureau of repairs of vessels. 4°. 3 pages, and strip of paper.

1809, November 9, Washington. Inclosing a requisition to prepare Navy estimates for 1810. To enable the Department to comply with them it is essential to know whether any addition or reduction of the number of vessels now in commission is to be made. Asks instructions. 4°. 2 pages.

Washington.

1811, November 8, Washington. Notifying Madison of the receipt of his and Mrs. Washington's wine imported in the *Dumfries*. Amount of duties and freight. 4°. 1 page.

——— to COLES, MR. *Washington.*

1811, December 21, Washington. Inclosing papers in respect to an importation of wine for the President. fol. 1 page.

——— to MADISON. *Washington.*

1813, January 7, Washington. Desiring the President to revoke an order on the Navy Department. 4°. 1 page.

1813, January 7, Washington. A list of vessels purchased and built since last session of Congress, with their cost. 4°. 1 page.

1813, January 21, Washington. The inferior quality of the powder from Dr. Ewells' mills put on board the *Constellation*. Suggests an investigation be made immediately. fol. 2 pages.

1813, January 22, Washington. Has received samples which confirm the correctness of the opinion of Mr. Catalano as to the inferior quality of the powder furnished the *Constellation* from Dr. Ewells' mills. fols. 1 page.

1814, June 18, Georgetown. Complaining of the injustice of the Navy Department towards him in dismissing him from his place on the false accusation of his enemies. Reviews his acknowledged satisfactory services from the organization of the Government and appeals to the President in submitting the case, to obtain justice. 4°. 3 pages.

1815, March 8, Georgetown. Acknowledgment of Thomas Ewell of the incorrectness of his publications about Mr. Goldsborough. Trusts this and the explanation of other injurious allegations will relieve Madison's mind unfavorable to himself. fol. 2 pages.

GOOCH, GIDEON. *Washington.*

1805, July 28. Remittances made and to be made to Madison. 4°. 1 page.

1809, October 8. Order on him to pay a sum of money to Richard Purdy. 8°. 1 page.

GOODLET, ADAM. *Washington.*

1805, December 8, Cane Run, Scott County, Ky. Asking Madison's influence in procuring for him the office of register of the land office for Indiana Territory. 4°. 1 page.

GORDON, DUFF & CO. *Washington.*

1803, December 31, Madeira. With circular from Hill, Bissets & Co., announcing Gordon, Duff & Co., as their successors and solicits the patronage of Madison. 4°. 2 pages.

GORDON, JAMES, JR. *New York.*

1788, February 17, Orange. Madison's friends are solicitous for his appointment to the convention to meet in Richmond in June, and that his presence in Orange is very desirable to secure his election. fol. 1 page.

Richmond.

1788, August 31, Germanna. Acknowledging letters of July 25 and 27. His views respecting the adoption of the constitution by different States. Conjectures respecting Virginia and New York, bearing on direct taxation. 4°. 3 pages.

GORDON, WILLIAM. *Washington.*

1814, January 7, Charleston. The expeditions of the U. S. Navy and the grand object which the pub-

GORDON, WILLIAM.

lic measures are calculated to accomplish, are well known to the writer, who, if he can be appointed to some civil employment near Washington, will communicate to the Cabinet a supplemental plan calculated to give the grand design a finished polish and gothic solidity.
fol. 2 pages.

GOUVERNEUR, SAMUEL L. *Montpellier.*

1833, January 2, New York. Transmitting certain papers given in his charge. 4°. 1 page.

1833, January 26, New York. Papers of Monroe's left with Madison and returned unopened after the former's return from his mission, relative to the investigation of the conduct of Gen. Hamilton. Asks him to communicate any facts bearing on the matter in order to do justice to the memory of Monroe. 4°. 1 page.

GRAHAM, GEORGE (Chief Clerk). *Washington.*

1814, August 1, Washington. Respecting the resignation of Mr. Garrard, of the Marine Corps, and other current business of the War Department. 4°. 3 pages.

Montpellier.

1815, March 30, Washington. Inclosing letters from Generals Winchester and Miller. The number of commissions to be signed. Will forward daily by mail a few of them to expedite business of the War Department. 4°. 1 page.

1815, April 20, Washington. Inclosing a blank brevet commission for Gen. Ripley, to be signed and returned. 4°. 1 page.

——— to WARD, WILLIAM. *Philadelphia.*

1815, May 9, Washington. Returns his bill not accepted, as the appropriation for subsistence is overdrawn. [Copy.] 4°. 1 page.

——— to HAWKINS, BENJ. (Creek agent).

1815, July 12, Washington. Sending a request of the President to report to the War Department his opinions on certain points indicated. Goods to be distributed among the Creek Indians and Cherokees. [Copy of extract.]
4°. 3 pages.

——— to MADISON. *Montpellier.*

1815, August 16, Washington. Amount appropriated for the local distribution of the pay of the Army and Navy. 4°. 1 page.

1815, August 22, Washington. Mr. Dallas will communicate his views respecting the pay of the Army. Mr. Crawford leaves to-morrow for Montpellier.
4°. 1 page.

1815, August 26, Washington. Forwarding extract of a letter from Mr. Dallas in which it states that an American commercial treaty is signed by Parliament. Gallatin and Clay on their way hither.
4°. 1 page.

1815, August 30, Washington. Current business of the War Department. 4°. 2 pages.

——— to PARKER, DANIEL (Adjutant-General).

1815, September 6, Washington. Inclosing copy of an opinion given by the Attorney-General respecting brevet commissions. 4°. 1 page.

GRAHAM, GEORGE, to MADISON. *Montpellier.*

1815, September 6, Washington. Fllling of vacancies in the medical staff. 4°. 1 page.

1815, September 12, Washington. Current business of the War Department. 4°. 2 pages.

——— to PARKER, DANIEL.

1815, September 12, Washington. Appointment of officers to the vacancies in the medical staff. 4°. 1 page.

——— to MADISON. *Montpellier.*

1815, September 12, Washington. Appointments to fill vacancies in the medical staff. 4°. 2 pages.

——— to BLOUNT, WILLIE (Governor of Tennessee).

1815, September 14, Washington. Authority given to agents residing with the Choctaws and Chickasaws to obtain the consent of the chiefs to the opening of a road from Reynoldsberg to Natchez. [Copy.] 4°. 2 pages.

——— to MADISON. *Montpellier.*

1815, September 14, Washington. Applications, appointments, and current business of the War Department. 4°. 3 pages.

1815, September 18, Washington. Acknowledging letter of 15th. Appointment of Dr. Elbyey as garrison surgeon's mate. Continuance of William Baylor on the peace establishment. C. A. Baylor left out. Several of the Kentucky delegation anxious for his reinstatement. 4°. 2 pages.

1815, September 20, Washington. Acknowledging letter of 17th. Business of the War Deparment relating to the filling of vacancies. 4°. 2 pages.

1815, September 20, Washington. Allowance of double rations to officers commanding posts. 4°. 2 pages.

1815, September 26, Washington. Forwarding a treaty at Spring Wells by the commissioners and chiefs of all the tribes of Indians with which they were authorized to treat. 4°. 1 page.

Washington.

1815, October 2, Washington. Current business of the War Department. 4°. 2 pages.

1816, July 16, Washington. Transmiting papers relating to Capt. Hamilton, discharged from the British service for refusing to do duty when the British forces landed in Louisiana, he being a native American. 4°. 1 page.

Montpellier.

1816, November 14, Washington. Appropriation of Congress for defences of the United States. Suggests changes in relation to the corps of engineers and the assignment of officers to particular districts. 4°. 2 pages.

1818, September 15, Washington. Acknowledging letter of 10th, respecting the recommendations of Mr. French for a commission in the Army. 4°. 1 page.

1823, November 5, Washington. Acknowledging letter inclosing money, dated October 30. Returns a receipt from Mr. Smith, who has applied a portion as directed and asks instructions as to the balance. 4°. 2 pages.

GRAHAM, GEORGE.

1824, April 7, Washington. Acknowledging letter of March 27. The board of directors of the branch bank has assented to Madison's proposition. 4°. 1 page.

1824, April 24, Washington. Acknowledging letter of 20th, and one inclosed for Mr. Smith. 4°. 1 page.

1827, March 31, Washington. Inclosing evidences of vindication from charges against his official conduct. 4°. 2 pages.

GRAHAM, JOHN. *Washington.*

1802, September 9, Madrid. Negotiations respecting the cession and evacuation of Louisiana between the French ambassador and Spain. Our claims for French spoliations. The rights and interests of the United States in the Mississippi River. Thinks Spain wishes to make some commercial arrangement with us. fol. 4 pages.

1803, May 7, Aranjuès, Spain. Unfriendly acts of Spain towards us and the small hope of gaining any redress for injuries done to our commerce by foreign nations under Spanish authority. Their desire to weaken our rights to the navigation of the Mississippi. Thinks the present is the opportunity to maintain our rights, as Spain has no means of resisting us. Is anxious to leave Spain, and should our Army be called into service, would be happy to join it in any capacity, where he could be useful. 4°. 10 pages.

1806, Februarg 13, New Orleans. Sends manuscript copy in Spanish of a work called the Geographical and Political Tables of Baron Humboldt, dated in Mexico, 1805. 4°. 1 page.

1807, August 10, Richmond. The names of those elected to serve on the jury to try Aaron Burr. Only four have not been objected to, the others having declared their belief that Burr's intentions were treasonable. 4°. 1 page.

Orange.

1807, August 14, Richmond. Acknowledging letter of 8th. Difficulty in procuring jurymen for the trial of Burr. 4°. 3 pages.

1807, August 30, Richmond. Judge Marshall's opinion on certain points on Burr's motion. 4°. 1 page.

——— (Chief Clerk, Department of State).

1808, May 10, Washington. Transmiting despatches from London and Paris, also newspapers. Memorandum inclosed on Department business. 4°. 3 pages.

1808, May 12. General business of the Department detailed. 4°. 3 pages.

——— to TURREAU, General (French Minister).

1808, May 13, Washington. Acknowledging letters to the Secretary of State of 5th, 6th, and 10th, which have been forwarded. Permissions will be granted on specific applications, except for persons in the service of the Emperor, which cases must receive the sanction of the President. 4°. 1 page.

——— to MADISON. *Orange.*

1808, May 16, Washington. Current business of the State Department concerning passports. 4°. 3 pages.

GRAHAM, JOHN.

1808, May 17, Washington. News of the abdication of Charles IV, of Spain, in favor of his son Ferdinand. The Prince of Peace experiences a reverse of fortune. 4°. 1 page.

1808, May 20, Washington. Acknowledging letter of 15th. Passport for the *Leonidas* received. Letter in cipher inclosed from Gen. Armstrong. The mission of Mr. Hill. He is elevated to the rank of envoy to make a treaty. 4°. 2 pages.

1808, May 24, Washington. Acknowledging letters of 16th and 20th. No vessel yet found to convey Mr. Hill on his mission. The *Leonidas* will sail soon. 4°. 2 pages.

1808, May 27, Washington. Acknowledging letter of 21st with inclosures. Sailing of the *Leonidas.* Passport for the vessel which will take out Mr. Hill to the Brazils. 4°. 4 pages.

1808, May 31, Washington. Acknowledging letter of 27th. Has given Mr. Hill the instructions sent. Passport for the vessel which takes Mr. Hill. 4°. 3 pages.

1808, June 3, Washington. Acknowledging letter of May 30. Has received passport from the French minister for Mr. Hill on the *Hamlet.* Mr. Rademaker to take passage in her. 4°. 2 pages.

1808, July 29, Washington. Transmitting letters from Gen. Turreau. Permission granted by Mr. Gallatin for the purchase of vessels, probably to be fitted out as privateers. fol. 2 pages.

1808, August 1, Washington. Dispatches from Admiral Cochrane, from which it appears that the Spanish will resist the French who are advancing to Cordova. "Juntos" in the name of Ferdinand VII. English have landed in Spain and will assist the Spanish people. 4°. 3 pages.

1808, August 11, Washington. Advice of a draft on Madison. Canvassing of the Federals for next Presidential election. The British consul asks permission to charter a vessel. 4°. 3 pages.

1808, no date, Washington. Current business of the Department of State. Prospect of the election in Maryland not favorable to us. 4°. 3 pages.

1808, August 5, Washington. Acknowledging letter of 2d. Current business of the Department. 4°. 2 pages.

1808, August 15, Washington. Acknowledging letter of 12th. Current business of the Department. 4°. 2 pages.

1808, August 19, Washington. Acknowledging letter of 16th, containing an accepted bill which will be paid when due at the Treasury. Mr. Gallatin receives his passports transmitted by Mr. Feronda. 4°. 2 pages.

1808, August 23, Washington. Acknowledging letter of the 19th. Has transmitted to Mr. Gallatin extract from Madison's letter to Gen. Turreau, who will give necessary orders concerning his vessels. Interesting intelligence from Spain. The King of Portugal raises the blockade of certain ports in Spain. 4°. 3 pages.

GRAHAM, JOHN.

1808, September 2, Washington. Acknowledging letter of August 30th. Incloses bill for Madison's signature. Remarks of Mr. Smith on the speech of Mr. Canning in the National Intelligencer. 4°. 2 pages.

1808, September 6, Washington. Inclosing letters for Madison's signature. General business of the Department. 4°. 2 pages.

1808, September 9, Washington. Acknowledging letter of 6th. No difficulty in getting a bearer of dispatches to England. Printers employed for the laws of Connecticut. 4°. 3 pages.

1808, September 13, Washington. Acknowledging letter of 6th. No cases to be particularly recommended to Gen. Armstrong. Case of the *Little William.* Capture of the *Commerce* by the Russians. Cipher for Mr. Short. Mr. Gibbon bearer of dispatches for Mr. Pinckney. 4°. 3 pages.

1808, September 16, Washington. Instructions to Mr. Short touching his drafts. Mr. Gibbon (bearer of dispatches) will go to Philadelphia and wait further orders. 4°. 2 pages.

1808, September 19, Washington. Acknowledging letter of 16th. Matters connected with Mr. Short's mission. Accident in the Senate chamber. 4°. 3 pages.

1808, September 20, Washington. Has forwarded instructions for the departure of dispatch vessel. 4°. 1 page.

——— to MASTER OF THE SHIP *Union.*

1808, September 20, Washington. Instructions in relation to the sailing of the ship bearing Mr. Short and Mr. Gibbon, bearer of dispatches. [Copy.] 4°. 2 pages.

——— to STEELE, Gen. (Collector of Philadelphia).

1808, September 20, Washington. Instructions relative to the sailing of the vessel conveying Mr. Short and Lieut. Gibbon, in charge of dispatches. [Copy.] 4°. 1 page.

——— to SHORT, WM. *Philadelphia.*

1808, September 23, Washington. Acknowledging letter of 20th. Instructions given to the captain of the vessel in which Mr. Short is to sail, subject to the discretion of Mr. Short. [Press copy.] 4°. 3 pages.

——— to MADISON. *Orange.*

1808, September 23, Washington. Instructions to Mr. Short and inclosing copy of letter to him. With bills of exchange for signature. 4°. 3 pages.

Washington.

1809, August 3, Willtown, S. C. Invention for destroying bridges over which the enemy is passing, safe for the operator who may be at a long distance from the spot. 4°. 3 pages.

Montpellier.

1809, August 23, Washington. Inclosing letters from Governor Claiborne to the Secretary of State. 4°. 1 page.

1809, September 1, Washington. Acknowledging letter of August 29. The gentlemen nominated

GRAHAM, JOHN.

for the legislative council of the Mississippi Territory. Their antecedents. Letter from Mr. Erwing has not been in possession of the Secretary of State. Pencil marks show that it has been in the hands of a printer. Letter to Napoleon. 4°. 3 pages.

1809, September 4, Washington. Incloses a letter from Mr. Daschkoff. Arrival of Mr. Jackson, Mr. Erskine, and Mr. Smith. 4°. 1 page.

1809, September 6, Washington. Acknowledging letter of 2d. Will send copy of the laws of the last session. 4°. 2 pages.

1809, September 11, Washington. A letter from Gen. Turreau missing, relating to a vessel building at Baltimore for the revolted blacks at St. Domingo. Thinks it was forwarded under cover to Madison. 4°. 1 page.

——— to RODNEY, ——.

1810, June 10, Washington. A work entitled, "Memoire of Moreau de Lislet," on the subject of the Batture, desired for Mr. Jefferson. It is not in the Department and think it may be with Mr. Rodney. [Press copy.] 4°. 1 page.

——— to LOWRY, ROBERT. *Baltimore.*

1810, July 12, Washington. Acknowledging letter of 10th. Papers which Lowry will require will be sent before the 20th. Instructions. [Copy.] fol. 1 page.

——— to MADISON. *Montpellier.*

1810, July 27, Washington. Inclosing papers from the Secretary of State. Has written for a book for Mr. Jefferson called "Memoire de Moreau de Lislet." Has been unable to procure it here. 4°. 1 page.

1810, August 3, Washington. Acknowledging letter of July 26, inclosing copy of communication from Governor Holmes and Mr. Robertson, concerning state of affairs in West Florida. 4°. 6 pages.

1810, August 6, Washington. Forwards English newspapers. Private letters do not mention any favorable change in our affairs in England. 4°. 1 page.

1810, August 8, Washington. Incloses copy of dispatches from Mr. Pinkney. Orders to Admiral Saumarer to not molest American vessels coming from certain forts and suffer them to leave Swedish ports with their cargoes. Partial relaxation of the blockade on the coast of Spain. Notice of the blockade of Elsineur. 4°. 2 pages.

——— to HOLMES, GOVERNOR.

1810, August 13, Washington. Inclosing a copy of a letter to the Secretary of War from the commandant of Fort Stoddart. The governor to maintain the laws of his Territory (Mississippi). [Press copy]. 4°. 1 page.

——— to MADISON. *Montpellier.*

1810, August 13, Washington. Acknowledging letter of 10th. Intention of Mr. Erving to go to Montpellier. Copy of Col. Spark's letter sent to Governor Holmes concerning the West Florida Territory. 4°. 2 pages.

GRAHAM, JOHN.

1810, August 15, Washington. Apologizing for a mistake at the post-office in not waiting for Madison's mail. A misunderstanding of orders. 4°. 2 pages.

1810, August 20, Washington. Acknowledging letter of 16th. Unsuccessful in his search for a paper desired by Madison, there being no Parisian file here. Mr. Skipwith's papers. 4°. 2 pages.

1810, August 22, Washington. Unable to find a missing paper. Statement that Messrs. Chew, Clarke, and Skipwith, in company, had purchased from Morales all the country in West Florida worth having between the Mississippi and Pearl River. Dispatches received from Mr. Pinkney. Thinks the British Government will soon send us a man of rank as envoy. 4°. 2 pages.

1810, August 24, Washington. Inclosing copies of letters from Governor Holmes and Mr. Robinson relative to affairs of West Florida. "Official Register" received from Mr. Skipwith, commencing 1797 and ending in 1808. 4°. 1 page.

1810, August 27, Washington. Acknowledging letter of 24th. Will attend to its instructions. Incloses copy of a letter from Mr. Shaler. 4°. 1 page.

1810, August 29, Washington. Acknowledging letter of 24th. Mr. Poinsett's papers sent to Baltimore for the Secretary of State's signature. Revolution in Buenos Ayres reported. Forwards Mr. Pinkney's dispatches. Returns Judge Toulmin's letter. Governor Holmes is apprised of the contemplated expedition against Mobile. 4°. 3 pages.

1810, September 3, Washington. Acknowledging letter of August 30. Our records do not show that any delegated power has been given by the President under the law of 1794. His orders have gone through the War Department and no particular form has been used there for calling out the militia. Incloses press copy of a letter to Governor Holmes. 4°. 2 pages.

1810, September 5, Washington. Has searched through the registers sent by Mr. Skipwith and has failed to find a paper Madison wants. Describes the character of the papers in the register. Sudden deaths of Col. Whiting and Maj. Rogers. 4°. 2 pages.

1810, September 10, Washington. Remitting the proceeds of Madison's check. Eastern end of the city sickly, but the west end and Georgetown not at all so. Newspaper articles about Mr. Pinkney's speeches. The story of the diamonds contradicted. 4°. 2 pages.

1810, September 21, Washington. Transmitting copies of letters received. Cautions the President about returning to Washington before a frost. 4°. 2 pages.

1810, September 21, Washington. Financial matters. American produce abundant at Liverpool. Since July 14 no impressments had taken place in Liverpool. 8°. 1 page.

1810, September 26, Washington. Inclosing a letter from Gen. Armstrong. 8°. 1 page.

1811, July 31, Washington. Inclosing papers from the Department of State. Arrest of the captain of

GRAHAM, JOHN.

the French privateer, the *Diligent*. Inclosures from Mr. Adams. 4°. 1 page.

1811, August 14, Washington. Acknowledging letter of 10th. Inclosing Mr. Adams's letter deciphered. Weather in Washington. 4°. 2 pages.

1811, August 16, Washington. Unable to find any one to translate the Portuguese letter sent to Madison. It appears to be a project for the President to enter into an alliance with England against France and to propose to all nations to make common cause against her. 4°. 3 pages.

1811, September 13, Washington. Has been ill. The city unusually sickly. Mr. Adams declines the appointment of judge and intends to remain a little longer in Russia. 4°. 3 pages.

1811, September 18, Washington. Acknowledging letter of 16th. Has been enabled to get Virginia notes for the amount of check sent. 4°. 2 pages.

1811, September 20, Washington. Acknowledging letter of 16th, covering a check which he has had cashed and sends proceeds as requested. The city continues sickly. Incloses memorandum of cash sent. 4°. 2 pages. 2 strips of paper.

1813, September 22, Washington. Inclosing a paper giving an account of the victory on Lake Erie. Congratulates him. 4°. 2 pages.

1813, September 29, Washington. Inclosing letters from Mr. Adams and Mr. Beasley, also English newspapers. The city very healthy. 4°. 2 pages.

1813, October 9, Washington. Inclosing interesting letters to be returned to the Secretary of State. Official report of our having possession of Malden. Republican victories in Maryland. 4°. 1 page.

1814, May 20, Washington. State of affairs in France. Napoleon's downfall. Pretensions of Great Britain on us. Termination of the Russian mediation. Character of the Emperor. Biased by our enemy, his ally. fol. 2 pages.

1815, April 18, Washington. Inclosing letters including one from Mr. Pinkney. 4°. 1 page.

1815 (?), no date, Washington. Mr. Barker (British minister) left the inclosed memorandum. Doubtful if the British vessels now in our ports will consider themselves as under any obligation to refrain from capturing our vessels after they get to sea. 4°. 1 page.

1816, June 25, Washington. Letters from Governor Cass stating that British naval officers at Malden board American vessels passing that place. Does not think they intend violating our rights. 4°. 3 pages.

1816, July 13, Washington. Inclosing a letter from Mr. Bagot. Sends papers, in Spanish, throwing light on the policy of Great Britain in relation to the dispute between Spain and her colonies. Mr. Hughes's opinion that the patriots must submit. 4°. 2 pages.

1816, July 15, Washington. In the absence of Mr. Monroe, sends letters from Mr. Wirt and Mr. Mitchell relating to important matters. 4°. 1 page.

Graham, John.

1816, July 29, Washington. Mr. Monroe's conversations with Mr. Bagot on the fisheries and naval armaments on the lakes. Mr. Bagot's reply will be forwarded. The letter from the Dey of Algiers not yet been translated. Thinks it can be done in Baltimore. 4°. 3 pages.

1816, August 3, Washington. Transmitting a letter from Mr. Monroe. Difficulty in procuring a translation of the letter from the Dey of Algiers. 4°. 3 pages.

1816, August 3, Washington. Inclosing letters from Adams, Shaler, and Montgomery. These are of importance as respects our affairs with Algiers. 4°. 1 page.

1816, August 6, Washington. Inclosing letters. Expects to receive the translation of the letter from the Dey of Algiers in a day or two. 4°. 1 page.

1816, August 8, Washington. Inclosing papers from Mr. Thomson, diplomatic agent from the Government of Buenos Ayres. Is charged with the delivery of a pair of pistols and other articles as specimens of art among his countrymen. 4°. 2 pages.

1816, August 9, Washington. Acknowledging letter of 7th. Mr. Bagot's letter to Monroe relative to the proposed arrangement on the Lakes. Not the intention of the Swedish Government to join in the combination of the European powers against Barbary. 4°. 3 pages.

1816, August 10, Washington. Unexpected delay in getting the translation of the Dey of Algiers' letter. No Arabic dictionary in Baltimore. Hope to have it accomplished shortly. 4°. 2 pages.

1816, August 26, Washington. Sends by postrider papers, including Mr. Daschkoff's official letter. Wishes for the copies sent Madison of communication from Crowninshield, and Judge Story relating to fisheries. 4°. 2 pages.

1816, August 28, Washington. Inclosing copies of official letters. 4°. 1 page.

1816, August 29, Washington. Inclosing copy of Monroe's official letter to Mr. Harris, chargé d'affairs in Russia, respecting the Kostoff affair. 4°. 1 page.

1816, September 9, Washington. Asks Madison to send Monroe copies of the papers respecting the Kostoff affair. 4°. 2 pages.

1816, September 20, Washington. Recommendation for the secretaryship of Illinois Territory. Inclosing papers respecting the Kostoff affair. 4°. 2 pages.

1816, September 28, Washington. Complies with a request on the cover of a letter which he did not discover before. 4°. 1 page.

Graham, John A. *Montpellier.*

1828, July 25, Washington. Presents a small volume entitled "Graham's Junius." 3°. 1 page.

Granger, Gideon. *Washington.*

1809, March 14, Ohio. Inclosing resolutions of the citizens of Muskingum, in Ohio, which have been sent to the Intelligencer for publication. 4°. 1 page.

GRANGER, GIDEON.

1809, March 28, Washington. The post route mentioned by Paul Verdier is discontinued. [*See* Verdier, Paul, March 25, 1809]. 4°. 1 page.

——— to IRWIN, NATHANIEL. *Newville, Pa.*

1811, March 23, Washington. Acknowledging letter of 14th, transmitted by the President. Respecting irregularities of the mails. [Copy]. 4°. 2 pages.

———, to MADISON. *Montpellier.*

1811, June 5, Washington. Mail arrangements for Barboursville. 4°. 1 page.

Washington.

1813, January 13, Washington. Inclosing the answer of Mr. Burrall, postmaster at Baltimore, to the interrogatories put to him by the House of Representatives of Maryland, respecting an attempted riot and assault on the post-office in August 1812. 4°. 1 page. Large fol. 7 pages.

GRANGER, R. *Washington.*

1813, November 17, Princeton. Explains the absence of his father from his office, which is owing to his having been extremely ill. 4°. 1 page.

GRAY & BOWEN. *Montpellier.*

1832, March 17, Boston. By request of Jared Sparks, has transmitted by mail a set of the "Life of Gouverneur Morris." 4°. 1 page.

GRAY, MICHAEL DE.

See DE GRAY, MICHAEL.

GRAY, PETER. *Montpellier.*

1834, November 10, Fredericksburg. Sends bill for subscription for the "North American Review" for 1834. 4°. 1 page.

GRAY, STEPHEN W. *Washington.*

1813, April 29, Washington. Solicits Government employment. 4°. 3 pages.

GRAY, VINCENT. *Washington.*

1803 (?), no date, Havana. Acknowledging letters of August 26, and April 6, and 9. Will procure such papers as may be attainable in the Foster claims. Has received official accounts of the war between England and France and captures of French and American vessels having French cargoes. Arrival of citizens of St. Domingo. Will supply all American vessels leaving with documents to secure them from capture and detention. 4°. 3 pages.

1804, April 28, Havana. Introducing Baron Humboldt, traveling for the purpose of advancing the progress of natural history, and on his return from South America and the United States. 4°. 1 page.

——— to SMITH, SAMUEL. *Baltimore.*

1810, July 31, Havana. Execution of a young man, a Mexican, as an emissary of Napoleon's at Havana. Seizure of his private papers, which may cause great injury to those concerned with him. [Copy.] 4°. 1 page.

GRAY, WILLIAM, to MADISON. *Washington.*

1813, July 6, Boston. Introducing Dr. Benjamin Waterhouse and recommends him as capable to fill office under the Government. 4°. 2 pages.

GRAY, WILLIAM.

1814, January 21, Boston. Introducing Moses Carleton, of Wiscasset. 4°. 1 page.

——— and others. *Washington.*

1814 (?), no date, Boston. Protest of citizens of Massachusetts against the order issued by the Secretary of War to Brigadier-General Boyd. Injustice of the order to repair to the extreme part of the United States after his gallant services on all occasions, and to report himself to an officer just elevated over his head. Thinks the President should countermand the order. 4°. 4 pages.

——— to EUSTIS, WILLIAM.

1815, January 10, Boston. Mr. Alex. H. Everett would think himself honored with the secretaryship of the embassy to the Netherlands. 4°. 1 page.

——— to MADISON. *Washington.*

1815, August 30, Boston. Suggesting the appointment of Hon. John Holmes, of Alford, in Maine, as commissioner in ascertaining the boundary line on the eastern part of the United States. 4°. 1 page.

GRAY, W. F. *Montpellier.*

1818, September 7, Fredericksburg. Mentions several scientific works which he will procure and send to him. 4°. 2 pages.

1821, June 6, Fredericksburg. Inclosing his account. 4°. 1 page.

1821, April 30. Bill for books and stationery. 4°. 1 page.

1823, March 20, Fredericksburg. Acknowledging letter of 17th. Has discontinued the "London Quarterly Review" and sends the "North American Review" for January, 1822. 4°. 1 page.

1823, May 17, Fredericksburg. Sends January number of the "North American Review." 4°. 1 page.

1823, May 28, Fredericksburg. Acknowledging letter of 24th, respecting certain numbers of the "North American Review" and other periodicals. 4°. 2 pages.

1823, October 21, Fredericksburg. Has procured a draft on New York, which he incloses with his account. Offers future services. 4°. 3 pages.

1823, October 27, Fredericksburg. Acknowledging letter of 24th, with check inclosed and placed to Madison's credit. 4°. 1 page.

1824, May 4, Fredericksburg. Asks if he has been furnished with the "North American Review" for last October; if not, will furnish it. 4°. 1 page.

1825, February 24, Fredericksburg. Proposes furnishing him with the Reviews. Incloses prospectus of "Malte Bruns's geography." Has gone into the book business again. small 4°. 2 pages.

1825, August 12, Fredericksburg. Respecting reviews and newly published works, which he may keep or return as he pleases. 4°. 2 pages.

1825, August 27, Fredericksburg. Acknowledging letter of 24th and books returned. 4°. 1 page.

1825, November 7; 1828, December 11, 16; 1830, November 19; 1832, January 17; 1833, February 6, Fredericksburg. Six letters with statements of account. 4°. 6 pages.

GRAYSON, WILLIAM. *Richmond.*

1785, May 1, New York. Hostile preparations of the Emperor of Austria and the Dutch. Treating with the Elector of Bavaria for an exchange of territories in the low countries for Bavaria. France privy to the negotiations. Those countries wishing to preserve the balance of power will unite with Prussia to prevent this accession to Austria. War seems probable. Influence of the Queen of France in the government in favor of Austria. Methods of Congress for disposal of the Western territory. The deed of cession from Virginia. Conditions for officers and men engaged in the war. Resolution of Mr. King, of Massachusetts, for preventing slavery in the new State. Means for protecting settlers. Appropriations in Congress for public buildings in Trenton. Treaty with Barbary to purchase their friendship. Treaties with the Cherokees, Chickasaws, etc. fol. 4 pages.

1785, May 28, New York. Arrival of Don Diego de Gardoqui at Philadelphia. Incloses copy of the land ordinance passed Congress. Difference of views of the Eastern and Southern States respecting sales of Western lands. Arrival of an American ship direct from Canton. Views of the writer respecting a direct commerce between China and Virginia. [Signature cut off.] fol. 3 pages.

1785, June 27, New York. Acknowledging letter of May 29. The proposed treaty with the Western Indians much canvassed. Emigration already commenced at the mouths of the Scioto and Miami. Measures to remove intruders. Congressional appropriations. Governor Livingston appointed to The Hague. Character of Gardoqui, minister from Spain. Not much progress made by commissioners to make commercial treaties. The Pope has opened Civita Vecchia and Ancona to American commerce. Treaty with the Barbary States in train. fol. 3 pages.

1785, August 21, New York. Acknowledging a letter (no date). Opposed to the doctrine of paper money in Virginia. The mint and post-office bills before Congress. Arrangement for transportation of the mails. Commission formed by Congress to negotiate with Gardoqui. Application of Kentucky to the Virginia legislature for independence. The negotiation should be carried on through Congress, as no State has a right to dismember itself without consent of the United States. Nothing as yet done respecting public buildings at Trenton. Monroe leaves for the Miami about the Indian treaty and from thence through the wilderness of Kentucky to Virginia. fol. 4 pages.

1785, September 16, New York. The question of requisitions for 1785 still discussed in Congress. Settlement of accounts subsisting between the several States and the United States. 4°. 3 pages.

1785, October 14, New York. Acknowledging letter from Philadelphia. War declared by Algiers against the United States. Thinks the best policy is to make peace. Report of the Secretary of Foreign Affairs, recommending the vesting the American ministers with consular powers. fol. 3 pages.

GRAYSON, WILLIAM.

1785, November 8, New York. Mr. Hancock talked of by the Southern States for President. Motion brought forward by Massachusetts and Virginia respecting the dismemberment of States. Contracts made for transportation of the mails.
4°. 2 pages.

1785, November 14, New York. Interview between Mr. Adams and a committee of merchants of Glasgow about the American debts to Great Britain. Acts of the Virginia legislature respecting the "requisition." Claims of the several States against the United States. American ministers vested with the powers of consuls-general.
fol. 4 pages.

Richmond.

1785, November 22, New York. Conference between Mr. Adams, in London, with Mr. Pitt. Question of the payment of interest on American-British debts during the war. On the settlement of accounts subsisting between the several States and the United States. fol. 3 pages.

1785, November 28, New York. Adams's correspondence with the Secretary of Foreign Affairs. Pressing the necessity of commercial restrictions, that no treaty can be had without them. Hancock chosen President of the Senate. Question whether Temple shall be received as consul-general from Great Britain. Inconvenience which members of Congress have to submit to in living in New York. Memorandum stating the number of negroes carried off by the British from New York during the war. 4°. 4 pages.

1786, March 22, New York. New Jersey's house of delegates declares to Congress they will not comply with the requisition of 1785. A greater prospect of the impost. Commission dispatched to negotiate with Barbary powers. The maritime powers will counteract all our measures in order to destroy our commerce. Contest in New Jersey about paper money. Members adverse to it burnt in effigy. The governor drawn to the stake and pardoned. Suggestion of certain members of Congress to call a convention to alter the terms of confederation of States. Weakness of a Federal Government. Monroe married.
4°. 7 pages.

1786, May 28, New York. Movements of Congress. Connecticut prevails on Congress to accept her cession. Virginia embarrassed with the Connecticut business. Mr. Adams's demand for the posts. Marquis of Caermarthen's refusal. General reflections on the state of the nation. Alterations in the land ordinance. Surveyors allowed to survey by magnetic meridian. Navigable waters made common highways for all of the States. No present prospect of forming treaties with Spain or Great Britain. Depredations and murders by the Indians in Kentucky.
fol. 8 pages.

1786, November 22, New York. Acknowledging a letter, date not stated. Has heard of his own reappointment to Congress. The affair of the Missisippi in suspense. Massachusetts delegation more conciliatory since their late insurrection. Vermont in league with a certain nation. Vote of the assembly on paper money. A commercial

GRAYSON, WILLIAM.

treaty said to be nearly formed between Spain and Great Britain. 4°. 3 pages.

1787, May 24, New York. Proposition as regards fixing upon Georgetown as Capital of the Federal empire. Farce by the Poet Tyler called May day, with local characters and incidents, not successful. Incloses a letter from France. 4°. 4 pages.

1787, August 31, New York. Promises to attend to the case of Maj. Turner. His chance for secretaryship desperate. May be nominated for a judge's seat. New Jersey locates her claim for the country between the Great and Little Miami. A committee appointed to draft an ordinance for indiscriminate locations. Claims of Virginia. 4°. 4 pages.

GRAYSON, W. S. *New York.*

1790, May 20, Dumfries. His father's death. Wishes a commission as ensign or lieutenant. small 4°. 3 pages.

GREEN, A. M. *Montpellier.*

1834, January 11, Washington. Claim of Col. Francis Taylor for bounty lands, for services. 4°. 2 pages.

GREEN, DUFF. *Montpellier.*

1827, October 15, Washington. Inclosing a cutting from the "Boston Sentinel" and asks permission to contradict the report that he is the writer of the essays published in the "Richmond Whig," over the signature of a farmer. 4°. 1 page, and cutting.

1828, May 1, Washington. Returning money received which was inadvertently charged by his clerk for a subscription for the United States Telegraph. [Memorandum on same sheet from Madison noting the remittance. small 4°. 1 page, and slip of paper.

1828, May 6, Washington. Apologizing for an error of his clerk in sending him a bill for the "United States Telegraph" as it was not intended to charge him with it. 4°. 1 page.

GREEN, JOHN W. *Montpellier.*

1818, January 10, Fredericksburg. Acknowledging letter of 7th, and subscription for the Central College. 4°. 1 page.

GREEN, WILLIAM D. *Montpellier.*

1825, August 6, Fredericksburg. Inclosing an account of E. D. Withers. 4°. 1 page.

GREENHOW, SAMUEL. *Washington.*

1804, December 7, Richmond. Request to forward a letter to Mr. Monroe. 4°. 1 page.

1813, September 17, Richmond. Notice from an insurance company to pay a premium on the revaluation of a building. 4°. 1 page.

1813, November 16, Richmond. Asks his aid towards the purchase and distribution of Bibles in Virginia. 4°. 2 pages.

GREETHAM, WILL, to GALLATIN, ALBERT. *Washington.*

1801, June 17, Washington. The collector of Alexandria refusing a pass for his vessel to go to the

GREETHAM, WILL.

Mediterranean as protection against Algerine cruisers, appeals to the Secretary of the Treasury and asks him to direct the collector to grant it.
4°. 2 pages.

GREGORY, E., to MADISON. *Montpellier.*

1824, August 21. Asks the favor of an interview.
4°. 1 page.

GRIFFIN, CYRUS. *Richmond.*

1788, March 17, New York. The Marchioness (*sic*) wishes to be present at the Indian treaty. Thinks the governor-general should take her in his train, but seems averse to it. The French minister too exclusive. 4°. 2 pages.

Orange.

1788, March 24, New York. Has fears that the constitution will never be adopted from the action of certain States. Daniel Shays and Eli Parsons have petitioned the Massachusetts legislature for pardon, and will succeed. 4° 4 pages.

1788, April 7, New York. Nonattendance of members. Rhode Island rejects the constitution. Hears of Madison's election as member of Congress with pleasure. Mr. Paradise will embark for Paris in the first French packet and will take charge of any letters to Jefferson. Asks Madison's opinion on the prospect of the new constitution. 4°. 4 pages.

Richmond.

1788, April 14, New York. Inclosing paper received from Jefferson. Letter from Adams from the Netherlands representing state of affairs there. The Russians at war with the Turks, and may soon be assisted by the Emperor of Austria. Peace between France and England may not continue long. Is pleased at Madison's election, as he will be the main pillar of the business on the right side. 4°. 4 pages.

1788, April 28, New York. Acknowledging letter of the 10th. Adoption of the constitution uncertain. The Emperor of Austria declares war against the Turks. His Ottoman Majesty shows no inclination for peace. France in strict unison with the Porte. 4°. 4 pages.

1788, May 5, New York. Inclosing a letter from St. Petersburg. Maryland accedes to the proposed constitution. South Carolina will adopt it soon. Virginia and New York is opposed to it; thinks, however, in twelve months we shall have the Government in operation. The war in Europe to be conducted with energy. Russia and Austria wish to demolish Turkey. French officers in the Turkish service are ordered to quit those dominions. Mr. Neckar to again be brought into the finances. He is not our best friend.
4°. 3 pages.

1788, May 19, New York. Acknowledging letters of 1st and 3d. Letters from Mr. Adams, who is mortified at taking leave without customary letters, and that Mr. Smith is not continued at the Court of London. Thinks the war will be general. Parting scene with the King, who declares friendly disposition. 4°. 4 pages.

GRIFFIN, CYRUS.

1788, May 26, New York. Jefferson and Adams have met at Amsterdam and can borrow a million of florins for the United States from the Dutch on the prospect of the new constitution. They think the war in Europe will be general. Courtiers ridicule our situation and say that when we shall assume some sort of Government, England will speak out. The intentions of Virginia respecting the constitution. 4°. 4 pages.

1788, May —, New York, Mr. Paradise embarks for France, carrying with him the papers for Jefferson. The trial of Hastings in London. The Dauphin continues very ill. 4°. 3 pages.

1788, June 18, New York. Regrets Madison's indisposition. Not sanguine upon the event of the proposed constitution in Virginia. Arrival of a brig from China. 4°. 2 pages.

Washington.

1801, April 5. Inclosing a medal as a testimony of his high consideration and friendship. 4°. 1 page.

1801, July 29, Williamsburg. Asks for a copy of the laws of the last session of Congress. Alludes to his sending a medal to Madison, which it appears was not acknowledged. 4°. 2 pages.

1809, March 3, Yorktown. Congratulating Madison on his elevation to the chief magistry. [Signature cut off]. 4°. 1 page.

GRIFFIN, JOHN. *Washington.*

1812, May 1, Albany. Wishes to supply the vacancy caused by the departure of Judge Stuart from Illinois Territory. If nominated and confirmed by the Senate, begs this letter may be considered as a resignation of the appointment he holds in the Michigan Territory. Prospects of the elections. small 4°. 2 pages.

GRIFFIN, ISAAC. *Washington.*

1817, March 2, Washington. Bids him farewell and wishes him happiness in his retirement. 4°. 1 page.

GRIFFIN, THOMAS. *Washington.*

1805, February 14, Washington. Patent of John Houston, of Williamsburg. 4°. 1 page.

GRIFFIN, THOS. LIGHTFOOT. *Washington.*

1811, February 26, Washington. Requesting an answer to his letter of 20th. Is ready and willing to answer any interrogatories that may be propounded. 4°. 1 page.

GRIFFITHS, ELIJAH. *Washington.*

1813, April 18, Philadelphia. Wishes to be appointed to fill the vacancy caused by the death of Dr. Rush in the mint establishment. Incloses recommendations. 4°. 1 page.

GRIFFITH, THOMAS W. *Montpellier.*

1831, September 16, Baltimore. Asking Madison to favor the public with his views in relation to the tariff. 4°. 1 page.

1831, December 1, Baltimore. Acknowledging letter September 22 on the Constitution and manufactures. Incloses his opinions on the present French revolution as sent to Lafayette. Asks Madison's approval. 4°. 2 pages.

GRIFFITH, THOMAS W.

1833, Januarg 25, Baltimore. Copy of a paper on the subject of amendment of the Constitution now agitating the people. Asks his opinion of it.
4°. 2 pages.

1833, February 13, Baltimore. Acknowledging letter of 5th. Asks his opinion whether the members of the Federal Convention in 1787, contemplated the immense growth of our country.
4°. 3 pages.

GRIFFITH, WILLIAM R. *Montpellier.*

1829, April 7, Orange C. H. Purchase of land in which Mr. Tapscott and Benjamin Bell were interested. Suggests the sale of the lands if offered in convenient lots. Asks Madison's views.
4°. 3 pages.

1829, May 16, Baltimore. Has examined records in the land office in Richmond of various grants of land in the Kentucky district previous to 1792 and find that a portion taken up in names of Madison, Moore, and Barbour remain. He also discovers tracts of land patented in the name of Madison's ancestor. Will cheerfully furnish information. 4°. 3 pages.

Richmond.

1829, December 25, Frankfort, Ky. Gives a list of lands in Kentucky in which Madison and his relatives are interested. Particulars of certain conveyances by Mr. Barbour. Talk of renominating Henry Clay as President. The list appended.
4°. 4 pages.

GRIMKE, THOS. S. *Orange C.H.*

1829, January 3, Charleston. Sends resolutions in testimony of gratitude and admiration for Madison's public services. 4°. 1 page.

Montpellier.

1830, October 11, Philadelphia. Asks Madison if he received two copies of the oration delivered before the Phi Beta Kappa Society of Yale. Incloses one for the University of Virginia.
4°. 1 page.

Charlotte, Va.

1830, October 14, Philadelphia. His son having been dismissed from Yale College, wishes to know if the fact will be a barrier to his admission in the Virginia University; what course of study is desirable, and the expense. 4°. 2 pages.

Montpellier.

1833, January 30, Charleston. Apologizing for sending his last pamphlet to Charlotte instead of Orange C. H. Compliments Madison on his public services. Asks for some autographs of distinguished characters. 4°. 1 page.

Orange.

1833, May 10, Charleston. Introducing Mr. Barnard, of Hartford. 4°. 1 page.

Montpellier.

1833, August 21, Charleston. Acknowledging letter of 10th. Asks Madison to indicate any errors in some of the political passages referred to in his letter. Respecting autographs requested from Madison of distinguished personages.
4°. 3 pages.

GRISCOM, JOHN. *Montpellier.*

1833, April 17, New York. Sends some volumes of his work as a testimonial of regard and esteem. [Signed J. G.] 4°. 1 page.

GRISWOLD, CHESTER, to JEFFERSON, THOMAS. *Washington.*

1808, October 14, Otsego, N. Y. Asking employment. 4°. 3 pages.

GRISWOLD, ROGER (Governor), to MADISON. *Washington.*

1812, September 1, Hartford. Transmitting copy of declarations and resolutions of the legislature of Connecticut on the subject of the present war with Great Britain, disapproving it and refusing to comply with the requisition of the General Government for a portion of the militia of the State and approving of the conduct of the governor. 4°. 11 pages.

GRISWOLD, STANLEY. *Washington.*

1804, November 26, Walpole, N. H. Result of the State election for electors of President and Vice-President. The amendment proposed by the legislature of Massachusetts to the United States Constitution rejected. 4°. 1 page.

1810, December 18, Cincinnati. Wishes the exchange of local situations with Judge Griffin, of Michigan Territory. Has seen the President's message and heartily approves of his measures relating to West Florida. 4°. 3 pages.

1811, February 16, Cincinnati. Introducing Aaron Greely, who is employed by the surveyor-general as his deputy in Michigan. Recommends his maps of that country and his performance of his duties. 4°. 1 page.

1812, December 1, Kaskaskia. Wishes to be made known, through Mr. Edward Hempsted, that he would like to fill the vacancy made by the resignation of Col. Mansfield, late surveyor-general. 4°. 1 page.

GROVER, MATTHEW C. *Washington.*

1810, June 3, Boston. Had written him March 28 last, and, having no response, requests him to return his letter to Mr. Jefferson and his answer, which were inclosed. 4°. 1 page.

GRUBB, RICHARD. *New York.*

1789, July 29, Richmond. Requests Madison to assist him in making the proper application for a patent for his invention of a circular car for carrying heavy loads. fol. 5 papes.

GRYMES, PEYTON, and others. *Montpellier.*

1834, January 28, Orange C. H., Va. Inviting Madison, in behalf of a portion of the Republican citizens of this district, to a dinner to be given to John M. Patton, Member of Congress, representing this district. 4°. 1 page.

GUESTIER, P. A. *Washington.*

1805, November 12, Baltimore. Inclosing a draft for acceptance. 4°. 1 page.

1805, November 20, Baltimore. Bill of freight, merchandise per brig *Lyon.* strip of paper.

GURLEY, J. W.

1807, November 26, New Orleans. Certificate of the register for the district of Orleans of the filing of a warrant for land by Armand Duplantier, agent for Gen. Lafayette. Describes the location.

GURLEY, R. R. *Montpellier.*

1831, November 21, Washington. Asks for an expression of Madison's views on the principles and measures of the American Colonization Society. 4°. 3 pages.

1833, February 12, Washington. Madison's election as president of the American Colonization Society, lately vacated by the decease of Charles Carroll, of Carrollton. 4°. 1 page.

1834, March 31, Philadelphia. Asks for a letter of introduction for the Rev. Charles Brooks, of Hingham, Mass., to the friends of the American Colonization Society. 4°. 1 page.

HACKLEY, RICHARD S.

1819, May 23, Madrid. Sends a parcel from the Royal Botanic Garden of Madrid, accompanied by a letter from Señor Mariano Lagaska. Recommends the latter to the Central College of Virginia. Inclosed is a memorandum in Madison's hand, and extract from Señor Lagaska's letter. 4°. 3 pages.

1821, February 9, Washington. Desirous of the appointment as collector at St. Augustine, Fla., asks a letter of recommendation to the Secretary of the Treasury. 4°. 1 page.

HAEVEL, MATTHEW ARNOLD. *Washington.*

1810, September 29, Santiago, Chile. Provisional Government of Chile. Wishes to be appointed as commercial agent and to treat with that government for a treaty of friendship and navigation. 4°. 3 pages.

HAFF, JOHN.

1814, January 28, New York. His efforts in detaining a quantity of specie at Morrisina on its way to Boston in the care of Tories. 4°. 4 pages.

HAGNER, PETER. *Montpellier.*

1833, August 27, Washington. Sends him some eyeglasses to select from. 4°. 1 page.

1833, September 6, Washington. Has procured a package of spectacles which he sends to select from. 4°. 1 page.

HAINES, HIRAM.

1822, June 4, State Mills, Culpeper County. Wishes Madison's autograph with a copper-plate likeness. 4°. 1 page.

HALE, MATTHEW. *Unknown.*

17th century. Some experiences extracted from his writings of the guidance and direction to be obtained in imploring aid of Divine wisdom. [On the back of this paper are some printed verses entitled "Hints to Young Statesmen."] 4°. 1 page.

HALL, B., to MADISON. *Washington.*

1813, July 8, Washington. Explains the cause of the recent defeats in Upper Canada which have attended our arms to incompetent officers and men inimical to the administration 4°. 2 pages.

HALL, CHAUNCY.

1811, September 2, Meriden, Conn. Submits 6 propositions on the methods of raising sunken vessels and their cargoes. 4°. 3 pages.

HALL, D. A., to BUTLER, PIERCE. *Philadelphia.*

1801, June 16, Charleston. Would like the appointment as chief judge of the fifth circuit now vacant by the resignation of Mr. Gaillard. Asks Mr. Butler's influence in securing the place. fol. 1 page.

——— to MADISON. *Montpellier.*

1834, March 28, Washington. Sends a volume of his own compilation. 4°. 2 pages.

HALL, EDWARD. *Washington.*

1809, March 3, Salem County, N. J. Offering congratulations on Madison's elevation to the Presidential chair, and incloses proceedings of a meeting of citizens at Salem approving of his measures respecting foreign relations, and promising support to the administration. 4°. 6 pages.

HALL, FRANCIS. *Washington.*

1810, February 22, New York. Sends bill for subscription to the "American Citizen" for two and one-half years. 4°. 1 page.

HALL, HEZEKIAH. *Washington.*

1810, March 6, Washington. Is confined in the city jail for an assault committed in self-defense. Asks Madison to assist him in procuring bail, he not being able to find it. 4°. 1 page.

HALL, JOHN H. *Montpellier.*

1823, October 10, Philadelphia. Appeal to several persons in behalf of M. M. Russell, formerly of the Army, who has lost his property by fire and is in ill health. 4°. 1 page.

HALLET, STEPHEN S. *Washington.*

1809, September 9, New York. Proposes an improvement on Montgolfier's hydraulic ram, for which he has obtained a patent, to be used at the President's house. 4°. 1 page.

HAMILTON, ALEXANDER. *Princeton.*

1783, July 6, Philadelphia. The public sentiment against Congress. Intends publishing explanations respecting the removal to Princeton in consequence of the mutinous soldiers of Pennsylvania. Asks Madison his ideas of his (Hamilton's) disposition respecting the removal. Wishes to vindicate his position. [Signature cut off.] fol. 1 page.

Philadelphia.

1788, April 3, New York. Acknowledging a letter from Philadelphia. Opinions respecting certain portions of the proposed new constitution. Sends copies of the "Federalist" containing commentary on the Executive branch. Is pleased at Madison's election to Congress. small 4°. 2 pages.

Orange.

1788, May 11, New York. The New York elections over; result not yet known. Has sent Madison the first volume of "Publius." Incloses letter to Mr. Van der Kemp. 4°. 1 page.

HAMILTON, ALEXANDER.

1788, May 19, New York. Thinks that there will be a majority against the constitution in the election in New York. Clinton leader of his party in opposition. Conjectures as to other States. His (Clinton's) declaration as to the instability of the Union. Asks Madison's views as regarding Virginia. Will forward, as directed, copies of the "Federalist." [Signature cut off.]
4°. 3 pages.

1788, June 8, Poughkeepsie. The elections in New York result favorably to the anti-Federal party. Majority of the convention oppose the constitution. Their measures and object. Dreads the consequences of nonadoption of the constitution—eventual disunion and civil war. Hopes Virginia will accede, as her influence will be great. Wishes to get, by express, any decisive result from Virginia. [Signature cut off.]
4°. 3 pages.

Richmond.

1788, June 19, Poughkeepsie. The convention make a house. To-morrow to go into committee of the whole on the constitution. Not easy to conjecture the result. A happy issue in Virginia will have considerable influence with New York.
4°. 1 page.

1788, June 21, Poughkeepsie. Acknowledging letter of 9th. Glad to think the chances in Virginia are favorable respecting the adoption of the constitution. Proceedings in the New York convention. New Hampshire most probably for adoption. small 4°. 2 pages.

New York.

1788, June 27, Poughkeepsie. Gen. Schuyler sends an express to Madison giving account of the adoption of the constitution by New Hampshire. Awaits, eagerly, accounts from Virginia as New York's only chance of success. Has a gleam of hope. [Signature cut off.] small 4°. 1 page.

Richmond.

1788, July 8, New York. Felicitating Madison on the event in Virginia. Proceedings in the New York convention at Poughkeepsie. Conjectures. Disturbances in Albany. Federalists victors. Tranquility restored. small 4°. 3 pages.

New York.

1788, July —, Poughkeepsie. Acknowledging letter of June 20. Regrets prospects are not certain in Virginia. Discussions in the convention at Poughkeepsie on taxation. The opposition wavering. The chief wishes to establish Clintonism on the basis of anti-Federalism.
small 4°. 1 page.

1788, July —, Poughkeepsie. Proceedings in the convention. Reservation of a right to recede in case the amendments have not been decided on in the mode pointed out in the constitution within five or seven years. small 4°. 2 pages.

1788, July 22, Poughkeepsie. The convention debating on the amendments. His fears diminishing.
4°. 1 page.
Richmond.

1788, November 23, New York. Acknowledging letter of 20th. Conjectures as to the candidates for

HAMILTON, ALEXANDER.

Vice-President. The majority probably for Adams. Hamilton proposes to support Adams, and gives his reasons. 4°. 3 pages.

1789, October 12, New York. Asking Madison's views in respect to means for addition to our revenues. °. 2 pages.

——— to JEFFERSON, THOMAS. *Philadelphia.*

1791, April 12, Philadelphia. Debt of the United States to France. 4°. 3 pages.

1791, April 15, Philadelphia. Correspondence relating to the debt of the United States to France. Inclosing a memorandum. 4°. 4 pages.

1791, June 8, Philadelphia. Asks that information from United States officers abroad may be sent to the Treasury Department respecting the state of the coins of foreign nations, specifying their respective standards, weights, and value, and periodically a state of market prices for gold and silver in coin and bullion, also the rates of different kinds of labor in manufactures and tillage. 4°. 2 pages.

1791 (?) Fragments of a memorandum about Hamilton's views respecting the national debt, and apparent change in Madison's opinion. Scrap of paper.

——— to JEFFERSON, THOMAS.

1792, June 29, Philadelphia. Payment of the debt of the United States to France. 4°. 2 pages.

1792, December 26, Philadelphia. Suggesting that consuls of the United States everywhere should be possessed of the laws of the United States respecting commerce and navigation in order to inform merchants' and owners and masters of ships. Also to direct them to transmit by every opportunity rates of exchange and values of assignats. 4°. 2 pages.

——— to SHORT, WILLIAM.

1792. Notes and memoranda in Madison's handwriting relative to the charges against the Secretary of the Treasury according to Mr. Giles's recollections. fol. 2. pages.

——— to JEFFERSON, THOMAS. *Philadelphia.*

1793, May 3, Philadelphia. Respecting an advance of money requested by M. Ternant, French minister of France, who should have made the application to the Secretary of State. Gives reasons for applying to the treasury. Trusts the Secretary of State will not consider what has been done an infringement of a rule of official propriety. Inclosed is a copy of the application from the French minister. 4°. 3 pages.

1793, May 9, Philadelphia. Acknowledging letter of 8th, respecting the issuing of passports. 4°. 2 pages.

1793-'94 (?), not dated, Philadelphia. His views as to a term of expression in an official document. 4°. 1 page.

——— to MADISON.

1793 (?), not dated. Requests the opportunity of an interview. 4°. 1 page.

HAMILTON, ALEXANDER.

1793 (?), not dated. A memorandum in Hamilton's handwriting on the funded debt. Suggestions as to imposts and taxes for revenue. 4°. 2 pages.

HAMILTON, ALEXANDER, JR. *Montpellier.*

1831, June 30, New York. Announcing the approaching death of Monroe. 4°. 1 page.

HAMILTON, A. *Washington.*

1811, June 12, Lisbon. The consulate office now vacant, applies to fill it. Importance of the station. Expected battle between Marshals Soult and Victor and Lord Wellington on the plains of Merida. 4°. 3 pages.

HAMILTON, A. W. *Montpellier.*

1822, April 10, Washington. His desire to be appointed to office in the Treasury or State departments. Has been employed as asistant deputy quartermaster-general in the Army. 4°. 1 page.

HAMILTON, ELIZ. *Washington.*

1809, January 25, Grange. Petition for the half pay to Maj. Gen. Hamilton's widow and children. 4°. 1 page.

1809, May 20, New York. Asks Madison's good offices towards the procuring of commutation of her husband's (A. Hamilton) half pay on account of services. fol. 1 page.

HAMILTON, J. C. *Montpellier.*

1833, June 20, New York. Acknowledging receipt of the extract from Madison's notes of the debates of the convention of 1787. 4°. 1 pages.

HAMILTON, JAMES.

1827, February 28, Washington. Acknowledging letter of December 30. Sends him copy of a speech. 4°. 1 page.

HAMILTON, JOHN T. *Washington.*

1805, January 8, Orange C. H. Asks as a favor to rent him a field to cultivate in corn. 4°. 2 pages.

HAMILTON, PAUL.

1809, March 22, Branford, S. C. Acknowledging letter of 7th, accompanied by a commission appointing him Secretary of the Navy. Accepts, and will repair to the seat of Government as soon as practicable. 4°. 1 page.

1809, no date, Washington. Will wait on the President the next day and observe with fidelity his instructions. 4°. 1 page.

1809, May 29, Washington. Sends a list of officers in the Corps of Marines named for promotion. 4°. 1 page.

Montpellier.

1809, July 24, Washington. Will not leave his post for private considerations. The insults of Great Britain towards the United States will create a union of sentiment throughout our country. There will be no cause for fear for the issue. 4°. 2 pages.

1809, July 25, Washington. In view of the present aspect of affairs with England, he has thought it inexpedient to diminish any of our preparations for defense until Madison's sentiments are known. The Secretary of State agrees with Hamilton in this decision. 4°. 2 pages.

HAMILTON, PAUL. *Washington.*

1806 (probably 1809), November 25, Washington. In view of the inadequate quarters and provisions for sick and disabled seamen a marine hospital is recommended. [Unsigned.] 4°. 4 pages.

1809, December 4, Washington. Recommending Mr. John K. Smith to fill the vacancy of navy agent at New Orleans, in the place lately filled by Mr. Keith Spence, deceased. 4°. 1 page.

1809, December 8, Washington. Recommending Dr. Fraser, of South Carolina, as surgeon in the Navy. 4°. 1 page.

1809, December 22, Washington. Recommending the appointment of Dr. Julius R. Shumate as surgeon's mate in the Navy. His services are now wanted in New Orleans. 4°. 1 page.

1809 (?), not dated. Statement of debts due under the head of repairs of vessels. Navy Department. [Not signed.] 4°. 1 page.

1809 (?), not dated. Memoranda. Names of vessels in commission. Other vessels of the Navy. With the exception of those at New Orleans all the gunboats have been placed in a state of ordinary. [Not signed.] 4°. 3 pages.

1810, May 23, Washington. Appropriations for "Repairs" in the Navy Department exhausted. Suggests the propriety of a transfer of funds from the appropriation for "Provisions." 4°. 3 pages.

——— to NAVY AGENTS.

1810, March 22, Washington. Circular to Navy agents. Instructions to incur no expense whatever under the head of "Repairs" without special instructions. 4°. 1 page.

——— to MADISON. *Montpellier.*

1810, July 23, Washington. Account of the outrage of the commander of the British brig *Moselle* in firing upon the U. S. brig *Vixen*. Incloses copies of letters from the captain of the *Vixen* and the British commander's answer, also copy of a letter from Mr. Poindexter, a passenger on the *Vixen*. 4°. 3 pages.

1810, August 3, Washington. Acknowledging letter of July 26. Having been informed by Mr. Gaillard, U. S. Senator for South Carolina, of the illicit introduction of slaves, has issued orders to our vessels stationed in Charleston, Savannah, and St. Marys, also dispatched the brig *Syren* to New Orleans to observe instructions to prevent the practice. Annexed is extract from Mr. Gaillard's letter. 4°. 3 pages.

1810, August —, Washington. Inclosing a statement representing the appropriations for the Navy Department. Transfers, however, will be required in aid of "Repairs of vessels," from the appropriations for "Pay and subsistence of the Navy" and for "Provisions." Other transfers recommended. 4°. 2 pages.

1810, September 20, Washington. State of affairs in the Floridas. Recommends him to not return to Washington before cold weather on account of the prevalence of fever. Fears he will be unable to visit him. 4°. 3 pages.

1810, September 25, Washington. Incloses a paper from New York giving information of returning justice on the part of belligerents of Europe towards us. 4°. 1 page.

HAMILTON, PAUL.

1810, November 1, Washington. Incloses a statement respecting Navy appropriations. Recommends certain transfers of funds. 4°. 2 pages.

Washington.

1810, November 24, Washington. Incloses letters which illness prevented his delivering in person. 4°. 1 page.

1811, January 17, Washington. Loss of the U. S. schooner *Revenge.* Not an important loss, as she was unsound. 4°. 1 page.

1811, February 26, Washington. Transmits nominations for officers of the Navy and Marine Corps. 4°. 1 page.

1811, April 17, Washington. Inclosing papers vindicating Thomas Turner, accountant of the Navy, from the charges alleged against him in the memorial of Mr. Hanson. 4°. 1 page.

1811, May 3, Washington. Incloses a letter relating to Col. Butler, of South Carolina. Holds him in high estimation. 4°. 1 page.

——— to HANSON, SAMUEL (of SAMUEL).

Washington.

1811, July 16, Washington. Revokes the appointment of Mr. Hanson as purser in the Navy. fol. 1 page.

——— to MADISON. *Washington.*

1811, July 23, Washington. Statement of Navy appropriations. 4°. 2 pages.

Montpellier.

1811, July 24, Washington. Submits a statement of the Navy appropriations to July 23. Recommends transfers of funds from certain appropriations to pay deficiencies in others. 4°. 1 page.

1811, August 25, Washington. Heavy rains in Washington. Pennsylvania avenue overflowed. 4°. 2 pages.

1811, September 3, Washington. Arrival of the *John Adams* on August 28. His son brings dispatches which he will at once proceed to carry to Madison. Does not doubt the report of the revocation of the French decrees. 4°. 2 pages.

1811, September 4, Washington. Result of the elections in Maryland show Republican gains. 4°. 2 pages.

1811, September 9, Washington. Incloses copy of letter from Capt. Porter. His operations are approved of. Sitting of the court on the case of Commodore Rodgers. The going to sea of some of our ships will have a salutary effect in restraining the insolence offered by the British. Reports of a British squadron coming to our coast under Admiral Yorke. Suggests it may be proper to prepare gunboats for the service in the Chesapeake. 4°. 3 pages.

1811, September 11, Washington. Apologizes for having opened a letter addressed to him recommending a Mr. Smith as chaplain in the Navy, at Smith's repeated solicitations, as it was inconvenient for him to wait for Madison's return to Washington. The writer and Mrs. Hamilton hope to visit Montpellier. 4°. 2 pages.

HAMILTON, PAUL.

1811, September 17, Washington. Termination of the court of inquiry in the case of Commodore Rodgers, resulting in his being above the reach of censure or even suspicion. Has ordered gunboats to be equipped. Our frigates and other cruising vessels are disposed of in a manner best calculated to resent insults. 4°. 3 pages.

Washington.

1812, February 11, Washington. Incloses a sketch, to be used by the President if he thinks proper, to state his objections to certain parts of the proceedings in the case of the court-martial of Gen. Wilkinson. Is induced to confirm the sentence of the court so far as it acquits him of the charges against him, that he be released from arrest and that his sword be restored to him. 4°. 3 pages.

——— to GALLATIN, ALBERT.

1812, July 13, Washington. An order on the Treasury in favor of Thomas T. Tucker, treasurer of the Navy, to be charged to the appropriation of July 5, 1812, for purposes of fortifying and defending ports, harbors, and maritime frontier of the United States. [Gallatin's notes on back of letter.] 4°. 1 page.

——— to MADISON.

1812, December 30, Washington. Being about to resign his position as Secretary of the Navy, he wishes as a valuable legacy to his children, a statement from the President that in his opinion there has never been anything reprehensible in his course of conduct while occupying that position. 4°. 2 pages.

1812 (?), not dated, Washington. Memorandum of vessels worthy of repair and general condition. Contemplated expenditures. Our operations against the enemy. Vessels lost and captured. 4°. 3 pages.

HAMILTON, SAMUEL S., to MADISON.

1805, November 26, Washington. Notice from the Librarian of Congress to return certain books before the meeting of Congress. 4°. 1 page.

HAMPTON, WADE.

1801, July 12, Charleston, S. C. Applies for the consulship of Bordeaux for Mr. James Miller, of Charleston, if the place is vacant. 4°. 2 pages.

1802, March 16, Charleston. Introducing Mr. Read. 4°. 1 page.

HAND, CALEB.

1810, December 21, Philadelphia. Receipt for a pitcher from John Mullowny to be delivered to Madison. 8°. 1 page.

HANDS, JOHN.

1810, April 16, Washington. Bill of freight of copper, etc. Strip of paper.

HANSON, A. C. *Richmond.*

1788, June 2, Annapolis. Respecting a narrative promised to Mr. Daniel Carroll of the proceedings in the late convention of Maryland for the adoption of the constitution. Incloses an address to the people of Maryland. fol. 23 pages.

HANSON, SAMUEL (of SAMUEL). *Washington.*

1802, May 9, Washington. Solicits an appointment to a place lately made vacant by the resignation of Mr. Wagner. States his acquirements and fitness. small 4°. 2 pages.

1803, October 6, Washington. Asks Madison's influence with members of the Senate to procure the appointment of secretary of the Senate. 4°. 1 page.

1810, March 19, Washington. The probability of his dismissal from his office. Attempts to justify himself from the misrepresentations and malignity of his enemies. 4°. 12 pages.

1810, March 24' Washington. Has received his dismissal. Explains how he has been unjustly treated. 4°. 3 pages.

——— to TURNER, THOMAS.

1810, April 10, Washington. Demands of the accountant of the Navy to admit an inclosed document as a voucher for a claim. [Copy.] 4°. 1 page.

1811, April —, Washington. Resents the charge of being insane. Demands the publication of his letter to the comptroller. [Copy.] 4°. 2 pages.

——— to HAMILTON, PAUL (Secretary of the Navy).

1811, April 12, Washington. Complains of the oppression by the accountant of the Navy. His suspensions of charges in his accounts, which he specifies. Asks that justice be done him. [Copy.] 4°. 3 pages.

——— to MADISON.

1811, April 16, Washington. Petition to the President, complaining of partiality of Thomas Turner, accountant of the Navy, in relation to the petitioner's claim. Asks the President to cause an examination into the conduct of the accountant to be made. fol. 2 pages.

1811, April 29, Washington. Charges against the accountant of the Navy. Suggests the means of arriving at the truth of the matter by selecting referees, before whom the charges will be made. fol. 3 pages.

1811, July 20, Washington. Appeals to the President's sense of justice respecting the charges of the Secretary of the Navy, in which it is stated that he (Hanson) had been disrespectful toward the President. He is not conscious of such an act, and would like to have the instance pointed out. fol. 1 page.

HARDIN, M. D.

1817, January 17, Washington. Request of some members of the House of Representatives to the President to permit the commissioner of claims to give out certificates on those cases which he considers legal and of minor importance. Approves of this application. [Indorsed on the back of this letter, in approval, Isham Talbot.] 4°. 4 pages.

HARISON, RICHARD, to TODD, JOHN, JR.

1788, May 12, New York. Acknowledging letter of 6th, containing various papers. 4°. 1 page.

HARDING, SETH, to MADISON. *Washington.*

Not dated. Asks how he can obtain redress on account of the depreciation of Continental paper money which he obtained for his services in the Revolution. fol. 2 pages.

HARPER, SAMUEL H., to MEIGS, JOSIAH.

1816, July 15, New Orleans. Acknowledging letter of May 25. Location of the land of Lafayette. Lafayette's agent unwilling to accept the land outside the fortifications. Asks instructions whether he is authorized to issue a patent for land within the fortifications. [Copy.] 4°. 2 pages.

HARRIES, ETIENNE, to MADISON.

1810, March 21, Paris. Not being able to obtain letters from New Orleans, requests the President to allow M. L. Rousset to communicate with him to the care of his secretary. [In French.] 4°. 2 pages.

HARRIS, CHARLES.

1810, March 30, Savannah. Incloses a work by an old French officer dedicated to Madison. Requests that he write a few lines to this meritorious old man, approving the work. 4°. 1 page.

HARRIS, JAMES M.

1812, October 30, Pine *Hill.* Asks Madison to give him, by letter, the prominent articles of his religious creed. fol. 1 page.

HARRIS, JOHN C. *Montpellier.*

1830, July 27, Orang*e C. H.* Requests his views relative to the candidates for the fall election in this district. Rumors of statements relating thereto as expressed by him which he desires to verify or deny. 4°. 4 pages.

HARRIS, LEVETT. *Washington.*

1806, July 11, St. Pet*ersburg.* Introducing Joseph Allen Smith, of South Carolina. 4°. 1 page.

HARRISON, BENJAMIN. *Philadelphia.*

1782, November 30, Richmond. Thanks Madison for some books sent him. Has got a new Beau hat and wishes Madison to procure a cockade for it from his favorite milliner. Scarcity of money. Looks for the surrender or evacuation of Charleston in a week. small 4°. 2 pages.

1782, December 28, Richmond. The assembly rises today. Is concerned with the situation of Madison's finances. Charleston not evacuated on November 27. [Not signed.] small 4°. 1 page.

1783, January 4, Richmond. Acknowledging several letters. Vacillations and indolence in Congress. Coincides with Madison's views. 4°. 1 page.

HARRISON, CARTER B. *Orange.*

1798, November 9, Cabin Point. Wishes to buy some land in Orange County and asks Madison's views in relation to value. 4°. 1 page.

Washington.

1801, April 4, Maycox. Introducing Mr. Alexander Kerr, who wishes the appointment to some office. Recommends him as capable, and is a Republican. 4°. 1 page.

HARRISON, CARTER B.

1802, August 5, Richmond. Extracts from a letter received from his brother, William Harrison, in which he wishes him to ask Madison and Gen. Dearborn to advise him and assist him in a proposal he has made. 4°. 3 pages.

HARRISON, J. B. *Montpellier.*

1828, July 3, Lynchburg. The situation he desires to stand with the visiting board of the University of Virginia in reference to the professor's chair occupied by Mr. Long. His desire to go abroad in a year's time after his inauguration. 4°. 1 page.

HARRISON, L.

1829, August 24. Would like to be employed as manager on a portion of Madison's farm. 8°. 1 page.

HARRISON, R. *Washington.*

1796, June 1, Philadelphia. Claim of William Russell for compensation for wages in the commissary department. [*See* letter from William Russell to Madison, June 1, 1796.] fol. 1 page.

Philadelphia.

1796, June 1, Washington. Returns W. Russell's papers. The claim can not be admitted at the Treasury, interfering as it does with decisions by Congress of cases of the same kind submitted to it. fol. 1 page.

HARRISON, SAMUEL. *Washington.*

1812, May 11, Chittenden, Vt. Urges the President to pause before he declares war against Great Britain. It will be the destruction of himself and friends and country. fol. 3 pages.

1812, October 30, Chittenden, Vt. The reasons given last May why it was improper to go to war are yet powerful arguments against its continuance. Warns him to flee from the wrath to come. fol. 4 pages.

1812, November 23, Chittenden, Vt. War and its horrors. Relates an anecdote which he considers applicable to the present situation. Hopes the President will be enabled to discover the true interests of the United States before the nation is precipitated into remediless ruin. fol. 3 pages.

HARRISON, WILLIAM H., to EUSTIS, WILLIAM.

1810, June 26, Vincennes. Arrival of a deputation of Pottawattamies, giving information of the decision of a council held near St. Joseph, on Lake Michigan, attended by all the Indians of that quarter and deputies of the Delawares. Winamac, the chief, gives information of the "Prophet's" plans which were to surprise Detroit, Fort Wayne, Chicago, St. Louis, and this place. The Prophet's villainy. Anecdote about him. Proceedings and measures to be taken. Miserable and desperate condition of the Indians. [Copy.] 4°. 6 pages.

1810, July 4, Vincennes. Arrival of Brouillet from the "Prophet's" town, who gives an account of his interviews with him respecting his intentions. Denies that he intends to go to war against the whites. Complains that the Indians had been cheated of their lands and otherwise ill treated. Incloses a deposition of Mr. Brouillet. [Copy.] 4°. 4 pages.

HARRISON, WILLIAM H.

1810, July 11, Vincennes. Letter received from Mr. Johnson, Indian agent, containing information on subject of the hostile combinations of Indians against the United States. Thefts of horses a ruse to entice the whites to follow, and capture or kill them. Fears that all the Indian tribes will combine against us in six months after hostilities may commence. [Copy.] 4°. 3 pages.

1810, July 18, Vincennes. Col. Vigo returns from his mission to the Miamis being charged with ascertaining the fidelity of that tribe and to procure their consent to a conditional cession of land. The Miami chiefs are supposed to be faithful to the United States with one exception. Intends proposing that several chiefs should go to Washington to see our strength and deter them from being hostile. The Sacs and Foxes ready to attack when the "Prophet" signals. Defection of the Wyandottes only partial. [Copy.] 4°. 3 pages.

1810, July 25, Vincennes. Acknowledging letters of 3d, 5th, and 7th. Learns that the chiefs of the Pottawattamies are employed in forming a combination to disperse the banditti which the "Prophet" has collected at Tippecanoe. This chief is actively employed in poisoning the minds of the Indians. Conjectures as to his movements. Presents to various tribes. Arrivals of militia from Ohio and Kentucky. [Copy.] 4°. 6 pages.

1810, August 1, Vincennes. Depredations of the Indians on the northern frontier of the Jeffersonville district. Driving off of the inhabitants. Reports from persons sent to investigate the truth. The alarm extends as far south as the Blue River. Movements proposed. A display of force necessary. [Copy.] 4°. 3 pages.

——— to the "PROPHET."

1810, no date. Speech sent by Harrison to the "Prophet." Attempts to show that hostile movements will end in misery and death. Our soldiers are too numerous for all their tribes combined. The red coats can not protect them. Promises to rectify any injury done them. [This is a translation from a French copy.] 4°. 2 pages.

——— to EUSTIS, WILLIAM. *Washington.*

1810, August 22, Vincennes. The designs of the "Prophet." Interviews with the "Prophet's" brother Tecumseh. His speeches insolent at first, pretentious, and arrogant. Would punish with death all the chiefs who were parties to the late treaty. Inconsistent statement that they would not go to war. Sends copy of a speech to the "Prophet." Does not think war inevitable. The friendly tribes. [Copy.] 4°. 6 pages.

1810, August 28, Vincennes. Interviews with Tecumseh relating to the sales of Indian lands. Impositions practiced on the Indians by designing white men. Delight of the British agent at the union of so many tribes against us. War feeling of the warriors. Error of the President in causing his agents to effect a peace between the tribes. The establishment of tranquility between neighboring tribes. A sure indication of war against us. [Copy.] 4°. 3 pages.

HARRISON, WILLIAM H., to MADISON.

1814, May 11, Cincinnati. Resigns his commission. Is convinced that his retiring from the Army is as compatible to the claims of patriotism as with those of his family and a proper regard to his own feelings and honor. 4°. 2 pages.

HART, ABIJAH.

1806, November 29, New York. Applies for the position of consul at Calcutta or at some other important English port. 4°. 2 pages.

HART, WILLIAM S.

1809, March 8, New York. Congratulating Madison on his election. 4°. 1 page.

HARTSHORNE, ——, to WENTWORTH, SIR JOHN. *Halifax.*

1805, June —, Halifax. Sends a bill of lading of articles for the President, Mr. Madison, and Senator P. Butler per brig *Adventurer* for New York. fol. 1 page. 8°. 1 page.

HASKELL, ABRAHAM, JR., and others, to MADISON. *Washington.*

1812 (?), not dated. Recommendation by citizens of Worcester County, Mass., of Philander Jacob Willard, of Ashburnham, for an appointment as captain in the Army. 4°. 2 pages.

HASKELL, E. *Princeton.*

1783, September 12, Philadelphia. Incloses a copy of the Institution of the Society of the Cincinnati. 4°. 12 pages.

HASSLER, F. R. *Montpellier.*

1825, November 24, New York. Presents a copy of his papers upon the Coast Survey, which had remained in manuscript since 1819. 4°. 1 page.

1827, January 18, New York. Presents a copy of his publication of his "Elements of Arithmetic." fol. 2 pages.

1828, February 28, Washington. Presents him with a copy of his new publication, "A Popular Exposition of the System of the Universe." 4°. 2 pages.

1828, September 8, New York. Presents him with two copies of his "Elements of Geometry." fol. 1 page.

1830, June 14, New York. Presents a copy of his logarithmic and trigonometric tables. Would like this work and others introduced into the University of Virginia. fol. 2 pages.

1833, February 6, Washington. Presents him with copies of his reports upon weights and measures, for the University of Virginia and Senator Cabell. Is again in charge of the work of survey of the coast of the United States. 4°. 3 pages.

1835, January 9, New York. Sends documents relating to his work on the Coast Survey. Unjust attacks upon him by the fourth auditor. His request for an inquiry refused. Is afraid he will be obliged to abandon the work unless the President interfere. 4°. 4 pages.

1835, July 27, Washington. Acknowledging letter of 2d. Thanks him for recommending him for the professorship vacant at the University of Virginia. The sacrifices and losses he has made in the Coast Survey. 4°. 2 pages.

HASWELL, ANTHONY, to JEFFERSON, THOMAS.
Washington.

1801, May 10, Bennington, Vt. Is publisher of a newspaper which, on account of political opinions, has incurred the secret and open enmity of men whom he esteemed as friends, and caused his ruin. Asks if his gazette can not be made the medium of necessary governmental communications of the United States. fol. 3 pages.

HAUMONT, CHARLES, to MADISON.

1809, April 25, Sapelo Island, Ga. Sends a manuscript with a request that he would read it, and give his approval of it, that it may be deemed worthy of the attention of the public. [In French.] fol. 3 pages.

1810, January 29, Island of Sapelo, Ga. Calls attention to a letter and manuscripts sent some time since, and which has never been acknowledged. Begs the President's attention to the manuscript and an answer. [In French.] fol. 1 page.

1810, April 1, Island of Sapelo, Ga. Again calls the President's attention to a manuscript sent him, and asks his opinion thereon. Speaks of his destitute condition and having been a Revolutionary soldier. [In French.] fol. 2 pages.

HAWES, AYLETT.

1814, December 5, Washington. Inclosing copy of the will of Martin Kaufman, deceased, in which there is a legacy to Madison to be expended in charities. Suggestion of the writer, by request of Madison, how this bequest shall be disposed of. 4°. 5 pages.

1815, June 18, Washington. Acknowledging receipt of a power of attorney for Martin Kaufman's legacy. The trust is committed to the widow of the deceased. 4°. 1 page.

Montpellier.

183—, not dated. Notifies him of a deposit to Madison's credit at the Farmer's Bank at Fredericksburg. small 4°. 1 page.

HAWES, JOHN, to COLES, EDWARD. *Washington.*

1815, March 16, New Bedford. Incloses bill of lading, two cases of wine, per schooner *Rose in Bloom,* for Madison's account. 4°. 2 pages.

———, to MADISON.

1815, July 7, New Bedford. Acknowledging letter of June 29, in which inquiry is made as to some wine. Hawes states the manner in which it was shipped to Alexandria. 4°. 1 page.

HAWKINS, BENJAMIN. *Princeton.*

1783, August 9, Princeton. Has letters from Mr. Dana up to April 14. Had communicated his mission to the vice chancellor, Count Osterman, but has not been received by the Empress of Russia, for several reasons which he communicates. 4°. 2 pages.

1784, September 4, Sweet Springs in Botetourt. Has been elected a representative for his county. The cession of Western territory was carried in the House of Commons. The reason why the writer was defeated at his election to Congress. 4°. 2 pages.

HAWKINS, BENJAMIN. *Richmond.*

1788, February 14, Warrenton. Questions propounded by a neighbor respecting Richard Henry Lee. The feeling in the community respecting the proposed new constitution. 4°. 2 pages.

New York.

1789, June 1, Warren. Acknowledging letter of May 5. His admiration for the character of the President. Madison's scheme of impost. The Indian department; difficulties in the way of designating a line of boundary between the whites and Indians. The Indians hope everything from Congress, and the whites fear their speculative views will be blasted. Sends congratulations to the President. 4°. 4 pages.

1789, June 3, Warren. Sentiments of the people in Virginia formerly opposed but now favorable to the new Government. Prediction in Virginia for paper money. The grasshopper and tobacco crop. 4°. 3 pages.

1789, August 27, Warrenton. Acknowledging letter of June 24. Results of the Virginia elections. Letters from Nashville relating to predatory and murderous excursions of the Indians. Maj. Morgan's settlements on the Mississippi. Overflow of the land. The adventurers returned disgusted. 4°. 1 page.

Washington.

1803, January 13, Fort Wilkinson. Introducing William Hill, an assistant in the Creek agency. 4°. 1 page.

1803, July 11, Creek *Agency.* Acknowledging a letter. Condition of the agency. Apprehension of Bowles and his disgrace. Concurs in the idea that it would have been unjust and premature to make war with Spain on the infraction of our right of deposit by the Spanish intendant at New Orleans. Is for peace on any terms. All are Quakers in the Indian agency. Improvements among the Indians; their contented condition. Labor no longer a disgrace. Hunting no longer profitable. Carried on solely for amusement of young people. 4°. 3 pages.

1811, March 11, Creek Agency. Arrival of Gen. Matthews, who seems confident in the success of his mission. Impressed with the reception given him by the President. States he (Matthews) was apprehensive of a party forming against him, and that Robert Smith, member of the Cabinet, was of it. Thinks he shonld be dismissed. Matthews not a Federalist. His record excellent. Thinks his present mission will lead up to his being called into service again. 4°. 2 pages.

1811, October 13, Creek *Agency.* His disgust for Mr. Smith, lately Secretary of State. Interview and correspondence with Felix O'Hanlon, bearing on Madison's character and measures. Extract from the correspondence. 4°. 3 pages.

HAWKINS, WILLIAM.

1811, December 20, Raleigh. Incloses a copy of the resolutions adopted by the general assembly of North Carolina in approbation of the President's message to Congress, attributing the evils which we have experienced wholly to the unprincipled conduct of the belligerent powers of Europe. 4°. 1 page.

HAWKINS, WILLIAM.

1813, November 30, Raleigh, N. C. Inclosing a memorial relative to the defenseless and unprotected situation of the State, by the general assembly of North Carolina.
4°. 1 page. large fol. 3 pages.

HAY, CHARLES (Clerk of House of Delegates, Virginia), to MARYLAND GENERAL ASSEMBLY.

1789, December 10. Resolution of the house of delegates of Virginia, and agreed to by the senate, respecting the cession of 10 miles square to the United States for the permanent seat of Government. [Copy.] fol. 1 page.

HAY, GEORGE, to MADISON. *Washington.*

1807, June 12, Richmond. Wishes an authentic copy of the President's proclamation in relation to Burr and his confederates. Also the orders issued from the War and Navy departments. 4°. 1 page.

1813, September 28. Incloses for consideration certificates offered by Mr. Coleman in support of his pretensions to office of collector. 4°. 1 page.

Montpellier.

1820, September 18, Oak Hill. On leaving Montpellier he carried away, inadvertently, some books belonging to Madison. Will return them soon by mail. 4°. 2 pages.

1821, April 23, Washington. Asks for the use of Valen's commentary on the "Ordonnances de la Marine." Has been investigating decisions and reasonings of the Supreme Court concerning the power of the House of Representatives to punish for contempt. 4°. 2 pages.

1823, August 11, Washington. Submits inclosed remarks for Madison's consideration, for the purpose of obtaining his views on a point of importance. 4°. 1 page.

HAYWARD, W. *Washington.*

1809, March 14, Easton, Talbot County, Md. An address in behalf of a committee of citizens of Talbot County, expressive of their approbation of and confidence in Madison as President of the United States and promising support.
fol. 3 pages.

HAZARD, WILLIAM.

1805, May 17, Stonington. Acknowledging payment of drafts. Asks Madison to forward the amount of the bill on Mr. Jefferson. Goes to the Mediterranean soon and will attend to any orders.
4°. 1 page.

HEATH, JOHN.

1801, July 8. Asks Madison's good offices with the President to obtain a place in the judiciary or customs. 4°. 1 page.

HEATH, JOHN D.

1812, February 19, Charleston. Application for the office of district judge for South Carolina.
4°. 2 pages.

1813, April 7, Charleston. Asks for the appointment of Thomas Lehre, of Charleston, as United States marshal of this district, in case the present marshal is removed, as is reported. 4°. 3 pages.

1814, January 29, Charleston. Acknowledging letter of 16th. Thanks him for his sympathy in anticipation of a malady which has now become a reality. small 4°. 1 page.

HEATH, WILLIAM.

1809, March 13, Roxbury, Mass. Congratulates Madison on his election. Heath, the only surviving general officer of the first provincial and Congressional appointment, and contemporary with Hancock, Adams, Warren, and others, and near the illustrious Washington in the Revolution. 4°. 2 pages.

HECKLE, LYDIA, and others, to JEFFERSON.

1808 (?), not dated. Petition of American citizens, prisoners at Carthagena, in South America (accomplices of Miranda), for assistance in their behalf and to procure amelioration of their condition. Signed by Lydia Heckle and many others. royal fol. 2 pages.

HELM, JOHN.

Not dated. Plat of a survey of property in litigation in a suit of Joseph H. Daviess *vs.* Madison's heirs, on the Panther Creek. large fol. 1 page.

HENCHMAN, NATHANIEL, to MADISON.

1813, May 29, Amherst, N. H. Lives in a Republican town; the inhabitants rejoice at success of our arms, but shudder at the thought of contributing money. fol. 1 page.

HENDERSON, THOMAS.

1812, September 10, Mecklenburg County, N. C. Proceedings of a meeting of citizens approving of the declaration of war against Great Britain and declaring their willingness to cooperate with the Government in rendering every assistance in their power to prosecute the war with vigor. fol. 2 pages.

HENDRY, THOMAS.

1810, March 5, Gloucester, N. J. As presidents of the Democratic association sends a record of the resolutions adopted by them approving of the conduct of the President in dismissing Jackson, the British minister, and promising support to the administration. 4°. 2 pages.

HENING, WILLIAM W. *Philadelphia.*

1799, July 29, Albemarle. Incloses proceedings upon the claim of Dr. Inglis before the board of commissioners under the sixth article of the treaty of amity and commerce between Great Britain and the United States. 4°. 1 page.

Washington.

1809, January 19, Richmond. Approves of the wise measures of the administration. Wishes him success. small 4°. 2 pages.

HENRY, ——— (Captain).

No date. His record, by an unknown person. fol. 1 page.

HENRY, JAMES, to MADISON.

1801, July 24, Northumberland. Calls to Madison's notice a friend, name not mentioned, who desires a position in the Government service. His good character described. 4°. 1 page.

HENRY, JAMES M.

1806, February 25, New York. Asks Madison's acceptance of a pipe of Madeira. [Note in Madison's hand. "Answered by a refusal."] 4°. 1 page.

HENSHAW, JOHN. . *Montpellier.*

1824, April 10. Madison's man Jesse wishes to be purchased in order to go with his wife, and the writer offers $300 for him if Madison approves of it. 4°. 1 page.

HERBERT, WILLIAM. *Washington.*

1803, March 18, Alexandria. Acknowledging letter of 16th. Presumes the sum remitted is to meet the discount at the bank of Monroe's notes. Has no claim against him and any money remitted will be placed to his credit. 4°. 1 page.

HERRICK, S.

1809, February 25, Muskingum, Ohio. In behalf of the citizens of this place transmits, as secretary of a meeting, resolutions approving the measures of the General Government. fol. 2 pages.

HERSAUT, (French Consul). *Montpellier.*

1830, June 22, New York. Pamphlets remitted by Baron Hyde de Neuville, and a letter from Madame de Neuville to Mrs. Madison. 4°. 1 page.

HERTTELL, THOMAS.

1819, November 11, New York. Presents a pamphlet entitled "An exposé of the causes of intemperate drinking and the means by which it may be obviated," and asks his opinion on it. 4°. 1 page.

1829, October 13, New York. Transmits by mail a copy of a pamphlet entitled "The Demurrer." Has read with pleasure Madison's memorial and remonstrance on the religious rights of man, addressed to the general assembly of Virginia in 1784-'85. 4°. 2 pages.

HETH & RANDOLPH to MCGRAW, THOMAS. *Washington.*

1812, August—. Shipment of coal for the use of the President's house. 4°. 1 page.

——— to MADISON.

1812, August 20, James River. Bill of lading of coal for Washington. 8°. 1 page.

HETH, HENRY, to COLES, ISAAC.

1812, September 1, Black Heath. Wishes the explanation of Thomas Magraw's refusal to pay a bill of coal ordered for Madison by Col. Coles. 4°. 1 page.

HETH & RANDOLPH to MAGRAW, THOMAS.

1812, September 4, Manchester. On refusal of Magraw to accept a draft in payment of coal furnished Madison. Sends copy of letter from Col. Coles ordering the same. 4°. 1 page.

HEWITT, THOMAS, and others, to MADISON.

No date. Petition of citizens of the first ward of Washington to appoint Richard S. Briscoe a justice of the peace. 4°. 2 pages.

HICHBORN, BENJAMIN.

1803, April 3, Dorchester. Introducing Mr. Nathaniel F. Fosdick, late collector of Portland. Has been unjustly deprived of his office and wishes to have him retained in office. 4°. 1 page.

HICKLEY, JAMES, to UNKNOWN.

17 6, March 7, Baltimore. Order of Madison's for the purchase of millstones and inquiries relative to a miller. 4°. 1 page.

HILL, BISSETS & CO., to MADISON. *Washington.*

1803, December 31, Madeira. Circular recommending Gordon, Duff & Co., as their successors in business in Madeira, [This is annexed to a letter filed of Gordon, Duff & Co., of this date.] 4°. 1 page.

HILL, MARK LANGDON. *Montpellier.*

1820, April 17, Washington. Regrets that owing to press of business he was unable to visit Madison and Jefferson. Sends a letter from Jefferson to Governor Langdon, and the latter's answer, to be returned after perusal. 4°. 3 pages.

HILLHOUSE, JAMES, and others. *Washington.*

1811, March 11, New Haven, Conn. Petition of the inhabitants of New Haven for the President to convene Congress to enable them to grant relief to the petitioners, who are suffering from the non-importation law, and repeal it. 4°. 4 pages.

HILTSHEIMER, JACOB.

1791, September 2. Receipted bill for horse keeping. strip of paper.

HINDE, THOMAS S. *Montpellier.*

1829, July 23, Urbana, Ohio. The critical state of our national affairs. Compliments Madison on his administration. Hears Madison is writing a political history of our country. When a youth the writer was the organ of the first disclosure in the West of the plot for dismemberment of the Union. fol. 3 pages.

Richmond.

1829, September 26, Urbana, Ohio. Incloses two bundles of papers containing a condensed sketch of the transactions of a national affair important in its day. Trusts Madison's labors at Richmond may be crowned with success. fol. 1 page.

Montpellier.

1830, January 26, Urbana, Ohio. Acknowledging copy of the new constitution of Virginia. Hopes it will be adopted. Is preparing a weekly paper as a compiler for western researches, antiquities, western sketches, etc. fol. 1 page.

1832, August 20, Urbana, Ohio. Remarkable coincidence of the death of three Presidents occurring on July 4. Reflections on the better state of existence beyond the tomb. Reviews Madison's life and administration. The triumph of religious liberty in our country. fol. 3 pages.

HIORT, HENRY. *Washington.*

1807, November 17, Washington. Solicits the influence of Madison for the appointment of marshal of this district, Mr. Brent having notified his intention of resigning. 4°. 1 page.

HITCHCOCK, J. *Montpellier.*

1825, June 24, Richmond. Bill for a pump receipted. strip of paper.

HITCHCOCK, J. IRVINE.

1830, October 20, Baltimore. Bill for subscription to the "American Farmer." fol. 1 page.

HITE, GEORGE, to UNKNOWN. *Washington.*

1809, February 23, Charleston. Wishes the person to whom this letter is addressed to confer with Madison respecting a Government situation for his son Robert. fol. 2 pages.

HITE, JAMES M., to MADISON. *Montpellier.*

1825, September 10, Guilford. On sheep-raising.
4°. 1 page.

HOFFMAN, DAVID.

1833, February 14, Baltimore. Contemplates traveling in Europe and would like letters of introduction.
4°. 1 page.

HOGAN, ——. *Washington.*

1810, March 14, Washington. Incloses a pamphlet as a tribute of respect. 4°. 1 page.

HOLLAND, EDWIN C. *Montpellier.*

1822, November 15, Charleston. Incloses a pamphlet recently published. 4°. 1 page.

HOLLAND, LORD, to JOY, GEORGE. *London.*

1806, November 17, London. Acknowledging letter of August 25. Did not find Joy's letter of July 4, among Mr. Fox's papers. [*See* Joy's letter to Lord Holland of November 20, 1806.]
4°. 1 page.

1806, November 21, London. Acknowledging letter of November 20. Thanks him for the extract which accompanies it. [*See* letter from George Joy to Lord Holland, dated November 20, 1806.] [Copy.]

HOLLEN, H. VON, to UNKNOWN.

1807, October 13, 27, and November 3, Hamburg. Extracts from three letters, unsigned, relative to goods consigned per the vessel *Eleanora* and the cargo detained at the custom-house. Also relative to the seizure by the Government of cargo of ship *Julius Henry* and her detention. [Copy.]
4°. 3 pages.

HOLLEY, HORACE, to MADISON. *Montpellier.*

1827, February 2, Lexington, Ky. Intending to travel in Europe as a literary and philosophical inquirer. Ask for letters of introduction.
4°. 1 page.

HOLLINS, JOHN. *Washington.*

1808, March 1, Baltimore. Order of the governor of Bermuda to not allow any vessel touching there with provisions to proceed to any other place, consequently the ship *Monticello* must have a particular pass. Practice of covering by insurance companies, British, French and Spanish property. Annexed is extract of a letter being an order for insurance on ship *Monticello.*
4°. 3 pages.

HOLLINSHEAD, BENJAMIN.

1816, February 3, Charleston. Petitions the President to order the Secretary of State to record his new adopted name. He changes his practice of medicine to Divinity, also intends to be admitted to the bar. 4°. 2 pages.

1816, February 27, Charleston. Is desirous of corresponding with the President. Asks him to interest himself in procuring subscriptions to reprinting the assemblies and catechism.
4°. 1 page.

HOLLOWAY, PETER.

1803, December 10, Shelburn, Mass. Submits an inclosed article on the raising of wheat by the Siberians, and why the wheat fly does not affect their wheat berry, while it does ours.
fol. 2 pages, and 2 strips of paper.

HOLMES, CHARLES. *Washington.*

1811, July 27, Charleston. Irregularties in the revenue department in Charleston. large fol. 3 pages.

HOLMÈS, JOHN.

1814, February 24, Boston. Albert Smith not being confirmed by the Senate as collector of Plymouth County, recommends Aaron Hobart, of Hanover, as a suitable person for the office. 4° 1 page.

1815, October 26, Alfred, Me. Introducing A. K. Paris. 4°. 1 page.

HOMANS, BENJAMIN.

1801, August 10, Bordeaux. Unjust removal of Mr. Isaac Cox Barnet from the consulate at Bordeaux to give place to Mr. Lee, who is less deserving. 4°. 6 pages.

——— and others.

1810, July 12, Boston. In behalf of the Bunker Hill Association, a copy of the oration delivered on July 4, is presented, with wishes that he may enjoy the satisfaction of seeing our country flourish in peace and union under the happy influence of his wise and salutary administration. 4°. 1 page.

———.

1814, December 13, Washington. Sends the brevet commission for Capt. Sevier for the President's signature. Also sends warrants for midshipman. 4°. 1 page.

Montpellier.

1815, August 11, Washington. Submits for the President's consideration a letter from Capt. Arthur Sinclair. 4°. 1 page.

HOMER, BENJAMIN.

1815, September 12, Washington. Appropriations for "Ordnance" and "Purchase and equipment of captured vessels" being expended, requests the President to direct a transfer to their aid from other appropriations. 4°. 1 page.

HONYMAN, ROBERT.

1812, June 23. Apologizes for his abrupt departure from Madison's mansion, which was owing to his feeling of the approach of an infirmity which required seclusion. 4°. 2 pages.

HOOE, J. H. *Washington.*

1810, May 4, Alexandria. Importation of Merino sheep. Some are intended for Madison and some for Jefferson. Asks instructions with regard to them. 4°. 2 pages.

1810, October 13, Alexandria. Has received another parcel of sheep from Lisbon from which Madison is to select two ewes. Requests him to send for them. 4°. 1 page.

1810, October 14, Alexandria. Respecting two ewes received from Mr. Jarvis from Lisbon for the President, the cost and expenses. 4°. 2 pages.

1810, October 19, Alexandria. Acknowledging letter of 17th, respecting prices to be paid for Merino sheep imported from abroad. 4°. 1 page.

HOOE & CO., ROBERT.

1804, December 13, Alexandria. Notice of shipment of goods received per the *Unity*. 4°. 1 page.

HOOMES, JOHN. *New York.*

1789, July 27, Bowling Green, Va. Thinks of moving to Kentucky. The lands there finest in the world. Asks Madison's opinion as to the prospect of trade down the Mississippi and whether New Orleans will be made a free port. fol. 2 pages.

Washington.

1803, January 4, Richmond. Incloses a receipt from Col. Newton for $100.
4°. 1 page, and strip of paper.

New York.

1790, May 18, Bowling Green, Va. Recommends Capt. Twining, who has a memorial before Congress.
4°. 1 page.

HOPKINS, B. B. *Washington.*

1813, August 3, Philadelphia. Resolution of the Philadelphia Bible Society, transmitting a copy of the Scriptures for himself and one to each House of Congress. 4°. 2 pages.

HOPKINS, JOHN. *Orange.*

1784, January 3. Receipts of lottery tickets to be sent to Philadelphia to procure certificates for them for account of Thomas Underwood. Numbers given. 8°. 1 page.

——— to MADISON. *New York.*

1789, April 10, Richmond. Wishes to retain the office he now holds, as loan officer of the United States in the State of Virginia and receiver of Continental taxes. 4°. 2 pages.

Philadelphia.

1797, January 3, Richmond. Incloses a draft for $200 by direction of Gen. Jonathan Clarke.
4°. 1 page.

HORSE-BREEDING.

1803, March 16. Memorandum of bills to certain parties for services. [Apparently by Madison's overseer.] 4°. 1 page.

HOSACK, DAVID, to MADISON. *Montpellier.*

1824, September 29, New York. Notice of his election as honorary member of the New York Horticultural Society. 4°. 1 page.

HOTZ, PETER, JR.

1829, December 8, Washington. Sends Madison the President's message. 4°. 1 page.

HOUGEWORTH, V. M.

1829, June 10, Fredericksburg. Asks Madison to remit the amount of a draft due. 4°. 1 page.

HOUSE, WILLIAM. *Washington.*

1813, November 11, Philadelphia. Solicits a removal from his present station to one more congenial to his wishes and where he can more effectually serve his country. 4°. 1 page.

HOUSTON, JAMES.

1804, April 10, Philadelphia. Presents him with a pamphlet. Contemplates a lottery for a fund to reward discoveries in medicine. 4°. 1 page.

HOUSTON, SAMUEL.

1809, February 14, Natural Bridge. In view of the straits and perils of the present condition of our country, recommends the appointment of a day of prayer and fasting when he enters the new station of President. fol. 3 pages.

HOWARD, CHARLES P.

1806, June 5. Incloses amount of subscription to Mr. Smith for his paper. A worm has appeared which attacks wheat and most kind of grasses and Indian corn. [Signature torn off.] 4°. 1 page.

1807, April 27. Insurance on Madison's house. 4°. 1 page.

1811, April 1, Woodly. Announcing the death of Dr. Willis. Suggests that it be announced in Gale's paper. 4°. 1 page.

1811, May 30, Mowbray. Having been chosen a director for constructing a turnpike between Fredericksburg and Swift River Gap, asks Madison's advice as to the best means of construction and whether he thinks the stock will be a good investment. fol. 2 pages.

Montpellier.

1818, March 8. Sends a file of Franklin's newspapers prior to 1740, having belonged to his grandfather. 4°. 1 page.

HOWARD, J., MARCH & CO. *Washington.*

1816, February 22, Madeira. Invoice of a pipe of Madeira by ship *Mary and Frances*, with bill of exchange attached. 4°. 1 page. 8°. 1 page.

HOWELL, DAVID.

1801, March 30, Providence. Incloses a paper from an old and capable officer of the Government, requesting that he may not be removed from office. Another from the writer's son who wishes to be a candidate as surveyor of customs. 4°. 2 pages.

1810, November 26, Providence. The office of judge. Does not approve of Mr. Asher Robbins, who is advocated by the Federalists, who are inimical to Governor Fenner, and whose political character as a monarchist and speculator unfit him for the place. Thinks the present district judge (having been previously district attorney) is more worthy of promotion. 4°. 3 pages.

1810, November 28, Providence. Incloses a letter from the late Governor Sullivan to himself showing the high trust confided to him by Gen. Washington. Whatever the President intends to do towards rendering his future days comfortable and happy, will receive a candid and liberal consideration. 4°. 1 page.

1811, October 12, Providence. Introducing his son, lately elected U. S. Senator from Rhode Island. [Signature cut off.] 4°. 1 page.

1812, October 22, Providence. The state of politics in the State of Rhode Island. Depression of the Republican party. Its cause, a schism. 4°. 3 pages.

HOWELL, JOSEPH. *Philadelphia.*

1790, December 28, Philadelphia. Respecting the claim of Wm. O'Callis for lands allowed by Congress for pay for services in the Army. fol. 1 page.

1792, February 23, Philadelphia. Statement of the paymaster in the Army of the account of Col. Alexander Spotswood. His claim barred by act of limitation. [*See* letter of Alexander Spotswood, February 11, 1792.] 4°. 1 page.

HOWELL, JOSEPH.

1792, November 21, Philadelphia. Incloses papers with notes by himself at the Army accountant's office. fol. 1 page.

HOYT, MOSES. *Washington.*

1810, September 28, New York. Appeal from a prisoner to the President for a pardon. small 4°. 2 pages.

HUBBARD, J. *Montpellier.*

1826, July 15, Norwich. Sends copy of a dirge written on the occasion of the simultaneous death of Adams and Jefferson on July 4, 1826. 4°. 2 pages.

HUBBARD, SIMEON.

1826, July 12, Norwich, Conn. An article which the writer calls a dirge, a paper complaining of the present administration. 4°. 3 pages.

1833, July 25, Norwich, *Conn.* Our defective Constitution. Requests Madison to draw articles for a new constitution, predicated on the "let alone" system. That Congress may not have the power to lay countervailing duties. Does not approve of the protective system. 4°. 2 pages.

HUGER, BENJAMIN. *Washington.*

1815, March 27, Georgetown, S. C. Introducing Lieut. Kinlock. 4°. 2 pages.

HULL, ANDREW, JR.

1812, August 7, *Cheshire, Conn.* Denies the representations of those unfriendly to the Government that the declaration of war is unpopular, even among Republicans. The determined stand of the Republican party. Is ready to volunteer as a private if necessary. fol. 2 pages.

1812, August 7, New Haven. The governor and council have refused to comply with the requisition of the Secretary of War in calling out the militia. fol. 1 page.

HULL, ISAAC, to JONES, WILLIAM.

1814, May 11, Portsmouth, N. *H.* Incloses copy of a letter from New Haven, by a respectable gentleman, giving information of an expedition of the British against Capt. Hull's force. Defenseless state of Portsmouth Harbor. [*See* Wm. Jones's letter to Madison, dated June 6, 1814, lettered G and H. Copy.] fol. 3 pages.

1814, May 29, Portsmouth, N. *H. See* Wm. Jones' letter to Madison, dated June 6, 1814, lettered F. [Extract.] fol. 1 page.

HULSHOFF, M. A., to MADISON.

1814, June 1, New York. Depicting the horrors of war, appeals to the President to make peace. 4°. 4 pages.

HUMBERT, JONAS.

1811, July 8, New York. As a victim, he has been sacrificed to gratify the Clinton faction of this city. He held the office of assistant to the inspector-general of flour and meal. Appeals for appointment to a Government position. fol. 4 pages.

HUMBERT, JONAS, JR.

1813, January 22, New York. Appeals to the President from the order of Gen. Armstrong to stop a

HUMBERT, JONAS, JR.

portion of his pay. Also relates the injustice done his father by the Clinton party and urges him to give him Government employment. fol. 5 pages.

HUMBOLDT, ALEXANDER VON.

1804, May 24, Philadelphia. Forwards a package for Madison from the U. S. consul at Havana. Has been traveling in South America and intends returning to Europe with the fruits of his scientific labors. After witnessing the physical grandeurs of nature in those countries, he is desirous of the moral spectacle of a free people worthy of their grand destiny. [Signature cut off. In French.] 4°. 3 pages.

1804, June —, Philadelphia. Assures Madison of the enjoyments he has experienced in his visit to Washington. Intends sailing for Bordeaux on the 28th. Requests some alterations to be made in his passport. In making his adieus he hopes to return to this country and make extensive explorations. [In French.] 4°. 4 pages.

1804, June 21, Philadelphia. Change in his passport for himself and secretary. [In French.] 4°. 3 pages.

1804, June 27, Philadelphia. Acknowledging letter of 24th, with his passport. Possibilities of communication from sea to sea at the isthmus. Indicates the possible routes. [In French.] 4°. 2 pages.

1810, September 23, Paris. Recalls Madison's kind attentions to him while in the United States in 1804. Sends him the result of his geographic works on Mexico. Recommends to the President Mr. Warden, who carries this letter, and to render justice to him who seems to have displeased some prominent personage. [In French.] 4°. 3 pages.

1813, August 26, Paris. His admiration for Mr. Barlow, whose wife takes this letter. Recalls with pleasure his friendly intercourse, while in this country, with Madison and Jefferson. Recommends Mr. Warden, late consul-general at Paris, who has displeased Gen. Armstrong, American minister, and asks Madison to interest himself in this talented and worthy man. [In French.] 4°. 4 pages.

1813, November 13, Paris. Introduces a young American, Mr. Dickens. Renews his request that Madison would interest himself in Mr. Warden, who is suffering under unjust charges. [In French.] 4°. 2 pages.

HUME, CHARLES.

1806, February 13, Elkrun, Va. Offers for sale to Madison a piece of land in Orange county. 4°. 1 page.

HUMPHREYS, DAVID.

1807, September 26, New York. Incloses a letter from Gen. Lafayette and sends dispatches from Monroe. Asks that attention may be paid to his accounts which, with documents, vouchers, etc., are deposited in the Department of State. 4°. 2 pages.

1812, January 10, Humphreysville. New machine for spinning yarn of various kinds. 4°. 2 pages.

HUMPHREYS, DAVID.

1813, February 19, Boston. Introducing Jacob Perkins, of Newburyport, author of several ingenious and useful inventions. Gives his own views in respect to the political state of the country, and the probability of narrowing the breach existing between Great Britain and the United States. Claims against France for spoliations committed. 4°. 7 pages.

1813, March 20, Humphreysville, Conn. Awkward situation of the British fleet now at this station. Were we prepared there would be little danger of loss on our part. Incloses a paper respecting this matter. In case of a speedy peace, a glorious opportunity will be presented for aiming an effectual blow at Algiers, and overthrow that viperous nest of haughty and contemptible pirates. 4°. 3 pages.

1816, March 5, New Haven. Introducing Mr. Pollard, of Boston. 4°. 1 page.

HUMPHREYS, HOSEA.

1815, December 31, Providence. Incloses a pamphlet containing his political sentiments. 4°. 2 pages.

HUNT, ABRAHAM. *New York.*

1790, July 9, Boston. Appeals to Madison to advocate back pay due him as a Revolutionary soldier, and compensation for seizure of his property by the British. 4°. 2 pages.

HUNT, G. J. *Montpellier.*

1821, May 1, New York. Incloses the prospectus of a new work which he requests Madison to sign and return. 4°. 1 page.

HUNTER, JOHN. *Washington.*

1801, April 16, Huntsville. Giving account of the state of politics in South Carolina, and his own views. 4°. 8 pages.

HUNTER, JOHN D. *Montpellier.*

1824, October 15, Philadelphia. His publishers neglected to send Madison a copy of his book as directed. Has brought seeds from England; will furnish Madison a few if he wishes. 4°. 2 pages.

HUNTINGTON, EBEN.

1817, December 30, Washington. Incloses a copy of the documents presented by the officers of the Revolutionary Army accompanying their petitions to Congress for half pay from 1793. Asks whether the proposition was suggested by Congress to the Army to commute the half pay, or by the Army to Congress. 4°. 2 pages.

HUNTINGTON, HEZ. *Washington.*

1812, August 29, New Haven. Proceedings of the Connecticut legislature respecting the organizing of volunteers. 4°. 3 pages.

HUNTINGTON, H., JR. *Montpellier.*

1833, April 12, Hartford. Proposes to Madison to write a history of the United States, particularly that portion of it subsequent to the war of the Revolution. Thinks it will prove acceptable to the community as well as pecuniarily advantageous. Will make liberal compensation for such a work. 4°. 2 pages.

HUNTINGTON, JED. *Washington.*

1805, May 16, New London. The drafts of Mr. Cathalan has been paid to William Hazard. 4°. 1 page.

HUNTINGTON, SAMUEL.

1809, February 13, Chillicothe. Inclosing resolutions of the general assembly of Ohio, approving the measures of the General Government. Acknowledging a letter to the legislature recommending the prevention of selling spiritous liquors to Indians. fol. 1 page. 4°. 3 pages.

1810, February 22, Chillicothe, Ohio. Transmits a resolution of the general assembly of the State of Ohio, approbating the measures of the General Government. 4°. 1 page. fol. 1 page.

HURLBUT, M. L. *Montpellier.*

1830, April 25, Charleston. Incloses a pamphlet. Asks Madison, as the surviving member of the convention which formed the Federal Constitution, to set him right on certain questions. Considers the present a momentous period, and asks his opinion as to the relative powers and duties of the Federal and State governments. 4°. 3 pages.

1830, June 15, Charleston. Thanks Madison for his letter (without date). Concurs in his opinion relative to his interpretation of certain portions of the Constitution. Does not believe that it is a mere compact or league between sovereign States. It would be insufficient to hold them together. 4°. 3 pages.

HURT, JOHN (Reverend).

1790, June —. Notes on David Ramsey's History of the American Revolution. fol. 8 pages. 4°. 2 pages. 8°. 2 pages.

HURT, JOHN. *Philadelphia.*

1795, May 12. Price of a horse that Madison wishes to buy. Would like to know the price of Mr. Smith's tract of land, if he will agree to take in part payment some Kentucky land. fol. 2 pages.

HUTCHINS, HENRY J. *Washington.*

1809, February 13, Philadelphia. Advice as to the measures Madison is to pursue when he exchanges his duties as Secretary of State for that of President. To place reliance on his own judgment, and to keep his own counsel. 4°. 3 pages.

1814, March 14, Philadelphia. Solicits the nomination for a suitable station in the post-office, either of this or some other State. 4°. 1 page.

HUTTON, JOSEPH.

1815, October 9, Philadelphia. Solicits the patronage of Madison for a poem on the subject of the victory at Plattsburg, and gives a specimen of it. Wishes to dedicate it to the President, with his signature at the head of the subscription list. 4°. 2 pages.

Montpellier.

1818, October 2, Petersburg, Va. Solicits his name to the inclosed prospectus of a literary work. 4°. 1 page.

HUTTON, NICHOLAS.

1817, June 25, Laverick Hall, Durham, England. Wishes for encouragement in making such arrangements as might lead to the execution of a project for the improvements of agriculture in this country. large fol. 3 pages.

IHLEY, D., and others. *Washington.*

1809 (?), not dated. Proposal that Mr. Granger should be advanced to one of the Cabinet departments under the next administration. small 4°. 1 page.

ILLINOIS, TERRITORY OF, to CONGRESS, U. S.

Not dated. Proposition to purchase of the U. S. Government, a valuable saline on Saline Creek, near the Ohio River, on certain terms as specified. Signed by Speaker of the House of Representatives and president of the council. fol. 8 pages.

——— to MADISON.

1812, December 4. (*See* Fisher, George, Speaker of the House of Representatives.)

INDIANS, CONNISSTOGA, to PENN, JOHN (Governor of Pennsylvania).

1763, November 30, Connisstoga. An address, signed by Sohay, Cuyanguerricosa, and Saguyasotha, asking the friendly aid and protection of the Government. large fol. 1 page.

INDIAN SPEECH.

1776 (?). Speech of an Ottawa chief delivered early in the Revolution, promising hospitality and friendship. fol. 1 page.

INDIANS, PEACE WITH. *Unknown.*

1790 (?), not dated. Hints to bring about a peace with all the Indians and to extend the trade of Virginia to the West. fol. 1 page.

INDIANS, DEPREDATIONS OF, to MADISON. *Washington.*

1812. Talks of a deputation of Indians at Washington at the commencement of the war, followed by a memorandum of the points which it is probable the President will take notice of. 4°. 19 pages.

INDIAN TALKS.

1812. Talks of chiefs of several tribes of Indians at Washington at the commencement of the war of 1812. 4°. 24 pages.

INGERSOLL, CHARLES J.

1808, November 26, Philadelphia. Forwards a pamphlet on the foreign relations of the United States. Since the *Chesapeake* affair no true Americans can oppose the measures of the Government. 4°. 2 pages.

1811, January 10, Philadelphia. The author of "Inchiquin's" letters on the United States begs the President to accept one of the earliest copies of that work. Asks that he may not make the author's name known. [Unsigned.] 4°. 1 page.

1811, February 26, Philadelphia. Removes the injunction to conceal his authorship of a pamphlet sent him. The "Inchiquin letters." His object in its publication. 4°. 2 pages.

1813, April 24, Philadelphia. Recommends the appointment of Dr. James Rush as treasurer of the Mint. 4°. 2 pages.

1814, January 5, Washington. Recommends the appointment of Richard Bache as postmaster at Philadelphia. 4°. 1 page.

1814, January 18, Washington. Incloses a letter from a lieutenant who states the Army is jeopardized for want of a competent number of officers. 4°. 1 page.

INGERSOLL, CHARLES J.

1814, February 15, Washington. Incloses a letter, and has received others, and verbal communications complaining of gross frauds which are practiced by the Postmaster-General, or his immediate agents, in contracts for carrying the mails. 4°. 1 page.

1814, July 18, Philadelphia. His advocacy of the principle that free ships make free goods. Is fortified in his reasoning by the perusal of a treaties published in Amsterdam. Has translated it into English and will use it in Congress next session. The mistake of Americans in not reading anything but English books, on the supposition that they are acknowledged authorities on law and politics by all nations. fol. 3 pages.

1814–'15 (?). Quotes Smollet's continuation of Hume of an account of the dispute with Spain in 1737 respecting the right of search. 4° 1 page.

1815, March 7, Philadelphia. Appointment of Commodore Bainbidge to the command of the expedition against Algiers. Has no opinion of his professional talents. His ill luck is invariable. fol. 3 pages.

1817, January 16, Philadelphia. Particulars of the illness and death of A. J. Dallas. 4°. 2 pages.

Montpellier.

1817, December 25, Philadelphia. Intending to write a history of the late war with England. Asks Madison to furnish him with materials. 4°. 3 pages.

1829, July 21, Philadelphia. Introducing Count Ney, son of Marshal Ney. 4°. 1 page.

1831, January 21, Harrisburg, Pa. His opinion on the incorporation of State banks. Asks Madison whether there is any State power to make paper banks. 4°. 2 pages.

1831, November 31, Philadelphia. Incloses an address, of which he asks Madison's opinion. Does not despair of visiting Montpellier. 4°. 1 page.

1834, August 13, Philadelphia. Introducing his son Charles. 4°. 1 page.

1835, January 27, Philadelphia. Incloses a notice he had just published on a constructive power of each House of Congress. 8°. 2 pages.

1836, April 28, Washington. Announces his intention to visit Madison in company with his daughter. 4°. 1 page.

1836, May 9, Philadelphia. His pleasant visit at Montpellier. Regrets that he could not make a longer one. Promises himself to make another visit. His instructive conversations there. The Texas contest. Fears a collision between Mexico and the United States. 4°. 3 pages.

INGERSOLL, JARED. *Washington.*

1810, January 28, Philadelphia. Introducing his son Charles. Awaiting anxiously the result of the deliberations of Congress on measures of defense. English depredations. 4°. 1 page.

1810, March 21, Philadelphia. Introducing his son Joseph. [Only a small part of this letter remains.] Strip of paper.

INGRAHAM AND SON, NATHANIEL.

1809, March 27, Charleston. Acknowledging the receipt of a commission as Navy agents. 4°. 1 page.

INNERARITY, JAMES, to TOULMIN, HENRY.

1810, November 22. Mobile. Acknowledging letter of 20th. Arrival of Governor Folch. Conversations with him on the critical situation of affairs in West Florida. Efforts to maintain peace. [Answer to this letter on last sheet.] 4°. 3 pages.

Mobile.

1810, November 24, Mobile. The governor desirous of bringing the present discontent to a happy issue with a view of making arrangements for putting the country under the protection of the United States. Asks Toulmin to exercise all his influence to induce Col. Sparkes to prevent a wanton and useless effusion of blood. 4°. 2 pages.

INNES, HARRY, to MADISON. *Washington.*

1801, June 11, Cincinnati. Objects to the appointment of John Smith as marshal of this district and recommends Dr. Richard Allison. For district attorney he prefers Jacob Bennet to the other aspirants. 4°. 3 pages.

1813, April 25, Frankfort. Has sued Humphrey Marshall for villainous and virulent attacks. To rebut certain charges as to his complicity with Gen. Wilkinson in carrying on illicit and traitorous correspondence with Spanish officers, would like to procure from the State Department an official copy of the specifications which were exhibited to the court-martial at Fredericktown. Asks the President to have the copy made. 4°. 2 pages.

INNES, JAMES. *New York.*

1789, August 27, Richmond. Holds lands as a bounty, by Virginia, being a late officer in Continental service. A resolution of Congress, if carried into effect, will probably deprive him of his lands. Asks Madison's endeavors to have the obnoxious and oppressive act rescinded. 4°. 1 page.

INTERNAL IMPROVEMENTS.

1831, August. (*See* Parks, Andrew, Chairman.)

INNES, JAMES, to UNKNOWN.

No year, November 9. Excuses himself to keep an appointment on account of the wish of the President to meet him at that time. 4°. 1 page.

IRWIN, NATHANIEL, to MADISON. *Washington.*

1801, March 31, Bucks County, Pa. Congratulating him as Secretary of State. Has a son who wishes a Government clerkship. Gives a sketch of his own life, in which he is devoted to the cause of republicanism. large fol. 3 pages.

1802, October 1, Bucks County, Pa. Organization of a post-road from Philadelphia to New York. Suggests appointments of Republicans which he names for postmasters. Calls attention to the appointment of his son as ensign in the Army, which did not pass the Senate. large fol. 3 pages.

1811, March 15, Bucks County, Pa. Asks that the President transmit an inclosed letter to Mr. Granger (Postmaster-General). An indorsement at foot in Madison's writing of the respectability and character of Irwin. fol. 1 page.

IRVINE, WILLIAM, to DAVIES (Colonel).

1792, July 18. Acknowledging letter of June 26. Respecting certain accounts connected with State and Federal debts. [Copy.] 4°. 2 pages.

IZARD, GEORGE, to MADISON. *Washington.*

1814, July 18, Camp near Plattsburg. Has delivered the note, covering a letter for Col. Lear, to him in person. 4°. 1 page.

JACKSON, ANDREW, to CRAWFORD, W. H.

1816, September 7, Chickasaw Nation. Incloses an account of the capture of the negro fort on the Apalachicola. Anticipates war with Spain. Is prepared for what may occur. The command of the lower country, including Orleans and the Mississippi, important for us. Suggests certain movements of troops. 4°. 3 pages.

JACKSON, G., to MADISON. *Orange.*

1801, February 5, Washington. Conjectures as to the result of the Presidential election. Voting to commence on the 11th in the House. 4°. 2 pages.

1801, March 3, Washington. Acknowledging letter of February 14. Has no doubt Madison will be called to a high office, probably Secretary of State. Recommends Col. William Lowther as collector of public money. Sales of Northwestern lands. 4°. 1 page.

Washington.

1810, November 24, Zanesville. Application of the writer for the office of marshal for the State of Ohio, and Samuel Herrick for the office of district attorney. small 4°. 3 pages.

JACKSON, HENRY.

1816, April 26, Paris. Incloses an address relating to Mr. Williamson, the inventor of the Congreve rocket. Suggests the importance to this country of obtaining his practical experience. 4°. 3 pages.

JACKSON, JAMES. *Philadelphia.*

1795, November 17, Savannah. His resignation as a member of the Senate. Displeasure of the people of Georgia with the late Mississippi sale. Wishes Madison's influence in the House to restrain the Executive power and to have the act repealed. 4°. 8 pages.

Washington.

1801, May 15, near Savannah. Has been reelected as Senator of the United States. Politics of the State of Georgia. Disgust occasioned by recent appointments under the late administration. Suggestions as to appointments. 4°. 8 pages.

——— to GALLATIN, ALBERT.

1802, March 27, Washington. Asks him to deliver to the bearer the map of Georgia. Matters respecting the Georgia commissioners and the act authorizing the establishment of a government on the Mississippi. Impatience of the Georgia people for the delay in either paying for the territory or of restoring it. 4°. 2 pages.

——— to MADISON.

1803, March 6, Baltimore. Asks Madison's good offices in procuring from the Marquis d'Yrujo a letter of

JACKSON, JAMES.

recommendation for Mr. Thomas Collier to the governor of East Florida, to enable him to collect a sum of money due him from a Mr. Atkinson, now holding a commission under the Spanish governor. fol. 2 pages.

JACKSON, JOHN G.

1799, May 14, Clarksburg. Incloses a letter to Miss Polly Paine. Madison's election to the State legislature. Republicanism gaining in this district. fol. 1 page.

1800, September 25, Clarksburg. Auspicious appearance of political events. Thinks Jefferson will be the next President. Liberty will shine refulgent, etc. fol. 2 pages.

1805, April 29, Clarksburg. Acknowledging letters of March 21 and April 1. Rupture between England and Spain. The elections in Virginia. 4°. 2 pages.

1805, October 28, Clarksburg. Surveying of, and titles to land belonging to Mr. Lovel's relatives. 4°. 2 pages.

1806, June 15, Clarksburg. Has unlimited confidence in the Executive government. Conjectures as to Monroe's course on his return from England. Are we destined to engage in the contest in Europe? 4°. 3 pages.

1806, August 25, Clarksburg. Distress in his family and death of his children caused him to neglect a remittance of money which he now remits to pay a loan. 4°. 2 pages.

1807, June 21, Clarksburg. Acknowledging several letters inclosing foreign and domestic news. Sees with indignation the efforts made to defend Burr by attacking the Executive. Trusts he will have justice done him. 4°. 2 pages.

1807, July 5, Clarksburg. Surprised and indignant that he has been made the subject of a criminal prosecution at the instance of Burr. The court suffers the charge to be abandoned without investigation. Judge Marshall's dishonest partiality to the accused (Burr). Our tame submission to the outrages of Great Britain. We must not show weakness or pusilanimity. Our system the strongest on earth. 4°. 3 pages.

1807, August 2, Clarksburg. Resolutions of the people of this county to the President on the subject of the British outrage. No distinctions of party. Never any event better calculated to unite all parties and swallow up schismatics which have disgraced us so long. Anti-British spirit predominates. The wisdom of the Cabinet will shine conspicuous in its decision. 4°. 1 page.

1807, October 11, Clarksburg. Illness of himself and Mrs. Jackson has prevented his attending Congress on the first day of the session. Feels great solicitude on the subject of our national concerns. Asks Madison to inform him of the state of affairs. 4°. 2 pages.

1807, October 18, Clarksburg. Extreme illness and probable death of Mrs. Payne. Its bad effect on Mrs. Jackson, who has had an attack of paralysis. Situation alarming. 4°. 1 page.

JACKSON, JOHN G.

1807, October 25, Clarksburg. Death of Mrs. Payne. Mrs. Jackson extremely ill—fears she can not recover. 4°. 1 page.

1807, November 20, Clarksburg. Continued illness of Mrs. Jackson prevents their traveling. Snow 2 feet deep on the mountains. 4°. 1 page.

1807, November 29, Clarksburg. Acknowledging a letter. Is of opinion that the British pretensions would be supported at the risk of a war. Conjectures as to action of the House of Representatives. Hopes soon to be at his post in Washington. Mrs. Jackson no better. 4°. 2 pages.

1807, December 10, Clarksburg. Is ill from effects of an attempt to assassinate him by two criminals whom he was about to commit for trial. Is now convalescent. His wife better. 4°. 2 pages.

1807, December 25, Clarksburg. Is recovering from the effects of his attempted assassination. Describes the effects of his wounds. Is well enough to attend court. His curiosity as to the action of Congress, who are sitting with closed doors. Hostile appearance of the British proclamation. 4°. 1 page.

1808, January 7, Clarksburg. Serious apprehensions for the life of Mrs. Jackson. A relapse. 4°. 1 page.

1808, January 15, Clarksburg. Extreme illnesss of his wife. His accumulated trials and disappointments. 4°. 1 page.

1808, July 17, Clarksburg. Alluding to the death of his wife. His incalculable and unparalleled misfortunes. Contemplation of his country's affairs. The perfidy of our countrymen has been the chief cause of our embarrassments, with their ruinous measures. The mercantile cupidity. Disaffection in Massachusetts. fol. 2 pages.

1808, September 4, Clarksburg. Acknowledging letter of August 23. Has returned from a tour in West Pennsylvania. Thinks there will be a Republican majority there in the next election. False representations by the Federalists. Apprehensions about the health of his children. His deep melancholy. 4°. 2 pages.

1808, October 8, Harewood. Arrived at this place and found his children sick with bilious fever. Political excitement at Winchester. Federal stories of Secretary Smith, who boasts of opposing the President in the matter of the embargo. 4°. 1 page.

1809, March 24, Clarksburg. Exertions of the Federalists to elect their candidates. Believes, however, the Republican majority will not be diminished. 4°. 1 page.

1809, April 8, 18, Clarksburg. Elections in Virginia. 4°. 2 pages.

1890. May 15, Clarksburg. His calculations as to results of the elections in Virginia realized. Intends to go to Washington. 4°. 1 page.

1809, July 28, Harewood. President's proclamation. Will be glad if Congress will not be called. Authority of the President to reprohibit intercourse. Legality of nonintercourse. Is about to order a new carriage. Will buy Madison's if price is acceptable. 4°. 2 pages.

JACKSON, JOHN G. *Montpellier.*

1809, August 17, Clarksburg. The President's renewal of the nonintercourse with Great Britain. Insulting State paper of Canning's. Trusts that the people will express their indignation at this outrage. Congress should be goaded on by the people. 4°. 2 pages.

1809, October 12, Clarksburg. Apathy and indifference succeed the excitement produced by British perfidy. We must be cautious and not yield any important rights. Elections favorable. Advocates war or to lay embargoes. fol. 1. page.

Washington.

1810, January 9. The guardianship of his child. 4°. 1 page.

1810, September 13, Clarksburg. Accepts Madison's congratulations on his marriage. Intends resigning on account of ill health from an accident. 4°. 2 pages.

1810, September 29, Clarksburg. Recommends the appointment of Samuel Herrick as district attorney of Ohio. Was surprised at the appointment of Mr. Cass as marshal. His conversion to republicanism too recent. His abuse of Jefferson. 4°. 2 pages.

1810, November 17, Clarksburg. Majority of the Republican candidate, McKinley, as United States Representative, at the late State election. False assertion relating to McKinley. Asks for a copy of Washington's proclamation, relating to the Western insurrection, in order to refute the charge. Another false charge that Congress made an appropriation for no specific object, and divided it among the members. 4°. 3 pages.

1810, December 4, Clarksburg. Wishes to procure a pair of Merino sheep or a ram. 4°. 1. page.

1811, April 1, Clarksburg. Conjectures that Monroe is to fill the office vacated by Mr. Smith (Secretary of State). Announces the birth of a daughter. 4°. 2 pages.

1811, April 5, Clarksburg. Is mentioned as a successor to Judge Nelson, who has resigned his judicial office. Would like to be named by Madison to some friend at Richmond who would favor his views. 4°. 1 page.

1811, April 19, Clarksburg. Acknowledging letter of 12th. The Federal candidate elected over McKinley as Member of Congress. Jackson voted in as a member of the Virginia assembly. He hoped he would have been appointed to the office vacated by Judge Nelson. Will oppose any appointment to that place by his influence in the legislature, if he is not a native lawyer. His success in sheep-raising and domestic manufactures, etc. 4°. 3 pages.

1811, April 26, Clarksburg. Sheep-raising and wool. Sends a sample of a peculiar kind and wishes Madison's opinion. Public opinion will support Madison against factions of disappointed expectants in his public measures. 4°. 1 page.

1811, December 8, Washington. Arrival of Harrison at Vincennes after the battle at Prophet's town. A proper display of force and decision will pre-

vent concentration of the tribes next year. Is apprehensive that Congress will disappoint Madison's hopes and the nation's just expectations. They are too tardy for decision and vigor.
fol. 1 page.

1811, December 27, Richmond. Some particulars of the burning of the Richmond theater, when Jackson narrowly escaped with his life. Names of many of the killed. 4°. 3 pages.

1812, March 30, Clarksburg. Illness and death of Jackson's mother. Gloomy reflections on the inveterate hostility of the opposition. Proofs of British perfidy. Great Britain counts upon a party amongst us. Advocates a declaration of war. 4°. 2 pages.

1812, April 13, Clarksburg. The embargo laid by Congress; conjectures that the next step will be war. Is rejoiced that the national honor has demanded it. The war will become popular. Noble ends are pursued with noble means. Knows that Madison's administration has no other object.
4°. 1 page.

1812, June 26, Clarksburg. Is gratified at the declaration of war. Signifies his desire to be of service in the Army. The war will separate the partisans of England from the honest Federalists, and tar and feathers will cure their penchant for the enemy. 4°. 2 pages.

1812, July 24, Clarksburg. Acknowledging receipt of a commission from the executive of Virginia to superintend the line between the Virginia military reservation and the lands ceded to the United States by Virginia. Asks that the meeting of the commissioners be delayed three weeks on account of important business in the courts confided to him. 4°. 1 page.

1812, October 21, Franklinton. On his way to join the Northwestern army destined to Detroit. Application to Gen. Harrison for forage and rations for his mounted rifle corps. Finding Harrison not authorized to do so, volunteers to advance the sums required for compensation. Wishes to know if he can expect indemnity. For himself, he would refuse any compensation. Intentions of Harrison. The force described. Has resigned his office as commissioner to ascertain the boundary line of Virginia's military reservation. fol. 3 pages.

1813, May 3, Clarksburg. Has been elected member of Congress from his district. Is satisfied that the conduct of Great Britain is influenced more by a consideration of the power of their party here than a belief there is justice or policy in their profligate and wicked measures. Shall go to Washington when the session commences.
4°. 1 page.

1813, June 11, Washington. Requests that his father, George Jackson, may be appointed marshal for the State of Ohio. 4°. 1 page.

Montpellier.

1813, September 4, Clarksburg. Cautions Madison about returning too soon to Washington on account of prevailing bilious fever. Recommends persons for certain offices in Virginia.
4°. 2 pages.

JACKSON, JOHN G. *Washington.*

1815, January 10, Washington. Sufferings of the Twentieth Brigade of Virginia under his command at Norfolk. Victims of the bad climate. Asks if they may not be discharged or sent elsewhere. 4°. 2 pages.

Montpellier.

1815, May 8, Clarksburg. Events in Europe. Return of Bonaparte to the throne of France. Hopes the ministry of Great Britain will listen to the just maritime pretentions of the United States, and that a treaty of commerce will result from it. No danger of their provoking a new war with us. Virginia's assumption of the direct tax. No doubt she will be reimbursed for her advances to the militia. Assessments should stop. Too burthensome on the people. Congress should dispense with the tax. 4°. 3 pages.

1816, October 15, Clarksburg. Asks that the contract of Johnson & Co., for supplying rations to the military forces in the Southwest, should be continued. Hostility to the compensation bill. Political life not to be coveted. Hopes to retire from it when Madison's term closes. Has erected a blast furnace for making iron metal, with all the necessary buildings. Prospects of the crops. 4°. 2 pages.

JACKSON, JOSIAH. *Washington.*

1809, June 1, Charlotte C. H. Information respecting collateral branches of Madison's family. fol. 3 pages.

1810, April 23, Charlotte C. H. Asks Madison's advice where he can purchase good land in Virginia for a moderate sum. fol. 3 pages.

JACKSON, MATTHEW W. *Orange C. H.*

1836, February 6, Danville. In view of Madison's declining years, the writer, a Presbyterian minister, and distantly connected with his family, asks him if he has faith in God through Christ, and a lively hope of immortality, etc. 4°. 3 pages.

JAMES, DANIEL. *Washington.*

1809, July 31, Madison County, Va. Asks Madison whether there is a probable chance for a negotiation taking place with Great Britain, or are we to have no trade at all. Crops of wheat uncommonly good. small 4°. 2 pages.

JAMISON, JAMES, to CRAWFORD, WILLIAM H.

1816, August 27, Nachitoches (Indian Agency). Showing the advisability of removing the agency with the garrison and factory. Merchants here plunder the unsuspecting Indian after plying him with whisky. Assurances of a powerful tribe called the Comanchies of their friendship and hatred to the Spanish. Advises the cultivation of their friendship and giving them an idea of our importance, of which they are ignorant. Descriptions of other tribes. Intends to invite a few of the principal men of each station to bury the hatchet. 4°. 4 pages.

JARVIES, JAMES, to MADISON.

1816, July 30, London. From a boy whose blood swells in his veins when Madison is abused. 4°. 1 page.

JARVIES, WILLIAM, to MADISON.

1807, August 18, Lisbon. Acknowledging letter of June 17, inclosing a present. Sends some brandy, also a pipe of wine and some citrons per brig *Maria* for Alexandria. Will draw on Mr. Gallatin for the amount. "Private". 4°. 3 pages.

1807, August 20, Lisbon. Introducing Col. Sparhawk and his daughter. 4°. 1 page.

JAY, JAMES, to MADISON.

1808, May 11, New York. Change in politics in this State attributed to the unwearied exertions of the Federalists and the apathy of Republicans. Thinks' the Republicans will have a majority in the House of Representatives. The Senate sure for a large one. The embargo grossly misrepresented. Respecting the use of the vessel carrying messengers to England. fol. 2 pages.

1808, October 19, New York. Wishes to send his son to Paris to pursue his studies as engineer, he having a turn for military life. Asks whether his sending him to a military school will be attended with any difficulty. fol. 2 pages.

1811, June 7, New York. Acquaints him that there are persons in New York who are taking measures on a large scale to introduce British goods from Canada into the adjacent States. Trusts from this hint he may be enabled to defeat or diminish the impending evil. 4°. 1 page.

1811, July 1, New York. Intends going to Europe to reestablish his fortune. From his political opinions and course, he is apprehensive of difficulties in his pursuits. He asks for a passage for himself and son in the frigate which is to take out Mr. Barbour, he paying the expense of passage. fol. 2 pages

1811, July 11, New York. Disappointment in not being allowed to take passage in the frigate which takes Mr. Barbour to France. fol. 3 pages.

JAY, JOHN, to UNKNOWN.

1780, November 6, Madrid. Contents of a letter respecting his negotiations with the Spanish Government for a loan and a proposed treaty. [Copy.] small 4°. 35 pages.

——— to BARCLAY, THOMAS.

1787, October 5, New York. Incloses an act of Congress approving of his conduct in the late negotiations with Morocco. [*See* letter from Jefferson to Barclay, dated August 3, 1787.] [Copy.] 4°. 2 pages.

——— to MADISON. *New York.*

1789, December 2, New York. Intention of Mr. Jefferson to sail from the Isle of Wight for the Chesapeake. Incloses a bill of lading. The packages mentioned therein will be deposited in public store, where they will be perfectly safe. [Signature cut off.] 4°. 1 page.

———. *Philadelphia.*

1794, November 19, London. Treaty of amity, commerce, and navigation between Great Britain and the United States, with a resolution of the Senate ratifying the same. 4°. 29 pages. fol. 1 page.

JEFFERSON, GEORGE, to MADISON. *Washington.*

1805, September 14, Richmond. Acknowledging letter of 9th. Respecting the price of tobacco and prospects of crop. Advises Madison to hold his tobacco. Will advance on it if desired, and gives the necessary instructions as to drafts. 4°. 2 pages.

1805, October 29, Richmond. Advises him of the sale of his tobacco. 4°. 1 page.

1805, November 9, Richmond. Acknowledging letter of 4th. Incloses a draft for balance of account. 4°. 1 page.

1806, October 22, Richmond. Acknowledging letter of September 7. Supplying him with coal. 4°. 1 page.

1806, December 26, Richmond. Supplies the President and Madison with coal. 4°. 2 pages.

1807, October 24, Richmond. Shipment of coal for the President and Madison. Incloses a receipt of the captain of the sloop *Unity.* 4°. 1 page, and strip of paper.

1808, January 8, Richmond. Acknowledging letter of 4th, inclosing a check. 4°. 1 page.

——— to MONROE, JAMES.

1812, March 11, Lisbon. Difficulty in obtaining books and papers from the late consul, Mr. Green. Matters relating to the consular office charges. Charges for clearing and entering freights. 4°. 4 pages.

JEFFERSON to FRANKLIN, BENJAMIN. *Versailles.*

1781, October 5, Virginia. Introducing Col. James Monroe, a distinguished officer in the Revolution, intending going abroad to complete his studies. He will give details of the surrender of Cornwallis, etc. small 4°. 1 page.

1781, October 5, Virginia. Duplicate of the foregoing. small 4°. 1 page.

———, to MONROE, JAMES.

1781, October 5, Monticello. Incloses three letters of introduction to Benjamin Franklin, John Adams, and John Jay, respectively. Advises Monroe as to the place of residence in France and England to pursue his studies Mentions books left at Richmond, which may be of service to him. Wishes Monroe to correspond with him when abroad. small 4°. 1 page.

——— to MADISON. *Philadelphia.*

1783, January 31, Baltimore. Arrived in Baltimore after a fatiguing journey of five days and nights from Philadelphia. Relates an anecdote (in cipher, with translation) of Dr. Franklin and an unfortunate person who desired information of Franklin's negotiations with the Court of France. 4°. 2 pages.

1783, February 7, Baltimore. Attempts a passage in the ice to communicate with the Chevalier du Villebrun. Is informed of the strength of the British naval force. Jefferson's delayed departure on account of the bad condition of the ship selected. Suggests several means of getting abroad. Idle report of peace being actually concluded. Suggests Congress' interference to expedite his

JEFFERSON.

departure, and Madison's aid towards it. Postscript added on February 8, relating to a passport. 4°. 4 pages.

1783, February 14, Baltimore. Acknowledging letter of 11th. His views on the characters of Adams and Franklin as negotiators in the present commission (written in cipher). Extract of a letter in French of the Chevalier du Villebrun respecting the sailing of his ship, the *Romulus*. Abandons the idea of sailing in her. Conjectures as to the best means of going abroad. 4°. 3 pages.

1783, February 14, Baltimore. Incloses a package from Patsy. Her hieroglyphical writing. Friendly messages to his friends. 4°. 1 page.

1783, April 14, Susquehanna. Gives some directions for Mr. Ingles about sending books to Richmond. The last part of this letter in cipher. 4°. 1 page.

1783, May 7, Tuckahoe. Acknowledging letter of April 22. Respecting the impost. Conversion of State into Federal debts. A portion of this letter in cipher with a translation in Madison's hand relating to the state of parties in the Virginia legislature. The leaders criticised. Patrick Henry. Mr. Short wishes to be secretary of legation. small 4°. 5 pages.

1783, June 1, Monticello. Acknowledging letter of May 6. Patrick Henry declares in favor of the impost. Alludes to the family of Floyd, and Madison's interest in it. small 4°. 2 pages.

1783, June 17, Monticello. Acknowledging letters of May 13 and 20. Patrick Henry's course on the impost. Jefferson's ideas as to a new State constitution or amendments. small 4°. 2 pages.

Princeton.

1783, August 31, Monticello. Acknowledging letters of July 17. An allusion to an affair of the heart in which Miss Floyd was (probably) the object. Asks for a perusal of Madison's Congressional notes. His quarters in Philadelphia on the return of Congress thither. 4°. 4 pages.

——— to MONROE, JAMES. *Annapolis.*

1783, November 18, Philadelphia. Acknowledging letter of 9th. Thanks him for making arrangements for his residence. The President leaves for Annapolis on the 23d. 4°. 1 page.

——— to MADISON. *Orange.*

1783, December 11, Annapolis. Reception of the definitive treaty with a joint letter of our commissioners. The riot in Philadelphia and removal of Congress from thence makes a serious impression in Europe, and have excited doubts of the stability of our confederacy. Respecting Mr. and Mrs. Trist. 4°. 2 pages.

1784, January 1, Annapolis. Acknowledging letter of December 10. Views respecting Buffon's theory of the heat of the globe. Conjectures as to the ratification of the definitive treaty. European affairs. 4°. 2 pages.

JEFFERSON.

1784, February 20, Annapolis. Acknowledging letter of 11th. The procuring of some books for Madison. Bones of certain animals found in South America. Query as to their existence there before the advent of Spaniards. Question as to the ratification of the definitive treaty. No Secretary of Foreign Affairs yet appointed.. Plan to appoint Adams, Franklin, and Jay to conclude treaties with several European powers. (A passage in cipher not deciphered). Question of the residence of Congress. Cession of Virginia lands. Navigation of the Potomac and Ohio. The Virginia delegates to Congress. Criticisms on recent books. Offers Madison the use of his library. Monroe is buying land adjoining Jefferson's. Short also. 4°. 8 pages.

1784, March 16, Annapolis. Acknowledging letter of February 17th. Trembles at the idea of Mazzei coming to Annapolis. Asks Madison to exert himself to prevent it, he being a violent enemy of Franklin. Seven States only represent Congress. Advices from Franklin and Lafayette that North and Fox are out, and Pitt and Temple are coming in. The whole British nation indisposed towards us, not having lost the idea of reannexing us. The Marquis coming to America. Our ratification of the treaty on its way. Asks Madison to keep a diary. 4°. 2 pages.

1784, April 25, Annapolis. Act of Congress respecting the cession of land from Virginia. Clauses relating to hereditary powers and slavery. Votes of the States. Discussions relating to the place of next meeting of Congress. Dr. Lee appointed Indian commissioner. [A passage in cipher.] The question of empowering persons to privately buy up Virginia's quota of old Continental money. British debtors refuse to pay interest during the war. Difficulty of delegates getting their pay. Postscript dated April 30, giving English news. 4°. 4 pages.

1784, May 11. First part of this letter wanting. His determination to go to Boston and take shipping thence. Expects to be in Boston June 3. 4°. 1 page.

1784, May 25, Philadelphia. Acknowledging letters of 8th and 15th. Offers to purchase books for Madison abroad. Washington would accept the superintendence of the navigation of the Potomac. Assault of a Frenchman on Mr, Marbois. Question as to his punishment or giving him up to France. 4°. 4 pages.

1784, July 1, Boston. After visiting the New England States to acquire knowledge of their commerce, etc., returns to Boston, from whence he sails to London in the *Ceres*. His purpose is to take boat on the coast of France and proceed to Paris. The lower house of legislature of Massachusetts have passed a bill giving Congress power over their commerce. Draft in favor of Madison. 4°. 2 pages.

1784, November 11, Paris. Acknowledging letters of August 20 and September 7 and 15. Madison's observations on the navigation of the Mississippi approved of. Denies having any interest in speculative western lands. Books purchased in

JEFFERSON.

Paris for Madison. Account of a novelty in phosphorus matches; also, a new lamp with a hollow wick in the form of a cylinder giving the light of 8 candles. The lamp of war is kindled, not to be extinguished but by torrents of blood. Movements of troops in Holland. The hostility of England to us. Their Irish affairs will trouble them extremely. 4°. 6 pages.

1784, December 8, Paris. Acknowledging letter of October 11. His reasons for wishing to center our commerce at Norfolk to reduce the army of tax gatherers. The proposition for a convention in Virginia. (Here follows a cipher.) Trusts Virginia will do something for Paine. Looks anxiously for the approaching improvement of the navigation of the Potomac and Ohio. Urges Madison to take a trip to Europe. Wishes he would buy land in his vicinity. Monroe was trying to do. European intelligence. 4°. 4 pages.

1785, March 18, Paris. Acknowledging letter of February 1. (Many parts of this letter in cipher undeciphered). European politics, particularly to Holland. England sends a consul to America. We must show that we are capable of foregoing commerce with them before they will consent to an equal commerce. We have all the world to choose from and to buy our tobacco, and they depend upon us for it, and for transportation in their ships. Question of exempting Ireland from prohibition of commerce. Purchase of some books. [A lead pencil note on back of the sheet alludes to a proposed foreign appointment for Madison.] 4°. 4 pages.

1785, May 11, Paris. Acknowledging letter of January 9. Has made a cipher which he will transmit by Mr. Doradour. Has finished printing his notes. Will send Madison some copies. Not intended for general publicity. Thinks they will be useful for students in the William and Mary College. 4°. 2 pages.

1785, September 1, Paris. Acknowledging letters of January 22 and April 27. The Emperor and Dutch are agreed. The German confederation. Its object. The brig *Betsey* taken by the Emperor of Morocco given up to the Spanish Government. The only American vessel taken by the Barbary States. The Emperor of Morocco shows his friendly feeling for us. The late proceedings in America have produced a wonderful sensation in England in our favor, namely, the disposition to invest Congress with the regulation of our commerce. The misrepresentations of the London press prejudiced all Europe against us. The defeat of the Irish propositions is also in our favor. The purchase of valuable books for Madison. Procures a plan for the capitol in Virginia. The copying press. 4°. 4 pages.

1785, September 20, Paris. Manner of payment for the purchase of books abroad. Madison to do what best pleases him. Plans for public buildings in Virginia. Regrets that unavoidable delay has prevented sending designs and urges Madison to exert his influence to delay building before these plans are seen. The model taken for the capitol is from the Maison carré of Nismes.

4°. 3 pages.

JEFFERSON.

1785, October 28, Fontainebleau. Describes Fontainebleau and surroundings. Conversation with a laboring woman. Extreme low wages and poverty of the people. The rich proprietors of this part of France. His views on uncultivated lands and unemployed poor. Small landholders the most precious part of a State. Describes the deer, hares, and rabbits. Their habits differing from ours. Fruits of the country compared with ours. 4°. 4 pages.

1786, February 8, Paris. Acknowledging letters of August 20, October 3, and November 15. Sends bill of lading for books. Thanks him for the copy of the remonstrance against the assessment. Regulation of our commerce to Congress. Should other States concur it would produce a respect for us abroad. Annoyance at a publication of his notes in France without his permission. His purchases of books for Madison. Georgia's cession of land to Count d'Estaing. Hopes Virginia will present lands to Lafayette and Rochambeau. The inscriptions on the monument of Houdin's Washington. 4°. 6 pages.

1786, February 9, Paris. Inclosing a letter from Dr. Edward Bancroft respecting a debt of Virginia to Mr. Paradise. Asks Madison's aid in having justice done him. 4°. 1 page.

1786, April 25, London. Is in London for objects of the joint commission. Returns to Paris. Nothing done with this nation. The King against a change of measures, as are also the ministers and people. The merchants, though valuing our commerce, are persuaded they will enjoy it on their own terms. Interest on debts during the war not admitted. Asks Madison to use his influence to obtain the payment of Mr. Paradise's claim on Virginia. 4°. 4 pages.

1786, December 16, Paris. Acknowledging letters of January 22, March 18, May 12, June 19, and August 12. Incloses copy of letter from the minister of finance respecting regulations for our commerce. Lafayette a useful auxiliary. Suggests the organization of our General Government into legislative, executive, and judiciary powers. Question if Congress will have self-denial enough to go through with this distribution. The Western States and the navigation of the Mississippi. Their interests to remain united with us. Religious freedom in Virginia approved of in Europe. The first legislature which has had the courage to declare that the reason of man may be trusted with his own opinions. The punishment for rape indecent and unjustifiable. The British debts. Reflections on the natural history of the earth. Orders a watch to be made for Madison. Loans for the improvements of the Potomac. European affairs and politics.
4°. 6 pages.
New York.

1787, January 30, Paris. Acknowledging letters of November 25 and December 4. Has no fear of serious consequences in the late troubles in New England. Trusts they will provoke no severities. A little rebellion now and then is a good thing, as necessary in the political as storms are in the

JEFFERSON.

physical world. A medicine necessary for the sound health of the Government. Apprehends the possibility that the navigation of the Mississippi may be abandoned to Spain. An act of separation between the Eastern and Western country. An abandonment of the fairest subject for the payment of our public debts. A war with Spain preferable so as to unite the whole people. The French minister to be sent to the United States. ,Count de Moustier would give satisfaction. Jefferson is going to the south of France. [The greater part of the rest of this letter is in cipher, giving his estimate of the character of J. Adams, Carmichael, Bingham, Lafayette, Count de Vergennes, Reyneval, and Hening. The cipher to be found in the Monroe papers and Jefferson's series 5, vol. 11.] 4°. 8 pages.

1787, February 7, Paris. An inclosure for Madison's perusal and of his colleagues not to be copied or extracts taken, and after perusal to send it to the governor. Introduces Mr. Bannister. 4°. 1 page.

1787, June 20, Paris. Acknowledging letters of February, March, April, and May. Has returned from a journey in the south of France. His views at length on the subject of the separation of the executive business of the confederacy from Congress. Is uneasy at seeing the sale of our Western lands is not yet commenced. A precious fund for the extinction of our public debt. Wishes to know the decision of Congress respecting the continuance of his mission in order to make preparations for quitting his house, selling his furniture, etc. [A large portion of this letter is in cipher and to found in Monroe's correspondence and Jefferson's.] 4°. 7 pages.

1787, August 2, Paris. Acknowledging letters of May 15 and June 6. Private business in the purchase of books and shipment and settlement of accounts. Loans effected by Mr. Adams in Holland to pay interest due in Paris. Political news of France but in cipher [which is to be found in the Monroe papers and Jefferson's series 5, vol. 11, No. 35]. 4°. 11 pages

——— to BARCLAY, THOMAS.

1787, August 3, Paris. Character and abilities of Mr. Barclay, consul-general for France and minister to the Court of Morocco. [This letter is on a sheet on which are copies of testimonials from John Jay, Benjamin Franklin, and John Adams. Copy.] 4°. 3 pages.

——— to MADISON. *New York.*

1787, August 15, Paris. Popular enthusiasm in Paris. The parliament house surrounded by 10,000 people. The principal speakers drawn in their chariots by the people. The English squadron sailed. Another move towards war. 4°. 1 page.

1787, September 17, Paris. Shipment of boxes containing books. Sum of money to be collected for a Mr. John Burke, deceased. Asks him to send him some Newtown pippins and grafts of them. Also some red birds for the ladies and opossums for naturalists, if means can be found. 4°. 3 pages.

JEFFERSON.

1787, October 8, Paris. Introducing the Count de Moustier, successor to Mons. de la Luzerne, the French minister. Also recommends Madame de Brehan, who accompanies de Moustier, as a charming acquaintance. Sends Madison a watch. Describes de Moustier's character in cipher.
4°. 2 pages.

1787, December 23, Paris. Acknowledging letters of July 18, September 6, and October 24. Thanks Madison for the information in cipher about himself. Thanks him for the investigations he is making about Mr. Burke's affairs. Is much pleased at the success of the sale of Western lands. His opinions on the constitution proposed by the Virginia convention. Likes the organization of the Government into legislative, executive, and judiciary. Dislikes the omission of a bill of rights providing for freedom of religion, freedom of the press, protection against standing armies, etc. Dislikes the abandonment of the necessity of rotation in office, particularly in the case of President. On the whole he approves of the convention. Predicts that our governments will remain virtuous for centuries as long as they are chiefly agricultural, etc. 4°. 7 pages.

1788, February 6, Paris. Acknowledging letters of December 9 and 20. Private matters relating to cuttings, seeds, and agriculture. Specimens received and sent. Jefferson's opinion on the new Federal constitution proposed by the Virginia convention. European politics. On the law proposed in Virginia prohibiting the importation of brandies [in cipher]. 4°. 3 pages.

1788, March 8, Paris. Introducing Francis Adrian Van der Kemp, a late victim of patriotism in Holland. 4°. 1 page.

1788, May 3, Paris. Acknowledging letters of February 19 and 20. Our national credit compared with the credit of foreign nations. Suggestions as to methods of paying the interest on our debts. Foreign money dealers look forward to our new Government with interest and have much confidence in it. The first acts of our new Government should be some operation by which we may obtain better credit than any nation, the English not excepted, and not borrow money to pay interest. Warville's business in America [cipher]. Asks to be sent copy of Governor Randolph's reports on the navigation of the Mississippi. Sends Madison a pedometer with instructions for using it. 4°. 6 pages.

——— to JAY, JOHN (Secretary of Foreign Affairs).

1788, May 15, Paris. His salary and outfit. Asks Jay's and Madison's good offices before Congress to regulate his claims. [Press copy.]
4°. 5 pages.

——— to MADISON.

1788, May 25, Paris. Incloses press copy of a letter to John Jay, relating to his claim for outfit and salary as minister to France. Inadequate sum allowed to live as befits his position. Asks Madison's good offices in advocating his claims particularly. 4°. 4 pages.

1788, July 31, Paris. Acknowledging letter of April 22. The first two pages of this letter mostly in

JEFFERSON.

cipher on the abilities of Lafayette, Montmorin, and others. Sends a book of Dupont's on the commercial treaty with England, and pamphlets by Condorcet on the great questions which agitate France. Rejoices at the acceptance by 9 States of the new constitution. His opinions upon it. His approvals and disapprovals. Directions about letters of introduction, to discriminate between recommending personally and recommendations from others which he can not refuse. 4°. 6 pages.

1788, August 4, Paris. Introducing Mr. Dobbyns, of Ireland, who contemplates removing to America. 4°. 1 page.

1788, November 18, Paris. Acknowledging letters of July 24, August 10, and 23. Has read the "Federalist" with care, pleasure, and improvement. Still thinks the bill of rights should be added to the new constitution. State of affairs in France. The people not yet ripe for receiving the blessings to which they are entitled. Jefferson's wish to visit America for the summer Sends estimates for the funding of the foreign debt. Hopes the new Government will make provision for payments. 4°. 4 pages.

1789, January 12, Paris. Acknowledging letters of September 21 and October 8, with a pamphlet in the Mohican language. Is collecting vocabularies of American Indians and those of Asia, persuaded they have a common origin. Is pleased at the vote of Congress on the subject of the Mississippi. Movements of Lafayette. He takes part with those who demand a constitution. Among the foremost of patriots. Anxiety for the captives in Algiers. New books mentioned. 4°. 3 pages.

1789, March 15, Paris. Acknowledging letters of October 17, December 8 and 12. Has viewed Madison's thoughts on the subject of declaration of rights with great satisfaction. His own ideas on the subject. Trusts it will be added to the Constitution. European affairs commented upon. The new Constitution in France. The funding of their public debts. New bickerings with The Hague. Insanity of the King of England. 4°. 7 pages.

1789, May 11, Paris. Is expecting hourly his leave of absence. The madness of the King of England gone off, but left him imbecile and melancholy. The King of Prussia more moderate, throws cold water on the fermentation he had excited in Poland. Caprices of the King of Sweden. Denmark will aid Russia. France occupied with internal arrangement. The war in Europe will probably be confined to those actually engaged. The revolution in France. Mobs in Paris. The nobility coming over to side with the people in the question of voting by persons or orders. They abandon their pecuniary privileges only. The clergy divided. Purchase of books for Madison. 4°. 4 pages.

1789, June 18, Paris. Acknowledging letter of March 29. Has not received an answer to his application for his leave of absence. Is ready to depart. The Russian campaign. Death of the Grand

Seignior. Imbecility of the King of England. Proceedings of the States General. The question of voting by persons or orders. The States General declare themselves the National Assembly. Proposition about taxes. Question of bankruptcy or civil war. All the talent in the nation in the commons. No great talent among the noblesse. The clergy waiting to profit of any incident to secure themselves. The curés with the commons. The bishops and archbishops bribe them away from the commons. Detestation of the people for their carriages and equipages. The soldiers will follow their officers, the lower nobility. 4°. 5 pages.

1789, July 22, Paris. Acknowledging letter of May 9. Events in France. The King decides the question of voting by persons or orders. The tiers étât declare his proceedings a nullity. Mobs about the palace. The French guards mixed with the people. The foreign troops march towards Paris. The King states to the States General that it was to preserve tranquility. Necker dismissed. Ministry changed. People attack and rout cavalry. Retaliation by a French guard. The insurrection becomes universal. The people free a prison and takes arms. Committee of safety resolve to raise militia of 48,000 men. People attack the Invalides, obtain arms, and attack and carry the Bastile, cut off the governors' heads. The council propose to march the foreign troops to suppress tumults. Fifty to sixty thousand men in arms. The King orders away the troops. Lafayette named commander-in-chief. Tumults continued. The court alarmed at Versailles. Necker recalled. Foulon, a fugitive minister, killed by the mob. Other ministers fled. Still waiting his leave of absence. 4°. 4 pages.

1789, July 29, Paris. Acknowledging lette. of May 23. Ridiculing [in cipher] the President's title to be proposed by the Senate. The tranquillity of Paris not disturbed since the death of Foulon and Berthier. Supplies of bread scarce. Expect new wheat in ten days. The harvest late. The sun shines only five hours a day during the year. 4°. 1 page.

1789, August 28, Paris. Acknowledging letters of May 27, June 13, and 30. Dissensions between the French and Swiss guard. Scarcity of bread. Bakers allowed to go into the country to buy flour Declaration of rights finished; will send copy. Distress for money; no taxes paid, nor can money be found. Necker's memoir on the subject to the Assembly. The new French constitution. Various propositions based upon that of the United States. The Duke of Orleans faction caballing with the populace and intriguing in London, in view of the transfer of the Crown to the Duke of Orleans. His vile character. Mirabeau their chief. Does not believe in their ultimate success. The Assembly well disposed towards us. His opinions upon the declaration of rights, copy of which Madison sent him. Proposes to sail from Havre on October 1. 4°. 9 pages.

1789, September 6, Paris. An essay on the question whether one generation of men has a right to bind another, on the ground that "the earth belongs in usufruct to the living." The national debts and method of paying interest. Successions of individuals compared with those of a whole generation. 4°. 8 pages.

1789, September 17, Paris. Notifies Madison of the shipment of 4 boxes from Havre, containing books, busts of Paul Jones, and medals. 4°. 1 page.

1789, October 3, Havre. Copy of a bill of lading of books shipped, per *Cato*, for Madison. 4°. 1 page.

1790, January 9, Monticello. Incloses a letter written to Madison before leaving Paris. Expects with anxiety the President's ultimate determination as to what is to be done with him. 4°. 1 page.

1790, February 14, Monticello. Acknowledging letter of January 24. Reluctantly accepts the appointment of Secretary of State. Is delayed in going to New York by the marriage of his daughter to Mr. Randolph. Asks Madison to procure suitable residence for him in New York. 4°. 1 page.

1790, September 23, Monticello. Purchase of a horse from Madison. 4°. 1 page.

1790 (?), not dated, New York. Asks Madison's opinion as to the mode of conveying official communications from the States through the channel of the President to the two Federal Houses. 4°. 1 page.

Philadelphia.

1791, January 1, Philadelphia. Communication to Mr. Otto, the French chargé d'affairs, respecting our commerce and the will of the French nation. 8°. 1 page.

1791, January 10, Philadelphia. Asks to know the amount of his debt to Madison for traveling expenses, the horse, and bill of freight. Sends a Connecticut newspaper with an article at Jefferson's expense. 8°. 1 page.

1791, January 12, Philadelphia. Exonerates Madison from all responsibility respecting a disorder of the horse lately purchased of Madison, and sends him a check. 4°. 1 page.

1791, May 9, Philadelphia. Acknowledging letter of 1st. His indorsement of Paine's "Rights of Man." Hamilton and Beckwith open-mouthed against him as likely to give offense to the Court of London. 4°. 2 pages.

New York.

1791, June 21, Philadelphia. Private business—financial. The President to leave Mount Vernon on the 27th. Col. H. Lee in Philadelphia. Botanical remarks. 4°. 2 pages.

Orange.

1791, June 28, Philadelphia. Acknowledging letter of 23d. Respecting books. The French proceedings against our tobacco and ships very eccentric and unwise. The author of "Publicola." Thinks peace will ensue between Russia and Turkey. Thinks the President will contrive to be on the road July 4, to avoid ceremonies. 4°. 2 pages.

1791, July 6, Philadelphia. Acknowledging letters of June 27 and July 1. Incloses money to pay bills.

JEFFERSON.

Arrival of the President. Subscriptions to the bank exceed the amount of capital stock. Incloses a memorandum of stock subscribed.
4°. 2 pages, and scrap of paper.

1791, July 10, Philadelphia. Lafayette resumes his command on a ground which strengthens him and the public cause. Subscriptions to the bank. Proposes Paine for postmaster. 4°. 1 page.

1791, July 21, Philadelphia. Acknowledging letters of July 10 and 13. Freneau declines coming here. Paine will not be appointed postmaster. European intelligence. France going on steadily with her work. Constitution of her colonies.
4°. 3 pages.

1791, July 24, Philadelphia. Acknowledging letter of 21st. Time of his journey to Virginia doubtful. The President indisposed with a blind tumor. Merchants from Richmond here to dabble in Federal filth. 4°. 1 page.

1791, July 27, Philadelphia. Incloses pamphlets on weights and measures. Jefferson's journal of his travels through France and Italy. Insinuates that Hamilton gives out that Madison and himself are hostile to everything not Southern. The President much better. 4°. 1 page.

1791, August 3, Philadelphia. Acknowledging letters of July 31 and August 1. The President has recovered and will probably go to Mount Vernon in October. Jefferson leaves sooner. His carriage horse dangerously ill. Incloses a map belonging to his journal during his tour. 4°. 1 page.

1791, August 18, Philadelphia. Acknowledging letter of 16th. Incloses copy of the census, including that of Virginia. Urges him to come to Philadelphia. Jefferson wishes him to go with him to Virginia. One of his horses sick and Madison's will be a fortunate aid. The President continually inquires after him. Is charged to carry him to the President's to dinner. 4°. 1 page.

——— to TERNANT, (Minister Plenipotentiary of France). *Philadelphia.*

1791, August 31, Philadelphia. Is instructed by the President to inform him that the Government of the United States have no idea of paying their debt in depreciated medium, avoiding all benefit from depreciation, assignats of France having been the medium of payment before their depreciation from gold and silver. 4°. 1 page.

——— to MADISON.

1791, November 11. On the practice made by individuals to get the President to hand in their petitions to the legislature, which he constantly refuses. Every person should address himself directly to the department to which the constitution has allotted his case. Asks if Madison approves. 4°. 1 page.

1792, January 12, Philadelphia. Proposition that Monroe makes concerning Mr. Hawkins.
small 4°. 1 page.

1792, March 16, Philadelphia. On the exchange of criminals between free and arbitrary governments. England never would agree to a convention with any state on the subject and has hitherto been the asylum of all fugitives from oppressions of other governments. Asks his observations on the subject. 4°. 1 page.

1792, May 13, Philadelphia. His ideas on the distinction between bonds and simple contracts. 4°. 1 page.

1792, June 4, Philadelphia. Interview with Mr. Hammond, the British minister, relating to the delivering up the posts in the Northwest, the line of boundary and the navigation of the Mississippi. Asks Madison's aid in a list of names that he may make a comprehensive table of the debts and numbers of all modern nations to show the President, without naming his authority, how high we stand indebted by the poll in that table. 4°. 2 pages.

1792 (?), no date. Has just received a Northern hare and a common one. Wishes him to come and examine the difference. Scrap of paper.

1792, June 21, Philadelphia. The New York State election. Some returns. Gives a table of the national debts and revenues of foreign countries. The United States debts and revenues. The youngest nation and most indebted. Brandt, the famous Indian. 4°. 2 pages.

1792, June 29, Philadelphia. Hamilton's defense of the bank. Dares to call the Republican party a faction. Hamilton's desire that Marshall should come into Congress from Richmond. Thinks he should be made judge. An attack to be made on the residence act. Brandt has left with best dispositions for peace. Short gives flattering results of conversations with Claviere and Dumourier with respect to the United States. Description of the Jacobin party. 4°. 2 pages.

Orange.

1792, July 3, Philadelphia. Acknowledging letters of June 24 and 25. Conjectures as to changes in the next Congressional elections. A branch bank will be established at Richmond. Suggests that a counter-bank be set up to befriend the agricultural man. The President leaves the 12th. Jefferson leaves the 14th. Hopes to be with Madison in Orange the 20th. 4°. 2 pages.

Philadelphia.

1792 (?), August 26, Philadelphia. Requests an interview and to dine with him. The President wishes that he (Jefferson) and Madison would examine a plan of L'Enfant's. 4°. 1 page.

1792, September 17, Monticello. The plans for payment of the national debt and interest. Members of his family ill. 4°. 1 page.

1792, October 1, Georgetown. Confidential conversation with the President, who is undecided about his retirement. small 4°. 1 page.

Orange.

1792, October 2, Baltimore. Elections in Maryland. 4°. 1 page.

1793, January 3. A paper in Jefferson's handwriting, not dated, on the report of the Secretary of the Treasury of the above date, with an account of the funds provided in Europe, and an account of the funds provided in America. Receipts and disbursements. 4°. 3 pages.

JEFFERSON to WASHINGTON. *Philadelphia.*

1793, January 4, Philadelphia. Our commercial relations with St. Domingo. Conversation with M. Payan, one of the St. Domingo deputies. [Copy.] 4°. 1 page.

—— to HAMILTON, ALEXANDER.

1793, March 27, Philadelphia. Gives his views as requested of the destination of the loan of three million of florins obtained by our bankers in Amsterdam previous to the acts of the 4th and 12th of August, 1790. [Draft.] 4°. 2 pages.

—— to MADISON. *Orange.*

1793, March 31, Philadelphia. Acknowledging letter of 24th. Incloses draft of a letter to Hamilton, on the destination of the loan for 3,000,000 florins in Amsterdam. 4°. 1 page.

1793, April 7, Philadelphia. Declaration of war between France and England. An impeachment ordered here against Nicholson, the comptroller-general. Threatenings of Duer. Jefferson moves into the country. 4°. 1 page.

1793, April 28, Philadelphia. Acknowledging letter of 12th. Will attend to the commission about plows. Genet, the French minister, expected soon. Proposition to declare our treaties with France void. Neutrality requisite to keep us out of the calamities of war. 4°. 1 page.

1793, May 5, Philadelphia. Acknowledging letter of April 12. Model of a threshing-mill. Madison's plows will be done in a week. Incloses a Boston paper respecting political parties. 4°. 1 page.

1793, May 12, Philadelphia. Acknowledging letter of 29th April. Anglophobia seizes violently on the Cabinet. Questions of neutrality. Hamilton's circular to collectors. System of espionage objected to. Indecisive and suspicious course of Edmund Randolph. A manly neutrality would have given satisfaction to our allies. A classification of political parties. Hints a wish to retire to private life. 4°. 2 pages.

1793, May 19, Philadelphia. Acknowledging letter of 8th. Notes on the general plan of a house. Arrangements of the people to receive Genet, the French minister. Ternant's letter of recall. Genet presents his letter of credence. His exposition of the liberal spirit of his mission. Disposition of a part of the Cabinet to make a part in a confederacy of princes against human liberty. Excitement in Western Pennsylvania against the excise offices. Scotch threshing machine. 4°. 3 pages.

1793, May 27, Philadelphia. Disposition of the Cabinet towards France relating to a treaty of commerce. Conflicting accounts about Dumourier. Wishes an intelligent correspondent to reside in New Orleans with a salary. 4°. 1 page.

1793, June 2, Philadelphia. Privateers fitted out in Charleston by French citizens commissioned by that nation. Dumourier's address. Internal combustion in France gives Jefferson uneasiness. Edmund Randolph visits Virginia. Trusts that he may fall into hands that will not deceive him about the dispositions of that State. Suggests Madison's writing to certain friends relative

JEFFERSON.

thereto. Question of the treaty with France. Lowering disposition perceivable in England and Spain towards us. Seeds of the Kentucky coffee tree desired. 4°. 2 pages.

1793, June 9, *Philadelphia.* Acknowledging letters of May 27 and 29. Gives reasons for his fixed determination to resign. Washington's sensitiveness on the attacks on him in the public papers. Genet's conversations. Tull's horse-houghing plows. 4°. 4 pages.

1793, June 23, Philadelphia. Acknowledging letter of 13th. History of the proclamation of neutrality. Unfriendliness of Spain. Her desire to pick a quarrel. The President goes to Mount Vernon. 4°. 2 pages.

1793, June 29, *Philadelphia.* Acknowledging letter of 17th. Affairs in France. Nothing can shake their republicanism. Dumourier the popular commander. The English trying to stop the current of their bankruptcies by the emission of exchequer bills, inferior to assignats. Jefferson's general plan of farming. Postscript, June 30. The paper signed "Pacificus," in defence of the neutrality proclamation. Jefferson's objections to it. 4°. 4 pages.

1793, July 7, *Philadelphia.* Hamilton's papers signed "Pacificus." Urges Madison to answer his most striking heresies and cut him to pieces. The calamitous appointment of the minister of France (Genet). Jefferson's opinion of his character. Passionate, disrespectful, and even insulting to the President. 4°. 1 page.

1793, July 14, Philadelphia. Acknowledging letter of June 29. Wishes to see Madison before Congress convenes. Afraid of an open rupture between the French minister and the United States. 4°. 1 page.

1793, July 21, Philadelphia. Engagements between the combined armies and the French. France having the worst of it in the first engagement. She sends commissioners to England to sound for peace. Edmund Randolph returned; he reports on the loyalty of the people of Virginia to the General Government; their indisposition against Hamilton personal, not against his measures. 4°. 1 page.

1793, August 3, Philadelphia. Recall of Genet decided upon. The loan agreed to. The President uneasy at the doctrines in "Pacificus." Authorities on the construction of treaties. Genet's ignorance astonishing. Has informed the President of his intention to resign on the last day of September. Incloses a cipher deciphered. 4°. 2 pages. Scrap of paper.

1793, August 6, *Philadelphia.* Conversations with the President respecting the filling the vacancy on Jefferson's retirement. Names of persons suggested and objections. Washington's wish that Jefferson would delay the time until December. Meeting of the Cabinet at the President's, when Jefferson's letter to Gouverneur Morris was discussed and a phrase therein decided upon to be left out. The letter in question related to the conduct of Mr. Genet, the French minister. [Memorandum. Press copy.] 4°. 7 pages.

JEFFERSON. *Orange.*

1793, August 11, Philadelphia. Acknowledging letter of July 30. Intention of the President's proclamation. Hamilton under signature of "No Jacobin." Incloses a newspaper article from the pen of Edmund Randolph, on the indictment of Gideon Henfield for enlisting on board a French privateer. 4°. 3 pages.

1793, August 11, Philadelphia. Writes a second letter, which is confidential, respecting the desirability of the Republicans sustaining the President in his proclamation. The popular feeling against Genet, the French minister. Determination of the Government to request his recall. Character of Edmund Randolph, a chameleon who has no color of his own and reflecting that nearest him. The President desirous of knowing Madison's sentiments on the proclamation. Evasive answer by Jefferson. 4°. 4 pages.

1793, August 18, Philadelphia. Acknowledging letters of 5th and 11th. Respecting privateering. General support of the President's proclamation. Feeling against Genet. Incloses part of a speech of Lord Chatham's in a debate on the Falkland Islands, on the monied interest. 4°. 2 pages.

1793, August 25, Philadelphia. Disapproval of the mass of Republicans to Genet's conduct and intermeddling. The President leaves for Mount Vernon and Jefferson for Monticello. 4°. 1 page.

1793, September 1, Philadelphia. Actions of a French consul in Boston for rescuing with an armed force from a French frigate a prize vessel in the hands of the marshal. The English orders in council. General disapprobation of Genet. A manuscript of Franklin. Malignant fever breaks out in Philadelphia. A threshing machine. The maker coming to America. 4°. 3 pages.

——— to PINCKNEY, THOMAS. *London.*

1793, September 7, Philadelphia. Instructions to obtain explanations of the order of counsel of June 8, issued by the British Government, relative to articles in said order as manifestly contrary to the law of nations. [Press copy.] 4°. 5 pages.

——— to MADISON. *Orange.*

1793, September 8, Philadelphia. Has been reading the Franklin manuscripts with great pleasure. Genet's conduct in New York in overawing and obstructing the law by an armed force. Yellow fever increasing in Philadelphia. Hamilton's illness and fear of the epidemic. Jefferson the only member of the administration remaining in Philadelphia. Does not like to exhibit the appearance of panic. The Indians refuse to meet our commissioners. 4°. 3 pages.

1793, September 15, Schuylkill. Acknowledging letters of August 27 and September 2. Continuance of the yellow fever. Names of persons who have died. His intended departure for Virginia. 4°. 1 page.

1793, November 2, Germantown. Arrangements for the meeting of Congress. Difficulty in getting lodgings in Germantown. Johnson, of Maryland, refuses to be Secretary of State. Other persons proposed to be nominated. Rumored engagement of Genet to Clinton's daughter. Hamilton ill again. 4°. 1 page.

JEFFERSON.

1793, November 9, Germantown. The fever disappearing in Philadelphia. Inhabitants returning. The President goes to Reading. European news. Has engaged beds for Madison at Bockin's tavern. 4°. 1 page.

1793, November 17, Germantown. Has engaged good lodgings for Madison and Monroe. The President remains here until the meeting of Congress. The yellow fever disappears. Attack on Wayne by the Indians. Genet's conduct. 4°. 1 page.

——— to TAYLOR, GEORGE. *Philadelphia.*

1793, December 31. Certificate as to Taylor's faithful and careful administration of his duties while employed as clerk and chief clerk in the Department of State. [Press copy of a copy.] 4°. 1 page.

——— to WASHINGTON.

1793, no date. Opinion given to Washington respecting the stipulations in our treaties with the French, Dutch. and Prussians, that when either party is at war and the other neutral, the neutral shall give passports to the vessels belonging to their subjects. Distinction between vessels owned and built, and owned only. [Among Madison's letters to Washington. Copy, partly in Jefferson's hand.] 4°. 6 pages.

——— to MORRIS, GOUVERNEUR. *Paris.*

1793, (?) not dated, Philadelphia. A review of the conduct of Mr. Genet, the French minister. [Press copy.] 4°. 24 pages.

——— to MADISON. *Philadelphia.*

1794, February 25, Monticello. Rumors of Genet's recall. Is closely occupied with his own affairs. Prices of produce, etc. 4°. 1 page.

1794, October 30, Monticello. Asks for the amount of Mazzei's claim against Dohrman for information of the Van Stophorsts. Has had an attack of rheumatism. Alludes to a speech on an appeal to arms. 4°. 1 page.

1794, November 6, Monticello. Asks Madison's aid in forwarding him books from Philadelphia. A long drought, and abundant rains. Prices of produce. Scarcity of cash. 4°. 1 page.

1794, December 28, Monticello. Denunciation of the Democratic societies by the monocrats. The society of the Cincinnati, a self-created one, carving out for itself hereditary distinctions. The changes in the House of Representatives encouraging. Discouraging Madison's retirement. 4°. 4 pages.

1795, February 5, Monticello. Commissions which he asks Madison to attend to. The weather and crop prospects. Local politics. Choosing of members of the House of Representatives. The taxes very unpopular. 4°. 1 page.

1795, February 23, Monticello. Sends two open letters to the President and Secretary of State. If he disapproves, to return them; if not, to deliver them. Sends letter to a fresco painter. 4°. 1 page.

1795, March 5, Monticello. Acknowledging letter of 15th. Incloses a letter to Mr. Christie on obtaining the vetch (a plant) from England. Rotation of crops. The low practices of the competitor of F. Walker (House of Representatives), in buying votes with grog. 4°. 1 page.

1795, April 27, Monticello. Acknowledging letter of March 23d. Only one change of Madison's position which he ever wished to see him make, as he is the only person in the United States, who, being placed at the helm of our affairs, his mind would be so completely at rest for the fortune of our political barque. As for himself his retirement from office had been meant from all office, high or low. Intends to never permit himself to think of the office (presidency (?)). The delight he feels in the society of his family and his agricultural pursuits. Feels the absence of Monroe. Agricultural plans. 4°. 3 pages.

1795, July 13, Monticello. Incloses him a paper to return after reading. Has not seen the treaty. Randolph's (his son-in-law) health bad. 4°. 1 page.

1795, August 3, Monticello. Incloses a paper showing that Hamilton supports the treaty. He is attacked by the Livingston party in New York and beat off the ground. Richmond decides against the treaty. 4°. 1 page.

Orange.

1795, September 21, Monticello. Acknowledging receipt of six dozen volumes to be divided between Madison, himself and others. Writings by Hamilton and Beckley. Hamilton a colossus to the anti-Republican party. His great talents. The Republicans have only middling talent to oppose him, with the exception of Madison. Urges him to give a fundamental reply to the papers of Curtins and Camillas. Restored health of Mr. Randolph. Invites Madison with his bride to visit him. 4°. 3 pages.

Philadelphia.

1795, December 3, Monticello. Incloses a letter from Madame de Chastellux to the Duke of Liancourt. Death of Dr. Gilmer. 4°. 1 page.

——— to WYTHE, G. (chancellor). *Richmond.*

1795, January 16, Monticello. Sends him inclosed a statement of papers forwarded him, consisting of his collection of the printed laws of Virginia, and manuscripts which were not sent, but in his possession. 4°. 9 pages.

——— to MADISON. *Philadelphia.*

1796, February 21, Monticello. Acknowledging letters of January 31 and February 7. Incloses a letter of J. Bringhurst. Considers payments for his honor as debts of honor, whether right or wrong. 4°. 1 page.

1796, March 6, Monticello. Acknowledging letter of February 21. The finances of the United States. Hamilton's object in throwing them into forms which would be undecipherable. If Gallatin would undertake it, he might reduce this chaos to order. Claims of the Count de Grasse. Disagreeable features of the Spanish treaty. Respecting post roads. 4°. 3 pages.

1796, March 27, Monticello. Acknowledging letter of 13th. Is much pleased at Gallatin's speech on the treaty-making power. Jefferson's comments upon it. 4°. 1 page.

JEFFERSON.

1796, April 17, Monticello. Acknowledging letter of the 4th. Incloses copies on the subject of the journals of the convention for forming the Constitution, and relating to the commerce of the Mediterranean and the measures for the relief of the prisoners at Algiers. 4°. 4 pages.

1796, April 24, Monticello. A supply of rod iron. Directions as to the remittance of money to Mazzei. 4°. 1 page.

1796, December 17, Monticello. Acknowledging letter of the 5th. Wishes that anybody rather than himself had been proposed for the administration of the Government. Hopes his name will come out second or third. Begs Madison to solicit on his behalf that Adams may be preferred. Aspect of foreign affairs gloomy. Severe weather in Virginia. 4°. 2 pages.

1796, not dated. Notes on the alloy of the dollar. suggested by the vote in the Senate for reducing the dollar. 4°. 1 page.

1797, January 1, Monticello. Acknowledging letter of December 19. The event of the election has never been a doubt in his mind. His disinclination to honors. His only view in which he would have gone into the first office would have been to put our vessel on the Republican tack. As to the second office, he thinks with the Romans that the general of to-day should be a soldier to-morrow if necessary. Incloses a letter to Mr. Adams for Madison's perusal, if not approved of to return it. Reflecting on a work called "Political Progress". 4°. 1 page.

1797, January 8, Monticello. Acknowledging letters of December 25. Fears the issue of the present dispositions of France and Spain. Our commerce is destroyed through the wrongs of the belligerents and our own follies. The bank and paper money our ruin. Severe weather in Virginia. 4°. 1 page.

1797, January 16, Monticello. Probability of the choice of Vice-President has fallen on Jefferson. Incloses a letter to Tazewell. Doubts expressed of the validity of the Vermont election. 4°. 1 page.

1797, January 22, Monticello. Acknowledging letter of 8th. Intends going to Philadelphia as a mark of respect to the public. His confidence in Adams's integrity and solid affection for him. Does not wish to participate in the Executive councils. Hopes war will be avoided with France. The boundary of Maryland. 4°. 2 pages.

1797, January 30, Monticello. Acknowledging letter of the 15th. His friendship for Mr. Adams. Thanks Madison for the discretion he has used in relation to Jefferson's letter to Adams. Is going to Philadelphia to qualify himself for his office. Hopes he will not be made a part of any ceremony. 4°. 2 pages.

Orange.

1797, May 18, Philadelphia. Excitement in the administration on receipt of Mr. Pinckney's dispatches. Rumors of the failure of the Bank of England. Members of Congress concur that negotiation or anything rather than war was the wish of their constituents. Action of Congress in supporting the Executive. A majority it is believed will be for arming merchantmen, finishing frigates, fortifying harbors, and making all other military preparations as an aid to negotiation. France has asked Holland to send away our minister without success. Presumes France has made the same application to Spain. Spain's discontent with us. Monroe returning. 4°. 2 pages.

1797, June 8, Philadelphia. The amendment for putting France on an equal footing with other nations clogged with another requiring compensation for spoliations. Discussion in the House on the restriction of the merchants from arming their vessels. Determination of the Senate on the purchase of vessels. 4°. 2 pages.

1797, June 15, Philadelphia. The last great victory of Bonaparte. Peace between France and Austria. The victories on the Rhine. Meeting on the English fleet. Armies of the Rhine destined for England. Action of the Senate respecting dragoons and bill for manning frigates and buying vessels. The fortification bill before the House of Representatives. New newspapers to be issued. 4°. 2 pages.

1797, June 29, Philadelphia. Congress will probably rise on the 3rd or 4th of July. Senate rejects their own bill authorizing the President to lay embargoes. Other bills in both Houses which will probably not pass. Monroe and family arrived. 4°. 1 page.

1797, August 3, Monticello. Jefferson's letter to Mazzei, which being translated from English into Italian and from Italian into French and from French back to English, has considerably varied in its diction. Question of taking the field of the public papers. Fear of embroiling himself with the late administration and nine-tenths of the people. Asks Madison to come to him with Monroe to discuss the latter's business and other matters. 4°. 3 pages.

Orange.

1798, January 3, Philadelphia. Acknowledging letter of December 25. The Fredericksburg post. Extension of the stamp act. Foreign currency. Tench Coxe displaced for his activity in the last election. Bill for arming private vessels. Answer to Monroe's book under signature of "Scipio". Foreign intelligence. Letter from Talleyrand to the French consul here noting arrival of our envoys, who would find every disposition on the part of his Government to accommodate with us. 4°. 3 pages.

1798, January 24, Philadelphia. Acknowledging letter of December 25. Letter received by an individual from Talleyrand which says our envoys have been heard, their pretensions so high that possibly no arrangement may take place, but there will be no declaration of war by France. Bill in the House for foreign intercourse. Bill in the Senate for regulating proceedings on impeachments. Marshall, of Kentucky, proposes in the Senate some amendments to the Constitution. Prices of produce. 4°. 2 pages.

1797, February 8, Philadelphia. Articles of impeachment given in against Blount. The question of arming. Inflammatory message from the President against French depredations. 4°. 1 page.

1798, February 15, *Philadelphia*. The question of arming. Public sentiment against it. Dayton expects to be appointed Secretary of War in room of McHenry, who will retire. Question of the jury in cases of impeachment. Impeachment an engine of passion rather than of justice. Incloses acts of Parliament passed on the subject of our commerce. 4°. 2 pages.

1798, February 22, *Philadelphia*. Acknowledging letter of 12th. We hear nothing from our envoys. The countervailing act will put American bottoms out of employ in our trade with Great Britain. News from the Natchez of the delivery of the posts. The great contest between Israel and Morgan is to be decided this day. The impeachment question. The cutting machine. 4°. 2 pages.

1798, March 2, *Philadelphia*. Acknowledging letter without date, probably February 18. The new partition of Europe sketched. The French busy in their preparations for a descent on England. Gossip about the late birthnight. Not attended by the Adamites. The Washingtonians went religiously. Disposition to repeal the stamp act. No talk yet of adjourning. 4°. 2 pages.

1798, March 15, *Philadelphia*. Acknowledging letter of 4th. The French decree making the vessel friendly or enemy according to the hands by which the cargo was manufactured. Sensation among the merchants. The plan of arming. In case of war, changes in the Cabinet will ensue. J. Q. Adams named commissioner plenipotentiary to renew the treaty with Sweden. Tazewell's objections. Nothing yet said about adjournment. 4°. 2 pages.

1798, March 21, *Philadelphia*. Acknowledging letter of 12th. Excitement of the war party among the Representatives on the French decree. Probable adjournment in order to consult with their constituents. No reason for war, either of interest or honor. Views of the grand convention. 4°. 2 pages.

1798, March 29, *Philadelphia*. Resolution on the inexpediency of resorting to war against the French Republic. Rumors of a treaty of alliance, offensive and defensive, with Great Britain. Purchase of vessels to be armed and used as convoys. Money required for the buildings at Washington. Adams against the Government being there. 4°. 2 pages.

1798, April 5, *Philadelphia*. Bill for the Federal buildings in Washington before the Senate. Private letters assure us that France, classing us in her measures with the Swedes and Danes, has no more notion of declaring war against us than with them. Sprigg's resolutions on the expediency of war debated. Papers signed "Marcellus," attributed to Hamilton. Urges Madison to answer them. The Senate vote the publication of the communications from our envoys. The House against it. 4°. 2 pages.

1798, April 6, *Philadelphia*. Communications from our envoys. Mr. Adams's speech to Congress is deemed a national affront (to France). No explanations can be entered upon until that is disavowed or acknowledged. Overtures through informed agents. Base propositions on the part of Talleyrand. Misrepresentations of the newspapers. 4°. 2 pages.

1798, April 12, Philadelphia. Acknowledging letter of 2d. Incloses copies of instructions to our envoys and their communications. In view of coming State elections, suggests that Madison should write articles to place things in their just attitude. Question as to the modification of the land tax. 4°. 1 page.

1798, April 19, Philadelphia. Petitions to Congress from merchants and trades against arming. Expenses of preparation. Means to pay these expenses. Tax on salt. The land tax. Stoppage of public interest. Col. Innes ill with gout and dropsy. Madison probably elected to the State legislature. 4°. 2 pages.

1798, April 26, Philadelphia. Acknowledging letter of 15th. Bill for naval armament passes the House of Representatives. Bill for establishing a Department of the Navy. Motion for modifying the citizen law, which points at Gallatin. Sedition bill to be proposed; object, to suppress Whig presses. Committee of Ways and Means vote for a land tax. An additional tax on salt will be proposed in the House. Hamilton coming as Senator from New York. War addresses pouring in. 4°. 2 pages.

1798, May 3, Philadelphia. Acknowledging letter of April 22. War spirit kindled in the towns. These and New Jersey pouring in addresses offering life and fortune. Chances of peace lost by the President's answers. Conjectures as to bills to be passed to answer the passionate purposes of the war gentlemen. A committee of the Representatives have struck out the discretion of the President over the raising of armies. Proposed taxes for these expenses. The alien bills alarm the native French, who are going off in a ship chartered for the purpose. Cabot, of Massachusetts, appointed Secretary of the Navy. Hamilton, it is said, declines coming to the Senate. 4°. 2 pages.

1798, May 31, Philadelphia. Acknowledging letter of 20th. Corrects errors in his last letter. Bill for capturing French armed vessels on our coast passed both Houses. The alien bill ready for the third reading. A proviso saving the rights of treaties. A bill for suspending all communications with France. The land tax debated on. Volney and two shiploads of French depart soon. Volney impressed with the importance of preventing war. Incloses a poem on the alien bill by Mr. Marshall. The President refuses an exequatur to Dupont, the new French consul-general. 4°. 2 pages.

1798, June 21, Philadelphia. Acknowledging letter of 10th. Arrival of Marshall (from France) in New York with great éclat. Gerry remains in Paris. The French have no idea of a war with us. Dr. Logan sails for Europe. His secret mission. A panic among the citizens owing to an announcement of a traitorous correspondence between the

JEFFERSON.

Jacobins here and the French Directory. Many people implicated, Jefferson among the number. Message to both Houses from the President, with communications from Pinckney to the envoys, Talleyrand to Gerry, and Gerry to Talleyrand and to the President. The President will not send another minister until he be received with the respect due to a great nation. A bill to declare treaties with France void. 4°. 3 pages.

1799, January 3, Philadelphia. The President's speech written, probably, by Hamilton. The Republican spirit gaining ground in Pennsylvania and Massachusetts. The tax-gatherer excites discontent. Gerry's correspondence with Talleyrand kept back. France's conciliatory actions. If their overtures for reconciliation fail, to admit the mediation of the Dutch Government. Raising of the Army goes on and it is proposed to build twelve seventy-fours. Impressment of seamen by a British man-of-war from one of our armed vessels excites Mr. Pickering. Capture by the French of the *Retaliation*. Gen. Knox becomes a bankrupt. Gen. Lincoln suffers from it. Petition from Vermont to remit Lyons's fine.
4°. 2 pages.

1799, January 16, Philadelphia. Forgery of a pretended memorial, presented by Logan to the House of Representatives, exposed. Gerry's communications still kept back. Sincerity of the French Government to avoid war with us. Still an addition to our Army and Navy is intended. Expenses of a loan. Bankrupt bill rejected. Determination of the British commissioners under the treaty are extravagant. Bonaparte will probably succeed in Egypt. Ireland more organized in her insurrection. Prices of tobacco. Desire expressed that Madison should publish his debates of the convention. Suspicions against the Government on tampering with letters in the post-office. 4°. 2 pages.

1799, February 5, Philadelphia. Acknowledging letter of January 25. The bill for the eventual Army. Estimates. Bill for suspension of intercourse with France before the Senate. Toussaint's clause. Probable separation of St. Domingo from France. Probable English action respecting commerce with that island. Urges Madison to write for the press. He can render incalculable service to the country.
4°. 2 pages.

1799, February 19, Philadelphia. Bill for the eventual Army passes the Senate. Liberation of the *Retaliation* and her crew. Sincerity of France for a reconciliation. Consul-general named for St. Domingo. Overtures to our minister, Murray, at The Hague, by Pichon, French chargé d'affaires, approved by Talleyrand, who assures Murray that any plenipotentiary sent by our Government to France to end our difficulties will be received with the respect due to the representative of a free, independent, and powerful nation. Asks him to transmit these expressions to our Government. Murray appointed minister plenipotentiary to France. Dismay of Federals in both Houses at this intelligence. This silences all arguments against the sincerity of the French Government. 4°. 2 pages.

JEFFERSON.

1799, February 26, Philadelphia. The nomination of Murray minister plenipotentiary to France. Mortification of the war party. The President nominates O. Ellsworth, Patrick Henry, with W. Vans Murray, envoys extraordinary to France, but declaring the two former should not leave this country until they should receive from the Directory assurances that they should be received with the respect due, by the law of nations, to their characters. Scandalous scene in the House of Representatives. Interruptions of Mr. Gallatin's speech on the alien and sedition laws. 4°. 2 pages.

1800, March 4, Philadelphia. Acknowledging letters of December 29, January 4, 9, 12, 18, and Febru- 14. Mr. Pinckney's proposed amendment to the Constitution. Stagnation of commerce. Landing of our envoys at Lisbon. Conjectures as to the coming State elections and condition of parties. 4°. 3 pages.

1800, May 12, Philadelphia. The rising of Congress. The Federals have been unable to carry a single strong measure in the lower House. Tide of public opinion too strong against them. The Senate undismayed, however. The furnishing of Madison's house. 4°. 2 pages.

1800, July 20, Monticello. Money accounts with Madison. A Fourth-of-July dinner at Rawleigh. The toasts drank. 4°. 1 page.

1800 (?), not dated. On the act of Congress of March 3, 1800, entitling a citizen, owner of a vessel, to restitution until the vessel has been condemned by competent authority on paying salvage to the captor. Spoliations by the French. 4°. 2 pages.

1801, February 1, Monticello. Acknowledging letter of January 10. Does not dare to hazard a word on subject of election. The interception and publication of his letters exposes the republican cause as well as himself personally to much obloquy. Suggests to Madison a change of climate and in the habits and mode of life, for his health. 4°. 1 page.

1801, April 30, Washington. Gives directions to Madison as to the route he should take in coming to Washington. The badness of the roads described. 4°. 1 page.

Washington.

1801, June 20, Washington. Contracts for carrying the mails. The expediency for making them for one year only. 4°. 1 page.

1801, June 20, Washington. Asks Madison's and Gallatin's opinions on the application for a Mediterranean pass for a vessel owned here, though built abroad. 4°. 1 page.

1801, June 24, Washington. Approving of Mr. Erving as consul to London. Question as to who shall be his successor for Lisbon. Respecting other offices to fill, he refers them to his cabinet. scrap of paper.

1801, July 15, Washington. Fragment of a letter. Respecting an act authorizing the capture of French armed vessels, and dividing and appropriating their proceeds. French captures considered. 4°. 1 page.

JEFFERSON.

1801, July 19, Monticello. Prosecutions against Thomas and others for a misdemeanor at common law. Thinks the Executive should not interfere. The prosecution against Duane being under the sedition law should be withdrawn. 4°. 1 page.

1801, August 22, Monticello. Acknowledging letter of 18th. Case of the British scow *Windsor* taken by the prisoners she was carrying and brought into Boston. Mr. Poinsett's application for a passage in the frigate conveying Mr. Livingston, the U. S. minister. Question as to Mr. Clay of Philadelphia for consul to Lisbon. Asks whether it were advisable to propose to Russia through Mr. Livingston to exchange the new articles inserted in our late treaty for the old ones.

4°. 2 pages.

1801, August 28, Monticello. Acknowledging letter of 26th. Respecting applications for office. Our affairs with the Bey of Tunis. Thinks nothing will stop the increase of demands from the Barbary pirates but the presence of an armed force. Enormities of the British courts of admiralty.

4°. 2 pages.

Orange.

1801, September 12, Monticello. Acknowledging letter of 11th. The letter of credence for Mr. Livingston. Delay in the ratification of the treaty with France. Suggests that Livingston be instructed to propose the article concerning restitution of prizes, and that we are willing to trust without a treaty to the mutual interests of the two countries, for dictating terms for our commercial relations. Arrearage from the Department of State to our bankers in Holland. Advance to Gen. Lloyd. 4°. 2 pages.

———to the CABINET. *Washington.*

1801, November 6, Washington. A circular addressed to the heads of departments as a uniform course of proceedings in the mode and degrees of communication, particularly between the President and heads of departments. Adds that his confidence in them is unlimited, unqualified and unabated. "Private" [Press Copy]

4°. 2 pages.

———to MADISON.

1802, May 9, Monticello. Describes the state of the roads to Monticello and directs him how to proceed. Report of the arrival in New Orleans of a French governor. 4°. 1 page.

Orange.

1802, May 24, Monticello. Incloses letters. A recommendation for pardon in Jackson's case. Directs him to prepare the papers which he will sign on arriving in Washington. 4°. 1 page.

Washington.

1802, August 16, Monticello. Measures for taking care of the mint on shutting it up. Respecting commissioners of bankruptcy. 4°. 1 page.

1802, August 27, Monticello. Incloses letters apprehensive that the negroes taken from Guadaloupe will be pushed in on us. Asks Madison to write a friendly letter to M. Pichon and Governor Clinton. Commissioners of bankruptcy. Sickness in Washington. 4°. 1 page.

JEFFERSON.

1802, August 30, Monticello. Acknowledging two letters of the 25th. Detailed instructions should be sent to Mr. Pinckney relating to the dissatisfaction of the Chickasaw chief with the Spanish governor. Wishes that the European powers would give instructions to their diplomatic representatives to control the conduct of their governors in what relates to us. Commissions to be made out. Suggests a call for a docket of cases decided in the last twelve months in the Federal courts to be laid before Congress. 4°. 1 page.

1802, September 3, Monticello. Acknowledging letter of 1st. Returns letters of Higginson, Davis & Co., praying that a public vessel may be sent to demand their vessels of the viceroy of La Plata with indemnity for detention, etc. Sees no reason for departing from the regular course and committing our peace with Spain. Want of information as to facts. Mr. Pinckney be desired to look into these cases, and if right, to ask redress. 4°. 1 page.

1802, September 6, Monticello. Acknowledging letter of 3d. Questions relative to commissioners of bankruptcy. The British scow *Windsor*. The war against Tripoli. Detention of the *John Adams*. 4°. 1 page.

1802, September 10, Monticello. The letter to Higginson and others approved of. The consulate at Nantes. Mr. Patterson's claims for that office. Expects a visit from Madison and family and directs him the road to take. 4°. 1 page.

1802, September 13, Monticello. Negotiations by Chancellor Livingston with France and Spain. Letter from the mayor of New York, who asks a guard to prevent the French blacks from escaping into the country. Thinks it should be left to Gen. Dearborn's discretion, and suggests that Madison explain measures to Mr. Pichon (French minister). Expects a visit from Madison before Monroe goes away. 4°. 1 page.

1803, March 22, Monticello. Acknowledging letter of 17th. Request of the Bey of Tunis for a frigate should be refused. Gun carriages for the Emperor of Morocco and stores for Algiers should be sent with dispatch. These two powers must be kept friendly. Question of sending more ships to the Mediterranean. A newspaper in Kentucky advocating separation. 4°. 1 page.

1803, July 31, Monticello. Pardon of Samuel Miller. Mr. King's letter respecting the abandonment of the colonial system and emancipation of South America, and impressments of seamen. England will never yield and can not be forced. Suggests Sumpter as governor of Louisiana. Wishes to find an eligible diplomatist or two for Europe. 4°. 1 page.

1803, August 8, Monticello. Wishes the opinion of the Cabinet as to the propriety of consenting to give a passage in a frigate to Jerome Bonaparte. It would confer an obligation on the First Consul, but might give offense to Great Britain. 4°. 1 page.

1803, August 13, Monticello. Incloses letter and papers from Governor Mercer, of Maryland, requesting the President's approbation of the relinquishment of a part of claim to bank stock in England in order to obtain the residue. Asks Madison's advice on the matter. Jonathan E. Robinson to be a commissioner of bankruptcy for Vermont. 4°. 1 page.

1803, August 16, Monticello. Acknowledging letter of of 13th. Returns several letters and two protests on impressment by a British and a French armed vessel. The latter will serve as a set off against French complaints on the British trespassers on us. Remedies proposed. Indian affairs. Thinks Congress should authorize the sending of embassies to the Indian tribes of Louisiana to explore the country and ascertain its geography. Consular appointments. 4°. 1 page.

1803, August 29, Monticello. Received and forwarded Madison's letter to Duane. Case of Cloupet and the contraband negroes. Vessels sailed for Tripoli. Visit of Governor Page. Hopes to see Madison soon. 4°. 1 page.

1803, September 14, Monticello. Respecting the action of Spain on the cession of Louisiana. Suggests that Clarke be trusted with a hint of possible opposition from Spain and an instruction to sound, with caution, the force there and how the inhabitants are likely to act if we march a force there. 4°. 1 page.

1804, April 9, Monticello. Asks Madison to consult with the other members of the administration on the allowance to be made to Governor Claiborne, and to settle the term at which Gen. Wilkinson's authority as commissioner ceased. 4°. 1 page.

1804, April 27, Monticello. Acknowledging letter of 19th. The squadron for the Mediterranean. Question as to course to pursue with Tripoli in case our prisoners have been liberated at solicitations of foreign governments. Unwarrantable commitment of us by our agents at Paris and St. Petersburg on the loss of the *Philadelphia.* 4°. 2 pages.

1804, May 14, Monticello. Acknowledging letters of 7th and 11th. On the conduct of Leclerc. Insult to the Spanish flag. Commitment of a whole crew by the sheriff and posse, and their taking possession of the ship. 4°. 1 page.

1804 (?), not dated. On the law recognizing the right of a sheriff to use his posse comitatus without consulting anybody. 4°. page.

1804, June 15, Washington. Mr. King's dispatches. Money for the secret service. Susceptible of abuse. Directs a commission to be sent to Peter P. Schuyler as collector at Fort Schuyler. 4°. 1 page.

1804, June 24, Washington. Construction of a treaty. 4°. 1 page.

1804, July 5, Washington. The case of St. Julien. The local judge must decide whether the crimes committed against Louisiana under its former government can be punished under its present one. Differences between the governor and the Roman Catholic priests. Course to pursue when a belligerent privateer brings one of our vessels within our jurisdiction. Governor Claiborne's expenses. He should be liberally treated. 4°. 1 page.

1804, July 5, Washington. Our rights to the Perdido River. Boundaries of Louisiana. Conferences respecting Florida, and navigation of the Mississippi. 4°. 1 page.

1804, July 6, Washington. Conversation with Mr. Gallatin respecting the conferences concerning proposed acquisition of Florida. 4°. 1 page.

1804, August 3, Monticello. Incloses the South Carolina ratification of the amendment to the Constitution. Provost judge of Orleans Territory. Proposes Dickerson as attorney-general. Appointments for collector and inspector of revenues for Marietta. 4°. 1 page.

1804, August 7, Monticello. Acknowledging letter of 4th. Mr. Livingston's letter on the conduct of the commissioners incomprehensible. Hopes that the next Congress will give to the Orleans Territory a legislature to be chosen by the people. Asks Madison's aid in making a list respecting principal officers for the Orleans government. 4°. 1 page.

1804, August 19, Monticello. Establishment of a post line from Natchez to New Orleans. Suggests that Governor Claiborne be instructed to communicate with the Marquis Casa Calvo for making this establishment for mutual convenience. Incloses a letter from a Mr. Damen, of Amsterdam. 4°. 1 page.

1804, August 23, Monticello. Acknowledging letters of 18th and 21st. Complaint of the Bey of Tunis. The winding up of the affairs of Spain in New Orleans. Everything ready for the arrangement of the government of Orleans. 4°. 1 page.

1804, September 6, Monticello. Query as to whether we should not write to the governors of South Carolina and Georgia relative to the irregularities in their harbors by French privateers. 4°. 1 page.

Orange.

1804, September 25, Monticello. Arrival of M. and Madame Yrujo. Expects to be with Madison the next day. 4°. 1 page.

Washington.

1805, March 23, Monticello. Acknowledging letter of 17th. Monroe's negotiations respecting the right of navigating the Mobile. Lee and Claiborne pestered with intriguants. Their conduct without blame. 8°. 1 page.

1805, March 29, Monticello. Acknowledging receipt of packet containing letters from various persons. Proclamation of Governor Harrison. Persons to be named as counselors. Armstrong's correspondence. Land to be located in Louisiana for Lafayette. Dupont and Lafayette's probable visit to this country. 4°. 1 page.

1805, April 1, Monticello. Acknowledging letter of 27th. Pinckney's letter gives the true design of Great Britain to be to oust the French and Dutch from our quarter and leave the Spaniards and Portuguese. The western boundary of Louisiana. The navigation of the Mobile and Mississippi we reserve as a right. 8°. 1 page.

JEFFERSON.

1805, April 11, Monticello. Acknowledging letter of 5th. Will be in Washington next week. His daughter ill. The weather and season. 8°. 1 page.

1805, July 25, Monticello. Acknowledging letter of 22d. Departs for Bedford. Hopes Madison will not be obliged to remain long in Washington on account of Mrs. Madison's condition. The climate at Monticello cool and pleasant. 4°. 1 page.

1805, August 4, Monticello. Acknowledging letter of July 24. Regrets that Mrs. Madison's situation requires her going to Philadelphia. Letter of Charles Pinckney respecting the refusal of Spain to settle a limit. Suggests proposing to Great Britain an eventual treaty of alliance in case of a war with Spain or France. Convicts (black) from Surinam at Philadelphia. Thinks they should be sent to England. 4°. 2 pages.

1805, August 25, Monticello. Incloses a letter from Turreau the French minister. His offensive manner in dictating how we should receive Moreau. The style of the French Government in the Spanish business calculated to excite indignation. The United States are not of those powers which will receive and execute mandates. Is impressed with a belief of hostile and treacherous intentions against us on the part of France. We should lose no time in securing more than a neutral friendship from England. 4°. 1 page.

1805, December 22, Washington. Correspondence with the Bey of Tunis. Indignation of the Tunisian ambassadors against Davis. 4°. 1 page.

1806, May 19, Monticello. Hires an express to deliver letters to Mr. Smith, attorney-general, in time for the sailing of a ship. 4°. 1 page.

1806, May 30, Monticello. Acknowledging letter of 26th. Returns letters received of Madison from several persons. Gives directions relative thereto. Asks that Ryland Randolph may be appointed some consulship in the Mediterranean. The weather and caterpillars. 4°. 1 page.

1806, July 26, Monticello. Wishes Madison to bring him his great coat, which he left in Washington. Excessive drought in his section. Rivers and creeks dry. Considerable sickness. 4°. 1 page.

1806, August 2, Monticello. Respecting correspondence with the Ottoman Government relating to the case of the ketch *Gheretti*. 4°. 1 page.

1806, August 8, Monticello. Thinks it better to not appoint a consul for St. Thomas at present. Queries whether we have a convention with Spain for the mutual surrender of fugitives from justice in cases of murder and forgery. Question as to the giving up the murderer of a negro. Asks an investigation by Gen. Dearborn as to the fact of the British having a fort on the isthmus near Carleton or Buck island. Thinks a new marshal should be appointed for New York. 4°. 2 pages.

1806, August 15, Monticello. Sends papers for the Department of State, and to Mr. Gallatin. Leaves for Bedford. 4°. 1 page.

JEFFERSON. *Orange.*

1806, August 17, Monticello. A commission to be made to Mr. Page for the loan office made vacant by the death of Merewether Jones. 8°. 1 page.

Washington.

1806, August 28, Monticello. Acknowledging letter of 15th. Suggests that particular attention be shown to the Russian ships expected in Philadelphia, and instructions given to customs officers. French privateers. Plan of the middle part of the Capitol. Meade's conduct to wards Yznardi. Suggests the arrest of Capt. Lewis, of the *Leander*. 4°. 2 pages.

1806, September 2, Monticello. Acknowledging letter of August 30. Returns letters from various persons sent him. Instructions as to arrest of Capt. Lewis. Certificates of citizenship. Directs Madison the road to take when he visits him. 4°. 1 page.

1806, September 16, Monticello. Returns letters and papers. Directions respecting refractory Tunisians. Case of an impressed American seaman. 4°. 1 page.

Orange.

1806, September 23, Monticello. Acknowledging letter. Recommends an alteration in Madison's draft of a letter to Turreau. The loan of the navy-yard. Counts on being with Madison October 1. Death of Judge Patterson requires the nomination of a successor. 4°. 1 page.

1806, September 26, Monticello. Letter to Mr. Merry (British minister) respecting a murder committed on the high seas by a British subject. The prisoner can not be given up. Haumont's letter; we can not interfere. 4°. 1 page.

Washington.

1806 (?), not dated. Notes on Mr. Eaton's accounts. Consul-general at Tripoli. 4°. 2 pages.

1807, April 14, Monticello. Witnesses at Burr's trial. Rainy weather. 4°. 1 page.

1807, April 25, Monticello. Acknowledging letter of 20th. Returns letters sent for perusal. Witnesses for Burr's trial. Gives instructions. Great rains in Virginia. 4°. 1 page.

1807, May 8, Monticello. Returns Monroe's letter of March 5. Burr's enlistments. Expects to leave on the 13th. 4°. 1 page.

——— to NORVILL, JOHN.

1807, June 11, Washington. Acknowledging letter of 9th. Gives his views respecting a course of reading. Recommends several works on Government and history. Manner in which newspapers should be conducted. Asks that this letter should not be made public. [Copy.] 4°. 3 pages.

——— to CABELL, WILLIAM H., Governor of Virginia.

1807, August 7, Monticello. Acknowledging letters of July 31 and August 5. States the practice of nations to meet cases which may arrive in the neighborhood of Norfolk respecting armed British vessels and intercourse with them according to usages of war and cases of suspended amity. 4°. 4 pages.

JEFFERSON to MADISON. *Orange.*

1807, August 7, Monticello. Incloses letters from Governor Cabell, of Virginia. Asks that a commission be sent to Madison from the Department, sealed, for Bolling Robertson as secretary for the Territory of Orleans, and to forward it to Jefferson for signature. strip of paper.

1807, August 7, Monticello. Asks Madison to examine the inclosed letter to Governor Cabell and make any corrections it may need. Hopes to have a visit from himself and Mrs. Madison. 8°. 1 page.

1807, August 9, Monticello. The regulation of flags which should be confided to Commodore Decatur. Gen. Dearborn's plan of a war establishment. 4°. 1 page.

1807, not dated, Monticello. Importance of the careful selection of the consul-general for the Danish Islands. Erskine's demand respecting the water casks. 4°. 1 page.

1807, August 11, Monticello. Asks Madison to read and consider an inclosed letter of Governor Cabell and his answer and to forward it if no corrections are necessary. Respecting a spring lock. 4°. 1 page.

1807, August 18, Monticello. Complaints of Mr. Erskine of a want of communication between the British armed vessels in the Chesapeake or off the coast. Statement of a British sergeant that he saw British deserters enlisted in their uniforms by our officer. Recommends that the Secretary of the Navy make inquiries. 4°. 1 page.

1807, August 20, Monticello. Meade's persecutions of Yznardi. Annihilation of the allied armies by Bonaparte. The result will be peace on the continent. The British authorities withdrawing all their cannon and magazines from Upper Canada to Quebec as their only fasthold. Deserters should not be enlisted. 4°. 1 page.

1807, August 25, Monticello. Acknowledging a letter without date. Prosecution commenced in Connecticut against a clergyman for preaching or praying defamation against Jefferson. Jefferson's wish that the prosecution be dropped, if possible, that the tenor of his life could support his character more than the verdict of a jury. On the compelling of testimony by the judge of one district on another. 4°. 2 pages.

1807, August 30, Monticello. Foronda's claim for money advanced to Lieut. Pike. Pike's mission was for the purpose of ascertaining the geography of the Arkansas and Red rivers. The mails in Virginia. 4°. 1 page.

1807, September 1, Monticello. Thinks we had better secure peace with Algiers while war with England is probable. As to Spain, it is the precise moment when we should declare to the French Government that we will seize on the Floridas as reprisal for spoliations. Reasons for discontinuance of the daily post in Virginia to save expense to the Government. Reasons why those who receive annual salaries can not be constantly at their posts. 4°. 1 page.

1807, September 2, Monticello. Incloses letters, copies and extracts for perusal. 4°. 1 page.

JEFFERSON.

1807, September 3, Monticello. Incloses Mr. Smith's letter. The proposition of apprising our East India commerce of their danger. Desires Madison to give necessary instructions without delay. 4°. 1 page.

1807, September 4, Monticello. Letter from Mr. Crowninshield on the subject of notifying our East India trade [of probability of war with Great Britain]. Nothing but an exclusion of Great Britain from the Baltic will dispose her to peace with us. Hopes to receive a visit from Madison and Mrs. Madison next day. Directs him as to the róad to take. 4°. 1 page.

1807 September 18, Monticello. The orders to Commodore Rogers, at New York, on the late or similar entry of that harbor by the British armed vessels. Our Indian affairs in the Northwest, on the Missouri and at Nachitoches, wear an unpleasant aspect. The prosecution in Connecticut [against the slanderous parson] will be dismissed. 4°. 1 page.

1807, September 22, Monticello. Capt. Hewes's demand of indemnification from Great Britain a proper acknowledgment of the violation of jurisdiction. 4°. 1 page.

1808, May 19, Monticello. The Attorney-General's opinion on the right to the batture. Mr. Livingston's printed memoir thereon. 4°. 1 page.

1808, May 24, Monticello. Returns letters and papers with his observations thereon. Navigation of the Mobile. Lieut. Pike's mission. 4°. 2 pages.

1808, May 31, Monticello. Returns papers. Appointments below field officers are made. Turreau's letters complains of French deserters enlisted by us. Woodward's scruples relating to administration of oaths. Directions concerning postriders. 4°. 2 pages.

1808, June 3, Monticello. Returns Pinckney's and Graham's letters. Forwards passport for Hill's vessel. Gallatin's circular orders relative to the trade to New Orleans. Intends being with Madison on the following Tuesday. 4°. 1 page.

1808, July 29, Monticello. The proposed mission to St. Petersburg. Secrecy of the mission essential during the recess of the Senate. Suggests terms of letter of credence. The transaction at New Orleans between Ortega and the British office with the prize sloop *Guadaloupe.* The habitual insolence of British officers. Suggests proceedings of the court be sent to Mr. Erskine. 4°. 2 pages.

1808, August 5, Monticello. Acknowledging letter of 3d. A letter from B. R. Randolph. He is totally unconnected with others of that name. Shall not answer it. On anonymous letters. Productions of cowards which never merit a moment's attention. 4°. 1 page.

1808, August 9, Monticello. Acknowledging letter of 7th. Suggests whether it is worth while to send Erskine a copy of Bailey's letter and to observe to him that this disrespect by the officers of his Government, if not corrected, may urge us to retaliate in the same manner. The spirit of the

JEFFERSON.

Boston Tories. Bonaparte finds a limit to his power in Spain. 4°. 1 page.

1808, August 16, Monticello. Acknowledging letter of 14th. Letters from Mr. Short. The season too late for navigation of the Baltic and return. Wishes to consult with Madison on the subject. Permission to be given to Turreau to send his two vessels, but on certain conditions. 4°. 1 page.

1808, August 19, Monticello. Acknowledging letter of 17th. On the permission granted to send French subjects home caught here by the embargo. Petition of shipmasters from Philadelphia. 4°. 1 page.

1808, September 5, Monticello. Incloses counter addresses relating to the embargo. Employment of a bricklayer. He is at Madison's service. Expects to be in Washington October 1. 4°. 1 page.

1808, September 6, Monticello. Returns Pinckney's letter. If the British Government repeals their orders, we must repeal our embargo; if they make satisfaction for the *Chesapeake*, we must revoke our proclamation; if they keep up impressments, we must adhere to nonintercourse, etc. The anonymous rhapsody in Morris's style. 4°. 1 page.

1808, September 13, Monticello. Sends letters for perusal. Gen. Armstrong's letter recommending the taking possession of the Floridas. Turreau's letters unintelligible. Vessels to convey home French seamen. If he wishes to buy vessels here and man them with French seamen and send them elsewhere, to permit it would be a breach of neutrality. His remedy is to repeal the decrees. 4°. 1 page.

1808, September 20, Monticello. Erving's opinions influenced by French versions at Madrid. Difficulty in answering Erskine's letter. The haughty style of his Government. Soderstrom to be reprimanded. A foreign agent to not embody himself with the lawyers of a factious opposition to influence the opinions of the Government. 4°. 1 page.

1808, September 23, Monticello. Acknowledging letters of 20th and 21st. Has sent the letter to Turreau without alteration. Sends a bricklayer. Suggests an improvement to Madison's house. 4°. 1 page.

Washington.

1809, March 17, Monticello. Extracts of a letter from Mr. Short. Fatiguing journey from Washington. Backward spring. Feels great anxiety for the next four or five months. If peace can be preserved it will be a smooth administration. No Government so embarrassing in war as ours. Wonderful credulity of members of Congress. Lying and licentious character of the press. The present maniac state of Europe. Our avoidance of it to our credit. War may be a less losing business than unresisted depredation. 4°. 2 pages.

1809, March 24, Monticello. Incloses several letters intended for the office and not the person named on the back. Recommends Thomas Page for office.

JEFFERSON.

Mr. Ray, author of the "War of Tripoli." Names Gen. Dearborn's son for a military commission. 4°. 1 page.

1809, March 31, Monticello. Acknowledging letters of 27th and 28th. Directions about a bronze time piece. Newspapers for the President. Matters relating to Erving, minister to Spain. 4°. 1 page.

1809, April 19, Monticello. Acknowledging letter of 9th. If the British ministry are changing their policy towards us, it is because the nation is shaken by the late reverses in Spain. Her claim to dominion of the seas by conquest and to levy contributions on all nations; her resources being inadequate. Our nonimportation law. This conquest of Spain will force a delicate question on Madison as to the Floridas and Cuba. Mr. Hackley's affair. Suggests for him the vacant consulship at Lisbon in case Jarvis goes to Rio Janeiro. Conduct of Meade denounced. 4°. 3 pages.

1809, May 22, Monticello. Madison's indorsement on his note at the Bank of United States. States his resources. Trusts that no section of Republicans will countenance the suggestions of the Federalists that there has ever been any difference at all in their (Jefferson's and Madison's) political principles. The weather. 4°. 2 pages.

1809, June 16, Monticello. Acknowledging letter of 12th. The new order in council, and the official exposition of it by the Lords of trade to the London American merchants. Erskine's arrangement. Settlement of financial matters with Madison. The weather and crops. 4°. 2 pages.

1809, July 12, Monticello. Acknowledging letters of 4th and 7th. Incloses draft of a letter to the Emperor of Russia. Bonaparte's successes. Expects to visit Bedford. 4° 1 page.

Orange.

1809, August 17, Monticello. Acknowledging lettter of 8th. The chicanery of Anglomen in consequence of the disavowal of Erskine. The perfidy of England. The British minister assured that the orders in council would be revoked before June 10. Considers war with England as inevitable. We should take Baton Rouge to secure New Orleans. Has confidence in Erskine's integrity. The unprincipled rascality of Canning. The most shameless ministry which ever disgraced England. 4° 2 pages.

Washington.

1809, October 9, Monticello. Acknowledging letter of 6th. Mr. Dupont's and Dr. Prestley's ideas respecting a university in Virginia. Disposition of Jefferson's books eventually. Conjectural establishments of a university at Washington. Dupont to be president or professor. The corn crop. 4°. 1 page.

1809, October 25, Monticello. Acknowledging letter of no date, covering check for balance of account. Should Rodney (Attorney-General) resign Wirt would accept the vacancy. Mentions John Monroe as governor of Illinois should the present incumbent resign. 4°. 1 page.

JEFFERSON.

1809, November 6, Monticello. Acknowledging letter of October 30. Sends copy of paper to Thomas Monroe. The weather. 4°. 1 page.

1809, November 26, Monticello. Acknowledging letter of 6th. Returns letters from Mr. Short and Romanzoff, with a letter from Gen. Armstrong. Infatuation of the British Government; they still proceed with the same madness and increased wickedness. Thinks that Jackson should have been sent off. The rejection of Onis expedient. Lafayette's anxiety to receive his formal titles to his lands in Louisiana. Effects of the unfortunate Governor Lewis with official documents; their disposition. 4°. 2 pages.

1809, December 7, Monticello. Gives a general statement of a plan for establishing Father Richards' School, an agricultural school, and for the trades, in the neighborhood of Detroit, for the benefit of the Indian youth. The land is now in possession of the Treasury Department. 4°. 3 pages.

1810, March 25, Monticello. Improved plow which he wishes to send to Paris; and expected arrival of some Merino sheep, in which both he and Madison are interested. Prospect of the crops. 4°. 1 page.

1810, April 16, Monticello. Acknowledging letter of 2d. Incloses a letter from Mr. F. X. Martin, who wishes a judgeship in Louisiana. His improved plow. Backward spring. 4°. 1 page.

1810, May 13, Monticello. Importation of Merino rams. Suggestions as to the disposition of their descendants, so that their friends in all parts of the State may be supplied with rams and ewes of this valuable breed. 4°. 3 pages.

1810, May 30, Monticello. Wishes to procure papers from the Departments of War, Treasury, and State, in his defense of the action brought against him by Edward Livingston relative to the batture. Asks Madison to furnish him with his copy of Moreau del' Isle's Memoir. 4°. 1 page.

1810, June 27, Monticello. Acknowledging letters of 8th, 15th, and 22d. Will acquiesce in any arrangement Madison may make relative to the debt to Mr. Hooe. The want of rain and crop prospects. Great Britain's real object the exclusive use of the ocean. A return to embargo can alone save us. 4°. 1 page.

Montpellier.

1810, July 13, Monticello. Early works on the history of Virginia. On Merino sheep and their raising. Livingston's case against Jefferson. Has furnished his counsel with the grounds of his defense. A clear case. Submits it to Madison. Shepherd dogs. 4°. 2 pages.

1810, July 26, Monticello. Acknowledging letters of 17th, and last mail. Unable to find a letter of Hamilton's which Madison mentions. Will copy it from the conventional debates. The batture case. 4°. 1 page.

1810, August 16, Monticello. Acknowledging letter of 15th. Describes the character and capabilities of Mr. McGehee, an overseer. Relates all that is good and bad of him. 4°. 1 page.

JEFFERSON.

1810, August 20, Monticello. Referring to his case of the batture respecting the Nile and Mississippi not being sufficiently clear, he states their analogies more clearly. 4°. 1 page.

1810, September 10, Monticello. Has just returned from Bedford. Hopes to see Madison and Mrs. Madison at his place. Bidwell's flight on account of fraud committed by him in his office of county treasurer. 4°. 1 page.

Washington.

1810, December 8, Monticello. Incloses a survey of Lafayette's lands adjacent to New Orleans. Also a MS. from Dupont on our system of finance. Has had a visit from Mr. Warden, of whom he has a good opinion, and suggests the finding of some Government employment for him. 4°. 2 pages.

——— to WARDEN, DAVID BAILIE. *New York.*

1811, January 11, Monticello. Acknowledging letters of December 11 and 19, and January 2, with packets accompanying. Hears with pleasure his prospects of a return to France in the character he wishes. Asks him to notify him on his arrival that he may write to his friends there concerning him. [*See* letter from Warden to Madison, April 23, 1811.] 4°. 1 page.

——— to MADISON. *Washington.*

1811, March 8, Monticello. Congratulates him on the close of the session of Congress. Our only chance as to England is the accession of the Prince of Wales to the throne. Difficult to understand what Bonaparte means towards us. Advocates taking possession of East Florida. Bad winter for the farmers. 4°. 1 page.

1811, October 10, Monticello. A request of Mrs. Lewis to mention the name of a Mr. Wood, an applicant for a commission in the Army. The old king dying; he hopes the successor will give us justice and peace, but thinks it barely possible relying on his former habits. 4°. 1 page.

1811, December 31, Monticello. Contrary to his inclination he sends applications for office from persons it is difficult to refuse, but he wishes Madison to consider him only as a postrider bearing these letters. The prospect of the death of George III still keeps up a hope of avoiding war. Compliments him on his message. 4°. 1 page.

1812, March 26, Monticello. Acknowledging letter of 6th. Has published explanations of the case of the batture. Declaration of war expected. 4°. 1 page.

1812, May 2, Monticello. Solicitation of Archibald C. Randolph for command in the new Army. States what he knows about him. 4°. 1 page.

1812, May 30, Monticello. The triangular war, the idea of the Federalists and malcontents. Arguments against it. The preventing Eastern capitalists and seamen from employment, and thereby taking away the most powerful weapon we can employ against Great Britain. It would shut every market for our agricultural productions and engender discontent. Quixotic to choose to fight two enemies at a time. 4°. 1 page.

JEFFERSON.

1812, August 10, Monticello. A private communication respecting the applicant for the office of consul at Lisbon. His unfitness. 4°. 1 page.

1813, April 10, Monticello. Incloses a letter from Thomas Lehré to himself soliciting the office of marshal of the district of Charleston, S. C. Wish of Dr. Barton to be appointed to the medical department of the Army. Intends to communicate with Madison his views on the defences of the Chesapeake. 4°. 1 page.

1813, August 23, Monticello. The selection of principal assessor in his county. Mentions Peter Minor as an excellent person for the office. 4°. 1 page.

1814, February 16, Monticello. Incloses copy of a letter to Col. Elias Earle, relative to the latter's call on the Government to reimburse expenses in which Jefferson thinks it is not liable. Scheme of the new loan. The creation of new banks will facilitate it. His views on the banking system. New taxes are paid with cheerfulness. The public mind is made up to a continuance of the war. 4°. 1 page.

——— to EARLE, ELIAS.

1814, February 16, Monticello. Establishment of iron works on the lands of the Cherokees. As it was a private enterprise, does not think the Government liable for expenses of explorations. Will be glad to hear Gen. Dearborn's views and will acquiesce in his statement that the Government was liable for the expenses. 4°. 1 page.

——— to MADISON. *Washington.*

1814, March 16, Monticello. Incloses two letters from Mr. Charles Burrall, postmaster at Baltimore. The removal of Mr. Granger, Postmaster-General, will induce efforts to be made for Burrall's removal. Jefferson gives his testimony as to his good character and abilities. 4°. 1 page.

Montpellier.

1814, May 17, Monticello. Incloses a paper sent him, probably for his signature, to recommend a certain person (not named) for office. Has not a good opinion of the person. Congratulates Madison on the success of the loan. Asks him to return Wynne's life of Jenkins if it is in the office of State Department. 4°. 2 pages.

Washington.

1814, October 15, Monticello. Acknowledging letter of 10th. The war declared by Great Britain to have become a war of conquest until she reduces us to unconditional submission. Means to be pursued as a counterchange. Reorganization of the militia into classes and the ways and means. On the emission of treasury notes and their redemption. Gives a tabular statement of the amount of emissions, taxes, redemptions, and balances left in circulation every year on the plan sketched. [Signature cut off.] 4°. 3 pages.

1815, March 23, Monticello. Acknowledging receipt of letter of 12th, with the pamphlet on the causes and conduct of the war. Thinks it should be published and sent to Europe to set them right as to our character and conduct and to remove

JEFFERSON.

false impressions. Congratulates Madison on the peace and the éclat with which the war was ended. England should concur in a convention for relinquishing impressment. That the present is but a truce, determinable on the first act of impressment of an American seaman. Respecting the removal of his library. 4°. 4 pages.

Montpellier.

1815, March 24, Monticello. Is laboriously employed in arranging his library to be ready for its delivery. Wishes much to see him and will try to visit him. 4°. 1 page.

1815, March 25, Monticello. Has received the "Aurora," beginning the publication of the "Causes and conduct of the war." Thinks the Government should reprint it immediately, so that it will go to Europe as the edition published by the Government. 4°. 1 page.

1815, May 12, Monticello. Incloses a letter from Francis de Masson and Lafayette. Newspapers begin the war for the European powers. Can not believe that these powers can force a sovereign upon France. The financial difficulties of England will deter her from attempting it single-handed. 4°. 1 page.

Washington.

1815, July 16, Monticello. Receives a letter from Governor Nicholas, asking his testimony as relates to the character of his son, late a colonel in the army, who wishes to be appointed consul at Leghorn. Sends a copy of his answer to Madison, in which he regrets he can not recommend him for that office during the occupancy of the present consul, who is his friend and has held the office for thirty years with credit and ability. 4°. 2 pages.

1815, July 23, Monticello. Inclosing applications for office, the persons not named. 4°. 1 page.

1815, December 22, Monticello. Incloses a letter from Robert Patterson, asking the influence of Jefferson to secure the appointment of Mr. Hassler as a surveyor of the Government. Also commending Samuel Francis Dupont, who wishes to be midshipman in the Navy. A letter from his father, Victor Dupont, relating to it, also inclosed. Also inclosed a letter from H. G. Spofford, who wishes to be postmaster at Albany. 4°. 1 page.

1816, August 15, Monticello. Incloses a letter from William Duncanson, nephew of Jefferson's old friend, Maj. Duncanson, one of the pioneers of Washington, and an honest, honorable man. 4°. 1 page.

1817, February 8, Monticello. Incloses a paper from Mr. Spofford, of Albany, for Madison's perusal, with a request to return it to Spofford. Commissions received for the visitors of Central College. State of the weather and agricultural items. 4°. 1 page.

Montpellier.

1817, November 15, Monticello. Wishes to borrow a copy of Palladio if Madison has one. Respecting the building of the college and engaging professors. Sketch of a bill for establishing ward schools, colleges and university. 4°. 1 page.

JEFFERSON.

1818, January 2, Monticello. Signature by the President and others of a paper relating to the University of Virginia, to be presented to the governor. 4°. 1 page.

1818, April 11, Monticello. Acknowledging letter of March 29. Financial matters connected with the University. Introduces Mr. Coffee, a sculptor, who is to take Madison's and Jefferson's busts. 4°. 1 page.

1818, June 28, Monticello. Proposed meeting at Rockfish Gap of the visitors of the University to consult on a report to be made to the House of Representatives. Questions to be discussed as to the location. Suggestions as to the course they intend to travel. 4°. 2 pages.

1819, February 19, Monticello. Acknowledging letter of 12th. Meeting of the board of visitors of the University of Virginia. Arrangements for meeting Madison. Accident to his grandson, Jefferson Randolph. 4°. 1 page.

1819, March 8, Monticello. Returns a letter from Mr. Watson. Matters concerning Mr. Cooper and the University. 4°. 1 page.

1819, July 7, Monticello. Describes the present state of things at the University of Virginia. Proposed changes of plans in building. Progress of the work slow. Preparation of subjects for the University. 4°. 4 pages.

1819, September 23, Monticello. Annual report to be made of the disbursements, funds on hand, and general statement of the condition of the University. 4°. 1 page.

1820, February 16, Monticello. The finances of the University. Subscriptions in arrear. 4°. 1 page.

1820, April 11, Monticello. Preparations for brewing. Leaves for Bedford, to return May 1. 4°. 1 page.

1820, May 17, Monticello. Measures adopted by the board of visitors of the University. Incloses a letter to Gen. Taylor to read and forward to him. Suffers from a stiffening of the wrist. 4°. 1 page.

1821, January 28, Monticello. Introducing his physician and friend, Dr. Watkins. 4°. 1 page.

1821, August 15, Monticello. A circular letter relating to the resolution of the visitors of the University of Virginia at their last session on the ascertaining of the state of accounts under contracts made and expense of completing the buildings begun and contemplated. 4°. 1 page.

1821, September 16, Monticello. Endeavor to get the duty repealed on the importation of books. Propositions to make a combined movement by the Northern and Eastern colleges, with a request for the Southern and Western to to cooperate. Mr. Ticknor's able views on the subject. 4°. 2 pages.

——— to JAMES LEANDER CATHCART.

1821, September 10, Monticello. Gives his testimony as to his character for his ability and integrity while consul on the Barbary coast. [Copy.] 4°. 1 page.

JEFFERSON to MADISON. *Montpellier.*

1821, September 30, Monticello. Cost of the buildings finished at the University and a review of the state of the funds. Conjectural estimates. Appended is a view of the whole expenses and of the funds of the University.
4°. 4 pages.

1821, October 30, Monticello. Incloses the sketch of a petition to Congress. The November report of the University on the basis of Mr. Brockenbrough's settlement. 4°. 2 pages.

1822, April 7, Monticello. Acknowledging letter of March 29. Meeting of visitors of the University. Question of the removal of the seat of government of Virginia. Building of the rotunda discussed. 4°. 2 pages.

1822, November 22, Monticello. Introducing a person who was taken prisoner by the Indians when 3 or 4 years old. Is a student of medicine and wishes to attend the medical lectures in Philadelphia. Has broken the small bone of his left fore-arm. It is doing well. Will prevent a visit to Madison. Financial matters of the University. 4°. 1 page.

1823, February 16, Monticello. The legislature authorizes the literary board to lend another $60,000. Thinks, with others of the board of visitors, it should be accepted and, if Madison concurs, will authorize the engagement of workmen and provide materials for the library. 4°. 1 page.

1823, February 24, Monticello. Incloses a letter from Mr. Cox which he can not answer on account of crippled hands. Will not meddle in a Presidential election nor express a sentiment on subject of candidates. Asks Madison to write Mr. Cox for him. The acceptance of the loan by five of the visitors of the University. Intends proceeding immediately to engage the workmen.
4°. 1 page.

1823, March 12, Monticello. Has authorized the erection of the rotunda at the University.
4°. 1 page.

1823, April 30, Monticello. The University of Virginia. Size of the lecture rooms. Apparatus for natural philosophy. Arrangement of the seats for the students. Financial matters. 4°. 2 pages.

1823, August 30, Monticello. The Declaration of Independence. Corrects certain statements of Timothy Pickering, describing the incidents of that occasion and the fact of Jefferson's original draft.
4°. 3 pages.

1823, October 24, Monticello. Forwards two important letters sent to him by the President. Receives Trumbull's print of the Declaration of Independence. Pythagorus first taught the true position of the sun in the center of our system; his doctrine was a long time after restored by Copernicus. 4°. 1 page.

1823, November 6, Monticello. Belief that the legislature will dispose of the University debt. Provisional preparations should be made to send an agent to England to procure professors. Cabell declines the mission. Recommends F. Gilmer. Query as to salaries. 4°. 1 page.

JEFFERSON.

1824, January 7, Monticello. Incloses two letters from Dr. Cooper. Question as to offering him a place in the University of Virginia. 4°. 1 page.

———, to BARBOUR, JAMES. *Washington.*

1824, January 20, Monticello. Recommending J. L. Cathcart. [*See* Cathcart, James Leander]. [Copy]. 4°. 2 pages.

——— to MADISON. *Montpellier.*

1824, April 9, Monticello. Statement of account of the University of Virginia. Income and expenses. [Circular]. 4°. 1 page.

——— to GILMER, FRANCIS W.

1824, April 26, University of Virginia. Power of attorney to Gilmer to proceed to Europe and select and engage professors for the different schools of the University. [Copy]. 4°. 1 page.

——— to MADISON. *Montpellier.*

1824, August 8, Monticello. Incloses a letter from Mr. Gilmer. Endeavors to secure a professor of mathematics in England for the University—Mr. Ivory. Catalogue of books for the library of the University. Has devoted much time to it. Asks Madison's assistance in selection of theological works. 4°. 1 page.

1824, September 3, Monticello. Is near closing his catalogue and would like Madison's theological supplement. 4°. 1. page.

1824, October 6, Monticello. Disappointment in the endeavor to secure professors for the University. The amounts paid for salaries are higher in England than the University of Virginia can afford. Importance of immediate action to secure the best that can be had, that the legislature and public may not think the enterprise as failed. 4°. 2 pages.

1824, November 15, Monticello. Was unable to accompany the General (Lafayette?), who will leave Madison on Friday to go to a dinner and ball at Fredericksburg. No letter yet from Gilmer. 4°. 1 page.

1824, November 20, Monticello. Arrival of Gilmer in New York. He has engaged five professors, whom he names, for the University. 4°. 1 page.

1824, November 30, Monticello. Appointments of professors for the University. 4°. 1 page.

1824, December —, Monticello. Professors, Long and Batterman, of ancient and modern languages. Inquiries respecting Mr. Preston in case Mr. Gilmer should decline. 4°. 1 page.

1825, February 15, Monticello. Meeting of the visitors of the University to be called as soon as the professors arrive. Henry St. George Tucker proposed as professor. 4°. 1 page.

1825, March 22, Monticello. George Tucker and Emmet accept and Henry St. George Tucker declines professorships. Preston and Robertson suggested. Number of students coming. [Signature cut off]. 4°. 1 page.

1825, April 15, Monticello. Proposition from Mr. Perry to sell lands separating two tracts of the

JEFFERSON.

University. Incloses sketch of the grounds, and statement of the financial estimates of expenses and receipts. 4°. 6 pages.

1825, May 13, Monticello. Difficulty in filling the chair of law professor. False rumors as to appointment of Judge Dade. His qualifications and character. Suggests offering him the position. 4°. 2 pages.

1825, September 10, Monticello. The state of his health makes uncertain his attendance at the University, so invites the board of visitors to meet at Monticello, and drive with him and then ride to the University, pro forma, for attesting the proceedings. [Circular]. 4°. 1 page.

1825, October 18, Monticello. Everything going on smoothly at the University. His experience with Browere, the sculptor, in sitting for his cast. Recommends Bernard Peyton as his commission merchant. 4°. 1 page.

1825, December 24, Monticello. General opinion in favor of the question of internal improvements. Is willing to adopt anything that Madison may advise. Suggests heads of consideration to propositions to submit to Congress, under injunctions as to secrecy. 4°. 7 pages.

1826, February 17, Monticello. Apointment of Terrill to the chair of law. Number of students at the University. Vote of the house of representatives against giving another dollar to the University. Course to be pursued relating to the library. Importance of political principles in the selection of the law professor. Virginia must follow the lead of New York and South Carolina in vindication of the Constitution. Jefferson's financial difficulties and suggestions as to extricating himself. Gloomy thoughts lessened by communicating them with a friend such as Madison is and always has been. 4°. 3 pages.

Not dated. Incloses some loose notes on the bankrupt bill and a plan of American finance. 4°. 3 pages.

Not dated. Notes in an unknown hand relating to Jefferson's memoirs. strip of paper.

——— to MADISON. *Washington.*

Not dated. Fragment of a letter of instructions to the Secretary of State respecting captures of vessels after and before the signature of a treaty. [Not signed]. 4°. 1 page.

Not dated. Statement and suggestions respecting consulates and appointments. 4°. 4 pages.

Not dated. Fragment of a letter alluding to the presenting of facts to European governments on yellow fever. 8°. 1 page.

JERFRY & CO., JOHN. *Philadelphia.*

1794, June 27. Accounts of the schooner *Sally.* fol. 2 pages.

JERVEY, JAMES, and others, to MADISON. *Washington.*

1813, April 26, Charleston, S. C. Inclosing a copy of an oration delivered before the "Seventy-six" Association on March 4. 4°. 1 page.

JEWELL, R. GEO. WASHINGTON. *Montpellier.*

1835, July 4, Cincinnati. Asks Madison's advice as to his future path in life (Jewell's). 4°. 3 pages.

1835, August 10, Cincinnati. Thanks him for answering his letter. 4°. 2 pages.

JOHNSON, C.

1827, October 3, Bear Wallow. Acknowledging letter of September 24, respecting the resignation of Prof. Long from the University of Virginia. Incloses a copy of a letter from Dr. Robert M. Patterson concerning the fitness of Dr. Jones to fill the vacancy in the chair of natural philosophy. He is recommended for the place by Dr. Horner. 4°. 2 pages.

1827, October 5, Bear Wallow. Appointment to the vacant chair of natural philosophy at the University of Virginia. 4°. 2 pages.

1827, October 29, Richmond. James Renwick, of New York, highly recommended to fill the vacancy in the chair of natural philosophy at the University. 4°. 2 pages.

1827, December 15, Richmond. Acknowledging letter of 9th, respecting the provisional appointment of Mr. Harrison. His qualifications. The appointment of professor of natural philosophy remains in *statu quo*. Thinks Mr. Renwick will not accept an appointment.

1828, March 8, Richmond. Acknowledging letter of December 19. The vacant chair of natural philosophy at the University of Virginia. The quarterly appointment of their chairman. 4°. 3 pages.

1828, April 21, Richmond. Acknowledging letter of March 24, inclosing testimonials in favor of Mr. Ritchie and Mr. Dodd to the vacant chair. The subject of salary. Policy of not refusing Ritchie on account of his religion. 4°. 3 pages.

1828, August 3, near Staunton. Has written to Dr. Harrison about the professorship of ancient languages. He will accept the appointment for a year. 4°. 2 pages.

JOHNSON, EDWARD. *Washington.*

1813, February 18, Baltimore. As chairman of meeting of citizens of Baltimore incloses a memorial on the subject of a proposed repeal or modification of the nonimportation acts of the United States. 4°. 1 page.

Washington.

1813, February 18, Baltimore. Memorial of a committee of citizens of Baltimore, protesting against the partial repeal of the nonimportation act of Congress, presented to the President and Congress. royal fol. 3 pages.

1815, April 10, Baltimore. Congratulations of a meeting of Republican citizens of Baltimore on the conclusion of peace, with complimentary remarks on the patriotic measures of the President during his administration. [Signed by William Pinkney and many others.] 4°. 4 pages.

JOHNSON, F., to BARBOUR, JAMES.

1821, January 8, Washington. Offers for sale for Madison a selection of riding horses. 4°. 2 pages.

JOHNSON, JAMES, to MADISON. *Washington.*

1815, June 4, Great Crossing. The exhaustion of the appropriation for provisioning the Army, and a large sum being due him for contracts for Louisiana and Mississippi. Appeals to the President for relief. 4°. 4 pages.

1815, June 12, Great Crossing. Renews his appeal to the President respecting his situation by reason of the exhaustion of the appropriation for provisioning the Army. 4°. 4 pages.

1815, July 4, Great Crossing. Another appeal to the President for relief. The want of funds in the appropriation for provisioning the Army, causes the writer's bills to go to protest. 4°. 5 pages.

1815, July 9, Great Crossing. Appeals to the President for assistance in getting through the Secretary of War the amounts due for contracting for Jackson's army. 4°. 4. pages.

1815, July 16, Great Crossing. Expresses his gratitude for Madison's good offices with the Secretary of War in procuring the relief desired, which saves him from bankruptcy. 4°. 2 pages.

1816, September 15, Great Crossing. Political matters in his section. Discomfiture of the Federalists. 4°. 5 pages.

JOHNSON, JAMES B. *Washington.*

1815, June 15, Waynesville. Showing the evils of slavery. 4°. 3 pages.

1816, December 17, Chillicothe. Appeal of a youth for the abolition of slavery. 4°. 3 pages.

JOHNSON, JOSEPH, and others.

1811, August 29, Charleston. The standing committee of the "Seventy-six" Association of South Carolina transmits a copy of an oration delivered on the Fourth of July by Benjamin A. Markley. 4°. 1 page.

JOHNSTON, ORRAMEL, to UNKNOWN.

1812, May 17, Natchez. Request to forward a letter to the President in great haste, as it contains something of a serious nature. 4°. 1 page.

JOHNSON, RICHARD M., to MADISON. *Washington.*

1812, July 24, Blue Spring, Ky. Impatience of the Kentucky troops to be called into service. A well-organized force of 6,000 men. Anxious to take Malden this year, a post of rendezvous for Indians to get supplies of arms. Excellence of the troops. 4°. 3 pages.

1812, September 18, Fort Wayne. Commands a battalion of mounted riflemen. Recommends giving Gen. Harrison the command of the Kentucky forces destined for Canada. His unequalled capacity. Has destroyed the Elkhart village. Commends an expedition against the savages. The Miamis are enemies. His men serving without pay. small 4°. 2 pages.

1813, January 21, Washington. Resignation of Governor Harrison. Hopes he will be appointed major-general. He now acts under his brevet commission from the governoı of Kentucky. His capacity and merit. 4°. 3 pages.

JOHNSON, RICHARD M.

1813, July 14, Camp on road to Piqua. Order to Gen. Harrison for militia regiment to go to Kaskaskia. Attempt to execute the order with dispatch. Describes the intended route of march. fol. 1 page.

1813, August 9, Great Crossing, Ky. Movements of the regiment under his command. Protests at the War Department of Ward & Taylor's drafts for contracts under Gen. Flournoy in Louisiana. Injustice of the proceeding. Details the facts in the case. fol. 4 pages.

1813 (1814?), January 22, Great Crossing. Indisposition of Gen. Howard to be placed within the command of the Northwestern army. Usefulness and capacity of Gen. Howard. Johnson's painful wounds. Indignantly denies the reports reflecting on his character during his absence. His money transactions explained. 4°. 3 pages.

1814, June 4, Great Crossing. Appointment from the Secretary of War as associate with Gen. Harrison and Jeremiah Morrow to treat with the Northwest Indians. 4°. 1 page.

1814, July 15, Great Crossing. Acknowledging receipt of the communication of the War Department substituting his appointment of commissioner by some other person. Advocates the proposals of his brother, James Johnson, to carry mails. 4°. 2 pages.

1814, November 22, Washington. Raising of a militia regiment, with a regular regiment, to serve during the war. Recommends the appointment of Col. Mason to the regular Army. 4°. 2 pages.

1814 (?), not dated, Camp near River Raisin. Recommends for tax collector of his district William Brown, of Cynthiana. Has just received marching orders from Gen. Harrison, who is expected to land in Canada, below Malden, with 4,000 men. Takes prisoner an important man of the Shawnee tribe. Difficulty in restraining his men from killing him. Obtains important information. fol. 2 pages.

1815, May 14, Great Crossing. Appeal to the President to avert the ruin which must fall on the house of Ward & Taylor for nonacceptance by the Secretary of War of their drafts as contractors for the Army. Incloses copy of a letter from Mr. Brown, agent of Ward & Taylor. 4°. 4 pages.

1815, June 4, Blue Spring, Ky. Incloses a letter to Secretary of War urging a transfer of appropriation to pay the just demands of Ward & Taylor, contractors for the Army, the appropriation for provisions, etc., being exhausted. 4°. 3 pages.

Montpellier.

1815, June 12, Great Crossing. Renews his appeal to the President to prevent the ruin of the house of Ward & Taylor by ordering the payment of their just dues. 4°. 3 pages.

——— to DALLAS, A. J. *Washington.*

1815, June 15, Great Crossing. Urgent appeal to the Secretary of War to save the firm of Ward & Taylor from failure. [Copy.] 4°. 3 pages.

JOHNSON, RICHARD M., and others, to MADISON.
Washington.

1816, April 26, Washington. Recommendations for the appointment of Samuel Lane as commissioner to superintend the public buildings. 4°. 1 page.

———.

1816, June 12, Great Crossing. Recommendations of Joel Haden for chaplain in the Army, and John T. Mason as deputy commissary. Incidents of local politics. 4°. 3 pages.

1816, October 10, Great Crossing. The judicial vacancy occasioned by the death of Judge Innes. Names of the candidates to fill the place. His choice would be John T. Mason. His qualifications. 4°. 3 pages.

1816, December 19, Washington. Calls attention of the President to Mr. Lee, who makes deductions in the pay of troops under Governor Shelby till their final discharge. 4°. 3 pages.

1816, ——— 26, Washington. Recommends Col. Lane, who is an applicant for commissioner to superintend the public buildings. 4°. 1 page.

1817, January 16, Washington. Joseph Hawkins requests to have his name withdrawn from the Senate for the office of surveyor on account of objections of some members from Louisiana for want of residence. He will be a resident in February. 4°. 1 page.

Montpellier.

1824, April 4, Washington. Acknowledging letter of 2d. On imprisonment for debt. 4°. 1 page.

1828, May 13, Washington. Acknowledging letter of 9th. Respecting Mr. Emmons. 4°. 1 page.

1829, September 4, Blue Spring, Ky. Introduces Mr. William Emmons, brother of Dr. Richard Emmons, the author of the "Fredoniad." Deep interest in the coming Virginia convention. 4°. 2 pages.

Richmond.

1829, September 15, Blue Spring, Ky. Introducing Robert W. Scott. 4°. 1 page.

Montpellier.

1830, December 27, Washington. Is extremely sorry that Mr Emmons is troubling Madison about his books. 4°. 1 page.

No date. A memorandum relating to certain land purchases by Mr. McKee and others. (Unsigned.) 4°. 1 page.

JOHNSON, ROBERT. *Richmond.*

1786, September 23, Fayette County. Expeditions against the Wabash Indians and Shawnees. Convention to sit in a few days to determine on a separation. Asks Madison's advice on the subject. [Memorandum on this sheet in Madison's handwriting, relating to paper money.] fol. 2 pages.

Washington.

1802, December 5. Abuse of Jefferson; Burr suspected of it. Hears that Rufus King intends offering for the next Presidency. Louisiana to be given up to the French Government. Understands that the Indians about Port Vincennes agree to cede territory to the United States that Salt Licks may be worked. Concerning Salt Licks. small 4°. 4 pages.

JOHNSON, THOMAS B.

1810, February 11, New Orleans. Thanks the President for sanctioning the recommendation of his friends in nominating him to the Postmaster-General for the post he holds. 4°. 1 page.

JOHNSTON, P.

1801, October 30, Prince Edward. Introduces Elijah Hendrick, who seeks employment in Washington. small 4°. 1 page.

JOHNSTONE, G. W.

1811, December 11, Vincennes, Indiana Territory. Inclosing a joint memorial of the two branches of the legislature of Indiana Territory to Congress on the subject of the Army, and praying relief for the soldiers' families by granting a section of land. 4°. 6 pages.

JOHONNOT, G., to STORY, ISAAC. *Marblehead.*

1801, November 22, Hampden. Value of land in Maine. Asks Mr. Story to write Mr. Gerry to influence the President in his favor and appoint him to the office of collector. small 4°. 2 pages.

JONES, JESSE, and others, to MADISON. *Washington.*

1811, April 27, Cumberland County. Address of the Baptist church of Neels Creek, disapproving of the proceedings of the Baptist church at Salem, Miss., and assures Madison of their high sense and confidence in him. fol. 1 page.

JONES, JOSEPH, to Unknown.

Not dated. Fragment of a letter bearing signature of Joseph Jones. Scrap of paper.

——— to GOODWYN, PETERSON. *Washington.*

1812, June 5, Petersburg. Recommends Mr. Mordecai Barbour, who wishes an appointment in the Army. War seems inevitable. If France will not do us justice, advises the President to recall our minister and have nothing to do with her. Flour scarce. fol. 1 page.

JONES, THOMAS, to CHEW, JOSEPH.

1794, June 21, Bourbon County. A survey of land and plat. fol. 2 pages.

JONES, WALTER, and others, to MADISON. *Orange.*

1799, February 7, Philadelphia. Expression of their confidence in Madison and justice of his motives. Hope that the obstacles to his serving in the State legislature may be less imperious than those by which he was withdrawn from that of the Union. Invite him with earnestness to take part in the councils of his State. 4°. 2 pages.

JONES, WALTER, JR., to EUSTIS, WILLIAM J. (Secretary of War). *Washington.*

1811, September 11, Fredericktown. Asks for the orders to be taken in the War Department upon the subject of certain witnesses in the court-martial of Gen. Wilkinson. 4°. 3 pages.

JONES, WALTER, to MASON, J. (President Bank of Columbia).

1812, July 7, Washington. Respecting James Stewart, Thomas and Mark Winslow, prisoners on a charge of counterfeiting. Is disposed to be lenient in their punishment. [*See* letter of Mason, J., June 9, 1812.] 4°. 1 page.

JONES, WALTER, to MONROE. *Washington.*

1819, September 9, Washington. Recommending Alexander Scott as a candidate for an appointment under Government. [*See* letter of A. Scott to Madison, dated January 2, 1820. Copy.] 4°. 1 page.

JONES, WILLIAM, to MADISON.

1807, March 28, Philadelphia. Acknowledging letter. Regrets his incompetency, yet will do his best to investigate the matter desired with as little delay as possible. 4°. 1 page.

1811, February 11, Philadelphia. Incloses translation of a French circular respecting American vessels, prizes of the French. 4°. 1 page.

1811, February 21, Philadelphia. Incloses a translated extract from a letter from Jonathan Jones, of Bordeaux, respecting circular letters from the grand judge and minister of finances in France, ordering the tribunal of prizes to suspend all further business respecting American prizes, and announcing that the decrees of Berlin and Milan are withdrawn. American interests will be terminated advantageously. 4°. 2 pages.

1813, January 14, Philadelphia. Acknowledging letter of 12th. Accepts the appointment of Secretary of the Navy. Will leave for Washington in a few days. 4°. 2 pages.

1813, February 19, Washington. Announcing the capture and destruction of the British frigate *Java* by the *Constitution*, Commodore Bainbridge. 4°. 1 page.

1813, February 26, Washington. Disapproves of the existing instructions from the Navy Department rendering the naval commanders on certain stations subordinate and obedient to military commanders. Officers of talent and character will not submit to the degradation and will decline or resign. 4°. 2 pages.

1813, March 27, Washington. Object of the attempt of the British to ascend James River is to draw the gunboats from Norfolk. Shall give instructions to Capt. Stewart to confine his attentions to Norfolk. 4°. 1 page.

1813, April 1, Washington. Conjectures as to the movements of the British fleet. 4°. 1 page.

——— to GORDON, CHARLES (Captain). *Baltimore.*

1813, April 15, Washington. Instructions respecting the security of the trade of Baltimore and its intercourse with the waters of the Chesapeake. Authorizing the purchase of schooners to be fitted out and armed for service, the men and officers to be paid the same rations and prize-money as other officers and crews of the Navy. Instructions as to the cooperation with the military in case of the approach of the enemy. [Copy.] 4°. 3 pages.

——— to MADISON. *Washington.*

1813, April 17, Washington. Returns from Baltimore where they are much gratified at the arrangements made. Secures three or four fine privateer schooners, a prompt and effective force. They will be ready for service to-day. Hopes to recapture the fine schooners the enemy had taken and to restrain the depredations of schooners and barges. 4°. 2 pages.

JONES, WILLIAM.

1813, April 26, Washington. Recommends the appointment of Dr. James Rush for the position lately occupied by his father, Dr. Benjamin Rush, as treasurer of the Mint. 4°. 1 page.

1813, May 12, Washington. Attack upon Commodore Murray in the Democratic press. Incloses a letter from him. His party prejudices warm, but could not commit a dishonorable act. 4°. 1 pages.

1813, May 15, Washington. Proceedings of the court-martial at Sacketts Harbor for the President's decision in the sentence of dismissal of Sailing-master Hutton. Suggests the sentence of 500 lashes in the case of Fitzgerald be mitigated to 200, as being too severe. 4°. 1 page.

1813, May 16, Washington. Extract from a letter of Capt. Sinclair, at Norfolk, enumerating the British vessels at the capes. 4°. 1 page.

1813, May 28, Washington. Incloses letters from Commodore Chauncey. Capt. Sinclair goes to Sacketts Harbor to take command of the new ship there. No marines to send. Lieut. Brooks recruiting in vicinity of Erie. Capt. Wainwright daily expected from Charlestown with marines for the Lakes. Lieut. Trenchard goes to New York with seamen. Sloop of war launched at Erie. Desires the President to designate Mobile as the port of entry. fol. 2 pages.

1813, June 6, Washington. James T. Leonard next in command to Commodore Chauncey under arrest waiting investigation of a court-martial. Some of the Razees armed on our coast. News from Boston, stating a British frigate came into Boston Bay and Capt. Lawrence, of the *Chesapeake*, slipped his cables, went out to attack her. Result not yet known. fol. 2 pages.

1813, June 6, Washington. Incloses a report prepared for the chairman of the Senate Naval Committee, of the number of gunboats in service. Additional special defense of Baltimore. Exhibits a general view of our coast and harbor defence. fol. 1 page.

1813, June 7, Washington. Exhibit showing the number of gunboats and vessels substituted for gunboats in service for harbor and coast defense at the several naval stations and elsewhere in the United States. fol. 2 pages.

1813, June 8, Washington. Incloses official letters of Commodore Chauncey. Also incloses a letter from Commodore Bainbridge, covering Commodore Brooke's challenge to Capt. Lawrence. Also incloses letter from Commodore Decatur. Secretary of War orders cannon from New York to New London. fol. 1 page.

1813, June 21, Washington. Incloses letters showing that Commodore Chauncey determines on the course the President was solicitous he should have done, thereby greatly elevating his character. Few naval officers would have resisted the temptation to exalt their fame. 4°. 1 page.

——— to PERRY, OLIVER H. *Erie.*

1813, July 3, Washington. Acknowledging letters of June 19 and 24. Instructions as to his cooperation with Commodore Chauncey, and general orders as to the fleet under his command on Lake Erie. [Copy.] 4°. 5 pages.

JONES, WILLIAM, to CHAUNCEY, ISAAC (Commodore). *Lake Ontario.*

1813, July 3, Washington. General orders and instructions respecting the campaign on lakes Ontario and Erie. [Copy.] fol. 8 pages.

——— to MADISON. *Washington.*

1813, July 15, Washington. Details of the preparations for defence at the navy-yard in Washington. fol. 3 pages.

1813, July 24, Washington. Asks to be relieved from the duties of Acting Secretary of the Treasury. His duties as Secretary of the Navy occupying his whole time and mind. fol. 2 pages.

——— to DENT, JOHN H. *Charleston, S. C.*

1813, November 8, Washington. Acknowledging letter of October 25. Communications with the enemy. Instructs him to prohibit all intercourse except the commanding military general or naval officer. Should a flag of truce be found necessary, gives the necessary instructions as to the method. 4°. 2 pages.

——— to MADISON. *Washington.*

1813 (?), not dated. Incloses a sketch of our financial means to sustain the credit and provide the money to carry on the war with energy and effect. 4°. 9 pages.

1813 (?), not dated. Commodore Chauncey thinks that two ships of the line and one frigate can be built at Sacketts Harbor in due time. Expediency of seizing a point on the St. Lawrence to intercept supplies going to Kingston. Transportation of heavy articles. Asks the President's decision as to the heavy equipments. [Memorandum]. small 4°. 1 page.

1813 (?), not dated. Memorandum respecting Mr. Fox. No man more conversant with banking institutions, moneyed operations, and stocks. His record as a financier. [Unsigned. Draft.] 4°. 1 page.

———.

1813 (?), not dated. Memorandum respecting blocks and iron work for the Navy. Strip of paper.

——— to MADISON. *Washington.*

1813 (?), not dated. Impoverished condition of the Navy Department. Destitute of money; seamen unpaid and recruiting service at a stand. Not a dollar to transport seamen. Articles contracted for are withheld until funds appear. [Unsigned]. Scrap of paper.

——— to NAVY DEPARTMENT.

1814, April 15, Washington. General orders. Proceedings of the court-martial on James T. Leonard, a master commandant in the United States Navy with sentence of the court. [Printed document with written signature.] fol. 2 pages.

——— to MADISON. *Washington.*

1814, April 25, Washington. Announces his intention of resigning his position of Secretary of the Navy. Nothing but patriotic motives induced him to accept it. His pecuniary sacrifices, now demand his attention as they have greatly embarrassed his fortune, and it is necessary that he should engage in business to try to recover his losses. 4°. 4 pages.

JONES, WILLIAM.

1814, May 6, Washington. Acknowledging letter of 4th. Rumored preparations of the enemy at Mockodash on Lake Huron. Construction of boats for transportation. Contemplated operations on Lake Erie. Instructions to Capt. Sinclair. All apprehensions for the safety of Sacketts Harbor have subsided. New vessels of the enemy, their force exaggerated. Commodore Barney's force in the bay. The Army bounty deprives us of seamen. Frigates waiting for men. The new loan. Mortifying fact that the nation has to depend on individual speculators. 4°. 4 pages.

1814, May 10, Washington. Congratulations on the brilliant achievements of the United States ship *Peacock* in capturing the British sloop of war, *Epervier* with $200,000 in specie. Is embarrassed by the absence of the comptroller. Requisitions on the Secretary of Treasury laying over. Requests the appointment of an acting comptroller. 4°. 1 page.

1814, May 14, Washington. Inclosing proceedings of a court-martial held on board U. S. ship *United States*, for trial of officers and seamen, late of the ship *Chesapeake*, for charges of crimes committed by them in action between the *Chesapeake* and *Shannon*. fol. 1 page.

1814, May 16, Washington. Incloses letters from Commodore Chauncey. Attack by the enemy on Oswego. Desperate effort of the enemy to intercept our cannon and naval stores. 4°. 2 pages.

1814, May 18, Washington. The enemy's force and operations at Oswego. Capture of our guns and naval stores. Accounts from Europe of a gloomy nature as respects our prospects of negotiation. The pretensions of Great Britain that we renounce all trade beyond the Cape of Good Hope and to West Indies and abandon the fisheries. Impressment she adheres to. Query, if the northern powers exert their friendly influence from a feeling of common interest. The vindictive desperation of the enemy may unite and purify this country. The subjugation of France a great calamity. Incloses copy of Admiral Cochran's proclamation exciting the blacks to revolt. 4°. 2 pages.

1814, June 6, Washington. Inclosing documents lettered from A to E, containing all the information in this Department on subjects of the President's inquiry as to the naval force. 4°. 10 pages.

1814, June 6, Washington. Copies and extracts of letters addressed to the Secretary of the Navy from the officers on the several stations and others, exhibiting all the information obtained by them respecting the naval force of the enemy, near and in the Atlantic waters of the United States. [Lettered F and H.] fol. 8 pages.

1814, June 8, Washington. Asks the President to name the three seventy-fours now building. 4°. 1 page.

——— to MONROE, JAMES, Secretary of State.

1814, June 17, Washington. Disapproves of the proposed instructions to military commanders, giving them exclusive control and direction of all communications from the enemy's naval forces on our coast. [Copy.] 4°. 2 pages.

JONES, WILLIAM, to MADISON.

1814, June 18, Washington. Incloses a letter on an important matter not mentioned. It also relates to an important appointment. fol. 1 page.

1814, July 26, Washington. Incloses a paper supposed to be from a personal enemy of Commodore Chauncey. Asks Madison to compare the writing with that sent to him by Mr. Gales. The brother officers of Chauncey entertain the highest opinion of him. 4°. 1 page.

1814 (?), not dated, Washington. Submits proceedings of a court-martial, and asks his decision on the sentence of Joseph Wallace. The robbery in the public magazine on the Eastern Branch. Public property stolen by Ewell. [Draft.]
Strip of paper.

1814, July 30, Washington. Regrets having commenced the new ship at Vergennes. Does not know where the money is to come from. Rumors of the capture of the *Rattlesnake* by the *Leander*. It is not believed to be true. 4°. 2 pages.

1814 (?), not dated, Washington. Asking what answer to give Mr. Gray to his petition respecting a capture. Distinction in Gerard's case alluded to as analogous. [Signed W. J.] 4°. 1 page.

1814, August 1, Washington. Incloses letter from Dr. Buchanan, of the Navy, Commodore Chauncey's physician. Delicacy of proceedings in the order given to Decatur, should Chauncey recover. Asks if he shall send Chauncey a copy of the order, which sufficiently explains the motive.
4°. 2 pages.

——— to DECATUR, STEPHEN, (Commodore).
New York.

1814, August 8, Washington. In view of the powerful force with which our country is menaced by the enemy, he charges Decatur with the naval defence of the harbor and city of New York, and instructs him to take command of the whole naval force there, whether in service or in ordinary, and to cooperate with the military commander, the governor of the State, and corporate authorities. [Copy.] 4°. 3 pages.

——— to CHAUNCEY, ISAAC, (Commodore).
Sackett's Harbor.

1814, August 13, Washington. Acknowledging letter of July 31. Orders to cooperate with Gen. Izard, who is on his way to the St. Lawrence, in the plan of a joint attack on Kingston. In the event of his health not being sufficiently restored, he is instructed to commit the command of the squadron to Capt. Jones. [Copy.] 4°. 3 pages.

——— to MADISON. *Washington.*

1814, August 15, Washington. Showing the gratifying result of a change from the hospital establishment at Charleston to a floating hospital in the open harbor. 4°. 2 pages.

1814, August 18, Washington. Inclosing a letter from Commodore Bainbridge respecting the irregularity and serious evil arising from communications by flag of truce. If the Government has occasion to communicate with the enemy's naval force it is invariably done through the naval commander of the station. 4°. 3 pages.

JONES, WILLIAM.

1814, September 5. Suggestions offered to the President on the recent destruction of the public buildings in Washington, and how accommodations for Houses of Congress and the other offices can be substituted and improved. 4°. 8 pages.

1814, September 11, Washington. His private affairs compel him to again tender his resignation as Secretary of the Navy. Incloses the letter of resignation. "Private." fol. 2 pages.

1814, September 11, Washington. Letter of resignation subject to the President's decision between this time and December 1 ensuing. fol. 1 page.

Washington.

1814, September —, Washington. Communication in lead pencil announcing glorious news. (Probably the defeat and capture of the English squadron on Lake Champlain.) [Signed W. J.) fol. 1 page.

——— to CHAUNCEY, ISAAC. *Sackett's Harbor.*

1814, October 24, Washington. Instructions as to measures to be pursued towards increasing the naval force on Lake Ontario. [*See* letter of William Jones to Madison, dated October 26, 1814. Copy.] 4°. 2 pages.

——— to ANDERSON, SAMUEL T., naval storekeeper. *New York.*

1814, October 24, Washington. Instructions as to the transportation of public stores to Sackett's Harbor preparatory to the increase of the naval force on Lake Ontario. [*See* William Jones's letter to Madison, dated October 26, 1814. Copy.] 4°. 8 pages.

——— to MADISON. *Washington.*

1814, October 26, Washington. Details of preparatory steps to be taken for increasing the naval force on Lake Ontario. Inclosing copies of letters to Commodore Chauncey and S. T. Anderson, agent of transportation, on the measures to be pursued. 4°. 25 pages.

1814, November 14, Washington. Proposed promotions from masters commandant to captains. Case of Master Commandant Leonard. 8°. 1 page.

1814, November 15, Washington. Reports in obedience to a resolution of the Senate, a system of the better organization of the Navy Department. [Copy.] 4°. 29 pages.

1815, December 15, Philadelphia. Describes a fine collection of mathematical and astronomical instruments by the invitation of Prof. Patterson, president of the mint. Recommends Mr. Hassler to Madison's patronage and favor. 4°. 4 pages.

1814, December 22, Baltimore. Requests the appointment of E. W. Duval to more important duties than those in which he has been engaged in the Navy Department. 4°. 1 page.

1816, January 1, Philadelphia. Answer to an inquiry of Madison's how a general circulating medium is to be obtained independently of a national bank. Views as to the creation of a national bank. [Copy.] 4°. 12 pages.

1816, January 13, Philadelphia. Project of a bank to be established in Philadelphia, with branches

JONES, WILLIAM.

at Boston, New York, Baltimore, and Washington, and, if required by the Treasury Department, at Norfolk, Charleston, and New Orleans. [Unsigned.] fol. 3 pages.

1816, January 13, Philadelphia. State of the national currency and its effects upon the public and private property. 4°. 1 page.

1816, July 29, Philadelphia. Progress and prospects of the subscriptions to the Bank of the United States. 4°. 2 pages.

1816, August 25, Philadelphia. Vindication of the character of Mr. Clarke against a vile and groundless calumny in a paper under the prostituted name of "Americanus." 4°. 3 pages.

1817, February 27, Philadelphia. Proposition to appoint Mr. E. W. Duval solicitor of the treasury. 4°. 1 page.

Montpellier.

1828, May 12, Philadelphia. Acknowledging letter of April 26, covering letters directed to our chargé d'affaires in London. Has forwarded them. 4°. 1 page.

JORRE, ——. *Philadelphia.*

1791, November 5, Philadelphia. Asks his good offices with the President in submitting his desires for Government employment. 4°. 3 pages.

JOURDAN *et fils.*

[*See* CATHALAN, STEPHEN, JR.]

JOY, BENJAMIN, to MADISON, *Washington.*

1809, December 20, Boston. Incloses a printed copy of a memorial which has been committed in the House of Representatives to the Committee of Claims, respecting a transaction in which purchasers in Boston were in no measure accessory to any fraud committed in Georgia. 4°. 1 page.

JOY, GEORGE, to PINCKNEY, CHARLES (Governor). *South Carolina.*

1791, October 16, London. Wishes information relative to a claim on the State of South Carolina, standing in the names of Nicholas and Jacob Van Stophorst, of Amsterdam. fol. 4 pages.

——— to MADISON. *Philadelphia.*

1791, November, London. Enclosing copy of a letter to Governor Pinckney, of South Carolina, respecting a claim against that State of N. and J. Van Stophorst, of Amsterdam, in which he is interested. Asks Madison's and Jefferson's aid to hasten the settlement. large fol. 3 pages.

1794, May 1, London. Acknowledging letter of May 17, 1792. The diplomatic correspondence of Mr. Jefferson. The subject of free ships making free goods. Affairs on the Continent. Enthusiasm and numbers on the side of the French. Discipline on the part of the allies. Intemperate and sanguinary measures of the French cause the allies to hope a return to monarchy. Sends books to Jefferson and himself. 4°. 6 pages.

1795, August 10, London. Acknowledging letter of April 3, with books sent by Madison. Tench Coxe's collection discussed. His views respecting

JOY, GEORGE.

Jay's treaty. Death of Mrs. Joy. Thinks of devoting the rest of his life, which he can no longer enjoy, to the public. 4°. 6 pages.

Washington.

1803, August 3, London. Acknowledging letter of June 12. Respecting Mr. Williams, American agent in the mixed commission in London, to determine British claims for violation of neutrality and of American claims for illegal capture. Vindication of his character. On the balance of power in Europe and the policy of America's abstaining from all European complications. Letter from Lafayette. 4°. 10 pages.

1804, February —, London. Incloses a letter apologizing for its length. 4°. 1 page.

1804 (?), not dated. Intervention of the United States with the belligerent powers by mediation. State of European affairs. Offers his services in an embassy to Spain. Gives an account of his antecedents and offers recommendations.
large fol. 20 pages.

1805, July 26, London. Acknowledging letter of November 10. Has communicated to Monroe the information he possessed relative to South American claims. Conversation with Monroe about the recent adjudication in the court of admiralty. Monroe's negotiations. Incloses the opinion of the court of admiralty in the case of the *Enoch*, Capt. Doam, before the Right Honorable Sir William Scott. 4°. 10 pages.

——— to SCOTT, Sir WILLIAM. *London.*

1805, October 24, London. On his adjudication in the admiralty court in the case of the *Enoch*. [Annexed is answer by Sir W. Scott.] [Copy.]
4°. 6 pages.

——— to MADISON. *Washington.*

1805, December 31, London. Decisions of Sir William Scott in the court of admiralty. Wishes to be considered a candidate for the office of consul at Rotterdam, in case of its being vacant. [Copy.]
4°. 9 pages.

1806, January 15, London. Incloses copy of a letter dated December 31. Thinks the British Government may bring the subject of the neutrality laws to a favorable regulation. 4°. 2 pages.

——— to "MORNING CHRONICLE," EDITOR OF THE. *London.*

1806, March 27, London. Asks if an article signed "A Constant Reader" will be published. [*See* letter to Madison, April 20, 1806.] [Copy.]
4°. 1 page.

——— to "ORACLE," THE EDITOR OF THE. *London.*

1806, April 4, London. Asks him to insert copies of two letters to the editor of the "Morning Chronicle," which he has not thought fit to notice, on a question of litigation between the two countries, tending to ease apprehensions of many individuals. [*See* letter to Madison, April 20, 1806. Copy.] 4°. 2 pages.

——— to MADISON. *Washington.*

1806, April 20, London. Incloses report of a decision made in the court of appeals, and copies of let-

JOY, GEORGE.

ters sent to the editors of the "Chronicle" and the "Oracle." Newspapers in London will not admit pieces opposed to individual or particular interests. Alludes to a pamphlet, attributed to Madison, relating to belligerent rights. Will send him copy of a pamphlet erroneously attributed to Lord Holland, as showing the feelings of the present administration. 4°. 7 pages.

——— to FOX, C. J. (Right Honorable). *London.*

1806, July 4, London. Incloses an extract of a letter from Madison, Secretary of State, showing his earnest desire to maintain the relations of amity between the two nations. [Copy.] 4°. 2 pages.

——— to HOLLAND, LORD. *London.*

1806, August 25, London. Incloses copy of a letter written to C. J. Fox, dated July 4, in which he inclosed extract of a letter from Madison, expressing the sentiments of amity existing between the two nations. Having no answer, he thinks Fox's ill-health may have been the cause of his silence. Offers his services. 4°. 2 pages.

1806, November 20, London. Acknowledging letter of 17th, relating to a letter of Madison's, extracts of which were sent to Mr. Fox. Sends a copy. 4°. 2 pages.

——— to MADISON. *Washington.*

1807, February 10, London. The late Mr. Fox. His professions of friendship for the United States. Estimates of amounts paid for British manufactures by the United States. Importance of the fisheries to England. Abstains from intercourse with Monroe and Pinckney to show that his suggestions did not originate with them. The next Presidential election. Randolph endeavoring to set up Monroe in opposition to Madison. 4°. 8 pages.

1807, August 25. London. The *Chesapeake* and *Leopard* affair. Disavowal of the British Government of its being their measure. Monroe's belief that apologies and reparation will be made, should it be found the British officer was wrong. Conversations with Monroe on the necessity of adjustment of subject of impressments. The West India trade. Mr. Marryatt's pamphlet. Would accept the consulate at Rotterdam. 4°. 12 pages.

1807, August 26, London. Duplicate of the foregoing. 4°. 8 pages.

1807, October 5, London. Interview with Monroe. The negotiations with the British Government respecting impressments remain as yet undecided. Incloses extracts from notes on the report from the committee of the House of Commons on the commercial state of the West India colonies. Pamphlet entitled, "Concessions to America the Bane of Britain," by *Conciliator*. 4°. 4 pages.

1807, October 11, London. Monroe's late interview with Canning. Is trying to collect official information on the proportion of income of this country (England) from the neutral trade. Incloses extract from a work from the West India Committee signed "Conciliator." 4°. 6 pages.

1808, January 28, London. His views on the embargo. Approves of it as do the other Americans abroad. Reports concerning Monroe's standing for the

JOY, GEORGE.

Presidency as opposing Madison. Describing the sentiments of Americans. 4°. 5 pages.

1808, February 12, London. Accepts the consulate at Rotterdam. [This is appended to the foregoing letter dated January 28.] 4°. 1 page.

1808, March 12, London. Has handed Lord Holland duplicate of calculations on the fallacy of the testimony before the West Indian Committee respecting necessary articles furnished by the British settlements in America. Lord Holland will avail himself of these statistics. 4°. 1 page.

1808, March 27, London. Document called for by Lord Auckland relating to the defalcation of trade during the last quarter of 1807, compared with corresponding quarters of 1805 and 1806. Custom-house clerks quite unoccupied. [This letter is appended to the foregoing dated March 12.] 4°. 1 page.

1808, March 31, London. Incloses documents and duplicates of previous letters. The British orders in council. Uniform opinion of the press of the gross impolicy of a war with America. Lords Holland and Hawkesbury's ideas of extra-territorial jurisdiction. The way to preserve peace with us is to show they are not afraid to go to war with us. Object of Mr. Rose's mission. Encloses copy of letter to Lord Holland. 4°. 2 pages.

——— to HOLLAND, LORD. *London.*

1808, not dated. Alluding to the treaty signed by Lords Holland and Auckland, mentions a provision respecting the coasting trade of India. Also on the proportion of supplies to the West Indies, drawn from the United States, and the scanty supplies from all the British colonies in America. [This letter is on the same sheet as the foregoing from Joy to Madison, of March 31. Copy.] 4°. 1 page.

——— to MADISON. *Washington.*

1808, April 18, London. Inclosing marginal notes on Madison's letter to Mr. Erskine, March 25, 1808. 4°. 1 page. fol. 7 pages.

1808, May 2 London. An article which was sent to the "Times" for publication under the head of "Prize Cause". It was not published, but a sarcastic article appeared ridiculing the honorable scruples of the judge. Incloses another article written by Joy from the "Star" on neutral rights. Reports that Bonaparte will not retire from the rigid letter of his decrees. 4°. 4 pages.

1808, May 24, London. Judgment of the court in the case of the *Missouri*, Capt. Reid. Was present and took notes, which he details. [Duplicate.] 4°. 4 pages.

1808, May 24, London. Triplicate of the foregoing. 4°. 3 pages.

1808, May 31, London. Report by Capt. Hopkins, of Boston, just arrived from Cadiz, that the Algerians are fitting out cruisers, doubtless against the Americans. 4°. 2 pages.

1808, June 10, London. Corroboration of the report mentioned in the foregoing letter of May 31,

JOY, GEORGE.

Acquittal of New Orleans ships by virtue of the order in council extending the time of notice of blockade. 4°. 3 pages.

1808, September 17, London. A change in the face of Europe. Movements in Spain. Accession of force to England. An opportunity for adjusting on liberal terms our differences with England. Conjectures as to Great Britain's policy. The West India interests not duly represented. Advantages of our seclusion from Europe. Growth of manufactures and self dependence. 4°. 24 pages.

1808, October 14, London. Sends the substance of an order in council. Thinks it contains symptoms of a gradual retreat from the orders in council of last November. Neutrality laws discussed. Is more and more satisfied that the measures adopted by our Government, independent of the embargo, have saved to the mercantile interests, millions. 4°. 4 pages.

1808, December 13, London. Negotiations with Great Britain and Madison's letter to Joy, of July 21, manifesting the magnaminity of the United States Government, and to sacrifice all but honor to the maintenance of harmony. Joy's article signed "Conciliator" for publication in the "Chronicle." His interviews with Mr. Pinckney. folio. 3 pages.

1808, December 19, London. On our system of seclusion. Importance of strengthening all our vulnerable points of attack and building a respectable navy. Too much higgling for pence. fol. 4 pages.

1808, December 19, London. Duplicate of the foregoing. fol. 3 pages.

1808, December 20, London. Relating to the Treasury. His early project of a speculation in the American funds. Estimates showing our ability to pay our debts, comparing it with Europe. His conversation with Hamilton as to the measures to be pursued and the latter's difference with Madison. fol. 7 pages.

1808, December 20, London. Duplicate of the foregoing. fol. 4 pages.

1808, December 22, London. On the power of the people to pay taxes and of a government to raise them. Observations on the payment of the national debt. Measures recommended. His disappointment in not procuring the consulate at Rotterdam. fol. 5 pages.

1808, December 22, London. Duplicate of the foregoing. fol. 4 pages.

1809, January 2, London. Transcribing his short-hand notes of Madison's letter of March 25, to Erskine. Has not collected the documents for making the estimates mentioned in his last letter. 4°. 1 page.

1809, February 23, London. Copies of articles written for publication in the "Chronicle." Thinks that the symptoms of conciliation on the part of the administration were far short of what they were twelve months ago. Mr. Pinckney thinks differently. fol. 2 pages.

JOY, GEORGE.

1809, March 8, London. On the inconsistency of the Lord Chancellor with Lord Liverpool in the debate on the subject of priority of aggression. Joy's account of the question of imports and exports, and supplies for the West Indies. Canning's speech. His consummate impudence. [Duplicate.] 4°. 3 pages.

1809, May 24, London. Grateful news received of the close of the embargo. Reflections on the cause and effect of this measure. 4°. 3 pages.

1809, May 24, London. Duplicate of the foregoing. 4°. 4 pages.

——— to CANNING, RT. HON. GEORGE. *London.*

1809, May 29, London. On the necessity of maintaining a good understanding with the United States and to show the gross fallacy of unfounded pretensions that the interests of rapacity had set up relative to the partiality of the United States for France. [Copy.] fol. 13 pages.

——— to MADISON. *Washington.*

1809, May 29, London. Inclosing copy of the foregoing. fol. 8 pages.

1809, May 31, London. Refers Madison to the debates in Parliament of the last night, as published in the "Chronicle," which he incloses. He also incloses copy of the instructions that have been printed in conformity with the order in council of April 26. 4°. 1 page.

1809, June 10, London. Refers to the letter of Canning to Erskine. Madison's asperity reprehensible, but shows the difficulty of doing anything satisfactory through such an organ (Erskine). Contemplates sending an extract of Joy's letter to Canning, to headquarters. Reflections on the measures of the British Government. 4°. 10 pages.

1809, June 27, London. Incloses a letter from Mr. Bourne to Mr. Williams. Joy's wish to be at his post in Holland. Question of passport. 4°. 2 pages.

——— to WALKER, ——— (Col.). *London.*

1809, June 30, London. Wishes to know if his communication to the head of the church and state was directly or indirectly committed to him, as it happened that immediately after, measures were determined on precisely meeting those suggestions in view of reconciliation between the two governments. [Annexed to this letter is copy of a note from Joy's nephew (not named), saying he had delivered the letter to Walker. Copy.] 4°. 2 pages.

——— to MADISON. *Washington.*

1809, July 15, London. Incloses copy of a letter to Col. Walker relative to the delivery of a paper addressed to the Duke of Cambridge, copy of which is also inclosed. [Copy.] 4°. 1 page.

1809, July 15, London. Duplicate of the foregoing copy. 4°. 2 pages.

1809, July 25, London. Has ascertained that his efforts to have his assertions and opinions canvassed have been effectual. On what small events the affairs of nations sometimes hang. 4°. 2 pages.

JOY, GEORGE,

1809, July —, London. An order in council antecedent to November, 1807, in which the blockade of Tonningen was decreed, and the removal forgotten. The advocate-general's orders. [This letter is copied on same sheet with that dated July 15. Copy.]

1809, July 29, London. Sends third copy of his letter to the Duke of Cambridge. 4°. 6 pages.

——— to CAMBRIDGE, The DUKE OF. *London.*

1809, not dated. Inclosing a letter to George Canning of May 27, relating to a letter from the secretary of foreign affairs to Mr. Erskine, of January 23. The differences between the two nations and suggestions as to measures to bring about reconciliations. 4°. 6 pages.

——— to MADISON. *Washington.*

1809, August 3, London. Depredations on American trade by the cruisers of Denmark and Norway. Thinks it an object for interference and to open the way for him to Holland. Has prepared a memorial such as the occasion requires and submits a draft of it. The intercourse with Holland is not to be obstructed on the part of the British Government. 4°. 4 pages.

1809, August 3, London. Duplicate of the foregoing. 4°. 4 pages.

1809, September 9, Harwich. On his way to Denmark. J. Q. Adams appointed minister to Russia. The motive and measures he proposes to pursue in the matter of Danish and Norwegian depredations on our commerce. fol. 26 pages.

1809, September 9, Harwich. Duplicate of the foregoing. 4°. 21 pages.

1809, October 5, Gottenburg. Sends duplicates of letter of September 9. Is waiting for arrival of documents necessary for the support of his pretensions in the matter of Danish depredations. Should the matter take an official turn he will communicate with the proper organs of the Government. 4°. 23 pages.

1809, October 27, Gottenburg (?). Gives the substance of a long conversation with Count Bernstorff on the question of depredations by Danish and Swedish cruisers. [Copy]. 4°. 10 pages.

1810, April 28, Copenhagen. Claims of the heirs of a Mr. Gerard to lands or the value of them presented to him by the Illinois and Wabash Company. Regulations by which a minister of the United States is prohibited from accepting presents. Conversations with and views of Mr. Didelot, the French minister at Copenhagen. 4°. 10 pages.

——— to SAABYE, H. R. (U. S. Consul). *Copenhagen.*

1810, August 22, Gottenburg. Acknowledging letter of last post. Commissions on ships and cargoes. Captures of our vessels after paying sound dues. Explanations of correspondence with the Secretary of State. Emoluments of consuls. Explanations concerning Joy's intercourse with Mr. Erickson, of a rival house. 4°. 8 pages.

1810, August 22, Gottenburg. Duplicate of the foregoing. 4°. 8 pages.

JOY, GEORGE.

1810, September 1, Gottenburg. Explanations obtained from conversations with Mr. Marsh and others respecting captures and detention of ships by cruises. Examinations by prize courts. 4°. 2 pages.

1810, September 1, Gottenburg. Duplicate of the foregoing. 4°. 2 pages.

——— to MADISON. *Washington.*

1810, September 2, Gottenburg. Conjectures as to measures of the allies, France and England, relative to neutrality in commerce. The commerce of England never fails to influence our politics. She is now suffering under inconvenience of obstructed trade. A modification of her orders in council may be looked for. Bonaparte's measures. 4°. 14 pages.

1810, September 8, Gottenburg. Particulars of his interviews and correspondence in his negotiations for the adjustment of our claims against the Danish Government. Character of the King described as an honest and well disposed man. 4°. 12 pages.

1810, September 14, Gottenburg. Has numerous communications for Madison which contrary winds delay. Wishes him to wait the receipt of them before taking measures relative to the consulship at this place. 4°. 1 page.

1810, September 16, Gottenburg. On the inconveniences arising from the informality of negotiations without a direct commission. The protection granted him exclusively by the King gives rise to mortifying rumors against him. Qualifications for a consul for this post. 4°. 17 pages.

1810, September 16, Gottenburg. Duplicate of the foregoing. 4°. 14 pages.

——— to SMITH, ROBERT, Secretary of State.

1810, September 24, Gottenburg. The attempt to turn the difficulties incurred in the case of the ship *Unicorn* notwithstanding the interference of the King, to the benefit of the remaining cases. [Press copy] 4°. 2 pages.

——— to MADISON.

1810, October 7, Gottenburg. Incloses a letter from Mr. Saabye and copies of letters to him. Is satisfied with the honesty and integrity of Mr. Saabye. New cases of confiscations of vessels. Hopes to obtain restitution. Leave for Copenhagen on the 9th. 4°. 5 pages.

1810, October 7, Gottenburg. Duplicate of the foregoing. 4°. 4 pages.

1810, October 8, Gottenburg. Relative to Mr. Saabye; his character, etc. Is undecided whom to recommend as consul for Gottenburg. Situation of affairs in Sweden and Denmark. Remuneration for his own service alluded to. Solicits an appointment with sufficient salary. 4°. 17 pages.

1810, October 8, Gottenburg. Duplicate of the foregoing. 4°. 17 pages.

1810, October —, Copenhagen. Interview with the French minister. Conversations relating to prize cases. Offers his services under any appointment Madison sees fit to charge him with. Views

JOY, GEORGE.

of Count Rosencrantz respecting the *certificat d'origine.* 4°. 7 pages.

1810, November 16, Copenhagen. Is informed his letters have been put ashore at Gottenburg, so incloses copies. Report of an armistice between the Turks and Russians. 4°. 3 pages.

——— to ROSENKRANTZ, Court Minister of Parliamentary Affairs. *Copenhagen.*

1810, December 8, Copenhagen. Protection of American property. His previous communications with the Danish Government and his address to the King. Specifies the case of, the *Julian,* Capt. Abbott, and action of the prize court. Application of this case to others. 4°. 7 pages.

——— to MADISON. *Washington.*

1810, December 19, Copenhagen. Is unadvised of the fate of his letters that were put on shore at Gottenburg, therefore incloses duplicates which he specifies. 4°. 1 page.

——— to LAW, WILLIAM. *Copenhagen.*

1811, February 23, Copenhagen. Wishes to be informed of what is expected of him in the management of the case of the *Swift.* [Press copy.] 4°. 2 pages.

——— to ERVING, GEORGE W.

1811, May 11, Copenhagen. Americans, who have employed him in prize cases, are satisfied with him. All vessels confided to his management have been acquitted, and that sufferers by detention have obtained through him particular privileges. Has memorialized the King respecting convoy cases. Will be glad to be of any service. [Copy.] 4°. 3 pages.

1811, May 25, Copenhagen. Has obviated a difficulty interposed by the court of admiralty. Thinks that the object of the memorial to the King on the 18th will be obtained. [Copy.] 4°. 1 page.

1811, June 2, Copenhagen. Requests that a delay in the proceedings in American prize cases may be applied for. [Press copy.] 4°. 2 pages.

1811, June 5, Copenhagen. Informs him about points of etiquette in his visits to officials, etc. [Copy.] 4°. 1 page.

——— to ADAMS, JOHN QUINCY. *St. Petersburg.*

1812, May 8, London. Details at length his negotiations in Denmark concerning the release of captured vessels and his relations with Mr. Erving, the U. S. minister. Mentions certain distinguished officials of rank with whom it would be desirous that Mr. Adams should become acquainted, when he goes to Denmark. Defends himself from malicious remarks of his enemies. 4°. 47 pages.

——— to MADISON. *Washington.*

1815, February 23, London. The delay by contrary winds allows him to add more numbers of his "Conciliator" to those already sent. small 4°. 1 page.

——— ("Conciliator").

1815 (?). Extracts from notes on the report from the committee of the House of Commons on the commercial state of the West India colonies and the minutes of evidence appending thereto,

JOY, GEORGE.

with a short notice of the pamphlet, entitled "Concessions to America the Bane of Great Britain," by "Conciliator." [Copies and press copies.] 4°. 105 pages.

—— to ADAMS, JOHN QUINCY. *London.*

1817, January 14, London. An appointment as consul-general to Holland. Conditions of his acceptance. 4°. 3 pages.

—— to MADISON. *Montpellier.*

1817, May 10, London. J. Q. Adams's appointment as Secretary of State and his acceptance. Uncertainty as to time of departure. Report of the death of Mr. Bourne at Amsterdam. Probability of Dr. Eustis (U. S. minister at Netherlands) desiring Joy's presence there. Offers his temporary services also if required when Adams leaves London. Asks an appointment. 4°. 3 pages.

1817, June 17, London. Correspondence with Dr. Eustis respecting the consul-generalship of Holland. Mr. Parker's temporary services there. Incloses copy of his letter to J. Q. Adams of May 8, 1812. 4°. 3 pages.

—— to ADAMS, JOHN Q. *Washington.*

1817, November 4, London. The interest of Great Britain in the emancipation of South America. Shilly-shally measures in the foreign enlistment bill. [On same sheet as letter from Joy to Madison, of March 16, 1824.] [Extract.] 4°. 1 page.

—— to MADISON. *Montpellier.*

1822, January 2, London. A letter written on April 16, 1804, and Madison's answer. If he has preserved copies would like to have them, as they are not to be found in the archives of the Department of State. Incloses copy of letter from his brother. 4°. 4 pages.

1822, January 2, London. Duplicate of the foregoing. fol. 3 pages.

1822, January 9, London. Relating to the letters mentioned in the foregoing letter of 2d instant. 4°. 2 pages.

—— to POTT (captain of ship *Henry Clay*).

1822, February 2, London. Books sent to Madison. Directs Capt. Pott how to forward them. 4°. 1 page.

—— to MADISON. *Montpellier.*

1822, February 2, London. Sends, per ship *Henry Clay*, a book entitled "Histoire de l'esprit révolutionnaire des nobles en France." Commends it and thinks it will interest Mr. Jefferson also. 4°. 1 page.

1822, August 27, London. Loss of the packet ship *Liverpool*. Fears that the letters and dispatches to Mr. Rush are lost, which were duplicates of another vessel also lost. Mr. Maury. 4°. 2 pages.

1823, January 30, Brighton. Annexing a copy of letter written in October last respecting the forwarding of some books which miscarried. Has been ill with a contusion of his arm, and mistaken remedy by a chemist. State of affairs in Europe. Spoliation claims by the United States. 4°. 8 pages.

JOY, GEORGE.

1823, February 5, London. The speech of the King of France sent, per Mr. Maury, on the 1st instant. The packet of the 8th will take out the King of England's speech relating to the Spaniards and Portugese. Explains a difficulty with the custom-house. fol. 4 pages.

1823, April 26, London. Sends him two prints of the battle of Bunker's Hill and Quebec, with books. Political measures of European governments. 4°. 5 pages.

1823, June 27, London. Acknowledging letter of November 10. Sends him the third time copies of books which have previously miscarried or been lost. Discouraging news from Portugal. Apathy in the friends of freedom. Relations between France and Spain. 4°. 3 pages.

1824, February 4, London. Sends a newspaper with marked article. Refers to an article in the "North American Review," entitled "England and America," in answer to the same. 4°. 1 page.

1824, March 8, London. Sends a paper containing a too true picture of France. Ignorance of the people. Does not wonder that Lafayette abandons them in despair. Speech of Sir James Mackintosh. South American affairs. 4°. 2 pages.

1824, March 16, London. Incloses copies of the Marquis of Landsdowne's motion; also copies of two letters to Mr. Adams, of November 4, 1817, and July 16, 1819, respectively. 4°. 1 page.

1830, June 22, London. English politics. Incloses a letter relating to an error of the press respecting a letter from Jefferson to Madison, of December 23, 1794, in which Mr. Jay is disparaged by having his name substituted for Mr. Joy. 4°. 2 pages.

1833, March 7, London. Introducing James C. Fuller of the Society of Friends. Annexing a letter from J. C. Fuller. 4°. 2 pages.

1834, October 21, London. Acknowledging letter of September 8. Reminiscences of Mr. Adams. Respecting Mr. Alcedo Thompson. The question of free ships and free goods. Concerning his friend Mr. Fuller. 4°. 4 pages.

JOY, M., to JOY, GEORGE. *London.*

1822, January 1, London. Splendid project of the Erie Canal. Publication to the "North American Review." Bryant's poems criticised. Irving's "Sketch Book" and "Knickerbocker." [Copy.] 4°. 3 pages.

JUNE, ZABUEL, to MADISON. *Washington.*

1812, September 27, North Salem, N. Y. Wishes for a prosecution of the war with vigor. To make no peace until Canada is ours. His life and fortune at the service of his country. 4°. 2 pages.

JUSTUS, JAMES.

1814, January 4, Cross Roads, Pa. Submits the plan of a steamboat called the *Grizzly Bear of the West*, calculated (with pecuniary aid) to destroy British ships of the largest size. fol. 4 pages.

1814, January 18, Cross Roads, Washington County, Pa. Distrusts the conduct of the British nation in

JUSTUS, JAMES.

their overtures to peace. Advocates the vigorous prosecution of the war. To put Gen. Harrison in full command of all the forces we can raise, and under Providence we will have victory. Is ready to volunteer. fol. 3 pages.

KEEMBE, JOHN.

1810, January 11, Philadelphia. In behalf of the surviving Revolutionary characters residing in Philadelphia, incloses an address approving of the measures of the administration in repelling hostile attacks of foreign powers upon the neutral and natural rights of the United States and promising support. [Signed by himself and 27 others.] 4°. 2 pages. fol. 4 pages.

KEIONTZ, JOHN.

1815, March 25, Harrisonburg, Va. Informs the President of his having been reinstated in his command by the executive of Virginia. 4°. 1 page.

KELSALL, CHARLES.

1817, February 15, London. The author of "Phantasm of a College," etc., sends Madison his book on the suggestion of the raising of a university in Virginia, which may be of use. Wishes him success in his efforts. 4°. 3 pages.

KELSO, WILLIAM.

1812, September 4. Expresses his antipathy for Gen. Hull. Asks as a favor that he (Hull) be sent to Kentucky and allow him (Kelso) to dispose of him as he thinks proper. Intends to enlist in the Army next spring. fol. 2 pages.

KEMPER, REUBEN, to SPARKS, RICHARD (Lieutenant-Colonel). *Fort Stoddert.*

1810, November 27, Bunkers Hill. Acknowledging letter of 26th. Is unable to wait upon him in person at Fort Stoddert at present. Delivers up two soldiers as requested. [Copy.] fol. 1 page.

KENNEDY, JOHN P., to MADISON. *Montpellier.*

1834, June 19, Baltimore. Sends by this mail a copy of his discourse on the life and character of William Wirt. 4°. 1 page.

1834, July 28, Baltimore. Sends Madison a copy of his book "Swallow Barn." 4°. 1 page.

KENNEDY, JOSEPH P.

1815. Statement in pamphlet form given in vindication of his character and honor from charges of his being instrumental in the loss of Mobile Point. 8°. 14 pages.

KENNEDY, PHILIP PENDLETON.

1830, November 22, Baltimore. Sends a pamphlet of his own upon the doctrine of nullification. 4°. 1 page.

KENTUCKY LEGISLATURE.

1812, December 22. *See* SHELBY, ISAAC (Governor).

1814, February 6. *See* SHELBY, ISAAC (Governor).

KER, JAMES. *Washington.*

1803, August 13, Philadelphia. Incloses a bill for a chariot of Thomas Ogle. Asks directions about delivering. fol. 1 page.

KERCHEVAL, SAMUEL.

1810, February 7, Stevensburg, Va. Solicits a subscription in order to proceed with the buildings for the institution at this place. 4°. 1 page.

Montpellier.

1829, August 27, Newtown, Stevensburg, Va. Transmits by mail a copy of Jefferson's letters on the amendments of the State constitution. Asks Madison's opinion. 4°. 1 page.

KERR, JOSEPH. *Washington.*

1808, Georgetown. Resigns a commission under act of Congress for laying out a road from Cumberland to the Potomac to the Ohio River. 4°. 1 page.

——— and others. *Montpellier.*

1835, April 18, Washington, Pa. Notification by a committee of the Washington Literary Society of Madison's election as an honorary member of the association. 4°. 2 pages.

KERSEY, JESSE. *Washington.*

1810, April 9, Downingtown. Refers to a conversation when a bill was before the Senate respecting some emigrants from Cuba. Sends him a pamphlet intended to reform the habits of our country. fol. 1 page.

KITELTAS, WILLIAM.

1812, March 9, New York. Gives the extract of a letter from a friend respecting a mission to Quebec, in which terms are proposed concerning the revoking of the orders in council, and a general pacification. 4°. 1 page.

1812, March 9, New York. Gives his opinion as to the causes of our present difficulties with the two great belligerents. The duplicity of artful demagogues. Incloses extract of letter relating to England's projects. 4°. 3 pages.

1812, May 17, New York. Feels hurt at receiving no acknowledgment of his previous letters. Thinks it may be the uncertainty of the mails. 4°. 1 page.

1812, September 2, New York. Hull's defeat at Detroit. Causes and effects. Counsels dismissal of other officers who are known enemies of the administration. Attempt of the Clintonians to throw the blame for Hull's defeat on the administration. Thinks this the proper time to press our claims on France. 4°. 3 pages.

1812, October 11, New York. Release of the schooner *Industry*. Has received no answer to his application for a commission of colonel and to raise a regiment of horse. Feels hurt that Col. De la Croix, a Frenchman, has been appointed to command a regiment. Americans should not be commanded by foreigners. Thinks the war against Great Britain holy and just. She must yield sooner or later to our just claims. 4°. 3 pages.

1812, November 14, New York. Repeats his offer to serve his country if he may be given the command of a regiment of horse or foot. Asks for appointment of marshal of this district. 4°. 2 pages.

KEY, F. S., and DORSEY, W. H.

1807-8 (?), not dated, Georgetown. As counsel for S. Swartwout, a prisoner confined in the Marine barracks, solicit an order for an interview with him, which has been refused by the commandant and the Secretary of War. 4°. 2 pages.

KEYSER, GEORGE.

1811, June 25, Baltimore. Forwards copy of an address to the people of the United States, over the signature of Robert Smith, late Secretary of State. 4°. 1 page.

KIDD, ALBERT J. *Montpellier.*

1835, November 12, New Boston, Ala. Means for erecting a suitable monument in honor of Washington. 4°. 2 pages.

KIDD, JAMES. *Washington.*

1816, March 29, Aberdeen. Sends him some books, one of his own writing. Importance of the instruction of the rising generation, particularly in the doctrines of religion. Shows how seals of dispatches are useless and how they are counterfeited. Importance of creating a formidable fleet for the safety of the union. To depend, also, on our own manufactures in case of war. 4°. 4 pages.

KILTY, JOHN.

1809, March 20, Annapolis. Solicits an appointment under Government. His long public services, military and civil. large fol. 4 pages.

KILTY, W., to SMITH, S.

1814, August 23, Bath. Recommends Alexander Scott for the office of secretary of the Senate. [*See* letter of Alexander Scott to Madison, dated August 20, 1816. Copy.] 4°. 1 page.

——— to MONROE.

1819, September 16, Annapolis. Recommending Alexander Scott as a candidate for Government office. [*See* letter of Alexander Scott to Madison, dated January 2, 1820.] [Copy.] 4°. 2 pages.

KING, BENJAMIN, to MADISON. *Montpellier.*

1836, June 22, Philadelphia. Asks his good offices in procuring an increase of pay after thirty years' services in the navy-yard. Relates his services at Bladensburg. Incloses copies of letters from Commodore Barron and Col. Miller and other documents. 4°. 2 pages.

KING, CHARLES, to LATTIMER, WILLIAM. *Natchez.*

1805, September 20, Natchez. Asks his good offices with the President to reclaim the men who were taken by the Spaniards, when Knowland was killed in 1800 or 1801, and who are now prisoners. 4°. 2 pages.

1806, September 10, Natchez. Gives the names of Knowland's men who were captured by the Spaniards in 1800 or 1801. 4°. 2 pages.

——— to MADISON. *Washington.*

1817, January 1, Washington. Regrets his health will not permit him to accept an invitation to dinner. 4°. 1 page.

KING, JOHN. *Montpellier.*

1830, August 14, Richmond. Asks his aid in prosecuting his claim in aid of the heirs of Thomas Bullett, a Revolutionary officer. The papers proving his claim were burned at the War Office. Madison's personal recollection of this officer may be of assistance to the heirs. 4°. 3 pages.

KING, MILES. *New York.*

1789, March 3, Hampton, Va. Congratulates him on his election as Representative in Congress. Suggests names of persons to be retained in office, and others to be appointed in Government positions in Virginia. 4°. 3 pages.

Washington.

1816, June 29, Mathews County Va. On the subject of Christianity. 4°. 8 pages.

KING, N.

1809, March 31. List of trees and shrubs for the President's garden, and where to be procured. royal fol. 1 page.

KING, RUFUS, to MADISON and Colonel GRAYSON, jointly. *Philadelphia.*

1787, March 11. Transmits an extract of a letter to himself from a gentleman in Boston, respecting the news which alarmed the Virginia delegates that the Massachusetts commissioners, who settled the Territorial controversy between Massachusetts and New York, were for a monarchy, and that those delegates wrote to their legislature of it. Asks Madison and Grayson if it were true. 4°. 2 pages.

——— to MADISON. *New York.*

1788, January 6, New York. Sends copy of the confederation between the New England colonies. Asks if he will inform him if anything interesting occurs from the Southern States relating to the proposed constitution. [Part of this letter cut off.] 4°. 1 page.

1788, January 16, Boston. Deliberations of the assembled convention in Boston, on the question of the constitution. Terms on which Mr. Gerry takes a seat in the convention. 4°. 3 pages.

1788, January 20, Boston. Proceedings of the convention at Boston. Jealousy of the opposition. Mr. Gerry's charges against Mr. Dana. 4°. 2 pages.

1788, January 23, Boston. Gloomy prospects at the convention. Gerry not returned; will not be invited to a seat. Proposed amendments to their ratification of the constitution. 4°. 1 page.

1788, January 27, Boston. Jealousy of the opposers of the constitution. The wealth and talent of the State are in favor of it. Hence the jealousy of the ignorant and poorer classes who fear the establishment of two orders in society. [Signature cut off.] fol. 3 pages.

1788, January 30, Boston. Mr. Hancock takes his seat as president of the convention. If he does not disappoint present expectations our wishes will be gratified. 4°. 1 page.

1788, February 3, Boston. Mr. Adams approves of Hancock's propositions. Thinks the result will be favorable. fol. 2 pages.

1788, February 6, Boston. The question of assenting to and ratifying the constitution is decided in the affirmative by the Massuchusetts convention. New Hampshire will probably decide in favor of the constitution. fol. 2 pages.

Richmond.

1788, May 25, New York. Asks to be informed of the determination of the Virginia convention. Large

KING, RUFUS.

majority of the people in Massachusetts in favor of the Federal constitution. Results of the late State elections confirm the decision of the convention. Intelligence from New Hampshire favorable. 4°. 3 pages.

New York.

1788, July 20, Boston. Congratulates Madison on the decision of the Richmond convention. The results of the New York convention undecided. Prospects in other States. 4°. 2 pages.

Washington.

1801, May 25, London. Introducing Prince Ruspoli. 4°. 1 page.

1801, October 20, London. Inclosing continued report of his conferences with the Lord Chancellor and Lord Hawkesbury, respecting the negotiations on articles in the treaty with Great Britain. 4°. 16 pages.

KING, WILLIAM. *Montpellier.*

1819, May 10, Bath. Separation of Maine from Massachusetts. Asks how the separation between Virginia and Kentucky was managed. 4°. 1 page.

KINGSTON, JAMAICA.

1794. See American vessels.

KINLOCK, FRANCIS. *Washington.*

1803, February 8, near Georgetown, S. C. Intending to travel in Europe, he asks to be furnished from the Department of State with a general letter of introduction to ministers and agents of the United States in the countries he proposes visiting and which he specifies. 4°. 3 pages.

1803, May 7, near Georgetown, S. C. Acknowledging receipt of his passport and the letter accompanying it. His intentions in traveling abroad. Offers to carry dispatches. His political opinions. 4°. 3 pages.

1809, March 27, near Georgetown, S. C. Although a Federalist, he expresses his satisfaction of the inaugural speech. The exclusion of Federalists from the honors and emoluments of public life. The class of talented people and those possessed of property, who have submitted to the operations of laws which have reduced them to distress, cannot submit much longer to partialities. 4°. 3 pages.

Year *not dated, March 26, near Georgetown, S.* C. Introducing his son, who goes to Washington to retain his employment in the Army. 4°. 1 page.

KINNEY, THOMAS T.

1809, March 6, Newark, N. J. As secretary of a meeting of citizens in Essex County, forwards an address congratulating Madison as President, and promising support to his administration. fol. 5 pages.

KINSEY, CHARLES.

1815, October 19, Paterson, N. J. Appeal in behalf of the cotton manufacturers of New Jersey to the President to advocate measures in Congress to protect them against the unbounded importations of cotton fabrics which threaten destruction to our infant establishments. 4°. 3 pages.

KIRBY, E., to CALHOUN, JOHN C.

1823, August 22, Washington. Memorandum for the Secretary of War from the Adjutant-General's Office stating the practice of the War Department in issuing commissions to officers of the Army. 4°. 2 pages.

KIRK, WILLIAM, to MADISON.

1814, February 14, Orange County, N. C. Offers his services in the Army. fol. 2 pages.

KIRKPATRICK, WILLIAM.

1805, March 22, Malaga. Filling an order for wine and fruit, with the bill of expense. 4°. 3 pages.

KNAPP, JOHN. *Orange, Va.*

1800, July 9, Washington. Solicits his good offices with the new administration towards obtaining a position under Government. 4°. 1 page.

Washington.

1801, March 29, Washington. Congratulations on the election of Jefferson. Solicits Madison's influence in procuring a Government appointment. 4°. 2 pages.

KNOX, JAMES.

1812, February 24, Giles County, Tenn. Memorial protesting against the conduct of Gen. Nathaniel Taylor and Col. Robert Love, touching a dispute about surveying lands bordering the States of Tennessee and North Carolina and defying the General Government. fol. 4 pages.

KNOX, THOMAS. *Philadelphia.*

1795, December 12, New York. Requests that some letters, among Monroe's papers in Madison's possession, relating to a suit in chancery with J. Kortright respecting lands bought of his (Monroe's) father, be sent to him. 4°. 1 page.

KONKAPOT, JOHN, JR., an Indian. *Washington.*

1806, March 27, Washington. Appeals to Madison and the President to be released from jail, that he may be of service to the country in some way. 4°. 3 pages.

KUCH, A. *Montpellier.*

1827, March 28, Waverly. Introducing J. F. Shepherd. who would like the appointment of tutor of Latin and Greek in the University of Virginia. 4°. 1 page.

LACOCK, ABNER. *Washington.*

1812, April 7, Washington. Unarmed and defenseless condition of the people on Lake Erie. Asks if a supply of arms can be furnished by the Government for the militia or to call out the Pennsylvania militia. Requests an interview. 4°. 2 pages.

1812, April 11, Washington. Incloses a copy of a letter to the Secretary of War which was unanswered. Requests the information desired of him be given by the President. 4°. 1 page.

1812, May 18, Washington. Supplying of arms to the militia of Pennsylvania should they tender their services to the President. Requests that the militia on the lake when called into service, that it be on their own frontier. 4°. 2 pages.

LACY, JOHN D. DE.

See DE LACY, JOHN D.

LAFAYETTE.

1803, July 3, Aubray, France. Has been confined to his bed from the results of an accident. Monroe's negotiations with Spain. Expects to meet him next day at Livingston's. 4°. 2 pages.

1806, November 18, La Grange, France. Asks if a further sum may be raised on mortgage of his property in Louisiana, in order to pay a creditor a sum due. 4°. 1 page.

1815, February 11, La Grange. Recommends Mr. Masson for a consular appointment in France. 4°. 1 page.

——— to JEFFERSON. *Monticello.*

1815, February 11, La Grange. Recommending Mr. Francis de Masson, formerly engineer at West Point, who desires a consulship. 4°. 1 page.

——— to MADISON. *Washington.*

1815, August 20, Paris. Introducing Regnauld de St. Jean d'Angely, who intends visiting the United States. 4°. 1 page.

——— to PARISH, DAVID.

1816, January —. Letter relating to the sale of his Point Coupée lands. [*See* letter of David Parish, January 24, 1816.] [Copy.] 4°. 2 pages.

——— to EASTON, DAVID.

1821, October 28, La Grange. Incloses a copy of a letter expressing affectionate remembrances of Col. Robert H. Harrison, distinguished for important services to his country during the war of the Revolution. 4°. 3 pages.

See GURLEY, J. W. (register Land Office).

LAMMOND, ALEXANDER.

1805, November 20, Baltimore. Receipt of packages from Robert Purviance to be delivered to Madison. 4°. 1 page.

LAFFITE, JEAN, to MADISON.

1815, December 27, Washington. In view of the services he, his officers, and men and vessels did for the country, requests that restitution of his property be made by the Government. 4°. 3 pages.

LAFON, B.

1810, May 12, New Orleans. Observations accompanying his plat of lands adjacent to New Orleans granted by Congress to Lafayette. The plats of surveys were given to Lafayette. 4°. 3 pages.

LAIRD, JOHN.

1811, March 22, Georgetown. Incloses money by direction of Robert Patton. 4°. 1 page.

LAKANAL, ——.

1816, June 1, Gallatin county, Ohio. Intends to occupy his time in the cultivation of the soil and writing a history of the United States. Incloses a printed article from the "Moniteur Universelle," under the title "Lakanal", which gives a record of his literary works. [In French.] 4°. 8 pages.

LAMBERT, JOHN.

1809, June 10, Washington. Incloses some lines by Phillip Freneau, the poet, at his request. 4°. 1 page.

LAMBERT, JOHN.

1810, April 19, Washington. Sends grafts of the St. Germain pear. small 4°. 1 page.

LAMBERT, WILLIAM. *New York.*

1789, November 2, New York. Wishes him to use his good offices with Jefferson to procure a situation in the Department of State for Mr. Reuben Burnley. 4°. 2 pages.

Washington.

1805, December 23, Washington. Desires a position in the Department of State. 4°. 1 page.

1806, April 2, Washington. Inclosing a circular letter, addressed to members of both Houses of Congress, respecting the treatment he has received from John Beckley on the statements made respecting the payment of salary. 4°. 2 pages.

1809, January 7, Washington. Congratulates him on his election as President. 4°. 1 page.

1809, December 5, Washington. Incloses a letter to Bishop Madison relating to the geography of the United States. Thanks him for past favors. 4°. 1 page.

1810, February 19, Washington. Incloses a letter received from Bishop Madison relative to Lambert undertaking to fix a first meridian for the United States. 4°. 2 pages.

1810, May 25, Washington. Incloses copy of an ode which he composed for the Fourth of July, in which is a testimonial of respect for Madison and Jefferson. 4°. 1 page.

1811, February 16. Collection of precedents authorized by a resolution of the House of Representatives. Gives some examples. large 4°. 3 pages.

1811, June 10, Washington. Incloses for inspection and transmission a communication to Bishop Madison, relating to the longitude of William and Mary College from Greenwich, by computation from the end of the solar eclipse of June 16, 1806. large 4°. 2 pages.

1811, July 8, Washington. Astronomical matters. Calculations of longitude, etc. 4°. 1 page.

1811, October 23, Washington. Incloses a communication to several Members of Congress. 4°. 1 page.

1815, February 18, Washington. Difficulty in bearing up under false accusations of unseen enemies against his habits and character. Declares them base and malicious. 4°. 2 pages.

1813, March 10, Washington. Declines, with thanks, the appointment of commissary of prisoners at the British Island of Barbadoes. Some other appointment within the limits of the United States he would be better qualified to fill. 4°. 1 page.

1815, February 20, Washington. Resolution passed the House of Representatives for ascertaining the exact longitude of the Capitol. Mentions persons capable for making these observations. 4°. 2 pages.

LAMBERT, WILLIAM. *Montpellier.*

1822, April 8, Washington. Incloses two printed copies of a report relative to the latitude and longitude of the Capitol. 4°. 1 page.

1829, March 10, Washington. Appeal for his aid in obtaining some office under Government. Small 4°. 2 pages.

LAMMOND, ALEXANDER, *Washington.*

1805, November 20, Baltimore. Receipt of packages from Robert Purviance of certain articles to be delivered to Madison at Georgetown per *Betsy and Charlotte.* 8°. 1 page.

LANDON, JAMES. *Richmond.*

1829, not dated. Appeal for pecuniary assistance, having been induced to come to this country, from England, under false pretenses. [Memoranda on back of the letter in Madison's hand, stating suspicions of man's appearance and manner]. 4°. 3 pages.

LANE, SAMUEL. *Washington.*

1816, July 5, Washington. Mr. Hassler's plans and drawings for the observatory. Is anxious for a decision as to the site selected by him. As commissioner of public buildings, asks instructions. 4°. 1 page.

1816, October 15, Washington. Reports the progress of building the President's house and the Capitol. 4°. 2 pages.

LANG & TURNER. *Washington.*

1809, May 13, New York. Asks for a copy of the next message at the extra session of Congress before any competitors, to publish in the "New York Gazette." Gives reasons why this preference should be given. 4°. 2 pages.

LANGDON, JOHN, to HAMILTON, ALEXANDER. *Poughkeepsie.*

1788, June 21, Concord, N. H. Announcing the adoption of the Federal Constitution by the State of New Hampshire. [At foot of a letter from Phillip Schuyler to Madison, June 24, 1786.] [Copy.] fol. 1 page.

——— to MADISON. *Philadelphia.*

1796, April 28, Portsmouth. Opposition to the treaty with Great Britain. 4°. 2 pages.

Washington.

1801, June 24, Portsmouth. Gives reasons why he declined the President's offer of the Secretaryship of the Navy. 4°. 2 pages.

1805 ,February 22, Portsmouth. Incloses a letter to the "Federalist" by his son-in-law, McElroyn. 4°. 1 page.

1808, November 30, Wiscasset. British influence and venality of the press. Suggests means for rectifying the evil. fol. 3 pages.

1811, July 16, Portsmouth. Acknowledging a late letter which recalls the many years of anxiety, tribulation, and pleasant ones, spent together. 4°. 1 page.

1814, September 19, Wiscasset. Incloses a proposition which he thinks will tend toward the termination of the war. A proposition agreeing to subscribe

LANGDON, JOHN.

to a fund to be distributed among British seamen who will desert and a guarantee to find employment here, and to merchant sailors a bounty, or division of proceeds of vessels they may capture. fol. 6 pages.

LANGDON, WOODBURY. *Washington.*

1802, February 6, Portsmouth. Appointment of printers of the laws of the United States. Federals and opposers to the administration have been appointed and he suggests it should be given to true Republicans. 4°. 2 pages.

LANGHAM, ELIAS. *New York.*

1789, March 15, Point of Fork. Appointment as a commissary of military stores by Congress. Incloses letters to Madison, he being Representative of his district, to read and send to their destination if he thinks proper. small 4°. 1 page.

1789, April 11, Richmond. Incloses recommendations for his appointment as commissary of military stores. fol. 1 page.

1790, June 1, Point of Fork. Incloses a letter from Col. Carrington. If his appointment as commissary of military stores can not be made, he would like the management of the magazine arsenal in Virginia. The people do not approve of disciplining the militia. State of the crops. Howell Lewis would like an army appointment. small 4°. 3 pages.

LANSING, ABRAHAM G. *Washington.*

1812, September 23, Albany. Requests that his son, John Y. Lansing, who is a surgeon in a regiment of detached militia, may be transferred in the same grade to the regular army. 4°. 2 pages.

——— to CUTTS, RICHARD.

1813, April 12, Albany. Acknowledging letter of 6th, requiring him to make returns as quartermaster-general. Has received no information of his appointment. [Copy.] 4°. 1 page.

——— to ARMSTRONG, JOHN.

1813, April 12, Albany. Incloses a letter from Mr. Cutts instructing him as quartermaster-general to make a report. Not having been officially informed of the appointment, requests to know if it is so. [Copy.] 4°. 2 pages.

——— to MADISON.

1813, April 18, Albany. Thanks him for the appointment of surgeon for his son. Proposals made to Lansing by supposed friends of Madison to aid in promoting the election of Clinton to the Presidency, and on his refusal, their animosity is shown by appointing Swartwout quartermaster-general instead of himself. Incloses copies of letters from Mr. Cutts and Gen. Armstrong relating to the subject. 4°. 3 pages.

LAPSLEY, SARAH W.

1809, December 26, Paris. Solicits Madison's aid in securing a claim on Congress for services rendered by her father, Capt. Samuel Lapsley, in the war of the Revolution. 4°. 2 pages.

LATHAM, WILLIAM, to MAURY, WILLIAM. *New Orleans.*

1821, January 25, Liverpool. Appointment of consul at Liverpool, of William Maury, in case his

LATHAM, WILLIAM.

father should resign the office. Suggests a consultation with Madison and President Monroe and other friends in relation thereto. [See letter of William Maury to Madison, April 6, 1821.] [Copy.] 4°. 2 pages.

LATROBE, BENJAMIN H., to RODNEY, CAESAR A.

Washington.

1807, June 2, Philadelphia. Inconvenience of immediately obeying his summons to Washington to testify in Burr's trial. A memorandum of his evidence is in the hands of the President. Will call on Rodney as soon as he arrives in Washington. 4°. 4 pages.

—— to MADISON.

1809, March 10, Washington. Has made arrangements to provide the most necessary articles required for the President's house. Enumerates various articles and solicits an advance out of the fund appropriated. 4°. 2 pages.

1809, March 14, Washington. Planting of the grounds of the President's house. small 4°. 1 page.

1809, March 12, Washington. Expenses of the direction of the public buildings. Asks that his son may be appointed his assistant. 4°. 2 pages.

1809, March 14, Washington. Asks directions as to the adaptation of rooms in the President's house. 4°. 2 pages

1809, May 29, Washington. With an account of expenditures for the furniture of the President's house. fol. 2 pages.

1809, July 5, Washington. List of payments for furnishing the President's house. fol. 2 pages.

1809, July 7, Washington. Asks instructions respecting seeds for the grounds of the President's house. Appropriations for public buildings. Solicits instructions as to payment. 4°. 1 page.

1811, July 19 and 20, Washington. One receipted bill and two accounts rendered. 4°. 3 pages.

Montpellier.

1809, September 8, Washington. Report on the present state of the public buildings. The Capitol and President's house. 4°. 8 pages.

Washington.

1809, November 23, Washington. Sends sketch of expenditures on the furniture of the President's house. fol. 3 pages.

1809, December 15, Washington. The more detailed specifications of the estimate for the public buildings. 4°. 4 pages.

1810, January 18, Washington. Arrangements of seats in the Senate and House of Representatives. 4°. 3 pages.

Montpellier.

1810, September 1, Washington. Progress of the public buildings under his charge. Regrets he can not avail himself of Madison's invitation to visit him. Thinks of going into the cotton manufacturing business in Baltimore. 4°. 3 pages.

Washington.

1810, October 5, Washington. Construction of the fireproof vault of the office of the State Department. 4°. 1 page.

LATROBE, BENJAMIN H.

1811, January 6, Washington. Returns a letter of Madison's of September 29, 1809. Manner of fitting up the court room. 4°. 1 page.

1811, January 18, Washington. Outstanding claims and estimates of the sum necessary to finish the Capitol. Requires more clerical assistance. Account of amount drawn for finishing the President's house. 4°. 3 pages, and strip of paper.

——— and MURRAY, GEORGE, jointly.

1811, January 27, Washington. Invites Madison in behalf of the Society of Artists at Philadelphia, to accept the distinction of patron of that establishment. 4°. 2 pages.

———.

1811, February 1, Washington. Receipt for $1,000 on account of the fund for furnishing the President's house. 8°. 1 page.

1811, February 11, Washington. Letter in the hands of a committee which he has asked to be transmitted to Madison. 4°. 1 page.

1811, February 23, Washington. Estimates for expenditures for public buildings required by a resolution of the House of Representatives. Submits a list of outstanding claims. Will send drawings if permitted to the House of Representatives the next day. 4°. 2 pages.

1811 (?), not dated. Glass to be sent to the President's house. Dissuades Madison from using ornamental molding of composition for his house in the country. Repairs for the President's house. 8°. 3 pages.

1811, June 28, Washington. Wishes an interview with the President and the Secretary of the Navy, in order to explain the merits of his claims in the direction of the construction of the public buildings. 4°. 2 pages.

Montpellier.

1811, July 19, Washington. Accounts of expenditures for glass and sheet iron for his place in Montpellier. 4°. 3 pages.

1811, September 6, Washington. Refuses the office of engineer of the State of New York on account of his engagements at the Navy Department. Preparations at the President's house. Hopes to arrange affairs that he may pay Madison a visit. 4°. 3 pages.

Washington.

1811, November 18, Washington. Asks for a warrant on the Treasury on account for furnishing the President's house. 4°. 1 page.

1812, March 30, Washington. Objects to the lowering of his salary, on the principle of justice and equity. 4°. 3 pages.

1812, March 31, Washington. His original appointment as superintendent of public buildings. Corrects an error of Jefferson's in respect to salaries of former persons. 4°. 1 page.

1812, June 10, Washington. Incloses copy of an account of expenditures for the President's house. Asks for an order for a warrant for $200 of moneys remaining in the fund. 4°. 3 pages.

LATROBE, BENJAMIN H.

1816, April 24, Washington. Complains of the course and offensive manner of the commissioners of public buildings. States his general usefulness. Solicits the office of commissioner of public buildings under the new arrangement directed by Congress, or that of surveyor with the salary formerly annexed to the same. Annexed is copy of letter from Jefferson on his former appointment. 4°. 7 pages.

1816, December 30, Washington. Inconveniences of the present system respecting the completion of the Capitol. Interference of the commissioners with the architects. Impossibility of making estimates of time or cost owing to that circumstance. Reviews past experience of his own under Jefferson's administration. Solicits that the President will take the subject into his consideratien that position of public architect may be rendered respectable and worthy the acceptance of men of talent and science. 4°. 3 pages.

LAURENS (Lieutenant-Colonel).

See CONGRESSIONAL COMMITTEE, 1782.

——— to MADISON.

1815, March 25, Paris. Asks the President to accept a flute made of glass, of his invention. [In French.] 4°. 1 page.

LAVAL, JOHN. *Montpellier.*

1821, February 19, Philadelphia. Transmits by mail the first volume of "Nature Displayed." 4°. 1 page.

LAW, THOMAS. *Philadelphia.*

1797, October 18, Washington. Wishes to hold lands in Virginia and requests his advice if he approves of a foreigner petitioning the legislature for that purpose. 4°. 4 pages.

Washington.

1801, May 12, Washington. Asks Madison if he will occupy a house on Capitol Hill for the coming summer. 4°. 3 pages.

1804, July 15, Washington. Submits for his perusal imaginary speeches to the Indians now here. Suggests establishment of a school. fol. 15 pages.

1804, July 18, Washington. On the importance of encouraging Indians in the pursuit of agriculture. fol. 3 pages.

1813, March 28, Washington. Recommends the inclosure of 200 acres or more of the public grounds for the purposes of agriculture and the propagation of valuable trees and plants. fol. 2 pages.

——— and others.

1814, September 15, Washington. The citizens offer for the temporary House of Representatives the church near the Capitol and buildings contiguous for the Senate and offices requisite for both Houses. fol. 2 pages.

LAW, THOMAS.

Not dated. Submits a proposition and plan for the erection of a national monument to the memory of Washington. 4°. 9 pages.

1814, not dated. Suggestions in view of the late destruction of the Capitol and public buildings,

LAW, THOMAS.

that the reputation of parsimony and neglect exhibited in this city in relation to public buildings should no longer be continued. The advice of Washington respecting a university and military school. Hopes every edifice will arise with superior convenience and splendor.
fol. 3 pages.

1814, not dated. A paper headed "Anticipation." Relating to a scheme for a national bank. His doubts as to its practicabiliiy to aid in the approaching campaign. fol. 13 pages.

1814, not dated. Suggestions as to the means of rendering the city of Washington comfortable with pavements, lamps, and a compact population. Inconvenience of the great distances between public buildings and residences.
4°. 4 pages.

1817, February 1, Washington. Inclosing letters containing arguments to insure the establishment of a national currency. fol. 1 page.

1817, February 1, Washington. Transmits letters on the subject of finance and other matters.
fol. 1 page.

Not dated. Situation of creditors and means of relief to be applied for debtors.
fol. 1 page.

Not dated. Scheme proposed for the establishment of a permanent asylum for disabled decrepit naval officers, seamen, and marines, according to act of Congress, passed February 6, 1811.
4°. 4 pages.

Not dated. Financial scheme for the purpose of raising revenue for the general defense with the least inconvenience to the community. [Not signed.] [Copy.] fol. 4 pages.

Montpellier.

1823, December 22. Introducing Mr. Chapman, a British officer, and Mr. Ralston, of Philadelphia.
4°. 1 page.

1824, July 11, Washington. Incloses a paper on the national currency. fol. 1 page.

1829, August 3. In order to allay malignant feelings at elections, suggests a mode to prevent demagogues from forcing voters to elect contrary to their real sentiments. 4°. 1 page.

Not dated. Transmits a pamphlet which is the key to a greater one which may perhaps be posthumous. 4°. 1 page.

LAW, WILLIAM, to JOY, GEORGE. *Copenhagen.*

1811, February 24, Copenhagen. Acknowledging note of 23d. Has petitioned to the King for a delay of decision in the business of the *Swift*. As soon as the results of this petition is known will better judge of what may be prudent and necessary. [On same sheet with letter to Law from George Joy of 23d.] [Press copy.]
4°. 2 pages.

LAWS OF THE UNITED STATES, ERRORS IN.

Not dated. Communication unsigned, proposing for a stated recompense, to give the Government the results of a discovery for correcting errors in Sunday laws, whereby much can be saved to the Government. 4°. 1 page.

LAY, JOHN, to MADISON. *Montpellier.*

1822, January 12, Richmond. Proposal to receive Madison's tobacco to dispose of, giving prices in the Richmond market. 4°. 1 page.

LAY, JOHN O.

1822, July 17, Richmond. Sends a box of seed. Offers his services in sending parcels to him. 4°. 1 page.

1824, May 11, Richmond. Reporting the state of the Richmond tobacco market. 4°. 1 page.

1825, May 14, Richmond. Acknowledging letter of 12th. Excitement in the tobacco market. Suggests selling Madison's tobacco and authorizing him to draw on account. Prices of cotton. 4°. 2 pages.

1825, May 20, Richmond. Inclosing sales 8 hogsheads tobacco. Suggestions as to a better plan of grading. 4°. 3 pages.

1825, June 20, Richmond. Transmits sales of tobacco. The price for wheat. 4°. 2 pages.

1825, July 2, Richmond. Transmits account current and certificate for balance. Prices of wheat and tobacco. 4°. 2 pages.

1825, July 5, Richmond. Sales of tobacco. 4°. 1 page.

1825, July 15, Richmond. Private financial matters respecting sales of tobacco. 4°. 1 page.

1825, August 2, Richmond. Transmits account sales of tobacco. 4°. 2 pages.

LEA, ISAAC.

1828, March 30, Philadelphia. Asks if he has any recollection of the fact of the brig *Diligence*, Capt. Wilder, having been sent from Virginia in 1772 for the purpose of discovering a north-west passage. 4°. 2 pages.

LEAR, BENJAMIN L. *Montpellier.*

1822, December 14, Washington. Asks for statement by Madison if he recollects whether it was stipulated that Gen. Hull was to receive the pay of governor of Michigan as well as that of brigadier-general, in order to close the account which his relatives claim of the Treasury Department. 4°. 3 pages.

LEAR, TOBIAS. *Washington.*

1803, July 19, Boston. Acknowledging letter of 11th, respecting his outfit and part of advanced salary as consul at Algiers. Suggests the idea of a cypher. Thinks he will sail with Commodore Preble, about August 10. Entertainment at New York given to Mr. King, at which he was present. Patriotic toasts, etc. 4°. 3 pages.

1803, July 19, Boston. Acknowledging letter of 12th, received since writing this day. The *Constitution*, in which he sails for Algiers, described. Will not be ready to sail before August 10. "Private." 4°. 1 page.

——— to MARSHALL, JOHN (Chief-Justice).

1803, August 13, Boston (on board U. S. frigate Constitution). Injurious reports circulated in Boston, that he had suppressed certain papers forming

LEAR, TOBIAS.

part of the diary of Washington, said to have originated from Judge Marshall. Declares his innocence of the charge and relates an interview with a clergyman in Boston who spread the said report and who refuses to name the person who informed him. [Copy.] 4°. 3 pages.

——— to MADISON.

1803, August 23, at sea. Particulars of his voyage and describes the ship *Constitution* and Commodore Preble. Adds a postscript dated September 5, off Cape St. Vincent, and incloses copy of a letter to Chief-Justice Marshall declaring his innocence of a scandalous report of his having suppressed certain papers, a part of Gen. Washington's diary, to prevent publication. "Private." 4°. 3 pages.

1804, July 16, Algiers. Acknowledging a private letter of January 23. Appreciates Madison's approbation of his conduct in the business in Morocco. Expenses of living in Algiers. Inadequacy of salary, considering enhanced expenses of all articles of the first necessity. Describes his residence and of other consuls. Respecting Mr. Robert Hurley, a midshipman in the Navy, who expects preferment. Details his services. "Private." 4°. 4 pages.

1807, March 15, off Algiers. Base and false aspersions which have appeared in the public prints upon his conduct in the Tripoli business. The Government has been imposed upon by false representations about Barbary affairs. Is grateful to Madison and the President for the confidence placed in him to negotiate the Tunis business. "Private and confidential." 4°. 3 pages.

1810, July 12, Algiers. Congratulations on his election to the Presidency. Would like to return to his native country or to find more congenial employment. Full details of his official business have been given to the Department. Sends wheat for seed, also some rams of the best breed, and other products. "Private." 4°. 3 pages.

1812, August 31, Gibraltar. Difficulty in sending articles to the United States. Breeds of sheep of Barbary. Wine of the country, its excellence and cheapness. Particulars of events in Algiers sent in official letters to the Department of State. Hurried manner of leaving Algiers. Conjectures as to future negotiations. Shall remain in Gibraltar until further instructions are given. 4°. 4 pages.

1813, April 9, New York. Just arrived from Cadiz. Has forwarded to the Secretary of State a copy of a communication in the Spanish language by the regency of Spain to the cortes on the subject of the conduct of the United States toward Spain and her American colonies. His son has made a translation, but it may be imperfect. As soon as possible will go to Washington and report details respecting Algiers and Spain. Offers his services in the present conflict. "Private." 4°. 2 pages.

1814, July 17, Plattsburg. Declines the appointment of accountant of the War Department on account of his inexperience in that line. Transmits to the Secretary of State the modification of the convention as executed by the Barbary commissioners and himself on exchange of prisoners. fol. 1 page.

LEAR, TOBIAS.

1815, March 18, Washington. Statement from the accountant's office of the War Department, showing the amounts appropriated under each head of expenditures for the years 1814 and 1815, including balances on December 31, 1813.
royal fol. 1 page.

LEE, CHARLES CARTER. *Montpellier.*

1831, May 9, New York. Incloses a letter from his brother. Unable to find the wine he alludes to. Recalls old associations and is grateful for past favors. 4°. 3 pages.

LEE, EDMOND J., to DALTON, T.

1809, July 24. Gives his opinions respecting the removal of slaves from Virginia into the District of Columbia and their freedom on returning to Virginia. 4°. 2 pages.

LEE, EDM. J., and others, to MADISON.
Washington.

1816, March 23, Alexandria, Va. Remonstrance of the mayor and common council of the town of Alexandria on behalf of the citizens against the bill depending before the Senate to limit the right of appeal from the circuit court of the District of Columbia to the Supreme Court. 4°. 6 pages.

LEE, HENRY. *Richmond.*

1785, February 16, New York. Incloses a report passed by Congress on the situation of the country. Advices from Madeira affording grounds to hope for success in our negotiations with the Barbary powers. Indian affairs not promising.
4°. 2 pages.

1786, October 19, New York. Letter of the Virginia delegates to the assembly on the subjects of finance. Advocates the establishment of a well-disciplined and well-appointed militia. The Eastern commotions becoming serious. Madison's expected marriage. 4°. 4 pages.

1786, October 27, New York. The discontents in the Eastern States. Fears the contagion may spread to Virginia. Object of the malcontents.
fol. 2 pages.

1786, December 28, Alexandria. Expressing with bitterness the mortification of his defeat as delegate to Congress. Complains of Madison's abandonment of him in connection with his own (Madison's) election to the office. fol. 3 pages.
New York.

1787, not dated. Returns from a visit to Judge Pendleton. His firmness to the Federal constitution. Different parties in Virginia. Patrick Henry, leader of the one opposed to any system which tends to confirm the union of the States; another party friendly to the constitution, and a third wishing amendments to the proposed constitution. Suggests means to secure Madison's election as delegate. fol. 2 pages.

1787, December 7, Stratford. The Virginia assembly hostile to the new constitution, owing to the art and talents of Henry for declamation. Gen. Washington, the Pages, R. Wormley, and F. Lightfoot Lee are firm for the constitution. Thinks Madison should return to secure his election. Offers himself as delegate from Westmoreland, but it is doubtful if he succeeds.
4°. 3 pages.

LEE, HENRY.

1788, January 14, Stratford. To aid Mr. Twining he indorses his bill, to be paid by the Postmaster-General as the contract is performed. Asks Madison to see that it is paid. fol. 1 page.

1788, October 29, Alexandria. On a project for securing land at Great Falls. Describes the location and probable future advantages. 4°. 3 pages.

1788, November 19, Alexandria. The advantages of securing the property at Great Falls. Madison's defeat in the election for State senator. Virginia politics. Washington's love of domestic repose and unwillingness to engage in public life, but will come forward if the public happiness demands it. fol. 4 pages.

1788, December 8, Alexandria. Has visited Great Falls. Was disappointed in not meeting Gen. Washington there, as expected. Great advantages of the place. Navigation of the river. Anxious for Madison to interest himself in the purchase. Virginia politics. Patrick Henry's influence. Madison will probably be elected delegate. 4°. 4 pages.

1788, December 17, Alexandria. Madison's decision for standing for his district. Transmits a plat of the canal with Col. Griffin's observations. Suggests they be published in the monthly magazines. Is pleased that Madison has become interested in the property. Thanks him for some fruit trees. fol. 2 pages.

1789, June 10, Alexandria. General satisfaction of the people for the new Government and the President, Debates in Congress relative to the title of the Chief Magistrate. The impost bill discussed. Management of the public money. Matters relating to the Great Falls lands. 4°. 6 pages.

1789, January 14, Marmion. Mrs. Lee's illness prevents his return to Richmond. Reports concerning Madison's election as Member of Congress. Thinks it certain. Virginia elections. 4°. 3 pages.

1789, March 8, Alexandria. European project about the Great Falls scheme and navigation of the Potomac. 4°. 2 pages.

1789, March 14,, Alexandria. Applications for purchase of lots at the Great Falls. On back of sheet is a memorandum relating to the proposed titles of the President, Vice-President, and other officials. 4°. 1 page.

1789, June 9, Richmond. Appointment of a friend to official position, it is understood that the public good must combine with the views of the gentleman recommended. 4°. 2 pages.

New York.

1789, September 8, Berkley. Ultimate location of the Federal Government. Advantages of the Potomac Valley. Queries the policy of the early adjournment of Congress when so much important business is to be done. 4°. 5 pages.

1789, November 23, Richmond. Proposed amendments to the Constitution. Opposition to the Federal Government in Virginia as great as ever. fol. 2 pages.

LEE, HENRY.

1789 (?), not dated. Incloses a letter on which was founded his to the President and his answer. 4°. 2 pages.

New York.

1790, January 25, Stratford. Introducing Dr. Morrow, who wishes to resume his old employment as naval surgeon. Asks his good offices to secure it. small 4°. 2 pages.

1790, March 4, Stratford. His disapproval of the report of Hamilton on the funding system. On the subject of the Great Falls scheme. Jefferson's gloomy views on the subject. Mrs. Lee's continued ill health. fol. 8 pages.

1890, April 22, Alexandria. Acknowledging letter of 4th. Laments that the Great Falls scheme should be locked for want of £3,000. Suggests means of raising the sum by mortgage. 4°. 4 pages.

1790, March 13, Alexandria. Acknowledging letter of 1st. Has read Madison's debates in Congress. The Government, he fears, will prove ruinous to Virginia. Nothing can alleviate our suffering, but the establishment of the permanent seat near the center of territory and direct taxation. 4°. 2 pages.

1790, April 3, Berry Hill. Introducing a son of Thomas J. Lee, who wishes a place in some department. Gloomy views in respect to the sectional legislation of Congress. Sees no prospect of alteration or alleviation. No cure but to change the seat of Government to the territorial center, direct taxation, and the abolition of the gambling systems of finance. fol. 3 pages.

Philadelphia.

1791, July 29. Dines with the President and Jefferson. Has no longer fears of the happiness of the United States from the event dreaded in New York. Respecting corn which Madison thought well of. Sedgwick, of Massachusetts, defendant in a suit before the Federal court. Describes the case. 4°. 3 pages.

1791, August 3, Philadelphia. Describes with minuteness the illness of Col. Fisher, and wishes Madison to procure the advice of Dr. McKnight in relation thereto. 4°. 6 pages.

1791, August 6, Philadelphia. Hopes to raise the money to pay Fairfax and secure the Great Falls property. Asks Madison's aid, as he is interested one-fourth. 4°. 1 page.

1791, August 24, Alexandria. The prevailing rage of stock gambling and speculation. 4°. 2 pages.

Philadelphia.

1791, December 8. Incloses list of subscribers to Freneau's "Gazette." The late defeat of our Army in the Northwest by the Indians. [Signature cut off.] 4°. 1 page.

1791, December 22, Richmond. Asks for letters of introduction for Mr. James Marshall, who goes to Europe. 4°. 2 pages.

1792, January 8, Richmond. Acknowledging letters of December 18 and 1st instant. The disaster in the west disgraceful to the military reputation of the United States. Denounces the financial schemes

LEE, HENRY.

of the Treasury. Does not approve of Madison's reply to the President's speech. Thinks Madison has treated him ill in respect to the Great Falls scheme. 4°. 7 pages.

1792, January 17, Richmond. Acknowledging letter of the 8th. Condemns the leading measures of the administration. Changes must be made in the arrangements for the next campaign against the Indians, or the late disgraceful defeat will be repeated. Suggestions as to means. 4°. 4 pages.

1792, January 29, Richmond. Acknowledging letter of 21st. Urges vigorous and open opposition to the financial measures of the administration. Suggestions as to the conduct of the campaign against the Indians. 4°. 5 pages.

1792, February 6, Richmond. His interest in Freneau's paper. Disapproves of the principle which governed the first Congress of intrenching on the rights of their successors in relation to the funding system. Congress too slow in deliberations relative to the military measures for the next campaign. 4°. 3 pages.

1792, April 4, Richmond. Acknowledging letter of March 28. Depreciation of Hamilton's financial schemes. Impression on the coin. 4°. 3 pages.

1792, April 18, Richmond. Acknowledging letters of 6th and 11th. Appointment of Gen. Wayne to the command in chief of the United States Western army. Expresses his surprise. 4°. 2 pages.

1792, September 10, Richmond. His late domestic calamity. Branch of the United States Bank to be established at Richmond. 4°. 3 pages.

1794, January 23. Acknowledging a letter brought by Mrs. Adair. Approves of Madison's commercial proposition. [Signature cut off.] 4°. 3 pages.

1794, September 23, Alexandria. Congratulates Madison on his marriage. Is appointed to take command of the troops to restore order in Pennsylvania. 4°. 2 pages.

Washington.

1801, February 1, Alexandria. Asks into whose hands he can intrust some private papers of a pecuniary nature, which he intended to send to Monroe, but hears he is to return. 4°. 2 pages.

1807, July 19, Shirley. Probability of war. Suggestions as to immediate preparations and manner of defensive and offensive proceedings. 4°. 6 pages.

1808, January 18, Stratford. Sincerely hopes peace may be preserved. Nothing but a sense of honor will reconcile the people of Virginia to war. If the British Government shall make amends for the Chesapeake insult Virginia will pour forth her indignation on the promotors of war. Thinks our differences can be easily adjusted. 4°. 3 pages.

1808, February 3, Alexandria. The solicitude he feels at this portentous moment. In Madison's hands is committed our destiny. Wishes to have a private interview. 4°. 2 pages.

LEE, HENRY.

1808, February 10, Washington. Project for removing the seat of government to Philadelphia, growing out of the wish of those preferring Clinton to Madison as Presidential candidate, and the drawing of Pennsylvania to the support of Clinton. Should Madison's present negotiations with Great Britain be brought to a happy issue the efforts of his opponent will be completely overset. Asks to be sent as Government agent to the Brazils on account of his wife's health. 4°. 4 pages.

1808, March 21, Alexandria. Failure of Mr. Rose's mission. Asks if any renewal of negotiations can take place. Lee's desire to go to the Brazils. 4°. 3 pages.

1808, April 21, Alexandria. Recommends Dr. Wellford for a position in the medical department of the U. S. Army now raising. 4°. 2 pages.

1808, April 22, Alexandria. Asks his aid in the case of Mr. Clark with Mr. Rodney, the Attorney-General. 4°. 2 pages.

1808, not dated, Alexandria. The British decrees. Is of opinion the continuance of the embargo will influence his chances of election and the Government placed in the hands of a man whose administration will be woeful. fol. 4 pages.

1808, December 17, Prince George County, Md. His anxiety to go to Bermuda. Want of conveyance thither. Asks if he can not procure some means of getting there in a Government vessel. Importance of securing an interview with a Col. Brown whose deposition is necessary to the safety of his estate. The state of his health requires a sea voyage. 4°. 3 pages.

1808, not dated. His great anxiety to go to a climate recommended by his physician on account of his wife's and his own health. Would like Government employment at the Brazils. Has no fears of a war with Great Britain. 4°. 3 pages.

1809, February 11, Baltimore. On the responsibilities, at a period of difficulty and danger, attending his position as President. Advice and suggestions as to his conduct in the administration of the office. 4°. 4 pages; and fol. 4 pages.

1809, March 5, Baltimore. Has read his inaugural speech and criticises it and gives advice. Recommends as Secretary of State Judge Washington. 4°. 2 pages.

1809, March 6, Baltimore. Recommending John Fitzhugh for a consulate or place in the custom-house. 4°. 3 pages.

1811, June 24, Alexandria. Petition of Mr. Yeaton for remittance of a fine for evasion of custom-house regulations. fol. 3 pages.

1811, July 19, Alexandria. Trial of Gen. Wilkinson. Lee satisfied of his innocence. His wish to change the place of his trial. 4°. 4 pages.

——— to STODDERT, ——.

1811, August 14, Alexandria. Acknowledging letter of 7th. Corrects a misunderstanding of statements relating to the President's negotiations with the Government of Great Britain. [Copy.] 4°. 2 pages.

LEE, HENRY, to MADISON.

1811, August 19, Alexandria. Inclosing copy of a letter to Mr. Stoddert, correcting a misconception of a statement respecting Madison's negotiations with the Government of Great Britain. Lee's unceasing desire for the peace and amity of the two nations, but thinks it better to fight our way to future peace than to drag on in the present state of disputation and imitation. Mr. Davis and his pretended assurance of his future cordial coalition and support of the administration. Gossip of Mrs. Madison's intercession with Monroe in favor of Colvil. 4°. 7 pages.

1811, November 8, Alexandria. Expresses his pleasure at Madison's message, but it will be vain unless followed by appropriate measures which Lee specifies. Suggests a manifesto from the President or Congress announcing our longsuffering, patience, hope of amicable settlement, our disappointment, and our determination to make the last appeal, as all other efforts had failed. 4°. 2 pages.

1811, December 27, Baltimore. Introducing Maj. Clarke, of Little York, Pa., a brother soldier in the Revolutionary war. 4°. 1 page.

1812, February 27, Washington. Incloses a letter from Gen. Wilkinson and requests Madison to say if he is satisfied with it without further explanation. 4°. 1 page.

1812, April 24, Washington. Learns that Congress may possibly send a present of provisions to the distressed inhabitants of the Caraccas; suggests that he might be entrusted with its presentment. Wishes no emolument. 4°. 2 pages.

1812, June 6, Alexandria. Inclosing papers from Richmond. 4°. 1 page.

1812, June 21. Begs him to hold back ships of war and privateers until further news from England is received, as the latest indications were of a disposition to repeal the orders in council and to show disinclination to wade in human blood. fol. 1 page.

1813, January 15, Alexandria. Apprehensions for the safety of a corps under command of Brigadier-General Smith, stationed at Queenstown, and which should be removed from the danger of a sudden nocturnal attack. 4°. 2 pages.

1813, August 4, Barbadoes. Improvement of his health and strength. Has accomplished his object, the obstacles to which seemed insurmountable. Sends a cask of Madeira and a large green turtle. 4°. 3 pages.

1813, November 17, Barbadoes. His health not improving. Thinks the climate not so beneficial as the South of Europe. Describes his residence there and the people he meets. Deplores the war, and wishes for its honorable termination. 4°. 8 pages.

Not dated. A memorandum in Madison's handwriting respecting the evidence of Gen. H. Lee's disaffection to the policy and measures of the Federal Government during several of the early years of Washington's administration. 4°. 1 page (torn edges).

LEE, HENRY (author). *Montpellier.*

1824, May 4, Fredericksburg. Acknowledging letter of April 22. Proposes to write a second edition of his father's memoirs, and asks if Madison can contribute any documents or observations in connection, confirmation, or illustration of that work. 4°. 4 pages.

1824, June 18, Fredericksburg. Wishes to obtain Madison's sentiments in regard to the style and principles of a prospectus inclosed. fol. 1 page.

1824, August 5, Fredericksburg. Transmits a copy of an address reported to the Jackson convention. His political views. Proposes to write biographies of Virginia's great men, including Jefferson, Madison, Monroe, and Marshall. Asks Madison's aid in furnishing him materials. 4°. 8 pages.

1824, August 24, Washington. Proposes to write a history of the campaign of 1814 on the Niagara. Asks Madison's assistance in furnishing materials. 4°. 5 pages.

1825, January 6, Washington. Incloses a paper on the Constitution, which he will be glad to hear he approves of, he being the chief architect of our political temple. Has abandoned the project of a work unsuccessfully suggested to Madison for want of materials. 4°. 3 pages.

1825, December 13, Washington. Thanks him for offer of materials in a work he proposes to write on the campaign of 1814. Incloses copy of a letter from Gen. Armstrong on same subject. 4°. 3 pages.

1827, February 2, Westmoreland C. H. Asks if Madison can recollect why certain plans in the campaign in 1814 were not carried out, and how to account for the singular infelicity of many of Madison's appointments in the Cabinet during that period. 4°. 4 pages.

1827, August 24, near Nashville. Wishes information respecting the provisional order to Gen. Jackson of July 18, 1814, authorizing him on certain conditions to take possession of Pensacola. large fol. 2 pages.

1829, March 12, Westmoreland C. H. Acknowledging letter of February 16. Introduces Mr. Clarke, an English gentleman. 4°. 2 pages.

1829, May 30, Washington. Introducing Mr. Alfred Langdon Elwyn, grandson of the New Hampshire patriot. fol. 2 pages.

1833, June 5, Paris. Wishes copy of a certain letter of Jefferson's to Madison, in order to vindicate his father's memory from a gross and virulent blunder in the writings of the late Mr. Jefferson. 4°. 3 pages.

1833, September 15, Paris. Acknowledging letter of August 14. Strictures on the conduct of Jefferson as a man or a statesman in censuring the policy and measures of the first administration, and admitting that the object of Jefferson himself and party was to restore and act on the principles of that administration. 4°. 5 pages.

1833, November 14, Paris. Asks if it is true that he declined to accept the office of Secretary of State, tendered by Washington, as successor of Mr. Jefferson. 4°. 2 pages.

LEE, HENRY (author).

1834, January 14, Paris. Acknowledging letter covering copies of his father's letters to Madison. Incloses copy of a letter to his brother Carter, requesting him to furnish Madison copies of his letters to his father, and tells him where to find them. 4°. 2 pages.

Not dated. Draft of an ordinance for the government of the District of Columbia. 4°. 12 pages.

LEE, JOHN H. *Montpellier.*

1829, July 30, Daviess City. Suit against Bell & Tapscott in Madison's favor. Endeavors to secure property in payment of the debt. Recommends commencing a suit in chancery. 4°. 2 pages.

1830, November 12, Daviess City. Incloses answers of Bell & Tapscott in a bill in chancery for Mr. Willis and Madison. Directs Madison to state the manner in which he derives title, as the papers are in his brother's name. 4°. 2 pages.

1831, April 23, Daviess City. Interview with Mrs. Bell and Mrs. Tapscott in relation to the chancery suit. The anger of Mrs. Tapscott. Final agreement on terms and withdrawal of defense. Asks Madison's wishes as to the future management. 4°. 1 page.

LEE, LUDWELL.

1831, September 19, Belmont. Apologizes for not sooner answering his letter asking for copies of letters which he informs him are in the possession of the University of Virginia, from whence he can procure copies. 4°. 3 pages.

LEE, RICHARD BLOND. *Washington.*

See Van Ness, John P., August 28, 1815; November 20, 1815, March 25, 1816.

LEE, RICHARD BLOND and TENCH RINGGOLD, jointly to MADISON. *Washington.*

1816, February 15, Washington. Incloses contract with Bank of Washington for an additional loan authorized by act of Congress for rebuilding public buildings, for the President's approbation. 4°. 1 page.

LEE, RICHARD HENRY. *Richmond.*

1784, November 20, Trenton. Retention of the British posts owing to the fact that Virginia has not repealed her laws that impede the recovery of British debts. Incloses copy of a treaty made at Fort Stannix with the six nations. Emigrations from Virginia to Georgia and North and South Carolina. Causes assigned. Reflections on taxes and the revenue. 4°. 3 pages.

1784, November 26, Trenton. Acknowledging a letter informing him of the proceedings of the Virginia legislature. Suggests that Congress should call upon the States to form a convention for revision of the confederation. 4°. 4 pages.

1784, December 27, Trenton. Acknowledging letter of 11th. Congress decides to make New York their temporary residence, and the permanent one to be on the banks of Delaware, and federal buildings to be erected. Apprehensions of a war with the Southern Indians. Probable appointments of Ministers to Spain and London. The navigation of the Mississippi. [Signature cut off.] 4°. 3 pages.

LEE, RICHARD HENRY.

1785, May 30, New York. Acknowledging letter of 20th. Navigation of the Potomac in the legislature of Virginia. The separation of Kentucky from Virginia. Disposal of public lands northwest of the Ohio for extinguishing the debt. Dr. Franklin has leave to retire. Jefferson will remain in France and John Adams to be sent to London. Arrival of Gardoqui in Philadelphia Negotiations about the navigation of the Mississippi. [Signature cut off.] 4°. 3 pages.

LEE, RICHARD. *Montpellier.*

1834, March 6, Philadelphia. Is engaged in publishing a memoir of his grandfather, Richard Henry Lee. Sends Madison some of his original correspondence for inspection and asks permission to publish same. fol. 2 pages.

LEE, ROBERT. *Washington.*

1815, February 6, Rahway, N. J. Incloses a paper originally intended for publication in the "National Intelligencer," signed "An American" proposing a financial plan for the national requirements. 4°. 9 pages.

Montpellier.

1829, December —, Rahway, N. J. Gives his own and asks Madison's opinion whether an amendment to the Constitution of the United States limiting the office of President to a single term would not be an eligible amendment. fol. 7 pages.

LEE, THEODORICK. *Washington.*

1817, February 26, Washington. Application for the promotion of his son serving in the U. S. Navy. 4°. 2 pages.

LEE, WILLIAM. *Washington.*

1803, July 2, Bordeaux. Bill and two bills of lading of 13 cases wine shipped for Norfolk; also bill of freight. 4°. 4 pages.

1803, July 4, Bordeaux. Inclosing bill of lading of wine shipped to Norfolk. 4°. 1 page.

1803, August 3, Bordeaux. Annexing copy of letter, dated July 4, 1803, notifying shipment of some cases of wine to Norfolk. Notice of draft for payment of the same. 4°. 2 pages.

1803, October 25, Bordeaux. Has been visiting the Pyrenees for his health. Apologizes for having caused the wrong kind of wine shipped for the President, owing to a mistake of his partners. Affairs in Spain and Portugal. Said to have purchased of France their neutrality to which England has consented. Describes flat-bottomed boats in the port of Bordeaux destined to carry troops and heavy ordnance. 4°. 5 pages.

1803, December 20, Bordeaux. Sends by the *Good Intent* for Philadelphia, fruits in brandy, almonds, and prunes. 4°. 1 page.

1804, May 12, Bordeaux. Explains a financial difficulty with Messrs. Porter & King, thinking the matter may be misrepresented. Dissatisfaction with the Emperor of France. 4°. 3 pages.

1804, June 20, Bordeaux. Notifies him of a shipment of wine. 4°. 1 page.

1804, June 20, Bordeaux. Copy of the foregoing. 4°. 2 pages.

LEE, WILLIAM, to DAVIS, WILLIAM (collector). *Norfolk.*

1804, June 20, Bordeaux. Ship per brig *Maria* for Norfolk 10 cases wine for account of Madison. Incloses bills of lading, account and duplicate of account. 4°. 4 pages. 8°. 3 pages.

——— to MADISON. *Washington.*

1804, July 10, Bordeaux. Ships 9 cases of wines and liquors per ship *Sheffield* for Norfolk. Incloses bill of lading and account. 4°. 2 pages. 8°. 1 page.

1805, January 5, Bordeaux. Calumnies respecting his action in respect to the *Joseph and Phebe* attributed to *jalousies de metier* which he explains. "Private." 4°. 4 pages.

1805, January 5, Bordeaux. Duplicate of the foregoing. 4°. 4 pages.

1805, January 8, Bordeaux. Seizure of the ship *Easter*, of New York, claimed to be the property of Stroebel & Martini. Evasion of the custom-house laws. Charging a Mr. Wigginton as being an accomplice in the fraud. 4°. 4 pages.

1805, January 20, Bordeaux. Explaining how the ship *Easter*, pretending to be American property, and procuring papers of the consul, proves to be French property, and the course he has pursued in consequence. 4°. 4 pages.

1805, February 12, Bordeaux. Sends Madison and the President two boxes of paté de Perigord. 4°. 1 page.

1805, September 14, Bordeaux. Incloses bill of lading and invoice of wine, etc., shipped per brig *Lyon* for Baltimore. 4°. 2 pages. 4°. 1 page.

1805, September 18, Bordeaux. Ships wine per brig *Lyon* for Baltimore. Incloses French newspapers. 4°. 1 page.

1806, September 10, Bordeaux. Acknowledging letters of July 25 and 26. Incloses newspapers containing European political news. 4°. 1 page.

1806, October 29, Bordeaux. Rumors of a battle between Wiemer and Jena, in which the Prussians lose many prisoners and ordnance. The Duke of Brunswick and Prince Henry of Prussia were killed. Rumors of another battle in which the Emperor is said to have been wounded and the King of Prussia killed. Wants confirmation. Ships per brig *Jacob* wine and nuts. 4°. 2 pages.

1806, October 31, Bordeaux. Confirmation of reports of successes of the Emperor. Reports that the Emperor has entered Berlin, the Saxon army joins the French, and that the Russian army has entered the Prussian territory. Spain and Austria prepared to join the allies. 4°. 2 pages.

1806, November 5, Bordeaux. Incloses invoices of wine per brig *Jacob* for Baltimore. Transmits bulletin of the grand army, announcing arrival of the French at Berlin. Proceedings in Spain. 4°. 2 pages.

1806, November 5, Bordeaux. Inclosing invoices and bill of lading, with duplicates, of wine and nuts per brig *Jacob* for Baltimore. 4°. 4 pages. 8°. 2 pages.

LEE, WILLIAM.

1807, September 15, Bordeaux. Acknowledging letter of June 28, requesting a supply of wine and cordials to be shipped. 4°. 1 page.

1807, October 4, Bordeaux. Shipments of wine and other articles, and notice of drafts in payment. Fears of a war with Great Britain, and our commerce shut out of Europe from the Dardanelles to the Baltic. [Duplicate.] 4°. 2 pages.

1807, October 19, Bordeaux. Invoice and bill of lading of a pipe of brandy shipped per sloop *Susan* to New York, also account of charges.
4°. 2 pages. 8°. 1 page.

1807, November 27, Bordeaux. Invoice of articles shipped per ship *Lorenzo*, and consigned to David Gelston for account of Madison, with duplicates.
4°. 2 pages.

1807, November 30, Bordeaux. Ships nuts and liquors. Regrets his brandy is detained by an embargo. The President's address received and gives great satisfaction. 4°. 1 page.

1807, December 10, Bordeaux. Notice by the British squadron at the mouth of this river, warning vessels from entering any port in France, Portugal, Spain, Italian, and Mediterranean ports. Measure considered hostile to the United States. European affairs. 4°. 3 pages.

1807, not dated, Bordeaux. Invoice of merchandise consigned to the collector of New York per ship *Calypso* for Madison's account, with bill of lading. Also bill of lading schooner *Laurel*, from New York to Alexandria, of the same merchandise.
4°. 1 page. 8°. 1 page. 8°. 1 page.

1808, November 1, Bordeaux. Difficulty in shipping articles. The Emperor in Bordeaux on his way to join the army. The conquest of Spain and Portugal doubtless will soon be achieved. Apprehensions for the safety of Mr. Irving. An attempt to assassinate him in Madrid. 4°. 3 pages.

1811, February 11, New York. Denies the statement that he brought with him from France a number of licenses under which he has been expediting a number of vessels. 4°. 1 page.

1812, January 1, Paris. Mr. Barlow's negotiations do not appear to be favorable. The hopes of French merchants and manufacturers will be disappointed. If Congress should lay similar restricting duties on brandy, wine, and manufactured goods as the Emperor has on imports from the United States, it would have a good effect. Lee's good opinion of Mr. Barlow as a diplomat.
fol. 3 pages.

1812, April 12, Paris. Incloses a letter from Gen. Desfourneaux. 4°. 1 page.

1812, April 22, Paris. Licenses granted to vessels for importation of colonial produce. The business greatly increased. No remedy except to place restrictions on importations of French silks. Mr. Barlow's exertions continual. Scarcity of bread. Incloses a letter from Mr. Meyer.
fol. 3 pages.

1812, May 24, Paris. Conjectures on the policy of the British Government towards us. The Prince Re-

LEE, WILLIAM.

gent's manifesto. Licenses for exportation under American colors in the name of French houses. Proclamation of the Emperor, who promises to conduct his army into St. Petersburg in July. The Emperor Alexander's declaration that all Russians who take up arms shall be free.
4°. 6 pages.

1813, August 20, Bordeaux. Correspondence with Mr. Crawford and Mr. Warden, touching Lee's controversy with the latter. Is convinced that his explanation will be satisfactory to the President. Shall transmit the correspondence, and asks the President's indulgence until he receives it and the whole subject is laid before him.
fol. 2 pages.

1813, November 10, Bordeaux. Incloses receipt for a shipment of wine per schooner *Engineer*.
fol. 1 page.

1814, January 28, Bordeaux. Incloses invoice and bill of lading of brandy, wine, and fruits per brig *Rambler*, consigned to the captain, who will enter the articles and send the amount of freight and charges. fol. 1 page.

1815, September 6, Bordeaux. A box containing some French lamps in Mr. Hughe's possession. It is Madison's property, and asks him to direct it to be sent him. Asks if his wine arrived safe with other articles. fol. 2 pages.

1815, September 15, Bordeaux. Sends per schooner *Manlius* a barrel of vinegar and box of sweet oil. Wines and brandy are higher in price ever known and can be bought cheaper in the United States.
4°. 2 pages.

1816, January 23, Bordeaux. Forwards a packet from Mr. Espec, president of the college at St. Foy, who intends dedicating one of his works to Madison. fol. 1 page.

1816, February 16, Bordeaux. Party rancor in Bordeaux. Insults to himself and Americans. Wishes to return home, and, during his absence, to have Mr. Stroebel appointed agent.
fol. 3 pages.

1816, February 27, Bordeaux. Repeats his desire to return to America, and requests the appointment of Mr. Stroebel as consul. fol. 2 pages.

1816, November 8, New York. Is informed that the President had appointed him accountant in the War Department. Is grateful, but declines on account of manufacturing projects in New York, and in establishing a deaf and dumb school. Does not like the occupation of accountant.
4°. 4 pages.

1816, November 17, New York. On reconsideration decides to accept the appointment of accountant of the War Department, as he has abandoned his plans of manufacturing in New York.
fol. 1 page.

Montpellier.

1818, February 27, Washington. Sends an account of articles forwarded from Bordeaux, from which is to be deducted a sum sent out for articles purchased for Mrs. Madison in Paris. Intends visiting Montpellier with Mrs. Lee and daughters in the course of the year. 4°. 2 pages.

LEE, WILLIAM.

1818, February 27, Bordeaux. Account to date. 4°. 1 page.

1830, November 9, Boston. Announces his marriage with Mrs. Ann McLean, and states who were present at the ceremony. 4°. 2 pages.

LEGARE, J. B., and others.

1818, July 24, Charleston. In behalf of the "'76 Association" sends copy of an oration delivered by one of its members on the 4th instant. 4°. 1 page.

LEGG, JOHN.

1797, January 18. Account sales of beef and pork sent to vendue by D. and J. Blair to sell for account of Madison. 4°. 1 page.

LEHRÉ, THOMAS. *Washington.*

1808, December 7, Columbia, S. C. Announces that the 10 electors of both branches of the legislature voted unanimously for Madison as President and George Clinton as Vice-President. Congratulates him and Mr. Jefferson on the prospect of so able a successor. fol. 1 page.

1812, March 30, Charleston, S. C. Incloses a letter of introduction from Charles Pinckney. Wishes the permission to correspond with him on political matters. 4°. 3 pages.

1812, May 20, Charleston, S. C. Sends copy of resolutions and proceedings of a meeting of citizens at Circular Church. fol. 1 page.

1812, May 21, Charleston, S. C. Incloses proceedings of citizens. Great exertions made by the Federalists to reject the whole of the resolutions, but not agreed to. 4°. 2 pages.

1812, June 6, Charleston, S. C. The patriotic spirit of our citizens. Review of drafted men of the Twenty-ninth Regiment. Appearance among them of a "Scotch bonnet." Danger of a riot in consequence. The bonnet given up and torn to pieces. 4°. 2 pages.

1812, June 27, Charleston, S. C. Meeting of citizens at St. Nicholas Church, who solemnly pledge themselves to support him and the Government to the last extremity, and approve of the act of Congress in declaring war against Great Britain. Protection promised to British subjects. fol. 2 pages.

1812, June 29, Charleston. Numerous meetings of citizens in St. Nicholas Church; incloses a paper containing their proceedings. Governor Middleton states that the offers of volunteers are almost incredible in numbers, and it is with difficulty he could get rid of them without offense. Opposition to Madison in the next Presidential election. 4°. 2 pages.

1812, November 10, Charleston, S. C. The President's message received, and has raised the spirits of his friends and depressed his enemies. Gross misrepresentations circulated which this message will undeceive. Attempts to defeat his election, but they will be unsuccessful. fol. 2 pages.

1812, December 4, Columbia. John Gaillard elected Senator in Congress, a supporter of the administration. 4°. 1 page.

LEHRÉ, THOMAS.

1813, March 16, Charleston, S. C. Applies for the position of marshal of this district.
4°. 2 pages.

——— to JEFFERSON. *Monticello.*

1813, March 23, Charleston. Asks Jefferson's good offices towards his application for the position of marshal for his district. States his claims.
4°. 3 pages.

——— to MADISON. *Washington.*

1813, March 26, Charleston, S. C. Meeting of citizens to deliberate on the best mode of defending the city. Incloses resolutions. Violent attacks on the Government by the Federalists. Suggests that the amounts of the sums expended on the different forts, gunboats, barges, and amounts placed in the military chest here, be furnished to the friends of the administration here to refute falsehoods. fol. 2 pages.

1813, April 12, Charleston, S. C. Wishes to be marshal of this district. States his qualifications and claims. fol. 4 pages.

Montpellier.

1819, July 10, Charleston, S. C. Acknowledging letter of June 25, which adds to the obligations already conferred on him. Should the President honor him with the appointment he seeks, he will faithfully discharge its duties. 4°. 1 page.

1828, July 21, Charleston, S. C. The tendency towards dissolution of the union. Thinks the next session of the legislature will be a stormy one. Hopes that Virginia will not be for dissolution.
4°. 2 pages.

1834, September 15, Bradford Springs, S. C. Happy to hear Madison's health is better. Fears we are on the eve of a revolution. Hopes the evil will be averted. Thanks him for his unvarying kindness, and expresses his love and respect.
4°. 2 pages.

LEIB, MICHAEL. *Washington.*

1809, May 3, Philadelphia. Suggests the policy of pardoning Gen. Bright and his associates for resisting the process of the district court.
4°. 2 pages.

1811, February 7, Washington. Denies the calumnies made on him. Wishes Madison to state that he has not made any application to him for the office of marshal of the district of Pennsylvania.
4°. 1 page.

1811, April 18, Philadelphia. Solicits the office of commissioner of loans, made vacant by the death of Gen. Maylan. 4°. 1 page.

LEIGWOOD, JR. ——. *New York.*

1789, July 25, New York. Solicits an appointment to office in the new Government. 4°. 2 pages.

LEIPER, THOMAS. *Washington.*

1805, December 15, Philadelphia. Has received a twist of tobacco from Mrs. Madison. His opinions on the preparing of tobacco. 4°. 3 pages.

LEIPER, THOMAS.

1808, August 9, Philadelphia. Questions the propriety of keeping certain persons in office, detrimental to the Republican party. Offers to sell Madison's crop of tobacco. 4°. 5 pages.

1808, May 5, Philadelphia. The sentence against Gen. Bright undoubtedly just, but it would give general satisfaction if he were pardoned. 4°. 2 pages.

1808, October 6, Philadelphia. Acknowledging letter of August 20. The appointment of Gen. Steel to the collectorship gives satisfaction. Matters relating to tobacco. 4°. 3 pages.

1809, June 14, Philadelphia. Does not approve of the appointment of Mr. Alexander, of New York, as consul to Dublin. Recommends instead Mr. English. Duncan McIntosh wishes to be consul at Aux Cayes. Federalists puffing Madison at the expense of Jefferson. 4°. 3 pages.

1811, January 14, Philadelphia. Charges against John Smith, the marshal of this district. Defends him. Wilkinson to be persecuted for preventing Burr's treason. 4°. 3 pages.

1812, August 16, Philadelphia. The appointment of Capt. Callender Irvine to the office of commissary-general gives satisfaction. Recommends William Leonard to the place lately filled by Capt. Irvine. Men in office inimical to the country. 4°. 2 pages.

1812, December 27, Philadelphia. His high estimation of Captain Callender Irvine. Disapproves of Gen. Dearborn as head of the Army. He is too old. Thinks the rank and file should be from 18 to 30 years of age and officers 20 to 40. Thinks Wilkinson should be made head of the Army. His experience and qualifications. Thinks Armstrong is better qualified to command than Dearborn. fol. 3 pages.

1814, January 5, Philadelphia. Recommends Gen. John Barker to be postmaster in Philadelphia. Thanks him for offering office for his son, which he did not accept. 4°. 2 pages.

1814, February 22, Philadelphia. Memorial requesting the removal of Gideon Granger from office; the cause assigned is for his appointment of Michael Leib as postmaster. John Binns and company the projectors of this memorial. 4°. 2 pages.

——— and BROWN, LIBERTY.

1814, August 29, Philadelphia. Inclosing copy of a resolution of the select and common councils of the city of Philadelphia, offering accommodations for the President, Congress, and the Departments, provided they should think it proper to accept the same in the present unfortunate situation of the city of Washington. small. 4°. 2 pages.

1814, September 1, Philadelphia. Superior advantages of the city of Philadelphia for the residence of Congress and President. Incompetency of persons in command. They should be turned out. Regrets the resignation of General Armstrong. fol. 2 pages.

LEIPER, THOMAS.

1815, December 1, Philadelphia. Recommends the repeal of the excise law. Its depression on the tobacco interests. 4°. 1 page.

1815 (?), not dated. Observations on the law of excising snuff. 4°. 16 pages.

LELAND, JOHN, to BARBER, THOMAS.

1788. Objections to the Federal constitution. fol. 2 pages.

——— to MADISON. *New York.*

1789, not dated. Congratulating Madison on his election as Representative to Congress. Asks him to inform him of all that occurs in this trial of the new Government. 4°. 2 pages.

LENOX, D. *Washington.*

1801, October 12, London. Inclosing abstract of applications made by him for the discharge of seamen representing themselves to be citizens of the United States, and detained on board British fleets from July 1 to October 1, 1801. 4°. 5 pages. fol. 1 page.

LENOX, JAMES.

1808, January 28, Queen Anne, Md. Position of the Republican party. Questions its unanimity in respect to the Presidential election. Asks Madison's views on the situation. 4°. 2 pages.

LEONARD, DAYTON.

1810, December 21, Tompkins, N. Y. Is an invalid for twenty years and has invented a machine which he claims to be of perpetual motion. All he requires is cash to finish it, and appeals to Madison for aid. Describes the plan. fol. 4 pages.

LEONARD, JAMES I.

1814, November 22, New York. Resents the promotion of Commander Cram over senior officers who have served with much greater distinction. Gives a record of his own services. Is not related to the Capt. Leonard who surrendered Niagara. 4°. 4 pages and strip of paper inclosed.

LE RAY DE CHAUMONT.

1807, July 12, New York. Incloses a letter of La Fayette, also one from Madame de Stael. The latter has sent a book for Madison. Dispatches from Gen. Armstrong. News from France of the expectation of a general battle to take place between the French and Russian armies. Few people doubt the Emperor's success. Rumors of parleys between belligerents. fol. 2 pages.

Montpellier.

1824, September —, Le Raysville. Asks Madison's questions relating to agricultural societies. 4°. 2 pages.

1832, June 2, New York. Is about sailing for France to attend to claims on the French and American Governments. Sends proceedings of the convention at Albany for incorporating a State agricultural society. 4°. 1 page.

LEROY, LEWIS, to JEFFERSON. *Washington.*

1809, January, Washington, N. C. Petition for redress for seizure of the schooner *Union* for having on board a slave, not knowing it was contrary to the laws. large fol. 1 page.

LESCALLIER, ——, to MADISON. *Montpellier.*

1817, November 6, New York. Transmits a publication, a translation from the Persian language. Congratulates him on his retirement from public affairs. 4°. 2 pages.

LÈTOMBE, ——. *Washington.*

1802, April 7, Paris. Acknowledging letter of August 25 last, which has been of great service to him. Thanks him for his kindness to himself and other Frenchmen. [In French.] 4°. 2 pages.

LEWIS, ADDIN, to BACON, EZEKIEL (Comptroller of the Treasury).

1814, September 8, Mobile. The collector of Mobile states that the public service requires that an attorney should be appointed without delay. 4°. 2 pages.

LEWIS, E., to MADISON.

1810, December 10, Fort St. Stephens. Complaints of lawless exactions of duties on trade. Settled personal hatred of Judge Toulmin and some of his party. His partial administration. Prays that a worthy American lawyer should replace him. 4°. 3 pages.

LEWIS, EVAN.

1810, January 8, Wilmington. Incloses a pamphlet as a tribute of respect for our chief magistrate. Trusts the President will not set his signature to the bill before Congress for incorporating religious societies in the District of Columbia. 4°. 2 pages.

LEWIS, GEORGE.

1815, July 14, New York. The National Bank. Thinks it will become a powerful engine in the hands of the opposition to prostrate the present administration. 4°. 2 pages.

LEWIS, J.

1803, April 13, New York. Acknowledging letter of March 5. Thanks him for the offer it contained, but can not accept, as he has made arrangements to go to the Mississippi River. Offers his services in that quarter. 4°. 1 page.

LEWIS, JACOB, to JONES, WILLIAM.

1814, May 29, New York. See William Jones's letter to Madison, dated June 6, 1814, lettered F. [Extract.] fol. 1 page.

LEWIS, JAMES, to MADISON.

1803, May 20, Albemarle County. Is authorized by Monroe to draw on Madison for money. Asks him to send the bills cut in two and retain one half for a post or two for fear of miscarriage. small 4°. 1 page.

1803, August 16. Receipt for $250, remitted for account of James Monroe. fol. 1 page.

Orange.

1803, September 11, Albemarle County, Va. Respecting furniture belonging to Col. Monroe, which Madison can use. Requests that an amount due from Monroe to his overseer, McGhee, may be paid by Madison. small 4°. 1 page.

Washington.

1804, April 10, Albemarle County. Incloses a letter to be forwarded to Col. Monroe. Asks him to pay

LEWIS, JAMES.

an amount due from Monroe, if his account is not squared up. Offers the use of any of Monroe's furniture. 4°. 1 page.

LEWIS, J.

1814 (?), not dated. Notifying the presence of the British fleet off Montauk point. A plan of defence transmitted. fol. 1 page.

LEWIS, JESSE V.

1800, April 28, New York. Asks Madison to use his influence with the Secretary of the Navy to appoint James Ferguson as midshipman. fol. 2 pages.

1806, December 15. Appeal for place as a printer, also for pecuniary assistance. 8°. 3 pages.

LEWIS, MORGAN.

1808, January 9, New York. Effects of the embargo. Thousands thrown out of employment. Suggests employing them in the navy-yards in the construction of gunboats and to man the flotillas. The discontent of these people place in the hands of the enemies of the administration a powerful weapon, not only with the Federalists, but the Clinton faction of Republicans who advocate him for the Presidency. His total unfitness. 3°. 3 pages.

1808, May 16, Staatsburg, N. Y. State of parties in the State of New York. Increase of Federal strength. Misrepresentations respecting the embargo, and charges of French influence. Violence of the Clintonians in removing all from office not devoted to their views. His intentions to write essays on our commerce and wishes copy of a report of the Secretary of the Treasury on the imports and exports of the last year. 4°. 7 pages.

1808, December 29, Staatsburg, N. Y. Offers his congratulations on his probable election as President. Exceptionable conduct of Clinton's friends. Importance of having a skillful agent in Spain Immense quantities of specie passing through New York State to Canada. Mischievous effects of this traffic. 4°. 2 pages.

1811, May 12, New York. The State election favorable to views of Clinton. Support of Federalists hostile to the administration. Conjectures as to Clinton's ulterior objects. All the offices of the Government in the hands of Clintonians. Abuses by the District marshal and Post-Office Department. Detention before the election of newspapers and letters favorable to the administration. 4° 2 pages.

1812, August 21, Albany. Suspension of the orders in council. Gen. Hull not included in the armistice. His views on the plan of campaign. Great disadvantages in taking the field. Inferiority of force and ill supplies, and defective organization. 4°. 3 pages.

LEWIS, NICHOLAS. *New York.*

1786, November 26, Albemarle County. Acknowledging letter of 4th. Board and tuition of Peter Carr at Mr. Maury's school. Asks instructions as to payment of the same. small 4°. 1 page.

LEWIS, NICHOLAS.

1789, January 9, Albemarle County. Application from Peter Carr for money which he states Jefferson placed in Madison's hands for the purpose of discharging expense of tuition and board. Asks for instructions small 4°. 1 page.

LEWIS, ROBERT. *Montpellier.*

1824, November 8, Fredericksburg. Invitation of the chairman of the committee of arrangements to be present at the dinner in honor of Lafayette. 4°. 1 page.

LEWIS, SAMUEL S.

1829, February 3, Hartford. Announces his election as honorary member of the Washington College Parthenon Society. 4°. 1 page.

LEWIS, SETH, and others. *Washington.*

1809, March 7, Mississippi Territory. Communication from 17 lawyers, remonstrating against the ap pointment of George Poindexter as one of the judges of this Territory, as being unfit for the position. A certificate added, as to signatures, by Walter Leake. fol. 3 pages.

LEWIS, WILLIAM. *Washington.*

1806, November 30, Philadelphia. Character, qualifications, and conduct of Mr. Smith, the marshal of the Pennsylvania district. 4°. 3 pages.

1807, September 28, Philadelphia. Highly recommending to Madison's notice, Mr. Nicholas Biddle, a young gentleman of singular worth and who bids fair to be an ornament to his country. 4°. 2 pages.

1809, February 20, Philadelphia. Receipt for forming a rough coating or casting for the outside of a wall or even for pillars, that will bear all weather, harden by time, and last forever. 4°. 1 page.

1809, December 30, Philadelphia. Asks Madison, as a member of the convention for forming the Constitution of the United States, about the views of Alexander Hamilton, who was also a member, as to the establishment of a monarchy. Hamilton's attachment to a republican form of government. Lewis's high opinion of Dr. Mason. 4°. 4 pages.

LIMOZIN, ANDREW. *New York.*

1788, January 10, Havre de Grace. Incloses a bundle of papers sent to his care by Jefferson, at Versailles, France. 4°. 1 page.

1788, January 26, Havre de Grace. Acknowledging letter of December 8. The fruit was delivered, but rotten. The fruit trees were sent to Jefferson, at Versailles. Inclosing copy of a letter to Benjamin Franklin with a petition to Congress for certain recompense or indemnity which he promised to present. Asks Madison's assistance in behalf of this petition. 4°. 4 pages.

1788, February 26, Havre. A French and English bill of lading of goods sent Madison per ship *Juno* and *King's Packet.* fol. 1 page. 8°. 1 page

1788, February 27, Havre de Grace. Sends a bill of lading per *King's Packet,* of two cases from Jefferson for himself. 4°. 2 pages.

LINCOLN, LEVI. *Washington.*

1801, April 16, Washington. Incloses a letter from the author of the "Farmer's Letters." Sends a pamphlet on the agriculture of the United States. It contains neither facts, principles, nor invention. Republicanism prevails in New England. Massachusetts State election. 4°. 2 pages.

1801, April 17, Washington. Inadvertently opened a letter to Mrs. Madison. Apologies. 4°. 1 page.

1801, July 5, Worcester. Acknowledging letter inclosing papers in the Bingham and Cerbalt cause. Is pleased to hear that Mr. Wagonner is to remain with Madison. The laurels of Federalism withering. Republicanism growing. Celebration of the Fourth of July. 4°. 4 pages.

1802, November 1, Worcester. Application of John Waldo for a consulate. Is a Federal. Lincoln tells him that it is necessary that the administration in order to not embarrass their measures, must give offices to friends. Mr. Joy wishes the consulate at Antwerp. small 4°. 1 page.

1804, December 28, Washington. His office (Attorney-General) becoming vacant at the end of the year, he offers his services, should there be anything in the Department of State requiring immediate attention. Thanks Madison for courtesies and attentions to himself and family. 4°. 1 page.

1809, December 25, Worcester. Introducing Maj. Cogswell. small 4°. 1 page.

1810, April 12, Worcester. Congratulations on the result of recent elections in Massachusetts and New Hampshire. Triumph over the mad and helpless cause of the Northern confederacy. Judge Cushing to resign as judge of the Supreme Court. Recommends Mr. Bidwell as his successor. fol. 1 page.

1810, November 27, Worcester. Declines the appointment of judge of the Supreme Court made vacant by the death of Judge Cushing. 4°. 4 pages.

1811, January 20, Worcester. Is compelled to decline the appointment of successor to Judge Cushing, owing to his difficulty in seeing, being afflicted with cataracts. Is grateful for the distinguished honor. 4°. 3 pages.

1811, February 15, Worcester. Nomination of Alexander Wolcott, as an associate judge of the Supreme Court of the United States. Speaks of him in the highest terms. Introduces his son, Daniel Waldo Lincoln. 4°. 1 page.

LINDSAY, REUBEN. *Philadelphia.*

1791, December 9, Richmond. Acknowledging letter of November 10. Has disposed of the interest of Thomas and John Dickenson in the certificates of registered debt to Robert Pollard, and granted power of attorney to John Vaughan, of Philadelphia, to negotiate the business. Incloses a letter of T. and J. Dickenson, and annexes receipt of John Vaughan. 4°. 2 pages, and strip of paper.

LINDSAY, WILLIAM. *New York.*

1789, March 2, Port *Royal, Va.* Is elected to the place of naval officer for the district of Norfolk by the executive of the State. 4°. 1 page.

LINN, JAMES. *Washington.*

1801, June 22, Trenton. Appointment of George Maxwell as district attorney for New Jersey. 4°. 1 page.

LINSEY, JAMES.

1812, March 13. Petition to Congress on account of a purchase of land at a public sale for discharge of taxes on it. Asks Madison's aid in obtaining his title and redress. 4°. 2 pages.

1812, March 29. Purchase of land sold by the Government for taxes and his difficulty in obtaining titles and redress from persons now holding it. 4°. 4 pages.

Montpellier.

1819 (?), not dated. His unsuccessful attempts in obtaining justice respecting title to lands purchased by him at a public sale for non-payment of taxes. Asks his good office with the President to get justice. fol. 4 pages.

LIPPENCOTT and HUDDY.

No year, August 19. Draft of a resolution of a committee to whom was referred a letter from the commander-in-chief, Sir Guy Carleton, and the proceedings on the trial of Capt. Richard Lippencott for the murder of Capt. Joshua Huddy. [Unknown handwriting.] 4°. 1 page.

LIQUORS, SUCCEDANEA for foreign.

Not dated. A substitute for foreign liquors drawn from native products. A paper from an unknown writer with notes. 4°. 12 pages.

LIST, FREDERICK, to MADISON. *Montpellier.*

1829, January 21, Reading, Pa. Submits some of his essays on political economy. 4°. 2 pages.

LISTON, ROBERT. *Washington.*

1802, October 12, The Hague. Introducing Capt. Murray of the Royal Navy, son of the Earl of Denmore. 4°. 1 page.

LITTELL & HENRY. *Montpellier.*

1821, July, Philadelphia. Printed prospectus for the publication of a new edition of "Blackstone's Commentaries," by Thomas Dunlap and William M. Meredith, of the Philadelphia bar. 4°. 1 page.

1821, September 24, Philadelphia. Incloses a prospectus of an edition of "Blackstone's Commentaries." Asks Madison's favorable comments. 4°. 1 page.

LITTLE, PETER. *Washington.*

1813, March 3, Washington. Is under the necessity of leaving Washington and is unable to take personal leave of the President. Wishes him prosperity and happiness. 4°. 1 page.

LIVERMORE, ARTHUR (?).

Not dated. On the state of the territorial claim of New Hampshire. [Not signed.] fol. 1 page.

LIVINGSTON, BROCKHOLST. *Washington.*

1809, December 7, New York. Introducing William Cutting of New York. 4°. 1 page.

——— to MONROE, JAMES.

1817, September 24, New York. Recommending Mr. Hamilton for some position under Government.

LIVINGSTON, BROCKHOLST.

He was formerly officer in the British army but resigned his commission at the time of the invasion of New Orleans, not wishing to draw his sword against his country. [Copy.]
4°. 3 pages.

LIVINGSTON, CHARLES, to MADISON. *New York.*

1789, April 12, Norfolk. Asks his friendly aid on the subject of Col. Lee's letter, inclosed.
4°. 2 pages.

LIVINGSTON, EDWARD. *Washington.*

1801, March 25, New York. Introducing Mr. Ysnardi.
4°. 1 page.

1801, April —, New York. Regrets at not seeing Madison when he left the seat of government. Views on the present condition of political parties. Recommends, in case of vacancy of the office, Thomas Tillotson as collector of the port of New York. 4°. 2 pages.

1801, July 22, New York. Recommends Dr. George Davis, of the United States Navy, as consul to Algiers. 4°. 1 page.

1814, October 24, New Orleans. On public opinion in New Orleans. Recommends the policy of a general pardon for smugglers and privateers and for acts against the revenue laws under French and Carthagenian flags which might be construed into piracy. These experienced men would be of service should there be a rupture with Spain.
4°. 2 pages.

Montpellier.

1822, May 19, New Orleans. Incloses a pamphlet on the defects of the system of criminal jurisprudence. Asks Madison's observations.
4°. 1 page.

1825, March 13, Washington. Offers for his acceptance a part of the penal code of Louisiana. Is convinced of its utility and asks Madison's views. [Signature cut off.] 4°. 1 page.

1830, April 29, Washington. Unwarranted attempts made in Congress to put upon Madison's and Jefferson's writings to cover dangerous doctrines. He endeavors to expose this fallacy, but stands alone among the speakers. Asks Madison to communicate with him on the subject (nullification) with or without permission to make them public. 4°. 2 pages.

1833, January 19, Washington. Thinks the publication of Madison's opinions respecting nullification will be of use. Will not take the liberty without permission. Sends Mrs. Madison his bust. 4°. 3 pages.

1834, February 8, Paris. The politics and character of all Europe are undergoing a radical change, particularly in France. The present political condition of France detailed. Its attitude in relation to England. 4°. 3 pages.

Not dated. Introducing Mr. M. L. Davis.
4°. 1 page.

——— *v.* STORY, BENJAMIN.

Not dated. Fragment relating to the above case in an unknown handwriting. fol. 2 pages.

LIVINGSTON, HENRY B., to MADISON.

Philadelphia.

1794, March 20, Rhinebeck, N. Y. Has written to Mr. Bailey, M. C., of this State, to present a petition in his behalf, an old soldier, and not hearing from him, has requested him to deliver it to Madison that he will be persuaded to introduce it. fol. 1 page.

——— to JEFFERSON. *Washington.*

1809, February —. Acknowledging letter with inclosures. Did not tender his services from any "fondness" or "familiarity" with scenes of successful warfare, but that he might be successful at a critical juncture. 4°. 2 pages.

LIVINGSTON, J. R., to MADISON.

1802, February 26, New York. Gives extract of a letter of the American minister at Paris, showing the improbability of the French Government doing anything at present towards the adjustment of American claims. fol. 2 pages.

LIVINGSTON, R. R.

1783, July 19, Clermont. Is informed that the definitive treaty is concluded. If Congress should not make an appointment of Secretary of Foreign Affairs before it is received, it would give him pleasure to sign the treaty as Secretary and thus conclude his political career. 4°. 4 pages.

Philadelphia.

1793, October 20, Clermont. Introducing Mr. Adair. fol. 2 pages.

1795, January 30, New York. Intelligence by private correspondence in Philadelphia, from Mr. Jay, respecting the treaty. The evacuation of the posts, free intercourse of traders in and through those posts and adjustment of debts due to Great Britain. As we pay sacrifices, the essential interests of this country, it is suggested, as we have not as yet the official account of the treaty, that a law be brought before Congress prohibiting exports or imports to or from Canada into our Western frontiers. 4°. 6 pages.

Washington.

1801, July 1, Clermont. In accepting the appointment of minister to France he gives his views and suggestions as to the powers he is to be intrusted with in his negotiations. Waits instructions and expresses his readiness to depart. [Signature cut off.] 4°. 5 pages.

——— to MONROE, JAMES. *London.*

1803, September 7, Paris. The question of the guarantee of the payment for the Louisiana purchase prior to the ratification of the treaty. [Copy.] 4°. 3 pages.

1803, September 7, Paris. Duplicate of the foregoing. 4°. 3 pages.

1803, September 11, Paris. Explains his hesitation in his acquiescence to Monroe's promise to guarantee the loan of Hope & Baring to the French Government in anticipation of the ratification of the treaty for the purchase of Louisiana. [Copy.] 4°. 7 pages.

1803, September 11, Paris. Duplicate of the foregoing. 4°. 7 pages.

Livingston, R. R., to Marbois, Barbé. *Paris.*

1803, September 13, Paris. Powers vested in him and Monroe to guarantee the loan of Hope & Baring, based on the ratification of the convention for the purchase of Louisiana. [Copy.] 4°. 3 pages.

——— to Madison. *Washington.*

1803, September 17, Paris. Explanation of the hesitation of his acquiescence in Monroe's agreement to the guarantee, in advance, of the ratification of the treaty of the loan of Hope & Baring, respecting the Louisiana purchase. 4°. 7 pages.

1803, September 17, Paris. Duplicate of the foregoing. 4°. 5 pages.

1803, September 18, Paris. Preparations of France for the descent on England or Ireland. Spain will not be permitted to retain her neutrality. Her prince of peace a partisan of England. The northern powers' jealousy of England will eventually drag them into the war. Our flag is now respected. If Spain goes into the war it would be favorable for us to press for East Florida. Conversation with the Spanish ambassador about acquisition. Monroe displeased at Livingston's interference, which the latter now avoids. 4°. 4 pages.

1803, September 18, Paris. Duplicate of the foregoing. 4°. 5 pages.

1804, March 12, Paris. Acknowledging letter of October 28. Marriage of Jerome Bonaparte. Interview with Joseph Bonaparte, in which he negotiates for Jerome's establishment in America or France. The first consul extremely irritated. Arrest of two sons of the Duke of Polignac, Pichegru, George, La Riveeu, and 30 others, in Paris, for avowed object of some of them to assassinate the first consul. Livingston wishes to return to America. 4°. 6 pages.

1804, March 12, Paris. Duplicate of the foregoing. "Private." fol. 4 pages.

1804, March 24, Paris. Arrest and execution of the Duc d'Engheiu. 4°. 1 page.

1804, May 5, Paris Disagreeable state of his relations with the commissioners. Monroe's correspondence with himself to be made public or not, at the option of the Secretary of State. His friendly feeling towards Monroe. The marriage of Jerome Bonaparte. Views of the Emperor since his elevation. Conversations with Marbois. The Emperor insists Jerome should return to France alone. Talleyrand all powerful. Livingston's resignation and his wish for his successor as named in a previous letter. The Emperor's esteem for Jefferson. [Signature cut off.] "Private." 4°. 5 pages.

1804, May 5, Paris. Duplicate of the foregoing. 4°. 5 pages.

1804, May 5, Paris. Triplicate of the foregoing. 4°. 4 pages.

1804, June 20, Paris. Written entirely in cipher. "Private and confidential to be deciphered only by the Secretary of State himself." 4°. 3 pages.

LIVINGSTON, R. R.

1804, June 20, Paris. Press copy of the foregoing deciphered in pencil. Suggests the means of acquiring the desired boundary of West Florida, either by occupation or negotiation, and eventually the acquisition of East Florida, with the aid of the French emperor, and the outlay of a moderate douceur. [With the translation.] 4°. 6 pages.

1805, November 16, Baltimore. The new orders in council in England relative to colonial commerce. How all countries will be injured by being driven from the West India markets. Suggests sending ministers to Russia and Austria to engage all Europe in compelling England to change her system. To avow to France the object of these embassies. 4°. 2 pages.

1806, December 24, Clermont. The consulate at Havre. Two commissions existing at the same time. Adjustments of Livingston's accounts at the Treasury. The new coalition in Europe. Enlargement of Holland's boundaries. Great Britain's ultimate fall. The Emperor's ambition and resentment. Our negotiations respecting our differences with Spain, with the Emperor require great delicacy of management, as we are at the same time negotiating with his greatest enemy. Reviews his conduct while minister to France. Misrepresentations of his enemies. Resentment of the British Government to Livingston for his attentions to French exiles in America. fol. 8 pages.

1807, March 22, Clermont. Acknowledging letter of January 28. Congratulates him on the defeat of Burr's plans. Conjectures as to his motives. Anxiety for the success of negotiations with Spain and France. Everything depends on the will of the Emperor. His continued increase of power in Europe. The policy of the interposition of France in our affairs. Will consent to go abroad for a few months as special envoy. fol. 4 pages.

1807, May 17, Clermont. Desire of his son-in-law, Col. Livingston, to carry dispatches to Europe. The state elections. Forged report of a coalition between the friends of Gov. Lewis and the Federalists. The loss of the election to the Republican party attributed to it. [Signature cut off.] 4°. 3 pages.

1808, January 8, Clermont. Asks Madison to inclose letters to his daughters under cover to Gen. Armstrong. The embargo, although necessary, is a calamity to American citizens abroad, they being cut off from all resources. Suggests the commissioning of ships to bring them home with their effects. Conduct of the Federalists and their press in misrepresentations as to the embargo. 4°. 2 pages.

1808, February 5, Clermont. Introducing Mr. Jasper Livingston, who wishes to be agent for seamen at Jamaica, as successor to Mr. Lenox. Congratulates him on his nomination to the Presidency. Wishes him success. 4°. 2 pages.

1808, July 12, Clermont. Incloses a letter to Gen. Armstrong covering letters to his daughters whom he wishes to return home. The change

LIVINGSTON, R. R.

in the Emperor's views towards Americans. Pride and not avarice is his predominant passion and it must be flattered. 4°. 2 pages.

1808, November 23, Clermont. Introducing his sons-in-law, Robert L. and Edward P. Livington. Incloses samples of woolen cloth of his manufacture from imported Spanish wool. Wishes Madison's aid in a shipment of Merino sheep in some Government vessel from Bordeaux. 4°. 3 pages.

1809, January 17, Clermont. Acknowledging letter of 11th. Is indifferent to the measures of the belligerents. Our continued prosperity, as seen by himself in a tour through New England. Suggests that Congress regiment our seaman as artilleryists. Discharge them when our ports are open. Is desirous of encouraging the importation of Spanish sheep. Sends Madison a coat of E. Livingston's manufacture. 4°. 4 pages.

1809, January 24, Clermont. Sends a roll of cloth of E. P. Livingston's manufacture from Spanish wool, superior to English broadcloth. Livingston the first to import the Spanish wool stock. Anticipates great results from the manufacture of this kind of wool. 4°. 2 pages.

1809, October 25, Clermont. Incloses a treatise to remove prejudices respecting the importation of Merino sheep. The great increase in New York and neighboring States from his flock. Appeals to the President through Madison for justice in regard to the eviction of his brother from a property without the forms of law. 4°. 4 pages.

1810, January 8, Clermont. Interest of the farmers in his vicinity in the raising of Merino sheep. Difficulty in supplying the demand for rams. Respecting the conduct of Mr. Jackson, the British minister. The hatred of the King and people of that nation to us. Suggests means for our coast defences. The money spent in reducing the debt would have been far better employed in forts and cannon. 4°. 3 pages.

1812, May 15, New York. Introducing Mr. Budd. 4°. 2 pages.

LIVINGSTON, CHARLES.

1811, July 12, Boston. As chairman of a private committee expresses his views on Mr. Smith's late unwarrantable attack on Madison's character. Recommends Rufus L. Barrus, of Boston, to Madison's favor. fol. 1 page.

LLOYD, THOMAS.

1813, August 29, Alexandria. Appeal for pecuniary aid. Is a teacher of shorthand writing. 4°. 1 page.

LOBSTEIN, J. F. D., M. D. *Montpellier.*

1822, October 19, Lebanon, Pa. Sends him the prospectus of a work entitled, "Topography of the City of Philadelphia, and Observations of the United States of America." 4°. 6 pages.

1824, August 9, Philadelphia. Asks Madison to subscribe for one of his works. A nonpaying subscriber. [In French.] 4°. 2 pages.

LOGAN, GEORGE. *Washington.*

1809, June 17, Staunton. Introduces Silvain Godon, a mineralist from Paris, who wishes to be employed in the service of the United States. 4°. 2 pages.

LOGAN, GEORGE.

1810, January 10, Staunton. Advocates as a sound policy of our Government to act with forbearance towards other nations. Recommends renewing negotiations for a treaty of friendship and commerce. 4°. 6 pages.

1810, January 14, Staunton. Sails for England in a few days. Will take any communication to our minister in London. 4°. 1 page.

1810, January 19. Has decided to not go to England at present. Has conversed with Mr. Onis, who regrets that he was not received at Washington, as he had full powers to settle all misunderstandings between Spain and the United States. 4°. 1 page.

1810, January 24, Staunton. Acknowledging letter of 17th. Wishes our country to remove every obstacle to peace and appeal to the magnanimity, sound policy, and permanent interest of Great Britain. Recommends Mr. Onis to Madison's more particular notice. Expects to sail for England in about two weeks. 4°. 3 pages.

1810, February 19, New York. Conversation with Mr. Jackson, who does not consider his dismissal will cause a rupture with his government and ours. He considers our friendship of importance to his own country. 4°. 1 page.

1810, May 6, London. General anxiety prevails in England to preserve peace. The foreign and domestic affairs of Great Britain are in a deplorable situation. Our relations with Spain and France. 4°. 3 pages.

1810, July 17, London. The magnanimous act of the United States in renewing commerce with the belligerents. The ministry and parliament express in private conversation a desire to preserve peace with the United States. The sentiment general among the people. Sentiments expressed at agricultural dinners to that effect. 4°. 3 pages.

1811, December 17, Staunton. The melancholy spectacle of discord and disorder the present barbarous system of commercial warfare has produced. Appeals to the President to make use of his influence to prevent war. 4°. 7 pages.

1812, March 31, Staunton. Regards the contemplated invasion of Canada with horror. The present time propitious to preserve peace. The Prince of Wales' accession to the throne. He is a Whig and his associates friends of the United States. Suggests a mission to England to congratulate him on the event, and to point out the mutual interest of the countries to maintain peace. 4°. 5 pages.

1813, January 18, Staunton. Approves of the proposition for excluding foreign seamen from the public and private vessels of the United States. Peace may yet be obtained equally honorable and beneficial to both countries by friendly negotiations. 4°. 4 pages.

1816, February 9, Staunton. Introducing his nephew, Joseph P. Norris. 4°. 1 page.

LOGAN, WILLIAM. *Montpellier.*

1819, July 28, Charleston. In behalf of the standing committee of the '76 Association, sends copy of William Condy's oration delivered before that society on June 5. 4°. 1 page.

LOMAX, J. T.

1827, March 5, University of Virginia. Jefferson's bequest of his library to the university. The number of students at present. 4°. 2 pages.

LONG, G.

Year not dated, September 21, London. Appointment of Mr. Harrison to the chair of ancient languages in the University of Virginia. Other matters relating to the University. 4°. 2 pages.

——— to the RECTOR AND VISITORS OF THE UNIVERSITY OF VIRGINIA.

Not dated. A fit person for teaching the ancient languages in the University. Desirous of having an assistant. What compensation should be given him. 4°. 1 page.

LONG ISLAND SOUND.

Not dated. Sketch of a chart of the entrance of Long Island Sound. 4°. 1 page.

LONGSTRETH, JONATHAN, to TOULMIN, HENRY.

1810, October 14, Pinckneyville. Instances connected with the capture of Baton Rouge fort, and the sentiments and conduct of the people who wish to become United States citizens. Insincerity of the governor of West Florida. 4°. 2 pages.

LOVE, JOHN, to MADISON. *Washington.*

1813, February 6, Alexandria. Solicits subscription to stock in the road-making from Washington to the Kanhawa country. fol. 2 pages.

1814, January 10, Washington. Applies for the office of postmaster at Alexandria. 4°. 1 page.

1814, March 30, Washington. Assures the President no disrespect was intended in the manner in which his application for the place of postmaster of Alexander was made. 4°. 2 pages.

——— and others.

Not dated. Certificate of the political conduct of Dr. James H. Blake, of Washington, and of his talents and rectitude. Signed by John Love, Thomas Gholron, and W. A. Burwell. 4°. 1 page.

——— *Montpellier.*

1817, July 15, Buckland. Asks if Monroe's order to supply Madison with the Lawler wheat is still open; if so, notify him (Love) at once. Its superior quality. 4°. 3 pages.

LOVE, RICHARD H.

1824, May 4. Applies for one of the boarding houses of the University of Virginia. fol. 1 page.

LOVELL, JAMES. *Washington.*

1805, March 29, Boston. Error in a remittance which he rectifies. 4°. 1 page.

1806, January 27, Boston. Acknowledging the closing of a business which regarded his grandchildren, with gratitude. 4°. 1 page.

1809, May 5, Boston. Retention of his place as naval officer. 4°. 2 pages.

LOVELL, JOHN E. *Montpellier.*

1832, March 22, New Haven. Recommendation of Mr. Cardella for an instructor in the fine arts in the University of Virginia. 4°. 3 pages.

LOWE, ENOCH M. *Washington.*

1809, December 5, Washington. Wishes to communicate verbally or in writing upon an important and delicate matter, and to indicate the time. 4°. 1 page.

LOYALL, GEORGE. *Montpellier.*

1827, May 20, Norfolk. Introducing Hugh B. Grigsby. 4°. 1 page.

1827, May 28, Norfolk. Choice of a successor to the chair lately made vacant by Mr. Key's retirement from the University of Virginia. 4°. 2 pages.

LUCAS, JOHN B. C. *Washington.*

1804, June 25, Pittsburg. Recommending Anthony Soulard as a surveyor. 4°. 2 pages.

1810, March 22, St. Louis. Wishes that an inquiry be made into his official conduct as one of the board of commissioners for ascertaining titles and adjusting claims in the Territory of Louisiana. 4°. 1 page.

1813, February 27, Washington. Gives his testimony as to the character and standing of Col. Samuel Hammond. 4°. 1 page.

LUCKEY, GEORGE.

1809, June 12, Harford County, Maryland. Congratulates him and recalls their youthful days. Thinks a law should be enacted by Congress to prevent duelling. small 4°. 3 pages.

1809, August 10, Harford. Acknowledging an answer to a former letter. Recalls early acquaintance. The custom of duelling. fol. 2 pages.

1810, August 26, Harford County. Suggests the idea of forming an armed neutrality by sea of all European powers for defense against the tyrants of the ocean and disturbers of the peace of the world, and unite with them. small 4°. 2 pages.

1811, July 1, Harford County. In the present condition of affairs suggests whether it were not good policy to confine our trade entirely within the limits of the United States, as we have here the best productions of every clime. We lose by intercourse with foreign nations. small 4°. 2 pages.

1811, October 17, Baltimore. The injustice and cruelty of England toward this country. Suggests that our merchants arm their vessels and that Congress authorize them to not only defend but attack, and permit them to share the spoils equally with the Government. Trusts that God will be on our side and justice prevail. [In Latin.] small 4°. 3 pages.

1812, April 1, Baltimore. Deplores the condition of affairs. Thinks justice on our side, and that with God's help we will be victorious. [In Latin.] small 4°. 3 pages.

1812, December 8, Hartford. On the present condition of our country. Congratulates our country on Madison's election. Predicts a happy issue over our enemies. Incloses an essay entitled "Maxims in Politics." small 4°. 5 pages.

1813, April 25, Hartford. Reflections on our condition. We are forced to resent the aggressions of the most covetous, corrupt, and revengeful nation, and are encouraged in the belief that Heaven

LUĆKEY, GEORGE.

will frown upon the tyrants, that our inestimable liberties and privileges may be preserved inviolate. Annexed is a paper entitled "Bonaparte, the Tyrant." small 4°. 4 pages.

1814, November 8. Expresses patriotic sentiments and trusts in our deliverance from the nefarious designs of our enemies abroad and at home. fol. 2 pages.

LUDLORY, DANIEL.

1802, November 30, New York. Incloses receipt for a box received from Leghorn and directed to Madison, with bill of expenses. 4°. 1 page. 8°. 1 page.

LUDLOW, BENJAMIN (President).

1812, July 10, Trenton, N. J. In behalf of the convention of Republican delegates from several counties of New Jersey, gives assurances of the approval of the measures of the President toward a vigorous prosecution of the war, and promises their support. 4°. 1 page.

LUDLOW, DANIEL, JR., to VERPLANCK, DANIEL C.

1809, February 17, New York. Asks his influence with President Madison for the appointment of private secretary. 4°. 2 pages.

LUFBOROUGH, NATHAN to MADISON.

1802, January 28, Washington. Mr. Payne wishes to be appointed to the vacancy in the Department of State. Recommends him. 4°. 1 page.

1814, September 26, Washington. Copies an extract from a letter from Mr. Bacon, giving the reasons for his absence from his place in the comptroller's office. fol. 2 pages.

——— to DALLAS, A. J. (Secretary of Treasury).

1814, October 17, Washington. Incloses a letter from the collector at Mobile. 4°. 1 page.

LUSHINGTON, R., to MADISON. *New York.*

1789, June 4, Charleston. Sends a paper containing an account of the exports and tonnage of shipping, and the nations to which they belong; also amount of imports. small 4°. 2 pages.

LYMAN, WILLIAM. *Washington.*

1804. December 6, Washington. Waited on Madison several times at the Office of State. Leaves for New York, where he will remain until he hears from him. 4°. 1 page.

1805, January 12, New York. Has been waiting for his promised appointment as consul to London and is still without communications. Asks to be informed. 4°. 2 pages.

LYNCH, D., JR. *Montpellier.*

1817, June 14, New York. Announces his election as a member of the American Society for the Encouragement of Domestic Manufactures. 4°. 1 page.

LYNCH, M. *Virginia.*

1783, February 15, Nantes, France. Offers his services as a merchant for sale of tobacco or purchaser of anything required in America from France. 4°. 1 page.

LYON, ISAAC S. *Montpellier.*

1834, April 20, Boonton Falls, N. *J.* Is collecting, in pamphlet form, to be bound together, celebrated orations, addresses, speeches, etc., and would like to be supplied with one of Madison's. 4°. 1 page.

LYON, J. *Washington.*

1801, July 2, Washington. Explains reasons for the delay in printing the laws of Congress. Proposes a new plan, which he intends to apply for next Congress, for the printing of the laws, which will be much more advantageous than the present. 4°. 4 pages.

LYON, JAMES, and DINSMORE, R.

1802, April 21, Washington. Solicits the publication of the laws of Congress in their paper, the "American Literary Advertiser." fol. 1 page.

LYON, M.

1804, January 21, Washington. Incloses a letter from Mr. Dinsmore. 4°. 1 page.

——— to JEFFERSON.

1808, December 24, Washington. On the discoveries of copper on the shores of Lake Superior. Congressional action suggested in order to investigate and develop. 4°. 8 pages.

——— to MADISON.

1809, January 22, Washington. About leaving for England. Asks if he can take passage in any vessel about to be sent there by the Government. 4°. 2 pages.

1809, January 24, Washington. Has requested a friend to take passage for him by the *Pacific,* and offers to take letters. 4°. 2 pages.

MCCALL, JAMES, and others, to VIRGINIA HOUSE OF DELEGATES.

Not dated. Petition of the house of McCall, Denniston & Co., and debtors of that firm, respecting British debts. royal fol. 1 page.

MCCARAHER, A., and others, to MADISON. *Montpellier.*

1834, June 29, Fountain Green. Invitation of a committee, by Democrats of the party of '98, to a dinner on July 4. 4°. 1 page.

MCCLURE, DAVID. *Washington.*

1815, March 7, Philadelphia. Offers himself as a candidate for a place as professor in one of the naval schools now under consideration in Congress. States his experience and qualifications. 4°. 3 pages.

MCCLURE, DAVID. *Montpellier.*

1834, February 6, Philadelphia. Sends a system of education for the Girard College. 4°. 1 page.

MCCLURE, GEORGE. *Washington.*

1814, February 14, Bath, N. *Y.* Inclosing a handbill published in order to exculpate himself from blame in relation to the late disaster on our frontiers. 4°. 1 page.

MCCLURG, JAMES. *Philadelphia.*

1787, August 5, Richmond. Thinks his attendance at the convention would be useless. P. Henry's disapprobation of the circular letter of Congress

MCCLURG JAMES.

respecting payment of British debts, and that the interests of this State can not be trusted with that body. The doctrine of three confederacies, or great republics, has its advocates.
4°. 2 pages.

1787, August 22, Richmond. An association in Greenbrier County to oppose payments of the certificate tax and of all debts, and will stop forcibly the proceedings of the next court. The ringleader, Adonizah Matthews. The dangerous tendency and unsoundness of John Adams' doctrines to be exposed by a newspaper writer, supposed to be P. Henry. 4°. 2 pages.

1787, September 5, Richmond. European news. French march into the United Provinces. A general European war expected, a benefit to us. Regrets we have not a government established to inspire Dutch merchants with confidence and seek a retreat here. Adonizah Matthews is lodged in jail. 4°. 2 pages.

1787, September 10, Richmond. Reported tendency to insurrection in this State. Expectation of a remedy for discontents in the next Assembly.
small 4°. 2 pages.

1787, October 31, Richmond. Acknowledges receipt of copy of the new Constitution. Discusses its merits and objections. small 4°. 3 pages.

MCCONNELL, MATHEW, and others. *Washington.*

1816, September 26. A committee in behalf of officers of the Pennsylvania line of the Revolutionary Army sends memorials and resolutions. Asks the President's just and prompt interference to their relief at the next session of Congress.
4°. 2 pages.

MCCOY, W.

1812, May 13, Washington. Expected appointment of Mr. Joseph Nevill as a captain of infantry.
4°. 3 pages.

MCCREERY, WILLIAM.

1807, January 25. Claim of Messrs. Hoffman's for supplies furnished the French Government. Incloses their letter and asks the favor of a letter to Gen. Armstrong in favor of their claim.
4°. 2 pages.

1809, March 2, Washington. Recommends Tench Ringgold for an appointment under Government.
4°. 1 page.

MCCULLOCH, JAMES H., to CALHOUN, JOHN C.

1823, January 18, Baltimore. Introducing and recommending James Madison Bunn to be received into the Military Academy at West Point.
4°. 1 page.

MCDONOUGH, THOMAS, to MACOMB, ALEX.
Lake Champlain.

1814, September 11, U. S. Ship Saratoga. Requests that surgeons be sent him. Has gained a great victory. 4°. 1 page.

MCGOWTY to MADISON. *Washington.*

1809, March 19, Windham, Conn. Congratulates Madison on his elevation to the Presidency. Respecting the embargoes being partly taken off. Has no faith in any favorable negotiations with England, and thinks war with her would be better than the present state of affairs.
4°. 3 pages.

MCHENRY, JAMES. *Richmond.*

1788, June 17, Baltimore. Sends him authentic information as to the present state of opposition to the constitution in Pennsylvania. Hopes Virginia will adopt the constitution. 4°. 1 page.

1788, July 26, Baltimore. Asks him to communicate the views or plan of the anti-Federalists. Wishes P. Henry's declaration in his own words as to the basis of the new opposition to the constitution. small 4°. 2 pages.

1788, August 14, Baltimore. Asks his opinion respecting State taxes on transfers of debts by their own citizens to those of another State or to foreigners. [Signature cut off.] 4°. 1 page

Baltimore.

1789, March 5, Baltimore. Col. Ballard is desirous of seeing Madison on some business with Congress. 4°. 1 page.

New York.

1789, June 21, Baltimore. Laws on the collection of the revenue. Thinks when the imports are considerable that the office of naval officer and collector should not be lodged in a single person. small 4°. 1 page.

MCINTOSH, J. *Washington.*

1809, October 6, McIntosh County, Ga. Inclosing resolutions of citizens of county of McIntosh expressive of their approval of the measures of the President. fol. 1 page.

MCINTOSH, LACHLAN, to TELFAIR, EDWARD, and JONES, W. W. (Delegates for the State of Georgia). *Philadelphia.*

1781, November 15, Philadelphia. Boundaries and territorial claim of the State Georgia. large fol. 4 pages.

MACKAY & CAMPBELL to MADISON. *Montpellier.*

1820, September 4, December 18; 1821, May 16, July 19, 23, 30, October 4, November 1; 1822, January 16, 24, February 7, Fredericksburg. Series of 11 letters on private business. 4°. 14 pages.

MACKAY, ROBERT.

1821, February 23, Fredericksburg. Respecting a saw which Madison returned; it not answering the purpose desired. 4°. 1 page.

1822, May 2, Fredericksburg. Acknowledging letter of April 24. Price of merino wool and advice as to disposing of it. Quotations of produce. 4°. 1 page.

1823, February 6, Fredericksburg. Incloses his account. 4°. 1 page.

1827, May 4, Fredericksburg. Inclosing a letter from John Myers asking a letter of recommendation for his father, Moses Myers, who wishes to be appointed collector of Norfolk. 4°. 1 page.

MCKEEHAN, DAVID.

1809, August 15, Baltimore. Appeals to the President for an appointment under Government. 4°. 5 pages.

MACKENZIE & GLENNIE to GLENNIE, R., & SONS. *Baltimore.*

1809 (?), July 25, London. Extract of a letter stating that according to English instructions the British

MACKENZIE & GLENNIE to GLENNIE, R., & SONS.

cruisers are bringing into port for condemnation all American vessels bound direct to ports in Holland and France with colonial produce on board. Thinks it contrary to the laws of nations. fol. 1 page.

MCKENNEY, THOMAS L., to MADISON.

Washington.

1814, September 2, Camp Windmill Point. The call for mounted riflemen is not complied with, owing to the impossibility of procuring but a partial number of horses. Wishes to know if the corps shall proceed on foot. The enemy has dropped down below Alexandria. 4°. 2 pages.

——— to HAMILTON PAUL (Secretary of Navy).

1814, November 25, Georgetown. Appeal for reinstatement to office and favor of Mr. Ritchie, accessory to a fatal duel between two officers of the *Constellation* frigate at Norfolk. [Indorsed on the outside "Respectfully submitted to the President."] 4°. 3 pages.

——— to MADISON.

1817, March 4, Weston (Georgetown). Complimentary sentiments on Madison's retirement and reviewing the wise measures of his administration. 4°. 3 pages.

Montpellier.

1821, February 7, Weston. Incloses a pamphlet. 4°. 1 page.

1822, June 11, Weston. Incloses a prospectus of the "Washington Republican" and "Congressional Examiner." 4°. 1 page.

1824, March 20, Weston. Refers to accompanying papers, being in vindication of his conduct from attacks made on him while superintendent of the United States trade with the Indians. 4°. 4 pages.

1825, April 7, Washington. Inclosing papers on the subject of locating the Indians now within our States and Territories west of the Missouri and Arkansas. 4°. 1 page.

——— to MADISON, Mrs.

1825, April 7. Has seen her son, Mr. Todd, occasionally. He is well. strip of paper.

——— to MADISON.

1825, April 26, Washington. Inclosing the "National Journal," which contains his notice of the "Quarterly Review," which he hopes Madison will approve of. 4°. 1 page.

1825, May 10, Washington. Acknowledging letter of 2d inclosing Madison's "Talk," which, after loaning to the printer, he passed to the files of the Department of War. Remarks on the subject. 4°. 1 page.

1826, February 4, Washington. Asks his good offices with the President to recommend him as a special commissioner to negotiate a treaty with the Chippeway Indians and all business relating to Indian concerns. 4°. 4 pages.

1826, March 18, Washington. Inclosing a document relating to the civilization of the Indians. 4°. 1 page.

1828, August 4, Washington. Wishes to justify himself from the attacks upon him in the Telegraph apparently sustained by Mr. Cutts. 4°. 2 pages.

McKENNEY, THOMAS.

1829, September 4, Washington. Transmits a pamphlet containing proceedings of a board recently organized in New York. 4°. 1 page.

McKIERNAN, GEORGE S.

1834, October 8, Wheeling, Va. Asks for his autograph. 4°. 1 page.

McKIM, A. *Washington.*

1811, not dated. Detention of the schooner *Friendship*, Capt. Snow, at Bordeaux. [*See* letter of Sullivan, Jeremiah, February 5, 1811.] 4°. 1 page.

1813, April 13, Baltimore. Introduces his nephew, Maj. Isaac McKim, who goes to Washington for the express purpose of representing the near approach of the enemy's squadron in the Chesapeake and the defenceless situation of Baltimore. 4°. 2 pages.

1813, May 5, Baltimore. Solicitude for the safety of Baltimore. How it is defended. Difficulties in the construction of the powers of those appointed to command. A general head necessary. The militia constantly on duty and may soon grow tired. Suggests that a regiment of twelve-months men be raised. fol. 2 pages.

McKINLEY, JOHN.

1812, March 27, New York. His disappointment in not being appointed to a captaincy. His character assailed by foes of the present administration. 4°. 3 pages.

1812, April 1, New York. Has learned the source from which his disappointment originated in his expectation for an appointment as captain. Vindictiveness of the Clintonians, who could not persuade him to influence the Irish voters, against the administration. 4°. 2 pages.

1812, June 1, New York. The causes of interference and persecution of himself by Clintonians. Regrets the appointment of so many inefficient men, the minions and sycophants of Dewitt Clinton. The renomination of Clinton supported by Federalists. 4°. 3 pages.

1812, June 10, New York. The arts and intrigues of the De Witt Clinton faction. Regrets of Madison's friends of the continuance in office of persons hostile to the administration. 4°. 2 pages.

McKINLEY, WILLIAM.

1804, May 14, West Liberty, Ohio County, Va. A publication in the U. S. Gazette, of April 20, relating to Jefferson's impiety. Suggests that it be contradicted as it may affect Republican interests. fol. 1 page.

1809, May 1, West Liberty. Inclosing addresses to show how to be able to form a correct idea of Madison's friends and enemies. fol. 1 page, and strip of paper.

1809, September 13, West Liberty. Adds his name to the list of those who have recommended Thomas Kenedy, of Pittsburg, for a commission in the Army. 4°. 1 page.

1809, November 16, West Liberty. Withdraws his name as being in favor of Thomas Kenedy, of Pittsburg, for a commission in the Army. Disapproves of certain places on the Ohio being ports of entry. 4°. 1 page.

McKinley, William.

1811, February 18, Washington. Has no information to give on foreign affairs. Asks to be furnished with such information as Madison may deem proper. 4°. 1 page.

McKinney, James.

1809, April 5, Chenango Point, N. Y. Advisability of acquiring Canada as the inhabitants would be better reconciled to the customs and manners of the Americans than they now are to the British Government. fol. 1 page.

Montpellier.

1822, December 23, Madison's Mills. Proposed purchase of Madison's mills. small 4°. 3 pages.

1823, January 6, Madison's Mills. Proposes to call and see Madison when Mr. Feray returns. small 4°. 1 page.

McKnight, John. *Washington.*

1813, June 11, Middleway, Va. Wishes a reappointment in the Navy, from which he retired, the Government not having use for his services. 4°. 3 pages.

McLane, A.

1814, January 25, Wilmington, Del. Scheme to prevent the approach of the enemy's shipping by erecting works and obstructions. Trusts Madison will not believe in the sincerity of proposals from the enemy for peace. Will lay down his life for his country. 4°. 2 pages.

McLane, Louis. *Montpellier.*

1834, February 13, Washington. Acknowledging note of 6th, inclosing a letter for Mr. Vail, which has been forwarded. 4°. 1 page.

McLean, John. *Washington.*

1809, September 14, Sandy Hill, Washington County, N. *Y.* Address of the chairman of a meeting of Republican citizens of Washington County, approving the course of the President in counteracting the late overtures of the British Government and promise their support. 4°. 4 pages.

Montpellier.

1824, January 28, Washington. The President asks Madison's advice respecting the appointment of Mr. Wagner, as to his ability and integrity. 4°. 1 page.

1827, August 20, Nassau Hall, Princeton. Announces Madison's election as president of an association with the request that he should address them at its first annual meeting. 4°. 2 pages.

McMahon, Bernard. *Washington.*

1809, June 27, Philadelphia. Inclosing a bill for garden seeds and giving descriptions of roots and plants which he can furnish if desired. fol. 2 pages.

McMahon, Thomas P. *Montpellier.*

1822, January 30, Philadelphia. Asks him to settle the account due to the estate of B. McMahon for for seeds. 4°. 1 page.

McMillen, Hugh. *Washington.*

1809 (?), not dated, New Boston, N. H. Proposal for Government aid to erect a labaratory for the manufacture of medicines for the Army. fol. 3 pages.

MACOMB, ALEX. (General).

1814, September 11, Fort Moreau, Lake Champlain. A note written in pencil on the letter from Commodore McDonough of this date wishing him to send him surgeons and announcing the victory of Plattsburg. Gives details of the victory briefly. 4°. 2 pages.

MACON, EDGAR. *Montpellier.*

1818, September 12. Thanks his uncle for the course of reading he has laid down for him. Mentions the books he has read and gives his impressions. 4°. 2 pages.

1818, October 28, Princeton. Acknowledging letter of 3d. Thanks for Madison's opinions respecting the study of Latin and Greek. Has been reading English history, and gives his views respecting different authors. 4°. 2 pages.

1823, June 29. Returns Chancellor Taylor's journal of the moot school, and papers loaned him. scrap of paper.

MACON, THOMAS. *Washington.*

1803, January 24, Somerset. Will draw on Madison for a balance for a purchase of lime. Death of Madison's sister Hite. 4°. 1 page.

1804, July 30. Accepts terms for land from off Winslow's tract, which Madison offers for an interest which Macon had in Madison's father's will. small 4°. 1 page.

1810, May 28, Orange. Wishing to place his son Madison in a wholesale store in New York. Asks Madison to procure him such a position through some of his friends there. Concerning family matters. 4°. 2 pages.

1810, June 13, Orange. Thanks for endeavoring to procure a situation for his son in New York. Respecting sheep, farming, and the crops. 4°. 1 page.

MCPHERSON, CHRISTIAN. *Orange.*

1800, April 13, Louisa, Va. Thanks him for the use of his horses. fol. 1 page.

MCPHERSON, W. *Washington.*

1807, May 13, Philadelphia. Application of his brother, John Montgomery McPherson, for the place lately made vacant by resignation of Henry Hill, late commercial agent in Jamaica. 4°. 1 page.

MCRAE, ALEXANDER, to JEFFERSON. *Monticello.*

1809, July 22, Richmond. Incloses a letter from Mr. Wirt. Maj. Clarke and himself about to leave for Europe in pursuit of an object mentioned therein. Offers to carry dispatches or any other communications. Wishes the object of the trip to be kept private. 4°. 2 pages.

——— to MADISON. *Washington.*

1809, August 11, Richmond. Object of the visit of Maj. Clarke and himself to Europe On explanation Mr. Jefferson is satisfied that the fears he first expressed of violation of the laws of those countries are unfounded. Foreign capital is desirable to carry out the plans of a great manufacturing project in the vicinity of Richmond. 4°. 3 pages.

1809, December 8, Washington. Returns letters with a request to write new ones to the same effect but with the present date. 4°. 1 page.

McRae, Alexander, to Madison.

1809, December 8, Washington. As Maj. Clarke can not accompany him to Europe, he requests the President to substitute letters to ministers at London and Paris for others in which Maj. Clarke's name is not mentioned. 4°. 2 pages.

1809, December 26, Philadelphia. Extraordinary conduct of Mr. Bond, the British consul, in refusing to certify his passport. McRae refuses to apply to Jackson (British minister), on account of his strained relations with our Government.
4°. 6 pages.

1810, January 7, New York. Interview with the British consul in New York, Mr. Barclay, who refused to certify the passport of the Secretary of State at Washington. McRae refuses to apply to Mr. Jackson on account of the relation existing between him and the Government. Incloses a memorandum of Jos. D. Fay. 4°. 9 pages.

1811, January 26, Paris. The wish of Judge Cooper to obtain certain publications, which he is endeavoring to comply with. Incloses a French work. 4°. 3 pages.

McRae, Richard.

1814, July 2, Washington. Rejection of his account at the War Department. Universal complaint of the conduct of the accountant, Mr. Simmons. The interest of the country calls for his dismissal.
4°. 2 pages.

1814, July 5, Washington. His claims on the War Department as adopted by Mr. Simmons, the accountant, and asks that his account may be taken out of Simmons's hands and submitted to more correct authority. 4°. 3 pages.

Madison, Mrs. Dolly, to Todd, John P. *Orange.*

1848. Private papers, consisting of an indenture between Mrs. Dolly P. Madison and Richard D. Cutts. [Draft or copy.] Letter to John P. Todd requesting him to sign and return a paper, and to find out whether the President (Monroe) will pay a sum due her. Draft of a note to unknown. fol. 3 pages. 4°. 1 page. 2 scraps of paper.

Madison, James (Sr.), to Madison.

Richmond.

1784, June 4. Private financial business. 4°. 1 page.

New York.

1788, January 30. Sentiments of the Virginia Delegates respecting the constitution. Private business matters and family concerns. Annexed is a letter from Wm. Moore. fol. 1 page.

Philadelphia.

1791, May 11, Orange. Acknowledging letter of April 23. Tobacco and subscription to a loan. Farming and domestic matters. Reports that Madison is a partner in the Yazoo Company in a grant for lands which is looked on as being obtained in a dishonest manner. Thinks if it is not so he should authorize Gen. Mathews to contradict it.
4°. 2 pages.

1796, February 11, Orange, Va. Affidavit of William Russell respecting the alteration of the date of a certificate signed by John Robinson, of the commissary department of Virginia. fol. 1 page.

MADISON, JAMES (Rev.). *Philadelphia.*

1780, August 3. Acknowledging letter of July 18. Anticipation of an early peace. Arrival of the French fleet. Hears that Madison refuses an important foreign appointment. Attempts a course of lectures on Natural History.
small 4°. 4 pages.

1781, January 18, Williamsburg, Va. The raid of Arnold on Richmond and the destruction of the capitol in Williamsburg and public buildings in Richmond. Families suffering from losses of property and slaves. Fears this is only the prelude to something more important. The spirit of Virginia, however, is not sleeping. The militia turn out with readiness. The university a desert. Pupils and professors warriors. Thinks of changing his profession. small 4°. 2 pages.

1781, March 9, Williamsburg. Is pleased at the more favorable intelligence received from abroad. Our naval superiority or at least equality. The people of Virginia willing to risk all in the cause, but the assembly has lost its respect. Iniquitous laws. Zeal in resisting the approach of Cornwallis. Want of guns. Asks Madison to procure certain law books. small 4°. 3 pages.

——— RANDOLPH, EDMUND. *Richmond.*

Not dated. Questions in geology and chemistry.
small 4°. 1 page.

——— to MADISON. *Philadelphia.*

1782, March, Williamsburg. Has returned to this place a spectacle of misery and ruin. Is with his old friend, Bellini, who will write. Congratulates Madison on the glorious events that America has lately experienced. Is tired of the war. [Annexed is a letter from C. Bellini.]
4°. 2 pages.

——— to RANDOLPH, EDMUND. *Richmond.*

1782, May, Williamsburg. Has declared his intention to appear in the court of admiralty. Asks that he will permit George Hay to send him a transcript of laws of Congress relative to that court. Matters relating to the William and Mary College. small 4°. 3 pages.

——— to MADISON. *Philadelphia.*

1782, June 15, Williamsburg. Acknowledging letter of April 22. General anxiety as to the result of the action in the West Indies. Good behavior of our allies in this part of the country. Their respect to private property. Interest of the French officers in the university and the natural history of Virginia. Letter of the president of Yale College respecting the theory of the Phœnecians having visited Narragansett Bay.
small 4°. 3 pages.

1782, August 2, Williamsburg. Acknowledging letter and books. Proceedings of the court of admiralty. Fossil remains of the mammoth found upon the Ohio, as mentioned by Buffon. Respecting the arcana of the opossum. Departure of the French. Sailing of the French fleet, supposed for New York. small 4°. 3 pages.

1782, September 18, Williamsburg. Acknowledging letters of August 13 and 14. Conjectures as to the probability of recognition of our independence by European powers. Our attitude towards

MADISON, JAMES (Rev.).

France. High prices of everything except provisions. Respecting Gen. Chastellux. His literary intentions respecting the United States.
fol. 2 pages.

1782, October 3, Williamsburg. Acknowledging a letter respecting acquaintance with French officers. Conjectures as to an early peace. Asks Madison to request Mr. Rittenhouse to furnish him with one of the new cakes for electrical experiments.
small 4°. 2 pages.

——— to GOVERNOR OF VIRGINIA.

Not dated. Inquiries respecting land warrants.
fol. 1 page.

——— to MADISON. *Philadelphia.*

1783, January 16, Williamsburg. Acknowledging letter of December 24. The commission for negotiating for peace. Obstacles. Reports that a majority of members of Congress are under the influence of the French minister. 4°. 2 pages.

1783, April 15, Williamsburg. Letter from Jefferson relating to expected confirmation of the peace. Jefferson's expected visit to Europe. An expected convention to reforming the constitution of Virginia. small 4°. 1 page.

1783, June 4, Williamsburg. Inclosing a receipt for payment of a seal by Robert Scott, engraver, of the university at Williamsburg.
small 4°. 1 page and 8°. 1 page.

Princeton.

1783, August 27, Williamsburg. The residence of Congress. Asks if there is the least probability of its fixing on Williamsburg as its residence.
fol. 1 page.

1785, November 15, Williamsburg. Matters connected with the college. The separation of Kentucky from Virginia. 4°. 2 pages.

——— to RANDOLPH, EDMUND (Governor of Virginia).

1787, April 23, Williamsburg. Incloses a paper to be given out for a Thesis or oration to be delivered on Foundation Day at the college. 4°. 4 pages.

——— to MADISON. *New York.*

1787, June 11, Williamsburg. Reviews John Adam's books which Madison has sent him. Interprets his views as advocating a government in opposition to our Republican form, similar to the English. His residence abroad has weakened his optics so that he can not withstand the glare of European courts. Thinks Congress should speedily give him the opportunity of breathing a purer American air. 4°. 4 pages.

1787, (?), not dated, Williamsburg. His views on the new Federal Constitution. Small 4°. 4 pages.

Philadelphia.

1787, August 1, Williamsburg. Wishes to be informed of the Conventional Deliberations. fol. 2 pages.

New York.

1788, February 9, Williamsburg. Respecting the "Federalist." Views on the Constitution.
small 4°. 4 pages.

MADISON, JAMES (Rev.).

1788, November 22, Williamsburg. Suggests that Madison be a candidate for member of Congress from the Williamsburg district. small 4°. 3 pages.

1789, March 1, Williamsburg. Is satisfied at Madison's election. Predicts the population of the United States in a century to be 60,000,000. small 4°. 2 pages

1789, May 5, Williamsburg. Notifies him of the intention of Peter Carr to visit New York. Acknowledging letter of April 19. The question of import. Solicits an appointment for Mr. Ellicott. small 4°. 2 pages.

1789, May, Williamsburg. Recommending Mr. Ellicott for the place of Geographer General to the United States. small 4°. 1 page.

1789, August 15, Williamsburg. On the question of amendments to the Constitution. On the union of the legistative and executive branches. 4°. 4 pages.

1790, March 12, Williamsburg. Acknowledging receipt of a letter. Has accepted the appointment of Bishop of Virginia. 4°. 2 pages.

Philadelphia.

1791, April 10, Williamsburg. Acknowledges a letter by Col. Griffin. Chemical publication. 4°. 3 pages.

1791, November 25, Williamsburg. Introducing Otway Bird, who wishes to obtain Madison's assistance in some business with Congress. 4°. 1 page.

1794, November 12, Williamsburg. Congratulates Madison on his marriage. Suggests the scheme as proposed by Jefferson respecting the establishment of a university. 4°. 3 pages.

1794, December 24, Williamsburg. The proposed establishment of a university. Thinks the application had better be postponed until either Madison or Jefferson be placed in the state legislature in order to better influence the assembly. 4°. 3 pages.

Not dated. Has undertaken a map of Virginia. Asks aid in procuring a copy of the one by Col. Francis Deakens, in the possession of George Fenwick, of Washington. Also would thank Jefferson for any assistance which he may give him in respect to latitude and longitude of certain places. 4°. 1 page.

Philadelphia.

1795, July 25, Williamsburg. Apologizes for having inadvertantly opened a letter intended for Madison. Gives his views respecting the treaty with Great Britain. 4°. 3 pages.

Richmond.

1800, January 9, Williamsburg. Invites Madison and Mrs. Madison to pay him a visit. His views on the present measures of the Federal Government. Advocates a university for Virginia. Approves of Madison's report on the resolutions of the last assembly. 4°. 3 pages.

Orange.

1800, October 9, Williamsburg. Incloses extract of a letter bearing on the remedy for the ravages of

MADISON, JAMES (Rev.)

the Hessian fly on wheat. Purchase of land. Approves of Jefferson as a candidate for the Presidency. Conduct of our envoys relating to spoliations. Adams's declaration as to the necessity of an hereditary chief magistrate.
4°. 2 pages.

1800, December 28, Williamsburg. Acknowledging a letter from Richmond giving information respecting purchase of land by Mr. Patterson. Describes an invention, with a small diagram, of an application of water for the purpose of creating a current of air. The nomination of Burr for the President's chair. [Signature cut off.]
4°. 3 pages.

1801, February 23, Williamsburg. Acknowledging a letter inclosing one from Mr. Patterson respecting land offered for sale. Possibility of obtaining the presidency of New York College. Rejoices at Jefferson's election. Finds the water machine before mentioned is not a new invention.
4°. 2 pages.

Washington.

1802, October 29, Williamsburg. Introducing his son James Catesby. Denies the assertion in Davis's paper that he had declared Jefferson had deceived him with respect to money sent Mr. Calender. Is indignant at this abuse of the first magistrate.
4°. 2 pages.

1802, December 17, Williamsburg. Introducing Dr. Barraud, with a request that the post that he now holds under Government may be secured to him. 4°. 1 page.

1803. October 27, Williamsburg. Acknowledging a letter inclosing $400. The treaty of Louisiana seals the prosperity of the Western country, yet Jefferson has but few friends, as he discovered in his excursion to Kanawha. Introduces his son James Catesby. 4°. 2 pages.

1803, November 14, Williamsburg. Incloses a bond. The pretentions of Maryland to a part of Virginia. Is appointed with others to examine into the grounds of those pretensions and report to the assembly. 4°. 1 page.

1803, November 18, Williamsburg. Remits cash to supply his son John, who is on his way to Baltimore to commence business. The awkward opposition made in the Louisiana business anticipated, but has no doubt about the issue, which will be popular. 4°. 1 page.

1803, December 11, Williamsburg. Incloses paper for Dr. Thornton. Has framed a report and forwarded it to Richmond, demonstrating the invalidity of the pretensions of Maryland to a part of Virginia. Attributes the opposition of the Louisiana treaty not to stupidity but to a miserable anxiety to detract from the popularity which the Administration party merits. 4°. 2 pages.

1803, December 13, Williamsburg. Acknowledging letter of 4th. Is not a candidate for the presidency of the Philadelphia University. Is anxious for retirement. 4°. 1 page.

1804, April 8, Williamsburg. The new bank. Gives directions about private money matters.
4°. 1 page.

MADISON, JAMES (Rev.)

1804, April 18, Williamsburg. Prospects of the Virginia bank. Wishes to add Mr. Mansfield, now employed as surveyor or geographer, to the number of professors in the William and Mary College. Thinks it will be better for him to accept the appointment. 4°. 2 pages.

1804, August 2, Williamsburg. Asks for the loan of his father's meteorological observations. Wishes to know the inclination of Mr. Mansfield in réspect to the offer to him of the professorship of of mathematics. Invention for the sharpening of razors. John Houston wishes to obtain the patent. 4°. 3 pages.

1804, September 3, Williamsburg. Wishes Madison to remit proceeds of his note due him that he may invest in shares of the Virginia bank. Asks Madison's opinion of the bank. 4°. 1 page.

1806, July 26, Williamsburg. Establishment of his son John in business. Our foreign negotiations. The new map of Virginia. 4°. 2 pages.

1809, February 8, Williamsburg. Congratulates him on the issue of the Presidential election. Mr. Crittenden wishes an introduction to secure Madison's interest in procuring a military commission. Thinks, from the debates in Congress, that war is inevitable. fol. 1 page.

1809, May 14, Williamsburg. Introducing Mr. Greenhow. The wisdom and sound policy of the measures of our Government with respect to our foreign relations. 4°. 1 page.

1810, December 14, Williamsburg. Acknowledging letter of 8th. Respecting an applicant for aid, who is not entitled to it. The measures adopted with respect to West Florida approved of by all parties. 4°. 1 page.

1811, July 13, Williamsburg. The late publication of R. Smith. Thinks it abundant justification for his dismissal. 4°. 1 page.

1812, February 1, Williamsburg. Solicits the appointment of his son-in-law, Robert G. Scott, as collector of revenue. His own declining health. Is ill with dropsy. 4°. 1 page.

MAGRATH, THOMAS. *Montpellier.*

1812, September 7, Washington. Incloses a letter from Heth & Randolph, respecting a purchase of coal, and a draft on him for payment. 8°. 1 page.

MADISON, JOHN, to MADISON, JAMES (Sr.).

1735 or 7155, August 19. Precarious situation of himself and family. Apprehension of attacks from Indians. Flight of families. Distressing scenes of women and children crying after their murdered husbands and fathers. small 4°. 3 pages.

MAGRUDER, PATRICK, and others, to MADISON. *Washington.*

1808, October 15, Georgetown. Certificate by Magruder and other persons as to the character of Dr. James H. Blake, and recommending him for a Government appointment.

4°. 2 pages.

MAGRUDER, PATRICK.

1811, February 26, Washington. Resolution of Congress that the report of the committee appointed to inquire into the conduct of General Wilkinson be presented to the President.

4°. 2 pages.

MAIN, JAMES.

1808, March 7, New York. Suggests the plan of establishing a new daily paper in New York to counteract the schemes and intrigues of the Clinton party, who have subjugated the State. 4°. 2 pages.

1808, April 18, New York. Local prejudices will be sacrificed by our Presidential electors and their votes given to Madison. The "Public Advertiser" will vindicate the cause of the administration. Predicts Madison's election and congratulates him. Asks Madison's good offices for the pardon of Philip M. Topham. 4°. 2 pages.

1808, May 11, New York. Prospect of the total overthrow of Clintonism in the State. Thinks Madison will be the people's choice. 4°. 1 page.

1808, June 21, New York. Application for the consulship at Tunis defeated through the hatred of Clinton and his followers. Would like a clerkship in one of the public offices. 4°. 2 pages.

1808, July 13, New York. Asks to be messenger of Government to the continent of Europe or England. A general meeting to be called to support the Congressional nomination of Madison for President. 4°. 1 page.

1808, October 31, New York. Has taken the direction of the "Daily Advertiser". Asks the patronage of Madison and his friends. 4°. 1 page.

MALCOM, HOWARD. *Montpellier.*

1826, October —, Philadelphia. Appeal for aid in support of the "American Sunday School Union". 4°. 2 pages.

1830, June 3, Boston. Transmits copy of report of the Prison Discipline Society. 4°. 1 page.

1831, April 4, Boston. Asks for a letter of introduction to Lafayette, as he goes to Europe shortly for his health. 4°. 1 page.

1834, December 22, Mowbray. Sends a specimen of wrought anthracite. Avows his affection and admiration for Madison's personal worth and his eminent services. 8°. 2 pages.

MALIN, DAVID, and SEDGWICK, C. B.

1832, November 5, Clinton. The committee announces to Madison his election as honorary member of the Phi Gamma Alpha Society of Hamilton College. 4°. 1 page.

MALLORY, ROBERT.

1818, February 7, Richmond. Informs him of his election to the board of public works. 4°. 1 page.

MANNING, JAMES. *New York.*

1789, August 29, Providence, R. I. Introducing Benjamin Bourne, who is to present a petition to Congress that Rhode Island may be exempt from the tonnage imposed on foreigners to which they are subjected by acts of Congress. In all probability by the next session Rhode Island will come into the Union. Asks Madison's interest in favor of the petition. 4°. 3 pages.

MANNING, T. S. *Washington.*

1811, November 15, Philadelphia. Sends the seventh number of the "Freemason's Magazine," and wishes him to read the article entitled "Valley Forge." 4°. 1 page.

MANSFIELD, GEORGE.

1792, November 16. . Cover of papers on which is indorsed "George Mansfield's claims for land at Gen. Knox's office, lodged by Hon. Mr. Madison, November 16, 1792. The powers for land left with Mr. Audibert at War office. M."
4°. 1 page.

MANSFIELD, JARED.

1816, November 26, West Point. Recommending the appointment of Peyton S. Symmes as register of the land office in Cincinnati in the place of Daniel Symmes, his brother, who is about to resign.
4°. 1 page.

1817, February 7, West Point. Showing the disadvantages of the application of certain of the laws regulating the Military Academy in respect to the appointment of instructors from the corps of engineers or from cadets. Suggests that Congress repeal those restrictions. 4°. 2 pages.

MARBOIS, FRANCOIS DE BARBÉ. *Richmond.*

1785, May 31, New York. Acknowledging letter of June 3, 1784. Respecting Mr. Mazzei. Thinks that Jefferson's appointment as minister to France will give satisfaction to that court. Thinks that peace will continue in Europe. Mesmer keeps his ground, and Marbois sees sufficient reasons to doubt before pronouncing him to be a quack.
4°. 1 page.

1785 (?), not dated. Notes on the boundaries between the Spanish settlements and the United States (Louisiana). [Mutilated and incomplete. Copied in Madison's handwriting.]
fol. 2 pages.

——— to LIVINGSTON, R. R. *Paris.*

1803, August 12, Paris. Respecting Madison's letter of April 20. Livingston's acquiescence necessary respecting the question of guarantee in the purchase of Louisiana. [In French. Copy.]
4°. 1 page.

1803, September 13, Paris. Guarantee of the loan of Hope & Baring before the ratification of the Louisiana purchase and treaty. The acquiescence of Livingston to Monroe's decision is necessary, and he asks Livingston to inform him this day. [In French. Copy.] 4°. 1 page.

MARCH & CO., J. HOWARD, to MADISON.
Washington.

1816, February 22, Madeira. At request of Col. R. H. MacPherson, ships a pipe of Madeira wine per *Mary and Frances* for Alexandria. 4°. 1 page.

MARION, J., and DESGRANGES, F.

1815, September 26, Paris. Proposal of two professors of mathematics to erect a Government observatory. Annual expense of the French establishment. large fol. 2 pages.

MARSH, CAPEN & LYON. *Montpellier.*

1830, May 4, Boston. Proposes to compile and publish Madison's writings under his directions, allowing a price for copyright. 4°. 2 pages.

MARSHALL, E. F.

1820, February 23, Saratoga. Sends a copy of the "American Tutor's Assistant." Asks him to examine it and send his opinions. 4°. 1 page.

MARSHALL, HERBERT.

Not dated. Asks for letters of introduction, as he sails shortly for South America, and to be informed about a passport. 4°. 1 page.

MARSHALL, JAMES. *Richmond.*

Not dated. Fears of serious acts of hostility between the Spaniards of Louisiana and our citizens in the West. The Spanish trade on the Mississippi. fol. 3 pages.

MARSHALL, JOHN. *Philadelphia.*

1790, November 29, Richmond. Introducing Mr. Giles. small 4°. 1 page.

MARSHALL, JOSEPH, to BLOOMFIELD, S. F.

1807, February 14, Cowita. Delays in forwarding the mails. Copy of a letter from Postmaster-General Graham. 4°. 2 pages.

MARSHALL, W., to MADISON. *Washington.*

1801, June 16, Charleston. Incloses a certificate in recommendation of Dominick Augustin Hall for the office of chief judge of this circuit, in consequence of the resignation of Mr. Gaillard. 4°. 2 pages.

1801, June 19, Charleston. Incloses a note from Charles Pinckney, to accompany the letter of 16th instant, recommending Mr. Hall for the office of chief judge of this circuit. Expresses his admiration for the present administration. fol. 2 pages.

1802, March 3, Charleston. Introducing Mr. Read. 4°. 1 page.

MARTIN, F. X., to JEFFERSON. *Monticello.*

1810, February 11, New Orleans. Soliciting the office made vacant by the death of Judge Thompson at New Orleans. 4°. 3 pages.

——— to MADISON. *Washington.*

1810, February 11, New Orleans. Wishes the appointment of the office of judge in the Orleans Territory made vacant by the death of Judge Thompson. 4°. 3 pages.

MARTIN, JOHN B. *Montpellier.*

1829, December 22. Incloses a lithographic portrait of Mr. Randolph from Mr. Harding's picture. 8°. 1 page.

MARTIN, ROBERT. *Washington.*

1812, July 17, Caswell County, N. C. Claim for a sum of money due his grandfather from Madison's father for land occupied by him. Asks him, as executor of his father's will, if he knows anything about it. fol. 1 page.

MARTIN, SAMUEL. *Montpellier.*

1829, January 12, Campbell Station. Has received Madison's letters on the constitutionality of a protecting duty on imports. Intends printing them. Suggests the propriety of having the whole mail establishment of this nation supported from the general fund. The Treasury can well support the charge. fol. 1 page.

1829, February 26, Campbell Station. Acknowledging letter of January 30. Reduction or abolition of postage. Asks Madison's opinions. fol. 2 pages

1833, April 10, Campbell Station. Advocates a bill to be presented to Congress for reduction of post-

MARTIN, SAMUEL.

age. Advocates rotation in office under Government, also for not extending the charter of the United States Bank. 4°. 2 pages.

MARTIN, WHEELER. *Washington.*

1808, June 28, Providence, R. I. Candidate for President by the electors of Rhode Island. The Federalists exerting themselves for George Clinton. The Republicans determined on Madison. Suggests that John Langdon, of New Hampshire, be nominated as Vice-President. Suggests that timely action be made respecting the embargo, which is an obstacle to success of the Republican party. 4°. 3 pages.

MARYLAND GENERAL ASSEMBLY.

1811, November 19, Annapolis. See THOMAS, WILLIAM.

MASON, ARMISTEAD T.

1816, April 26, Washington. Testifies to the merits of Col. Samuel Lane, who wishes to be appointed commissioner to superintend the public buildings. 4°. 1 page.

1817, January 20, Washington. District judgeship of Kentucky. Advocates the appointment of Mr. Trimble in preference to his own brother, who would not accept it were it not given freely. 4°. 5 pages.

Montpellier.

1817, September 15, Selma. Acknowledging a letter covering a subscription paper for the Central College of Virginia. Will make every exertion to promote its success. 4°. 1 page.

1818, March 21, Selma. Regrets he has not been very successful in respect to subscriptions to the Central College of Virginia. Sends the subscription paper with his subscription to it, and a check for the first installment. 4°. 2 pages.

MASON, GEORGE.

1776. First draft of the Declaration of Rights made by the representatives of the people of Virginia with alterations and corrections. 4°. 3 pages.

Philadelphia.

1780, August 2, Gunston Hall. Should Congress appoint a consul in Spain, he recommends Mr. Richard Harrison for the place. His sentiments respecting the back lands communicated to Mr. Jones. Col. The. Bland elected to succeed Mr. Griffin as judge in the new court of admirality. small 4°. 3 pages.

——— to VIRGINIA DELEGATES IN CONGRESS, *Philadelphia.*

1781, April 3, Gunston. Advising a duty on British trade, to be applied to the reparation of the wanton destruction of private property by their troops in the United States. [Duplicate.] fol. 3 pages.

——— and ALEXANDER HENDERSON, jointly, to SPEAKER OF THE HOUSE OF DELEGATES OF VIRGINIA. *Richmond.*

1785, March 28, Mount Vernon. Result of the deliberations of the commissioners of Virginia and Maryland appointed to settle the navigation and jurisdiction of that part of the Chesapeake Bay within the limits of Virginia, and the rivers Potomac and Pocomoke. Inclosing the compact of the commissioners. [Copy.]
fol. 6 pages, and a scrap of paper.

MASON, GEORGE, and others, TO PENNSYLVANIA, THE PRESIDENT OF THE EXECUTIVE COUNCIL OF.

1785, March 28, Mount Vernon. Letter from the commissioners of the States of Maryland and Virginia, respecting the navigation of the Potomac. [*See* letter of this date to the speaker of the house of delegates of Virginia.] fol. 1 page.

MASON, GEORGE. *Orange.*

1785, August 9, Gunston Hall. Acknowledging letter of June 2. Incloses copy of the proceedings of the commissioners of Maryland and Virginia respecting the boundaries and navigation of the Potomac. small 4°. 3 pages.

Richmond.

1785, December 7, Gunston Hall. Incloses the compact of the commissioners appointed to settle the navigation and jurisdiction of the Potomac River. Apologizes to the assembly for having exceeded his instructions on a certain point. small 4°. 4 pages.

Montpellier.

1826, July 6, Green Spring. Incloses a paper which came into his possession by accident. Is impressed with its valuable truths and profound views. Wishes to know if it is Madison's composition. 4°. 2 pages.

1827, December 10, Green Spring. Incloses copies of a memorial. Asks if he has papers in his possession written by his grandfather, Col. George Mason, and if he will allow him to make use of them in a biography he is preparing. 4°. 2 pages.

——— to VIRGINIA GENERAL ASSEMBLY.

Not dated. "A private citizen" submits queries to the assembly respecting the port bill, and protesting against it. [Printed document.] fol. 1 page.

Not dated. Observations of George Wilson on the caveats entered by George Wilson against the Orange companies and George Mason's surveys on Panther Creek. 4°. 2 pages.

——— to MADISON. *Washington.*

1801, November 2, Georgetown. Asks if Madison will pay an indorsed engagement of Mr. Orr's for money advanced. 4°. 1 page.

1804, March 28, Georgetown. Renewal of a note falling due at bank. 4°. 1 page.

1804, July 18, Georgetown. Incloses Madison's note to be signed by him in renewal of one coming due soon. 4°. 1 page.

1805, April 24, June 19, August 26; 1807, April 8; 1808, July 14, Georgetown. A series of letters relating to business with the Bank of Columbia, Georgetown. Also an account for interest April 9, 1807. 4°. 7 pages.

1808, July 14, Georgetown. Account current. Inclosing canceled note of Madison's. 4°. 2 pages. 8°. 1 page.

1808, October 28, Georgetown. Testifies to the integrity and assiduity of Dr. James H. Blake, a decided Republican and zealous supporter of the administration. 4°. 1 page.

MASON, GEORGE.

1812, July 8, Indian Office, Washington. Statement showing the salary and subsistence money in lieu of rations paid to Indian agents at trading houses from April 1811 to March 1812. fol. 1 page.

1812, July 8, Washington. Incloses a statement of salaries to Indian agents. 4°. 3 pages.

1812, August 10, Washington. Recommends the appointment of Robert B. Bayly as agent at the trading house on Chickasaw bluffs. Also recommends Wm. M. Stewart for assistant agent at Fort Madison. 4°. 2 pages.

1812, August 27, Washington. Recommends Robert B. Belt as assistant agent at Fort Madison in the place of William M. Stewart, resigned. 4°. 2 pages.

——— to JONES, WALTER.

1812, June 9, Washington. Respecting Stewart and the two Winslows, prisoners, on charge of counterfeiting. Recommends leniency. 4°. 1 page.

——— to MADISON.

1812, September 4, Georgetown. Suggests that Monroe be appointed in command to relieve the despondency created by Hull's infamous conduct if he can be spared from the Cabinet, and appoint Jefferson as Secretary of State. 4°. 3 pages.

1813, April 21, Georgetown. Incloses a letter from J. T. Ricketts, relating to the inattention of Government to place Alexandria in a state of defense. 4°. 1 page.

——— to MONROE.

1819, September 3, Georgetown. Recommending Alexander Scott as a candidate for an appointment to office. [*See* letter of Alexander Scott to Madison, dated January 2, 1820. Copy.] 4°. 2 pages.

MASON, J. M., to MADISON.

1810, January 29, New York. Acknowledging note of 12th, inclosing an important document. Asks for further materials relating to the acts of the Federal convention. 4°. 2 pages.

1810, December 20, New York. Acknowledging receipt of two notes relative to a constitution for the United States drawn up by Gen. Hamilton. Asks for a copy. 4°. 2 pages.

MASON, JOHN T.

1802, July 16, Georgetown. Application of S. Hansen for the place of chief clerk in the Department of State. Suggests his appointment for a temporary period on trial. 4°. 2 pages.

MASON, S. T. *Montpellier.*

1800, March 7, Philadelphia. Acknowledging a letter. Actions of Congress respecting the bankrupt bill. Prospect of its success. Ross's bill for deciding elections for President and Vice-President. Arrival of our envoys to France at Lisbon. System of procrastination. 4°. 3 pages.

1800, April 2, Philadelphia. Incloses copy of the bill concerning the Presidential elections as passed the Senate. The order to arrest Duane. fol. 1 page.

MASON, S. T. *Washington.*

1802, May 8. Recommending Lund Washington as a clerk in the Department of State should a vacancy occur. 4°. 1 page.

1802, October 29, Rasberry Plain. Introducing Charles Fenton Mercer, about to sail for England. small 4°. 1 page.

MASON, THOMSON.

1808, April 26, Fairfax County. Recommending Dr. James H. Blake as a man of integrity and a firm and decided republican. small 4°. 1 page.

——— and others.

1808, May 18, Fairfax County. Testimony of persons in Fairfax County, Va., to the character and abilities of Dr. James H. Blake, who seeks Government employment. 4°. 2 pages.

MASON, W.

1809, June 14. Bacon and hams to be furnished Madison. 4°. 1 page.

MASSACHUSETTS, COMMONWEALTH OF.

1790. Report of the committee of both houses of the legislature appointed to consider further amendments in the Constitution of the United States. [Printed document.] fol. 3 pages.

MASSACHUSETTS GENERAL ASSEMBLY.

1814, January 29, Boston. Report of the committee to whom was referred the memorial and petition of the president, etc., of the New England Bank, complaining of an arbitrary, illegal, and unwarrantable seizure and detention of their property by the collector of the customs of the United States for the district of New York, with resolutions of the legislature and accompanying documents. royal fol. 13 pages.

MASSACHUSETTS LEGISLATURE.

1815, February 23, Boston. *See* Austin, Benjamin and others.

MASSIE, GEORGE (senior), to MADISON. *Montpellier.*

1828, July 3, Louis County, Va. An ox left on his premises by Madison's wagoners to die. Has resuscitated him and he can be had when sent for. fol. 1 page.

MASSON, FRANCIS DE, to JEFFERSON. *Monticello.*

1815, February 9, Paris. Formerly of the Corps of Engineers at West Point, solicits Jefferson's good offices in the procurement of a place in the legation at Paris or a consulate at Nantes or any other place. 4°. 3 pages.

1815, February 9, Paris. Has served twenty years in the United States. Is recommended by M. de Malesherbes and Lafayette, and wishes to obtain a Government position in the American legation in Paris or as consul to Nantes. 4°. 3 pages.

MATHEWS, GEORGE, to MADISON. *Washington.*

1812, April 16, Moosa, Old Fort, East Florida. His duties as commissioner of the United States for East and West Florida approaches a close. Transmits to the Secretary of State the official papers. The inconveniences and delays occasioned by Maj. Lavals in disobedience of orders. Recommendations of several persons for positions. Requests

MATHEWS, GEORGE.

that two companies of artillery and one of infantry to fortify Amelia and Cumberland islands and Point Petre. Thinks it advisable to erect a Territorial government here as soon as possible. 4°. 5 pages.

MATHEWS, THOMAS. *Washington.*

1801, November 3, Norfolk. Introduces Lieut. Saunders. 4°. 1 page.

1808, March 19, Norfolk. Recommends William Hamilton, of North Carolina, for a commission as lieutenant. fol. 1 page.

MATTHEWS, WILLIAM. *Montpellier.*

1827, February 8, Everettsville, Va. The furnishing of arms to the students. Has applied to Gen. Cocke and has received no definitive answer. 4°. 1 page.

MAURY, FONTAINE. *New York.*

1789, April 18, Fredericksburg. Acknowledging two letters with inclosures. Asks information respecting imposts. Has forwarded Madison's tobacco for Liverpool and authorizes him to draw on him for the proceeds. fol. 2 pages.

1789, June 14, Fredericksburg. Shipments of tobacco and directions about drafts. 4°. 1 page.

1790, July 20, Fredericksburg. Acknowledging letter of 4th. Authorizing drafts for shipments of tobacco. Sends copy of account. Local politics. 4°. 2 pages.

1790, July 20. Account for sundry articles. 4°. 1 page.

1790, May 26, Fredericksburg. Petition presented to Congress by the inhabitants of Fredericksburg and Falmouth praying the removal of the naval office to Urbana. Requests Madison to interest himself to cause a delay in the matter. 4°. 1 page.

Philadelphia.

1791, July 10, Fredericksburg. Sends statement of account. Notice of shipment of tobacco to Liverpool. 4°. 2 pages.

1791, July 10, Fredericksburg. Bill of exchange on Madison in favor of Phillips, Cramond & Co. 8°. 1 page.

Orange.

1801, February 19, Fredericksburg. Announces the election of Jefferson. 4°. 1 page.

1801, February 19, Fredericksburg. Announcing the election of Jefferson and copy of a handbill addressed to the editor of the "Times" giving the particulars. 4°. 2 pages.

Washington.

1801, May 17, Fredericksburg. Solicits the appointment of collector of imposts at Alexandria. 4°. 1 page.

1802, June 1, New York. Incloses a pamphlet. Has established himself in a commission business in New York and offers his services. 4°. 1 page.

1804, January 10, New York. Asks for a letter of introduction for Mr. Hugh Pollock to Governor Claiborne, of Louisiana. 4°. 1 page.

MAURY, FONTAINE.

1804, November 6, New York. Introducing Mr. Destrihan, of New Orleans. 4°. 1 page.

1804, November 6, New York. Introducing Mr. Sauve, of New Orleans. 4°. 1 page.

——— to GILSTON, DAVID (Collector).

New York.

1804, November 20, New York. On his failure to make the necessary entry for drawback on a consignment of coffee, from ignorance of the law, he applies for the duties paid to be returned. 4°. 2 pages.

——— to MADISON. *Washington.*

1805, January 2, New York. Correspondence with the collector of New York about a return of duties paid on a cargo of coffee entitled to drawback. Asks Madison's aid, as it is well understood no fraud was attempted. 4°. 2 pages.

1805, January 20, New York. Acknowledging letter of 10th. Incloses to Mr. Dawson the necessary documents relating to the matter of drawback on a cargo of coffee. 4°. 1 page.

1810, June 25, Fredericksburg. Requests Madison to suspend his opinions on the unfair and unfounded representations made with a view to injure the reputation of his brother James in his official character. 4°. 2 pages.

Montpellier.

1819, February 14, Washington. Sends a sample, as experiment, of Talevara wheat imported from England. It matures ten or fifteen days earlier than most other wheats. 4°. 1 page.

MAURY, JAMES. *New York.*

1786, July 10, Fredericksburg. About to embark for Liverpool. Trusts that Madison will intimate to his friends in Congress that he still considers himself as a candidate for a consulate. London his first choice; would not object to any of the ports on the continent provided the salary be competent to a support and not debar him from trade. 4°. 1 page.

1789, January 24, Liverpool. Acknowledging letter of July 3, with copy of the "Federalist." Sends account sales of tobacco per the *Venus.* 4°. 1 page.

1789, February 19; March 16; 1791, October 11, 11, December 29; 1794, March 1, 1, 1, 1; 1804, October 25, 25, 25; 1814, March 8, 8, 16, Liverpool. Series of letters concerning private business. 4°. 15 pages.

1789, August 21, Liverpool. Has received tobacco by the *Cyrus* and *Venus*, but not yet sold. Authorizes him to draw on it. Congratulates him on the regeneration which goes on so wonderfully in France. fol. 1 page.

1789, October 6, Liverpool. Wishes the appointment of consul at Liverpool. Incloses a letter to the President on the subject. Gives directions as to shipments of tobacco. 4°. 3 pages.

1790, February 13, Liverpool. Acknowledging letter of June 21. Shipments of tobacco. 4°. 1 page.

MAURY, JAMES. *Philadelphia.*

1791, July 29, Liverpool. Acknowledging receipt of State papers. Mob at Birmingham on the occasion of the celebration of the festival of the French revolution. Respecting tobacco. 4°. 2 pages.

1791, November 12, Liverpool. Arrival of shipments of tobacco. American funds popular in England. Purchases at advanced prices. Duties of the consular office. 4°. 2 pages.

1791, December 31, Liverpool. Account current. 4°. 2 pages.

1792, February 3, Liverpool. Acknowledging paper and a pamphlet. Letter of introduction extorted from him by Mr. Jorne. Incloses account sales of tobacco. Offers his services in the purchase of material used in the building of public offices. 4°. 3 pages.

1792, May 26, Liverpool. Fall in British stocks. Fears that the United States may become involved. The consular bill. 4°. 1 page.

1793, April 9, Liverpool. Introducing the Rev. Mr. Toulmin. 4°. 1 page.

1793, September 26, Liverpool. Capture of American vessels on the suspicion of having French property on board. Intelligence from the continent. Accounts of advantages gained by the anti-revolutionists counter-balanced by those over the combined armies before Dunkirk. Quotations of consuls. 4°. 1 page.

1794, March 1, Liverpool. Incloses sales of tobacco. Immense warlike preparations, yet thinks peace in Europe is not remote. 4°. 1 page.

1796, November 28, Liverpool. Prospects not favorable to peace. Has disbursed for relief of distressed Americans beyond the line prescribed by the consular act. Will memorialize Congress. Asks Madison to present and patronize it. Tobacco in great demand at high prices. 4°. 2 pages.

Washington.

1801, October 7, Liverpool. Signing the preliminaries of peace between the United States and France. 4°. 1 page.

1801, October 24, Liverpool. Acknowledging letter of August 1, containing instructions relative to the duties of the consulate respecting purchase of foreign ships by Americans, quarantine regulations and other details. fol. 3 pages.

1801, October 24, Liverpool. Duplicate of the foregoing. fol. 3 pages.

1803, September 5, Liverpool. The prohibitions of France and Holland to all commercial intercourse with this country added to the blockade of the Elbe and Weser cause the markets to be in a most depressed state. Low price of wheat and flour. [Duplicate.] 4°. 1 page.

1804, February 28, Liverpool. Has been ill with rheumatism. Arrival of the *Atlantic* with Madison's consignment. The king said to be alarmingly ill. 4°. 1 page.

1804, July 21, Liverpool. Has honored his draft. Has nearly finished the sale of tobacco. His old claim on the Secretary of the Treasury. Talk of invasion. 4°. 2 pages.

MAURY, JAMES.

1804, August 22, Liverpool. Acknowledging letter of July 2. Incloses particulars of clearances of vessels. Advance in price of grain.
4°. 2 pages.

1804, September 19, Liverpool. Repeated seizures of our vessels at this port for smuggling tobacco by sailors. Submits the propriety of publishing the fact which is a serious evil. 4°. 2 pages.

1804, October 25, Liverpool. Acknowledging letter of July 22. The results of a consignment of tobacco. "Private." 4°. 1 page.

1804, November 28, Liverpool. Notices the acceptance of drafts. State of the market. "Private."
4°. 1 page.

1807, August 5, Liverpool. Incloses invoice and bill of lading of cheese and parcels. 4°. 1 page.

1807, August 5, Liverpool. Invoice of two boxes of cheese per ship *Leonidas* with a bill of Leicester & Gouthwaite. 4°. 1 page. 8°. 1 page.

1809, May 3, Liverpool. Congratulations on his becoming President. The partial repeal of the embargo and revocation of orders in council unexpected. Prices of cotton and tobacco.
4°. 1 page.

1810, October 11, Liverpool. Consignment of tobacco. Large quantity on hand and price low.
4°. 2 pages.

1810, November 14, Liverpool. Arrival of the *Adeline* with tobacco in a damaged condition. State of trade. Immense influx of produce since the expiration of the nonintercourse law. Many failures. Low prices of tobacco. 4°. 2 pages.

April 11, Liverpool. Unparalleled distresses in the trading interests. Loan by the Government for relief of sufferers. Stock of tobacco large and unsaleable. 4°. 2 pages.

1812, March 20, Liverpool. Advance in wheat and flour. Tobacco still on hand. Quotations of grain. 4°. 1 page.

1812, April 20, Liverpool. Not a good prospect for amicable adjustment between Great Britain and the United States. Determination of the British administration to continue the orders in council. Petitions for their revocation increase. High price of wheat. 4°. 1 page.

1812, July 29, Liverpool. Sends two cheeses. Still has his tobacco on hand. Will sell at first opportunity. 4°. 1 page.

1813, August 20, Liverpool. Notes the sale of tobacco.
4°. 1 page.

1814, September 17, Liverpool. Notes a balance due him for sale of tobacco. Quotations of tobacco.
4°. 1 page.

1815, January 2, Liverpool. Peace being agreed on, continues his offer of services in the situation of consul. State of the tobacco market.
4°. 2 pages.

1815, January 18, Liverpool. Repeats the tender of his services as consul in Liverpool. Information respecting tobacco. 4°. 2 pages.

MAURY, JAMES.

1815, April 19, Liverpool. Is grateful for the President's anticipating Maury's desire to be continued as consul. Activity in business. Prices of tobacco. 4°. 1 page.

1816 March 2, Liverpool. Thanks for his re-appointment as consul. Madison's account with him, on tobacco sales. 4°. 1 page.

——— *Montpellier.*

1817, April 22, Liverpool. Is gratified in reading Madison's message. Incloses newspapers. Quotations and information respecting grain and tobacco. 4°. 2 pages.

1818, September 29, Liverpool. Acknowledging letter of July 24. Information respecting walnut. The wheat crop and prospects as to prices. 4°. 2 pages.

1818, October 26, Liverpool. Observations of a gentleman respecting Talevera wheat. Extract from a letter to Maury. 4°. 1 page.

1821, April 7, Liverpool. Acknowledging letter of February 20. Respecting prices of articles ordered by Madison. Information about tobacco. 4°. 2 pages.

1821, September 25, Liverpool. Acknowledging letter of April 5. His son's attachment to America. The farmers in England and the wheat crop. Has no intention of resigning his office as consul. 4°. 2 pages.

1822, June 24, Liverpool. Inclosing newspaper containing the bill for opening intercourse with the United States, in parliament. 4°. 1 page.

1822, July 20, Liverpool. The bill regulating the opening of intercourse between the United States and the British colonies in vessels of each nation has become law. Acknowledging letter of May 23. Maury's son to return to the United States. Recommends him to Madison's notice. 4°. 1 page.

1823, May 21, Liverpool. Acknowledging letters of September 28, and March 20 and 24. Indignant feeling in all parties in England at the unprovoked invasion of Spain by France. Comparative value of imports of produce in England from the United States. Cotton versus tobacco. Petitions to Parliament for abolition of slavery in the British colonies. The advocates confident of success. 4°. 2 pages.

1823, July 3, Liverpool. Notifies Madison of the shipment of a cheese. 4°. 1 page.

1825, June 22, Liverpool. Introduces his son Matthew, who goes to the United States. High price of tobacco. 4°. 1 page.

1827, February 24, Liverpool. Acknowledging letter of November 25. Sends newspapers with articles on negro slavery in Virginia. Lord Liverpool visited by a paralytic stroke. 4°. 1 page.

1828, January 29, Liverpool. Introduces James Hagerty. Jefferson's death. Decline of imports of tobacco. France consumes her own growth. Activity and energy of the writer, also of Mr. Carroll in their old age. 4°. 3 pages.

MAURY, JAMES.

1828, March 31, Liverpool. Use of American tobacco for the manufacture of snuff. Repeal of the test and corporation acts, forerunners of the removal of disabilities of the Catholics. Unsettled account with John Walker, a lawyer.
4°. 2 pages.

1828, September 16, Liverpool. Acknowledging letters of April 5 and May 13. Arrival of Mr. Barbour and family. An instance of longevity in Madison's region. 4°. 1 page.

1829, June 19, Liverpool. Settlement of account with John Walker. Prospects of the crops. Incloses circular about tobacco. Alludes to the death of Madison's mother in February. Madison in his 80th year. 4°. 2 pages.

1831, February 10, Liverpool. Acknowledging letter of December 10. Receives Madison's portrait. Consumption of American flour in England. Remarks on tobacco and other produce. The writer is 85 years old, and is not disqualified for the luxury of cold baths. Death of his wife.
4°. 2 pages.

1831, June 7, Laurel Hill, Spottsylvania. Acknowledging letter of April 29. His intention to visit Madison, also to go to the mountainous region to get rid of a nervous cough. 4°. 2 pages.

1831, July 13, near Charlottesville. Regrets indisposition prevents Madison from coming to Charlottesville. 4°. 1 page.

1832, February 12, Richmond. Extreme cold weather in Richmond. The writer in his 87th year and in perfect health. 4°. 2 pages.

1832, July 19, Schooley's Mountain, N. J. Salubrity of the air at Schooley's Mountain. The writer 87 years old and walks with ease 5 miles a day.
4°. 2 pages.

MAURY & LATHAM.

1819 (?), not dated, April 27; 1820, September 13, 27, October 24; 1821, March 22, September 28, October 2, 6, 19, November 1; 1822, January 2, February 1; 1829, May 20, June 16; 1831, September 30, Liverpool. Sixteen letters relating exclusively to private business. 4°. 23 pages.

MAURY, MATTHEW.

1826, January 24, Richmond. Incloses a letter from his father, James Maury. Hopes to be able to call on Madison in the summer. 4°. 1 page.

1829, August 11, Richmond. Newspaper attacks on his father respecting his consulate in Liverpool. Interview with the President relative thereto. His father's robust health at the age of 84. Memorandum of the income of the Liverpool consulate from 1790. 4°. 4 pages.

1833, June 8, New York. Change which the reform bill has worked in the relative position of minister and Parliament. 4°. 1 page.

MAURY, THOMAS W.

1820, October 23, Orange, C. H., *Va.* Asks for letters of introduction for his relative, William Maury, to a few distinguished persons in Kentucky, Tennessee, Mississippi, and New Orleans.
4°. 2 pages.

MAURY, WILLIAM.

1819, December 4, Charleston. Second crop of clover. Explanation by a Boston gentleman why clover causes salivation in horses. Cotton manufactures. 4°. 2 pages.

1820, June 19, Richmond. Asks Madison to ship his crop of tobacco by the *Arethusa* from Bermuda Hundred to his father's address. Asks Madison to invite his father to visit him in Virginia. 4°. 2 pages.

1821, March 8, New Orleans. Thanks for letters of introduction. A visit to Henry Clay. His jocular observations. Trip down the river to New Orleans. Describes the city. Attentions from the governor. American inhabitants improving New Orleans. Cotton planting; its profits. 4°. 4 pages.

1821, April 6, New Orleans. Asks Madison to consult with the President about the appointment of himself as consul at Liverpool in the event of his father's resignation. Annexed copy of a letter from his father's partner, William Latham, in reference thereto. 4°. 2 pages.

1821, July 9, Richmond. Madison's crop of tobacco. Authorizing him to draw on it. Will send Mrs. Madison his promised present of Natchitoches snuff. 4°. 2 pages.

1831, September 17, Liverpool. Sends strawberry plants to Mrs. Madison, with directions as to planting. Thanks for Madison's kind reception of his father. Madison's predictions relative to the corn laws to be verified. The tariff. Accepts the position of the vice-consulship of France in Liverpool. 4°. 4 pages.

MAXCY, VIRGIL.

1822, November 10, Tulip Hill, near Annapolis. Incloses a pamphlet written in defense of the Maryland resolutions relative to appropriations of public lands for the purposes of education. 4°. 1 page.

MAZZEI, PHILIP. *Williamsburg.*

1779, June 13, Hob's Hole. Cypher given him by Madison. Deposits papers in a 4-pound ball to throw overboard should prudence require it. Suggestions about a loan to be negotiated abroad. In a postscript, dated 17th, states the vessel is stopped near Urbana on account of privateers reported in the bay. Is uneasy about clothing for the Army. 4°. 3 pages.

1779, June 18, Urbana. The captain and crew of the vessel in which he goes abroad. Is not well satisfied. Expense of the undertaking. Asks Madison's good offices that justice be done him in regard to his expenditures and salary. Recounts the pecuniary difficulties. Suggestions. 4°. 4 pages.

1779, June 19, Yorktown. Asks Madison to ride over to Yorktown to consult with him on matters which he can not communicate on paper, prior to his departure for Europe on the mission from the State of Virginia. 4°. 1 page.

Philadelphia.

1780, November 30, Florence. Prefers to write in Italian, as it is easier for him and will be a good

MAZZEI, PHILIP.

Italian lesson. Hears with pleasure Madison's election as Delegate to Congress, although it will be a loss in the councils of the State of Virginia. Relates injustice done him, and especially so receiving no answers to his letters to the governor. Asks Madison's good offices in obtaining justice to his claims with his friends in Virginia. [In Italian.] fol. 3 pages.

1780, December 7, Florence. Complications in European affairs and death of the Queen of Hungary. [In Italian.] fol. 2 pages.

1782, March 15, Florence. Acknowledging letter of September 28, 1781. Political matters in Europe. Matters connected with his mission to Europe by the government of Virginia. [In Italian.] fol. 3 pages.

——— to BLAIR, JOHN.

1782, March 22, Florence. Complains of the neglect of his friends in not answering his communications, particularly because the object of his mission from the State of Virginia is delayed thereby. Recommends Mark Lynch to those of his friends who have commercial business commissions. [Copy.] fol. 3 pages.

1782, April 5, Florence. Extract of a letter to the governor of Virginia, wishing to know if he is to be employed in the public service; that it is necessary he should have an ostensible letter showing the probability of the payment of the interest on the loan, and that his expenses should be paid by remittances. 4°. 2 pages

——— to MADISON.

1782, April 5, Florence. Letters written to Mr. Blair on the question of the neglect of the governor in not informing of what is expected of him in the matter of his mission from Virginia to negotiate a loan, the payment of his necessary expenses, and necessity of a letter of credence. [In Italian.] 4°. 1 page.

——— to LOMAX. *Caroline County, Va.*

1782, April 5, Florence. Debates in the British Parliament on the question of prohibiting an offensive war in America. No confidence to be placed in their pretense of friendship. Wishes to return to Virginia. It appears that the executive of Virginia sent him over merely to starve and as if they do not even intend to furnish him with the means of returning home. 4°. 3 pages.

——— to MADISON. *Richmond.*

1784, November 15, Willlamsburg. Reasons why he still remains in Virginia. Wishes to see Lafayette before his departure. His views respecting religious liberty in an article annexed, which he authorizes Madison to have translated and published. Small 4°. 4 pages.

1784, December 5, Williamsburg. Asks the favor of letters of introduction to Mr. Marbois and Members of Congress. [In Italain.] fol. 1 page.

1785, June 3, New York. Will deliver the letters for Jefferson and the marquis in person. Leaves his adopted country with regret. America is his Jove and Virginia his Venus. His views on the measures to be adopted in relation to the proposed constitution of the State. fol. 2 pages.

MAZZEI, PHILIP.

1785, June 15, New York. On the necessity of establishing two ports in Virginia. Will write on this subject, and Monroe will have it translated. Objections of Col. Mason. [In Italian.] small 4°. 1 page.

New York.

1786, August 14, Paris. Acknowledging letter of March 18. Is indignant at the representations made relative to our Government by French writers. Has written some confutations. Intends his book to be translated with the assistance of Mr. Short into English. Respecting the rascally act of Mr. Bohrman in reference to a bill of exchange, and other pecuniary matters. [In Italian.] small 4°. 3 pages.

——— to BOHRMAN, ANT., HENRY.

1787, February 3, Paris. Acknowledging letter of August 15. Does not agree with him in his statement that his disappointment was not his fault. Is confident from declarations of his friends that when he made the draft in Mazzei's favor he knew it would not be paid. Has desired Madison to attend to the matter. small 4°. 1 page.

——— to MONROE, JAMES.

1787, February 3, Paris. Acknowledging letter of August 19. On the subject of Mr. Bohrman's transaction with him. Knows his credit was not good and that his draft would not be paid. Extract from letter from Amsterdam giving directions in regard to the matter which he desires Monroe to act upon in order to make the satisfactory settlement of his obligations with his creditors. small 4°. 3 pages.

——— to MADISON. *Philadelphia.*

1787, February 5, Paris. Incloses letters relating to his business with Bohrman. Informs Madison about his future publication and desires his opinion. [In Italian]. small 4°. 2 pages.

1787, June 22, Paris. In regard to the Bohrman matter, it will be a relief to him when Congress settles its account with Bohrman, for he will then be able to satisfy his creditors, the brothers Van Staphorst in Holland. Asks Madison's kind offices in regard thereto. Refers to Madison's kind assistance concerning his book. [In Italian.] small 4°. 2 pages.

1787, August 6, Paris. Acknowledging letter of April 24. Respecting his book. Relies on Madison's friendship in using his good offices towards the settlement of the Bohrman affair. [In Italian.] small 4°. 3 pages.

1787, December 21, Paris. Acknowledging letter of 5th ultimo. Respecting the matter with Bohrman. Directs Madison about remitting him bills. The progress of his new book. [In Italian.] 4°. 2 pages.

Richmond.

1788, February 4, Paris. His book finally printed. Disposition of some copies for his friends. Thanks Madison for his aid in terminating the Bohrman affair. Review of the matter. Incloses his remarks (in French) in confutation of several publications from distinguished authors in France to

MAZZEI, PHILIP.

the disadvantage of the United States with a request that they be translated and printed. [In Italian and French.] small 4°. 10 pages.

1788, February 7, Paris. Sends copies of his book to be distributed to persons named. [In Italian.] small 4°. 1 page.

1788, May 9, Paris. Sends another case of his books by way of Havre. The conduct of Foster Webb in the management of his affairs. Begs Madison to procure a remittance for him in order to protect himself from the persecution of a bad woman. Settlement of Bohrman's affairs. [In Italian.] small 4°. 2 pages.

1788, July 4, Paris. Asks Madison's aid in procuring assistance from Messrs. Blair and Edmund Randolph, and to regulate the affair with Bohrman. small 4°. 1 page.

New York.

1790, March 23, Paris. Introduces Count Paolo Andreani to Madison's kind notice. He is the first Italian who has made a balloon ascension. Hopes Madison will not hesitate to recommend any of his friends to him if he can be of service. Bohrman has only paid one half of what he owes, and a sequestration has been made in Lisbon on his effects and he will be able to pay his creditors. Asks Madison to send him money from sale of his books. [In Italian.] 4°. 1 page.

Washington.

1803, December 28, Pisa. A long and friendly letter, marked private, recounting some episodes in his history while in Poland and Russia. fol. 4 pages.

1804, August 30, Pisa. Incloses a letter of Guiseppi Timpanari Vijano, not dated. Containing an account of his business with Mr. Jefferson, and of yellow fever in Leghorn. Desirous of obtaining a piece of land near Jefferson's place in Albemarle on which to build a small house and kitchen garden. Asks if he received a letter dated December 10, 1803. In a postscript dated July 24, 1805, he states he has not received any replies to the letters written December 10, 1803, and December 15, 1804. [Copy in his own handwriting. In Italian.] 4°. 2 pages.

1804, December 15, Pisa. Asks if he received a letter from him inclosed in one to the President. Incloses copies two bulletins sent to Petersburg relative to the malady which caused so many deaths at Leghorn and in other parts of Tuscany. Respecting his book. Incloses a letter from Mr. Appleton. [In Italian.] 4°. 1 page.

MEAD, COWLES.

1811, November 20, Washington, Michigan Ter. Incloses, by instruction of the House of Representatives of Michigan Territory, a copy of a presentment by the grand jury against Harry Toulmin, judge of the superior court, enumerating the charges against him of betraying the trust confided in him by the Government, etc. fol. 1 page. 4°. 4 pages.

——— (Speaker of House).

1812. Resolutions of the Mississippi Territory general assembly, approving of the war and promising support. large fol. 2 pages.

MEAD, JOEL K. *Montpellier.*

1820, October 12, Washington. Advocates the establishment of an institution for the instruction of indigent youth of native genius and talents, in the higher branches of literature, science, and the liberal arts. 4°. 6 pages.

MEADE, R. W., to CATHCART, J. L.

1816, February 2, Cadiz. Statement of the present state of Spain, which he wishes made known to our Government. A violent case of transgression on the part of an English brig of war, on the neutrality of the Spanish territory on the American brig *William and Mary*, Capt. Jacob Smith. Importance of our Government being represented by a firm character, invested with full and ample powers. Mr. Morris not a proper person to manage the Spaniards. small 4°. 4 pages.

MEASE, JAMES, to MADISON. *Washington.*

1811, April 5, Philadelphia. Application of Charles Swift for the office of commissioner of loans. States the reasons why he should not be appointed. Gives a sketch of his antecedents. 4°. 3 pages.

1814, October 14, Philadelphia. The means likely to obtain funds to prosecute the struggle now making for our rights. 4°. 4 pages.

MECHANIC.

1814, May 8, Charlottesville. Work to be done at Madison's house. 4°. 1 page.

MEDALS, GOLD.

1814, November 3. Proposed resolution that the President of the United States be requested to cause gold medals to be struck and presented to Gens. Ripley, Miller, and Porter, in testimony of their gallantry, etc., by Congress. 4°. 1 page.

MEIGS, JOSIAH, to MADISON.

1814, April 3, Cincinnati. The subscriber, the surveyor-general, proposes to exchange offices with the commissioner of the general land office. 4°. 3 pages.

1814, September 20, Washington. Suggests the employment of Andrew Ellicott to designate the western and northern boundaries of the State of Ohio. 4°. 2 pages.

1815, March 6, Washington. The surveyor-general to take measures for carrying into effect the law of Congress of May 6, 1812, entitled an act to provide for designating, surveying and granting the military bounty lands. Inclosing a memorandum. 4°. 4 pages.

1815, April 25, Washington. Incloses a letter from Mr. Kerr relative to the road from the foot of the rapids of the Miami of Lake Erie to the western line of the Connecticut reserve. Incloses a plat. 4°. 2 pages.

1815, April 27, Washington. Recommends the exposing at public sale the lands in the district east of Pearl River. Has prepared a proclamation for the President to sign should the measure be approved, which he incloses. Also incloses a letter from the register of the land office at St. Stephens. 4°. 1 page.

1815, August 8, Washington. Incloses a communication from Edward Tiffin, surveyor-general. 4°. 1 page.

MEIGS, JOSIAH.

1816, February 13, Washington. Incloses Mr. Clay's letter to Madison relative to Lafayette's lands. Statement of the lands granted and the patents already issued. 4°. 2 pages.

1816, February 17, Washington. Transmits a letter, recommending Israel Pickens as receiver of public moneys in the land office about to be opened for the sale of the public lands ceded by the late treaty with Gen. Jackson. Has no doubts of his integrity and capacity. 4°. 1 page.

1816, March 5, Washington. Dr. Daniel Drake requests Meigs to present the President with a copy of his book entitled "Picture of Cincinnati." 4°. 1 page.

——— to FREEMAN, THOMAS. *St. Stephens.*

1816, May 15, Washington. The alteration of the plan of survey in the country acquired by the treaty of August 9, 1814. Submits a sketch of the intended survey. 4°. 2 pages.

——— to MADISON. *Washington.*

1816, July 25, Washington. Incloses a letter from Speaker Clay. Has just returned from an excursion to the northward, where he meets some of Madison's friends. 4°. 1 page.

1816, July 8, Washington. Incloses a sketch copied from a vignette which is proposed to be impressed on the patents for bounty lands to the soldiers of the late Army. Suggests an inscription. 4°. 2 pages.

1816, July 19, Washington. Incloses a letter from Mr. Wolcott. 4°. 1 page.

——— to CRAWFORD, WM. H. *Washington.*

1816, August 20, Washington. The facts obtained from the register of the land office at New Orleans about the land claims of Lafayette. [Copy.] 4°. 2 pages.

——— to MADISON.

1816, November 20, Washington. Incloses the copy of a letter from the register of the land office at New Orleans, dated July 15, 1816, and a copy of a letter addressed to the Secretary of War, dated August 20, 1816, relating to Lafayette's land claim. 4°. 1 page.

——— to CUTTS, Mrs. R.

1819, August 5, Washington. Excessive heat in Washington. Record of the thermometer for July. 4°. 2 pages.

MEIGS, RETURN JONATHAN, to MADISON. *Philadelphia.*

1792, February 1, Marietta. Discrimination between the adventitious holders of public securities, and the original proprietors. The injustice of Congress towards the soldiers. 4°. 3 pages.

——— to EARLE, ELIAS.

1807, June 20, Southwest Point. Acknowledging letter on the subject of his claim, and erecting iron works in the Cherokee Nation. Has communicated the design to a large number of the chiefs, who will give further advice after communicating it to the other chiefs. [Copy.] 4°. 2 pages.

MEIGS, RETURN JONATHAN.

1807, December 2. Articles of a treaty between the United States, by their commissioner, R. J. Meigs, and the Cherokee chiefs, to purchase a tract of land, a site for iron works, at the mouth of the Chickamauga Creek, on the south side of Tennessee. [Copy.] 4°. 3 pages.

——— to DEARBORN, HENRY. *Washington.*

1807, December 3, Highwasser. Inclosed, transmitted by Col. Earle, a cession made to the United States by the Cherokee Nation, of a tract of land at the mouth of the Chickamauga Creek for the purpose of an establishment of iron works. Describes the locality and difficulty in procuring the cession. [Copy.] 4°. 2 pages.

——— to MADISON.

1812, January 1, Zanesville, Ohio. Transmits a resolution of the general assembly of the State of Ohio, relating to the foreign affairs of the United States, in which they express their approval of the course of the President, and promise to support him. 4°. 3 pages.

1812, January 18, Zanesville. Transmits copy of a resolution of the legislature of Ohio on the subject of the contemplated canal between the River Hudson and the Great Lakes. [The printed resolution annexed, also a duplicate of the above letter.] 4°. 3 pages.

1813, January 10, Chillicothe, Ohio. Inclosing a printed copy of a declaration and resolves of the general assembly of Ohio approving of the war and promising support to the General Government in sustaining the honor of the nation. 4°. 2 pages.

1815, December 22, Cherokee Agency. Relates to an interview with Correa de Serra. Congratulates Madison on his having successfully conducted the nation through an arduous struggle. 4°. 2 pages.

MEIGS, RETURN JONATHAN, Jr.

1812, November 24, Chillicothe. Report that Gen. Harrison is suspended or superceded in the command of the Northwest Army. Hopes that arrangements may be made to reconcile any difficulties which may oppose his retaining the command, as he fears the objects of the campaign may be lost. 4°. 2 pages.

MELISH, JOHN.

1813, January 5, Philadelphia. Acknowledging letter of December 30. Sends by mail, a copy of the "Travels." Trusts the work will be approved of. 4°. 1 page.

1814, November 12, Philadelphia. Incloses a map accompanied by the documents relative to the negotiations and remarks on the British pretensions, and the effect they would produce if acceded to. Monroe's instructions to the plenipotentiaries an admirable production. fol. 1 page.

MELVILL, THOMAS, to MOLLIEN, ——— (Minister de Tresor Public). *Paris.*

1806, January.—An article written in French, giving his views on public credit. [Copy.] fol. 13 pages.

1816, January 10, Pittsfield. Transmits a diploma of honorary member of the Berkshire Agricultural Society. fol. 1 page.

MENARD, PIERRE. *See* Illinois Territory.

MERCER, HUGH, to MADISON. *Montpellier.*

1825, August 22, Fredericksburg. Expresses his gratification in his late visit to Montpellier, and in meeting Jefferson. 4°. 1 page.

1828, January 17, Fredericksburg. Refusal of Monroe and Madison to serve on the electoral ticket for nominating the President at the convention in Richmond. Wishes they would not decline to serve, as he does not think Gen. Jackson fit for the elevation to that office. Has written Monroe to that effect. 4°. 2 pages.

1833, November 2, Fredericksburg. Takes pleasure in declaring that the board of directors at the bank will make the loan to Mr. Allen, and will always have particular gratification in granting to Madison any and every accommodation he may ask for. 4°. 1 page.

MERCER, JAMES. *Orange.*

1786, May 19, Fredericksburg. Solicits his patronage to the Fredericksburg Academy. The superiority of Fredericksburg for such an institution over other places. 4°. 1 page.

New York.

1790, May 12, Fredericksburg. Acknowledging letter to Mr. Page of April 27. Negotiations respecting the appointment to fill a vacant professorship in the Fredericksburg Academy. Progress of the institution. 4°. 2 pages.

MERCER, JOHN. *Montpellier.*

1834, January 14, Washington. His sister and himself are making an effort to obtain from Congress the half pay of their father, the late John Francis Mercer, who served as an officer in the State of Virginia during the Revolutionary war. Actual proof of the fact from Madison's personal recollections will be of great use. 4°. 4 pages.

MERCER, JOHN F. *Philadelphia.*

1783, August 14. A bill drawn on him (Mercer). Requests Madison to pay it. The question on the return of Congress to Philadelphia. No prospect of Mr. Hartley's mission to terminate either in a commercial or definitive treaty. 4°. 3 pages.

1784, November 12, Trenton. Incloses an order on the treasury of Virginia on account of salary due in payment of a loan from Madison. Regrets the relaxation and inattention of members of Congress. Bad effect abroad. Nothing more ardently desired by the British nation than a renewal of the war with us. Col. Monroe's opinion after a visit to Canada. The scanty and irregular supply of money. The contributions of Virginia to the General Government alone keep the wheels in motion. 4°. 5 pages.

——— to AMBLER, JACQUELIN.

1784, November 12, Trenton. Order on the treasury of Virginia to pay Madison $400. scrap of paper.

——— to MADISON.

1784, November 26, Trenton. Expects an early commencement of business in Congress. Complains of the failure of the legislature to pay members during the recess of Congress. 4°. 2 pages.

MERCER, JOHN F.

1785, February 8, Annapolis. Announces his recent marriage. 4°. 2 pages.

Richmond.

1786, March 28, Marlboro'. Acknowledging receipt of a letter from Richmond. Has sent Madison a statement of his political doctrines to be circulated among his constituents. Desires a strong Government. 4°. 2 pages.

1786, December 23, Annapolis. His opinions on the British debt bill. small 4°. 3 pages.

1787, January 16, Annapolis. Invites Madison to come by Annapolis on his way to Philadelphia. Maryland appoints no delegates to the general convention this session. The question of paper emission. 4°. 1 page.

Philadelphia.

1795, February 11, Marlboro. Introduces his nephew, John Fenton Mercer. Asks his good offices in getting an appointment in the French army. Congratulates Madison on becoming a "Free Mason," (alluding to his marriage.) small 4°. 2 pages.

Orange.

1799, November 14, West River. Apologizes for having neglected to pay a debt to him. Has made arrangements for a settlement by selling some slaves and other property. small 4°. 3 pages.

1799, December 20. Has only realized $200 on a sale of $5,000 of property. If not paid in two days will go to Baltimore and try to get a discount on some drafts, and forward Madison the money. 4°. 1 page.

1800, January 6, West River. Has been taken ill and prevented going to Baltimore. Will lose no time and try to forward money. small 4°. 1 page.

1800, November 10, Annapolis. His pecuniary difficulties. Thinks he will be able to pay Madison this month. His political enemies. Position of affairs in the Maryland legislature. 4°. 2 pages.

1801, January 5, Baltimore. Has the money to pay Madison his debt to him. Asks instructions how he wishes it paid. Prospects of the election. Thinks Burr will be elected by the States. For the good of the Republican party he should withdraw. 4°. 2 pages.

1801, February 8, Baltimore. Pecuniary matters between them. Hopes to be before long entirely out of debt to him. Political opinions. 4°. 3 pages.

Washington.

1802, February 15, Annapolis. Fears for the popularity of the administration on account of certain financial measures. Thinks Madison is deceived in respect to the State of Maryland that its wealth and talents are against it. 4°. 1 page.

1802, November 12, Annapolis. Hears nothing from Madison respecting his promise to inform him of any communications received from Mr. King relating to the bank stock of Maryland. This is to remind him of the promise, and that it would be peculiarly interesting. [Signature cut off.] "Private." 4°. 1 page.

MERCER, JOHN F.

1804, March 20, Baltimore. A French gentleman desires a letter to Madison in reference to a collegiate institution in New Orleans. small 4°. 2 pages.

1805, April 7, Annapolis. In the event of the disturbance in our foreign relations, he offers his services to the Government. 4°. 2 pages.

1805, May 23, West River. Is mortified at a report current that he had applied for a commission in the Army. His letter was soberly predicated on a supposed immediate rupture with France. 4°. 2 pages.

1808, March 8, West River. Gives reasons why he has not before this settled the debt due to Madison. Incloses some money which will be handed him by his nephew, Landon Mercer, whom he recommends to Madison's good offices. His political views. 4°. 3 pages.

1810, February 15, West River. Information received by an eminent French emigré concerning the arrival here of a conspicuous personage from Spain with other supposed agents of Bonaparte. The French gentleman promises information relative to these intriguers. 4°. 1 page.

MERINO SHEEP.

1809, December 28, Badajor. Certificate from notaries public, authenticating a breed of Merino sheep. [Copies.] 4°. 2 pages.

MERRY, ANTHONY, to MADISON. *Washington.*

1804, July 8, Baltimore. Explains his delay in going to Philadelphia. 4°. 1 page.

1804, July 13, Baltimore. Non-receipt of a letter which Madison had directed to be sent to Baltimore. Asks for a duplicate, if necessary. 4°. 1 page.

1805, June 30, Washington. Incloses extracts of two letters from the Governor of Nova Scotia, stating that the effects of the President and Madison, seized by Capt. Nairn, will be forwarded soon. 4°. 3 pages.

1805, August 19, Philadelphia. Transmits extracts of a letter from Sir John Wentworth, governor of Nova Scotia, on the subject of the effects belonging to the President and Madison, with the bill of lading. 4°. 2 pages.

MERRY, PRETTYMAN.

1816, October 17, Buckingham County, Va. Solicits the appointment of Dr. Samuel Merry to the place of surgeon or surgeon's mate in the Navy. 4°. 1 page.

METCALFE & PARKER to MAURY, JAMES. *Liverpool.*

1812, July 28, Liverpool. Bill for two cheeses [for Madison]. 4°. 1 page.

METCALFE, SAMUEL L., to MADISON.

No year, July 19, University of Virginia. A stranger from Louisiana is desirous of seeing the father of our constitution. 8°. 1 page.

MEYER, CHRISTOPHER, to LEE, WILLIAM. *Paris.*

1812, April 16, Bordeaux. Injustice of Great Britain in restricting the trade with her colonies. Gives list of names of those who have obtained licenses. 4°. 2 pages.

MEYER, CHRISTOPHER.

1812, April 16, Bordeaux. Annexes a list of names of licenses of Americans to import colonial produce. 4°. 2 pages.

——— to MADISON. *Washington.*

1813, January 19, Bordeaux. Applies for the position of consul at the port of Bayonne. 4°. 1 page.

MEYER, GEORGE.

1814, May 6, New York. Declaration of Great Britain of the blockade of the American coast, with orders to burn, sink and destroy all that sails under the American flag. Armistice concluded between Bonaparte and the allies. Peace immediately expected. [Unsigned.] 4°. 1 page.

MICHAUX, ANDRE, to JEFFERSON.

1808 August 1, Philadelphia. Has been making researches during the last three years for the object of science. He leaves for France soon and recognizes the kind permission to take passage in a Government vessel, and states the number of parcels he wishes to take. [In French.] 4°. 1 page.

MICHIE, DAVID, to MADISON. *Montpellier.*

1831, December 16, Buck Island. Incloses a paper giving an account of the Belgian and Holland question. Will send pamphlets or papers procured from Washington, which may afford interest or amusement to Madison. 4°. 1 page.

MIDDLETON, HENRY. *Washington.*

1812, November 25, Columbia, S. C. Incloses his last communication to the State legislature. South Carolina is willing to go all lengths in the prosecution of the just objects of the war. Adds that Madison will obtain the undivided vote of the State for his reelection. 4°. 1 page.

MILLAR, JOHN.

1811, June 6, Darien, Ga. Appeal for pecuniary aid. Gives a sketch of his past life. 4°. 2 pages.

MILLEDGE, JOHN (President of Senate *pro tempore*).

1808, February 8. Certificate of the President of the Senate of the United States *pro tempore*, that James Madison, of Virginia, is elected President of the United States. royal fol. 1 page.

MILLER, GEORGE A. *Montpellier.*

1835, February 16, Manchester, Vt. Asks Madison for his autograph. 4°. 1 page.

MILLER, ROBERT.

1829, December 8, Glasgow, Ky. Gives a specimen of writing English words in Greek characters and mathematical signs. Evidently from an insane person. 4°. 1 page.

MILLER, SAMUEL.

1822, January 11, Princeton. Asks his acceptance of a copy of a work by him just published. 4°. 1 page.

1835, January 8, Princeton. Introduces Rev. Daniel Newell, the general agent appointed by the society of the alumni of the college of New Jersey to raise funds for enlargement of the institution. Asks Madison's kind offices and patronage and invites him to their next anniversary meeting. 4°. 2 pages.

MILLER, SAMUEL.

1836, April. Appeal in behalf of Benjamin King, a soldier in the late war. [Copy.] 4°. 1 page.

MILLIGAN, JOSEPH to JEFFERSON. *Monticello.*

1815, March 20, Georgetown. Acknowledging letter of February 27. States his readiness to go to Monticello to pack the books for removal of his library. Directions about packing cases. 4°. 1 page.

——— to MADISON. *Montpellier.*

1818, October 30, Georgetown. Sends a book containing two distinct treatise on gardening and on the cultivation of native vines, and directions about making domestic wines. 4°. 1 page.

1821 (?) not dated. Incloses a letter to Mrs. Madison and a small book for her subscription. Is about to publish a new and correct edition of Jefferson's notes on Virginia. 4°. 2 pages.

1821, May 4, Georgetown. Sends parcels containing 5 copies of historical letters for Mrs. Madison. 4°. 1 page.

MILLS, ROBERT. *Washington.*

1814, March 5, Philadelphia. Asks Madison's good offices towards securing for him the place of surveyor of public buildings. 4°. 2 pages.

——— to MONROE, THOMAS.

1814, September 22, Philadelphia. Recommending the President to have the Capitol roofed temporarily for the purpose of preserving the work that still remains good internally. 4°. 1 page.

MILLS, SAMUEL F., to MADISON.

1817, January 3, Washington. Appeal for funds for a scheme of the directors of an African school in New Jersey for educating free blacks. Asks for an interview at the President's house. 4°. 3 pages.

MINOR, JOHN.

1801, March 31, Fredericksburg. Applies for an appointment under Government for Henry Coleman. States what he knows about him. 4°. 2 pages.

1808, April 25, Fredericksburg. Payment of a claim of the Mutual Assurance Company against fire, for a quota due on his buildings in Orange. 4°. 1 page.

MINOR, PETER. *Montpellier.*

1818, September 15, Ridgeway. Acknowledging letter of 7th. Sends copies of rules and regulations of an agricultural society. 4°. 1 page.

1821, March 7, Ridgeway. Asks him to affix his signature as President of the Agricultural Society of Albemarle to the papers of Mr. Skinner, the society's agent, who goes to Spain. Apologizes for having opened a letter for Madison from Matro de la Serna, supposing that it related to the business in question. 4°. 2 pages.

1822, January 12, Ridgeway. Box of seed sent by Mons. Thouin at Paris. Questions as to the distribution of them. Asks Madison's opinion, and requests his attendance at a meeting of the society. 4°. 3 pages.

1822, October 9, Ridgeway. Incloses an extract of the proceedings of the agricultural society.

MINOR, PETER.

Request of the society that Madison would prepare a circular address to the other societies of the State of Virginia. 4°. 4 pages.

1822, November 5, Ridgeway. Sends copies of the printed address to be franked by Madison and sent to agricultural societies. Asks Madison's suggestions as to a suitable answer to Mr. Thouin for his present of seeds.
small 4°. 2 pages.

MINOR, STEPHEN. *Washington.*

1804, February 20, Natchez. Statement of facts relative to State land speculations in which Col. Cato West was concerned. [See Claiborne, Wm. C. C., February 20.] 4°. 2 pages.

MIRANDA, FRANCISCO DI.

1805, December 10, Washington. Reasons for not calling on Madison at the time designated and asks an interview the next day. 4°. 1 page.

1806, January 22, New York. Thanks him for his kind attentions in Washington. Asks that the important matters, communicated to him be kept secret until the final result of the delicate affair. Has followed and observed with exactness and discretion, and in conforming to the intentions of the Government in all cases. [In French.]
4°. 2 pages.

MISSISSIPPI TERRITORY, HOUSE OF REPRESENTATIVES.

1809, July 8. See Claiborne, Ferdinand L.

MISSISSIPPI TERRITORY to CONGRESS.

1810. Memorial to Congress of the legislative council and house of representatives of the Mississippi Territory, praying the time of preemption claims may be extended. Note attached signed A. G. (Albert Gallatin) remarking that the delay can apply only to the Mobile district. The petition agreed to November, 1810.
large fol. 2 pages, and scrap of paper.

———, to MADISON.

1812, August 12. Adams County, Mississippi Territory. [*See* SESSIONS, JOSEPH.]

1812, November 19. [*See* BARNES, THOMAS.]

1812, [*See* MEADE, CHARLES, Speaker of the House of Representatives.

1814, December 29. [*See* BURNETT, DANIEL, Speaker of House.]

1814, January 11. [*See* BURNET, DANIEL, Speaker of the House of Representatives.]

MITCHELL, JOHN.

1803, April 10, Havre. Forwards dispatches from Livingston. Arrival of Monroe, who was shown much attention from the authorities and has set out for Paris. 4°. 2 pages.

MITCHELL, SAMUEL L., to JEFFERSON.

1801, July 23, New York. Recommends Dr. George Davis as consul to Algiers. 4°. 1 page.

MITCHELL, SAMUEL L., to MADISON.

1803, January 15, Washington. Incloses a letter from John S. Roulet, recommending a Mr. Currey to fill the post of consul at Fayal. 4°. 1 page.

1803, April 28, New York. Third day of the State election. Has great hopes of a victory for the Republican party. fol. 2 pages.

1803, October 20, Washington. Asks for aid and information toward framing a proper bill for restraining evils alluded to in the President's message relating to "regulations to be observed by foreign vessels within the jurisdiction of the United States, etc." 4°. 2 pages.

1804, May 3, New York. Gives the results of the State election. Victory for the Republicans. 4°. 1 page.

1805, May 5, New York. At the solicitation of a member of the board of health in New York, he suggests the importance of instructing consuls and agents abroad concerning endemic distempers in cities or countries where they reside, and to forward to the Department publications relating to the diseases which are called contagious. 4°. 3 pages.

1805, May 28, New York. Introduces Mr. Ewell, of Virginia. 4°. 1 page.

1805, June 12, New York. Introduces Robert L. Patterson, who visits Washington in the view of soliciting a renewal of the commission of his brother, William D. Patterson, as consular agent at Nantes. 4°. 1 page.

1806, May 2, New York. The State election carried by Republicans. Importance of Congressional action on the subject of defences in the harbor of New York. Desires Madison's good offices toward this object. 4°. 2 pages.

1806, July 17, New York. The opinion of Judge Patterson on the requiring the testimony of Madison and the other officers of the executive. (The Miranda expedition.) 4°. 1 page.

1806, July 17, New York. Reports the proceedings of the circuit court, sitting in New York, relative to the Miranda expedition. Question as to the necessity of Madison's testimony and of others in the executive departments. Sensational stories in New York, and difficulty in persuading the people that the administration did not approve or connive at Miranda's and his associates' intentions. 4°. 3 pages.

1811, February 26, Washington. Petition of Capt. John O'Brien for clemency for the penalty incurred in consequence of violation of the embargo laws. 4°. 1 page.

1813, January 23, Washington. Judge Tiffany's description of the peninsula of Upper Canada. He can rely upon its genuineness and authenticity, and thinks it may be useful on the opening of the campaign. 4°. 2 pages.

1 16, December 23, New York. Introducing Dr. Alexander McLeod. 4°. 1 page.

MIX, ELIJAH.

1813 (?), not dated. Plan of a torpedo, which can be explained by the Secretary of the Navy. 4°. 2 pages.

MIX, ELIJAH.

1813, April 8, Washington. Has resolved, with Frederick Weedon, to undertake, by means of four torpedos, to destroy enemy's ships. The first attempt will be made on the seventy-four-gun ship lying off Newpoint. Wishes an appropriation to carry out his scheme. 4°. 2 pages.

1814, January 8, Washington. Claim for services rendered and money advanced for machines to destroy enemy's ships. 4°. 1 page.

1814, January 10, Washington. States that his demand on the Navy Department has not been satisfied. If he did wrong in not applying to the Secretary before he attempted the defence of the harbor he hopes to be forgiven. 4°. 1 page.

MOHAWK, PLAT OF LAND ON THE.

Not dated. Sketch of a plat of land on the Mohawk. [With notes in Madison's handwriting.] fol. 2 pages.

MONROE, ANDREW, to MADISON. *Washington.*

1806, March 25, Laytons. Incloses a letter to his brother James, informing him of the bad management of his farm during his absence abroad, and wishes Madison to forward it. 4°. 1 page.

MONROE. *Richmond.*

1784, November 7, Trenton. Incloses a cipher for correspondence. 4°. 1 page.

1784, November 15, Trenton. Variance between the Indian commissioners of the United States and those of New York. Question whether Indians are to be considered members of the State of New York, or simply living within its bounds. Variance between Great Britain and United States. Surrender of the western posts. Question of removal of Congress to New York or Philadelphia. 4°. 4 pages.

1784, December 6, Trenton. Representation of the States. It is supposed Mr. Jay will accept the office of foreign affairs. Conduct of Spain respecting the Mississippi. 4°. 1 page.

1784, December 14, Trenton. Acknowledging letter of November 27. Question in Congress of appointing a minister to Great Britain. Franklin wishes to return home. Question of impost. Connecticut lays a duty on goods imported from a neighboring State, which affects Rhode Island very sensibly. Whether other States will accede will soon be decided. fol. 2 pages.

1784, December 18, Trenton. Acknowledging letter of 4th. Question of the appointment of a minister to Great Britain. The wish of Franklin to return will be granted. Claim of Spain to the exclusive navigation of the Mississippi. Appointment of a minister there discussed. Nominations for the Treasury. Proposal to invest Congress with the power to regulate commercial intercourse of the States, with other powers, and regulate duties on imports. fol. 2 pages.

1785, February 1, New York. Question of a successor to Franklin as minister. Extract of a letter from John Jay respecting his ideas of his duties in the office of foreign affairs to conform with those of Congress. The nomination of Mercer for the Treasury is withdrawn. 4°. 3 pages.

MONROE:

1785, March 6, New York, Appointment of John Adams as minister to Great Britain. Has letters from Jefferson relative to European affairs. Gives reasons why England will keep out of war. 4°. 4 pages.

Orange C. H.

1785, May —, New York. Acknowledging letter of April 12. Appointments of Adams to Great Britain and Jefferson to France. [Paragraph in cipher.] Recommendation of certain States to raise men for protection on the frontier settlements. Question whether it were not better by requisition and upon the Union. Ordinance regulating the mode of survey and sale of lands ceded in Virginia, dicussed in Congress. Treaty with Indians. On the payment of interest on foreign loans. 4°. 3 pages.

1785, July 12, New York. State debts and requisitions of commissaries, quartermasters, etc., of the United States. Claims of individuals which have been satisfied, should be transfered to the States of which they were citizens. Arrival of Don Diego de Gardoqui from Spain. Suggests a trip to attend the Indian treaty to be held on the Ohio, or to Boston, Lake George, Champlain and Montreal. 4. 6 pages.

1785, July 26, New York. Proposition to invest Congress with powers to regulate trade externally and internally. Arrival of Adams in London and his presentation to the King. Gardoqui here and the Secretary of foreign affairs authorized to treat with him on the object of his mission. Incloses a treatise by Mazzei, in Italian, in favor of the port bill. Has not time to translate it. fol. 3 pages.

1785, August 14, New York. The proposed trip to Boston and Canada, or to attend the Indian treaty. The requisition bill. State debts against the Union. Proposition for a navigation act. [Several paragraphs in cipher.] fol. 3 pages.

Richmond.

1785, December 19, New York. Only six States represented in Congess. Expects the arrival of Mr. Hancock, who has accepted the chair. Objection to the dismemberment of States and doubtful of the propriety of admitting a single new one into the confederacy. 4°. 2 pages.

1785, December 26, New York. Acknowledging letter of 9th. Expediency of Congress regulating the trade of the United States. Monopoly of the trade in the Mediterranean by France, Great Britain and Holland. Mr. Jay's controversy with Mr. Littlepage. 4°. 3 pages.

Near Fredericksburg.

1786, February 9, New York. Subject of the impost taken up and report made by Congress. Has conferred with Mr. Scott on the subject of his lands on the Mohawk. 4° 2 pages.

Orange

1786, February 11, New York. Inclosing a paper containing the report on the impost. Alludes to his approaching marriage. 4°. 1 page.

1786, March 19, New York. Objections of New Jersey to the impost. Impost act passed by Rhode Island and Georgia. Marriage of Monroe. 4°. 2 pages.

MONROE.

1786, May 31, New York. Mr. Jay's difficulty in negotiating with Mr. Gardoqui relative to navigation of the Mississippi. 4°. 4 pages.

Philadelphia.

1786, July 15, New York. Acknowledging a letter from Philadelphia. Trusts to seeing him soon in New York. Purchase of land from Mr. Taylor. 4°. 2 pages.

1786, August 10, New York. Mr. Jay's proposition respecting the Mississippi. 4°. 2 pages.

1786, August 14, New York. Suggestions respecting the negotiations with Spain on the Mississippi question. 4°. 1 page.

1786, August 30, September 1, New York. Proceedings in Congress respecting the Mississippi. 4°. 4 pages.

1786, September 3, New York. Design of the Eastern States in certain contingencies to dismember the Union by the line of the Potomac. fol. 3 pages.

Annapolis.

1786, September 12, Philadelphia. Thinks Pennsylvania will reject the proposition of the separation of the impost from the supplementary funds. Strange indisposition of Col. Grayson. 4°. 3 pages.

Philadelphia.

1786, September 29, New York. Richard H. Lee and Arthur Lee in favor of Jay's project. fol. 2 pages.

Richmond.

1786, December 16, Springhill. Financial private affairs. 4°. 2 pages.

Philadelphia.

1787, May 23, Fredericksburg. Convention at Philadelphia. Private financial matters. 4°. 2 pages.

New York.

1787, October 13, Richmond. Conjectures as to the action of the Virginia legislature respecting the convention in Philadelphia. [Signature cut out.] 4°. 3 pages.

1787, December 6, Richmond. Course of the Virginia legislature respecting the proposed constitution of the United States and the subject of British debts. Mr. Henry's course. 4°. 3 pages.

1788, February 7, Fredericksburg. The course of Virginia respecting the adoption of the constitution. The revenue act and the resolution of the legislators respecting cession. 4°. 2 pages.

1788, September 24, Fredericksburg. Acknowledging letter of 14th. Agrees to the propriety of yielding to the majority respecting the place of residence of Congress. The drawing of a lottery. 4°. 2 pages.

1788, October 26, Richmond. Approves of the conduct of Congress respecting the Mississippi. Has purchased land of Col. Nicholas in Charlottesville and contiguous for a residence. fol. 2 pages.

MONROE.

1788, November 22, Richmond. Acknowledging letter of 5th. Question of the right of the judiciary to declare a law unconstitutional and void. The revenue laws. 4°. 2 pages.

1789, April, Fredericksburg. Acknowledging receipt of a letter on his arrival from a visit to Staunton and Charlottesville. Both branches of the legisture in session. Drawing of a lottery in which he had secured to Madison some tickets. 4°. 2 pages.

1789, June 15, Richmond. Mr. Jefferson's expected return to Virginia soon. Intends removing to Albemarle. 4°. 2 pages.

1789, July 19, Fredericksburg. Acknowledging letter advising of the passage of the tonnage and impost bills by both houses of the Virginia legislature. Conduct of England and France towards the United States. Speculation in the Mohawk lands. Madison draws a small prize in a lottery. 4°. 2 pages.

1789, August 12, Fredericksburg. Acknowledging letter of July 27. Intends moving in a few days to Albemarle. 4°. 1 page.

1790, March 5, Richmond. His inability at present of remitting a balance due Mr. Taylor for purchase of land. Hopes to do so, shortly. Mr. Jefferson in Richmond. The marriage of his daughter to Mr. Randolph. Measures of the house of representatives respecting the public debt. 4°. 2 pages.

1790, June 7, Fredericksburg. Leaves for Albemarle. Introduces Mr. Garnett. fol. 1 page.

1790, July 2, Richmond. Acknowledging letter of June 17. Recommends the appointment of Mr. Dawson as a commissioner for settling the accounts of the United States with individual States. 4°. 2 pages.

1790, July 25, Charlottesville. Acknowledging letter of July 4. Assumption and the temporary and permanent residence of the seat of Government. 4°. 2 pages.

Philadelphia.

1792, May 14. Receipt for money received from Madison. Memorandum of an account. 8°. 1 page.

1792, June 27, Albemarle. Condition of his farm. Clinton elected governor of New York. Disaffection at Richmond on the measures of the Government. The excise tax. 4°. 3 pages.

1792, September 18, Albemarle. Papers sent from Madison to be published. His review and criticisms thereon. Measures of the Secretary of the Treasury. 4°. 2 pages.

1792, October 9, Fredericksburg. Candidates for election of Vice-President. His preferences and reasons. 4°. 4 pages.

Orange.

1793, May 18, Albemarle. Col. Taylor's writings on the subject of the bank. small 4°. 3 pages.

1793, September 25, Albemarle. Doubtful if he goes to Fredericksburg; if he does he will call on Madison on the way. Local politics in Staunton. Jefferson has arrived; will see him. 4°. 2 pages.

MONROE. *Philadelphia.*

1794, February 8, New York. Mr. Kortright's health. Sentiment of the people friendly to France and inimical to Great Britain. 4°. 2 pages.

1794, May 26, Philadelphia. Has given Mr. Randolph no final answer to the President's message to him respecting his appointment to France. Requests Madison's and a few friends' approval or he will decline it. 4°. 1 page.

1794, June 17, Baltimore. Authorizes Madison to receive from or draw on Gen. Wilkinson for money; also to obtain from Gen. Bradley what is due from a sale of Vermont property. Matters respecting the claim under the will of Mr. Kortright, his late father-in-law. 4°. 1 page.

1794, September 4, Paris. Describes his voyage and reception by the convention, where he addressed them, and the effect of it. [The latter part of the letter missing.] 4°. 4 pages.

1794, September 20, Paris. Introduces Mr. Swan, of Boston, agent of the French Government in America. 4°. 1 page.

1794, November 30, Paris. Tranquility in Paris since the fall of Robespierre. Carrère yielded up by the convention to trial before the revolutionary tribunal. Prospects brightening up for France. Probability of their taking possession of Holland. The present is the moment for our Government to act with energy in putting the British beyond the Lakes and opening the Mississippi. The mission of Jay embarrasses Monroe's movements in France. Letter from Gardoqui. Monroe urges France to not make peace with Spain until the Mississippi be opened. Suggests a loan to France. Skipwith recommended as consul for Paris and Provost to fill his place. Cautions Madison about Mr. Swan. Offers his services to him and friends in procuring any articles from Paris. Gives directions about his land property. T. Paine is visiting him. 4°. 8 pages.

1794, December 18, Paris. Transmitting letter to the Secretary of State, and two others to be addressed by Madison if he thinks proper. 4°. 1 page.

1794, December 18, Paris. Incloses three letters, one for Mr. Randolph (Secretary of State), and two for whom Madison may think best to direct them, they being left open for his inspection, to to be delivered or suppressed as he may decide. The French Republic in a flourishing conditon. Wise, humane and just in its councils and eminently successful in its armies. fol. 2 pages.

——— to RANDOLPH, EDMUND, Secretary of State.

1794, December 18, Paris. Statements in the British papers that Mr. Jay had adjusted the points in controversy between that country and the United States. Expresses his uneasiness that this accommodating disposition in the cabinet of St. James, if it exists, is owing to the successes of the French arms. 4°. 7 pages.

1794, December 18, Paris. Duplicate of the foregoing. 4°. 7 pages.

1795, February 12, Paris. Defence of Monroe on Randolph's criticism of his address to the national convention of the French. [Copy.] 4°. 8 pages.

MONROE to MADISON.

1795, February 18, Paris. Acknowledging letter of December 4. Randolph's severe criticism on Monroe's address to the national convention. Defends his conduct. fol. 4 pages.

1795, February 25, Paris. Inclosing a copy of his defense on Randolph's criticism of his address to the national convention. 4°. 3 pages.

1795, June 13, Paris. Acknowledging letter of March 4. Awkward position in which he is placed on account of the withholding from him the facts relating to Jay's treaty. Mr. Jay's conduct. Changes in the French constitution of 1793, based on our principle, a division of the legislature into two branches. Asks Madison to show all his communications to Jefferson and others. 4°. 4 pages.

1795, June 30, Paris. Inclosing a copy of the [French] constitution reported by the committee of 11, to be discussed in a few days. The character of Americans doing business in Paris. Character of Swan—his monopolies. The conduct of Great Britain. We should retaliate by seizing their vessels and property. fol. 2 pages.

1795, July 26, Paris. Sends portion of a letter in cipher by private hand, not being able to finish it in time. It is a defence against unjust attacks. To be shown to Jefferson and Mr. Jones. 4°. 1 page.

1795, September 8, Paris. Acknowledging letter of May 2. Comments on the Jay treaty, followed by a portion of the letter in cipher. Remarks on the constitution reported by the committee of 11 of the convention of the French Republic. 4°. 7 pages.

1795, October 24, Paris. Incloses copy of a letter to Mr. Randolph and of correspondence with Mr. Jay relative to the treaty. The French obtain a naval victory in the Mediterranean. Denunciation of Tallien in the convention against Boissy d'Anglas and others. Change in the government expected. Situation of Paris. Attempt to vindicate Mr. Jay for his misconduct in the negotiations with Mr. Gardoqui. The French receive a check on the Rhine. 4°. 6 pages.

——— to WALCOTT, OLIVER.

1796, January 14, Paris. Extract of a letter to the Secretary of the Treasury exculpating Fulwer Skipwith from any negligence in relation to the robbery of money belonging to the United States from his house. [Not signed. Copy.] 4°. 1 page.

——— to MADISON.

1796, January 20, Paris. Thomas Paine's residence with Monroe in Paris since his release from prison. Monroe's request to him to not write political articles while accepting his hospitality is unheeded. Affairs in France and the continent. China and furniture purchased for Madison. The request of an English subject for passports from the French Government declined by Monroe. Etiquette as to first visit. Suggests the importance of a fleet, and to fortify our coasts so that we may have our just weight upon the scale of nations and be respected. 4°. 6 pages.

MONROE.

1796, May 7, Paris. Resentment of France caused by our treaty with Great Britain. The successful campaign in Italy. 4°. 2 pages.

1796, July 5, Paris. A great portion of this letter in cipher and untranslated. Italy entirely subjugated and peace made with all the powers. Considerable sums of money and works of art to be delivered up to France. State of Europe. Conduct of Thomas Paine respecting articles written while enjoying Monroe's hospitality calculated to compromise him. [Unsigned.] fol. 4 pages. 4°. 1 page.

——— to SKIPWITH, FULWAR. Paris.

1796, July 23, Paris. Acknowledging letter of 20th. From Monroe's knowledge of facts he takes pleasure in inclosing an extract of his letter to the Secretary of the Treasury, giving an account of the robbery of money belonging to the United States, exculpating him from the charge of not taking proper precautions. [Copy.] 4°. 1 page.

——— to PICKERING, TIMOTHY. *Philadelphia.*

1796, September 10, Paris. Acknowledging letter of June 13. In vindication of the charges of neglect of duty in omitting, as stated, to dissipate by a timely and suitable application of the lights in his possession of the discontent of the French Government on account of our late treaty with England. [Unsigned.] 4°. 10 pages.

——— to MADISON.

1796, September 1, Paris. Entirely in cipher, undeciphered. 4°. 2 pages.

1796, September 26, Paris. Bonaparte's continued success in Italy. Remarks in cipher respecting Pickering's letter to himself and an insolent one to Skipwith. 4°. 2 pages.

——— to FRANCE, MINISTER OF FOREIGN AFFAIRS OF.

1796, October 12, Paris. Acknowledging letter of 7th, announcing that the directoire executif had suspended Mr. Adet's functions as minister plenipotentiary to the United States, also that orders had been given that the armed ships of the Republic should treat our vessels in the same manner as the English treat them. Awaits instructions from our Government. [Copy.] 4°. 3 pages.

——— to MADISON.

1796, November 15, Paris. Inclosing correspondence with Timothy Pickering, Secretary of State, relating to the complaints of the French Government against that of the United States. Considers the measures of Pickering precipitate. Alludes to the address of American citizens resident in Paris, expressive of their favorable sentiments towards Monroe. Asks Madison's opinion respecting the publication of this correspondence. Conjectures as to Pickering's motives. Probabilities of France and England making peace. 4°. 2 pages.

1797, January 8, Paris. Received notice of his recall in November and took leave of the French Government on January 1. Intends returning home in April. Incloses copy of his address and the

MONROE.

President's reply. Intends going to Holland before returning. 4°. 2 pages.

——— to JEFFERSON.

1797, July 12, New York. Arrived two days since. Proposes to go to Philadelphia and stay a fortnight and then return home. Will retain the result of an interview with the friend of Mr. and Mrs. R. (?) when he sees him. Suggestions respecting correspondence with Mazzei. 4°. 2 pages.

——— to MADISON. *Orange.*

1797, September 24, Albemarle. Is occupied in preparing his narrative to be printed by Mr. Bache. Invites Madison and Mrs. Madison to pay him a visit. 4°. 2 pages.

——— to EDWARDS, E.

1798, February 12, Albemarle. Wishes him, who was in Paris at the time, to state what he knows of Monroe's conduct at a dinner at which it was stated the health of President Washington was not drunk, also of his general conduct while representing this country in Paris, in order to vindicate him from malicious and untrue charges. [Annexed is Mr. Edwards's reply. Copy in Monroe's hand. Unsigned.] 4°. 1 page.

——— to MADISON.

1798 June 24, Albemarle. Incloses a letter from Dr. E. Edwards in reply to a request to furnish Monroe with evidence respecting his conduct while minister to France, in order to vindicate himself from untrue and malicious charges. 4°. 4 pages.

1799, July 13, Albemarle. Assumpsit in favor of Mr. Brooke. The different persons and sums mentioned as concerned. Asks Madison to pay him a visit. 4°. 3 pages.

1799, September 20, Albemarle. Alexander Stewart, brother of Archibald, asks Madison's friendly aid in his pretentions to a seat in the legislature. Is a sensible young man, sound in morality and political principles. 4°. 1 page.

1799, November 22, Albemarle. Suggests that Madison will come to visit him where he can meet Jefferson, who intended to meet Madison at his place, and thereby silence any compromising rumors. 4°. 2 pages.

1799, December 7, Albemarle. In reference to his election as governor he incloses papers on vindication of his conduct while minister to France and authorizes Madison to do what he thinks proper as to their publication. 4°. 3 pages. fol. 2 pages.

Orange.

1800, August 6, Albemarle. Arrival of his family. His child sick with a fever. Shall go to Richmond in a day or two. 4°. 1 page.

1800, August 13, Albemarle. On his return from Richmond he finds his child better. Incloses papers for Madison's perusal and to return them. Fatigue and his public duties will prevent his visiting Madison at present. Invites him and his wife to visit him in Richmond. 4°. 2 pages.

MONROE.

1800, August 14, Albemarle. Inquiries respecting an overseer for his plantation. Has no command of his time. Returns immediately to Richmond. 4°. 1 page.

1800, September 9, Richmond. Acknowledging letter of 27th August. Respecting the engagement of Mr. Macgee as overseer of his plantation. Reports of a negro insurrection not entirely subsided. About 25 have been committed for trial. 4°. 2 pages.

1800, October 8, Richmond. Loan of money from Madison. State of our negotiations with France. Execution of negroes for attempted insurrection. 4°. 2 pages.

1800, November 3, Richmond. Publication of a pamphlet by Hamilton decrying Adams in order to throw the British or anti-Republican vote on Pinckney. [Signature cut off.] 4°. 1 page.

Washington.

1801, May 20, Richmond. Introducing Mr. Davis, from Kentucky, with a request to furnish him with letters of introduction to friends in the Eastern States. 4°. 1 page.

1801, June 6, Richmond. Mr. Callender and the remitting of his fine. Callender's project in entering on the practice of law. 4°. 2 pages.

1802, May 13, Richmond. Introducing Mr. Garevain (?). 4°. 2 pages.

1802, July 2, Richmond. Recommends Maj. Scott to be appointed marshal of the State of Virginia. 4°. 2 pages.

1803, February 22, New York. Preparing for his departure for France. Reports that Bonaparte is to be made Emperor. 4°. 1 page.

——— to LIVINGSTON, ROBT. R. *Paris.*

1803, August 20, London. Guarantee to be paid to France to secure the purchase of Louisiana. Urges Livingston's cooperation. [Copy.] 4°. 7 pages.

——— to MARBOIS, BARBÉ.

1803, August 20, London. Guarantee for the purchase of Louisiana. [Copy.] 4°. 2 pages.

1803, August 20, London. Guarantee of the loan of Hope & Baring in the Louisiana purchase. [The important part of this letter being in cipher, without a key, it is impossible to give its purport. *See* duplicate letter of Livingston to Madison, September 18, 1803. Copy.] 4°. 2 pages.

——— to LIVINGSTON, R. R.

1803, August 20, London. Explains the matter of his agreement to guarantee the loan of Hope & Baring for advance of money to the French Government, in respect to the acquisition of Louisiana, prior to the ratification of the treaty, and asks his acquiescence. [*See* duplicate of Livingston's letter to Madison, September 18, 1803. Copy.] 4°. 7 pages.

——— to MADISON. *Washington.*

1803, December 15, London. Acknowledging letter of 10th October. Part of a letter relating to furni-

MONROE.

ture and plate sold to Madison, and private financial arrangements which he asks Madison to manage. [No signature.] 4°. 2 pages.

——— to SCOTT, ALEXANDER.

1812, May 14, Washington. Letter of instructions for the duties to perform with the Government of Venezuela. [Copy of extract.] 4°. 2 pages.

———to MADISON. *Montpellier.*

1817, April 27, Washington. Intends to visit him the next week. 4°. 1 page.

1817, May 16, Washington. Incloses a letter to Mrs. Madison. Mr. Correa's arrival. His visit to counteract the movements of the Pernambuco ambassador who has not arrived. Mr. Correa expresses himself in strong terms against the insurgents. 4°. 1 page.

1817, October 17, at Mr. Gordon's. Intended to visit Madison, but hearing Mr. Bagot, the British minister, was with him, declines calling. Incloses a copy of a private letter to Gen. Jackson. 4°. 2 pages.

1817, November 24, Washington. Is busily occupied in preparing his message for Congress. The question respecting canals and roads, and proposals to institute seminaries of learning. Intends to recommend breaking up the establishments at Amelia Island and Galveston. Improved condition of the Treasury. 4°. 2 pages.

1817, December 22, Washington. Acknowledging letter of 9th. Breaking up of the piratical establishments at Amelia Island and Galveston. Respecting Indian titles. Roads and canals. 4°. 3 pages.

1818, February 13, Washington. Proceedings in Congress. Affairs of the Spanish colonies and the conduct of the Government towards them. The recognition of Buenos Ayres. The suppression of Amelia Island establishment. The cession of East Florida to the United States. Spain applies to the principal powers of Europe to mediate between the United States and Spain, and Great Britain intimates her willingness to interpose. Our affairs with Holland. 4°. 3 pages

1818, April 28, Washington. Proceedings of the late Congress. Questions involving the right of Congress to make roads and canals. The policy of the Executive respecting South America. The Emperor of Russia's instructions to his ministers to designate the manner in which he wishes the disputes between Spain and Portugal to be settled. Our commissioners to Buenos Ayres. Reports in Rio Janeiro that the diplomatic corps and the court had circulated reports that recognizing the independence of Buenos Ayres was the object of the mission. 4°. 3 pages.

1818, May 18, Washington. Sends papers giving full account of the views of the allies respecting South America. 4°. 1 page.

1818, July 10, Little River, Loudoun County. Gen. Jackson's report of his proceedings in Florida. He imputes the whole cause of the Semniole war to the interference by the Spanish authorities in the Floridas of the Indians, together with that of foreign adventurers. Our commissioners at Bue. nos Ayres well received; have left for home- Victory of the patriots. Royal army destroyed at Val Ravassi. 4°. 2 pages.

1818, July 20, Washington. Acknowledging letter of 17th. His intention to visit Madison. Onis demands whether the Spanish ports were taken by Gen. Jackson on the order of this Government; if not, they should be surrendered and the general punished. No answer given yet. Jackson not authorized. He charges the governor of Pensacola with a breach of neutrality in stimulating the Indians to war and furnishing the means. This furnishes an opportunity to charge the governor with aggression. 4°. 2 pages.

1818, July 22, Washington. Sends copy of his letter to Gen. Jackson which gives the Executive's views on the subject of the Spanish ports. 4°. 1 page.

1818, July 23, Washington. Omitted to send copy of his letter to Gen. Jackson which he now incloses. Probably sent some other paper. 8°. 1 page.

1818, September 27, Highland. Incloses a letter from Mr. Rush giving a view of our present relations with England. Hopes to visit Madison on his way to Washington. 4°. 1 page.

1818, October 5, Highland. Acknowledging letter of 2d. Will visit Madison in a day or two. Will go to Washington as soon as possible. Mr. Crowninshield, Secretary of the Navy, has resigned. Thinks of offering the office to Mr. Snider, of Pennsylvania. 4°. 1 page.

1818, November 23, Washington. Incloses papers from Mr. Rush giving the latest intelligence from England. Also copy of papers relating to our affairs with Spain. Our attitude with the allies in respect to South America favorable. 4°. 2 pages.

1818, December 21, Washington. Introducing Gen. King, of the district of Maine, in Massachusetts. 4°. 1 page.

1819, March 18, Washington. Introducing Mr. Vaughan, of Kennebec, Maine, a confidential friend of the Marquis of Landsdown and Franklin. 4°. 1 page.

1819, September 10, Oak Hill. Rival candidates for a Government position in South Carolina. A vacancy in the office of collector in Alexandria applied for by the son of Col. Simmes, the late collector. 4°. 4 pages.

1819, October 20, Oak Hill. Settlement of his administration on the estate of the late Judge Jones. Incloses three receipts of money. The King of Spain declines to ratify the treaty, but will send a minister to ask explanations. 4°. 3 pages, and 3 strips of paper.

1819, November 24, Washington. Settlement of the accounts of the late Judge Jones. The treaty with Spain unsettled. If the King does not ratify we can not decline taking possession of Florida. 4°. 2 pages.

1819, December 7, Washington. Sends copy of the message to Congress. Affairs with Spain have been placed on the best ground and hopes to secure the object desired without war. 4°. 1 page.

MONROE.

1820, May 3, Washington. Our troubles with Spain not ended. The minister not authorized to do more than ask explanations respecting the treaty. States his Government will not be satisfied unless the United States stipulates that they will not recognize the South American colonies until recognized by other powers. 4°. 1 page.

1820, December 18, Washington. Reports from Mr. Rush in London that the treaty with Spain had been ratified by the King. 4°. 1 page.

1821, January 19, Washington. Introducing Mr. Laurence and Mr. Jones, of New York. 4°. 1 page.

1821, March 31, Washington. Receives quantities of newspapers from all parts of the Union which he never reads. Understands that Madison also received them, and on his retirement bills of subscription were presented for the eight years. Asks him if that was a fact, and, if so, will stop them. The troubles in organizing a government in Florida. Has only appointed the governor, Gen. Jackson. 4°. 3 pages.

1821, May 19, Washington. Appointment of Gen. Pegram as marshal. Would have appointed Robert Taylor had he known of his desiring it. Has at length made the arrangements and appointments for carrying into effect the treaty with Spain. Names the appointments. Baron de Neuville has been negotiating a commercial treaty with Mr. Adams without any prospect of success. Termination of the Neapolitan movement. 4°. 4 pages.

1822, March 9, Washington. Acknowledging a letter and excuses himself for not writing oftener on account of want of time. Refers him to the "Intelligencer," in which is printed his message to Congress. 4°. 1 page.

1822, August 4, Highland. Will be with Madison the next day. Asks him to examine the subject of preliminary nominations between the Senate and himself. Sends him the material papers. 4°. 1 page.

1823, June 28, Washington. Allowances for expenses of Mr. Morris in Spain. Gallatin arrived in New York. Nothing done in favor of our claims against the French Government. Affairs in Spain. Commodore Porter suppresses the pirates in the West Indies. 4°. 2 pages.

1823, August 29, Oak Hill. His visit to Albemarle prevented by illness of Mrs. Monroe. 4°. 1 page.

1823, September 3. Sale of his land. Late intelligence from Spain by way of Gibraltar. Mr. Rodney speaks in desponding terms of the affairs of Spain. small 4°. 2 pages.

1823, September 20, Highland. Expects to be with Madison the next week. Incloses a letter from Judge Nelson respecting affairs in Spain. 4°. 1 page.

1824, January 18, Washington. Introducing Richard H. Lee, grandson of the Revolutionary character of that name. Is writing a biography of his ancestor and thinks Madison may give him useful information. 4°. 1 page.

1824, January 26, Washington. South American affairs. It is presumed that the allied powers will

MONROE.

make no attempt in favor of Spain for their subjugation. The correspondence between the Secretary of War and Gen. Jackson. Jackson's feelings towards Madison are friendly.
4°. 2 pages.

1824, March 27, Washington. The Senate confirms the nomination of Mr. Conway to a land office in Alabama. Nomination of James Robertson to the vacancy at Petersburg. Percival nominated to the professorship of chemistry at West Point.
4°. 2 pages.

1824, April —, Washington. The claim of Virginia for the payment of the interest paid by her for moneys borrowed, and paid to the militia in the late war. Refers him to a letter to Jefferson respecting a movement of Georgia members of Congress relating to the compact of 1802 extinguishing the Indian rights to lands within the limits of that State. The Missouri compromise.
4°. 2 pages.

1824, May 10, Washington. Introducing Mr. Sullivan, son of the late governor of Massachusetts.
4°. 1 page.

1824, August 2, Washington. Arrival of Gen. Clark with 20 Indian chiefs to consult on points relating to the new government to the South. The connection with Russia for adjustment of differences respecting the Northwest coast. Mrs. Monroe's poor health. French agent at Bogota to treat respecting its independence. The convention with Russia will be satisfactory to the nation—describes some of its articles.
4°. 4 pages.

1824, October 18, Washington. Visit of Lafayette. Describes him. If possible Monroe will visit Madison soon. The accounts from Russia are favorable. The late treaty relating to the Northwest coast all that we could desire.

4°. 2 pages.

1824, November 11, Washington. Introducing Col. and Mrs. Sullivan of Massachusetts whose intention it is to visit the University of Virginia.
4°. 1 page.

1824, December 9, Washington. Introducing Mr. Ticknor and Mr. Webster, who intend to visit the University. Asks Madison to show them attention.
4°. 1 page.

1824, December 13, Washington. Sends copy of the message and documents relating to negotiations with the French Government for the suppression of the slave trade. Items in his account for compensation in his missions to Europe. The reception by Congress of Lafayette. 4°. 2 pages.

1825, March 9, Washington. Introducing Mr. Owen.
4°. 1 page.

——— to SCOTT, ALEXANDER. *Georgetown.*

1825, July 5, Oak Hill. Expresses his opinion that his compensation for services in Venezuela should have been precisely the same as that of Mr. Poinsett. [Certified copy]. 4°. 2 pages.

——— to MADISON. *Montpellier.*

1825, March 20, Washington. Mr. Wheaton sends a packet through Monroe to Madison. Has been detained by ill health of Mrs. Monroe, but expects to be with Madison in May. 4°. 1 page.

1826, June 16, Albemarle. Proposes to advertise the sale of his lands in this county for the benefit of his creditors. Hopes to pass a day with Madison on his return. 3°. 1 page.

1827, January 22, Oak Hill. Has recovered from a fever. Mr. Causten and French spoliation claims. Offers his land to the bank at a price they will not accept. 4°. 1 page.

1827, April 2, Oak Hill. Acknowledging letter of March 19, with a circular to visitors of the University. Vacancy caused by the retirement of Mr. Key from a professorship. Advises the appointment of a native and gives reasons therefor. Desire of Capt. Partridge to connect his military academy to the University. 4°. 2 pages.

1827, September 23, Oak Hill. Incloses a letter from a gentleman of Bladensburg, applying for the professorship held by Mr. Long. Mr. Gallatin's views respecting the source from which instructors in colleges should be brought. Qualifications of Dr. Jones of Philadelphia. Sale of Monroe's slaves to take place in November. 4°. 2 pages.

1827, October 3, Oak Hill. Acknowledging letter of September 22. Armstrong's provisional letter to Gen. Jackson of July 18, 1814, to take possession of Pensacola. Refers to a communication of Judge White, of Tennessee, respecting an attack on Monroe, charging him with neglect of duty in not furnishing supplies to troops for defence of New Orleans. The deposit of arms in New Orleans. 4°. 3 pages.

1827, November 2, Oak Hill. Acknowledging letter of October 29. Continuation of the subject of Armstrong's letter to Gen. Jackson respecting the order to take Pensacola, and Monroe's defence to charges of neglect to support him at New Orleans with supplies. 4°. 3 pages.

1827, December 1, Oak Hill. Incloses letter to Gen. Jackson of October 21, 1814, and one from Mr. Ingersoll relating to Madison's views respecting the power of Government to encourage domestic manufactures. Has received a letter from Col. Mercer referring to nomination of himself and Madison as delegates to the convention for nominating candidates for the Presidential election. Approves of their neutrality. 4°. 1 page.

1827, December 10, Oak Hill. Acknowledging letter of 2d, with papers relating to the application of J. B. Harrison to obtain the appointment held by Mr. Long in the University. Inclosing letters from Col. Mercer respecting the contemplation of appointing himself and Madison on the electoral ticket. Monroe's views on the subject. 4°. 2 pages.

1828, January 18, Oak Hill. Himself and Madison placed on the electoral ticket. He will decline to serve, and wishes to know what course Madison will take. 4°. 2 pages.

1828, January 29, Oak Hill. In reference to their nomination to the electoral ticket on which they both decline to serve. 4°. 2 pages.

MONROE.

1828, February 13, Oak Hill. Acknowledging letter of 5th. In absence of the official notification of his and Madison's nomination on the electoral ticket, proposes to address a communication to the public declining to serve. 4°. 2 pages.

1828, February 15, Oak Hill. Thinks it advisable to communicate their refusal to serve on the electoral ticket to Judge Brooke and have their letters published. Mrs. Monroe very seriously indisposed. 4°. 2 pages.

1828, March 28, Oak Hill. Acknowledging letter of the 20th. Mrs. Monroe's indisposition. Embarrassments at the University relating to the vacant professorship. Sends copy of his memoir. Has sold his slaves, and obtained with the proceeds a release of a debt to J. J. Astor, who loaned him money during the late war. 4°. 2 pages.

1828, May 31, Oak Hill. Incloses letters from Mr. Tracie soliciting the professorship at the University, and the other from Mr. Duponceau in support of his application; also one from Mr. Peters to the same effect. Proposes to accompany Mrs. Monroe to New York to visit Mr. Gouverneur and their daughter, and will stop in Washington to pay his respects to the President. 4°. 2 pages.

1828, June 16, New York. Acknowledging letter of 3d. Proposes to return in time to attend the meeting of the board of visitors of the University. Incloses letter from Mr. Hassler, a candidate for the professorship of natural philosophy. Mrs. Monroe's health being restored. [Signature cut off.] 4°. 1 page.

1828, August 5, Oak Hill. Mrs. Monroe's health improved. Sends Madison some buckles. Asks to be sent a plan of police for the University. The weather and crops. 4°. 2 pages.

1828, December 24, Oak Hill. Introducing Mr. Elliott Cresson. [Signature cut off.] fragment of 4°. 1 page.

1829, March 20, Oak Hill. Lately recovered from a fever arising from his horse's falling and injuring him severely. Mr. Giles's attacks on Madison will do him no injury. Hears Madison has been nominated as a candidate for the Richmond convention and declined. A like nomination has been made of himself, and thinks he will follow his example. 4°. 2 pages.

1829, April 28, Oak Hill. Answers an application from citizens of Leesburg to know if he would act in the convention, if elected; that he would with conditions. His health improving as well as Mrs. Monroe's. 4°. 2 pages.

1829, June 25, Oak Hill. Has been indisposed, but hopes to be able to attend the meeting of visitors at the University. His granddaughter to be married on February 5 to Mr. Rogers, of Baltimore. Proposes to meet Madison on February 8 at the latter's house to attend the meeting of visitors. [Signature cut off.] 4°. 1 page.

1829, September 10, Oak Hill. Hopes Madison will be able to attend the convention, and to meet him there if he goes himself. Thinks it will have a useful effect. Mrs. Monroe will be unable to accompany him. 4°. 1 page.

MONROE, JOHN. *Washington.*

1806, October 15, Paris, Ky. Incloses a letter for Col. Monroe. Gives his views on the state of the country. Its prosperity owing to the acquisition of Louisiana. Suggests the importance of obtaining the Floridas. Jealousy of France and Great Britain towards the United States.
4°. 3 pages.

MONTAGUE, ABRAHAM.

1815, October 21, Middlesex County, Va. Appeal for pecuniary aid. fol. 2 pages.

MONTGOMERY, JAMES.

1807, July 13, Philadelphia. Deposition of James Montgomery respecting his son, William Griffith Montgomery, an American citizen, impressed on board a British ship, in the India seas, called the *Alfred*. Attached is certificate of British consul-general at Philadelphia.
4°. 2 pages. small 4°. 1 page.

MONTGOMERY, JOHN. *Philadelphia.*

1795, November 28, Carlisle. Introducing Rev. David Beard. 4°. 1 page.

Washington.

1808, April 29, Belle Air. Incloses an extract of a letter to Mr. Pinckney. The subject of the extract is about the approaching election and his opinions as to the merits of Madison.
4°. 2 pages.

1812, August 9, Baltimore. The origin, extent, and progress of the late disturbances in this place. Now no occasion for alarm for the safety of the post-office. 4°. 2 pages.

MONTGOMERY, WILLIAM.

1812, August 25, Philadelphia. Thinks we can make an honorable peace. Believes that Great Britain is at this moment disposed to it. The conduct of France very unfriendly. Privateers preying on our commerce. 4°. 3 pages.

1810, August 28, Philadelphia. Critical state of our foreign trade. Calls for the spirited interference of our Government. Suggests the arming of merchant vessels, but try conciliation with Spain and other powers. 4°. 2 pages.

1814, January 5, Philadelphia. Satisfaction at the prospect of peace. Distress in our cities.
4°. 2 pages.

MONTLEZUN-LABARTHETTE, BARON DE.

1817 (?), not dated. Appeal from a friend of Lafayette, from whom he brings a letter, for Madison's assistance in obtaining a land grant, he having served, as did his father, in the Revolution. Has a scheme for establishing a poste-volante, by the means of which communications in writing may be conveyed in twenty-four hours from the Capital to our principal frontiers and seaports. [In French.] 4°. 4 pages.

MOODY, JOHN.

1798, January 7, Richmond. Newspaper article implicating a number of his friends, Madison among the number. Asks if he thinks it is worth noticing. fol. 1 page.

MOODY, JOHN.

1802, February 8, Richmond. Asks for the position of postmaster at Richmond. 4°. 1 page.

MOOERS, BENJAMIN, and PETER SAILLY.

1814, March 19, Plattsburg. Reports that Gen. Wilkinson will be arrested or recalled from his command. Some of the principal inhabitants of these Northern counties contemplate addressing Madison on this subject, and express sentiments favorable to the general. 4°. 2 pages.

MOORE, ANDREW.

1800, September 14. Introducing Col. Alexander Mc Nat. small 4°. 1 page.

MOORE, GABRIEL. *Montpellier.*

1832, February 28, Washington. Incloses a letter from his brother, Matthew Moore, and requests that if he possesses any information touching the subject to which the letter refers that he will intimate that information to him and his brother. 4°. 1 page.

MOORE, ISAAC. *Washington.*

1810, January 9, Bridgetown, Rahway, N. J. Inclosing a genealogical tree showing that his grandfather had 192 descendants, and whose names he gives. fol. 1 page. royal fol. 1 page.

MOORE, JOHN. *Philadelphia.*

1792, March 17, Carlisle. Money in Madison's hands, to be paid to himself, deposited by his father. small 4°. 1 page.

1792, May 1, Carlisle. Asks him to send him money as authorized by his father. 8°. 1 page.

1794, January 9, Carlisle. Asks him to send him some money. [Note at foot in Madison's hand "the money sent."] small 4°. 1 page.

MOORE, MATTHEW. *Montpellier.*

1832, February 17, Stokes County, N. C. Asking information relative to a transfer of land of Samuel Dalton, in a land speculation company, to Madison. fol. 2 pages.

MOORE, ROBERT.

1830, March 13, Buckingham County. Tobacco seeds sent Madison. fol. 1 page.

MOORE, THOMAS. *Washington.*

1802, April 2, Retreat, Brookeville. Pamphlet deposited in Madison's office relating to agriculture. Requests Madison to read it and if he approves, to mention it to members of Congress to promote its circulation. 4°. 1 page.

1802, August 8, Retreat. Incloses a certificate from the farmers society in this neighborhood. 4°. 1 page.

MOORE, WILLIAM. *New York.*

1788, January 31, Orange. Impresses on Madison the disadvantage of his being absent at the time of the election; urges him to return certainly by March 1 [On same sheet as letter from J. Madison (Senior) to Madison, January 30, 1788.] fol. 1 page.

MOREAU, CESAR.

1830, April 5, Paris. Printed notice of Madison's appointment as a member of the "Société française de statistique universelle." 4°. 1 page.

MORFIT, HENRY M., to MADISON *Montpellier.*

1834, January 22, Washington. Settlement of Robert C. Jennings's accounts with the Government. Asks Madison to review a copy of Gen. Armstrongs' evidence and to add such information as he can. 4°. 4 pages.

MORRIS, ANN C.

Not dated. Asks Madison to get some of his friends to see Edmund Randolph; to read inclosed letters respecting Mr. Ogden, who has swindled her innocent babe of half his patrimony, and also wishes to deprive him of his name, also. 4°. 1 page.

Washington.

1815, May 22, Morrisania. Recommends as consul at Gibraltar, Mr. Samuel Larned, of Providence. 4°. 1 page.

MORRIS, ANTHONY.

1812, July 20, Philadelphia. Wishes the appointment of consul at Lisbon. 4°. 1 page.

1813 April 29, Philadelphia. Admiral Warren's objections to Morris's Bermuda mission. 4°. 1 page.

1813, May 10, Bristol. Acknowledging letter of 5th. Will see him in a few days. 4°. 1 page.

1813, 1814, 1815, and 1816. Account with the United States of the contingent expenses of his agency to Spain in 1813, 1814, 1815, and 1816. 4°. 1 page.

1816, March 12. Statement of account with the Government at agency to Spain 1813, 1814, 1815, 1816. 4°. 1 page.

Montpellier.

1826, January 24, Washington. Finds a balance in Madison's favor on the books relative to unclaimed dividends on the stock of the United States. If he can be of service to obtain it for him, to give instructions. [Incloses a memorandum of Monroe's relation to the matter.] 4°. 1 page, and strip of paper.

1826, January 31, Washington. Incloses a statement from an abstract of dividends on the stock of the United States, originally declared at the office of the commissioners of loans in the State of Virginia, returned as unclaimed. 4°. 1 page.

1826, September 6, Bolton Farm. Acknowledging letter of August 31. Has no doubt that the unclaimed dividends of the United States stock belongs to the estate of Madison's father, whose executor will be entitled to receive the amount. 4°. 1 page.

1826, September 20, Bolton Farm. Incloses a letter and blank form from the register of the Treasury to enable Madison to obtain the claim of the executors of his father's estate for a dividend of the United States stock. 4°. 1 page.

1827, May 9, Washington. Invites Madison's attention to some short sketches of the Fellenburg system of education. 4°. 1 page.

1827, May 31, Washington. Incloses a letter from an octogenarian farmer and friend on the subject of Fellenburg institutions of education in the United States. 4°. 1 page.

MORRIS, ANTHONY.

1828, December 2, Washington. Acknowledging letter of 27th. The final payment of a loan certificate. 4°. 1 page.

MORRIS, CHARLES (Commodore), to JONES, WILLIAM (Secretary of Navy). *Washington.*

1813, July 15, U. S. Frigate Adams, Washington's Reach. The wind fair for the enemy to ascend the river. Intends, at daylight, to proceed to Fort Warburton and there await orders. Enumerates the force of the enemy. 4°. 1 page.

1814, May 6, Off Tybee. See William Jones's letter to Madison, dated June 6, 1814, lettered F. [Copy.] fol. 1 page.

MORRIS, GEORGE P., to MADISON. *Montpellier.*

1833, April 13, New York. Intends publishing a national engraving containing likenesses of the Presidents. Asks Madison to lend him his portrait, from which Durand will make the engraving. 4°. 1 page.

1833, September 19, New York. Introducing A. B. Durand, who goes to Montpellier for the sole purpose of painting Madison's portrait, and afterwards engraved for the New York "Mirror," if he may be permitted. 4°. 2 pages.

MORRIS, JAMES P.

1823, July 19, Bolton Farm, near Bristol, Pa. Incloses an address which, if it merits Madison's approval, will encourage him to believe may be conducive to the improvement of the agricultural class. 4°. 1 page.

MORRIS, RICHARD. *New York.*

1789, March 10, Green Springs. The post at the Point of fork (*sic*) it is supposed will be sold to the Government as a place of arms. Wishes to be made victualler for the men to be engaged to keep the arms in proper order. Asks Madison's good offices. small 4°. 1 page.

MORRIS, THOMAS. *Washington.*

1814, June 27, New York. His nephew, Thomas W. C. Moore, would like to be bearer of dispatches for France. 4°. 2 pages.

MORRISON, JAMES, to TODD, THOMAS.

1814, March 23, Lexington, Ky. Attack of Indians on the settlers near Saline. The governor declines to call on the militia to suppress them. Wishes the Secretary of War to order Gen. Howard back to St. Louis, with unlimited powers, to protect the inhabitants against the tomahawk and scalp ing knife. 4°. 4 pages.

MORROW, JOHN, to MADISON.

1809, March 2, Washington. Recommends Robert Hite to be secretary of the Illinois Territory. Incloses a letter from Capt. George Hite. 4°. 2 pages.

MORROW, JOHN, Jr.

1811, March 7, Pittsburg. Is shunned by his relatives and friends, as they say he has a disordered mind. Would like to be sent to any of the Territories and live secluded the rest of his life. fol. 1 page.

MORSE, JEDEDIAH. *Philadelphia.*

1792, February 28, Charlestown. Intends to put in press the second edition of his geography. Asks

MORSE, JEDEDIAH.

Madison to correct any statements he has made in his account of Virginia. small 4°. 2 pages.

Washington

1814, November 25, Woodstock, Conn. Is an old man of 89. Protests against Congress' purchasing Jefferson's library, which consists of deistical and heterodox works. Suggests another method of establishing a public library. fol. 1 page.

Montpellier.

1822, February 16, Washington. Transmits, as corresponding secretary, a copy of the constitution of a society just established, which recognizes the general system of measures which Madison pursued during his administration. Hopes it will meet with his approbation. 4°. 1 page.

1823, February 20, New Haven, Conn. Has read, in Niles's Register, Madison's letter to Lieut.-Gov. Barry on the subject of "A general system of education." Approves of his sentiments. 4°. 3 pages.

1823, April 9, New Haven. Thanks Madison for his valuable answers to the questions sent him relative to the treatment of negroes. 8°. 1 page.

MORTON, J. *Montpellier.*

1826, June 16, New York. Transmits a note from a committee of the corporation of the city of New York. 4°. 1 page.

MORTON, JEREMIAH.

1828, April 2, Fredericksburg. Wishes him to exercise his influence with the executive of Virginia to commute the sentences of three slaves of Mrs. Smith, convicted of murder of a slave. 4°. 2 pages.

MORTON, JOHN A., to MORTON, NATHANIEL.

Baltimore.

1804, February 18, Bordeaux. In view of the possible dismissal of Mr. Lee from the consulate at Bordeaux, owing to the failure of his house, he applies for that post. [*See* letter of Samuel Smith to Madison, May 4, 1804. Copy.] 4°. 2 pages.

MORTON, PEREZ, to MADISON, *Washington.*

1803, July 18, Dorchester. Acknowledges receipt of a letter covering the penal laws of Georgia. His opinions respecting the Georgia claims. 4°. 7 pages.

MOULDER, WILLIAM.

1815, August 28, Philadelphia. Affidavit of Nicholas Thosloff that James Alexander threatened personal injury to him. Warrant issued by Justice Moulder to bring Alexander before him to answer. 4°. 1 page.

MOUNTFLORENCE, J. C.

1796, July 27, Paris. Certificate respecting the robbery of money deposited with Pulwar Skipwith belonging to the United States. [*See* letter of Pulwar Skipwith, July 27, 1796.] fol. 2 pages.

MOUSTIER, COUNT DE. *Richmond.*

1788, March 2, New York. Regrets Madison's departure from New York. Trusts his absence, however, will not prevent his seconding him in his

MOUSTIER, COUNT DE.

search in conciliating the interests of France and the United States. With this view he propounds questions relative to the proceedings of the British Government in a case similar to that of Ferrier, whether he should have been punished according to the laws of England or sent to France, his native country, to be tried there. [In French and English.] 4°. 3 pages.

Washington.

1810, August 2, Well Walk, Hampstead County, England. Recommending B. F. Fauche as consul of the United States at Gothenburg. [In French.] 4°. 2 pages.

MOYES, JAMES, to SMITH, J. ADAM.

1818, February 17, London. Has not seen Mr. Kelsall for two years. Tried in vain to find his address. 4°. 1 page.

MOYLAN, STEPHEN, to MADISON.

1798, April 25, Philadelphia. Will pay the tax gatherer, but must deduct the sum from the rent. Will honor his bill whenever convenient to Madison. fol. 1 page.

1798, June 4; 1799, December 11; 1800, February 18, April 11; 1801, May 20; 1803, May 10; 1804, March 7; 1805, February 11; 1807, January 1, December 3, Philadelphia. Ten letters, relating to the occupation, lease, and payments of rent of Madison's house. 4°. 12 pages.

MUHLENBERG, FREDERICK. Orange C. H.

1798, January 17, Philadelphia. Acknowledging letter of December 28. Claim of Barbara Peters to the house she sold, and the finding of a deed which he copies. Instructions about planting. 4°. 2 pages.

MUHLENBERG, PETER. *Washington.*

1801, July 18, Philadelphia. Solicits the appointment of Henry Irwin for a commission in the Army. fol. 1 page.

MULHALLER, JOHN.

1812, May 3, Easton. The present crisis. Publication of treasonable documents by enemies of the administration. Incloses one for Madison's perusal. 4°. 2 pages.

MULLIGAN, FRANCIS.

1806, October 14, Charleston, S. C. Congratulates him on the result of the South Carolina election. Republican majorities. 4°. 2 pages.

——— to COXE, TENCH.

1813, June 28, Charleston Neck. Soliciting the office of supervisor of the revenue. 4°. 3 pages.

MULLOWNY, JOHN, to MADISON.

1810, October 26, Philadelphia. Sends a pitcher manufactured by the Washington Pottery in Philadelphia, whereof he is proprietor. Asks Madison's patronage. fol. 1 page.

MUMFORD, BENJAMIN B., to MEIGS, R. J.

1814, June 25, Newport, R. I. Arrival of Swedish brig, *Oscar*, Capt. Stewart, with American prisoners. Expedition fitting out at Bermuda, bound to the coast of America with a body of troops. Admiral Cockburn to command the fleet. Thinks their destination is New Orleans. 4°. 1 page.

MUMFORD, GURDON SALTONSTALL, to MADISON.
Montpellier.

1825, August 23, New York. Has published a pamphlet composing a brief view of the honors tendered to Lafayette in New York city and State, the proceeds to be applied to alleviate the unfortunate Frenchmen who have been overtaken by misfortunes beyond their control. Asks Madison to contribute. 4°. 3 pages

MUNROE, ISAAC.

1824, August 13, Baltimore. Republishes the celebrated embargo letter of John Quincy Adams, and sends a copy to Madison. Is zealously engaged in promoting the election of Adams to the Presidency. 4°. 1 page.

MUNROE, THOMAS. *Washington.*

1814, September 23, Washington. Recommending Mr. Mills, an architect. 4°. 1 page.

1814, October 3, Washington. Incloses a requisition for the President's signature for money to pay expenses incurred in consequence of fire and storm of August 24 and 25, to public buildings and property. [Memorandum attached.] 8°. 2 pages.

1816, February 27, Washington. Transmits a general abstract account of receipts and expenditures "in the City of Washington under authority of the United States," under act of Congress of 17th instant, with a statement of the probable value of the public property remaining on hand. 4°. 2 pages.

Montpellier.

1821, December 20, Washington. His son Thomas, wishing to take service in the Russian army, requests Madison's aid in furtherance of this object by addressing a letter recommending him either directly to the Emperor, or to Chevalier de Politica. Incloses copy of a letter from J. Q. Adams to Chevalier de Politica. 4°. 2 pages.

MURDOCK, YUILLE, WARDROP & CO.
Washington.

1807, January 10, Madeira. Ships per schooner *Three Sisters* bound for Norfolk, two pipes wine. Incloses bill of lading and statement of cost. 4°. 3 pages.

1807, January 10, Madeira. Duplicate of the foregoing. 4°. 3 pages.

1807, January 10, Madeira. Bill of lading, 2 pipes of wine per ship *Three Sisters*, for Norfolk and Baltimore. Baltimore collector's certificate. Madison's custom-house entry of same at Georgetown. fol. 3 pages. 8°. 2 pages.

1815, May 13, Madeira. Ships per *Fair American* 2 pipes wine. Inclosing memorandum of insurance and bill of freight and charges. 4°. 4 pages.

1816, February 16, Madeira. Notice of shipment of 2 pipes of wine with statement of cost. 4°. 1 page.

MURRAY, ROBERT, & CO *Philadelphia.*

1795, December 29, New York. Incloses invoice of furniture to be shipped to Philadelphia. 4°. 2 pages.

MURRAY, ROBERT, & CO.

1796, January 11, New York. Incloses bill of lading of furniture for Philadelphia per schooner *Ariel.* 4°. 1 page.

1796, January 20, New York. Acknowledging letter of 13th. Notifying him of the payment of drafts for sundry expenses, attending the importation of furniture from Havre. 4°. 1 page.

MUSE, HUDSON. *New York.*

1789, February 13, Urbanna. Asks Madison's good offices in continuing him in his present situation as naval officer for the district of Rappahannock River. 4°. 2 pages.

1789, February 22, Urbanna. Renews his request to be continued in his office of naval officer. 4°. 2 pages.

Philadelphia.

1794, February 8, Port Tappahannock, Va. Has been imprudent in granting indulgences and by returns from the naval office made himself liable for money, expecting it to be ready when called for. Asks Madison's good offices with the President and Secretary of the Treasury, assuring them that the money will be ready when called for in the course of the next month and will never again be in like situation. 4°. 1 page.

MUSSI, JOSEPH.

1794 (?), not dated. Gives estimates of the cost for marble work. 4°. 2 pages.

1794, June 9. Mentions his brother, Stephen Mussi, a partner in houses in Frankport and Amsterdam, who is disposed to lend any sum to the United States and mentions the terms. 4°. 1 page.

MUTER, GEORGE. *Orange.*

1785, January 6, Mercer, Ky. Incloses some questions proposed by Caleb Wallace, when a form of government is to be adopted. 4°. 3 pages.

New York.

1786, September 23, Mercer, Ky. The convention for deciding on the act of separation [from Kentucky]. 4°. 4 pages.

1787, February 20, Mercer, Ky. Acknowledging letter of January 7. Respecting the act of separation. Navigation of the Mississippi. Irritation of the Indians. Their depredations. Fears of the inhabitants. 4°. 7 pages.

MYER, SOLOMON. *Washington.*

1809, November 9, Washington. Transmits a political paper for Madison's perusal and opinions. 4°. 1 page.

MYERS, JOHN, to MACKAY, ROBERT. *Fredericksburg.*

1827, May 2, Washington. Asks him to communicate with Madison respecting his wish for the nomination of his father for the office of collector of Norfolk. 4°. 1 page.

——— to MADISON. *Montpellier.*

1827, May 2, Washington. Solicits a letter in the behalf of his father, Moses Myers, who is put in nomination for the office of collector of the port of Norfolk. 4°. 1 page.

NAVY, COMMISSIONERS OF THE, to CROWNINSHIELD, B. W. *Washington.*

1815, May 19, Washington. Acknowledging letter of 18th. The board of commissioners only claim the execution of the law constituting their powers over all matters connected with the Naval establishment. [Copy.] 4°. 4 pages.

NAVY DEPARTMENT.

1809, August 19. Balances of the appropriations for the support of the Navy and Marine Corps unexpended August 19, 1809. 4°. 1 page.

——— to MADISON.

1810, October 31, Washington. Statement of Navy appropriations showing balance in the hands of the Secretary of the Treasury and the Treasurer. 4°. 2 pages.

1812, July 24, Washington. Statement of the naval appropriations, showing balance in the hands of the Treasurer and Secretary of the Treasury. fol. 2 pages.

NEILSON, JAMES, to MADISON.

1811, February 5, Baton Rouge. Titles to lands in West Florida. fol. 2 pages.

NELSON, HUGH.

1812, January 28. Recommends the nomination of Joseph Jones Monroe to the bench in the Mississippi Territory, the vacancy being caused by the resignation of Judge Fitts. 4°. 2 pages.

NELSON, R., and others.

1809, March 3, Washington. Testimonials as to character and qualifications of Tench Ringgold, who wishes a Government appointment. Signed by the above and Senators and members of the House from Maryland. 4°. 1 page.

NETHERLANDS.

1667–'68, February $\frac{7}{17}$, Hague. Article 11 of the treaty between Charles II, of England, and the States General of the United Netherlands, concluded at The Hague, February $\frac{7}{17}$, 1667–8. [Copy.] 4°. 1 page.

NEUVILLE, HYDE, DE to MADISON. *Washington.*

1816, January 24, Paris. Letter of credence (signed Louis) as minister plenipotentiary from France. [In French.] fol. 2 pages.

Montpellier.

1818, December 3, Washington. Inclosing an extract from the official paper, the "Moniteur," of October 12, respecting convention between the Minister Duc de Richelieu, and the ministers of Austria, England, and Russia, that the army of occupation will leave France on November 30. Gives the sum which France will pay. [In French.] fol. 3 pages.

1819, November 25, New York. Announces his approaching departure for France, and expresses his thanks with kindly sentiments to Madison. [In French.] fol. 2 pages.

NEVIL, F., and others, to MADISON.

1830, February 10, Prince *Edward County, Va.* Announcing the election of Madison as honorary member of the Union Society of Hampden Sidney

NEVIL, F., and others.

College. The objects of the society. The communication signed by Fayette Nevil, Robert Southgate, and Benjamin P. Burwell.
4°. 1 page.

NEVILL, JOSEPH. *Philadelphia.*

1795, December 8, Hardy. Is disappointed in his election as member of Congress. Is devoting his leisure time to astronomy. Is constructing an orrery. Hopes Congress will not follow the example of the Virginia legislature in censuring the President for ratifying the treaty with Great Britain. Thinks he (the President) has done wisely. Andrew Ramsey's claim for services. fol. 3 pages.

NEW ENGLAND BANK.

1814, January 29, Boston. See Massachusetts General Assembly.

NEW HAMPSHIRE GRANTS.

Not dated. Report of a committee to whom was referred the letter of Governor Clinton, relative to certain acts of hostility which had taken place in the county of Cumberland by an armed force under the order of Ethan Allen. Resolution appointing a day to determine on the report relating to the dispute concerning the jurisdiction of said district, called the "New Hampshire grants." [Draft.] fol. 1 page.

NEWMAN, JOHN F., to MADISON. *Montpellier.*

1833, August 16, Woodland, Tipton County, Tenn. Announcing the death of his wife's father, Dr. Robert H. Rose. 4°. 1 page.

NEW ORLEANS CITY COUNCIL. *Washington.*

1:09, June 10. See Trudeau, Charles.

NEW ORLEANS. PLAT OF LAND.

Not dated. A plat of land in the vicinity of New Orleans. Without explanations. fol. 1 page.

NEWTON, THOMAS, to MADISON.

1801, July 1, Norfolk. Capt. Dutton requests him to send Madison a box of cigars. 4°. 1 page.

1802, June 22, July 19, November 28, Norfolk. Three letters relating to private business. 4°. 5 pages.

1804, May 5, Norfolk. The collector about to resign. He recommends his (Newton's) son as his successor. 4°. 1 page.

NEWTON, THOMAS.

1806, November 28, Norfolk. Incloses a receipt for a hogshead of old Brazil wine. Gives his method of fining wine. small 4°. 2 pages.

NEWTON, THOMAS, to MADISON.

1808, June 23, Norfolk. Inclosing a letter from J. H. Fernandez, informing Madison of the arrival at Falmouth of the *Osage*, having on board as passengers, Messrs. Nourse and Lewis. Rumor of the departure of Mr. Armstrong from Paris.
4°. 1 page.

NEWTON, THOMAS, Jr.

1803, July 30, Norfolk. Unsuccessful attempt to procure some crab cider for Madison. Renewed practices of the British men-of-war of pressing our seamen. 4°. 2 pages.

1803, September 12, Suffolk. Order for wine and cider. The British ships of war continue to impress our seamen. small 4°. 2 pages.

NEWTON, THOMAS, Jr.

1804, May 19, Norfolk. Acknowledging receipt of a draft. Offers choice cider and wines for sale. 4°. 2 pages.

1804, September 26, Norfolk. Sends two quarter casks of wine. Dr. Fernandez, of the house of Oliviera, has received a cargo of excellent Madeira. Also port wines. fol. 2 pages.

1805, January 28, Washington. Sends Dr. Fernandez' account for wines. 4°. 1 page.

——— to DUVALL, GABRIEL.

1808, February 24. Introducing James H. Blake. [Copy.] fol. 1 page.

——— to MADISON.

1813, March 12, Alexandria. Objects to appointments of Federalists to office. 4°. 2 pages.

1813, December 29, Washington. Objects to Mr. Corbin as collector at Norfolk on account of his being a Federalist. Thinks no Federalists should be appointed to office. His reasons. 4°. 4 pages.

1814, April 18, Norfolk. Defenseless condition of Norfolk. Thinks in the War Department a right apprehension of its situation is not entertained. The militia should be looked upon as a mere auxiliary force. 4°. 3 pages.

1814, June 27, Norfolk. Sends a box of salt made in Princess Anne County. Republicans pleased at the appointment of Gen. Porter to command at this port. 4°. 2 pages.

NEW YORK CITY, COMMITTEE OF CORPORATION OF. *Montpellier.*

1826, April 26, New York. The city of New York transmits a gold medal in commemoration of the completion of the Erie Canal. 4°. 2 pages.

NEW YORK, HIGH SCHOOL SOCIETY OF.

1827, November 12, New York. Pamphlet containing the third annual report of this society. 8°. 16 pages.

NEW YORK LEGISLATURE to MADISON. *Washington.*

1814, November 5. [*See* Tompkins, Daniel D. (Governor).]

NEY, P. S., to MADISON. *Montpellier.*

1831, October 1. On the gradual extinction of slavery and transportation of blacks across the Rocky Mountains. 4°. 4 pages.

NICHOLAS, GEORGE. *Orange.*

1785, April 22, Charlottesville. The bill in the Virginia legislature respecting the clergy. Asks Madison to write remonstrance and Nicholas will get it sent to various counties. 4°. 2 pages.

1785, July 7. Has received the remonstrance and has caused it to be sent to respectable freeholders for signature. small 4°. 1 page.

1785, July 24, Sweet Springs. Remonstrance to the bill before the assembly of Virginia containing a general tax to support Christianity. small 4°. 1 page.

NICHOLAS, GEORGE. *Richmond.*

1788, April 5, Charlottesville. Conjectures as to the adoption of the Constitution. Importance of the decision of Virginia bearing on the other States. Patrick Henry the almost avowed enemy to the Union. 4°. 4 pages.

1788, May 9, Charlottesville. Navigation of the Mississippi. 4°. 1 page.

Orange.

1788, December. Acknowledging letter of 23d. The Congressional election and suggestions as to Madison's course to secure it. small 4°. 2 pages.

1789, January 2. Acknowledging letter of December 29. Madison's election to the House of Representatives in Congress. Suggestions as to his course respecting a second convention. fol. 3 pages.

New York.

1789, May 8, Kentucky. Accounts of Madison's election to Congress. State of things in Kentucky. Advances made by England and Spain towards Kentucky's seceding and becoming an independent country. Navigation of the Mississippi. Danger of secession if Congress does not defend them from Indians and secure their rights. 4°. 4 pages.

1789, November 2, Kentucky. Acknowledging letter of July —. State of things in Kentucky. Intrigues of Spain and England. Inadequate provisions of the Government for the security of the inhabitants from attacks of Indians, etc. 4°. 4 pages.

1790, May 3, Richmond. Acknowledging letter of February 27. The last act of Virginia assembly on the subject of separation of Kentucky satisfactory. Seductions of Spain. Depredations of Indians. Suggests means to secure relief. 4°. 3 pages.

Orange.

1791, June 20, Spring House. Account of the successes of our volunteer expedition in Kentucky against the Indians. Anticipated success of St. Clair's movements. 4°. 2 pages.

Philadelphia.

1791, September 14, Kentucky. Gen. St. Clair calls for a body of militia. The excise bill will be unjust and unequal in its operation in this country. Thinks it unconstitutional. Asks Madison's aid in getting Gen. Wilkinson on the military establishment. 4°. 2 pages.

1792, February 1, Kentucky. Acknowledging letter of November 24. Constitutionality of the militia laws. Unjustness of the excise law. The tax on foreign rum. The French constitution. John Adam's advocacy of a hereditary monarch and nobility. Remarks on St. Clair's unfortunate campaign. 4°. 4 pages.

1792, May 2, Kentucky. Formation of the new government in Kentucky. The total disregard of property qualifications for voters. The question of slavery. St. Clair's defeat. The Kentucky legislature will probably make application to Congress for change in her judiciary in relation to land disputes. 4°. 3 pages.

NICHOLAS, GEORGE.

1792, September 5, Kentucky. The new government. Movements of the troops. Gen. Wilkinson's appointment. 4°. 3 pages.

1793, November 15, Kentucky. Acknowledging letters dated March and August. His opinion on French affairs. Our relations with France. An attempt in Kentucky to raise an army to go against the Spaniards. Gen. Clarke's proposition to the French agent. Our attitude with foreign nations. small 4°. 4 pages.

1794, February 9, Kentucky. Acknowledging letter of December 15. The situation of America critical and interesting. The conduct of Great Britain and France. The attempts of a body of men in Kentucky to go against the Spaniards fail for want of money. Conjectures as to the course of Congress respecting the Indian war. Gen. Wayne's intentions. Mr. Randolph, the new Secretary of State. Has placed himself in a bed of thorns. Our foreign relations.
small 4°. 4 pages.

1794, November 29, Kentucky. The Northwestern campaign ended. Reported brilliant success exaggerated. Disapproves of the Executive's calling 20,000 American citizens into the field to act against their fellow-citizens. (The Pennsylvania insurrection.) Nicholas's political creed.
fol.. 3 pages.

NICHOLAS, JOHN. *Washington.*

1804, January 1, Geneva, N. Y. Introducing Mr. Moffatt, who obtained a patent and was stopped by a pretended right to the same discovery of prior date set up by Dr. Thornton, a clerk in the Department of State. Wishes an investigation made. 4°. 3 pages.

1807, August 2, Geneva. Inclosing a memorial for the President respecting the probability of war with Great Britain and asking for aid in procuring a depot of arms in this country. Hopes the President will choose to make offensive war.
4°. 2 pages.

1807, August 22, Washington. A summons on himself, Mr. Madison, and others as witnesses in a libel case. Suggests that the annoyance in this case may possibly be avoided by Madison's aid and the matter settled. 4°. 3 cases.

1807, September 7. Has to determine on disobeying a precept of one of the U. S. courts, or attending on a business as inconvenient as disagreeable. Asks Madison to decide on the subject. (Alluding to his testimony in a libel suit.) 4°. 2 pages.

1807, September 8. Acknowledging a letter, which relieves him from a disagreeable dilemma.
4°. 1 page.

1813, May 4. On the subject of taxation. The actual necessity for it at the present time. Tax on distilled spirits. fol. 6 pages.

1815, March 18. An essay on protection to home manufactures, and agricultural productions.
fol. 8 pages.

1816, February 28, Geneva, N. Y. Informs Madison that the court to which he belongs has no cognizance of the causes of the United States. Re-

NICHOLAS, JOHN.

specting the appointment of Dixon to office and matters connected therewith. fol. 4 pages.

1816, May 20. Objects to the appointment of Solomon Southwick as postmaster at Albany. Gives his reasons at length. fol. 4 pages.

Montpellier.

1823, June 20, Milton, Va. Horse-breeding and terms for service. small 4°. 1 page.

1826, February 9, Albany. Introducing Mr. Hallett. 4°. 1 page.

NICHOLAS, PHILIP N. *Orange.*

1800, May 23, Richmond. Since the assembly of Virginia has risen the Executive has appointed him Attorney-General. Asks Madison to make his pretensions known to members of the legislature as is compatible with his ideas of delicacy and propriety. fol. 1 page.

NICHOLAS, W. C. *Washington.*

1801, May 8, Warren. Introducing Joseph Daviess, the district attorney for Kentucky. fol. 1 page.

1802, January 27. Thanks him for his assistance in procuring an accommodation at the bank. 4°. 1 page.

1802, February 4, Washington. Has received from Virginia a remittance which will prevent the necessity of availing himself of Madison's goodness to him. He only requires a part of the sum. Returns the note indorsed by Madison, cancelled, and sends a new one. 4°. 1 page.

Albemarle.

1804, September 14, Warren. Hears with pleasure that Madison and Mrs. Madison will be in his neighborhood soon. Hopes they will visit him. 4°. 1 page.

Washington.

1809, October 19, Warren. Introducing Maj. Morrison, of Kentucky. 4°. 1 page.

No date. Mail day for Detroit. Madison may avail himself of it. Appointment of a general. 4°. 1 page.

1814, December 18, Richmond. Acknowledging letter of November 27. Apologizes for addressing this letter to him rather than the usual way, to heads of departments, as of being of unusual interest. Describes the destitute condition of the militia in Virginia. Perishing on the highways. Trusts that means will be found to defend the State without relying so much on the militia. Suggests means of reducing hardships. 4°. 4 pages.

1815, July 28, Richmond. Applies in favor of his son, Robert Carter Nicholas, to be consul at Leghorn. 4°. 2 pages.

1815, August 14, Warren. When he applied for the appointment of his son, Robert Carter, as consul to Leghorn he supposed the office vacant. He would on no account desire a competent man to be removed in his favor. Thanks him for his kindly disposition. 4°. 1 page.

1816, April 2, Richmond. The State of Virginia, to insure the judicious application of an appropria-

NICHOLAS, W. C.

tion for internal improvements, wishes the services of a civil engineer. Requests Madison to send the name of a gentleman lately arrived from France, of whom Commodore Decatur had heard Madison speak. 4°. 1 page.

1816, April 28, Richmond. Thanks him for his information relating to a civil engineer for the State of Virginia. Asks, in confidence, if he thinks Mr. Latrobe should be employed. Taxation in Virginia. 4°. 2 pages.

1816, May 10, Richmond. Asks if there exists a survey of the sea coast, bays, and harbors of the United States, and whether the services of Mr. Hassler, with the use of the instruments belonging to the United States, could be obtained. An act of the assembly directs an accurate map of the State to be obtained. 4°. 2 pages.

1816, September 30, Richmond. Applies for a clerkship for Mr. Armisted. 4°. 2 pages.

1816, October 18, Richmond. Announces the appointment of Madison as one of the visitors of the Central College in Albemarle. 4°. 2 pages.

1816, November 23, Richmond. An insult to his nephew by Gen. Bissel, to whom Col. Nicholas applied for the hand of his daughter. Difficulties arising between them may result in the inferior officer's disgrace, and he begs Madison's interference, as the general was undoubtedly the aggressor. 4°. 2 pages.

NICHOLLS, ROBERT H.

1809, April 5, New Orleans. Solicits employment. 4°. 2 pages.

NICHOLS, J., Jr.

1810, January 19, near Boston. In view of probable war, he proposes to submit to the War Department an invention of a portable battery properly illustrated. fol. 2 pages.

NICHOLSON, JOHN. *New York.*

1790, February 17, Philadelphia. Incloses letters on the subject of the practicability of discriminating between original and assigned holders of the public debt. 4°. 1 page.

Philadelphia.

1792, October 3, Philadelphia. Candidates for the Vice-Presidency in the ensuing election. Thinks the people prefer Burr to Clinton. 4°. 1 page.

NICHOLSON, JOSEPH H. *Washington.*

1802, November 19, Centerville. Recommends the appointment of Col. Thomas Rodney as one of the commissioners under the late convention with Spain. 4°. 1 page.

1812, May 22, Baltimore. Transmits resolutions of the Democratic citizens of Baltimore. 4°. 1 page.

NICOLSON, THOMAS.

1807, February 26, Richmond. Incloses by mail the third volume of "Callo Reports" and the price thereof to be remitted. Small 4°. 1 page.

NILES, HEZEKIAH. *Montpellier.*

1817, July —, Baltimore. Publication of the "Weekly Register." A new arrangement proposed. Asks Madison's opinion. 4°. 3 page.

NILES, HEZEKIAH.

1818, March 6, Baltimore. Sends the "Weekly Register" from March last. Apologizes for the neglect. 4°. 1 page.

1823, January 19, Baltimore. Will insert in the next week's "Register" Madison's communication respecting the proceedings during the Revolution as to the navigation of the Mississippi. 4°. 1 page.

NIROTH, LOUIS B. de. *Washington.*

1812, October 1, Washington. Is imprisoned for jail fees to the amount of $20, for which he appeals to Madison for assistance. Says he has an important communication to make to the Secretary of War. fol. 2 pages.

1812, October 7, Washington. Has received no answer to his former communication and can not reveal on paper the important information alluded to, as he has taken an oath to that effect, and must perish in this bastile, which is kept by one of the greatest of barbarians. fol. 1 page.

1813, January 15, Washington. Claims he has important information to reveal of benefit to this country. The Secretary of State favors his project, but the Secretary of War does not comprehend. Is in financial difficulties, and requires aid to procure his papers and effects now seized for debt. 4°. 2 pages.

NOAH, MORDECAI M. *Montpellier.*

1818, May 6, New York. Takes pleasure in saying that to Madison and his colleagues the Jews in this country owe many of the blessings they now enjoy. Hopes the impression that his recall was owing to irregularity of his accounts may be removed and attributed solely to his religion. 4°. 3 pages.

NORTH CAROLINA GENERAL ASSEMBLY. *Washington.*

1810, January 1. *See* STONE, DAVID.

1813, November 30, Raleigh, N. C. *See* HAWKINS, WILLIAM (Governor).

NORTHUP, HENRY. *Montpellier.*

1834, July 13, Washington. Asks information concerning the family of the late Samuel Findley, president of Princeton College. 4°. 1 page.

NORTON, J. H. *Orange.*

1785, October 1, Winchester. Acts of the Virginia legislature touching British debts. Submits the matter to Madison's serious consideration. fol. 2 pages.

1785, October 2, Winchester. Continuation of the subject of the foregoing letter and praying Madison's good offices in advocating relief and recovery of British debts due from the State. fol. 1 page.

NORVELL, JOHN. *Washington.*

1814, August 13, Washington. Asks Madison's opinion of the elegibility and utility of a publication at Washington of a "Weekly Political Recorder." 4°. 1 page.

Montpellier.

1826, June 14, Philadelphia. Inclosing Madison's account for the "Franklin Gazette." 4°. 1 page.

NORVELL, JOHN.

1826, June 27, Philadelphia. Acknowledging receipt of letter of 20th with inclosure of amount of subscription to a paper. 4°. 2 pages.

NOURSE, CHARLES J.

1823, November 22, Washington. Asks to whose address he may forward a few Seckel pear trees for himself. 4°. 1 page.

NOURSE, JOSEPH, to MORRIS, ANTHONY.

1820, September 15, Washington, Treasury Department. Official notice of unclaimed dividends from the loan office at Richmond to the credit of James Madison (senior), and authorizing payment to his executor or administrator. 4°. 1 page.

——— to MADISON. *Montpellier.*

1823, April 16, Washington. Items of account presented by Anthony Morris under head of Contingent expenses incident to his mission or agency to Spain. Submitted to Madison's consideration, as Morris was appointed by him as confidential agent. 4°. 2 pages.

O'BRYAN, JOHN. *Washington.*

1811, February 23, New York. Asks a release from prison, he being led into an involuntary infraction of the embargo laws, for which he now suffers for no fault but of his ignorance. 4°. 3 pages.

O'CONNOR, THOMAS. *Montpellier.*

1819, June 11, New York. Solicits Madison's subscription to the "Globe," of which he is editor. 4°. 1 page.

O'CONNOR, JOHN M.

1824, April 29, New York. Transmits a copy of a translation of a "Treatise on the science of war and fortifications." Expresses himself violently against the existing administration. 4°. 2 pages.

OGDEN, ISAAC, to DUANE, WILLIAM. *Philadelphia.*

1808, February 18, Germantown, N. J. Is informed that smuggling flour is practiced in the bay of Passamaquoddy from English vessels to scows. Asks information from Mr. Duane relative thereto. 4°. 1 page.

OGILVIE, JAMES, to MADISON. *Washington.*

1804, March 9, Richmond. Announces himself as a candidate for the presidency of the university about to be organized in South Carolina. Has written to Col. Wade Hampton and requests Madison to converse with him on the subject. 4°. 2 pages.

1808, July 15, Alexandria. Introducing Dr. William Daingerfield, of Alexandria. 4°. 1 page.

1809, June 20, Portland. Has the profoundest respect and esteem for Madison's principles, motives, and talents, and congratulates him on his elevation to the Presidency. Enlightened persons of all parties are disposed to cooperate with Madison in his policy. 4°. 4 pages.

No year, May 18, Augusta, Ga. His intenton to remove to a village in Kentucky to prosecute his literary pursuits. 4°. 4 pages.

OGILVIE, JAMES.

1816, August —, Philadelphia. Transmits a synopsis of a book shortly to be published. Has decided to continue his literary pursuits. 4°. 1 page.

OGLE, THOMAS.

1803, May 16. Agreement to furnish a chariot and the price. Description. Small 4°. 1 page.

1803, August 13, Philadelphia. Bill for a chariot and charges for delivering. 4°. 1 page.

OHIO RIVER, PLAT OF LAND ON THE.

Not dated. Memorandum with a plat showing the situation of property on the Ohio. fol.

OHIO GENERAL ASSEMBLY, to MADISON. *Washington.*

1810, February 22. *See* HUNTINGTON, SAMUEL.

1812, January 1. *See* MEIGS, RETURN J.

1813, January 10. *See* MEIGS, RETURN J.

OHIO, STATE OF.

1809, February 11. *See* HUNTINGTON, SAMUEL, February 13.

OLIVER, JULIUS.

1809, June 3, Marseilles. *See* CATHALAN, STEPHEN, Jr.

OLIVIERA, FERNANDEZ & CO.

Not dated. Bill of three casks of wine and three cases. 8°. 1 page.

———, to NEWTON, THOMAS. *Norfolk.*

1806, November 27, Norfolk. Bill for 1 hogshead Brazil wine, and receipt of Job Palmer of the hogshead, which he promises to forward to Madison. 8°. 1 page. Strip of paper.

OLIVIERA & SONS, to MADISON. *Washington.*

1810, October 25, Norfolk. Acknowledging letter of 14th. Ships Madison a hogshead of old L. P. Madeira wine. 4°. 1 page.

1810, October 26, Norfolk. Orders for Madeira and Lisbon wine. 4°. 2 pages.

1810, November 3, Norfolk. Acknowledging letter of October 29 covering a draft. Inclosing bill of lading of wine. 4°. 2 pages and strip of paper.

OLSEN, P. BLEICHER.

1803, June 21, Philadelphia. Has engaged passage for Bordeaux, to sail on 1st or 2d of July. Offers to take charge of anything intrusted to his care. Thanks Mrs. Madison for her hospitality and gift of an elixer, without which he would have been poisoned. 4°. 3 pages.

1804, December 4, Copenhagen. Has charged the bearer of this letter, Mr. Eikard, Danish consul at Philadelphia, to give full account of all that concerns himself. Sends a small packet to Mrs. Madison containing trifles for the toilet. His attachment and admiration for the President. 4°. 4 pages.

OPIE, LEROY, to WILKINSON, JAMES. *Fredericktown.*

1811, October 9, Fredericktown, Md. Inclosing statement of a conversation between himself and Mr. Simmons respecting a report that Dr. Mitchell was to be appointed Secretary of War, and that Dr. Eustice did not intend to resign unless Wil-

OPIE, LEROY.

kinson was to resume command of the Army. [*See* letter of Wilkinson to Madison, this date.] [Copy.] 4°. 2 pages.

O'REILY, HUGH, to MONROE. *Washington.*

1819, May 2, Fort Alert. Wishes an honorable discharge from service. Recommends himself for a commission in the First Regiment. Gives his references. Recommends to the President his two sons, now in Cincinnati. 4°. 2 pages.

ORR, BENJAMIN GRAYSON, to MADISON.

1801, July 27, Washington. Lease of a slave named Plato to Madison for five years. 4°. 2 pages.

1802, June 25, Georgetown. A servant called Plato in his possession claimed by Mr. Merewether. Leaves it to Madison and Mr. Jones's decision. 4°. 1 page.

1802, June 28, Georgetown. Incloses a letter from Walter Jones respecting the negro Plato. Begs Madison to consult his own convenience in his determination in this business. 4°. 1 page.

OSBORNE, A. L.

1805, May 3, Salisbury. Asks Madison's good offices with the President to procure Government employment. 4°. 2 pages.

———, to SMITH, SAMUEL H.

1805, July 24, Salisbury. Incloses a letter for Madison respecting an application he had made for his good offices with the President to secure a Government clerkship. 4°. 2 pages.

OSGOOD, SAMUEL, to MADISON.

1801, April 24, New York. Suggestions as to appointments to office by the President, and doubts as to republicanism of Mr. Burr, the Vice-President. Should removals be contemplated recommends Governor Clinton. 4°. 2 pages.

O'SULLIVAN, B., MRS. *Montpellier.*

1827, June, Montpellier. Appeal for pecuniary aid. 4°. 5 pages.

1827, not dated. Statement of her life and adventures, to be seen by none but Madison. An appeal for aid. fol. 5 pages.

OTIS, GEORGE ALEXANDER.

1820, June 20, Philadelphia. Presents the first volume of his translation of Botta. Asks for his encouragement in prosecuting the work. 4°. 3 pages.

1820, December 5, Philadelphia. Thanks him for his letter expressing his opinion of the first volume of his translation of Botta. Transmits the second volume, asks his opinions, and requests that he may publish his letter. 4°. 2 pages.

1821, January 4, Philadelphia. Acknowledging letter of December 29. Thanks for permitting him to publish his letter of July 5. Criticisms of John Adams and others on his Botta's, American war. 4°. 4 pages.

1821, January 31, Philadelphia. Acknowledging letter of 17th. Transmits the last volume of the translation of Botta for Madison's approbation. John Adams waives his objections entirely and compliments him in high terms. Other favorable opinions received. 4°. 1 page.

OTIS, GEORGE ALEXANDER.

1823, June 14, Boston. Transmits a work by Mr. Beyle, formerly private secretary of Napoleon, on the subject of fine arts. 4°. 1 page.

OTIS, SAMUEL A. *Orange.*

1789, February 4, New York. Applies for a clerkship in either the Senate or House of Representatives. [Signature cut off.] 4°. 3 pages.

New York.

1789, March 16, New York. Gives a summary of his pretensions to the public favor, and relying on Madison's good offices. Applies for Government employment. 4°. 6 pages.

OTTO, ——— (French minister), to RAYNEVAL, ——— DE.

1791, April 5, Philadelphia. Extract of a letter respecting the valuation of the territory bought by the Illinois and Wabash companies. Immigrations are commencing to give great value to the land. Disposition of shares. Action of Congress in the next session probable. [In French. *See* letter of Wilson, James, to Madison (?), January 1, 1781. Copy.] fol. 2 pages.

OVERTON, SAMUEL, to MADISON. *Washington.*

1811, May —, Nashville. Does not write for an office, but reminds Madison that they were both born in the same district from which Madison was elected to Congress, and that he is now President and himself a private citizen. fol. 1 page.

OWINGS, DAVID, and WOODS, DAVID. *New York.*

1791, December 12, Albemarle. Asks Madison's aid in securing their claims before Congress. They were both Revolutionary soldiers. fol. 1 page.

OYLEY, DANIEL D'. *See* D'OYLEY DANIEL.

PACKARD, FREDERICK A. *Montpellier.*

1830, November 20, Philadelphia. The life of Washington published by the American Sunday School Union. Asks Madison the circumstances which attended the final vote on the Declaration of Independence, and in what sense, if in any, was it unanimously adopted. 4°. 2 pages.

PAGE, EDWARD P.

1820, September —, Marietta. The first part of this letter illegible. The remainder relates to religious matters and evidently from an insane person. 4°. 3 pages.

PAGE, JOHN. *Washington.*

1814, January 24, Boston. Has been disappointed in not being appointed collector. Frauds in the custom house detailed. 4°. 6 pages.

1814, January 26, Boston. Is of the opinion that the officers and men now stationed in different posts in Massachusetts should be ordered to the headquarters of the Army, and the forts be garrisoned by men enlisted during the war and mechanics out of employment. Relates the manner in which the Navy agency is conducted, and which should be remedied. 4°. 3 pages.

Montpellier.

1831, March 2, Williamsburg. The vacant professorship of mathematics in William and Mary College.

PAGE, FRANCIS.

1832, October 8, Hanover County. Asks Madison's good offices with the President to have his son, Francis Mann Page, appointed midshipman in the Navy. 4°. 1 page.

1833, October 28, Woodlawn, Hanover County. Incloses a petition by the heirs of Gen. Thomas Nelson for remuneration for his services. Asks Madison's opinion and approbation. fol. 1 page.

PAINE, ROBERT TREAT. *Montpellier.*

1832, March 19, Boston. Transmits copy of the oration delivered on February 22 by Hon. Francis C. Gray in Boston, also the third edition of his letter to Governor Lincoln on Harvard University. Gives the latitude and longitude of Montpellier and of the University of Virginia. 4°. 1 page.

PALMER, AARON H. *Washington.*

1809 (?), not dated. Asks for the appointment of a Government position, particularly one in which a knowledge of several languages would be requisite. 4°. 1 page.

1809, April 20, New York. Transmits copy of minutes of the proceedings of the twelfth American convention for promoting the abolition of slavery and improving the condition of the African race. 4°. 1 page.

1809, May 9, New York. Acknowledging a letter with a pamphlet. Incloses a publication of his own entitled an "Analytical Development of the 214 Elementary Characters of the Chinese Language." 4°. 2 pages.

1810, June 25, New York. Incloses a parcel and letter for Mrs. Madison. 4°. 1 page.

PALMER, THOMAS H.

1813, April 20, Philadelphia. Incloses the prospectus of a work which he proposes to publish. Asks his opinion of it. 4°. 1 page.

Montpellier.

1825, March 10, Philadelphia. Sends a few copies of a plan of education for a small class of young ladies, to give to his friends who may have daughters to educate. 4°. 2 pages.

PARISH, DANIEL. *Washington.*

1810, May 13, Philadelphia. Embarks for Europe in ten days and will take charge of the deeds Madison wishes to transmit to Lafayette. Offers his services abroad. 4°. 1 page.

1810, May 21, Philadelphia. Has received two packets transmitted by Madison containing land patents for Lafayette, which he will deliver into his own hands at La Grange in August. 4°. 1 page.

1814, July 10, Philadelphia. Transmits a deposition of Joseph R. Paxson as to the good treatment he had received in England. England desires that the liberality shown to American citizens should be made known to the President as an inducement for our Government to reciprocate. 4°. 3 pages.

1816, January 24, Philadelphia. Transmits an extract from a letter from Lafayette stating that his Point Coupée lands have been disposed of. Parish inquires whether the location of land Madison

PARISH, DANIEL.

wished to secure to Lafayette near New Orleans had been effected. 4°. 2 pages.

1816, March 5, Ogdensburg. Acknowledging two letters respecting Lafayette's concerns. Intends to embark for Europe in June. 4°. 1 page.

PARKER, DANIEL.

1814, October 29, Washington. Is chief clerk in the War Department. Applies for the appointment of adjutant and inspector-general. Details his past services and qualifications. Incloses a note to Mr. Cutts. 4°. 11 pages.

——— to CUTTS, ——.

1814, October 31, Washington. Inclosing his letter to Madison, dated 29th, and, after reading it, asks him to deliver it. 8°. 1 page.

——— to MADISON.

1815, April 8, Washington. Gives an estimate of the troops in service on February 16, 1815. fol. 1 page.

1815, April 15, Washington. Application of Gen. Smith for office. Suggests that of agent to the Creek Indians. Indian affairs in the War Department. Mr. Boyd's and his own application for the consulate at London. "Private." 4°. 6 pages.

1815, August 31, Washington. Applicants for vacancies in the Army. 4°. 1 page.

1815, September 7, Washington. Incloses copies of papers relating to the government of the Army, also the form of an order which he submits for further instructions. 4°. 1 page.

1815, September 13, Washington. Inclosing a form of a general order. 4°. 1 page.

——— to WHEATON, HENRY (Army Judge-Advocate).

New York.

1816, May 6, Washington. By order of the Secretary of War he is requested to make a selection between his military and civil appointments. [Copy. *See* letter from Wheaton to Madison, May 24.] 4°. 1 page.

1816, May 21, Washington. Acknowledging letter of 9th. Is instructed by the Secretary of War to inform him that it is considered as vacating the office of Judge-Advocate on the day of its date. [*See* letter from Wheaton to Madison, May 24, 1816.] 4°. 2 pages.

——— to MADISON.

1816, July 28, Washington. Sends a communication from General Gaines, respecting the summoning of witnesses. 4°. 2 pages.

1831, May 17, Washington. Introducing Dr. R. Harlan and William Norris, of Philadelphia. 4°. 1 page.

PARKER, SAMUEL.

1804, June 21. Appeal for pecuniary aid. small. 4°. 1 page.

PARKER, THOMAS.

1813, April 23, Winchester. Applies for promotion. 4°. 1 page.

PARKER, THOMAS B. *Montpellier.*

1821, January 18, Boston. On the separation of Maine and the amendment of the Massachusetts constitution. Asks Madison's opinion respecting the manner of apportioning the Senate and on the question of the supporting of public teachers of morality and religion. 4°. 2 pages.

PARKS, ANDREW. *Washington.*

1807, March 14, Baltimore. Arrival of schooner *Three Sisters* with wine from Madeira. Asks directions as to forwarding. 4°. 1 page.

1807, March 26, Baltimore. Will send his wine as directed. Has entered it in bond. Incloses copy of the entry. 4°. 1 page.

1808, February 25, Baltimore. Incloses account of duties, insurance, freight, etc., on two pipes of wine. Requests Madison to qualify to the entry before the collector at Georgetown or Alexandria. 4°. 1 page.

Montpellier.

1824, January 22, Kanawha County, Va. Incloses the account of John Payne Todd. 4°. 1 page.

1826, November 1, Burning Spring. An old account of John Payne Todd's. Is desirous of its settlement. 4°. 2 pages.

PARKS, E. L. *Washington.*

1815, January 3, Lawrenceburg. Was appointed by Madison in 1813 as attorney for Indiana. This appointment is now revoked and a successor named. Has never had any intimation of any dissatisfaction. Thinks he has been misrepresented. Informs him of trespassers on public lands. A remedy should be provided. small 4°. 3 pages.

PARTRIDGE, A. (Captain).

1816, May 26, West Point. A roll of the cadets at the Military Academy at West Point, embacing their ages and dates of appointment. Also list of applications for cadet appointments from the several States. A statement of the branches of science and instruction comprising a complete course of education at the academy. fol. 5 pages. 4°. 18 pages.

PATTERSON, ROBERT.

1807, April 27, Philadelphia. Asks a letter from Madison to the consul at Canton for Mr. R. Morrison, who goes to China for the purpose of studying Chinese. He is sent by the "Missionary society of London for propagating the gospel among the heathen." 4°. 2 pages.

1807, May 4, Philadelphia. Is informed that there is no British consul in Canton. Mr. Drummond, the chief agent of the East India Company, will permit no person unconnected with the company to take passage in any of their vessels For this reason he applies to the American Government to assist him in his praiseworthy undertaking, and would like a letter to Mr. Carrington, our consul there. 4°. 2 pages.

1813, April 20, Philadelphia. Announces the death of Dr. Rush, treasurer of the Mint. No inconvenience in the operations of the institution will be experienced for two or three weeks should not the vacancy be supplied sooner. 4°. 1 page.

PATTERSON, ROBERT, to JEFFERSON. *Monticello.*

1815, December 2, Philadelphia. Recommending Mr. Hassler to be employed by the Government as a surveyor and engineer. Details his abilities and character. 4°. 2 pages.

——— to MADISON. *Washington.*

1815, December 2, Philadelphia. Respecting Mr. Hassler. Asks the President to use his interest with the Government to secure the services of Mr. Hassler either in the contemplated survey of the coast, the running of boundary lines or superintendence of a national observatory. 4°. 2 pages.

1816, January 11, Philadelphia. Fire in the mill house in the mint. Origin unknown. No serious damage. 4°. 1 page.

PATTERSON, ROBERT M., to JOHNSON, C.

1827, September 8. Extract of a letter giving information and recommending Dr. Jones as professor of natural philosophy and chemistry, in the University of Virginia. [Copy.] 4°. 2 pages.

——— to MADISON. *Montpellier.*

1830, July 5, Charlottesville. Was prevented from visiting Madison by the extreme hot weather. During the vacation he hopes with Mrs. Patterson to make the visit. Invites Madison and Mrs. M. to stay at his pavilion during the session of the board of visitors at the University. 4°. 2 pages.

1830, October 15, Charlottesville. Hugh A. Garland, lately professor at Hampden Sydney College, wishes to become a student at the University of Virginia, with certain privileges. Asks Madison's consent and views. Condition of the university. Dismissal of one of the students for gambling and disobedience to rules. 4°. 3 pages.

1831, April 21, Charlottesville. Has been nominated by the medical faculty of the University of Maryland for the chair of chemistry in the Baltimore school. Everything goes on smoothly and prosperously at the University of Virginia. 4°. 2 pages.

1832, March 7, Charlottesville. Asks Madison as a member of the executive committee of the university, if he will consent that certain students over the age of 20 may be allowed to board at a private table and lodge in a house outside the precincts of the university. 4°. 2 pages.

1832, April 27, Charlottesville. Death of Arthur S. Brockenbrough. The office of patron of the students of the University thus becoming vacant, proposes to the executive committee that Thomas Brockenbrough, of Richmond, be appointed to that place. 4°. 3 pages.

PATTERSON, WILLIAM.

1833, August 20, Baltimore. Proposes to send as a present to Mrs. Madison a pair of calves, bred from celebrated Devon cattle belonging to Mr. Coke, M. P. 4°. 1 page.

1833, October 14, Baltimore. Sends Mrs. Madison two pair of Coke-Devon calves, and gives directions as to their conveyance. 4°. 1 page.

PATTON, JAMES.

1820, April 10, Alexandria. Acknowledging letter of 6th. Shipment of some wild turkeys, at request of Admiral Sir Isaac Coffin, to Liverpool.
4°. 2 pages.

1820, April 18, Alexandria. Shipment of wild turkeys to Liverpool. 4°. 2 pages.

PATTON, JOHN M.

1826, March 17, Fredericksburg. Claim against Benjamin J. Porter in behalf of the legatees of John S. Wood. Is obliged to decline acting, as he is retained by Porter in a claim precisely similar.
4°. 1 page.

1826, April 10, Fredericksburg. Gives the papers in the claim against Porter to his brother, Robert Patton, who is at liberty to advocate the claim.
small 4°. 1 page.

1831, March 9, Fredericksburg. Takes charge of a parcel given him by Mr. Verplanck to be delivered to Madison, which he will forward when opportunity occurs. 4°. 1 page.

1834, March 27, Washington. Expresses his gratification and pride on receiving a letter which will be treated as strictly confidential on a topic of public discussion. 4°. 1 page.

PATTON, LOUISA M.

1833, September 8, New Orleans. Asks Madison's influence with the Secretary of War that her eldest son may be a successful candidate for West Point.
4°. 1 page.

PATTON, ROBERT. *Philadelphia.*

1792, March 30, Fredericksburg. Incloses copy of an affidavit recorded in the public office at Charleston, respecting the forgery on his name to a bond given Gen. Greene by Banks and Hunter. Relates the manner in which the discovery was made. 4°. 4 pages.

Washington.

1806, January 6, Philadelphia. A letter from New York is in the post-office for Madison, asks him if he shall forward it to Washington. 4°. 1 page.

1806, January 24, Philadelphia. Acknowledging letter of 21st, inclosing a draft in payment of a pair of horses. Incloses Thomas Allen's receipt.
4°. 1 page and scrap of paper.

1808, August 11, Philadelphia. Acknowledging letter of 7th respecting an order for the purchase of a pair of horses. Promises to get him a good pair. 4°. 1 page.

1808, October 15, Philadelphia. Has purchased a pair of horses for Madison. Has sent them forward.
4°. 2 pages.

1808, October 22, Philadelphia. Acknowledging letter of 19th with a draft in payment for a pair of horses purchased by him for Madison.
4°. 1 page.

No year. October 12, Philadelphia. Results of the elections in the city of Philadelphia.
4°. 1 page.

——— to LATROBE, B. H.

1809, July 11, Philadelphia. Acknowledging letter of 14th respecting a coach which was badly fin-

PATTON, ROBERT.

ished. Has represented to Mr. Harvey the faults. [Part of this letter torn and illegible.]
4°. 2 pages.

——— to MADISON, Mrs. D. P.

1809, September 19, Philadelphia. Incloses receipt for payment of a chariot and harness. Decides to send it by land to Washington and gives directions to Mrs. Madison's coachman.
4°. 1 page and strip of paper.

——— to FORREST, RICHARD.

1809, September 30, Philadelphia. Acknowledging letter of 28th inclosing a draft in payment for a chariot for the President's use. 4°. 1 page.

——— to MADISON, Mrs. D. P.

1810, April 22, Philadelphia. Has purchased a pair of horses as leaders for her other pair. If they do not suit on trial will try to procure another pair. 4°. 1 page.

——— to MADISON.

1810, May 24, Philadelphia. Sends bills for a pair of gray horses with the expense of sending them to Washington. Hopes the horses will suit.
4°. 1 page.

1810, May 31, Philadelphia. Acknowledging letter of 28th inclosing a draft in payment for a pair of horses. 4°. 1 page.

1810, November 8, Philadelphia. Acknowledging letter of October 29. Is sorry to hear Madison has lost one of his horses. It will be difficult to match the other, but will do his best.
4°. 1 page.

1810, December 6. Settlement of an account.
4°. 1 page.

1811, May 9, Philadelphia. Has purchased a gray horse and incloses receipt of Samuel Paul.
4°. 1 page, and strip of paper.

1811, May 27, Philadelphia. Acknowledging a letter with a draft to pay for a horse. Is glad the horse matches the other so well. 4°. 1 page.

1811, August 12. Statement of account.
fol. 2 pages.

1813, September 11, Philadelphia. Acknowledges letter of 8th with a check for the use of James M. Macon and incloses his receipts.
4°. 1 page and strip of paper.

1814, December 20, Fredericksburg. Has paid installments on Madison's turnpike stock which he will remit at convenience 4°. 1 page.

Orange.

1818, March 17, Fredericksburg. Sends certificate of shares in the Potomac Steamboat Company and notice of dividend. 4°. 1 page. 8°. 1 page.

——— to MADISON, Mrs.

Not dated. White mice sent to Mrs. Madison.
8°. 1 page.

PAVIA, JOSE MARIANA.

1822, July. Account of coinage of the mint of Mexico from 1802 to 1821. small 4°. 1 page.

PAYNE, G. WOODSON, to MADISON. *Montpellier.*

1830, January 16. Asks Madison and Mrs. Madison to visit him on his return from the convention. small 4°. 1 page.

PEALE, C. W., to MADISON. *Washington.*

1809, April 30, Philadelphia. Is proprietor of Peale's museum, which is in good condition and well managed. Suggests that it ought to be national property. His son, Rembrandt Peale, wants an opportunity to go to Paris to paint portraits and would like to take passage on a public ship. 4°. 2 pages.

PECK, ABIJAH.

1812, October 23, Warwick, N. Y. Is a bridle bit manufacturer. Foreign competition will ruin him unless the embargo will protect him. Opinions of political parties in reference to the matter. Merchants inimical to American manufacturers. fol. 3 pages.

PEERS, B. O. *Montpellier.*

1833, March 22, Lexington, Ky. As president of the Transylvania University is engaged in making a thorough review of the laws, course of studies, etc. Asks Madison to inform him by letter the experience of the University of Virginia respecting her system of discipline, and any other points connected with education which he supposes may be of service. 4°. 2 pages.

PEMBERTON, EBEN. *Washington.*

1814, January 8, Boston. Applies in behalf of Rev. Daniel Oliver for the place of chaplain to the Navy Hospital in Charlestown and to Fort Independence. fol. 2 pages.

PENDLETON, JOHN. *Philadelphia.*

1787, April 24, Richmond. Error rectified at the Auditor's office respecting the amount advanced Madison for attendance in Congress. Small 4°. 1 page.

New York.

1789 February 11, Richmond. Introducing William Lambert, who wishes employment in some department under the first arrangements of Congress. 4°. 1 page.

Washington.

1805, July 15, Richmond. Asks Madison to intercede with the Secretary of War for a discharge of his son from the army in which he precipitately enlisted and is totally unfit for a soldier's life. 4°. 2 pages.

1805, August 12, Richmond. Acknowledging letter of 20th ultimo. Thanks him for his kind attention to the subject of his last letter. 4°. 1 page.

PENDLETON, PHIL. *New York.*

1790, March 1, Berkeley. Applies for the vacancy in the Supreme Court for the western territory owing to the death of Gen. Parsons. small 4°. 1 page.

PENN SOCIETY. *Montpellier.*

1830, October 1, Philadelphia. Invitation to Madison to their anniversary dinner. 4°. 1 page.

PENN, S., Jr. *Washington.*

1815, February 22, Georgetown, Ky. Presenting a bill for subscription to the "American Statesman,"

PENN, S., Jr.

which he admits was never subscribed for. His impudent remarks on Madison's and his own politics. 4°. 3 pages.

PENNOCK, WILLIAM.

1804, September 12, Norfolk. Notice of entry of wines etc., per *Brig. Maria* from Bordeau for himself and Mr. Gallatin. Incloses bill of freight and duties. 4°. 2 pages.

1808, July 1, Norfolk. Presents bill for duty paid on wine with interest from 1804. 4°. 1 page.

PENNSYLVANIA IMPORTS.

1734. Memorandum of imports into the State of Pennsylvania in the year 1734. Strip of paper.

PENNSYLVANIA GENERAL ASSEMBLY to MADISON. *Washington.*

1810, June 9. See SNYDER, SIMON.

PENNSYLVANIA, STATE OF.

1813, April 14, Harrisburg. Supplement to an act to incorporate a company for the purpose of cutting and making a canal between the River Delaware and the Chesapeake Bay, with an extract from the act of the general assembly passed February 19, 1801. [Copy.] 4°. 6 pages.

PEPOON, BENJAMIN F. *Montpellier.*

1833, April 13, Charleston. Incloses a circular to the effect that if exertions are not made to the contrary, our young people will grow up with cold feelings toward the general Government. 4°. 1 page.

PERCIVAL, LIEUT.

1819, January 31, Washington. Asks information respecting the power of the executive to change the order in which names of individuals for promotion in the Navy had been presented to and confirmed by the Senate. fol. 2 pages.

PERPETUAL MOTION. *Washington.*

1815, January 5, Walpole, N. *H.* Claimant to an invention which he presents to the nation and cuts out his signature to be revealed in the future, by producing it, and fitting it to the original. 4°. 2 pages.

PERPIGNAN, PETER. *Montpellier.*

1823, February 26, Philadelphia. Incloses the smallest representation of Gen. Washington ever presented to our countrymen. 4°. 1 page.

PERRON, CHARLES DE.

1817, June 22, New York. Wishes to be permitted to embark on board the ship *Franklin* and admitted among its officers, he paying his share of the table expenses. Is recommended by La Fayette and wishes to obtain instruction in so excellent a school as the American Navy. Asks for a letter to Capt. Steward. 4°. 2 pages.

1817, November 18, Annapolis. Expresses his thanks to Commodore Stewart for his admission as volunteer on the *Franklin* which has resulted in success. 4°. 2 pages.

PERRY, LILBURN P.

1830, March 8, University of Virginia. Asks to be allowed a dispensation from the uniform prescribed by one of the enactments of the University. 4°. 1 page.

PETERS, RICHARD. *New York.*

1789, August 24, Belmont. Acknowledging letter of 19th. Believes in adhering to the Constitution. Sends copy of the "Aunsiente Balladdes." 4°. 1 page.

Philadelphia.

1790, March 31, Philadelphia. Sends a pamphlet on finance by Mr. Herman Husbands. Calls it "balderdash". fol. 1 page.

1792, December 31. Remarks on the bill Congress is about to establish touching fees in the admiralty side of the district court. 4°. 2 pages.

1793, February 26. His opinions respecting a bill in Congress respecting circuit and district courts. Suggests a short clause to give the power of appointing commissioners to take bail. The affidavit business. 4°. 2 pages

1796, February 4. Incloses a memorial accompanied by a translation. Recommends Monsieur Perret as deserving a better situation. Asks Madison's good offices respecting Perret. 4°. 1 page.

Washington.

1803, May 18, Belmont. Has received a letter from Gen. Ternant respecting Lafayette, who is in need of assistance. Suggests a spontaneous act of Congress to do something for him. Asks Madison's aid in furthering this object. The favorable disposition of the First Consul toward this country. It is said there is more submission than voluntary agreement to the present regime in France. [Signature cut off.] 4°. 1 page.

1810, March 18, Belmont. Incloses letters to several French savans who have corresponded with the Philadelphia Agricultural Society. Has reason to believe that former letters have miscarried and requests Madison to have the letters sent with the public dispatches. small 4°. 1 page.

1811, March 11, Belmont. Seeds of a remarkably fine rye sent him by Gen. Armstrong as a sample. Requests Madison to endeavor to have some sent to him from France by a public ship, as the only means of getting them. Recommends the rye as particularly fine. 4°. 1 page.

1811, April 6, Belmont. Breeding of sheep. Causes and remedies of their diseases, particularly of the imported kinds. 4°. 2 pages.

PETERS, SAMUEL.

1806, May 2, Washington. Apologizes for not waiting upon Madison, his letters of introduction from distinguished persons not having reached him. Has been falsely called an English spy, which is another reason for not making himself known for fear of compromising himself and the President. Asks for a position for his son. An Indian deed claimed by the heirs of Jonathan Carver. Suggests a plan for the settlement of Western lands. Gives his experience in settling townships in Vermont. fol. 3 pages.

PETTIT, CHARLES.

1801, October 11, Philadelphia. Applies for the filling of any vacancy in the office of collector of the port of Philadelphia or in the general post-office. Enumerates his qualifications and services. 4°. 2 pages.

PHILE, FREDERICK, TO HENRY, JOHN.

1789, March 23, Philadelphia. Wishes to be retained under the new Government in the office which he has filled for thirty-five years, that of naval officer for the port of Philadelphia.
4°. 3 pages.

PHILLIPS, CHARLES H., TO MADISON. *Montpellier.*

1821, March 30, Baltimore. Appeal for pecuniary aid.
4°. 3 pages.

PHILLIPS, HENRY.

1834, September 14, Canton, Miss. Wishes to be informed on various political subjects, as he considers Madison the great oracle of our constitutional rights and liberties. fol. 2 pages.

PHILLIPS, JOHN R. *Washington.*

1801, November 27, Newport, Del. Hears that Madison or one of his brothers has a mill in Madison County on the Rapidan for sale or rent. Wishes to be informed on the subject as he wishes to rent or purchase. 4°. 1 page.

1818, January 27, Wilmington, Del. Printed circular soliciting patronage for the Madison Woolen Cloth Manufactory. 4°. 1 page.

PHILLIPS, N., to MADISON. *Montpellier.*

1827, July 9, New York. Is making a few historical memoranda and would like to know on what day Madison was born. 4°. 1 page.

PHILO, CLASSIC.

1826, April 4, Charlottesville. Qualifications of a professor at the University of Virginia to be appointed to fill the vacancy which will probably occur after the close of the session.
4°. 5 pages.

PHYSICK, PHILIP S., to MADISON. *Washington.*

1812, September 18, Philadelphia. Recommends as a candidate his nephew, Dr. John Syng Dorsey, now adjunct professor of surgery in the University of Pennsylvania, as surgeon-general to the Army. 4°. 3 pages.

1813, April 21, Philadelphia. Announces the death of Dr. Rush, treasurer of the Mint. Recommends his son, Dr. James Rush, as his successor in the office. 4°. 2 pages.

1814, December 27, Philadelphia. Robert Ralston is desirous of sending his ship, called the *Pacific,* to France, as a cartel, if she can be licensed as such. In such case Dr. Physick might take passage in her,as a change of climate would be beneficial for his health, as his health is bad.
4°. 1 page.

PICHON, L. A. (French chargé d'affairs).

1803, January 6, Georgetown. Informs Madison that he believes that the aid-de-camp of Gen. Leclerc, from St. Domingo, is now on his way to Washington, bringing dispatches relating to Louisiana. 4°. 1 page.

1803, March 11, Georgetown. Asks permission that an unsealed letter may be inclosed in the dispatches preparing for Marquis D'Irujo for New Orleans. 4°. 1 page.

1803, November 2, Georgetown. Asks Madison to inform him of the resolutions of the President on

PICHON, L. A.

the subject contained in the memorial of Pichon of the 27th October, it being connected with the unforeseen interference of Spain. 4°. 2 pages.

1804, July 9, Washington. Apologizing for leaving Washington for Philadelphia without taking leave. Mrs. Pichon's state of health required this sudden resolution. Hopes to pay a friendly visit to Mr. and Mrs. Madison in Virginia. 4°. 2 pages.

1804, October 1, Philadelphia. Reports of sickness in Washington and Mrs. Pichon's health prevents him from waiting on Madison. Wishes him to forward all communications to Philadelphia for the present and to inform him as to time of Gen. Turreau's departure from Paris. 4°. 2 pages.

1804, November 1, Philadelphia. Acknowledging letters of 20th and 26th October. Expects to be in Washington the next week. Mrs. Pichon's illness. 4°. 2 pages.

1805, April 11, Philadelphia. Acknowledging letter of 8th, with inclosures. Requests Madison to authenticate an inclosed certificate stating time of arrival here of the vessel in which his letters came from Washington. Leaves for France in a week. Thanks Madison and the President for the marked attention to him and Mrs. Pichon. 4°. 4 pages.

1809, July 1, Paris. Congratulates Madison on his election to the Presidency. Is now practicising law. Reviews his past occupation in this country and states his intention to print his memoirs. 4°. 8 pages.

PICKERING, TIMOTHY. *Philadelphia.*

1796, May 12, Washington. Accounts of Monroe for sums paid for books for the War Department. 4°. 1 page.

1796, August 19, Philadelphia. Claims of Mr. Mazzei. Incloses Mazzei's letters to Madison. 4°. 2 pages.

——— to MONROE. *Paris.*

1796, August 22, Philadelphia. Letter of recall of Monroe from Paris and announcement of his successor, Charles Cotesworth Pinckney. 4°. 2 pages.

——— to MADISON. *Philadelphia.*

1797, February 16, Philadelphia. Forwarding to Jefferson of the certificate announcing his election to the Vice-Presidency. 4°. 2 pages.

Washington.

1813, August 3, Washington. Asks for the discharge of a minor of the name of Chase from the Navy. 4°. 2 pages.

Montpellier.

1825, September 7, Salem. Articles on agriculture printed in the "American Farmer." Is obliged to correct misrepresentations of John H. Powel. [Signature cut off.] 4°. 1 page.

PICKET, ALBERT, and others.

1821, September 10, Baltimore. Asks Madison's opinion of the establishment of a female college to be conducted on an extensive scale, and the course of instruction to be adopted. 4°. 2 pages.

PICKET, WILLIAM. *Washington.*

1811, October 18, Charlestown, Mass. Explains that his son, William S. Picket, just arrived in Boston from Naples, had a packet for the President which was broken open by cruisers of one of the belligerents, which he hopes will be a sufficient excuse for their condition. fol. 1 page.

PIERCE, WILLIAM. *Richmond.*

1788, December 6, Savannah. Wishes the appointment to the office of collector of the port of Savannah. fol. 1 page.

PINCKNEY, CHARLES.

1788, May 16, South Carolina. Proposed alteration of the mode of electing electors of a President of the United States in Virginia. fol. 2 pages.

New York.

1789, March 28, Charleston. Apologizes for his long silence. His opinions respecting certain provisions of the Constitution. Recommends George Abbott Hall to be continued as collector of the impost for South Carolina. Recommends Mr. Smith to Madison and his friends, he being lately elected member of the House of Representatives from South Carolina. His future intentions. Is married and has a son. 4°. 8 pages.

Orange.

1789, September 30, Charleston. Importance of the Virginia legislature's passing an act like the South Carolina act, to declare that the electors of a President and Vice-President shall be elected by joint ballot. Calls attention to papers written by himself over signature of a "Southern Planter." [Private and in confidence.] fol. 3 pages.

New York.

1790, June 14, Charleston. Incloses proceedings of the South Carolina convention for amending the State constitution. fol. 2 pages.

Philadelphia.

1791, August 6, Charleston. Expresses his wish for a foreign appointment. States his qualifications. "Private." fol. 4 pages.

Orange C. H.

1800, October 26, Charleston. Incloses a package for Jefferson which he wishes forwarded. Congratulates Madison on the prospects on the next election. The writer's efforts to carry it by his writings. Describes his domestic life with his children. fol. 2 pages.

Washington.

1801, September 22, The Hague. Arrival at the Hague. Proposes to leave for Paris. The people he has met since his arrival. Proposes taking notes for the private inspection of his friends. 4°. 2 pages.

1802, March 14, Madrid. Has removed from the Escurial to Madrid. Negotiations for the cession of the Floridas at the court of Spain. The influence of France necessary; also that of the Prince of Peace, who is all powerful. Corresponds with Mr. Livingston on the subject. His wish for leave of absence to visit Rome. Instructions to consuls respecting releases of our vessels. Sug-

gests the appointment of commissioners to decide questions of captures and compensation. His desire to remain two years longer abroad.
fol. 4 pages.

1802, March 20, Madrid. Sends copy of a book on the duties and commercial regulations of Spain. Wishes Madison to send him a likeness of Jefferson at full length to decorate his "salle." Has commenced housekeeping and intends to receive two nights in the week and endeavor to make the "Casa de America" equal to any, and to make our nation and himself as agreeable as possible to Spain. [Private.] 4°. 2 pages.

1802, March 28, Madrid. Sends the book on duties and commercial regulations of Spain. Increased difficulties in the acquisition of the Floridas. The Spanish want of money may tempt them. The King of Spain goes to Barcelona and during his absence with his minister not much can be accomplished, and Pinckney would like a few weeks of absence to go to Rome; suggests it might be a good occasion to congratulate the new King of Etruria, as we have no minister to Italy. [Duplicate. Private.] fol. 4 pages.

1802, May 20, Madrid. Submits his account of contingent expenses. Incloses a letter to his daughter which he wishes Madison to read. Enormous expenses of living in Spain. High rates of postage. The definitive treaty. The business of Spanish spoliations. Can not persuade the Spanish Government to consent to a consul or agent from the United States residing at New Orleans. Recommends Mr. Isaac Cox Barnet to a consulate. [Private.] fol. 5 pages.

1802, May 24, The Sitio, Spain. Incloses a letter to the President in cipher; reports that France is to declare Bonaparte first consul for life. Squadron with troops under Gen. Bernadotte to sail for Louisiana to take possession. Negotiations still pending to that effect. Wishes instructions respecting the sum to fix upon should Spain be inclined to the sale of either of the Floridas. The subject of spoliations before the minister. Difficulties with consuls in settlements of their accounts. Will return to Madrid about June 30. [Private.] fol. 5 pages.

1802, July 8, Madrid. The Spanish court influenced by France respecting the Floridas. Correspondence with Livingstone. Mr. Cervallos' verbal promise that Louisiana will only be delivered to France subject to the conditions of our treaty with Spain. Our claims on Spain. Has adopted a mild course. Endeavors to obtain from the minister a declaration of our rights of navigation of the Mississippi and of deposit in Louisiana. Celebration of the Princesses weddings. [Private.]
fol. 4 pages.

1802, August 28, Madrid. His account for the past three months. High rates of postage. Enormous expenses attending the wedding of the King's daughter to the heir of the two Sicilies. Suggestions as to the extra expenses for which he has made no charge in "contingent expenses." [Private.] 4°. 2 pages.

1802, November 6, Barcelona. Inclosing copy of a letter from Mr. Cervallos requesting a passport for

PINCKNEY, CHARLES.

a Spanish vessel to enter the port of Tripoli, which he did not refuse to give. Proposes to take advantage of the King and courts absence to take his proposed tour in Italy. Enormous expense attending the court on the occasion of the marriage of the Princess. Numerous retinue. [Private.] fol. 3 pages.

1802, November 8, Barcelona. Movements of the King and court. Pinckney leaves for Italy. Mr. Graham will remain in Madrid to attend to any business during his absence. Question of Mr. Graham's compensation and the continuation of Pinckney's salary during his absence on leave. Asks instructions as to transmitting original vouchers or keep them among the papers of the office. [Private.] fol. 4 pages.

1802, December 20, Rome. Incloses an open letter to his daughter which Madison may read and show it to the President; it gives an account of his travels in Italy. His interviews with our consuls at Rome, Naples, and Leghorn. [Private.] 4°. 2 pages.

1803, February 28, Madrid. Conduct of the intendant of New Orleans. Quarantine on vessels from America. Fears of yellow fever by the Spaniards and other European countries. Incloses letter to his daughter, open, which Madison and the President may read, relating to his travels. Reserves his comments about people and foreign affairs until he sees him. Nothing has been done respecting claims during the absence of the King and court. [Private.] fol. 3 pages.

1803, March 2, Madrid. Incloses duplicates of former letters. Politeness and dispatch of Mr. Cervallos on the conduct of the intendants of New Orleans. Causes why the Spaniards are so afraid of yellow fever. Deaths from that cause in Andalusia in 1800. Conversations with Cervallos on French condemnations. Doubts about the ratification of the convention. Expects to see the Prince of Peace on the subject of Madison's last letter. fol. 2 pages.

1803, March 30, Aranjuez, near Madrid. Touching the orders of the Spanish Government to the intendant of New Orleans. Pinckney's conference with the Secretary of State respecting indemnity. State of affairs in Europe. Precarious situation between France and England. War imminent. Monroe's expected arrival. [Signature cut off.] fol. 3 pages.

1803, May 14, Madrid. Acknowledging letter of March 22. Restoration of the deposit at New Orleans. Secret article of the treaty of St. Ildefonso, which restores Louisiana to the French, to be made use of by Livingston and Monroe in their negotiations with France. French captures and condemnations. The quarantine taken off on our vessels. "Private." fol. 4 pages.

1803, August, Madrid. Transmits duplicate of contingent account. Excessive postage. 4°. 3 pages.

——— to CERVALLOS, DON PEDRO. *Madrid.*

1803, August 28, Madrid. Acknowledging letter of 23d. On our claims against Spain for not suppressing the injuries we have suffered in her ports from

PINCKNEY, CHARLES.

the citizens or subjects of a foreign nation. A pleasant task to be the instrument of preventing misunderstandings between our two countries. [Copy.] fol. 4 pages.

——— to MADISON. *Washington.*

1803, September, Madrid. Pinckney's reply to Cervallos. Copy remitted for approval. Spain's agreement to grant a passage to the French army against Portugal. War between Great Britain and France inevitable. Policy of our remaining neutral. 4°. 2 pages.

——— to LIVINGSTON, R. R. *Paris.*

1804 (?), not dated. Acknowledging two letters. Recommends writing in cipher in future. Urges him to endeavor to obtain the assistance of the French Government in our negotiations with Spain. Is pleased to hear that Jefferson will not be opposed to in the coming election. Comparison of the condition of our countrymen and the people of those countries he has visited in Europe. "Private." [Copy.) 4°. 5 pages

——— to MADISON. *Washington.*

1804, July 30, Madrid. Change of his conduct towards the Court of Spain, owing to their continued ill-usage and neglect of the claims of our citizens. Has decided to send Capt. Dalton as private messenger of his dispatches, and who will be able to inform Madison of state of affairs. Force or fear is the only method of dealing with Spaniards since the cession of Louisiana. His desire to return home. The corps diplomatique approve of Pinckney's conduct. "Private and confidential." fol. 4 pages.

1804, December 8, Madrid. Probability of war with Great Britain and its results to Spain; ruin to its commerce and marine. Anxiety to leave Spain. The Spaniards much alarmed at the prospects of war. Incloses prices of articles of necessary consumption in Madrid. "Private." 4°. 5 pages.

1805, February 28, Aranjuez, near Madrid. Unfriendly interference by the French Government preventing the ratification of our treaty with Spain and acknowledgment of spoliation claims. Abject solicitations of Spain to England to obtain peace. The coalition in 1793–'94 (had the Bourbon's been restored), to attack the United States; to clip the wings of this new and rising Empire of Liberty. "Private." 4°. 7 pages.

1806, February 10, Charleston. Arrival from Lisbon. Is occupied in the management of his private estate, which has suffered from his long absence. Will probably go to Washington in the spring. Sends his account up to 25th of October, the day of leaving Spain. Farewell interview with the King and Queen. fol. 3 pages.

1808, October 12, Charleston. Incloses a paper and requests him to instruct Gen. Armstrong, touching the matter of Mr. Macline, an American citizen. Actions of the State legislature. Madison's constant friends. 4°. 1 page.

1808, December —, Columbia. Announces the unanimous vote of South Carolina legislature for electors in favor of Madison for President. 4°. 1 page.

PINCKNEY, CHARLES.

1808, December —, Columbia. Announces his signing of official papers, showing that Madison had received the unanimous vote of the electors of President, who were also unanimously elected by the legislature of Virginia. Congratulates him on the certainty of his election. 4°. 1 page.

1809, January 2, Charleston. Congratulating Madison on his election to the Presidency. Transmits his (Pinckney's) communication to the South Carolina legislature. Expiration of his term as governor of South Carolina. 4°. 1 page.

1809, September 6, Charleston. Incloses resolution of the inhabitants of the city of Charleston, expressing their approbation of Madison's conduct and pledges of their support. Thinks if we are firm, Great Britain will yield, as she has more reasons for peace than we have. It is twenty-two years since he has seen Madison but hopes to do so before long. fol. 2 pages.

1809, November 18, Charleston. Transmits intelligence of the immense amount of smuggling, despite the blockade by way of Amelia, in Florida, of British goods. The whole country is stocked with them, and British goods are cheaper than ever known. fol. 3 pages.

1809, November 28, Charleston. On the subject of smuggling on the coasts of Florida and Georgia. Actions of Mr. Jackson, the minister from Great Britain. 4°. 2 pages.

1810, January 10, Charleston. Introducing Maj. Noah. Hopes soon to send his son to Washington in order to pay his respects to Madison and Monroe. 4°. 2 pages.

1811, December 18, Columbia. Incloses a report he made to the Virginia house of representatives which passed unanimously. The spirit of the State is fully equal to that of our first revolutionary year. Progress of manufactures in the South. Many of the planters dress in homespun. fol. 2 pages.

1812, February 18, Charleston. Acknowledging letter of 10th, announcing the death of the judge of his district and recommending John D. Heath to fill his place. Has received a letter from Jefferson describing his happiness in his retirement. 4°. page.

1812, March 18, Charleston. Introducing Col. Letrue, of Charleston. Development of Henry's agency with the British. 4°. 2 pages.

1812, December —, Charleston. Unanimous vote of the electors of South Carolina and North Carolina which fixes Madison in the chair for four years more. Congratulates him and the country. Laments extremely Clinton's conduct. Capture of the *Macedonian*. Trusts Congress will increase our vessels of war. 4°. 3 pages.

1820, September 2, Charleston. It is thirty-three years since they have seen each other. Relates early reminescenses. Growth of our country Opinions on the tariff. Members who signed the Constitution; only seven of them alive and three of them from "unhealthy" South Carolina. Asks to be remembered affectionately to Jefferson. 4°. 4 pages.

PINCKNEY, CHARLES.

Not dated. Portion of a paper relating to the cession or dismembering of a province or town, according to the law of nations—giving authorities. Also in the free navigation of rivers. fol. 6 pages.

PINKNEY, WILLIAM, to MADISON.

1807, October, London. Explanitory of his position as Minister in the place of Monroe, who returns to the United States. He waits the orders of the President. "Private." 4°. 4 pages.

1808, February 22, London. Incloses a copy of Mr. Percival's bill to Parliament for carrying the late orders of council into effect. Touching the export duty on cotton and salt. Postcript added February 25th, stating that Mr. Percival had abandoned his proposed duty on salt. "Private." 4°. 8 pages.

1808, February 22, London. Duplicate of the foregoing. "Private." 4°. 7 pages.

1808, April 2, London. Incloses duplicates of former letters. The bill for carrying into execution the orders in council has passed the House of Lords and received the assent of the King and become a law. Respecting a Mr. Swartwout, who was implicated in Burr's treason, asks to be sent a copy of Burr's trial. [Duplicate.] "Private." 4°. 3 pages.

1808, April 25, London. Acknowledging a private letter of March 21. Is gratified to hear through Madison that the President never suspended for a moment the purpose of nominating him to the permanent legation at London. Incloses instructions to British cruisers and gives his views upon them. Will attend to Madison's commission about books. Sends Bingham's speech on the orders in council. Have just received his credentials. "Private." 4°. 6 pages.

1808, April 25, London. Duplicate of the foregoing. "Private." 4°. 7 pages.

1808, April 26, London. Intended to have sent duplicates of yesterday's letter, but had no time to copy it. Transmits a newspaper of instructions to British cruisers. "Private." 4°. 1 page.

1808, April 27, London. Interview with Mr. Canning touching his (Pinkney's) dispatch of November 23, on the orders in council. "Private." 4°. 3 pages.

1808, April 27, London. Duplicate of the foregoing. "Private." 4°. 3 pages.

1808, June 6, London. Introduces John Lloyd Halsey, who desired of him (Pinkney) to aid him in procuring a license as soon as the embargo should be repealed for commercial expeditions to South America. 4°. 3 pages.

1808, August 2, London. Conjectures as to Burr's motives in England. He had just arrived. Question as to our ability to sustain the embargo whether the orders in council are repealed or not. Incloses extracts from a private letter relating to France. Condemnation of American vessels. Worthington, an American, found on board a French privateer, arrested and imprisoned at Plymouth. ffairs in Spain. The destinies of South America. Pinkney's refusal to attend the Spanish dinner. "Private." 4°. 9 pages.

PINKNEY, WILLIAM.

1808, August 17, London. Second interview with Mr. Canning respecting the orders in council concerning Spain in opening her ports, not in the occupation of France, to direct trade with the United States. [The last part of this letter with the signature cut off.] "Private." 4°. 3 pages.

1809, January 16, London. Acknowledging public letter of December 5, and private letters of December 5 and 9. Madison need feel no concern as to the publicity given of his (Pinkney's) letter of September. Should it lead to his recall it would give him no pain. Burr at Edinborough. Extract of a letter relative to him by one of his friends. The embargo. Incloses extracts of letters from Mr. Maury. "Private." 4°. 6 pages.

1809, May 4, London. Introducing Robert Walsh, jr., of Baltimore. 4°. 3 pages.

1810 June 13, London. The violence and injustice of France towards the United States inexplicable, and England does not profit of the occasion. Mr. Ewing, agent for claims, presents his accounts. Speaks in high terms of him. 4°. 3 pages.

1810, November 27, London. Refers to a letter of 24th explaining his motive in wishing to return to America. 4°. 2 pages.

1811, January 22, Baltimore. Application to Mr. Dallas to assist in the cases in the Supreme Court in which Pinkney is to argue, and in which Dallas agrees to. The mass of business in the Supreme Court he hopes to be able to get through with by the ensuing term. The Beaumarchais cause perplexes him. Hopes to be in Washington on the following Tuesday. 4°. 3 pages.

1811, December 17, Annapolis. Acknowledging letter of 12th and the commission as Attorney-General of the United States. Will not delay repairing to Washington. Expresses his thanks for the appointment. 4°. 2 pages.

1811–12 (?) not dated, Washington. Incloses letters from Mr. Brougham. Leaves for Baltimore on business, but will attend to any duties that may be transmitted to him. 4°. 2 pages.

1811–14, no date, Washington. In view of the probability of Mr. William Hilt losing his office of chancellor of Maryland, and his worth and business habits, recommends him for the station of comptroller, said to be vacant. 4°. 3 pages.

1811–14, not dated. Case of Livingston *v.* Dorgenoy before the Supreme Court, which he is to argue. Would like the district attorney to join him in the argument. 4°. 2 pages.

1812, April 21, Baltimore. Excuses for his absence from Washington. Recommends Mr. Elias Glenn to the office of district attorney for Maryland made vacant by the resignation of Thomas B. Dorsey. 4°. 2 pages.

1812, May 14, Baltimore. Incloses a letter from Alexander Baring. 4°. 1 page.

PINKNEY, WILLIAM.

1812, July 17, Baltimore. Recommends his son, William, for the consulate at Lisbon, if the place is vacant. 4°. 2 pages.

1812, August 7, Baltimore. Does not think the General Government could well interfere in the matter of the riots. Thinks also it will be unnecessary, for the authorities, aided by the militia, will be able to suppress a mere handful of low people. 4°. 2 pages.

1813 (?), not dated. Had just received the President's invitation to dinner for two days previous. 4°. 1 page.

1814, January 25, Baltimore. Tenders the resignation of the office of Attorney-General. 4°. 1 page.

PINKNEY, WILLIAM E., to PINKNEY, Mrs.

1816, May 24, Annapolis. At the request of his father he asks Mrs. Pinkney's good offices with Mrs. Madison, to interest herself in his behalf with the Secretary of War towards his appointment as attending surgeon to the troops stationed at Annapolis. 4°. 2 pages.

PITMAN, JOHN, JR., to MADISON.

1811, October 24, Providence, R. I. Objects to the appointment of David L. Barnes to fill the vacancy occasioned by the death of Judge Cushing. 4°. 3 pages.

PLEASONTON, STEPHEN, and others.

1802, July 1, Washington. Appeal of three clerks in the Department of State for increase of compensation, signed by the above and William Crawford and Christopher S. Thorn. 4°. 2 pages.

1807, September 19, Washington. Asks instructions respecting the way and from what fund the sum of $3,000 can be paid, which the Secretary of the Navy was stipulated to pay for services rendered by the consul at Batavia. 4°. 2 pages.

1815, January 4, Washington. Presents a petition of Mr. Shipley, of Delaware, that the remission granted for a forfeiture in the Pennsylvania district should also be applied to the district of Delaware. 4°. 1 page.

1815, May 18, Washington. Apologizes for opening his letter to Mr. Graham, during the latter's absence, relating to private business. Will attend to the business. Arrival of the frigate *Constitution* at New York. fol. 1 page.

1815, August 7, Washington. Inclosing letters from Mr. Russell and Mr. Baker. Crawford accepts the appointment to the War Department. Shall prepare a commission to Mr. Cathcart as consul to Cadiz. Captures by the *Algerine* squadron. 4°. 2 pages.

1815, August 18, Washington. During the absence of Monroe he forwards his letters to the President directly. Should he wish to communicate with Monroe oftener than is practicable by the mail, the Postmaster-General has given directions to forward them as often as is desirable. Incloses letter from Daschkoff and Pinkney. Asks information respecting the *Neptune*. Recommends the sale of a Government vessel. 4°. 3 pages.

PLEASONTON, STEPHEN, and others.

1817, January 27, Washington. Submits the propriety of nominating to the Senate a number of persons to be consuls at different places. 4°. 1 page.

Montpellier.

1826, April 12, Washington. Sends copy of a report of a select committee of the House of Representatives on items of claim of Monroe, which arose out of his missions abroad. 4°. 1 page.

PLEASANTS, JAMES B.

1819, April 6, Brookeville. Incloses projects of improving internal navigation, addressed to the president of the board of public works of Virginia. 4°. 1 page.

——— to PRESTON, JAMES P.

1819, April 6, Brookeville, Md. On the method of improving the navigation of James River. 4°. 3 pages.

——— to MADISON.

1820, January 15, Brookeville, Md. Inclosing a letter to the Governor of Virginia respecting internal improvements, alludes to a conversation respecting a method of destroying the enemies' ships of war. 4°. 2 pages.

PLEASANTS, JAMES, Jr., and others. *Washington.*

1813, February 22. Recommendation by a part of the Virginia Representatives in Congress of Capt. Bankhead for promotion to the rank of colonel. 4°. 1 page.

PLEASANTS, JAMES, Jr. *Montpellier.*

1817, May 18, Goochland. Introducing his son, John H. Pleasants. 4°. 1 page.

1820, March 25, Washington. Incloses letters and documents by Mr. Robert S. Rose, member of the New York legislature. Asks Madison's opinion upon them. The subject not mentioned. 4°. 1 page.

1824, March 1, Richmond. Notifying Madison of the appointment of seven visitors for the University of Virginia. Commission constituting Madison as one of the visitors. 4°. 2 pages.

1824, March 22, Richmond. Acknowledging letter of 11th with an inclosure. Is unable to find the letter, a copy of which Madison wished to be made. 4°. 1 page.

PLEASANTS, ROBERT. *Philadelphia.*

1791, June 6, Virginia. Asks if he would be willing to present a memorial of the Humane or Abolition Society on the subject of the slave trade. Suggests action also of Congress for the gradual abolition of slavery. Also asks if he will present a memorial on the subject of the militia bill. 4°. 2 pages.

1791, August 8, Richmond. Transmits papers relating to the abolition of the slave trade and of slavery; also the militia bill to Mr. Pemberton to deliver to Madison. 4°. 1 page.

PLEASANTS, THOMAS.

Not dated. A series of queries and answers relating to the trade with France to be encouraged or not with Virginia. royal fol. 1 page.

PLEASANTS, THOMAS, JR. *New York.*

1788, June 26, Richmond. Claim of Capt. Charles Connor. 4°. 2 pages.

1788, July 25, Raleigh. His views on commercial treaties. Recommends Thomas Thompson to some office under the new Government. 4°. 4 pages.

1789, April 23, Raleigh. Introduces William Vannerson. Asks Madison's friendly interposition to prevent measures respecting Mr. Ross and himself, which would inconvenience them both. Vannerson will explain the business. 4°. 1 page.

1790, July 10, Raleigh. Acknowledging letter of 2d. Opened the letter addressed to Sterling Pleasants inclosed therein, as there is no such person in America by that name. Recommends a consulship for Mr. Thomas Thompson. State debts. The national debt. Its increase impolitic. Reciprocal trade between Great Britain and United States. The foreign debt. The slavery question. Its gradual abolition. 4°. 12 pages.

Philadelphia.

1791, January 6, Raleigh. Continues his application for the consulship at Madeira for Thomas Thompson. Incloses abstract of the present state of the navy of Great Britain. Asks for an abstract of the articles of export from the United States and imports within the period of a year. 4°. 3 pages.

1791, March 4, Raleigh. Acknowledging letter of February 13. Refers again to the consulship which he desires Mr. Thomas Thompson to obtain. On the national finances. 4°. 3 pages.

PLUMER, WILLIAM. *Washington.*

1812, June 6, Concord, N. *H.* Incloses his speech delivered to the New Hampshire legislature. A Republican majority in both branches of the legislature. 4°. 1 page.

1812, September 23, Epping, N. *H.* Imputes the want of success in enlistments to the low pay to the soldier. Suggests their being raised. Success of the Republican election in Vermont. The war grows more popular. 4°. 2 pages.

1812, November 18. Pamphlet containing the speech of the governor of New Hampshire to both houses of the legislature on the present status of the country and states. 8°. 8 pages.

——— to MADISON.

1813, March 27, Epping, N. *H.* The recent elections in New Hampshire in favor of the Federalists by small majorities, caused by absence of Republicans who are in the Army and privateers. The war more popular. Still considers New Hampshire as a Republican State. Remains in office (governor) until June 1. 4°. 2 pages.

1816, November 25, Concord, N. *H.* Success of Republicans in choice of electors and Representatives in Congress. Presents a copy of his speech to the legislature. 4°. 1 page.

Montpellier.

1819, June 8, Epping, N. *H.* Presents a copy of his valedictory address to the legislature of New Hampshire. 4°. 1 page.

1821, November 6, Epping, N. *H.* Presents an address delivered by his son to the Rockingham Agricultural Society. 4°. 1 page.

PLUMER, WILLIAM, Jr. *Washington.*

1815, June 8, Epping, N. *H.* Is preparing for publication a history of the late war with Great Britain. Asks Madison's permission to address inquiries necessary in the course of the work to the War and Navy Departments for brief statements of events. 4°. 3 pages.

POINDEXTER, GEORGE.

1809, February 11, Washington. Is informed that Governor Williams, of the Mississippi Territory, will resign on March 4. As to the appointment of his successor, he recommends the Hon. David Holmes. Secretary Williams not suitable, in view of his political opinions, to succeed Governor Williams. The condition of parties in that Territory. 4°. 6 pages.

——— to HAMILTON, PAUL (Secretary of the Navy).

1810, June 30, Havana. Relates the incident of the firing upon the *Vixen,* near the Bahama Banks, by the British brig *Moselle.* [Copy.] 4°. 3 pages.

POINDEXTER, JAMES, to MADISON.

1807, September 11. Certificate by the above-named justice of the peace of the citizenship of David Yancey. 8°. 1 page.

POINSETT, J. R.

1801, July 24, New York. Applies for permission to accompany Mr. Livingston and suite on their voyage to France. 4°. 1 page.

POLITICA, P. *Montpellier.*

1819, June 10, Washington. Asks if he may pay him a visit at his residence, in company with a countryman of his, who is ambititious of being introduced to him. 4°. 1 page.

POLK, CHARLES P. Or*ange* C. *H.*

1800, June 20, Fredericktown. Is prevented from establishing a newspaper, and returns the subscription. Election of electors of President and Vice-President. Is pleased that Madison is nominated for one of them. Incloses proceedings of his county meetings on the subject. [Part of the letter torn off with signature.] fol. 4 pages.

1800, ——— *10, Fredericktown.* Acknowledging letter of August 5. The people of Maryland will exercise the right of suffrage in the choice of electors in districts. Republicans have a majority in the lower house. Thinks Jefferson will most probably have 7 votes from Maryland. 4°. 1 page.

Washington.

1801, April 2, Fredericktown. Solicits a situation here or elsewhere under Government. 4°. 3 pages.

1801, May 14, Fredericktown. Acknowledging letter of April 19, respecting his application for a Government office. Thanks Madison for his prompt attention to his letter. small 4°. 2 pages.

1801, November 10, Fredericktown. Continues his appeal for a subordinate appointment under the Government. 4°. 2 pages.

1802, January 7, Georgetown. Asks Madison's good offices with the Postmaster-General for his appointment to a subordinate position in the Post-Office. 4°. 2 pages.

POLK, CHARLES P.

1809, October 12, Washington. Asks permission to use a letter of Madison's, written in 1801, which may serve in procuring an increase of salary for himself. 4°. 2 pages.

POLK, ROBERT.

1815, March 10, Washington. Asks Madison's influence with Mr. Dallas to obtain the appointment of principal clerk to the Secretary of the Treasury, which is about to be vacated. States his qualifications. 4°. 2 pages.

POLLOCK, ALLAN, Jr. *Montpellier.*

1830, June 4, Fredericksburg. Sends a copy of the life of Arthur Lee. 4°. 1 page.

POLLOCK, OLIVER. *Washington.*

1801, October 22, West Hanover, Pa. Solicits the consulship at New Orleans. 4°. 2 pages.

POLLARD, ROBERT. *Montpellier.*

1823, September 18, Richmond. Sends account of charges on a cheese forwarded from Liverpool by James Maury. 4°. 1 page.

POLLARD, ROBERT, AND SON.

1823, November 17, Richmond. Have forwarded a cheese by wagon to Fredericksburg. 4°. 1 page.

POLLARD, THOMAS. *New York.*

1789, March 20, Fairfax County, Va. Asks for information respecting the redemption of continental currency. Offers himself as a candidate for the office of collecter of the Potomac district. small 4°. 1 page.

POMEROY, J. W. *Montpellier.*

1820, February 7, Brighton, Mass. Sends last number of the "Massachusetts Agricultural Journal," calls attention to an article therein on "dairy stock," hinting at the expediency of spaying heifers to fit them for farm work as a substitute for horses. 4°. 3 pages.

POMEROY, S. W.

1821, August 12, Brighton, Mass. Acknowledging letter of July 21, with samples of flax. Is desirous of obtaining models of flax machines. The French and English methods of manufacturing the article. Sends seeds of Yellow Aberdeen turnip. 4°. 2 pages.

1822, July 25, Brighton, Mass. On machines for the manufacture of flax and hemp. 4°. 3 pages.

POOL, JOHN.

1824, August 30, Woodlawn, Ky. Asks Madison's interpretation of a clause in the Constitution. 4°. 2 pages.

POPE, JOHN.

1817, July 20, Frankfort, Ky. Asks if he has retained a letter written to him about April 1, 1812, the day preceding Madison's message to Congress commending an embargo, and, if so, to send him a copy. 4°. 2 pages.

POPE, PHILIP C., to JEFFERSON, *Washington.*

1809, January 5, Crowsville, Hanover, Va. Complaints of the improper administration of affairs in Virginia by Judge Marshall, George Hay, as district attorney, and Mr. Gibbon, the collector, respecting the embargo laws. 4°. 3 pages.

POPE, WILLIAM, to MADISON.

1808, October 31, Montpellier, Powhatan County, Va. State of parties in Virginia. Mentions several of Madison's inveterate enemies who should be turned out of office. Thinks Madison will get three votes to one for Monroe in the approaching election. 4°. 4 pages.

1808, November 9, Montpellier. The election in Virginia. A complete victory for the republican patriots. Mentions the names of opposing factions. Considers the embargo a wise measure, and his friends are unanimous in support of it and would recommend him to bring forward again the non-importation bill introduced in Congress in 1794. 4°. 3 pages.

1812, July 12, Virginia. Popularity in Virginia of the declaration of war. Will tend to unite all parties except the Randolphists. John Randolph as a leader appears to be proscribed. Madison's communication to Congress highly commended. William Wirt's popularity. Recommends Madison to take a journey to the Eastern States to conciliate them. 4°. 4 pages.

1812, July 30, Virginia. Regrets the great inactivity observed in the enlistment of men in Virginia by the Secretary of War. Suggests plans of attack on the enemy. 4°. 3 pages.

PONTOIRE, H.

1812, December 22, Nantes. Offers his services as engineer in the War or Navy Departments. [In French.] 4°. 1 page.

PORTEEN, STANIER, (Sir), to WEYMOUTH, LORD.

Not dated. Correspondence to and from Mr. Stanley and the Duke of Bedford respecting the articles in the Treaty of Utrecht touching the New Foundland fisheries and articles agreed upon in the definitive treaty signed February 10, 1763. Sends extract of a letter of the Earl of Egrement to the Duke of Bedford of March 1, 1763. [Copy.] Small 4°. 2 pages.

PORTER, DAVID, to HAMILTON, PAUL. *Washington.*

1811, August 31, Gosport. Had received information of the arrival in Hampton Roads of the British sloop of war *Tartarus*, not having complied with the conditions of the nonintercourse law. While preparing his force agreeable to orders of July 16 to drive her from that place, she had cut her cables and departed during the night. Commends the zeal and activity of his officers, seamen, and marines. 4°. 2 pages.

——— to MADISON.

1815, January 12, New York. Presents Madison with a copy of the journal of his cruise in the *Essex*. 4°. 1 page.

1815, October 31, Washington. Proposes to undertake a voyage of discovery to the North and South Pacific oceans. Remarks on the importance attached to similar voyages by other nations. 4°. 8 pages.

1819, August 8, Washington. Acknowledging letter of July 20. Expresses gratification at Madison's and Mrs. Madison's friendly sentiments, and if in his power will visit them at Montpellier, accompanied by Mrs. Porter. 4°. 2 pages.

1822, November 28, Meridian Hill. Sends him a volume of his book. 4°. 1 page.

PORTER, DAVID (Commodore).

Not dated. Rules of etiquette touching military honours and ceremonies. fol. 2 pages.

PORTER, JOHN, Jr. *Orange Court House.*

1802, August 13, Louisa County. Acknowledging letter of November 25, 1801. Claim before Congress for services during the Revolution. fol. 1 page.

PORTER, JOHN.

1806, October 1? Albemarle. Claim before Congress which has been strengthened by vouchers. Asks Madison's advice in the case. fol. 2 pages.

Washington.

1809, July 31, Louisa. Claim before Congress for services in the Revolutionary war. Asks Madison's advice. fol. 2 pages.

POSEY, THOMAS. *New York.*

1790, July 5, Fredericksburg. Inquires if money due him for arrears of subsistence can be obtained at New York by giving a friend a power of attorney for drawing it. fol. 2 pages.

POTTS, THOMAS. *Montpellier.*

1822, September 7, New York. Informs him of a parcel containing books which he brought from London. It can be obtained at Mr. Williamson's Fountain Inn. 4°. 1 page.

PORTMAN, JOHN. *Washington.*

1814, August 2, Madison, Tenn. Incloses a memorial signed by many settlers praying protection against officials who threaten to drive them off lands which they have reclaimed and cultivated. fol. 7 pages.

POTTER, EBEN.

1803, June 23, Charlestown, Va. Declines the purchase of a mill. Wishes to return to Mississippi and to obtain one of the registers of claim's offices, if any are vacant. 4°. 1 page.

1803, August 25, Charlestown, Va. Acknowledging letter of June 30. Asks an appointment in some office growing out of the cession of Louisiana. Should prefer a situation in Mississippi. 4°. 1 page.

POTTER, S.

1813, February 7, Washington. Considers it a great indignity for our chief ruler to hold slaves. That it is Madison's duty to emancipate his own. Lengthy remarks on the evils of slavery. small 4°. 20 pages.

POULSON, L.

1813, May 1, Philadelphia. Gives his reasons why he sends in his account for forwarding the "American Daily Advertiser," the President never having authorized him to do so and refusing to pay it. 4°. 1 page.

POUTINGON, J. A. P.

1813, June 1, Washington. A series of letters and papers requesting audience with the President and petitions Congress to cause his removal from the "criminal residence" or be brought to trial. Pretends he has an important discovery to impart for the safety of our country. Evidently from a poor insane person. fol. 10 pages.

POTOWMAC, THE EXPOSTULATIONS OF.

1789, November 20. A printed circular respecting the proposed residence of Congress on the Potomac, touching its advantages. Addressed to the Virginia general assembly. fol. 2 pages.

POWELL, JAMES, to MADISON. *Washington.*

1809, March 17, New York. Asks if the President can give him any information or redress concerning an entailed property of which he is an heir, now in the possession of Colen Leben Powell, esq. 4°. 4 pages.

1809, March 17, New York. Duplicate of the foregoing, with a postscript. 4°. 4 pages.

PRATT, HENRY.

1803, January 25, Baltimore. States that a shipment of goods was seized at Gonaives, in 1796, by the French and for which he has never been paid. Asks that inquiry be made of the French minister if there was any provision made for the payment of such debts: 4°. 2 pages.

PRAY, JOHN G.

1814, September 12, New York. The great importance of an efficient navy. Communicates his plans for the building of one and the enlisting of seamen. 4°. 3 pages.

PREBLE, EDWARD, to MONROE. *London.*

1803, November 12, Gibraltar. Requests that the British Government and ministers and consuls of neutral powers in law shall be notified of the blockade of Tripoli by ships under his command. 4°. 2 pages.

PRENTIS, JOSEPH, to MADISON. *Washington.*

1807, April 5, Williamsburg. Asks him to cause to be delivered a letter from Mr. Basset to Mr. Fox of the navy-yard to place under his care the son of David Mead, of Kentucky, to learn the trade of shipbuilding; also, asks Madison's good offices in furthering the project. 4°. 1 page.

PRENTISS, J., Jr., and others, to GERRY, ELBRIDGE.

1814, July 13, Marblehead. Asks his aid in obtaining from the proper departments, in causing a competent force of gunboats and armed schooners to cruise between Boston and Cape Ann in order to keep off the enemy's cruisers. Also for the enlistment of 40 or 50 men as United States troops to be stationed at Marblehead. [Signed by the select men and committee of public safety of Marblehead.] 4°. 2 pages.

PRENTISS, JOSHUA, 3d.

1814, July 14, Marblehead. Asks Gerry's influence in procuring for him the place of sailing master's warrant in the U. S. Navy. Should the petition of the town to Congress be granted for a number of gunboats to be stationed in Marblehead, would prefer to have command of one of them. 4°. 2 pages.

PRENTISS, WILLIAM, to MADISON.

1816, November 23, Washington. Asks his patronage in support of a reading room in Washington. 4°. 1 page.

1817, March 7, Washington. Incloses a prospectus of a reading room and solicits his patronage. 4°. 1 page.

PRESTON, JAMES P., to ARMSTRONG, JOHN (Secretary of War).

1813, August —, Fort George, N. C. Acknowledging receipt of notification of promotion. Wishes to be continued in the command of the 12th Regiment. 4°. 3 pages.

PRESTON, JAMES P. (Governor), to MADISON. *Montpellier.*

1817, June 14, Richmond. Acknowledging the receipt of a letter of last May. Respecting the request of Valentine Gill for the place of engineer to the board of public works. 4°. 2 pages.

1818, May 20, Richmond. Qualifications of F. R. Hassler, who proposes to be employed as engineer to the board of public works. 4°. 2 pages.

1819, February 13, Richmond. Official appointment of Madison as one of the visitors of the University of Virginia. 4°. 1 page.

1819, February 27, Richmond. Inclosing his appointment as one of the visitors of the University of Virginia, with notice of the first day of meeting. 4°. 2 pages.

1828, May 9, Richmond. Wishes to be appointed Treasurer of the United States. Asks Madison's good offices with the President, as he is acquainted with his (Preston's) qualifications and integrity. 4°. 1 page.

PRICE, ALEXANDER POPE.

1799, November 25, Orange C. *H.* Solicits the appointment of clerk to serve in the house of delegates. fol. 2 pages.

PRICE, CHANDLER. *Washington.*

1804, March 30, Philadelphia. Notice of receipt of a barrel of wine per ship *Hindostan* from Cadiz, which he holds subject to order. Incloses bill of lading, two casks per sloop *Sally* for Georgetown. 4°. 1 page. 8°. 1 page.

1804, December 14, Philadelphia. Acknowledging letter of 7th. Respecting the forwarding of two casks of wine, one for himself and the other for the President. 4°. 1 page.

PRICE, DAVID (P. M.).

1805 (?), May 12, Surry County, Va. Incloses a letter believing that he should be informed of his enemies. 4°. 1 page.

PRICE, JOHN, Jr.

1805, August 31, Baltimore. Arrival of two pipes of wine which he has directed to be sent to the public store. 4°. 1 page.

1806 December 29, Baltimore. Is informed that the vessel in which wine was shipped had put into Guadeloupe, where it will probably be condemned as unfit for sea. The wine will be forwarded by the first conveyance. 4°. 1 page.

1807 March 7 Baltimore. The cargo of the wreck of brig *Jacob* has been saved and held by the collector of Newbern, N. C., until the owners pay duty. The wine is probably safe. 4°. 1 page.

1807, May 11, Baltimore. Ships boxes and barrel per schooner Cri*spin*, being part of the goods on the brig *Jacob*, cast away in North Carolina. 4°. 1 page.

PRICE, JOHN F., (Capt.)

1809, September 18, Richmond. Tenders the services of the Washington and Jefferson Artillery whenever the exigencies of the country require military aid. 4°. 2 pages.

PRICE, WILLIAM. *Montpellier.*

1827 (?), not dated. At the request of Rufus Stone, who is desirous of emigrating to Texas, he asks letters from Madison and Monroe recommending him to the government of that province, that he may not be considered a fugitive from justice, as most of the inhabitants of that province are. fol. 1 page.

PRICE, JOHN HARVIE.

1832, May 1, Richmond. Asks if Madison has any papers or vouchers which would be useful in authenticating a claim of Mr. French for land bounty granted to officers and soldiers of the Revolution. 4°. 1 page.

PRICHARD, WILLIAM. *Washington.*

1805, October 21, Richmond. Shipment of books to Mr. Mazzei at Leghorn, Italy. 4°. 1 page.

——— to MAZZEI. *Leghorn, Italy.*

1805, October —, Richmond. Bill of lading of two boxes merchandise. 8°. 1 page.

PRINGLE, JAMES R. (President of Senate) to MADISON. *Washington.*

1817, January 25, Charleston, S. C. Inclosing copy of resolutions passed by the legislature of South Carolina, expressing a tribute of respect in approbation of the wisdom, firmness and patriotism exercised by him during his administration. 4°. 1 page. fol. 2 pages.

PRINGLE, JOHN J.

1812, June 30, Charleston. Transmits as chairman resolutions of a meeting of citizens of Charleston, unanimously expressing confidence in the executive and promise support in carrying into effect their firm and energetic measures for prosecuting the war against Great Britian. fol. 2 pages. 4°. 1 page.

PURCELL, JAMES.

1809, March 17, Philadelphia. Wishes employment under Government. 4°. 4 pages.

PURDY, RICHARD.

1809, October 16, Orange C. H. Asks Madison to send him the amount of a draft which he incloses by mail. small 4°. 1 page.

PURVIANCE, JOHN HENRY.

1800 (?), not dated. Asks if sums received of the commissioners in London should be inserted as a credit in accompanying statements. [Private.] 8°. 1 page.

1813, April 5, Baltimore. Declines on account of ill health to accept the appointment to the intended legation to France. 4°. 1 page.

PURVIANCE, ROBERT.

1805, October 4, Baltimore. Account for duties and charges on 2 pipes of wine, with a receipt of Zachary Main of the same, which he promises to forward. 4°. 1 page. 8°. 1 page.

PURVIANCE, I. H.

1805, April 29, Baltimore. Transmits a letter and bill of lading from Mr. Lee, consul at Bordeaux. Will forward the boxes as soon as they are discharged from on board the vessel. 4°. 1 page.

1805, April 30, Baltimore. Forwards 2 boxes. 4°. 1 page.

1805, October 4, Baltimore. Forwards 2 pipes of wine. 4°. 1 page.

1805, November 11, Baltimore. Incloses letters from Mr. Lee from Bordeaux accompanied by invoice and bill of lading. Asks instructions about transportation of the goods. 4°. 1 page.

1805, November 20, Baltimore. Forwards articles imported in brig *Lyon* and gives statement of expenses. 4°. 1 page.

QUINN AND FITZGERALD.

1803, October 7, Washington. Asks the favor of lending them $100 for fifteen days. small 4°. 1 page.

RADCLIFF, WILLIAM S.

1816, April 30, Washington. Has been disappointed in not being appointed as judge-advocate. Would like Madison to make a selection of some position, now vacant, which his education and capacity entitle him to. 4°. 2 pages.

RADFORD, WILLIAM.

1802, February 9, Richmond. Asking his influence with the President to obtain for him the office of postmaster of Richmond. 4°. 2 pages.

RAGGI, GIACOMO. *Montpellier.*

1830, November 4, New York. Inclosing a letter from from Lafayette which he promised to deliver personally, but was unable to do it. 4°. 1 page.

1830, December 1, Charlottesville. Proposed monument in honor of Jefferson. Asks his assistance towards completing a subscription for that purpose. He is recommended by Lafayette as the artist. [In French.] 4°. 3 pages.

RAMSAY, ANDREW.

1820, August 5, Washington. Arrival of John Graham from Rio Janeiro in very ill health. Engraving of Jefferson to be sent to Madison. 4°. 1 page.

1820, August 30, Washington. Acknowledging letter of 13th. Is much gratified at the expressions of condolence to Mrs. Graham on the death of Mr. Graham. 4°. 2 pages.

RAMSAY, DAVID. *New York.*

1788, October 8, Charleston. Is authorized by Jefferson to draw on Madison for a specified sum, which he now does. The draft inclosed and indorsed after payment by the payee. 4°. 1 page, and scrap of paper.

1789, April 4, Charleston. Eligibility of an elected Representative to Congress, he having been absent from the country during the war. Asks Madison to support his memorial to Congress stating his opinion of the ineligibility of one of the Representatives from South Carolina. 4°. 2 pages.

RAMSAY, DAVID. *Washington.*

1805, May 20, Charleston. Introducing John C. Calhoun. 4°. 1 page.

1805, December 1, Charleston. Introducing Dr. Alexander Garden. [Signature cut off.] 4°. 1 page.

1809, May 17, Charleston. Introducing Thomas Heyward, of South Carolina. 4°. 1 page.

1809, September 5, Charleston. Incloses resolutions of citizens of Charleston expressing confidence in the administration and pledging their support. 4°. 2 pages. fol. 3 pages.

1812, February 20, Charleston. Recommending John D. Heath as an able lawyer. 4°. 1 page.

RAMSEY, THOMAS.

1817, February 22, St. Louis. Expresses his respect and esteem and hopes to meet him in the happy world to come. 4°. 1 page.

RAND, B. H. *Montpellier.*

1821, December 16, Philadelphia. Presents him with an elegant edition of Washington's farewell address, which he has just published. small 4°. 1 page.

RANDOLPH, BEVERLEY. *Philadelphia.*

1787, May 28, Richmond. Asks Madison to bring before Congress the matter of salary to be paid to one of the commissioners appointed to adjust the matter of cession of Western Territory. fol. 2 pages.

——— to VIRGINIA REPRESENTATIVES IN CONGRESS. *New York.*

1787, June 2, Richmond. Incloses copy of letter from Gen. Shelby, of North Carolina, to Gen. Russell, of Virginia, respecting that tumults may be excited by the temerity of the Franklinites [citizens of Tennessee], and Shelby's call for aid on Virginia. Requests the matter to be laid before Congress. [Copy] fol. 1 page.

——— to MADISON.

1790, April 27, Richmond. Requests his assistance in procuring the establishment of a regulation by Congress or Secretary of the Treasury to prevent the exportation of goods not duly inspected. Suggests a certain method to prevent frauds by inspectors. 4°. 3 pages.

1790, May 26, Richmond. Thanks him for his attention to the inspection laws of Virginia. Assumption of State debts. Thanks him for newspapers. fol. 1 page.

1790, June 4, Richmond. Settlement of accounts of individual States with the United States. Report of the commissioners appointed to settle these accounts. Asks Madison the sentiments of the members who spoke on the subject of Virginia's claims. fol. 2 pages.

1790, July 12, Richmond. The assumption bill unpopular in Virginia. The vote on the permanent residence of the General Government unexpected. fol. 1 page.

1790, August 10, Richmond. Acknowledging letter of July 25. On the appointment of more commissioners for settlement of accounts between individual States and the United States. Is sorry

RANDOLPH, BEVERLEY.

the efforts for augmentation of commissioners were unsuccessful. The assumption act as now modified will be more favorably received.
fol. 1 page.

RANDOLPH, D. M. *Washington.*

1803, September 27, Richmond. Asks that an inclosed letter for France may be forwarded. 4°. 1 page.

1807, June 12, Richmond. Asks Madison's advice respecting titles to lands in the Mississippi country.
4°. 3 pages.

——— to UNKNOWN.

1810, January 3. Part of a communication relating to an invention respecting carriage wheels and gun carriages, certified to by D. M. Randolph.
fol. 7 pages.

——— to MADISON.

1811, June 14, London. Soliciting the appointment of the consulship in Lisbon, or in case there should be a vacancy, in London. 4°. 4 pages.

1811, September 26, London. The event which his letter of June 14 anticipated has arrived. Refers to John Marshall as reference to his responsibility and integrity. 4°. 1 page.

1811, September 26, London. Duplicate of the foregoing. 4°. 1 page.

1811, December 16, London. New improvements in the art of shipbuilding and economy of force in navigating. 4°. 4 pages.

1812, November 10, London. Excitement caused by the statement in English papers of the building of privateers after a certain model in America. Refers to a previous letter respecting improved system of naval architecture, and hopes the adoption of his views, and of the inventors, will be remunerated by Congress. 4°. 3 pages.

1812, December 26, London. Seeing that 20 new frigates are to be built, he is anxious that that opportunity may be improved by testing his improvements, as described in his prospectus.
4°. 4 pages.

1815, June 15, Richmond. Naval concerns. Anxious to know the result of investigations as to the invention he is concerned in. 4°. 2 pages.

Montpellier.

1829, December 7, Washington. Asks his and Monroe's good offices with the President, to promote his purpose of being reinstated in the confidence of his country, by giving testimony as to his integrity. small 4°. 2 pages.

Washington.

Not dated. Application for a patent for certain improvements in the construction of wheel carriages of every description. [Last part of document torn off.] fol. 4 pages.

RANDOLPH, MARY. *Montpellier.*

1825, March 17, Washington. Presents Madison with the second edition of her cookery book.
4°. 1 page.

RANDOLPH, R. B. *Washington.*

1808, July 25, Petersburg. Appeal of an unfortunate mariner for pecuniary aid. 4°. 1 page.

RANDOLPH, R. B. *Montpellier.*

1833, April 24, Alexandria. Surrenders his commission, which he received from Madison, as lieutenant in the Navy. Enumerates his long and faithful services, and expresses his detestation of the present administration for the injustice done him, and for the spirit of persecution and gross tyranny. Is the victim of base and heartless injustice. 4°. 4 pages.

RANDOLPH, T. J.

1830, August 3, Edgehill. Inclosing a letter from Maj. Crozet recommending his brother as an assistant in the school of modern languages. 4°. 1 page.

1830, September 13, Edgehill. Appointment of assistant to the professor of modern languages at the University of Virginia. 4°. 2 pages.

RANDOLPH, T. M. *Richmond.*

1799, December 28, Charlottesville. Eligibility of Mr. Woods as a member of the house of delegates, he never having ceased to perform the functions of a minister of the Gospel. Question of the policy of his exclusion. 4°. 3 pages.

Washington.

1813, December 11, Georgetown. Accepts the appointment of collector of direct taxes, but in case the place should become a void one by the assumption of the legislature, he would be mortified at losing his post in the Army. 4°. 1 page.

Montpellier.

1817, October 14, Monticello. Organization of an agricultural society. Tenders the position of "honorary head" to Madison. 4°. 2 pages.

1820, December 28, Richmond. Introducing his brother-in-law, Mr. Hackley. 4°. 1 page.

RANDOLPH, W. B.

1824, November 20, Washington. Asks testimonials as to his character and qualifications to be used in support of an application for the appointment of Sergeant-at-Arms of the House of Representatives. 4°. 2 pages.

RAWDEN & BALCH.

Not dated. Transmits a sample of diploma for agricultural societies calculated for any State or county, with the terms for engraving. 4°. 1 page.

RAY, MOSES. *Washington.*

1816, October 30, Philadelphia. His intention to settle with 200 or 300 families on the Ohio or Mississippi rivers. Asks Madison's aid in prosecuting so laudable an undertaking. 4°. 2 pages.

RAY, WILLIAM, to JEFFERSON. *Melton, Va.*

1809, March 7, Amsterdam, N. *Y.* Acknowledging letter of 14th December. Publication of his book, "The Horrors of Slavery." Solicits the loan of $100 to secure the publication, now in the hands of the printer. fol. 2 pages

——— to MADISON. *Washington.*

1809, March 22, Amsterdam, N. *Y.* Asks for a place under Government. Incloses an original poem. fol. 1 page.

RAY, WILLIAM.

1809, March 22, Amsterdam, N. Y. A poem complimentary to Madison on his elevation to the presidential chair of state. fol. 4 pages.

1809, October 4, Amsterdam, N. Y. Asks if he ever received a book entitled "Horrors of Slavery" and a poem. Is hurt at receiving no acknowledgment. fol. 1 page.

1812, July 27, Elizabethtown, N. Y. Solicits Government employment or the loan of a small sum of money. fol. 1 page.

RAYMOND, D. *Montpellier.*

1829, January 26, Baltimore. Sends a pamphlet entitled "The American System." Commends Madson's letters on the constitutional powers of Congress to protect American manufacturers. 4°. 2 pages.

RAYNOLDS, WILLIAM. *Washington.*

1809, September 30, Muskingum County, Ohio. In behalf of the commissioned and staff officers of Ohio militia, expresses their confidence in the measures of the President in meeting the approaching crisis touching Great Britain's disregard of national obligations, and promises their support. fol. 2 pages.

READ, G. C., to MORRIS, CH., (Captain).

1813, July 14, U. S. Cutter Scorpion Informs him of the enemy's having a strong force, consisting of ships, principally war, got up as far as Ragged Island. 4°. 2 pages.

READ, JACOB, to MADISON. *Orange.*

1785, August 29, New York. Asks if he knows of any one in his vicinity who wishes to sell a gang of slaves, and the price of them. Inactivity of Congress. Contrasts the ability of the present delegation of Virginia with that of 1783. Madison's abilities and experience greatly missed in that body. 4°. 4 pages.

Washington.

1809, May 8, Charleston. Congratulates the President on his election to the office. Asks for the position of district judge. 4°. 4 pages.

READ, LUTHER H. *Montpellier.*

1832, October 4, Eastville, Va. Asks for information of a claim of the heirs of Lewis Perrault for advances of provisions, clothing, etc., made by him to the Illinois (*Sic.*) regiments in the Revolutionary war. 4°. 2 pages.

READ, THOMAS.

1820, November 1. Introducing Mr. Helme of Rhode Island. Small 4°. 2 pages.

REED, AARON (chairman). *Washington.*

1814, February 15, Hillsdale, N. Y. Address of Republican citizens of the town of Hillsdale, assuring the President of their patriotism and their readiness at the call of their country to vindicate her violated rights. fol. 2 pages.

REICHARD, F.

1815, November 2, New York. Incloses a letter from France. If there is an answer to be made to it, requests him to send it to him, as he leaves for France shortly. [In French.] 4°. 1 page.

REED, WILLIAM. *Montpellier.*

1818, February 14, Norway. Commission while acting as deputy collector in Massachusetts. 4°. 1 page.

REILY, THOMAS B.

1834, October 2, Washington. Introducing Mr. Crabb, of Philadelphia, who brings with him a lithographic portrait of Amos Kendall. small 4°. 1 page.

RENT ACCOUNT.

1800. Account for moneys advanced to sundry persons charged to Madison and credited by rents due him. [Name not stated.] 4°. 1 page.

REYNOLDS, ENOCH.

1820, February 8, Washington. The two copies of the splendid edition of the Declaration of Independence, for which Madison subscribed, are ready for delivery. Asks if he prefers them framed. States the price. 4°. 1 page.

REYNOLDS, H. G.

1834, May 15, Montpellier, Vt. Asks his views on the question: "Ought the Bank of the United States to be rechartered?" this subject being before the Montpellier Lyceum. 4°. 1 page.

REYNOLDS, J. B.

1818, November 18, Clarksville, Tenn. Anticipates a new field for speculation in the late purchase from the Chickasaw Nation. Is engaged in the pursuit of farming. Prices of produce. 4°. 2 pages.

1830, December 15, Clarksville, Tenn. Is much pleased at Madison's last public effort in putting down the Nullifiers. Trusts his example will not be lost. Political affairs in Europe threatening. Is now a farmer on a small scale. Lost his seat in Congress because he would not join the hue and cry against Clay. State of the crops and prices. 4°. 2 pages.

RHEA, JOHN. *Washington.*

1810, May 4, Washington. Sends a copy of a letter to his constituents. 4°. 1 page.

1813, August 5, Washington. Incloses a paper. [Subject not stated.] 4°. 1 page.

1815, August 16, Sullivan C. H. Has been defeated in the election for Representative to Congress from Tennessee. Has consented to offer his name for the next general assembly for a Senator of the United States. 4°. 1 page.

1815, November 24, Sullivan C. H., Tenn. Is no longer a member of the legislature of the United States. Submits to the decision of the majority, but regrets his defeat. 4°. 1 page.

1816, March 30, Washington. The great subjects under consideration of this Congress, internal improvements, expatriation and Spanish patriots, progress of the United States since the war with Great Britain, diminishing of the debt, and happiness and peace of the people. His views on these subjects. 4°. 3 pages.

1816, May 30, Sullivan C. H. Tenn. Thanks Madison for his appointment as one of the commissioners to superintend, at Nashville, subscriptions towards constituting the capital of the Bank of the United States. 4°. 1 page.

RHÉA, JOHN.

1816, July 1, Nashville. Is gratified at his appointment as one of the commissioners to inquire into and decide definitively upon claims set up by the Choctaw Nation to lands supposed to have been ceded to the United States. His views respecting this national policy. 4°. 2 pages.

1816, July 14, Nashville. Will be ready to attend to the business of the intended treaty with the Choctaw tribe that is confided to him as soon as the business of subscriptions for the national bank is finished. 4°. 1 page.

1816, September 6, Chickasaw Nation. Negotiations for the treaty with the Choctaws soon to begin. A spirit of amity and friendship prevails. Trusts that negotiations here will terminate so that a complete continuity of settlement of citizens of the United States will be from Tennessee to Mobile. 4°. 1 page.

1816, September 24, Chickasaw Agency. States the particulars of the treaty accomplished by the commissioners on behalf of the United States and chiefs of the Cherokee tribe of Indians attending the council in the Chickasaw Nation. Also the conclusion of the treaty with the Chickasaws. Gen. Jackson as an able negotiator. The commissioners to treat with the Choctaws. Will leave for the Choctaw factory in a few days. 4°. 2 pages.

1816, October 25, Choctaw trading house. The treaty made and concluded with the Choctaw Nation. Terms specified. 4°. 1 page.

1816, December 31. Blountville, Tenn. Hopes the treaty concluded with the Choctaws meets with his approbation. Gives it as his opinion that our country is in no danger of serious difficulties with any European power. 4°. 1 page.

1817, January 14, Blountville, Tenn. Hopes to see him in Washington before the 3d of March. Is informed that the treaties with the Chickasaws and Choctaws are ratified. The great benefits which will ensue. 4°. 1 page.

1817, January 16, Blountville. Expresses his gratitude for Madison's two appointments. Compliments him on the success of his administration. 4°. 1 page.

Montpellier.

1818, April 23, Washington. Acknowledging letter of 6th. Regrets being unable to visit him on his way to Tennessee. 4°. 1 page.

1820, May 17, Washington. Regrets not being able to visit him and Mrs. Madison. Incloses copy of a speech and a circular relating to agriculture and manufactures. 4°. 1 page.

1821, March 13, Washington. Inclosing a circular to his constituents. 4°. 8 pages.

RICAUD, MARY, to Mrs. MADISON. *Washington.*

1816, October 20, Baltimore prison. Appeal to Mrs. Madison to exercise her influence in obtaining a pardon for her husband, who is in prison on an action in favor of the United States which he is unable to pay. 4°. 3 pages

RICE, ALEXANDER (President), to MADISON.

1812, ——, Alfred, York County, Me. Proceedings of the York County Convention, declaring approval of the declaration of war, and for prosecuting it with vigor, and promising support.
4°. 19 pages.

RICHARD, GABRIEL, to JEFFERSON. *Monticello.*

1809, November 9, Detroit. School for the education of Indians. Plan of the institution. Government assistance required. Asks Jefferson to give directions relative to his correspondence with the Government. Intends to make his instructions a kind of amusement and recreation for children. fol. 4 pages.

RICHARDSON, ANSTIS E., to MADISON.
Washington.

No date. Appeal in favor of the father of the writer, who is to be removed from the office of postmaster of Newport, which he has held for thirty years.
4°. 2 pages.

RICHARDSON, R. D., to MORTON (Captain).

1813, October 14, Detroit. Extract of a letter relating to the council held with Pottawatomie and Miami Indians. An expedition intended to Mackinac and Long Point. Flag of truce sent by Gen. Proctor on the subject of private papers. Gen. Harrison's action in the case. fol. 1 page.

RICHARDSON, WILLIAM, to UNIVERSITY OF VIRGINIA, BOARD OF VISITORS OF.

1830, December 13, Greenwich, England. Applies for the position of assistant professor of mathematics, should there be such an office. Incloses testimonials. 4°. 2 pages.

RICHARDSON, W. H., to MADISON. *Montpellier.*

1824, March 1, Richmond. Notification of the appointment of the board of visitors of the University of Virginia, by the governor. Appointment of the day of meeting. 4°. 1 page.

RICHMOND CONVENTION, PRESIDENT OF.

1828, February 8, Richmond. Circular transmitting copy of proceedings and address to the people of Virginia, informing Madison of his appointment on the electoral ticket. 4°. 1 page.

RICKETTS, JOHN T. *Washington.*

1803, June 11, Cameron Mills, Va. Incloses a letter from a friend in New Orleans representing the present order of things there. Requests Madison to show it to the President and return the letter, which is confidential. 4°. 1 page.

——— to MASON, JOHN. *Georgetown.*

1813, April 20, Cameron Mills, Va. Unprotected state of the district against the probable movements of the enemy. The inattention of the Government. Suggestions. fol. 3 pages.

RIDGELY, CHARLES G., to MADISON. *Montpellier.*

1834, February 8, Navy-Yard, N. Y. As president of U. S. Naval Lyceum, announces the election of Madison as an honorary member of the institute. Inclosing a list of the officers of the U. S. Naval Lyceum and a list of honorary members.
4°. 4 pages.

RIDGELY, JOHN. *Washington.*

1808, December 21, Annapolis. Thinks he is entitled to the continuance of his salary as consul at Tripoli, and explains his unavoidable delay in reaching the United States. 4°. 4 pages.

RIDGWAY, COATS.

1802, February 24, Washington. Wishes an appointment as clerk in the Department of State. 4°. 1 page.

RIGAUD, AUGUSTE.

1813, June 11, Montpellier. Incloses a discourse in verse to Americans on the war of Independence. [In French.] 4°. 2 pages. fol. 7 pages.

RIKER, R., and others. *Montpellier.*

1826, June —, New York. Invitation of the committee of arrangements of the corporation of New York to attend the celebration of the Fourth of July. 4°. 1 page.

1827, February 26, New York. In behalf of the corporation of the city of New York, sends a copy of Mr. Colden's memoir on the New York canals. 4°. 1 page.

RILEY, JAMES.

1818, December 19, New York. As agent of James Stimpson, late consul at Morocco, he incloses copy of his representations and petition for settlement for arrearages of pay. Asks Madison's good offices with the Secretary of State to favor the claim. 4°. 3 pages.

RIND, N. B. S. *Washington.*

1813, October 13, Trenton, N. J. Communication from a young man of 17. Rambling and incoherent; evidently insane. fol. 3 pages.

RIND, W. A., to WHEATON, JOSEPH.

1820, April 24, Georgetown. Makes a statement, duly certified, respecting an interview with his brother, showing how he (Joseph Wheaton) had been disinherited for taking part of the rebels in the Revolutionary war, and against the British Government in the war of 1812, and disgraced by his family, who held positions in that Government. [*See* letter of Wheaton to Madison, July 1, 1820.] fol. 2 pages.

RIEUX, P. DE, to MADISON.

See DE RIEUX, P.

RINGGOLD, TENCH.

1816, February 18, Georgetown. Desires an appointment in the District of Columbia. 4°. 3 pages.

See VAN NESS, JOHN P., November 20, 1815.
See LEE, RICHAD BLOND, February 15, 1816.

1816, February 20, Washington. Applies for the place of superintendent of Indian affairs, which is to be vacated by resignation of Gen. Mason. States his reasons for the application. 4°. 5 pages.

1816, March 28, Washington. Withdraws, by advice of his friends, his application for the appointment of superintendent of Indian affairs. 4°. 1 page.

1816, May 23, Leesburg, Va. Incloses letters from Mr. Pinckney respecting his application for the office held by Mr. Boyd, who he supposed intended

RINGGOLD, TENCH.

resigning; that not being the case, trusts Mr. Pinckney's letter of recommendation may serve in obtaining another appointment.
fol. 2 pages.
Montpellier.

1817, December 24, Washington. As the office of marshal of this district is soon to be vacated, he requests Madison to return Mr. Pinckney's letter of recommendation, as it may be useful in his proposed application for that place.
4°. 2 pages.

1827, August 5, Orange C. H. Regrets he will not be able to visit him and Mrs. Madison. Incloses a letter from S. L. Southard, expressing regrets to same effect. 4°. 2 pages.

1831, July 4, New York. Announcing Monroe's death. Remarkable coincidence of the deaths of three of our venerable revolutionary patriots and Presidents. 4°. 1 page.

1831, July 7, New York. The last illness and death of Monroe described. Monroe's affectionate regard and esteem for Madison. 4°. 2 pages.

1831, September 23, Washington. Incloses answer of L. Lee for the information desired respecting his father's papers. Expresses gratitude for Monroe's numerous acts of kindness to him.
4°. 1 page.

1831, November 29, Washington. Mr. Lee's papers. Judge McKean's opinion in the Cobbett case, on the subject of nullification. fol. 1 page.

RIPLEY, E. W. *Washington.*

1814, March 29, Pittsfield. Solicits the appointment of attorney for the district of Maine.
4°. 2 pages.

RITTENHOUSE, DAVID. *New York.*

1790, January 19, Philadelphia. Recommends Francis Bailey, printer, of Philadelphia.
small 4°. 1 page.

RIVES, ALEXANDER. *Montpellier.*

1832, December 28, Charlottesville. Sends him two newspaper essays of his own, attempting to vindicate Madison's State papers, given to Virginia, on the subject of nullification and secession. [Signed, A Friend of Union and State Rights.]
4°. 1 page.

1833, January 7, Charlottesville. Acknowledging letter in answer to the anonymously-signed letter "A Friend of Union and State Rights." Will consider it confidential, and will show it only to a few friends who share his sentiments relating to secession and State rights. 4°. 2 pages.

ROANE, JOHN. *Washington.*

1810, April 17. Presents a few bottles of wine as samples of the product of native grapes of Virginia. Asks his opinion whether in our land may not be found not only necessaries, but all the comforts and luxuries of life, by suitable application and perseverance. small 4°. 2 pages.

ROANE, SPENCER.

1813, January 18, Richmond. Recommends George Hay for the appointment of Federal judge of the district of Virginia, made vacant by the death of Judge Tyler. 4°. 2 pages.

ROANE, SPENCER. *Montpellier.*

1819, August 22, Richmond. Incloses articles written by himself, published in the "Inquirer" on a subject as cardinal as that which involved our independence. 4°. 1 page.

ROBBINS, ASHER. *Washington.*

1811, June 3, Newport, R. I. Nomination of the successor to Judge Cushing. Denies the accusation that he (Robbins) was a monarchist in principle. 4°. 2 pages.

Montpellier.

1818, July 17, Newport, R. I. Has read Madison's essay, addressed to the Horticultural Society of Albemarle. Disagrees with him on one point in the application of the Theory of Tull as a system of incessant cropping by means of incessant tillage; states his own views at length. 4°. 6 pages.

1824, August 5, Newport, R. I. Applies for the office of judge of the district of Rhode Island, which has become vacant by the death of Judge Howell. Asks him to communicate with the President in view of this appointment. 4°. 2 pages.

1832, March 15, Washington. Incloses a copy of his speech in the U. S. Senate. 8°. 1 page.

ROBERTS, JONATHAN. *Washington.*

1812, July 6, Washington. Col. Anderson's pretensions to a brigadier-generalship. 4°. 2 pages.

1814, September 29, Washington. Protests against the appointment of Mr. Clarke in the place of Mr. Charles Bidde (signer of Treasury notes), removed. 4°. 2 pages.

ROBERTSON, A. *New York.*

1796, April 16, New York. Wishes him to think seriously as to the matter of the treaty with Great Britain, in which the peace and tranquility of the country depends. 4°. 4 pages.

ROBERTSON, ISAAC. *Washington.*

1804, March 17, Jefferson County, Ky. Desires a federal appointment in Orleans connected with the law, either one of the judiciary or attorney for that district, to not interfere too much with his practice as an attorney. fol. 3 pages.

ROBERTSON, JOHN, to RUSSELL, WM.
Surrey C. H.

1781, September 25, Richmond. Instructs him to proceed to Surrey, old court-house, and take charge of the duty of assistant commissary of issues. fol. 1 page.

1781, November 10, Yorktown. Official instructions from his chief, the deputy commissary of issues. 4°. 1 page.

1782, January 18, Yorktown. Certificate that Russell was employed by the superintendent commissary of issues, and for which he has received no salary. [Copy.] 8°. 1 page.

1796, February 16, Amherst County, Va. Certificate that Russell was appointed by him as assistant commissary of issues department. Wishes compensation for his services. 4°. 1 page.

ROBERTSON, J., jr., and others, to MADISON. *Washington.*

1814, February 11, Richmond. Recommendation and certificate as to character and conduct of Zachariah Brooks. 4°. 1 page.

——— *Montpellier.*

1831, March 8, Clifton, Amelia County. Asks information respecting the resolutions offered to the Virginia assembly in 1798, by John Taylor, of Carolina. Is engaged in writing a history of the Constitution of the United States. 4°. 2 pages.

1831, April 3, Amelia. Acknowledging letter of 27th March. Has nearly finished his history of the Constitution, but wishes to add something to make a volume of 300 pages. Asks Madison his views on certain portions of the work. fol. 2 pages.

ROBERTSON, J. (cashier.)

1831, May 24, Richmond. Notifies Madison of the receipt of a sum of money, which he has deposited, as requested, to credit of Edward Coles. 4°. 1 page.

ROBERTSON, THOMAS B., to SMITH, ROBERT. *Washington.*

1810, August 26, New Orleans. Incloses copy of an address to the Governor of West Florida, accompanied with a private letter to the effect that unless the United States shows some disposition to countenance the English who hold most of the offices there, a proposition would be made for an alliance with England.
[Copy.] 4°. 2 pages.

ROBERTSON, WILLIAM, to MADISON. *Montpellier.*

1819, February 13, Richmond. Appointment of the day of meeting of the visitors of the University of Virginia. 4°. 1 page.

ROBINS, JAMES B. (Chairman). *Washington.*

1812, September 8, Snow Hill, Worcester County, Md. Address of citizens of Worcester County, Md., declaring their readiness to cooperate with the General Government in carrying on the war in which we are engaged. large fol. 4 pages.

ROBINSON, DAVID H.

1813, January 27, Bowling Green, Ky. Efforts of the friends of Capt. Anthony Butler to make him the successor of W. H. Harrison in his gubernatorial seat. Reasons given why he is not suitable for the office. fol. 3 pages.

ROBINSON & HARTSHORNE.

1805, August 6, New York. Arrival of some packages from Halifax for the President and himself. Requests to be reimbursed for the necessary expenses incurred. 4°. 2 pages.

ROBINSON, W. D. *Montpellier.*

1820, December 28, Washington. Transmits by mail a volume of his Memoirs of the Mexican Revolution. fol. 1 page.

ROCHESTER, N. *Washington.*

1809, March 6, Hagerstown, Md. As chairman of a meeting of the citizens of Washington County, transmits resolutions approving of the measures of the administration and denouncing its enemies. fol. 6 pages.

1810, January 25, Hagerstown, Md. Inclosing proceedings of a meeting of citizens of Washington

ROCHESTER, N.

County, Md., approving the measures of the administration in repelling the insult of Mr. Jackson, the British minister. 4°. 3 pages.

RODGERS, JOHN, HULL I., and PORTER, D., to CROWNINSHIELD, B. W.

1815, April 25, Washington. Official information that the above named have met and formed a board of Navy commissioners and are ready to receive any communications relative to the Navy Department. [Copy.] 4°. 1 page.

RODGERS, JOHN.

1815, May 1, Washington. Acknowledging letter of April 29. Transmits a copy of rules and regulations which the board of commissioners of the Navy Department have established. The board propose to act with perfect unanimity with the other branches of the Navy Department. They desire that communications may be made in writing. [Copy.] 4°. 3 pages.

1815, May 16, Washington. Regrets that want of information as to the disposition of the naval force of the United States has embarrassed the board of commissioners in making their report, as requested by the Secretary of the Navy. They lament the appearance of reserve, which does not comport with the law authorizing the establishment of the board, in their opinion. 4°. 2 pages.

1815, May 16, Washington. Duplicate of the foregoing. 4°. 2 pages.

1815, May 19, Washington. Acknowledging letter of 18th. In respect to the Secretary of the Navy's belief of the "erroneous opinion" of the board of Navy commissioners, he gives an exposition of the law authorizing the establishment of the board, to relieve themselves of any responsibility which may result from a failure in the execution of it. 4°. 5 pages.

1815, May 23, Washington. Difference of opinion between the Secretary of the Navy and the board of commissioners, on the definition of the law authorizing the latter's powers. The board propose to adjourn until June 1, to await the President's decision on the question. 4°. 3 pages.

1815, May 23, Washington. Copy of the foregoing. 4°. 3 pages.

RODGERS, JOHN, HULL, I., and PORTER, D. to MADISON.

1815, May 25, New York. Construction of the law constituting the board of Navy commissioners, as interpreted by the Secretary of the Navy, and the board's opinion. 4°. 11 pages.

RODGERS, JOHN, to CATHCART, JAMES LEANDER.

1819, June 9, Washington. Acknowledging letter of May 28. The Navy board of commissioners testify that the duties performed by Mr. Cathcart were satisfactory. [Copy.] 4°. 1 page.

——— to CATHCART, J. L., and HUTTON, JAMES. *Georgetown.*

1819, August 6, Washington. Acknowledging receipt of his communication to the Navy board of commissioners, with a summary. The commissioners have derived much information from a perusal of it. [See letter from the same, June 19, 1819.] [Copy.] 4°. 1 page.

RODNEY, CESAR A., to MADISON. *Washington.*

1801, October 5, Wilmington, Del. Results of the election in the State of Delaware for governor, Senator, and Representatives. fol. 3 pages.

1801, December 20, Wilmington, Del. The opposers of the Republican ticket for governor dispute his election. The course to be taken to prevent it. 4°. 2 pages.

1801, December 25, Wilmington, Del. Fears that the fair prospect of increase of Republicans in Delaware will be destroyed without firmness and exertion in supporting the voice of the people. [Referring to the attempt to set aside the election of governor.] Asks Madison's views and advice. fol. 2 pages.

1802, January 18, Dover, Del. Acknowledging letter of 1st. Success of the Republicans in preventing the setting aside of the election of Governor Hall and substituting Gen. Mitchell. Describes the method in which the matter was managed. Postscript.—December 19, stating that Governor Hall has been qualified, and delivered an address. 4°. 7 pages.

1805, January 2, Wilmington, Del. Incloses a letter from Maxwell Bines relating to the appointment of a Mr. Watson as consul at Martinique. 4°. 1 page.

1807, January 7, Wilmington, Del. Merchants eluding the embargo. Regrets that Mr. Gallatin's amendment preventing it did not succeed. 4°. 1 page.

1807, March 21, Richmond. Acknowledging receipt of a note. Burr's case argued before Marshall, C. J., and his subsequent speech. Wirt has written that he will serve the United States as their counsel. Opinion generally expressed that the Government will be successful. 4°. 2 pages.

1807, April 1, Richmond. Burr held to bail on the charge of preparing and setting on foot an expedition against Mexico. The Chief Justice's statement. Gave Mr. Hay a list of witnesses to be summoned. 4°. 2 pages.

1807, April 21, Wilmington. Acknowledging letter of 17th. Anticipates the President's wishes on the subject of witnesses in White's case. Burr's men imprisoned, not being able to procure bail. 4°. 1 page.

1807, May 31, Wilmington. Acknowledging letters of 21st and 29th. Matters connected with the trial of Burr for treason. 4°. 4 pages.

1807, June —, Wilmington. Agreeable to request remits certain sums of money to be applied as directed. Judge Toulmin's salary. Original letter of Burr's on his pretended Washita tract. 4°. 1 page.

1807 (?), July 7. Introducing Mr. White, editor of the "Public Advertiser", of New York. 4°. 1 page.

1807, September 18, Wilmington. Acknowledging letter of 2d, inclosing letter from Judge Davis, respecting the trial of Floyd. Acquittal of Burr by Chief Justice Marshall, to the surprise of every lawyer. He may still be indicted in Kentucky. 4°. 2 pages.

RODNEY, CESAR A.

1808, January 7, Wilmington. This interpretation of certain points in common law. The Irish trade and failure of crops. The embargo. fol. 4 pages.

1808, November 19, Wilmington. The President requested to lay before Congress the orders and decrees of the belligerent powers which have isolated our neutral rights. Sends some information to contribute aid and assistance. Mr. Pickering's report criticised. Cause of the issuing of the Berlin decree. 4°. 3 pages.

1808. November 23, Wilmington. Has been occupied in Clark's case and decided in favor of the United States. Effects of the embargo. Very little difference in prices here of flour, etc., since the embargo. Suggests the publication by Congress of a complete collection of all the orders, decrees, and proclamations of the belligerent powers affecting the rights of neutrals. 4°. 3 pages.

1809, April 17, Wilmington. Acknowledging letter of 14th with inclosures. Approves of Madison's letter to Governor Snyder, of Pennsylvania, in the effectual mode of restoring the authority of the laws. Inclosing extract of a letter relating to White's case. The embargo. Its results. 4°. 3 pages. 8°. 1 page.

1809, September 6, Washington. Gives his opinion as to the receiving of Mr. Jackson the British minister. Incloses the authority for his decision. fol. 4 pages. 4°. 1 page.

1809, October 17, Wilmington. The printing of Mr. Lisley's work. Does not consider it sufficiently temperate and dignified for the Government to sanction. Does not anticipate any favorable termination in negotiations with Mr. Jackson, the British envoy. fol. 3 pages.

1810, June 7, Wilmington. Is detained from going to Washington by the confinement of Mrs. Rodney. Large shipments by the merchants of Philadelphia since the nonintercourse act expired. Fears that they are rash ventures. fol. 2 pages.

1810, September 26, Wilmington. Incloses letters from Capt. R. C. Dale relating to his resignation. He (Dale) has been selected as candidate for Congress. Conjectures as to the result of the State election. The Methodists will revolutionize the State. 4°. 2 pages.

1810, September 27, Wilmington. Inclosures received this day containing ample testimony of Col. Monroe's principles and qualifications. Suitable candidates to succeed Judge Cushing. 4°. 1 page.

1810, November 2, Washington. Draft of a proposed proclamation by the President, removing restrictions to commerce on the revoking of the decrees of Berlin and Milan. fol. 2 pages.

1811, May 10, Wilmington. Doubtful state of our prospect of reconciliation with France, supposed to be reported by the merchants in order to effect sales of imports at high prices. 4°. 4 pages.

1811, August 24, Wilmington. Incloses a letter from Mr. Kentzing. Is highly spoken of. Mr. Smith's publications beneficial to the administration. Reports of British vessels and a French privateer within our capes. 4°. 2 pages.

RODNEY, CESAR A.

1812, January 20, Dover. Acknowledging letter of 15th, unsealed. The "Mirror" the paper desired in which to print the laws. Asks information about our consul at St. Jago. 4°. 1 page

RODNEY, THOMAS.

1801, August 7, Dover. Acknowledging a letter. Reminiscences of the time when their services were combined in the councils of the nation to rescue our country from the vindictive hand of foreign despotism. 4°. 1 page.

1801, November 17, Dover. Wishes the position of clerk in one of the departments for his nephew, Caesar R. Wilson. fol. 2 pages.

ROE, E. MCDERMOTT. *Montpellier.*

1831, May 7, Mobile, Ala. Compares the assumption of infallibility of the Roman Catholic Church with the power created by any union of the United States for other purposes than those of external defence and international duties. 4°. 3 pages.

ROGERS, ALLEN, to MADISON, MRS. *Washington.*

1810, May 2, Philadelphia. Bill for horse keeping, shoeing, and sending a pair to Washington. 4°. 1 page.

ROGERS, JOHN, and others to MADISON.

1814, September 3, New London. Petition of John Rogers, Jeremiah Chapman, William Brudick, and Joshua Holt for a bounty for capturing a midshipman and two sailors of the enemy's squadron in Long Island. Annexing a certificate signed by the collector of New London and other Federal officers as to the truth of the statement. fol. 4 pages.

ROGERS, MAURICE.

1809, January 26, St. Jago de Cuba. On the political situation of Cuba. Is persuaded that the island should be placed under the protection of the United States in preferment to Great Britain. Incloses an account of the entries and clearances of American vessels. 4°. 3 pages.

ROGERS, THOMAS J. *Montpellier.*

1823, December 14, Washington. Incloses a volume, intended for the use of schools, on the causes and principles of the Revolution. 4°. 2 pages.

1826, January 5, Easton, Pa. Transmits by mail the third edition of his biographical dictionary. 4°. 1 page.

ROGERS, WILLIAM. *Washington.*

1810, October 4, Philadelphia. Introducing Dr. Baldwin and his daughter, from Boston. 4°. 2 pages.

ROMAINE, BENJ. *Montpellier.*

1822, January 11, New York. Sends by mail two pamphlets on the constitution of the State of New York. 4°. 1 page.

1829, March 30, New York. Transmits three pamphlets on the controversy between the late President (J. Q. Adams) and Harrison G. Otis and company. Also sends three pamphlets written by himself in opposition to the adoption of the State constitution of New York in 1822. His views on the subject of State rights. 4°. 2 pages.

RONALDSON, JAMES.

1828, July 28, Philadelphia. Cultivation of hemp in Virginia. Sends a specimen of New Zealand hemp. 4°. 2 pages and specimen.

ROSS, COLIN & JAMES. *Washington.*

1802, October 21, November 4, December 19; 1803, February 19, July 13; September 14; 1804, September 19; 1806, June 5; 1814, February 15, Fredericksburg. [Nine letters relating to shipments of tobacco and accounts of sales, etc.] 4°. 10 pages.

ROSS, DAVID.

1811, March 23, Washington. Accounts of George Webb, deceased, agent in the State of Virginia and receiver of her quota of revenue for the General Government. 4°. 6 pages.

1811, March 25, Washington. Acknowledging letter of this date. Thanks him for the information respecting the award in 1783 contained therein, which accords with the views of Mr. Tazewell. 4°. 1 page.

ROSS, JAMES.

1816, February 19, Pittsburg. Sends by Lieut. Stewart a specimen of woolen cloth manufactured at the Steubenville woolen factory, established by Mr. Wells, Mr. Baldwin, and himself. The machinery and engine made in the Western country. 4°. 1 page.

ROSS, WILLIAM.

1800, March 24, Washington. His occupation of printing laws of Congress given to another. Appeals to Madison's sense of justice. 4°. 1 page.

ROTCH, WILLIAM, Jr.

1813, June 17, Newport, R. I. Appeal of the Society of Friends to the President and Congress to restore peace. 4°. 2 pages.

ROYEZ, GABRIEL. *Orange.*

1785, May 24, Paris. Agrees to furnish the future publications of the encyclopedia at a stipulated sum. [In French.] 4°. 1 page.

RUELLE, ——. *Washington.*

1811, March 26, Paris. Political party in Mexico formed for the emancipation of that country and for declaring her independence. [In French.] fol. 2 pages.

ROULET, JOHN S., to MITCHELL, SAML. L.

1803, January 11, New York. Recommends Mr. Currey for the post of consul at Fayal. 4°. 2 pages.

ROUX BORDIER, ——, to MADISON.

1804, February 1, Lyons. The person to whom Mr. Adet had given a letter of recommendation sends it directly to Madison, as he was prevented from leaving Europe. [In French. *See* letter from P. A. Adet.] 4°. 1 page.

ROUX, PIERRE.

1816, November 20, Washington. Asks for a loan in order to establish a public tavern in Washington. [In French.] fol. 1 page.

ROXAS, Mr.

1810 (?), not dated. The writer proposes to wait upon the President, and incloses a letter from Dr. Rush introducing him. 4°. 1 page.

ROZER, F. H.

1801, October 25. States the terms which he will expect for the services of his servant to Madison, who wishes to hire him. 4°. 2 pages.

1802, October 2. The hiring of his negro man by Madison. 4°. 1 page.

RUSH, BENJAMIN, to JEFFERSON.

1783, January 24. Sends Jefferson a packet to be delivered to Benj. Vaughan, to whom he introduces. [A memo. on the back of this letter in Madison's writing.] 4°. 1 page.

——— to MADISON. *New York.*

1790, February 27, Philadelphia. Public credit and assumption of State debts. Congratulates Madison for his motion respecting the question on the prevention of wars. A proposition from the United States to the courts of Europe advocated, in the appointment of umpires, to decide national disputes without appealing to arms. On the subject of abolition of slavery. fol. 7 pages.

1790, April 10, Philadelphia. Is pleased at the prospect of the funding system being delayed until the next session, the elections intervening. Question of the temporary residence of Congress. Dishonorable influences used by the British minister to carry a measure. Has committed to press a pamphlet entitled "Information to Europeans disposed to migrate to the United States." 4°. 3 pages.

1790, May 4, Philadelphia. Madison's proposition in Congress for doing justice to the late Army of the United States both popular and practicable. Requests that Rush's opinions respecting the funding system may not be communicated to Mr. Coxe. 4°. 2 pages.

1790, July 17, Philadelphia. Count Andreani, as described in Madison's letter. The natural productions of the United States explored and described only by foreigners who are imperfectly acquainted with our language and who derive first impressions of us through British publications. The "residence" bill gives general satisfaction in Philadelphia. Our domestic debt. 4°. 3 pages.

Washington.

1805, December 3, Philadelphia. Introducing Gen. Miranda. 4°. 1 page.

1806, April 7, Philadelphia. Introducing Capt. John McDougal, who will petition to Congress respecting the loss of a ship. Rush has received acknowledgments and a gold medal from the King of Prussia for answering queries respecting the origin of the yellow fever. 4°. 1 page.

1808, May 6, Philadelphia. Dr. Thomas Clark, who contemplates becoming a citizen of the United States, and desires the interposition with the Government of France by our Government for his release as a prisoner on parole, at Verdun, France. 4°. 2 pages.

1808, June 21, Philadelphia. Has written to Gen. Armstrong in favor of his friend, Dr. Clark, and wishes Madison to forward the letter. Communicates the great satisfaction which Madison's late correspondence on public subjects has given. 4°. 1 page.

RUSH, BENJAMIN.

1809, March 13, Philadelphia. Congratulates Madison on his elevation to the Presidential chair. 4°. 2 pages.

1809, May 20, Philadelphia. Introducing his son, Dr. James Rush. 4°. 1 page.

1809, October 6, Philadelphia. Incloses a pamphlet by his son, Richard Rush, on the administration of justice in Philadelphia. Sends also copy of three lectures of his own on a new edition of his medical inquiries. 4°. 1 page.

——— to JONES, WALTER.

1810, February 6, Philadelphia. Introducing Mr. Joseph Roxas, of the City of Mexico. 4°. 2 pages.

——— to MADISON.

1810, October 29, Philadelphia. Sends report of the directors of the African institution in London. 4°. 1 page.

1810, December 9, Philadelphia. Informs Madison of a successful operation performed on his nephew. Refers to Dr. Physick's letter for particulars. 4°. 1 page.

1810, December 13, Philadelphia. Madison's nephew continues to exhibit all the marks of relief which he discovered on the evening after the operation was performed on him. 4°. 1 page.

1811, January 30, Philadelphia. Informs Madison of the death of his nephew. 4°. 1 page.

1811, March 30, Philadelphia. Introducing Mr. Caldwell and Maj. Plenderleith, officers under the British Government. 4°. 1 page.

——— and others.

1813, February 12, Philadelphia. Memorial of the Pennsylvania Society for Promoting the Abolition of Slavery, praying that measures may be adopted to prevent American citizens from participating in the African slave trade. Royal fol. 2 pages.

RUSH, JAMES.

1813, May 2, Philadelphia. Expresses his obligations for the appointment under Government received at Madison's hands. 4°. 2 pages.

RUSH, RICHARD, to CRAWFORD, W. H.

1815, September 1, Washington. Gives his opinion [as Attorney-General respecting brevet commissions. [Copy.] 4°. 2 pages.

——— to MADISON.

1816, June 29, Washington. Inclosing remarks relating to the act of March 3, 1815, "to vest more effectually in the State courts, and in the district courts of the United States, jurisdiction in the cases therein mentioned." Relates an anecdote connected with the recently asserted doctrines of British allegiance. 4°. 6 pages.

RUSSELL, JONATHAN.

1811, January 2, Paris. Conversation with the Marquis Almanara (minister of interior to King Joseph, of Spain) respecting the purchase of Florida. 4°. 4 pages.

RUSSELL, JONATHAN.

1815, February 15, Paris. Certain diplomatic arrangements in which he considered himself slighted. 4°. 11 pages.

1815, February 20, Paris. Is dissatisfied with the present American consul in Paris. Recommends Mr. Joseph Russell for the post. 4°. 2 pages.

1816, January 9, Stockholm. Wishes a suspension or termination of his mission to Sweden, for causes already communicated. Independent of these causes, he wishes to get married. 4°. 2 pages.

1816, May 21, Stockholm. Application of Reuben C. Peasley for the office of consul at Bordeaux. Statements concerning his character are unjust, according to the writer's opinion. 4°. 3 pages.

Montpellier.

1819, October 18, Mendon, Mass. Introducing Bernon Helme, of Rhode Island. 4°. 2 pages.

RUSSELL, WILLIAM. *Philadelphia.*

1796, February 22, Orange. Incloses letters relative to a claim for compensation for wages in the commissary department when supplying provisions for United States troops. [Remarks of R. Harrison, auditor, appended to this letter.] fol. 2 pages.

1796, October 24, Orange C. H. Incloses papers relative to his claim against the United States. Asks Madison to petition Congress in his behalf. fol. 1 page.

RUSSIA, ALEXANDER, Emperor of. *Washington.*

1811, July 20, St. Petersburg. Letter of credence of Count Frederick de Pahlen, envoy extraordinary and minister plenipotentiary. [Copy.] fol. 2 pages.

RUTGERS, HENRY (chairman).

1812, June 25, New York. Inclosing copy of proceedings of citizens of New York approving of the measures of the Government in declaring war and promising support. 4°. 1 page. fol. 1 page.

RUTLEDGE, JOHN.

Not dated. Notes on the proclamation of 1763, preventing the granting of lands by certain colonies within the limits of their respective governments. fol. 2 pages.

RUTHERFORD, J. to MADISON. *Montpellier.*

1827, May 25, Richmond. Advises him of the sale of Farmers' Bank stock standing in the names of Edward Coles and his sister Betsey and the deposit of the proceeds to Madison's credit. 4°. 1 page.

RUTHERFORD, ROBERT. *New York.*

1789, August 22, Berkeley County, Va. Gives his views on the Constitution. 4°. 4 pages.

1795, March 30, Berkeley County, Va. Is elected Representative from Virginia. Gives his political opinions. 4°. 4 pages.

RUTHERFORD, W. *Washington.*

1813, August 29, Washington County, Ga. Complains that Madison divides with the Federalists the lucrative offices of our Government. fol. 3 pages.

SAABYE, H. R., to JOY, GEORGE. *Gottenburg.*

1810, September 11, Copenhagen. Acknowledging letters of August 22 and 1st instant, respecting the payment of a service which was supposed to be rendered gratis. Has no fears of rivalship in trade with Mr. Erickson. Is an old friend.
4°. 2 pages.

1810, September 11, Copenhagen. Press copy of the foregoing. 4°. 2 pages.

SADLER, H., and others (American citizens in Paris), to SKIPWITH, FULWAR. *Paris.*

1795, November 23, Paris. Certificate showing that the robbery committed in the office of Mr. Skipwith, consul-general, was not owing to any negligence on his part. [*See* Letter of Fulwar Skipwith, July 21, 1796, to James Monroe. Copy.]
fol. 1 page.

SAGE, E., to MADISON. *Washington.*

1816, January 14, Sag Harbor. Recommends the appointment of Nicoll Fosdick as collector of the port of Sag Harbor. Gives testimony as to the worth and fitness of Mr. Fosdick for the place.
4°. 2 pages.

SALTONSTALL, ROSEWELL.

1812, July 31, New York. Expresses his indignation on the attacks of the press on our rulers. Incloses two articles, signed "An American of 1776," written in relation thereto. fol. 7 pages.

SANDERSON, JOSEPH M. *Montpellier.*

1820, December 9, Washington. Sends the first volume of the Biography of the Signers of the Declaration of Independence. 4°. 1 page.

SANDFORD, THOMAS. *Washington.*

1806, August 1, Campbell County, Ky. Asks that a patent be issued and forwarded to him. Great drought in Kentucky. Thinks that nineteen-twentieths of the people of Kentucky will support Madison at the next Presidential election.
4°. 2 pages.

SANFORD, JONAH.

1814, June 21. Litchfield, Conn. In view of the probable amicable adjustment of all difficulties among the contending nations for restoration of peace and tranquility, suggests measures to be adopted to prevent further effusion of human blood. fol. 3 pages.

SANFORD, NATHAN. *Montpellier.*

1821, January 19, Washington. Introducing William Beach Lawrence and John Q. Jones.
4°. 2 pages.

1826, April 27, Washington. Introducing Jeromus and Henry Ashley, of New York. 4°. 2 pages.

SANSOM, JOSEPH. *Washington.*

1813, December 16, Philadelphia. Suggests that if it were known at London to be the President's pleasure to make peace, effect might be given to the Russian mission by a friendly invitation to the American commissioners to make the British capital the seat of negotiation in the spring.
4°. 3 pages.

1814, February 5, Philadelphia. Suggestions as to the measures to be adopted for an armistice to prevent the calamity of another campaign.
4°. 2 pages.

SANSOM, JOSEPH.

Not dated. Presents to the President-elect a proof impression of the medal which completes his historical series upon the American Revolution. It commemorates the peace of 1783.
4°. 1 page.

SARGENT, JOHN HENRY. *Washington.*

1813, July 4, Charleston, S. C. Gives his views on the financial affairs of our country.
large fol. 3 pages.

SARTORI, JOHN B.

1801, December 15, Philadelphia. Introduces Prince Ruspoli, of Rome. 4°. 1 page.

Montpellier.

1821, June 21, Trenton. Acknowledging a letter. Directs him to send a statue, if he has no use for it, to Philadelphia, subject to the order of Mr. Cattarina. 4°. 1 page.

SAWYER, LEMUEL. *Washington.*

1807 (?), December 15, Washington. Apologizes for having caused the confidential letters of Pinckney and Armstrong to get into print. Takes the responsibility upon himself to lessen the public mischief. 8°. 2 pages.

1810, January 2, Washington. Applies for the office of collector of New Orleans. 4°. 1 page.

1811, April 13, Jonesburg, N. C. Would like the appointment of the office of consul of Tunis. Should it not be vacant would be glad to succeed to some post in Philadelphia or Baltimore. 4°. 2 pages.

SAY, BENJAMIN.

1806, February 3, Philadelphia. Recommends the use of cold bathing for a dislocated ankle. Sends pamphlets to Washington respecting yellow fever. 4°. 2 pages.

1806, November 24, Philadelphia. Asks Madison's good offices for his appointment as collector of the port of Philadelphia. 4°. 3 pages.

1807, February 13, Philadelphia. Introducing his nephew, William Collins, and Robert J. Murray, of New York. 4°. 1 page.

SAYRE, STEPHEN.

1801, May 16, Baltimore. Appeals to the justice of the Government in respect to a claim for debts incurred while in the service of the Government abroad. 4°. 3 pages.

1801, June 9, Philadelphia. Acknowledging letter of 23d of May, respecting his claims; their history; injustice of Congress in not remunerating him for his acknowledged services; unfairness of Arthur Lee in superseding him by his brother William, an alderman of London, to the place of assistant in the commission at Berlin in 1777. Lee's family influence in Congress inimical to himself. 4°. 4 pages.

1801, October 30, Philadelphia. Asks Madison to remind the President of his extensive and extraordinary services, long since. Have never been compensated. Appeals for the place of post-master in Philadelphia. 4°. 2 pages.

1802, March 10, Philadelphia. Asks to be restored in a position he occupied. Recapitulates his services.
4°. 4 pages.

SAYRE, STEPHEN.

1809, January 20, Point Breeze. Enumerates his qualifications and experiences, entitling him to a position in the Navy Department; can point out means by which the British navy may be rendered useless and contemptible. 4°. 3 pages.

1810, May 12, Bordentown. Appeals to the President for a position which was promised by Jefferson in compensation for past services, which he neglected to give. 4°. 2 pages.

SCHAEFFER, F. C. *Montpellier.*

1819, December 30, New York. Asks Madison's opinion on a "Report on Idleness and Sources of Employment," made to the managers for the prevention of pauperism in this city, which he sends him. 4°. 1 page.

1821, November 19, New York. Offers Madison an exemplar of his address pronounced at the laying of the corner stone of St. Matthew's church, New York, October 22, 1821. 4°. 2 pages.

SCHENCK, RALPH. *Washington.*

1815, August 24, New York. Congratulates and expresses gratitude for Madison's successful efforts in obtaining peace, and asks him to accept of an accompanying cup. 4°. 3 pages.

SCHMIDT, J. W.

1814, February 7, New York. Transmits a letter from the Chevalier de Wieberking, intrusted to his care, and asks how to forward the books and prints which accompany it. 4°. 1 page.

SCHOOLCRAFT, HENRY R. *Montpellier.*

1822, January 5, Albany. Presenting a geological memoir. 4°. 1 page.

SCHRUSTOV, ——, to SIMPSON, WILLIAM. *Gibraltar.*

1802, July 9, Tangier. Acknowledging letter of 5th respecting Simpson's letter to the Governor of Tangier and the latter's remarks. [*See* Simpson to Madison, July 3.] 4°. 2 pages.

SCHULTZ, C., to MADISON. *Montpellier.*

1828, October 11, Schultz's Range, Va. Asks Madison to transmit Schultz's late communication concerning the prosperity of Virginia to some printer. Strip of paper.

1829, January, Schultz's Range, Va. Extracts from his review on the Five Books of Moses. His views on revealed religion. 4°. 7 pages.

SCHULTZ, WILLIAM. *Washington.*

1815, January 11, New York. Will communicate in a private interview a scheme to annually raise $60,000,000 in a way that would cause no public clamor or be sensibly felt by the community. His only compensation is that his expenses may be paid to Washington and return. 4°. 2 pages.

SCHUYLER, PH. *Richmond.*

1788, June 24, Poughkeepsie. Announces by express the adoption of the constitution by the State of New Hampshire. [Annexing copy of a letter from John Langdon to Alex. Hamilton, to the same effect.] fol. 2 pages.

SCOTT, ALEXANDER, to SENATORS OF UNITED STATES. *Washington.*

1816, August 17, Port Tobacco. Circular letter denying charges made by one Law, that he sold negroes entitled to their freedom, and intemperance, which caused his rejection by the Senate to his nomination as Secretary of the Senate. 4°. 3 pages.

——— to MADISON.

1816, August 20, Port Tobacco, Md. In vindication of himself from misstatements made, which caused his rejection by the Senate to his nomination of the President to an appointment. Incloses a circular letter addressed to Senators and copies of letters from R. Brent and William Kelty, recommending him as candidate for the office of Secretary of the Senate. 4°. 2 pages.

Montpellier.

1819, April 7, Georgetown. Termination of his suits against John Law in Scott's favor. Sends copy of extract from the court record, showing its decision. Thanks Madison for his patronage and his friendly disposition. 4°. 2 pages and scrap of paper.

1819, August 11, Georgetown. Acknowledging letter of 2d of July. Thanks him for having written a letter to the President on a subject which Scott suggested. 4°. 1 page.

1820, January 2, Georgetown. Asks for a letter of introduction from Senator Barbour. Incloses letters from William Wirt, W. Kelty, and J. Mason, recommending him for an appointment under Government. Also would like a letter to the Secretary of State. 4°. 2 pages.

1821, March 10, Georgetown. Asks Madison's good offices with the President for an appointment under the Spanish treaty (secretary to board of commissioners). 4°. 2 pages.

1821, March 12, Georgetown. Requests his appointment as secretary to the board of commissioners of the Spanish treaty. 4°. 2 pages.

1825, March 24, Georgetown. Applies for office. His appointment to Pensacola was unsatisfactory. Asks for letters to Mr. Adams or Mr. Clay, recommending him. 4°. 2 pages.

1825, September 10, Georgetown. Claim for compensation for unusually heavy expenses incurred in a mission to South America which should be on the same footing as that of his contemporary, Mr. Poinsett. Incloses copies of letters to and from Monroe. 4°. 4 pages.

1826, August 22, Georgetown. His claim disallowed by Mr. Clay, the Secretary of State, on the plea of its being a settled account. Asks a small pecuniary loan. 4°. 2 pages.

1827, March 8, Georgetown. Acknowledging a letter containing some money. Failure of his claim. Asks Madison's good offices with the president to obtain a Government office. fol. 4 pages.

1827, August 8, Washington. Asks for a further pecuniary loan. fol. 1 page.

1829, June 6, Washington. The House Committee of Foreign Affairs reported a bill in his favor but was not acted on for want of time. Asks for a small loan of money. 4°. 2 pages.

SCOTT, ALEXANDER.

1831, November 10, Washington. Has obtained a land warrant on account of military services of Mrs. Scott's father. Asks information of certain military documents as evidence in other claims. 4°. 1 page.

SCOTT, CHARLES. *Washington.*

1807, January 31, Canewood, Ky. Introducing Henry C. Gist and Jesse Bledso, who go to Washington to report the discovery of a lead mine in the Indian Territory. . small 4°. 1 page.

——— and others to JEFFERSON.

1808, December 16, Kentucky. Resolutions signed by the governor and speakers of the house and senate of Kentucky, approving of the measures of the administration. Addressed to the President, Senators, and Representatives in Congress. [Certified copy.] 4°. 1 page.

1809, April 23, Frankfort, Ky. Inclosing copy of resolutions passed by the legislature of Kentucky at their last session. 4°. 1 page.

——— to MADISON.

1809, November 30, Frankfort, Ky. Incloses copy of a letter from Dr. J. Speed, relating to affairs in Louisiana. 4°. 1 page.

1812, July 30, Frankfort, Ky. Gives his views of what may contribute to the success of our contest with Great Britain. Suggests that William H. Harrison be promoted to an efficient command. Impatience of the militia of the State for immediate active service. 4°. 5 pages.

SCOTT, GUSTAVUS, to UNKNOWN. *Washington.*

1789, May 22, Cambridge. Acknowledging a letter of 5th. Would not object to an appointment to a district judgeship. Thinks Madison may be disposed in his favor. 4°. 4 pages.

SCOTT, JOHN, to MADISON. *Washington.*

1803, October 19, Orange. Wishes to have the lines drawn between his and Madison's land and to appoint some person to act for him in this matter. 4°. 1 page.

SCOTT, ROBERT G.

1812, February 9, Williamsburg. Wishes to be usefully employed in the service of his country. Would like to be appointed collector of revenue to the district in which Williamsburg may lie. Bishop Madison's health. 4°. 1 page.

1813, November 13, Williamsburg. Destitute condition of the discharged regiment commanded by Col. Mason, which has not been paid for six months' services. Recommends Samuel Travis for the command of the marine and barge force. 4°. 3 pages.

1816, March 15, Williamsburg. Application for the place of attorney for the United States, just vacated by Mr. Hay's resignation. Incloses a letter from St. George Tucker. 4°. 2 pages.

Montpellier.

1824, September 27, Richmond. In behalf of the volunteer companies of this State, invites Madison to attend the celebration at Yorktown on October 19, to which Lafayette has been invited. 4°. 1 page.

SCOTT, ROBERT G.

1831, July 12, Richmond. Acknowledging letter of 7th, inclosing copy of a letter from Robert Walsh relative to the late Bishop Madison. Will give all the information he is possessed of to aid Mr. Walsh in his biographical sketch to be introduced into the "Encyclopedia Americana."
4°. 2 pages.

SCOTT, WILLIAM (Sir), to JOY, GEORGE. *London.*

1805, October 27, London. Acknowledging receipt of letter of 24th, in which he declines entering into a private correspondence relating to subjects of the nature requested. [Annexed to copy of letter of George Joy, dated October 24, 1805, which see.]
4°. 1 page.

SEAGROVE, JAMES, to MADISON. *Washington.*

1805, September 2, St. Marys, Ga. Misunderstanding between the United States and Spain. In view of a rupture he gives his views as to the policy of taking immediate possession of the Floridas. Describes the manner in which it can be accomplished. 4°. 4 pages.

SEAVER, E.

1810 (?), not dated. Extract of a letter to the Hon. Levi Lincoln, urging him to accept the position of one of the judges of the Supreme Court of the United States. 4°. 2 pages.

SEDGWICK, THEODORE, JR. *Montpellier.*

1831, January 27, Stockbridge, Mass. With view of collecting materials for a memoir of the late Governor William Livingston, of New Jersey, asks information respecting the part he took in the debates in the convention held in Philadelphia in 1787, of which he was a member. 4°. 3 pages.

SELBY, SAMUEL. *Washington.*

1808, October 25, Somerset. Congratulates him on the prospect of his election to the Presidency.
4°. 1 page.

SELLMAN, J.

1808, June 8. Conversation between Mr. John Smith, Col. James Taylor, and Gen. Carbery, relating to a separation of the Union. [Copy.]
4°. 1 page.

SENF, CHARLES.

1804, January 24, Rocky Mount, S. C. Asks him to forward letters to relations abroad. The new establishment for the armory under his superintendence is making as much as the season and circumstances permit. 4°. 2 pages.

SERGEANT, ELIZABETH.

1813, March 22, Philadelphia. Application in behalf of Mr. and Mrs. Henry Gardiner, who come under the alien law, to procure his return.
fol. 2 pages.

SERURIER, —, to SMITH, ROBERT.

1811, February 17, Washington. Was unable on account of indisposition to call on Mesdames Smith and Madison this morning. If not prevented, asks the honor of presenting himself the next day. [In French.] 4°. 2 pages.

SESSFORD, JOHN, to MADISON. *Montpellier.*

1829, January 13. Gives details respecting the growth of the city [place not stated]. 4°. 1 page.

SESSIONS, JOSEPH. *Washington.*

1812, August 12, Adams County, Mississippi Territory. Resolution of citizens of Adams County, approving the act of the General Government, declaring war against Great Britain, and promising support and expressing confidence in the President. 4°. 2 pages.

SEVENTY-SIX, OLD CITIZEN OF.

1810 (?), not dated. Lessons in public administration being an inquiry into the present state of our maritime defence, the deficiencies in the means of our protection coastwise, the practicability of rendering our system more perfect, with a view of our national powers and resources in this particular. small 4°. 20 pages.

SEVIER, JOHN. *Philadelphia.*

1792, October 30, Knoxville. This country is wholly invaded by Creek and Cherokee Indians. A tolerably well-directed force speedily employed would suppress and check the hostile part of these nations. fol. 1 page.

1795, February 13, Greenville. Introducing Rev. Mr. Balch, president of Greenville college. fol. 1 page.

Washington.

1803, October 24, Knoxville. Capt. Richard Sparks, of the Third Regiment, stationed on the Mississippi for several years and greatly suffered in health, asks that he may be stationed in Tennessee. fol. 1 page.

1803, November 29, Knoxville. Acknowledging letter of 14th. Gives information respecting land in which Madison is interested. fol. 1 page.

1804, February 8, Knoxville. The troops from this country return after a long and tedious march from Natchez. Trusts that Government will pay off these men. 4°. 1 page.

1804, May 9, Knoxville. Has forwarded to Gen. Dearborn a letter respecting the subject of his inquiries. 4°. 1 page.

SEWALL, THOMAS. *Montpellier.*

1825, November 7, Washington. Sends a circular of the medical school recently instituted with copy of an introductory lecture. 4°. 1 page.

SEYBERT, ADAM. *Washington.*

1812, July 6, Washington. Appointment of William Anderson, of Philadelphia, as a brigadier-general. Gives his approbation of his appointment as colonel. 4°. 2 pages.

SHALER, WILLIAM.

1814, February 19, New York. Incloses an account of an action between the privateer *Governor Tompkins* and a British frigate. 4°. 1 page and a newspaper cutting.

Montpellier.

1818, December 18, Marseilles. His intention of forwarding a *paté de Perigorde.* Expresses gratitude for Madison's patronage and disinterested consideration. 4°. 1 page.

SHARPE, WILLIAM. *Philadelphia.*

1782, May 25, My own seat (sic). Acknowledging letter of January 21. Measures adopted in North

SHARPE, WILLIAM.

Carolina for completing her quota of continental troops. Finances of the State.
small 4°. 3 pages.

Washington.

1801, June 1, Iredell County, N. C. Has taken up the practice of law. Would like to be appointed one of the commissioners for making a treaty with the Indians south of the Ohio river.
fol. 1 page.

1804, March 11. Would like to be appointed one of the commissioners for a treaty or treaties between the United States and sundry nations of Indians on the Western waters. fol. 1 page.

SHECUT, J. L. E. W.

1813, June 8, Charleston. Asks his patronage in behalf of the Antiquarian Society of Charleston.
4°. 1 page.

Montpellier.

1817, December 11, Charleston. Presents Madison with a copy of an "Essay on the yellow fever of Charleston." 4°. 1 page.

SHELBY, EVAN, to RUSSELL (Brigadier-General).

1787, April 27, Sullivan County, N. C. Asks him to hold himself in readiness to assist the citizens of North Carolina against the conduct of the self-erected State of Franklin (Tennessee). [*See* letter of Beverly Randolph, June 2, 1787. Copy.]
fol. 2 pages.

SHELBY, ISAAC (Governor), to MADISON.

Washington.

1812, December 22, Kentucky. Resolutions of the Kentucky legislature approving of the measures of the President and the declaration of war against Great Britain, and declaring their readiness to support the General Government to the best of their ability. large fol. 1 page.

1814, January 25, Frankfort, Ky. Transmitting a letter signed by officers of this Government and most of the members of the general assembly of Kentucky. 4°. 1 page.

1814, February 6, Frankfort, Ky. Inclosing resolutions adopted by the general assembly of Kentucky expressing confidence in the General Government and approving the restriction on our commerce enforced by an embargo. 4°. 2 pages.

SHELDON, D. to GRAHAM, JOHN (Chief Clerk Department of State).

1808, June 2, Washington. State of the accounts of the bankers in London and the Department of State. 8°. 1 page.

——— to MADISON.

1815, February 20, Washington. Applies for the appointment as secretary of legation in Paris, should Mr. Gallatan be appointed minister.
4°. 3 pages.

SHEPHERD, ALEXANDER.

1801, October 8. Is informed by his connection, James Madison, jr., that he intends commencing business, and has recommended him to go to Stevensburg as a good opening. 4°. 1 page.

SHERBURNE, JOHN HENRY. *Montpellier.*

1825, April 23, Washington. Presents a copy of the life and character of John Paul Jones. Asks Madison's candid opinion of his conduct during our Revolutionary struggle. 4°. 1 page.

1833, June 12, Washington. Sends him a portrait of his father. 4°. 1 page.

SHEYS, J. B., and PETER LUDLOW, JR.

1819, February 11, New York. Proposed history of events which have grown out of the late Seminole war, and the conduct of Gen. Jackson. Asks Madison's aid in furnishing materials. 4°. 2 pages.

SHORE, JOHN. *Washington.*

1801, May 8, Petersburg. General conduct of Mr. Thomas Field, of Petersburg. Gives him a good character. 4°. 2 pages.

SHORT, WILLIAM. *Philadelphia.*

1787, March 23, Paris. Jefferson absent on a tour in France. Lafayette constantly occupied at Versailles at the *assemblee des notables.* The fire at Richmond may effect the question of the foundation of the capital of Virginia. 4°. 2 pages.

1787, May 7, Paris. Introducing Mr. Crevecœur, the French consul at New York. We will explain the present ideas of France towards America better than himself. America's credit treated with contempt in the *assemblee des notables.* Lafayette's exertions to prevent unfavorable ideas from increasing. Short's opinion respecting the means of paying the interest on our debt to France. The action of the State of Virginia relating to her debt commended. Mr. Jefferson crosses the Alps to Genoa and is now returning. 4°. 3 pages.

1787, August 1, Paris. Acknowledging letters of May 16 and June 6. Jefferson has returned from his journey and will write him an account of it. Lafayette's friends expected he would be made President of the assembly. His youth prevented his nomination. The inclosed papers will give an account of public affairs in France. Pecuniary embarrassment of France. Urges Madison to return to the next assembly in Virginia as there is nobody but himself who can oppose the dangerous influences of Mr. Henry. 4°. 2 pages.

New York.

1787, December 21, Paris. Acknowledging letter of 24th. Attitude of the advocates and opponents to the new Constitution in Virginia, Rhode Island, New York, and Maryland. Foreign opinions respecting the result of the Philadelphia convention. War or peace in Europe for the ensuing spring will depend on the arrangement of finances of France. Predicts a revolution. 4°. 2 pages.

1789, November 17, Paris. Confusion and disorder in Paris. The King and royal family brought back to Paris. Bread riots. The people believe the scarcity brought about by the clergy and nobility. Violence against these orders. The future government of France. Equal laws made by representatives legally chosen. Hereditary and dignified orders abolished. The constitution

SHORT, WILLIAM.

about to be made the best in Europe. Proceedings of the assembly. Jefferson left Paris in October for America. Arguments in Congress on subject of titles give pleasure to Madison's friends in Paris. Changing of titles in France. 4°. 2 pages.

——— to MONROE. *Paris.*

1795, May 4, Madrid. Wish of Spain for pacification with the French Commonwealth. Friendly interference of the United States desired. Asks instructions. Incidental remarks between the Duke de la Alcuda and himself. [Unsigned. Copy.] fol. 6 pages.

——— to MADISON. *Montpellier.*

1808, September 14, Philadelphia. Acknowledging private letter of 9th. Engagement of a vessel to be used for Government service and in which he is to take passage to France. Hopes to have a cipher with his dispatches. 4°. 2 pages.

Washington.

1808, September 18, Philadelphia. Destruction of the vessel commissioned to carry the Government agents to France and England. Waits instructions from the Secretary of State. Detention on account of the equinoctial storms. 4°. 2 pages.

1809, September 15, Paris. Annexes a copy of letter from Count Romanoff. The Emperor's determination to establish a close connection with the United States. Incloses a letter for Mr. Jefferson. 4°. 2 pages.

1810, February 7, Paris. Acknowledging letter of December 3. Intends to return soon. Difficulty and risk in procuring a safe passage. 4°. 2 pages.

1810, June 19, Liverpool. His intention to embark for America delayed. Sends dispatches by Mr. Erving. Reports the delay. 4°. 1 page.

SHOTWELL & KINDER,

1813, December 24, New York. Invention for the manufacture of a fabric composed of hair of cattle from the tanneries and wool. Sends a pattern for an overcoat, two parts hair and one of wool, and sample of carpeting. 4°. 2 pages.

SILLIMAN, B. *Montpellier.*

1818, March 3, New Haven. Asks Madison's countenance and favor in a scheme to concentrate American science on a general plan. [Alluding probably to the publication of the "American Journal of Science and Art."] 4°. 1 page.

1820, June 9, New Haven. Thanks him for his handsome treatment of the subject of his Journal of Science. Will send him the first number of Vol. 2 when it appears, disclaiming any additional remuneration. 4°. 1 page.

SIMMONDS, JAMES. *Washington.*

1812, October 26, Cumberland, Va. Expresses his confidence in Madison's reelection. fol. 3 pages.

SIMMONS, WILLIAM.

1814, September 23, Washington. Complains of having been discharged from office under Government after twenty years of faithful service without notice of any charge against him, at the instance

SIMMONS, WILLIAM.

of John Armstrong, late Secretary of War, from personal and fraudulent motives. Expects to be called on for evidence against Armstrong. Meanwhile would like to be restored to an official station. fol. 2 pages.

1816, January 30, Washington. Requests a personal interview in order to expose the extortions practiced on the cadets at West Point and the degrading manner in which they are treated for trifling offenses. Has papers to prove charges against Capt. A. Partridge, one of the professors. small 4°. 2 pages.

1816, May 10, Washington. Incloses report of the committee to inquire into the settlement of the accounts of James Thomas, quartermaster-general on the Niagara frontier. Expects to be called upon to give his evidence. Exposes to Madison facts in the case. fol. 4 pages.

SIMMS, CHARLES.

1802, July 1, Alexandria. Hears that he is to be superceded in the office of collector by Dr. Rose. Protests against his removal after the satisfactory manner in which he has filled it. 4°. 2 pages.

1807, October 30, Alexandria. Notice of entry at custom-house of articles per brig *Maria* from Lisbon for Madison's account, with a bill of charges and bill of lading. 4°. 2 pages. 8°. 1 page.

1815, March 27, Alexandria. Notice of receipt of wine, etc., per brig *Wanderer*, from Boston, with bill of lading. 4°. 1 page. 8°. 1 page.

SIMONS, ROBERT. *Philadelphia.*

1796, February 28, Mount Gerrezzem. Inclosing a memorial to Congress urging the impeachment of the President and 20 Senators for having violated the Constitution. fol. 3 pages.

SIMPSON, HENRY. *Washington.*

1815, January 17, Philadelphia. Has established a wool warehouse in Philadelphia for the sale and purchase of wool and solicits Madison's custom. Advances made on consignments. 4°. 1 page.

SIMPSON, JAMES.

1802, July 3, Gibraltar. Has received a letter from the governor of Tangier, advising that he might be permitted to remain there six months. As his majesty has declared war against the United States and caused the consul to be expelled something besides a letter from the governor will be necessary. Does not care to decide upon the matter without consulting with Commodore Morris. Suggests that Morris could show himself in force off the Emperor's ports, to act in case of need. [Copy]. 4°. 3 pages.

———, to TANGIER, GOVERNOR OF.

1802, July 5, Gibraltar. Acknowledging letter of June 29, advising him of the Emperor's permission to remain in Tangier six months. On the arrival of the frigate expected from America he will write to the Emperor. [*See* letter to Madison dated July 3. Copy.] 4°. 2 pages.

——— to MADISON.

1802, July 16, Gibraltar. Incloses extract of a letter from Mr. Schruston, Danish consul-general at Tangier, respecting the letter to the governor of Tan-

SIMPSON, JAMES.

gier, which he took upon himself to forward to the Emperor. Awaits instructions as to his return to Tangier. The *Adams* not yet arrived [*See* letter to the same of July 3.] 4°. 2 pages.

SIMPSON, ROBERT. *Montpellier.*

1823, December 1, St. Ferdinand, Mo. Announces Madison's unanimous election as honorary member of the St. Louis County Agricultural Society. 4°. 1 page.

SITMAN, JOHN, and others. *Philadelphia.*

1795, January 22, Marblehead. Acknowledging letter of May 28, 1794, respecting petitions to Congress on the laws relating to the fishing business, the chief occupation of the natives of Marblehead. 4°. 4 pages.

SIX NATIONS, TREATY WITH THE.

1784, October 22, Fort Stanwix. *See* Wolcott, Oliver, and others.

SKINNER, J. L., to MADISON. *Montpellier.*

1829, March 24, Washington. Sends him, at the suggestion of the Speaker of the House of Representatives, a set of the "American Journal" to examine at his leisure and express his opinion. 4°. 1 page.

SKINNER, J. S. *Washington.*

1814, August 13. Incloses a pamphlet given him by Admiral Cockburn. Query, whether they were furnished by his Government to be circulated with Admiral Cochrane's proclamations to the blacks of the South and Tories of the East? Conversation with Admiral Cockburn respecting prospects of peace. 8°. 1 page.

Montpellier.

1822, August 3, Baltimore. Comparison of Virginia and Maryland tobacco. Inclosing a sample of tobacco. 4°. 1 page.

1822, November 18, Baltimore. Transmits a specimen of northern corn exhibited at the agricultural exhibition at Brighton. Asks Madison to communicate with him on agricultural topics. 4°. 1 page.

SKINNER, TIMOTHY. *Washington.*

1809, March 14, Litchfield, Conn. Transmits in behalf of a Republican meeting resolutions adopted by it sustaining the measures of the General Government. large fol. 4 pages.

SKIPWITH, PULWAR, to MONROE. *Paris.*

1796, July 21, Paris. Loss of money belonging to the United States deposited with him to be remitted to Holland, and stolen. Asks Monroe for a statement of facts, which he is able to give, to vindicate him against aspersions on his conduct. 4°. 2 pages.

——— to ———.

1796, July 26, Paris. Robbery of money belonging to the United States placed in his charge. Transmits papers proving that the utmost possible care was taken of the money, as a means of vindicating himself against any calumnies. Gives liberty to the person to whom this letter is to be addressed to give publicity to the documents if it is found necessary. [*See* letter to Madison, July 27.] 4°. 2 pages.

SKIPWITH, FULWAR, to MADISON. *Philadelphia.*

1796, July 27, Paris. Incloses a letter addressed in blank from himself, to be filled up by Madison, inclosing documents exculpating him from any negligence respecting the robbery of money belonging to the United States placed in his care to be sent to Holland. The inclosures are a certificate of J. C. Mountflorence, T. Davis, and proces verbal of Denis Carpentier, commissary of police. 4°. 1 page.

SKIPWITH, HENRY, Sr. *Washington.*

1815, April 10, Williamsburg. Illness of Judge Tucker, who apprehends his speedy dissolution, and in case he dies recommends his son Henry to succeed him in the office he now holds under Madison's appointment. 4°. 1 page.

SLAUGHTER, PHIL. *Montpellier.*

1818, January 23, Springfield. His inability to get subscriptions to the paper he holds for the Central College. He hopes to raise something, however. 4°. 1 page.

SLAUGHTER, PHIL, and LONG, GABRIEL.

1825, August 16, Culpeper. Invitation of the committee of arrangements to a dinner to be given to Lafayette by the citizens of Culpeper County. 8°. 1 page.

SLAUGHTER, R.

1820, March 20, Culpeper. Death of Alex. Shepherd. Appeal for aid for his family. small 4°. 3 pages.

SLOAN, JAMES.

1829, November 18, Southport. Sends a small treatise on the "Baneful effects of priestcraft." 4°. 1 page.

SMALL, ABRAHAM.

1826, February 2, Philadelphia. Asks Madison to remit $5 for the volume of "Philosophical Transactions", as the society wants a settlement. 4°. 1 page.

SMITH, BERNARD. *Washington.*

1804, November 29, Washington. Forwards paper which contain writings of his own under the signature of "Franklin." Thanks him for employing him in the Department. 4°. 1 page.

1806, September 29, Washington. Request for increase of salary as an employé of the Department, extra work having been apportioned to him. 4°. 2 pages.

1808, June 29, Washington. Declares that the depositions made by one Gardner that he (Smith) was the author of certain communications which appeared in the "Democratic Press" in Philadelphia, on the subject of the approaching Presidential election, are false in every particular. 4°. 3 pages.

1811, March 12, New Brunswick, N. J. Transmits a newspaper containing an oration delivered on the 4th. 4°. 1 page.

1813, January 11, New Brunswick. Inclosing a letter from Robert Eastburn, who belongs to the Society of Friends and an advocate of peace, but a decided Republican and a supporter of the administration since the commencement of Jefferson's. fol. 1 page.

SMITH, BERNARD.

1814, March 10, New Brunswick, N. J. Inclosing a newspaper containing an account of a Republican festival in this city, showing they remain firm to the administration. 4°. 1 page.

Montpellier.

1820, September 6, New Brunswick, N. J. Opposition to his reelection as Representative to Congress, he having voted against the proposed restriction on Missouri. Thinks a letter from Madison, showing his appreciation of his services in the Department of State, and subsequent services, would be of great service to him. 4°. 2 pages.

1820, September 20, New Brunswick, N. J. Acknowledging letter of 13th. Madison's reasons for not wishing publicity to be given to his opinion as to the manner in which he discharged his official duties during his administration are satisfactory. The excitement respecting the Missouri question still kept up in New Jersey.

4°2. pages.

SMITH, DANIEL. *Washington.*

1813, May 10, Sumner County, Tenn. Introducing Maj. Howell Tatum, who desires the appointment of collector of revenue for this State.

4°. 1 page.

SMITH, DENNIS, A. *Montpellier.*

1825, February 21, Baltimore. Reviews his own services to the Government in the last war with Great Britain in loaning money at a critical period, and having an opportunity to be engaged in important fiscal operations in Mexico, asks if he will furnish him with a letter as evidence of having been useful in his own country in that particular department. 4°. 4 pages.

SMITH, ELISHA.

1832, August 24, Mount Vernon, Ky. Asks his opinion on certain points respecting the national bank charter. fol. 3 pages.

1832, May 1, Mount Vernon, Ky. Acknowledging receipt of the answer to his inquiries as to his opinion on the United States Bank. Inquiries about the decisions of the Supreme Court relating to the Georgia and Cherokee question.

fol. 2 pages.

SMITH, GEORGE W. *New York.*

1789, July 10, Tappahannock. Wishes Government employment. small 4°. 3 pages.

1789, September 22, Tappahannock. Acknowledging letter of August 15. Wishes government employment. small 4°. 1 page.

SMITH, ISRAEL. *Washington.*

1802, May 19, New York. Introducing William Albert Straus. 4°. 1 page.

SMITH, JAMES.

1809, June 18, Baltimore. Plan for the preservation and distribution of genuine vaccine matter for the prevention of smallpox. 4°. 12 pages.

1813, February, 26, Baltimore. Asks permission to forward a supply of genuine vaccine matter to the several surgeons now in the actual service of the United States. 4°. 2 pages.

1813, July 24, Georgetown. Has furnished supplies for the Army, and desires the Government to discharge the certified accounts. 4°. 2 pages.

SMITH, JOHN.

1801, August 12, Frederick, Va. Requests that John Boyd, surveyor of the second district of Pennsylvania, may not be removed from office. His services as a soldier. fol. 2 pages.

——— (Chief Clerk War Department), to JEFFERSON.

1809, February 22, Washington. Order for removal of intruders from the Cherokee lands. Inclosing press copy of the letter to Col. Meigs, requiring him to give notice to intruders on the Cherokee and Chickasaw lands, dated October 29, 1808. 4°. 1 page.

——— to MADISON.

1809, March 6, Washington. List of names of persons to be appointed agents of fortifications. 4°. 2 pages.

1810, August 7, Washington. Inclosing copy of letter from Lieut. Col. Sparks. 4°. 1 page.

1810, August 7, Washington. Inclosing a copy of a letter from Lieut. Col. Sparks. 4°. 1 page.

——— to SMITH, ROBERT.

1811, January 14, Philadelphia. Applies for the office of marshal of the Pennsylvania district. 4°. 1 page.

——— to MADISON.

1814, January 24, New York. Suggests that a relaxation of the law laying an embargo, which will operate so hard on a large portion of the inhabitants of Long Island, may be considered, as almost the sole occupation of those on the south side consists in supplying cord wood for the city of New York. 4°. 3 pages.

——— to GALLATIN, ALBERT.

1816, April 5, New York. Asks that John Jacob Astor be appointed one of the commissioners for receiving the subscriptions to the bank. He contemplates becoming a large stockholder. 4°. 1 page.

SMITH, JOHN ADAMS, to MADISON.

1815, May 18, New York. Solicits the appointment of secretary of legation to the Court of St. James. 4°. 1 page.

SMITH, JOHN B. *Richmond.*

1784, June 21, Hampden-Sydney. Protesting against the incorporation of the Episcopal Church in Virginia. fol. 2 pages.

1785, May —. Respecting a dispute between Carter H. Harrison and himself in Madison's presence. Asks if he recollects a remark of Harrison's about Dissenters. 8°. 1 page.

1786, December —, Hampden, Sydney. Acknowledging letter by Mr. Allen. Has serious alarm for the situation of our country. Tyrannical usurpations on the rights of man. Matters respecting Madison's nephew. Mr. Smith agreeably disappointed in him. fol. 1 page.

1787, May 26. Receipt for money received on account of Madison's nephew. strip of paper.

1788, June 12, Hampden, Sydney. Expresses his indignation as to Henry's opposition to the Federal Constitution. small 4°. 4 pages.

SMITH, J. H. *Montpellier.*

1825, June 27, Montpellier, Hanover County. Sends proposals for publishing a weekly paper in Richmond. Solicits Madison's subscription.
4°. 1 page.

SMITH, J. K. *Washington.*

1810, March 18, New Orleans. Certificates of land located for the Marquis Lafayette. fol. 1 page.

1810, May 15, New Orleans. Acknowledging letter of April 12. Information respecting the location of the lands presented by Congress to Lafayette.
4°. 3 pages.

1810, July 14, New Orleans. Acknowledging letter of May 28. On the location of Lafayette's land.
4°. 2 pages.

SMITH, JOHN R.

1808, January 29, Philadelphia. Transmits a pamphlet, the work of Mr. Rose, father of the British envoy, on the financial affairs of the British during the administration of Mr. Pitt.
4°. 1 page.

1810, February 3, Philadelphia. Introducing Robert Smith, one of the directors of the Bank of the United States. 4°. 2 pages.

SMITH, LARKIN. *Philadelphia.*

1791, November 10, King and Queen, Va. Asks his advice respecting a claim for commutation from which he was deprived under peculiar circumstances. fol. 2 pages.

Washington.

1801, August 14, Ricohoe, King and Queen County, Va. Recommends Lawrence Muse as collector of Norfolk in case the present incumbent is removed.
4°. 3 pages.

1809, May 3, King and Queen, Va. Suggests the appointment of an officer of intelligence and correct political principles to command in the garrison of Norfolk. 4°. 1 page.

1813, January 13, Norfolk. Recommends Littleton W. Tazewell to supply the vacancy made by the death of Judge Tyler. 4°. 2 pages.

SMITH, M.

Not dated. Wishes to visit Madison and his mother, who he hears is religious. Is a Baptist minister. 4°. 1 page.

1814, January 30, Richmond. Giving his views respecting the war. Suggests a method of conducting a campaign in the Canadas.
fol. 3 pages.

SMITH, O'BRIEN.

1802, June 10, Charleston. Recommends John O'Hara to be appointed consul at Kingston, Jamaica.
4°. 1 page.

SMITH, ——, Rev. *Montpellier.*

1829, (?), not dated. Thanks for books loaned him.
small 4°. 1 page.

SMITH, ROBERT (Secretary of Navy).
Washington.

1802, August 3, Washington. Acknowledging letter of July 29. Has instructed Lieut. Chauncey to

SMITH, ROBERT (Secretary of Navy).

receive money from the Secretary of the Treasury and to deliver it to the U. S. consul at Algiers. 4°. 2 pages.

1806, (?), not dated. Memorandum respecting the naval force in the Mediterranean, repairs, expenses, and condition. [Unsigned.] 4°. 2 pages.

1807, April 17 Washington Mentions the sum to be paid for the passage of Mr. Purviance in the *Wasp.* 4°. 1 page.

1809, March 6, Washington. Submits two papers containing nominations of Navy agents and officers in the Corps of Marines. 4°. 1 page.

1809, March 6, Washington. Requests the President's signature to blank warrants inclosed. 4°. 1 page.

1809, March 6, Washington. Sends the names of persons to be appointed surgeon and surgeon's mates in the Navy. 4°. 1 page.

1809, September 6, Washington. Inclosing a communication from Governor Claiborne. Asks instructions respecting it. Incloses a letter from Gen. Turrean, as requested. Accounts of a second battle on the Danube not authenticated. Mr. Jackson, British minister, arrived in Annapolis. 4°. 2 pages.

1809, September 8, Washington. Incloses the only original dispatch received by Mr. Jackson. It indicates something like a change of temper on the part of the British Government. 4°. 1 page.

1809, (?) not dated. Recommending Mr. Lowry as a good Republican, who understands French and Spanish. [In pencil.] 4°. 1 page.

1809, (?) not dated. Has seen Col. McKee, who will immediately proceed to the country in question but not in the character of a secretary. Asks the President to designate a proper person as secretary to Matthews. [In pencil.] 4°. 1 page.

SMITH, SAMUEL. *Orange C. H.*

1799, September 3. Acknowledging letter of August 25. Transmits a copy of a circular letter to answer such inquiries as Madison makes in the name of his friend. Wishes Madison would return to public life. 4°. 1 page.

Washington.

1801, June 30, Baltimore. Incloses a letter received by his house. The writer, a gentleman of intelligence, doubts the treaty being confirmed in any other way than *in toto.* News of a complete victory by the French in Egypt. Thinks there will be peace if the King of England dies, not otherwise. 4°. 1 page.

1801, July 9, Baltimore. Change of route of the mails from Philadelphia to Pittsburg. Thinks this has been done to make the administration unpopular, or from improper motives. 4°. 2 pages.

1801, July 9, Baltimore. John Dumeste, about to go to the Isle of France, wishes a passport for himself and family. By him he wishes to send a commission to William Buchanan as commercial agent for the Isles of France and Bourbon. 4°. 2 pages.

SMITH, SAMUEL.

1801, July 12, Baltimore. Introducing Mr. O'Mealy, who wishes the commercial agency at Havre. 4°. 1 page.

1801, July 17, Baltimore. Thinks that Mr. Patterson should not be appointed consul at Nantes. Edward Jones's appointment to Guadeloupe is said to be a bad one. Mr. Gautt's nomination to Nantes may gratify his friends. The appointment of Capt. Neill to the *Boston* is unfortunate. His brother (Robert Smith) would have preferred a post as judge or attorney-general to the Navy Department. 4°. 2 pages.

1801, July 21, Baltimore. Troublesome demands of Mr. Pichon, the French minister, respecting captures of French vessels condemned in British ports. 4°. 2 pages.

1801, December 3, Baltimore. Acknowledging receipt of two letters. Has mislaid or lost an order if not in the Department. 4°. 1 page.

1801, December 29, Baltimore. Has found and incloses Mr. Dawson's orders for balances due him from the United States. Gives facts relating to weights of tobacco, rice, and freights. 4°. 2 pages.

1803, April 1, Baltimore. Names a firm as agents in London. Is informed that all the frigates, except two, are ordered home from the Mediterranean. Thinks it will raise insurance rates and interfere with commerce. Suggests that more frigates be sent out. 4°. 2 pages.

1803, April 6, Baltimore. Presses the appointment of Mackensie & Glenisie, of London, merchants, as agents. 4°. 1 page.

1804, May 4, Baltimore. Calls attention to an inclosed letter from John A. Morton to Nathaniel Morton, respecting his application for the consulship at Bordeaux, in case Mr. Lee is dismissed from that post on account of the failure of his house (Perrot & Lee). 4°. 1 page.

1804, May 17, Baltimore. Is informed that Government intends sending armed vessels to the neighborhood of Hispaniola to protect our commerce. Republican merchants protest against this measure, it being a breach of neutrality to prevent trade with revolted slaves, as all know the risk. 4°. 2 pages.

——— to GALLATIN, ALBERT.

1804, June 20, Baltimore. Claims submitted by Capt. Barney, in which his (Smith's) name appears among others. Denies that he has any claims whatever against the French nation on the contract alluded to. [Copy.] 4°. 1 page.

——— to BARNEY, JOSHUA.

1804, October 26, Baltimore. States that no inquiry has ever been made, nor has he given any information respecting items of his claims against the French nation, except as to that alluded to in his letter to Mr. Gallatin. [Copy.] 4°. 2 pages.

——— to MADISON.

1804, October 27, Baltimore. Incloses letter from Capt. Barney and copy of his answer to it. 4°. 1 page.

1805, May 25, Baltimore. Introducing Mr. Barclay and Mr. Davis. 4°. 1 page.

SMITH, SAMUEL.

1805, September 28, Baltimore. Inclosing extract of a letter from Mackenzie & Gleinsie respecting a new Government order relating to vessels and their cargoes bound from an enemy's port direct to the East or West Indies as good prize. 4°. 2 pages.

1805 (?), not dated. Suggesting a change in the laws relating to imports and exports. Incloses a sketch of a proposed act of Congress. 4°. 3 pages.

1806, July 21, Baltimore. Introducing William Duer, lately from New Orleans. 4°. 1 page.

1806, July 21, Baltimore. Introducing Dr. Davizeau, lately arrived from New Orleans. 4°. 1 page.

1807, August 20, Baltimore. Debates in Parliament respecting the American intercourse law. Thinks publicity should be given them. 4°. 1 page.

1809, March 20, Baltimore. The business of the Navy agent in Baltimore has been transferred from the Bank of Baltimore to the Branch Bank. The former had a Republican president and very few Republicans have any business with the latter. Thinks it not too late for the order to be changed. 4°. 1 page.

1810, June 7, Baltimore. Late surrender of American property by the King of Holland to the Emperor of France. Suggests retaliation by seizing Dutch property in the United States. 4°. 3 pages.

1810, August 17, Baltimore. Incloses extract of a letter from Vincent Gray from Havana respecting the execution of a young man from Mexico as an emissary of Napoleon's. 4°. 1 page.

1810, December 12, Washington. Notes on the commerce of Russia with the United States, by his son. 4°. 1 page.

1811, February 4, Baltimore. Incloses copy of a letter from the supercargo of the schooner *Friendship*, of her arrival in Bordeaux and subjected to quarantine, and ordered by the authorities to land her cargo. 4°. 2 pages.

1811, not dated. Inclosing copies of letters from Jere. Sullivan to Solomon Etting and from A. McKim, relating to the schooner *Friendship*. [*See* Sullivan, Jere., February 5, 1811.] 4°. 1 page.

SMITH, SAMUEL H. *Orange.*

1800, August 27, Philadelphia. Proposes to publish a newspaper at the seat of Government to advance the best interests of the Government. Asks Madison's approval and cooperation. 4°. 2 pages.

——— to CALLENDER, JAMES T. *Richmond.*

1801, April 15, Washington. States how he procured information from the Department of State respecting Callender's case. [Annexed is an answer from Callender.] 4°. 1 page.

——— to WASHINGTON CRIMINAL COURT.

1811, June 15, Washington. Statement by the foreman of the grand jury respecting Nancy Gerry, a free mulatto girl sold as a slave, and supposed to have been carried to Georgia. Asks that she be reclaimed. [Certified copy.] 4°. 1 page.

SMITH, SAMUEL H., to MADISON. *Washington.*

1801, June 24, Washington. Offer of the appointment of Mr. Caldwell to the consulate at St. Domingo. 4°. 1 page.

1813, July 29, Washington. Will accept the appointment tendered him by the President of Commissioner of the Revenue. fol. 1 page.

1814, May 12, Washington. On the resignation of William Ward as collector for the Tenth district of Massachusetts. He writes to Mr. Gerry, who recommends Mr. Levi Thaxter for the place. Incloses Gerry's answer, also one to Mr. Cutts from Mr. Gorden, who has been rejected by the Senate. 4°. 2 pages.

1814, May 20, Washington. States that Mr. Dolton, collector of the Ninth district of Massachusetts, has not furnished the bond required by law. Incloses letters recommending Robert Farley, should there be a vacancy in that office. fol. 2 pages.

1815, April 4, Washington. Joseph Dougherty, whom Madison selected to transport Jefferson's library, is not satisfied with the proposed compensation. 4°. 1 page.

Montpellier.

1826, October 25, Washington. Has undertaken, at the request of the Columbian Institute, to prepare a memoir of Jefferson. Asks Madison's assistance. 4°. 2 pages.

1827, January 24, Sidney. Presents Madison with a copy of his memoirs of Jefferson. Thinks this the proper time for Madison to publish with the sanction of his name the debates of Congress and those of the general convention. 4°. 2 pages.

1834, September 11, Washington. Transmits an inclosed letter to Mrs. Madison. 4°. 1 page.

SMITH, SAMUEL STANHOPE. *Orange.*

1778 (?), not dated. Congratulates him on his election to the executive council of Virginia. Contains a long philosophical essay on liberty and necessity. fol. 16 pages.

1778, September 15, Hampden Sidney. Discussion on moral liberty. Distinction between desire and volition. fol. 5 pages.

New York.

1787, December 12, Princeton. Mr. John Fitch about to make application to Congress for assistance to complete his steamboat. Recommends that Madison should assist him. 4°. 2 pages.

1789, March 26, Princeton. Introducing John Churchman, who believes he has discovered a method for readily ascertaining the longitude. small. 4°. 2 pages.

Philadelphia.

1795, January 4, Princeton. Ask if he can copy any notes Madison may have of his discussion on the Federal Constitution, as he is to introduce into the philosophic course of his college some general observations on that subject. 4°. 2 pages.

Orange.

1799, November 28, Princeton. Acknowledging letter of August 25; gives items for tuition, rooms, rent, board, and other expenses at Princeton College. 4°. 2 pages.

SMITH, SAMUEL STANHOPE. *Washington.*

1809, April 14, Princeton. Dismissal of his son, John W. Smith, from the position of clerk of the supreme court in New Orleans, by Governor Claiborne. Ask Madison's opinion, or decision, as to the powers of the governor. 4°. 2 pages.

SMITH, THOMAS S., and others. *Montpellier.*

1834, April 2, Philadelphia. Invitation of a committee in behalf of the Jefferson Democratic Society to a dinner to be given on 14th April. 4°. 1 page.

SMITH, THOMAS R., to IRVING, WILLIAM and JOTHAM POST, JR., jointly. *Washington.*

1814, October 1, New York. Is directed by the committee of defense to inclose copy of a memorial to the President on the subject of the removal of the commander of this military district, and substituting some able and efficient officer. Urges their immediate attention to the subject. 4°. 2 pages.

SMITH, WILLIAM, to MADISON.

1806, April 25, Baltimore. Acknowledging receipt of the Treasurer's draft for amount of draft inclosed for acceptance. Asks if there is any probability that the Floridas will be purchased by the United States. 4°. 2 pages.

Montpellier.

1822, March 31. Wishes to have the boundary line settled between their two estates, as he wishes to build a fence. fol. 1 page.

1822, April 9. Settlement of the boundary line between their estates. Makes an offer to purchase Madison's interest of a portion. 4°. 1 page.

SMITH, WILLIAM H. *Washington.*

1806, April 20, Baltimore. Asks the favor of Madison to present an inclosed draft for acceptance on H. Dearborn. 4°. 1 page.

SMITH, WILLIAM S., and SAMUEL G. OGDEN.

Not dated. Refusal of the heads of Departments to testify before a special circuit court for the district of New York on the part of William S. Smith and S. G. Ogden, severally, in certain issues of traverse between the United States and said Smith and Ogden. The President can not dispense with their services. [Unsigned.] 4°. 3 pages.

SMITH, WILLIAM S., to MADISON.

1815, May 17, New York. His son, W. S. Smith, secretary of legation at the court of Russia, is at home on a visit, and does not wish to return as secretary of legation. His son, John Adams Smith, would like to be appointed secretary of legation at the Court of St. James. 4°. 1 page.

SMOCK, JAMES.

1814, April 13, Fredericksburg. Asks Madison to accept the present of a saddle as a token of his respect and approbation of his course during the late war. 4°. 1 page.

SMOOT, A. S.

1805, May 7. Wishes to be appointed clerk in the Department of State. 4°. 1 page.

SMYTH, ALEXANDER.

1812 (?), not dated. Hears that his promotion will be objected to. He will undertake to justify the

SMYTH, ALEXANDER.

appointment by proving that he is incorruptible, disinterested, patriotic, and brave as any man in the nation. [Annexed to this is a duplicate.] 4°. 3 pages.

1812, April 23, Washington. Presents evidence justifying himself. [Probably lost or misplaced.] 4°. 1 page.

SMYTH, WILLIAM.

1814, February 5, New Glasgow, Va. Complains that he was wounded in the same battle with Capt. Moor, who was honorably mentioned, and he (himself) was not. Asks for a clerkship under Government. 4°. 2 pages

SNODGRASS, WILLIAM, to CONGRESS.

1809, January, 7. A petition by a committee of the Baptist Church at Salem meetinghouse, Mississippi Territory, to secure the title to some land annexed to the meetinghouse. 4°. 2 pages.

SNOWDEN & McCORKLE, to MADISON.

Philadelphia.

1797, August 9, Philadelphia. Transmits 13 copies of a history of the United States and wishes him to remit the amount of subscription. Asks him to subscribe for a weekly paper fol. 1 page.

1798, June 25, Chambersburg, Pa. Again requests payment for 12 copies of a history of the United States, which were sent by authority of John Beckley. [Madison writes in the margin, "Not authorized."] 4°. 1 page.

SNYDER, SIMON. *Washington.*

1809, June 20, Lancaster. Incloses copy of a resolution of the legislature of Pennsylvania, instructing their Representatives in Congress to procure the passing of a law establishing weights and measures. 4°. 2 pages.

1810, June 9, Lancaster, Pa. As governor of Pennsylvania, sends a copy of the resolutions of the general assembly of Pennsylvania, approving the course of the administration in their conduct respecting the insolence of the British minister, and promising support. 4°. 4 pages.

1813, April 14, Harrisburg. Transmits an act of the legislature of Pennsylvania, entitled, "A supplement to an act to incorporate a company for the purpose of cutting and making a canal between the river Delaware and the Chesapeake Bay." Also copy of an act incorporating the Delaware & Chesapeake Canal Company. 4°. 1 page.

1814, February 8, Harrisburg. Transmits a resolution of the Pennsylvania legislature approbating the decisive spirit evinced by the national authority in securing hostages for the safety of the defenders of the Republic, who are threatened with the penalties of treason against Great Britain. 4°. 1 page.

SODERSTROM, RICHARD.

1808, July 28, Philadelphia. Asks to be informed of the nature of the charge against him which he is informed has been made to the President by one Mr. Fahlberg, who he is convinced is an impostor. fol. 3 pages.

SOMERVILLE, WILLIAM C. *Montpellier.*

1823, May 9, Baltimore. Presents him with a volume of the "Past and Present state of France." 4°. 1 page.

SOUTHARD, SAMUEL L., to RINGGOLD, TENCH.

1827, August 1, Washington. Is obliged to go to Norfolk, and will be unable to visit Madison. Will try to see him on his return. 4°. 1 page.

SOUTHCOMB, THOMAS, to MADISON. *Philadelphia.*

1796, April 8, Fredericksburg. Asks to be informed about some money to be paid on some bonds he holds of Monroe in Paris. 4°. 1 page.

SOUTHWICK, SOLOMON, to MADISON, Mrs. *Washington.*

1816 (?), not dated. Presents her with a periodical of which he is author and editor. Will send the missing numbers. Also begs her to accept a poem or drama. 4°. 2 pages.

——— to MADISON.

1816, May 30, Albany. Proposes to send to Mrs. Madison a perfect set of the "Christian Visitant." 4°. 1 page.

Montpellier.

1821, April 12, Albany. Sends an address. States that when he went to Washington he had formed political prejudices against him. He left Washington his friend and admirer. 4°. 3 pages.

SPAFFORD, H. G. *Washington.*

1810, July 12, Albany. Congratulates him on the return of the State of New York to Republicanism. Asks to be relieved of the expense of postage. His correspondence has yielded to the Government $1,000 within three years. 4°. 1 page.

1811, January 7, Albany. Asks Madison's advice as to the subject of his proposition for embodying in a volume of convenient size the details which the Third Census will afford. Thinks of going to Washington for that purpose. 4°. 1 page.

1814, December 16, Albany. Has made an important discovery, and asks Madison's aid in obtaining an exclusive right by a special law for a longer term than is authorized by ordinary patents. 4°. 2 pages.

1814, June 15, Albany. Rumors of the designs of circles to change the form of government to a limited monarchy. Relates in confidence a conversation with a noted British partizan, in which it was asserted that in a few weeks Baltimore was to be burned, and that he was going to the lines, toward Canada, for a certain purpose. 4°. 2 pages.

1814, September 13, Albany. Is a Quaker, and it is against his conscience to take human life, but if he could in any way, consistent with his conscience, serve his country he would do so, at the hazard of his life, with alacrity and zeal. 4°. 1 page.

1815, February 18, Albany. Congratulations on prospects of peace. Incloses certificate of a single right to make use of his improvement in the construction of wheel-carriages. Refers to the information he gave to Madison on the conversation he had with a British spy. 4°. 1 page.

SPAFFORD, H. G., to JEFFERSON. *Monticello.*

1815, November 15, Albany. Wishes to be appointed postmaster at Albany. 4°. 1 page.

——— to MADISON. *Washington.*

1815, November 18, Albany. Solicits the office of postmaster of Albany. 4°. 1 page.

1815, December 25, Albany. Sends to Jefferson to examine, and after to be sent to Madison, a long essay on the propriety of establishing a "National school of science and the mechanic arts in Washington," and a "Reform of the patent system." Has made an invention which will save to the people of the United States a million per annum, if he can obtain an exclusive patent right for thirty years. Despotism of theological opinions in the East. 4°. 3 pages.

1816, April 18, Albany. Jefferson approves of his essays on the project of establishing a national school of science and the mechanic arts, and the new modeling of the patent system. At present does not dare to trust his invention with the officers who have charge of that office. 4°. 2 pages.

1817, January 23, Albany. Essay on the revision of the patent system. 4°. 1 page.

Montpellier.

1818, August 9, Venango County, Pa. Asks him to send him a copy of his address to the Albemarle Agricultural Society, respecting agricultural subjects. Contemplates forming an agricultural society in this part of the country, and wishes a copy of the constitution and by-laws of the Albemarle Agricultural Society. 4°. 2 pages.

1822, March 15, Ballston Spa, N. *Y.* Presents a copy of his proposals for a second edition of the "Gazetteer" of this State. Is preparing a sort of American Plutarch for the youth of the two Americas. Wishes the booksellers would encourage him to write a gazetteer of Virginia. States his terms. 4°. 1 page.

1822, June 11, Ballston Spa, N. *Y.* Acknowledging letter of April 16. His "Geography" and "Gazetteer" will soon be ready for the press. Would like Madison to suggest to Mr. Ritchie the idea of writing a geography and gazetteer of Virginia. Thinks the potato indigenous to West Pennsylvania. Describes a species. 4°. 2 pages.

1822, November 25, Troy, N. *Y.* Invention for the manufacture of cast steel. Asks Madison's advice about securing his patent for a specified period or selling his invention to the Government. States his process of manufacture. fol. 3 pages.

1824, April 8, Troy, N. *Y.* Wishes instructions how to send his "Gazetteer and Geography" of New York in view of his desire to publish a gazetteer of Virginia. Is soon to engage in a history of our canals. 4°. 1 page.

1825, March 8, Troy, N. *Y.* Has undertaken a work intended as a handbook for tourists and travelers for places of public resort in the United States. Asks information about certain places in Virginia. 4°. 1 page.

1825, May 10, Lansingburg, N. *Y.* Acknowledging letter of March 23. His work on public resorts

SPAFFORD, H. G.

in the United States is advancing. Will be published soon. Has collected materials for a history of the canals of New York. Sends memoranda of his account. 4°. 1 page.

1825, July 29, Lansingburg, N. Y. Acknowledging letter of 22d, inclosing $10 for settlement of account. Sends Madison, to read and return to him, "Swedenborg's treatise on the doctrine of the New Jerusalem concerning the Lord." 4°. 2 pages.

SPAIN, NEGOTIATIONS WITH.

Not dated. Drafts and notes relating to negotiations with Spain towards making a treaty. [Unknown handwriting.] fol. 14 pages. 4°. 2 pages.

SPALDING L., to MADISON. *Washington.*

1810, April 13, Portsmouth. Sends the Portsmouth bill of mortality for 1809. 4°. 1 page.

SPARKS, JARED. *Montpellier.*

1827, April 12, Mount Vernon. Incloses a letter of introduction from Mr. Randolph. Will wait on Madison in a few days. Is preparing for publication Washington's life and letters. A plan of his intended work. Asks his aid in establishing facts which came under his personal knowledge. Contemplates also a history of the Revolution and other intended publication. 4°. 5 pages.

1827, May 22, Washington. Sends list of letters from Washington to Madison. Asks to be furnished with copies of those not comprised in this list. Respecting Washington's letter of January, 1789, relating to the message to the First Congress. Asks Madison's advice as to publishing it. His object in writing the life. Has access to the papers at Mount Vernon. Will thank Madison for any remarks or hints. 4°. 5 pages.

1827, August 25, Boston. Acknowledging letters of May 3 and August 6. Washington's letters. Expects to go to England for the purpose of examining manuscripts pertaining to our Revolutionary history. Will also consult the diplomatic correspondence of the English ministers in Holland, France, and Spain during that period. Mr. Grahame's history of North America, collected from materials in the library of Göttingen. 4°. 4 pages.

1827, December 29, Baltimore. His object in going to Europe already explained. Asks Madison for letters of introduction. Inquires whether Madison believes that the leaders of the period prior to the assembling of the First Congress were resolved on independence? Washington's declaration on the subject. 4°. 4 pages.

1828, February 27, Washington. Acknowledging letter of January 7. Thanks him for his hints respecting the opinion of the early actors in the cause of independence. His voyage delayed. Will probably sail about the 1st of April. Bill reported to Congress for procuring copies of papers in England. 4°. 2 pages.

1828, March 23, New York. Acknowledging letter of 13th, with a letter inclosed for Lafayette. Expects to sail the next day. The bill not yet called up in Congress to procure historical papers abroad. 4°. 1 page.

SPARKS, JARED.

1830, March 8, Boston. Acknowledging letter of March 28 (?). The confidential correspondence between Washington and Madison. Madison must decide what parts are proper to be submitted to Sparks's perusal. The first draft of the farewell address. Madison's assistance therein. Correspondence with Madison on the same subject. His voyage to Europe successful. Reluctance of officials overcome. His access to papers relating to the American Revolution. Was also successful in France, owing to courtesy of Marquis de Marbois. 4°. 4 pages.

1830, May 5, Washington. Conversation with Mr. Adams respecting Charles Pinckney's draft of a Constitution. 4°. 1 page.

1830, July 16, Boston. Inclosing a copy of the extract contained in the draft of Washington's farewell address as first transmitted by him to Hamilton. 4°. 6 pages.

1831, March 30, New York. Is engaged in writing a life of Gouverneur Morris. Asks information as to the part he took in the convention of 1787. Asks for the confirmation of an anecdote in which Morris was the means of restoring harmony to the violent discussions of that body. Madison's views of the Constitution ably defended at a dinner given to Daniel Webster. 4°. 4 pages.

1831, June 16, Boston. Pinckney's draft of the Constitution. Asks Madison's views of the letter accompanying the draft. 4°. 1 page.

1831, May 24, Boston. Gouverneur Morris and the part he took in the convention of 1787. His pamphlet on the repeal of the law of Pennsylvania, which had been passed in order to support the Bank of North America. Asks Madison to indicate whatever articles or pamphlets in Morris's writing he knew of. Respecting Pinckney's draft of the Constitution, and Madison's explanation. 4°. 3 pages.

1831, November 14, Boston. Question as to the origin of Pinckney's draft of a Constitution. The life of Gouverneur Morris is in press. 4°. 4 pages.

1831, January 17, Boston. Acknowledging letter of 7th and November 25. Pinckney's draft of a Constitution. Morris's life is now in the printer's hands. The Washington papers will go to press in the summer. Is engaged in a work entitled "A History of the Alliance between France and the United States during the American Revolution." Restrictions in Paris by the Government in respect to copying papers. The present Government removing restrictions. Discovery of papers in Canada respecting correspondence between Duc de Choiseul and Baron de Kalb in 1768, to ascertain whether the colonies were ready to revolt. 4°. 7 pages.

1835, April 16, Cambridge, Mass. Asks information respecting a letter from Madison to Washington of December 9, 1786. Would like a copy of it. Five volumes of "Washington's Writings" published. Two more in the press. 4°. 1 page.

SPARKS, R. (Lieut. Col.), to EUSTIS, WILLIAM (Secretary of War). *Washington.*

1810, January 12, Fort Stoddert. Reported hostile movement against Mobile and Pensacola. Sup-

SPARKS, R. (Lieut.-Col.).

posed causes. State of the garrison. Suggests the necessity of strengthening the post. Supposed leader of the plot a Joseph P. Kennedy. His character and capabilities. [Copy.] 4°. 8 pages.

1810, August 10, Washington. Return of two regiments of infantry stationed at summer cantonment near Fort Stoddert, commanded by R. Sparks. [Copy.] royal fol. 1 page.

"SPECTATOR" to MADISON. *Montpellier.*

1828, November 12, University of Virginia. Informs him of the state of this institution. The hotels the root of all dissatisfaction. Wishes the present regulations repealed and Jefferson's renewed. 4°. 1 page.

SPENCER, JAMES. *Fredericksburg.*

1788, February 28, Orange County, Va. Opposition in Orange County to the Federal Constitution. Suggests that Madison should come to Orange and explain away their prejudices. He also thinks it will aid in obtaining his election. fol. 2 pages.

SPOONER, ALDEN B. *Washington.*

1813, December 17, Norfolk. Complaints of discharged militia at not receiving their pay. Are obliged to either sell their wages due or beg their way home. Speculators making money out of the needy soldiers. Relates his own experience. Gives the causes of his complaint. 4°. 4 pages.

SPOTSWOOD, ALEXANDER. *Philadelphia.*

1791, December 4, Nottingham, Va. Solicits a berth in the Navy for his son, who has received a thorough education in navigation in the merchant service, and is willing to have a thorough examination as to his capabilities. fol. 2 pages.

1792, February 11. Asks what is necessary to do to establish his claim for pay due for services while in the Army. Gives a record of his services. Incloses a certificate of Joseph Howell of the pay office. 4°. 4 pages.

1792, April 9. Acknowledging letter of 2d. His claim for pay in the Army. Relates facts respecting his services. fol. 4 pages.

1792, April 23. Denies the statement that he had been paid £120.10, according to the accounts of depreciation of pay, from Virginia. Incloses copy of a letter from Mr. Hopkins to Dykes & Gray, respecting the matter. Asks Madison's aid in obtaining his dues. 4°. 3 pages.

1792, May 1. Acknowledging letter inclosing information from Col. Parker respecting the drawing of his pay. 4°. 1 page.

1794, October 30. Proposes to move to Kentucky. Has lands for sale particularly adapted for establishing public foundry for cannon and small arms. Describes the iron mine and situation. 4°. 2 pages.

SPOTSWOOD, GEORGE W. *Montpellier.*

1823, February 17. Applies for the situation of a stewardship in the University of Virginia. 4°. 1 page.

1823, November 29, University of Virginia. Illness of his family. Complains of the unhealthy condi-

SPOTSWOOD, GEORGE W.

tion of his house. Requests remedies, by the rector and visitors, to cause the drains to be improved and enlarged. Thinks he should be allowed to raise the price for his boarders, as it is impossible to make his expenses. Other matters relating to his stewardship. 4°. 4 pages.

1829, March 23, University of Virginia. Is compelled to seek a more favorable situation. Solicits Madison's assistance and thanks him for his many acts of kindness. 4°. 1 page.

1829, October 29, Richmond. Leaves the university and asks Madison to write him, correcting the malicious report that he had been dismissed. 4°. 2 pages.

1831, June 8, Charleston, Va. Advantages and beauty of Charleston. Is obliged for pecuniary reasons to leave for Cincinnati, Louisville or Pittsburg. Asks Madison to supply him with letters of recommendation. 4°. 4 pages.

1833, November 11, Coal Ridge, Va. His present home and its advantages. Intends leaving for Washington to investigate his father's and his wife's father's claims before Congress for commutation of pay in the Army. Gives some particulars of the claim. Asks Madison to give him information in relation to the matter. 4°. 4 pages.

1834, August 10, Kan*awha Salines, Va.* The salt works in this place Deaths from cholera. Imprudence in eating generally the cause. Death of Dr. Cabell, of Lynchburg, from eating cucumbers and buttermilk. Intends starting for Washington on foot to look after Capt. Spotswood's claims. 4°. 4 pages.

SPRAGUE, WILLIAM B.

1828, July 5, West Springfield, Mass. Wishes to obtain, for a friend, autographs of distinguished persons. Asks Madison to send him something in his own handwriting with his signature. Also autographs of other Presidents or signers of the Declaration of Independence. 4°. 2 pages.

1828, August 18, West Springfield, Mass. Acknowledging letter of 11th. Thanks Madison for having furnished him with the desired autographs, and wishes for others which he designates, or whence they can be obtained. Is struck with the beauty of Madison's writing and asks his age. 4°. 2 pages.

1828, September 18, West Springfield, Mass. Thanks for information granted in his last letter. Sends him a 4th of July address before the Colonization Society. 4°. 1 page.

1828, December 5, West Springfield, Mass. Thanks him for Patrick Henry's autograph and others. Asks if he will procure for him the autograph of Bishop Madison. Asks him to accept a small volume consisting of letters relating to his late tour in Europe. Wishes to know about the franking privilege. 4°. 2 pages.

1829, April 4, West Springfield, Mass. A volume, which he sends to Madison, of a tour in Europe. 4°. 1 page.

1830, March 8, Albany. Is engaged in preparing for the press a genealogical account of distinguished men of this country. Asks to be furnished with

SPRAGUE, WILLIAM B.

an account of Madison's ancestors, including residences and interesting facts in respect to them. 4°. 1 page.

1830, November 14, Savannah. Introducing J. K. Tefft, of Savannah. 4°. 1 page.

1831, December 12, Albany. Wishes to obtain the autographs of Button Guinnett, signer of the Declaration of Independence, and John Blair, of Virginia, signer of the Federal Constitution. 4°. 2 pages.

1833, February 6, Albany. Wonderful success of the temperance movement. Asks his views expressing approbation of this object in view of publication. 4°. 2 pages.

SPREAD. WILLIAM. *Washington.*

1816, August 24, New York. William Walsh's invention for cleaning and dressing flax. Asks if he received Walsh's letters in which were inclosed samples of flax, and if he could expect any encouragement from Government were he to come to this country with his family. Incloses samples. 4°. 2 pages.

SPROGELL, MARY.

1814, May 9, Woodstown, N. *J.* Her husband, Lieut. Sprogell, has recently died. Thinks he is entitled to a pension. Her son, a midshipman in the Navy, was lately drowned. Appeals to Madison for advice and information. Wishes Mrs. Madison to take her daughter under her protection. 4°. 2 pages.

SPROGELL, THOMAS *Y.*

1801, May 22. Applies for a clerkship in the Department of State. fol. 1 page.

SPROUT, ZEBEDEE and others.

1809, July 4, Pittsfield, Rutland County, Vt. Address of citizens of Pittsfield expressing confidence in his measures and congratulations on his elevation to the Presidential chair. fol. 2 pages.

STAATS, CUYLER. *Montpellier.*

1829, November 10, Albany. Presents Madison with a memorial of the late De Witt Clinton. 4°. 1 page.

1830, January 14, Albany. Sent Madison recently a "Tribute to De Witt Clinton," and has received no answer. 4°. 1 page.

STADLER, JOHN. *Philadelphia.*

1791, October 22, Fredericksburg. His services in the Army as engineer. Complains that his accounts were never satisfactorily settled and that money is due him. Wishes the letter laid before Congress. fol. 4 pages.

STANARD, JOHN. *Montpellier.*

1819, February 12, Fredericksburg. Asks Madison to oblige him by acknowledging the service of an inclosed notice. Asks him to remit the cash for the amount. 4°. 1 page.

1819, July 7, Fredericksburg. Sends bill of expenses of sale of land. 4°. 1 page.

STANARD, Mrs.

1829, August 14. Informs him that she can accommodate him with apartments for the approaching convention. 4°. 1 page.

STANSBURY, ——.

Not dated. Incloses notes of his last plea for peace. 4°. 1 page.

STANTON, JOSEPH. *Washington.*

1808, January 30, Charlestown. The Tammany Society in their address to the President spoke the sentiments of his heart. Trusts that Madison will be the successful candidate for the Presidental chair. 4°. 2 pages.

STARK, JOHN, to BENTLEY, WILLIAM. *Salem.*

1809, December 6, Derryfield. Acknowledging letter of November 4. Expresses his opinion of Madison. [This letter is filed with the letter of William Bentley to Madison, dated December 11, 1809. Copy.] 4°. 2 pages.

——— to MADISON. *Washington.*

1810, October 12, Derryfield. Introduces his son-in-law, Franklin Stickney, who wishes to be employed in some Government office should there be a vacancy. 4°. 2 pages.

1811, July 13, Derryfield. Describes the personal appearance of his son-in-law, Franklin Stickney, who has made a tender of his services. 4°. 1 page.

STATE, DEPARTMENT OF.

1800. A list of the officers of the Department of State, together with their salaries. fol. 1 page.

1808. A list of the officers of the Department of State for the year 1808, with their respective salaries. fol. 1 page.

——— to MADISON.

1816. List of the officers of the Department of State for the year 1816, together with their respective salaries. fol. 1 page.

1820. A list of the officers of the Department of State for the year 1820, together with their respective salaries. fol. 1 page.

STEELE, JOHN.

1802, July 19. Incloses a letter from Gen. Davie, recommending Mr. Barnet and Mr. Mountflorence to the notice of the Government. 4°. 1 page.

1808, April 25, Salisbury. Recommends Maj. Jesse A. Pearson, who wishes to make an offer of his services in one of the new regiments, provided he can obtain the same rank which he now holds in the militia. 4°. 1 page.

STEELE, JOHN.

1813, April 26, Philadelphia. Recommends Col. Hugh Ferguson, of this city, for the office of Treasurer of the mint. 4°. 1 page.

Not dated. A private memorandum submitted to Madison respecting Dr. Stephens' appointment as consul-general at a place not stated. Relating to certain claims. 8°. 3 pages.

STEELE, JONATHAN (chairman).

1812, October 7, Gilmanton, N. H. At a convention of delegates of the friends of peace, holden at Gilmanton, the committee prepared an address on the calamitous situation of the nation, which is inclosed by the chairman, declaring the inutility of war under the circumstances. 4°. 18 pages.

STEPHEN, ADAM. *Philadelphia.*

1787, November 25, Martinsburg, Berkeley County, Va. Intention of the "Wild Men" of Franklin, State [Tennessee], to drive out the Cherokees. They are well-behaved and faithfully observed the treaty. Our people broke it. Fears that should they be forced into war all the Southern Indians will be against us. Suggests means to prevent it. Advantages of the Western territory. Approves of the general convention. Hopes the plan will be adopted. fol. 2 pages.

New York.

1789, April 12, Berkeley County, Va. Permanent seat of Government. The Western country daily growing into more importance. Apathy of Congress. Parallel between Russia one hundred years ago and the West. The Middle States could do better without the territory east of the Hudson than without the friendship and ultimate coalition of the Transappalatian country. Disadvantages of a coast city for a seat of Government. Algerine Corsairs and Rhode Islanders, excellent navigators, well calculated to exact tribute from our coast cities. fol. 2 pages.

1790, April 25, Berkeley County, Va. Acknowledging letter containing sentiments on the assumption of State debts. Variance of views between New England and the Southwest. Confidence of the people lessened in our Congress. Reported death of the Secretary of the Treasury (Hamilton). Incloses the "Expostulations of Potomac."

fol. 1 page.

Philadelphia.

1790, March 3, Martinsburg, Va. Hamilton's report. Funding the debts of the individual States with the others a masterly stroke of policy.

fol. 1 page.

STEPHENS, W. *Washington.*

1801, October 22, Washington. Applies for the appointment of district judge of Georgia should the place be considered vacant. 4°. 2 pages.

STERLING, M. *Montpellier.*

1819, May 7, Washington. Transmits, in behalf of the Agricultural Society of the County of Jefferson, N. Y., a diploma of honorary membership conferred upon Madison by unanimous vote.

4°. 1 page.

STEVENS, ALBERT. *Washington.*

1802, June 8, Washington. Asks for employment in the Department of State. small 4°. 2 pages.

STEVENS, ALEXANDER H.

1813, August 10, Washington. Is a messenger from Mr. Warden, acting chargé d'affaires at Paris. Explains his delay, which was caused by the capture of the vessel in which he was a passenger. The papers intrusted with him were sunk before the flag was struck to the enemy. 4°. 3 pages.

STEVENS, EDWARD. *Virginia.*

1789, January 31, Culpeper C. H. Suggests that Madison should be present at the election, with Monroe, the other candidate. May be unable to be present himself, but hopes to. 4°. 1 page.

New York.

1789, March 16, Culpeper, Va. Solicits the appointment as collector of the district of Norfolk.

4°. 1 page.

STEVENS, EDWARD.

1789, June 25, Fredericksburg, Va. Acknowledging letter of May 11. Approves of Madison's porposed amendment to the Constitution. Procedure of the Senate on the subject of a new title to the President. 4°. 1 page.

Philadelphia.

1791, January 21, Culpeper, C. *H.* The law of Congress respecting the lands given to the officers and soldiers by Virginia will tend to deprive him of a bounty in lands given by a resolution of the general assembly. Necessary steps to be pursued to have justice done. Tax on stills. 4°. 2 pages.

Washington.

1802 March 19, Philadelphia. Introducing Mr. Perkins, of Boston. 4°. 1 page.

1808, April 20, Culpeper C. H. Recommending Col. William Campbell, who served with him in the Revolutionary war. small 4°. 1 page.

STEVENS, JOHN, to CRAWFORD, WILLIAM H.

1815, November 21, Washington. Contract for supplying the Government with "elongated shells." Should further experiments be required, would like to know how many shells would be required in the contract. 4°. 1 page.

——— to MADISON.

1815, November 22, Washington. Incloses a copy of a letter from himself addressed to the Secretary of War, from whom he has received no answer. It relates to his invention of a shell and fears it will be pirated unless he is shielded by the countenance and patronage of the Government. 4°. 3 pages.

STEWART, CHARLES, to CROWNINSHIELD, B. W. (Secretary of Navy). *Salem, Mass.*

1815, September 17, Philadelphia. Declines the office of a member of the navy board on account of his health. Would accept any situation attached to his profession requiring activity or enterprise. 4°. 3 pages.

STEWART, JOHN, to MADISON. *Washington.*

1805, February 4, Washington. Conduct of the Postmaster-General in changing the route of the Southern mails. 4°. 1 page.

STEWART, D.

1805, May 8, Philadelphia. Asks information respecting a claim against France by her husband, Gen. Stewart. States some particulars and asks Madison's good offices. 4°. 3 pages.

1806, May 15, Philadelphia. Her agent in Paris neglected her interests in her husband's claim for French spoliations and her only resource is to go in suit of them herself. Asks Madison to give her letters of introduction (not in his official capacity) to Gen. Armstrong or other friend whom he thinks proper to aid her. 4°. 2 pages.

STICKNEY, B. F., to B. W., Rev.

1810, January 19, Bow. Acknowledging a letter covering a letter from Madison to Gen. Stark. Respecting the propriety of printing Madison's letter. Will suspend the publication until he

STICKNEY, B. F.

hears from him. Annexed is copy of an answer (unsigned) advising him to publish the correspondence. 4°. 3 pages.

STILLEY, ISAAC N., to MADISON.

1831, November 20. Bill of freight 4 pipes wine. Strip of paper.

STILWELL, SILAS M. *Montpellier.*

1831. September 14, New York. Submits for Madison's consideration and opinion the report of a committee of the New York legislature, together with an act to abolish imprisonment for debt and to punish fraudulent debtors. 4°. 1 page.

1832, May 19, New York. The law relative to imprisonment for debt has taken effect and accompanied with cheering consequences. Sends report and bill on the subject of capital punishment. Asks his opinion. 4°. 2 pages.

STITH, GRIFFIN. *New York.*

1789, April 22, Northampton County, Va. In behalf of Mrs. Grace Bowdoin, who keeps a ferry, asks Madison's interposition to prevent the route of a post road being changed. fol. 1 page.

STODDERT, BENJAMIN, to TINGEY, THOMAS. *Washington.*

1809, January 18, Bladensburg. Mr. Jefferson's intentions must be to promote his country's good, but thinks further perseverance in the embargo will produce open and effectual resistance to the laws of nations. Advocates abandoning the foreign carrying trade and to declare we will trade in our own productions with whoever will trade with us. [Signed, B. S. Copy.] 4°. 2 pages.

STODE, JOHN, to MADISON.

1810, July 7, Culpeper. Has executed a mortgage deed to Madison as security for payment of a penal bond. 4°. 1 page.

STODERT, BEN, and others. *Philadelphia.*

1794, February 18, Georgetown. Inclose proceedings of inhabitants of the Territory of Columbia in relation to the establishment of a college in the city of Washington or its vicinity. Gives a list of persons solicited to receive subscriptions, Madison's among them. 4°. 1 page.

STOKELEY, JOHN.

1799, December 29, Wood County. On the lamentable condition of Wood County. Asks Madison to assist in devising means to arrest the progress of the growing evils therein. Thinks that Madison's influence in the assembly will be respected. fol. 2 pages.

Washington.

1807, (?) December 13, Georgetown. The increasing insolence of Great Britain. Advocates war rather than sacrifice our independence and patriotism. Defends the President against the charge of pusillanimity and trusts he will support the dignity of his station. 4°. 3 pages.

Philadelphia.

1807, December 15, Georgetown. The extraordinary insolence of Great Britain. Is opposed to the repeal or modification of the nonintercourse law. 4°. 1 page.

STOKELEY, JOHN. *Washington.*

1807, December 17, Georgetown. The atrocious and overbearing insult of Great Britain in assuming dominion over the seas. The duty of all nations to resist Our cities should be put in defense and the nonintercourse law fully enforced. 4°. 3 pages.

1807, December 31, Georgetown. Suggests the policy of conciliating the Indians on the frontiers Message of the President relating to the Indians and British in Upper Canada. In case of war the British would let them loose on our territory. Suggests that gunboats be built on the Little Kanawha, every facility being on the spot. Offers his services. 4°. 3 pages.

1814, October 24, Richmond. Bill now before the Virginia Assembly, permitting any Virginian to purchase and bring negroes from other parts of the Union into this State. His disapproval of the measure. Good policy to colonize free negroes by laying out a territory for their special use, between the 32° and 36° of north latitude. [Signed "A Western Virginian."] 4°. 3 pages.

1815, January 29, Georgetown. A bill establishing the United States Bank. Thinks its principles are illy suited to the relief of the falling credit of our country. Incloses a project, which he desires Madison to read before he signs the bill. 4°. 2 pages

STOKES, MONTFORD. *Montpellier.*

1831, July 26, Raleigh, N. C. Acknowledging letter of 15th, with "Lawson's History of North Carolina." Thanks him in behalf of the State. 4°. 1 page

STONE, BENJAMIN. *Washington.*

1812, October 9, Warren, N. H. An address on the conduct of the war. Causes of Hull's defeat. Suggestions as to the invasion of Canada. Inadequate pay of soldiers. Experienced officers necessary. His opinion of General Dearborn. fol. 7 pages.

STONE, DAVID.

1807, February 10, Washington. Leaves Washington on his return to North Carolina and expects to be near the place where the *Jacob* was wrecked. Will aid in recovering and forwarding to Madison his articles on board the *Jacob.* 4°. 1 page.

1807, February 24, Windsor. The wine and nuts for Madison and Jefferson from the wreck of the *Jacob* have been placed in the hands of James Taylor, collector of Ocracoke. 4°. 1 page.

1810, January 1, Hope, near Windsor, N. *C.* Transmits an address of the General Assembly of North Carolina, adopted unanimously, declaring confidence in the Chief Magistrate of the United States; and approval of his course, and promising their support. 4°. 2 pages. fol. 2 pages.

STONE, WILLIAM L. *Montpellier.*

1832, June 17, New York. Incloses a volume by himself on "Masonry and Anti-Masonry". 4°. 2 pages.

STORROW, S. A.

1827, April 16, Farly. Introducing Mr. Sparks. Storrow is unable to visit Madison at present. 4°. 2 pages.

1828, February 18, Farly. Acknowledging note of 12th. The package given him by Mr. Sparks he hopes to forward soon. 4°. 2 pages.

1828, March 10, Farly. Mr. Carter will deposit the bundle of books safely in Madison's hands. 4°. 1 page.

1828, July 6, Farly. Respecting Mr. Higginson, son of a gentleman who served with Madison in the Congress of the Revolution. Was opposed to Madison and his views in politics, but wished his son to visit him and express himself in the terms of highest respect. 4°. 3 pages.

Richmond.

1829, September 26, Fredericksburg. Wishes Thomas B. Baxter to be presented to the notice of the convention as its clerk. 4°. 1 page.

Montpellier.

1830, March 24, Farly. Asks his good offices in respect to his application for the office of Comptroller or Register of the Treasury, should there be a vacancy. 4°. 3 pages.

STORY, ISAAC. *Philadelphia.*

1794, October 27, Marblehead, Mass. Appeal for his influence to secure the payment for services of his father as clerk and cashier of the navy board in Boston. 4°. 2 pages.

Washington.

1802, January 11, Marblehead. Asks his influence in securing the place of collector and searcher for the district of Penobscot, for Col. Johannot, of Hampden. In case it should be refused, he would like the office himself. 4°. 2 pages.

STOUGHTON, JOHN.

1809, March 14, Boston. Congratulating him on his election to the Presidency. 4°. 1 page.

STOUGHTON, WILLIAM.

1813, April 23, Philadelphia. The office of treasurer of the Mint having become vacant by the death of Dr. Rush, solicits the appointment of Gen. William Duncan, late superintendent of military stores of Philadelphia, to fill the vacancy. 4°. 2 pages.

STOW, JOSHUA. *Montpellier.*

1817, September 20, Middleton, Conn. Results of the semiannual election in Connecticut prove to be in the hands of the friends of the General Government. 4°. 1 page.

STREET, PARKE.

1810. Serves a process on Madison in a suit which he asks him to acknowledge and also to present it to Mr. Jackson, who he hopes will also acknowledge it. small 4°. 1 page.

Washington.

1814, July 10, Hanover. Subpœna to be served on Mrs. Madison in a chancery suit. 4°. 1 page.

STREET, P. *Montpellier.*

1817, November 25, Hanover. Paper to give Mrs. Madison to sign and return by post. Has not been answered, and sends a copy to acknowledge the serving of it. She has no interest in the suit in chancery, merely a nominal party.
fol. 1 page.

STRICKER, JOHN, to GOLDSBOROUGH, CHAS. W. *Washington.*

1811, November 5, Baltimore. Incloses receipt for 4 pipes of wine for the President. Gives amount of the charges and asks him to remit.
4°. 1 page and strip of paper.

STRODE, JOHN, to MADISON. *New York.*

1789, January 20, Culpeper. Scheme of Col. Morgan's. Lands to be settled. Boundary line between Spanish possessions and United States. His acquaintance in iron-mining and manufacture of iron. Advantage to be gained by him in this unsettled portion of the country. Desires privilege under Government respecting iron-manufacturing. fol. 3 pages.

Philadelphia.

1792, March 9, Culpeper, Va. Intended road to be made through this county to the Federal City. Suggests the advantage of extending it to the capital of Georgia. Asks his influence with Jefferson and Members of Congress to effect this plan.
4°. 3 pages.

Orange.

1801, April 9, Culpeper. Invites Madison and Mrs. Madison to visit him on his way to the seat of Government. small 4°. 2 pages.

Washington.

1801, May 30, Culpeper. Recommends Thomas Field, of Petersburg, to be appointed postmaster of that town. 4°. 2 pages.

1802, April 5, Culpeper. Invites him and Mrs. Madison to visit him on their way to Orange from Washington. 4°. 2 pages.

1808, June 13, Richmond. Incloses copy of an article in the "Virginia Gazette" and a letter to the editor denying the statement that Madison had dunned him for the payment of a crop of wheat. Asks him to befriend Mr. Barbour. 4°. 1 page.

——— to "VIRGINIA GAZETTE" (Editor of). *Richmond.*

1808, June —, Richmond. Denies a statement published in his newspaper. [Copy. *See* letter to Madison June 13, 1808.] 4°. 1 page. 8°. 1 page.

——— to MADISON. *Washington.*

1808, October 15, Culpeper. Asks his advice and aid in procuring an order that his son, who has made up a company, be ordered to Norfolk instead of a distant place. Mr. Barbour asks for the vacancy in the loan office. 4°. 1 page.

1808, November 19, Culpeper. Acknowledging letter of October 18. Thanks him for his attention to his request respecting his son. Promises to pay his obligations to him at the first favorable opportunity, with interest. 4°. 1 page.

STRODE, JOHN.

1809, November 2, Fredericksburg. Urges his appointment to command at Norfolk. 4°. 2 pages.

1810, February 7, Culpeper. Offers him a mortgage on some landed property to secure him for his debt to him. Asks for Government employment for Mr. Robert Voss. 4°. 2 pages.

1813, August 9, Fredericksburg. Asks for Government employment. fol. 1 page.

Montpellier.

1819, October 6, Fredericksburg. Order of the clerk of chancery court (J. J Ford) rescinding a decree; also an order of J. B. Barton, commissioner, for parties interested to attend at his office to support their pretentions. [Madison *v.* Strode *et al.*] fol. 1 page.

STRODE, THOMAS. *Washington.*

1808, June 11, Culpeper. Thanks him for his friendly attention on his application at the War Office. Thinks he can easily raise a company equal to any on earth. 4°. 1 page.

1808, October 3, Stevens, Va. Gives reasons why he wished the post of command of Fort Norfolk. 4°. 2 pages.

1808, November 16, Culpeper. Acknowledging letter of 8th. Thanks him for his kindly attention in procuring his command at Norfolk. Is gratified at the prospect of his election as President. 4°. 1 page.

STRONG, CALEB (Governor).

1814, January —, Boston. Transmits a resolution of the legislature of Massachusetts with evidence in support of a complaint of the outrage committed by the collector of New York on one of the corporations of this State. Demands that the collector return the money and be removed from his office. 4°. 1 page.

STRONG, NATHANIEL W., to DAVIS, M. L.

1812, June 3, Lisbon. Great scarcity of bread. Reliance on American flour. Should the embargo continue the armies can not remain. Thinks our Government should, if it acts with decision, obtain a speedy redress for our complaints against England. Wishes to be appointed consul at Lisbon. 4°. 4 pages.

STROTHER, FRENCH, to MADISON.

1799, April 22. Will not be able to see him before the election, and relates certain reports calculated to injure him. 4°. 1 page.

STUART, ALEXANDER. *Orange.*

1799, July 20, Lynchburg. Has determined to become a candidate for a seat in the council the ensuing assembly. Asks for Madison's patronage. 4°. 1 page.

STUART, ARCHIBALD. *Philadelphia.*

1787, October 21, Richmond. Proceedings of the house of delegates in Virginia. Additional tax on tobacco exports. Amending of militia law. Calling of a convention on the subject of the Federal Constitution. Patrick Henry's opposition. The doctrine of installments. Commutation of tobacco for specie in payment of taxes to be proposed. Query as to amendment of the State constitution. small 4°. 2 pages.

STUART, ARCHIBALD. *New York.*

1787, November 2, Richmond. Incloses resolutions of Virginia on the subject of the Federal Government. Urges Madison to be of the convention in order to adopt the constitution. Proceedings in the house of delegates. Debate on the petition to repeal the port bill. small 4°. 2 pages.

1787, November 9, Richmond. Acknowledging letter of October 30. Probability that most of the Northern States will adopt the Federal Constitution. Received the paper signed "Publicus." Wishes subsequent papers to be sent him. Incloses resolutions occasioned by petitions for paper money from the southern counties, drawn up by Mason. Debates on the installments. The British debts. Henry's opposition. fol. 2 pages.

1787, December 2, Richmond. Vote taken in the legislature on the subject of payment of the British debts. Patrick Henry's active part in the discussion. Acts of the assembly. Prohibition of further importation of distilled spirits. Receipts of tobacco for taxes. Money in the treasury counted. Resolutions for paying salaries of members of the convention. Madison's friends wish him to come into the State convention. 4°. 4 pages.

1788, January 14, Richmond. Acts of the Virginia legislature. The anti-constitutional fever abating. "Publicus" in general estimation; his greatness acknowledged universally. Arthur Campbell would like the appointment of superintendent of Indian affairs. 4°. 3 pages.

STUART, PHILIP (General). *Washington.*

1814, July 29, Camp at Yates'. Complains of the apathy of the War Department in not protecting the peninsula. The enemy's vessels in the Patuxent. Fears of the inhabitants for their unprotected situation. Abandonment of their homes and property and fleeing into the woods. Dreading the enemy's possible allies, the negroes. Appeals to the Executive to prevent the enemy from occupying the neighborhood of the capital. Thinks the flotilla should be dismantled and a protecting force be sent to protect them from ruin. fol. 2 pages.

STUART, THOMAS, to SMITH, ROBERT (Secretary of State.

1810, March 16, Nashville. Is informed that his letter tendering his resignation of the office of district attorney for west Tennessee has never been received. Sends a copy of it dated December 5, 1809. Recommends John E. Beck to fill the vacancy. fol. 3 pages.

STUBBLEFIELD, JAMES, to MADISON. *Montpellier.*

1819, July 16, Harpers Ferry. Has invented a machine in the U. S. armory for turning musket stocks. Sends a sample and describes the method. Sends another for Jefferson. 4°. 2 pages.

SULLIVAN, G.

1825, May 12. Regrets he had no opportunity to deliver inclosures. [Subject not stated.] 4°. 1 page.

SULLIVAN, JAMES. *Washington.*

1804, July 8, Boston. Suggests reasons why it would be impolitic to remove Gen. Lincoln from the office of collecter of the revenue. 4°. 3 pages.

SULLIVAN, JAMES.

1804, October 8, Boston. Wishes that the controversy with Spain may be settled, even at any disadvantage rather than by hostilities. fol. 1 page.

1804, November 5, Boston. Introducing Mr. Russell, who goes to Washington in behalf of Sullivan and others concerned in the purchase of Georgia lands and the titles. 4°. 1 page.

1805, January 26, Boston. Asks information respecting the qualifications of voters in Virginia. 4°. 1 page.

1808, May 31, Boston. Has been qualified as governor. Wishes Madison's aid in procuring a schedule of the procedures of the States in each Presidential election since the Government has existed. Comprising the manner in which votes for the President have been taken in each State. 4°. 2 pages.

SULLIVAN, JERE, to ETTING, SOLOMON.

1811, February 5, Baltimore. Inclosing extract of a letter respecting the schooner *Friendship*, Capt. Snow, by the supercargo detained in Bordeaux. Annexed note from A. McKim, who states that the vessel was laden with colonial produce and that she had no license. S. Smith incloses the above extracts; date not mentioned. [Copy.] 4°. 3 pages.

SUMNER, W. H., to MADISON. *Montpellier.*

1823, June 5, Boston. Inclosing a printed letter to Mr. Adams on the importance of the militia as a civil as well as a military institution. [Paper missing.] 4°. 1 page.

1824, February 22, Boston. Inclosing a pamphlet containing letters of distinguished citizens. [Missing. 4°. 1 page.

1834, February 27, Boston. Sends from the adjutant-general's office a report on the militia to the governor of this Commonwealth. 4°. 2 pages.

SUMTER, THOMAS. *Washington.*

1802, June 13, Statesburg, S. C. Asks permission to convey communications to his son in Paris through the Department of State. Had sent previously to the President the names of several persons well qualified to act as commissioners in cases of insolvency. Wishes to know if he received them and if he approved. Great drought in Virginia. 4°. 2 pages.

SUMTER, THOMAS, JR.

1801, August 6, Washington. Inclosing a letter from J. R. Poinsett, who desires to accompany Mr. Livingston and suite on their voyage to France. 4°. 3 pages.

1802, May 18, Paris. Tenders his resignation of the commission of secretary of legation. 4°. 1 page.

1808, April 12, Statesburg, S. C. Asks Madison to forward letters to France and England to members of his family and friends. Compliments him on communications to Mr. Rose, the British envoy. 4°. 3 pages.

——— to MONROE.

1818, February 10, Rio de Janeiro. Acknowledging letter of July 20. His various occupations as minister and consul. His views on the recognition of South American independence and the

SUMTER, THOMAS, JR.

policy of our Government toward South America and Europe. Although desirous of the Southern colonies' independence, does not approve of the Cæsarian operation in national births. His desire to return home. Gives his reasons. 4°. 6 pages.

——— to MADISON. *Montpellier.*

1820, June 9, Rio de Janeiro. Offers to present Madison with a portrait of Jefferson. 4°. 2 pages.

SURVEYORS' FEES.

Not dated. Statement of surveyors' fees on vessels, foreign and domestic. 4°. 1 page.

SUTTON, LEWIS, to MADISON. *Washington.*

1816, March 17, Hunting Town, Md. Is desirous of being Postmaster-General. small 4°. 2 pages.

SWAN, JAMES. *Philadelphia.*

1797, February 10, Boston. Recommends to Madison and the Virginia Delegates the cause of Mrs. De Neufville, widow of John De Neufville, merchant, of Amsterdam, who was ruined by his blind zeal for the support of the liberty and independence of this country. She has claims on this Government. 8°. 1 page.

SWANN, THOMAS. *Washington.*

1804, May 6, Alexandria. Note of Monroe's, now due at the bank. Asks his advice about its renewal. 4°. 1 page.

1804, October 12, Alexandria. Debt of Monroe's to the bank. Asks Madison if a part of his salary can be applied for payment. 4°. 1 page.

1805, June 28, Alexandria. Payment of a protested note of Monroe's at the bank Asks if Madison can furnish the money. 4°. 1 page.

1815, June 8, Washington. Inclosing a report of the award of the board of commissioners upon the subject of claims exhibited under the Tennessee Company. 4°. 1 page.

——— and others.

1815, not dated. Inclosing a final report on the case of claimants under the Upper Mississippi Company, and a report relative to a part of the claim of claimants releasing under the Georgia and Mississippi Company. fol. 1 page.

SWANWICK, JOHN. *New York.*

1789, April 22, Philadelphia. Introducing James B. Nickolls, of Portsmouth, Va., who solicits the appointment of collector of customs at Norfolk. Asks Madison's good offices. 4°. 2 pages.

Orange.

1795, June 14, Philadelphia. Acknowledging letter of 7th. Describes a house offered to rent to Madison, and terms, on Spruce street Philadelphia. European affairs. England's attitude toward us since the treaty. 4°. 4 pages.

1795, July 26, Philadelphia. Acknowledging letter of June 30. Has secured a house for Madison in Spruce street. The general town meeting sends memorial to the President disapproving of the treaty. fol. 1 page.

SWARBRECK, EDWARD, to HARRIS, CHARLES.

1815, January 12, Savannah. Sends a sample of sugar and molasses manufactured by Mr. Spalding from sugar cane of his own raising. Describes the works and capacity of the mill. 4°. 2 pages.

SWIFT RUN TURNPIKE.

Not dated. "Statement showing amount of the original subscription to the Swift Run Turnpike of the concern of James Madison & Co., the amount of discounts paid thereon to the bank, the loss sustained by the insolvency of three of its members; and also the sums paid by each, and what is now respectively due." fol. 3 pages.

SYMMES, DANIEL, to MADISON. *Washington.*

1812, December 14, Cincinnati. As first sachem of the Tammany Society, belonging to Wigwam No. 3, State of Ohio, expresses his opinion relating to the present crisis. Approval of the war and promise of support. fol. 3 pages.

TAIT, C. *Montpellier.*

1827, May 24, Culpeper. Has been making the tour of the United States. On his return will pay Madison a visit, accompanied by his wife. 4°. 1 page.

TALIAFERRO, BALDWIN.

1819, March 26, Wood Park. Asks Madison to give a letter to his son giving his impressions as to his (T's) family, its respectability, etc., generally. 4°. 2 pages.

TALIAFERRO, LAU. *New York.*

1787, December 16, Rose Hill, Orange. Acknowledging a letter giving him information about his nephew John, at Princeton. Is informed that Washington has offered himself for the spring convention. Hopes Madison will also be present, and that he will come before the elections, as it is reported that he is opposed to the Federal system of government. 4°. 2 pages.

Philadelphia.

1797, January 4, Rose Hill, Orange. Gives names of persons who offer to present themselves for the next Congress. Urges Madison to agree to do the same. Does not doubt his reelection. 4°. 2 pages.

TALIAFERRO, W. F. *Montpellier.*

1831, November 14, Peckatone. Asks information as to connections of his wife, in order to prove a title by inheritance to shares in the Loyal Company. His wife (Taliaferro's) is only third in descent of Henry Willis, an original shareholder. 4°. 2 pages.

TALLEYRAND to RAYNEVAL, —— DE.

1803, May 2, Paris. Assures him that he will recommend the French minister at Washington to use his good offices with the United States Government to satisfy his claims, but thinks an act of Congress will be necessary, notwithstanding the good intentions of the President. Respecting the Illinois and Wabash land companies. [*See* letter of Wilson, James, to Madison (?), January 1, 1781. Copy in French.] fol. 2 pages.

TAMMANY SOCIETY, to MADISON. *Washington.*

1811, June 14, Chillicothe. *See* TOFFEN, EDWARD.

TAMMANY SOCIETY, Ohio.

1812, December 14, Cincinnati. *See* SYMMES, DANIEL.

TATHAM, WILLIAM.

1808, October 24, Princess Anne County, Va. Inward coastwise navigation. Has proposed an act of the Virginia legislature in relation thereto. Asks Madison's personal aid. Hopes to go to Washington to lay before the Executive detailed surveys as will throw light on his design. 4°. 5 pages.

1809, August 18, Washington. Applies to the Government for some employment in the line of civil engineering. His qualifications, and the valuable collection of works in that science which he possesses. 4°. 8 pages.

1810, March 10, Norfolk. His need of Government aid. The Secretary of the Treasury will vouch for his unremitting devotion to public prosperity and safety. fol. 2 pages.

1810, May 18, Norfolk. Announces the death of Miss Tatham, the daughter of his father's elder brother. Is her heir, and also to Mr. Marsden, of Hornby Castle. Reserves the question of expatriation for deliberate determination and advice of his friends. "Private." 4°. 3 pages.

1810, May 18, Norfolk. Acknowledging answer to his letter of March 10. Has hopes of getting over his embarrassments without sacrificing any part of his collection. Has had no response to his letter to the Secretary of the Treasury relating to coastwise improvements. Wrote to the Secretary of the Navy about certain maritime improvements, and was taken ill next day. Trusts that his project may not be supplanted, if meritoriously reported upon, and that he may be put on a right road to a just remuneration. 4°. 3 pages.

1810, July 10, Norfolk. On the subject of fire-rafts and defense of Lynnhaven and Norfolk and environs. Has been occupied all summer in completing topographical surveys of this intricate country. Unprotected and penniless condition of his children at Harbour Island. 4°. 2 pages.

1811, January 1, Norfolk. Details certain evidences for the Executive tending to strengthen our pretentions to the claim of the United States to Florida. Wishes to dispose of his valuable collection of Florida charts and surveys at the value Congress stamped on them in 1806. 4°. 2 pages.

1811, January 1, Norfolk. Duplicate of the foregoing. 4°. 2 pages.

1812, March 16, Norfolk. Offers to mutilate his valuable collection of documents for the benefit of the Government on any terms of accommodation, to counteract any schemes of Great Britain in endeavoring to sow dissension and arming negroes and Indians against the United States. These papers contain official surveys, military and naval manuscripts, fortifications, etc., and are very valuable. 4°. 2 pages.

1812, June 26, Norfolk. Makes a last effort in persuading Government to purchase the accumulated documents relating to military and topographical plans, manuscript charts, topographic and ichnographic surveys of Canada, Nova Sco-

TATHAM, WILLIAM.

tia and maritime archives, for a fair consideration. His extreme poverty compels him to this sacrifice. 4°. 2 pages.

1812, December 7. His offer to Congress to dispose of his valuable collection of topographical manuscripts, and plans. Transmits his memorial and vouchers. Will give every facility for their examination. If required will give copies. fol. 2 pages.

1814, April 18. Bills before Congress for authorizing the examination and purchase of his manuscripts laid over until next December. Offers his services in the general survey of post roads or any other public agency. His annual allowance insufficient for the increasing heavy duties of his topographical employments. 4°. 3 pages.

1815, April 1, Washington. Delay in the War Department in settling his accounts. Asks Madison to transmit an authority to instruct immediate attention. 4°. 1 page.

TARRANT, CARTER.

1815, July 25, New Orleans. Is chaplain in the Southern army. Would like to be transferred to another station. His salary not equal to his expenditures. fol. 2 pages.

1815, October 25, New Orleans. If the President thinks proper to continue a chaplain in the Southern army, he is willing to serve. 4°. 1 page.

TARASCON, L. A. *Montpellier.*

1824, July 3, Shippingport, Ky. Transmits an address to the people at large, in view of the prosperity and permanency of our Union. If he approves of it, wishes he would induce the editors of newspapers to publish it. fol. 1 page.

1824, August 20, Shippingport, Ky. Acknowledging letter of July 24. The propriety and necessity of a good road to unite our Western coasts with our old States. 4°. 3 pages.

TAVERN BILL.

1786, September 15. Bill sent to Madison for board and lodging, place not stated. fol. 1 page.

TAYLOE, JOHN. *Washington.*

1807, July 25, Mount Airy, Va. Acknowledging letter in reply to his of 12th. His application for commissions for officers in a military corps. Makes a tender of their services to the President, as a regiment of associated volunteers. 4°. 3 pages.

1809, July 16, Mount Airy. His hopes of nomination to the command of a regiment of light dragoons, being frustrated, he now tenders his services in any way they can be useful. Would like to reside in or near Washington and be the President's military secretary or aid. 4°. 4 pages.

1812, January 22. Tenders his services in any way Madison may think most serviceable to his country. Would prefer being appointed his aid-decamp or military secretary. Pay or emoluments no object. 4°. 2 pages.

1812, March 9. Petition of the cavalry officers of this district. In behalf of them he addresses the President to know his determination about accepting their services. Asks that two infantry

TAYLOE, JOHN.

companies be added to them, and that a separate regiment be formed. 4°. 3 pages.

Montpellier.

1820, December 1, Washington. Asks him to send his proxy as a stockholder of the steamboat *Washington* to vote at the ensuing meeting for a board of directors. [Copy of Madison's answer, dated December 4, at foot, complying with his request.] 4°. 2 pages.

1824, August 4, Washington. Introducing his son, Edward J. Tayloe. 4°. 1 page.

TAYLOR, CHARLES. *Washington.*

1807, August 26. Inclosing his account with a request for payment. 4°. 2 pages. fol. 2 pages.

Montpellier.

1818, August 27. Physician's bill for services. 4°. 1 page.

TAYLOR, CREED (Chancellor).

1822, December 21, Needham. Sends a copy of the journal of the law school, and asks his opinion in relation to it. Regrets to decline an invitation to visit him at present. 4°. 2 pages.

TAYLOR, E. H.

1833, June 5, Frankfort, Ky. Asks for information respecting his great uncle, Francis Taylor, a major in service at the close of the Revolutionary war. Also asks information respecting his uncle, John Taylor, a lieutenant in the Continental Navy 4°. 2 pages.

TAYLOR, FRANCIS. *New York.*

1790, November 7. Incloses a memorial to present to Congress, in relation to his claim for half pay. Will forward vouchers and commissions here after. 4°. 2 pages.

TAYLOR, F. S. *Washington.*

1804, May 22, Norfolk. Applies for the office of collector of the port of Norfolk should Mr. Nicholas, the new collector, decide to not accept. 4°. 1 page.

TAYLOR, GEORGE, Jr. *Philadelphia.*

1796, January 30, Philadelphia. Thinks the position of chief clerk of Department of State should be placed upon a different footing than in the other departments in respect to salary. The duties much more laborious and attended with more responsibility. Incloses copy of a letter from Jefferson. 4°. 2 pages.

1797, January 11, Philadelphia. Applies for increase of salary as chief clerk of the Department of State. 4°. 1 page.

TAYLOR, HUBBARD.

1791, December 17, Lexington, Ky. Acknowledging letter of November 23. Gen. St. Clair's defeat. Is nominated as a member of the convention. Trusts that Col. Nicholas will be elected. fol. 2 pages.

1792, January 3, ———, Ky. Acknowledging letter of September 23. Was defeated in his election as Representative to Congress. A vigorous war to be carried on against the Indians the coming

TAYLOR, HUBBARD.

spring. Action of the legislature respecting taxation. The year's crops. Prices of products. small 4°. 5 pages.

1792, April 16, Danville, Ky. Acknowledging letter of February 22. Incloses resolutions passed by the convention on which the Kentucky constitution is to be based. Debates on the emancipation of slaves. 4°. 14 pages.

Orange.

1792, May 8, Spring Hill. Incloses copy of that part of the Kentucky constitution that provides for the establishment of the judiciary. Discusses the capacities of the members of the legislature. Raids of Indians on the frontiers. fol. 3 pages. 4°. 2 pages.

1792, May 17, Lexington, Ky. Incloses a return of governor and Senators. Indians continue their thefts of horses. The collection of the excise keeps up animosities. Meetings of distillers to protest to Congress. small 4°. 2 pages, and slip of paper.

1792, July 9. Acts passed by the legislature relating to the revenue and judiciary. Mr. Brown and Col. Edwards chosen Representatives of the State of Kentucky in the Federal Senate, and mentions candidates, including himself, to the lower House. Conjectures as to the plans of the Indians. Appointment of judges and militia field officers. 4°. 4 pages.

1792, August 6, Fayette. Has been defeated in his election as Representative to Congress. Sends an account of the proceedings of the first session of the Kentucky assembly. Question of the land tax and tax on negroes. Asks Madison's influence in getting his relative, Edmund Taylor, into the Army. 4°. 3 pages.

Philadelphia.

1793, May 23, Clark County, Ky. Acknowledging letter of March 16. The question on the conduct of the Secretary of the Treasury. Indian affairs in a bad way. Inefficiency of the military. Great improvements in this State in regard to trade, inhabitants, and agriculture. small 4°. 4 pages.

1794, January 13, Kentucky. Incloses papers respecting the navigation of the Mississippi. Gen. Clark's appointment under the French Government. He is supposed to have money to raise troops in the spring to go against the Spanish settlements on the Mississippi. Tax on lands and negroes acted on in the assembly. Iron works in Kentucky. Salt licks. Cultivation of cotton. small 4°. 4 pages.

1794, March 10, Clark County, Ky. Alarm felt at the probability of a British war and Clarke's intended expedition. Its interference with commerce. Conduct of the Indians. Wayne still in winter quarters. Progress in iron manufactures in Kentucky. Smallpox in Kentucky. fol. 2 pages.

1795, January 16, Clark County, Ky. Madison's land on Sandy River. Reported evidences of silver mines thereon. Mrs. Payne's land supposed to be very valuable. small 4°. 3 pages.

TAYLOR, HUBBARD.

1795, February 3, Spring Hill, Ky. Incloses papers respecting a decision of the court of appeals respecting claims of settlements and preemptions granted by the commissioners in 1779 and 1780. Great individual distress apprehended. Supposition that the judges were actuated from impure and corrupt motives. Introducing Dr. Ridgely. Lands held by Madison and his brother in Kentucky. Offers to protect them.
small 4°. 4 pages.

Orange.

1795, August 9, Orange. Incloses copy of a memorandum of Ambrose Madison's relating to Madison's and Mrs. Payne's lands. Asks him to remit for the taxes. fol. 2 pages.

Philadelphia.

1796. March 1. Incloses a letter from Jonathan Taylor, who wishes to be employed as an Indian agent. Speaks favorably of his character as an officer and paymaster. small 4°. 1 page.

——— to MADISON, JAMES, Sr. *Orange.*

1796, June 14, Spring Hill, Ky. Acknowledging letter of May 28. Gives particulars respecting Mr. Chew's land in Kentucky. fol. 4 pages

——— to MADISON. *Philadelphia.*

1796, not dated. Mrs. Payne's lands. Gives particulars as to title and location. Madison's claim on the Sandy. The person who claims to have found a mine thereon refuses to divulge the place. Increase of population in Kentucky. The weather and crops. small 4°. 5 pages.

Orange.

1796, July 16, Spring Hill, Ky. Kentucky lands. Peace with the Indians. Approaching election for electors for the President. Will probably be unanimous for Jefferson. The mode of disposing of lands on the northwestern side of the Ohio not approved of by the people of Kentucky.
fol. 3 pages.

1796, September 12. Acknowledging receipt of money to be applied as directed. H. Marshall threatened with tar and feathers since his return from Congress. John Towler elected to Congress.
small 4°.. 4 pages.

Philadelphia.

1796, November 14, Frankfort. Is collecting materials for claims against the Mays. small 4°. 1 page.

——— to MADISON, JAMES, Sr. *Orange.*

1797, March 15. Grant of land in Joseph Chew's name. Statement of expenses. 4°. 2 pages.

——— to MADISON.

1797, May 1. Acknowledging letter of March 27. Locating of Mrs. Payne's lands. Interference of Madison's land with John May's estate. Will endeavor to settle the matter. Is concerned at the situation of our affairs with France. Unfounded report that Madison had gone as envoy to France. Is sorry that he is soon to quit political life.
small 4°. 3 pages.

1797, October 8, Clark County, Ky. Sales of lands in Kentucky. small 4°. 3 pages.

TAYLOR, HUBBARD.

1797, November 24, Clark County, Ky. Ambrose Madison's land in Kentucky. Location of Madison's land. His opinion of it. Kentucky titles to land. small 4°. 3 pages.

1799, January 3, Kentucky. United sentiments of the people of this State respecting the measures of the General Government. Is anxious to have the result of deliberations on that subject in the Virginia assembly. The assembly of Kentucky have passed a law to call a convention to amend, alter, or readopt the constitution of the State. The taxes on Madison's and his father's lands in Kentucky. 4°. 2 pages.

Washington.

1801, May 20, Clark County, Ky. Had drawn a draft on Madison's late father, which he asks him to protect. Congratulations on the election of Jefferson as President. Madison's acceptance of the Secretaryship of State adds greatly to the confidence of all Kentuckians. Suggests the propriety of resurveying Madison, Senior's, lands. 4°. 2 pages.

1801, June 21, Clark County, Ky. Solicits the appointment of marshal of this State. fol. 1 page.

1803, January 16, Clark County, Ky. Settlement of taxes on the lands of Madison, senior's, estate. Asks information respecting his brother's estate. Gives information respecting Madison's lands. 4°. 3 pages.

1803, March 6, Lexington, Ky. Introducing John Jordan. The people of Kentucky have full confidence in the Executive on the Mississippi business. 4°. 1 page.

1804, December 12, Clark County, Ky. Introducing Capt. Richard Taylor, who will apply for an additional pension from the Government. Respecting the lands of Madison's father in Kentucky. Will be in Washington shortly and give a full statement respecting Madison's and brother's interests in Kentucky lands. small 4°. 3 pages.

1805, April 20, Caroline, Va. Inclosing statement of disbursements for Kentucky land purposes. Asks information about Madison's niece's land. Is unable to go to Washington. small 4°. 4 pages.

1806, November 12, Frankfort, Ky. Introducing Mr. Marlin Harden. small 4°. 1 page.

1807, January 31, Clark County, Ky. Introducing Jesse Bleadsoe and Henry Gest. small 4°. 2 pages.

1808, December 10, Clark County, Ky. Introducing Commodore Richard Taylor, bearer of votes of the electors of Kentucky, which were unanimous. Great unanimity in this State as to the embargo, and approbation of the measures of the administration. small 4°. 2 pages.

1809, April 15, Clark County, Ky. The Hon. John Allen, of Kentucky, is willing to fill the office of governor, now vacant by the nonacceptance of the Hon. John Bayle, for the Illinois Territory. 4°. 1 page.

1809, June 16, Clark County, Ky. Introducing Maj. Jonathan Taylor, who visits Washington with a

TAYLOR, HUBBARD.

view of making propositions for renewal of the lease of the Saline salt works. 4°. 3 pages.

1809, October 5, Winchester, Clark County, Ky. Respecting the Saline salt works. Increase of supply and reduction of price in the United States. 4°. 2 pages.

1812, December 6, Clark County, Ky. Approves of his message to Congress. Gen. Hopkins' failure in his first expedition against the Indians. Trusts his present expedition will result more favorably. Difficulty in supplying the Northwest army with provisions and clothing. Mismanagement in regulations. Has had the satisfaction again of being an elector. Unanimous vote for Madison and Gerry. His son Hubbard in the Army. George Shannon takes on the votes of the electors. 4°. 6 pages.

——— to TAYLOR, ROBERT. *Orange.*

1813, August 30, Clark County, Ky. The proposed sale of Mrs. Willis's lands in Kentucky. small 4°. 3 pages.

——— to MADISON. *Washington.*

1813, November 5, Lexington, Ky. The governor returns from Canada. He says the Indian warfare is at an end in the Northwest unless the British again get possession. On the subject of Mrs. Willis's and Madison's lands in Kentucky. 4°. 3 pages.

1814, February 15, Clark County, Ky. Inclosing a bill for 10 mules purchased for Madison. Has hired a man to take them to Madison's place in Orange. The citizens of Kentucky will pay the Federal tax without a murmur. The embargo popular. Joseph Hawkins will supply the place of Mr. Clay in Congress. 4°. 4 pages.

1816, September 25, Clark County, Ky. Death of Hon. Harry Innes, the Federal district judge. Recommends Robert Trimble to fill the vacancy. Claims of Judge Todd for the place. 4°. 3 pages.

1816, October 17. Contradicts the report that Mr. Trimble did not contemplate holding the position of district judge permanently should he be appointed. 4°. 2 pages.

Montpellier.

1823, April 2, Clark County, Ky. Inclosing a pamphlet, at request of Judge Todd, published by James Smith, giving an account of his captivity with the Indians. small 4°. 2 pages.

1823, May 26, Spring Hill, Ky. Acknowledging letter of April 25. Interfering claims on land sold by Madison and Mrs. Willis. Will investigate the matter. fol. 2 pages.

1830, April 15, Spring Hill, Ky. The closing up of Madison's accounts show a balance in the latter's favor. The people of Virginia will adopt the constitution submitted to them by the late convention. fol. 1 page.

TAYLOR, JAMES. *Washington.*

1801, February 26, Jefferson, Ky. Anxiety of the people to know of the results of the election. His nephew, William Taylor, desires the appointment of marshal in this State, if a new one is to be appointed. fol. 1 page.

TAYLOR, JAMES.

1801, June 14, Campbell C. H., Ky. Plat and certificate of land on a military warrant, lying in the Northwest Territory. Thinks it was burned in Washington. Requests a duplicate unless the original is found. Asks Madison's aid in having it looked up. Recommends Dr. John Sellman, of Cincinnati, for the office of marshal for the Northwest Territory. fol. 3 pages.

1803, September 25, Bellevue, Campbell, Ky. Introducing Col. Thomas Sandford, M. C., from this district. Will attend to the superintendence of erecting the public buildings at this place. Thanks Madison for the appointment. The people in Kentucky are much interested in the rumored cession of Louisiana. fol. 2 pages.

1804, October 28, Norfolk. Acknowledging a letter of 20th, inclosing a check. 4°. 1 page.

1805, November 12, Jefferson County, Ky. Introducing Dr. Nicholas, of this neighborhood, who will inform Madison of his connections here. small 4°. 1 page.

1806, February 3, Newport, Ky. Sends a package of strawberry vines and nectarine and peach cuttings. Directions about planting. Has made inquiries about his land in Kentucky and estimates their value per acre. Marriage of Margaret Bell and Col. Sandford. fol. 3 pages.

Orange.

1806, August 18, Jefferson County, Ky. Introducing Dabney Strother Taylor. small 4°. 1 page.

Washington.

1806, October 13, Newport, Ky. Acknowledging letter of April 20. Reports a scheme in agitation to separate the Western from the Atlantic States. Movement of Aaron Burr and Mr. Blennerhassett. Building of gunboats at a navy-yard on the Muskingum. fol. 5 pages.

1807, April 3, New Port, Ky. Applies for the appointment of James W. Moss to be surveyor of the port of Limestone (or Maysville) in Mason County, Ky. Madison's relations in Kentucky. The robbery committed on the public money in Gen. Findlay's hands. His enemies will seize the occasion to endeavor to get him removed from office. His dismissal would be very unpopular. 4°. 7 pages.

1807, April 13, New Port, Ky. Incloses a Cincinnati newspaper relating to Wilkinson and Burr, written by Capt. Stoddard. Asks whether his lands on Sandy have been surveyed. Estimates the value of the lands on Panther Creek. 4°. 2 pages.

1807, April 27, Belle Vue, Ky. Introducing Gen. Carbery. 4°. 1 page.

1807, April 27, Belle Vue, Ky. Incloses surveys of land. Charles Vottier, who robbed Gen. Findlay, has been convicted and sentenced. William D. S. Taylor's appointment to the Army. Thinks it will be declined. Col. Isaac Shelby a candidate for governor. 4°. 4 pages.

1807, July 13, New Port, Ky. Acknowledging a letter by Gen. Carbery, respecting the Burr trial at Richmond. Candidates for the governorship of Kentucky. 4°. 3 pages.

TAYLOR, JAMES.

1807, September 27, Richmond. Survey, in the name of Francis Taylor, of land, sent to Madison. Asks if he received it. Thinks the trial of Burr will close this week. Gen. Wilkinson's evidence. No idea can be formed of the result. [Signature torn off.] 4°. 3 pages.

1808, March 19, New Port, Ky. Incloses papers, about which he asks Madison's advice. Regrets having given a letter of introduction to Gen. Carbery. His questionable attitude in respect to Aaron Burr. Relates some particulars respecting him. 4°. 3 pages.

1808, June 13. The settlement of a misunderstanding. [See Carbery H. Copy.] 4°. 1 page.

1808, July 16, New Port, Ky. Explaining his position in regard to his differences with Gen. Carbery and their reconciliation. Incloses copy of their mutual settlement and a statement of J. Sillman. 4°. 5 pages.

1808, November 13, Belle Vue, Ky. Acknowledging letter of August 20. Is pleased that he approves of the adjustment of the affair with Gen. Carbery. Corrects a statement as to his family relation to Dr. Sillman. Their estrangement. Gives a detailed statement of his difficulties with J. H. Daviess. Matters respecting the Miami Exporting Company and their arrangement with Gen. Findlay in Cincinnati respecting deposits. Application of William Taylor for office of marshal. 4°. 8 pages.

1808, November 29, New Port, Ky. Incloses a letter to Mr. Graham containing a draft for Taylor's father. Names given of the electors. Respecting the embargo. No repeal can take place under existing circumstances. 4°. 1 page.

1809, February 26, Belle Vue, Ky. Congratulating him on his election to the Presidency. Is occupied in erecting barracks at this place for the troops recruited in this State and Ohio and providing boats for their transportation down the river. Speaks of Lieut. Zachary Taylor as a valuable officer. Death of Gen. Sandford by drowning. His son, Alfred Sandford, is desirous of a captaincy. John Weaver wishes an appointment in the Army. Col. William Mountjoy solicits an appointment in the volunteers, should they be raised. [The last part of this letter in the War Office.] 4°. 4 pages.

1809, April 2, Belle Vue, Ky. The President's speech just arrived and is much admired. Federalists speak well of him. It is in Madison's power to be the most popular man on earth by uniting all parties. Movement of troops. Delays on account of weather in procuring boats to embark. Reports of the loss of a flotilla in the Mississippi by a tempest, with all the officers and men. Gives no credit to it. 4°. 3 pages.

1809, April 29, New Port, *Ky.* An order from the Secretary of the Treasury respecting Judge Colburn. His family averse to his removing to Louisiana. His popularity and usefulness. 4°. 3 pages.

1809, May 26, New Port, Ky. Calls his attention to claims of officers for land located north of the Indian boundary. Asks for information about locating land warrants. 4°. 3 pages.

TAYLOR, JAMES.

1809, —— 9, New Port, *Ky.* In behalf of Capt. Jervis Cutler, asks information as to cause of his dismissal from office as captain in the Seventh regiment. Thinks him a worthy and efficient officer. 4°. 3 pages.

1809, August 11, New Port, *Ky.* Introduces Hezekiah Johnson, of the U. S. Army, who wishes to procure a furlough. Conduct of England in the case of the late adjustment between our ministers. The Hon. John Monroe would gladly accept office in any of the Territories. He is a supporter of the administration. 4°. 3 pages.

1809, October 20, Belle Vue, Ky. Gives accounts of his vineyard and the fine quality of his grapes. Hopes to make his own wine in a few years. Will make some the next year. Anxious to know what propositions Mr. Jackson, the British envoy, has to make to our Government. Our people indignant at the conduct of the British Government. 4°. 2 pages.

1810, October 16, Belle Vue, Ky. Satisfactory result of the State elections. Is much pleased at the prospect of an accommodation with France and England. 4°. 2 pages.

1810, November 28, Belle Vue, Ky. Is pleased to understand that our differences may probably be adjusted with the belligerents. 4°. 1 page.

1810, November 28, Belle Vue, Ky. Incloses pamphlet by Gen. James Findlay. Query as to its effects. Scarcity of money in the Northwest. 4°. 3 pages.

1811, January 10, Zanesville, Ohio. The legislature of this State has done nothing of importance, except to elect a senator to the United States. The question of the spot for the permanent seat of government of Ohio is to come on to-morrow. 4°. 2 pages.

1811, February 20, New Port, Ky. Judge Colburn's commission as judge of Louisiana expires during a recess of Congress. Suggests that his commission be renewed. High character, abilities, and popularity of Colburn. 4°. 4 pages.

1812, May 30, Camp Meigs. Has been honored by the Secretary of War with the charge of furnishing transportation and supplies for the Ohio troops to Detroit. Has concluded to accompany them. Incloses Gen. Meig's address to the troops on delivering up the command to Gen. Hull, and Hull's answer. Hears that Madison renominated him to the Senate as one of the purchasing commissaries, and the Senate had rejected him. Wishes to know the reason. Has personal enemies in the Senate. Is confident of always having done his duty. States in a postscript the condition of his brigade. 4°. 5 pages.

1812, June 7, Belle Vue, Ky. Hears from his friend H. Clay that the Senate has rejected his renomination as commissary, and that Maj. Morison is to be nominated. Expresses his indignation and mortification. Attributes it to underhand schemes by his and Madison's enemies and relatives in power. 4°. 7 pages.

1812, not dated. Suggests that Governor Howard be appointed to the command of all the troops in

TAYLOR, JAMES.

his territory with the rank of brigadier-general. Recommends that Gen. Harrison, as the only competent general to command the Northwest Army, be raised to the rank of major-general. fol. 2 pages.

1812, July 7, Detroit. Arrived in Detroit on the 6th. Have been so unfortunate as to have all our stores taken by the British with four officers and twenty-three noncommissioned officers and privates. States the particulars. Is confident of our troops taking Malden. Thinks the loss is a fortunate circumstance, as it has created such an antipathy that it will be worth five times the amount taken. But the loss of hospital and quartermaster's stores can not be replaced here. 4°. 3 pages.

1812, September 10, Cleveland, Ohio. Introducing Gen. James Findlay whose regiment from this State was unfortunately compelled to surrender prisoners of war at Detroit on August 16. Refers to Gen. Findlay for additional circumstances that may have transpired during the stay at Detroit and Fort Malden. Gen. Hull's endeavor to embarrass Taylor by drawing orders on him for large amount in favor of two men in Canada, which he refused to do and was threatened with military and civil detention. fol. 2 pages.

1812, September 23, Newport, Ky. Occurrences attending the surrender of Gen. Hull at Detroit so far as his personal knowledge is concerned. 4°. 3 pages.

1813, January 31, Belle Vue, Ky. Congratulating Madi- on his re-election. Hopes that Gen. Harrison will be more fortunate with the present N. W. army. The circumstance of Hull's surrender prevented many from participating in the honors which await our arms in that quarter. Laments that he can not be actively employed. His numerous relatives in the army, and how employed. Taylor Berry he recommends for appointment as a lieutenant; also, recommends Alfred Sanford for promotion. Highly recommends Dr. Hosea Blood, who was wounded by a cannon ball at Detroit. 4°. 7 pages.

1813, March 30, Washington. Recommends for positions in the U. S. Army, Dr. Charles Taylor, jr., nephew of Col. F. Taylor, and John Taylor, son of Maj. William Taylor. 4°. 3 pages.

1813, April 7, Washington. Has recommended to the Secretary of War for the appointment of Hubbard Taylor, jr., as captain in the U. S. Army, and Nathaniel Pendleton Taylor for the same appointment should there be vacancies. 4°. 3 pages.

1813, January 12, Mount Sion, Caroline County. Thanks him for informing him of the safety of his son. Recommends Capt. Reuben Tankoesley to command a company. Has written to Monroe about his qualifications. fol. 1 page.

1813, September 20, Mount Sion, Caroline County. Recommends Capt. William Jones, an applicant for the appointment of collector for the district of which Caroline is a part. small 4°. 1 page.

1814, January 13, Belle Vue, Ky. Has made arrangements with his brother, Hubbard Taylor, to pur-

TAYLOR, JAMES.

chase mules for Madison. Reports from Fort Wayne that the Indians are peaceful in that quarter. Gen. Harrison making arrangements to guard the frontier toward Detroit and the town of Erie. 4°. 2 pages.

1814, August 8, Belle Vue, Ky. Conversations with Gen. Harrison relative to the necessity of breaking up the party of Indians collected at Chicago and vicinity and destroying their crops of corn. Suggests that Gen. Adair would command such an expedition with great credit to himself and benefit to his country. 4°. 3 pages.

1814, September 6, Belle Vue, Ky. Rumors of the possession by the British of the city of Washington. Offers of assistance of mounted regiments to repair to the city, by Gens. Harrison and Findlay. Offers himself to do everything in his power to assist. Thinks several regiments will volunteer at once. Instructions necessary as to supplies of rations and forage. 4°. 2 pages.

1815, February 21, Belle Vue, Ky. Purchase of a horse for the President. Gives his pedigree. Congratulates him on Jackson's victory at New Orleans. Is gratified at the restoration of peace; it having gained for us a high national character. 4°. 3 pages.

1815, March 27, Belle Vue, Ky. Introducing Dr. Cauly who brings Madison a horse purchased by Taylor. Incloses a certificate of the pedigree of the horse "Speculator." 4°. 2 pages.

1815, April 19, Belle Vue, Ky. Forwarded some weeks since a horse by Dr. Cauly. Hopes he got to Washington safe and that he pleased him. Recommends Gen. McArthur to some active employment under Government. He is a practical surveyor and woodsman. 4°. 3 pages.

1816, July 16, Belle Vue, Ky. Introducing Lieut. Joseph P. Taylor. If he and Maj. Zachary be induced to accept the appointments recently offered them, thinks they will be an acquisition to the service. 4°. 2 pages.

Montpellier.

1818, November 7, Lexington Ky. Introducing Richard Taylor, jr. Is about building a house and asks Mrs. Madison to procure a rough draft of Mrs. Carter's house near Green Mountain, and suggest any improvements. 4°. 3 pages.

1823, April 12, New Port, Ky. Sent some horses a month ago to Virginia. Wishes Madison and Mr. Todd to see them. Acounts from Virginia unfavorable for prices for horses, but disturbances in Europe may make money more plentiful and enhance the price of horses. Crops of wheat unpromising, owing to the severity of the winter. Family intelligence. 4°. 3 pages.

——— to TODD, PAYNE.

1823, April 12, Newport, Ky. Has sent some horses to Virginia and the proceeds of sales of them will be paid to him for the paintings purchased by Mr. Todd for him. Incloses a note which he wishes Mr. Todd to present for payment. 4°. 3 pages.

——— to MADISON.

1827, July 9, Columbus, Ohio. Introducing Chapman Coleman, marshal of the State of Kentucky. fol. 1 page.

TAYLOR, JAMES.

1828, March 17, Belle Vue, Ky. Introducing his son James, who was prevented delivering a letter of introduction 2 years ago, by the kick of a horse. General family intelligence and reminiscences of old times. 4°. 4 pages.

1830, May 17, Frankfort, Ky. Incloses a letter to Mrs. Madison. Felt great interest in the deliberations of the late convention in Richmond. Thinks the new constitution a good one and hopes it will be ratified. Family matters. 4°. 2 pages.

1830, December 15, Washington. Has been making a tour via Philadelphia, New York, the canal, Niagara, the Lakes, and through Ohio to this place. Has been trying to procure a Government clerkship for Robert Macon. Speaks of his visit at Montpellier with pleasure. Several accidents to Senators and Members from oversetting of coaches. Impeachment of Judge Peck. Little business in Congress. Thinks Mr. Clay will come to the Senate. Politics in Ohio. Blair's new paper, "The Globe." 4°. 3 pages.

1831, January 2, Washington. New Year's reception at White House; no lady to preside. Gossip respecting the relations between the President and Maj. Donaldson owing to the conduct of Mrs. D. towards Mrs. Eaton. Breach between the President and Vice-President. No good feeling between certain members of the Cabinet, Van Buren, Eaton, and Gov. Barry, because Barry and family refuse to hold intercourse with Mrs. Eaton. The claims of Monroe being urged by Gouverneur. T. J. Randolph's impudence in publishing certain letters of Jefferson and Burr. Confidential communication respecting the contest between Jefferson and Burr. Other gossip, political, social, and personal. 4°. 4 pages.

1831, March 13, Belle Vue, Ky. Incloses a letter to Mrs. Madison giving all the occurrences of his family and friends in this quarter. Congratulates Madison on his reaching his four score years. fol. 1 page.

Washington.

1807, February 14, North *Carolina.* Wreck of the brig *Jacob*, with articles on board for Madison and the President. Has secured them and requests invoices to be sent that returns may be made to the Treasury Department. Will forward the articles. 4°. 1 page.

1807, April 8, Newbern, N. C. Acknowledging letter of February 28. Articles to be forwarded from the wreck of the brig *Jacob*. 4°. 1 page.

1807, April 28, Ocracoke, N. *C.* Forwards wine and nuts cast away from the brig *Jacob*. Will send bill of expenses. 4°. 1 page.

1807, April 29, Ocracoke District. Bill of duties and charges of articles from wreck of brig *Jacob*. 4°. 1 page.

——— (of North Carolina).

1813, March 12, Washington. Solicits Government employment. 4°. 2 pages.

TAYLOR, JAMES, JR.

1803, September —. Annexing bill of a hogshead of wine secured from T. Newton, of Norfolk. 4°. 1 page.

TAYLOR, JOHN. *Orange.*

1793, May 11, Caroline, Va. At the next session of Congress a direct, firm. and resolute attack should be made upon the bank law. Has written a pamphlet on the subject. small 4°. 2 pages.

1793, June 20, Caroline, Va. A humorous description of a pamphlet which he had lately written respecting certain laws recently discussed in Congress, and which he submits to Madison for perusal and correction, if he thinks proper, with a view to publication. fol. 3 pages.

1793, August 5, Caroline, Va. Giles and Venable, who were visiting him, recommend Madison to publish Taylor's pamphlet on the proposed repeal of the bank law. Its effect on the Virginia assembly. small 4°. 2 pages.

1793, September 25, Bowling Green, Va. Acknowledging letter of 20th. Approves of his emendations of his paper on the bank law. A meeting was formed and resolutions made in approval. Hopes Madison will approve. small 4°. 2 pages.

1800, September 10, Caroline, Va. Recommends Mr. F. Taylor as naval officer at Norfolk, the place being vacant by death of Mr. Byrd. small 4°. 2 pages.

Washington.

1812, July 7, Washington. Asks for a young gentleman of Virginia, to whose family he is under obligations, a position as a Government clerk. Incloses a book written by the young man. [His name not mentioned.] 4°. 2 pages.

1815, January 4, Washington. Recommends the appointment of Edmund J. Lee as judge of this district. 4°. 1 page.

1815, May 6, Albany. Recommends that Samuel S. Connor be appointed a commissioner to ascertain to which power (Great Britain or United States) certain islands in the Bay of Passamaquoddy belong. [In reference to an article in the late treaty.] 4°. 1 page.

TAYLOR, JONATHAN, to TAYLOR, HUBBARD.

1796, February 3, New Port, Ky. Contemplates resigning his commission in the Army, finding the pay inadequate to his support and no hope of promotion. Asks for the appointment of storekeeper in the Indian department, and his influence in obtaining it. small 4°. 2 pages.

TAYLOR, RICHARD, to MADISON. *Orange.*

1794, October 10, Jefferson, Ky. Wishes to be informed how he can obtain the title to land conveyed by Ambrose Madison, who died without giving him a deed. fol. 2 pages.

1795, July 11, Jefferson, Ky. The surveying of lands purchased of Madison's brother Ambrose. Propositions respecting conveyance of the same. fol. 2 pages

1798, June 1, Beargrass, Ky. Asks him to take the necessary steps that a title may be procured to the lands purchased of his brother Ambrose. Has sold the property and the purchasers are restless. small 4°. 2 pages.

Washington.

1804, December —, Sailor's Retreat, Jefferson County, Ky. Introducing his son, who desires increase of

TAYLOR, RICHARD.

pension for wounds received in service against the Indians. fol. 1 page.

1805, March 3, Louisville, Ky. Asks his influence with the Secretary of the Navy to get an appointment for his son, William D. S. Taylor, as a midshipman in the Navy. fol. 1 page.

1808, January 25, Louisville, Ky. Asks his influence with the Secretary of War to promote his son William to a higher rank. 4°. 1 page.

1816, July 23, Louisville, Ky. His son Joseph visits Washington, as he has business with the War Department. Asks Madison to advise him of the course to be taken. If he rejoins the Army it should be with the rank he formerly held. fol. 1 page.

1816, September 26, Frankfort, Ky. Has claims before Congress for additional pension. Sufferings from his old wounds. Asks his advice and influence in order that he may defray the expenses of the frequent and expensive surgical operations which he is obliged to undergo. His numerous family who depend on him. Asks advice about disposing of military lands. fol. 2 pages.

——— to CROGHAN, WILLIAM.

Not dated. Receipt of money from William Croghan, in payment for land on the Ohio River. [Copy.] 4°. 1 page.

TAYLOR, ROBERT, to MADISON.

1801, October 24. Deed devising lands to Mrs. Rose. small 4°. 1 page.

1802, August 31. Deeds which accompany this letter. The manner of authenticating deeds in Kentucky described. small 4°. 1 page.

1802, September 17. Conveyance of a deed to Mrs. Rose. 4°. 1 page.

1803, December 23. Acknowledging letter of 6th. Agreement of Dr. Rose to sign a deed. Is glad to hear our dispute with Morocco is accommodated. Does not think Spain will resist our taking possession of Louisiana. small 4°. 2 pages.

1804, February 17. Acknowledging letter of 22d January. Explains delay in giving his opinion respecting a deed to be drawn for Miss N. Madison to execute, transferring a part of lands in Kentucky held in her father's name. small 4°. 2 pages.

1804 (?), September 16. Has not prepared the paper for Madison to execute, as it appears to be necessary to confer with Madison's brother, William. Has sketched the condition of an arbitration for Madison's approval or emendation. Thinks it may give his brother, William, an advantage in the settlement. small 4°. 2 pages.

1808, January 30, Richmond. Acknowledging letter of 26th respecting a money transaction; subject not stated. Incloses some letters for H. Buckley, to be forwarded to Ireland or England. 4°. 1 page.

1808, April 21, Orange. Applies in behalf of Lewis Madison, of Caroline, for a position in some public office. small 4°. 2 pages.

TAYLOR, ROBERT.

1808, November 16. Asks if he is to pay a bond by Gideon Gooch assigned to Taylor by the late James Pulliam. small 4°. 1 page.

1809, January 8, Richmond. Gives statement of amount to be paid for Gooch's bond. 4°. 1 page.

1809, October 30. Acknowledging receipt of a letter, inclosing money, which will be paid to his brother. 4°. 1 page.

1812, August 31, Orange. Application on behalf of Gen. Moses Green, who wishes a regimental command in the Army should there be a vacancy. He now holds office as adjutant-general of the State. 4°. 2 pages.

1815, March 4, Orange. A negro girl bound to Samuel Harrison Smith by Dr. Willis. Asks Madison to take charge of her and to permit her to remain among his servants until he can send her, when occasion offers, to Orange. 4°. 1 page.

Montpellier.

1824, December 25. Suit between Mr. Harrison and Madison. Harrison refuses to settle by reference and will only accept principal and interest, or principal and costs, referring the subject of interest. small 4°. 2 pages.

1825, January 15. Harrison's suit against Madison. Agrees to accept Cowherd's order for the principal and leave the question of interest to reference, provided Madison pays cost of suit. He refuses to submit the whole matter to reference. small 4°. 2 pages.

1825, February 8. Harrison's suit against Madison. Mr. Cowherd volunteers the statement that Madison will be obliged to pay the whole. small 4°. 2 pages.

1826, January 26, Washington. Incloses a resolution from the Senate for amending the Constitution of the United States. The question of Presidential electors or a direct vote of the people. 4°. 1 page.

1827, November 30, Washington. Col. William Grayson's claim for services investigated at the bounty-land office. No evidence in this office that he served until the termination of the war. Asks him if he can give the desired information. 4°. 2 pages.

1833, June 20. A. M. Greene, of Richmond, has undertaken to investigate and present the claim of Col. Francis Taylor. John Taylor's naval-service claim is also with Mr. Greene, for a contingent recompense. 4°. 2 pages.

TAYLOR, R. ST. C.

1833, January 26, Louisville, Ky. Asks information about the circumstances of his uncle John Taylor's services in the Revolution, as the heirs think they are entitled to some land scrip due him. The family has not sufficient evidence. 4°. 1 page.

1833, May 1, Louisville, Ky. Claim of his father, William Taylor, against the State of Virginia for services rendered in the Revolutionary war. Relates certain evidence and desires further information. Also for his uncles, Francis and John, who served in the Revolution. fol. 2 pages.

TAYLOR, R. W. *Washington.*

Not dated. Was a midshipman on an English sloop-of-war. Left the service on account of cruelty and ill-treatment. Wishes to become an American citizen and serve in the American Navy.
4°. 2 pages.

TAYLOR, WALLER.

1816, December 5, Washington. Asks him to lend him his copy of the constitution of the new State of Indiana for a few days. 4°. 2 pages.

TAYLOR, WILLIAM.

1802, May 20, Jefferson County, Ky. Asks Madison's recommendation of himself and son to Michael Krafft, the inventor of an improvement on stills, in order to use his (Krafft's) patent right, and to pay him when his fall remittances come in.
4°. 1 page.

Montpellier.

1817, November 3, Washington. Acknowledging letter of August 25 with a letter to the President. The consulship at Amsterdam which he wished was disposed of, but the letter will serve in another point of view. 4°. 1 page.

1822, July 19, Mexico. Appointed consul at Vera Cruz. Remains at Mexico at present on account of epidemic of "black vomit" at Vera Cruz. Iturbide, Emperor. Describes his character and conduct. The intelligent, wealthy, and honorable part of the army oppose him; the clergy and rabble support him. His coronation takes place on 21st. It will be the commencement of strife. Mr. Sosaya appointed minister to United States. Describes the country, beggary and filth of the people. Low state of Government finances and stagnation in commerce. The shooting of Gen. Long. Ruin of bankers who have made advances of money. Twenty-second July—describes the coronation of the Emperor and Empress. Coins of the country. August 2—confusion and alarm. Republican standard raised by Gen. Guadaloupe. Risings in other provinces. Introducing Mr. N. Rocofuerte
4°. 10 pages.

1823, November 15, Washington. Fall of Iturbide in Mexico. Republican form of government established. Proceedings of the Mexican Congress. To form a constitution. Little practical political wisdom in the country. Mexico freed forever from Spanish supremacy unless forced upon her by foreign influence. His circumstances not improved by his trip to Mexico. The President allows him a salary. Will embark for Vera Cruz in December. French intriguers in Mexico to place one of the royal family of France on the throne of Montezuma. 4°. 4 pages.

1823, December 13, New York. On the eve of his departure for Vera Cruz. Spain single-handed can do nothing against Mexico. With the aid of France she would instantaneously regain that country. The President's message carries a threatening attitude on that subject.
4°. 1 page.

1824, April 3, Alvarado. Describes Tampico and other towns in Mexico, the people, primitive style of manufacture, manners and customs, and politics. Great want of men of talent in

TAYLOR, WILLIAM.

Mexico. The Iturbide party gathering strength again by the injudicious measures of the ruling party. 4°. 7 pages.

1824, October 1, Alvarado. Execution of Iturbide. Description of the banditti chief Gomez. His defiance of the Government. Civil war in Yucatan. Reinstating Spaniards in office. Treachery of the governor-general of Yucatan. The two political parties, the Republicans and Bourbon ists. The clergy and friars go in a body to the Bourbonists. This party composed of the wealth and learning of the country, no army, but great intriguers. Gen. Victoria candidate for President. Character and merits of Dr. Pablo Obregon, the Mexican minister to the United States. 4°. 7 pages.

1825, August 7, Alvarado. The Mexican Government completely organized. Gen. Guadalupe Victoria President. Tranquility and peace will continue until Government shall have spent all the money raised from loans of English Jews, who will demand the payment of the bond to the last shilling. Predicts difficulties and trouble. Incapacity of the officials. Sends a likeness of Iturbide. Castle of San. Juan de Ulua still in Spanish hands. They have no supplies and will soon capitulate. English capitalists purchase large mining interests. Baring's purchase an immense tract of land. Dislike of foreigners inculcated by the clergy. 4°. 4 pages.

1826, August 10, Vera Cruz. Mr. Poinsett has concluded a treaty with the plenipotentiaries of the Mexican Government. The boundary line not settled or defined. Commodore Porter enters the Mexican service. Intrigues in Mexico with a view of getting present ministers out of office. Our commercial intercourse with Mexico decreasing rapidly on account of direct imports from Europe. 4°. 4 pages.

——— (of Point Coupé).

1824, October 10, Culpeper, Court House. A horse purchased of him. Recommends him to swap him off for two good plow horses. 4°. 1 page.

TAYLOR, W. D. L. *Washington.*

1807, January 17, Louisville, Ky. Has resigned his appointment in the Navy for family reasons. Would like an appointment in the Army for a position not below a captaincy. fol. 2 pages

TAXES ON LAND—CONGRESS, CONTINENTAL, RESOLUTIONS OF.

1783, February 6. Vote of Congress on the resolution to require the legislatures of States to pass laws to procure accurate estimates of the value of lands; that sums of money be raised by taxes on such lands to defray the expenses of the United States service. Resolution lost. [Copy.] fol. 4 pages.

TAZEWELL, HENRY, to MADISON. *Orange.*

1795, June 26, Philadelphia. The Senate adjourns. The treaty not yet made public. Will communicate with Madison in Fredericksburg in July. 4°. 1 page.

Philadelphia.

1796, April —, Philadelphia. Remarks on certain articles contained in the British treaty. 4°. 2 pages.

TAZEWELL, LITTLETON W. *Washington.*

1803, December 8, Norfolk. Loan obtained at the bank for Col. Monroe. small 4°. 3 pages.

1803, December 26, Norfolk. Acknowledging letter of 18th inclosing a check, which was placed to credit of Monroe. Asks for the appointment of collector of this port. small 4°. 2 pages.

1804, April 28, Norfolk. Obligations due from Monroe to the bank which the latter is obliged to refuse to renew. Suggests measures to be taken to take them up without inconveniencing Madison or Monroe. Alarm existing among commercial men respecting captures of trading vessels by Spanish and French privateers. 4°. 3 pages.

TEACKLE, LITTLETON DENNIS.

1813, May 13, Baltimore. Introducing Monsieur De Nard, who wishes to be concerned in the establishment of a military school under the auspices of Government. 4°. 1 page.

1814, January 31. On the subject of a national bank. Submits his views. 4°. 4 pages.

Montpellier.

1823, February 4, Annapolis. As chairman of the committee of public instruction submits a bill reported at the house of delegates. 4°. 1 page.

1824, June 12, Baltimore. An association being formed to conduct a work on political economy, with intent to discover causes of the retarding the progress of our prosperity. Solicits Madison's aid in furthering the object. 4°. 1 page.

1826, March 22, Baltimore. Sends a newspaper containing an act of the general assembly of Maryland relating to public instruction. Gives his views respecting a scheme for introducing higher branches of education, such as agricultural schools. 4°. 1 page.

1828, January 21, Annapolis. Transmits the first annual report of the superintendent of public instruction to the legislature of Maryland. 4°. 1 page.

1830, January 20, Annapolis. Transmits a report to the house of delegates of a proposition to establish a financial bank in this State. The benefits to be derived described. 4°. 1 page.

1832, March 1, Annapolis. Sends several legislative documents and a report to the house of delegates. 4°. 1 page.

1834, July 13, Annapolis. Plan for adjusting the financial question now pending in Congress. 4°. 1 page.

TEBBS, GEORGE.

1817, November 8, Stevensburg. Proposes establishing a female boarding school. Asks Madison's opinion, but particularly as regards public patronage. The plan to raise a sufficient sum will be the subject of future communication. 4°. 3 pages.

1817, December 1, Stevensburg. Communicates his plans for the establishment of a boarding school. 4°. 3 pages.

TECUMSEH, ———, to HARRISON, Governor.

1810, August 20. Tecumseh's speech to Governor Harrison. [Copy.] fol. 9 pages.

TEFFT, J. K., to MADISON.

1830, November 17, Savannah. Requests Madison's autograph, also those of any distinguished American which he can spare. 4°. 2 pages.

1832, July 31, Savannah. Inclosing a letter purporting to be an original from Washington. Asks Madison's opinion as to its genuineness. 4°. 1 page.

TEMPLE, ROBERT, and others. *Washington.*

1813, December 14, Richmond. In behalf of the Dover Baptist Association, expressing satisfaction in Madison as Chief Magistrate and recommending appointments of days of fasting and prayer in these times of national distress. 4°. 1 page.

TENNESSEE GENERAL ASSEMBLY.

1812, —, Nashville. Proceedings of the general assembly approving of the declaration of war and promising support. 4°. 4 pages.

TERNANT, Col. (French minister), to HAMILTON, ALEXANDER. *Philadelphia.*

1793, April 13, Philadelphia. Application for an advance of money on account of the debt to France. [In French. *See* letter from A. Hamilton to Thomas Jefferson, dated May 3, 1793. Copy.] 4°. 1 page.

1793, April 30, Philadelphia. An order of the French minister for 20,000 livres tournois on account of the debt of the United States to France. [In French.] 4°. 1 page.

TERRELL, RICHARD, to MADISON. *Orange.*

1799, September 24, Albemarle. Bills in chancery from Col. Taylor and Mr. Croghan, asks instructions, after correcting any impropriety in the bill. 4°. 1 page.

THASHER, STEPHEN. *Washington.*

1812, September 20, Kennebunk, York County, Me. As chairman of the Republican committee of the county of York, transmits the proceedings of a late convention of the Republican citizens of that county, in support of the measures of the administration. 4°. 2 pages.

THOM, CHRISTOPHER S.

1807, June 10, Boston. On account of a complaint in his eye, thinks it advisable to resign his office. 4°. 1 page.

THOMAS, DAVID.

1808, December 5, Albany. Introducing Mr. Jenkins, secretary of State of New York, and Mr. Bloodgood, clerk of the supreme court. 4°. 1 page.

THOMAS, E.S.

1807, October 23, Baltimore. Sends for deposit in the Department of State "Ramsey's Life of Washington." Incloses a bound copy for himself with a request for his opinion of it as a reading book for schools and academies. 4°. 1 page.

THOMAS, PHILEMON, and others, to CLAIBORNE, W. C. C. (governor of Louisiana).

1814, January 24, New Orleans. *See* CLAIBOURNE, W. C. C. (governor).

THOMAS, WILLIAM, to MADISON. *Washington.*

1812, January 7, Annapolis. Transmits as president of the senate of Maryland, resolutions passed by

THOMAS, WILLIAM.

the general assembly approving of the measures of the President respecting our relations with France and England and promising support. 4°. 4 pages.

1815, July 25, Williamsville. Complains that after seven years' service, his name, which was second on the list of hospital surgeons, was erased by the President to make room for Dr. Waterhouse, who is totally unfit for the place and whose character is detestable. fol. 2 pages.

THOMPSON, BENJAMIN.

1801, March 31, Delaware. Application for a clerkship or consulate. fol. 2 pages.

New York.

1789, August 7, Morristown. Applies for an appointment as consul in one of the ports of France or French islands. small 4°. 2 pages.

THOMPSON, GEORGE.

1790, June —, Fluvanna County. Has lately returned from Kentucky. Gives details of murders and outrages by the Indians. Thinks Congress should lose no time in preventing these outrages. Recommends extirpating the Indians from the face of the earth. fol. 3 pages.

Montpellier.

1825, June 3, Shawanee Springs, Ky. Deplorable state of State legislation in Kentucky respecting the laws of debtor and creditor. fol. 3 pages.

THOMPSON & HOMANS.

1831, July 1, Washington. Transmiting a copy of a new edition of the "Federalist." 4°. 1 page.

THOMPSON, H., jr.

1828, February 26, Uniontown, Pa. Announces his election as honorary member of the Madison Literary Society. 4°. 1 page.

THOMPSON, JOHN. *Washington.*

1816, March 28, Georgetown, D. C. Is an old soldier of the Revolution and has never been reimbursed for his services. Asks for an appointment in a land office or any other which he may be capable of filling. 4°. 1 page.

THOMPSON, JOHN R.

1813, November 6, Abbeville, S. C. Commends the President for having appointed a day of general humiliation and prayer in September last. In view of the distinguishing interpositions of Divine Providence in our favor as a nation he recommends a thanksgiving day. fol. 2 pages.

THOMPSON, JONATHAN. *Montpellier.*

1821, June 14, New York. Informs him that there is in the public store of this port a box directed to him, said to contain garden seed from the royal gardener, near Paris. Asks instructions about sending it to him. 4°. 1 page.

1821, June 29, New York. Two bills of lading of a box of seeds to care of Mackay & Campbell, of Fredericksburg, per schooner *Tell Tale.* 8°. 1 page.

1821, June 30, New York. Has forwarded from the custom-house his box of seeds to Fredericksburg. 4°. 1 page.

THOMPSON, JONATHAN.

1823, April 26, New York. Has received, per ship *Howard*, from Havre, a box of seeds, which he has forwarded via Fredericksburg. 4°. 1 page.

1824, May 7, New York. Has received, per ship *Stephania*, from Havre, a box of seeds to Madison's address, which he has forwarded to Fredericksburg. 4°. 1 page.

THOMPSON, PISHEY.

1831, March 22, Washington. Is about to publish a new edition of the "Federalist." It has been suggested to him that a valuable companion to it might be made from a compilation of political disquisitions, essays, etc., which appeared previous and during the publication of the "Federalist," and asks Madison's opinion and assistance as to means of collecting them. 4°. 2 pages.

THOMPSON, THOMAS. *New York.*

1789, March 8, Fair Hill, Va. Asks Madison's influence with Gen. Washington, should the new government be adopted, for the appointment of the consulate to the Kingdom of Portugal. 4°. 2 pages.

THOMPSON, W. *Washington.*

1809, February 14, Elberton, Ga. Transmits the proceedings of a meeting of citizens of Elbert County, approving the measures of the General Government. 4°. 1 page.

THOMPSON, WILLIAM.

1816, June 13, Baltimore. Applies for a Government position. 4°. 2 pages.

Montpellier.

1823, December 28, Morrisville. Deed which he was to send to William Stone and which has not been received. Thinks it must have miscarried, and desires Madison to execute one and forward it. 4°. 1 page.

THOMSON, CHARLES. *New York.*

1786, September 15. As Secretary of Congress, transmits a copy of proceedings of Congress in the appointment of a court of hearing and determining a question between the States of South Carolina and Georgia, by which Madison will be informed he is a member. Incloses a circular. fol. 4 pages.

Washington.

1808, December 13, Harrison. Introducing Thomas Amies, a paper manufacturer. Sends by him the first two volumes of his own translation of the Bible. 4°. 1 page.

THORNTON, A. *Montpellier.*

1825, June 18, Fredericksburg. Appeal for pecuniary aid from a person who apparently is insane. small 4°. 1 page.

THORNTON, EDWARD. *Washington.*

1801, May 12, Philadelphia. Congratulates him on his appointment as Secretary of State. Asks him to inform him of the probable time of Mr. Lear's sailing for St. Domingo as consul. "Private." 4°. 2 pages.

1802, March 17, Philadelphia. The publication of "Phillidor's Game of Chess" suspended on ac-

THORNTON, EDWARD.

count of want of subscribers. Suggests that he and the President should subscribe, and others whom he may induce, to insure the publication. "Private." 4°. 2 pages.

1803, July 12, Philadelphia. Asks for copies of Gallatin's letter of 1801 to transmit to England and British consuls here. Asks to be informed as to the time of Mr. Merry's probable departure from England. 8°. 3 pages.

THORNTON, FRANCIS.

1812, July 6, Fall Hill, near Fredericksburg. Tenders his services. Would prefer a position in the volunteer Army. 4°. 1 page.

THORNTON, HENRY.

1814, March 19, Saco, Me. States that the appointment of Col. Learned would be unsuitable for the position of district attorney. Mentions several other names who would be preferable to the community. 4°. 1 page.

THORNTON, WILLIAM.

1801, March 16, Washington. Is pleased that Madison has arrived in this city. Thinks the climate will be beneficial. The virtue and talents of the country, irrespective of party, will approve of his appointment as Secretary of State. Invites him to stay with him. 4°. 3 pages.

——— to THOMPSON & VEITCH. *Alexandria.*

1801, August 15, Washington. Informs them that Madison, having taken a house, declines renting theirs. [*See* Letter to Madison of this date.] [Copy.] 4°. 1 page.

Orange.

1801, August 15, Washington. Acknowledging letter of 8th, respecting the engagement of renting a house belonging to Nicholas Voss. Incloses copy of engagement signed by Voss, that the house will be ready on October 1, and states the terms. Thornton engaged in making highways. 4°. 4 pages.

1803, August 17, Washington. M. Lançat expected as ambassador to this country instead of Gen. Bernadotte. The French will have occasion for all their generals in Europe. Movements of France. Arrival of Rochambeau in this country after escaping from St. Domingo. Madison's carriage arrived and nailed up in his carriage house. Mrs. Law's dashing movements. 4°. 3 pages.

1803, August 26, Washington. Acknowledging letter of 19th, respecting the exchange of a pair of horses. 4°. 2 pages.

1803, September 9, Washington. Fever in Alexandria. Is pleased with the horses after trying them. 4°. 1 page.

Washington.

1804, November 19. States terms on which he will let brood mares. Specifies certain mares with pedigree. Two strips of paper. 4°. 1 page.

Orange.

1805, October 3, Washington. Insults and injuries received from the Spanish and English. Thinks that if we do not receive prompt satisfaction from

THORNTON, WILLIAM.

both we could take the Floridas and Cuba by volunteers and do the English greater injury by armed vessels than France and Spain combined. The office made vacant by the death of Mr. Grainger would be gratefully accepted by himself. Asks his good offices with the President to procure it. 4°. 3 pages.

Washington.

1806, February 11, Washington. Asks him to lend him $200 for a few days, as he has an obligation to pay at the Bank of Columbia. 4°. 1 page.

1806, August 6, Washington. Requests him to inform the President of Mr. Latrobe's deviation from the original plan of a portion of the Capitol. 4°. 2 pages.

1807, November 27, Washington. In view of the increasing business of the Patent Office, he recommends the propriety of Congress granting a reasonable salary for the superintendent and to appoint a clerk, a proper office, and an assistant. Thinks a national establishment of such importance ought to have no connection with an undignified parsimony. 4°. 3 pages.

Orange.

1808, May 9, Washington. Respecting a filly which he is to receive from Madison. Appointment of a son-in-law of Gen. Steele to a commission in the Army. Is informed the only vacancy is filled. Will communicate with Gen. Steele on the subject. 4°. 2 pages.

Washington.

1809. Account rendered respecting horse-breeding. 4°. 2 pages.

1808, December 17, Farm. Gives his reasons for his absence from Washington. Pecuniary losses and financial business actually require it at present. Hopes to return soon. 4°. 2 pages.

1810, July 27, Washington. Application of Mr. Joseph Cerneau, a French citizen of the United States, to send a vessel to France, but is afraid of the Rambouillet decree. The Secretary of State refuses and gives his reasons. Suggests a plan. 4°. 1 page.

1811, August —, Washington. Explanation of a seeming want of respect in not paying a farewell visit to Madison and Mrs. Madison before their departure. Has had to lament a marked distance and coldness towards him, for which he can not account. 4°. 1 page.

Orange.

1811, August 3, Washington. Is very ill in bed. Is grateful for his and Mrs. Madison's kind attention at the time of their departure from Washington. Mentions particulars about a horse which he is willing to take at a fair valuation, if Madison does not wish to keep him. 4°. 1 page.

1811, August 12, Washington. Still remains sick in bed with rheumatic fever. Severe rains. People hereabouts think a double crop of corn will be raised. Drouth in Jefferson County. 4°. 1 page.

THORNTON, WILLIAM. *Washington.*

1814, January 28, Washington. The great benefits to be derived from a national botanic garden. Calls attention to the advantage of the importation of Merino sheep. Suggests that the President, if he approves, to further these subjects in recommending Congress to act on them.
4°. 5 pages.

——— to MADISON. *Montpellier.*

1817, June 18, Washington. Introducing to Madison and Jefferson Mr. Thomas Freeborn.
4°. 1 page.

1821, January 20, Washington. Applies for the position of agent to the Republic of Colombia, now vacant. His particular object in obtaining this position is to write a natural history of that country. Has valuable acquaintances there. Has served this Government twenty-six years. Asks Madison's good offices to obtain the place.
4°. 3 pages.

1823, September 2, Washington. Complains of the conduct of Mr. Cutts, who owes him a large sum and which he considers a debt of honor. As Madison is a connection of Cutts's, he begs his influence in inducing him to fulfill his promises.
4°. 3 pages.

1824, March 1, Washington. Introducing Mr. John Finch. 4°. 1 page.

THORNTONE, D'ALEMBERT.

1834 (?), not dated. On the unconstitutionality of the United States Bank and the right of Congress to grant corporate privileges. 4°. 3 pages.

1834, February 25. Respecting the Bank of the United States. Suggests amendments to the new charter. 4°. 3 pages.

1834, April 20. On the unconstitutionality of the United States Bank. 4°. 3 pages.

1834, April 22. Suggests ideas respecting a national bank. 4°. 1 page.

THOSDOFF, NICHOLAS.

1815, August 28, Philadelphia. [*See* MOULDER, WILLIAM.]

THRUSTON, B., to MADISON.

1833, February 13, Washington. Transmits a Latin epitaph on John Adams and Thomas Jefferson. Mr. Clay's tariff act. 4°. 2 pages.

THURBER, SAMUEL. *Washington.*

1815, November —, *Providence, R. I.* Objects to the petition of cotton-manufacturers for Congress to secure them greater prospects for gain, although a cotton-manufacturer himself. Thinks it unfair to grant exclusive benefits. 4°. 1 page.

THURMON, WILLIAM.

1814, October 6, Lynchburg, Va. Submits a plan to meet the expenses of the nation. Scheme for a national bank. 4°. 1 page.

TICKNOR, GEORGE. *Montpellier.*

1825, March 29, Boston. He and Mrs. Ticknor express gratitude for hospitalities received from him and Mrs. Madison while in Virginia. Sends an

TICKNOR, GEORGE.

engraving and memoir of Lafayette to Mrs. Madison. Expresses his interest in the University of Virginia. 4°. 2 pages.

1825, April 14, Boston. Presents a second copy of "Outlines of the Life of Lafayette," the first not having reached its address. 8°. 1 page.

1825, November 21, Boston. Sends a pamphlet which he recently published on the changes in Harvard College in mode of instruction. 4°. 2 pages.

TIFFANY, J. H., to TOMPKINS, DANIEL D. governor of New York. *Albany.*

1812, January 30, Albany. Scheme for the invasion of Canada and to proclaim their independence and establishment of a republic. fol. 3 pages.

1813, January 3, Albany. Inclosing remarks on the soil, produce, climate, geography, population. manners, policy, and government of upper Canada. Prepared in view of a scheme for invasion. fol. 27 pages

TIFFIN, EDWARD, to MADISON. *Washington.*

1811, June 14, Chillicothe, Ohio. As grand sachem of the Tammany Society, approves of the President's measures respecting our relations with France and England, and promises support. 4°. 2 pages.

1813, May 31, Washington. The two commissioners appointed to ascertain titles and claims to land in Louisiana, east of the Mississippi and New Orleans. Mr. Crawford, one of the commissioners. is discharging his duties satisfactorily, but Mr. Cosby, the other, has never made his appearance. It is suggested that another appointment be made, and asks instructions. 4°. 2 pages.

1813, July 12, Washington. Explanation from Mr. Cosby for delay of arrival to attend to the duties of his appointment. He is progressing in a satisfactory manner towards that object. 4°. 1 page.

1813, August 7, Washington. Submits, for the President's approbation, instructions to commissions for ascertaining the titles and claims to lands in Louisiana east of the Mississippi and island of New Orleans, pursuant to act of Congress of April 25, 1812. 4°. 1 page.

1814, March 28, Washington. Asks for an exchange of situations with Josiah Meigs, Surveyor-General. Thinks he is competent and will give satisfaction. 4°. 2 pages.

1814, October 10, Washington. Josiah Meigs sends in his resignation as Surveyor-General and Tiffin that of Commissioner of General Land Office. Meigs is ready to start from Ohio and Tiffin is ready to go there. Madison will confer a great obligation in attending to their mutual wishes. 4°. 1 page.

——— to GRAHAM, GEORGE (Commissioner General Land Office).

1827, February 17, Chillicothe. Charges of a Mr. Wilson before the House of Representatives for improper conduct as Commissioner of the General Land Office. Declares that the duties of Commissioner were never discharged with greater fidelity, ability, and circumspection than when under his control. 4°. 2 pages.

TILGHMAN, EDWARD, to MADISON.

1806, November 30, Philadelphia. Agrees with Mr. W. Lewis's views respecting the qualifications and conduct of Mr. Smith, the marshal of the Pennsylvania district. [Written on same sheet with W. Lewis's letter to Madison of this date.] 4°. 1 page.

TILGHMAN, C. J., and JUDGE SMITH.

1807, July 20. See DUMAS, HIPPOLITE.

TILLOTSON, THOMAS, to MADISON.

1803, December 20, Albany. Burr's attempts to vilify and blacken the characters of those he can not control. In a pamphlet published by him or under his auspices charges Tillotson as coming to Washington seeking the office of collector and ridiculing his pretentions. Asks Madison to state whether he ever applied to him for that or any other office. 4°. 2 pages.

TILTON, JAMES.

1802, January 17, Wilmington. Disturbed condition of Delaware on account of the governor-elect. Incloses copies of the proceedings of the Republican representatives, showing a true state of the case. Apprehends a desperate effort will be made to displace Col. Hall and usurp the government. 4°. 2 pages.

TIMPANARI to JEFFERSON.

Not dated. Respecting the yellow fever in Leghorn. Suggestions as to the prevention of its spreading. [This letter inclosed in one from Philip Mazzei, dated Piza, August 30, 1804. In Italian. Copy.] 4°. 3 pages.

TINGEY, THOMAS, to HANSON, SAMUEL (of SAMUEL).

1808, August 26, Washington. Declines approving of his account left at the navy-yard, as it is not his duty, and would be an improper interference with the duty of another officer. [Copy.] 4°. 1 page.

——— to MADISON.

1809, January 21, Washington. Incloses an extract of a letter from Benjamin Stoddert. As an officer under Government, Tingey thinks it his duty to communicate such opinions to the President, and hopes he does not err in judgment in so doing. 4°. 2 pages.

1811, March 25, Washington. Acknowledging letter of 18th with Col. Hanson's account. Declines to act in the matter, as he sees no reason to deviate from his former opinion. [Copy.] 4°. 1 page.

——— to REED, WILLIAM.

1814, December 10, Washington. Acknowledging letter of 26th November. His views and opinions respecting the expediency and practicability of a reform of the Naval Department in conformity with a report to the Senate. 4°. 6 pages.

TODD, SAMUEL S., to MADISON.

1809, March 13, Philadelphia. Applies for a Government office. 4°. 1 page.

TOMKINS, JOSEPH Y.

1814, May 25, Baltimore. Inclosing a letter from D. M. Randolph, relating to a plan by which a ship of the line can use her lower-deck guns in a heavy sea. 4°. 1 page.

TOMPKINS, DANIEL D. (governor of New York).

1813, January 12, Albany. Enclosing a letter from Mr. Tiffany, with accompanying documents respecting Upper Canada, an account of its population, productions, etc. 4°. 2 pages.

——— to ARMSTRONG, JOHN.

1814, January 2, Albany. The destruction of Buffalo. Capture of Fort Niagara. Makes suggestions to counteract these winter expeditions. Will cooperate and support any other propositions or arrangements which may be devised. To attempt to retake Fort Niagara with militia alone and without ordnance would be folly. [Copy—unsigned.] 4°. 4 pages.

——— to MADISON.

1814, January 3, Albany. Distressing state of things on the Niagara frontier. Destruction of Buffalo. Burning of Lewiston, Manchester, and all the buildings near the Niagara River from Lake Ontario to Lake Erie, and massacre and scalping of inhabitants. Panic general among the inhabitants. The British force. Recommends immediate operations by our army, in which the State militia will cooperate. The taking of Prescot should be attempted without delay. The occupation of Prescot and Sacketts Harbor, and strongly garrisoned, will reduce Kingston immediately. 4°. 3 pages.

1814, March 30, Albany. Introducing Col. Anthony Lamb, late deputy quartermaster-general, who visits Washington on business. 4°. 1 page.

1814, April 6, Albany. Introducing Horatio G. Spofford. 4°. 1 page.

1814, October 14, Albany. Introducing Col. Jenkins, quartermaster-general of this military district. 4°. 1 page.

1814, November 5, New York. Transmits a resolution of the senate and assembly of New York, that the extravagant and disgraceful terms proposed by the British commissioners at Ghent be not received, and recommends to the national legislature the adoption of the most vigorous and efficacious measures in the prosecution of the war. 4°. 3 pages.

1814, December 31, Albany. Introducing William D. Cheever, of Troy. 4°. 1 page.

1815, February 27, Albany. Introducing John Champlin. 4°. 1 page.

1815, May 16, New York. Introducing John A. Smith. 4°. 1 page.

1815, June 5, New York. Introducing A. Clark. 4°. 1 page.

TONE, MATILDA, to WARDEN, DAVID BAILIE. *Paris.*

1812, January 8, Paris. Is much affected to hear that her brother-in-law, Arthur Tone, is still living. Gives a sketch of his life and adventures. [*See* Letter of WARDEN to PAUL HAMILTON, January 10, 1812.] 4°. 7 pages.

TONGUE, JAMES, to MADISON. *Washington.*

1814, June 17, Anne Arundel County. The British fleet are as far up as the Patuxent. Fears that the warehouses will be burned by them. Suggests that if it

TONGUE, JAMES.

were made known that Sir Francis Baring holds tobacco in those warehouses the property may be respected. Suggests means of defense on the Patuxent and describes its position.
Small 4°. 2 pages.

TORRES, MANUEL.

1815, February 11, Philadelphia. On the financial situation of the United States. Suggests a plan of internal taxation bearing equally on all sorts of capitals, as well as on those proceeding from industry and professions. folio. 4 pages.

1815, February 15, Philadelphia. On the establishment of a National Bank, one of the branches of his new plan of finances. Also a plan for a new sinking fund calculated to extinguish the national debt gradually. 4°. 3 pages.

TORREY, JESSE, Jr. *Montpellier.*

1822, January 15, Chambersburg, Pa. Apologizes to Madison and Mrs. Madison for the enthusiasm and eccentricities displayed at their residence and in Washington with his rhapsodies on the subject of African slavery. Was suffering with fever and his head was affected. Incloses a copy of the "Moral Instructor," designed to advance the progress of knowledge and virtue. Asks Madison's approbation of his views. [Confidential.]
folio. 3 pages.

1822, February 12, Washington. Has finished an address to the citizens of the United States on the subject of education and free libraries. Asks for a contribution to aid in the expense of publishing it. 4°. 2 pages.

Richmond.

1829, October 19, Germantown, Pa. Inclosing a tract on the subject of free and universal diffusion of education and useful knowledge, for the consideration of Madison and members of the convention now in Richmond. Hopes they will adopt a system of general, free, and universal education at the session. folio. 3 pages.

Montpellier.

1833, March 3, Philadelphia. Forwards the first number of the "National Library." Wishes to devote the rest of his life to the diffusion of useful knowledge. To effect this, the publication of books in periodical numbers and free circulating libraries are the cheapest and most expeditious means. Appeals for aid in publishing. Will consider it a loan to be refunded in a year.
4°. 5 pages.

TOULMIN, HENRY. *Orange.*

1793, October 11, Alexandria. Asks for letters of introduction to Madison's friends in Kentucky, where he intends to go shortly with a view to instruct youth in classical knowledge and other branches of liberal education. 4°. 3 pages.

Washington.

1803, April 5, Frankfort, Ky. Transmits a copy of a collection of the laws of the general assembly of this Commonwealth. Contradicts the reports circulated that it was in contemplation in this country to proceed to New Orleans unauthorized by Government. The project of a union with France and Spain was that of a conceited and cracked-

TOULMIN, HENRY.

brained man. Imprisonment of Dr. Speed by the governor at New Orleans. Subsequent report that the account is unfounded. 4°. 7 pages.

1803, July 25, Frankfort, Ky. Is gratified with the intelligence respecting the treaty between France and Spain recognizing the rights of Americans. The happy issue of the embassy to France will silence the clamors of faction in regard to the Mississippi. If it is contemplated by the President to send an agent to acquire information respecting Louisiana, he would like to be appointed, as he is familiar with the country and people. fol. 5 pages.

1803, August 12, Frankfort, Ky. Acknowledging letter of July 20. Recent elections in Kentucky resulted in being Republican. A meeting at Lexington to celebrate the cession of Louisiana. Conspicuous Federalists attended and drank Republican toasts. fol. 2 pages.

1804, November 15, Frankfort, Ky. Acknowledging letter of August 30. Thanks the President for his appointment as U. S. judge of district court of Mississippi. Is preparing to move. Asks to be furnished with letters of introduction. 4°. 4 pages.

1807, April 14, Fort Stoddert. Examination of Mr. Willie, who had been in the employ of Aaron Burr. Burr's real objects and conduct. Inclosing a memorandum of depositions taken in Washington, Mississippi Territory, relative to the conduct of Aaron Burr, with a receipt signed by George Hay of an affidavit of Charles Willie. 4°. 11 pages.

1807, December 6, Fort Stoddert. Has read Madison's treatise on neutral rights with satisfaction. The bloated selfconceit of Great Britain and her ridiculous ideas of her own power. The ignorance of our country by the upstart Englishmen who settle at our seaports and their influence at home. Describes the country in West Florida. Sends Madison an essay on evidence. folio. 4 pages.

——— to MOBILE, (commandant of Post of).

1809, February 21, Mobile. Petition to remove restrictions as to the removal of powder and lead to Fort Stoddert. [Copy of translation.] 4°. 2 pages.

——— to FOLCH (governor).

1809, February 21, Mobile. Memorial in behalf of George S. Gaines, factor of the Choctaw trading house at St. Stephens, praying the removal of restraints laid on the transit of gunpowder and lead from New Orleans to said trading house. [Copy.] 4°. 3 pages.

1809, February 21, Mobile. Memorial removing restraints imposed on the transit of gunpowder and lead toward the factory at St. Stephens. [Copy.] 4°. 2 pages.

——— to MADISON. *Washington.*

1809, February 25, Fort Stoddert. Temper and conduct of the public officers of foreign governments stationed adjacent to United States territories. Detention of a vessel containing goods for the Choctaw nation detained in Mobile Bay by Span-

TOULMIN, HENRY.

ish officers, notwithstanding duties were ready to be paid. Details of the whole affair.
fol. 7 pages.

1810, October 31, Fort Stoddert. Acknowledging letter of September 5. Efforts employed to injure him by false reports as to his being a Spanish pensioner. Panic in west Florida. The people of Mobile packing up their valuables on the rumor of a convention army being on its way from Baton Rouge. Some of the French ask asylum in American limits. Incloses a letter from a friend relating to the state of affairs in west Florida. Address of the convention to the people of Mobile. Governor Folch's correspondence with the governor-general of Havana.
4°. 4 pages. fol. 4 pages.

1810, November 22, Fort Stoddert. Certainty that some rash act inconsistent with the duty of American citizens and injurious to the cause of peace will take place in this district. Describes the population who think the proper time has arrived to free themselves from Spanish oppression. Doubts whether a sufficient opening is given for judicial interference. Advocates our taking possession of the country. Incloses letters respecting the state of parties at Baton Rouge. fol. 7 pages.

——— to INNERARITY, JAMES. *Mobile.*

1810, November 23, Mobile. Acknowledging letter of 22d. Endeavors to get rid of the oppressive duties. The good citizens will use every means and go any length under the authority of Government. Believes that the leaders of the expedition are influenced by personal popularity and power. [Copy of this letter written on last page of one from Innerarity to Toulmin, November 22.]
4°. 3 pages.

——— to MADISON. *Washington.*

1810, November 28, Fort Stoddert. Critical situation of this country. The judicial arm so feeble that the violators of the law boast there is no danger of being convicted by a jury of their countrymen. Officers of the militia join the insurgents. Details of movements by the governor of Mississippi Territory and other officials. Supposed force of the insurgents. Anxiety at Mobile.
fol. 6 pages.

1810, December 6, Fort Stoddert. No force yet appeared from Baton Rouge. Unsuccessful attempt of Governor Folch to disperse the assembled party from this district from a bluff opposite Mobile. Threats of death against any public officer who shall institute prosecution against any of the individuals concerned in the enterprise. Will execute a warrant against Maj. Buford. His own personal danger. Supplies received by the patriots. Fears that they will stop supplies for the troops; has, accordingly, applied to Col. Sparks for an escort. Thinks that Governor Folch is firmly attached to the interests of the United States. 4°. 5 pages.

1811, January 23, Fort Stoddert. Hopes of our obtaining possession of the residue of Louisiana. Governor Claiborne's plan of laying off parishes as far as Bayou Battrie, and sending a parish judge to Pascagoula. Stealing of his cattle on the pretext of their being Spanish property. Fears of

TOULMIN, HENRY.

the inhabitants of Mobile allayed by Col. Cushing's movements. 4°. 4 pages.

1811, February 6, Fort Stoddert. Quotes from a letter from Judge Cumming of his failure to establish civil government in the settlement on the Pascagoula. Plundering of slaves by Maj. Dupree on pretext of orders from Col. Jas. Collier. Indignation of the individuals of predominant parties. Talk to the Indians by the Spaniards who anticipate a war by Spain against the United States. Rumors of the expectation of a British force at Pensacola. The Spanish governor indignant towards the United States, in the belief that the revolt of their subjects was countenanced and abetted by the United States. Col. Cushing's orders to remove the troops from Mobile to Fort Stoddert. 4°. 5 pages.

1811, February 27, Fort Stoddert. Acknowledging letter of December 22d. Timely arrival of Col. Cushing with a competent force; thinks it has saved the country from a scene of plunder and desolation. The court for trial of the offenders commences the next Monday. Doubtful if any indictment will be found. Threats of personal violence have been made against him should he presume to hold a court. 4°. 3 pages.

1811, May 14, Fort Stoddert. His impressions of the dispositions existing towards the U. S. Government in the country lately taken possession of adjacent to the Mississippi. Great increase of population. Intends going to Pascagoula to strengthen the people in their allegiance. Has suggested to Governor Claiborne the propriety of extending the jurisdiction of the territorial government as far as the Perdido. 4°. 4 pages.

Not dated. Giving a description of a threshing machine at Charles Mordant's, Halsal, near Omskirk, Lancashire, England. small 4°. 7 pages.

TOWLES, O. (Lt. Col.)

1787, November 26. Certificate that John Turnley served in his company of regular troops in the continental army. Statement indorsed by I. Howell, of his discharge. Scrap of paper.

Philadelphia.

1791, November 8, Virginia. Asks Madison's attention to certain representations which are to be laid before Congress in his behalf, in order to expedite the business. small 4°. 1 page.

TOWNES, JOHN.

1792, January 21, Easton. Asks his advice and opinion upon a claim which he proposes to lay before Congress for pay for services during the Revolutionary war. fol. 1 page.

TRACIE, M. L. *Montpellier.*

1828, August 7, Washington. Asks to know the precise reasons why his application for the vacant chair of ancient languages at the university was objected to. 4°. 1 page.

TRACY, ELISHA. *Washington.*

1809, January 31, Norwich, Conn. No combination in New England to resist the embargo laws. Congratulates him upon his election. Wishes to be appointed collector of customs at New Haven. 4°. 3 pages.

TRACY, ELISHA.

1809, February 20, Norwich, Conn. Can vouch for the enforcement of the laws in this State respecting the embargo. Thinks it will be more difficult for the Government to enforce nonintercourse with France and Great Britain, owing to the clamors of the Federalists. 4°. 2 pages.

1812, June 26, Norwich, Conn. Finds the people are better disposed to acquiesce in the declaration of war than he expected. Inquiry made whether blank commissions for privateers will be forwarded to collectors. 4°. 1 page.

1816, December 30, Washington. Anxiety respecting the issue of the bank bill. Suggests the propriety of providing by law that all Treasury notes issued or to be issued be made a legal tender in any action at law or in chancery. 4°. 1 page.

TRADE, REGULATION OF.

1786 (?). Acts of the thirteen States, respectively, giving Congress regulation of trade. fol. 2 pages.

TREASURY DEPARTMENT.

1790. A paper giving estimates of tonnage duty as paid in the year 1789 and 1790 on American and foreign vessels; also relating to seamen. With various papers touching same subjects, with memoranda in Madison's handwriting. 4°. 3 pages. small 4°. 1 page. 9 papers, various sizes.

TREASURY WARRANTS.

1780, May 9. Entries of land on Panther Creek by Madison and William Moore. Copies by J. H. Daveiss, November 4, 1801. fol. 2 pages.

TREDWELL, SAMUEL. *Washington.*

1807, February 24, Edenton. Acknowledging letter of 8th. Brig *Jacob Easton*, which was wrecked. Has written to the collector of Newbern, giving instructions how to forward the saved articles to Madison. 4°. 2 pages.

TRESCOT, JOHN S.

1813, September 7, Charleston. Notifies him of his election as honorary member of the Literary and Philosophical Society of South Carolina. 4°. 1 page.

TRIPLETT, JOHN R. *Montpellier.*

1821, May 26, Norfolk, Va. Forwards some salt to care of Mackay & Campbell, of Fredericksburg, with account of charges, duty, etc., paid here. 4°. 1 page.

TRIPPE, JOHN (Captain), to commander of British brig *Moselle.*

1810, June 24, U. S. brig Vixen. Demands his reasons for firing on his brig and received an answer that it was not done with hostile intent and the shot was not aimed at the vessel. [Copy. Not signed.] 4°. 1 page.

——— to HAMILTON, PAUL, Secretary of Navy. *Washington.*

1810, June 30, Havana. Circumstance of the firing upon the U. S. brig *Vixen* by the commander of the British brig *Moselle.* [Copy.] 4°. 3 pages.

TRIST, E., to MADISON.

1810, July 7, Philadelphia. Suit before the superior court at New Orleans, Mary Jones against the

TRIST, E.

United States, claiming certain articles of property belonging to her former husband, H. B. Trist. Inclosing papers relating to this case, with the verdict of the jury.
4°. 6 pages. fol. 1 page. 3 strips of paper.

Montpellier.

1810, August 27, Mount Holly. Wishes to know if Mr. Pinckney has communicated to the Government anything respecting William Brown's arrest at Pinckney's suit. 4°. 2 pages.

TRIST, H. B. *Orange.*

1801, February 13, Charlottesville. Intention of Peter Dobell, in case of a Republican administration, to apply for the consulate at Bordeaux.
4°. 2 pages.

TROUP, GEORGE M. *Washington.*

1808, March 4, Washington. Incloses a paper signed by himself and others recommending Dr. Kirkpatrick for office under Government.
4°. 2 pages.

TRUDEAU, CHARLES.

1809, June 10, New Orleans. As president of the city council, congratulates Madison on his elevation to the Presidental chair and approves of his measures. [In French and English.]
large fol. 3 pages.

TRUXTUN, THOMAS, to SMITH, ROBERT (Secretary of Navy).

1805, September 7, Philadelphia. It was never his intention to write an ambiguous letter, but was simply to communicate his desire to relinquish command of the Mediterranean service without a second captain being furnished him as was promised. Incloses letters to and from Charles Biddle and Commodore Dale. [Copy.]
4°. 2 pages.

——— to BIDDLE, CHARLES. *Philadelphia.*

1805, September 7, Philadelphia. Asks him to state if he understood that when he declined to command the squadron in the Mediterranean, that he intended to resign his commission, as it has been stated that his expressions were ambiguous and desires to have the matter cleared up. [*See* letter of this date to Smith, Robert. Copy.]
4°. 2 pages.

——— to SMITH, ROBERT. *Washington.*

1805, September 14, Philadelphia. States his views as to how an honorable peace with Tripoli might have been effected at the period when circumstances prevented his going to the Mediterranean in 1802. "Private." [Copy.] 4°. 4 pages.

——— to MADISON.

1805, September 15, Philadelphia. Incloses copies of correspondence relating to misunderstandings and misconceptions in consequence of his not having a captain assigned to command of his flagship. Asks his opinion of his case, as the suspense is injurious to him, it preventing pursuits of a pecuniary kind. 4°. 3 pages.

1808, March 17, Philadelphia. Incloses a letter from himself to Thomas Tingey, unsealed, for Madison to read and forward. 4°. 1 page.

TRUXTUN, THOMAS, to TINGEY, THOMAS.

1808, March 17, Philadelphia. Acknowledging letter of 14th. The great interest at the present crisis respecting the Presidential candidates. Respecting the movements of Mr. Duaine [of the "Aurora."] The influence of his paper. The embargo a salutary measure. Thinks we should prepare for war. Thinks vessels should be sent out by our Government to warn China and India vessels to keep out of the way of French privateers. 4°. 4 pages.

——— to MADISON.

1808, May 6, Philadelphia. Incloses a letter to Mr. Tingey, and, after reading it, requests him to seal and forward it. Clinton as a Presidential candidate. 4°. 1 page.

TSCHIFFEY, F. D. *Montpellier.*

1822, July 15, Orange C. H. Has been dismissed from the Treasury Department, where he has served for twelve years, for no reason or cause alleged. Asks pecuniary aid. small 4°. 3 pages.

TUCHERVILLE, (?) GEORGE W. *Philadelphia.*

1793, January 28, Richmond County, Va. Acknowledging letter of December 2. Confirmation of the French Republic. The reign of despotism will hardly survive the eighteenth century. America's agency therein. Our national finances touched upon. The revenue laws disapproved of. small 4°. 4 pages.

TUCKER, GEORGE. *Montpellier.*

1822, May 16, Lynchburg. Has requested his publisher to send Madison a copy of a work he has lately published. 4°. 1 page.

1827, February 19, University of Virginia. Returns Dr. Cooper's new work on political economy. Has a favorable opinion of it. Considers that Jay's political economy the best text-book. The new regulations of the visitors seem to work well. 4°. 1 page.

1829, September 19, University of Virginia. Acknowledges letter with a copy of the first draft of the Constitution. On the right of suffrage—his opinions. Relies on the convention to devise a mode of extension. 4°. 1 page.

1830, March 29, University of Virginia. Proposes to write a biography of Jefferson. Asks Madison's assistance. 4°. 1 page.

1831, October 21, University of Virginia. Has been unable to find among the papers of R. H. Lee that part of his correspondence relating to Federal judiciary. 4°. 1 page.

1832, September 17, University of Virginia. Desired change in the lecture hours. 4°. 1 page.

——— to DUNGLISON, Dr.

1833, June —, University of Virginia. Requests him to ask Madison to furnish him with his letters to Jefferson on subject of declaration of rights. Also Madison's letter to the same on the right of one generation to bind succeeding ones. Strip of paper.

——— to MADISON. *Montpellier.*

1833, July 12. Thanks him for his opinions respecting Jefferson's repeated reference to the political

TUCKER, GEORGE.

unity of the Federal Government. Leaves soon for Baltimore and will stop on the way to visit Madison. 4°. 1 page.

1833, July 23, Orange C. H. Sends him a part of his manuscript of his "Life of Jefferson. Asks him to make corrections of errors and omissions. His proposed additions. 4°. 1 page.

1833, October 13, University of Virginia. Asks him to return his manuscript of, if he does not care to keep it longer. Sends him specimens of a newly invented metallic pen. 4°. 1 page.

1833, November 9, University of Virginia. As he advances in his life of Jefferson he finds Madison's aid very valuable in communicating important unpublished facts. Sends him manuscripts to read and correct. 4°. 1 page.

1835, June 3, University of Virginia. Apologizes for keeping Madison's volumes of newspapers sc long. His opinion on some points of Congressional history has been modified and changed. His first volume of Jefferson's life is being transcribed to be sent to England to be published at the same time as in the United States. 4°. 1 page.

1836, April 2, University of Virginia. Introducing Prof. Palfrey, of Harvard College. 4°. 1 page.

1836, June 17, University of Virginia. Incloses a copy of the form in which he dedicates his life of Jefferson to Madison. Will send him a volume as soon as bound. 4°. 1 page. 8°. 2 printed pages.

TUCKER, HENRY ST. GEORGE.

1817, December 18, Washington. Sends a hasty sketch on a constitutional question. Is indebted to Madison for every principle of constitutional law which in early life was impressed on his mind. 4°. 2 pages.

1819, November 10, Winchester, Va. Claim of Madison's to bring suit on Messrs. Baldwin. They have declared themselves insolvent and he advises Madison to withdraw the suit to save costs. 4°. 1 page.

TUCKER, ST. GEORGE. *Washington.*

1812, July 8, Williamsburg. Arrest of a British officer on board the *Hampton.* His suspicious movements. 4°. 2 pages.

1812, July 27, Williamsburg. Acknowledging letter of 21st. Pernicious designs of a political faction in Boston to rule or dissolve the Union. 4°. 1 page.

1813, January 27, Williamsburg. Has written an official letter accepting the commission of U. S. district judge. Expresses his pleasure at this mark of friendship from Madison. 4°. 1 page.

1813, March 19, Williamsburg. Incloses a letter from William Coleman giving information of the enemy's vessels in the Chesapeake. Suggests the importance of communication by telegraph. Will send a model of one of his invention. 4°. 1 page.

1813, March 24, Williamsburg. Inclosing a note from W. Coleman. Acknowledges a letter of 22d. Will send model of a telegraph by next mail. 4°. 1 page.

TUCKER, ST. GEORGE.

1813, March 26, Williamsburg. Sends a model of his telegraphic invention, with explanation of the manner of using it. 4°. 5 pages.

1813, December 1, Richmond. Incloses a paper from James C. Cabell, copied from an original affidavit. If the subject is of sufficient importance will endeavor to procure the original and send it to him. 4°. 1 page.

Orange.

1815, April 15, Williamsburg. Is recovering from a severe illness and apologizes for the delay in acknowledging a service rendered. 4°. 1 page.

Washington.

1816, March 4, Williamsburg. Recommends the appointment of William Wirt for the office of U. S. attorney for this district. 4°. 1 page.

——— to SCOTT, R. G.

1816, March 15, Williamsburg. Acknowledging letter of this date. Would have complied with his request had he not already recommended a friend [William Wirt] for the office now vacant from Mr. Hay's resignation. 4°. 1 page.

——— to MADISON.

1816, June 28, Williamsburg. Imprisonment of two persons committed to jail on the charge of revolt and mutiny at sea on board the schooner *Romp*, of Baltimore, and of others charged with piracy committed on the high seas against vessels of Spain and Portugal, at peace with the United States. 4°. 7 pages.

Montpellier.

1818, March 11, Williamsburg. Sends him at the request of Joseph Delaplaine, a sketch prepared by himself of the life of the late Gen. Thomas Nelson, for his approval, and to return it to Delaplaine. 4°. 1 page.

1826, November 22, Richmond. Forwards a few short notes, in compliance with a request of Madison's, by Mr. Cabell. 4°. 1 page.

1826, December 22, Williamsburg. Incloses fragments of the journals of the house of delegates of Maryland. 4°. 3 pages.

1827, January 4, Williamsburg. Acknowledging letters of 23d and 30th December. Regrets his inability to furnish any further information from the journals in his possession. 4°. 1 page.

TUDOR, WILLIAM, jr. *Washington.*

1807, October 24, London. Inclosing a letter from his mother to Mrs. Madison requesting her good will with her friends in behalf of Madame de Vaudreuil, whose petition to the House of Representatives Mr. Monroe has kindly promised to deliver. Her husband's services to the United States during the Revolution.
4°. 3 pages [mutilated by mice.]

TUFTS, T.

1808, July 2. Regulations of the custom-house on proceeds of old cargoes and debts. 4°. 2 pages.

TURNER, G. *New York.*

1789, July 19, Philadelphia. Solicits a Government office. fol. 2 pages.

TURNER, G.

1789, August 2, Philadelphia. Continues his application for office, but would prefer a situation near Washington. fol. 2 pages.

1789, August 5, Philadelphia. Continues his application for office and relies on his friends to exercise their judgments to suit the office to his pretensions, as he has no knowledge of the nature and salaries of the several offices. fol. 2 pages.

TURNER, GEORGE. *Philadelphia.*

1791, December 20. Account of Indians inhabiting the northeastern parts of the Territory northwest of the Ohio. Annexing a copy in Madison's handwriting of distances on the Wabash, with observations on its navigation.
fol. 2 pages. 4°. 3 pages.

TURNER, PHILIP. *Washington.*

1813, July 28, Fort Columbus. Incompetency of high officers in the Army and enemies of the administration. Thinks Gen. Armstrong should be an active major-general of the field and Daniel Parker, his chief clerk, in his stead at the War Department. Wishes to have his own commission issued and sent on to him. 4°. 1 page.

1814, January 18, New York. Gen. Dearborn in command in New York. Generally supposed he will be called to the Cabinet as head of the War Department. Inefficiency of the Surgeon-General's Department. Thinks there should be a new system of appointments in that service. Would like to be appointed one of the surgeons of the First Regiment of Artillery on the peace establishments, to which he is entitled. 4°. 2 pages.

——— to ARMSTRONG, JOHN (Secretary of War).

1814, March 2, New York. Has been approved of as surgeon of the First Regiment of Artillerists by Gen. Dearborn and Dr. Eustis and would also like his approval. 4°. 1 page.

1814, March —, New York. Proposes a new arrangement of the medical staff for the armies of the United States. Is satisfied with his position as surgeon to the First Regiment of Artillerists, but will be ready to serve wherever he is placed.
4°. 1 page.

——— to MADISON.

1814, March 3, New York. Incloses copy of his letter to Gen. Armstrong and a plan for an arrangement of the medical staff. For himself he wants nothing but to be enrolled on the list of appointments and commissioned. 4°. 1 page.

1814, June 27, New York. Recommends a new system for the medical staff of our armies. Gives his views on the subject and a plan. He wished to be commissioned. Considers himself neglected.
4°. 3 pages.

TURNER, THOMAS, to TINGEY, THOMAS.

1811, March 18, Washington. Sends the account of Samuel Hanson of Samuel, for hospital stores for approval, with copy of his own disapproval.
4°. 2 pages. fol. 3 pages.

——— to DUVALL, GABRIEL.

1811, April 15, Washington. Acknowledging letter of 3d, relative to Samuel Hanson of Samuel's accounts as purser in the Navy. [Copy.]
4°. 3 pages.

TURNER, THOMAS, to MADISON.

1811, April 17, Washington. Remarks of the accountant of the Navy Department in reply to Mr. Samuel Hanson of Samuel's memorial to the President. 4°. 6 pages.

TURNLEY, JOHN. *See* TOWLES, O. (lieutenant-colonel.)

TURPIN, WILLIAM, to MADISON.

1812, May 29, Charleston. Gives reasons why a loan of $11,000,000 has not been fully subscribed. Makes suggestions. 4°. 1 page.

Montpellier.

1833, July 4, New York. Was sorry that Madison was a friend and supporter of the African Colonization Society. Strongly disapproves of it as not being beneficial to the blacks. Approves of Jefferson's plan of granting free blacks land in our own country and treating them as friends. Progress towards emancipation of slavery. 4°. 2 pages.

1833, December 25, New York. Incloses the declaration of representatives of ten States assembled in Philadelphia. Acknowledging letter of 9th August. Was for sixty years a resident of South Carolina and alone advocated the cause of oppressed Africans. Is now 80 years old and in perfect health in body and mind. 4°. 1 page.

TURREAU, Gen., to GALLATIN, ALBERT.

Washington.

1807, January 16, Washington. Requests that he will remit to his secretary of legation a sum of money for drafts to the French consul general from the United States. [In French.] 4°. 1 page.

——— to MADISON.

1807, October 30, Washington. Makes an appointment to call on Madison. 4°. 1 page.

TUTTLE, JEHIEL.

1810, April 24, Philadelphia. Receipt for payment for a pair of horses. 8°. 1 page.

TYLER, JOHN. *Philadelphia.*

1791, October 28, Greenway, Va. Claim of Mr. Mumford's father as commissary of issues for the Southern department. Asks Madison to aid him in this application. fol. 2 pages.

TYLER, JOHN (governor). *Washington.*

1809, February 25, Richmond. Application of Col. Miles Selden for the office of commissioner of loans. Congratulates him on his election. 4°. 2 pages.

1809, April 24, Richmond. Acknowledging a letter inclosing correspondence with the British minister, out of which a full redress for our injuries and insults may grow. Suggests, in case a messenger be sent to our minister in England, that Alexander McRae would be an excellent one. 4°. 2 pages.

1810, January 15, Richmond. Introducing George William Smith, lieutentant-governor of Virginia. Thinks Madison's hints to Congress to place our country in a proper state of defence will not be attended to. Deplores our national character which has degenerated. Recommends the inter-

TYLER, JOHN (governor).

diction of all British trade and seizure of British property if another impressment takes place. 4°. 2 pages.

1810, January 27, Richmond. Acknowledging letter of 13th on the subject of the purchase of a sword for Gen. Campbell. 4°. 1 page.

1810, January 29, Richmond. Draft on the Bank of Columbia to be applied to state use, but until he is informed on the subject by Madison will suspend the application of it. 4°. 1 page.

1811, January 7, Richmond. Acknowledging a confidential communication and transmits papers by consent of the council. Arrest of individuals in Tennessee for forging bank paper. 4°. 2 pages.

1811, October 28, Greenway, Va. The district courts. Suggests changes of periods of holding courts in Norfolk. 4°. 2 pages.

TYLER, SAMUEL.

1805, February 15, Williamsburg. Incloses a letter to Monroe, which he wishes Madison to forward. 4°. 1 page.

UNDERWOOD, JOHN. *New York.*

1790, January 4, Goochland, Va. Asks Madison's assistance in securing the payment of some lottery tickets in the hands of R. Claiborne, who has gone to Europe. Asks information about British debts. fol. 2 pages.

UNDERWOOD, S. *Washington.*

1816, April 2, Bristol, England. Is a dissenting minister and wishes to leave his present situation and leave for America. Is in the habit of instructing youth and wishes the President to point out a suitable situation. 4°. 2 pages.

UNDERWOOD, THOMAS. *New York.*

1789, June 20, Goochland, Va. Asks his opinion on the public debt. Also on certificates due to officers and soldiers of the Continental Army. The weather, and crop prospects of tobacco. fol. 2 pages.

UNDERWOOD, THOMAS, JR. *Montpellier.*

1829, October 4, Richmond. Applies for the office of doorkeeper to the convention at Richmond. 4°. 1 page.

UNIVERSITY OF VIRGINIA to JEFFERSON, THOMAS.

1824 (?). Resolution of the board of visitors of the university to authorize the rector to appoint a professor of ancient languages. [Copy.] 4°. 1 page.

1828. Memorandum of grants to the University of Virginia by the legislature of that State from 1817 to 1828, with list of annuities. 4°. 3 pages.

1828, July. Printed notice of the course of examination propounded in the several schools of the University of Virginia at the late public examination in July, 1828. fol. 3 pages.

UNKNOWN.

Not dated. A description of New Spain, with statistics as to population, extent, resources, productions, climate, etc. [Unknown handwriting.] fol. 7 pages.

UNKNOWN to DANDRIDGE, BART.
King William Co.

Not dated. Acknowledging letter of January 9, relating to an assignment of his son William's bond, with himself as security, and other matters respecting the payment of an obligation when he gets his tobacco to market. [No signature. *See* letter in same writing from Unknown to Unknown, dated Orange, February 26,1785. Draft.] small 4°. 1 page.

1785, not dated. Acknowledging letter of January 9. Business letter relating to the taking up of a bond. On the back of this is another letter dated Orange, February 26, 1785, from an unknown person, relating to a request for an advance of money. 4°. 2 pages.

——— to UNKNOWN.

1785, February 26, Orange. Acknowledging a letter of April 10, 1784, respecting certain money obligations. [Signature torn off as well as address. *See* letter without date or signature addressed to Bart. Dandridge. Draft.] small 4°. 1 page.

——— to JAY, JOHN (Secretary Foreign Affairs).
New York.

1786, —— *New York.* An unsigned protest against his proceeding upon any other plan than those of stipulating for the free navigation of the Mississippi and fixing of territorial limits agreeable to the treaty with Great Britain. 4°. 2 pages.

——— to PARKER, JOSIAH.

1790, June 18, Norfolk. On encouragement to American ship-building as advocated by Madison and Mr. Page before Congress. 4°. 11 pages.

1807, September 12. A printed pamphlet, entitled: "No. 2. Thoughts on the subject of naval power and on the means of protecting commerce, continued." 8°. 4 pages.

1800, December 1. A bill concerning the Protestant Episcopal Church in the town of Alexandria and District of Columbia, presented to the Senate and House of Representatives. 4°. 3 pages.

——— to LORD ——.

1808-9 (?). On the pernicious effects already derived and the more pernicious consequences expected from the orders in council, so strenuously and uniformly opposed by his lordship and his friends. [Copy.] fol. 14 pages.

1813 (?), *not dated.* A draft in lead pencil, probably intended for a letter to the Navy Department, stating the precarious situation of the squadron in Lake Erie. Strip of paper.

Not dated Respecting the issuing of commissions for letters of marque. Scrap of paper.

——— to MADISON.

Not dated. Canton, Mass. A mutilated letter without signature, apparently relating to public sentiment as to the war of 1812. fol. 1 page.

Not dated. Bill for duties and other charges on 2 pipes wine. 8°. 1 page.

UPHAM, TIMOTHY, to DEARBORN, H. *Boston.*

1815, July 2, Portsmouth, N. H. Asks his friendly assistance in obtaining for him the office of collector for the district of New Hampshire. 4°. 3 pages.

VAIDEN, THOMAS S., to MADISON. *Montpellier.*

1829, December 28, Petersburg. Anonymous letter written in 1828 by himself respecting the successor of Mr. Long's chair in the University of Virginia. small 4°. 2 pages.

VAIL, A.

1834, October 14, London. Acknowledging letter of 9th September. Has inclosed his former letter as an autograph for the Princess Victoria, which she desires, as well as those of Jefferson, Monroe, and John Adams. Has been unable to procure those three. 4°. 2 pages.

VAN AMRINGE, W. F., and others.

1834, March 25, Philadelphia. Expressions of high regard of a deputation of the Jefferson Democratic Society of Philadelphia and a request that he will accept the honorary office of patron of the society. 4°. 2 pages.

1834, July 14, Philadelphia. Expressions of concern of the Jefferson Democratic Society at the indisposition of Madison and pleasure at his recovery. Their great attachment to him on account of the principles advocated in his report on the Virginia resolutions of 1798 and practiced upon when afterwards in power. 4°. 2 pages.

VAN BUREN, MARTIN.

1820, March 15, Albany. Daniel D. Tompkins, the candidate for governor of New York. As great efforts have been made to detract from his merits, he wishes evidence of his devotion to the cause of his country while governor, and requests Madison to furnish for publication a copy of his correspondence relating to his refusal of the offer of a seat in his cabinet during the war of 1812, being better able to serve his country as chief magistrate of the State of New York. 4°. 3 pages.

1820, March 15, Albany. The Vice-President feels a delicacy to permit the publication of his correspondence with Madison without his consent. Incloses copies which have been taken from his letter-book to show that his services were estimated by Madison as well as by his friends. Renews his request to allow them to be published. 4°. 2 pages.

1826, April 22, Washington. Appreciates Madison's opinion on his remarks on the Panama mission. Action of the House of Representatives respecting the measure. Ratification of the Creek treaty. 4°. 3 pages.

1826, August 30, Albany. Asks Madison's advice and opinion on his proposed amendment to the Constitution respecting internal improvements, and the power of Congress over the subject. Would prefer to have the amendment worded by Madison. 4°. 3 pages.

1826, September 28, Albany. Washington's opinion on the power of Congress on the subject of internal improvements. 4°. 2 pages.

1830, June 9, Washington. Acknowledging note of of 3d instant, which he had showed to the President, who regrets he had misconceived his intentions in regard to his (Madison's) veto on the bill for internal improvements. Van Buren expresses his views on the subject. 4°. 7 pages.

VAN BUREN, MARTIN.

1830, July 30, Saratoga Springs. Acknowledging a letter containing suggestions respecting internal improvements and the President's misconstruction of Madison's veto. Asks Madison to give him hints about laying down and describing some general rules for our Government in sanctioning appropriations for light-houses, harbors, rivers, etc., connected with foreign commerce.
4°. 3 pages.

1830, December 13, Washington. With an inclosure, the nature of which, not mentioned.
4°. 1 page.

VAN NESS, JOHN P.

1808, May 12, Washington. Inclosing an application from a Mr. D——, for an appointment.
fol. 2 pages.

Washington.

1808, October 3, Washington. Inclosing a commission from the superior court of the State of New York with interrogatories annexed for the President and Madison, whose evidence is required.
large fol. 1 page.

1811, November 22, Washington. Reminds him of the wish of the friends of his brother, William P. Van Ness, that he should hold some respectable appointment under Government. The vacancy in the office of Comptroller affords that opportunity. 4°. 2 pages.

1814, July 28, Washington. Introducing Maj. Thos. L. McKenny, who wishes to suggest the project of calling into the field a battalion of militia of the District during the agitation and alarm produced by the menaces of the enemy.
4°. 2 pages.

—— and RICHARD BLAND LEE.

1815, August 28, Washington. Inclosing a duplicate contract for a loan for the office of commissioners of the public buildings. Gives information respecting the present progress of the public buildings. Discovery of a quarry of marble on the upper Potomac. 4°. 2 pages.

—— and RICHARD BLAND LEE, and TENCH RINGGOLD, jointly.

1815, November 20, Washington. On the refusal of the Secretary of the Navy to furnish yellow pine plank for work on the public buildings as requested by the commissioners of public buildings. 4°. 2 pages.

—— and others.

1816, March 14, Washington. Report inclosing abstracts of disbursements made by the commissioners of the public buildings in the city of Washington.
fol. 12 pages. Large fol. 8 pages.

—— and RICHARD BLAND LEE, jointly.

1816, March 25, Washington. Inlcosing a contract in duplicate for a loan with the Union Bank of Georgetown for the approbation of the President. Said loan authorized by act of Congress for repairing or rebuilding public buildings in Washington. 4°. 1 page.

——

1816, April 24, Washington. Recommends Dr. Wheaton, of Rhode Island, for an appointment in the

VAN NESS, JOHN P.

Army. Recommends John Jacob Astor and Peter H. Schenck, as commissioners for receiving subscriptions to the U. S. Bank in New York. Also as commissioners for Vermont, S. M. Mitchell and Guy Catlin. 4°. 3 pages.

VAN PELT, P. J.

1815, December 4, Washington. Congratulates the President on the termination of the war. Asks permission to pay his respects in person. 4°. 1 page.

VAN RENSSELAER, K. K. *Philadelphia.*

1794, November 14, Albany. Asks for letters of introduction for Robert S. Van Rensselaer, to Mr. Monroe and Mr. Pinckney in Europe. 4°. 1 page.

VAN RENSSELAER, STEPHEN. *Montpellier.*

1823, February 4, Washington. Incloses an address and asks his opinion of the project for establishing an agricultural school. Has offered a farm to the Board of Agriculture for a pattern farm if the legislature will sanction it. 4°. 2 pages.

VARDEN, CHARLES. *Washington.*

1809, July, 15. Bill for altering carriage. 8°. 1 page.

VARISH, HAZLEWOOD. *Montpellier.*

1820, May 3, Fredericksburg. Receives a box for Mrs. Cutts which will be immediately forwarded. 4°. 1 page.

VARNUM, GEORGE W., to SMITH, ROBERT. *Washington.*

1810, August 7, Lovingston. As commandant of the Nelson Cadets of Artillery transmits resolutions in approval of the administration and promises their support. 4°. 3 pages.

VARNUM, J. B., to MADISON.

1809, March 1, Washington. Suggests the appointment of Gideon Granger as Secretary of War. 4°. 2 pages.

VARNUM, JAMES M., to WASHINGTON. *Philadelphia.*

1787, June 18. Copy in Madison's handwriting. [*See* CONVENTION, FEDERAL, 1787. 4°. 2 pages.

VAUGHAN, BENJAMIN, to MADISON. *Montpellier.*

1824, November 6, Hallowell, Me. Introducing Miss Emma Jane Gardiner, who is traveling with Mr. and Mrs. Ticknor, of Boston. 4°. 2 pages.

VAUGHAN, JOHN. *Philadelphia.*

1791, December 19, Philadelphia. Receipt for certificates of registered debt from Thomas and John Dickinson. [Annexed to the letter from Reuben Lindsay to Madison of December 9, 1791.] 4°. 1 page.

Washington.

1810, September 24, Philadelphia. Publications bought in France by Mr. Thomas Cooper. Recommends Frederick Kinlock, to whom he has given a letter of introduction. 4°. 1 page.

1815, November 15, Philadelphia. Notices a sale of books purchased by Mr. Ticknor in Europe, rare and of best editions. Sends a catalogue. 4°. 1 page.

VAUGHAN, JOHN. *Montpellier.*

1828, June 20, Philadelphia. Introducing Dr. Robert M. Patterson and J. R. Kane, who intend visiting the University of Virginia. 4°. 1 page.

VAUGHAN, SAMUEL, JR. *New York.*

1789, April 17, Philadelphia. Sends him Mr. Le Trosne's work. Recommends it, especially the treatise on "L'interet social." Madison's speech on the extension of the import duty. Method of destroying the Hessian fly or weevil. 4°. 1 page.

1789, July 11, New York. Incloses an extract from a letter from a gentleman in London, respecting the insects infesting American corn. The matter brought before the House of Commons. The alarm serious. 4°. 3 pages.

1790, February 26, Jamaica. Returns a pamphlet borrowed of Madison, commending Madison's political sentiments. 4°. 3 pages.

Philadelphia.

1794, February 14, London. Introducing Monsieur Beaumé, a political refugee from the Constituent Assembly. 4°. 1 page.

1794, February 14, London. Introducing Talleyrand Perigord, Bishop of Autun. 4°. 1 page.

VAUX, ROBERTS. *Montpellier.*

1833, May 4, Philadelphia. Introducing the Marquis Charles Torrigiani, of Florence. 4°. 1 page.

VERDIER, PAUL. *Washington.*

1809, March 25, Orange. Applies for the contract for a post-route carrier. 4°. 1 page.

VERMONT GENERAL ASSEMBLY.

1812, November 7, Montpelier, Vt. [*See* GALUSHA, JONAS, Governor.]

VERPLANCK, DANIEL C.

1809, February 25, Washington. Incloses a letter recommending a young gentlemen of New York for an office as consul or commercial agent. 4°. 1 page.

VERPLANCK, GULIAN C. *Montpellier.*

1819, January 9, New York. Asks his acceptance of a copy of an anniversary discourse which he lately delivered before the New York Historical Society. 4°. 1 page.

1825, January 30, Washington. Ask his acceptance of a little volume recently published in New York by three gentlemen under an assumed name. 4°. 1 page.

1828, February 5, Washington. Sends copy of the last report of the New York High School Society. fol. 1 page.

1828, December 24, Washington. Sends a copy of the second statement of the London University, thinking it may afford some useful hint for the management of the University of Virginia. 4°. 1 page.

1829, January 1, Washington. Sends the "New York Annual" for 1829, with the compliments of the season. 4°. 1 page.

1831, March 3, Washington. Requests his acceptance, on behalf of the artists and authors of the publi-

VERPLANCK, GULIAN C.

cation, of a copy of proof impressions of the first number of "American Landscapes." 4°. 1 page.

No year, July 12, New York. Asks his acceptance of an accompanying address. 8°. 1 page.

VIARE, JOSEPH Y. *Washington.*

1801, May 20, Philadelphia. Congratulates him on being appointed Secretary of State. 4°. 1 page.

VIDAL, WILLIAM GEORGE.

1809, April 30, Urbanna, Va. The greater part of the circulating intrinsic value of coin in this continent comes from Spain and its colonies. Advocates an establishment similar to the Bank of England, which prohibits the circulation of foreign coin as legal tender, and would enable the Government to convert foreign into national coin, and adopt a standard. 4°. 2 pages.

VINING, JOHN. *Philadelphia.*

1792, December 18, Wilmington. Presents a memorial from merchants of Wilmington to Congress, praying amendments of the customs laws. Asks Madison to represent the case. fol. 3 pages.

VIRGINIA, CITIZENS OF, to VIRGINIA GENERAL ASSEMBLY.

Not dated. Memorial and remonstrance against a bill presented to the last session of the general assembly entitled "A bill establishing a provision for teachers of the Christian religion." In Madison's handwriting. royal fol. 2 pages.

Not dated. Petition of citizens of Virginia west of the Alleghany Mountains for a separate government. [Not signed. Copy.] fol. 1 page.

VIRGINIA, CLAIMS OF, *v.* UNITED STATES.

1789, December. Abstract of claims of Virginia against the United States. fol. 1 page.

VIRGINIA CONVENTION IN 1776, JOURNAL OF THE.

1776, May 10. Draft of proceedings of the convention, with the declaration of rights and a plan of government. [In handwriting of Madison.] 4°. 13 pages.

VIRGINIA DECLARATION OF RIGHTS.

1776. [*See* MASON, GEORGE.]

VIRGINIA GENERAL ASSEMBLY to MADISON.

1812, January 29, Richmond. *See* BARBOUR, JAMES (Governor).

VIRGINIA HOUSE OF DELEGATES to MADISON. *Washington.*

1814, February 17, Richmond. *See* BARBOUR, JAMES (Governor).

VIRGINIA LAND WARRANTS,

Not dated. Copy of a bill for confirming and establishing title to lands under actual surveys. fol. 2 pages.

VIRGINIA LEGISLATURE.

Not dated. Resolution that Edmund Randolph, James Madison, Walter Jones, St. George Tucker, and Merriwether Smith be appointed commissioners to meet commissioners of other States to consider the trade of the United States to arrange an uniform system in commercial regulations. 8°. 1 page.

VIRGINIA, PLAN OF GOVERNMENT FOR—

Not dated. A printed document entitled: "A plan of government laid before a committee appointed for that purpose, which they have ordered printed for the perusal of the members of the Virginia general assembly, followed by the declaration of rights, with written remarks and emendations in Madison's handwriting." fol. 4 pages.

VOLLINTINE, NATHANIEL, to MADISON. *Washington.*

1809, December 4, Weston, Mass. Christens his child by the name of James Madison. 4°. 1 page.

VOSBURGH, HERMAN.

1811, May 31, New York. Is a manufacturer of paint articles from metallic substances. Shows the advantages to be gained by the Government selling tracts of mineral lands (unlocated) to encourage settlers and to take metallic lead in payment, thereby not only furnishing the company's own supply, but also the whole market of the Atlantic States. 4°. 4 pages.

VOSS, NICHOLAS.

1801, August 15, Washington. Engagement to rent a house to Madison on 1st October, giving the terms. [*See* Letter from William Thornton to Madison, of this date. Copy.] 4°. 1 page.

1802, March 20, Washington. Receipts for acceptance of an order in favor of Thomas Tingey on account of rent of a house. 4°. 1 page.

1802, June 2, Washington. Terms of an agreement for renting a house and building a stable thereon. [Signed by Voss and Madison.] 4°. 1 page.

1804, July 12, Washington. Asks for an advance on account of rent. small 4°. 1 page.

1805, May 8, Washington. Asks for amount of rent due. 4°. 1 page.

VOWELL, JOHN and THOMAS.

1803, December 9, Alexandria. Notifies him of the arrival of the brig *Celia* from Malaga with wine and fruit. 4°. 1 page.

1804, June 12, Alexandria. Charges of freights and duties for wine shipped Madison by Gringoire & Co., of Malaga. 4°. 1 page.

1804, June 18, Alexandria. Acknowledging letter of 15th, inclosing bill of charges on wine and fruit from Malaga. 4°. 2 pages.

VOWLES, ZACH.

1805, June 19, Falmouth. Sends his account for Irish linen, omitted in a previous one. 4°. 1 page.

WAGNER, JACOB (Chief Clerk, Department of State). *Orange.*

1801, August 3, Washington. Incloses various letters, with sketches, for answers. Suggests action respecting French privateers and prizes, printing of the laws, passport for a vessel chartered for Tunis. Question of demurrage. 4°. 4 pages.

1801, August 10, Washington. Discharged seamen at Jamaica. Mr. Thornton's letter relating to French privateers and their prizes. American seamen imprisoned on the British frigate *Andromache.* Wrote to the British consul at Norfolk re-

WAGNER, JACOB (Chief Clerk, Department of State).

questing his interposition, which he has done. Current business of the Department.
4°. 3 pages.

1801, August 17, Washington. Acknowledging letter of 8th. Current business of the Department of State. Settlement of a demurrage case. Printing of the laws of Congress. Question of publishing them in the German language in Pennsylvania. Claims of Danish subjects against the United States. Demands of the Dey of Algiers. Detailed statement respecting his annuities. Questions the measures of Mr. Eaton in hiring a vessel from Tunis to go to the United States and return. 4°. 7 pages.

1801, August 17, Washington. Asks instructions about the cattle mentioned in Mr. Eaton's letter.
4°. 1 page.

1801, August 24, Washington. Acknowledging letter of 15th. Inclosing documents respecting the tonnage and countervailing duties imposed by the British Government on our shipping. Suggests Congress should impose a light-house duty upon foreign vessels. Mr. Blake accepts the office of attorney for Massachusetts. Incloses report of the collector of Boston relating to Mr. Thornton's complaint respecting the *Beguine.* Question as to its being a Spanish or French privateer.
4°. 2 pages.

1801, August 31, Washington. Privateer *Beguine,* which proves to be Spanish. Incloses dispatches from France. 4°. 3 pages.

1801, September 7, Washington. Acknowledging letter, with inclosures, of signatures of patents from the President. Arrival of our squadron in the Mediterranean. Two naval combats between the French, Spanards, and British. Current business of the Department of State. 4°. 3 pages.

1801, September 12, Washington. Acknowledging letter of 4th. Incloses a commission and letter of credence for Mr. Livingston; instructions; a letter of credit for him and Sumpter; a letter to Mr. Pinckney, with additional letter of credit and his instructions. Expunging the second article of the convention; asks instructions. Intention of Mr. Graham to visit Madison. 4°. 3 pages.

1801, September 14, Washington. Incloses weekly dispatches. Has received two or three complaints of Spanish captures. Mr. Livingston's mission requires additional funds. His outfit.
4°. 1 page.

1801, September 25, Washington. Extract of a letter from Mr. Mountflorence, dated Paris, August 3, stating that ratifications were exchanged August 31, and Thomas Appleton, our consul for Leghorn, has been intrusted with that of the French Government, and is to embark for Philadelphia via Dieppe. Arrival at Algiers of Commodore Dale. 4°. 2 pages.

Washington.

1802, March 30, Baltimore. The change of air from that of Washington has been of benefit to his health. fol. 1 page.

1802, July 22, Philadelphia. Has had a relapse of his complaint. He is unable yet to promise when to

WAGNER, JACOB (Chief Clerk, Department of State).

return to resume his functions, but hopes to by the meeting of Congress. In the meantime, he can not expect his salary to continue.
4°. 2 pages.

1802, November 1, Baltimore. Acknowledging letter of 26th. Is on his way to Washington to resume the duties of his former station. 4°. 1 page.

Orange.

1803, August 10, Washington. Incloses private letters and public communications. Transmits copy of the protest respecting the imprisonment of William Blake, to Mr. Thornton. Respecting franks for another Department, which he incloses.
4°. 2 pages.

1803, August 17, Washington. Acknowledging a letter covering Miller's pardon. Current business of the Department. 4°. 2 pages.

1803, August 24, Washington. Acknowledging letter of 19th. Current business of the Department.
4°. 2 pages.

1803, August 26, Washington. Acknowledging letter of 18th. Incloses letter from Governor Claiborne and newspapers. Orders of the War Department respecting stationary detachments of troops on the Tennessee River and at Duck River for giving protection to travelers; also, measures taken for establishing houses of entertainment on the Wilderness road which will afford security. Proclamation offering reward for apprehension of robbers. 4°. 2 pages.

1803, August 31, Washington. Mr. Pichon in possession of orders to Mr. Laussat to receive possession of Louisiana and deliver it to the United States. Has received ratifications of the treaty and conventions. Monroe goes to London without going to Madrid at present. Complaints against British commanders on the Chesapeake. Current business of the Department. Incloses letter from Mr. Pinckney exhibiting the sensation produced at Madrid by the cession of Louisiana.
4°. 3 pages.

1803, September 2, Washington. Incloses private and official documents. Letter from the French minister of marine to Gallatin alluding to a contract made with Mr. Baring for sale of stock. He is coming to the United States. Mr. Fitzsimmons's criticisms respecting the convention for paying American claims on France. Other current business of the Department. 4°. 3 pages.

1803, September 7, Washington. Transmits copy of an award made by the commissioners against the United States under the seventh article of the British treaty. Appropriation made for the payment of such demands expired in the year 1800. Congress will doubtless make provision. The cession of Louisiana. Contract between the houses of Hope and Baring and the Government for purchase of the stock. Monroe's letter of 15th April containing the list of the commissioners. The amount received by Mr. Lear 4°. 4 pages.

1803, September 9, Washington. Transmits copy of a letter from the Spanish minister. Thinks that orders have been issued to Spanish officers in Louisiana to delay the delivery to France, who,

WAGNER, JACOB (Chief Clerk, Department of State).

having no troops there, will be unable to give us possession. Yellow fever reported at Alexandria. Current business of the Department.
4°. 2 pages.

1804, August 16, Washington. Amendment of the Tennessee constitution relating to choice of President, etc. Rescue of the *Eugenia*, of New York, by the former captain and others in Connecticut from her British captors. The commissioners will not act on any construction placed upon the convention concurrently by the French ministry and Mr. L[ivingston] where it may not accord with their own opinion. The bey of Tunis refuses to treat with the consul-general on account of his his residence in Tunis. 4°. 3 pages.

1804, August 21, Washington. Forebodings of Monroe as to what we have to expect from Pitts's administration. Mr. Merry's answer respecting the proceedings of the British ships at New York. Mr. Walton's letter suggesting the sending a vessel to St. Domingo to collect the suffering seamen and send them home. Mr. Merry takes up, on slender evidence, the conduct of the officers of the *Poursuivante* at Baltimore respecting impressment from a French vessel. 4°. 3 pages.

1804, August 23, Washington. Incloses passports and franks to sign, and an article from a newspaper relating to a disclosure of Miranda's plans.
4°. 2 pages.

1804, August 28, Washington. Acknowledging letter of 26th. Gen. Armstrong's new commission and letter of credence. Changes in the French Government. Mr. Lear satisfies the Dey of Algiers for the annuities due him. Mr. Barney's claim. Incloses letters and papers for Madison's signature. 4°. 4 pages.

1804, September 1, Washington. Incloses a letter from Monroe removing the unfavorable impression of the disposition of the British Government produced by his former letter. Mr. Merry's correspondence about passports and impressed seamen and the question of Wagner's authority to correspond with ministers of foreign nations during the Secretary's absence. 4°. 3 pages.

1804, September 8, Washington. Acknowledging letter of 5th with accompanying packages. Allusion to Merry's letter, in which he complains of irregularities committed by the French at Baltimore.
4°. 1 page.

1804, September 15, Washington. Acknowledging letter of 9th. Attack on Mr. Ellery by Mr. Rutledge respecting the recognition of Mr. Pedersen. Mr. Merry's assurances of not intending a want of respect to himself or doubting his authority to make the applications he has made. His explanations. The coronation of the Emperor to take place on the 9th November.
4°. 4 pages.

1804, September 18, Washington. Acknowledging letter of 15th. Post-office irregularities. Return of Mr. Gallatin. W. Jones's appointment. Respect and friendship of the Emperor of Russia.
4°. 2 pages.

1804, September 20, Washington. The Marquis Yrujo goes to Monticello. He mentions the terms on

WAGNER, JACOB (Chief Clerk, Department of State).

which the Spanish Government will alone ratify the convention. Incloses two drafts of letters respecting the imputed violations by the French ships at New York. Americans imprisoned on the *Leander*. 4°. 3 pages.

1804, September 23, Washington. Marquis Yrujo empowered to negotiate an exchange of the Floridas for part of Louisiana. He expressed surprise that a publication of the intended departure of Mr. Pinckney was made at Norfolk and Richmond before he received official advices. 4°. 1 page.

1804, September 25, Washington. Acknowledging letters of 20th and 22d. The wine received and stored in his house. Sends a cipher of Mr. Livingston's. 4°. 1 page.

1805, February 20, Washington. The Navy Department will furnish documents relating to the *Huntress*, to be inclosed in a letter to Monroe. London advices state that the court of apppeals has decided new precedents of rigor on the restraint of the colony trade. Capt. Bainbridge to be entertained at a public dinner. 4°. 1 page.

1805, July 28, Washington. Negotiations with Spain have failed, but care taken not to commit us to war. The Prince of Peace has declared that the deposit at New Orleans was formerly taken away by a written demand of the French Government as a preparation for its possession of Louisiana. 4°. 1 page.

1805, July 29, Washington. Transmits dispatches from Madrid. Copies also transmitted to the President. 4°. 1 page.

1805, August 5, Washington. Acknowledging letter of 30th July and 2d instant. Conversation with Mr. Merry about the privateer *Les Amies*. Capture of a brig belonging to Newbury Port. Nicklin & Griffith's claims. Mr. Lears's drafts on Baring & Co. Mr. Seymour's application for a consulate. Cannon for Algiers. Impressment of seamen from fishing vessels. Friendly interposition of British Consul Allen. 4°. 3 pages.

1805, August 7, Washington. Acknowledging letter of 3d. Mr. Gallatin disapproves of the descent of the revenue cutter on east Florida to seize coffee and sugar, and ordered it to be returned. Mr. Merry disapproves of the interposition of Consul Allen in favor of impressed seamen. 4°. 2 pages.

1805, August 8, Washington. Expects to procure a vessel to carry the brass guns to Boston, to be shipped for Algiers. Examination of O'Brien's accounts. 4°. 1 page.

1805, August 11, Washington. Acknowledging a letter of 6th. Incloses press copy of a statement of U. S. Consul Lee, of Bordeaux, respecting a fraud which it is alleged a Mr. Wigginton was a party to, but of which Wagner thinks he was merely a dupe. See letter of William Lee, dated January 8. 4°. 1 page.

1805, August 19, Washington. Money and presents for the Dey of Algiers. The outrages in Passamaquoddy Bay. As smuggling is much practiced in that quarter, and is being within British juris-

WAGNER, JACOB (Chief Clerk, Department of State).

diction, complaints to Mr. Merry ought not to be very animated. Will inclose a draft of a letter accommodated to this tone. 4°. 2 pages.

1805, August 28, Washington. Incloses drafts of letters to Mr. Prevost and Governor Claiborne respecting the government of Louisiana. 4°. 2 pages.

1805, September 5, Washington. Acknowledging letter of 2d. Mr. Merry to pay Dr. Rogers' services to English invalids at New Orleans. Rumors of settlement of our Mediterranean affairs. Attributes the event, if true, to apprehensions of attack from our maritime force. Exemption from duty of articles claimed for use of household by Mr. Merry. Fears that Philadelphia will not be exempt from yellow fever. Thinks that where Madison is situated it will be exempt. 4°. 4 pages.

1805, September 10, Washington. Liquidation of awards for French spoliations by Gen. Armstrong. Dispatches received from the Navy Office announcing details of cessation of hostilities with Tripoli and liberation of prisoners. 4°. 2 pages.

1805, September 13, Washington. Incloses copy of a letter from Monroe, who has arrived in London. Thus ends the negotiations with Spain. Has received a box through the post-office of phials of liquid resembling wine, unaccompanied by ex planations, per ship *Robert*. 4°. 1 page.

1805, September 16, Washington. Acknowledging letter of 13th from Gray's. Thinks it desirable to publish the list of bills of awards drawn by Gen. Armstrong, as it will contain useful information to French spoliation claimants. Respecting passports to inhabitants not citizens of the United States in Louisiana. Relaxation of the British navigation act to suit the exigencies of war, as it affects British commerce and manufacture. 4°. 2 pages.

1805, September 17, Washington. Arrival of the frigate *President*, Capt. Barron, with 100 late captives from Tripoli. Mr. Eaton is on his return in a private vessel. Has sent to the President Mr. Lear's dispatches and extracts of leading articles of the treaty. Capt. Bainbridge has had a court on his case and has been honorably acquitted from blame. Capt. Barron has returned ill. The officers from Tripoli speak favorably of their treatment except as to close confinement. 4°. 2 pages.

1805, September 24, Washington. Rigorous decision of the Lords of Appeal respecting the carrying of colonial produce. Has received from Dr. Sibley the book promised as calculated to throw light on the boundaries of Louisiana. Describes it. The appointment of Navy agents by commanders of United States ships. Thinks the practice should be checked. Remarks on Mr. Lear's treaty with Algiers. 4°. 3 pages.

1805, September 26, Washington. On the rights of belligerent powers to interfere in the commerce of neutral nations. Has investigated certain authorities and gives quotations. Massacre of Jews at Algiers. Mr. Cathcart desires the office of the Indian agency at Nachitoches. 4°. 3 pages.

WAGNER, JACOB (Chief Clerk, Department of State).

1805, September 28, Washington. Current business of the Department. 4°. 1 page.

1805, October 1, Washington. Incloses money drafts on banks in Philadelphia. 4°. 1 page.

1805, October 9, Washington. Acknowledging letter of 5th. Answers to correspondents on Department business chiefly concerning complaints and frauds in prize cases. Gives result of his investigations relative to coasting and colony trade, examples of acts of Parliament relaxing commercial and navigation laws of Great Britain in time of war, and free trade. 4°. 3 pages.

1805, October 14, Washington. With the concurrence of Gen. Dearborn he submits an article for publication respecting the interviews between Monroe and the British secretary of state subject to recent captures, when the latter states that there is nothing in the disposition of his Government to admit of an unfriendly measure against the United States. 4°. 2 pages.

1805, October 17, Washington. Incloses extracts from Sir J. Mainott's report, reference to treaties and other matters concerning navigation laws; communication from Yznardi's deputy respecting captures by the British under pretense of blockades of Cadiz and St. Lucas, and a letter to Mr. Merry respecting the *Hannah Maria* case. 4°. 2 pages.

Washington.

1806, March 12, Baltimore. On account of a marriage in his family he will be absent for two days. 4°. 1 page.

1806, June 8, Washington. Yrujo's recall. It is reported in Baltimore that he has a new commission to present, under which, if he is not permitted to act, he will retire and no successor be appointed. 4°. 2 pages.

1806, August 11, Washington. Opens a private letter, there being no mark to indicate it. Suggests that it should appear to have been opened by Madison. 4°. 1 page.

1806, August 8, Washington. No convention with Spain for the mutual delivery of offenders. 4°. 1 page.

Orange.

1806, August 15, Washington. Cases of British aggression. The forcible or deceptive detention of Mr. Harvey's son on the *Leander*, and case of the *Eliza* and that of Stoddert and Mason. Commission of the successor of Swartwout. 4°. 3 pages.

1806, August 19, Washington. Causes of the unexpected delay of the departure of the Tunisians. 4°. 2 pages.

1806, August 22, Washington. Case of the crew of the *Indefatigable.* Thinks it not improper to publish the substance of Mr. Merry's inclosed letter or to apprise the collector of Passamaquoddy of it. Acknowledging letter of 19th. 4°. 1 page.

1806, August 25, Washington. Has directed Mr. Cathcart not to pay the gratuity to the delinquent Tunisians at New York. Respecting Morales and the exactions of foreign consuls on United States.

WAGNER, JACOB (Chief Clerk, Department of State).

citizens. Suggests that collectors whose certificates Admiral Berkeley impeaches show the grounds upon which they were issued.
4°. 2 pages.

1806, August 29, September 5, 12, Washington. Current business of the Department. 4°. 6 pages.

1806, September 19, Washington. Mr. Erskine succeeds Mr. Merry, Lord Selkirk having declined the office. Jones' case gives authority that the sending back of offenders, except when required by treaty, by state policy, or peculiarity of circumstances, is gone into disuse. Conjectures respecting Yrujo's visit to Baltimore. 4°. 3 pages.

1806, September 26, Washington. Claims of three captains against *L'Eole.* Advises them to delay action at present and the case will be laid before the French minister. Current business of the Department. 4°. 3 pages.

1806, September 29, Washington. States that his quarter's salary will be left in bank. Correspondence of the commissioners in Paris, appealed to by Mr. R. 4°. 1 page.

1806, October 13, Baltimore. Applies for the office of collector of Baltimore. 4°. 1 page.

Washington.

1808, January 28, Baltimore. Resents the imputation in the President's message that he is accountable for a bundle of Mr. Clark's papers. Thinks it improbable that they were burned.
fol. 1 page.

1808, not dated, Washington. Apprises him of his intention of leaving Washington by the 1st of October with a view of improving his circumstances. 4°. 1 page.

Montpellier.

1824, January 15, Philadelphia. Shows the importance of the preservation of the archives of the old confederation and their accessibility to the public. Destruction of important documents by fire before and during the war of 1812. Proposes that he may be permitted to give to the public in volumes in regular order and in the text such of it as may serve for monuments of the transactions of an era so important. His long experience and capacity for doing it.
4°. 2 pages.

WADDELL, H. L. *Washington.*

1809, January 16, Philadelphia. Acknowledges a letter in answer to his own of 12th December respecting an opportunity for a passage to France. Thanks him for suggestions for precautions against interruptions. Will apply to Gen. Turreau for a passport. 4°. 2 pages.

1809, January 26, Philadelphia. Asks that a passport be sent him in the customary form.
4°. 1 page.

WALKER, SAMUEL P. *Montpellier.*

1830, January 10, Washington. Solicits the appointment as midshipman in the U. S. Navy. Asks Madison's good offices. Annexed is copy of a letter from Andrew Jackson, dated November 6, 1829, to John Branch, Secretary of the Navy, recommending Mr. Walker. 4°. 2 pages.

WALKER, WILLIAM. *Philadelphia.*

1796, April 28, Madison County. States that Col. George Hancock, on his way to Congress, prevailed upon him to dispose of the patents of some land in which they were partners, and to deposit his own share with Madison. Has never received an answer to a letter written him on the subject, and requests him to forward the money when he receives it to William Lovell, of Fredericksburg. 4°. 1 page.

WALLACE, CALEB. *Orange.*

1785, July 12, Lincoln County, Ky. Has settled in this remote county with his family. Fertility of the soil. Depredations of the Indians. Difficulty of exporting produce. Harmony among the settlers. Absence of crime. The land-jobbing business attended to with much villainy; it retards improvements. Petition of a convention to have this district formed into a State. Taxes burdensome, but not to be avoided. Fears the lack of wisdom and virtue to govern. Suggestions as to the form of government. Asks Madison's advice as to such a form as he thinks proper. fol. 3 pages.

1785, September 25, Lincoln County, Ky. Acknowledging letter of August 23. A deputy from the militia companies in this district assemble to discuss grievances which can not be redressed while in connection with Virginia; they recommend electing a convention to consider the propriety of separation, which they do, and unanimously adopt the plan. George Muter and Harry Innes appointed to wait on the [Virginia] assembly with the petition. Recommends these gentlemen. 4°. 2 pages.

Richmond.

1785, October 8, Kentucky. Discusses the question of separation and difficulties attending it. The remote situation deprives the people of the advantages of equal government while connected with Virginia, and the absence of an export trade will render them incapable of defraying expenses of separate government. Depredations of the Indians continue. Introduces Capt. Christopher Greenup. Inconvenience occasioned by the inattention or reluctance of the assembly to provide for the support of the court. 4°. 3 pages.

1786, September 30, Mercer County, Ky. Acknowledging letter of 15th March. Unanimity of sentiment respecting separation interrupted by the influence of misguided men. Discussion of the subject. fol. 3 pages.

New York.

1786, November 20, Danville, Ky. Depredations by the Indians. Expeditions by the militia. Impressments became necessary and were made not strictly agreeable to rules of law and propriety. Ask for an act of indemnity for articles necessary for the troops to prevent any advantages that might otherwise be taken at law and dampen their valor. Wishes the militia law were made more explicit, which would prevent irregularities. 4°. 2 pages.

WALLACE, CALEB. *Orange.*

1787, November 12, Fayette County, Ky. Acknowledging letter of 5th January. Navigation of the Mississippi. Indian affairs wear a serious aspect. Killing of inhabitants and theft of houses. Inadequacy of defense. Agency of English and Spanish partisans. The convention decides on separation. Gives his views on the subject.
fol. 3 pages.

WALLACE, GUSTAVUS B.

1789, March 4, Fredericksburg. Is a candidate for the appointment of office of collector for the port of Rappahannock. 4°. 1 page.

1790, March 25, Fredericksburg. Balances due to soldiers and officers of this and the North Carolina line. A man from New York is purchasing these balances at a great discount. Thinks a stop should be put to it, that the soldiers get the whole, which can be done by publishing a list of names and sums due them. 4°. 2 pages.

1790, April 20, Fredericksburg. Acknowledging letter of 10th. The speculation in balances due soldiers exposed. Explains the method.
large fol. 1 page.

Philadelphia.

1794, May 13, Fredericksburg. Acknowledging letter of 7th. Thanks him for mentioning him at the War Department. Would like to be garrisoned at Norfolk if Point Comfort is not fortified.
4°. 2 pages.

1795, January 12, Charleston. Introducing Mr. Harper, of South Carolina. 4°. 1 page.

WALLACE, JAMES W. *Montpellier.*

1823, September 2, Fauquier County. Sends him an inkstand made from the rock of Gibraltar.
4°. 1 page.

WALLER, A. *Washington.*

1813, November —, Caroline, Va. Extract from the minutes of the Baptist Association in the district of Goshen, Va., recommending the appointment of days of fasting, humiliation, and prayer in the present crisis of our public affairs.
4°. 2 pages.

WALLER, BEN. *Richmond.*

1785, November 28, Williamsburg. Explains his reasons for not attending the court of appeals at Richmond. Gives a short account of his experiences in 1779 and during the Revolution. Ignorant as to whom his resignation should be directed out of season, he asks Madison to seal and deliver it. fol. 3 pages.

WALN, JESSE. *Washington.*

1810, April 23, Philadelphia. Previous to his departure from Canton he received a small package from Poonqua Winchong for Mrs. Madison, which he will forward by first opportunity.
4°. 1 page.

Montpellier.

1831, July 22, Philadelphia. Applies for the vacant consulship at Tangier. 4°. 1 page.

WALSH, PETER.

1809, May 20, Cette. Congratulations on his election as President. 4°. 1 page.

WALSH, ROBERT, Jr.

1817, December 5, Washington. Sends the 2d volume of the "American Register." 4°. 1 page.

1819, September 30, Philadelphia. Sends a book which he had just published, a portion of which it will be found was gathered from Madison's observations. Will issue a second part when he can procure the materials. 4°. 1 page.

1826, November 16, Philadelphia. Calls attention to a prospectus for a new review. Solicits Madison's contributions. fol. 1 page.

1827, August 29, Philadelphia. Introducing N. Gilpin, of Philadelphia. 4°. 1 page.

1827, December 26, Philadelphia. Thanks him for his kind attention to his request for contributions to his review. Will accept any document of his choice. 4°. 1 page.

WALSH, ROBERT.

1831, February 14, Philadelphia. Introducing William Keating, of Philadelphia, a traveler and savant. 4°. 1 page.

1831, July 3, Philadelphia. Wishes to introduce into the "Encyclopedia Americana" a biographical sketch of Bishop Madison, of Virginia. Asks if Madison can give him information concerning his birth, education, and death, public stations and labors, and his general qualities. 4°. 1 page.

1831, September 4, Philadelphia. Thanks him for his memoranda concerning Bishop Madison. 4°. 1 page.

1836, April 22, Philadelphia. Intends going abroad. Intends to publish in Paris or London sketches, biographical and bibliographical, of eminent of living writers. Asks for a list of Madison's publications and stations he has filled. 4°. 1 page.

WALSH, WILLIAM J. *Washington.*

1816, May 17, Dublin. Had forwarded a package in September last and had never received an acknowledgment. The particulars are obtained in an inclosure in this letter. fol. 1 page.

WALTER, LYNDE, and others. *Montpellier.*

1821, January 15, Boston. Request of a number of persons friendly to a bankrupt act for Madison to use his influence to obtain its passage at the present session of Congress. 4°. 2 pages.

1821, February 3, Boston. Acknowledging letter of January 24, and thanks him for the candor with which he had given his views in respect to the bankrupt act. 4°. 1 page.

WALTON, MATTHEW. *Washington.*

1809, August 28, Washington County, Ky. Address of the citizens of Washington County, Ky., expressing their confidence in the President and pledging their support. fol. 2 pages.

WAR DEPARTMENT.

1813 and 1814. Return of arms made and repaired at Springfield, Mass., in 1813 and 1814. 4°. 1 page.

1815, September 9, Washington. Statement of approriations for the several divisions in the War Department on August 31 and September 9. fol. 2 pages.

WAR DEPARTMENT.

1815, September —, Washington. A list of doctors late of the Army of the United States that have been appointed to fill vacancies in it. fol. 1 page.

WAR OF 1812.

Record of events during the war up to the close in 1815. [Unsigned.] fol. 1 page.

WARD, RICHARD, to MADISON.

1816, November 15, Paterson. In behalf of the Manufacturing Association of New Jersey, an appeal is made for further protection of manufacturers, coincident with the great interest of agriculture. 4°. 2 pages.

WARDEN, DAVID BAILIE.

1809, May 1, Paris. Wishes to continue in his present office as consul. States his qualifications. 4°. 2 pages.

1809, July 2, Paris. Offers for Madison's acceptance the life of the Duke of Marlborough, lately published here by the Emperor's directions. small 4°. 1 page.

1809, September 17, Paris. Sends a memorial in the case of the *Jefferson,* prepared and published at Gen. Armstrong's request. Has transmitted to the Secretary of State a communication on the subject of prize cases. Hopes to have his provisional appointment as consul confirmed. 4°. 1 page.

1809, October 17, Paris. Again makes application for his continuance in office as consul. Is much occupied in prize causes. 4°. 2 pages.

1809, October 17, Paris. Duplicate of the foregoing.

1809, November *17,* Paris. Sends newspapers and memorials relating to prize cases. 4°. 1 page.

1810, January 26, Paris. Sends a copy of Botta's "American War." Hopes to be continued here as consul. The late orders of the Emperor concerning American vessels and their cargoes in Spain and Naples are extremely hostile and may prevent any speedy arrangement between this country and the United States. Coleman's attack upon him. fol. 1 page.

1810, January 26, Paris. Duplicate of the foregoing.

1810, May 25, Paris. Incloses newspapers and a brochure. Is occupied with prize causes. Defends cases not represented by any agent. The court regularly confiscates the property in all American cases; ratifies contracts between captors and captured. 4°. 1 page.

1810, June 16, Paris. Sends copies of his memoirs in defence of American vessels and cargoes. Trusts his zeal and industry will meet with the President's approbation. 4°. 1 page.

1810, August 18, Paris. Hears through Gen. Armstrong that Mr. Russel is appointed chargé d' affaires and he intimates he is to replace him as consul. Hopes to be continued in his office, having faithfully performed his duties, and if there is any charge against him of improper conduct it was prompted by falsehood and intrigue. fol. 2 pages.

1810, August 18, Paris. Duplicate of the foregoing.

WARDEN, DAVID BAILIE, to ARMSTRONG, JOHN.
Paris.

1810, September 7, Paris. Expresses surprise and regret at the accusations in Armstrong's letter of 6th. Denies the charges of disrespect and abusive language and declares his uniform and unalterable attachment to Armstrong and the administration. Declares he has been misinformed by his enemies. [*See* letter from Armstrong, John, September 6, 1810.] 4°. 10 pages.

1810, September 10, Paris. In answer to his note of this date he declares he neither had the cause or right to censure his private conduct. Has nothing to do with his ministerial acts except so far as relates to those which may regard himself in his present delicate situation. Declares his sincere attachment to him and his family. Hopes to still retain his regard and esteem. [*See* letter of Armstrong, September 6, 1810. Copy.] 4°. 3 pages.

——— to MADISON. *Washington.*

1811, February 21, Washington. Attempt to smuggle in a vessel purchased for the ostensible object as a parlementaire or flag vessel, in which, by permission of Gen. Armstrong, a person was allowed to send some mathematical instruments and machinery. Had been charged with participating in the fraud. Vindicates himself and shows how injustice has been done him by misrepresentation, and which resulted in his being removed from office by Gen. Armstrong. 4°. 7 pages.

1811, February 26, Washington. Makes explanations concerning his conduct as agent of prize causes, which had been represented to the President in an unfavorable manner. Has invariably declined to take fees for himself or charged a commission. Gives further particulars respecting the smuggling of silk in the *Happy Return*, and vindicates himself from any complicity with the fraudulent proceedings. 4°. 4 pages.

1811, March 18, New York. Waits for instructions respecting his departure for France. 4°. 1 page.

1811, April 23, Washington. Gives a detailed statement of facts concerning his conduct while consul in Paris in those affairs in which he has recently been attacked. Annexed are certificates from masters of vessels declaring that his conduct in prize cases merits the approbation and protection of our Government. Also annexed is a copy of a letter from Gen. Armstrong notifying him of his appointment as consul, and another of the appointment of Alexander McRae as his successor. 4°. 14 pages.

1811, April 23, Washington. Duplicate of the certificates mentioned in the foregoing with copy of a friendly letter from Jefferson. 4°. 3 pages.

——— to HAMILTON, PAUL (Secretary of Navy).

1812, January 10, Paris. Inclosing a letter from Matilda Tone, widow of Gen. Theobald Wolf Tone, respecting her brother-in-law, Arthur Tone, a common sailor on board an American ship-of-war. Thinks he deserves promotion. 4°. 2 pages.

——— to MADISON.

1812, July 21, Paris. Sends a brochure on the principles and laws of armed neutrality. The progress

WARDEN, DAVID BAILIE, to MADISON.

of the Emperor. It is conjectured that Russia will make but a feeble resistance. 4°. 1 page.

1813, January 26, Paris. The death of Joel Barlow places in Warden's hands the affairs of the legation. Sends Dr. Stephens as confidential messenger; carries current news and summary of facts which are not prudent to commit to paper. Sends outline of a treatise on consular establishment, which he proposes to publish. 4°. 1 page.

1813, August 25, Paris. Gives a copy of a communication from the U. S. consul at Havre respecting a list of Americans detained as prisoners of war. William Parrie's case. 8°. 1 page.

——— to CRAWFORD, WILLIAM H. *Paris.*

1814, June 6, Paris. Order for his removal from his consular duties by Mr. Crawford, and which he declines to obey before receiving authentic information of his authority. Followed by a letter to Monroe, Secretary of State, ceasing to act as consul, but awaiting instructions. [Copy.] fol. 6 pages.

——— to MONROE, Secretary of State. *Washington.*

1814, June 10, Paris. Incloses copy of his correspondence with Mr. Crawford to serve as a defense of his determination to wait for official instructions with respect to his consular powers, which he has been ordered to relinquish by Mr. Crawford, and, as he (Warden) thinks, without legal authority. fol. 2 pages.

1814, June 12, Paris. Being informed by Mr. Bayard that he had seen the instructions as to his suspension, of which Mr. Crawford had refused him communication, he ceases from consular functions, but remains in Paris for further orders. [*See* letter from Warden to Crawford, W. H., June 6, 1814.] fol. 1 page.

WARRELL, JAMES, to MADISON.

1816, May 27, Richmond. A letter covering a proposal for the establishment of a State museum, to be erected in Richmond. Terms of subscription. 4°. 3 pages.

Montpellier.

1818, June 25, Richmond. Acknowledging letter of 18th, inclosing a note of $100, which shall be forwarded to Mr. Vanderlyn. 4°. 1 page.

1824, November 23, Richmond. Incloses a letter of introduction from Dr. Rose, of Alabama, which he was unable to deliver in person. 4°. 1 page.

WARREN, SAMUEL (President of Senate), to MADISON. *Washington.*

1812, September 1, Columbia, S. C. Transmitting an address adopted unanimously by both branches of the legislature of this State, at an extra session, approving the declaration of war. 4°. 5 pages.

——— and GEDDES, JOHN, jointly.

1813, January 18, Charleston. In behalf of Mr. Noah, of this city, appointed consul at Riga, and who contemplates making application for a change in his place of destination, they highly recommend him for promotion. 4°. 1 page.

WASH, THOMAS. *Philadelphia.*

1791, February 22, Louisa County, Va. Power of attorney to Madison to collect sums of money due him for services during the late war. 4°. ½ page.

1791, February 22, Louisa County, Va. A narrative of his services during the war, with a request to collect any sums which may be due him, and for which he gives him a power of attorney.
small 4°. 2 pages.

WASHINGTON, BUSHROD. *Washington.*

1807, November 12, Mount Vernon. Apologizes for having neglected to settle with him for some wine he imported for him, and asks that the account be sent him. 4°. 1 page.

Montpellier.

1819, September 14, Mount Vernon. Acknowledging letter of August 28. Will furnish, as requested, certain letters as soon as they can be found. Many of them mutilated by rats and damp.
4°. 1 page.

1820, January 31, Mount Vernon. Acknowledging letter of December 18. Makes excuses for delaying sending certain papers on account of the cold, as they are stored in an outhouse. 4°. 1 page.

1820, March 23, Mount Vernon. Has carefully examined George Washington's papers in his possession and sends inclosed papers of Madison addressed to him. Others may be found and forwarded. Has written to the chief justice to look the bundles over and inclose all he can find.
4°. 1 page.

Philadelphia.

WASHINGTON, GEORGE, to JONES, JOSEPH.

1780, May 31, Morristown. Complains of the apathy of Congress. The ill-timed adoption of measures and delays in the execution of them. The powers of Congress declining too fast for the consequence and respect which is due to them. Sees no possibility of giving Gen. Weeden any command out of the line of his own State. [Copy.]
4°. 4 pages.

1781, March 24, New Windsor. Acknowledging letters of February 21 and 27. Neglect of Congress to conform with the wishes of distressed States. Delay by the French commander at Rhode Island prevented the destruction of Arnold's corps during the debilitated state of the British fleet. The critical situation of affairs in Virginia and North Carolina. Fears of the inability of the French fleet to cooperate with the militia in maintaining a position in Hampton Roads and preventing succors to the British. Importance of the controlling power of Congress and jealousy of States. Without the compliance of the thirteen distinct States each pursuing its local interests they will be annihilated in a general crash. [Copy.]
4°. 7 pages.

1781, July 10, Dobbs Ferry. Acknowledging letter of June 20. Scarcity of horses. Clamor against Gen. Steuben. The command (Lafayette's) in Virginia can not be in better hands. His uncommon military talents. Equivocal state of affairs in Vermont. Their neutrality is the most we have to expect. Does not think the people have evil intentions, but certain leaders there have and will prevent our deriving aid. [Copy.]
4°. 5 pages.

WASHINGTON, GEORGE, to JONES, JOSEPH.

1782, December 14, Newburg. Expects Congress will receive soon an address from the Army on the subject of their grievances. Their discontent at the continued state of inactivity. The dissatisfaction of the Army great and alarming. Combinations among officers to resign in a body. Thinks Congress should dictate soothing measures. Patience and fortitude of the community and their great hardships. Efforts of officers heretofore to prevent mutinies among the soldiers. Spirit of enthusiasm is done away. If the civil officers of Government and military could fare alike with respect to emoluments the military would not be the first to complain. [Copy.] 4°. 4 pages.

1783, March 12, Newburg. Acknowledging letter of February 27. Temper of the Army, irritated at their protracted sufferings. Reports that they would not disband until they had obtained justice. Anonymous summons circulated among officers. The postponement of settling of accounts gives great uneasiness. Appeals to Mr. Jones to push the matter to an issue in Congress, and if delegates are opposed to doing justice scruple not to tell them they must be answerable if matters come to an extremity for all the ineffable horrors which may be occasioned thereby. [Copy.] 4°. 7 pages.

1783, March 18, Newburg. Urges the liquidation of the accounts of the officers and soldiers of the Army. Their sufferings. Obliged to anticipate their pay and run in debt. To disband men before their accounts are liquidated would set open the doors of jails and close them on seven years of faithful and painful services. Cautions those gentlemen in Congress who have no disposition to compensate the services of the Army, for nothing is too extravagant to expect from men who conceive they are ungratefully and unjustly dealt by. [Copy.] 4°. 5 pages.

——— to GIBBS, CALEB.

1783, December 1, New York. Certifies to the services of Maj. Gibbs as volunteer and officer during the war, and his brave and discreet conduct. [Copy.] 4°. 2 pages.

——— to MADISON. *Orange.*

1784, December 28, Annapolis. Measures of the Virginia legislature about the establishment of tolls. [Copy.] 4°. 3 pages.

——— to EDWARD E. FRANKFORT.

1796, August 25, Philadelphia. Acknowledging letter of 24th March written in cipher. Thanks him for information contained in the letter in refutation of a charge against Monroe of his having neglected any concern in which the fame of the President was involved. [*See* Monroe's letter to E. Edward, April 21, 1798. Copy in Monroe's hand.] 4°. 1 page.

WASHINGTON, LUND, to UNKNOWN.

1780, August 26, Mount Vernon. Apparent error in the dates of certain loan certificates which he requests may be rectified. 4°. 1 page.

WASHINGTON, L. A., to MADISON. *Washington.*

1801, April 27, Rech Woods. Solicits the appointment of Andrew Parks as postmaster at Baltimore. fol. 3 pages.

WASHINGTON, P. G. *Montpellier.*

1833, November 16, Washington. Requests information respecting the services of Gen. William McPherson, of Philadelphia, during the Revolutionary War. 4°. 2 pages.

WALSH, ROBERT, jr.

1819, January 2, Philadelphia. Incloses a pamphlet on the subject of the Missouri question. 4°. 3 pages.

WATERHOUSE, BENJAMIN. *Washington.*

1813, April 24, Boston. Endeavors for his removal from the management of the Marine Hospital, by the misrepresentations and false charges of his political enemies, Gen. Dearborn and Dr. Eustis, and others under their influence. Appeals for justice in his case. 4°. 20 pages.

1813, April 29, Boston. Transmits a narrative, dated 24th, relative to his management of his office of physician to the Marine Hospital and Navy-yard at Charlestown, and the misrepresentations of his enemies, Gen. Dearborn and Dr. Eustice, which resulted in being deprived of his office. 4°. 3 pages.

1813, May 1, Boston. Applies for the appointment of the office Treasurer of the Mint, lately made vacant by the death of Dr. Rush. Accompanied by recommendation of 16 prominent Boston men to the notice of the President, for any office in which his professional knowledge and integrity which may comport with his years and rank in society. 4°. 2 pages.

1816, June 18, Cambridge. Sends him his story of "A journal of a young man of Massachusetts," who was captured by the British and confined during the war at Halifax, Chatham, and Dartmoor. Explains circumstances of its publication. 4°. 2 pages.

Montpellier.

1822, June 9, Cambridge. Sends him a copy from a new edition of his lecture on the pernicious effects of the too free use of tobacco and ardent spirits on young persons. 4°. 1 page.

1822, December 12, Cambridge. On the establishment of a professorship of agriculture at the University of Virginia. Sends some publications on that subject showing the progress in New England of that branch of science. 4°. 2 pages.

1825, June 30, Cambridge. Thanks for hospitality shown him in Virginia. Has just returned from Washington. General Hull treated with a public dinner. His opinion of him and his present situation. Waterhouse would not object to the appointment as minister to the Netherlands. Anecdote of Mrs. Waterhouse's jealousy of Mrs. Madison. 4°. 3 pages.

1829, February 14, Cambridge. Sends a production of his early life, an inaugural oration of his appointment as professor of physic in Cambridge University. Correspondence between the remnants of the Hartford Convention and President Adams. 4°. 1 page.

1831, May 9, Cambridge. Sends Madison to deposit, in the University of Virginia, after reading it, a copy of his latest publication, a work ascribing

WATERHOUSE, BENJAMIN.

the authorship of Junius to Lord Chatham. Holds up Samuel Adams as the file leader of our revolution. 4°. 2 pages.

1833, May 30, Cambridge. Sends copy of a book describing the adventures of a youth who started with twenty others for the Pacific coast on land. Describes the object in writing it as exposing the folly of the speculation of emigration, and danger of making too much haste to get rich. The New England people excited about President Jackson's visit. Hospitalities shown him. Compares the visits of Monroe and Lafayette. 4°. 3 pages.

1834, February 20, Cambridge. Madison's election as president of the temperance society. Criticises Mr. Dwight's history of the Hartford convention. 4°. 1 page.

1834, September 17, Cambridge. The beheading of Jackson's figure on the ship *Constitution*. Burning of the nunnery in Boston. Riot in Cambridge by students. The turbulence exorcised by John Quincy Adams. Waterhouse's admiration for his character. Commends Jefferson's writings, published by his grandson. Censures the press. 4°. 2 pages.

WATSON, DAVID.

1819, February 26, Louisa County. Excuses himself for not being able to meet Jefferson and Gen. Cocke at Madison's house on business of the University. Will assent to anything they approve of, and authorizes him to affix his signature to papers that may require it. 4°. 1 page.

WATSON, ELKANAH. *Washington.*

1812, October 12, Pittsfield, Mass. Sends, inclosed, a sample of cloth made of wool under his own directions. 4°. 2 pages.

1814, September 8, Pittsfield. Importance of conciliating parties. Universal satisfaction at the report that Mr. King is appointed Secretary of Foreign Affairs. Thinks the appointment of Gen. Brooks at the head of the War Department would conciliate all the Federalists of New England. 4°. 4 pages.

Montpellier.

1819, August 18, Albany. Asks him to transmit the inclosed to presidents of agricultural societies in Virginia and Maryland. 4°. 1 page.

1820, May 3, New York. Sends a work on canals and agriculture, just published. [Answer on same page acknowledging receipt of same.] 4°. 1 page.

1825, March 8, Albany. Plan before the New York legislature calculated to place our agricultural institutions on a permanent, useful, and reputable footing. Plan for a national board of agriculture, which could not fail to be accelerated by the American Exhibition of Manufactures at Washington. Incloses four numbers of papers on the subject. Sends him some seeds of a new variety of cabbage, the product of some imported from Naples. 4°. 3 pages.

WATTERSTON, GEORGE. *Washington.*

1813, October 28, Washington. Applies for the office of collector of this district. 4°. 1 page.

WATTERSTON, GEORGE.

1815, March 25, Washington. Has received the commission of Librarian of Congress. Suggests the apartment in the third story of the present Capitol as suitable. 4°. 1 page.

Montpellier.

1820, August 4, Washington. Contemplates writing a history of Madison's administration. Asks his aid in explaining certain events. 4°. 1 page.

1834, May 5, Washington. Incloses a certificate of membership of the Columbian Horticultural Society. 4°. 1 page.

WATSON, GEORGE. *Philadelphia.*

1800, January 23, Philadelphia. Bill for board and wines, etc. fol. 2 pages.

WATTSON, JAMES.

1796, February 10, Liverpool, England. In answer to his letter, informs him of the bounties on linen cloth granted by the Government of Great Britain. 4°. 2 pages.

WATTLES, JAMES. *Montpellier.*

1835, July 13, Baltimore. The bar of this city desire to procure a portrait of the late Chief-Justice Marshall. Asks Madison to send him a copy of a letter from him recommending Wattles to paint Madison's portrait. 4°. 1 page.

WATTS, JOHN. *Philadelphia.*

1796, December 16, New York. Power of attorney from Joseph Chew to Sir John Johnson, and a substitution from the latter to Watts respecting the sale of some Kentucky lands. As Madison had a power from Chew, wishes to know if he had sold it or whether there is any probability of selling it and at what price. 4°. 1 page.

WAUGH, ABNER. *Washington.*

1806, July 14, Fredericksburg. Asks for pecuniary aid. 4°. 2 pages.

WAUGH, CHARLES STUART.

1814, February 16, Culpeper, Va. Is extremely anxious to procure from Madison a Merino ram of the purest blood. fol. 2 pages.

Montpellier.

1817, August 30, Culpeper. Asks the loan of "Rollins' Roman History." fol. 2 pages.

1817, September 8, Culpeper. Asks for the loan of "Hook." Sends Madison a chemico-agricultural work by Sir Humphrey Davy. fol. 1 page.

1827, October 25, Culpeper. Solicits a clerkship in one of the Departments. 4°. 2 pages.

WEAVER, DAVID, to MADISON. *Orange.*

1833, August 29, Rockingham Co. Proposition to supply Madison with pork for the winter. 4°. 1 page.

WEBB, JAMES. *Washington.*

1814, April 13. Applies for the occupation of cabinet-maker to attend to and keep in repair the furniture of the President's house, Capitol, War and Treasury offices, also that on the U. S. vessels in the navy-yard. 4°. 2 pages.

WEBB, WILLIAM C. *Philadelphia.*

1790, November 22. Asks Madison's aid in securing a claim on Congress for supplies of cattle during the war to the army of General Gates.
fol. 2 pages.

WEBSTER, NOAH. *Orange, Va.*

1784, July 5, Hartford. Asks his assistance in securing a copyright to publish and sell in Virginia the "Grammatical Institute of the English Language." Accompanying the letter is an advertisement desiring copies of Smith's History of Virginia and works containing the charters, constitutions, ancient laws, etc., of that State, also other books or pamphlets relating to the settlement and progress of the State to the Revolution.
4°. 2 pages. small 4°. 1 page.

Washington.

1801, July 18, New Haven. Appointing officers of the Government as a reward for party services, regardless of ability and good standing, and removing tried and able incumbents to make room for them. States examples of appointments of incompetent people by the President, doubtless from misrepresentations of his political friends.
4°. 8 pages.

1809, February 20, New Haven. Is engaged in literary pursuits which require the purchase of books and a voyage to Europe to procure them, and for which he has not the means to spare. Suggests that he might be appointed to some foreign position in which he might be of service to the Government and be enabled to carry out his own plans. Is opposed to the present administration and its measures, but thinks that offices under Government should not be exclusively given to political partisans, but to deserving and capable persons, regardless of politics. States instances of very improper appointments to important offices in New England and elsewhere.
4°. 4 pages.

Montpellier.

1826, Mdrch 17, New Haven. Has returned from Europe, where he has been collecting material for his dictionary. His projects respecting the publication of the same. 4°. 2 pages.

WEDGE, The Entering.

Not dated. Verses entitled The Entering Wedge, a political satire. [Unknown writer.]
12mo. 3 pages.

WEEMS, M. L., to MADISON. *Washington.*

1812, January 17, Washington. Sends a pamphlet respecting gamblers. Thinks the people of this Republic will support the President in his measures to defend and support the Government.
4°. 4 pages.

——— to MADISON, Mrs.

1813, July 22, Dumfries. Wishes her patronage in the publication of a new edition of "Hunter's Sacred Biography." 4°. 4 pages.

——— to MADISON.

1814, January 1. Proposes to reprint the poem "Leonidas" as a motto to a subscription paper, in order to revive among us the old Spartan love of liberty and country. small. 4°. 2 pages.

WEEMS, M. L., to MADISON.

1814, October 24, Dumfries. Proposes a scheme for destroying the British army by laying in trenches in the roads where they must traverse canvas tubes filled with gunpowder and firing them. small 4°. 3 pages.

Montpellier.

1819, January 22, Richmond. Sends a copy of the "Life of Marion." Asks his commendation of the work as a schoolbook. His "Life of Washington" has gone through 21 editions. Sends also a paper for Dr. Hunter's work to Mrs. Madison. small 4°. 3 pages.

1820, May 18, Fredericksburg. Sends by stage a copy of his "History of the Great French War." Trusts he found Dr. Hunter's book amusing. Is about to publish a little work against dueling, illustrated with caricatures. 4°. 3 pages.

1823, February 20, Charleston, S. C. Sends a copy of his "Life of William Penn" to Mrs. Madison. Sends account of a religious book agency. fol. 2 pages.

WEIGHTMAN, R. C. *Washington.*

1808, December 30, Washington. Sends the seventh volume "Laws of the State of Pennsylvania," and a proposal for publishing an edition of the laws of the United States. 4°. 4 pages.

1814, September 6, Cool Springs. Is informed that the whole force of the enemy had gone down the bay. Thinks they will not go up the Potomac, as the enemy's ships have passed down that river. small 4°. 1 page.

Montpellier.

1826, June 14, Washington. As chairman of a committee to make arrangements for the fiftieth anniversary of American independence, is directed to invite Madison, as one of the former Presidents, to honor the city with his presence. A special deputation will be sent to accompany him here and back. fol. 1 page.

WELLS, SAMUEL ADAMS.

1833, January 26, Boston. With inclosures. [Subject not mentioned.] 4°. 1 page.

WENDOVER, P. H. *Washington.*

1815, January 30, New York. Incloses a small volume calculated to produce good at this important crisis. [Title not mentioned.] 4°. 1 page.

WERTENBAKER, WILLIAM. *Montpellier.*

1830, February 24, University of Virginia. Incloses letters from John S. Skinner, of Baltimore, respecting books sent to the university. Asks if they shall be retained in the library or returned to him. 4°. 1 page.

WESTON, J. (Collector). *Washington.*

1813, June 5, New Bedford. Has been informed that charges had been made against him for illegal practices in the custom-house, with request for his removal and to substitute John Hawes. Gives a list of the charges and his answers to them. Asks that his conduct may be investigated by some person or persons in whom the Executive has confidence. large fol. 3 pages.

WEST POINT CADETS.

1816, May 26. (*See* Partridge, A.)

WEYER, MICHAEL.

1810, March 7, Cumberland, Md. "Statutes noted in Holy Scripture, with some particular affairs of our time." Long quotations from Scripture, the application of which is conjectural. fol. 3 pages.

WHAM, WILLIAM (Cashier).

1808, September 23, Washington. Presents a draft for acceptance. 4°. 1 page.

Montpellier.

1818, December 15, Georgetown. Notice of a check of James Monroe placed to Madison's credit at the Bank of Columbia. 4°. 1 page.

WHARTON, JOHN A.

1821, February 12, Nashville. Asks information as to the university at Charlottesville; when it will go into operation, and the probable expense of a student, and the qualifications necessary to insure entrance into each class. 4°. 1 page.

1821, December 27, Bedford, Va. Request for information as to the necessary qualifications for entrance into the university and the cost of tuition and board. 4°. 1 page.

WHARTON, T. J.

1826, November 6, Philadelphia. Sends a copy of a discourse delivered on October 24 before the Society for Commemorating the Landing of William Penn. 4°. 1 page.

1828, April 18, Philadelphia. Sends copy of report of the commissioners to revise the penal code of this State. Thanks him for explaining his connection with the foundation of our present Constitution in his letter of August last. 4°. 2 pages.

WHEATON, HENRY, to PARKER, D. *Washington.*

1816, May 9, New York. Acknowledging letter of 6th respecting an order from the Secretary of War to select between his military and civil appointments. Is unable to make the selection at the present time. [*See* letter from Wheaton to Madison, May 24, 1816. Copy.] 4°. 2 pages.

——— to MADISON.

1816, May 24, New York. Incloses a correspondence between himself and the Adjutant and Inspector General, in which he complains that he has been injuriously treated. 4°. 1 page.

——— to PARKER, D.

1816, May 24, New York. Acknowledging letter of 21st, respecting the order of the Secretary of War to resign one of the civil and military offices which he holds, and upon his declining to do so for reasons, he is notified that the office of judge-advocate is vacated. Demands to know if he is removed from that office and for what cause. Protests against the course adopted by the Secretary of War. Appeals to the President from his decision. [*See* letter from Wheaton to Madison of this date. Copy.] 4°. 4 pages.

——— to MADISON. *Montpellier.*

1823, September 29, New York. Has undertaken to give to the public some account of the professional and political character of the late William

WHEATON, HENRY, to MADISON.

Pinkney. Asks Madison if he will allow him to publish some of his private correspondence with Pinkney, and to favor him with his own recollections of him. 4°. 3 pages.

1824, January 1, New York. Acknowledging letter of October 15, offering him the use of the letters of Mr. Pinkney. Asks him to lend him all of them. In his proposed work he intends to do justice to features of Madison's administration. His resistance to the exorbitant pretentions of Great Britain in 1812. 4°. 3 pages.

1824, March 6, Washington. Requests him to send the Pinkney letters to the care of the President, who will forward them. 4°. 1 page.

1825, February 27, Washington. Returns Mr. Pinkney's letters, from which he has made necessary extracts. Asks if Madison will supply him with copies of his own letters to Pinkney as necessary links in the chain of correspondence. 4°. 1 page.

1826, July 26, New York. Sends him a copy of his publication respecting Mr. Pinkney. 4°. 2 pages.

WHEATON, JOSEPH. *Washington.*

1808, August 24, Washington. Asks him to examine and present the inclosed to the President. A single line to the Deputy Postmaster-General will relieve him from great embarrassment. fol. 1 page.

1812, May 29, Washington. His desire for an appointment in the Army. Thinks his Revolutionary services and sacrifices will be recollected by Madison. 4°. 3 pages.

1812, June 27, Washington. Gives the geographical situation of St. Johns, New Brunswick, and the surrounding country, and its desirability, should that country be made an object of the war. 4°. 3 pages.

1812, December 10, Canton, Ohio. Has received the appointment of assistant deputy quartermaster. Hull's disaster. Describes the condition of troops at Pittsburg. Their disorders and desertions. Recommends an additional force of 30,000 infantry of regulars. Compensation of soldiers. Their addiction to ardent spirits. Movements of ordnance and military stores to join Gen. Harrison. [Confidential.] 4°. 3 pages.

1812, December 23, Wooster. The disastrous affair at Black Rock, opposite Queenstown. Insubordination and desertion. Requests that the officers of the Quartermaster-General's Department be given a military rank in proportion to their worth and experience. fol. 1 page.

1812, December 29, Mansfield. Arrived on the 27th after a difficult march. Bad roads and forage scarce. Broken wagons and poor horses. Complaints of the inhabitants of the insults of the troops. Desertions of troops. Recommends the enlargement of the regular system. [Confidential.] 4°. 4 pages.

1813, January 3, Camp. Describes the march of his command from Mansfield to the upper Sandusky. Bad roads, breaking of wagons, and heavy snow storms delay progress. Severe labor of the

WHEATON, JOSEPH.

troops. Complaints that Gen. Crooks with his force did nothing towards repairing roads or had out any pioneers; no discipline observed in his camp. Their robberies of cattle, hogs, and household furniture from the inhabitants. Cheating by contractors of axes not fit for use. Extreme difficulty of progress. [Confidential.]
fol. 4 pages.

1813, January 8, Camp. Describes the movement of his convoy on the route to Sandusky from Mansfield. Extreme difficulty in progressing, owing to snow and bad roads. Axes which will not cut. Describes the waste and destruction of Gen. Crooks' brigade. This system of militia is destructive of the best interests of the nation, and disgusting and distressing to the people wherever they march. [Confidential.] fol. 2 pages.

1813, February 10, Upper Sandusky. Defeat of Gen. Winchester at River Raisin and loss of 1,000 men. Movements of Gen. Harrison. Misrule at this post. Refusal of Capt. Dawson to furnish axmen to procure timber for the quartermaster's department. Incloses the order. Asks to be relieved from this quartermaster department, as his life is in danger from checking abuses on public property. This post extremely exposed. [Confidential.] 4°. 4 pages.

1813, February 26, Camp Miamie Rapids. Gen. Harrison's movements. Dislodgment of Indians from an island at entrance of this river. This post being strongly fortified. Safe arrival of wagons loaded with ammunition and quartermaster's stores. Preparation for an expedition to burn the *Queen Charlotte* under the guns of Malden. The distance on the ice is 60 miles. Wishes a different station in the army. 4°. 2 pages.

1813, February 12, Fort Freree, Upper Sandusky. Movements of Harrison to dislodge Indians from an island at the entrance of Miamie River, so placed as to interrupt all communication between lower Sandusky and his post at the rapids. Thinks he will not stop until he strikes Malden.
4°. 2 pages.

1813, March 4, Fort Meigs. Gen. Harrison's expedition to Malden to leave next day. Doubts the success of this forlorn hope. He (Wheaton) is doing all the duties of quartermaster without assistance. Is not in his element. His desire and ambition is to be in the line of the Army.
4°. 2 pages.

1813, March 8, Miamie Rapids, Fort Meigs. British troops sent in sleighs to Malden. The demoralized condition of our troops. Inexperienced officers. Undisciplined men. Does the whole duties of his department with the assistance of a young man. 4°. 3 pages.

1813, March 12, Camp Miamie Rapids. Describes his camp and surroundings. Ice breaking up. Idle curiosity and insubordination cause the death and scalping of a young officer by the Indians. Hopes soon to be able to advance on the enemy. Abundance of forage at upper Sandusky, yet a young deputy quartermaster refuses to send him any, and is now out. Speaks of Gen. Harrison in the highest terms as a commander. His indefatigable industry, labors, and zeal.
fol. 4 pages.

WHEATON, JOSEPH.

1813, June 20, Chillicothe. A written note, with printed circular from R. J. Meigs, governor of Ohio, asking for mounted volunteers, to serve for thirty-five to forty days. 4°. 1 page.

1814, May 9, Richmond. Regrets the successes of the allies in Europe, which will militate against us. Essential benefits experienced from the methods adopted for providing for movements of troops which the governor declined to furnish. Incloses an order of the Adjutant-General. 4°. 1 page.

——— to BRIGADE COMMANDER ———.

1814, May 9, Richmond. Circular in conformity with the Adjutant-General's order respecting the supplies of provisions for militia. [Appended, without signature, a memorandum giving an account of the action between the *Peacock* and *Epervier,* resulting in the prize of the latter with a large amount of specie. Copy.]
4°. 1 page. 8°. 1 page.

——— to MADISON.

1814, June 2, Richmond. Incloses a list of troops which he had fed and transported to Norfolk. Has acted on his own judgment, having received no orders. 4°. 2 pages.

1815, April 28, Richmond. As requested, he states what has been the deportment of Joseph Jones Monroe since he has been attached to the Quartermaster-General's Department. Gives him the highest character for sobriety, steadiness, and fidelity, and very useful officer. Advises his promotion. 4°. 2 pages.

Montpellier.

1820, July 1, Washington. Incloses copy of statement touching his appointment as Sergant-at-Arms when Madison was member of the House of Representatives. Desires a certificate or letter from Madison of his services during the war of 1812, as an heirloom for his children and grandchildren. fol. 1 page.

1821, October 20, Washington. An appeal to exercise his influence with Congress to favor his petition for payment of services due him in the war of 1812, for which he has never received compensation. 4°. 3 pages.

1824, November 16. Incloses an application for the office of Sergeant-at-Arms, which is vacant by the death of Thomas Dunn, with a request to advocate his claims. 4°. 1 page.

1824, October 9, Washington. Printed application for the office of Sergeant-at-Arms of the House of Representatives, enumerating his services in the Revolution and war of 1812. Appended request to use his influence with Senator Barbour to support him. 4°. 2 pages.

WHEATON, LEVI. *Washington.*

1812, November 6, Providence. Application of David Howell for the office of district judge. Describes his character and endeavors to show that he is totally unfit for the place. Recommends Samuel Eddy as a suitable person and well qualified to fill that office. 4°. 9 pages.

WHEATON, SETH, and others.

1810, not dated, Rhode Island. A letter signed by the above, Henry Smith, Thomas Coles, Christopher Ellery, and Henry Wheaton, protesting against the appointment of David L. Barnes, district judge, as a candidate for the office of judge of the Supreme Court, vacated by the decease of Mr. Cushing, as recommended by the governor of this State. 4°. 4 pages.

WHEELER, D. E. *Montpellier.*

1831, July 15, New York. The American Peace Society offer $500 for the best dissertation on the subject of a "Congress of nations for the amicable adjustment of national disputes, etc." Madison, Marshall, Calhoun, William Wirt, and Joseph Story appointed to judge of the relative merits of the several dissertations. Requests Madison to comply with the wishes of the society. 4°. 2 pages.

WHEELER, PHINEAS. *Washington.*

1810, October 13, Caldwell, N. Y. Demands pay for his services as a sergeant during the Revolution, from June, 1783, to the definitive treaty. fol. 4 pages.

WHEELOCK, JOHN.

1815, July 13, Dartmouth College. Attempts to civilize and Christianize the savage tribes by the employment of missionaries. Want of funds of the Moor's Indian Charity School. Applies to the precedents that a part of the annuities to the Indians be appropriated to the education of the Indian youths now in that school. 4°. 5 pages.

WHIPPLE, OLIVER.

1809, February 6, Hallowell, Me. Application for office. small 4°. 3 pages.

1811, October 22, Georgetown. Application for the office of Sergeant-at-Arms in the Senate. Asks his influence with Senators to obtain this office. 4°. 2 pages.

WHITE, ALEXANDER. *Richmond.*

1788, August 16, Bath. The new constitution of Virginia. 4°. 2 pages.

New York.

1788, December 4, Richmond. Thinks it necessary that Madison should be present at his own district to insure his election to Congress. The judiciary system in Virginia. fol. 2 pages.

1789, August 9, Philadelphia. Sentiments of the people in this city. They object to the salaries of our officers [in Congress] and of the President and Vice-President. Are satisfied with the revenue laws. Their childish anxiety for the removal of Congress to this city. They ridicule the idea of the Potomac. small 4°. 2 pages.

1789, August 17, Woodville. Satisfaction of the people in the proceedings of the House of Representatives. The pay of members and salaries generally are considered too high, and distinctions between the Senate and Representatives would be thought improper. The question of the temporary seat of Government of little importance; the permanent seat the great object. Lowness of the rivers. 4°. 3 pages.

WHITE, ALEXANDER.

1789, August 25, Woodville. Acknowledging a letter of yesterdays e'ennight. Question as to the adjournment of Congress. Want of money to complete the navigation of the Potomac. Thinks Congress should not adjourn to any other place until the permanent seat of Government can be fixed. Discrimination in pay of members of the two Houses reprobated. 4°. 2 pages.

Philadelphia.

1793, November 30, Woodville. Has retired from public life and returns to the bar, which he finds more agreeable occupation. Expresses his confidence in Madison's knowledge, soundness of judgment, coolness of temper, and love of country. Reports of the crops. 4°. 3 pages.

1793, December 28, Woodville. Fears no longer a schism in Congress by the influence of Genet (the French minister). Thinks it will be more difficult in future for a foreign minister to influence our Government or people. The importance of placing ourselves in a position of defence by establishing an effective militia, and by armed vessels and fortifications. fol. 3 pages.

1794, January 19, Woodville. Anxiety to hear of the result of the representations to the French Government on the conduct of Genet. 4°. 2 pages.

1794, February 1, Woodville. Acknowledging letter of January 20. Measures taken by England to obtain and retain the carrying trade of the United States and the whole world. We should put ourselves in a strong position of defence. Suggests the wisdom of delaying action until tranquillity is restored in Europe. 4°. 2 pages.

1794, February 17, Woodville. Acknowledging letter of 4th. Family details. Marriages of mutual friends. Report that Great Britain demands an answer to the question what part will America take in the war in Europe. 4°. 2 pages.

1794, March 1, Woodville. Acknowledging letter of February 17. The question of equipping a fleet to check the Algerines. It is of more importance to provide for the security of our own coasts and harbors with a militia well regulated and armed. Quarrel between Mr. Page and Mr. Vane in the Virginia assembly. A duel prevented by a Quaker alderman of Winchester. 4°. 2 pages.

1794, March 30, Woodville. Acknowledging letters of 2d and 17th. The question of laying an embargo. The right of Congress to lay it. Has no objection to vesting that power in the President, under proper regulations, during recess of Congress. Hears that Great Britain has released all our vessels and paid damages for detention. Thinks we should place ourselves in the strongest posture for defense. An effective militia desirable, and fortifying our harbors. 4°. 3 pages.

1794, April 7, Woodville. On the resolutions of Congress for laying an embargo, and the British King's instructions restricting those of the 6th November, 1793. 4°. 2 pages.

1794, April 26, Woodville. Acknowledging letter of 22d. Disapproval of Jay's appointment. Confesses he is pleased with it. 4°. 1 page.

1794, May 5, Woodville. Can not discover any constitutional ground of objection to the appoint-

WHITE, ALEXANDER.

ment of Mr. Jay, whatever impropriety there may be on his holding two offices at the same time. Fears that if the war continues against France, we shall not be able to avoid taking a part. Gen. Clarke's movements on the Ohio.
4°. 2 pages.

1794, May —, Woodville. Contradicts the report that Gen. Clarke had gone down the Ohio with 600 men. 4°. 1 page.

1794, May 19, Woodville. Acknowledging letter of 12th instant. Rumors that the embargo is not to be continued. His views respecting direct taxes and extension of excise. 4°. 1 page.

1794, November 2, Woodville. Was disappointed in not seeing him and Mrs. Madison on their passing through this country. The successes of France.
4°. 2 pages.

1795, January 17, Woodville. Acknowledging letter of December 28. Trusts that the result of Jay's mission will be favorable. The power of France to establish a free and independent republic is assured, if she does not risk her glory for the chimerical project of reducing all governments to her own standard. Unconstitutionality of the tax on carriages. The policy of encouraging immigration. The system of naturalization.
4°. 2 pages.

1795, February 14, Woodville. Acknowledging letter of 2d. Thinks the accounts of Jay's negotiations are well founded, and a general peace in Europe an event not remote. Trusts the present Congress will establish a mode of taxation in respect to the extinguishment of our national debt. 4°. 2 pages.

Near Charlottesville.

1796, September 26, Washington. Desirability of a national university at the National Capital. The President will make a donation toward its support and appropriate a handsome site for the buildings in the city of Washington. The establishment of a botanic garden also suggested. Progress of building the Capitol and President's House and private dwellings in Washington.
fol. 3 pages.

Philadelphia.

1796, December 2, Washington. Establishment of a national university in the city of Washington.
fol. 2 pages.

WHITE, E. D. *Montpellier.*

1832, February 16, Washington. In acknowledging a note of 14th apologizes for franking a pamphlet on the abolition of slavery he received from an unknown author and addressed to Madison.
4°. 2 pages.

WHITE, HUGH. *Washington.*

1812, July 18, Albemarle. Sends him a few of his meditations and mental discussions.
small 4°. 2 pages.

WHITE, JOHN, Jr.

1804, January 1, Orange. Wishes permission to extend his fence up to a certain point to improve the appearance of his plantation without injury to Madison's land. small 4°. 2 pages.

WHITE, THOMAS W., to GILES, W. B. (Governor of Virginia).

1827, December 4, Richmond. On application to the clerk of the Senate for the copy of the Senate Journal from 1777 to 1790, the result indicated the numbers specified herein. Gives the numbers. 4°. 1 page.

——— to MADISON. *Montpellier.*

1831, June 13, Richmond. Asks his views as to the policy of rechartering the present Bank of the United States. 4°. 2 pages.

1835, February 27, Richmond. Asks if he or Mrs. Madison may not have manuscripts which he would not object to seeing transferred to the "Literary Messenger." 4°. 1 page.

WHITE, WILLIAM. *Washington.*

1812, June 11, Philadelphia. Thanks for his appointment to the office of commissioner of loans. Promises to faithfully discharge his duties. 4°. 2 pages.

WHITE-HAIR (Osage chief).

1807, November 6, Osage Village. Proposition of chiefs of other tribes to meet in grand council to express enmity to the Americans, which he refused to do. [Written in bad French and difficult to decipher.] fol. 3 pages.

WHITEHILL, JOHN and JOHN LIGHT.

1812, July 1, Lancaster, Pa. In behalf of citizens of Lancaster County, transmit a copy of resolutions adopted at a public meeting expressive of their sentiments on the position of public affairs, approving of the war and promising support to the General Government. 4°. 1 page. fol. 3 pages.

WHITESIDE, J.

1811, January 17, Washington. Has received commissions for taking testimony in a case. [Mentions names of witnesses, but does not mention the subject of the case.] 4°. 2 pages.

WHITNEY, E.

1815 (?), not dated. Memorial representing a contract in 1812 with the Secretary of War to manufacture muskets for the use of the United States. Requests that the business should be placed in the hands of some other officer or agent of the Government than that of Callender Irvine, commissary-general of purchases, for reasons specified. 4°. 2 pages.

WHITTLE, CONWAY. *Montpellier.*

1835, January 26, Collector's Office, Norfolk. Has received from some unknown person a box which appears to have come from Havre for Madison's address. Sends it to the collector at Richmond to forward to him. 4°. 1 page.

WICHELHAUSEN, T. J. *Washington.*

1804, April 4, Bremen. Introducing his brother, H. D. Wichelhausen. Presents Madison with a box of old hock from his own wine cellar. 4°. 2 pages.

1805, December 7, Bremen. Acknowledging receipt of two boxes of old peach brandy. Thanks him for his kind attentions to his brother in Washington. 4°. 2 pages.

WICHELHAUSEN, T. J.

1809, February 2, Bremen. Congratulates him on his election. 4°. 2 pages.

WICKHAM, JOHN.

1807, May 15, Richmond. As counsel for Aaron Burr, requests that copies be furnished him of three affidavits, by Comfort Tyler, Luke Hill, and Frederick Haymaker, filed in the Department of State. 4°. 1 page.

WILBEKING, CHEVALIER DE.

1813, June 29, Munich. Sends documents relative to the construction of bridges. [In French.] fol. 1 page.

WIGFALL, A. THOMPSON. *Montpellier.*

1828, July 12, Edgefield, S. C. Asks his advice as to a course of reading. Is studying law at the University of Virginia. 4°. 3 pages.

WILDE, RICHARD HENRY.

1834, November 16, Augusta. Sends him a paper on his retiring to private life. 4°. 4 pages.

WILDS, SAMUEL. *Philadelphia.*

1796, March 28, Cheraw, S. C. Memorial to the Senate and House of Representatives on the evils of monopolies and oppression of rich proprietors, and praying legislation to remedy evils. fol. 10 pages.

WILKINSON, JAMES (General).

1787, February 22, Kentucky. Proposed colonial government. Habits, manners, and language of the French and Indians. Difficulty of bringing them to submit to taxation. They should be treated with lenity. 4°. 3 pages.

——— to MADISON, Mrs. *Washington.*

1808, November 9, Washington. Apologies for Miss Barrows's being unable to accept an invitation. 4°. 1 page.

——— to MADISON.

1809, May 1, New Orleans. Conversation with Governor Folch about ceding west Florida to the United States under certain circumstances. fol. 3 pages.

——— to EUSTIS, WILLIAM.

1810, July 14, Washington. Asks for the issue of orders necessary to procure the attendance of officers at the inspector's office to vindicate his conduct and character and substantiate facts and for repulsion of misrepresentations. Also to leave orders that he may obtain transcripts of official documents at the War Department. [Copy.] 4°. 1 page.

1810, July 14, Washington. List of witnesses called for by Gen. Wilkinson. [Copy.] 4°. 1 page.

1810, July 14, Washington. Rejection by the President of his application for a court of inquiry. Asks that certain officers be ordered to attend at the inspector's office as witnesses for the purpose of substantiating various facts essential to the vindication of his character. Also asks that orders be given for transcripts from official documents in the War Department, and that directions be given to furnish him his pay during his (Eustis's) absence. [Copy.] 4°. 1 page.

WILKINSON, J. (General), to MADISON.

1810, July 14. List of witnesses called for in his trial. [Copy.] 4°. 1 page.

1811, April 20, Washington. Report of the committee of the House of Representatives appointed to examine into the causes of the mortality among the troops on the Mississippi, with the professed object to ascertain truths for the information of Government, but in fact to criminate him. 4°. 4 pages.

1811, October 8, Fredericktown, Md. Complains that Mr. Simmons, the accountant of the War Department, in the double capacity of witness for the prosecution in his (Wilkinson's) case and paymaster to the officers of the court, attempts to excite and rivet injurious prejudices against him with a view to influence the impending trial. Incloses copy of a conversation between Lieut. LeRoy Opie and Mr. Simmons, and letter from the former. 4°. 5 pages.

——— to GALLATIN, ALBERT.

1812, January 27, Hagerstown. Recommends a commission as colonel to Capt. Christie, who had resigned to practice law at Wilkinson's suggestion and advice, but in view of a probable war with Great Britain thinks him well qualified to render service. 4°. 2 pages.

——— to MADISON.

1812, February 27, Washington. Declares that no language or sentiment recorded in his defence was intended either to affect his mind (the President's) or derogate from his character, and can with equal truth aver that no instance of his conduct (Wilkinson's) before the general court-martial was intended to apply to the President. 4°. 4 pages.

1812, February 29, Washington. Perceives by an indorsement on his defense before the general court-martial that he had reserved the right to correct it, and which will enable him to alter the manner without changing the matter. 4°. 1 page.

1816, April 5, Philadelphia. Is engaged in writing a narrative of his public life. During his last trial he petitioned the President for a prompt trial or for the temporary suspension of his arrest that he might resume his sword in the public cause. He wishes this document to have a place in his work, and desires a copy of it. 4°. 1 page.

WILKINSON, JOSEPH, to JEFFERSON.

1808, December 20, Calvert County, Md. Introducing Dr. James H. Blake. 4°. 1 page.

WILLARD, JACOB, to GERRY, ELBRIDGE.

1814, July 13, Marblehead, Mass. Applies for the appointment of Joshua Prentiss and a warrant as sailing master, to command a gunboat stationed in this bay. 4°. 1 page.

——— to MADISON.

1815, June 12, Marblehead, Mass. Inclosing a speech in the legislature of Massachusetts on the resolve for raising a State army as connected with the projects for holding a convention. He can not conscientiously vote for its adoption. 4°. 1 page. folio. 6 pages.

WILLARD, SIMON, JR.

1814, (?), not dated, Washington. Incloses a book on a system of government, the objects being the union of the people, restoration of their rights, establishment of the national finances, the consolidation of all North America, and freedom of the ocean from British danger. 4°. 3 pages.

1814, November 26, Washington. Repeats his request of a former letter to give his opinion on a book which he sent him on a system of government. 4°. 3 pages.

WILLETT, MARINUS.

1812, January 26, New York. Thinks that effectual measures should be taken to destroy the naval force of the enemy on the lakes as soon as the weather will permit. To insure its success, shipbuilders from Atlantic ports and sailors from our vessels of war should be ordered there. The easy conquest of Canada would ensue. 4°. 1 page.

——— to GALLATIN, ALBERT.

1812, October 14, New York. The appointment of Gen. Armstrong, of Evert, a banker, judge-advocate, he highly approves of. Criticises the mode of transports of stores from the southward to Albany. 4°. 1 page.

——— to MADISON.

1812, December 16, New York. Imbecility of some of his cotemporaries in the conduct of the late campaign. Recommends the appointment of young men to command, selected for patriotism, spirit, courage, and skill. Comparisons between the first compaign of the revolutionary war with this past campaign. Recommends Capt. Swartwout, now in the volunteer service, for the Regular Army. 4°. 4 pages.

1812, December 17, New York. Is informed by Mr. Swartwout, who has just returned from Niagara, that the health of the troops there is not properly attended to. He leaves for Washington and recommends him to the President and hopes he may be placed in the permanent army. 4°. 1 page.

1813, February 25, New York. Suggests the removal of the present marshal, on account of his opposition to the administration, and recommends Roger Strong as his successor. 4°. 2 pages.

1813, August 4, New York. In recommendation of the appointment of Gen. Giles to the command of a regiment for the defence of this place. 4°. 1 page.

1813, December 3, New York. Failure of the expedition of Gen. Wilkinson shows how the failure should have been prevented. Urges the completing as many vessels as will be deemed sufficient and have seamen ready for them, to control lakes George and Ontario. Recommends the employment of young men to command. Advantage of snow shoes in marching. 4°. 3 pages.

1814, February 7, New York. Urges the importance of increasing our force on the lakes. 4°. 1 page.

WILLIE, JAMES.

1813, April 20, Conway, N. H. Asks to be appointed assistant commissary or quartermaster, or even superintendent's clerk. fol. 2 pages.

WILLIAMS, C. D. *Montpellier.*

1820, January 29, Baltimore. Sends a pamphlet on the causes of the present commercial embarrassment of the United States, with a plan of reform of the circulating medium. Wishes Madison's opinion upon it. 4°. 2 pages.

WILLIAMS, DAVID R. *Washington.*

1812, June 12, Washington. Appointment solicited by Mr. Halsey, as consul at Buenos Ayres, contingent on the withdrawing of Mr. Poinsett. 4°. 3 pages.

1813, February 28, Washington. Declines an appointment tendered him for a command in the army. 4°. 2 pages.

1815, May 29, Center Hall. Financial embarrassments arising from his being security for his friend, Mr. Freneau. 4°. 3 pages.

1815 June 13 Center Hall. Thanks for a favor granted him. Congratulates him on the termination of the war. 4°. 1 page.

1816, December 6, Columbia S. C. Introducing Hon. William Smith, Senator from this State. 4°. 1 page.

WILLIAMS, JAMES.

1802, February 1, Orange. Introducing Morton Pannil. Requests Madison to furnish him with a letter of introduction to Prof. Smith, of Princeton, as he (Pannil) intends going there to study natural and moral philosophy. 4°. 2 pages.

1815, January 2, Battletown, Va. Our national finances, and suggestions respecting a national bank which will give great resources to the Government and to individuals. 4°. 2 pages.

WILLIAMS, JOHN. *Montpellier*

1822, January 21, Washington. Incloses an agreement in support of a claim of Massachusetts depending before Congress. 4°. 1 page.

WILLIAMS, JOHN W.

1825, April 5, Clarksburg, Va. Announces the death of a mutual friend, name not mentioned. 4°. 1 page.

WILLIAMS, JONATHAN. *Washington.*

1806, May 6, West Point. Notifying him of an assessment as member of the U. S. M. P. S. to be employed in premiums for scientific improvement and compensations for meritorious works of art. 4°. 1 page.

1809, February 23, Philadelphia. Introducing James Craig. Describes the condition of the West Point Military Academy. Suggests the plan of removing it to the seat of Government. 4°. 2 pages.

1809, July 19, New York. Acknowledging letter of 15. Intends to submit a report to the War Department suggesting an improvement in the methods of instruction at the Military Academy at West Point and placing the establishment on the most advantageous footing. 4°. 2 pages.

1811, February 27. On the bill before Congress for a new organization of the Military Academy. Urges Madison to exercise his influence in pressing the increase of appropriations. 4°. 2 pages.

WILLIAMS, M. D.

1807, January 5, Washington. Mr. Lockhart declines accepting the appointment of marshal for North Carolina. Requests that another person may be appointed to fill the place. 4°. 1 page.

WILLIAMS, NATHAN.

1806, September 5, Utica, N. Y. Extraordinary expedition in the Western Territories and down the Ohio. The promoter of this secret enterprise is a Mr. Comfort Tyler. He sates he is authorized by an association and mentions the names of Burr, Dayton, Bloomfield, Swartwout, and others, and is collecting young, active, and enterprising men to meet at Pittsburg in December. 4°. 3 pages.

1812, November 28, Utica, N. Y. Introducing Alexder Johnson. 4°. 1 page.

WILLIAMS, O. H.

1789, April 16, Baltimore. Statement of duties imposed in Maryland from May 1, 1786 to April 16, 1789, on imports and tonnage. [Copy.] fol. 1 page.

WILLIAMS, ROBERT, to EUSTIS, WILLIAM, *Secretary of War.*

1809, May 12, Boston. Applies for the pardon of William Stanwood, whose offense was for landing goods prior to entry, owing to his ignorance of the laws, and suffering from yellow fever. 4°. 3 pages.

——— to MADISON.

1811, November 2, Washington, Miss. Ter. Would consent to fill the vacancy occasioned by the death of Judge Matthews, of the Orleans Territory, in case the President should give him the appointment. (Confidential.) 4°. 3 pages.

1811, November 11, Washington. M. T. The reported death of Judge Matthews happily contradicted. 4°. 1 page.

WILLIAMSON, BASIL.

Not dated. Regrets that a mistake was made about forwarding him some books from London. 4°. 1 page.

WILLIAMSON, HUGH. *Richmond.*

1788, June 2, New York. Navigation of the Mississippi. 4°. 3 pages.

New York.

1789, May 19, Suffolk. Complaints of the tax on molasses. 4°. 2 pages.

1789, May 12, Edenton, N. C. Is informed that a treaty is to be held by the Indian agent for the Southern Department with the commissioners from Georgia, North and South Carolina. Sevier submits to the Governor of North Carolina and takes the accustomed oaths. Uneasiness of the people near the sea coast at the idea of being shut out from the Union. The alien duty will starve them and their families. 4°. 2 pages.

1789, May 24, Edenton, N. C. Conjectures as to the adoption of the Constitution by the State of North Carolina. Believes that the desire of eluding all taxes and defrauding the nation and leaving the burden on other shoulders is the great object of the anti-federals. Suggests the propriety for Congress to call upon this State very pointedly for its quota of the annual supplies. 4°. 2 pages.

WILLIAMSON, HUGH.

1789, July 2, Baltimore. Believes that unless Madison persuades Congress seriously to take up and agree to some such amendment as he had proposed, North Carolina will not consider the adoption of the Constitution. [Signature cut off.] 4°. 1 page.

WILLIAMSON, THOMAS. *Washington.*

1816, April 15, Paris. His purpose of settling in the United States. History of his life as an engineer and inventor. Tenders this letter under the possibility of Madison's perceiving an opening for his introduction into America .4°. 16 pages.

WILLIG, WILLIAM.

1812, August 11, Westminster, Vt. Sentiments of the people of Vermont respecting the war. In case of an invasion by the enemy, party distinctions would be forgotten and all would unite to repel it. 4°. 2 pages.

1815, February 27, New Bedford. On the mission of Otis and other agents from Massachusetts to Washington. Suggests the policy and justice for the administration to relieve the people of that State from burdens, but it should appear as emanating from the administration, without being influenced by Otis, etc. 4°. 2 pages.

WILLIS, BYRD C. *Montpellier.*

1825, April 7. Regrets that the badness of the roads will prevent his dining at Montpellier, having no means of locomotion but his chair. Asks his aid in procuring an appointment for his son George at the Military Academy at West Point. A letter to Col. Barbour (Secretary of War) will be of infinite service. 4°. 2 pages.

1826, September 15, Tallahassee. Respecting Madison's letter to the Secretary of War, applying for the appointment of his son George as cadet at West Point. As he has changed his residence from Virginia to Florida, he thinks an application from the latter State will meet with better success, owing to the greater number of applicants from the former State. Describes the country and products. Duel between Mr. Murat and Judge McComb. 4.° 3 pages.

WILLIS, CARVER.

1819, April 15, Jefferson. Funds left by Mr. William Tapscott with Capt. Richard Baylor for payment of his part of a purchase of land of Madison. Small 4°. 2 pages.

1827, January 16, Richmond. Purchase of land by William Tapscott, now deceased. His widow wishes to be released from the terms of the purchase, and proposes that a portion should be bought back, or some other satisfactory arrangement may be agreed on. 4°. 3 pages.

1829, March 23, Middleway, Va. Introduces W. R. Griffith, who wishes to make some arrangement satisfactory to Madison respecting his claim on Mrs. Tapscott for the payment of land purchased by her late husband. 4°. 2 pages.

WILLIS, PERRIN. *Washington.*

1813, September 11, Orange C. H. Is about to leave his native country. Submits a few thoughts on the science of war. The requisites of a good officer and soldier. Asks for a certificate that he has

WILLIS, PERRIN.

been in the Army, which may be of use to him in Mexico. 4°. 3 pages.

1816, May 4, Washington. Applies for an appointment. 4°. 1 page.

1816, July 12, Washington. Is desirous to be appointed agent to purchase the ground and erect the building for the intended observatory. 4°. 1 page.

WILLISTON, E. B. *Montpellier.*

1825, December 30, Middletown, Conn. Is preparing for publication the most celebrated speeches of American orators. Asks Madison to designate some of the most distinguished Congressional speeches delivered before 1800, and the source from which he can obtain copies. 4°. 1 page.

1828, December 24, Washington. Is engaged in the publication of a work, and sends prospectus. Asks him to subscribe for it. 4°. 1 page.

WILLISTON, C. FENNIMORE.

1836, May 6, Philadelphia. Alluding to Madison's correspondence with Jeremy Bentham, asks him if there have been any other proposers to codify the laws, who they were, and whether their works were ever published. 4°. 1 page.

WILLSON, JAMES R. *Washington.*

1813, June 1. Request to return papers sent him. [Filed as "Reverend, and insane."] 4°. 1 page.

WILLSON, RICHARD.

1804, February 22, Washington. Asks to be returned to him the letters written to the President in his favor by Robert Wright and Joseph H. Nicholson, as a testimony of the estimation in which he is held by his old acquaintances. 4°. 1 page.

WILMER, JAMES JONES.

1812, February 22, Chelsea, Md. Solicits Government employ. 4°. 1 page.

WILMER, JAMES S.

1809, September 16, Georgetown, D. C. Incloses an epitome of a work contemplated "A defence of Jefferson's administration." 4°. 1 page.

WILSON, ARCHIBALD, JR. *Orange.*

1804, April 13, Greenock, Scotland. Asks about regulations with respect to absence of American citizens for a length of time, and if there are any new regulations about shipping. The advisability of having a consul at Greenock rather than Glasgow to avoid detention and expense of shippers. 4°. 2 pages.

Washington.

1804, April 18, Greenock, Repeats his opinion and reasons why the residence of the American consul should be at Greenock rather than Glasgow. 4°. 1 page.

WILSON, ANDREW.

1813, June 5, New Jersey State Prison. Has made a series of discoveries and inventions in military and naval tactics, the effects of which on the enemy will be tremendously unerrable, awful, and terrific. If he can be liberated from prison, he feels sure, in the course of two or three months, some of the most signal and brilliant victories will be the result. fol. 3 pages.

WILSON, EBENR., and SWAN, JOHN, jointly.

1815, August 25, Paisley, Scotland. A new plan of maritime defence has been devised by them, so powerful that with the means now possessed by the United States it could completely defeat any effort and destroy the combined fleets of Europe. States the terms of confiding the secret.
4°. 3 pages.

WILSON, JAMES. *Philadelphia.*

1781, January 1, Philadelphia. Claims respecting lands granted by the Indians to the Illinois and Wabash companies. [Copy. Extracts from letters from various persons relating to this matter both in French and English.]
fol. 12 pages.

WILSON, JOHN. *New York.*

1790, June 28, New York. Petition to the House of Representatives for payment of services and wounds received in the service of his country. Asks Madison's aid in obtaining relief.
4°, 2 pages.

Washington.

1804, November 8, Washington. Desires Government employment. fol. 1 page.

[*Not dated.*] *War Department, Washington.* Submits a manuscript for his perusal and approval.
4°. 2 pages.

WILSON, JOSEPH, and others to GERRY, ELBRIDGE.

1814, July 14, Marblehead, Mass. Recommending Joshua Prentiss, third, who wishes to enter the U. S. Navy in the capacity of sailing master and command of a gunboat stationed here.
4°. 1 page.

WILSON, THOMAS.

1812, March 18, Erie, Pa. Is desirous of making a proposal to Government of importance, but wishes to be informed if it would be held strictly confidential and returned to him in case it should not be deemed improper, but inexpedient to approve or accede to it. 4°. 1 page.

1814, January 10. Improvements in French Creek and estimates of cost. Transportation of supplies inland. 4°. 2 pages.

WINDER, WILLIAM H.

1814, February 1, Washington. Incloses copy of the correspondence between Sir George Prevost and himself while prisoner of war and his permission to come to the United States upon certain terms. The rights of retaliation discussed.
4°. 4 pages.

1814, February 8, Washington. His reflections on the question of retaliation depending between the Governments of Great Britain and the United States. fol. 39 pages.

Montpellier.

1834, March 28, Philadelphia. In view of insinuations against his father's conduct at the battle of Bladensburg, for which he was acquitted by the court of inquiry, he asks Madison, who confirmed that decision, to give his approval of his measures in a letter. 4°. 2 pages.

WINGATE, JOSHUA, JR. *Washington.*

1813, March 1, Bath, Me. Wishes him to withhold commissions of J. D. Learned and Vinson as col-

WINGATE, JOSHUA, JR.

onel and major, respectively, of a regiment of volunteers, until the writer and others have an opportunity to confute base calumnies that have been made against them at the instance of those persons. 4°. 2 pages.

WINN, JOHN, and others. *Montpellier.*

1823, June 24, Milton, Va. As a committee they invite him to attend the celebration of the anniversary of American independence at Milton. 4°. 1 page.

WINSLOW, JOHN (Chairman). *Washington.*

1812, June 27, Fayetteville, N. C. Proceedings of a meeting of citizens of Fayetteville approving of the declaration of war and promising support to the General Government. Large fol. 2 pages.

WINSLOW, MARK; WINSTON, THOMAS; STEWART, JAMES, jointly.

1812, July. Petition for pardon. They have been convicted for perjury, acknowledged their guilt, and made reparation by disclosing every circumstance which could tend to stop the evils resulting from the crime and a powerful combination to carry it on with success. [Annexed are copies of sentences.] fol. 3 pages.

WINSTON, JOHN. *Philadelphia.*

1791, February 23, Hanover, Va. Certifies as to the character of Thomas Wash, who has presented a claim against the United States for services during the late war for independence. small 4°. 1 page.

WIRT, WILLIAM. *Washington.*

1809, July 10, Richmond. Introducing Alexander McRae and John Clarke, who are going to Europe. Requests Madison to give them letters as will insure them a favorable reception. 4°. 2 pages.

1812, July 17, Richmond. Does not desire a military appointment, which ill-judged officiousness of friends had recommended. 4°. 2 pages.

1815, June 7, Richmond. Recommending James Hagarty to fill the vacancy of the consulate at Cadiz. 4°. 1 page.

1816, March 10, Richmond. Recommending Abel P. Upshur to fill the vacancy caused by the resignation of Mr. Hay, district attorney for Virginia. 4°. 2 pages.

1816, March 23, Richmond. Accepts the appointment of district attorney for Virginia. 4°. 1 page.

1816, June 21, Richmond. Asks instructions respecting appointment of deputies in the State courts. 4°. 3 pages.

—— to MONROE. *Montpellier.*

1819, September 4, Washington. Recommending Alexander Scott as a candidate for some appointment within Monroe's gift. [*See* letter from A. Scott to Madison, dated January 2, 1820.] [Copy.] 4°. 1 page.

—— to MADISON.

1830, October 5, Baltimore. Acknowledging letter of the 2d. On the titles of Indians to their lands. 4°. 3 pages.

WISTAR, CASPAR, JR. *Washington.*

1804, May 29, Philadelphia. Introducing two distinguished travelers, Dr. Anthony Fothergill and Baron Humboldt. 4°. 2 pages.

1808, December 26, Philadelphia. Introducing C. Otto, who has lately returned from Europe. 4°. 2 pages.

1809, May 22, Philadelphia. Recommends Col. T. Matlack for some Government appointment in Washington. 4°. 3 pages.

1810, January 4, Philadelphia. Introducing Edward Tilghman, jr., of Philadelphia. 4°. 1 page.

1810, April 12, Philadelphia. Incloses a letter from a patient of his referring to interesting facts, the subject of which is not stated in Wistar's letter. 4°. 2 pages.

1811, April 13, Philadelphia. Gives his opinion, as requested by B. M. McClenachan, on his health and capability of attention to the office which he solicits of Madison. 4°. 2 pages.

1813, April 22, Philadelphia. Certifies as to the character, honor, and respectability of Dr. Samuel Conover, a candidate for the place of Treasurer of the Mint. 4°. 1 page.

WITHERELL, JAMES.

1808, July 4, Fairhaven, Vt. Asks to be informed as to whom he shall apply to administer the oath to him (Witherell) of the office to which he has been appointed. fol. 1 page.

WITHERS, E. D. *Montpellier.*

1823, November 19, Fredericksburg. Has received the agency of the "Edinburgh Review" and wishes to know if he wishes to continue the subscription, and that of the "Quarterly" or "North American Review." 4°. 1 page.

WOLCOTT, ALEXANDER. *Washington.*

1811, June 11, Middletown. Recommends Jacob Ogden, jr., as a suitable person to be appointed as consul at Buenos Ayres or Montevideo. Thanks him for his nomination to the office of Judge of the Supreme Court of the United States. 4°. 3 pages.

WOLCOTT, OLIVER; BUTLER, RICHARD, and LEE, ARTHUR.

1784, October 22, Fort Stanwix. Articles of a treaty concluded between the United States Commissioners, as above, and the sachems and warriors of the Six Nations. [Copy.] 4°. 2 pages.

WOLCOTT, OLIVER, JR., to HOWELL, JOSEPH. *Philadelphia.*

1792, July 13, Washington. Instructions to the accountant to the War Department respecting the settlement of accounts of the Treasurer of the United States of expenditures and warrants drawn by Walcott as accountant. fol. 3 pages. 4°. 3 pages.

WOLGER, CATHERINE, to MADISON. *Washington.*

1809, April 29, Washington. Petition for pardon. She is confined in the city goal for assault and battery and can not discharge the fines and fees. 4°. 1 page.

WOOD, ABIEL, to GERRY, ELBRIDGE.

1813, September 13, Wiscasset. Recommends Samuel Parker as a suitable person for the office of collector for the county of Lincoln. 4°. 1 page.

WOOD, JETHRO, to MADISON. *Montpellier.*

1823, March 3, Poplar *Ridge, Cayuga County,* N. Y. As corresponding secretary of the Cayuga Agricultural Society, asks for information on the subject of dressing flax without rotting. 4°. 1 page.

WOOD, JOHN H.

1820, December 22, Albemarle. Asks for a pecuniary loan, for which he will give security. small 4°. 2 pages.

1821, January 5, Albemarle. Application for a pecuniary loan. small 4°. 2 pages.

WOOD, WILLIAM.

1834, January 1, New York. The agent of the Naval Lyceum at the U. S. navy yard requests a volume from Madison's library with his autograph within. 4°. 1 page.

1834, March 6, New York. Madison's letter to the Naval Lyceum will appear in the "Evening Post." 4°. 1 page.

WOOD, WILLIAM B. *Washington.*

1811, June 19, Nashville, Tenn. Wishes to buy land in Mississippi Territory, and asks for a loan. 4°. 3 pages.

WOODS, WILLIAM.

1810, February 6, Washington. Asks Madison to accept of a cheese made at the place where the mammoth cheese was made which was presented to Jefferson. 4°. 1 page.

WOODWARD, A. B.

1809, May 27, New York. Intends to lay a memorial before the President on the subject of opening an intercourse between our Government and that of China. Should there be any mission from the Government to that country, he recommends Aaron H. Palmer as well qualified as a secretary. 4°. 2 pages.

1809 ,June 12, New York. Inclosing a paper entitled "Considerations addressed to the President of the United States on the subject of opening an intercourse between the American and Chinese governments." 4°. 8 pages.

1815, February 26, Michigan. Intelligence of peace authentic. Applies for the position of secretary of legation when a minister to Great Britain is appointed. 4°. 3 pages.

1817, January 25, Detroit. Submits to the President's perusal a discussion on the organization of the Executive Departments of the Government of the United States. fol. 1 page.

Montpellier.

1825, March 25, Washington. Acknowledging letter of September 11, 1824, on the subject of a standard of weights and measures. 4°. 3 pages.

WOOLLEY, A. R., to MORTON, JOHN.

1815, January 11, Fort Lafayette, Pittsburg. An abstract return of ordnance and stores forwarded by the U. S. Ordnance Department to the Seventh Military District, at Baton Rouge, New Orleans, and Mobile. [Certified copy.] fol. 4 pages.

WORTHAM and MCGRUDER to MADISON.
Montpellier.

1825, July 28, Richmond. Acknowledging letter of 23d with a check for balance of account. 4°. 1 page.

WORTHINGTON, VACHEL.

1819, May 10, Transylvania University. Announcing Madison's election as an honorary member of the Calliopean Society. 4°. 1 page.

WORTHINGTON, W. G. D., to ANDERSON, JOSEPH.
Washington.

1816, June 27, Washington. His health impaired by his monotonous life in his office. Requests that he will use his influence in obtaining for him an office adapted to his abilities in either foreign or domestic service. 4°. 3 pages.

——— to UNKNOWN.

1816, July 11. Acknowledging letter of 1st. Appointment to office. Supposes the President, knowing his pursuits and vocation, will feel no difficulty in assigning him a proper position. 4°. 1 page.

——— to MADISON.

1817, February 22, Baltimore. Is grateful for the honor conferred on him by his appointment to the mission to South America. 4°. 2 pages.

WRIGHT, FRANCES. *Montpellier.*

1820, June 28, Whitburn, Sunderland, Eng. Presents him with a copy of the "Tragedy of Altorf." Expresses her admiration of America and Madison's name and reputation. 4°. 2 pages.

——— to MADISON, MRS.

1825, July 26, Baltimore. Her plans for the emancipation of slaves. Asks her to obtain Madison's views on her scheme and address. 4°. 4 pages.

WRIGHT, MOSES, AND OTHERS, to MADISON.
Washington.

1813, April 12, Ashtabula County, Ohio. Memorial to the President of inhabitants of several towns of Ashtabula County deploring the existence of war, which they consider unwise and impolitic, and wishing for a speedy and honorable peace. The injustice of drafting militia to supply the place of regular troops, from the unprotected and defenceless state of their homes. fol. 4 pages. 4°. 1 page.

WRIGHT, ROBERT.

1809, January 27, Annapolis. Applies for the situation of private secretary for his son, Gustavus W. T. Wright. His qualifications. 4°. 2 pages.

1815, February 9, Washington. Solicits the appointment to the place lately occupied by Gabriel Duvall, who is appointed judge. 4°. 1 page.

Montpellier.

1823, June 26, Blakeford, Md. Incloses a letter from Samuel T. Anderson relative to a claim created under Madison's administration. 4°. 2 pages.

WYER, EDWARD.

1820, February 11, Washington. Presents him with two iron casts of Washington. 4°. 1 page.

YANCEY, CHARLES. *Philadelphia.*

1791, January 27, Louisa, Va. Asks his advice respecting the present and prospective value of certain State securities in Philadelphia. 4°. 2 pages.

Montpellier.

1822, December 21, Richmond. Solicits his subscription to a newspaper printed in Richmond by Mr. Crawford. 4°. 1 page.

1823, January 9, Richmond. Acknowledging letter of 4th, inclosing a check for subscription for Mr. Crawford's newspaper, the "Virginia Times." 4°. 1 page.

1823, January 30, Richmond. Receipt for subscription to Mr. Crawford's "Virginia Times." 4°. 1 page.

1823, March 11, Richmond. Incloses Mr. Crawford's receipt for his paper, as by Madison's request. 4°. 1 page.

1823, August 4, Richmond. Unfortunate difference between Mr. Crawford, editor of the "Virginia Times," and his foreman. Hopes Madison will give his support to Mr. Crawford, of whom he speaks in high terms. 4°. 1 page.

YANCEY, ——— (?) to VESTRY OF A PARISH.

1772, June 23, Louisa, Va. Offers himself as a candidate for minister. [Unsigned.] fol. 1 page.

YANCEY, DAVID, to MADISON. *Orange.*

1807, September 10, Yanceyville. Incloses a certificate of citizenship and asks for a passport, as he intends going abroad. small 4°. 2 pages.

Washington.

1807, September 12, Yanceyville. Relating to a letter of the 10th, which was directed to Orange, asking for a passport, which he requests may be forwarded to him. small 4°. 2 pages.

YANDELL, WILSON.

1814, February 22, Hartsville, Tenn. On the detention of troops after their time of service is expired. Extracts of letters from Gen. Jackson and Governor Blount relating to the militia of Tennessee. 4°. 4 pages.

YARD, JAMES. *Orange C. H.*

1796, September 9, Philadelphia. Private financial matter. Has received a box containing china, which he unpacked and is now at his house. 4°. 1 page.

Fredericksburg.

1800, October 28, Philadelphia. Has forwarded, by Schooner *Elizabeth*, 20 cases of Madeira wine to care of Mr. Wilson. His high opinion of its quality. 4°. 3 pages.

Washington.

1802, March 19, Philadelphia. Introducing Mr. Perkins, of Boston, who has a claim to recover property seized by Spaniards in South America. Yard has identical claims which he intends prosecuting in Spain, and if unsuccessful will appeal to our Government. Gives details and asks for a letter of recommendation to Mr. Pinckney. 4°. 4 pages.

1803, May 6, Lisbon. Has heard with surprise that he is to be appointed commissioner under the

YARD, JAMES.

treaty lately made with Spain. Considers himself disqualified to act on account of the interest he has in claims which will be made under the treaty. Is on his way to Spain. Thinks it important that the United States should have a minister in Lisbon. 4°. 3 pages.

1803, November 18, Philadelphia. Has lately arrived from Spain. The Spanish Government has positively refused to extend the provisions of the last treaty to the objects which the President so justly and positively insists on. It is to be regretted that Monroe did not go to Spain. 4°. 2 pages.

YATES. E. A. *Richmond.*

1829, October 17, Charleston. His views on the gradual emancipation of slaves. fol. 3 pages.

YOUNG, JOSEPH. *Washington.*

1810, April 23, New York. On the physical cause of the circulation of the blood. Sends a treatise for Madison's perusal, to be submitted by him to Secretary Custis and Joel Barlow, and if approved of will give a copy to the editor of the "National Intelligencer," and if he will publish it will be given the copyright. fol. 2 pages.

YORK COUNTY CONVENTION.

1812, ———. *See* Rice, Alexander, President.

YZNARDI, JOSEPH.

1811, August 29, Rota, Spain. His ineffectual attempts to get satisfaction from the authorities who are now controlled by the French respecting seizures of American vessels and property and detentions. His own arrest and property seized. Asks the Government's assistance and settlement of his account for losses sustained in carrying out his consular instructions. [In Spanish.] fol. 3 pages.

ZANE, EBENEZER. *Philadelphia.*

1795, November 17, Wheeling. Introducing Mr. McIntyre, who has established a land office for sale of Western lands. Asks Madison to inform him about certain particulars relating to the matter. 4°. 2 pages.

ZANE, ISAAC.

1795, June 17. His last will and testament. fol. 3 pages.

ZOLLICKOFFER, WILLIAM, to MADISON. *Montpellier.*

1822, December 25, Middleburg, Md. Sends copies of a treatise on the use of prussiate of iron in intermitting and remitting fevers. 4°. 1 page.

○

INDEX.

BULLETIN

OF THE

OF THE

DEPARTMENT OF STATE.

SUPPLEMENT TO No. 4.

AUGUST, 1895.

WASHINGTON:
DEPARTMENT OF STATE.

INDEX.

A.

Abbeville, sentiments of the citizens, 252.
Abolition of slavery, 236.
  Eventual, 294.
  Gradual, 581.
  Morbid sensibility on the question, 57.
  Plan for the, 129.
  Frances Wright's plan for the, 130.
  In the British colonies, 511.
Abolition of African slave trade, 135.
Aborigines of New and Old Continents, 124.
Accomac County, approbation of President's proclamation by citizens, 294.
Accomac Court-House, citizens, 24.
Accounts of officers and men, 141, 712.
Acheson, Thomas, letters from, 133.
Adair, John (General), letter from, 133.
  recommended, 662.
Adams and Clinton, contest for the Vice-Presidency between, 95.
Adams and Jefferson, coincidences in their lives and deaths, 114.
  Dirge on death, 364.
Adams, Charles Francis, letters to, 1.
Adams, Herbert, & Co., letters from, 133.
Adams, John, advocacy of an hereditary monarchy, 553.
  Antirepublican doctrines, 38.
  Appointment as minister to Great Britain, 528.
  Conduct not approved of at Mount Vernon, 45.
  Conference with Mr. Pitt, 335.
  Criticisms on, 45.
  Death, 96.
  Declaration as to an hereditary chief magistrate, 498.
  Difficulties thrown in the way of his successor, 47.
  Election as President, 43, 73.
    Vice-President, 194, 273.
  Enmity to banks and the funding system, 43.
  Hamilton's support of, as Vice-President, 344.
  Inconsistency and weakness, 44.
  Instructions to, 16.
  Integrity, 395.
  Interest in natural history, 127.
  Jefferson's affection for, 395.
    estimate of his character, 379, 383.
  Leave-taking at London, 337.
  Letter from, 133.
  Letters to, 1, 134.
  Memoir by Judge Cranch, 113.
  New England opposes the measures of (1798), 258.
  Opposition to a republican form of government, 496.
  Prejudices against the French court and Franklin, 34.
  Presentation to the King, 528.
  Rash measures, 44.
  Refutation of charge of monarchism, 280.
  Revocation of powers, 101.
  Speech to Congress considered an affront to France, 397.
  Unsoundness of doctrines, 488.
  Vice-President, policy of electing him, 273.
  Violent passions and heretical politics, 45.
Adams, John (mayor of Richmond), letter to, 1.
  letter from, 133.
Adams, John Quincy, 1, 214.
  Admiration of character, 714.
  Antirepublican sentiments, 236.
  Appointment as judge declined, 330.
    Secretary of State, 439.
  Appointments granted to him (1794–1821), 134.
  Controversy between Harrison G. Otis and, 605.
  Correspondence, 2.
  Embargo letter, 548.
  Lectures, 134.
  Letters from, 134.
    to, 1, 2, 438, 439.
  (Minister to Russia), 436.
  Nomination as commissioner to renew treaty with Sweden, 397.
  Renomination as minister to Russia, 48.
Adams, Samuel, approval of Hancock's propositions by, 125.
  File leader of the Revolution, 714.
Adams, Thomas B., letters from, 134.
Addison, J., letter from, 134.
Addison, Thomas G., letters from, 134.
Adet, Pierre Auguste (French minister), arrival of, 173.
  letter from, 134.
  remonstrance of, 73.
  suspensions of functions of, as French minister, 533.
Adlum, John, letter from, 134.
  letter to, 3.
Administration, Madison's, 1.
Admiralty, courts of, recent adjudications in the, 49, 82, 431.
Advantages, natural, 194.
Aeronautic expedition, 36.
African Colonization Society, disapproval of the, 689.
African race, the oppressed, 207.
African school in New Jersey, appeal for funds for the, 524.
African trade, attempts to open the, 208,
Age of officers and men, suggestions as to, 471.
Agg, ——, introducing, 246.
Aggression, priority of, 435.
Agriculture, American Board of, 135.
Agriculture and its incompatibility with slavery, 223.
Agriculture, convention for improvements in, 169.
  English prejudices against our system, 229.
  Improvements of, 367.
  National board of, plan for a, 714.
  Professorship of, 3, 713.
  Promotion of interests of, 112.
Agricultural products, high price of, 27
  Protection of our, 230.
Agricultural Society of Berkshire, letter from, 135.
Agricultural Society of the County of Jefferson, membership of the, 640.
Agricultural Society of the Valley, 236.
Agriculturalists, pernicious policy for our, 189.
Aguiar, Marquis de, letter from, 135.
Albany, disturbances in, 343.
Albemarle Agricultural Society, 3, 252, 524.
Albemarle, citizens of, invitation of, to a public dinner, 320.
Alcuda, Duke de la, 619.
Alden, Timothy, letter from, 135.
  Letter to, 3.

Alexander of Russia, his character and views, 84.
Count Czernicheff, his aide, 151.
Defense by, of arbitrary power, 56.
Proclamation to free all Russians who take up arms, 468.
Alexander, J. Addison, and others, letter from, 135.
Alexander, James, 546.
Alexander, —— (consul to Dublin), 471.
Alexandria, bank at, 255.
Citizens of, remonstrance against limiting the right of appeal, 457.
Defense of, 505.
Protestant Episcopal Church of, 135.
Algerine affairs, 250.
Algerine corsairs and Rhode Islanders, 640.
Algerines, British expedition against the, 308.
Cruisers of the, fitted out against Americans, 433.
Expedition against the, 71, 242, 723.
Madison's plans respecting the, 311.
"Algernon Sydney," papers of, on the suability of States against the District of Columbia, 105.
Algiers, annuity, 303.
Blockade, 249.
Brass guns for, 701.
Captives in, 385, 395.
Dey of, 19.
Demands of the, 698.
Disposition of the, to quarrel, 243.
Letter of the, 244.
Letter to, 3.
Satisfaction of the, 700.
Squadron to act against the, 241.
Letter of the Dey of, difficulty in obtaining translation of, 331.
Expense of living at, 456.
Opportunity of overthrowing, 366.
Orders to delay sailing of the expedition against, 242.
Payments to, 142.
Stores for, 402.
Treaty with, 72, 80, 96, 702.
Tribute to, or war with, 3.
War declared by, 334.
Alien and sedition laws, 30, 104, 116.
Efforts to repeal the, 258, 259.
Alien, holding of land by an, 453.
Alien law, 45, 228, 398.
Allan, William, letter from, 135.
Allegheny College, 3.
Allen, —— (British consul), friendly interposition of, 701.
Allen, Ethan, 551.
Allen, John (Honorable), desire of, to be governor, 656.
Allen, Monroe T., letter from, 135.
Allen, Thomas, 566.
Allen, William, letter to, 3.
Allen, William O. (Captain), 297.
Alliance with England against France proposed, 330.
Alliances, to form, to resist Great Britain, 138.
Allison, Richard (Dr.), recommended as marshal, 370.
Allston, Joseph, 46.
Letter from, 135.
Almanara, Marquis, 108, 608.
Alsace and Lorraine, 294.
Alston, Willis, letters from, 135.
Amalgamation, 56.
Ambler, J., letters from, 135.
Ambler, Jacquelin, letters to, 3, 520.
Amelia Island and Galveston, breaking up of piratical establishments at, 84, 536, 577.
"American Academy of Language and Belles Lettres," 12, 187.
American, an, letter from, 136.
American and European people compared, 576.
American and foreign bottoms, discrimination between, 194.
American Board of Agriculture, 169.
"American Citizen," 225, 342.
American citizens, length of absence of, 732.
American Colonization Society, principles and measures of the, 341.
American cruisers, recall of, 100.
"American Daily Advertiser," 586.
American Eagle, case of the, 308.
"American Farmer," editor of, letter from, 136.
Subscription to the, 359.
American funds, speculations in, 434.
"American Gazette and Literary Journal," 59.
American industry, 14.
"American Journal," 621.
"American landscapes," 696.
American Peace Society, 722.
American people, French observations on, 233.
American Philosophical Society, transactions of the, 277.
American property, forfeitures of, 307.
Protection of, 438.
Surrender of, by Holland to France, 628.
"American Quarterly Review," the, 122.
"American Register," 707.
American Revolution, history of, 22.
"American Society for Encouragement of Domestic Manufactures," election of Madison as member of, 486.
"American Statesman," 568.
"American Sunday School Union," appeal for aid of the, 500.
"American System, the," 594.
American vessels, condemnation of, 578.
French prizes of, 424.
American War, Botta's history of the, 164.
Americans in business in Paris, 532.
Americans in Canada, status of, 158.
Americans, longevity and physique of, 183.
Americans, relief of distressed, in Europe, 509.
Amherst memorial, 44.
Amies, Thomas, introduced, 672.
Amsterdam, specie from, 227.
Anarchy and despotism, nullification a choice between, 128.
Anatomy and natural history, professorships of, 178.
Ancestors, Madison's, 638.
Ancient languages, difficulty in conveying modern compositions into, 114.
Ancona open to American commerce, 334.
Anderson, —— (Colonel), pretensions of, 600.
Anderson, Elbert, letters from, 137.
Letters to, 3.
Anderson, Elbert, jr., letter to, 140.
Services, 137.
Anderson, G., son of, appointed to the Norfolk station, 321.
Anderson, Joseph, letters from, 137.
Letter to, 149, 737.
Anderson, Leroy, letters from, 138.
Anderson, Richard, letter from, 138.
Anderson, Samuel T., 737.
Claim, 138.
Letters from, 138.
Letter to, 429.
Anderson, William, appointment, 616.
Letter from, 138.
André, execution of, 91.
André, Francis, letter from, 138.
Andreani, Paolo (Count), introduced, 516, 607.
Andreani, Count, letter from, 138.
Andromache, British frigate. American seamen imprisoned on the, 697.
Anduaga, Joaquin de (Spanish Minister), 86.
Angeley, R. de St. Jean, letter from, 138.
Anglicans and Monocrats, action of the, 79.
Anglicism in New York, 38.
Anglomen, chicanery of, 410.
Anglophobia in the Cabinet, 390.
"Animal economy," 143.
Animals, strange American, 36.
Annapolis convention, 3, 77, 78, 138.
Annual Register, 163.
Anonymous letters, Jefferson's opinion of, 408.
"Anonymous," letters from, 138, 139.
Anthracite, wrought, specimen of, 500.
Anti-Federal views, 102.
Anti-Jackson convention, 146.
Antiquarian Society of Charleston, 617.
Anti-Tariff party, 180.
resolutions, 182.
Apalachicola, capture of negro fort on the, 371.
Appleton, John, introduced, 316.
Appleton, Th., letter from, 139.

Appointments, for party services, 716.
in recess of Congress, 3.'
in the Army, 290, 291.
of foreign courts, 58.
of incompetent persons to office, 716.
question as to dates, 86.
Suggestions as to, 371.
The law terminating, 52.
to office, 109.
Apportionment bill, 58, 70, 221.
Appropriations, transfer, 321, 346, 347, 361.
Arbitration of national disputes, 607.
Archives, preservation of the, 704.
Argus, the, 300.
Ariel, dismasting of the, 92.
Aristocracy, anglicism and mercantilism in New England, influence of, 41.
Arkansas and Red Rivers, geography of, 407.
Arkwright's cotton spinning mill, 227.
Armies, raising of, discretion of the President for the, struck out, 398.
Arming, petition of merchants and trades against, 398.
Arming the free population, necessity for, 233.
Armistead, 89.
Armisted, ——, application of, for clerkship, 556.
Armitage, George, 234.
Arms, furnishing of, to students, 507.
Return of, made and repaired, 707.
Armstrong, John (General), 186
Commission and letter of credence, 700.
Concerning ploughs and spinning wheel, 47.
Conduct of, toward General Dearborn, 265.
Excursion to northern frontier, 307.
Inconsistency of, 50.
Letters from, 139, 140.
Letters to, 3, 144, 145, 167, 168, 450, 588, 678, 688, 709.
Recommendation to take possession of the Floridas, 409.
Resignation in the Senate, 311.
Resignation as Secretary of War, 471.
Succeeds Livingston at Paris, 82.
Army, accounts, commissioner of, letter from, 140.
and militia laws, revision of, 292.
and Navy, intended addition to the, 399.
appointments to the, 289.
bill, provisional (1798), 258.
bounty deprives us of seamen, 427.
complaints of management of the, 141.
Condition of the (1812), 292.
consolidation, 3.
defeat of our, in the Northwest by the Indians, 459.
Disbandment of the (1815), 80, 248.
Discontent of the, 100.
Government of the, 563.
grievances, 99, 712.
jeopardized for want of competent number of officers, 368.
Mutinous (1783), 161.
Northern and southern division of the, 248.
Of the Rhine, destiny of the, for England, 396.
Officers and men of the, suggestions as to orders to the, 561.
Officers of the, nominations of, 86.
Organization of the, 247, 248, 249.
Pay of the, 168.
Provisioning of the, exhaustion of appropriation for, 420.
Standing, the question of a, 79.
Sufferings of the (1780), 92.
Temper of the, 712.
Arnold, Benedict, apostacy and plot of, 91.
Contempt of the enemy for, 91.
Sailing of, to New London, 92.
Success of, in his descent on New London, 92.
Arnold's Corps, destruction of, prevented by delay of French commander at Rhode Island, 711.
Arnold, Thomas, 187.
Letter from, 140.
Art, works of, to be delivered up to France, 533.
Removal from Paris, 294.
Artillery, Washington and Jefferson, 97, 589
Artists, society of, at Philadelphia, Madison invited to be a patron, 452.
Arworth, Samuel, claim of, for loss of a vessel, 140.
Letter from, 140.
Asgill, discharge of, 98.
Intercession for his life by Vergennes, 98
Ashley, Henry, introducing, 610.
Assessment, general, remonstrance against, 102.
Assize courts, 76.
Assize law, defeat of, 76.
Assize scheme, 68.
Assumption of State debts, 199, 221, 591, 607.
Astor, John Jacob, 186, 306, 624.
And the loan, 308.
Financial proposition, 305.
Monroe's payment of a debt to, 541.
Recommended, as commissioner, 694.
Astronomical matters, 284, 448.
Asylum for decrepit and disabled officers, seamen, and marines, 454.
Atherton, Boaz M., letter from, 140.
Atlantic Coast, climate, 178.
Atlantic waters, naval force of the enemy in, 427.
Atwater, Caleb, letters from, 140.
Letter to, 3.
"Aunsiente Balladdes," 580.
Aurora, The, 271.
Austen, Jonathan Loring, recommended, 317.
Austin, Benjamin, letters from, 140.
Letter to, 3.
Austin, Benjamin, and others, letter from, 140.
Austin, Charles, letter from, 140.
Austin, James T., 316.
Letters from, 141.
Letter to, 4.
Recommended, 314, 316.
Soliciting appointment of Comptroller of the Treasury, 141.
Austria, declaration of war against the Turks, 337.
Hostile preparations, 334.
Influence of the Queen of France with, 334.
Submission of, 139.
Authorship, profits, 24.
Autograph letters, 212.
Autographs of distinguished Americans, 30, 113.
Autographs, request for, 287, 637.
Award under seventh article of British treaty, 699.
Aydelot, Benjamin, letter from, 141.
Azuni, D. A., letter from, 141.
to, 4.

B.

Bache, Richard, letters from, 141.
Recommended, as postmaster, 368.
Backus, Azel, 282.
Bacon, E., letter from, 141.
Bacon, Ezekiel, 2.
Letter to, 473.
Badollet, John, 308.
Bagot, Charles (British minister), 536.
Conversation between Monroe and, on the fisheries, 331.
Interview with, 239.
Letter from, 142.
Bahama Islands, to replace destroyed buildings in the, 178.
Bailey, ——, letter from, 142.
Bailey, Francis, 165.
His appointment as public printer solicited, 300.
Letters from, 142.
Recommended, 599.
Bailey, Theodorus, 479.
Letter from, 142.
to, 4.
Baillie, George, 142, 170.
Baillie, John, letter from, 142.
Bainbridge, A., claim, 142.
Letter from, 142.
Bainbridge, William (Commodore), 425, 428.
Acquittal by court-martial, 702.
Capture of the *Java* by, 424.
Claim to command of navy-yard at Charlestown, 142.
Command of expedition against Algiers, 369.
Letters from, 142.

Baker, James, letter from, 142.
Baker, John, and others, letter from, 142.
Baker, John Martin, letters from, 142, 143.
Baker, Richard Bohun, 271.
Letter from, 143.
Bakewell, Page & Bakewell, letter from, 161.
Balch, Alfred, 148.
Balch, —— (Rev.), introduced, 616.
Baldwin, C., 255.
Baldwin, Ch. N., letter from, 143.
Baldwin, Daniel, letter from, 143.
Services offered, 143.
Baldwin, Thomas, letter from, 143.
Baldwin, —— (Dr.), introduced, 605.
Ball, B., letter from, 143.
Ball, Isaac, letters from, 143.
Ballard, James Hudson, letter from, 143.
Ballard, Robert, letters from, 143, 144.
Port surveyor, 144.
Ballinger, John, letter from, 144.
Balls, ——, letter to, 8.
Balmain, Alexander, letter from, 144.
Baltimore, alarm and distress of the people (1813), 160.
As seat of Government, 253.
Citizens of, congratulations on conclusion of peace, 419.
Defenseless condition, 491.
Democratic citizens of, resolutions, 556.
Disturbances at (1812), 542.
Inquiries on the assault on the post-office at, 332.
Prediction of burning, 632.
Riotous proceedings at, 176.
Baltimore American, the, 216.
Bancroft, Edward (Dr.), 382.
Letter from, 144.
Bank, bill for incorporating a, 69, 70.
Bank discounts, contraction of (1820), 107.
Bank, Hamilton's plan of a, 95.
report on the constitutionality of the, 104.
Bank law, the, 664.
Bank, National, institution of a, 272.
Organization of the, 250.
Proposition to establish a, 136.
Scheme for a, 675.
Subscriptions to the, 596.
Suggestions respecting a, 729.
Views as to creation of a, 429, 430.
Bank of England, reported failure of, 395.
Bank of Columbia, Georgetown, 504.
Bank of Washington, 168.
Contract with the, for loan for rebuilding public buildings, 464.
Bank of the United States, 200.
Constitutionality of the, 110.
Renewal of charter, 162.
Bank paper, forging, 660.
Bank stock, speculation in, 39.
Bankhead, James, letters from, 144.
Soliciting rank of colonel, 144.
Bankhead, ——, (Captain), 581.
Bankrupt act, passage of a, desired, 707.
Views on a, 122.
Bankrupt bill, 418, 505.
Rejection of the, 399.
Bankrupt laws, 258, 259.
Banks, deplorable condition of the, 223.
Linn, letter from, 144.
And others, letter to, 4.
Multitude and mismanagement of, 107.
Run on the (1814), 177.
State, 250.
State power to make, 33.
Views on, 300.
Banks, Ger., letter from, 144.
Banks, Henry, letter from, 144.
Banks, John, 144.
Banks, William, letter from, 144.
Barbados, climate and residence in, 462.
Barbary, chastisement of, 268.
Combination of European powers against, 331.
Treaty with, 334.
War declared by, 260.
Barbary affairs, misrepresentations as to the, 456.
Barbary commissioners, modification of the convention as executed by the, 456.
Barbary pirates, increased demands of the, 401.
Means for exterminating, 141.
Barbary powers, commission to negotiate with the, 335.
Barber, Abraham, application as captain, 145.
Letter from, 145.
Barber, Thomas, letter to, 472.
Barbour, Gabriel, application as lieutenant, 145.
Letter from, 145.
Barbour, James (Judge), 53.
Barbour, James, declination to accept the law professorship, 178.
Invitation to a dinner given to, 318.
Letters from, 145, 146, 147.
Letters to, 4, 5, 148, 417, 419.
Negotiations, 5.
Voyage and impressions of Europe, 147.
Barbour, James, and John Henshaw, letter to, 4.
Barbour, John S., letters from, 147.
Letter to, 5.
Payment of a note of, to Madison, 147.
Barbour, Mordecai, character and merits, 159.
Letters from, 148.
Recommended, 163, 178, 423.
Soliciting Government employment, 148.
Barbour, Philip, 146.
Letters from, 148.
Barbour, P. P., 147.
Letters from, 148.
Barboursville, mail arrangements for, 332.
Post-office at, 145.
Barclay, Thomas, letters to, 133, 299, 377, 383.
Negotiations with Morocco, 377.
Testimony as to conduct of, 133, 299, 383.
Barclay, ——, (British consul), refusal to sign a passport, 494.
Bard, David, letter from, 148.
Baring, Alexander, 579.
Baring Bros. & Co., letters from, 148.
Baring, Francis, (Sir) tobacco held by, 679.
Barker, Jacob, 186.
Contract with the Government, 149.
Letters from, 148, 149.
to, 148, 318.
Proposition to raise money, 149.
Suits against, by the Treasury Department, 149.
Barker, John, letter from, 149.
Letter to, 5.
Recommended, 471.
Barlow, Joel, death of, 192, 710.
Desire to be Secretary of State, 149.
Instructions to, 50.
Letters from, 149, 150, 151.
to, 5.
Life of, 278.
Negotiations, 467.
Recommended, as Secretary of State, 301.
Selection of, to fill vacancy in Department of State, 5.
Barlow, Thomas B., letter from, 151.
Barnard, Henry, letter from, 151.
Barnard, ——, introduced, 339.
Barnes, David L., 580.
Protest against appointment of, as judge of the Supreme Court, 722.
Barnes, Joseph, letter from, 151.
Barnes, Thomas, letter from, 151.
Barnet, Isaac Cox, recommended, 574.
Unjust removal as consul at Bordeaux, 361.
Barnett, William, letter from, 152.
Letter to, 5.
Barney, Joshua, claims, 627.
Letter to, 627.
Barney, Joshua (Commodore), force of, 427.
Suggestions, 51.
Barney, Joshua, and others, letters from, 152.
Letters to, 6.
Barataria, pirates and smugglers at, 249.
Baratarians, outrages by, 249.
Barrand, —— (Dr.), introduced, 498.
Barron, James, letter from, 152.
Barrow, William, 156.
Letter from, 152.
Barrus, Rufus L., recommended, 482.
Barry, James, letter from, 153.
Barry, W. T., letter from, 153.
Letter to, 6.

Barton, J. B., 646.
Barton, W., letters from, 153.
Barton, William A., 75.
Barton, —— (Dr.), letter to, 299.
Bayly, Robert B., recommended, appointment as Indian agent, 505.
Bascom, H. B., letters from, 153.
Letter to, 6.
Basin, proposition to form a, on unappropriated ground north of the Tiber, 160.
Bassett, Burwell, letter from, 153.
Bassett, George W., letter from, 153.
Letter to, 6.
Bassett, John, letter from, 153.
Bastile, taking of the, 386.
Batavia, consul at, services, 580.
Batavian Republic, friendly disposition of the, 120.
Bates, Stephen, letter from, 153.
Letter to, 6.
Bath, smuggling in, 155.
Baton, Benjamin Smith, letters from, 154.
Soliciting a place in the Mint, 154.
Baton Rouge, desire of inhabitants to become part of the United States, 153.
Independence of, 152.
Revolution at, 144.
State of parties at, 681.
Taking of, to secure New Orleans, 410.
Baton Rouge fort, capture, 484.
Battery, portable, illustrated invention, 556.
Battle of New Orleans, poem on the 301.
Battoile, H., letter from, 154.
Batture, the, 209, 328, 412.
Defense of Jefferson in the action relative to, 411.
Right to, the Attorney-General's opinion on the, 408.
Baudry, Peter, 277.
Bavaria, combination of powers to prevent the accession of, to Austria, 334.
Exchange of, for territories in the low countries, 334.
Baxter, Thomas B., 644.
Bayard, James, letter from, 154.
Bayard, J. A., letter from, 154.
Bayard, James A., vindication, 122.
Baylor, C. A., 324.
Bayle, John (Hon.), 656.
Baylor, Frances, letters from, 154.
Baylor, George, settlement of accounts, 154.
Baylor, John, letter from, 154.
Baylor, Richard (Captain), 731.
Baylor, William, 324.
Bayly, Thomas M., letter from, 154.
Bean, Phinehas, jr., letter from, 154.
Beard, David (Rev.), introduced, 542.
Beatson, A. (General), 137.
Beaumarchais, claim of, 81.
Beaumarchais cause, the, 579.
Beaumé, —, introduced, 695.
Beasley, Frederic, letters from, 155.
Letters to, 6.
Beasley, R. G., application for consulate at Bordeaux, 155.
Letters from, 155.
Beatty, James, letters from, 155.
Beck, John E., recommended, 647.
Beckley, John, 448, 631.
Letters from, 155.
Beckwith, Colonel, 39.
Bedford, Duke of, letter to, 283.
Bedford, J. R., letters from, 156.
Letter to, 152.
Bee, Thomas (Judge), 271.
Declines appointment as chief judge in circuit court, 156.
Letter from, 156.
Beguine, Spanish privateer, 698.
Belgian and Holland question, 523.
Bell Benjamin, 339.
Bell, Fanny, 13.
Bell, Henry, letter from, 156.
Soliciting appointment of superintendent of State arsenal, 156.
Bell, James M., letter from, 156.
Bell, Margaret, marriage of, and Colonel Sandford, 658.
Bell & Tapscott, covenant of, 241.
Suit against, 464.
Bell, William, appointment of, solicited, 156.
Belligerent powers, intervention of the United States with the, 431.
Orders and decrees of the, 604.
Rights of, to interfere with commerce of neutrals, 702.
Bellini, C., 495.
Letter from, 156.
Belt, Robert B., recommending, as assistant agent, 505.
Benger, Thomas, introduced, 229.
Bennet, Jacob, recommending, as district attorney, 370.
Bennett, William S., 135.
Bennington County, Vt., citizens of, sentiments of approbation of, 296.
Benson, Perry, letter from, 156.
Bentham, Jeremy, 2, 129.
Correspondence with, 732.
High character and learning, 171.
Letter from, 156.
Proposed code of laws of the United States, by, 156, 171.
Bentham, Robert, recommended, 271.
Bentley, John, 157.
Bentley, William, letters from, 156, 157.
Letter to, 6, 639.
Berkley (Admiral), 20.
Conduct of, 262.
Berkshire Agricultural Society, 157, 519.
Berlin decree, cause of the, 604.
Revoking, 604.
Berlin and Milan decrees, seizure of vessels under, 288.
Withdrawal of, 424.
Bermuda, English expedition fitting out at, destined for New Orleans, 547.
Order of governor of, relating to vessels with provisions, 360.
Trade with, 20.
Bermuda Hundred, exports, 157, 296.
Bernard, Simon (General), letter to, 6.
Services to this country, 6.
Bernardo, Joseph (Colonel), introduced, 214.
Bernadotte (General), 260, 673.
Sailing of, for Louisiana, 574.
Bernstoff, —— (Count), conversation with, on Danish depredations, 436.
Berry, Taylor, recommended, 661.
Betsey, brig, seizure of, 381.
Beverley, Carter, letter from, 157.
Bibb, ——, (Dr.), recommendation of, 239.
Bible Society, Philadelphia, 362.
Bibles, distribution of, in Virginia, 336.
Bickley, Robert S., letters from, 157.
Bidde, Charles, 600.
Biddle, Charles, letters from, 158.
to, 247, 684.
Biddle, Nicholas, letters from, 158.
Letters to, 7.
Recommended, 475.
Bidwell, ——, flight of, 412.
Bidwell, Barnabas, acceptance by, of office of attorney-general, 158.
Letters from, 158.
Recommended, as successor to Judge Cushing, 476.
Bigelow, Andrew, letter to, 7.
Bigotry, antiquated, countenanced by the legislature, 77.
Bill of exchange, 295.
Bill of rights, Jefferson's disapproval of the omissions of the, in the Constitution, 384, 385.
Billing, W. W., letter from, 158.
Billings, E. B., letter from, 158.
Complaint of arrest and trial, 158.
Billings, Jesse L., letter from, 158.
Bills payable and receivable, 7, 17.
Billy, slave, 68.
Punishment of, by disposing of him, 67.
Bines, Maxwell, 603.
Letter from, 158.
Bingham, Amos, letters from, 159.
Bingham and Cerbalt cause, 476.
Bingham, P. A., letter from, 159.

Bingham, William, letters from, 159.
Binney, Horace, speech of, 25.
Binns, John, 471.
Letters from, 159.
Biographies, materials for, 59.
Bioren, John. 272.
Birbeck, Morris, letter from, 159.
Birchett, Robert, letter from, 159.
Birckhead, Robert, letter from, 160.
Bird, John, judgment against, 170.
Bird, Otway, introduced, 497.
Bird's-nest soup, 214.
Birkbeck, Morris, letter to, 7.
Birmingham, mob at, 509.
Bishops, American, succession of, 247.
Bissell, Daniel (General), dispute between, and W. C. Nicholas, 556.
Black, J. R., letter from, 160.
Blackford & Co., Arthur, letter from, 160.
Blackledge, Benjamin, recommendation of, as consul to Guadeloupe, 162.
Blackledge, William, letters from, 160.
Black Rock, disastrous affair at, 719.
Blackstone's Commentaries, new edition of, 477.
Bladensburg, battle of, 130, 733.
Blair, F. B., letter from, 160.
Blair, James, letter from, 160.
Blair, John, 638.
Letter to, 514.
Blake, George, defense of, 314.
Letter from, 160.
Recommended, 314.
Blake, George (Mrs.), 314.
Blake, James H., certificate as to character of, 499.
Employment solicited by, 160.
Introduced, 552.
Letters from, 160, 161.
Letter to, 7, 225.
Blake, James H. (Dr.), political conduct, 484.
Recommended, 506.
Testimony as to character, 504.
Blake, William, imprisonment of, 699.
Bland, Theodorick, 196.
Bland, Theodorick (Colonel), election of, as judge, 503.
Bland, Theodorick, letters from, 161.
Letter to, 33.
Blatchly, Corn's. C., letter from, 161.
Blatterman, G., difficulties of, 181.
Bleadsoe, Henry, introduced, 656.
Bledsoe, Jesse, introduced, 614.
Bledsoe, J., letter from, 161.
Bledsoe, Pechy, letter from, 161.
Bleeding, cure by, 65.
Bleiherolsen, ——, letter from, 161.
Blocher, Jacob, letter from, 161.
Blockade, British, 230.
Blockade, mock, Great Britain's, 49.
Blockade of four German rivers, 83.
Blockade on coast of Spain, relaxation of the, 328.
Blockade, true principles of, 75.
Blockades and impressments, 19.
British doctrine of, 107.
Blockading system, irksome to France, 48.
Blodget, Rebecca, letter from, 162.
Petition of, in behalf of Aaron Burr, 162.
Blodget, S., letter from, 162.
Blood, circulation of the, cause of the, 739.
Blood, Hosea (Dr.), recommended, 661.
Bloodgood, ——, introduced, 670.
Bloodgood, Abraham, letter from, 162.
Letter to, 7.
Bloomfield, Joseph, 264.
Bloomfield, Joseph (General), introduced, 316.
Bloomfield, Joseph, letters from, 162.
Bloomfield, S. F., letter to, 502.
Blount, John, letter from, 162.
Blount, Thomas, letter to, 304.
Blount, Willie (Governor), 306.
Blount, Willie, letters from, 162.
Blount, Willie (Governor), letter to, 324.
Blount, William, 257.
Impeachment of, 396.
Report of the committee on the affair of, 257.
Blunt, E. M., letters from, 163.
Blunt, Joseph, letters from, 163.
Blunt, William, letter from, 163.
Boas, Jacob and others, letter from, 163.
Boats, flat-bottomed, destined to carry troops and heavy ordnance, 465.
Boggs, John, letter from, 163.
Bohrman affair, termination of the, 515, 516.
Bohrman, Ant. Henry, letter to, 515.
Transactions, 515.
Boissy d'Anglas and others, Tallien's denunciation in the convention against, 532.
Bolling, Robert, letters from, 163.
Bollman, Erick, letters from, 163.
Bonaparte. (*See* Napoleon.)
Bonaparte and the allies, armistice between, 523.
Bonaparte, annihilation of the allied armies by, 407.
Arrival of supposed agents of, 522.
Conjectures on the overthrow of, by the allies, 314.
Decrees of, 244, 433.
Designs toward the United States, 412.
Favorable disposition, 570.
First consul. 574.
In Egypt, 399.
Limit to power in Spain, 409.
Plot to assassinate, 480.
Reports of, being made Emperor, 535.
Return from Elba, 248, 293, 376.
Bonaparte's successes, 257, 396, 410, 533.
"Bonaparte the Tyrant," 486.
Bonaparte, Jerome, alias M. Dalbart, 260.
Marriage of, 480.
Question of passage to Europe in a frigate for, 402.
Bond, —— (British consul), refusal of, to sign a passport, 494,
Bonds and simple contracts, distinction between, 389.
Bones of animals found in South America, 380.
Bonnycastle, C., 213.
Bonnycastle, Charles. contract between, and Francis W. Gilmer, 319.
Bonnycastle, C., letter from, 164.
Bon wood of Louisiana, 211.
Books, importation of, endeavor to obtain repeal of duty on, 415.
Loss of, by Congress to be supplied by Jefferson, 51.
Preserving from dampness, 213.
Purchase of, 53.
Tax on imported, 52.
Bordeaux consulate, 212.
Consulship at, 627.
Party rancor at, 468.
Bordley, J. Beale, letter from, 164.
Bossange & Mason, letter from, 164.
Boston and Cape Ann, defense of coast between, 587.
Boston, citizens of, resolutions of, acquiescing in the embargo, 220.
Collector at, 23.
Constitutional convention at, 444.
Defenseless condition, 315.
Favorable result of the convention at, 125.
Malcontents in (1812), 315.
Political faction in, to rule or dissolve the Union, 686.
Sentinel, 336.
State Bank of, discharge of loan due the, 250.
Tories, spirit of, 409.
Botanic garden, establishment of a, suggested, 724.
National, benefits to be derived from a, 675.
Botanic Gardens, 164.
Botta, C. G. G., history of the American Revolution by, 8, 89, 90.
Botta, Carlo, letters from, 164.
Letter to, 8.
Botta's American War, translation of, 560.
Botts, Thomas, letter from, 164.
Boudon, David, letter from, 164.
Soliciting position of drawing-master, 164.
Boundaries defined, 72.
Boundaries of empires, natural, 297.
Boundary, line of, between the whites and Indians, 355.
Bounty for capturing prisoners of war, 605.
in lands for officers and soldiers, 641.
on wheat and flour, 42.
Bouriqueen (or Crab Island), proposed purchase of, as a naval station, 174.

Bourne, Benjamin, introduced, 500.
Bourne, George, letter from, 164.
Bourne, Silv., letters from, 164.
Bournonville, 80.
Bowditch, Nathaniel, 264.
  Letter from, 164.
    to, 8.
Bowdoin, Grace (Mrs.), 642.
Boyd, John, services of, 624.
Boyd, John Parker (General), 293.
  Conduct of, 264.
  Injustice to, 333.
Boyd, J. P., letters from, 165.
Boyd, John P. (General), pretensions to rank, 165, 317.
Boyd, Washington, letter from, 165.
Boyden, James, letter from, 165.
Bowie, Ralph, letter from, 165.
Brackenridge, H. H., letters from, 165.
Bradford, Alden, letter from, 165.
Bradford, David, complicity of, in the whisky rebellion, 165.
Bradford, James, letter from, 165.
Bradford, Samuel F., letter from, 165.
Bradley, Abraham, jr., letter from, 166.
Bradley P., letters from, 166.
Bradley, Stephen R., letter from, 166.
Brainard, —, 283.
Bramham, Thomas W., letter from, 320.
Bramham, V., letter from, 166.
Brand. C. J., letter from, 166.
Brandt and Indian warriors, movements of, 173.
Brandt, Joseph, 68.
Brandt, the Indian, 389.
Brandy, importations, 313.
  Importation of, prohibition proposed in Virginia of the, 384.
Brannan, John, letter from, 166.
  letters to, 8.
Bread, scarcity (1812), 646.
  Scarcity in Paris, 386.
Breadstuffs, exportation, 42.
  In Europe, scarcity, 72.
Breckenridge, James, letters from, 166.
  Letters to, 8.
Breed, Holton J., introduced, 244.
Breeze, Arthur, letter from, 166.
Brehan, Madame de, 38.
  Introducing, 384.
  Visit at Mount Vernon, 126.
Brennan, J., letters from, 166, 167.
Brent, Daniel, and others, letter from, 167.
Brent, Daniel, letters from, 167, 168.
  Position of, in the Department of State, 168.
Brent, R., 613.
Brent, Robert, letters from, 168.
Brent, William, letter from, 169.
Brevet commissions, 323, 608.
  In the peace establishment, 238.
Brevets, origin, 86.
Brewer, John, letter from, 169.
Brewery, establishment of a, 220, 221.
Bricks, making, 206.
Bridge, invention of a, 171.
  Stock, 8.
Bridges, construction, 726.
  Invention for destroying, over which the enemy is passing, 327.
Bridges, Isaac, letter from, 169.
Briggs, Isaac, letters to, 169.
Briggs, Joseph, 169.
Briggs, Robert, letters from, 169.
Briggs, R. (Dr.), letter to, 8.
Briggs, Wesson, claim, 169.
  Letter from, 169.
Bright, —— (General), policy of pardoning, 470, 471.
Bright, Michael, suggestions of clemency in case of, 272.
Bringhurst, J., 394.
Briscoe, Richard S., 168.
  Petition to appoint, justice of the peace, 358.
Bristow, Mary, claim, 169.
  Letter from, 169.
British aggression, cases, 291, 703.
British allegiance, 608.
British and Spanish Governments, claims on the, 303.
British armament in the West Indies, 42.
British armed vessels, entry of, into New York Harbor, 408.
  Intercourse with, 406.
British army, scheme to destroy the, 717.
British barbarities, 75, 114.
British blockade, 230.
British Cabinet (1811), folly and depravity of the, 50.
  Tergiversations of the, 81.
British captures, 330.
British cartel ship, permission for, to land and sell surplus stores, 249.
British claims, 288.
  For violation of neutrality, 182.
British colonies, navigation of the, 55.
  Trade with, 231.
British commanders, complaints against, 699.
British commerce, law prohibiting, 100.
British court, tricks of the, 34.
British courts of admiralty, enormities of the, 401.
British cruisers, instructions to, 578.
British debts, 67, 68, 71, 77 103, 169, 176, 196, 221, 228, 253, 380, 464, 521, 557, 647.
British decrees, the, 461.
British depredations, 71, 72, 73, 79, 83, 182.
British deserters, 203, 232.
British finances (1781), 92.
British fleet, arrival of the, 91.
  Awkward situation of the, 366.
  Capture of a, 91.
  Off Montauk Point, 474.
  Sufferings of the, 92.
British force in Canada, 306.
  To be sent to United States, 146.
British goods in Virginia, 205.
  Smuggled, 377.
British Government, conjectures of the, as to disaffection in maritime States, 273.
  Cooperation with the, in the struggle between liberty and despotism, 53.
  Diplomatic skill of the, 134.
  Hostility of the, 206, 272.
  Indignation against the, 660.
  Infatuation of the, 411.
  Intercourse between subjects of the, and our Indians, 249.
British hostility, 5.
British, inroads of the, on frontiers of New York (1780), 91.
British insolence, 347.
British intriguers, 133.
British, lost preeminence of the, 136.
British manufactures, prohibition, 306.
British minister, insolence of the (1810), 110.
British ministry, changing of policy of the, toward the United States, 410.
British navigation act, 702.
British nation, distrust of conduct of the, in overtures to peace, 441.
British naval force, plan for destruction of the, 220.
British officers, habitual insolence, 408.
  Refusal of, to deliver up posts, 248.
British orders in council, new, 47, 55, 231, 244, 392, 410, 433, 434, 481, 578, 579.
  Disposition to repeal the, 462.
  Revocation, 510.
  Suspension, 474.
British outrages, 40, 186, 232.
British partisans, efforts of, to embroil us with France, 73.
British perfidy, 374, 375.
British piracy, 142.
British policy, unfriendly, 40.
British posts, retention of the, 464.
British press, misrepresentations of the, 381.
British pretensions, negotiations and remarks on the, 519.
British proclamation, hostile appearance of the, 373.
British property, seizure of, recommended if impressment continues, 690.
British refugees, property, 161.
British seamen, enlistment, 212.
British ships, discrimination in favor, 47.
British, sinking hopes of the, 92.
British spy, conversation with a, 632.

British squadron, mode of communication between the, and British functionaries, 167.
British subject, murder committed by a, on the high seas, 406.
British subjects take oath of fidelity to Virginia, 256.
British trade, interdiction, recommended, 690.
Proposed duty on, 503.
British treasury, 170.
British treaty (1806), 230.
British vessels, captures by, 216.
Brobson, James, conduct of, as marshal, 280.
Defense, 170.
Letters from, 170.
Letter to, 280.
Brock, C. William, letter from, 170.
Brock, Isaac (Sir), 291.
Brockenbroug, William, introducing, 192.
Brockenbrough, A. S., complaint of, for ill treatment, 170.
Letters from, 170.
Letter to, 8.
Brockenbrough, Arthur S., death, 565.
Brockenbrough, John, letter from, 170.
Brockenbrough, Lucy, appeal of, in behalf of her husband, 170.
Letter from, 170.
Brockenbrough, Newman, letter from, 170.
Brockenbrough, Thomas, recommendation of, as patron of the students at the University of Virginia, 565.
Brodnax, William H., letter from, 171.
Brooke, Francis, letter to, 9.
Brooke, Walter, commission of, in Virginia State navy, 171.
Brooke, Walter T., letter from, 171.
Brooks, —— (Artist), 275.
Brooks, Charles (Reverend), 341.
Brooks, John (General), recommended, 714.
Brooks, Zachariah, letter from, 171.
Recommended, 601.
Broom, Jacob, application of, for collectorship at Wilmington, 171.
Letter from, 171.
Broom, John, letter from, 171.
Broome, (Alderman), 175.
Brougham, Henry (Lord), letter from, 171.
Broughton, Edward, letter from, 171.
Brouillet, ——, 351.
Brouillet, Michel, letter from, 171.
Brower, Garrett, letters from, 171.
Browere, Dolly Madison, 172.
Browere, J. H. J. (Mrs.), letter from, 172.
Browere, J. H. J., letters from, 171, 172.
Browere, ——, (Sculptor), 418.
Brown, ——, letter from, 172.
Brown, Ethan A., letter from, 172.
Brown, Harvey, introduced, 285.
Brown, J., letter from, 193.
Brown, Jacob, letter from, 173.
Brown, James, letters from, 172.
Retirement from public life, 172.
Brown, James T., letter from, 174.
Brown, John, 16.
Brown, John, and others, letter from, 173.
Brown, John, letter to, 9.
Brown, Liberty, letter from, 471.
Brown, Obediah B., letter from, 173.
Brown, William, arrest, 684.
Claim of United States against, 280.
Sale of estate, 280.
Browne, William, letter from, 174.
Brownstown and Detroit, treaties, 201.
Brudick, William, 605.
Brunt, Jonathan, letter from, 174.
Brussells, inauguration of the King at, 294.
Bryan, Joseph, letter from, 174.
Bryce, John, letter from, 174.
Bryson, James, letter from, 174.
Buchanan, —— (Dr.), 428.
Buchanan, J. A., letter from, 174.
Buchanan, William (commercial agent), 626.
Buck, Anthony, 261.
Buck, Daniel, letters from, 174.
Buckley, H., 665.
Buckminster's sermons, merits, 216.
Buel, Samuel, vindication, 175.
Letters from, 174, 175.
Redress for injustice to, and others, r 174, 175.
Buenos Ayres, independence, 84, 85.
Pistols manufactured at, 331.
Recognition, 536.
Revolution in, 329.
Buffalo, destruction, 678.
Buffon, theory of, on the heat of the glo
Works of, 36.
Buffon's theory of central heat, 35.
Buford, T., accounts of, 141.
Building for public offices, offer for sale
Bull, Epaphras, letter from, 175.
Bullett, Thomas, claim of heirs, 443.
Bullock, A. S., letter from, 175.
Bullus, John, letter from, 175.
Bumpass, Gabriel, letter from, 175.
Bunker Hill and Quebec, prints, 440.
Bunker Hill Monument Association, 24,
Bunn, James Madison, introduced, 488.
Burgoyne's defeat, 66.
Burke, John, 383.
Disposition of property, 171.
Information wanted, 175.
Burke, R., Letter from, 175.
Burke, Thomas, letter from, 175.
Letter to, 171.
Burke, Thomas (Mrs.), letter to, 175.
Burn, James Madison, 175.
Burn, James, letters from, 175.
Burnet, Daniel, letters from, 175, 176.
Burnett, Isaac Cox, letter from, 176.
Soliciting consulate at Lisbon, 176.
Application for consulship for, 251.
Burnley, Hardin, letters from, 176,
Burnley, Reuben, Government emplo quested for, 448.
Burr, conspiracy, 9.
Burr, Aaron, and Blennerhassett, move
And confederates, 356.
Acquittal, 603.
Attempt to vilify those he can not co
Defeat of plans, 481.
Designs of, speculations as to, 231.
Doubts as to the Republicanism of,
Enlistments, 406.
Motives of, in England, 578.
Nomination of, as President, 498.
Petition in behalf, 162.
Probable election of, by the States,
Projects of, to divide the United tween France and England not disliked by France or 151.
Real object and conduct, 680.
Treason, 32, 230, 231.
Trial, 325, 406, 603, 659.
Wilkinson the accuser of, 231.
Burrall, Charles, request of, to be retain master, 176.
Letters from, 176.
Postmaster, 413.
Burrill, James, introduced, 284.
Burtchett, William, application of, for o
Letter from, 176.
Burwell, Benjamin P., 551.
Burwell, William A., 484.
Letters from, 176, 177.
Bushby, William, letter from, 177.
Painter on public buildings, 177.
Busts and statues, National Gallery, 17
Butler, Anthony (Captain), 601.
Butler, —— (Colonel), 347.
Butler, Mann, introduced, 173.
Letter from, 177.
to, 9
Butler, Maria, appeal of, for assistance,
Butler, Pierce, letters from, 177, 178.
Letter to, 342.
Butler, Richard (General), appeal of wi assistance, 177.
Butler, R., letter to, 212.
Bynkershock's work, 276.
Byrne, James, letter from, 178.

C.

Cabaret, ——. letter from, 178.
Cabbage. new variety, 714.
Cabell (Doctor), death, 637.
Cabell, James C., 213, 687.
Claim, 86.
Letters from, 179-182.
to, 9-11.
Cabell, William H. (Governor), letter to, 406.
Cabinet, disinclination of Madison to position in the, 60.
Vacancy to be filled in the, 238, 239.
Cabinet of St. Cloud, book entitled, 165.
Cabot, George (Secretary of the Navy), 398
Cabot, Samuel, letter from, 182.
Salary, 182.
Cadena, Mariano V. de la, 182.
Cadets of the Military Academy, qualifications and course of study of the, 238.
Cadiz, combined force at, 92.
Cadwalader, Thomas, letters from, 182, 183.
Caermarthen, Marquis of, refusal of, to Mr. Adams's demand for the ports, 335.
Caffarena, Edward, letter from, 183.
Caines, Clem., letter from, 183.
Caldwell, ——, appointment, 629.
Caldwell, Charles, letters from, 183.
Letters to, 11.
Caldwell, James, letter from, 183.
Caldwell, Timothy, letter from, 183.
Calhoun, Hugh, introduced, 272.
Calhoun, John C., 11.
Attack on, 117.
Introduced, 591.
Letter from, 183.
Letters to, 446, 488.
Recommendation from, 225.
Callender, E., letters from, 183, 184.
Callender, James T., employment solicited by, 184.
Implacability, 81.
Letters from, 184.
Letter to, 628.
Remittance of fine, 535.
Calliopean Society, 737.
Callis, W. O., claims, 184.
Letters from, 184, 185.
"Callo Reports," 556.
Calves, present of, to Mrs. Madison, 565.
Calvin, A., letter from, 185.
Camara, José Manuel da, 135.
Cambreling, C. C., letter from, 185.
Letter to, 11.
Cambridge, Duke of, letters to, 435, 436.
"Camillo," poem by Botta, 164.
Campaign of 1814, history of, 140.
Campbell, Arthur, as superintendent of Indian affairs, 647.
Letters from, 185, 186.
Campbell & Britton, letter to, 271.
Campbell, G. W., letters from, 186.
Letter to, 11.
Recommendation, 137.
Campbell, Hugh G., letter from, 186.
Campbell, James, letter from, 186.
Campbell, John, letter from, 187.
Campbell, J. H., letter from, 186, 187.
Campbell, John K., request for appointment of, as district attorney, 288.
Campbell, William (General), letter from, 187.
Recommended, 641.
Sword voted for, by Virginia, 81, 118, 690.
Camps and intrenchments, 278.
Cambridge, riot in, 714.
Canada, acquisition, 492.
American citizens naturalized in, 158.
Annexation, 237.
British force in, 306.
Campaign in, 21, 51, 171.
Descent from, 91.
Description, 676.
Independence, 276.
Invasion, 50, 51, 186, 263, 483, 643, 676.
Military state, 182.
Not wanted by the United States, 108.
Possession, of no use to Great Britain in case of war, 85.
Proposed prohibition of exports or imports, 479.
Canal, contemplated, between the Hudson River and Great Lakes, 175, 519.
Canals, 62.
and agriculture, 128.
and roads, 536.
History, 633, 634.
Improvement in, 164.
New York, 104.
Treaties on, 127.
Canby, J. T., 140.
Letter from, 187.
Canby, William, letter from, 187.
Canning, George (Right Hon.), letter to, 435.
Canning, Stratford (Sir) (British minister), mysterious and ominous reserve, 86.
Unprincipled rascality, 410.
Cannon mounting, new construction, 271.
Cannon ball and swivel shot, historic, 271.
Cannon ball, papers to be deposited in a, to be thrown overboard, 513.
Cannon balls fired by British at Fort Moultrie, 143.
Cannon, Roquier, letter from, 187.
Capellano, Antonio, letter to, 11.
Cape of Good Hope, consul at, 151.
Capital and labor, 12.
Capital punishment, bill on subject, 642.
Views on, 19.
Capitol, funds required for finishing, 452.
Plan of middle part of, 406.
the, in Virginia, 381.
Temporary roofing of, 524.
and President's house, progress of building the, 724.
Captains, promotion of masters commandant to, 429.
Captured property while in military service, provision for, 240.
Captures and recaptures, code for, 99.
Epochs to limit, 101.
of vessels before and after signature of a treaty, 418.
Caracas, distressed inhabitants of, 462.
Carbery, H. (General), 615.
Introduced, 658, 659.
Letter from, and James Taylor, 187.
Settlement of a difficulty between, and James Taylor, 187, 659.
Carbery, Thomas, letter from, 187.
Cardell, W. S., letters from, 187.
Letters to, 12.
Cardelli, Peter, 2, 63.
Busts by, 187, 188.
Letters from, 187, 188.
Letter to, 12.
Recommendation of, 484.
Carey, John, letters from, 188.
Carey, Mathew, letters from, 188, 189, 190, 191.
Letters to, 12.
Carlisle College, 219.
Carleton, Guy (Sir), 34, 477.
Impatience of, for discharge of prisoners, 100.
Orders of, for evacuation of New York, 102.
Carleton, Moses, introduced, 333.
Carlton, Moses, jr., letter from, 191.
Carmichael, William, Jefferson's estimate of, 383.
Carpenter, Thomas, letter from, 191.
Carpentier, Denis, 622.
Proces verbal of, 191.
Carr, Dabney (Judge), 181.
Letters from, 191.
Qualifications of, 178.
Carr, Frank, letters from, 191.
Carr, M., letters from, 191.
Carr, Peter, 497.
Application of, for money due, 475.
Board and tuition, 474.
Letters from, 191, 192.
Carr, Samuel J., letter from, 192.
Carrère before the revolutionary tribunal, 531.
Carriage, purchase of a, 155.
Carriage wheels and gun carriages, 592.
Carriage tax, the, 42, 96, 724.
Carrington, Edward, 195.
Accepts office of supervisor, 196.
Letters from, 192-196.
Seat of, in House of Delegates, 254.
Solicitation of, for office, 194.
Carrington, Paul, jr., letters from, 196.

Carroll, Charles, of Carrollton, 198, 341.
Carroll, Daniel, 348.
    Claim, 239.
    Demolition of house, 197, 198.
    Exorbitant expectations, 198.
    Letters from, 196–199.
    Slanders against, 198.
Carroll, Henry, appointment as register and receiver solicited by, 199.
    Letter from, 199.
Carroll, James, and others, letter from, 199.
Carroll, James Cramsie, letter from, 199.
Carroll, John (Bishop), letter from, 199.
Carrying trade of the world, England's monopoly of, 723.
Carswell, Samuel, declining appointment of, as commissary-general, 200, 272.
    Letters from, 200.
Carter, Charles, letter from, 200.
    Sons of, 200.
Carter, C. H., letter from, 200.
Carter, Landon, letters from, 200.
Carthagena, South America, petition of prisoners at, 357.
Cartwright, John, letter from, 200.
    Letter to, 12.
Carver, Jonathan, 570.
Carver's land in Northwest Territory, 270.
Casa Calvo, Marquis de, 207, 404.
Cass, Lewis, appointment of, to command in Michigan and upper Canada, 301, 302.
    Letter from, 201.
Castine, post at, 248.
Cathalan, Stephen, 366.
    Letters from, 201.
Catalano, ——, 322.
Cathcart, James Leander, 212.
    Application of, for office, 202.
    Claim, 202.
    Letters from, 201, 202.
    Letters to, 12, 13, 415, 517, 602.
    Proposition of, to change consulates, 201.
    Recommended, 417.
    Services, 12, 134, 202.
Catholics, disabilities of, 512.
Catlin, Guy, recommended, 61.
    Commissioner, 694.
Cattle, new breeds, 26.
Causten, James H., 300, 540.
    Letters from, 202.
Cazenove, A. C., letters from, 202, 203.
    Letter to, 13.
Cazenove, Theophile, letter from, 203.
Census of Virginia, 195, 196.
    Details of the third, 632.
Central College, appointment of Madison as visitor at, 556.
    Commissions for visitors of, 414.
    Subscriptions for, 178, 336, 503.
    Titles of land purchased for, 310.
Century sermon, the, 216.
Ceracchi, importunities of, 118.
Cerneau, Joseph, 674.
Certificat d'origine, 438.
Cervallas, Don Pedro, 574, 575.
    Letter to, 575.
Cessions of territories of States, 35, 529, 578.
Chace, J. T., 279.
Chalamet, Charles, letters from, 203.
    Tribute in verse to Madison by, 203.
Chamberlain, James, letter from, 203.
Chamberlin, William A., letter from, 203.
Chambers, B. L., letter from, 203.
Champlin, John, introduced, 678.
Chancery suit, 13, 241.
Chandler, John B., letter from, 203.
Chantilly, purchase of, 80.
Chapman, —— (British officer), introduced, 454.
Chapman (Captain) and G. Ralston, letter from, 203.
Chapman, C. T., letter from, 204.
Chapman, Jeremiah, 605.
Chapman, N., letter from, 204.
Chapman, Reynolds, letters to, 13.
Chariot, price of a, 559.
    Purchase of a, 72, 567.
Charles IV, of Spain, abdication of, 299, 326.
Charleston, S. C., citizens of, approval of declaration of war and promise support, 98, 311, 469.
    Defenseless state, 312, 470.
    Evacuation, 99.
    Exports from, 296.
    Politics in, 80.
    Privateers fitted out at, 370.
    Republican society, 271.
    Revenue department of, irregularities in, 361.
    Surrender of, predicted, 350.
    Volunteers at, 469.
Charlton, Thomas B. (Judge), 302.
    Letter from, 204.
Charlton, Thomas U. P., letter from, 204.
    Letter to, 13.
Chase, Dudley, letter from, 20 4.
Chase, Samuel (Judge), acquittal, 119.
Chastellux, F. J. (Marquis de), literary intentions of, respecting the United States, 496.
    Travels of, in America, 8, 166, 167.
Chatham (Lord), speech, 392.
Chattahoochee, fort on the, 18.
Chaumont, Le Ray de, 204.
Chauncey, Isaac (Commodore), 3, 425, 428, 625.
    Declining seat at navy board, 204, 243.
    Gratuity to boatmen of barge, 243.
    Instructions to, 243, 426, 428.
    Letters from, 204.
    Letters to, 426, 429.
Chazotte, P. S., letters from, 204.
    Letter to, 13.
Cheat (deteriorated wheat), 96.
Cheese, mammoth, 736.
Cheever, William D., introduced, 678.
Chemistry, importance of knowledge of, 219.
Cheques, canceled, 13.
Cheriot, Henry, letter from, 204.
Cherokee and Chickasaw lands, intruders on, 624.
Cherokee Nation, appeal in behalf of the, 311.
Cherokee treaty, 204.
Cherokees, asking consent of, to cede lands, 262.
    Breaking of the treaty with, 640.
        cause of the, 130.
    Cession of land of, to Tennessee, 262.
    Chickasaws, etc., treaties with, 334.
    Good behavior of, 640.
    Treaty of 1807 with, 281.
Chesapeake, outrage on the, 1, 5, 55, 174, 232, 244, 261, 432, 460.
    Trial of officers of the, 427.
    and *Shannon*, action of the, 425.
Chesapeake and Delaware canal, 320.
Chesapeake Bay, defenses, 51, 152, 413.
    Navigation and jurisdiction, 503.
Chess, Phillidor's game of, publication, 672.
Chestnuts, planting, 224.
Chevallié, ——, claim of, on Virginia, 205.
    Letter from, 205.
Cheves, Langdon, letters from, 205.
Chew, John, letters from, 206.
    Letters to, 13.
Chew, Joseph, 66.
    Death, 206.
    Entry of land by, 217.
    Letters from, 205.
    Letter to, 422.
    Power of attorney from, 715.
Chickamauga, cession of land at the mouth of, 281.
Chickasaws, conference with, 206.
    Treaty with, 596.
Chief magistrate, title of the, 458.
China and India vessels, warnings to, 685.
China and Virginia, commerce between, 334.
China, intercourse with, 736.
Chinch bug, 108.
Chinese language, elementary characters of, 562.
Chisholm, Hugh, letters from, 206.
Choctaw chiefs, visit of, 290.
Choctaw Indians and negroes, destruction of fort occupied by, 212.
Choctaw Indians, commissioner to treat with, 104.
    Supplying, with cotton gin, 239.
    Trading post with, 261.
    Treaty with, 596.
Choiseul, Duc de, and Baron de Kalb, correspondence, 635.

Cholera, imprudence in eating cause of, 637.
Chouteau, Pierre, letter from, 206.
Christian religion, attempt of the Constitutionnel to subvert the, 277.
Bill establishing the, 77, 245.
Remonstrance against bill establishing, 696.
Christianity, tax to support, remonstrance to the bill to, 552.
Christian Visitant, 632.
Christie, —— (Captain), recommending, 727.
Christie, Gabriel, appointment of son of, as consul, 206.
Letters from, 206, 207.
Chrystie, John (Major), 306.
Recommendation, 307.
Church, Protestant Episcopal, bill for establishment of the, 245.
Churchman, George, letter from, 207.
Churchman, John, introduced, 629.
Cincinnati, the Society of the, 353, 392.
Cipher for correspondence between Madison and Monroe, 527.
Jefferson's, 383.
Circular car, invention of a, 340.
Circulating medium, plan of reform of the, 729.
Citizen law, motion for modifying the, 398.
Civil engineer for State of Virginia required, 556.
Civita Vecchia open to American commerce, 334.
Claiborne, Ferdinand L., letter from, 207.
Letter to, 13.
Qualifications, 210.
Claiborne, W. C. C., allowance to, 403, 404.
Death of wife and daughter, 208.
Death of second wife, 210.
Difficulties and embarrassments, 207.
Letters from, 207-211.
Letters to, 13, 14, 261, 670.
Livingston's attacks on, 249.
Marriage, 209.
Plan of, for laying off parishes, 681.
Request of, for reappointment, 210.
Claims and accounts of States, settlement, 78.
Claims on British and Spanish Governments, 303.
Clarke, ——, vindication of, against a calumny by "Americanus," 430.
Clark, Abraham, introducing, 678.
Letter from, 211.
Clark, Bushrod W., and Parks, G. D. A., letter from, 211.
Clark, Daniel, attempts of, to injure Claiborne, 208.
Enmity of, to the Government, 209.
Letter from, 211.
Speculations, 209.
Clark, G. R. (General) appointment of, by French Government, 654.
Movements of, on the Ohio River, 724.
Clarke, James, and others, letter from, 211.
Clark, John, letter from, 211.
Clarke, John, introduced, 734.
Letter from, 211.
Clarke, Jonathan (General) 362.
Clarke, —— (Major), introduced, 462.
Clark, Thomas, letter from, 212.
Petition, 607.
Clark, Thomas D., letters from, 212.
Clarke, William, intended expedition, 654.
Clarkson, Crolius, letter to, 14.
C——k, G., letters from, 211.
Letters to, 14.
Clason, J., letter from, 212.
Seizure by British of the property of, 212.
Clay, ——, question as to, for consul at Lisbon, 401.
Recommending, as naval officer, 306.
Clay, Henry, 146, 243.
Letters to, 14.
Opposition to, 238.
Renomination of, as President, 339.
Views of, on the tariff, 14.
Visit to, 513.
Clearance bill, the, 319.
Cleland, James, letter from, 212.
Clergy, bill in the Virginia legislature respecting the, 552.
Unwarranted opposition of the Northern, to the President's course, 294.
Clergyman, prosecution of a, for defamation against Jefferson, 407, 408.
Clerical misdemeanors, 102.
Climate of Atlantic Coast, 178.
Influences of, on the human race, 183.
Clinch, D. L., letter from, 212.
Clinton, De Witt, arts and intrigues of the faction of, 491.
Letters from, 212.
Memorial, 638.
Clinton, George, candidate for Vice-President (1792), 255.
Declaration of, as to the stability of the Union, 343.
Election as governor, 530.
Leader of the opposition, 343.
Letter from, 212.
Unfitness for office of President, 474.
Clintonians, partisanship of the, 474.
Clintonism, to establish, on the basis of anti-federalism, 343.
Overthrow, 500.
Clinton party, coalition of the Federalists with the, 315.
Cloth, American, students at New Jersey College dress in, 65.
Clothes, tailors' bill for, 191.
Clothing for the Army, 513.
British prisoners, seizure, 100.
Cloupet and contraband negroes, case, 403.
Clover, salivation in second crop of, causes 513.
seed, 166.
Clowes, Timo, letter to, 14.
Clymer, George, 16.
Letter to, 151.
Coaches, oversetting, 663.
Coal, shipments, 358.
Coalter, John, letters from, 212.
Coast defenses, 348, 482.
survey, by F. R. Hassler, 353.
Coasting and colony trade, 703.
Cobb, Matthew, letter from, 212.
Cobb, Thomas W., letter from, 213.
Cochrane, Sir A. F. I. (Admiral), proclamation of, exciting blacks to revolt, 427, 621.
Cochran, William E. (Dr.), character, 172.
Letter from, 213.
Cock, ——, appointment of, to agency at Martinique, 167.
Cockade, 350.
Cockburn, Sir George (Admiral), 234, 302, 621.
Cocke, John H., letters from, 213, 214.
Letters to, 14.
Cocke, William, impeachment, 214.
Letters from, 214.
Cocky, W., 287.
Code of Virginia, revised, 7.
Coffee and sugar, seizure, 701.
Coffee, W. J. (Sculptor), 415.
Letters from, 214.
Coffey, William A., letter from, 214.
Coffin, Alexander, jr., letter from, 214.
Coffin, Isaac (Sir), 566.
Letters from, 214, 215.
Coffin, Jared, letter from, 215.
Coghill, John, letter from, 215.
Cogswell, —— (Major), introduced, 476.
Cogswell, Nathaniel, letter from, 215.
Cogswell, William, letter from, 215.
Letters to, 15.
Coin, conversion of foreign, into national, 696.
Impression on, 460.
Intrinsic value, 696.
Mexican, 567.
Spanish, 696.
Coins of foreign nations, standards, weights, and values, 344.
Coke-Devon calves, 565.
Colburn, —— (Judge), 659.
Character and popularity, 660.
Colden, ——, 38.
Colder, Joseph, letter from, 215.
Coleman, Ambrose, letter from, 215.
Coleman, Chapman, introduced, 662.
Coleman, John I., letter from, 215.
Coleman, Samuel, appeal by, for office, 216.
Letters from, 215, 216.
Coleman, William, 686.
Letters from, 216.

Coles, Edward, 243, 601.
And Betsey, letters to, 609.
Letters to, 15.
Letters from, 354.
Coles, Isaac, letter to, 358.
Coles, Thomas, 722.
Coles, Walter (Lieutenant), wish of, to be appointed captain, 317.
Coles, William E., letter to, 295.
Collectors, appointments, 302.
Certificates of, 704.
Commissions for, 303.
Letters to, 306.
Profits of offices, 166.
Sureties for, 251.
College at Lexington, Ky., 155.
Establishment of a, in Washington, 642.
Female, 572.
Collier, James (Colonel), 682.
Collier, Thomas, 372.
Collins, Charles, introduced, 283.
Letter from, 216.
Collins, William, introduced, 611.
Coleman, Henry, application of, for office, 524.
Letter from, 216.
to, 15.
Colombia, Republic of, agent for the, 675.
Colonial commerce, England's system, 481.
Resentment of powers to, 481.
Restraint of the, 701.
Colonial government, proposed, 726.
Relations, reestablishment, 111.
Colonies, rights, 166.
Colonization of free negroes, 643.
people of color, 120.
society, 26, 30.
Colonna (Colonel), 181.
Columbia, District of, military events in, 11.
Columbia, S. C., citizens, 19, 241.
College, 27.
Columbia, District of, Territory of, and city of Washington, 197.
Columbian Chemical Society, 245.
Horticultural Society, 715.
Columbine, dispatch vessel, 167.
"Columbus" a pamphlet, 216.
Colvin, J. B., letters from, 215, 216, 217.
Solicitation of, for office, 217.
Comanche Indians, 376.
Comegys, Cornelius, letter to, 15.
Comet, orbit of the, 264.
Commerce, deplorable state of (1783), 35.
Extension, 53.
Exclusion, 32.
Freedom of external, 33.
Hostilities on our, 100.
Machinations of Great Britain on our, 36.
Reciprocity in, 381.
Stagnation, 400.
With Great Britain, 38, 107.
Commerce and manufactures, effect of wars and policy of other nations on, 64.
Commerce, capture of the, by the Russians, 327.
Commercial discontents, 77.
propositions, 123.
rights, British violation, 256.
system, a general, 196.
Commissioner of claims, certificates, 349.
of public buildings, interference of the, with architects, 453.
Commissions, brevets, 249.
Committee on agriculture, report of the, 310.
of citizens, dinner to J. M. Patton, 15.
of defense, communications to the, inculpating the governor and General Government, 234.
"Common defense and general welfare," 112.
"Common sense," author, 123.
Commonwealth Bank, 297.
Commutation of sentences of slaves convicted of murder, 546.
Compensation and claims law, 52, 376.
to soldiers, 719.
Comyn, ——, functions of consuls, by, 217.
Comtz, John, letter from, 217.
Conciliation, symptoms (1809), 434.
"Conciliator," 217.
Notes by, on the West India colonies, 438.
Pamphlets by, 432.
Condict, Lewis, letters from, 217.
Condorcet, murder of, in Paris, 255.
Condy, William, oration, 483.
Confederacies, ancient and modern, 16.
Three, doctrine, 488.
Confederacy made up of part of the United States and Spanish territories, 231.
Confederation, proposed change of the ninth article of the, 77.
Revision of the, 464.
Confiscated States, restitution, 99.
Confiscation of American captures, 708.
Congress, act of, the right of a State to arrest the execution of an, 115.
Apathy (1780), 711, 712.
Assembling of, at New York, 126.
Cautions to, respecting compensations for faithful services, 712.
Constructive power of each house, 369.
Continental, resolutions, 217.
Controlling power, 711.
Eastern Members of, policy of conciliation with, 177.
False charge of appropriations by, for division among Members, 374.
Houses of, and public offices, accommodations for (1814), 429.
Letter to, 161.
Members of, compensation for, 79.
Credulity, 409.
Failure to pay, during recess, 520.
Proposed method of choosing, 221.
Of nations for the amicable adjustment of national disputes, 86, 722.
Powers of, regulating trade, commerce, manufactures, and tariff, 9, 20, 26, 104, 225, 527, 529.
Proposed continuation of session (1810), 177.
Public sentiment against, 342.
Question of residence, 34, 67, 69, 101, 227, 380, 527, 529.
Regulation of our commerce by, 381, 382.
Removal of, to Philadelphia, 722.
Requisitions of, on the States, 93, 334.
Sectional legislation, 459.
Slowness of business in (1789), 103.
Suggesting a recess (1812), 237.
Trade regulated by, 77.
Unconstitutional course of, power of the President in checking, 58.
Vacillations and indolence, 350.
Work on the debates and proceedings, 302.
Congress, frigate, 19.
Congressional committee concerning Lieutenant-Colonel Laurens's report, 217.
Treaty of peace with United Provinces, 16.
Congressional privileges, 22, 25.
Congreve Rockets, 219, 371.
Conkling, Frederick (Captain), recommended, 317.
Connecticut, adoption of the Constitution in, 124.
Cession of lands, 335.
Legislature, letter from, 218.
Legislature of, disapproval of the, of the war and refusing the requisition of the General Government for militia, 68, 340, 364.
Organization of volunteers, 366.
Senators, 126.
Connor, Charles (Captain), claim, 582.
Letter from, 218.
Revolutionary services, 218.
Connor, Samuel S., recommended, 664.
Conover, Samuel F., letter from, soliciting office of treasurer of the mint, 218, 735.
Conspiracy, Blount and Siston's, 44.
Constable, William, letter from, 218.
Constantinople, burning, 99.
Constellation, frigate, duel between officers of the, 490.
Constitution, new French, 386.
of Virginia, 173.
Constitution of the United States.
Adoption of, conjectures as to, 322.
by Massachusetts, 444.
New Hampshire, 444, 449.
North Carolina, 176.
Virginia, 176, 221.
Amendments to the, 3, 16, 24, 31, 32, 94, 120, 227, 339, 343, 465.
Approval of the, by friends of America in England, 226.

Constitution of the United States—Continued.
As reported by committee of revision. 218.
Convention in Virginia on subject of the, 646.
Convention to adopt, 36, 37, 68.
Convention for forming a, at Philadelphia, 529.
Distinction between the authority of the, and public opinion, 115.
Formation of the, 30, 33.
Forms us into one State, 118.
Hamilton's plan of a, 49, 505.
History of the, 601.
Interpretation of the, 367.
Jefferson's approvals and disapprovals of the, 384, 385.
Merits and objections to the, 488.
Misrepresentations respecting the framers of the, 197.
Nonadoption of the, eventual disunion and civil war, 343.
Objections to the, 343, 472.
Origin of the, 15.
Preamble to the, by Jefferson, 130.
Printed, with notes and emendations by Madison, 218.
Probable adoption of the, 647.
Ratification of the, 69.
Reservation of rights to recede from the, 343.
Signers of the, 577.
Sitting of the convention for adopting, 37.
States aquiescing in the, 226.
The proposed, 93.
Washington's views on the, 25.
Constitution, capture and destruction of the *Java* by the, 424.
Constitution, frigate, cane cut from the, 286.
Constitutional drafts, 16.
reforms, 106.
"Constitutionel," the, 277.
Consul, England sends a (1785), 381.
Consular accounts, 16.
Consuls, emoluments, 436.
Foreign, exactions, 703.
Functions, 217.
Gratuity to, 164.
Requirements proposed for, 344.
Rights and powers, 164.
Settlement of accounts, 574.
Contee, Benjamin, friendship of, for Madison, 218.
Letter from, 218.
Contempt, power of House of Representatives to punish for, 356.
Continental currency, 584.
engagements, discharge, 99.
paper money, redress from depreciation, 350.
money, speculators in, of Virginia's quota, 380.
"Contracts," the term, in the Constitution, 116.
Convention, Federal (1787), 1, 2, 16, 60.
Acts of the, 505.
Assembling of the (1787), 68.
Copy of proceedings of the, 212.
Election of Virginia representatives to the, 123.
For forming Government (1787), 192.
Foreign opinions respecting the (1787), 618.
Origin of the, 112.
Proceedings of the, materials for publication, 104.
Proceedings of the Virginia legislature on subject of a (1788), 193.
Project of another (1788), 117, 221.
Publication of notes of the, 27, 46.
Conventions of States, debates in, 25.
For ratification of the Constitution, 93.
On the Constitution of the United States, 22.
Converse, Sherman, letter from, 218.
Conway, ——, appointment of, to the land office in Alabama, 539.
Cook, French, complaint of a, 270.
Cook, Orchard, soliciting collectorship of Newburyport, 218.
Letters from, 218, 219.
Cooke, A., letter from, 219.
Cooke, James, letter from, 219.
Cookery book, 592.
Cooley, Ebenezer, bill for relief, 217.
Claim, 219.
Cooley, Ebenezer, letter from, 219.
to, 217.
Cooledge, D., letter from, 219.
Coolidge, E. (Mrs.), letter to, 16.
Coolidge, Joseph R., letter to, 16.
Coombs, Griffith, letter from, 219.
Cooper, Thomas, 75, 694.
Advice to, to accept professorship at West Point, 286.
Application of for office, 220, 247.
Election of, as president of South Carolina College, 220.
Intended practice of law by, 220.
Letters from, 219, 220.
to, 17, 247, 286.
Qualifications, 53.
Question as to offering a place in the University of Virginia, 417.
Removal from his situation as judge, 219.
Cooper, Thomas (Dr.), unpopularity of, 178.
Cooper, John, letter from, 219.
Cooper, R., suit against, 303.
Cooper, William, letters from, 220.
Copeland, E., jr., letters from, 220.
Copper, discovery of, on shores of Lake Superior, 487.
Coppinger, Joseph, inventions of, 221.
Letters from, 220, 221.
Recommendation of, 273.
Corbin, Francis, appointment of, as director in bank, 205.
Director of United States branch bank at Richmond, 223.
Dislike of, to slavery, 221.
Ill health, 223.
Letters from, 221, 222, 223, 224.
Offer of, to be an agent to England, 222.
Reasons for declining visit to Montpelier, 223.
Corbin, G. L. (Major), merits of, 222.
Corbin, Robert B., letter from, 224.
Solicitation by, for foreign appointment, 222.
Corly, Thomas M., letter from, 223.
Soliciting position in the Navy, 224.
Corn, destruction of, belonging to Indians, 662.
Cornick, James, letter from, 224.
Cornick, Lemuel, supposed revolutionary services, 224.
Cornwallis, approach of, 495.
Situation of, 92, 93.
Surrender of, 378.
Troops under, to sail for New York, 66.
Corprew, Elizabeth Reed, complaint of, 224.
Correa de Serra, José, 135.
Appointment as Portuguese minister, 224.
Arrival, 536.
Departure, 319.
Diplomatic transactions, 85.
Impolitic course, 107.
Interview with, 519.
Introduced, 150.
Letters from, 224.
Correspondence, confidential matter in, 65.
Cosby, ——, 676.
Cosmeaux, Lekeel, letter from, 224.
Cotton, American, consumption of, 232.
And cotton fabrics, 17.
And silk manufactures, 75.
At Barbados, 226.
Benefits of, to the United States, 226.
Cultivation, sale, and employment, 235.
Cultivation in Kentucky, 654.
Duties on, 148, 227.
East India, 235.
East India, in England, 232.
Export duty on, 578.
Fabrics, importation of, destructive to home industry 445.
Goods, prohibition of foreign, 230.
In England, 17.
Machine, invention of a, 208.
Manufacture, 232, 675.
Manufactures, 513.
Manufacturers, protection for, 235, 284, 445.
Mills, list of, and estimated cost, 224.
Planting in Virginia, 226.
Planting, profits of, 513.
Trade, 12.

Counterfeiting, prisoners on charge of, 423.
Countervailing act, the, 397.
Duties, 364.
Couper, John, 221.
Letter to, 273.
Coupland, William R., letters from, 225.
Court of admiralty, proceedings of the, 495.
Appeals, decisions of, on taxes, 254.
Chancery, establishment of a, 203.
County, reversal of a judgment of a, by Federal court, 145.
Martial, proceedings of the, respecting Sailing-master Hutton, 425.
Courts, circuit, vote in Virginia to establish, 67.
In Virginia, 76.
County, reform of the, 68, 77.
District, bill for establishing, 123.
Federal, modification of the, 120.
Covington, Leonard, letter from, 225.
Cowper, Jonah, 225
Cowper, Josiah, letters from, 225.
Cox, John, 7.
Letter from, 225.
to, 17.
Petition for appointment as superintendent of the Capitol, 225.
Coxe, Charles D., letter from, 225.
Petition to be appointed head of the Marine Corps, 225.
Coxe, Tench, 188, 396.
(Assistant Secretary of the Treasury), 228.
Character and merits, 150.
Collection of books of, 430.
Desire for office, 85, 227, 233, 234, 235, 236.
Letters from, 225, 226, 227, 228, 229, 230, 231, 232, 233, 234, 235, 236.
Letters to, 17, 18, 547.
Memoir by, 52.
Obligations of the Republican party to, 228.
Political career, 4.
Proposals to, to enter public life, 227.
Request for promotion of his son in the Navy, 235.
Services of, and neglect of the Government, 233.
Services offered by, with his four sons, 234.
Soliciting warrants for his two sons as midshipmen, 234, 235.
Withdrawal from list of representatives, 226.
Crabb, ——, introduced, 595.
Crack, Jehu, letter from, 236.
Craig, Elijah, letter from, 236.
Craig, James, introduced, 729.
Craik, James, claim of, for services, 236.
Letter from, 236.
Cramer, Thomas, letter from, 236.
Cranch, W., letters from, 236, 237.
Letter to, 18.
Crane, —— (Commander), promotion of, over senior officers resented, 472.
Crane, Gabriel, letters from, 237.
Crawford's cotton machine, 208.
Crawford, William, 580.
Letters from, 237.
Crawford, William H., 21, 316.
Letters from, 237, 238, 239, 240.
to, 18, 19, 168, 172, 371, 376, 518, 608, 641, 710.
Refutation of slanders by enemies of, 240.
Request of, to delay nomination as Secretary of the Treasury, 240.
Crazy letters, 174.
"Creation du Monde," by Becourt, 274.
Credit, our national, 384.
Public, plan for supporting, 195.
Creditor for unclaimed interest, 240.
Creek agency, appointment of the governor of Georgia to the, 239.
Condition of the, 355.
Creek and Cherokee Indians, goods to be distributed among the, 323.
Creek Indians, invasion of the, 616, 616.
Treaty with the, 281.
Creek Nation, present from the speaker of the, 203.
Creek treaty, boundaries and execution of the, 135.
Ratification of the, 692.
Creek war, closing of the, 210.
Cresson, Elliott, introduced, 541.
Letter to, 19.
Crevecœur, ——, introduced, 618.
Creyon, John M., letter from, 241.
Letter to, 19.
Crimes, bill for punishing certain, 41.
Criminals, surrender of, 102.
Crittenden, ——, desire of, for a military commission, 499.
Crittenden, J. J., letters from, 241.
Crockett, G. F. H., letter from, 241.
Letter to, 19.
Croghan, William, 298.
Letters from, 241.
to, 665.
Croker, ——, letter to, 19.
Crolius, Clarkson, letter from, 241.
Crooks, ——, (Brigadier-General), destruction of brigade, 720.
Complaints against, and his command, 720.
Crowninshield, B. W., accepting the office of Secretary of the Navy, 241.
Declining office of Secretary of the Navy, 241.
Letters from, 241, 242, 243, 244.
to, 19, 142, 204, 239, 550, 602, 641, 537.
Crowninshield, George, & Sons, letter to, 153.
Crowninshield, George, jr., letter from, 244.
Crowninshield, Jacob, letters from, 244.
Crowninshield, John (Captain), exchange of, 157.
Crozet, A., letter from, 244.
Crozet (Major), 593.
Cruger, Daniel, letter from, 244.
Cuba, attempt of England to obtain, 305.
Emigrants from, 442.
Entries and clearances of American vessels in, 605.
Napoleon's object regarding, 47.
Political situation, 605.
Culpeper County, dinner to Lafayette at, 622.
Road from, to Washington, 645.
Cumberland and Ohio road, construction of the, 270, 306.
Protest against change of the, 161.
Cummins, Ebenezer H., letter from, 244.
Cunningham's letters, 146.
Currow, John G., letter from, 244.
Currency, national, arguments to insure the establishment of a, 454.
Disorder of the, 250.
State of the (1816), 430.
Currey, ——, recommended, as consul at Fayal, 526.
Curwin, Joseph, 320.
Cushing, Caleb, letter to, 19.
Cushing, ——, (Colonel), timely arrival of, with a competent force, 682.
Cushing, William (Judge), 314.
Death of, 476.
Custis, George W. P., letters from, 244, 245.
Custom-house laws, evasion of, in case of ship *Easter*, 466.
Customs laws, amendments of, petitioned for, 696.
Revenues, 240.
Cutbush, James, letters from, 245.
Cutler, Jervis (Captain), 660.
Cutting, Dr., letter to, 19.
Cutting, John Brown, claim of, 245.
Letters from, 245.
Cutting, Nathaniel, application of, for office, 246.
Letters from, 245, 246.
Cutting, William, introduced, 477.
Cutts, ——, letters to, 20, 563.
Cutts, Richard, letters from, 246.
Letter to, 450.
Recommended, 316.
Cutts, Richard D., 494.
Letter to, 20.
Cutts, R. (Mrs.), letter to, 518.
Cuyanguerricosa, Indian chief, 368.
Cyane, prize ship, purchase of the, 242.
Czermicheff, Count, 151.

D.

Dabbs, Richard, letter from, 246.
Dabney, William, letter from, 246.
Dade, Francis, letter from, 246.

Dade, Laurence T., 418.
Appointment solicited by, 247.
Letters from, 246, 247.
And others, letter to, 20.
Dagepau, Chevalier, letter from, 247.
Daggett, David, 269.
Letter from, 247.
Dailey, William, letter to, 20.
Petition for pension by, 247.
Daingerfield, William (Dr.), introduced, 558.
Dairy farms, 97.
Stock, 584.
Dalbart, ——, (alias Jerome Bonaparte), 260.
Dalcho, Frederick, letter from, 247.
Dale, Richard, letter from, 247.
Letter to, 158.
Dale, R. C. (Captain), 604.
Resignation of, 604.
Dallam, William S., letter from, 247.
Dallas, A. J. 20.
Death of, 220, 369.
Letters from, 247, 248, 249, 250, 251.
to, 20, 21, 203, 220, 421, 486.
Resignation as Secretary of the Treasury, 250.
Dallas, George M., letter to, 21.
Dalton, Samuel, 543.
Assignment from, to James Madison, 320.
Dalton, Tristram (inspector of port), 251.
Letters from, 251.
to, 457.
Soliciting office of postmaster, 251.
Dana, Francis, 124.
(Minister to Russia), nonreception of, by the Empress 354.
Dana, Samuel, letter from, 251.
Danæ, arrival of the, 99.
Dandridge, Bart. letter to, 691.
Dangerfield, John, heirship of mother of, 251.
Letters from, 251.
"Danger not over," paper entitled, 181.
Daniel, Peter V., letter from, 251.
Danish claim, the, 260.
Declaration, the, 92.
Government, claims against the, 437.
Islands, consul-general for the, 407.
Subjects, claims of, 698.
Dartmoor prison, sufferings at the, 250.
Daschkoff, André de (Russian minister), arrival, 48.
Hostility, 250.
Dauphin, illness of the, 338.
Dauphin, John, widow of, 169.
Dauphine, —— (Mrs.), 240.
Davidson, John, and others, letter from, 251.
Davie, William R., letters from, 251.
Davies, Thomas, letters from, 251.
Davies, William, letter from, 252.
Daviess, Joseph, introduced, 555.
Daviess, J. H., 659, 683.
Letters from, 252.
Suit of, against Madison's heirs, 357.
Davis, Abijah, letter from, 252.
Davis, Edward E. letter from, 252
Davis, Eli Simpson, letter from, 252.
Davis, George, application of, for consulship of Algiers, 252.
Letters from, 252.
Recommended, as consul to Algiers, 478, 525.
Davis, Isaac, letter from, 252.
Davis, J. A. G., 275.
Letter from, 253.
to, 21.
Davis, M. L., introduced, 478.
Letters from, 252, 253.
to, 646.
Davis, T., 622.
Davis, William (collector), letter to, 466.
Davison, Moses, and others, letter to, 21.
Davizeau (Dr.), introduced, 628.
Davy, William, letter from, 253.
Dawes, Thomas, letter from, 253.
Dawson, John, application of, for office, 253, 254, 255, 260.
Letters from, 253, 254, 255, 256, 257, 258, 259, 260, 261.
Recommended, as commissioner for settling accounts, 530.
Dawson, Joshua, letters from, 261.
Dawson, Moses, letter from, 261.
Day, Benjamin, letters from, 261.
Dayton, George, letter from, 261.
Deaf and Dumb Asylum of Danville, 191.
Deakens, Francis (Colonel), map of Virginia by, 497.
Dearborn, Henry, application of, for military position, 262.
Appointment, 315.
Character, 127.
Collectorship, 263, 293.
Court of inquiry asked by, 264.
Defense, 265.
Disapproval, 471.
Intentions (1812), 291.
Letters from, 261, 262, 263, 264.
to, 21, 140, 169, 519, 691.
Naming his son for a military commission, 410.
Nomination as Secretary of War, 21.
Plan for a war establishment, 407.
Recommended, 314.
Retirement, 140.
Suspension of command, 264.
Dearborn, H. A. S., letters from, 264, 265.
Soliciting the office of collector, 264.
Death of three Presidents on July 4, 359.
Deblois, Lewis, letter to, 21.
Deblois, ——, charges against, 288.
Debt, British, 229.
Foreign, estimates of the, 385.
National, 88.
Extinguishment of the, 724.
Payment of interest on the, 386.
Plan for paying the, and interest, 389.
Propositions relative to the, 101.
Public, a curse, 58.
Duties on imports to pay the, 217.
Discrimination between original and assigned holders of the, 556.
Extinguishment of the, 199.
Hamilton's report on the, 41.
Debts of the United States to France, 344.
Debtors, fraudulent, act to punish, 642.
Means of relief of, 454.
Debts, ability to pay our, 434.
American-British, payment of interest on, 335.
British, 487.
Payment of, 221.
National and State, 582.
Payment of, property receivable for, 253.
Public, 100.
Plans for contracting and providing for, 38.
Public and State, 227.
State, against the Union, 528.
Assumption of, 195, 196.
State and Federal, conversion of, 379.
Debts of modern nations, 389.
Decanters, domestic, 161.
Decatur, Stephen (Commodore), 242.
Appointment, 241.
Instructions to, 241, 428.
Letter to, 428.
Declaration of Independence, 21.
Biography of the signers of the, 610.
Draft of, and author, 104.
Jefferson's original draft of the, 416.
Origin of the, 53.
Senator Pope's proposition to rescind the, 149.
Share of George Mason in the, 74.
The final vote on the, 561.
Declaration of rights, 503, 685, 696.
Declaration of war (1812), acquiescence of the people in, 683.
Advocating, 375.
Gratification at the, 375.
Decrees, repeal, 150, 151.
Dedham, history, 61.
Defense, means for, 4, 273, 292, 345, 369, 396, 434, 492, 723.
De Gray, Michael, letter from, 265.
Delacroix, Charles (French minister of foreign relations), letter from, 265.
Delacroix, —— (Colonel), appointment, 442.
De Lacy, John D., letter from, 265.
De la Motta, Jacob, letter from, 265.
Letter to, 21.

Delambre, ——, astronomical observations by, 285.
Delaplaine, Joseph, letters from, 265, 266.
Delavan, Edward C., 214.
Letter from, 266.
Delaware, alien act of, 266.
Disputed election in, 603.
District judge in, 154.
Disturbed political situation, 677.
Legal characters in, 154.
Delaware and Chesapeake canal, 29, 569, 631.
Delegates, no provision for subsistence, 66.
Delegates to Congress from Virginia, 68.
Delivet, Peter, letter from, 266.
De Lormerie, ——, 287.
Delozier, D., letter from, 266.
Delpeaux, ——, appeal of, a refugee from San Domingo, 266.
Democracy of the United States, history of the, 277.
Democratic societies, the President's denunciation (1795), 79.
Scheme to connect the, with the whisky rebellion, 79.
Democrats, denunciations of the, by the Monocrats, 393.
Demoralization of troops (1813), 720.
Denmark, King of, character of the, 437.
Denmark and Sweden, naval equipments of, 71.
Denmark and Norway, cruisers of, depredations on American trade by, 436.
Dent, John H., instructions to, to prohibit intercourse with the enemy, 426.
Letter from, 267.
to, 426.
Department of State, allowance to clerks in the, 167.
Construction of a fireproof vault in the, 451.
Departments, heads of, modes of communication between, and the President, 401.
Refusal to testify, 630.
Depeyster, Frederick, jr., letter from, 267.
Deposit, right of, 355.
Deposits, removal of the, 2, 15, 105.
Restoration of the, 81.
Deposits of public money, 305.
Deposits of the Treasury, War, and Navy Departments, 306.
Depot of arms, proposed, 554.
Depredations, British, 23.
Deputies, appointment in State courts, 734.
Derbigny, ——, 208, 209.
Derby, Richard C., letter from, 267.
Soliciting a foreign appointment, 267.
Derieux, P., employment solicited, 267.
Letters from, 267.
Residence at Greenbrier, 267.
Descent, law of, 229.
Desert, the, tract of land called, 267.
Deserters, British, 232, 239, 310.
Enlistment, 407.
Desertions, 96, 719.
Desertions from Long Island, 92.
Desfourneaux (General), letter from, 267.
Permission asked for passage to France in a Government vessel, 267.
Desgranges, F., letter from, 501.
Desire and volition, distinction between, 629.
Despotism, tendency to promotion, 230.
Destrihan, ——, introducing, 508.
Detrion, ——, 208.
Detroit, possession by the British, 133.
Probability of regaining, 51.
Surrender of the army and post at, 292.
Devereux, J., letter from, 267.
Dew, Thomas R., letter from, 268.
Letter to, 22.
Diamonds, story of the, contradicted, 329.
Dickens, Ashbury, Government employment solicited, 268.
Letters from, 268.
Dickens, ——, introduction of, by Baron von Humboldt, 365.
Dickinson College, 219.
Dickinson, John, 694.
Dickinson, Thomas, 694.
Dickinson, Thomas and John, 476.
Letter from, 268.
Dickson, William, letter from, 268.
Dictionary, Webster's, 716.
Digges, Cole, Government employment solicited, 268.
Letter from, 268.
Digges, Thomas A., depredations on farm of, 268.
Letters from, 268.
Diligence, brig, 455.
Diligent, French privateer, arrest of the captain of the, 330.
Dillehay, James Madison, 268.
Dillehay, Thomas Jefferson, 268.
Dillehay, Th. L., letter from, 268.
Dillingham, James, letter from, 269.
Dillon, Robert J., letter from, 269.
Dinmore, R., letter from, 269.
Dinner of American products, 119.
Dinsmore, James, letters from, 269.
Dinsmore, R., letter from, 487.
Dinsmore, Silas, 230.
Diplomatic missions, policy and practice, 25.
Diplommatie Française, 19.
Discharges of enlisted men, 248.
Discontent and insubordination in Europe, 294.
Dislocations, cold bathing for, 611.
Dismal Swamp, project of a canal at, 227.
Dismemberment of States, objection to, 528.
Dismemberment of the Union, design of the Eastern States for the, 529.
Dismissals of good officers, 161.
Disputes, national, decision by arbitration, 607.
Disqualifying act, the, 193, 194.
Dissensions, State, 136.
Dissolution of the Union, 188.
Distilleries, tax on, 89.
Distillers, protests, 654.
District of Columbia, a university in, recommended, 110.
Draft of an ordinance for the government of the, 464.
The power of Congress to cede back the, to Maryland, 237.
Disunion, consequences, 100.
Dividends, unclaimed, to credit of Madison's father, 558.
Dixon, Henry St. John, letter from, 269.
Dixon, John, estate, 269.
Dixon, Thomas, appeal for assistance, 269.
Letter from, 269.
Dixon ——, appointment to office, 555.
Dobbyns, ——, introduced, 385.
Dobell, Peter, application for consulate at Bordeaux, 684.
Doctors, list of, in the Army, 708.
Dodge, Joshua, 157.
Dodge & Oxnard, letter from, 269.
Doddridge, Philip, 24.
Letter from, 269.
Letter to, 22.
Dogs, shepherd, 411.
Dohrman, A. H., letter from, 269.
Domestic industry, encouragement of, 138.
Domestic manufactures, powers of Congress to encourage, 540.
Donaldson (Major), relations between, and President Jackson, 663.
Donaldson, Thorburn & Co., letter from, 269.
Doolittle, J., letter from, 269.
Doolittle, ——, 278.
Dorsey, Benedict letter from, 270.
Dorsey, J., letter from, 270.
Dorsey, John Syng (Dr.), 571.
Dorsey, W. H., letter from, 442.
Dougherty, Joseph, 629.
Letters from, 270.
Proposed remittance of fine on, 169.
Dougherty, Mrs., letter to, 22.
Dover Baptist Association, 670.
Dox, Gerret L. (Postmaster), 244.
Letter from, 270.
Soliciting office of postmaster, 270.
Doyhan, H. S., letter from, 270.
D'Oyley, Daniel, letter from, 270.
Drafting of militia, complaints against, 737.
Drake, Benjamin, letter from, 270.
Drake, Daniel (Dr.), 518.
Letter to, 22.
Draper, Lyman C., letter from, 270.

Drawback on consignments, 508.
Drawback provision, 231.
Drayton, John, application for office of district judge, 271.
Appointment as district judge, 271.
Letters from, 270, 271.
Letter to, 22, 143.
Drayton, S., letter from, 271.
Drought in Virginia, 49, 648.
Drumegole, —— (Major), application in behalf of Cherokee Indians, 311.
Dry Tortugas and Florida Reefs, Gould's survey, 284.
Duane, James, 16.
Introduced, 272.
Letter from, 271.
Duane, William, attacks on Gallatin, 50.
Influence of the paper of, 685.
Letters from, 271, 272, 273.
Letters to, 134, 558.
Order to arrest, 505.
Prosecution against, 401.
Solicits the furnishing the Department of State with stationery, 271.
Dubourg, William, 221.
Letters from, 273.
Dubuisson, ——, letter from, 273.
Duck River, troops on, for protection to travelers, 699.
Dueling, custom of, 485.
Proposed law of Congress to prevent, 485.
Duer, of New York, failure, 95.
Duer, William, introduced, 628.
Letter from, 273.
Duer, W. A., letters from, 273, 274.
Letter to, 22.
Dufour, ——, introduced, 173.
Dufret, N. G., indictment against, 274.
Letter from, 274.
Duke, Alexander, letter from, 274.
Solicitation for assistance, 274.
Dumas, Hippolite, letter from, 274.
Release from imprisonment, 274.
Dumeste, John, passport requested, 626.
Dumourier, address by, 390.
Apostacy of, 39.
Dunbar, John R. W., letter from, 274.
Dunbar Robert, letter from, 274.
Duncan, A. L., 210.
Duncan, William (General), 183.
Appointment solicited as treasurer of the Mint, 644.
Duncanson, William, 414.
Letter from, 274.
Soliciting office, 274.
Dunlap, Andrew, 157.
Dunglison, Robley (Dr.), 181.
Letters from, 274, 275, 276.
Letter to, 685.
Resignation, 171, 275.
Dunlap, Thomas, 477.
Dunmore (Lord), arrival of ships to aid, 65.
Dunn, C. F., jr., application for office, 276.
Letters from, 276.
Dunn, Thomas, 721.
Dunn, William, application for assistance, 276.
Letters from, 276.
Dupin, ——, speech in Paris, 277.
Duplantier, Armand, 56, 209, 276, 341.
Letters from, 276.
Duponceau, Peter S., 75.
Letters from, 276, 277.
State papers, 228.
Dupont (French consul-general), exequatur refused to, 398.
Dupont, E. J., letters from, 277.
Dupont, Samuel Francis, application for appointment as midshipman, 414.
Soliciting place of midshipman, 278.
Dupont, Victor, 414.
Letter from, 278.
Dupont de Nemours, P. S., 48, 269.
Letters from, 277, 278.
Durand, A. B., portrait of Madison by, 545.
Introduced, 545.
Durand, W. J., 200.
Durham, J., letter from, 278.
Offer of services, 278.
Dutch Confederation, the want of un
the source of their calamities, 93
Dutch Government, mediation of i
Loan from the, 338.
Wretched situation of the, 124.
Duties, act relating to, 304.
Delinquency of merchants in payi
Discriminating, 38, 249.
Increase of, on sugar, molasses, tea
Reciprocal, 279.
Duties on imports, 278.
Duties paid, application for return
Proposed laying restricting, on br
and silks from France, 467.
Duty on imports to one State from ano
Duval, E. W., letters from, 279.
Proposition to appoint, Solicitor of
ury, 430.
Recommended, for promotion in of
Soliciting a clerkship, 279.
Duval, William P., letters from, 279.
Duvall, Gabriel, 737.
Letters from, 279, 280.
Letter to, 170, 552, 688.
Dwyer, J. H., letter from, 280.
Dykes & Gray, 636.
Dyster, Joseph Joshua, invention, 280.
Letter from, 280.
Eakin, ——, 264.
Eakin, James, 7.
Eakin, James H., 7.
Earle, Elias, 263.
Earle, Elias (Colonel), claim, 413.
Contract of, and cession of land, 28
Letter from, 281.
Letter to, 518, 413.
Early, Joel, letter from, 281.
Early, Peter (Governor), letter from, 28
Letter to, 22.
Earth, diameter and form of the, 35.
Earthquakes, 50.
Eastburn, James, letter from, 281.
Eastburn, Robert, 622.
Letter from, 281.
Easter, ship, seizure of, 466.
Eastern States, discontent in the, 457.
During the war of 1812, 128.
East Florida, cession of, to the United
Jefferson advocates taking posses.
East India commerce, apprising our, of
war, 408.
East India Company, renewal of chai
149.
East India trade, 230, 231.
East Indies, British census in, 234.
Easton, David, letter to, 447.
Letter from, 281.
East or West Indies, vessels from ene
for, good prizes, 628.
East Tennessee College, lottery for the
Eaton, J. H., letter to, 22.
Eaton, John Henry (Major), wife of, 66
Eaton, William, application of, to be
of Albany, 281, 282.
Letters from, 281, 282.
Offer of services, 281.
Soliciting employment as baker, for
Army and Navy, 160.
Eccleston, Daniel Belteschazzar Plant
ter from, 282. Presenting a m
Washington, 282.
Letter to, 22.
Eckard, J. F., letter from, 282.
Economy, national, and domestic ma
241.
Eden, Hancock County, Mass., resoluti
zens of, approving the Administ
Edgington, ——, introduced, 246.
Edrington, Edward, application of, for
Letters from, 282.
Education, Fellenburg system of, 544.
Free and universal diffusion of, 67
In America, views of Dupont de N
system of, 277.
In common schools, system of, 140.
Of indigent youth, proposed establ
an institution for the, 517.
Of young ladies, plan of, 562.

Education, public, 178.
For distinguished youths, 28
System of, in Kentucky, 6.
Edwards, Eno, letter from, 282.
Letter to, 534.
Monroe's request to, to state what occurred at a dinner at his house in Paris in vindication from malicious charges, 534.
Edwards, H. W., letter from, 282.
Edwards, Mirian, letter from, 282.
Edwards, Ogden, appointment as district judge, 309.
Edwards, Pierrepont, letters from, 282, 283.
Letter to, 22.
Edwin, David (engraver), 266.
Eels, Cushing, letter from, 283.
Egremont, Earl of, letter from, 283.
Egypt, victory by the French in, 626.
Eiland, Isaiah, letter from, 283.
Elbe and Weser, discontinuance of blockade at entrance of the, 75.
Elberton, Ga., approval of citizens of, of measures of the Government, 152.
Elbyey, —— (Dr.) appointment as surgeon's mate, 324.
Election for President and Vice-President (1796), 43.
Election, Presidential, balloting in the House of Representatives (1801), 259.
Election, Presidential (1800), efforts to prevent the, 259.
Election, Presidential (1800), inquietude as to issue of the, 81.
Election, Presidential (1800), to be in the House of Representatives, 46.
Elections for Presidents, bill for deciding, 53, 505.
Elections, State, not favorable to the Administration, 51.
Elector for President, 9, 126, 221, 255, 259, 573, 666.
Electoral bill, 46.
Electoral ticket (1827) Madison and Monroe nominated on the, 87, 597.
Electoral ticket (1827), Madison and Monroe decline to serve on the, 520, 540, 541.
Electrical experiments, cakes for, 496.
Eliza, case of the, 703.
Elledge, Thomas, letter from, 287.
Ellery, Christopher, 722.
Letter from, 283, 284.
Ellery, William, fears of removal of, from office, 284.
Letters from, 284.
Ellicott, ——, recommended for place of geographer-general, 497.
Ellicott, Andrew, claim of, for services, 284.
Difficulties and discomforts undergone by, 284.
Letters from, 284, 285, 286.
Offer of, to carry dispatches to France, 285.
Offer to, to be professor of mathematics at West Point, 285.
Refusal of, to oppose Jefferson, 284.
Suggesting the employment of, 517.
Ellicott, N., letter from, 286.
Elliot, Jonathan, asking loan of volumes and pamphlets, 286.
Letters from, 286.
Letters to, 22, 23.
Work of, on the Constitution, 286.
Elliott, J. D. (Commodore), letters from, 286.
Elliott, Robert, jr., letter from, 286.
Request of, to be retained as chaplain, 286.
Ellis, Thomas H., letter from, 287.
Ellsworth, Oliver, 130, 269.
Nomination of, as envoy to France, 400.
Elsineur, blockade of, 328.
Elskwata, the "prophet," 171.
Elsworth, Dorothy, letter from, 287.
Elwell, Jonathan, claim of, for seizure of vessel, 287.
Letter from, 287.
Elwyn, Alfred Langdon, introduced, 463.
Emancipation, 182.
Debates on, 654.
Progress toward, 689.
Quaker memorial relating to, 195.
Uncontrolled despersion of slaves favorable to, 85
Views on, 22, 24, 739.
Embargo, 41, 139, 185, 186, 220, 293, 396, 461, 579.
A calamity to American citizens abroad, 481.
Action of France relative to, 230.
Advocating (1796), 42.
An obstacle to the success of the Republican party, 503.
Approval of the, 617.
Appeal for removing the, 138.
Authorization of the President to lay an, during recess, 257.
Bill for, before Congress, 50.
Passage of, 40.
Close of, 435.
Continuation of, 71.
Counter addresses relating to, 409.
Disapproval of, 642.
Eastern discontent of, 2.
Effects of, 177, 474, 604.
England's dread of our, 47.
Evasions of, 603.
Fears of an, 168.
Measure, wisdom of, 233.
Misrepresentations of, 377, 481.
No combination in New England to resist, 682.
On the Lakes, 308.
Opposition of the Senate to, 210.
Popularity of, 657.
Proposed (1797), 257.
Question as to ability to sustain, 578, 723.
Recommending an (1806), 314.
Repeal of the, 41, 510.
Request for relaxation of, 624.
Suggestions of an, 237.
Emigrants, encouragement to, 7.
Information to, 607.
Emigration, speculation of, 714.
From Virginia to North and South Carolina and Georgia, 464.
Emlen, Samuel, jr., letter from, 287.
Emmons, Richard, 287, 422.
Letter from, 287.
Emmons, William, introduced, 422.
Emoluments, civil and military, 712.
Emporium of Arts and Sciences, 265.
Encyclopædia Americana, 707.
Encyclopédie Methodique, 150.
Enemy's ships, position of the, 717.
Engelbrecht, Jacob, letters from, 287, 288.
Letter to, 23.
Enghein, Duc d', arrest and execution of, 480.
Engineers, corps of, changes in relation to, 324.
England, alliance with, 43.
England and France, intercourse between, prohibited, 260.
Preliminaries of peace between, 509.
England and Holland, dispute between, 66.
England and the Greek cause, 57.
England and Virginia, common law of, 103.
England, anxiety in, to preserve peace (1810), 483.
Arrogance of, 232.
Commerce of, influence of, on our politics, 437.
Cost of living in, 147.
Elevation of, and degradation of France, 250.
Financial difficulties of, 414.
Hostility of, 381.
Injustice and cruelty of, 485.
Invasion of, by France, 260, 397.
Jealousy of, of the Northern powers, 480.
King of, insanity of the, 385.
rumors of death of, 260.
Power of, to destroy our trade, 231.
Preparations for the French invasion of, 480.
Sufferings of the poor in, 147.
The Whig party in, 108.
War with, probable (1807), 407.
Wealth, 147.
England's constitution produced and illustrated, 200.
English and French colonies, self-subsistence of, 107.
books not invariably authorities on law and politics, 369.
constitution, 12.
depredations, 44, 369.
property, condemnation of, on American vessels, 289.
vessels, facility of, obtaining provisions from "peace men" in Connecticut (1813), 283.

Englishmen, ignorance of, concerning this country, 680.
Enlisted men, pay and discharge of, 248.
Enlistment of British seamen in our Navy, 212.
Enlistments, illegal, 160.
Inactivity of, in Virginia in 1812, 585.
Of eighteen months, 292.
seamen, 587.
Term of, 100.
Ennalls, A. Skinner, letter from, 288.
Enoch, case of the, 431.
Eppes, Francis, letters from, 288.
Eppes, John W., letters from, 288.
Eppinger, John, recommended, 304.
Episcopal Church, act incorporating the, 67.
Remonstrating against establishment of the, 121, 288, 624.
Epitaph, Latin, on Adams and Jefferson, 675.
Erie Canal, completion of the, 552.
Opening of the, 185.
Proposed, 175. 440.
Erskine, David M. (British minister), 20, 48, 232, 289, 704.
Complaint of, of want of communication with armed vessels, 407.
Haughty style of the government of, 409.
Jefferson's confidence in integrity of, 410.
Letters from, 288.
Question of recall of, 83.
Erving, George W., attempt to assassinate, in Madrid, 467.
Letter from, 288.
Letters to, 23, 438.
Opinions of, influenced by French versions at Madrid, 409.
Espie, J. W., letter from, 289.
Essex County, address of citizens of, 55, 445.
Estaing, Count d', cession of lands to, by Georgia, 382.
Etiquette, breach of, 237.
Points of, in visits to officials, 289, 438, 532.
Rules of military, 586.
Etna, bomb-ketch, 167.
Etting, Solomon, 628.
Letter to, 648.
Eugenia, rescue of the, 700.
Europe, advantages of our seclusion from, 434.
Belligerent powers of, unprincipled conduct of the, 255.
Immense warlike preparations in, 509.
Maniac state of, our avoidance of the, 409.
New partition of, 397.
Probable general war in, 338.
Process of reformation in, 56.
Under control of France, 139.
War in (1784), 381.
European complication, abstention of America from, 431.
Powers, diplomatic representatives of, 402.
Eustervief, ——, complaints against, 250.
Eustis, Abraham, (Colonel) introduced, 293.
Eustis, William, 18, 23, 24.
Accepting office of Secretary of War, 289.
Appointment of, as minister to Holland, 293.
Commission tendered, 293.
Desire of, for a Government position at home, 294.
Letters from, 289, 290, 291, 292, 293, 294.
to, 23, 309, 333, 351, 352, 635, 726, 730.
Medical department directed by, 293.
Offer to nominate, as minister to United Netherlands, 114.
Prejudices of, 306.
Resignation of, 23.
Secretary of War, 23.
Tour of, in Virginia, 294.
Eustis, William J., letter to, 423.
Evacuation of New York, 67, 102.
Evacuation of posts, 34.
Evans, Oliver, invention of, for steam engines on board vessels, 294.
Letter from, 294.
Evans, Robert J., letters from, 294.
Letters to, 24.
Evans, Thomas, letter from, 294.
Letter to, 24.
Eve, George, letter from, 294.
Letter to, 24.
Everett, Alexander Hill, 293.
Application that, be appointed secretary of legation to Netherlands, 333.
Pamphlet by, 265.
Everett, Edward, letters to, 24.
Ewell, Maxcey, letter from, 294.
Services of, 294.
Ewell, ——, introduced, 526.
Public property stolen by, 428.
Ewell, James, recommendations, 294.
Letter from, 294.
Ewell, Thomas, 51.
Contract to, for the manufacture of gunpowder, 295.
Incorrectness of publications of, about C. W. Goldsborough, 322.
Appeal of, for protection from acts of the Secretary of the Navy, 295.
Application of, for position in the medical department of the University of Virginia, 295.
Inferior quality of gunpowder from mills of, 322.
Letters from, 295.
Ewing, F., letter from, 295.
Exchequer bills, emission by English of, 391.
Excise bill, 69, 70, 95, 553.
collection of, 654.
extension of, 724.
law, 196.
recommending repeal of the, 472.
system, 42.
tax, the, 530.
Executive Departments, organization of the, 736.
Executive, outcry against the, as violating law of nations (1806), 83.
power, exercise of, without intervention of judiciary, 33.
Executive powers of Government, encroachment on, 85.
Expenses of Government, 273, 307, 675.
Exportation, licenses for, under American colors, In the names of French houses, 468.
Exporting produce, difficulty in, 705.
Exports and imports, list of, 486.
to Europe in 1770, 296.
Expositor, the, 280.
"External relations," 233.
Extradition, 76, 389.
Extraterritorial jurisdiction, Lords Holland and Hawkesbury's ideas of, 433.
Eyeglasses and spectacles, 341.
Eyrien, Frères & Cie., letter from, 296.

F.

"Fabius," letters of, 296.
Fahlberg, ——, 631.
Fairfax, Denny, letter from, 296.
False accusations, difficulty in bearing up under, 448.
Farewell address, first draft of the, 635.
Farjon, Sœur de St. Xavier de, letter from, 296.
Farley, Robert, recommended, 629.
Farm, a pattern, 96.
Offered by Stephen van Rensselaer, 694.
Farmers' Bank of Virginia, 296.
Stock, 609.
Farley, Robert, application for office of collector, 296.
Letter from, 296.
"Farmers Letters,' author of, 476.
Farmers' Society, certificate of membership, 296.
Farms, Roman, diminutive size of, 7, 17.
Farrar, John (Professor), 25.
Fast day in Boston, 293.
Proclamation for a, in Massachusetts, 315.
Request for appointing a, 246, 362, 706.
Fauche, B. F., recommended to be consul at Gothenburg, 547.
Fauche, P., letter from, 296.
Fauchet, Joseph (French minister), 40, 71, 256.
Fauquier County, rents and profits of lands in, 147.
Fauquier Island, force of the enemy on (1814), 154.
Faure, Stans., letter from, 296.
Fay, David, letter from, 296.
Featherstonhaugh, G. W., letter to, 26.

Federal and Republican parties, attempt to harmonize (1814), 188, 189.
Federal City, plan of the, 197.
proprietors of land in the, 197.
sale of lots in the, 197, 199.
Federal compact, prediction of the destruction of the, 223.
Constitution, comments of Tench Coxe on the, 225.
Courts, change of system of the, 120.
Government, on the right of parties to the Constitution to individually annul the acts of the, 116.
Government, weakness of a, 335.
Leaders soured toward England, 47.
Offices, selection of, 226.
Power, exercise, 33.
"Federal" in contradistinction from "National," 17.
Federalism, associations to frustrate, 188.
New England, 262.
"Federalist" (newspaper), 20, 25, 90, 124, 318, 342, 343, 672.
Federalists, designs of the (1800), 259.
Exclusion of, from office, 445.
In command of regiments, 261, 263.
Measures of the, 162.
Objections to appointments to office of, 552.
Of New England, 24.
Public opinion against (1800), 400.
Fees, district court, 570.
Fellenberg Institution, 76.
Female college, establishment of a, 97.
Fendall, P. R., letter to, 26.
Fenner, James (governor of Rhode Island) 283.
Fenwick, George, 497.
Ferdinand VII, King of Spain, 299, 326.
Ferguson, Hugh (Colonel), recommended, 639.
Ferguson, James, application for appointment as midshipman, 474.
Fernandez, J. H., 551
Letter from, 297.
Ferrand, General, edict of, 118.
Fevers, bilious, in Washington, 375.
Intermitting and remitting, use of prussiate of iron in, 739.
Malignant, at New York, 92.
Ficklin, Joseph, letter from, 297.
Field, Thomas, conduct of, 618.
Recommended, 645.
Field officers, absence of, 290.
Fielding, Robert, letter from, 297.
Finance, views on, 51, 78, 135, 136, 679.
Finch, John, ingenious speculations, 26.
Introducing, 675.
Letters from, 297.
to, 26.
Findlay, James (General), 658.
Pamphlet, 660.
Findlay, Samuel, family of, 557.
Firearms, contract for, 157.
Fire rafts, 651.
Fisher, George, letter from, 297.
Fisheries, importance of the, to England, 432.
Newfoundland, 283, 585.
Question, 1, 51, 331.
Fishing business, petition relating to, 621.
Fitch, James, 269.
Fitch, John, application of, for completion of his steamboat, 629.
Claim of, to the invention of steamboats, 297.
Invention of, for application of steam for navigation (1788), 297.
Letters from, 297, 298.
Fitzgerald, ——, sentence of flogging of, mitigated, 425.
Fitzhugh, Denis, letter from, 298.
Fitzhugh, John, recommended for a consulate, 461.
Fitzsimmons, Christopher, introduced, 272.
Flags, Carthagenian, 478.
Flags of truce, communication by, 428.
Instructions as to, 426.
Flags, regulation of, 407.
Flax, culture of, 97.
Invention for cleaning and dressing, 97, 638.
Manufacture, 584.
Fleet, enemy's, scheme for destroying the, 266.
Success of our, in the Chesapeake, 92.
Fleets, French and English, situation of (1780), 91.
Fletcher & Toler, letter to, 26.
Flogging, sentence of, mitigated, 425.
Flood, William, letter from, 298.
Flood, W. (Dr.), character of, 172.
Florida, acquisition of, hopes for the, 85, 293, 298, 404.
and Cuba, suggested taking of, 674.
and Southern States, culture of coffee, vines, olives, etc., in, 204.
Boundaries, 34.
Claim of the United States to, 651.
Claims, 26.
Climate and fertility, 288.
Fears of contest in, 261.
Government for, trouble in organizing a, 538.
No duties on merchandise in, from United States citizens, 298.
Purchase, 608.
Resistance to enterprise against, 114.
Treaty, ratification of the, 236.
Floridas and Cuba, question as to the, 410.
Floridas, cession of the, 47.
Exchange of the, for part of Louisiana, 701.
Importance of obtaining the, 542.
Possession of the, General Armstrong's letter recommended, 409.
Proposed annexation of the, 615.
Seizure of the, as reprisal for spoliations, 407.
Spanish operations against, 91.
Flour, American, consumption of, in England, 512.
Reliance on, 646.
High price of, 42, 72, 96.
Floyd, ——, (Miss), 379.
Folch, V. (Governor), 207.
Letters from, 298.
to, 680.
Unsuccessful attempts, 681.
Fontainebleau, description of, 382.
Foord, James, letter from, 298.
Letter to, 26.
Foote, Samuel A., and others, letters to, 26.
Resolutions, 62.
Ford, J. J., 646.
Foreign Affairs, nominations for secretaryship, 101.
Foreign appointments, 76.
Intercourse, appropriations for, 258.
Nations, proposed discrimination between, 79.
Vessels, protection for, 306.
Foreigners and aristocrats, influx, 96.
Forman, E., 228.
Foronda, Valentine de, claim of, 407.
Spanish minister, letters from, 298, 299.
Forrest, Richard, 261.
Death, 168.
Letters from, 299.
Forrest, R., letters to, 216, 567.
Fort Defiance, military crisis near, 51.
Hood, important position, 145.
repairs and supplies for, 14.[illegible]
Michillimackinack, surprise and plunder of, 35.
negro, destruction of a, 239.
Niagara, capture of, 678.
post at, 248.
Powhatan, condition of, 146.
Stanwix, Indian treaty at, 67.
treaty at, with the Six Nation Indians, 464.
Stoddert, commanding officer at, letter to, 298.
public stores at, 290.
reinforcement of, 290.
Wayne, anxiety for, 291.
report of taking of, 291.
Fortification bill, 396.
Fortifications, agents of, 624.
On northern boundary, delay in commencing, 239.
Under control of the War Department, 306.
Fosdick, Nathaniel F., introduced, 358.
Fosdick, Nicoll, recommended, 610.
Fossil remains, 109, 297, 495.
Foster, Augustus John (British minister), character of the mission of, 50.
Foster claims, the, 332.
Fothergill, Anthony (Dr.), introduced, 735.
Foulton, Jesse, letter from, 299.

Foundation day, 496.
Foulon, death of, in Paris, 386.
Fowler, C. S., letter from, 299.
Fox, C. J. (Right Honorable), desire of, to maintain relations of amity, 432.
Letter to, 432.
Fox, British brig, dismantling of the, 232.
France, Adams's course relative to, 43.
A favored nation, 257.
Alliance with, 32, 308.
American claims on, 699.
American sentiment toward, 39.
and allied powers, engagements between, 391.
and Austria, peace between, 396.
and England, speculations on a triangular war with, 50.
temper of, toward each other, 230.
war declared between (1793), 390.
and Great Britain, failure of negotiations between, for peace, 73.
and Holland, prohibitions of, to commercial intercourse with the United States, 509.
and Italy, Jefferson's journal of his travels through, 388.
and Russia, symptoms of war between, 50.
and Spain, dispositions of (1797), 395.
negotiations between, respecting exchange of Florida for French islands, 254.
project of a union with, 679.
relations between, 440.
our relations with, 62.
and the Greek cause, 57.
and the Mississippi, 102.
and the United States, relations between (1796), 265.
Animals of, difference in habits, 382.
Army of occupation to leave, 550.
Attitude of (1812), 151.
Change of government in (1804), 167.
Claims of United States citizens against, 150, 303.
Coalition between King and Commons against the nobility, 126.
Combination in, against the Revolution, 95.
Clergy in, 386.
Conciliation with, 45, 399.
Condition of (1815), 294.
Conduct of, as respects the treaty with Great Britian, 79.
Conduct of, since repeal of decrees, 150.
Consulate of the United States in, new organization of the, 246.
Convention with (1801), 46.
Debt of the United States to, 344, 388, 618.
Delay in negotiations with, 46.
Delay in ratification of treaty with (1801), 401.
Dissatisfaction of, against the United States, 299.
Establishment of a republic by, 724.
Establishment of liberty in, 94.
Evacuation of, by occupying armies, 88.
Fears of rupture with, 43, 44.
Hereditary and dignified titles abolished in, 618.
Hopes of England to embroil us with, 47.
Hostile and treacherous intentions of, 405.
Hostility of British merchants to, 41.
Ignorance of the people in, 440.
Indignation against (1812), 5.
Injustice of, 423.
Internal combustion in (1793), 390.
Internal ferments in (1788), 93, 94.
Irresistible force of, and distress of the allies, 71.
Loans and donations of, detention, 217.
Low wages in, 382.
Mediation of, with Spain, 35.
Military schools in, 299.
Minister of foreign affairs of, letter to, 533.
Minister to, the President refuses to send a, 399.
Mission to, contingent account of the, 299.
New constitution in, 72, 221, 385, 619.
New form of government for (1804), 82.
Nobility and clergy, 385.
No declaration of war by, 396.
Nonintercourse with, 47, 259, 398.
France, Payment of the United States debt t
Peace with Prussia, 257.
Pecuniary embarrassment of, 618.
Political condition of (1834), 478.
Political and military leaders, 46.
Possible controversy with, 105.
Probable unsuccessful negotiations (1798), 80.
Proposed commercial treaty with, 5, 150.
Proposition to annul treaty with, 39.
Rage of Europe against, 257.
Ratification of convention with, 81.
Reconciliation with, 49, 604.
Relations with, 14.
Resentment of, the fruits of the B treaty, 73, 533.
Retaliatory measures, 232.
Revolution in, 385, 618.
Rich proprietors, 382.
Rumored war with, 44.
Rupture with, Gerry's letters on cause
Shipments to, 228.
Sincerity of, for reconciliation, 399.
Spanish allies of, 73.
Struggle in, between monarchy and ar racy (1788), 126.
Successes, 73, 258.
Subjection of, a calamity (1814), 427.
Suspended commerce with, 45.
Trade with, and Virginia, 581.
Treaties with, proposition to declare voi 390, 399.
Treaty with (1803), 74.
delays of the, 260.
Trophies of, to be returned to their o 250.
Uncultivated lands and unemployed po 382.
Unfriendly conduct of, 542.
Unsatisfactory relations with, 73.
Violence and injustice of, 579.
against the clergy and nobilit 618.
Voting by persons or orders in, 386.
War against, vigorous prosecution of, b gland, 66.
War with, no reason for, 397.
War office of, corruption in the, 151.
Francis, John W., letters to, 27.
Frankfort, Edward E., letter to, 712.
Frankland (Franklin?), State of, propose mission, 299.
"Franklin," papers signed, 622.
Franklin, Benjamin, 205.
and Vergennes, 100.
Anecdote about, by Jefferson, 378.
Excellent conduct of, 87.
Imitation of writing of, 23.
Letter from, 299.
Letters to, 378.
Memory of, 18.
Newspapers of, prior to 1740, 363.
No appointment of successor to, 56.
Political productions of, in the Departm State, 272.
The wish of, to return to America, 527.
Retirement of, 100, 465.
Views of Jefferson on the character negotiator, 379.
Vigor of intellect of, 100.
Franklin Literary Society, 199.
Franklin "Wild men," 640.
State of (Tennessee), self-erected, 617.
Franklinites (citizens of Tennessee), 591.
Frazer, Hubbart, discharge solicited by, 299
Letter from, 299.
Recommended, 346.
Fredericksburg Academy, progress of the,
Fredericksburg and Swift River Gap, tur between, 363.
Inhabitants of, petition of, praying remo naval office to Urbana, 507.
Fredericktown, court-martial at, 309.
"Fredoniad," The, 287, 422.
Freeborn, Thomas, introduced, 675.
Letter from, 300.
Free goods and sailors on neutral vessels, 3
Free ships and free goods, 369, 450, 440.

Freeman, Nathaniel, 1.
Freeman, Thomas, letter to, 518.
"Freemason," 521.
"Freemasonry," 153.
French, ——, recommended, 324.
French, Benjamin, letter from, 300.
French, J., letter from, 300.
  Return of papers to, 300.
French and Swiss guard, dissensions between the, 386.
French armed vessels, capture of, and appropriating proceeds, 400.
  decree concerning, 265.
  Army, money for the, 99.
  at Baltimore, irregularities of the, 700
  Brandy, wine, and silks, proposed restrictive duty on, 467.
  Budget, Lafayette's sentiments on the, 56.
  Cause, intemperate and sanguinary measures of the, 430.
  Colonies, trade of, with Virginia.
  Commander, delay of the, at Rhode Island, 711.
  Commissioners, instructions to our, 258.
  Condemnations, 575.
  Constitution of 1793, basis of the, 532.
    report of the committee of the convention on the (1795), 532.
  Consul in Boston, actions of a, 392.
  Creek, improvements in, 733.
  Decrees, 47 397.
    repeal of, 108, 347.
  Deserters, enlistment of, 408.
  Directory, friendliness of the, 258.
  Flag, scene produced by the, 80.
  Fleet, arrival of the (1780), 495.
    departure of the (1782), 495.
    inability of the, to cooperate with militia to prevent success to the British, 711.
    at Rhode Island, 66.
    off the coast (1780), 90.
  Guards fraternize with the people, 386.
  Government, indignation excited by the style of the, in the Spanish business (1805), 405.
    negotiations with the, for suppression of the slave trade, 539.
    sincerity of the, to avoid war with the United States, 399.
  Indemnity, 308.
  Minister to the United States, suspended functions of the, 265.
  Minister's coach and six, 102.
  Misrepresentations of the United States, 515.
  Officer, work by a, dedicated to Madison, 350.
  Prisoners taken from American vessels, 82.
  Privateers and prizes, 697.
  Irregularities of, in harbors of South Carolina and Georgia, 404.
  Republic, confirmation of the, 685.
  (1794), flourishing condition of the, 531.
  Situation of the (1794), 256.
  Retaliation against English on transgressions on rights of neutrals, 230, 231.
  Revolution, the, 94, 95.
  American sympathy with the, 39.
  Robbery, 49.
  Ships in Chesapeake Bay, 71.
  Ships of war, irregularities of, 75.
  Spoliation claims, 325, 479, 540,
  Spoliations, 23, 44, 73, 202, 300, 365, 400, 587, 641.
  Compensation for, 396.
  Indemnity for, 151.
  Liquidation of awards for, 702.
  Presidents message against, 397.
  Subjects, permission to, caught by the embargo, to return home, 408.
  Success of the, in Europe, 41, 71, 256.
Frenchman, a letter from, 300.
Frenchmen, trial of, in England or sent to France, 547.
  Unfortunate, aid to, 548.
Freneau, Philip, as translator, 38.
  Letters from, 300, 301.
  Lines by, 447.
  Newspapers of, 103.
  Printer, 300.
  Publication of poems of, 301.
Freneau, Philip, Retrospect of life of, 301.
  Schoolmaster and poet, 300.
Friends, Society of, appeal of the, 606.
Friendship, schooner, 628, 648.
Frigates and cruising vessels, disposition of, (1812), 348.
  Bill for building six, 71, 592.
Frontier settlements, protection of, 528.
Frontiers, defense of the, 133.
Froutté, ——, letter from, 301.
Fuller, ——, introduced, 260.
Fuller, James C., introduced, 440.
Fulton, Robert, application of, to be temporary Secretary of the Navy, 301.
  Complaints by, of unjust treatment, 301.
  Letters from, 301.
  Patent rights to steamboats, 301.
  Torpedo experiments, 262.
Funding bill, the, 69.
  System, 607.
  Hamilton's, disapproval of, 459.
Furlough of troops, 101.
Furniture received from Monroe, 119.
  Shipments, 215, 216.

G.

Gadsden, James (Lieutenant), 238.
Gaillard, John, election of, as Senator in Congress, 469.
Gaines, Edmund Pendleton, (General), 18, 238
  Appointment of, as major-general, 302.
  Complaints by, for injury done him by Mr. Crawford, 302.
  Court-martial of, 27.
  In command at New Orleans, 248.
  Letters from, 301, 302.
  Letter to, 27, 298.
  Services of troops under command of, 302.
Gales and Seaton, letters from, 302.
Gales, Joseph, letters to, 27.
  Political essays by, in the Intelligencer, 27.
Gales, Joseph, jr., letters from, 302.
  Letter to, 204.
Gallatin, Albert, 243.
  And the French mission, 250.
  Compensation and outfit for, 308.
  Departure of, for France, 308.
  Interview of, with the King of France, 308.
  Letters from, 302, 303, 304, 305, 306, 307, 308.
    to, 27, 28, 141, 162, 212, 280, 336, 348, 371, 624, 627, 689, 727, 728.
  Nomination of, as minister to Great Britain, 137.
  On the alien and sedition law, 400.
  Principles and capacity, 42.
  Refusal of, to furnish money to order of Secretary of the Navy, 306.
  Visit of, to Monticello, 48.
Galloway, Benjamin, appeal for votes as Member of Congress, 308.
  Letter from, 308.
Galusha, Jonas, letter from, 309.
  Letter to, 28.
Galvanism, experiments in, 274.
Gamble, James, letter from 309.
Gamble, R., letters from, 309.
Gamblers, pamphlet respecting, 716.
Gano, A. G., letter to, 28.
  And others, letters from, 309.
Gansevoort, P., letter from, 309.
Gantt, ——, nomination to Nantes, 627.
Gantt, Thomas John, letter from, 309.
Garden, Alexander (Dr.), introduced, 591.
Gardeneir, B., letter from, 309.
Gardiner, Emma Jane, introduced, 694.
Gardiner, Henry, application in behalf of, 615.
Gardiner, John, call by, for installments to a manufacturing company, 309.
  Letters from, 309, 310.
Gardner, Gideon, letter from, 310.
  Petition in behalf of citizens of Nantucket, 310.
Gardoqui, Diego de (Spanish minister), 9, 60, 528.
  Arrival, 334, 528, 465.
  Character, 334.
Garland, Hugh A., 565.
Garnett, ——, introduced, 530.

Garnett, James M., introduced, 311.
Letter from, 310.
Garnett, Robert S., letters from, 310.
Letters to, 28.
Garrard, ——, resignation of, of the Marine Corps, 323.
Garrett, Alexander, letters from, 310.
Gartland, James, letter from, 311.
Gasevain, ——, introduced, 535.
Gassaway, John, letter from, 311.
Gates, Horatio, letters from, 311.
Gaullier, J. F., Government position solicited by, 311.
Letter from, 311.
Gavrard, William, claim, 310.
Letters from, 310.
Gay, Payton, application of, for appointment in the Army, 311.
Letter from, 311.
Gazette, Freneau's, 459.
Gazetteer of Virginia, 104, 633.
Geddes, John, letters from, 311, 312.
Letters to, 28, 710.
Gelham, Henry M., proposed appointment of, as ensign, 289.
Gelston, David, 308.
Letters from, 312, 313.
Letter to, 305.
Gemme, C. D., letter from, 313.
General Government, assumptions of power, 104.
The people will support the (1809), 175.
General officers, the President's selection, 248.
General Ward, brig, 143.
Generals, Republican, appointment of, 315.
Generation, the right of one, to bind another, 386.
Genet, Edmond C. (French minister), American sentiment toward, 39.
Conduct, 39, 40, 79, 392, 723.
Description, 255.
Engagement of, to Clinton's daughter, 392.
Expected arrival, 390.
Indiscretions, 40.
Influence, 723.
Intermeddling of, 392.
Jefferson's estimate of character of, 391.
Recall of, decided upon, 391.
Resignation, 391.
Spirit of the mission of, 390.
Superceded by Fauchet, 71.
Geography, 76.
Geological survey of Virginia, 274.
Geology, knowledge of, 26.
George III, prospect of death of, 412.
Georgetown, proposition fixing upon, as capital of the Federal Empire, 336.
Georgia, advices from, favoring the Constitution, 225.
And Cherokee question, 623.
And Mississippi Company, 649.
And North Carolina, disputed boundaries of, 285, 489.
Claims, 546.
Compact with, 86.
Commissioners, 77, 371.
Electoral vote, 126.
General assembly of, approval of the Executive, 314.
Huet's history, 111.
Indian rights to lands in, 539.
Legislature of, disapproval of the terms of the British commissioners at Ghent by the, 281.
Proceedings respecting the tariff, 5.
"Georgia business," the, 120.
Georgian, the, 113.
German Confederation, the, 381.
troops in New York, discontent of the, 92.
Gerry, Elbridge, confirmation of, as minister to France, 257.
Death and services, 317.
Election as Vice-President, 316.
Impropriety of conduct, 124.
Letters from, 314, 315, 316, 317.
to, 157, 165, 168, 191, 293, 587, 727, 733.
Services, 4, 141.
Soliciting the collectorship of Boston, 315.
Gerry, Elbridge, jr., appeal of, for office, 317.
Application of, as secretary of legation, 293.
Letter from, 317.
Gerry, Nancy, free mulatto girl, sold as a slave, 628
Gest, Henry, introduced, 656.
Ghent, British commissioners at, extravagant and disgraceful terms offered by the, 678.
Negotiations at, 134.
Terms of peace proposed at, 114.
Treaty of, 2, 249.
Gholson, Thomas, 484.
Letter from, 318.
Gheretti, the ketch, 405.
Gibbon (Lieutenant), 327.
Gibbon, James, denial of abuse of the Administration, 318.
Letters from, 318.
Gibbs, Caleb, certifying to the services of, 712.
Letter to, 712.
Gibbs, Rowland, letter from, 318.
Gibraltar, blockage of, 92.
Naval force at, 243.
Relief of, 99.
Storming of, 99.
Gibson family in England, inquiry as to, 318.
Gibson and Jefferson, letters from, 318.
Gibson, Patrick, letter from, 318.
Gibson, Robert B., letter from, 318.
Gibson, Thomas, letter from, 318.
Gideon, Jacob, 20.
Letters to, 28.
Gideon, Jacob, jr., letter from, 318.
Giles, —— (General), recommended, 728.
Giles, I., letter from, 318.
Giles, William B., 196.
Calumnies of, 180.
Introducing, 502.
Giles, W. B. (Governor), invitation of, for Madison to visit him, 319.
Letters from, 319.
Letter to, 28.
Resolutions of, 46.
Gill, Valentine, 588.
Application of, for occupation as civil engineer, 319.
Letter from, 319.
Gilman, Nathaniel C., letter from, 319.
Loan solicited by, 319.
Gilmer, Francis W., contract between, and George Long, 319.
Introduced, 108.
Letters from, 319.
Letter to, 417.
Power of attorney to, from the University of Virginia, 319.
Recommended, 416.
Gilmer, Peachy R., letter from, 319.
Gilmer, Thomas W. (Prof.), 53.
Letters from, 320.
Letter to, 28.
Gilpin, H. D., letters from, 320.
Letters to, 29.
Permission asked by, to dedicate his life of Jefferson, to Madison, 320.
Gilpin, Joshua letters from, 320.
Letter to, 29.
Gilpin, N., introduced, 707.
Gilston, David, letter to, 508.
Gimbrede, Thomas, engravings of the four Presidents by, 320.
Letter from, 320.
Girard, Stephen, claim of, against France, 320.
Letter from, 320.
Girard College, system of education, 487.
Gist, Henry C., introduced, 614.
Gist, Nathaniel, claim of, 320.
Letter from, 320.
Glasgow, merchants of, committee, 335.
Glass, Franciscus, letter from, 320.
Letter to, 29.
Permission asked by (in Latin), to dedicate a life of Washington to him, 320.
Glass manufacture, 219.
Glassell, Andrew, letter from, 321.
Glassell, William, letter from, 321.
Glebes, and churches, Amherst memorial on, 44.
Glenn, Elias, recommended, 579.
Glen, Henry, application of, for reappointment as assistant deputy quartermaster, 321.
Appointment of, withheld, 292.
Letter from, 321.

Glennie, R., & Sons, letter to, 489.
Globe, the (newspaper), 89, 663.
God, the knowledge of the existence of, whence derived, 11.
Goddard, ——, 33.
Godefroy, Maxime, introduced, 203.
Godefroy, Maximilien, letter from, 321.
Godon, Silvani, introduced, 482.
Goetschius, John M., introduced, 212.
Gold and silver, coin and bullion, market prices for, 344.
Gold, British, corruption from, 138.
Goldsborough, Charles W., complaint of, on his dismissal, 322
Fraud and misrepresentations of. 295.
Letters from 321, 322.
Letter to, 187 645.
Goldsborough, Robert H., letter to, 29.
Gomez, the banditti chief, 668.
Gooch, Gideon, 666.
Letters from, 322.
Goodlet, Adam, application of, for office, 322.
Letter from, 322.
Goodwyn, Peterson, letter from, 423.
Letter to, 159, 163, 178.
Gordon, Charles (Captain), letter to, 424.
Gordon, Duff & Co., letter from, 322.
Gordon, James, jr., letters from, 322.
Gordon, William, application of, for Government employ, 323.
Letter from, 322.
Gordon, William, & Co., 7, 225.
Gospel, propagation of the, among the heathen, 244.
Gottenburg, consulate at, 437.
Gouverneur, Samuel L., letters from, 323.
Government, a virtuous, so long as agricultural, 384.
Boundary between general and local, 57.
Commencement of the Federal, 37.
Established, regrets at not having an, 488.
Federal, origin of the change in the (1788), 128.
General, organization of the, into legislative, executive, and judicial powers, 382.
Locality of the seat of, 69, 124, 126, 195, 197, 226, 254, 255, 464, 458, 459, 640, 722, 723.
Meeting of, to be in New York (1788), 126.
Of the United States, plan of, 2, 696.
Proposed reform in system of, 123.
Seat of, cession of land from Virginia for, 255.
Proposed removal of the, to Philadelphia, 461.
Temporary seat, 94.
The new, satisfaction of the people for, 458.
Governments, Federal and State, relative powers of, 367.
General and State, the boundaries between, 52.
United States and foreign, comparisons between, 293.
Governor Thompkins, privateer, action between the, and a British frigate, 616.
Graham, George, charges against, 29.
Letters from, 323, 324, 325.
to, 29, 676.
Vindication from charges against, 325.
Graham, John (chargé d'affaires), 575.
Death, 590.
(Inventor), 327.
Letters from, 325, 326, 327, 328, 329, 330, 331.
Letter to, 29, 617.
Offer of services, 325.
Salary, 575.
Graham, John A., letter from, 331.
Graham's Junius, 331.
Grain, high price (1790), 69.
Grand Menan Island, relinquishment of the, 83.
Granger, Gideon, illness of, 332.
Letters from, 331, 332.
Memorial praying for removal as Postmaster-General, 163, 471.
Proposal that, be advanced to a Cabinet Department, 368.
Recommendation of, 141.
Removal, 176, 413.
Suggested appointment as Secretary of War, 694.
Granger, R., letter from, 332.
Granville (Lord), 256.
Grasse, Count de, capture of, 136.
Claims, 394.
Grasse-Tilly, Count de, provision for daughters, 42.
Grasshopper and the tobacco crop, 355.
Graviora maneut, paper signed, 229.
Gray & Bowen, letter from, 332.
Gray, De. (*See* De Gray.)
Gray, Francis C., oration, 562.
Gray, Michael de. (*See* De Gray, Michael.)
Gray, Peter, letter from, 332.
Gray, Stephen W., Government employment solicited, 332.
Letter from, 332.
Gray, Vincent, 628.
Letters from, 332.
Gray, William, letters from, 332, 333.
Gray, William F., 8.
Assignee of, 164.
Books, stationery, etc., supplied by, 333.
Letters to, 29.
Grayson, William (Colonel), claim, 666.
Death, 254, 336.
Letters from, 334, 335, 336.
Letter to, 444.
Reappointment to Congress, 335.
Grayson, W. S., application for appointment as ensign, 336.
Letter from, 336.
Great Britain, a favored nation, 194.
Anxiety to secure our trade, 85.
Appointment of a minister to, 527.
Aristocrats who rule, 234.
Ascendency on the ocean, 56.
Balance of trade betwe n. and southern colonies, 189.
Change in colonial policy, 74.
Claim of, for dominion of the seas inadequate, 410.
Colonial policy, 112.
Conceit of, 680.
Conciliatory policy of, 47.
Commercial relations with, 48.
Retaliation for conduct of, 532.
Cooperation with, in the Mediterranean, 81.
respecting independence of South America, 86.
Declaration to destroy all that sails under the American flag, 528.
Depredations of, 49.
Desirable to secure from, more than a neutral friendship, 405.
Disposition of, to conciliate, 250.
toward the United States (1784), 380.
Disregard for our treaty, 76.
Distresses of the population, 115.
Encouragement of importations of breadstuffs, 72.
Exclusion from the Baltic, 408.
Expected revolution in, 240.
Hatred of the King and people toward United States, 482.
Hostile measures (1807), 467.
Increasing debt, 258.
insolence of (1807), 642, 643.
Insults toward the United States, 83, 345.
King of, declared friendly disposition of the, 337.
Mad policy of (1812), 50.
Minister to, 34.
More friendly disposition of (1801), 81.
Object of, the exclusive use of the ocean, 411.
Obstinacy of, 92.
On same footing as the most favored nation, 69.
Our tame submission to the outrages of, 372.
Policy of, respecting dispute between Spain and her colonies, 330.
to dissever the Union, 315.
Prejudices of, 12.
Preparations for war with, (1807), 83.
Pretensions of, 427.
Probable conflict with (1811), 174.
Probable disposition to cherish friendly relations, 75.
Proposed prohibition of commercial intercourse with, 257.
treaty with, 34, 115.
Proposition to place, on same footing as our allies, 94.
Resentment toward, 177.

Great Britain restrictions against our commerce, 256, 522.
Rumored alliance with, 44, 397, 405.
Satellite of, the United States not a 86.
Successes of enemies, 93.
Trade monopolized by, 77.
Treaty with (1796), 42, 43, 62, 80, 107, 115, 177, 250, 309, 377.
disapproval of the, 245.
inconsistent with treaty with France, 79.
not approved, 54.
(*See* Jay, John.)
the President withholds sanction, 83.
views on the, 231.
Views of, toward the United States (1795), 102.
Whole resources against France, 66.
Great Britain and Continental Powers, alienation between, 86.
Great Britain and France, war between, 576.
Great Britain and other nations, reciprocity with, 74.
Great Britain and Russia, no probability of war between, 70.
Great Britain and Spain, convention between, 95.
Peace between, 69.
Great Falls of the Potomac, advantageous situation of the, 58.
Purchase of land at, 126.
Applications for purchase of lots at, 458.
Great advantages, 458.
Project of securing land at, 458.
Scheme, 460.
Jefferson's views of the, 459.
Great St. Simons Island, protection of, 178.
Greece, the struggle in, 53.
Greek equipment at New York, 56.
Greek characters, English words in, 523.
Greeks, struggle of the, 56, 57.
Greely, Aaron, introducing, 340.
Green, A. M., letter from, 336.
Green, Duff, 22.
Letters from, 336.
Green, John W., letter from, 336.
Green, Moses (General), application for command in the Army, 666.
Green, William D., letter from, 336.
Greenbrier County, Association of, opposition of, to payment of tax, 488.
Insurrection in, 68.
Greene, A. M., 666.
Greenhow, Samuel, letters from, 336.
Greenhow, ——, introducing, 499.
Greenlanders, origin, 57.
Greenleaf, Thomas, 300.
Greenock, suggesting consulate at, 732.
Greetham, Will, letter from, 336.
Gregory, E., letter from, 337.
Gregory, ——, offer to sell a carriage, 155.
Grenville (Lord), communications with John Jay, 71.
Griffin, C., letter from, 193.
Griffin, Cyrus, letters from, 337, 338.
Griffin, Isaac, letter from, 338.
Griffin, John, application for appointment as judge, 338.
Letter from, 338.
Griffin, Thomas, letter from, 338.
Griffin, Thomas Lightfoot, letter from, 338.
Griffith, Thomas W., letters from, 338, 339.
Views on the French revolution, 338.
Griffith, William R., letters from, 339.
Griffiths, Elijah, letter from, 338.
Appointment recommended as treasurer of the Mint, 159.
Soliciting appointment as Director of the Mint, 338.
Grigsby, Hugh B., introducing, 485.
Grimke, Thomas, letters to, 29, 30.
Grimke, Thomas S., letters from, 339.
Request of, for autographs, 339.
Griscom, John, letter from, 340.
Griswold, Chester, asking employment, 340.
Letter from, 340.
Griswold, Roger (Governor), 218.
Letter from, 340.
Griswold and Lyon, encounter between House, 258.
Griswold, Stanley, letters from, 340.
Solicitation to be appointed surveyor 340.
Wish to exchange local situations wit Griffin, 340.
Grizzly Bear of the West, steamboat cal 440.
Grover, Matthew C., letter from, 340
Growth, rapid, of the States, 96.
Grubb, Richard, asking assistance in o patent, 340.
Letter from, 340.
Grymes, Peyton, in behalf of citizens of Court-House, invitation by, to a di John M. Patton, 340.
Invitation to dinner given in honor o
Letter from, 340.
Grymes, Philip, letter to, 280.
Grymes, —— (New Orleans), 209.
Guestier, P. A., letters from, 340.
Gurley, J. W., 276.
Letter from, 341.
Gurley, R. R., letters from, 341.
Letters to, 30.
Grammatical Institute of the English La 716.
Guadaloupe, negroes from, 401.
Guadaloupe, prize sloop, 408.
Guadaloupe, —— (General), republican s raised by, 667.
Guade, Francis, introducing, 256.
Gulf of Mexico, armed vessel to be sent t
Gunboats, advantage of, 263.
Building of, on the Muskingum, 658.
Equipping, 348.
Gunboats for the Chesapeake, 347.
Gunboats for harbor and coast defense, 4
Gunboats in state of ordinary, 346.
Gunpowder, contract for manufacturing,
Guns, lower-deck, plan for using, in a he 677.
Gwinnett, Button, 638.
Gymnasium and dancing hall at the Ur of Virginia, 115.
Hackley, Richard S., letters from, 341.
Request for appointment as collector,
Hackley, ——, 18.
Introducing, 593.
Haden, Joel, application for appointment lain, 422.
Haevel, Matthew Arnold, application to mercial agent to Chile, 341.
Letter from, 341.
Haff, John, letter from, 341.
Haggerty, James, introducing, 511.
Recommending, 734.
Hagner, Peter, letters from, 341.
Haines, Hiram, letter from, 341.
Hale, Matthew, extracts from writings of
Haley, Benjamin, arrest for disaffection, 6
Half pay, 101.
Commutations of, 32, 100, 366.
Opposition of New England to, 102.
Halifax, inspector-general at, 51.
Prisoners at, bad treatment, 157.
Hall (Governor), 603.
Hall, B., letter from, 341.
Hall, Chauncy, letter from, 342.
Hall, Dominick, 178.
Hall, D. A., letters from, 342.
Solicitation to be appointed judge, 34
Hall, Dominick Augustin, recommended of judge, 502.
Hall, Edward, letter from, 342.
Letter to, 30.
Hall, Francis, letter from, 342.
Hall, George Abbott, 573.
Hall, Hezekiah, appeal to procure bail, 34
Letter from, 342.
Hall, John H., letter from, 342.
Hallam, ——, introduced, 274.
Hallet, Stephen S., letter from, 342.
Hallett, ——, introduced, 555.
Halsey, ——, appointment solicited as c Buenos Ayres, 729.
Halsey, John Lloyd, introduced, 578.

Hamilton, A., application for consulate at Lisbon, 345.
Hamilton, Alexander, 61?.
Attachment to a republican form of government, 475.
Charges against, as Secretary of Treasury, 344.
of disunion projects of, 2.
Opinions concerning the proposed Constitution, 342.
Constitution delineated, 74.
Illness 392.
Jefferson's estimate, 394.
Letters from, 342, 343, 344, 345.
to, 30, 390, 449, 670.
Memorandum on the funded debt, 345.
On constitutionality of the bank, 30.
Plan of a Constitution, 49.
Publication of a pamphlet decrying John Adams, 535.
Report on the constitutionality of the bank, 104.
Retirement, 41.
Rumored appointment as minister to Great Britain, 40.
Speech, 2.
Treachery to Adams, 43.
Views as to the establishment of a monarchy, 475.
regarding the National debt, 344.
Hamilton, Alexander, jr., letter from, 345.
Hamilton, A. W. (Captain), 172.
Discharged from the British service, 324.
Refusal to take command under Pakenham, 298.
Hamilton, A. W., application for appointment to office, 345.
Letter from, 345.
Letter to, 213, 298.
Hamilton, —— (former British officer), recommending, for appointment, 477.
Hamilton, Eliz., letters from, 345.
Petition for half pay to Major-General Hamilton's widow and children, 345.
Hamilton, J., letter to, 30.
Hamilton, James, letter from, 345.
Hamilton, J. C., letter from, 345.
Hamilton, John T., letter from, 345.
Hamilton, Paul, acceptance of office of Secretary of the Navy, 345.
Letters from, 345, 346, 347, 348.
to, 30, 306, 349, 490, 583, 585, 683, 709.
Resignation, 348.
Hamilton, Samuel S., letter from, 348.
Hamilton, William, recommended, for commission as lieutenant, 507.
Hamiltonian system, soundness of the, 190.
Hammond, George (British minister), 39.
Arrival of, 70.
Hammond, Samuel (Colonel), character and standing, 485.
Hampden, author of, 180.
Letters of, 10.
Hampden-Sydney College, 32.
Union Society of, election of Madison as honorary member, 550.
Hampton, attack by gunboats on an English frigate near, 216.
Hampton, ship, arrest of a British officer on board the, 686.
Hampton, Wade (General), 264, 558.
Hampton, Wade, letters from, 348.
Hancock, George (Colonel), 705.
Hancock, John, 125.
President of Congress, 528.
the convention at Boston (1788), 444.
Southern States talk of, for President of Senate, 334, 335.
Hancock County, Mass., resolutions of inhabitants, 129.
Hand, Caleb, letter from, 348.
Hands, John, letter from, 348.
Handwriting, microscopic, 110.
Hannah Maria, case of the, 703.
Hanson, A. C., letter from, 348.
Hanson, Samuel (of Samuel), accounts, 280, 677, 688, 689.
Hanson, Samuel, application for an appointment, 349.
Complaints of injust charges, 349.
Dismissal of, claims unjust treatment, 349.
Letters from, 349.
Letter to, 347, 677.
Hanson, Samuel (Captain), introduced, 226.
Hanson, S., application for place of chief clerk, 505.
Happy Return, smuggling of silk in the, 709.
Harden, Marlin, introduced, 656.
Hardin, M. D., letter from, 349.
Harding, Seth, letter from, 350.
Hare, the northern and common, 389.
Hargrove, John (Rev.), 185.
Harison, Richard, letter from, 349.
Harlan, R. (Dr.), introduced, 563.
Harper, Robert G., character and abilities, 177.
Harper, Samuel H., letter from, 350.
Harpers Ferry, the armory at, 290.
Harpooning, experiments in, 301.
Harries, Etienne, letter from, 350.
Harris, Charles, letter from, 350.
Letter to, 650.
Harris, James M., letter from, 350.
Harris, John C., letter from, 350.
Harris, Levett, letter from, 350.
Harris, Richard Devens, introduced, 315.
Harrison, Benjamin (Governor), 93.
Letters from, 350.
Harrison, Carter B., letters from, 350, 351.
Harrison, Carter H., dispute between, and John B. Smith, 624.
Harrison, —— (Colonel), evidence wanting as to retirement, 281.
Harrison (Dr.), offer to, of professorship, 419.
Harrison, Gesner (Dr.), letters to, 30.
Harrison, Jesse B., 8, 54.
Application for professorship, 540.
Appointment to chair of Ancient Languages at the University of Virginia, 484.
Letter from, 351.
to, 31.
Harrison, L., application to be manager of Madison's farm, 351.
Letter from, 351.
Harrison, R., 609.
Letters from, 351.
Harrison, Richard, recommended as consul in Spain, 503.
Harrison, Robert H. (Colonel), 447.
Harrison, Samuel, letters from, 351.
Objections to declaration of war, 351.
Harrison, suit of, against Madison, 666.
Harrison, William H. (General), 519, 597.
At Lake Erie, 109.
Call for one-month men, 292.
Capacity, 420.
Charges against, 30.
Expedition under command, 168, 292.
Historical narrative of civil and military services, 261.
Hopes resting on, 51.
Indefatigable industry, labors, and zeal, 720.
Letters from, 351, 352, 353.
Letters to, 31, 669.
Movements, 720.
Recommended, 661.
Recommended to command of Kentucky forces, 420.
Resignation, 353, 420.
Speech to the "Prophet," 352.
Suggestion for the promotion of, 614.
Hart, Abijah, application to be consul at Calcutta, 353.
Letter from, 353.
Hart, William S., letter from, 353.
Hartford Convention, The, 128.
Criticism of Dwight's history of the, 714.
Correspondence between remnants of the, and President Adams, 713.
Hartshorne, ——, letter from, 353.
Harvard College, 676.
Theological professorships, 24.
Haskell, Abraham, jr., letter from, 353.
Haskell, E., letter from, 353.
Haswell, Anthony, letter from, 354.

Hassler, F. R., 588.
Application for, to be surveyor, 414.
Documents relating to his coast survey, 353.
Letters from, 353.
Letter to, 31.
Recommended, 429.
to professorship in the University of Virginia, 353.
as surveyor and engineer, 565.
Sending copies of papers and publications, 353.
Unjust attacks upon, by the Fourth Auditor, 353.
Hastings, the trial of, 338.
Hat, Cockade for a, 350.
Haumont, Charles, asking approbation of his manuscript, 354.
Letters from, 354.
Haurbury (Lord), 271.
Havre, consul at, complaints of the, 152.
Hawes, Aylett, letters from, 354.
Hawes, John, 717.
Application for appointment as collector, 318.
Letters from, 354.
Hawkins, Benjamin (Colonel), 185.
Letter to, 823.
Hawkins, W. (Governor), letter to, 31.
Hawkins, Benjamin, defeat of, at his election to Congress, 354.
Letters from, 354, 355.
Hawkins, —— (Colonel), attempts to injure, 285.
Hawkins, Joseph, 422, 657.
Hawkins, William, letters from, 355, 356.
Haws, John, recommendation of, 149.
Hay, Charles, letter from, 356.
Hay, George, 145, 584.
Letters from, 356.
Letter to, 31.
Recommended as Federal judge, 599.
Haymaker, Frederick, 726.
Hayne, Charles Eaton, letter to, 31.
Hayward, William, letter from, 31, 356.
Hazard, Thomas, jr., 149.
Hazard, William, 306.
Letter from, 356.
Heat, Buffon's theory of central, 35.
Heath, John, application for office, 356.
Letter from, 356.
Heath, John D., 577.
Application for office, 356.
Letters from, 356.
Recommended, 591.
Heath, William, letter from, 357.
Heckle, Lydia, and others, letter from, 357.
Hellespont, occupation of the, by the English, 289.
Helme, Benson, introduced, 609.
Helm, John, letter from, 357.
Helme, ——, introduced, 594.
"Helvidius," 40.
On proclamation of neutrality, 104.
Hemp and flax, machines for manufacture, 584.
Cultivation in Virginia, 606.
New Zealand, 606.
Hempsted, Edward, 340.
Henchman, Nathaniel, letter from, 357.
Henderson, Alexander, letter from, 503.
Henderson, Thomas, letter from, 357.
Hendrick, Elijah, introduced, 423.
Hendry, Thomas, letter from, 357.
Henfield, Gideon, indictment, 392.
Hening, William W., letters from, 357.
Henry IV, equestrian statue, 74.
National devotion to, 74.
Henry, —— (Captain), record, 357.
Henry, James, letter from, 357.
Henry, James M., letters from, 357.
Henry, John, letter to, 571.
Henry, Patrick, 126, 196, 379.
Avowed enemy to the Union, 192, 457, 553.
Course, 125, 529.
Declarations, 125.
Desperate measures, 102.
Disapprobation of the circular letter of Congress respecting British debts, 487.
Influence, 458, 618.
Opposition to the Federal Constitution, 489, 624, 646, 647.
Opposition to Madison, 38.
Henry, Patrick, nomination as envoy to France, 400.
Resolutions on the second convention, 221.
Henshaw, John, letter from, 358.
Herbert, Lady, the Prince Regent ruled by, 50.
Herbert, William, letter from, 358.
Hereditary Chief Magistrate, John Adams's declaration as to an, 498.
Hereditary powers, 380.
Hereditary titles, renunciation of, 96.
Herrick, S., letter from, 358.
Recommended for office of district attorney, 371, 374.
Hersaut (French consul), letter from, 358.
Hertell, Thomas, letter from, 31.
Letters to, 358.
Hervé, ——, recommended, 181.
Hessian fly, 51, 86, 96, 108.
on wheat, ravages of the, 498.
or weevil, method for destroying the, 695.
Heth, Henry, letter from, 358.
Heth & Randolph, 499.
Letters from, 358.
Hewes, —— (Captain), demand on Great Britain, 408.
Hewitt, Thomas, letter from, 358.
Heyward, Thomas, introduced, 591.
Hichborn, Benjamin, letter from, 358.
Hickley, James, letter from, 358.
Higginson, ——, 644.
Higginson, Davis & Co., claim of, 402.
Hill, ——, mission to the Brazils, 326.
Hill, Bissets & Co., 322.
Letter from, 359.
Hill, Henry, 493.
Hill, Luke, 726.
Hill, Mark Langdon, letter from, 359.
to, 21.
Hill, William, introduced, 355.
Hillhouse, James, letters to, 31.
And others, letter from, 359.
Hilt, William, recommended, 579.
Hiltsheimer, Jacob, letter from, 359.
Hinde, Thomas S., disclosure by, of the plot to dismember the Union, 359.
Letters from, 359.
to, 32.
"Hints to young statesmen," 341.
Hinds, Thomas (Brigadier-General of Militia), 238.
Hiort, Henry, application for office of marshal, 359.
Letter from, 359.
Hispaniola, disturbances at, 58.
Persons on vessels from, denounced as pirates, 118.
Trade with, 627.
History, plan for reading, 13.
History of the United States, proposition to Madison to write a, 366.
Transmitting copies of the, 631.
Hitchcock, J., letter from, 359.
Hitchcock, J. Irvine, letter from, 359.
Hite, George (Captain), 545.
Application for situation for his son Robert, 359.
Letter from, 359.
Hite, James M., letter from, 360.
Hite, Robert, appointment solicited for, 359.
Recommended to be secretary of Indian Territory, 545.
Hobart, Aaron, recommended as collector, 361.
Hoffman, David (Professor), 32.
Letter from, 360.
to, 32.
Hogan, ——, letter from, 360.
Hoge, Moses, letter to, 32.
Holland, American property in, French decree releasing, 27.
Bankers in, arrearages to, 401.
Civil war in, 68.
Consul-general to, 439.
Enlargement of boundaries, 481.
Intercourse with, 436.
King of, edict, 249.
Loan from, to pay debt to France, 383.
Negotiation of a loan in, 193.
Politics in, 293, 381.
Taking of, by France, 531.

Holland, Edwin C., letter from, 360.
Letter to, 32.
Holland (Lord), 254.
Letter from, 360.
to, 432.
Prime minister, 49.
Hollen, H. von, letter from, 360.
Holley, Horace, letter from, 360.
Hollins, John. letter from, 360.
Hollinshead, Benjamin, change of name, 360.
Letters from, 360.
Holloway, Peter, letter from, 360.
Holmes, Charles, letter from, 361.
Holmes, David, 583.
Letter to, 328.
Holmes, J., 152.
Holmes, John, 218.
Letters from, 361.
Suggesting the appointment of, as commissioner, 333.
Holt, Joshua, 605.
Holy Alliance, the, to aid Spain in subduing her colonies, 86.
Homans, Benjamin, introduced, 316.
Letter from, 361.
Homer's Iliad, translation, 164.
Homespun clothing, 577.
Honeyman, Robert, letter from, 361.
Apology for abrupt departure, 361.
Hooe, Francis H., court-martial against, 251.
Hooe, J. H., letters from, 361.
Hooe, Robert, & Co., letter from, 361.
Hoomes, John, letters from, 362.
Hope & Baring, guarantee of the loan of, 501, 535.
Houses of, contract with, 699.
Loan of, 479, 480.
Hope & Co. (Amsterdam), 205.
Hopkins, B. B., letter from, 362.
Hopkins, John, desire to retain office, 362.
Letters from, 362.
Hopkins, Samuel G. (General), failure of the expedition of, 657.
Horse keeping, 359, 605.
Horses, breeding of, 88, 362, 555, 673, 674.
Price of, 662.
Purchase of, 146. 387, 566 567.
by British agents, 257.
Riding, selection of, 419.
Scarcity of, 711.
Substituting, for oxen, 89.
Tax on, 199.
Thefts of, by Indians, 654.
Hosack, David, letter from, 362.
Hospital, establishment at Charleston, 428.
Hostages, securing of, 631.
Hostilities, cessation of (1783), 100.
Proposed suspension of (1812), 51.
Hotel keepers, depravity of, 213.
Hotz, Peter, jr., letter from, 362.
Hot water to prevent boarding of vessels, 294.
Houdon's statue, 36.
Hougeworth, V. M., letter from, 362.
House building, 269.
Building of Madison's, 206.
House of Representatives, a church offered for temporary occupation of the, 453.
Power of the, to punish for contempt, 356.
Scandalous scene in the, 400.
House, William, letter from, 362.
Houston, James, letter from, 362.
Houston, John, application for a patent, 499.
Patent of, 338.
Houston, Samuel, letter from, 362.
Howard, —— (General), recommended, 660.
Usefulness and capacity of (1813), 421.
Howard, Charles P., letters from, 363.
Howard University, 114.
Howe (Lord), fleet of, 98.
Howell, David, application for office of district judge, 721.
Death of, 600.
Letter from, 363.
to, 284.
Request of, to not remove from office an old officer, 363.
Howell, I., 682.
Howell, Jeremiah Brown, introduced, 363.
Ineligibility as Senator, 283.
Howell, Joseph, 636.
Letters from, 363, 364.
to, 735.
Hoyt, Moses, appeal of, for pardon, 364
Letter from, 364.
Hubbard, J., letter from, 364.
Hubbard, Simeon, complaint by, of t
Administration, 364.
Letters from, 364.
Huddy, Joshua (Captain), murder of,
Hudson River and Great Lakes, con
canal between the, 519.
Huger, Benjamin, letter from, 364.
Hull, Andrew, jr., letters from, 364.
Hull, Isaac (Captain), expedition of t
against force of, 364.
Letter from, 364, 602.
Victory over the *Guerrière*, 280.
Hull, William (General), 21.
Defeat of, 88, 133, 263, 273, 291, 310, 3
661, 719.
Downfall, 127.
Expedition, 51.
Incomprehensible conduct of, 292, 3
Not included in the armistice, 474.
Pay of, 455.
Recommended, 314.
Trial of, 141.
Hulshoff, M. A., letter from, 364.
Humbert, Jonas, appeal for Governn
tion, 364.
Letter from, 364.
Humbert, Jonas, jr., application for G
office, 364.
Letter from, 364.
Humboldt, Alexander von, intention t
tensive explorations in this coun
Introduced, 332, 735.
Letters from, 365.
Letter to, 32.
Opinion of, of possibilities of comn
from sea to sea at the Isthmus, 3
Travels of, in South America, 365.
Visit of, in Washington, 365.
Works of, 325.
Hume, Charles, letter from, 365.
Humphreys, David, letters from, 365, 3
Letter to, 32.
Humphreys, Hosea, letter from, 366.
Hungary, Queen of, death of the, 514.
Hunt, Abraham, claim of, 366.
Letter from, 366.
Hunt, G. J., letter from, 366.
Hunt, Henry, introduced, 212.
Hunter, John, letter from, 366.
Hunter, John D., letter from, 366.
Hunter's Sacred Biography, 716.
Hunting no longer profitable, 355.
Huntington, Eben, letter from, 366.
Letter to, 32.
Huntington, Hez, letter from, 366.
Huntington, H., jr., letter from, 366.
Huntington, Jed. letter from, 366.
Huntington, Samuel, letters from, 367.
Hurlbut, M. L., letters from, 367.
Letter to, 32.
Hurley, Robert (Midshipman), prefe
pected by, 456.
Hurt, John, letters from, 367.
Husbandry, essay on, 164.
Husbands, Herman, 570.
Huston (Surgeon's mate), court-martial
291.
Hutchins, Henry J., letters from, 367.
Soliciting situation of postmaster,
Hutchinson, Pemberton, recommended
Hutton (Sailing-master), court-martial
Hutton, James, letter to, 602.
Hutton, Joseph, letters from, 367.
Hutton, Nicholas, letter from, 367.
Hydraulic ram, Montgolfier's improven

I.

Ibley, D., and others, letter from, 368.
Illinois and Sacs Indians, accommodati
between the, 239.
Illinois and Wabash companies, 650.

Illinois and Wabash companies, lands granted by Indians to 733.
Illinois and Wabash campanies, valuation of territory bought by. 561.
Illinois and Wabash Company, claims of heirs of one Gerard to lands of the, 436.
Illinois, legislature of, letter from, 368.
Illinois, Territory, legislature of, petition to Congress for protection. 297.
Illinois, legislature of, memorial from the, 282.
Illinois regiments, 594.
Illinois Territory, military bounty lands of, 310.
Imbecility in conduct of last campaign (1812), 728.
Immigration, encouragement, 724.
Of Irishmen, 199.
Statistics on, 233.
Impeachments, bill for regulating proceedings on, 396.
Cases of, 45.
Question of jury in cases of, 397.
Of President and Senators proposed, 620.
Import duty, extension of the, Madison's speech on, 695.
Importers, profits of, 307.
Relief of, 307.
Imports and exports, taxation of, 124.
In England from the United States, 511.
Revenue from, 273.
Impost, 84, 98.
Act, passing of the, by Rhode Island and Georgia, 528.
Bill for establishing, 159.
Bills for collecting, 69.
Opposition of New York to the, 78.
Prospect of the, 335.
Recommendation of renewal, 100.
Repeal of the, 99.
Scheme, 355.
System, 227.
Imposts, question, 94, 103. 527.
Impressment question, 23, 54, 55, 73, 75, 82, 84, 85, 229, 232, 248, 293, 399, 402, 403, 406, 427, 432, 551, 701, 705.
Imprisonment for debt, 422, 642.
Improvements, promoting objects of, 108.
"Inchiquin's" letters, authorship of, 368.
Incomes, living beyond, 107.
Indefatigable, brig, case of the crew, 703.
Wreck of the, 109.
Indemnity, demands of, 52.
Independence, British acknowledgment of our (1783), 101.
Conjectures as to the probability of European recognition of our, 495.
Origin of American, 2.
India, shipment of wines to, 153.
Trade, 244.
Indian affairs, President's message on, 79.
agents, salaries in lieu of rations paid to, 505.
chiefs, as hostages, 291.
visit to Washington of, 240.
commissioners, variance between, of the United States and of New York, 527.
council, near St. Joseph, on Lake Michigan, 351.
Department, proposed transfer of the, 291.
hostilities, measures to prevent, 282.
no apprehension of (1810), 289.
hostility to Western posts, 58.
lands. (*See* Lands, Indian).
sale of, 352.
speech, (Ottaway chief), 368.
talks, (1812), 368.
treaties (1796), 80.
allotment of money for, 124.
treaty at Fort Stanwix, 67.
proposed trip by Monroe to attend the, 528.
Tribes, conciliation of, 185.
of Louisiana, embassies to, 403.
unsuspecting, plunder of the, 376.
war (1794), 554.
indications of, 352.
to be carried on (1792), 653.
youths, education of, 722.
Indiana claim, the, 255.
Company, the, 161.
Indians, activity of, on our frontiers, 51.
Address to, 32.
American and British conduct toward, contrasted, 64.
Attack of, near Saline, and protection asked, 545.
Civilization of the, 64, 65, 490.
Complaints of the, of ill treatment, 351.
Conduct of the (1794), 654.
Connistoga, letter from, 368.
Constitution of a society for the benefit of the, 76.
Depredations of the, 187, 352, 368, 549, 553, 654, 705.
Desirability of cultivating the friendship of the, 376.
Dispossessing, of their lands, 130.
Education of the, 185, 200.
Encouragement to, in pursuit of agriculture, 453.
Hostile combinations of the, 352.
Improvements and contented condition of the, 355.
Incursions of, instigated by British traders, 297.
Murders and outrages by, 671.
Peace with, 368.
Policy of conciliating the, 643.
Policy pursued toward, in the war of 1812, 64, 65.
Predatory and murderous excursions of the, 355.
Prevention of selling spirituous liquors to, 367.
Promises to the, to rectify injuries done, 352.
Proposal to, to sell their possessions east of the Mississippi, 265.
Provisions for the, 238.
Question whether, are members of the State of New York or simply living within its bounds, 527.
School for education of, 597.
Southern, apprehensions of a war with the, 464.
treaties with, 76.
Society for benefit of, 52.
Suggestions as to campaign against the, 460.
Supplies to, by British Government, 39.
Supplying, with mechanical instruments, 239.
Trading horses with the, 262.
Treaties with, 68.
Unquiet, instigated by Spaniards, 76.
Vocabularies of the American, 385.
West of the Missouri and Arkansas, location of the, 490.
Industry, schooner, release of the, 442.
Influenza, prevalence of, 69. 95.
Ingersoll, Charles, introduced, 369.
Ingersoll. Charles J., intention of, to write a history of the war of 1812, 369.
Letters from, 368, 369.
to, 32, 33, 159, 171.
Visit of, at Montpelier, 369.
Ingersoll, Jared. letters from, 369.
Ingersoll, Joseph, introduced, 369.
Inglis, —— (Dr.), claim of, 357.
Ingraham, Nathaniel, and son, letter from, 370.
Inland navigation, 56.
Innerarity, James, letters from, 370.
Letter to, 681.
Innes, Harry, 705.
Charges of complicity with Wilkinson, 370.
Death, 657.
Letters from, 370.
Insects, destroying of, on fruit trees, 215.
Inside Out, a publication, 214.
Instruction, public, of youth, 113.
Insurance case, 219.
on Madison's house, 363.
Intemperate drinking, 358.
Interest, unclaimed, on a stock to credit of Madison, 240.
Intercourse law, 46.
Internal defense, expenses providing for, 258.
Improvements, 62, 116, 120, 227, 418, 692.
Revenue, collector of, duties, 234.
Intoxicating drinks, use of, 31.
Introduction, letters of, discrimination in, 385.
Invalides, Hotel des, attack on the, 386.

Inventions in military and naval tactics, awful and terrific, 732.
Ireland, affairs in, a trouble to England, 381.
Insurrection in, 399.
People of, 228.
Vindication of, 12.
Irishmen, immigration of, 199.
Irish propositions, defeat of the, 381.
Trade, the, 604.
Iron manufactures in Kentucky, 654.
Mining and manufacture of, 645.
Works, etablishment of, 262, 263.
in Kentucky, 654.
in the Cherokee Nation, 413, 518, 519.
Irugo, Carlos M. de. (*See* Yrugo.)
Irvine, Callender, 725.
Appointment as commissary-general, 471.
Suggested as superintendent of military stores, 273.
Irvine, William, letter from, 371.
Letters to, 252, 630.
Irwin, Henry, application for appointment in the Army, 547.
Irwin, Nathaniel, application for clerkship for his son, 370.
Character, 370.
Letters from, 370.
Letter to, 332.
Israel and Morgan, contest between, 397.
Italy, subjugation of, 533.
Itching sensation, remedy for, 276.
Iturbide, Emperor, character of, 667.
Fall of, 667.
Execution of, 668.
Ivory, ——, 417.
Izard, George (General), charges against, 247.
Letter from, 371.

J.

Jackson, Andrew, 18.
Beheading of the figure of, on ship *Constitution*, 714.
Conduct, 85, 618.
Correspondence between, and the Secretary of War, 539.
Course, 5.
Dates of commissions granted to, 86.
Directions to, 239.
Estimate of, by Hugh Mercer, 520.
Important services, 211.
Jefferson and Madison's opinion of, 52.
Letter from, 371.
to, 33, 239.
Misunderstandings between, and executive authorities in Louisiana, 211.
Orders, 59.
Popularity, 248.
Prohibitory letter to, 87.
Report of the proceedings of, in Florida, 536.
Spanish posts taken by, 537.
Tariff policy of the Administration, 180.
Violent character of, 211.
Jackson, Francis James (British minister), 299, 411.
Arrival, 626.
Conduct, 482.
Dismissal of, not a rupture with his Government, 483.
Distrust of, by Canning, 48.
Insults, 602.
Jackson, George, application for office of marshal, 371, 375.
Letter from, 371.
Jackson, Henry, letter from, 371.
Jackson, James, letters from, 371.
Reappointment as Senator, 371.
Resignation, 371.
Jackson, John G., 48, 166, 271.
Acknowledging receipt of a commission, 375.
Attempt to assassinate, 373.
Desire to serve in the Army, 375
to be appointed judge, 374.
Election as Member of Congress, 375.
as member of the Virginia assembly, 374.
Letters from, 372, 373, 374, 375, 376.
Letter to, 33.
Jackson, John G., Marriage, 374.
Offer to advance sums for compensation of rifle corps, 375.
Resignation as commissioner, 375.
Sufferings of brigade of Virginia commanded by, 376.
Jackson, John G. (Mrs.), illness and death, 372, 373.
Jackson, Josiah, letters from, 376.
Jackson, Matthew W., letter from, 376.
Jackson party, confidence of the, 56.
Jacob, brig, cargo, 588, 643.
Wreck of the, 206, 663.
Jacobin party, description of the, 389.
Society, Monroe's official correspondence on, 79.
Jacobins, American, and French Directory, treasonable correspondence between, 399.
Jamaica, discharged seamen at, 697.
Prizes, seizures, 91.
James and Kanawha rivers, scheme of the, 182.
James River, attempt of the British to ascend, 424.
Defense, 145.
Navigation of the, 581.
James, Daniel, letter from, 376.
Jameson, ——, (Major), 240.
Jamison, James, letter from, 376.
Jarvies, James, letter from, 376.
Jarvies, William, letters from, 377.
Java, capture of the, by the *Constitution*, 424.
Jay, James, letters from, 377.
Request to take passage to France in a frigate, 377.
"Jay," misprint for "Joy," 59.
Jay, John, adjustment of points in controversy by, 531.
Affront put upon, by Congress, 77.
Appointment as minister to Great Britain, 41, 71.
As secretary of foreign affairs, 56, 67, 527.
Controversy with Mr. Littlepage, 528.
Delapaine's biography of, 111.
Disapproval of appointment of, 723.
Election as governor, 173.
Letters from, 377.
to, 384, 691.
Misconduct of, in his negotiations with Gardoqui, 532.
Misled as to the course of the French Government, 87.
Mission of, embarrassing to Monroe, 531.
Proposition of, respecting the Mississippi, 529.
Return to America, 67.
Treaty, 96, 377.
conjectures as to, 72.
discussion in Congress as to, 72.
in the hands of the Executive, 79.
object of, 45.
opinions on, 20, 24.
President's speech on, 42.
public opinion of, 41, 42, 43.
ratification of, in England, 72.
remonstrances against, 41.
withholding from Monroe facts relating to the, 532.
Jay, Peter Augustus, letter to, 33.
Jefferson, George, letters from, 378.
Jefferson, Thomas, ability of, and zeal for his country, 93.
Abuse of, 422.
Acceptance of appointment as Secretary of State, 387.
Administration of, a defense of, 732.
history, 164.
public sentiment toward (1801), 81.
Anachronisms, 2.
Jefferson and Adams, candidates for President and Vice-President, 80.
Jefferson's and Madison's political principles, no difference in, 410.
Jefferson, anecdote by, about Benjamin Franklin, 378.
Application for office from persons difficult to refuse, 412.
Appointment as minister to France, 35, 98, 528.
Secretary of State, 127.
Attempts of Government to defeat (1800), 279.

Jefferson, bequest, 113, 180, 484.
Biography, 117, 118.
Books to be supplied to Congress by, 51.
Charges of irreligion, 279, 280, 491.
Candidate for the Presidency, 498.
Correspondence, 115, 116.
Death, 56, 96, 511.
Delay of retirement, 391.
Delayed departure for Europe, 378.
Democratic Society, 692.
Desires the Presidency of Madison, 394.
Determination to resign (1793), 391.
Diplomatic correspondence, 430.
Disinclination of, for political honors, 395.
Dislike of, to be nominated to administration of the Government, 395.
Election, 43, 73, 122, 507, 572.
Embarcation, 34.
Estate of, embarrassments of, 54.
Eulogium on, 7, 158.
Expected visit to Europe, 496.
Expediency of inviting, to be Secretary of State (1812), 280.
Family of, destitute condition of, 56.
Financial difficulties, 418.
Gilpin's life of, 29.
Ideas as to a new State constitution or amendments, 379.
Inaugural address of, to be printed on satin, 260.
Letters from, 378, 418.
to Adams and Madison, 116.
to Kercheval, 55.
to Mazzei, 279.
Letters to, 33 to 54 inclusive, 142, 144, 160, 161, 176, 236, 262, 274, 279, 344, 354, 470, 472, 487, 493, 506, 523, 524, 534, 584, 593, 597, 607, 614, 624, 633, 627.
Library of, eventual disposition of, 410.
protest against the purchase of, by Congress, 546.
Manuscripts, publication of the, 75.
Marriage of daughter to Mr. Randolph, 387, 530.
Memoirs of, 418, 629.
results of publication of the, 57.
Mission of, to France, 34, 66.
as associate with Franklin and Adams, 67.
No desire to be President, 394.
Offering money arrangements to, 47.
Outfit, 37.
Plans of, for general farming, 391.
Preparation of memoirs, 110.
Proposed biography, 685.
mission, 98.
monument to, 590.
retirement (1793), 39.
statue, 172.
Query as to the present station (1792), 95.
Refusal to meddle in a Presidential election, 416.
Remarkable vigor, 107.
Salary and outfit, 384.
Serious illness, 274.
Settlement of financial matters with Madison, 410.
Sketch of life, 320.
Statue of, in plaster, by Coffee, 214.
Strictures on the conduct of, in censuring the measures of the first Administration, 463.
Suggestion that, be Secretary of State (1812), 505.
Tour in France, 383, 618.
Tribute to memory, 115, 172.
Undiminished friendship between, and Madison, 115.
Views on accepting the election of second office (1797), 395.
on a Dutch loan, 390.
on hereditary head of Government, 110.
Vindication, 122.
Visit to New England, 380.
Works of, prospectus, 54.
Jefferson, "Patsy," hieroglyphical writing of, 379.
Jena, battle of, 466.
Jenkins, —— (Colonel), introduced, 678.
Jenkins, —— (secretary of state of New Y introducing, 670.
Jennings, Robert C., settlement of accounts o
Jerfry, John, & Co., letter from, 418.
"Jerusalem delivered," translation of, 164.
Jesse (negro slave), offer to Madison to purc 358.
Jervey, James, and others, letters from, 418.
Jesup, Thomas S. (General), 18, 21, 239, 240.
Jewell, R. George Washington, letters from,
Jews, history of the, 21.
Massacre of, at Algiers, 702.
Johnson, Alexander, introduced, 730.
Johnson, Cabell, Loyall, and Breckinridge tors of the University), letters to, 54.
Johnson, Chapman, letters from, 419.
Letters to, 54, 565.
Johnson, Edward, letters from, 419.
Letter to, 54.
Johnson, F., letter from, 419.
Johnson, Hezekiah, introduced, 660.
Johnson, James, 421.
Appeal of, for payment of amounts due 420.
Letters from, 420.
Johnson, James B., letters from, 420.
Johnson, Jeromus, introduced, 610.
Johnson, John, recommended, 321.
Johnson, John (Sir), 205, 715.
Johnson, Joseph, letter from, 420.
Johnson, Richard M., denial by, of reports re ing on his character, 421.
Introduced, 294.
Letters from, 420, 421, 422.
Letter to, 172.
Services, 203.
Johnson, Robert, letters from, 422.
Johnson, Thomas B., letter from, 423.
Johnson, Valentine, 146.
Johnson, William (Judge), 52.
Letter to, 54.
Johnston, Orramel, letter from, 420.
Johnston, P., letter from, 423.
Johnstone, G. W., letter from, 423.
Johonnot, G. (Colonel), 644.
Letter from, 423.
Jones, —— (Dr.), appointment of, at the Ui sity, 213.
Recommended as professor of chemistry
Jones, Edward, appointment of, to Guadel 627.
Jones, Evan, resignation of, 208.
Jones, Jesse, and others, letter from, 423.
Jones, John Paul, life and character of, 618.
Jones, John Q., introduced, 610.
Jones, Jonathan, 424.
Jones, Joseph, 299.
Letter from, 423.
to, 711, 712.
Jones, Mary, suit of, against United States
Jones, Merewether, death of, 406.
Jones, Roger (Adjutant-General), letter to,
Jones, Thomas (Dr.), appointment of, 179.
Letter from, 423.
Jones, Walter, 696.
Letters from, 423, 424.
Letter to, 505, 608.
And others, letters from, 423.
Jones, Walter, jr., letter from, 423.
Jones, William, acceptance of, as Secretary c Navy, 424.
Announcement of his intention to resi Secretary of the Navy, 426.
Letter of resignation, 429.
Letters from, 424, 425, 426, 427, 428, 429, 4
to, 54, 149, 152, 175, 186, 204, 267, 364 545.
Request to be relieved from duties as A Secretary of the Treasury, 426.
Resignation as Secretary of the Navy, 5
Jones, William (Captain), recommended, 66
Jones, William, jr., 291.
Jones, W. W., letter to, 489.
Jordan, John, introduced, 656.
Jorre, ——, letter from, 430
Solicitation of, for Government employ 430.
Joseph and *Phœbe*, vessels, 466.

Jourdan, père et fils, letter to, 201.
"Journal of Science," 619.
Journals of Congress, preservation of the original, 61.
Journey with Monroe, postponed, 78.
Joy, Benjamin, letter from, 430.
Joy, George, 2.
Acceptance by, of the consulate at Rotterdam, 433.
Application for consulate at Rotterdam, 431.
Application for an appointment with sufficient salary, 437.
Death of wife, 431.
Defense from malicious attacks, 438.
Desire for consulate at Antwerp, 476.
Intention to devote his life to the public, 431.
Letters from, 430, 431, 432, 433, 434, 435, 436, 437, 438, 439, 440.
to, 54, 55, 289, 360, 440, 454, 610, 615.
Negotiations in Denmark, 438.
Offer of the services of, in an embassy to Spain, 431.
Offer of temporary services, 439.
Request for remuneration for services, 437.
Joy, M., letter from, 440.
Judge, removal of a, 145.
Judge-Advocate, office, 563.
Judicial act of 1789, 25.
Interpretation, 32.
Power, 15.
System, 56.
Judiciary act of 1789, authorship of the, 269.
Bill, 69, 94, 118.
Federal. 685.
National supremacy of the, 124.
Right of the, to declare a law unconstitutional, 530.
System, 196, 722.
reforms in the, 194.
Vacancy in the (1810), 49.
Julian, case of the, 438.
July Fourth, death of three Presidents on, 359.
The three days of, 57.
June, Zabuel, letter from, 440.
Offers his services in the prosecution of the war, 440.
Junius, authorship of, 128, 714.
Junto faction, 51.
"Juntos," 326.
Jurisdiction, civil, immunity of religion from, 62.
National, latitude of the, 105.
Jurisprudence, criminal, defects of the system, 478.
Jurors, drawing of, by lot, 46.
Grand, functions of, 44.
In Burr's trial, 325.
Justus, James, letters from, 440, 441.
Juvenile Library Company of Richmond, commends activity of founders, 75.

K.

Kalb, de (Baron), and Duc de Choiseul, correspondence between, 635.
Kane, J. R., introduced, 695.
Kaufman, Martin, legacy of, 354.
Kaskaskia, order to General Harrison to march to, 421.
Keating, William, introduced, 707.
Keembe, John, letter from, 441.
Letter to, 56.
Kelsall, Charles, letter from, 441.
Letter to, 55.
Kelso, William, letter from, 441.
Kelty, William, 613.
Kemper, Reuben, hostile projects of, 298.
Letter from, 441.
Kendall, Amos, 595.
Kenedy, Thomas, recommended for commission in the Army, 491.
Kennedy, John P., letters from, 441.
Letter to, 55.
Kennedy, Joseph P., character of, 636.
Letter from, 441.
Vindication of character, 441.
Kennedy, Philip Pendleton, letter from, 441.
Kenney, Thomas T., letter to, 55.
Kent, James (Chancellor), 274.
Kent, Joseph, recommendation from, 225.
Kentucky, admittance into the Union, 173.
and Tennessee called on for militia reinforcements, 210.
Application for independence, 334.
Attempt in, to raise an army to attack the Spaniards, 554.
Bill for admitting, 69, 70, 95.
Citizens of, bravery and patriotism, 109.
Constitution, 9, 654.
Convention, 173, 254.
Deed for tract of land in, 287.
Deplorable state of legislation in, 671.
Depredations and murders by Indians in, 335.
Factions in, 173.
Financial condition of (1825), 113.
Formation of a goverment in, 553, 705.
Formal application for independence, 123.
Great drought in, 610.
History, 173.
Improvements in, 654.
Inadequacy of defense in, 706.
Inefficiency of the militia in, 654.
Inroads of savages in, 78.
Iron manufactures in, 654.
Land disputes, 553.
Lands in, 205, 206, 339, 362, 656.
claim to, 13.
sale of, 715.
taxes on, 311.
titles to, 656.
Legislature of, acts of the, relating to revenue and judiciary, 654.
letters from, 441.
Proposed constitution, 173.
Proposed independence, 173.
Public schools in, 153.
Question of independence, 68.
Quota furnished by, 139.
Resolutions of 1799, 10, 25, 114, 116, 182.
Sale of land in, 205.
Scheme of Gardoqui to create an independent State, 9.
Secession, 553.
Separation of, from Virginia, 55, 60, 77, 465, 496, 549, 705, 706.
Services of militia, 168.
Smallpox in, 654.
Spanish intrigues to detach, 177.
System of education in, 6.
Taxes in, burdensome, 705.
Troops, impatience of, to be called into service, 420.
Ker, James, letter from, 441.
Kercheval, Samuel, letters from, 442.
Letter to, 55.
Kerr, Alexander, introduced, 350.
Kerr, Joseph, letters from, 442.
Resigns a commission, 442.
Kersey, Jesse, letter from, 442.
Keteltas, William, application for commission of colonel, 442.
Application for office of marshal, 442.
Letter from, 442.
Key (Professor), 16, 17, 25.
Resignation, 54, 118, 119.
Salary, 213.
Successor of, at the University of Virginia, 115.
Key, F. S., letter from, 442.
Keyser, George, letter from, 443.
Kidd, Albert J., letter from, 443.
Kidd, James, letter from, 443.
Kilty, John, appointment solicited by, 443.
Letter from. 443.
Kilty, W., letter from, 443.
King, Benjamin, appeal in behalf of, 524.
Letter from, 443.
Petition for increase of pay, 443.
King, Charles, letter from, 443.
King, —— (General), introduced, 537.
King, John, letter from, 443.
King, Miles, letters from, 444.
Letter to, 55.
King, N., letter from, 444.
King of England, convalescence of the, 50.
Disability of the, 94.

King, Rufus, appointment of, as minister to England, 302.
Entertainment at New York given to, 455.
Inflammatory conduct, 85.
Intention to offer himself for President, 422.
Letters from, 444, 445.
Report respecting negotiations with Great Britain, 445.
Sentiments as to conduct of Great Britain, 38.
King, William, letter from. 445.
Letter to, 55.
Kingly government, advocates of a, 197.
Kings Mountain, battle of, 91.
Controversy as to the participants in battle, 97.
King's speech, the (1783), 34.
Kingston, Jamaica, 445.
American vessels at, 136.
Approval of the Administration by shipmasters of, 152.
Kinlock, Francis, letters from, 445.
Requesting letters and passport, 445.
Request for his son's appointment in the Army, 445.
Kinlock, Frederick, recommended. 694.
Kinlock, —— (Lieutenant), introduced, 364.
Kinney, Thomas T., letter from, 445.
Kinsey, Charles, letter from, 445.
Kirby, E., letter from, 446.
Kirk, William, letter from, 446.
Kirkpatrick, —— (Dr.), recommended, 684.
Kirkpatrick, William, letter from. 446.
Knaggs, Whitman (Indian agent), claims, 239.
Knapp, John, appointment requested by, 446.
Letters from, 446.
Knowland, ——, killing of, 443.
Knox, Henry, bankruptcy, 399.
Knox, James, letter from, 446.
Knox, Thomas, letter from, 446.
Konkapot, John, jr., appeal of, for liberation from jail, 446.
Letter from, 446.
Koontz, John, letter from, 441.
Kortright, J., suit in chancery with, 446.
Kortright, L., will of, 531.
Kosloff affair, 331.
Complaints against, 250.
Krafft, Michael (inventor), 667.
Kuch, A., letter from. 446.

L.

Laboratory, proposal to the Government to erect a, 492.
Labor and agriculture, 128.
Rates of different kinds, 344.
Labouchere, John, introduced, 205.
Lacock, Abner, letter from, 446.
La Croix, (*See* De la Croix.)
Lacy. (*See* De Lacy.)
Lacy, John D. De, 446.
Lafayette, account of the journey of, through the United States, 277.
Adams's obituary of, 55, 120.
Affection for, 56.
At the *Assemblée des notables*, 618.
At the head of the militia, 94.
Bill for benefit, 81.
Busts, 76.
Career, 2.
Certificate of land located for, 625.
Character, 36.
Commander in chief at Paris (1789), 386.
Death, 62, 212.
Dinner and ball for, at Fredericksburg, 417.
Eulogy on, 25.
Expected visit of, to Orange, 146.
Extravagant honors and presents to, 265.
Incidents in life, 55.
In the Bastile 94.
Invitation to accompany, on his tour North, 67.
visit Madison, 56.
Madison to dinner in honor, 320, 475.
reception, 133.
Jefferson's estimate, 383.
Lafayette, land for, located in Louisiana, 219, 404, 411, 412, 518, 562, 563.
grants and debts, 49, 81.
titles. 48.
Letters from, 447.
to, 56, 57.
Life, 114, 676.
Loan to, 56, 303, 447.
Location of land, 56. 209, 217, 276, 304, 341, 350.
Movements (1789), 385.
Patriotic discretion, 57.
Pecuniary condition, 570.
Policy of selling land of. in Louisiana, 276.
Reception to, 1.
Recommendations by, for offices for consul, 260.
Reports concerning (1788), 37.
Sale of lands at Point Coupée by, 151.
Sentiments of, on the French budget, 56.
Situation (1793), 199.
Toasts at the dinner given to, 56.
Tour, 35.
Visit (1824), 113, 539.
Laffite, Jean, letter from, 447.
Petition of, for restitution of his property, 447.
Lafou, B., letter from, 447.
Plats of surveys of lands granted by Congress to Lafayette, 447.
Lagaska, Mariano, recommended. 341.
Laird, John, letter from, 447.
Lakanal, ——, letter from, 447.
Lake Champlain, victory of Commodore McDonough at, 242, 429, 488.
Lake Erie, contemplated operations on, 427.
Precarious situation of the squadron on, 691.
Unarmed and defenseless condition of the people at. 446.
Victory on, 330.
Lake Huron, preparations of the enemy on, 427.
Lake Ontario, increase of naval force on, 429.
Troops for, 264.
Lake Superior, discovery of copper on shores, 487.
Lakes, importance of increasing the force on the, 728.
Lamb, Anthony (Colonel), introduced, 678.
Lambert, John, letters from, 447, 448.
Lambert, William, introduced, 568.
Letters from, 448, 449.
Position in the Department of State desired by, 448.
Request of, for office, 449.
Undertaking of, to fix a first meridian for the United States, 448.
Lammond, Alexander, letter from, 447.
La Motta. (*See* De la Motta.)
Lamp, newly invented, 381.
Lancaster, tumultuous proceedings at, 155.
Lançat, ——, 673.
Land and rents, 5.
Bill, the Western, 70.
Conveyance, 4.
Divisions, 229.
In Virginia, decline in price, 116.
Jobbing business, 705.
Ordinance, change in the, 335.
Purchase, 36, 77, 78, 498, 731.
Sale of, on the Mohawk, 166.
Speculations in Louisiana, 207.
Tax for revenue, 309.
modification of the. 398.
Valuation, 34.
Warrants, 496.
Landed fund, 227.
Landon, James, letter from, 449.
Lands, Indian, removal of intruders on, 262.
In Kentucky, 205, 206.
Patents for, delay in issuing, 304.
Lands, Public. (*See* Public Lands), 15, 609.
Application to occupy, 159.
Appropriations of, for purposes of education, 513.
Disposal, 7, 37, 95.
Distribution, 106.
Enforcement of the laws on, 175.
Loans on the, 272.
Protection to settlers on, 586.
Rule of apportionment, 99.
Suit for adjusting share in, 72.

Lands, Public, survey and sale of, ceded by Virginia, 528.
Vacant, avidity of Western people for, 98.
Western, bills for selling, 42.
Sales, 334.
Lane, Samuel, letter from, 449.
Appointment of, as commissioner applied for, 422, 503.
Lang & Turner, letter from, 449.
Langdon, John, 193, 612.
Letter from, 449.
Pleasant reminiscences, 449.
Reasons for declining offer of secretaryship of the Navy to, 449.
Scheme of, to induce British sailors to desert, 449, 450.
Suggestions that, be candidate for Vice-President, 503.
Langdon, Woodbury, letter from, 450.
Langham, Elias, letters from, 450.
Request of, to be appointed commissary of military stores, 450.
Language, innovation in, 57.
Primitive structure, 37.
Languages, ancient, professor of, 30, 31.
Lansing, Abraham G., appointment, 139.
Letter from, 450.
to, 139, 246.
Lansing, John Y., wish to be transferred, 450.
Lanterns for artillery service, 272.
La Pena (Colonel), qualifications, 181.
Lapsley, Samuel (Captain), claim, 450.
Lapsley, Sarah W., letter from, 450.
Larned, Samuel, application for consul at Gibraltar, 544.
Latham, William, 513.
Letter from, 450.
Latrobe, Benjamin H., 47.
Complains of the commissioners of public buildings, 453.
Deviation of the plan of the Capitol by, 674.
Intention to go into the cotton manufacturing business, 451.
Letters from, 451, 452, 453.
Letter to, 57, 566.
Objections to the lowering of his salary, 452.
Progress of the public buildings under charge, 451.
Request that his son be assistant in direction of public buildings, 451.
Refusal of office of engineer of State of New York, 452.
Testimony in Burr's trial, 451.
Lattimer, William, letter to, 443.
Laurens, ——, letter from, 453.
Laurens, Henry (Lieutenant-colonel), 453.
Exchange, 98.
Imprisonment in the tower of London, 271.
Respecting the report concerning his mission to France, 217.
Laussat, ——, 207.
Laval, John, letter from, 453.
Law, common, of England and Virginia, 103.
Profession of the vile and vicious, 223.
Law, John, suit against, 613.
Law, —— (Mrs.), movements of, 673.
Law, Thomas, 19.
Essay by, 245.
Letters from, 453, 454.
Letter to, 57.
Law, William, letter from, 454.
Letter to, 438.
Lawrence, J., letter to, 318.
Lawrence, James (Captain), 425.
Challenge of Commodore Brooks to, 425.
Funeral, 157.
Lawrence, William Beach, introduced, 610.
Laws of Congress, printing of the, 606.
Publication, 269, 271, 272.
Suggestion as to publishing, in German language in Pennsylvania, 698.
Laws of nations, British order abrogating, 231.
Repeated violations of the, 232.
Laws of the United States and of the several States, proposed edition of the, 61.
Codification of the, 129, 732.
Errors in the, 454.
Lawson's History of North Carolina, 643.
Lay, John O., letters from, 455.
Lea, Isaac, letter from, 455.
Letter to, 57.
Leake, Walter, 475.
Leander, Americans imprisoned on the, 701.
Detention on the, 703.
Lear, Benjamin L., letter from, 455.
Lear, Tobias, conduct of, in the Tripoli business, 456.
Declining appointment in the War Department, 456.
Denial of reports of his suppression of part of the diary of Washington, 456.
Details of official business, 456.
Letters from, 455, 456, 457.
On leaving Algiers, 456.
Outfit and salary of, as consul at Algiers, 455, 456.
Sailing of, for Algiers in the *Constitution*, 455.
Learned, —— (Colonel), 673.
Learned, J. D., calumnies by, 734.
Leclerc (General), 403, 571.
Lee, Arthur, 529.
Unfairness of, 611.
Lee, Charles (Attorney-General), 80.
Lee, Charles Carter, letter from, 457.
Letter to, 57.
Lee, Edmond J., and others, letter from, 457.
Letter to, 457.
Recommended, 664.
Lee, Henry (General), 126.
Advice of, to Madison, as to his conduct as President, 461.
Anxiety of, to go to Bermuda, 461.
Appointment of, to take command to restore order in Pennsylvania, 460.
Blunder in the writing of Jefferson respecting, 463.
Censor of the policy of Washington's first term, 59.
Defeat of, as Delegate to Congress, 457.
Disaffection of, to the policy of Washington's administration, 462.
Indelicacy of the situation of, 57.
Letters from, 457, 458, 459, 460, 461, 462.
to, 57, 58.
Madison's treatment of, in the Great Falls scheme, 460.
Material for life, 59.
Memoirs of, by his son, 463.
Militia advocated by, 457.
Notes on, 60.
Offer of, as delegate from Westmoreland, 457.
Omission of, from the delegation to Congress (1786), 123.
Request of, to be sent to the Brazils as government agent, 461.
Residence of, in Barbadoes, 462.
Vindication, 59.
War preferred by, to continuation of disputation and irritation (1811), 462.
Lee, Henry (author), 140.
Letters from, 463, 464.
to, 59, 60.
Proposition of, to write histories of Virginia's great men, 463.
To write on the campaign of 1814, 463.
Lee, John H., 241.
Letters from, 464.
to, 60.
Settlement of a disputed land title by, 60.
Lee, Joseph (Captain), recommended, 317.
Lee, Ludwell, 599.
Letter from, 464.
Lee, Richard, letter from, 465.
Lee, Richard Bland, letter from, 464.
Letters to, 60, 240, 693.
Lee, Richard Henry, 96, 355, 529.
And Edmund Pendleton, correspondence, 118.
Election of, as Senator, 193.
Introducing grandson of same name, 538.
Letters from, 464, 465.
to, 60.
Memoirs, 60.
Memoirs of, by Richard Lee, 465.
Nomination for governor, 123.
Lee, R. H., jr., letters to, 60.
Lee, Robert, letters from, 465.

Lee, Silas, death, 218.
Lee, Thedorick, letter from, 465.
Lee, Thomas J., introducing a son, 459.
Lee, William (consul at Bordeaux), 260, 701.
Announcement of the marriage of, 469.
Controversy between, and David Bailie Warden, 468.
Decision of, to accept appointment in War Department, 468.
Desire of, to return to America, 468.
Letters from, 465, 466, 467, 468, 469.
Letter to, 61, 269, 289, 522.
Shipments of wine by, 465, 466, 467, 468.
Leeds, Henry M., introduced, 204.
Legal tender, Treasury notes to be made, 683.
Legaré, J. B., and others, letters from, 469.
Legg, John, letter from, 469.
Legislation, bench, and judicial interpretation, distinction between, 32.
Legislative action (1789), no precedent for, 38.
Addresses approving the Jefferson administration, 216.
And Judiciary Departments, memorandum on the, 61.
Executive branches, union of the, 497.
Lehré, Thomas, application of, for position of marshal, 470.
Appointment of, as marshal asked for, 356.
Introduced, 469.
Letters from, 469, 470.
Letter to, 61.
Recommended, 312.
Solicitation of, for marshalship, 413.
Leib, Michael, advocating, as postmaster, 273.
Application of, for office of commissioner of loans, 470.
Appointment of, as postmaster, 471.
Denial of the calumnies made on him, 470.
Letters from, 470.
Leigh, B. W., letters to, 61.
Leigwood, ——, jr., application of, for office, 470.
Letter from, 470.
Leiper, Thomas, letters from, 470, 471, 472.
Leland, John, letter from, 472.
L'Enfant, P. C., 197, 198.
A plan, 389.
Lenox, D., letter from, 472.
Lenox, James, letter from, 472.
L'Eole, vessel, claims against, 704.
Leonard, —— (Lieutenant), passport for, 303.
Leonard, Dayton, claim of, for invention of perpetual motion, 472.
Letter from, 472.
Leonard, James I., letter from, 472.
Military record, 472.
Leonard, James T., 425.
Proceedings of court-martial on, 426.
Leonard, Jonathan, letter to, 61.
Leonard, William, recommended, 471.
Leonidas, passport for the, 326.
"Leonidas," a poem, 716.
Le Ray de Chaumont, letters from, 472.
Leroy, Lewis, letter from, 472.
Relief, 162.
Lescallier, ——, letter from, 473.
Lesueur, ——, wish of, to assist in the trigonometrical survey of the United States coast, 308.
Letters, interception and publication, 400.
Of marque, commissions for, 691.
Letombe, ——, letter from, 473.
Letrue —— (Colonel), introduced, 577.
Levasseur, 57.
Leonis, Thomas C., letter to, 61.
Lewis, —— (Captain), instructions as to arrest of, of the *Leander*, 406.
Lewis, Addin, letter from, 473.
Lewis, E., letter from, 473.
Lewis, Evan, letter from, 473.
Lewis, George, letter from, 473.
Lewis, Howell, army appointment desired by, 450.
Lewis, J., letters from, 473, 474.
Offer of an appointment refused by, 473.
Lewis, Jacob, letter from, 473.
Lewis, James, letter from, 473, 474.
Lewis, Jesse V., appeal of, for pecuniary aid, 474.
Letter from, 474.
Lewis, Joshua, 209.
Lewis, Meriwether (Governor), disposition of effects, 411.
Lewis, Morgan (General), at Sacketts Harbor, 264.
Letters from, 474.
Lewis, Nicholas, letters from, 474, 475.
Lewis, Robert, letter from, 475.
Letter to, 61.
Lewis, Samuel S., letter from, 475.
Letter to, 61.
Lewis, Seth, and others, letter from, 474.
Lewis, W., 677.
Lewis, William, letters from, 475.
Lexington, Ky., college at, 155.
Liancourt, M., 42.
Libeling English goods, 307.
Liberty and despotism, struggle between, 53.
And necessity, essay on, 629.
The tree of, and its fruits, 87.
Librarian of Congress, appointment of George Watterston as, 715.
Libraries, free, 114.
Library, apprentices, 111.
Jefferson's, bequest, 484.
Eventual disposition, 410.
Removal, 414, 524, 629.
Of Congress, 20, 271.
Liet, Michael, dissatisfaction of, as postmaster, 159.
Limozin, Andrew, letters from, 475.
Petition of, to Congress for recompense, 475.
Lincoln, Benjamin (General), 399, 647.
Lincoln, Daniel Waldo, introduced, 476.
Lincoln, Levi, 615.
Appointment of, as successor to Judge Cushing, declined by, 476
Letters from, 476.
The office of, as Attorney-General to become vacant, 476.
Lindsay, Reuben, letter from, 476.
Lindsay, William, election of, as naval officer, 476.
Letter from, 476.
Linen cloth, bounties on, 715.
Linn, James, letter from, 477.
Linsey, James, letters from, 477.
Petition of, to Congress for title to land, 477.
Lippencott and Huddy, case of, 477.
Lippencott, Richard (Captain), trial of, for murder of Captain Joshua Huddy, 477.
Liquors, substitute for foreign, 477.
List, Frederick, letter from, 477.
Letter to, 61,
Liston, Robert, letter from, 477.
Litchfield, resolutions of Republicans at town of, 109.
Literary and Philosophical Society of South Carolina, election as member, 683.
Lithography, new art, 104.
Littell & Henry, letter from, 477.
Letter to, 61.
Little Kanawha, gunboats for, 643.
Little, Peter, letter from, 477.
Little, William, 316.
Littlepage, ——, Mrs., gossip about, 205.
Livermore, Arthur, letter from, 477.
Liverpool, American produce at, 329.
Consulate, memorandum of the income, 512.
Liverpool (Lord), 511.
Living, high cost of (1794), 72.
Livingston, Brockholst, letters from, 477, 478.
Livingston, Charles, letter from, 478, 482.
Livingston, Edward, case of the Batture claims, 209, 411.
Disapproval of the measures of the Government, 208.
Letters from, 478.
to, 62.
Memorial, 208.
Speculations, 209.
Livingston, Edward P., introduced, 482.
Livingston, Henry B., letters from, 479.
Services, 479.
Livingston, Jasper, introduced, 481.
Livingston, J. R., letter from, 479.
Livingston, Mathurin, recommendation of, as district judge, 301.
Livingston, Robert L., introduced, 482.

Livingston, R. R., acceptance of, as minister to France, 479.
Consent of, to go to France as special envoy (1807), 481.
Correspondence of, with Monroe, 62, 480.
Importation of Spanish sheep by, 482.
Letters from, 479, 480, 481, 482.
Letter of credence for, 401, 698.
Letters to, 62, 501, 535, 576.
Manufactures by, of woolen cloth, 482.
Misrepresentations by enemies, 481.
Monroe displeased at interference, 480.
Minister to France, 81.
Negotiation, 401.
Relations of, with the commissioners, 480.
Resignation of, as minister to France, 480.
Secretary of foreign affairs, resignation, 98, 99, 101.
Succeeded by General Armstrong at Paris, 82.
Livingston, William, appointment of, to The Hague, 334.
Politics of, and his part in convention of 1787, 109.
Proposed memoir, 615.
Lloyd, Thomas, experiments in a discovery by, 237.
Letter from, 482.
Lloyd's debates, 27.
Loan for war expenses (1813), 308.
Of $10,000,000, 186.
Loans, foreign, payment of interest on, 528.
On real estate for indeterminate periods, 158.
Lobstein, J. F. D. (Dr.), letters from, 482.
Lock for a carriage, invention of a new, 200.
Locust seed as food, 240.
Logan, George, appeal of, to the President to prevent war, 483.
Attempts of, to prevent war, 483.
Attempt to censure, 258.
Letters from, 482, 483.
Visit of, to England to negotiate for peace, 48, 398.
Lomax, ——, letter to, 514.
Lomax, John Tayloe, 181, 214, 275.
Letters from, 484.
London University, 275.
Long, ——, (General), shooting, 667.
Long, Gabriel, letter from, 622.
Long, George (Prof.), 8, 179, 213, 319, 351.
Appointment, 119.
Letters to, 63.
Resignation, 419.
Retirement, 63.
Longacre, James B., letter to, 63.
Longevity, instances of, 11, 512.
Long Island Sound, chart of entrance to, 484.
Longitude, method for ascertaining, 629.
Of the Capitol, 449.
Longstreth, Jonathan, letters from, 484.
L'Orient a free port, 102.
Lormerie, De. (*See* De Lormerie.)
Lottery and subscription for Jefferson, 56, 75.
Drawing of a, 529, 530.
In aid of education, 75.
Tickets, 362.
Payment, 690.
Louis XVI, acceptance by, of the constitution, 95.
Carte blanche given by, to the National Assembly to make a constitution, 94.
Execution, 39.
Louis XVIII, restoration, 23.
Louisa County, delegation, 148.
Louisiana, acquisition of, the seal of prosperity of the Western country, 498.
Appointment of commissioners to, 676.
Bank, establishment, 207, 208, 209.
Boundaries, 150, 229, 404, 501, 702.
Louisiana, cession of, 200, 576, 658.
Celebration, 680.
By Spain to France, 81, 257, 284, 422.
Citizens of, memorial of, to the President, 208.
Claims to lands in, 676.
Delay in delivering, owing to orders of Spanish officers, 699.
Differences between the governor of, and Catholic priests, 403.
Government, 62.
Louisiana, governor of, compensation, 200.
Hopes of obtaining the residue of, 681.
Ignorance of society in, 207.
Increase of crime in, 209.
Land speculations in, 207.
Monroe and Livingston's negotiations for transfer, 27.
Negotiations, France and Spain, 325.
Patriotic disposition, 210.
Penal code, 62, 478.
People of, describing, 208.
Pretext of France of our violation of treaty, 146.
Probable accession of, to France (1801), 229.
Prosperity, 208.
Punishment of crimes in, 403.
Purchase of, guaranty for the, 479, 480, 501, 535.
Ratification of treaty and convention for possession, 699.
Representative system for the people, 208.
Restoration of, to France, 574, 575.
Treaty, opposition to the, 498.
Troops ordered to (1804); 207.
Turbulent lawyers and printers, 209.
Louisianians, prejudices of the, 209.
Love, John, application of, to be postmaster, 484.
Letters from, 484.
Love, Richard H., letter from, 484.
Love, Robert (Colonel), dispute between, and Gen. Nathaniel Taylor, 446.
Lovel, ——, relatives of, surveying of land belonging to, 372.
Lovell, James, letters from, 484.
Lovell, John E., letter from, 484.
Letter to, 63.
Lovell, William, 705.
Lowe, Enoch M., letter from, 485.
Lowndes, William J., 20, 21.
Letter to, 63.
Offer to, of the position of Secretary of the Treasury, 63.
Lowrie, Walter, 266.
Lowry, ——, recommended, 626.
Lowry, Robert, letter to, 328.
Lowther, William (Colonel), recommended, as collector of public money, 371.
Loyal company, 75, 320, 650.
Loyall, George, 178.
Letters from, 485.
Lucas, John B. C. (Commissioner), inquiry desired by, as to his official conduct, 485.
Letter from, 485.
Lucas, Jonathan, jr., 271.
Luckey, George, letters from, 485, 486.
Ludlow, Benjamin, letter from, 486.
Letter to, 63.
Ludlow, Daniel, letter from, 486.
Ludlow, Daniel, jr., application of, to be private secretary, 486.
Ludlow, Peter, letter from, 618.
Ludlow, —— (Lieutenant), funeral, 157.
Lufborough, Nathan, letter from, 486.
Lupinella seed, 18, 240.
Lushington, R., letter from, 486.
Luxury, articles of, taxes on, 68.
Luzerne, Count C. A. de la, 34, 384.
Influence of, on Members of Congress, 496.
Lyman, William, application of, as consul to London, 486.
Letters from, 486.
Lynch, D., letter to, 63.
Lynch, D., jr., letter from, 486.
Lynch, Mark, letter from, 486.
Recommended, 514.
Lynchburg Star, the, 176.
Lynde, Walter, and others, letters from, 707.
Lyon and Griswold, debates in Congress relative to, 44, 45.
Lyon, Isaac S., letter from, 487.
Letter to, 63.
Lyon, J., letter from, 487.
Lyon, James, and Dinsmore R., letter from, 487.
Lyon, Joel (Lieutenant), court-martial in the case, 290.
Lyon, Matthew, circular, 208.
Letter to, 269.
McArthur, —— (General), recommended, 662.

McCall, Denniston & Co., petition of, respecting British debts, 487.
McCall, James, and others, letter from, 487.
McCaraher, A., and others, letter from, 487.
Letter to, 63.
McClenachan, B. M., 735.
McClure & Robertson, letter to, 64.
McClure, David, candidate as professor of naval school, 487.
Letters from, 487.
McClure, George, defense, 487.
Letter from, 487.
McClurg, James, letters from, 487, 488.
McConnell, Mathew, and others, letter from, 488.
McCoy, W., letter from, 488.
McCreery, William, letters from, 488.
McCulloch, Andrew, 289.
McCulloch, James H., letter from, 488.
McDonough, Thomas (Commodore), 493.
Letter from, 488.
Request of, that surgeons be sent, 488.
Victory, 488.
McDougal, John, introduced, 607.
McDowell, —— (Dr.), 217.
McDuffie, George, letters to, 64.
Macedonian, capture of the, 577.
McGehee (an overseer), character and capabilities, 411, 535.
McGowty, John, letter from, 488.
McGraw, Thomas, letter to, 358.
McHenry, James, letters from, 489.
Merits and talents, 123.
McIlvaine, Joseph, recommendation as district judge, 162.
McIntosh, Duncan, application to be consul at Aux Cayes, 471.
McIntosh, John, letter from, 489.
Letter to, 64.
McIntosh, Lachlan, letter from, 489.
McIntosh County, Ga., approval by citizens of the Administration, 64, 142.
McIntyre, ——, introduced, 739.
Mackay, ——, letters to, 64.
Mackay, Robert, letters from, 489.
Letter to, 549.
Mackay & Campbell, 219.
Letters from, 489.
to, 64.
McKee, ——, (Colonel), 626.
McKeehan, David, application for office, 489.
Letter from, 489.
McKenney, Thomas, application to be commissioner to the Chippewa Indians, 490.
Justification of, 490.
McKenny, Thomas L. (Major), introduced, 693.
McKenny, Thomas L., letters from, 490, 491.
Letters to, 64, 65.
Vindication of conduct, 490.
MacKenzie & Glennie, 627, 628.
Letter from, 489.
McKiernan, George S., letter from, 491.
McKim, A., 648.
Letters from, 491.
McKim, Isaac (Major), introduced, 491.
M'cKinley, John, interference and persecution by Clintonians, 491.
Letters from, 491.
McKinley, William, letters from, 491, 492.
McKinney, James, letters from, 492.
Mackintosh, James (Sir), 319.
Speech, 440.
McKnight, John, letter from, 492.
Solicitation for reappointment in the Navy, 492.
McLane, A., letter from, 492.
McLane, Lewis, letter from, 492.
McLean, Ann, marriage with William Lee, 469.
McLean, John, 158.
Letters from, 492.
Letter to, 65.
McLeod, Alexander (Dr.), introduced, 526.
McMahon, Bernard, letter from, 492.
McMahon, Thomas P., letter from, 492.
McMillen, Hugh, letter from, 492.
McNat, Alexander (Colonel), introduced, 543.
McPherson, Christian, letter from, 493.
McPherson, John M., application for commercial agency at Jamaica, 493.
McPherson, R. H. (Colonel), 501.
McPherson, W., letter from, 493.
McPherson, William (General), services, 7
McRae, Alexander, 139.
Appointment as consul, 709.
Introducing, 734.
Letters from, 493, 494.
Office of, to carry dispatches to Europ
Request for letters of introduction, 49
Suggested, as minister to England, 689
McRae, Richard, letters from, 494.
Macomb, Alexander (General), continuanc Army, 248.
Letter from, 493.
to, 488.
Macon, Edgar, commended, 279.
Course of studies suggested by Madis
Duel with son of Judge Smith, 279.
Habits, 279.
Letters from, 493.
Letter to, 147.
Persecution of, 279.
Macon, James M., 567.
Macon, Robert, clerkship solicited, 663.
Macon, Thomas, letters from, 493.
Requesting Madison's influence in ob a situation for the son of, 493.
Madison, administration of, history conten 715.
Agricultural essay, 223.
Ancestors of, 270.
Appointment as Secretary of State pı 371.
A snuff taker, 128.
At New Jersey College, 65, 74.
Attacks on, 18.
Biographical sketch, 217.
Bodily health, 55, 62, 105.
Calumnious charges against, 103.
Candidacy for Congress, 176, 194.
Chronicle of career, 63.
City assessment on personal property,
Claims in Congress, 146.
Congratulations to, on his retirement,
Constitutional convention, the part of, 129.
Contradiction of reports circulated 126.
Course of law reading, 102.
Death of father, 46.
sister, 493.
Defeat in election for State senator, 19
Election as member of the Washingto ary Society, 442.
Election as president of the American zation Society, 341.
Election as President of the United predicted, 500.
Election as President of the United 523, 577.
Election for the convention, 173.
to Congress, 194, 337, 444, 553.
to State legislature, 398.
Envoy to France, rumors of being an,
Expenses at college, 65.
Family of, collateral branches, 376.
Finances of, 350.
Handwriting, 19.
House of, building, 206.
in Philadelphia, rents and ta 547.
Invitation to take part in the council State, 423.
Last illness, 33.
Letters from, 1-130.
of, in the National Intelligenc
to, 133-739.
Lieutenant of the county, 66.
Life of, 266.
Manuscript debates on the adoption Constitution, 286.
Marriage, 300, 311, 457, 460, 497.
Microscopic handwriting, 110.
Mother of, death, 512.
Negotiations with Government of Gre ain, 462.
Nephew of, employment for sought, 3C
illness and death, 608.

Madison, old age, 4, 88.
Opposition to, 469.
Policy of, 222.
Popularity, 659.
Portrait, 266, 545.
Practice of law, 35.
Preference to seat in Congress (1788), 102.
Presidency of, desire of Jefferson for the, 394.
President of party, not to be a, 222.
Puffing of, at expense of Jefferson, 471.
Qualifications as minister of domestic affairs, 226.
Query whether, declined the office of Secretary of State tendered by Washington, 463.
Reelection of, congratulations on the, 485.
Religious creed, inquiry concerning his, 350.
Resolutions of (January 3, 1794), 6, 40, 256.
Retirement, 7, 24, 27, 161.
Secretary of State, 228.
Servants of, loss of, by a contagious disorder, 224.
Sole survivor of signers of the Constitution (1831), 111.
State papers, 599.
Study of the Bible, 116.
Summons to testify, 282, 554.
Merits of, 542.
Urged by Jefferson to write for the press, 399.
Views on nullification, 181.
Official appointment as visitor to the University of Virginia, 588.
Writings of, proposition to compile and publish, 501.
Madison and Monroe, declination to serve on the electoral ticket, 179.
Nomination to convention for selecting candidates for Presidential election, 540.
The long and uninterrupted friendship of, 88.
Madison and the *Miranda* affair, 261.
Madison v. Strade, case of, 151.
Madison, Ambrose, 241, 664.
Lands in Kentucky, 656.
Letters to, 65.
Madison College, 153.
Madison, Dolly. (*See* Madison, James, Mrs.)
Madison, James (Bishop), 8, 65, 247.
Acceptance of the appointment of bishop, 497.
Declining health, 499.
Health, 614.
Information asked concerning, 707.
Intention to appear in the court of admiralty, 495.
Letters from, 495, 496, 497, 498, 499.
Map of Virginia undertaken, 497.
Tribute to memory of, 122.
Views on the new Constitution, 496.
treaty with Great Britain, 497.
Madison, James, sr., congratulations on marriage, 205.
Letters from, 494.
to, 65–73, 205, 499.
Madison, James, jr., 617.
Madison, James (Mrs.), Christian name, 172.
Directions to, after burning of city of Washington, 74.
Letter from, 494.
Letters to, 73, 217, 490, 567, 596, 632, 716, 726.
Subpœna to be served on, in a chancery suit, 644.
Madison, James Catesby, introduced, 498.
Madison, John, 498.
Letter from, 499.
Precarious situation of, from Indian attacks, 499.
Madison, Lewis, application in behalf of, for office, 665.
Madison, Nellie, 241, 665.
Madison, William, 665, 666.
Letter from, 320.
to, 74.
Madison Literary Society, 671.
Madison woolen cloth manufactory, 571.
Madrid, prices of articles of consumption in, 576.
Sensation at, on cession of Louisiana, 699.
Magazine, public, robbery of the, at Eastern Branch, 428.
Magill, ——, (Dr.), 182.
Magnetic medium, surveying by, 335.
Magrath, Thomas, letter from, 499.
Magruder, Patrick, letter from, 499.
Magruder, Patrick, and others, letter from, 499.
Mails, contracts for carrying the, 400.
Irregularities of, 332.
Southern, change of route of the, 641.
Tampering with, 46.
Transportation of the, contracts for, 335.
Main, James, application for office, 500.
Character and antecedents, 252.
Direction of the Daily Advertiser taken by 500.
Letters from, 500.
Main, Zachary, 589.
Maine, admission of, 85.
District of, defense for, 264.
Separation of, 445, 564.
Value of land in, 423.
Maison Carrée of Nismes, 381.
Maitland, John, 159.
Majority government, 119.
Malcom, Howard, letters from, 500.
Request for letter of introduction to Lafayette, 500.
Malden, a post of rendezvous for Indians, 420.
Attack on, 21.
British troops sent in sleighs to, 720.
Capture of, 291.
Confidence in the taking, 661.
Possession, 330.
Malin, David letter from, 500.
Mallory, C. K., 145.
Mallory, Robert, letter from, 500.
Malthus, theory of, 24.
Manning, James, letter from, 500.
Manning, P., removal, 304.
Manning, T. S., letter from, 500.
Mansfield, ——, proposition to add, to the professors in William and Mary College, 499.
Mansfield, George, claim, 501.
Mansfield, Jared, letters from, 501.
Manufactures, British, estimate of amounts paid for, in the United States, 432.
Proposed prohibition of, 303.
Manufactures, domestic, encouragement to, 61, 63, 104, 116, 227, 594.
Growth of, and self dependence, 434.
Hamilton's report on, 95.
Home, preferable, 13.
In New England, growth, 234.
Protection for home, 9, 10, 11, 12, 62, 106, 189, 190, 199, 230, 233, 554, 594, 708.
Report of the Treasury on, 58.
Southern, 577.
Manufacturers, struggle of our, 27.
Manufacturing Association of New Jersey, 708.
Manufacturing enterprises, legislative action on, 169.
Manufacturing projects at Richmond, 493.
Manumission of slaves, 56, 123.
Manuscripts, Jefferson's, proposed publication 56.
Map of the United States, proposed, 284.
Marble quarry, discovery of a, on the Upper Potomac, 693.
Marble work, estimates for, 549.
Marblehead, defenseless state, 317.
Gunboats for defense of, 587.
Marbois, François de Barbé, 18, 227.
Assault by a Frenchman on, 380.
Letters from, 501.
Letter to, 74, 480, 535.
Marcellus, papers signed, attributed to Hamilton, 397.
March & Co., J. Howard, letter from, 501.
Marchioness, the, 337.
Marietta, appointments for collector and inspector of revenues for, 404.
Marigny's claim, 209.
Marine Corps, nomination of officers of the, 626.
Officers named for promotion, 345.
Marine hospital, recommended, 346.
Marion, J., letter from, 501.
Marion, Life of, 717.
Maritime defense, 616, 733.

Maritime law, questions of, 102.
Maritime powers, destruction of our commerce by the, 335.
Markets, want of adequate, for supplies, 107.
Markley, Benjamin A., 420.
Married men to procure substitutes in the militia 211.
Marriott, J. (Sir), report of, 703.
Marsh, Capen & Lyon, letter from, 501.
Marshal, office of, emoluments, 195.
Marshall, E. F., letter from, 501.
Marshall, Herbert, letter from, 502.
Marshall, Humphrey, suit against, 370.
Marshall, James, 459.
  Letter from, 502.
Marshall, John (Chief Justice), 282, 389, 584.
  Death, 236.
  Letter from, 502.
    to, 455.
  Partiality to Burr, 372.
  Portrait, 715.
Marshall, Joseph, letter from, 502.
Marshall, W., letter from, 502.
Martial law in New Orleans, 210.
Martin and Ware, deserters, 303.
Martin, F. X., application of, for office of judge, 411, 502.
  Letter from, 502.
Martin, John B., letter from, 502.
Martin, Robert, letter from, 502.
Martin, Samuel, letter from, 502.
Martin, Thomas (Rev.), letter to, 74.
Martin, Wheeler, letter from, 503.
Martinique, surrender of, to the British, 71.
Mary, schooner, case of the, 250.
Maryland accedes to the Constitution, 337.
  Census, 197.
  Convention of, proceedings of the, 348.
  Federalists in, 259.
  General assembly, 503.
    resolution of, respecting cession of land for the permanent seat of Government, 356.
  Imports and tonnage in, 730.
  Paper money, 167.
  Pretentions of, to a part of Virginia, 498.
  Public instruction in, 669.
Mason, A. T. (General), death of, 85.
  Letter from, 503.
Mason, —— (Colonel), destitute condition of regiment of, 614.
Mason, George (Colonel), biography of, 74.
  Letters from, 503, 504, 505.
    to, 74.
  Originator of the constitution of Virginia and declaration of rights, 130.
Mason, J., letter to, 423.
Mason, John, letter to, 597.
Mason, John T., letters from, 505.
  Qualifications of as judge, 422.
Mason, J. M., letters from, 505.
  Letter to, 74.
Mason, Sam, crimes of, 207.
Mason, S. T., letters from, 505, 506.
Mason, Thomson, letters to, 506.
Mason, W., letter from, 506.
"Masonry and antimasonry," 643.
  True character of, 6.
Massachusetts and Connecticut, seditious opposition of (1812), 51.
Massachusetts agents, mission of, to Washington, 731.
  Agricultural Society, 251.
  and New Hampshire, recent elections in, 476.
  and Virginia, motion of, respecting dismemberment, 335.
  Appointment of assessor of the district tax, 141.
  Change of rules in, 93.
  Claim of, before Congress, 9, 729.
  Commerce of, power of Congress over, 380.
  Commissioners of, in favor of a monarchy, 444.
  Commotions in, 68, 185.
  Delegation more conciliatory, 335.
  Disaffection in, 373.
  Governor of, refusal of the application of General Dearborn for militia by the, 315.
Massachusetts Horticultural Society, 265.
  Legislature of, amendment of the United States Constitution rejected by, 340.
    congratulations of, on peace, 140.
    opposition of the, to the Federal Government, 314.
    report of committee on amendments to the Constitution, 506.
    report of committee on seizure and detention of property of the New England Bank, 506.
  Militia of, 315.
  Peace Society, 253.
  Opposition to the Constitution in, 124.
  Political parties of (1811), 50.
  Ratification of the Constitution by, 444.
  Shay's rebellion in, 93, 123, 124.
  State army, resolution for raising a, 727.
  Temper of, as to the revenue propositions of Congress, 101.
Massias (Captain), services of, 204.
Massie, George (senior), letter from, 506.
Masson, Francis de, 414.
  Application of, for office, 506.
  Letters from, 506.
  Recommended for consulship, 447.
Masters, commandant, promotion of, to captains, 429.
Matches, phosphorous, 36, 381.
Mathematical and astronomical instruments, 429.
Matlack, T. (Colonel), recommended, 735.
Mathews, Thomas, letters from, 507.
Matthews, Adonizah, 488.
Matthews, George, acts of, in East Florida, 50.
  Commissioner for East and West Florida, 506.
  Letter from, 506.
  Record of, 355.
Matthews, William, letter from, 507.
Maury & Latham, 64.
  Letters from, 512.
Maury, Fontaine, application of, for appointment as collector of imports, 507.
  Establishment of, in business in New York, 507.
  Letters from, 507, 508.
Maury James, activity and energy of, in his old age, 511.
  Application for a consulate, 508.
  Claim on the Treasury, 509.
  Continuation of his office of consul, 510, 511.
  Death of wife, 512.
  In his eighty-seventh year, 512.
  Letters from, 508, 509, 510, 511, 512.
    to, 74, 75, 522.
  Newspaper attacks on, 512.
  Sales of tobacco by, 508.
  Unfounded representations to injure the reputation of, 508.
Maury, Matthew, introduced, 511.
  Letters from, 512.
Maury, Thomas W., letter from, 512.
Maury, William, 512.
  Acceptance by, of the vice-consulship of France in Liverpool, 513.
  Application for Liverpool consulate, 513.
  Appointment as consul at Liverpool, 450.
  Letters from, 513.
  Letter to, 75, 450.
Maxey, Virgil, letter from, 513.
Maxwell, George, appointment of, as district attorney, 477.
Mayhew, Matthew (Dr.), 2.
Mayo, Robert, and William A. Barton, letter to, 75.
Mazzei, Philip, 35, 380, 501.
  Affairs, 43.
  Cipher given, by Madison, 513.
  Claims, 572.
  Claim against Dahrman, 38, 393.
  Complaints of, that the executive of Virginia neglects him, 514.
  Desire of, to purchase land near Jefferson's place, 516.
  Expenditures and salary, 513.

Mazzei, Philip, injustice done, by the Virginia government, 514.
Letters from, 513, 514, 515, 516.
Letter to, 75, 139, 589.
Love for his adopted country, 514.
Mission from the State of Virginia, 513, 514.
Publication of his book, 515.
Suggestions by, as to a loan to be negotiated abroad, 513.
Respecting correspondence with, 534.
Treatise by, on the port bill, 528.
Mazureau, Stephen, letter to, 210.
Mead, Charles, 266.
Mead, Cowles, letters from, 516.
Mead, David, 587.
Mead, Joel K., letter from, 517.
Letter to, 75.
Meade, R., letter to, 75.
Meade, R. W., letter from, 517.
Mease, James, letters from, 517.
Mechanic [unsigned], letter from, 517.
Medal commemorating peace of 1783, 611.
Medallion of Washington, 22.
Medals, gold, proposed resolution that, be struck and presented to Generals Ripley, Miller, and Porter, 517,
Medical dictionary, 275.
Staff, new arrangement proposed of the, 688.
vacancies on the, 324.
Medicine, discoveries in, proposed lottery for a fund for, 362.
Mediterranean affairs, settlement of, 702.
Commerce of the, 395.
Naval achievements in the, 59.
establishment proposed at some island in the, 149.
force in the, 626, 627.
Squadron, 403.
for training and disciplining, 293.
captures by, 3.
destination of the, 242.
provisions for the, 243.
sailing of the, 248.
success of the, 249.
Trade, 81.
monopoly by France, Great Britain, and Holland, of the, 528.
Meigs, Josiah, letters from, 517, 518.
Letter to, 350.
Resignation, 676.
Meigs, R. J. (General), address of, 660.
Letter to, 244, 262, 547.
Meigs, Return Jonathan (jr.), letters from, 518, 519.
Melish, John, letters from, 519.
Melvill, Thomas, letter from, 519.
Views on public credit, 519.
Members of Congress, compensation of, 195.
"Memoire de Moreau de Lislet," 328.
Memoirs of the American Revolution, 271.
Menard, Pierre, 520.
Menon, Julius de, introduced, 200.
Mercantile cupidity, 373.
Mercantile interests, saving of, by Government's measures, 434.
Mercer, Charles Fenton, introduced, 505.
Mercer, Hugh, letters from, 520.
Visit to Jefferson, 520.
Mercer, James, letters from, 520.
Mercer, John, letter from, 520.
Mercer, John F., announcement of marriage, 521.
Claim to bank stock in England, 403.
for half-pay, 520.
Debt to Madison, 521.
Introduced, 521.
Letters from, 520, 521, 522.
Offer of services, 522.
Pecuniary matters between, and Madison, 521, 522.
Political doctrines, 521.
Mercer, Landon, recommended, 522.
Merchant and landowner, taxation of the, 309.
Merchant ships, arming, 396.
Merchant vessels, employment of, for convenience of foreign correspondence, 309.
Meredith, William M., 477.
Merida, expected battle on plains of, 345.
Merino, American, 244.
Merry, Anthony, complaints of, 700.
Departure, 83.
Discussions with, not advantageous, 75.
Exemption of duty on household effects, 702.
Letters from, 522.
to, 75.
Pretensions, 81.
Refusal to dine with the President, 81.
Merry, Mrs. Anthony, bad manners of, 81.
Merry, Prettyman, letter from, 522.
Merry, Samuel, (Dr.), appointment of, as surgeon's mate, 522.
Mesmer, ——, Marbois's opinion of, 501.
Message, the President's (1792), 95.
Committee of the Whole on the (1798), 258.
Improper and indelicate tone of the, 43.
Messengers, special, dispensing with, 150.
Metcalf & Parker, letter from, 522.
Metcalfe, Samuel L., letter from, 522.
Methodists, the, 604.
Mexican coinage, 567.
Mexican execution of a, at Havana, 332.
as emissary of Napoleon, 628.
Mexican revolution, memoirs of the, 601.
Mexico and United States, fears of a collision between (1836), 369.
Commercial intercourse with, decreasing, 668.
Coins of, 667.
Confusion and alarm in, 667.
Coronation of the Emperor and Empress, 667.
Freed from Spanish supremacy, 667.
French intrigues in, 667.
Mining interests in, purchase by English bankers of, 668.
Independence of, 210.
Party for declaring independence, 666.
People of, description of the, 667.
Republican form of government established in, 667.
Meyer, Christopher, application of, for consulate at Bayonne, 523.
Letter from, 522.
Meyer, George, letter from, 523.
Meyer, Jacob, introduced, 228.
Meyers, John, 489.
Meyers, Moses, recommended to be collector of Norfolk, 489.
Miami chiefs, fidelity of, 352.
Miami Exporting Company, 659.
Mice, white, 567.
Michaux, André, letter from, 523.
Michie, David, letter from, 523.
Michilimackinack, hopes to redeem, 51.
Micketts, George G. M., application of, for office of consul, 316.
Microscopic writing, 88, 117, 121.
Midas, privateer, 178.
Middleton, Henry, letter from, 523.
Migration or importation, 85, 122.
Milan, decree of, revoking the, 604.
Military Academy at West Point, roll of cadets at, 564.
Selection of instructors at the, 501.
Captain Partridge's, 540.
Military bill, disagreements in the Senate on the, 58.
bounty lands, 517.
code, the, 247.
establishment, 41, 93.
force, additional, act of April, 1808, for raising an, 292.
lands in Ohio, location of Virginia, 304.
operations, narrative, 75.
schools, the, 305.
schools in France, 299.
vacancies, filling, 86.
Militia, arming and organizing the, 292.
Bill, 69, 70, 95, 97, 581.
Calling out of the, 329.
Complaints of discharged, 636.
Dependence on the, 51.
Detention of, after expiration of service, 738.
Disciplining of the, not approved, 450.
Expeditions by the, 705.
Expenses, reducing, 307.
Firearms for the, 235.
Importance of, 113, 648, 723.

Militia, law, amending of the, 646.
defects of the, 315.
irregularities of the, 705.
Laws, constitutionality of the, 553.
President's message on, 79.
Reorganization of the, 232.
Service, the, 185.
The safeguard of republican government, 281.
To assist in effecting embargo, 308.
Mill, a new, 73.
Millar, John, appeal of, for aid, 523.
Letter from, 523.
Milledge, John (President of the Senate pro tem.), 523.
Miller, George A., letter from, 523.
Miller, James, application of, to be consul at Bordeaux, 348.
Miller, Robert, letter from 523.
Miller, Samuel, letters from, 523, 524.
Pardon, 402.
Milligan, Joseph, letters from, 524.
Mills, Madison's, purchase of, 492.
Mills, Robert (architect), 170.
Application for surveyor of public buildings 524.
Letter from, 524.
Mills, Samuel F., letter from, 524.
Millstones, purchase of, 358.
Mina, Xavia (General), 239.
Mineralogy, science of, 219.
Ministers, American, vesting of, with consular powers, 334, 335.
British, unmarried men not to be, 232.
Prohibition of, to receive presents, 436.
Minor, John, letters from, 524.
Minor, Peter, letters from, 524, 525.
Mention of, as assessor, 413.
Minor, Stephen, 207.
Letter from, 525.
Mint bill, the, 58, 70.
Mint, care of the, 401.
Miranda, Francisco di, accomplices of, prisoners at Carthagena, 357.
Case of, 260, 261.
Expedition, 282, 526.
Introduced, 607.
Letters from, 525.
Plans of, 700.
Recommending secrecy, 525.
Mississippi and Missouri rivers, exploration of the, 138.
Mississippi, cession of, to Spain, 123.
River, conduct of Spain respecting the, 527.
Establishment of a colony beyond the, 126.
Establishment of a government on the, 371.
Intentions of Congress concerning the, 124.
Navigation of the, 36, 56, 60, 72, 76, 77, 78, 81, 108, 161, 187, 227, 254, 325, 380, 382, 383, 389, 404, 464, 465, 529, 531, 549, 553, 557, 574, 654, 691, 706, 730.
Navigation of, by steam, 297.
Obstructions to Spanish stores bound up the, 167.
Prospect of trade on the, 362.
Mississippi Territory, depredations on the inhabitants of, 298.
Governor of, details of movements of (1810), 681.
Indemnification of claimants for public lands in, 240.
Lands in, ceded by Georgia, 240.
Legislative council of, 328.
Letter from, 525.
Legislature of the, memorial to the, 175.
Resolutions of the legislature of, to support the Government, 152, 207, 516.
Resolution repelling the aggressions of the enemy, 175.
The governor to maintain the laws, 328.
Treasonable conspiracy in, 314.
Missouri, the admission of, 85, 146.
Compromise, the, 56, 85, 539.
Question, 4, 31, 107, 122, 146, 235, 236, 623, 713.
Missouri, case of the, 433.
Mitchell, —— (General), 603.
Mitcchell, Francis, 159.
Mithell, John, letters from, 525.
Mitchell, Samuel L., letters from, 525, 526.
Letter to, 606.
Mitchell, Samuel M., recommended as commissioners, 694.
Mix, Elijah, claim of, for services, 527.
Letters from, 526, 527.
Mobile and Missisippi rivers, right of navigation, 404, 408.
Mobile and New Orleans, fortifications at, 238.
Mobile and Pensacola, hostile movement against, 635.
Mobile, commandant at post of, letter to, 680.
Expedition against, 329.
Mobile River, revenue district on, 14.
Right of navigation, 404.
"Modern Chivalry," 165.
Moffatt, ——, invention, 554.
Mohawk, land purchase on the, 36, 78, 166, 527, 528.
Molasses, tax on, 730.
Mole, natural history of the, 36.
Mollieu, —— (Minister de Tresor Public), letter to, 519.
Monarch, dethroned, substitute for, 57.
Monarchial party, the spirit and views of the, 80.
system, change of, in England, 18.
Monarchy, a feature, 58.
Constitutional, adoption in Europe, 57.
Limited, designs to form a, 632.
In France, hope of a return (1794), 430.
Parties for, 93.
Money, difficulty of procuring, without taxing, 51.
Hard, scarcity, 253.
Paper, advocates for, 78.
Paper, 98.
in the States, 36, 37.
depreciation, 66.
objections to, 68.
petitions for, 647.
Plans for raising, 66, 237, 272, 315, 426, 612.
Scarcity of, in Paris, 386.
the Northwest, 660.
Moneyed and mercantile affairs, perplexed condition (1819), 107.
Monopolies, evils, 726.
Monroe, Andrew, letter from, 527.
Monroe, James, Adams's assault on, 45.
Address of, defense of the, to the French national convention, 531, 532.
Administration of, harmony of sentiment toward, 84.
Against Madison, John Randolph's endeavors to set up, in next Presidential election, 432.
Alleged speculations of, in Paris, 80.
Appointment as minister to France, 531.
Secretary of State, 49.
Approaching death, 345.
Attentions shown to, 525.
Calumniators of, put in their true light, 80.
Claim for reimbursement and compensation, tion, 87, 530, 581.
Claim to land in Middlesex, N. Y., 166.
Commendatory of, 247.
Condition of the farm of, 527, 530.
Correspondence with Pickering, 44.
Correspondence between, and John Jay relative to treaty, 532.
Death, 27, 30, 104, 509.
Defense of, against charges of neglect to support General Jackson, 540.
Defense of, against unjust attacks, 532.
Demands of, for reasons of his recall, 80.
Departure of, for the Miami River, 334.
Difficulties to contend with, 83.
Dislike to Paris, 177.
Election to Congress, 253.
Exaggerated complaints, 44.
Faithfulness and ability, 83.
Friendship of, to William Eustis, 24.
Furniture belonging to, 473.
Governor of Virginia, 259.
Intention of, to remove to Albemarle, 530.
Introduced to Franklin, 378.
Letters from, 527, 528, 529, 530, 531, 532, 533, 534, 535, 536, 537, 538, 539, 540, 541.
Letters to, 76 to 88, 137, 170, 171, 183, 253, 378, 379, 427, 433, 477, 505, 515, 560, 572, 621, 648, 710.
Life and character, 2.
Loan obtained for, 669.

Monroe, James, Madison's affection for, 27, 30.
Marriage, 77, 335, 528.
Marriage of the daughter of, 541.
Mission of, to France, 71, 81.
to England of, to negotiate for prevention of impressments, 82.
Northern tour, 84.
Note of, at bank, 649.
Notice of recall, 533.
Official correspondence of, on Jacobin Society, 79.
Pamphlet of, 44, 80.
Papers, 323.
Patriotic conduct of, in Paris, 282.
Pecuniary affairs, 104.
Political hostility of, to Madison, 194.
Proposed mission of, to Spain (1804), 82.
Proposition of, to sell his lands in Albemarle, 540.
Publication by, in vindication of his conduct while minister to France, 534.
Purchase of land by, near Charlottesville, 529.
Recall, 43, 80, 572,
Reception of, by the convention, 71, 79, 531.
Refusal to renew a loan, at bank, for, 6.
Refutation of a charge against, 712.
Residence of, in New York, 88.
Sale by, to Madison of plate and furniture, 536.
Sale of slaves, 540.
Secretary of State, 84.
Secretary of War, 114.
Suggesting the appointment of, to command of Northwestern Army, 280.
Suggesting that Madison and Jefferson visit, in order to silence compromising rumors, 534.
Suggestions that, take command in place of Hull, 505.
Supposed appointment as Secretary of State, 374.
Willingness to take seat in Cabinet, 48.
Monroe, John (Hon.), 660.
Letter from, 542.
Naming, as governor of Illinois, 410.
Monroe, Joseph Jones, promotion of, recommended, 721.
Recommended, to be judge in Mississippi Territory, 550.
Monroe, Thomas, 411.
Letter to, 524.
Monroe, Thomas, jr., 134.
Monopolists, jealousy, 219.
Montague, Abraham, letter from, 542.
Montgomery, James, letter from, 542.
Montgomery, John, letters from, 542.
Montgomery, William, letters from, 542.
Montgomery, William Griffiths, 232.
Impressment of, on board a British ship, 542.
Montlezun-Labarthette, Baron de, appeal from, to obtain a land grant, 542.
Letter from, 542.
Montmorin, abilities, 385.
Moody, John, asking the place of postmaster at Richmond, 543.
Letters from, 542, 543.
Mooers, Benjamin, letter from, 543.
Moore, Andrew, letter from, 543.
Moore, Gabriel, letter from, 543.
Letter to, 75.
Moore, Isaac, genealogical tree showing that the grandfather of, had 192 descendants, 543.
Letter from, 543.
Moore, John, letters from, 543.
Moore, Matthew, 543.
Letter from, 543.
Moore, Robert, letter from, 543.
Moore, Thomas, letters from, 543.
Moore, Thomas W. C., request of, to be bearer of dispatches to France, 545.
Moore, William, 494, 683.
Letter from, 543.
Moor's Indian Charity School, 722.
Morale, ——, describing, 207.
Morales, 13.
Morales, —— (Consul-General), 260.
Mordant, Charles, 682.
Moreau, —— (General), 186.
Moreau, Cæsar, letter from, 543.
Moreau, Judge, unjustifiable charge to 209.
Morfit, Henry M., letter from, 544.
Morgan, George, project, 126.
Morgan's settlements on the Mississipp
Morning Chronicle, editor of the, letter
Morocco, American prisoners held at, fo 109.
Emperor of, declaration of war by tl
seizure and restoration l *Betsey*, 381.
Gun carriages for, 402.
Morril, David Laurence, 143.
Morris, Anne C., letter from, 544.
Morris, Anthony, accounts of, 544.
Application of, for consulship at Li 545.
Claim, 86, 558.
Letters from, 544.
Letters to, 76, 558.
Testimony to the intelligence, inte respectability of, 86.
Morris, Charles (Captain), 19.
Letter to, 594.
(Commodore), letters from, 545.
Morris, George P., letters from, 545.
Morris, Gouverneur, letter to, 393.
Minister to France, 58.
Life, 332, 635.
Morris, James P., letter from, 545.
Morris, Richard, 180, 181.
Application to be made victualer, 54
Letter from, 545.
Morris, Robert, death, 162.
Resignation, 100.
Morris, Thomas, letter from, 545.
Morrison, James, letter from, 545.
Morrison, —— (Major), introduced, 555.
Morrison, R. (Chinese Student), 564.
Morrow (Dr.), introduced, 459.
Morrow, Jeremiah, 421.
Morrow, John, letter from, 545.
Morrow, John, jr., letter from, 545.
Request to be appointed to any of t tories, 545.
Morse, Jedediah, letters from, 545, 546.
Letters to, 76.
Second edition in press of the geog 546.
Mortgage, foreclosure of a, 147.
Morton, —— (Captain), letter to, 597.
Morton, J., letter from, 546.
Morton, Jeremiah, letter from, 546.
Morton, John, letter to, 736.
Morton, John A., 627.
Application for consulship of Bord
Letter from, 546.
Morton, Nathaniel, 627.
Letter to, 546.
Morton, Perez, letter from, 546.
Moscow document, the, 84.
Moselle, British brig, firing of, on th States brig *Vixen*, 346, 583.
Reasons demanded for firing on t States brig *Vixen*, 683.
Moses, —— (Inventor), 284
Moss, James W., recommended, 658.
Moulder, William, letter from, 546.
Mounted volunteers asked for, 721.
Mountflorence, J. C., application for c for, 251.
Certificate, 622.
Letter from, 546.
Mountjoy, William, appointment solicit the volunteers, 659.
Moustier, Count de (French Minister),
Arrival, 124.
Character, 384.
Introduced, 384.
Letters from, 546, 547.
Letter to, 88.
Unpopular behavior, 37, 38.
Visit to Mount Vernon, 126.
Moyes, James, letter from, 547.
Moylan, Stephen, letters from, 547.
Muhlenberg, Frederick, letter from, 547

Muhlenberg, J. P. G., letter from, 547.
Speaker of the House, 94, 126.
Supervisor of the Revenue, 228.
Mules, purchase, 661.
Mulhaller, John, letter from, 547.
Mulligan, Francis. application for office of Supervisor of the Revenue, 547.
Letters from, 548.
Mullowny, John, 348.
Letter from, 547.
Mumford, Benjamin B., letter from, 547.
Mumford, Gurdon Saltonstall, letter from, 548.
Mun, —— de, introduced, 321.
Munroe, Isaac, letter from, 548.
Munroe, Thomas, application for letters of introduction, 548.
Letters from, 548.
Murat, ——, and Judge McComb, duel between, 731.
Murdock, Yuille, Wardrop & Co., letters from, 548.
Murray, —— (Captain of Royal Navy), introduced, 477.
Murray, Alexander (Commodore), attack upon, 425.
Murray, George, letter from, 452.
Murray, Robert, & Co., letters from, 548, 549.
Murray, Robert J., introduced, 611.
Murray, William Vaus, appointment as minister plenipotentiary to France, 399, 400.
Muse, Hudson, asking time to make his accounts good, 549.
Letters from, 549.
Request to be continued in situation of naval officer, 549.
Muse, Laurence, recommended, 625.
Museum, Peale's, 568.
State, proposal to establish a, at Richmond, 710.
Musket stocks, invention for turning, 647.
Muskingum County, citizens of, approval of the, of the Administration, 299, 331, 358.
Mussell Shoals, assemblage of troops at, 290.
Mussi, Joseph, letters from, 549.
Mussi, Stephen, offer of, to loan money to United States, 549.
Muter, George, 705.
Letters from, 549.
Mutinies among soldiers, efforts of officers to prevent, 712.
Mutinous remonstrance (1783), 101.
Mutiny, imprisonment of two persons for, 687.
On the English fleet, 396.
Myer, Solomon, letter from, 549.
Myers, John, letter from, 549.
Myers, Moses, application for collectorship at Norfolk, 549.

N.

Nagel, Baron de, 23.
Nancrede, introduced, 151.
Nantes, the consulate at, 402.
Nantucket, citizens of, petition of, to follow vocation of whaling prohibited by the embargo laws, 310.
No flour in, 310.
Naples, domestic struggles of, 56.
Napoleon. (*See* Bonaparte.)
Alabaster statue, 183.
Ambition, 481.
Audience with, 150.
Change of views of, toward Americans, 482.
Cooperation with, 174.
Commercial policy, 48.
Coronation, 700.
Downfall, 330.
Emissary of, execution of a Mexican, 332.
Entry of, into Berlin, 466.
Esteem of, for Jefferson, 480.
Hostile orders of, concerning American vessels in Spain and Naples, 708.
His want of money (1811), 49.
In Russia, disasters to army, 51.
Negotiations with, 151.
Power of, a benefit to this country, 174.
Promise of, to enter St. Petersburg, 468.
Proposed alliance with, that the United States may control this continent, 174.
Situation (1815), 249.
Speculations on projects and career, 151.
Successes, 466.
Views of, since his elevation, 480.
Nard, ——, de, introduced, 669.
Narragansett Bay, theory of the Phœnecians having visited, 495.
Nashville, citizens of, approval of conduct of the President by, 268.
Nassau, British ship, 735.
Nassau Hall, appeal for aid for, 217.
Natchez and surrounding territory, views of people in, 133.
to New Orleans, establishment of a post line from, 404.
Nathan, case of, 101.
National Assembly, the States-General in France declare themselves to be the, 386.
Bank, the, 196, 473.
appointment of John Rhea to receive subscriptions for the, 104.
charter of the, 623.
scheme for a, 454.
debt, payment of the, 434.
views of Hamilton on the, 344.
Library, 679.
Philological Academy, 12.
University, establishment of a, 245.
"National" in contradistinction from "Federal," 17.
National Intelligencer, 27.
Madison's letters in the, 180.
Naturalization law, 41, 96.
System, 724.
Terms, 124.
Nautical Almanac, 163.
Naval armament, taxes for expenses, 71.
Combats between French, Spanish, and British, 698.
Commanders subject to military commanders, disapproval, 424, 427.
Force on the lakes, measures to destroy the, 728.
History of the United States, 212.
Officer, office of, 489.
Power, balance of, 234.
Schools, proposed, 487.
Superiority, our, 495.
Navigable waters, common highways, 335.
Navigation act, 72, 146, 528.
Free, of rivers, 578.
Inland, 56.
Internal, improvements to, 581.
Inward coastwise, 651.
Supremacy of, 11.
Navy agency, manner in which the, is conducted, 561.
Agents, appointment, 702.
nomination of, 626.
and Marine Corps, nomination of officers for the, 347.
Board and Navy Department, altercation between the, 242, 243.
consolidating, 242.
British, condition of the, 582.
means for rendering the, useless, 612.
Commissioners, differences between, and the Secretary of the Navy, 602.
of the, letters from, 241, 242, 550.
reports, 602.
Department, appropriations and deficiencies of the, 321, 346, 347.
bill for establishing, 398.
deficits of the, 303.
impoverished condition of the, 426.
letters from, 550.
letter to, 426.
reforms in the, 677.
report on better organization of the, 429.
statements of balances of the, in Treasury, 550.
Establishment of a, to protect our coasts, 314.
Estimates of 1810, 321.
Extraordinary course of the Commissioners of the, 242, 243.
Heavy equipments for the, 426,

Navy, importance of building a, 434, 532, 587.
Operations of the, against the enemy, 348.
Powers of the Commissioners and Secretary of the, 250.
Promotions in the, 569.
Secretary of the, duties, 242.
nomination of the, 19.
Success of our, 312, 316.
Yard at Washington, preparations for defense at, 426.
Neapolitan movement, termination of the, 538.
Necker, dismissal of, 386.
Recall of, 94, 337, 386.
Negotiations, inconveniences of, without direct commissions, 437.
Negro, hiring of a. 607.
Insurrection, reports of a, 535.
Sale of a, to meet arrearages, 66.
Slave Jesse, offer to Madison to purchase his, 358.
Slavery in Virginia, 511.
Negroes carried off by British during the war, 335.
Compensation for abduction, 221.
Execution of, for insurrection, 535.
Low price of, 253.
Purchase of, in other States, to bring into Virginia, 643.
The enemy's allies, 647.
Transportation of, across the Rocky Mountains, 552.
Treatment of, 546.
Neill, —— (Captain), appointment of, 627.
Neilson, James, letter from, 550.
Nelson Cadets of Artillery, support offered by the, 694.
Nelson, Hugh, letter from, 550.
Nelson, R , and others, letter from, 550.
Nelson, Roger, 308.
Nelson, Thomas (General), heirs and representatives of, 90.
Petition of heirs of, for remuneration for his services, 562.
Sketch of life, 687.
Nervous system, essay on the, 274.
Netherlands, article 11 of the treaty between Charles II of England and States-General (1667, 1668), 550.
Criticism on text of treaty with the, 99.
State of affairs at (1788), 337.
Neufville, John de, widow of, claims, 649.
Neutral commerce, rights of, 75.
Vessels, colonial produce in, 48.
free goods and sailors on, 33.
trade, income to England from the, 432.
Neutrality, armed, principles and laws, 709.
Suggestions of an, with European powers for defense against tyrants of the ocean, 485.
British claims for violation, 182.
President's proclamation on (1793), 39.
of, history of the, 391.
Questions of, 390.
Neutrals, dictation of England and France to, 231.
Rights of, 230.
Spoliation of, 231.
Trade of, prohibition by the British of the, 276.
Neuville, Hyde de (Baron), 538.
Departure of, for France, 88, 550.
Letters of credence of, as minister from France, 550.
Letters from, 550.
to, 88.
Nevernois, Duke of, 282.
Nevil, F., and others, letter from, 550.
Nevill, Joseph, appointment of, as captain, 488.
Letter from, 551.
Newburyport, support of Madison's Administration by, 215.
Newcastle County, citizens of, sentiments in support of the Administration, 160.
Newell, Daniel (Reverend), introduced, 523.
New England Bank, 551.
Colonies, confederation of, 444.
Conduct of, respecting the war (1814), 89.
Elections in, against the Administration (1803), 81.
Manufactures in, 234.
New England, prosperity of, 482.
Society of New York, 26.
State of parties in, 188.
Troops to quell mutiny in Philadelphia, 101.
New England Farmer, 97.
Newfoundland fisheries, 585.
Rights claimed by the French to the, 283.
New Hampshire, adoption of the Constitution in, 124, 343, 449, 612.
Attitude of, respecting the Constitution, 193.
Convention in, 94.
Political condition of, 582.
Ratification of the Constitution by, 444.
Result of election of electors for State of, 340.
Territorial claim of, 477.
"New Hampshire grants," dispute concerning district called the, 551.
New Haven, petition of inhabitants of, 31, 359.
New Jersey, adoption of the Constitution by, 124.
Address of Republican delegates, 63.
Claims of, 336.
College commencement at, 65.
Contest in, about paper money, 335.
Republican delegates from, approving measures of the President, 486.
New Jersey, ship, case of, 83.
New London, court martial at, appointment of judge advocate, 140.
Newman, John F., letter from, 551.
New Netherlands, natural and topographical history, 153.
New Orleans and Mobile, custom-house business, 305.
New Orleans, citizens of, approval by, of the Executive, 117.
City council, 551.
Collegiate institution in, 522.
Conduct of the intendant at, 269.
The deposit of arms in, 540.
Deposits at, 575.
Description, 513.
Desertions of troops in, 288.
Determined spirit of all classes in (1815), 235.
French governor in, 401.
General Jackson's victory at, 662.
Great mortality at (1804), 82.
Invasion of, by a Spanish force, 240.
Local government, 208.
Martial law in, 210.
Plat of land in vicinity, 551.
Supplies to the Army in 1814 at, 87.
Newport, exposed situation of (1812), 284.
Newport News, captures at, by British vessels, 216.
New Spain, description of, 690.
Newspaper war in Pennsylvania, proposal to end, 141.
Newspapers, bills presented for, not ordered or read, 538.
Carriers of, 174.
Jefferson's views as to the conduct of, 406.
in London, practice of, to not admit pieces opposed to individual interests, 432.
Newton, Thomas, 663.
Letters from, 551.
Letter to, 297, 559.
Newton, Thomas, jr., letters from, 551, 552.
"New Views," criticism on, 28.
New York and New England rallying to Republican ranks, 48.
New York Board of Agriculture, 26.
British embarkation from, destined for Virginia or South Carolina, 91, 92.
Canals, 104.
City, committee of corporation of, transmittance of a medal, 552.
Collector at, complaint of the governor of Massachusetts against, 646.
College, possibility of Bishop Madison's obtaining presidency of, 498.
Corporation of city of, 17.
Election (1814), 51.
Evacuation of, 67, 102.
High School Society, 121, 552.
Harbor, military works in, 290, 292, 526.
Historical Society, collections of the, 96, 267.
Horticultural Society, 362.
Incorporations in, 90.

New York Journal, The, 300.
Living in, inconvenient to Members of Congress, 335.
Opposition of, to the Constitution, 337.
Legislature, letter from, 552.
Negotiations of, with the indians, 76.
Reported evacuation of, 98.
Republican committee of, address of the, approving the Administration's course, 162.
Sentiments of people of, respecting the new Constitution, 173.
State Agricultural Society, 472.
State constitution, 605.
State Temperance Society, 214.
Territorial cession, 98.
University, dissatisfaction at appointments of officers of the, 308.
Washington's preparations against (1781), 66.
Ney, —— (Count), introduced, 369.
Ney, P. S., letter from, 552.
Niagara, campaign of, 59.
Frontier, condition of the (1814), 678.
Occupation by British of post, 35.
Unfortunate event at, 263.
Unpopular commanding officer at, 263.
Nicholas, G., attorney for Kentucky, 254.
Nicholas, George, letters from, 552, 553, 554.
Political creed of, 554.
Nicholas, George W., letter to, 88.
Nicholas, John, letters from, 554, 555.
Letters to, 88, 89.
Testimony of, on a libel suit, 554.
Nicholas, Philip N., appointment of, as attorney-general, 555.
Letter from, 555.
Nicholas, Robert Carter, application to be consul to Leghorn, 555.
Introduced, 201.
Nicholas, W. C., 39.
Letters from, 555, 556.
to, 89.
Son, wishes appointment as consul at Leghorn, 414.
Respecting a loan to, 555.
Nicholls, Robert H., employment solicited by, 556.
Letter from, 556.
Nichols, J., jr., letter from, 556.
Nicholson, —— (Comptroller-General), impeachment ordered against, 390.
Nicholson, John, letters from, 556.
Nicholson, Joseph H., 732.
Letters from, 556.
Nicklin & Griffith, claims of, 701.
Nickolls, James B., appointment as collector solicited by, 649.
Nicolson, Thomas, letter from, 556.
Niles, Hezekiah, letters from, 556, 557.
"Ninety-eight," party of, dinner of, 487.
Niroth, Louis B. de, appeal of, for release from prison, 557.
Letters from, 557.
Noah, ——, (consul at Riga), 710.
Noah, M. M. (Major), introduced, 577.
Letter from, 557.
to, 89.
Religious views, 89.
Noon, Darby, 238.
Nonimportation law, 40, 71, 288.
Effect of, 149.
Inconveniences of, 31.
Pressure of, 51.
Protest against repeal, 419.
Sufferers from, 359.
Suspension of, 231.
Nonintercourse, adherence to, unless satisfaction is made for the *Chesapeake* affair, 409.
Advantages, 485.
Difficulty of enforcing, 683.
Legality, 373.
Renewal, 374.
Nonintercourse law, 642, 643.
Enforcement of the, 48.
Noninterference policy, 230.
Nonresidents, appointment to offices in this District, 149.
Nore, mutiny on the, 257.
Norfolk, defense, 177.
Defenseless condition, 552.
Intimacy of French and English consuls at, 256.
Suggesting a commander of the garrison at, 625.
Normonds Ford, proposed road to, 286.
Norris, Joseph P., introduced, 483.
Norris, William, introduced, 563.
North America, consolidation of, 728.
North American Review, Madison's letters to the, 182.
North Carolina, adoption of the Federal Constitution by, 176.
Approval by the executive (1810), 112.
Balances due officers and men of line of, and Virginia, 706.
Baptist churches of, letter to, 89.
Conjectures as to the adoption of the Constitution by, 730, 731.
Convention, 37.
Course of, in appointing electors, 259.
General assembly of, letter from, 557.
to, 89.
Grants by, on vacant lands west of the reservation, 175.
Lawson's history of the library of, 112.
Legislature of, approval of the Administration by, 355.
Opposition of, to the new Constitution, 69.
Patriotic resolutions, 31.
Protection by the General Government to seacoast, 89.
Quota, 617, 730.
Reconciliatian of, to the Constitution, 195.
Rejection of the Constitution by, 253.
Right of, to perfect titles to lands in Tennessee, 162.
Unanimous vote of, for Madison electors, 577.
Unprotected situation, 356.
Northern Neck, protection of inhabitants, 162.
North pole, Wilder's expedition to the, 57.
Northern States, votes of the (1800), 46.
Northup, Henry, letter from, 557.
Northwest, botany, zoology, and mineralogy of the, 154.
Expedition to the, 154.
Northwest coast, convention with Russia relating to the, 539.
Northwest passage, brig *Diligence* sent to discover a, 455.
Northwestern campaign, end of the, 554.
Norton, J. H., letters from, 557.
Norvell, John, 116.
Letters from, 557, 558.
Norville, John, letter to, 406.
Norway, paper currency, 304.
Notes on Virginia, 36.
A correction, 215.
Printing of Jefferson's, 381, 382.
Nourse and Lewis, detention of, at L'Orient, 297.
Nourse, Charles J., letter from, 558.
Nourse, Joseph, letters from, 558.
Nullification, 31.
Absurdity of, 10.
Authorship of term, 25.
Doctrine, 10, 11, 12, 14, 15, 89, 105, 106, 112, 116, 117, 128, 441, 478, 599.
Jefferson's opposition to, 117.
John Randolph's views on, 182.
Madison's views on, 181.
Proceedings of Virginia on the subject, 119.
Nullifiers, defeat, 595.
Fallacy and deception, 191.
Nullify, Jefferson's meaning of the term, 114.
Nunnery, burning of a, in Boston, 714.
Nutall, ——, refusal to furnish passport to, 299.
Passport for, 154.

O.

Oak bark for dyeing, 229.
Oak Hill, residence of Monroe, 88.
Oaths, administration of, 408.
O'Bryan, John, appeal of, for release from prison 526, 558
Claim, 85.
Letter from, 558.

Observatory, Government, proposal to erect a, 501.
Hassler's plans and drawings for the, 449.
New, at the University of Virginia, 213.
Site for, 20.
O'Callis, William, claim, 363.
O'Connor, —— (Major), discontent of, 249.
O'Connor, John M., letter from, 558.
O'Connor, Thomas, letter from, 558.
Letter to, 89.
Office, appointments to, of opposing politics, 257.
Removals from, 1, 90.
Tenure of, 1, 44, 85, 90.
Officers and soldiers, allowance to, 140.
Conditions for, 334.
Payment to, 254.
Army, incompetency of, 688.
Issuing of commissions to, 446.
Commissioned and noncommissioned, calling into the field of, for instruction, 292.
Discontent of, at promotion of juniors over them, 293.
For important command, appointment of, 264.
General, confirmation of nomination, 58.
Discharge of Board of, 248.
Inexperienced, 720.
Jealousies and illiberality of, 247.
Of the Eastern States, total loss of pay, 102.
Officers, public, classification of, 503.
Offices, two, incompatibility in holding, 235.
Ogden, ——, charges against, 544.
Ogden, Aaron (Governor), 301.
Ogden, Isaac, letter from, 558.
Ogden, Samuel G., letter from, 630.
Trial of, 282, 283.
Ogilvie, James, announcement by, that he is candidate as president of a South Carolina university, 558.
Congratulations of, on Madison's election as President, 558.
Letters from, 558, 559.
Ogle, Thomas, 441.
Letters from, 559.
O'Hanlon, Felix, 355.
O'Hara, John, recommended, 625.
Ohio, anniversary celebration of settlement, 28.
Boundaries of, 517.
Common schools in, 3.
Company, 205.
General assembly of, approval by the, of war (1812) and promising support, 519.
Invitation of citizens of, to celebrate anniversary of settlement in 1788, 309.
Permanent seat of government, 660.
River, plat of land on the, 559.
State of, 559.
Old age, debilitating effects of, 15.
Oliver, Daniel (Rev.), 568.
Olivier, Julius, 201, 559.
Oliviera & Sons, 219.
Letters from, 559.
Oliviera, Fernandez & Co., letters from, 559.
Olsen, ——, 282.
Olsen, P. Bleicher, letters from, 559.
O'Mealy, ——, introduced, 627.
Recommending, as consul at Havre, 152.
Onis, Luis de (Spanish minister), 248, 483.
Demand by, of surrender of the Spanish posts, 537.
Intrigues, 18.
Rejection of, expedient, 411.
Opie, Le Roy (Lieutenant), 727.
Letter from, 559.
Opossum, arcana of the, 59[illegible].
Oracle, editor of the, letter to, 431.
Orange County, value of land in, 350.
Orders in council, British, 2, 5.
England prefers war to repeal, 50.
Pernicious effects derived from the, 691.
Question of repeal, 49.
Repeal, 149.
Ordnance and stores, return of, for Baton Rouge, 736.
O'Reilly, Hugh, application of, for discharge from service, 560.
Letter from, 560.
Organized matter, elements, 26.
Orleans, Duke of, vile character of the, 386.
Orleans Territory, government, 404.
Governor, 14.
Orne, Azor, application of, for captaincy, 315.
Orr, Benjamin Grayson, letter from, 560.
Letter to, 89.
Osages, ceded territory of the, 206.
Osborne, A. L., application of, for clerkship, 560.
Letter from, 560.
Oscar, Swedish brig, arrival of, with American prisoners, 547.
Osgood, Samuel (Postmaster-General), 227.
Letter from, 560.
O'Sullivan, B. (Mrs.), appeal of, for aid, 560.
Letter from, 560.
Oswald, Richard, commission empowering, to treat with commissioners of States, 99.
Oswego, attack by the enemy on, 427.
Proposed floating battery at, 220.
Otis, George Alexander, approval by John Adams of Botta's American War, translated by, 560.
Letters from, 560, 561.
to, 89, 90.
Otis, Harrison G., controversy between, and J. Q. Adams, 605.
Otis, —— (portrait painter), 266.
Otis, Samuel A., application by, for a clerkship, 561.
Letter from, 561.
Otto (French chargé d'affaires), letter from, 561.
Otto, C., introduced, 735.
Ottoman Government, correspondence with the, respecting the *Gheretti*, 405.
Overton, Samuel, letter from, 561.
Owen, ——, introduced, 539.
Owings, David, claim of, as a revolutionary soldier, 561.
Letter from, 561.
Ox, a resuscitated, belonging to Madison, 506.
Oxen, superiority of, over horses on farms, 89, 97.
Oyley, Daniel D', 561.

P.

Pacific, ship, 571.
"Pacificus," 39, 40.
Heresies in, 391.
Packard, Frederick A., letter from, 561.
Page, ——, and Vane, ——, a quarrel in the Virginia legislature between, 723.
Page, Edward P., letter from, 561.
Page, Francis, letters from, 562.
Letter to, 90.
Page, Francis Mann, application for appointment of, as midshipman, 562.
Page, John (Governor), 246.
Disappointment of, in not being appointed as collector, 561.
Letters from, 561.
Page, Thomas, recommended for office, 409.
Pahlen, Count Frederick de, letter of credence of, 609.
Pahlen, Theodore de, 1.
Paine, Robert Treat, letter from, 562.
Paine, Thomas, attack on, by "Publicola," 38.
Compensation for, 123.
Conduct of, while a guest of Monroe, 533.
Enmity of, to Washington, 282.
Harsh letter of, to the President, 80.
Residence of, at the house of Monroe in Paris, 532.
Visit of, to Monroe, 531.
Paintings, purchase of, 662.
Revolutionary subjects for, 117.
Paint, metallic, manufacture of, 697.
Palfrey, ——, (Prof.), introduced, 686.
Palmer, Aaron H., application of, for Government position, 562.
Letter from, 562.
Recommended, 736.
Palmer, George, 159.
Palmer, Thomas H., letters from, 562.
Panama, Isthmus of, possibilities of communication from sea to sea, 365.
Panama mission, the, 692.
Pannill, McRae, and Pollard, captains, letter to, 90.
Pannil, Morton, introduced, 729.
Panther Creek lands, 252.
Entries on, 683.

Paper currency, 123, 129, 135.
Address on, 57.
Contest in New Jersey about, 335.
Predilection for, in Virginia, 355.
State, 36. 37.
Vote on, 335.
Paper, repeal of duty on, 258.
Pardon, petition for, of Mark Winslow, Thomas Winston, and James Stewart, 734.
Pardons by the President, 303.
Paris, A. K., introduced, 361.
Paris and London, expense of living in, 308.
Paris, barbarities prevailing in (1792), 95.
Confusion and disorder in (1789), 618.
Foreign troops march toward (1789), 386.
Insurrection in (1789), 386.
Mobs in, 385.
Our commissioners at (1797), 258.
Popular enthusiasm in (1787), 383.
Scarcity of bread in, 386, 467.
Situation in (1795), 532.
Tumults in (1789), 94.
Parish, David, letters from, 562, 563.
Letter to, 447.
Parker, Daniel, application of, for appointment of Adjutant and Inspector General, 563.
Application for the consulate at London by, 563.
Letters from, 563.
to, 323, 324, 718.
Recommended, 688.
Parker, Josiah, letter to, 691.
Parker, Richard (Captain), 165.
Parker, —— (Colonel), 636.
Parker, Samuel, 191.
Appeal of, for pecuniary aid, 563.
Letter from, 563.
Recommended, 317, 736.
Parker, Thomas, application of, for promotion, 563.
Letter from, 563.
Parker, Thomas B., letter from, 564.
Parks, Andrew, appointment of, as postmaster solicited, 712.
Letters from, 564.
Parks, E. L., letter from, 564.
Revocation of appointment, 564.
Parrie, William, case, 710.
Parsons, Eli, petition of, for pardon, 337.
Parsons (General), 568.
Parties, balance of, in Congress, 126.
Political, what a history of, should be, 52.
Partridge, —— (Captain), desire of, to connect his military academy with the University of Virginia, 540.
Partridge, A. (Captain), charges against, 620.
Letter from, 564.
Party spirit, 62.
Downfall of, 314.
Pascagoula, parish judge at, 681.
Passamaquoddy Bay, outrages in, 701.
Companies required for, 291.
Question of proprietorship of islands in bay of, 664.
Passport of protection against Algerines, 337.
Refusal to grant, to an English subject, 532.
Passports, how granted, 325.
Issuing, 344.
To inhabitants of Louisiana, 702.
To United States vessels not built in the United States, 303.
Patent Office, proposed superintendent and clerk for, 674.
Patent system, proposed remodeling of the, 633.
Patents, term of, extension of, 632.
Patterson, Robert (Professor), 54.
Patterson, Robert L., introduced, 526.
Patterson, Robert M., 419.
Dissatisfaction, 181.
Introduced, 695.
Letters from, 564, 565.
Qualifications, 213.
Patterson, William, letters from, 565.
Patterson, William D., application for renewal of office, 526.
Patton, James, letters from, 566.
Patton, John M., 15.
Dinner to, 4, 144.
Patton, John M., Letters from, 566.
Letter to, 90.
Patton, Louisa M., letter from, 566.
Patton, Robert, 447.
Death, 234.
Letters from, 566, 567.
Patuxent, enemy's vessels in the, 647, 6
Paul, Samuel, 567.
Paulding, James K., biographical under
Letters to, 90.
Pauperism, means for preventing, 108,
Pavia, Jose Mariana, letter from, 567.
Paxson, Joseph R., deposition, 562.
Paxson, William, 169.
Pay of the Army, appropriations for, to
to clothing department, 292.
Pay of the Army and Navy (1815), 323.
Pay of soldiers, inadequate, 643.
Paymasters, appointment, 168.
Payne, G. Woodson, letter from, 568.
Payne, J. C., 33.
Payne (Mrs.), illness and death, 372, 37
Valuable land of, 654.
Peace, anticipation of an early (1780), 4
A truce only, determinable on con
impressments, 414.
Commissioners, return of the, 249.
Congratulations on the, 3, 414.
Dawn of (1783), 99.
Establisment, organization of the,
In Europe, temporary, 294.
Negotiations for, 51, 66, 93, 496.
Overtures for, 610.
Preliminary articles, 34, 100.
Provisions for security in time of,
Ratification of the (1783), 35.
Tokens of preliminaries, 34.
Peacock and *Epervier*, action between,
Peale, C. W., letter from, 568.
Peale, Rembrandt, 568.
Pearl River, sale of lands in district e
Pearson, Jesse A., recommended, 639.
Peasley, Reuben, application, 609.
Pecan nuts, order for, 110.
Peck, Abijah, letter from, 568.
Peck, —— (Judge), impeachment, 663.
Pecuniary follies, 107.
Pedometer, 384.
Peers, B. O., letter from, 568.
Pegram, —— (General), appointment a
538.
Pemberton, 128.
Pemberton, Eben, letter from, 568.
Pen, metallic, specimen of a, 686.
Pencil, self-pointing, 275.
Pendergrast (Dr.), 138.
Pendleton, Edmund, 11.
And R. H. Lee, correspondence, 118
Introductory discourse of, in the
at Philadelphia, 94.
Letters to, 90 to 96.
Pendleton, John, letters from, 568.
Pendleton, Phil., letter from, 568.
Peninsula, unprotected situation of th
Penitentiary discipline, 129.
Penn, S., jr., letter from, 568.
Penn Society, dinner of the, 33.
Letter from, 568.
Penn, William, discourse on landing of
Introducing a descendant of the
Pennsylvania, 288.
Life, 717.
Society for the commemoration o
ing of, 277.
Tribute to, 120.
Pennock, William, letters from, 569.
Pennsylvania and Connecticut, contr
tween, 98.
Pennsylvania assembly, proceedings
specting the Constitution, 225.
Pennsylvania, bill against erecting a
within charter limits, 98.
Call of a convention to alter the co
227.
Constitution, 227.
Opposition to, 489.
Demands of, on Virginia, 221.
Discharge of the regiment of mili

Pennsylvania, elections to Congress in (1788), 38.
Electors, choice of, 259.
Exports from, 228.
General assembly, 569.
Imports, 569.
Insurrection, 554.
Judiciary system, mischief arising from the, 234.
Law in, for election of general ticket, 37.
Laws of State, 717.
Line of the Revolutionary Army, memorials and resolutions, 488.
Militia of, readiness of the, 133.
supply of arms for the, 446.
Mineral resources, 219.
Mutinous soldiers, 342.
Payment of creditors, 98.
Petitions for a new State in, 99.
Political intolerance under, 285.
President and executive council of, letter to, 504.
State convention. debates, 225.
State of, letter from, 569.
Treaty and antitreaty candidates in (1795), 42.
Troops at Pittsburg, 293.
Western, excitement in, against excise offices, 390.
Pensacola, authorization of the seizure of, by General Jackson, 87, 463, 540.
Governor of, charges against the, for inciting Indians to war, 537.
In hands of patriots, 239.
Spanish force at, 209.
Pensioner, injustice to a, 148.
Pensions, invalid, 58.
Pepoon, Benjamin F., letter from, 569.
Letter to, 96.
Pepper, white Sumatra, 244.
Percival, assassination, 50.
Percival, —— (Professor), nomination of, at West Point, 539.
Percival (Lieutenant), letter from, 569.
Perdido River, foreign powers averse to our obtaining territory west of the, 229.
Jurisdiction extended to, 682.
Our rights to the, 404.
Perkins, ——, claim of, 738.
Perkins, Jacob, introduced, 366.
Perpetual motion, 569.
Perpignan, Peter, letter from, 569.
Perrault, Lewis, heirs of, claim, 594.
Perret, ——, 570.
Perrin, Willis, application for an appointment, 732.
Perrine, Daniel, recommended, 304.
Perron, Charles de, letter from, 569.
Perrot & Lee, 627.
Perry, Lilburn P., letter from, 569.
Perry, Oliver H., instructions to, as to the fleet under his command on Lake Erie, 425.
Letter to, 425.
Perry's victory, 330.
Persian language, a translation from the, 473.
Peter, Robert, 198.
Peters, Barbara, claim, 547.
Peters, Richard, letter from, 570.
Letters to, 96.
Peters, Samuel, letter from, 570.
Petersburg, collector at, 319.
Volunteers, 90, 301.
Petitions to Congress, proper mode of presenting, 388.
Pettit, Charles, letter from, 570.
Peyster, Frederick, letter to, 96.
Peyton, Bernard, 418.
"Phantasm of a college," author of, 441.
Phi Gamma Alpha Society of Hamilton College, election of Madison as honorary member of the, 500.
Philadelphia, advantages of, as residence of Congress, 471.
Citizens of, loyalty of, 101, 149.
City council of, offer of the, accommodations for Congress (1814), 471.
Exodus of people from, 257.
Grievances of soldiers at, 101.
Instense heat in (1801), 178.
Meeting in, to discuss British outrages, 232.
Philadelphia, Mortality in (1780), 91.
Proposed removal of Government to (1787), 78.
Society of Arts, letter to, 97.
Supposed movement against, 92.
Topography of the city, 482.
University, Bishop Madison not a candidate for the presidency of, 498.
The riot in, 379.
Yellow fever in, 71, 257, 392.
Philadelphia, loss of the, 403.
Phile, Frederick, letter from, 571.
Phillips, Charles H., letter from, 571.
Phillips, Cramond & Co., 507.
Phillips, Henry, letter from, 571.
Phillips, John K., letters from, 571.
Phillips, N., letter from, 571.
Philo Classic, letter from, 571.
Philolexian Society of Columbia College, 27.
Phrenology, science of, 183.
Physick, Philip S., letters from, 571.
Physicians and surgeons for Army and Navy, incompetent, 252.
Physiology, mental, 116.
Piano, present of a, 225.
Pichegru, ——, arrest of, 480.
Pichon, L. A. (Chargé d'affaires), letters from, 571, 572.
Demands of, concerning capture of French vessels, 627.
Pickens, Israel, recommended, 518.
Pickering, Timothy, letters from, 572.
Letter to, 97, 533.
Motives of, respecting Monroe, 533.
Paper by, bearing unfavorably on Washington, 236.
Secretary of State, 80.
Vindication of Monroe of charges by, 533.
Picket, Albert, and others, letter from, 572.
Letter to, 97.
Picket, William, letter from, 572.
Picket, William S., 573.
Pictou, —— (General), 260.
Pierce, William, letter from, 573.
Pieton, murder of, in Paris, 255.
Pike (General), character, 31.
Pike, Zebulon M., mission, 407, 408.
Pikes, efficacy of, 278.
Pilgrim fathers, principles and virtues, 26.
Pillars, durable coating of, receipts for, 475.
Pinckney, Charles, 270, 502.
Desire for a foreign appointment, 573.
Domestic life, 573.
Draft by, of a constitution, 635.
Letters from, 573, 574, 575, 576, 577, 578.
Letter to, 430.
Negotiations of, for cession of Florida, 573.
Publication of a pamphlet by, 90.
Recall, 82.
Residence of, in Madrid, 574.
Travels in Italy, 575.
Pinckney, Charles Cotesworth, 572.
Minister to France, 257.
Not admitted, 73.
Pinckney, —— (Dr.), 238.
Pinckney, Thomas, letter to, 392.
Minister to Great Britain, 58, 95.
Pinkney, William, 206, 419.
Appointment as Attorney-General, 579.
Leaves Naples, 52.
Letters from, 578, 579, 580.
Letter to, 97.
Minister to Great Britain, 83.
Papers, 719.
Penetration and patriotism, 129.
Professional and political character, 718.
Proposed biography, 129.
Publication of private communication, 290.
Resignation as Attorney-General, 97, 580.
Unfriendly language held by, toward Jonathan Russell (1811), 108.
Pinkney, William E., letter from, 580.
Piracy, book on, 4.
Charges of, 687.
Pirates and smugglers at Barrataria, 249.
Barbary, means for exterminating, 141.
In West Indies, suppression of, 538.
Smugglers and negroes, the enemy intriguing with, 210.

Pistols, pair of, manufactured at Buenos Ayres, 331.
Pitman, John, jr., letter from, 580.
Pitts, administration of, forebodings of Monroe as to, 700.
Pittsburg, disorders and desertions of troops at, 719.
Militia to rendezvous at, 292.
Plants, formation and food of, 26.
Plato, negro servant, 89, 560.
Plattsburg, victory at, details, 493.
Poem on the, 367.
Pleasanton, Stephen, and others, letters from, 580, 581.
Pleasants, James B., letters from, 581.
Pleasants, James, jr., letters from, 581.
And others, letter from, 581.
Pleasants, John H., introduced, 581.
Pleasants, Robert, letters from, 581.
Letter to, 97.
Pleasants, Sterling, 582.
Pleasants, Thomas, letter from, 581.
Pleasants, Thomas, jr., letters from, 582.
Plenderleith (Major), introduced, 608.
Plows, 39, 40, 47.
Horse-houghing, 391.
Improved, 411.
Plumer, William, 2.
Governor, congratulations to, on retiring to private life, 97.
Letters from, 582.
Letter to, 97.
Plumer, William, jr., letter from, 582.
Letter to, 97.
Proposed history by, of war of 1812, 97.
Poindexter, George, 137.
Letters from, 583.
Remonstrance of lawyers against appointment as judge, 475.
Poindexter, James, letter from, 583.
Poinsett, ——, introduced, 260.
Poinsett, Joel R. (Commercial Agent), 305, 648.
Letter from, 583.
Recommendation of, 305.
Point Coupee lands, sale of Lafayette's, 447.
Poland, American interest in the fate of, 57.
Polignac, Duke of, arrest of sons of, 480.
Politica, Pierre de, letter from, 583.
Chevalier, letter to, 134.
Political opinions, B. Smith declines giving, in which a local bias may be suspected, 110.
Parties, classification, 390.
In 1794, the question which divided, 112.
Political system, lack of confidence in the (1787), 68.
"Political Recorder, Weekly," publication of the, 557.
Polk, Charles P., applications of, for office, 583, 584.
Letters from, 583.
Polk, Robert, letter from, 584.
Pollard, ——, introduced, 366.
Recommended, 261.
Pollard, Robert, 476.
Letter from, 584.
Pollard, Robert, & Son, letter from, 584.
Pollard, Thomas, letter from, 584.
Pollock, Allan, jr., letter from, 584.
Pollock, Hugh, 507.
Pollock, Oliver, letter from, 584.
Pomeroy, S. W., letters from, 584.
Letter to, 97.
Pontoire, H., letter from, 585.
Pool, John, letter from, 584.
Poor, the, in Europe, 36.
Poorer classes, distress of the, 37.
Pope, John, (Senator), 149.
Letter from, 584.
Pope, Philip C., letter from, 584.
Pope, William, letters from, 585.
Population, black and white, 107.
Increase of, 107.
Of the United States, prediction of a century's increase, 496.
Treatise on, 24.
Port bill, the, 123, 504.
Repeal of, 68, 647.
Porteen, Stanier (Sir), letter from, 585.
Porter, Benjamin J., claim against, 566.
Porter, David, 20.
Character, 19.
Correspondence, 23.
Enters the Mexican service, 668.
Letters from, 585, 586, 602.
Merits and services, 137.
Suppression of pirates in the West Indies by, 538.
Porter, John, claim, 586.
Porter, John R., letter from, 586.
Porter, Moses (Colonel), 315.
Portland, citizens of, compensation for losses from British piracy requested, 142.
Portman, John, letter from, 586.
Portraits, new method of making, 171, 172.
Portsmouth, bill of mortality of, for 1809, 634.
Portsmouth harbor, defenseless state of, 364.
Portugal and Spain, treaty between, 260.
Portugal, closing of ports of, to British prizes, 91.
Neutrality of, 92.
Portuguese letter, difficulty in translating a, 330.
Portuguese sailors, advances to, 302.
Port Vincennes, Indians about, agreement of, to cede territory, 422.
Posey, Thomas (General), 239.
Letter from, 586.
Post, Jotham, jr., letter to, 630.
Postage, expense of, 632.
Reduction or abolition of, 502.
Postage in Spain, 574, 575.
Postmaster-General, frauds practiced by the, 171, 369.
Removal of the, 227.
Postmasters, Federal, triumph of Federalism attributed to, 140.
Post-office bill, 58.
Post-office, complaints of delays in the, 46, 700.
Opening of, on the Sabbath, 200.
Phials of liquid received through the, 702.
Support of the, 502.
Tampering with letters in the, 399.
Post riders, directions concerning, 408.
Post road, organization of a, from Philadelphia to New York, 370.
Posts and stations, 289.
Posts, British retention of northwestern, 67.
Delivery of the, 397.
Evacuation of, 34.
In Canada, delay in surrender, 248.
Maritime, recruits for, 292.
Proposed chain of, on the frontiers, 249.
The western, possession, 185.
surrender of, 527.
Potato, the, indigenous to west Pennsylvania, 633.
Potomac and Ohio, navigation of the, 380.
Potomac, Great Falls of the, 58.
Improvements of the, 382.
James, and Ohio rivers, business before the legislature concerning the, 123.
Potomac Navigation Company, 199.
Potomac, navigation of the, 36, 37, 121, 465, 504, 723.
South side of the, the healthier, 233.
Potomac Steamboat Company, 166, 567.
Potomac Valley, advantages of the, 458.
"Potowmac, the Expostulations of," 587.
Pott, —— (Captain), letter to, 439.
Pottawatomie and Miami Indian council, 597.
Pottawattamies, deputation of, 351.
Potter, Eben, letters from, 586.
Potter, S., letter from, 586.
Potts, Thomas, letter from, 586.
Poughkeepsie, proceedings at (1788), 125.
Poulson, L., letter from, 586.
Poursuivante, conduct of officers of the, 700.
Poutington, J. A. P., letter from, 586.
Powder and lead, petition to remove restrictions on removal of, 680.
Powel, John H., 572.
Powell, Colen Leben, 587.
Powell, James, letters from, 587.
Power of attorney to the Madisons, revoking, 205.
Pratt, Henry, claim of, 587.
Letter from, 587.
Pray, John G., letter from, 587.
Preble, Edward, letter from, 587.
Preemption claims, 525.
Prentis, Joseph, letter from, 587.

Prentiss, Joshua (Captain), application of, for command in the Navy, 317.
Appointment of, as sailing master, requested, 727.
Recommending, as sailing master, 733.
Prentiss, Joshua 3d, letter from, 587.
Prentiss, J., and others, letter from, 587.
Prentiss, William, letters from, 587.
Presidency, animated contest for next (1823), 108.
President, new title to the, 641.
Title of the, ridicule of the proposed, 386.
President and Vice-President, candidates for, 37, 80, 146, 259.
Counting of ballots for (1789), 94.
Method of choosing, 64.
Preparations for reception of (1789), 94.
Titles to, 38, 103.
and other officials, proposed titles of, 458.
and eventual successor, bill for election of, 95.
President's House, articles required for, and planting of grounds at the, 451.
Expenses for furnishing the, 451.
and Capitol, progress of building the, 449.
Presidents of the United States, proposed work on the lives of, 270.
Press, attacks of the, on our rulers, 610.
License of the, 116.
Lying and licentious character of the, 409.
New England, corruption of the, 188.
Venality of the, 449.
Preston, Francis, letter to, 97.
Preston, James P., application of, to be appointed Treasurer of the United States, 588.
Letter from, 588.
to, 581.
Preston, William, 24.
Pretender, success of the (1745), 205.
Prevost, George (Sir), correspondence of, 733.
Price, Alexander Pope, letter from, 588.
Price, Chandler, letters from, 588.
Price, David (postmaster), letter from, 588.
Price, John F. (Captain), letter from, 589.
Price, John H., 300.
Letter from, 589.
to, 97.
Price, John, jr., letters from, 588.
Price, William, letter from, 589.
Prichard, William, letters from, 589.
Priestmann's case, 303.
Prince, James, 141.
Prince, —— (Marshal), defense, 317.
Prince of Peace, a partisan of England, 480.
and the deposit at New Orleans, 701.
Influence of the, 573.
Power of the, 82.
Reverse of fortune of the, 326.
Prince of Wales, accession of, to the throne, 483.
Habits, 412.
Regent, 94.
Prince Regent, manifesto of the, 468.
Princeton College, tuition and expenses at, 629.
Princeton, congress at, 34.
Removal of Congress to, 101, 342.
Pringle, James R., letter from, 589.
Pringle, John J., letter from, 589.
Printers of laws of the United States, 450.
Printing, the public, 301.
Prison Discipline Society, 500.
Prisoner by Indians when a child, introducing a person taken, who has assumed the name of —— Hunter, 416.
Prisoners as traitors, threat of the Prince Regent to treat, 159.
Prisoners at Halifax, bad treatment of, 157.
Prisoners at Tripoli, liberation of, 702
Exchange of, 91.
Reclaiming of, 443.
Treatment of (1813), 317.
of war, Americans detained as, 710.
Private confidence, publication of, 17.
Privateer, belligerent, course to pursue with, with American prize, 403, 404.
Privateers, commissions for, 683.
Fitting out, 424.
French, law for capturing, 45.
Spanish and French, 669.
Prize causes, defense of, 708.
Prizes, laws on selling, 803.
Sale of, in our ports, 80.
Produce, colonial, importation, 467.
Large amount of, in hands of farmers, merchants, and millers, 50.
Products, prices of, 147.
Professor, qualifications of a, 571.
Prometheus, brig, 243.
Promotions, 290, 317.
Property and slaves, families suffering from loss of, 495.
Property, legislation respecting bequeathing, 90.
Rights of, in Virginia, 10.
"Prophet, The" (Elskwatawa), 171.
Attack of, on General Harrison, 214, 217.
Designs of, 171.
Interview between, and Brouillet, 351.
Letter to, 352.
Plans of, for destruction of Detroit, Fort Wayne, Chicago, St. Louis, and Vincennes, 351.
Prophetstown, battle of, 374.
Prorogation of legislature, 44.
Protection against savages in Illinois Territory, 297.
Protection to American industry, 9, 10, 11, 12, 62, 106, 189, 190, 199, 230, 233, 554, 594, 708.
Constitutionality of, 502.
Protective system, essays on the, 190, 191.
Protestant Episcopal Church, 227.
Bill for the establishment of the, 245, 691.
Opposition to petition of the, 277.
Provisions, supplies of, for militia, 720.
Prussia and Russia, rumors of declaration of war between, 254.
Prussiate of iron, use of, in fevers, 739.
Psalms of David, American version of, 252.
"Public Advertiser," vindication of the Administration by the, 500.
Public buildings, expenditures for, 452.
Parsimony and neglect in relation to, 454.
Rebuilding of the, 693.
Public buildings and property, payment of damage to, 548.
Public debt, discrimination between original and purchasing holders of the, 107.
Duties on imports to pay the, 217.
Public lands, disposal of, for extinguishing the debt, 465.
Intrusion on, 239.
Law for relief of intruders on, 238.
Public officers, delinquencies of, in Charleston, 312.
Public property, value of, 548.
Public securities, holders of, 518.
Madison's discriminating plan respecting, 254.
Public works, board of, election of Madison to the, 178, 500.
"Publicola," 38, 39.
Author of, 387.
"Publius," 342.
Authorship of, 226.
Papers, the, 226.
General estimation of, 647.
Pulliam, James, 666.
Pump, patent, 246.
Purcell, James, letter from, 589.
Purdy, Richard, 322.
Letter from, 589.
Purviane, John Henry, letters from, 589.
Purviane, Robert, letters from, 589, 590.

Q.

Quaker memorial, debates on the, 103.
Quaker, patriotism of a, 632.
Quakers in the Indian agency, 355.
Quamer, Alexander (Captain), 256.
Quarantine in Spain of American vessels, 575.
Quartermaster-general, returns of the, 246.
Quartermaster's division, nominations in the, 291.
Quartermasters, government of commissioners of claims on, 238.
Quebec, British authorities withdrawing their cannon and magazines from Upper Canada to, 407.
Fleet, prizes of the, carried into New England, 91.

Quebec, ordinance of, for regulating commerce with the United States, 193.
Queen Caroline, trial of, 107.
Queen Charlotte, preparations for an expedition to burn the, 720.
Queenstown, defeat of troops at, for want of support, 292.
Quotas, respective, of the States, 292.
Quicksilver, to find water by aid of, 184.
Quinn & Fitzgerald, letter from, 590.

R.

Radcliff, William S., letter from, 590.
Rademaker, ——, 326.
Radford, William, letter from, 590.
Ragged Island, enemy's ships at, 594.
Raggi, Giacomo, letters from, 590.
Raisin, Samuel, letter to, 162.
Ralston, Robert, 571.
Ralston, ——, introduced, 454.
Ramsay, Andrew, letter from, 590.
Ramsay, David, letters from, 590, 591.
Letter to, 98.
Ramsey, Thomas, letter from, 591.
Rand, B. H., letter from, 591.
Randolph, Archibald C., solicitation of, for appointment, 412.
Randolph, Beverley, letters from, 591, 592.
Letter to, 98.
Randolph, B. R., 408.
Randolph, D. M., 677.
Appointment to a consulship solicited by, 592.
Letters from, 592.
Randolph, Edmund, 39, 696.
Character of, 392.
Letters to, 98–103, 185, 495, 496, 531.
Nomination for governor, 123.
Resignation, 177.
(Secretary of State), 554.
Suspicions, cause of, 390.
Vindication, 80.
Visit to Virginia, 390.
Randolph, Edward, soliciting appointment of, as collector, 224.
Randolph, John, as a leader, 585.
Letter to, 103.
Views on nullification, 182.
Randolph, Mary, letter from, 592.
Randolph, Peter B., berth of midshipman solicited for, 222.
Randolph, Ryland, proposed appointment of, as a consul, 405.
Randolph, R. B., letters from, 592, 593.
Resignation, 593.
Randolph, Thomas Jefferson, Jefferson papers in possession of, 110.
Letters from, 593.
Publication of confidential correspondence by, 663.
Report of the stabbing of, 224.
Randolph, Thomas Mann, named for command of a regiment, 51.
Letters from, 593.
Suggesting appointment as colonel, 177.
Randolph, W. B., letter from, 593.
Solicitation for appointment of Sergeant-at-Arms, 593.
Randolph, ——, lithographic portrait by Harding, 502.
Rank, priority, 86.
Rape, punishment for, 382.
Ratifications exchanged (1801), 698.
Rations for United States troops, price, 137.
Rations, double, officers commanding posts allowed, 324.
Rattlesnake, capture of the, by the *Leander*, 428.
Rawden & Balch, letter from, 593.
Ray, Moses, letter from, 593.
Ray, William, letters from, 593, 594.
Raymond, D., letter from, 594.
Rayneval, Gerard de, Jefferson's estimate of, 383.
Letter to, 561, 650.
Mission, 19.
Statement, 87.
Reynolds, William, letter from, 594.
Razors, sharpening of, invention for the, 499.
Read, G. C., letter from, 594.
Read, Jacob, letter from, 594.
Read, Luther H., letter from, 594.
Read, Thomas, letter from, 594.
Reading, course of, suggestions of a, 406
Reading room, prospectus of a, 587.
Rebellion, advantages of a little, 382.
Rebello, José Selvestre (Brazilian ch faires), 168.
Receipts and expenditures (1810), 305.
Reciprocal commerce, the President's tion conferring, 250.
Reciprocity in trade, 52, 74, 85, 86, 107, 58
Recruiting officers, incompetency, 293.
Recruiting service, bad management of
Reed, Aaron, letter from, 594.
Reed, Joseph, unpatriotic remarks, 234.
Reed, William, letter from, 595.
Letter to, 677.
Reform bill, 512.
Regiments, additional, necessity for rai
Regulus, Lucubrations of, 115.
Richard, F., letter from, 594.
Reily, Thomas B., letter from, 595.
Reenforcements from England (1780), 91
Religion and civil government, practic tion between, 89.
Religious establishment, memorials ar strances against, 74.
Religious freedom, bill for establishing,
Religious liberty, 68, 74, 89, 227, 358, 359, 3
Mazzei's views on, 514.
Religious societies in the District of incorporations, 473.
Removals and appointments, 15.
Removals from office, 94, 108, 165.
Removals of able incumbents to make partisans regardless of ability, 71
Removal of officers of the executive de power of the President, 194.
Rent account, 595.
Renting houses, 697.
Renwick, James, 419.
Representation, change in, 124.
Question of basis of, 10, 180, 181.
Reapportionment of 94, 95.
Representation bill, 58.
Failure of the, 198.
Representative, obligations to his con 59, 61.
Representatives and electors, choosing
Republic, French, establishment of the,
Republican Advocate, 215.
Republican and Federal parties, distin 24.
Republican form of government, 33.
Republican party, a faction, so called ton, 389.
Middling talent in the, excepting Ma
Question as to unanimity of the, r the Presidential election (1808), 47
Schisms in the (1806), 83.
Triumph of the, 200.
Republicanism, attack on, by Democra ties, 41.
Prevalence in New England, 476.
Tendency in Europe, 278.
Republics, ingratitude of, 218.
Opposition in Europe to, 229.
Residence act, the, 389, 607.
Residence of Congress, 227, 591.
Resignations of officers, 712.
Resorts, public, 633.
Retaliation, rights of, 733.
Retaliation on British piracy, license fo
Retaliation, capture of the, 399.
Liberation of the, 399.
Retaliatory duties on England and Fran
Retaliatory measures toward Great Brit
Revenge, U. S. schooner, loss of the, 347
Revenue, collection of the, 250, 251.
Frauds on the, 200.
Imports and taxes for, 345.
Laws on collection of, 489.
Plans for, 38, 100, 101, 102.
Questions of, 123.
Requisition on States for, 161.
Rhode Island's view as to, 101.
Revenue duties, 180.

Revenue laws, a system of, 199.
Disapproval of, 685.
Revenues, increased, 41.
Means for adding to our, 344.
Revolution, publication of the archives of the, 65, 86.
Revolutionary army officers, petitions for half pay, 366.
Revolutionary army, speech in behalf of the surviving officers of the, 120.
Revolutionary characters, address approving the measures of the Administration and promising support, 441.
Surviving, 56.
Revolutionary times, reminiscences, 96.
Reynolds, Enoch, letters f. om, 595.
Reynolds, H. G., letter from, 595.
Reynolds, J. B., letters from, 595.
Reynolds, ——, 8.
Reynoldsburg to Natchez, road from, permission to be obtained of the Choctaws and Chickasaws to open a, 324.
Rhea, John, commissioner to treat with the Choctaw Indians, 104.
Defeat of election of, 595.
Indian commissioner, 596.
Letters from, 595, 596,
Letter to, 104.
Rhetoric and oratory, lectures on, by J. Q. Adams, 134.
Rhine, French checks on the, 72.
Rhode Island, an inlet for clandestine trade (1784), 76.
General agitation in, cause assigned (1812), 283.
Legislature of, 16.
Madison candidate for Presidency by electors, 503.
Object in not adopting the Constitution, 227, 228.
Perversity of, 98, 99.
Petition for exemption from tonnage imposed on foreigners, 500.
Politics of (1812), 363.
Probable entry into the Union, 500.
Rejects the Constitution. 68, 69, 192, 337.
Retired from Congress, 125.
Ricaud, Mary, letter from, 596.
Ricaud, ——, appeal for pardon of, 596.
Rice, Alexander, letter from, 597.
Rice from the South Seas, 69.
Richard, Gabriel, letter from, 597.
Richard, ——, (Rev.). introduced, 199.
Richards, Father, agricultural school of, 411.
Richardson, Austis E., letter from, 597.
Richardson, Benjamin P., introduced, 204.
Richardson, R. D., letter from, 597.
Richardson, William, letter from, 597,
Richardson, W. H., letter from, 597.
Richmond, branch bank at, 389.
Defense of, 153.
Destruction of public buildings at, 495.
Disaffection at, 530.
Manufacturing project at, 493.
Plan of the capitol at, 36.
Proceedings of the convention at, 125.
Raid of Arnold on, 495.
The fire at. 375. 618.
Richmond and Petersburg, defense of, 145.
Richmond convention, 33, 58, 253.
Madison's friends desire his presence at, 322.
Monroe declines the nomination for candidate at the, 541.
President of the, letter from. 597.
Richmond Enquirer, letter to, 104.
Richmond Whig, 336.
Ricketts, John T., 505.
Letter from, 597.
Ridgely, Charles G., letter from. 597.
Ridgely, C. S., recommending, 238.
Ridgely, John (consul at Tripoli). 598.
Letter from, 598.
Ridgway, Coats. letter from, 598.
Rieux, P, de, 598.
Riflemen, mounted, the call for, 490.
Rigaud, Auguste, letter from, 598.
Right of one generation to bind succeeding ones, 685.
Right of search, dispute with Great Britain on the. 369.
Rights of Man, Paine's, Jefferson's indorsement, 387.
Riker letter from. 598.
Letter to, 104.
Riley, James, letter from, 598.
Rind, N. B. S., letter from, 598.
Rind, W. A., letter from, 598.
Ringgold, Tench, applications by, for appointments, 598. 599.
Letters from, 464, 598, 599.
to, 104, 632, 693.
Recommended, 488.
Testimonials as to character of, who wishes Government employment, 550.
Ringgold, ——, claim 239.
Ripley, E. W. (General). 248.
Brevet commission for, 323.
Letter from, 599.
Ritchie, Thomas, letters to, 104.
Ritchie, ——, appeal for reinstatement, 490.
Ritchie, —— (Professor), 214.
Rittenhouse, David, cakes for electrical experiments by, 496.
Letter from, 599.
Rives, Alexander, letters from, 599.
Rives, William C., 28, 56.
Letters to, 104, 105.
Minister to France 88.
Roads, public, keeping in repair, 98.
Roads and canals, 52, 53, 84, 86, 117, 120.
Roane, John, letter from, 599.
Roane, Spencer, correspondence, 11.
Letters from, 599, 600.
to, 105.
Robbers, rewards offered for apprehension, 699.
Warrant for arrest, 318.
Robbery of United States money in France, 191.
Robbins, the case of, 33.
Robbins, Asher, application for an appointment, 600.
David Howell's estimate of, 363.
Letters from, 600.
to, 105, 106.
Roberts, Jonathan, letters from, 600.
Letter to. 106.
Roberts, William J.. letter to, 106.
Roberts, —— (Dr.), court-martial on, 242.
Robertson, A., letter from. 600.
Robertson, Bolling, secretary to the Territory of Orleans, 209 407.
Robertson, Isaac letter from, 600.
Robertson, J. (cashier), letter from. 601.
Robertson, James, nomination to the vacancy at Petersburg, 539.
Robertson, James, jr., letters to, 106.
Robertson, James jr., and others, letters from, 601.
Robertson, John, letter from, 600.
Letter to. 106.
Robertson, Thomas B., letter from, 601.
Robertson, William, letter from. 601.
Robertson, —— (New Orleans), 209.
Robespierre, fall of, 531.
Robins, James B., letter from, 601.
Robinson, David H., letter from, 601
Robinson, John, certificate signed, 494.
Robinson, Jonathan E., 403.
Robinson, W. D., letter from, 601.
Robinson & Hartshorne, letter from, 601.
Rochambeau, ——, arrival of, 673.
Rochester, N., letters from, 601.
Letter to, 106.
Rockingham Agricultural Society, 582.
Rocky Mountains, animal from the, 48.
Rocofuerte, N., introduced, 667.
Rodgers, John (Commodore), 134.
Affair with British vessel (1811), 50.
Court of inquiry in the case of, 347, 348.
Letter to, 242.
Rodgers, John; Hull, J., and Porter D. (Navy Commissioners), joint letter from, 602.
Rodney (Admiral), at Sandy Hook with fleet, (1780) 90, 91.
Rodney, Cæsar A., letters from, 603, 604, 605.
Letter to, 158, 328, 451.
Loss of furniture and books, 49.

Rodney, Thomas, letter from, 605.
Recommending as commissioner under convention with Spain, 556.
Reminiscences, 605.
Roe, E. McDermott, letter from, 605.
Rogers, Allen, letter from, 605.
Rogers, John, and others, letter from, 605.
Rogers, Maurice, letter from, 605.
Rogers, Thomas J., biographical remembrances, 106.
Letters from, 605.
Letter to, 106.
Rogers, William, letter from, 605.
Romaine, Benjamin, letters from, 605.
Letters to, 106.
Romanoff, —— (Count), 619.
Ronaldson, James, letter from, 606.
Roots and plants, descriptions, 492.
Rope making, 245.
Rose, (British minister), 83.
Failure of mission, 84, 461.
Letter to, 107.
Mission, 174.
Notes on negotiations of, on grievances respecting impressments and *Chesapeake* affair, 107.
Rose, H., and others, letter to, 106.
Rose, —— (Mrs.), conveyance of deed to, 665.
Rose, Robert H., death, 551.
Rose, Robert S., 581.
Rosenkrantz, (Count), letter to, 438.
Ross, Colin and James, letters from, 606.
Ross, David, letters from, 606.
Ross, James, letter from, 606.
Ross, William, letter from, 606.
Rotation in office, 384, 503.
Rotch, William, jr., letter from, 606.
Roulet, John S., 526.
Letter from, 606.
Rousset, M. L., 350.
Roux, Pierre, letter from, 606.
Roux-Bordier, M., 134.
Letter from, 606.
Rowson, ——, defense of, 265.
Roxas, Joseph, introduced, 608.
Letter from, 606.
Royez, Gabriel, letter from, 606.
Rozer, F. H., letters from, 606.
Ruelle, ——, letter from, 606.
Rum and molasses, 38.
Imported, duties on, 65, 69, 553.
Rumsey, James, inventions, 151.
Rural Magazine, the, 294.
Rush, Benjamin, death, 159, 564, 571.
Gold medal to, by King of Prussia, 607.
Letters from, 607.
Letter to, 107.
Rush, James (Dr.), 159.
Appointment, 608.
Introduced, 608.
Letter from, 608.
Recommending the appointment of, as treasurer of the Mint, 368, 425, 571.
Rush, Richard, letters from, 608.
Letters to, 107, 108.
Pamphlet by, 608.
Ruspoli (Prince), introduced, 445, 611.
Russell, ——, introduced, 648.
Russell, ——(Brigadier-General), letter to, 617.
Russell, Jonathan, 188.
Letters from, 608, 609.
to, 108.
Proposed resignation, 609.
Slights to, 609.
Soliciting appointment as consul, 262.
Russell, Joseph, recommended, 609.
Russell, William, affidavit, 494.
Claim for services, 351, 600, 609.
Letters from, 609.
Letter to, 600.
Russia and France, armies of, 231.
Russia and Holland, exclusion of British trade by, 48.
Russia and Turkey, peace between, 387.
Probable war between, 150.
Russia, armaments, 56.
At war with Turkey, 337.
Commerce with, 628.
Russia, Convention with, 87, 539.
Emperor Alexander of, character a 107, 330.
French campaign in, 289.
Gigantic growth, 56.
Mediation, 66, 88, 92.
Proposed alterations in treaty wit
Respect of France and England fo
Rumored defeat of the army of, 23
Russia, Emperor of, friendly attitude o 619, 700.
Instructions of the, to his minist ing Spain and Portugal, 536.
Letter from, 609.
Russian and French armies, general ba place between (1807), 472.
Russian campaign, the, 385.
Defeat (1807), 303.
Government, Hawkins's account o the, 101.
Mediation, termination, 330.
Ruble, depreciation of the, 305.
Ships, particular attention to be sh
Rutgers, Henry (Chairman) letter fro
Rutherford, J., letter from, 609.
Rutherford, Robert, letters from, 609.
Rutherford, W., letter from, 609.
Ruthy, schooner, 143.
Rutledge, John, letter from, 609.
Rye, specimens of seeds, 570.

S.

Saabye, H. R., honesty and integrity, 4
Letters from, 610.
Letter to, 436.
Sabbath breaking, disasters to the cou by, 163.
Sabbath, keeping of the, 159.
Sabine River, recrossing of the, by the 209.
Sacketts Harbor, building of ships at,
Critical situation, 51.
Defense, 264.
Occupation, 678.
Transportation of public stores to
Sacs and Foxes, readiness of the, to
Saddle, offer of a, as a present, 630.
Sadler, H., and others, letter from, 610
Sage, E., letter from, 610.
Saguyasotha, Indian chief, 368.
Sailly, Peter, letter from, 543.
St. Aubin, ——, introduced, 274.
St. Clair, Arthur (General), act for rel
Campaign, 553.
Defeat, 553, 653.
St. Domingo, commercial relations wit
Danger of European occupation, 2
Distress in, 70.
Negroes, 402.
Probable separation of, from Fran
Prohibition of trade with, 47.
Schemes of American and Englis at, 228, 229.
Suffering seamen at, 700.
Trade with, 227.
Vessel building for the revolted bl
St. Idlefonso, treaty, 575.
Saint Jean d'Augely, Regnauld de, i 296, 447.
St. John, New Brunswick, geographica 719.
St. Kitts, capitulation, 136.
St. Lawrence River, command of the, 2
Navigation of the, 108, 196.
St. Louis County Agricultural Societ
St. Mathews Church in New York, la ner stone, 108, 612.
St. Petersburg, mission to, 1, 27, 408.
Negotiations at, for mediation, 23
Salaried officers, impossibility of, to be at their posts, 407.
Salaries of President and Vice-Pre Members of Congress, objection
Salem Baptist Church, petition of the title, 631.
Salem, citizens of, congratulations of, tion, and promising support, 342

Saline, purchase of a, 368.
Works, 657.
Salt, export duty on, 578.
Licks, 422.
In Kentucky, 654.
Tax on, proposed, 398.
Water, search for, near the United States saline, 148.
Works, 657.
Saltonstall, Rosewell, letter from, 610.
Sanderson, Joseph D., letter from, 610.
Sandford, —— (District Attorney), 307.
Sandford, —— (General) death, 659.
Sandford, Alfred, captaincy solicited by, 659.
Sandford, Thomas (Colonel), introduced, 658.
Letter from, 610.
Sandy Creek, capture of enemy's boats at, 204.
Sandy River, evidences of silver on, 654.
Madison's land on, 654.
Sanford, Alfred, recommended, 661.
Sanford, Jonah, letter from, 610.
Sanford, Nathan, letter from, 610.
San Juan de Uloa, 668.
Sansom, Joseph, letters from, 610, 611.
Sardinia, friendly sentiments, 143.
King of, interview with the, 143.
Navy agent for, 143.
Sargent, John Henry, letter from, 611.
Sartori, John B., letters from, 611.
Saul, Joseph, introduced, 211.
Saunders, —— (Lieutenant), introduced, 507.
Saunderson, John, 190.
Sauvé, —— 208.
Introduced, 508.
Savannah, city council of, congratulatory address from, 204.
Sawmill, 64.
Improved, 284.
Sawyer, Lemuel, application for office, 611.
Letters from, 611.
Say, Benjamin, application for collectorship, 611.
Letters from, 611.
Say, J. B., letter to, 108.
Sayre, Stephen, claims 611, 612.
Letters from, 611, 612.
Schaeffer, F. C., letters from, 612.
Letters to, 108.
Schenck, Ralph, letter from, 612.
Schmidt, J. W., letter from, 612.
Schoharie, burning of, 91.
School, agricultural, project for the establishment of an, 694.
Female boarding, proposed establishment of a, 669.
Schoolcraft, Henry R., letter from, 612.
Letter to, 109.
Schools, primary, law providing for, 113.
Schooners, armed, permission to, 424.
Schrusbor, —— (Danish Consul-General), 620.
Letter from, 612.
Schultz, C., letters from, 612.
Schultz, William, letter from, 612.
Schuyler, Peter P. (Collector), 403.
Schuyler, Ph., 193.
Letter from, 612.
Scioto and Miami, mouths of the, immigration commenced at the, 334.
"Scipio," signature of, 396.
Scotch bonnet, appearance of a, causes a riot in Charleston, 469.
Scott, Alexander, appointment solicited by, 613.
Claim, 613.
Compensation for services, 539.
Letters from, 613, 614.
Letter to, 536, 539.
Recommending, 168, 424, 443, 505, 734.
Request for a pecuniary loan, 613.
Suit by, against John Law, 613.
Scott, Charles, letters from, 614.
Scott, Gustavus, appointment requested by, 614.
Letter from, 614.
Scott, John, boundary line between land of, and Madison's, 614.
Letter from, 614.
Scott, —— (Major), recommended, to be marshal, 535.
Scott, Robert, 496.
Scott, Robert G., application for appointment to office, 614.
Letters from, 614, 615.
to, 109, 687.
Soliciting the appointment as collector, 499.
Scott, Robert W., introduced, 174, 422.
Scott, William (Sir), decisions of, in court of admiralty, 431.
Letter from, 615.
to, 431.
Scriptural prophecy, 252.
Scripture texts, notes on, 109.
Seacoast, bays, harbors, etc., survey of, 556.
Exposed condition of our, 312.
Seagrove, James, letters from, 615.
Seal, proposed, for impressing on bounty-land patents, 518.
Seals on dispatches, counterfeited, 443.
Seamen, American, detention of, in British squadron, 167, 472.
Seaman, army bounty deprives us of, 427.
Desertion, 96.
Discharged, at Jamaica, 697.
Distressed, relief, 249.
Enlistment, 587.
Foreign, exclusion of, from public and private vessels of the United States, 483.
Impressment, 314, 551, 697.
Proposition to regiment, as artilleryists, 482.
Scarcity, 427.
Unpaid, 426.
Seat of Government, location of the, 58, 94, 102, 106, 107, 356, 530.
Seaver, E., letter from, 615.
Secession and State rights, 599.
Secession, disorganizing doctrine of right of, 10, 12.
Of Western States advocated, 83.
Threatened in South Carolina, 61.
Seckel pear trees, 558.
Secret Service, money for the, 403.
Sectarian seminaries, 24.
Sedgwick, C. B., letter from, 500.
Sedgwick, Theodore, speech, 40.
Sedgwick, Theodore, jr., letter from, 615.
Letter to, 109.
Sedition bill, 42, 80, 258, 259.
Seditious party, the, 93.
Selby, Samuel, letter from, 615.
Selden, Miles (Colonel), application for office of commissioner of loans, 689.
Self-government, doctrines, 116.
Selkirk (Lord), 232.
Sellman, John, letter from, 615.
Recommended for marshal, 658.
Seminaries of learning, proposals in Congress to institute, 536.
Seminole war, 618.
Causes of the, 536.
Seminoles, attempt to promote hostility of the, 238.
Senate and House of Representatives, letter to, 292.
Senate Chamber, accident in the, 327.
Senate of the United States, letter to, 109.
Publication by the, contrary to sense of the House, 258.
Senator, recall of a, 145.
Senators, election, 226.
Letters to, 283, 613.
Senf, Charles, letter from, 615.
Separate government, petition of citizens of Virginia west of Alleghany Mountains for a, 696.
Sequestration bill, 256.
Sergeant, Elizabeth, letter from, 615.
Serurier (French Minister), intemperate zeal and complaints, 150.
Letter from, 615.
Sessford, John, letter from, 615.
Sessions, Joseph, letter from, 616.
Settlers, protection to, 334.
"Seventy-six" Association of South Carolina, 420, 469.
Old citizens of, letter from, 616.
Sevier, ——, brevet commission, 361.
Sevier, John, 137.
Letters from, 616.
Submission of, to the governor of North Carolina, 730.
Sewall, Thomas, letter from, 616.

Seybert, Adam, letter from, 616.
Seymour, ——, 283.
Shaler, William, letter from, 616.
Shannon, George, 657.
Sharks, crocodiles and cetaceous animals, fossil remains of, discovered, 297.
Sharpe, William, application for Indian Commissioner, 617.
Letters from, 616, 617.
Shaumberg, Bartholomew, services, 211.
Shays, Daniel, petition of, for pardon, 337.
Shay's rebellion, 68, 93.
Shecut, J. L. E. W., letter from, 617.
Shells, elongated, 641.
Sheep, Barbary, 456.
Sheep, breeding, 570.
Broad-tailed, 154.
Merino, certificate authenticating a breed, of 522.
Importation, 48, 49, 361, 411, 675.
Premiums for, 245.
Raising, 245, 360, 374.
Rambouillet merino, 245.
Spanish, importation, 482.
Shelby, Evan, letter from, 617.
Shelby, Isaac (Colonel), candidate for governor, 658.
Governor, 168.
Letters from, 617.
Letter to, 109.
Military services, 109.
Sheldon, D., application of, as secretary of legation, 617.
Letters from, 617.
Shenck, Peter H., recommended as commissioner, 694.
Shepherd, Alexander, death, 622.
Letter from, 617.
Shepherd, J. F., application for appointment of tutor of Latin and Greek, 446.
Shepperd, William (Dr.), 140.
Sherburne, John Henry, letters from, 618.
Sheriff, rights, 403.
Sherman, Converse, letter to, 109.
Sheys, J. B., and Peter Ludlow, jr., letter from, 618.
Shipbuilding, encouragement, 691.
Improvements in, 592.
Shipmasters of Kingston, approval of the Administration by, 152.
Ships and cargoes, commissions on, 436.
Ships, enemies', destruction of, by torpedoes, 527.
Foreign, purchase of, by Americans, 509.
Officers as special messengers, 150.
Of war, our ports open to French and English, 47.
Naming, 241.
Propelling, against wind and tide, 280.
Proposal to build twelve 74-gun, 399.
Shoes collected for the Army, 65.
Shore, John, letter from, 618.
Shore, Thomas, 319.
Short, William, 48.
Desire of, to be secretary of legation, 379.
Letters from, 618, 619.
Letter to, 344.
Minister to The Hague, 58.
Sailing of, 327.
Shorter, ——, misfortune, 22.
Short, Jack, illness, 270.
Shotwell & Kinder, letter from, 619.
Shrapnel shells, 219.
Shorthand writing, 482.
Shumate, Julius R. (Dr.), recommended, 346.
Siberia, subterranean city in, 35.
Sidney, arrival of the, 174.
Silliman, B., letters from, 619.
Sillman, J., 659.
Simmes, ——, application for office of collector by, 537.
Simmonds, James, letter from, 619.
Simmons, ——, complaint of the conduct of, accountant, 494.
Removal of, from the War Department, 262.
Simmons, William, letters from, 619, 620.
Letter to, 141.
Simms, Charles, letters from, 620.
Protest of, against his removal, 620.
Simons, Robert, letter from 620.
Letter to, 109.
Simpson, Henry, letters from, 620.
Simpson, James, letter to, 109.
Simpson, Robert, letter from, 621
Simpson, William, letter to, 612.
Sims, Edward, recommended, 321.
Sinclair, Arthur (Captain), 361, 425.
Sinclair, Sir John, 127.
Sitman, John, and others, letter from, 621.
Six Nations, confederacy of all the tribes of the, 192.
Treaty with the, 621, 735.
Skinner, J. L., letter from, 621.
Skinner, John S., 717.
Letter to, 109.
Skinner, Timothy, letter from, 621.
Letter to, 109.
Skipwith, Pulwar, 7, 64, 139, 191.
Certificate respecting robbery at house of, 546.
Claim of 260.
Letters from, 621, 622.
to, 533, 610.
Recommended as consul at Paris, 531.
Robbery of United States money deposited with, 252, 532, 533, 610, 621, 622.
Skipwith, Henry, sr., 622.
Slaughter, Phil., letters from, 618, 619.
Slaughter, R., letter from, 622.
Slave labor, 190.
Slave, lease of a, to Madison, 560.
Slave question, the, 268, 553.
Slave trade, 108, 228.
Abolition of the, 581.
Infraction of the law prohibiting the, 304.
Negotiations with France for the suppression of the, 539.
Prevention of, 122, 346, 608.
Slavery, abolition of, 236, 294, 552, 562, 607.
African, 679.
Bill for abolition, 97.
Evils, 223, 420, 586.
Horrors of, publication of the, 593.
Negro, a blot, 57.
Proposed prevention, in a new State, 334.
Society for the amelioration and gradual abolition, answers to the questions of the, 76.
Slaves, act of Virginia legislature relative to, 8.
Convicted of murder, requested commutation of sentence, 546.
Dependence on labor of, 102.
Duty of the chief magistrate to emancipate his, 586.
Importation of, authority of Congress to prohibit, 85.
Laws respecting, 221.
Plundering of, 682.
Produce of, abstaining from consumption, 216.
Removal of, from Virginia into the District of Columbia, and their freedom on returning, 457.
Representation in consideration of, 234.
Sale of, 15.
Sloan, James, letter from, 622.
Small arms, improvements in, 292.
Smallpox infection, prevention of, by vaccination, 298.
In Kentucky, 654.
Prevention, 623.
Smiley, William, 159.
Small, Abraham, letter from, 622.
Smith & Ogden, 22.
Smith, Bernard, 159.
Application of, for increase of salary, 622.
Letters from, 622, 623.
Letter to, 110.
Recognition of services of, asked, 623.
Smith, Daniel, letter from, 623.
Smith, D. A., 186.
Letter from, 623.
Services of, 623.
Smith, Elisha, letters from, 623.
Letter to, 110.
Smith, George W., Government employment applied for by, 623.
Introduced, 689.
Letters from, 623.

Smith, Henry, 722.
Smith, Israel, letter from, 623.
Smith, Jacob (Captain), 517.
Smith, James, 657.
Smith, John, letters from, 624.
Smith, John Adams, application of, to be secretary of legation, 630.
Introduced, 678.
Letter from, 624.
to, 547.
Smith, John B., letter from, 624.
Smith, Joseph Allen, introducing, 350.
Smith, J. H., letter from, 625.
Smith, J. Kelty (navy agent), delinquent, 304.
Letters from, 625.
Recommended, 346.
Smith, John R., letters from, 625.
Smith John W., dismissal of, 630.
Smith, Larkin, claim of, for commutation, 625.
Letters from, 625.
Smith, M., letters from, 625.
Smith, Merriwether, 696.
Smith, Margaret H. (Mrs.), letter to, 110.
Smith, O'Brien, letter from, 625.
Smith, Robert, address, 443.
Appointment desired by, 627.
Dislike to, 355.
Introduced, 625.
Letters from, 625, 626.
to, 110, 246, 437, 601, 615, 624, 647, 684, 694.
Resignation, 110.
Turpitude, 50.
Smith, Samuel, gossip about (1750), 205.
Letters from, 626, 627, 628.
to, 152, 174, 332, 443.
Smith, Samuel H., acceptance by, of an appointment, 629.
Letters from, 628, 629.
to, 110, 560.
Negro girl bound to, 666.
Smith, Samuel Stanhope, letters from, 629, 630.
Smith, Thomas R., letter from, 630.
Smith, Thomas S., letter from, 630.
Smith, William (Honorable), introduced, 729.
Smith, William, letter from, 630.
Settlement of boundary line between estates, 630.
Smith, William H., letter from, 630.
Smith, William S., letters from, 630.
Secretary of legation, 630.
Trial of, 282, 283.
Smith, ——, letter to, 110.
Smith, —— (Rev.), letter from, 625.
Smock, James, letter from, 630.
Smoot, A. S., letter from, 630.
Smugglers and privateers, policy of pardoning, 478.
Smuggling by Swedes, 212.
Seizures of American vessels for, by sailors, 510.
Smuggling, importance of suppressing, 210.
Smuggling of British goods in Florida and Georgia, 577.
flour in Bay of Passamaquoddy, 558.
silk in the *Happy Return*, 709.
Smyth, Alexander (General), 263, 264.
Letters from, 630, 631.
Promotion desired by, 630.
Smyth, Anna (Mrs.), 301.
Smyth, William, clerkship desired by, 631.
Letter from, 631.
Snodgrass, William, letter from, 631.
Snow Hill, proceedings of Republicans of, 171.
Snowden & McCorkle, letter from, 631.
Snuff, American tobacco in the manufacture, 512.
Snuffbox, amateurs of the, 128.
Snuff, Natchitoches, 513.
Snyder, Simon, letters from, 631.
(Governor), letter to, 110.
Soap, vegetable, 214.
Soderstrom, Richard, letter from, 631.
Reprimand of, 409.
Société Française de Statistique Universelle, notice of Madison's appointment as member of the, 543.
Society of Friends, appeal of the, 606.
Sohay, Indian chief, 368.
Solar system, original doctrine of the, 416.
Soldiers' families, memorial for relief, 423.
Soldiers, low pay of, 582.
Mutinous, of Pennsylvania, 342.
Somerville, William C., letter from, 632.
Soulard, Anthony, recommending, 485.
Southard, S. L., 599.
Letter from, 632.
South America, bones of animals found in, 380.
Claims of, 82.
Destinies, 578.
Emancipation, 85, 402, 439
Proposed treaty of cooperation with Great Britain against the resubjugation of, 4.
The revolution in, 85.
South American affairs, 56, 107.
South American claims, 431.
independence, 649.
Provinces and the allied powers, 108.
Southard, Samuel L., letter to, 110.
South Carolina, adoption by, of the Constitution, 337.
Anamalous doctrines, 57.
Approval of, in the prosecution of the war (1812), 111, 523.
Code of laws for, 29.
Debt, 228.
Discontent, 15.
Electoral vote, 126.
Exposition and protest, 147.
Ferment in, respecting the tariff, 5.
Huet's History, 111.
Headlong course, 117.
Legislature, approval of declaration of war and promise of support (1812), 312.
Legislature, letter to, 111.
Nullification in, 61.
Ratification of, to amendments of the constitution, 404.
Representative of, ineligibility in Congress, 590.
Tendency in, toward dissolution of the Union, 470.
Unanimous vote of, for Madison electors, 469, 576, 577.
View of, by John Drayton, 270.
Violent doctrines, 75.
South Carolina and Georgia, irregularities in the harbors of, by French privateers, 404.
South Carolina, capture by British of the ship, 99.
Southcomb, Thomas, letter from, 632.
Southern army, movement of, in 1781, from Deep River to the Santee, 59.
Ascendency, 17.
States, British invasion of the, 91.
Southern Planter, 573.
Southgate, Robert, 551.
Southwick, Solomon, letters from, 632.
Letter to, 111.
Objections to appointment of, as postmaster, 555.
Sovereignty of the people, 104.
Spafford, H. G., 104.
Application for office of postmaster by, 414, 633.
Introducing, 678.
Invention of, 633.
Letters from, 632, 633, 634.
Letter to, 111.
Spain, action of, in cession of Louisiana, 403.
Affairs with, concerning the Floridas, 248.
Anticipation of a war with, 371.
Claims against, 325, 575, 576.
Concessions to, 34.
Credit and finances, 91.
Enormous expenses of living in, 574.
Failure of negotiations with, 701.
France, England, and United States, attitude of, 150.
French invasion, 53, 511.
Hauteur and reserve of, dismissed (1783), 101.
Independence of, speech of the French King against, 74.
Interference of, 572.

Spain, jealousy of, in connection with our South American trade, 85.
King of, wedding of daughter of, 574.
Menaces of, 244.
Misunderstanding between, and the United States, 615.
Negotiations with, 481, 634.
delay in, 52.
probable satisfactory termination, 52.
Neutrality of, not permitted, 480.
No reliance on, for cash, 91.
Offensive conduct of, 250.
Perverseness, 23.
Question of an extradition treaty with, 405.
Refusal of, to settle a limit, 405.
Remonstrance of, against our acquisition of Louisiana, 82.
Restitution for illegal seizures by, 250.
Selfish projects of, 92.
Settlement of controversies with, 648.
Spain not desirous to quarrel, 82.
Tractability of, since British acknowledgment of our independence, 34.
Treaty with, 72, 79, 80, 96, 538.
Troubles with, 538.
Unfriendly acts, 325, 391.
War with, avoided by peace with England, 52.
preferable to separation of East and West, 383.
Spain and Algiers, treaties with, 42.
her American colonies treatment of the United States toward, 456.
Austria join the allies, 466.
Great Britain, commercial regulations with, 60.
dispute between, respecting right of search, 369.
relations of, 83.
other powers, concurrence of, against us, 73.
Portugal, probable conquest of, 467.
the people of, require example of Americans, 52.
South America, determination of Great Britain to prevent foreign interference between, 87.
Spalding, L., letter from, 634.
Spaniards of Louisiana, fears of conflict between, and United States citizens, 502.
Spaniards, pretensions of, to be masters of the Mississippi to the Ohio, 148.
Reprehensible conduct of the, 243.
Transportation of, from Baltimore to Havana, 298.
Spanish America, delay in recognizing, 86.
Trade with, 47.
Equivocal conduct of Great Britain respecting, 84.
Independence of, 5.
Spanish and English, insults received from, 673.
Spanish and French privateers, capture of trading vessels by, 669.
Spanish and United States Governments, friendly feeling existing between, 298.
Spanish claims, 167.
Spanish colonies, attempt of England to govern, 305.
Conduct of the Government toward, 536.
Interference of the allied powers in the concerns of the, 146.
Spanish flag, insult to the, 403.
Spanish intruders, 185.
Spanish invasion intended, 239, 240.
Spanish Government, John Jay's negotiations with the, 377.
Refusal of the, to extend provisions of last treaty, 739.
Reparations by the, in New Orleans, 81.
Spanish governor, indignation of the, 682.
Spanish officers at New Orleans, conduct of, 13.
Spanish people, English assistance, 326.
Spanish possessions and United States, boundary line between the, 645.
Spanish posts taken by General Jackson, 537.
Spanish seizures in the Mediterranean, 81.
Spanish spoliations, 574.
Sparhawk, —— (Colonel) and daughter, int duced, 377.
Sparks, Jared, correspondence with, concerni material for publication, 635.
Intended Life of Washington by, 634.
Letters from, 634, 935.
to, 111.
On the negotiations for peace, 86.
Sparks, Richard (Captain) 616, 624.
(Lieut. Col.) letter from, 635, 636.
Letters to, 298, 441.
Specie, detention of, at Morrisania for use Tories, 341.
From Amsterdam, 227.
Payments, resumption, 18, 27, 89, 250.
Scarcity of (1782), 136.
"Spectator," letter from, 636.
Speculation in balances due soldiers exposed, 7
Speculation, rage for, 58.
Speculative purchase, 58.
Speculator, horse, pedigree of, 140, 187, 662.
Speculators, individual, the nation depending for money, 427.
Speed, J. (Dr.), 614.
Imprisonment of, 680.
Spence, Keith, 346.
Spencer, James, letter from, 636.
Spies in the Departments, 224.
Spinning machine, 227, 365.
Spinning wheel, 47.
Spirits and wines, duties on, 199.
Spirits, distilled, excise on, 65.
Prohibition of importation, 647.
Tax on, 554.
Spirits, foreign, prohibition of, 89.
Spoliation claims by the United States, 439.
Spontaneous productions, 96.
Spooner, Alden B., letter from, 636.
Spotswood, Alexander, a berth in the Navy so ited by, for his son, 636.
Claim, 363, 636.
Letters from, 636.
Spotswood, George W., letters from, 636, 637.
Unhealthy state of house of, at Universit Virginia, 637.
Stewardship of, at University of Virginia.
Sprague, Peleg, speeches, 25.
Sprague, —— (Reverend), 113.
Sprague, William B., letters from, 637, 638.
Spread, William, letter from, 638.
Spring, S. (Reverend), letter to, 111.
Spring, curious, in Pennsylvania, 253.
Spring Wells, treaty with Indians at, 314.
Sprogell, Mary, letter from, 638.
Sprogell, Thomas Y., application by, for cl ship, 638.
Pension applied for by wife, 638.
Sprout, Zebedee, and others, letter from, 638.
Squatters, 18.
Staats, Cuyler, letters from, 638.
Stadler, John, claim, 638.
Letter from, 638.
Staff appointments, 238.
Staff of the Army, new organization of the, 26
Stallion, Barbary, present to Bey of Tunis, 174
Stamp act, disposition to repeal the, 397.
Extension of the, 296.
Proceedings in Virginia during the crisis the, 95.
Repeal of the, 45.
Stamp of head of the President, 58.
Stanard, John, letters from, 638.
Stanard, —— (Mrs.), 638.
Standing army, innovation of a, 41.
Stansbury, ——, letter from, 639.
Stanton, Joseph, letter from, 639.
Stanwood, William, application for pardon of,
Stark, John (General), 6.
Congratulations to, 156.
Effect of Madison's letter to, 157.
Letters from, 639.
Letter to, 112.
Sketch, 157.
The hero and patriot, 112.
State and Federal debts, 371.
State Bank of Boston, 250.
State bank, project of a, 81.

State banks, incorporation of, 369.
State claims, 112.
State debts, assumption, 58, 69, 79, 94, 95, 103, 106, 254, 607, 640.
State Department of, officers of the, with their salaries, 639.
State rights and government usurpations, 269.
State securities, value, 738.
State sovereignty, 106.
States, defection of the, from means of supporting the confederacy, 100.
States-General, Adams's memorial to the, 92.
States individual, the right of, to annul the acts of the Federal Government, 116.
  Jealousy, 711.
  Local interests, 711.
  New, admittance, 106, 234.
    objections to the, 528.
  Rapid growth of the, 96.
  Requisition on, for revenue, 161.
  Requisitions by Congress on, to defray expenses of war, 217.
  Sovereignty, 112.
Steamboat, project for a (1788), 297.
Steamboats, claim of John Fitch to the invention, 297.
Steam frigate, proposed building of a, 242.
  Frigates, economy in use, 301.
Steel and iron, process for purity and cheapness, 111.
  Cast, invention for manufacture, 633.
Steele, John (General), letter to, 327.
  Letters from, 639.
  Letter to, 251.
Steele, Jonathan, letter from, 639.
Stephen, Adam, letters from, 640.
Stephens, —— (Dr.), appointment, 639.
Stephens, W., application for appointment as district judge, 640.
  Letter from, 640.
Sterling, M., letter from, 640.
Steuben, F. W. A. (Baron), clamor against, 711.
  The grant of land to, 176, 196.
Steubenville Woolen Factory, 606.
Stevens, Albert, application of, for clerkship, 640.
  Letter from, 640.
Stevens, Alexander H., letter from, 640.
Stevens, Edward, appointment as collector at Norfolk solicited by, 640.
  Letters from, 640, 641.
Stevens, John, letters from, 641.
Stevens's Thesaurus, 214.
Stevenson, Andrew, letters to, 112.
Stewart, Alexander, request of, to aid him in his pretensions to a seat in the legislature, 534.
Stewart, Charles, letter from, 641.
  Seat at the Navy Board offered to and declined, 243.
Stewart, D., letters from, 641.
Stewart, (General), claims, 641.
Stewart, James, 423.
  Letter from, 734.
Stewart, John, letter from, 641.
Stewart, William M., recommending appointment of, as assistant agent, 505.
Stewart, ——, prisoner, on charge of counterfeiting, 505.
Stickney, B. F., 157.
  Letter from, 641.
Stickney, Franklin, introduced, 639.
Stills, improvement on, 667.
  Tax on, 641.
Stilley, Isaac N., letter from, 642.
Stilwell, Silas M., letters from, 642.
Stimpson, James, claim, 598.
Stith, Griffin, letter from, 642.
Stock, fluctuations of, 69.
  Gambling and speculations, the rage for, 459.
Stocks, sale of, 148.
Stoddert & Mason, case of, 703.
Stoddert, Benjamin, 677.
  Letter from, 642.
Stoddert, ——, letter to, 461.
Stode, John, letter from, 642.
Stodert, Ben, and others, letter from, 642.
Stokeley, John, letters from, 642, 643.
Stokes, Montford, letter from, 643.
  Letter to, 112.
Stone, Benjamin, letter from, 643.
Stone, David, letters from, 643.
  Letter to, 112.
Stone, Rufus, 589.
Stone, William L., letter from, 643.
Stone, William S., 174.
  Letter to, 219.
Storey, Joseph, introduced, 244.
Storrow, S. A., application for office, 644.
  Letters from, 643.
  Letter to, 112.
Story, Benjamin, 478.
Story, Isaac, application for office by, 644.
  Letters from, 644.
  Letter to 423.
Stoughton John, letter from, 644.
Stoughton, William, letter from, 644.
Stove, kitchen, 42.
Stow, Joshua letter from, 644.
Strahan, John (seaman), 167.
Straus, William Albert, introducing, 623.
Street Parke, process served on Madison by, 644.
Stricker, John, letter from, 645.
Strode, John, application for Government employment, 646.
  Letters from, 645, 646.
Strode, Thomas, application for post of command at Norfolk, 646.
  Letters from, 646.
Stroebel & Martini, owners of ship *Easter*, 466.
Stroebel, ——, recommending appointment of, as consul, 468.
Strong, Caleb (Governor), 264.
  Letter from, 646.
  Refusal to turn out the militia, 263.
Strong, Nathaniel W., application for consulate at Lisbon, 646.
  Letter from, 646.
Strong, Roger, recommended as marshal, 728.
Strong, ——, merits of, who applies for consulship at Lisbon, 253.
Strother, French, letter from, 646.
Stuart, Archibald, letters from, 646, 647.
Stuart, Philip (General), letter from, 647.
Stuart, Thomas, letter from, 647.
Stubblefield, James, letter from, 647.
Subsistence and clothing, want of money for (1781), 92.
Subsistence and pay, appropriations for, 219.
Subterranean city in Siberia, 35.
Sufferers, loan by the British Government for relief, 510.
Suffrage, the right of, 112.
Sugar and molasses, manufacture, 650.
Sugar, molasses, tea, etc., increase of duties on, 73.
Sullivan, G., letter from, 647.
Sullivan, James, letters from, 647, 648.
Sullivan, Jere, 628.
  Letter from, 648.
Sullivan, ——, introduced, 539.
Sumner, W. H., letters from, 648.
  Letter to, 113.
Sumter, Thomas, letter from, 648.
Sumter, Thomas, jr., letters from, 648, 649.
  Resignation, 648.
Supplies, refusal of Parliament to grant, 66.
Supremacy, national, of the judiciary, 124.
Supreme Court, organization of the, 52.
  The Executive unauthorized to prevent action of the, 110.
Surgeon and mates of Navy, nomination, 626.
Surgeon-General's Department, inefficiency, 688.
Surinam, black convicts from, 405.
Surveying by magnetic medium, 335.
Surveyors' fees, 649.
Surveys, bill for confirming, 67.
Sutton, Lewis, application to be postmaster, 649.
  Letter from, 649.
Swan, James, letter from, 649.
Swan, William (Captain), recommended, 289.
Swan, ——, character of, and his monopolies, 532.
Swan, ——, introduced, 531.
Swan, John, letter from, 733.
Swann, Thomas, letters from, 649.
Swanwick, John, letters from, 649.
Swarbreck, Edward, letter from, 650.
Swartwout, S., prisoner in the Marine barracks, 442.

Swartwout, ——, 578.
Swartwout, —— (Captain), recommended, 728.
Sweden, King of, caprices of the, 385.
Minister from, 316.
Renewal of treaty with, 396.
Swedes, smuggling by, 212.
Swedish ports, permission for American vessels to leave, 328.
Swedish vessels, expulsion of, from Spain, 299.
Swelled neck, prescription for, 274.
Swift, Charles, application for office of commissioner of loans, 517.
Swift, case of the, 438, 454.
Swift Run turnpike condition, 650.
Sword for State of Virginia, 27.
Swords, purchase of, for Virginia, 304.
Sydney, Algernon. (*See* Algernon Sydney.)
Symmes, Daniel, 501.
Letter from, 650.
Symmes, Peyton S., recommending appointment of, as register of the land office in Cincinnati, 501.

T.

Tait, C., letter from, 650.
Talbot, Isham, 349.
Talbot County, Md., address of citizens, 31.
Citizens of, confidence of the, in the Administration, 156, 356.
Taliaferro, Baldwin, letter from, 650.
Taliaferro family, 650.
Taliaferro, Lau., letters from, 650.
Taliaferro, W. F., letter from, 650.
Talleyrand, Perigord, 396, 398.
And Gerry correspondence, 399.
Extraordinary conduct, 45.
Introduced, 695.
Letter from, 650.
Overtures, 399.
Power, 480.
Views of, on United States envoys' pretensions (1798), 80.
Tammany Society, 14.
Address of the, 241.
Of Ohio, 650, 651.
approval of the Executive's measures, 114.
Tampico, description, 667.
Tangier, governor of, 612.
Letter to, 620.
Tankoesley, Reuben (Captain), recommended, 661.
Tapscott, William, 731.
Tapscott, ——, 339.
Tarascon, L. A., letter from, 652.
Tariff, the, 75, 108, 116, 117, 134, 189, 190, 303.
Tariff act, Clay's, 675.
Tariff agitation (1820), 107.
And taxes, the, 223.
Constitutionality of the, 13, 179.
Effects of the, in Liverpool (1828), 147.
For protection, 10.
Henry Clay on the, 182.
Jefferson's letter on the, 180.
Madison's views on the, 179, 180, 182.
Notes on the, 113.
On articles of luxury, 300.
Views on the, 5, 9, 10, 11, 13, 14, 17, 64.
Tarleton and Sumter, encounter between, 92.
Tarrant, Carter, letters from, 652.
Tartarus, British sloop of war, 585.
Tatham, William, collection of documents, offered for sale, 651, 652.
Government employment solicited by, 651.
Letters from, 651, 652.
Tatum, Howell (Major), introduced, 623.
Tavern bill, 652.
Tax, carriage, 96.
Newspaper, 95.
Still, 84.
Taxation, direct, 73, 113, 226, 376, 724.
Taxation, unconstitutional British, 2
Taxes and the revenue, 464.
Taxes, bill for reducing, 194.
Federal, 222.
For 1831, 246.
On land, 36, 44, 136, 258, 668.
and negroes, 654.
Taxes, on manufactures, horses, slaves, a proposed, 224.
Postponed in Virginia, 67.
Power of the people to pay, and the ment to raise, 434.
State, on transfers of debts, 489.
Suggesting the lessening of (1817), 8
Tobacco receivable for, 68.
Tayloe, Edward J., introduced, 653.
Tayloe, John, letters from, 652, 653.
Letter to, 113.
Offer of services to command a ı 652.
Petition in behalf of cavalry officers
Taylor, C., 92.
Taylor, Charles, letters from, 653.
Taylor, Charles, jr., recommended, 661.
Taylor, Creed (Chancellor), letter from, 6
Taylor, Dabney Strother, introduced, 658
Taylor, Edmund, Madison's influence ask him into the Army, 654.
Taylor, E. H., letter from, 653.
Taylor, Francis, 659.
Application for appointment of, as 321.
Claim for bounty lands, 336.
for half pay, 653, 666.
Letter from, 653.
Major, close of Revolutionary War,
Recommended, 664.
Taylor, F. S., letter from, 653.
Taylor, George, faithful services, 393.
Letter to, 393.
Taylor, George, jr., application of, for in salary, 653.
Letter from, 653.
Taylor, Hubbard, appointment solicite marshal, 656.
Defeat as Representative to Congres
Letters from, 653, 654, 655, 656, 657.
Letter to, 664.
Taylor, Hubbard, jr., recommended, 661.
Taylor, James (Colonel), 160, 615, 643.
Letters from, 187, 657, 658, 659, 660, 661
Taylor, James (of North Carolina), em solicited by, 663.
Rejection by the Senate of nomin commissary, 660.
Taylor, James, jr., introduced, 663.
Letter from, 663.
Taylor, John, 96, 601.
Letters from, 664.
Letter to, 296.
(Lieutenant, Continental Navy), 653.
Naval service, 666.
Recommended, 661.
Taylor, Jonathan, contemplated resign 664.
Introduced, 656.
Letter from, 664.
Taylor, Joseph, 665.
Taylor, Joseph P., introduced, 662.
Taylor, Nathaniel (General), dispute bet Col. Robert Love, 446.
Taylor, Nathaniel Pendleton, recommen
Taylor, Richard, 241, 298.
Claims for additional pension, 664.
(Captain), introduced, 656.
Letters from, 664, 665.
Taylor, Richard, jr., introduced, 662.
Taylor, Robert, 538.
Letters from, 665, 666.
Letter to, 657.
Taylor, R. St. C., letters from, 666.
Taylor, R. W., desire of, to serve in the Navy, 667.
Letter from, 667.
Taylor, Waller, letter from, 667.
Taylor, William, 661.
Application for consulate, 84.
Appointment as consul at Vera Cruz
Appointment as marshal solicited by
Letters from, 667, 668.
Taylor, William D. S., appointment soli to be midshipman, 665.
Appointment to the Army, 658.
Letter from, 668.
Resignation, 668.

Taylor, Zachary (Lieutenant), 659.
Taylor, —— (Colonel), "New Views of the Constitution," by, 310.
Tazewell, Henry, letters from, 668.
Remarks on the British treaty (1796), 668.
Speech, 44.
Tazewell, Littleton, letters from, 669.
Tazewell, L. W., 180.
Recommended, 625.
Teakle, Littleton Dennis, letters from, 669.
Letters to, 113.
Tebbs, George, letters from, 669.
Tecumseh, biographical sketch of, 270.
Interview with, 352.
Letter from, 669.
Request of, to General Brock, 291.
Tefft, J. K., introduced, 638.
Letters from, 670.
Letter to, 113.
"Telegraph," newspaper, 22.
Telegraph, model of a, 686, 687.
Telescope, refusal of Government to lend its, to Ellicott, 285.
Telfair, Edward, letter to, 489.
Temperance movement, 638.
Temperance societies, 128.
Temperance, subject of, 33.
Temple, Robert and others, letter from, 670.
Templeman, John, 266.
Tennessee and Kentucky, sentiments of people of, concerning the embargo, 186.
Tennessee and North Carolina, surveying the lands bordering, 446.
Tennessee company, claims under the, 649.
Tennessee constitution, amendment to the, 700.
Tennessee general assembly, address of the, promising support (1811), 113.
Letter to, 113.
Tennessee General Association, 670.
Tennessee, lands in, perfection of titles to, 306.
Right of North Carolina to perfect titles to, 162.
Legislature of, resolutions promising support, 162.
Militia, 738.
Navigable streams of, 113.
River, troops on, for protection to travelers, 699.
Troops, 616.
Tents, arrival from France of, 66.
Tenure of office, 94.
Ternant (French minister), application of, for advance of money to France, 670.
Letter from, 670.
to, 388.
Recall, 390.
Request of an advance of money by, 344.
Terrell, Richard, letter from, 670.
Terrestrial globes, prices of, 134.
Territorial fund, mode of surveying and selling, 77.
Territories, authority of Congress over, 62.
Territories of States, cessions of, 35.
Test and corporation acts, repeal of the, 512.
Testimony, compelling, by the judge of one district on another, 407.
Texado, Manuel, conveyance of land by, 207.
Texas contest, the, 369.
Texas, invasion of, 310.
Revolutionists in, 210.
Thasher, Stephen, letter from, 670.
Thaxter, Levi, recommended, 629.
Thom, Christopher S., 580.
Letter from, 670.
Thomas, David, letter from, 670.
Thomas, E. S., letter from, 670.
Thomas, James, accounts of, 620.
Application for Army appointment, 316.
Thomas, Philemon, and others, letter from, 670.
Thomas, William, complaint of, for removal from office, 671.
Letters from, 670, 671.
Thomas, ——, and others, prosecutions against, for misdemeanor, 401.
Thomason, ——, claim of, 161.
Thompson, Alcedo, 440.
Thompson & Homans, letter from, 671.
Thompson & Veitch, letter to, 673.
Thompson, Benjamin, application of, for a clerkship, 671.
Letters from, 671.
Thompson, George, letters from, 671.
Thompson, H., jr., letter from, 671.
Thompson, John, application of, for office, 671.
Letter from, 671.
Thompson, John R., letter from, 671.
Thompson, Jonathan, letters from, 671, 672.
Thompson, J. W., 159.
Thompson, Pishey, letter from, 672.
Thompson, Thomas, application of, for consulate in Portugal, 672.
Letter from, 672.
Recommended, 582.
Thompson, W., letter from, 672.
Thompson, William, application of, for Government office, 672.
Letter from, 672.
Thomson, Charles, letters from, 672.
(Translator of the Bible), 672.
Thomson, George, letter to, 113.
Thornton, A., letter from, 672.
Thornton, Edward, letters from, 672, 673.
Thornton, Francis, letter from, 673.
Offer of services in the Army by, 673.
Thornton, Henry, letter from, 673.
Thornton, William, 300.
Application for agency at Colombia, 675.
Illness, 674.
Letters from, 673, 674, 675.
Thornton, —— (Dr.), pretended invention of, 554.
Thorntone, D'Alembert, letters from, 675.
Thosloff, Nicholas, 546.
Letter from, 675.
Threshing machine, 392, 682.
Threshing mill, model of a, 390.
Thruston, B., letter from, 675.
Thruston, John Buckner, letter to, 113.
Thurber, Samuel, letter from, 675.
Thurmon, William, letter from, 675.
Ticknor, George, 415.
Introduced, 539.
Letters from, 675, 676.
to, 114.
"Tiers-Etat," grants of the King to the, 227.
Tiffany, J. H., 678.
Letters from, 676.
Tiffin, Edward, 517.
Letter from, 676.
(Grand sachem), letter to, 114, 201.
Tiger skins, 267.
Tilghman, C J., 274, 677.
Tilghman, Edward, letter from, 677.
Tilghman, Edward, jr., introduced, 735.
Tillotson, Thomas, complaints of, concerning Aaron Burr, 677.
Letter from, 677.
Recommended as collector of New York, 478.
Tilton, James (Surgeon-General), 293.
Letter from, 677.
Timpanari, ——, letter from, 677.
Tingey, Thomas, letters from, 677.
Letter to, 642, 685, 688.
Tingley, Thomas, 7.
Titles to Indian lands, 734.
Titles to President and Vice-President, 103.
Toast, offering a, 33.
Toasts at the Lafayette dinner, 56.
Tobacco and ardent spirits, use of, 127, 713.
Tobacco and hemp, defeat of Henry's project of, as commutables for taxes, 126, 127.
Tobacco, comparison between Virginia and Maryland, 621.
Culture, 14, 29, 75.
Dependence of England on the United States for, 381.
Exports, tax on, 646.
For specie, commutation of, 98, 646.
For taxes, 68, 123.
French regulations concerning, 38.
Planters, advice to, 75.
Preparation, 470.
Sales, 455.
Samples, 109.
Shipments, 64, 261, 606.
Tax on, 66.
Todd, John (Colonel), 136.

Todd, John, jr., letter to, 349.
Todd, John Payne, account of, 564.
Letter to, 494.
Todd, Payne, letter to, 662.
Todd, Samuel S., application of, for a Government office, 677.
Letter from, 677.
Todd, Thomas (Judge), claims of, 657.
Letter to, 545.
Tokay wine, 134.
Tolls, establishment, 712.
Tomkins, Joseph Y., letter from, 677.
Tompkins, Daniel D., 23.
Candidate for governor of New York, 692.
Correspondence, 119, 120.
Government's neglect of services, 265.
Letter from, 678.
to, 114, 676.
Office of Secretary of State offered to, and declined, 114.
Tone, Arthur, 678.
Promotion of, petitioned, 709.
Tone, Matilda, 709.
Letter from, 678.
Tone, Theobald Wolf (General), 709.
Tongue, James, letter from, 678.
Tonnage bill, the, 195.
Tonnage duty, estimates of, 683.
Tonnage, statistics on, 233.
Tonningen, blockade of, 436.
Topham, Philip M., application for pardon of, 500.
Topographical manuscripts and plans offered to Government, William Tatham, 651, 652.
Tories, treasonable conduct of the, 263.
Torpedo attack, experiments in, 301.
Experiments, 262.
Plan of a, 526, 527.
Torpedoes, 252.
Torres, Manual, introduced, 203, 273.
Letters from, 679.
Torrey, Jesse, letter to, 114.
Torrey, Jesse, jr., apologies of, 679.
Letters from, 679.
Torrigiani, Charles (Marquis), introduced, 695.
Torry, Dr. (professor of chemistry), 86.
Toulmin, Harry (Judge), 473.
Appointment of, as district judge, 680.
Desired appointment of, to be sent as agent to Louisiana, 680.
False reports concerning, 681.
Letters from, 679, 680, 681, 682.
Letters to, 114, 144, 370, 484.
Presentment by the grand jury against, 516.
Stealing cattle from, as Spanish property, 681.
Threats of personal violence against, 682.
Toulmin, —— (Rev.), introduced, 509.
Toulon, military executions at, 40.
Recapture of, 71.
Republican forces advancing to recover, 70.
Tourists and travelers, handbook for, 633.
Towles, O. (Lieutenant-Colonel), letters from, 682.
Townes, John, claim of, for services, 682.
Letter from, 682.
Towns, incorporating, law for, 253.
Townsend, C. C., letter to, 114.
Townsend, David (Captain), services of, and reasons for appointment, 317.
Tracie, M. L. 190.
Letter from, 682.
to, 115.
Tracy, Elisha (Captain), 283.
Application for collectorship of New Haven, 683.
Letters from, 682, 683.
Trade and shipping, notes on, 115.
Trade, balance of, 11, 12, 14, 107, 189.
Defalcation of, in 1807 compared with 1806, 433.
Foreign, critical state of our, 542.
Internal, 36.
Monopolized by Great Britain, 77.
Of the United States, commissioners to be appointed to arrange an uniform system of, 696.
Power of Congress to regulate, 26, 77, 78, 104, 105.
Regulations of Congress, 77, 78, 124, 205, 683.
Restraints and impediments affecting our, 232.
Trade, with the United States, proposi British Parliament to allow (1781
Trading interests, unparalleled distre 510.
Tranquillity and harmony in public fe
Tranquillity and prosperity (1823), 108.
Translations, ludicrous, 114.
Transportation, construction of boats f
Transylvania University, 183, 568.
Travis, Samuel, recommended, 614.
Treasonable documents, publication. 5
Treasurer of the United States, settlen accounts of the, 735.
Treasury Department, estimates of tc ties, 683.
Practice of the, forbidding review (ings of a predecessor, 240.
Treasury, inquiry into the administra (1793), 96.
Overflowing (1817), 84.
Federal, payments of the, ceasing,
Treasury notes at par, 250.
Depreciation, 20.
Emission, 413.
To be made legal tender, 683.
Receipts and disbursements, 307, 3
Treasury warrants, 683.
Treaties, commercial, 101.
Constitutional rights of Congress to, 42, 43.
Made by States, 118.
Treaty, definitive, 66, 67, 121.
Conclusion of the, 479.
Conjectures as to the ratification 380.
Delay of the, 102.
Notes on the, 115.
Reception of the, 379.
Unpopularity of, in House of Comn
Questions in interval between p and definitive, 34.
Treaty, Jay's, objections to, 177.
Reading of, in the Senate, 177.
Signing of, 177.
Treaty-making power, 394.
Treaty of commerce with France, pro
Treaty of Ghent, 2.
Treaty of Peace, fourth article of th tions in favor of, 76.
Question of, 123.
Our violations of the, 93.
Treaty of St Ildefonso, 575.
Treaty of 1794, jealousy of France, 230.
Treaty with France (1803), 74.
Treaty with Great Britain (1807), vie 231.
Tredwell, Samuel, letter from, 683.
Trees and plants, encouragement for p 453.
Trees and shrubs for the President 444.
Trenton, appropriations in Congress buildings in, 334.
Trescot, John S., letter from, 683.
Trident, the, to ultimately belong to tl Hemisphere, 107.
Trimble, Robert, recommended, 657.
Trimble, ——, advocating the appoint judge, 503.
Triplett, John R., letter from, 683.
Tripoli, blockade of, 587.
Cessation of hostilities with, 702.
How a peace with, might have bee 684.
Prisoners from, arrival, 702.
The course to pursue with, 403.
War declared by, 260.
Trippe, John (Captain), letter from, 683
Trist (Mr. and Mrs.), 379.
Trist, E., letters from, 683, 684.
Trist, H. B., 684.
Letter from, 684.
Trist, Nicholas P., letters to, 115, 116, 11
Troops in service, estimate (1815), 563.
Movement of, from Carlisle to Pit in the West (1810), 2
On the Mississippi, mortality of, 72
Troup, George M., letter from, 684.

Trudeau, Charles, letters from, 117, 684.
Trumbull divorce case, 221.
Trumbull, John, letter to, 117.
Paintings, 117.
Truxtun, Thomas (Commodore), 247.
Correspondence of, relating to misunderstandings, 684.
Letters from, 684, 685.
Resignation, 158, 684.
Tschiffely, F. D., dismissal, 685.
Letter from, 685.
Tuberville, G. L., letter to, 117.
Tucherville, George W., letter from, 685.
Tucker, George, 53, 54, 417.
Letters from, 685, 686.
to, 117, 118.
Tucker, Henry St. George, 417.
Letter from, 686.
to, 117.
Tucker, St. George, 696.
Acceptance of commission of district judge, 686.
Death, 179.
Letters from, 686, 687.
to, 118, 216.
Tucker, Thomas T., treasurer of the Navy, 348.
Tudor, William, jr., letter from, 687.
Tufts, T., letter from, 687.
Tull, theory of, 105.
Tunis ambassador, visit of the, 12.
Tunis, Bey of, 401.
Complaint of the, 404.
Correspondence with the, 405.
Present of a Barbary stallion to the, 174.
Request of, for a frigate, 402.
Tunis, ship and presents for, 149.
Tunisians, delay of departure of the, 703.
Delinquent, not to pay gratuity to the, 703.
Refractory, directions respecting, 406.
Turgot, M., works of, 277.
Turkey, no signs of peace by, 337.
Turkeys, live wild, 214, 215.
Wild, present of, 566.
Turkish service, French officers in the, 337.
Turks and Russians, armistice between the, 438.
War between, 124.
Turks, English sympathy with the, 147.
Turnbull divorce case, 255.
Turner, G., letter from, 687, 688.
Solicitation of, for office, 687, 688.
Turner, Philip, appointment, 688.
Letters from, 688.
Soliciting appointment as surgeon, 688.
Turner, Thomas, letters from, 688, 689.
Letters to, 280, 349.
Vindication, 347.
Turnip, yellow Aberdeen, 584.
Turnley, John, 689.
Certificate of service, 682.
Turnpike, construction of a, 363.
Turnpike stock, 4, 567.
Turpin, William, letters from, 689.
Turreau (French minister), letter from, 689.
Letters to, 118, 303, 325.
Missing letters from, 328.
On purchase of drafts on the French consul-general, 303.
Rudeness of, 29, 405.
Tuttle, Jehiel, letter from, 689.
Twining, —— (Captain), 362.
Twining, Nathaniel, 255.
Typhoid fever, prevalence, 107.
Typhus fever, 52, 85.
Tyler, Comfort, 726, 730.
Tyler, John, letters from, 689, 690.
Letters to, 118.
Speech of, relating to the Federal Convention of 1787, 118.
Tyler, Royall, farce by, called "May Day," 336.
Tyler, Samuel, letter from, 690.

U.

Uncertainty and speculation (1780), 91.
Underwood, John, letter from, 690.
Underwood, S., asks situation as a school teacher, 690.
Letter from, 690.
Underwood, Thomas, 362.
Letter from, 690.
Underwood, Thomas, jr., application of, for office of doorkeeper to convention at Richmond, 690.
Letter from, 690.
Uneducated people, prejudices, 219.
Unemployed, discontent of the, 474.
Suggesting construction of gunboats and manning flotilla, by the, 474.
Unicorn, case of the ship, 437.
Union, and its members, questions between the, 120.
Dismemberment of the, 359.
Political faction to rule or dissolve the, 686.
Purposes of the, 605.
Question as to the perpetuation of the (1788), 93.
Separation of the, 230, 615.
Union of States essential, 60.
Union, master of ship, letter to, 327.
Schooner, seizure of the, for having a slave on board, 472.
Uniontown, college at, 6.
United Provinces, French march into the, 488.
Treaty with, 16.
United States, a consolidated empire, 185.
And British colonies, bill regulating intercourse between the, 511.
And individual States, questions of jurisdiction between, 119.
And Spanish territories, confederacy made up of, 231.
United States Bank, 134.
Bill establishing the, 643.
Expiration of charter, 21, 306.
Loan from the, 304.
Objections of J. J. Astor to the, 305.
Renewal of charter of the, 311.
Shares, subscriptions for, 222, 223.
Subscriptions to stock of the, 388.
Unconstitutionality of the, 675.
United States, codification of laws for the, 129.
Conduct of, toward Spain and her American colonies, 456.
United States creditors, funds for paying, 99.
United States, debts and revenues, 389.
United States Government, a compound one, 118.
Immense growth of the, 339.
Increasing respect for the, by foreign nations, 55, 85, 235, 293.
Judicial powers of the, in respect to local legislation, 105.
Natural productions of the, 607.
United States Naval Lyceum, officers and members of the, 597.
Plan of government of the, 2.
Proposed code of laws of the, 171.
United States receive and execute no mandates, 405.
Settlement of accounts between the, and the several States, 334, 335.
United States stock, dividends on, 544.
United States telegraph, 336.
Ultimate ascendancy of the, on the ocean, 56.
United States, frigate, to join the Mediterranean squadron, 243.
Unity of the Federal Government, 686.
University and military school, advice of Washington respecting a, 454.
University at Washington, conjectural establishment of a, 410.
University in District of Columbia, recommending a, 110.
University in Virginia, ideas respecting a (1809), 410.
University, Jefferson's scheme of a, 497.
National, establishment of a, 103, 245, 724.
Phantasm of a, 55.
University of Virginia, 3, 6, 8, 9, 10, 14, 16, 22, 24, 26, 52, 53.
Appointment of a professor at, 166, 690.
Appointment of visitors to the, 581.
Building of, and engaging of professors, 414, 415, 416, 417, 418.
Candidate for classical professorship of, 75.
Complaints against the expenses, 213.
Condition of the, 56, 636.

University of Virginia, course of study, expense, and admission to the, 135, 339, 690.
Debt of the. 178, 179.
Educating and promoting to, from primary schools, 320.
Estimates of cost of the, 416.
Fever at the. 10.
Financial matters of the, 416.
Finishing of the buildings of the, 178.
Grants to the, 690.
Gymnasium and dancing hall at, 115.
Hotels and keepers at, 8.
Income and expenditures of the, 417, 418.
Information desired concerning, 155.
Law professorship of the, 53, 54.
Letters from the, 690.
Letter to, 597.
Library of the, 178, 417.
List of officers and students of the, proposed, 275.
Location of the, 415.
Matters concerning the, 170, 181.
Meeting of visitors of the, 87, 170.
Methods for raising funds for the, 178.
Plan of police for the, 541.
Political character of the, 181.
Proposed loan for, 52.
Proposed lottery for the, 179.
Qualifications for applicants for vacancies in 28.
Rector and visitors of the, letter to, 484.
Religious instruction at, 215.
Remittances to the, 310.
Report of the visitors of the, 118, 119.
Salaries of professors of the, 28, 417.
Securing professors for the, 108.
Selection of professors for the, 541.
Vacancies of chairs in the, 87, 213, 419.
Unknown, letters from, 690, 691.
Letters to, 119, 358, 359, 360, 377, 592, 614, 712, 737.
Unmarried men to serve in militia, 211.
Upham, Timothy, collectorship wanted by, 691.
Letter from, 691.
Upper Canada, cause of defeats in, 341.
Inhabitants of, acknowledging allegiance to the United States, 291.
Judge Tiffany's description, 526.
Upper Mississippi Company, claims under the, 649.
Upshur, Abel P., recommended, 734.
Ursuline Convent of New Orleans, congratulations of the superior, 296.
Usurpation, public will to prevent, 47.
Utrecht, treaty of, 585.

V.

Vacancies, filling, 14, 15.
Vaccination, 26, 623.
Vaccine matter, direction for use, 274.
Vaiden, Thomas S., letter from, 692.
Vail, A., letter from, 692.
Val Ravassi, royal army destroyed at, 537.
Van Amringe, W. F., letters from, 692.
Van Buren, Martin, correspondence, 120.
Letters from, 692, 693.
to, 119, 120.
Request of, to publish his correspondence with Madison, 692.
Secretary of State, 168.
Van der Kemp, Francis Adrian, introduced, 384.
Vanderlyn, John, remittance for, 710.
Vaudreuil, Madame de, petition, 687.
Vann, ——, prompt apprehension and punishment of, demanded of the Cherokee Nation, 262.
Vannerson, William, introduced, 582.
Van Ness, John P., letters from, 693.
Letter to, 243.
Van Ness, William P., desire of friends of, for an appointment, 693.
Van Pelt, P. J., letter from, 694.
Van Polanen, R. G., letter to, 120.
Van Rensselaer, K. K., letter from, 694.
Van Rensellaer, Robert S., letters of introduction for, requested, 694.
Van Rensellaer, Stephen, farm offered by, as a pattern, 694.
Letter from, 694.
Van Renselaer, ——, (General), 263.
Van Rensselaer, Solomon (General), defeat of, near Niagara, 292.
Van Stopherst, Nicholas and Jacob, claim, 430.
Vanuxem, Lardner Clark, recommended, 220, 277.
Van Wart, Isaac, interview with, 294.
Varden, Charles, letter from, 694.
Varish, Hazlewood, letter from, 694.
Varnum, George W., letter from, 694.
Varnum, J. B., letter from, 694.
Varnum, James M., 16.
Letter from 694.
Vaughan, Benjamin, 607.
Letter from, 694.
Vaughan, John, 476.
Letters from, 694, 695.
Vaughan, Samuel, jr., letters from, 695.
Vaughan, ——, introduced, 537.
Vaux, Robert, letter from, 695.
Letter to, 120.
Vellum, stamped, repeal of duty on, 258.
Vera Cruz, epidemic of black vomit at, 667.
Verdier, Paul, letter from, 695.
Vergennes, Count de, 98.
Jefferson's estimate, 383.
Vermont, admittance, 99.
Application for admittance to the Union, 70.
Bill for admitting, 95.
Equivocal state of affairs in, 711.
General assembly of, letter from, 695.
Resolution of the, to support the declaration of war (1812), 309.
Relinquishment of, by New York, 124.
Sentiments of people, 731.
Verplanck, Daniel C., letter from, 695.
Letter to, 486.
Verplanck, Gulian C., letters from, 695, 696.
Letter to, 121.
Versailles, alarm of the court at (1789), 386.
Versailles County, 236.
Vessel, armed, cooperation with land forces in Gulf of Mexico. 240.
Vessels, list of, purchased and built (1813), 322.
Names of, in commission, 346.
Owned and built and owned only, distinction between, 393.
Purchase as convoys, 397.
for privateers, 326.
Repairs, 346.
Seizure under Berlin and Milan decrees, 288.
American, boarding by British naval officers at Malden, 330.
British seizure of, 40.
Capture with French property, 509.
Documents supplied to secure them from capture, 332.
List of captured, at Kingston, 136.
Napoleon's hostile orders concerning, in Spain and Naples, 708.
Search on, for French goods, 39.
Seizure by British cruisers, 489.
Treatment by the French Republic, 533.
American and French, captures by English, 332.
Armed merchant, 1, 5.
Advocating authorization of, to defend and attack and share spoils with the Government, 485.
Enemy's, in Chesapeake Bay, 686.
Foreign, regulations to be observed by, within the jurisdiction of the United States, 526.
Merchant, arming, 542.
Private, bill for arming, 396.
Sunken, methods of raising, and their cargoes, 342.
Vessels in commission, urgent demands for, 321.
Vessels to China and India, warnings to, 685.
Veto, Madison's, on bill for internal improvements, 692, 693.
President's, 95.
Veto of 1817, 116, 120.
Viare, Joseph Y., letter from, 696.
Vice-President, candidates for, 226, 255, 344, 530. 556.
Inauguration, 316.

Vice-President, oath before a district judge, 136.
Votes for, 103.
Victoria, Guadaloup (General), President of Mexico, 668.
Victoria, Princess, autograph letters sent to, 692.
Victory, predictions of (1812), 485, 486.
Vidal, William George, letter from, 696.
Videre, Charles (Count), introduced, 277.
Vienna and St. Petersburg, mediations, 121.
Vijano, Guiseppe Timpanari, 516.
Villebrun, de (Chevalier), attempt by Jefferson to communicate with, 378.
Vine, cultivation of the, 3, 13, 17, 134, 235.
Vining, John, letter from, 696.
Virginia, accurate map wanted, 556.
Adoption of the Constitution, 176, 343.
Advances to the militia, 376.
for naval defense and supplies for Army, 252.
Amendment of constitution of, 74.
Appointments to office from, 78.
Assembly of, bill for increased pay of members, 46.
Influence of Patrick Henry in the, 457.
Resolution to appoint commissioners to convention at Philadelphia, 36.
Unfriendly complexion of the (1788), 102.
Bill for election of electors from, 193.
British goods in, 205.
Capital of, 618.
Census of, 196.
Cession of lands from, 102, 334.
Charters, 121.
Claims of, 9, 34, 86, 155, 178, 336, 539, 696.
Constitution of, origin of the, 117, 130.
proposed amendment, 57.
Contributions to the General Government, 520.
Convention of 1776, 9.
Journal of the, 696.
Convention of 1788, 121, 251.
Convention for reforming the constitution of, 496.
Cotton planting in, 226.
Debt, 618.
Defense of, 146.
Defenseless state of the maritime frontier, 145.
Deficiencies for proportion of men (1781), 93.
Delegates to Congress, 503.
Deputies to the convention of 1787, attacks on the, 105.
Duties imposed in, 279.
Expected adoption of the Constitution by, 196, 197.
Friends and foes of the constitution of, 173.
General assembly of, 121.
Letter to, 504.
Reprinting of the journals of the, 319
Governor of, letter to, 496.
Great drought in, 68.
History of, early works on the, 411.
House of delegates of, journal of the (1798, 1799), 117.
Letter to, 487.
Importation of negroes into, from other States, 643.
Impost in, 60.
Improper administration of affairs in, concerning embargo, 584.
Jefferson's draft of a constitution for, 9.
Legislature of, course respecting the Constitution, 529.
Failure of the, respecting memory of Jefferson, 9.
Leaders of the, 379.
Of 1798–99, proceedings, 62.
Location of miliiary lands of, in Ohio, 304.
Map of, 497.
Militia in, destitute condition of the, 555.
Military debt, 196.
Mineral resources, 26.
Negro slavery, moral character, religion, and education in, 121.
New constitution of, 75, 722.
Notes on, new edition, 524.
Opposition in, to the Federal Government, 458.
People of, willingness of the, to risk all in the cause (1781), 495.
Virginia, plan for public buildings in, 381.
Plan of government for, 697.
Political parties in, 457.
Position of the enemy in (1814), 153.
Property of, seized by Mr. Nathan, 92.
Proposed reduction of, by the British (1782), 136.
Purchase of swords for, 304.
Qualification of voters in, 648.
Question of removal of seat of government of, (1822), 416.
Quota of, on requisitions of Congress, 93.
Ratification of the Constitution by, 37, 125, 445.
Readiness of, in event of war, 145.
Reflections on the politics of, 194.
Repair of roads in, 121.
Reported tendency to insurrection in (1787), 488.
Republication of original journals of the legislature, 105.
Resolutions of 1798, 25, 106.
Speech on the, 90.
Revisal of constitution of, 5, 10, 35.
Revised Code of, 7, 93, 123.
Securities of the State, 144.
Sentiments of, respecting the adoption of the Constitution, 192, 193.
Sentiments of the people of, toward the new Government, 355.
Separation and boundaries, 185,
Speaker of house of delegates of, letter to, 503.
State government of, E. Randolph's plan, 254.
State of parties in (1808), 585.
Survey and sale of lands ceded by, 528
Tariff resolutions adopted by, 181.
Taxation in, 556.
Territorial cession of, 34.
Treasurer of State of, letter to, 121.
Volunteers of, declining invitation of, 109.
Virginia Agricultural College, 183.
Virginia and Kentucky, separation of, 445.
Virginia and New York opposed to the Constitution, 337.
Virginia and North Carolina, critical situation of, 711.
Virginia Bank, prospectus of the, 499.
Virginia bounty lands, 370.
Virginia charters, 121.
Virginia Family Physician, the, 295.
Virginia Gazette (editor of), letter to, 645.
Virginia land warrants, 696.
Abuse of, 102.
Virginia lands, cession of, 380.
Virginia Representatives in Congress, letter to, 591.
Virginia Times, subscription to, 738.
Virginia wine, 599.
Virginians, vanity of, 221.
Visscher, Manning I., proposed appointment as, captain, 289.
Vixen, attack on the, 290, 346, 583.
Reasons demanded for firing on the, 683.
Vollentine, Nathaniel, letter from, 697.
Voltaire on intolerance, anecdote, 285.
Volunteer act, 51.
Volunteer companies, organization, 251.
Volunteer force, disapproval of raising a, on unrecognized principles, 307.
Volunteers, bounty for, 293.
Enlisting for local and special services, 307.
Pay, 263.
Petersburg, 302.
Vosburgh, Herman, letter from, 697.
Voss, Nicholas, 7, 673.
Letters from, 697.
Voss, Robert, letter to, 646.
Votes, buying with grog, 394.
Compulsory, means for preventing, 454.
Plurality of, evidence of will of majority, 59.
Voting for President, mode, 31.
Vottier, Charles, conviction and sentence, 658.
Vowell, John and Thomas, letters from, 697.
Vowles, Zach, letter from, 697.

W.

Wabash, military movements on the, 291.
Navigation of the, 688.
Wabash and Shawnee Indians, expedition against, 422.
Waddell, H. L., letters from, 704.
Passport requested, 704.
Wadsworth (Colonel), 70.
Wadsworth (General), movements, 291.
Wagner, Jacob, 492.
Application as collector at Baltimore, 704.
Authority to correspond with foreign ministers, 700.
Illness of, 698, 699.
Letters from, 697-704.
Wait, John, notes of a conversation with. 292.
Waldo, John, application for consulate, 476.
Walker, John, 254, 300, 512.
Walker, Samuel P., appointment as midshipman solicited, 704.
Letter from, 704.
Walker, William, letter from, 705.
Walker —— (Colonel), letter to, 435.
Wall, Benjamin (Marshal), misbehavior of, 304.
Wallace, Caleb. 549.
Letters from. 705, 706.
Wallace, Gustavus B., letters from, 706.
Solicits collectorship of Rappahannock, 706.
Wallace, James W., letter from, 706.
Wallace, Joseph, trial by court-martial, 428.
Waller, A., letter from, 706.
Waller, Ben, experiences, 706.
Letter from, 706.
Waln, Jesse, application for consulship at Tangier, 706.
Letter from, 706.
Walsh, Peter, letter from, 706.
Walsh, Robert, 615.
Intention to publish sketches of eminent writers, 707.
Letters from, 707.
to, 121, 122.
Walsh, Robert, jr., introduced, 579.
Letters from, 707, 713.
Walsh, William, invention, 638.
Walsh, William J., letter from, 707.
Walter, Lynde, and others, letter to, 122.
Walton, Matthew, letter from, 707.
Letter to, 122.
War, a paper, 138.
A triangular, 412,
Congratulations on the close of the, 321.
Declaration of, 45, 50, 145, 315.
Fears of, (1810), 54.
Horrors of, 364.
Possibility of a foreign (1797), 73.
Probabilities of (1807), 460.
Prospects of (1794), 256.
Remedy to end. 161.
War a less losing business than unresisting depredation, 409.
War and Navy, Secretaries of, letter to, 307.
War and Navy Departments, monthly expenditures, 306.
War Department, expenditures of the, 457.
Finances of the, 248.
Mr. Clay declines the, 20.
Statements of the, 707.
War establishment, General Dearborn's plan, 407.
War in Europe, termination (1801), 229.
War of 1812, approval of the, 617.
Attempts to prevent, 151.
Characters and capabilities of officers in, 59.
Conduct of the Executive at opening of, 88.
Declared by Great Britain to be a war of conquest, 413.
Events, 59.
English history of the, 244.
Exposition of the causes and character of the, 52, 63, 249, 413, 414.
History of the, 33.
Hopes of avoidance, 170.
Opposition to the, 111.
Popularity of the, 364.
Protests of Federalists against, 50.
Record of events during, 708.
Unpopularity of the, in England, 51.
War spirit (1798), 398.
War with America, opinions of the British press on the impolicy of, 433.
War with England inevitable (1809), 410.
War with Great Britain, fears of a (1807), 467.
Ward & Taylor, protested drafts at War Department, 421.
Sums due, 172.
Ward, Richard, letter from, 708.
Ward, William, 629.
Letter to, 323.
Warden, David Bailie, 49, 224, 412.
Appointment as consul, 139.
Ceasing of consular functions, 710.
Controversy between, and William Lee, 438.
Explanations demanded of, 139.
Injustice done, by misrepresentation, 709.
Letters from, 708, 709, 710.
to, 122, 139, 412, 678.
Private character censured by General Armstrong, 709.
Recommendation by Baron Humboldt, 365.
Solicits the continuance of his consulship, 708.
Statement by, concerning his conduct, 709.
Vindication from unjust charges, 709.
Warder, William S., 169.
Warrell, James, letters from, 710.
Warren, Samuel letters from, 710.
Wash, Thomas, claim, 734.
Letters from, 711.
Services of, in the Revolutionary war, 711.
Washington, Bushrod, concerning George Washington's papers, 711.
Letters from, 711.
Washington, city of, avowed object of the British to destroy, 152.
Conflagration, 74, 268.
Commissioners for the, 198.
Corporation of, taxes due to, 158.
Destruction of public buildings at, 429.
Fall of (1814), 210.
Flooding of Pennsylvania avenue in, 347.
Long distances in, 454.
Money required for buildings at, 397.
Objections to, by President John Adams, 45, 397.
Sickness in, 330.
Suggestions as to improvement of the, 454.
Washington College Parthenon, 61, 475.
Washington County, resolutions of inhabitants, 106, 122, 158, 492.
Criminal court, letter to the, 628.
Washington, George, 16.
Acceptance of the Presidency, 103.
Address prepared for, in 1792, 111.
Washington and Carleton, interview between, 101.
Washington and Lafayette, arrival of, at Trenton, 76.
Washington and Rochambeau in Virginia, 92.
Washington's birthday (1798), 397.
Refusal of House to adjourn on, 80.
Washington's birthnight, nonattendance of Adamsites, 45.
Washington chairman of the convention for adopting the Constitution, 37, 68.
Conversation between, and Jefferson as to (W.'s) retirement, 389.
Correspondence with, 111.
Diary of, Tobias Lear's denial of having suppressed a part of, 456.
Washington's Farewell Address, authorship, 52.
draft of, in Hamilton's handwriting, 294.
Washington, Houdin's statue of, inscriptions on, 382.
Illness (1790), 79.
Iron casts, 737.
Letters from, 711, 712.
to, 123, 124, 125, 126, 127, 173, 393.
Little inaccuracies in hastily written, 111.
Life of (Sparks's), intended publication of, 111, 634.
In Latin, 29.
Love of, for domestic repose, 458.
Medallion, 22, 227.
Menaces against, on subject of the bank, 38.
Miniature representation, 569.

Washington, mother of, monument to memory of, 6, 153.
Proposed monument to, 443, 453.
Papers, 711.
Prudence and virtue, 100.
Retirement (1792), 127.
Selection of, as head of the Virginia deputation to the Federal Convention, 123.
Sensitiveness of, on newspaper attacks, 391.
Shares voted to, 36.
Statue of, voted by Congress, 101.
Unanimous votes for, as President (1789), 94.
Voice of Virginia for, as President, 193.
Washington, Lund, letter from, 712.
Recommended, as clerk in Department of State, 506.
Washington, L. A., letter from, 712.
Washington, P. G., letter from, 713.
Washington National Monument Association, 18, 236, 237.
Washington pottery in Philadelphia, 547.
Washington Union Society, constitution of the, 189.
Washington, steamboat, 113, 653.
Wasp, schooner, desertion of crew of the 299.
Water, application of, to create a current of air, 498.
Water casks, Erskine's demand respecting the, 407.
Waterhouse, Benjamin, 671.
Abilities and learning, 51.
Application for appointment as treasurer of the Mint, 713.
Minister to the Netherlands, 713.
Age of, a detriment for public service abroad, 128.
Defense, 314.
False charges of political enemies, 713.
Inaugural discourse, 128, 713.
Introduced, 332.
Letters from, 713, 714.
to, 127, 128.
Recommended, 316.
Waterhouse, Benjamin (Mrs.), jealousy of, of Mrs. Madison, 713.
Watkins, —— (Dr.), 238.
Introduced, 415.
Watson, ——, applicant for consulate at Martinique, 158.
Watson, David, letter from, 714.
Watson, Elkanah, letters from, 714.
Letters to, 128.
Watson, George, letter from, 715.
Watterston, George, application for collector, 714.
Appointment as Librarian of Congress, 715.
Letters from, 714, 715.
Wattles, James, letter from, 715.
Watts, John, 205.
Letter from, 715.
Watts, Robert, power of attorney to, 205.
Wattson, James, letter from, 715.
Waugh, Abner, letter from, 715.
Waugh, Charles Stuart, clerkship solicited by, 715.
Letters from, 715.
Wayne, Anthony (General), appointment of, to command the Western army, 460.
Weasel, natural history of the, 36.
Weaver, David, letter from, 715.
Weaver, John, appointment in the Army solicited by, 659.
Webb, Foster, 516.
Webb, George, accounts, 606.
Webb, James, letter from, 715.
Recommendation requested by, 715.
Webb, William C., claim for supplies for Army, 716.
Letter from, 716.
Webster, Daniel, introduced, 539.
Letters to, 128.
Speech, 25, 128.
Webster, Noah, application for a foreign position, 716.
Letters from, 716.
to, 128.
Webster's Dictionary, prospectus, 109, 218.
Wedge, the Entering, 716.
Weekly Register, publication of the, 556.
Weems, M. L., letters from, 716, 717.
Life of Washington by 717.
Weightman, R. C., letters from, 717.
Weights and measures, law establishing, 631.
Standard, 130, 227, 736.
Wellford, —— (Dr.), introduced, 260.
Recommended, 461.
Wellington, Duke of, conversation with the, 147.
Policy of, toward the United States, 5.
Wells, Samuel Adams, letter from, 717.
Wendover, P. H., letter from, 717.
Wentworth, John (Sir), 522.
Letter to, 353.
Wertenbaker, William, letter from, 717.
West, Aaron, petition for pardon, 247.
West, Cato (Colonel), 525.
Land conveyed to, 207.
West, military enterprise in the (1806), 83.
Western and Atlantic States, scheme for separating, 658.
Western calamities (1792), 58.
Western country, severance of the, from the Atlantic States espoused, 83.
Frontiers, means of protecting the, 95.
Lands, a fund for the extinction of the public debt, 383.
Lands, speculative, 380.
Territories, extraordinary expedition in the, and Ohio River, 730.
Western Virginian, 643.
Western Volunteer, periodical, 144.
West Florida, acquisition of, means for the, 481.
Alliance of, with England, 601.
And Louisiana, boundaries of, 82.
Approval of President's message relating to, 340.
Cession, 726.
Description, 680.
Essential to the United States, 82.
Independence and ultimate destiny of, 152.
Inhabitants of, desire to become American citizens, 156.
Measures adopted with respect to, 499.
Purchase of, 303.
part of, 329.
Question of placing, under protection of United States Government, 49, 290, 370.
Situation of affairs at, 49, 156, 370, 681.
Territory, 328.
Titles to lands in, 550.
West India markets, all countries driven from the, 481.
Navigation, reciprocity of British, 27.
West Indies, British armament in the, 72.
Imports and exports, 435.
Our commercial intercourse with the, 193.
Supplies to the, drawn from the United States, 433.
Trade with the, 5, 17.
Westgate, Davis, letter to, 129.
Weston, J., demand by, for investigation of charges against him, 717.
Letter from, 717.
West Point Military Academy, admittance of students at, 285.
Cadets at, 718.
Treatment, 620.
Condition, 729.
Deficiency in the branch of art of engineering at, 286.
Flourishing condition of the academy at, 285.
Qualifications and course of study of cadets of the, 238.
Weyer, Michael, letter from, 718.
Weymouth (Lord), letter to, 585.
Whaling vessels, seizure of, 250.
Wham, William, letters from, 718.
Wharton, John A., letters from, 718.
Wharton, Robert, unpatriotic toast of, 234.
Wharton, T. J., letters from, 718.
Letters to, 129.
Wheat, American, in Europe, 127.
And flour, high price of, 79.
Foreign, British bounty on importation of, 96.
Invention for gathering, 200.
In Virginia, prices, 5.
Siberian, 360.
Talavera, 511.

Wheat, white, 179.
Wheaton, ——. (Dr.), recommended, 693.
Wheaton, Henry. 722.
Injurious treatment, 718.
Letters from, 718, 719.
Letter to, 129, 563.
Recommended, as marshal, 283.
Wheaton, Joseph, application for office of Sergeant-at-Arms, 721.
Appointment, 719.
Description of the march of the command of, 719, 720.
Desire to be in the line of the Army, 720.
Letters from, 719, 720, 721.
Letter to, 129, 598.
Record. 129.
Services in war of 1812, 721.
Solicitation for appointment in the Army, 719.
Wheaton, Levi, letter from, 721.
Wheaton, Seth, letter from, 722.
Wheel carriages, construction, 632.
Wheeler, D. E., letter from, 722.
Wheeler, Phineas, claim for services, 722.
Letter from, 722.
Wheelock, John, letter from, 722.
Whig party in England, 108.
Whigs, appeal from new to old, 1.
Whipple, Oliver, application for office, 722.
Letters from, 722.
Whisky rebellion, 79.
White, Alexander, letters from, 722, 723, 724.
Retirement from public life, 723.
White, E. D., letter from, 724.
Letter to, 129.
White hair (Osage chief), letter from, 725.
White, Hugh, letter from, 724.
White, John, jr., letter from, 724.
White, Thomas W., letters from, 725.
Whitehill, John, and John Light, letter from, 725.
White House, New Year's reception at the, 663.
White, Samuel, 228.
White, William, appointment as commissioner of loans, 725.
Letter from, 725.
Whiteside, J., letter from, 725.
Whiting, John (Colonel), death 329.
Whitney, E., memorial concerning a contract for manufacture of muskets, War of 1812, 725.
Whittle, Conway, letter from, 725.
Whooping cough, contagion from, 274.
Wieberking, Chevalier de, 612.
Letter from, 726.
Wichelhausen, H. D., introduced, 725.
Wichelhausen, T. J., letters from, 725, 726.
Wickham, John, counsel for Aaron Burr, 726.
Letter from, 726.
Wigfall, A. Thompson, letter from, 726.
Wigginton, ——, charges against, 466.
"Wild men" of Franklin, 640.
Wilde, Richard Henry, letter from, 726.
Wilder (Captain), expedition of, in 1772 to the north pole, 57.
Wilds, Samuel, letter from, 726.
Wilkinson, James (General), 9, 553.
Appointment, 554.
Attempts to excite prejudices against, 727.
Character, 238.
Complicity with Burr, 49, 177.
Court-martial, 264, 291, 348, 423.
Defense, 50.
Experience and qualifications, 471.
Failure of movements of, toward Montreal, 293, 728.
Incident in the trial by court-martial, 237.
Jealousy, 207, 208.
Letters from, 726, 727.
Letter to, 559.
List of witnesses called for by, 726, 727.
Orders of, in disobedience of those of Secretary of War, 288.
Orders to, to repair to Washington, 289.
Persecution, 471.
Public sentiment against, 288.
Question as to the right of, to command, 290.
Rejection by the President of application by, for court of inquiry, 726.
Release from arrest, 348.
Wilkinson, James (General)—Continued.
Reports that, is to be arrested, 543.
Request of, to obtain attendance of officers to vindicate his conduct, 726.
Resolution of Congress to inquire into the conduct of, 499.
Sentiments of, toward Madison, 727.
Suspicions, 231.
Term of commissioner, 403.
Trial, 461.
Willard, Jacob, letter from, 727.
Willard, Philander Jacob, recommendation to appoint as captain, 353.
Willard, Simon, jr., letters from, 728.
Willet and Lindsey, apprehension of, for counterfeiting, 254.
Willett, Marinus, letters from, 728.
Success, 92.
William and Mary, brig, 517.
William and Mary College, 36, 53, 495.
Longitude of, by computation from solar eclipse, 448.
Williams, C. D., letter from, 729.
Letter to, 129.
Williams, David R., appointment to command in the Army declined by, 729.
Financial embarrassments, 729.
Letters from, 729.
Williams, James, letters from, 729.
Williams, John, letter from, 729.
Williams, John W., letter from, 729.
Williams, Jonathan, letters from, 729.
Williams, M. D., letter from, 730.
Williams, Nathan, letters from, 730.
Williams, Otho H., letter from, 730.
Williams, Robert, letters from, 730.
Williams, Samuel, commissioner to determine British claims, 431.
Williamsburg, convention at, 65.
Destruction of the capitol at, 495.
Proposed location of a national university at, 103.
Question as to the probability of, as residence of Congress, 496.
Removal of college from, 53.
Spectacle of misery and ruin (1781), 495.
University at, seal for the, 496.
Williamson, Basil, letter from, 730.
Williamson, Hugh, letters from, 730, 731.
Williamson, Thomas, letter from, 731.
Willie, Charles, examination of, 680.
Willie, ames, appointment requested by, 728J
Letter from, 728.
Willig, William, letters from, 731.
Willis, Byrd C., letters from, 731.
Willis, Carver, letters from, 731.
Suit in chancery of, and Madison, 241.
Willis, —— (Dr.), death of, 363.
Willis, George, appointment of, to Military Academy requested, 731.
Willis, Henry, 251, 650.
Willis, John, 251.
Willis, Mrs., 60.
Sale of Kentucky lands of, 657.
Willis, Perrin, letters from, 731, 732.
Williston, C. Fennimore, letter from, 732.
Letters to, 129, 130.
Williston, E. B., letters from, 732.
Willson, James R., letter from, 732.
Willson, Richard, letter from, 732.
Wilmer, James Jones, letter from, 732.
Solicitation for Government employ, 732.
Wilmer, James S., letter from 732.
Wilmore (Lieutenant), dismissal of, 238.
Wilson, ——, Commissioner of the General Land Office, 676.
Wilson, Andrew, letter from, 732.
Wilson, Archibald, jr., letters from, 732.
Wilson, Cæsar R., 605.
Wilson, Ebenezer, letter from, 733.
Wilson, George, caveats entered by, 504.
Surveys by, 145.
Wilson, James, letter from, 733.
Wilson, John, application of, for Government employment, 733.
Letters from, 733.
Petition of, for payment of services, 733.

Wilson, Joseph, 157.
And others, letter from, 733.
Wilson, Thomas, letters from, 733.
Winamac, chief of Pottawatomies, 351.
Winchester, James (General), defeat of, 264, 720.
Winder, William, letter to, 130.
Winder, William H. (General), acquittance of, by court of inquiry, 733.
Conduct of, at battle of Bladensburg, 130, 733.
Letters from, 733.
Windsor, British scow, capture of the, by prisoners she was carrying, 401.
Wine, American, 3.
Culture of, in Kentucky, 173.
Importations of, 206, 220, 312, 313, 588, 589, 590, 697.
Native, 660.
Orders and shipments of, 559, 564.
Shipment of, to India, 153.
Virginia, 599.
Wingate, Joshua, jr., letter from, 733.
Winn, John, and others, letter from, 734.
Winslow, John (chairman), letter from, 734.
Winslow, Mark, 423.
Winston, Thomas; and Stewart, James, jointly, letter from, 734.
Winslow, Thomas, 423.
Winslows, —— ——, prisoners on charge of counterfeiting, 505.
Winston, John, letter from, 734.
Winston, Thomas, letter from, 734.
Winthrop, John, anniversary of the arrival of, 25.
Wirt, William, acceptance of, of appointment as district attorney, 734.
Letters from, 734.
to, 130.
Life and character, 55, 441.
Popularity, 585.
Recommendation of, as district attorney, 687.
Wiscasset, address of merchants of, for cessation of arms (1812), 218.
Wise, George D. (Lieutenant), 154.
Wistar, Caspar, jr., letters from, 735.
Witherell, James, letter from, 735.
Withers, E. D., 336.
Letter from, 735.
Witherspoon, Matthew, 169.
Wolcott, Alexander, letter from, 735.
Nomination of, as associate judge of the Supreme Court of the United States, 476.
Wolcott, Oliver, 621.
Letter to, 532.
Wolcott, Oliver, Richard Butler and Arthur Lee, joint letter from, 735.
Wolcott, Oliver, jr., letter from, 735.
Wolger, Catherine, letter from, 735.
Petition of, for pardon, 735.
Wood, Abiel, letter from, 736.
Wood County, lamentable condition of, 642.
Wood, Jethro, letter from, 736.
Wood, John H., application of, for a loan, 736.
Letter from, 736.
Wood, John S., legatees of, 566.
Wood, Joseph, letter to, 130.
Wood, William, letters from, 736.
Wood, William B., application of, for a loan, 736.
Letter from, 736.
Woods, David, claim of, as a Revolutionary soldier, 561.
Letter from, 561.
Woods, William, letter from, 736.
Woodward, A. B., application of, to be secretary of legation, 736.
Letters from, 736.
Letter to, 130.
Wool, American, manufactures of, 245.
And hair fabric, manufacture of, 619.
Merino, 489.
Smiths Island, 244, 245.
Wool, Spanish, 228.
Woolen cloth, manufacture of domestic, 714.
Specimen of domestic, 606.
Woolley, A. R., letter from, 736.
Wortham & Magruder, letter from, 737.
Worthington, Thomas, letter from, on appointment of a district judge, 319.
Worthington, Vachel, letter from, 737.
Worthington, W. G. D., application of, for office, 737.
Character of, 137.
Letter from, 737.
Wright, Frances, experiment of, concerning manumission, 56, 737.
Letters from, 737.
Letter to, 130.
Wright, Gustavus W. T., application as private secretary by, 737.
Wright, Moses, and others, letter from, 737.
Wright, Robert, 732.
Appointment solicited by, 737.
Letter from, 737.
Writers, pensioned, by British Government to misrepresent, 316.
Wyandottes, defection of the, 352.
Wyer, Edward, letter from, 737.
Wythe, George, letter to, 394.
Political sentiments of, 40.

Y.

Yancey, Charles, letter from, 738.
Yancey, David, 191, 583.
Letter from, 738.
Request of, for a passport, 738.
Yancey, ——, letter from, 738.
Yandell, Wilson, letter from, 738.
Yard, James, appointment of, as commissioner to Spain, 738.
Letter from, 738.
Yates, E. A., letter from, 739.
Yazoo claims, 247, 271.
Yazoo Company in Massachusetts, 315.
Report that Madison is a partner in the, 494.
Transaction, the, 70.
Yazooism, 49.
Yellow fever, deaths by, 392, 418.
At Leghorn, 516, 677.
In New Orleans, 209, 210.
In Philadelphia, 155, 392, 702.
In Spain, 575.
Origin of the, 607.
Reported at Alexandria, 700.
York County convention, 739.
York County, Republican committee of, 670.
Yorktown, celebration at, 614.
Young, Joseph, letter from, 739.
Yrujo, Carlos M. de (Spanish minister), 47, 261.
And Miranda, 83.
Arrival, 404.
Conduct, 82.
Intercepted dispatches of, 83.
Recall, 703.
Sustains pretensions of Anthony Merry, 81.
Yucatan, civil war in, 668.
Political parties in, 668.
Yznardi, Joseph, and Hackley, 47.
Yznardi, Joseph, claim of, 739.
Introducing, 478.
Letter from, 739.
Meade's conduct toward, 406, 407.

Z.

Zane, Ebenezer, letter from, 739.
Zane, Isaac, last will and testament of, 739.
Zollickoffer, William, letter from, 739.

○

Lightning Source UK Ltd.
Milton Keynes UK
UKHW010321120219
337137UK00004B/383/P

9 780331 677713